BASIC FINANCIAL MANAGEMENT
Frequently Used Symbols

α_t	Certainty equivalent coefficient in period t		MCC	Marginal cost of capital
ACF_t	Annual after-tax expected cash flow in time period t		MIRR	Modified internal rate of return
AROR	Accounting rate of return		NPV	Net present value
ß	Beta of an asset, the slope of the regression or characteristic line		PMT	Periodic level payment of an annuity
			P/E	Price/earnings ratio
DCL	Degree of combined leverage		PV	Present value
DFL	Degree of financial leverage		PVIF	Present value interest factor
DOL	Degree of operating leverage		PVIFA	Present value interest factor for an annuity
EAA	Equivalent annual annuity		R	Investor's required and/or expected rate of return
EBIT	Earnings before interest and taxes			
EOQ	Economic order quantity		R_f	Risk free rate of return
EPS	Earnings per share		ROA	Return on assets
FV	Future value		ROE	Return on common equity
FVIF	Future value interest factor		RP	Risk premium
FVIFA	Future value interest factor for an annuity		SML	Security market line
g	Annual growth rate		σ	Standard deviation (lowercase sigma)
IO	the initial cash outlay		σ^2	Variance (standard deviation squared)
IRR	Internal rate of return		TIE	Times interest earned
Kc	Cost of internal common equity (also Kc)		T	Tax rate
Kd	After-tax cost of debt		WCC	Weighted cost of capital
Ko	Weighted cost of capital		W_d, W_c	Percentage (weights) of funds provided by debt and common equity respectively
Kp	Cost of preferred stock			
M/B	Market-to-book ratio		YTM	Yield to maturity

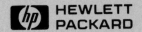
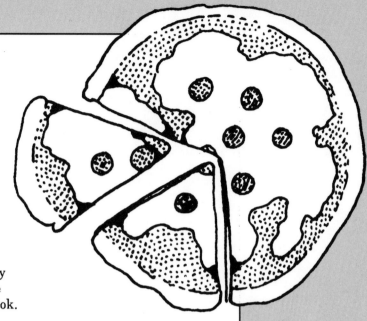

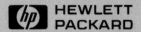

Rebate Terms and Limitations

Purchases made before November 1, 1992 or after December 31, 1993 are not eligible for this rebate. Offer good on HP 17BII only. Offer limited to one rebate per product purchased, and one rebate per customer. This coupon may be used for only one rebate claim. Offer is not redeemable at retailer. All purchases must be made in the U.S.A. Rebate will be sent only to U.S.A. addresses. Purchases must be valid only in accordance with terms set forth. If these terms and conditions are not met, rebate checks will not be issued. Offer is not valid in conjunction with any other Hewlett-Packard offer. HP employee orders are ineligible. Hewlett-Packard is not responsible for requests lost, damaged, or delayed in shipping. Void where prohibited, taxed, or restricted by law. All rebates will be paid in U.S. dollars. Rebate checks are void if not cashed within 90 days of issuance, and cannot be reissued. All incomplete or illegible claims will be returned for resubmission. All resubmitted claims are subject to these same terms and conditions, including postmark and receipt restrictions. Hewlett-Packard reserves the right to confirm identification. All documentation submitted with this claim becomes the property of HP and cannot be returned. Additional restrictions may apply to government agencies.

Yes! I want $10 back on my purchase of the HP 17BII.

6th Edition
BASIC FINANCIAL MANAGEMENT

J. William Petty
Baylor University
Professor of Finance
and the W. W. Caruth Endowed Chair
of Entrepreneurship

Arthur J. Keown
Virginia Polytechnic Institute
and State University
R. B. Pamplin Professor of Finance

David F. Scott, Jr.
University of Central Florida
Holder, Phillips-Schenck Chair
in American Private Enterprise

John D. Martin
University of Texas at Austin
Margaret and Eugene McDermott
Professor of Banking and Finance

PRENTICE HALL, Englewood Cliffs, NJ 07632

Library of Congress Cataloging-in-Publication Data

Basic financial management/J. William Petty . . . [et al.]—6th ed.
  976 pp.   cm.
  Includes index.
  ISBN 0-13-059635-3
    1. Business enterprises—Finance.   2. Corporations—Finance.
I. Petty, J. William.
HG4026.B318   1993
658.15-dc20   92-32701
                                                        CIP

Acquisitions Editor: LEAH JEWELL
Development Editor: TRISH NEALON
Production Editor: ANNE GRAYDON
Interior design: MAUREEN EIDE and MERYL POWESKI
Page layout: MERYL POWESKI
Cover design: RICHARD STALZER, RICHARD STALZER ASSOC., LTD.
Prepress Buyer: TRUDY PISCIOTTI
Manufacturing Buyer: PATRICE FRACCIO
Editorial/Production assistance: COLETTE CONBOY,
    EILEEN DEGUZMAN, RENEE PELLETIER, and ADAM VELTHAUS

Publisher: GARRET WHITE
Senior Managing Editor: JOYCE TURNER
Managing Editor: FRANCES RUSSELLO
Supplements Editor: DAVID SHEA
Marketing Manager: PATTI ARNESON

© 1993 by Prentice-Hall, Inc.
A Simon & Schuster Company
Englewood Cliffs, New Jersey 07632

Printed in the United States of America

10 9 8 7 6 5 4 3 2 1

ISBN 0-13-059635-3

Prentice-Hall International (UK) Limited, *London*
Prentice-Hall of Australia Pty. Limited, *Sydney*
Prentice-Hall Canada Inc., *Toronto*
Prentice-Hall Hispanoamericana, S.A., *Mexico*
Prentice-Hall of India Private Limited, *New Delhi*
Prentice-Hall of Japan, Inc., *Tokyo*
Simon & Schuster Asia Pte. Ltd., *Singapore*
Editora Prentice-Hall do Brasil, Ltda., *Rio de Janeiro*

The sixth edition of
Basic Financial Management
is dedicated to
our families—the ones who love us the most.
Donna, Krista, Katie, and Carter
Barb, Emily, and Artie
Peggy
Sally, David, and Jess

and in memory of
Richard James Scott,
a beloved brother

CONTENTS

PREFACE

Historical circumstances are a driving force underlying the development and practice of financial management. For example, in the 1970s volatile energy prices, interest rates, and exchange rates dominated both the financial press and the economic environment within which financial decisions were made. These factors led to the development of new commodity and financial futures markets in which firms could hedge their risk exposure and speculate on the directions of anticipated price movements. Similarly, in the 1980s corporate control contests have resulted in the restructuring of corporate America. This unprecedented wave of transactions has included corporate divestitures, leveraged buyouts, joint ventures, spinoffs, split-ups, employee stock option plans (ESOPs), partial public offerings, project financings, and a host of other types of truncations that have filled the financial press during the 1980s.

Some have characterized this latest wave of corporate control contests simply as evidence of the continual tug-of-war between the capital markets and corporate management for control over financial resources. If this be true, then it would appear that the 1980s have been a time of unparalleled victory for the capital markets. Many of the largest corporations have fallen victim to the "bust-up merger" as they have been bought up and their assets sold to the highest bidder. This, in turn, means that the investment and financing decisions of even the very largest firms are subjected to an unusual amount of scrutiny by the capital markets.

Some practicing financial managers have cried foul, saying that investors in the capital markets are too short-term oriented or myopic. This, they argue, has placed undue pressure on the corporate manager to produce short-term profits to the exclusion of making long-term commitments. The evidence from the academic community, however, has not supported this contention. Furthermore, as the pressures of international competition continue unabated, serious consideration must be given to the effect the capital markets have on the firm's competitiveness in world markets through their influence on the firm's investment and financing choices. Consequently, it is our belief that the events of the 1980s and early 1990s have *heightened* the importance of corporate finance in the overall formula for corporate competitiveness and success.

In the text, we provide an introduction to financial decision making that is rooted both in current financial theory and in the current state of world economic conditions. This focus is evident in a number of ways, perhaps the most obvious being the increased attention to the capital markets and their influence on corporate financial decisions. We have expanded our discussion of the concepts of risk and return and the related notion of opportunity costs. We believe the added emphasis on capital markets is consistent with their influence on corporate financial decisions.

A Note to the Teacher

Basic Financial Management, 6th edition, provides the reader with an overview of financial management as intended for an introductory course in the subject. Such a course might be taught in one semester or two quarters. The orientation continues to be managerial, with an emphasis on the identification and solution of the financial problems confronting the business enterprise. Decision making within an *enterprise valuation framework* is stressed throughout the text and, thereby, provides a unifying theme across all discussions. In the preparation of the manuscript, three primary standards were used. First, we have made a strong effort to offer *completeness* in the treatment of each topic. Second, we have given *readability* a high priority; we have taken extra care to use a clear and concise writing style, especially in the treatment of concepts requiring the use of mathematics. Third, complete, *step-by-step* examples are used frequently to increase clarity and to crystallize the critical issues in the student's mind. In summary, the pedagogical approach taken, particularly for the more difficult topics, progresses from an intuitive presentation of the problem to the introduction and illustration of the appropriate decision-making framework.

A number of other changes have been made in the 6th edition. Besides the expanded emphasis on the role of the capital markets in corporate financial decision making, we have also made a number of significant changes throughout the text that might not be so obvious.

1. We continue to work at adding life to the presentations by increasing the number of *Basic Financial Management in Practice* boxes. Because these practical application inserts proved to be a very popular feature of previous editions, we have expanded them in this edition.

2. Given the constant need to address ethical issues in the workplace, we have made a concerted effort to identify some of the important ethical issues as they relate to financial decision making. We have added material throughout the text in the form of *Ethics in Financial Management* boxes and provided four ethics cases that afford a means for constructive dialogue.

3. In view of the continued globalization of world markets, we have integrated international finance throughout the text in the form of *International Financial Management* boxes.

4. One of the difficulties students frequently encounter comes in transferring knowledge into live situations. It is one thing to understand how to work an end-of-chapter problem, but quite another to apply that understanding to an actual company. We are therefore pleased that Prentice Hall has developed an agreement with Disclosure, Incorporated, for the users of *Basic Financial Management*, 6th edition, to have access to the academic edition of Compact D™/SEC. This database, designed for the personal computer, contains financial and management information on 100 publicly traded firms. Company data is taken from annual and periodic reports filed with the Securities and Exchange Commission. The firms have been selected for their diversity and appropriateness for the classroom. Approximately one half of the chapters have suggested uses for the database relative to the material in the respective chapter. The use of the database truly takes the student to a higher level of learning.

5. The use of the financial calculator has been integrated throughout the text, especially with respect to the time value of money. A separate appendix has been added that demonstrates the use of the Hewlett-Packard HP 17BII, the latest addition to the HP product line. We have also designed an insert card to the text that shows how to find the compound value interest factors and present value interest factors without the use of the table values. Finally, in the student study guide, we provide a complete article on the use of all the popular financial calculators.

6. The end-of-chapter problems have been expanded, as has the test item file.

7. In prior editions, the transparency acetates have been limited to figures from the text. In the 6th edition, not only do we provide these acetates, but we have also designed acetates that present the main issues of the primary chapters, along with examples that may be used in class presentations.

8. We have added section openers to each of the major parts of the text. These section openers allow the student to see the "big picture" before delving into the details of the individual chapters.

9. To enhance the use of the selected ABC News video tapes, a written introduction to each video follows each section opener; and at the end of each section is a concluding discussion, questions, and suggested readings. These introductions and conclusions will greatly improve the effectiveness of the videos in the classroom.

We believe the foregoing will greatly enhance the student's learning experience.

Besides the broader changes just mentioned, modifications have also been made in each chapter. The following list includes the major additions that are new to *Basic Financial Management* in the 6th edition:

1. In our introduction to the capital markets (Chapter 2), we have significantly expanded our presentation on the term structure of interest rates.

2. Chapter 3, entitled Mathematics of Finance, has been simplified. In addition, we have adopted the more conventional notations of PVIF and FVIF in the equations.

3. We have divided the former chapter on valuation and rates of return into two chapters, one entitled Risk and Rates of Return (Chapter 4) and the other entitled Bond and Stock Valuation (Chapter 5). The division is part of our effort to give more attention to the influence of capital markets on financial decisions.

4. We have developed a clearer presentation of the capital asset pricing model and beta (Chapter 4).

5. We have moved the discussion on the arbitrage pricing model to an appendix in Chapter 4 to give the teacher added flexibility.

6. In Chapter 6, Capital Budgeting, we have simplified the presentation on how to measure a project's benefits and costs. Consequently, the student will find the concept of "relevant cash flows" easier to understand.

7. The former chapter entitled Capital Budgeting Under Uncertainty, Chapter 7 in this edition, is retitled Advanced Topics in Capial Budgeting. It now includes other important practical matters in capital budgeting analysis, such as "equivalent annual annuities," a measurement often used in practice.

8. In Chapter 8, we have expanded the material on determining the weighted marginal cost of capital and increased significantly the number of problems dealing with measurement of the weighted cost of capital.

9. Chapter 10, Planning the Firm's Financing Mix, contains new material on (a) how managers feel about capital stucture theory; (b) business cycles and financing behavior; and (c) agency theory, free cash flows, and the control hypothesis for debt issuance.

10. Chapter 15, Cash and Marketable Securities Management, includes new material from the Federal Reserve Banks of Atlanta and Richmond that focuses on the Fed's role in determining interest rates and the topic of monetary policy.

11. In Chapter 16, we have simplified the presentation on marginal or

incremental analysis of credit policy and moved the material from the appendix to the main body of the chapter.

12. Chapter 18 now contains material that demonstrates how financial managers were net buyers of common equity (rather than issuers) during the 1980s and how this trend reversed with the rise in stock prices that occurred into 1992. A case considering the ethics of insider trading is also included.

13. The former chapter on convertibles, warrants, options and futures has been separated into two chapters: Convertibles and Warrants, and The Use of Futures and Options to Reduce Risks. The material on futures and options is discussed in a financial management setting and has been expanded.

14. For teachers who make a copy of the problem solutions available to their class, you will be pleased to know that a selected group of problem solutions (from Problem Set B only) have been added to the *Study Guide*. These solutions in the *Study Guide*, along with check figures for many of the Set A problems provided at the back of the text itself, should meet your needs in this regard; so that copies may no longer be necessary.

The preceding list of changes is not comprehensive. However, it does highlight the kinds of changes we have committed ourselves to making in order that *Basic Financial Management* continue to reflect the very best thinking that financial scholars have to offer.

As a final, but important, comment to the teacher, we know how frustrating errors in a textbook or instructor's manual can be. Thus, we have worked diligently to make certain that any errors are virtually eliminated. Not only did we check and recheck the answers ourselves, but Prentice Hall hired faculty members at other universities to check the accuracy of the problem solutions. We therefore make the following offer to users of *Basic Financial Management*, 6th edition:

> Any professor or student identifying an error of substance (e.g., an incorrect number in an example or problem) in *Basic Financial Management*, 6th edition, in either the text or the instructor's manual, that has not been previously reported to the authors will receive a $10 reward. If a series of related errors occur resulting from an original error, the reward will be limited to a maximum of $20 for the group of errors.

A Note to the Student

As the authors of *Basic Financial Management*, we realize that our success ought to be measured by the level of effectiveness in our presentation to you, the end-user. Although you may not be involved in the process of selecting which text will be used in your finance class, we still consider you to be our customer. For this reason, we have made every effort to make the material understandable and to be sensitive to your needs in learning finance. Also, we have taken seriously our efforts to develop the *Study Guide* that assists and complements your learning. Two examples deserve note:

1. In addition to providing some sample problems with solutions in the *Study Guide*, we have added worked-out solutions to some of the end-of-chapter problems from Problem Set B.

2. We have made a first effort to provide outside material that may be helpful: In this edition of the *Study Guide*, we have included a complete article from *Financial Practice and Education* on the use of financial calculators. We believe you will find it quite helpful.

As our end-user, we would like very much to hear from you: Did you encounter anything in our presentation that was not clear or was confusing? We sincerely want to know what you think. While we cannot pay for your services, we would be willing to include your name and institution in the list of acknowledgments for your assistance in making the next edition of *Basic Financial Management* a better text for the student. Let us hear from you.

Acknowledgments

We gratefully acknowledge the assistance, support, and encouragement of those individuals who have contributed to the successful completion and revision of *Basic Financial Management*. Specifically, we wish to recognize the very helpful insights provided by many of our colleagues. For their careful review of the text, we are indebted to:

Kamal Abouzeid, *Lynchburg College*; V. T. Alaganan, *Hofstra University*; Michael T. Alderson, *University of Missouri at St. Louis*; Dwight C. Anderson, *Louisiana Tech University*; Nasser Arshadi, *University of Missouri*; Gary Benesh, *Florida State University*; Sam G. Berry, *Virginia Commonwealth University*; Randy Billingsley, *Virginia Polytechnic Institute and State University*; Russell P. Boisjoly, *Simmons College*; Virgil L. Brewer, *Eastern Kentucky University*; Jozelle Brister, *Abilene Christian University*; John Byrd, *Washington State University*; Don M. Chance, *Virginia Polytechnic Institute and State University*; Albert H. Clark, *Georgia State University*; David W. Cole, *Ohio State University*; Bernard C. Dill, *Bloomsburg University*; Mark Dorfman, *University of Arkansas—Little Rock*; Marjorie Evert, *Xavier University*; Sidney R. Finkel, *Canisius College*; Frederick G. Floss, *Buffalo State University*; Lyn Fraser, *Texas A & M University*; John Gilster, *University of Ohio*; Sharon S. Graham, *University of Central Florida*; Dennis A. Gribenas, *Data Systems International, Inc.*; Jack Griggs, *Abilene Christian University*; Samuel C. Hadaway, *Financo, Inc.*; Nancy Lee Halford, *Madison Area Technical College*; William R. Henry, *Georgia State University*; Keith Howe, *DePaul University*; Charles R. Idol, *Idaho State University*; Vahan Janjigian, *Northeastern University*; Nancy Jay, *Gannon University*; Jeff Jenkins, *Security National Corporation*; William Jens, *Stetson University*; Steve A. Johnson, *University of Texas at El Paso*; Djavad Kashefinejad, *California State Polytechnic University*; James D. Keys, *Florida International University*; David R. Klock, *University of Central Florida*; Howard C. Launstein, *Marquette University*; Leonard T. Long, *American International College*; Abbas Mamoozadeh, *Slippery Rock University*; Terry S. Maness, *Baylor University*; Surendra K. Mansinghka, *San Francisco University*; Barry Marks, *University of Houston at Clearlake*; K. Gary McClure, *University of Central Florida*; James E. McNulty, *Florida Atlantic University*; James A. Miller, *University of Arkansas*; Naval Modani, *University of Central Florida*; Eric J. Moon, *San Francisco University*; Shalini Perumpral, *Radford University*; John M. Pinkerton, *Virginia Polytechnic Institute and State University*; Jack H. Rubens, *Cleveland State University*; Todd Schank, *University of Portland*; Peter A. Sharp, *California State University at Sacramento*; Jackie Shu, *University of Central Florida*; Michael Solt, *San Jose State University*; Raymond F. Spudeck, *University of Central Florida*; Suresh Srivastava, *University of Maryland*; Donald L. Stevens, *University of Colorado—Denver*; L. E. Sweeney, *Ball State University*; Amir Tavakkol, *Kansas State University*; John G. Thatcher, *Marquette University*; Gary L. Trennepohl, *Texas A & M University*; Ronald Tsang, *University of Central Florida*; Kenneth L. Westby, *University of North Dakota*; Lawrence C. Wolken, *Texas A & M University*; Kevin Woods, *University of Central Florida*; Steve B. Wyatt, *University of Cincinnati*.

We also thank our friends at Prentice Hall. They are a great group of folks. We offer our personal expression of appreciation to Garret White, the editor who originally signed the first edition of *Basic Financial Management;* to Leah Jewell, of whom there is no equal as an encourager and advisor; to Patti Arneson, for her marketing genius; to Anne Graydon, for her attention to quality and detail and for her patience and understanding during the production process; and to the Prentice-Hall field representatives for their input based on their interaction with teachers from across the nation. We also thank Trish Nealon for her work as the developmental editor and Janet Cryer at Hewlett-Packard Company for helping to integrate the use of the calculator into the text.

As a final word, we express our sincere thanks to the many teachers who use *Basic Financial Management* in the classroom, in both academic as well as professional settings. We thank you for letting us serve you. Always feel free to give any of us a call when you have questions or needs. We view ourselves as partners in this venture, and we will be sensitive to your wishes and desires whenever possible.

J.W.P
A.J.K.
D.F.S.
J.D.M.

BASIC
FINANCIAL
MANAGEMENT

SCOPE AND ENVIRONMENT OF FINANCIAL MANAGEMENT

Financial management is largely about making decisions. Decisions about what assets or products to invest in, how to manage cash, and how to raise funds for growth. Part 1 sets the stage for the remainder of the text by describing the basic concepts on which financial decisions are based, the *language* and *arithmetic* used to make these decisions, and the world in which financial managers operate and how it influences financial decision making. We begin by discussing the objective of the financial manager, as well as some important concepts that will appear many times later in the text: market efficiency, the relationship between risk and return, the importance of prices as indicators of value, and the potential conflicts of interest that arise in business firms (Chapter 1). The decisions facing financial managers often are affected by forces outside the firm, such as taxes and the current sentiment in financial markets, so it is important to have some understanding of the business environment (Chapter 2). Finance has its own language and arithmetic. Many financial decisions are based on data from a firm's accounting statements: the balance sheet and income statement. One task of the financial manager is to bring accounting numbers to life; sometimes this means figuring out the rationale behind the entries on the financial statements or predicting how next month's or next year's number will look under various scenarios. Distinctions between the information needs of financial managers and accrual accounting also are basic to our study (Appendix 1A). The arithmetic of finance is built on the concept of the time value of money or *present value*: The value of money varies depending on when it is received (Chapter 3). This crucial concept underlies many of the ideas presented in this text. An investment in understanding the mechanics of present value early in the course will pay dividends later.

INTRODUCTION

VIDEO CASE 1

CEO Compensation: Corporate Governance in Inaction?

from ABC News, *Nightline*, May 20, 1991

The chief executive officers (CEOs) of America's largest corporations earn, on average, 85 times the amount earned by factory workers at those same corporations. In Japan this multiple is 17 and in Germany 23. Possibly more surprising than the magnitude of the salaries is the fact that CEO compensation often does not seem to be linked to the performance of the firm. As the participants in this video segment demonstrate, concern about this inequity is growing. Critics of large compensation packages for corporate CEOs are Professors Bud Crystal and Robert Reich, who are spokesmen from two shareholder rights groups, the Institute of Shareholder Partners and United Shareholders Association. Ben Cohen, CEO of Ben and Jerry's Ice Cream, describes the compensation system in their firm: CEO compensation is limited to about 10 times the salary of the lowest paid employee. Hicks Waldron, a compensation consultant and the former CEO of Avon Products, argues that looking at a few extreme cases does not imply that all CEOs are overpaid. He also argues that cultural differences make comparisons between the compensation packages in different countries inappropriate.

- Are American executives worth these large salaries and bonuses, or are they overpaid?
- If CEO salaries are out of line, do shareholders have the power to do anything about it?
- Should CEO pay be tied to firm profits or the firm's stock market performance?
- Do stock options solve the problem of CEO compensation?

To discuss these questions we need to understand something about the structure of the modern corporation, the conflicts of interest inherent in corporate business organization, and how those conflicts can be mitigated. Chapters 1 and 2 provide this background information. We will apply some of the concepts from these chapters when we complete our discussion of the CEO compensation video at the end of Chapter 2.

CHAPTER *1*

The Role of Financial Management

Development of Financial Thought • Goal of the Firm • Financial Decisions and Risk–Return Relationships • Why Prices Reflect Value • Ethics and Ethical Behavior in Financial Management • Overview of the Text • Appendix 1A: The Language of Finance: Accounting Statements • Appendix 1B: Glossary of Accounting Terms

Financial management during this century has undergone dramatic changes. Whereas financial managers were once limited to some bookkeeping, cash management, and the acquisition of funds, they now have a major voice in all aspects of raising and allocating financial capital. This book will introduce you to specific problems and areas that concern the financial manager. In this chapter we will explain the environment surrounding the problem, then propose a method of dealing with the problem. We will also stress the interrelationships among the financial manager's various concerns and decisions. To develop a proper perspective on the role of the financial manager and the financial decision-making process, we will look first at the development of financial thought. As a review we will provide a brief overview of the firm's basic financial statements in the appendices to this chapter.

Development of Financial Thought

At the turn of the century, financial thought focused on the legal environment within which the firm operated. The topics receiving the most attention were mergers, formation of new companies, investment banking, government regulation, and the process of raising funds in the capital markets. The economic and business activity of the time determined what was of primary importance in the finance field. During the early 1900s financial and economic news emphasized consolidations, mergers, and government regulation of the new business giants. This was the era when the great oil, auto, and steel firms were being formed and Teddy Roosevelt was making his name as a corporate trust buster.

In the 1920s the economy began to expand, and raising new funds in the capital markets became more important. As a result, the emphasis shifted from mergers and regulation to methods and procedures for acquiring funds. Arthur Stone Dewing devoted about a third of his landmark financial text *The Financial Policy of Corporations* (1920) to the description of methods and procedures for acquiring funds. The remainder of the book dealt primarily with consolidations, mergers, and a legalistic look at corporate bankruptcy.

Business failures during the Great Depression of the 1930s helped change the focus of finance. While it continued to be taught as a descriptive, or "how to" discipline, increased emphasis was placed on bankruptcy, liquidity management, and avoidance of financial problems. The political changes that dominated the thirties also influenced the field of finance, bringing more government regulation and control of both business and the securities market, and increased requirements to disclose large volumes of corporate financial data. These data allowed analysts to more effectively assess potential corporate performance, stirring new interest in financial analysis.

During the 1940s and early 1950s financial theory continued to be taught as a descriptive discipline. The major financial texts of the day continued to emphasize methods and instruments for fund raising, corporate bankruptcy and reorganization, and mergers and consolidations. Greater emphasis was given, however, to liquidity management, financial planning, and cash budgeting.[1]

During the mid-1950s the field of finance underwent drastic changes. First, the point of view shifted from that of an outsider assessing the condition and performance of a firm to that of an insider charged with the management and control of the firm's financial operations. The work of Joel Dean promoted the area of capital budgeting as a major topic in finance. This led to an increased interest in related topics, most notably firm valuation. Interest in these topics grew and in turn spurred interest in security analysis, portfolio theory, and capital structure theory. In effect the field of finance evolved from a descriptive discipline dealing primarily with mergers, regulation, and the raising of capital funds to a more encompassing one dealing with all aspects of acquiring and efficiently utilizing those funds.

The evolution of the field of finance continues at a lively pace. Economic activity, financing innovations, and new theoretical developments are constantly reshaping financial thought. For example, the October 1987 stock market crash forced a rethinking of how stocks are priced. In addition, the opening of markets abroad has created new and exciting opportunities for internationalizing firms' operations. This has, in turn, created a need for financial managers to better understand the financial systems of other countries and the role of the financial manager in the multinational corporation. Finally, the downturn in the economy in the early 1990s has created new challenges for the financial manager. For example, at IBM, which reported a $1.38 billion loss in the fourth quarter of 1991, financial managers are faced with the task of cutting costs and turning around earnings.

Before discussing the financial decision-making process, we will examine the appropriate goal of the firm. This will enable us to better understand the role and significance of financial decision making.

Goal of the Firm

In this book we will designate the goal of the firm to be *maximization of shareholder wealth*, or maximization of the total market value of existing shareholders' common stock. As we will see, this is an extremely inclusive goal, since it is affected by all financial decisions. To better understand this goal, we will first discuss profit maximization as a possible goal of the firm. Then we will

---

[1] Among the major financial texts of this period were Dewing's *Financial Policy of Corporations*, which went through five revisions between 1920 and 1953, and Charles W. Gerstenberg's *Financial Organization and Management of Business*, first published in 1939.

INTERNATIONAL FINANCIAL MANAGEMENT

U.S./Japanese Competition: The Race to Shape Our Brave New Biotechnological World

Today, business reality is that international economic boundaries no longer exist. In financial management when we ask questions like Where can funds be raised least expensively? Where can this new product be produced least expensively? and Where will our major competition come from? the answer will quite likely involve a foreign country. If we are going to be successful in business, we must have an international perspective in our decision making.

Typical of how the internationalization of business coupled with recent technological breakthroughs have created both competition and opportunities for U.S. firms is the case of the biotechnology industry. Here, we as financial managers must be able to look at new projects and see both their potential and risks from an international perspective.

Japanese industry's success in selling innovative, well-made consumer goods in the United States is well known. Now Japanese corporations are mounting a powerful new challenge to American dominance in biotechnology products. Although we are only beginning to see the applications of this new technology, it is already a multibillion-dollar industry, with products ranging from genetically improved farm animals and grains to cancer treatments and biodegradable plastics. The real focus in this rapidly growing field, however, is a battle between Japan and the United States for prominence in research and development (R&D).

The United States has been at the forefront of biotechnology, but Japanese companies are quickly gaining ground. Drawing on a strategy that has served them well in other industries, the Japanese are heavily relying on "piggybacking." The key to this strategy is to use their considerable financial assets to supply needed cash to biotechnology laboratories around the world, which then grant the Japanese access to technological breakthroughs. By riding "piggyback" on basic research conducted in other countries, the Japanese companies, in effect, augment their own research budgets, freeing resources for perfecting products that have the best chance of dominating markets around the world. Takeda, for example, which has a joint venture with Abbott Labs and alliances in West Germany, France, and Italy, funds research at Harvard University. Fujisawa acquired LyphoMed and a former joint venture with SmithKline. Chugai bought Gen-Probe, Inc., for $110 million and has stakes in Genetics Institute, Inc., and British Bio-technology.

The speed with which the Japanese have moved is startling. Beginning essentially from scratch ten years ago, they have used their vast financial resources to gain access to American and European technology and to develop their own impressive biotechnology industry, which grossed over $9 billion in 1989. This push was unavoidable—Japanese drug companies had to expand beyond their own markets and develop new technologies because of fierce competition and declining domestic profits—but it was not accomplished alone. Three-quarters of their $2 billion R&D budget for 1990 did come from private sources (many outside the drug industry), but the rest came from the Japanese Ministry of International Trade and Industry, which is actively supporting a variety of promising new projects for the twenty-first century. The Japanese now dominate the American market in anticancer drugs and growth hormones, and they are working on other biotech products such as anti-Alzheimer's drugs, cosmetics, biosensors, and agricultural seeds, fertilizers, and pesticides.

The downside for the Japanese is that the United States is spending over $6 billion per year on biotech R&D (three times the Japanese investment) and still holds a considerable lead in most areas of research. In addition, Japan's drug imports are still three times greater than their exports. Despite their success in gaining access to several smaller companies and research facilities in the United States, Japanese interests appear unable to swallow the European and U.S. giants. Moreover, the Japanese are concerned about a potential market backlash, especially in the United States, to biotech foods (grains, fish, vegetables, fruits, etc.)—an area of biotechnology in which they have invested heavily.

Sources: Roger E. Shamel and Joseph J. Chow, "Biotechnology: On the Rebound and Heading for a Boom," *Chemical Week* (September 27, 1989), 31–32; Jacob M. Schlesinger, "One High-Tech Race Where U.S. Leads Personal Computers," *Wall Street Journal* (October 31, 1989), A1, A12; Neil Gross, "Japan's Next Battleground: The Medicine Chest," *Business Week* (March 12, 1990), 68–72; "Strategic Challenges in Commercializing Biotechnology," *California Management Review* (Spring 1990), 63–72; Barbara Buell et al., "A Shopping Spree in the U.S.," *Business Week* (Innovation 1990 Issue), 86–87. Adapted by permission from James A. F. Stoner and R. Edward Freeman, *Management*, 5th ed., p. 81. © copyright 1992 by Prentice Hall, Inc.

compare it to maximization of shareholder wealth to see why, in financial management, the latter is the more appropriate goal for the firm.

Profit Maximization

In microeconomics courses profit maximization is frequently given as the goal of the firm. Profit maximization stresses the efficient use of capital resources. It ignores however, many of the real-world complexities that financial managers try to address in their decisions. Profit maximization functions largely as a theoretical goal; economists use it to prove how firms behave rationally to increase profit. In the more applied discipline of financial management, however, firms must deal every day with two major factors: uncertainty and timing.

Uncertainty of Returns

Microeconomics courses ignore uncertainty and risk to more easily present theory. Projects and investment alternatives are compared by examining their expected values or weighted average profits. Whether or not one project is riskier than another does not enter these calculations; economists do discuss risk, but only tangentially.[2] In reality projects differ a great deal with respect to risk characteristics, and to disregard these differences in the practice of financial management can result in incorrect decisions.

To better understand the implications of ignoring risk, let us look at two mutually exclusive investment alternatives (that is, only one can be accepted). The first project involves the use of existing plant to produce plastic combs, a product with an extremely stable demand. The second project uses existing plant to produce electric vibrating combs. This latter product may catch on and do well, but it could also fail. The possible outcomes (optimistic prediction, pessimistic prediction, and expected outcome) are given in Table 1–1.

No variability is associated with the possible outcomes for the plastic comb project. If things go well, poorly, or as expected, the outcome will still be $10,000. With the electric comb, however, the range of possible outcomes goes from $20,000 if things go well, to $10,000 if they go as expected, to zero if they go poorly. If we look just at the expected outcomes, the two projects appear equivalent. They are not. The returns associated with the electric comb involve a much greater degree of uncertainty or risk.

The goal of profit maximization, however, ignores uncertainty and considers these projects equivalent in terms of desirability. Later in this text we will examine the relationship between risk and expected return. The element of risk, we will discover, has everything to do with determining expected returns and correctly making investment decisions.

Timing of Returns

Another problem with the goal of profit maximization is that it ignores the timing of the project's returns. To illustrate, let us reexamine our plastic comb versus electric comb investment decision. This time let us ignore risk and say

	Profit		TABLE 1–1.
	Plastic Comb	Electric Comb	Possible Project Outcomes
Optimistic prediction	$10,000	$20,000	
Expected outcome	10,000	10,000	
Pessimistic prediction	10,000	0	

---

[2]See, for example, Robert S. Pindyck and Daniel L. Rubenfeld, *Microeconomics*, 2d ed. (New York: Macmillan, 1992), pp. 244–46.

TABLE 1–2.
Timing of Profits

	Profit	
	Plastic Comb	Electric Comb
Year 1	$10,000	$ 0
Year 2	0	10,000

that each of these projects is going to return a profit of $10,000 for one year; however, it will be one year before the electric comb can go into production, while the plastic comb can begin production immediately. The timing of the profits from these projects is illustrated in Table 1–2.

In this case the total profits from each project are the same, but the timing of the returns differs. As we will see later, money has a definite time value. Thus, the plastic comb project is the better of the two. After one year the $10,000 profit from the plastic combs could be invested in a savings account earning 5 percent interest. At the end of the second year it would have grown to $10,500. Since investment opportunities are available for money in hand, we are not indifferent to the timing of the returns. Given equivalent cash flows from profits, we want those cash flows sooner rather than later. Therefore the financial manager must always consider the possible timing of returns in financial decision making.

Overall, the real-world factors of uncertainty and timing force us to look beyond a simple goal of profit maximization as a decision criterion. We will turn now to an examination of a more robust goal for the firm: maximization of shareholder wealth.

Maximization of Shareholder Wealth

In formulating the goal of maximization of shareholder wealth we are doing nothing more than modifying the goal of profit maximization to deal with the complexities of the operating environment. We have chosen maximization of shareholder wealth—that is, maximization of the total market value of the existing shareholders' common stock—because the effects of all financial decisions are thereby included. The shareholders react to poor investment or dividend decisions by causing the total value of the firm's stock to fall and they react to good decisions by pushing the price of the stock up.

Obviously, there are some serious practical problems in direct use of this goal and evaluating the reaction to various financial decisions by examining changes in the firm's stock value. Many things affect stock prices; to attempt to identify a reaction to a particular financial decision would simply be impossible. Fortunately, that is not necessary. To employ this goal, we need not consider every stock price change to be a market interpretation of the worth of our decisions. Other factors, such as economic expectations, also affect stock price movements. What we do focus on is the effect that our decision *should* have on the stock price if everything else were held constant. The market price of the firm's stock reflects the value of the firm as seen by its owners. It takes into account uncertainty or risk, time, and any other factors that are important to the owners. Thus, again, the framework of maximization of shareholder wealth allows for a decision environment that includes the complexities and complications of the real world. As we follow this goal throughout our discussions, we have to keep in mind one more question: Who exactly are the shareholders? The answer: Shareholders are the legal owners of the firm.

The Agency Problem

While our goal of the firm will be maximization of shareholder wealth, in reality the agency problem may interfere with the implementation of this goal. The *agency problem* is the result of a separation of management and the ownership of the firm. For example, a large firm may be run by professional managers who have little or no ownership position in the firm. As a result of this separation between the decision makers and owners, managers may make decisions that are not in line with the goal of maximization of shareholder wealth. They may approach work less arduously and attempt to benefit themselves in terms of salary and perquisites at the expense of shareholders. The exact significance of this problem is difficult to measure. However, while it may interfere with the implementation of the goal of maximization of shareholder wealth in some firms, it does not affect the goal's validity.

The costs associated with the agency problem are also difficult to measure, but occasionally we can see the effect of this problem in the marketplace. For example, if the market feels that the management of a firm is damaging shareholder wealth, we might see a positive reaction in the stock price to the removal of that management. On the day following the death in 1989 of John Dorrance, Jr., chairman of Campbell Soup, Campbell's stock price rose about 15 percent. Some investors felt that Campbell's relatively small growth in earnings might be improved with the departure of Dorrance. There was also speculation that Dorrance was the major obstacle to a possibly positive reorganization.

Financial Decisions and Risk–Return Relationships

Much of the discussion to come in this book centers on evaluation of risk–return tradeoffs available to the financial manager. We will, in fact, find that almost all financial decisions involve some sort of risk–return tradeoff. The more risk the firm is willing to assume, the higher the expected return from the given course of action. For example, in general, the less inventory held on hand, the higher the expected return, but also the greater the risk of running out of inventory. We will see similar examples turn up in the areas of financial structure and management of long-term assets.

Figure 1–1 on page 10 is a graphic presentation of the financial decision-making process. Given risk–return tradeoffs available to the financial manager, he or she makes various decisions assuming the firm's goal of maximization of shareholder wealth. The owners of the firm then evaluate the decisions, and their evaluation is reflected in changes in the firm's price per share.

Why Prices Reflect Value

Throughout this text we have adopted shareholder wealth maximization as our goal. Let's take a closer look at this goal. First, let's define what we mean by shareholder wealth with respect to a business. For a corporation, the wealth of the shareholders at any point in time is simply the market value of the their common shares. Thus, decisions that maximize shareholder wealth are those that lead to an increase in the market price of each shareholder's shares. To understand why good financial decisions are reflected in positive stock price adjustments, as well as how securities are valued or priced by the financial markets, it is necessary to have an understanding of the concept of efficient markets.

Efficient Markets

The efficient market hypothesis actually deals with the speed with which information is impounded into security prices. Under the efficient market

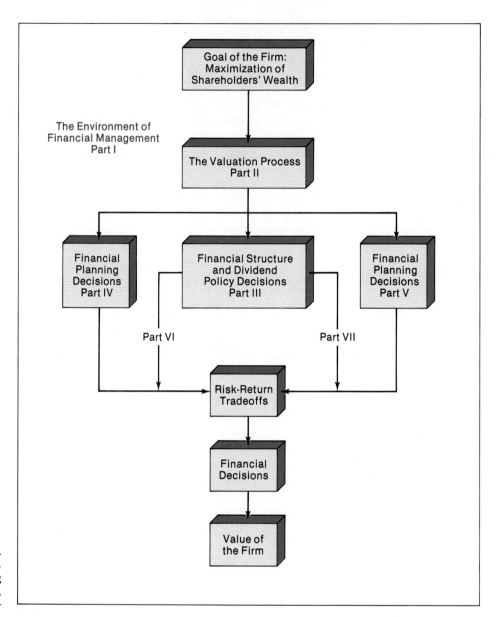

FIGURE 1–1.
Financial Decision-Making
Process

hypothesis, information is reflected in security prices with such speed that there are no opportunities for investors to profit from publicly available information. In effect, an efficient market is one characterized by a large number of profit-driven individuals who act independently of one another. In addition, new information regarding securities arrives in the market in a random manner. Given this setting, investors adjust to this new information immediately and buy and sell the security until they feel that the market price correctly reflects the new information. Whether or not the price adjustment turns out to be correct is not important, but it is important that the price adjustment not be biased—that is, that investors cannot predict whether or not it is an over- or underadjustment.

Just how quickly and what types of information are immediately reflected in security prices determine how efficient the market actually is. For our purposes, the point is that it is investors competing for profits that ensures that security prices will appropriately reflect the expected earnings and risks involved, and thus the true value of the firm.

Ethics and Ethical Behavior in Financial Management

Defining ethics and ethical behavior is simple. Ethical behavior means "doing the right thing." A difficulty arises, however, in attempting to define what we mean by "doing the right thing." The source of the problem lies in the fact that each of us has his or her own unique set of values. These values, in turn, form the basis for our personal judgments about what the right thing to do is. After all, the very essence of personal freedom lies in each individual's right to make choices. However, individuals in a society are not completely free. Every society adopts a set of rules or laws that prescribe what it believes to be "doing the right thing." In a sense, we can think of laws as a set of rules that reflect the values of the society as a whole, as they have evolved up to the present time. There are some who would argue that ethical behavior is more than simply obeying the law. However, for the purposes of this text, we recognize that individuals in a free society have a right to disagree about what constitutes "doing the right thing." For this reason, we will seldom venture beyond the basic notion that ethical conduct involves abiding by society's rules. However, we will endeavor to make you aware of some of the ethical dilemmas that have arisen in recent years with regard to the practice of financial management. These dilemmas generally arise when some form of individual behavior is found to be at odds with the wishes of a large portion of the population, even though that behavior is not prohibited by law. Ethical dilemmas can therefore provide a catalyst for debate and discussion, which may eventually lead to a revision in the body of law. So, as we embark on our study of finance and encounter ethical dilemmas, we encourage you to think through the issue and form your own opinion.

At this point you might want to look at the Ethics in Financial Management box titled "Is It Wrong to Tell a Lie?" As you will see, many times ethical questions are not easily answered, but they are something that we have to deal with on a day-to-day basis.

Discussion of ethics predominates in business and finance sources today, but this is a relatively new phenomenon. The question that many students ask is, "Is ethics really relevant to my career in business?" This is a good question and deserves an answer.

First, while business errors can be forgiven, ethical errors tend to end careers and terminate future opportunities. Why is this so? Because unethical behavior eliminates trust, and without trust businesses cannot interact. Second, the most damaging event a business can experience is a loss of the public's confidence in its ethical standards. In finance we have seen several recent examples of such events. It was the ethical scandals involving insider trading at Drexel, Burnham, Lambert that brought down that firm. Then, in 1991 the ethical scandals involving attempts by Salomon Brothers to corner the treasury bill market led to the removal of its top executives and nearly put the company out of business. So, as we embark on our study of finance we encourage you to keep ethics in mind and keep your internal compass handy while thinking through the issues and forming your own opinions.

Beyond the question of ethics is also the question of social responsibility. In general, corporate social responsibility means that a corporation has responsibilities to society at large beyond the maximization of shareholders' wealth. In effect it asserts that a corporation answers to a broader constituency than shareholders alone. As with most debates that center around ethical questions, there is no definitive answer and strong opinions abound. One opinion is voiced by Milton Friedman in the Ethics in Financial Management box, "Milton Friedman on the Social Responsibility of Corporations." Friedman takes the position that since financial managers are employees of the corporation, and the corporation is owned by the shareholders, the financial managers should run the corporation in such a way that shareholder wealth is maximized and then allow the shareholders to decide if they would like to pass on any of the profits to deserving causes. While Friedman presents a strong case, very few corporations consistently act in this way. For example, in 1992 Bristol–Myers Squibb Co. announced it would start an ambitious program to give away heart medications to those who cannot pay for them. This announcement was in the wake of an American Heart Association report that showed that many of the nation's working poor face severe health risks because they cannot afford heart drugs. Clearly, Bristol–Myers Squibb felt it had a social responsibility to provide this medicine to the poor at no cost—a decision with which Friedman would have no doubt disagreed. How do you feel about this decision?

Overview of the Text

This text is divided into seven parts, each dealing with one major area of financial concern:

- The Scope and Environment of Financial Management
- Valuation and the Management of Long-Term Investments
- Financial Structure and Dividend Policy

ETHICS IN FINANCIAL MANAGEMENT

Is It Wrong to Tell a Lie?

A teacher might not be able to change ethical standards in a college classroom, but he or she can teach students how to analyze questions so that they can bring to bear whatever ethical standards they have when they make decisions.

If you haven't already done so, there is no better time than now to develop a rule or set of rules against which you can measure the "rightness" or "wrongness" of your decisions and actions. It may be nothing more provocative than "Do unto others as you would have them do unto you." Or it might be a question or set of questions that you consistently ask: How would I feel about explaining to my parents or children what I did? How would I feel if the action I took were described, in detail, on the front page of my local newspaper? Have I avoided even the appearance that there might be a conflict of interest in my decision? Would my action infringe on the liberty or constitutional rights of others?

Let's begin our look at ethical dilemmas in finance by asking this question: Is it wrong to tell a lie?

One of the roles of the financial manager is to transmit financial information to people outside the company. Occasionally, the facts that the financial man-ager must transmit and explain aren't particularly flattering to the firm. This presents the dilemma of whether or not it is unethical to tell a lie.

For example, at the annual stockholders' meeting a senior financial manager is reviewing her company's financial performance for the previous year. The news is not good. Sales dropped 30 percent, and profits are down 50 percent. A stockholder asks the manager, "What caused this drastic decline and has it been corrected?" The manager knows that the primary cause of the decline was a series of poor top-management decisions made over the past several years, but she also knows that that's not what her colleagues want her to say. Furthermore, she personally believes that the de-cline is far from over, but she recognizes that that's not what the stockholders want to hear.

Should this financial manager lie? Is lying always wrong, or is it acceptable under certain circumstances? What, if any, would those circumstances be? What do *you* think?

Adapted by permission from Stephen P. Robbins, *Management*, 3d ed., p. 11. © copyright 1991 by Prentice Hall, Inc.

ETHICS IN FINANCIAL MANAGEMENT

Milton Friedman on the Social Responsibility of Corporations

In a free-enterprise, private-property system, a corporate executive is an employee of the owners of the business. He has direct responsibility to his employers. That responsibility is to conduct the business in accordance with their desires, which generally will be to make as much money as possible while conforming to the basic rules of the society, both those embodied in law and those embodied in ethical custom. Of course, in some cases his employers may have a different objective. A group of persons might establish a corporation for an eleemosynary purpose—for example, a hospital or a school. The manager of such a corporation will not have money profit as his objective but the rendering of certain services.

In either case, the key point is that, in his capacity as a corporate executive, the manager is the agent of the individuals who own the corporation or establish the eleemosynary instruction, and his primary responsibility is to them.

Needless to say, this does not mean that it is easy to judge how well he is performing his task. But at least the criterion of performance is straightforward, and the persons among whom a voluntary contractual arrangement exists are clearly defined.

Of course, the corporate executive is also a person in his own right. As a person, he may have many other responsibilities that he recognizes or assumes voluntarily—to his family, his conscience, his feelings of charity, his church, his clubs, his city, his country. He may feel impelled by these responsibilities to devote part of his income to causes he regards as worthy, to refuse to work for particular corporations, even to leave his job, for example, to join his country's armed forces. If we wish, we may refer to some of these responsibilities as "social responsibilities." But in these respects he is acting as a principal, not an agent; he is spending his own money or time or energy, not the money of his employers or the time or energy he has contracted to devote to their purposes. If these are "social responsibilities," they are the social responsibilities of individuals, not of business.

What does it mean to say that the corporate executive has a "social responsibility" in his capacity as a businessman? If this statement is not pure rhetoric, it must mean that he is to act in some way that is not in the interest of his employers. For example, that he is to refrain from increasing the price of the product in order to contribute to the social objective of preventing inflation, even though a price increase would be in the best interests of the corporation. Or that he is to make expenditures on reducing pollution beyond the amount that is in the best interests of the corporation or that is required by law in order to contribute to the social objective of improving the environment. Or that, at the expense of corporate profits, he is to hire "hard-core" unemployed instead of better-qualified available workmen to contribute to the social objective of reducing poverty.

In each of these cases, the corporate executive would be spending someone else's money for a general social interest. Insofar as his actions with his "social responsibility" reduce returns to stockholders, he is spending their money. Insofar as his actions raise the price to customers, he is spending the customers' money. Insofar as his actions lower the wages of some employees, he is spending their money.

The stockholders or the customers or the employees could separately spend their own money on the particular actions if they wished to do so. The executive is exercising a distinct "social responsibility," rather than serving as an agent of the stockholders or the customers or the employees, only if he spends the money in a different way than they would have spent it.

But if he does this, he is in effect imposing taxes, on the one hand, and deciding how the tax proceeds shall be spent, on the other.

Source: Milton Friedman, "The Social Responsibility of Business Is to Increase Its Profits," *New York Times Magazine* (September 13, 1970), 33, 122–126. Copyright © 1970 by The New York Times Company. Reprinted by permission.

- Financial Analysis, Planning, and Control
- Working Capital Management
- Long-Term Financing
- Special Topics in Financial Management

Figure 1–1 relates these sections to the financial decision-making process, indicating where each decision is discussed in the text. We describe these sections briefly here.

Part 1: The Scope and Environment of Financial Management

Part 1 begins by discussing the history and role of financial management and develops the goal of the firm, a goal that is to be used in financial decision making. Chapter 2 presents the legal and tax environment in which these decisions are to be made. Since this environment sets the ground rules, it is necessary to understand it before decision principles can be formulated. We will then examine the mathematics of finance and the concept of the time value of money. An understanding of this topic allows us to compare benefits and costs that occur in different time periods.

Part 2: Valuation and the Management of Long-Term Investments

Part 2 examines how the firm and its assets are valued. It looks at valuation models that attempt to explain how different financial decisions affect the firm's stock price. After the valuation principles are established we will discuss the capital budgeting decision, which involves the financial evaluation of investment proposals in fixed assets. We will then introduce methods to incorporate risk into the analysis. Finally, we will examine the financing of a firm's chosen projects, looking at what costs are associated with alternative ways for raising new funds.

Part 3: Financial Structure and Dividend Policy

Part 3 examines the firm's capital structure along with the impact of leverage on returns to the enterprise. Once these relationships between leverage and valuation are developed, we will examine the process of planning the firm's financing mix. This part closes with a discussion of the determination of the dividend–retained earnings decision.

Part 4: Financial Analysis, Planning, and Control

Part 4 introduces the basic financial tools the financial manager uses to maintain control over the firm and its operations. These tools enable the financial manager to locate potential problem areas and plan for the future. Also introduced are the preparation of the cash flow statement and ratio analysis, which allow the financial manager to achieve greater control over ongoing operations.

Part 5: Working Capital Management

The fifth part of the book deals with working-capital management, the management of current assets. We will discuss methods for determining the appropriate investment in cash, marketable securities, inventory, and accounts receivable, as well as the risks associated with these investments, and the control of these risks.

Part 6: Long-Term Financing

Part 6 describes and analyzes the various sources of long-term funding available to the firm, examining both the pros and cons of these sources and their particular characteristics.

Part 7: Special Topics in Financial Management

The final part of the book begins with a discussion of corporate restructuring, including mergers, spinoffs, and leveraged buyouts. It goes on to discuss international financial management, focusing on how financial decisions are affected by the international environment. Finally, the last chapter examines financial management from the perspective of the owner–manager of a small firm.

SUMMARY

This chapter outlines the framework for this book by first tracing the development of financial thought from the turn of the century to the present. During the early part of this century the field of finance reacted to and changed with the prevailing economic environment. Business failures and the Great Depression of the thirties created concern and interest in working-capital management and bankruptcy. More recently, financial innovations and new theoretical developments have continued to reshape financial thought.

Given this historical framework, the chapter examines the goal of the firm. The commonly accepted goal of profit maximization is contrasted with the more complete goal of maximization of shareholder wealth. Because it deals well with uncertainty and time in a real-world environment, the goal of maximization of shareholder wealth is found to be the proper goal for the firm.

Finally, the financial decision-making framework is presented and the format of the book is related to this process. The seven parts of the book are briefly previewed.

STUDY QUESTIONS

1–1. How has financial thought developed over the past century? What factors have affected it?

1–2. What are some of the problems involved in the use of profit maximization as the goal of the firm? How does the goal of maximization of shareholder wealth deal with those problems?

1–3. Compare and contrast the goals of profit maximization and maximization of shareholder wealth.

1–4. Firms often involve themselves in projects that do not result directly in profits; for example, IBM and Mobil Oil frequently support public television broadcasts. Do these projects contradict the goal of maximization of shareholder wealth? Why or why not?

1–5. What is the relationship between financial decision making and risk and return? Would all financial managers view risk–return tradeoffs similarly?

Suggested Application for *DISCLOSURE*®

Access the *Disclosure* database and locate information about Pepsico and Coca-Cola. Read the president's letter and the management discussion for each company. Compare what you learn about both companies. Were you able to determine what management has set as each firm's goal?

CASE PROBLEM

LIVING AND DYING WITH ASBESTOS

WHAT HAPPENS WHEN YOU FIND YOUR MOST PROFITABLE PRODUCT IS DANGEROUS—AN ETHICAL DILEMMA FOR THE FINANCIAL MANAGER

Much of what we deal with in financial management centers around the evaluation of projects—when they should be accepted and when they should be terminated. As new information surfaces regarding the future profitability of a project, the firm always has the choice of terminating that project. When this new information raises the question of whether or not it is ethical to produce a profitable project the decision becomes more difficult. Many times ethical dilemmas pit profits versus ethics. These decisions become even more difficult when continuing to produce the product is within the law.

Asbestos is a fibrous mineral used for fireproofing, electrical insulation, building materials, brake linings, and chemical filters. If you are exposed long enough to asbestos particles—usually ten or more years—you can develop a chronic lung inflammation called asbestosis, which makes breathing difficult and infection easy. Also linked to asbestos exposure is mesethelioma, a cancer of the chest lining. This disease sometimes doesn't develop until forty years after the first exposure. Although the first major scientific conference on the dangers of asbestos was not held until 1964, the asbestos industry knew of the dangers of asbestos sixty years ago.

As early as 1932, the British documented the occupational hazards of asbestos dust inhalation.* Indeed, on September 25, 1935, the editors of the trade journal *Asbestos* wrote to Sumner Simpson, president of Raybestos–Manhattan, a leading asbestos company, asking permission to publish an article on the dangers of asbestos. Simpson refused and later praised the magazine for not printing the article. In a letter to Vandivar Brown, secretary of Johns–Manville, another asbestos manufacturer, Simpson observed: "The less said about asbestos the better off we are." Brown agreed, adding that any article on asbestosis should reflect American, not English, data.

In fact, American data were available, and Brown, as one of the editors of the journal, knew it. Working on behalf of Raybestos–Manhattan and Johns–Manville and their insurance carrier, Metropolitan Life Insurance Company, Anthony Lanza had conducted research between 1929 and 1931 on 126 workers with three or more years of asbestos exposure. But Brown and others were not pleased with the paper Lanza submitted to them for editorial review. Lanza, said Brown, had failed to portray asbestosis as milder than silicosis, a lung disease caused by long-term inhalation of silica dust and resulting in chronic shortness of breath. Under the then-pending Workmen's Compensation law, silicosis was categorized as a compensable disease. If asbestosis was worse than silicosis or indistinguishable from it, then it too would have to be covered. Apparently Brown didn't want this and thus requested that Lanza depict asbestosis as less serious than silicosis. Lanza complied and also omitted from his published report the fact that more than half the workers examined—67 of 126—were suffering from asbestosis.

Meanwhile, Sumner Simpson was writing F. H. Schulter, president of Thermoid Rubber Company, to suggest that several manufacturers sponsor further asbestos experiments. The sponsors, said Simpson, could exercise oversight prerogatives; they "could determine from time to time after the findings are made whether they wish any publication or not." Added Simpson: "It would be a good idea to distribute the information to the medical fraternity, providing it is of the right type and would not injure our companies." Lest there should be any question about the arbiter of publication, Brown wrote to officials at the laboratory conducting the tests:

> It is our further understanding that the results obtained will be considered the property of those who are advancing the required funds, who will determine whether, to what extent and in what manner they shall be made public. In the event it is deemed desirable that the results be made public, the manuscript of your study will be submitted to us for approval prior to publication.

Industry officials were concerned with more than controlling information flow. They also sought to deny workers early evidence of their asbestosis. Dr. Kenneth Smith, medical director of a Johns–Manville plant in Canada, explained why seven workers he found to have asbestosis should not be informed of their disease:

> It must be remembered that although these men have the X-ray evidence of asbestosis, they are working today and definitely are not disabled from asbestosis. They have not been told of this diagnosis, for it is felt that as long as the man feels well, is happy at home and at work, and his physical condition remains good, nothing should be said. When he becomes disabled and sick, then the diagnosis should be made and the claim submitted *by the Company*. The fibrosis of this disease is irreversible and permanent so that eventually compensation will be paid to each of these men. But as long as the man is not disabled, it is felt that he should not be told of his condition so that he can live and work in peace and the Company can benefit by his many years of experience. Should the man be told of his condition today there is a very definite possibility that he would become mentally and physically ill, simply through the knowledge that he has asbestosis.

*See Samuel S. Epstein, "The Asbestos 'Pentagon Papers,'" in Mark Green and Robert Massie, Jr., eds., *The Big Business Reader: Essays on Corporate America* (New York: Pilgrim Press, 1980), pp. 154–65. This article is the primary source of the facts and quotations reported here.

When lawsuits filed by asbestos workers who had developed cancer reached the industry in the 1950s, Dr. Smith suggested that the industry retain the Industrial Health Foundation to conduct a cancer study that would, in effect, squelch the asbestos–cancer connection. The asbestos companies refused, claiming that such a study would only bring further unfavorable publicity to the industry and that there wasn't enough evidence linking asbestos and cancer industry-wide to warrant it.

Shortly before his death in 1977, Dr. Smith was asked whether he had ever recommended to Johns–Manville officials that warning labels be placed on insulation products containing asbestos. He provided the following testimony:

> The reasons why the caution labels were not implemented immediately, it was a business decision as far as I could understand. Here was a recommendation, the corporation is in business to make, to provide jobs for people and make money for stockholders and they had to take into consideration the effects of everything they did, and if the application of a caution label identifying a product as hazardous would cut out sales, there would be serious financial implications. And the powers that be had to make some effort to judge the necessity of the label vs. the consequences of placing the label on the product.

Dr. Smith's testimony and related documents have figured prominently in hundreds of asbestos-related lawsuits, totaling more than $1 billion. In March 1981, a settlement was reached in nine separate lawsuits brought by 680 New Jersey asbestos workers at a Raybestos–Manhattan plant. Several asbestos manufacturers, as well as Metropolitan Life Insurance, were named as defendants. Under the terms of the settlement, the workers affected will share in a $9.4 million court-administered compensation fund. Each worker will be paid compensation according to the length of exposure to asbestos and the severity of the disease contracted.

By 1982 an average of 500 new asbestos cases were being filed each month against Manville (as Johns–Manville was now called), and the company was losing more than half the cases that went to trial. In ten separate cases, juries had also awarded punitive damages, averaging $616,000 a case. By August, 20,000 claims had been filed against the company, and Manville filed for bankruptcy in federal court. This action froze the lawsuits in their place and forced asbestos victims to stand in line with other Manville creditors. After more than three years of legal haggling, Manville's reorganization plan was finally approved by the bankruptcy court. The agreement set up a trust fund valued at approximately $2.5 billion to pay Manville's asbestos claimants. To fund the trust, shareholders were required to surrender half the value of their stock, and the company had to give up much of its projected earnings over the next twenty-five years.†

Claims, however, soon overwhelmed the trust, which ran out of money in 1990. With many victims still waiting for payment, federal Judge Jack B. Weinstein ordered the trust to restructure its payments and renegotiate Manville's contributions to the fund. As a result, the most seriously ill victims will now be paid first, but average payments to victims have been lowered significantly—from $145,000 to $43,000. Meanwhile, the trust's stake in Manville has been increased to 80 percent, and Manville has been required to pay $300 million to it in additional dividends.‡

QUESTIONS

1. Should the asbestos companies be held morally responsible in the sense of being capable of making a moral decision about the ill effects of asbestos exposure? Or does it make sense to consider only the principal people involved as morally responsible—for example, Simpson and Brown?

2. Simpson and Brown presumably acted in what they thought were the best profit interests of their companies. Nothing they did was illegal. On what grounds, if any, are their actions open to criticism?

3. Suppose that Simpson and Brown reasoned this way: "While it may be in our firms' short-term interests to suppress data about the ill effects of asbestos exposure, in the long run it may ruin our companies. We could be sued for millions, and the

†See Robert Mokhiber, *Corporate Crime and Violence* (San Francisco: Sierra Club Books, 1988), pp. 285–86; and Arthur Sharplin, "Manville Lives On as Victims Continue to Die," *Business and Society Review* 65 (Spring 1988), 27–28.

‡"Asbestos Claims to Be Reduced Under New Plan," *Wall Street Journal*, November 20, 1990, p. A4; and "MacNeil–Lehrer Newshour." December 18, 1990.

Adapted by permission: William Shaw and Vincent Barry, *Moral Issues in Business*, 5th ed., pp. 227–30. © 1992 by Wadsworth, Inc.

reputation of the entire industry could be destroyed. So we should reveal the true results of the asbestos-exposure research and let the chips fall where they may." Would that be appropriate?

4. If you were a stockholder in Raybestos–Manhattan or Johns–Manville, would you approve of Simpson and Brown's conduct? If not, why not?

5. "Hands of government" proponents would say that it is the responsibility of government, not the asbestos industry, to ensure health and safety with respect to asbestos. In the absence of appropriate government regulations, asbestos manufacturers have no responsibility other than to operate efficiently. Do you agree?

6. Does Dr. Smith's explanation for concealing from workers the nature of their health problems illustrate how adherence to industry and corporate goals can militate against individual moral behavior? Or do you think Dr. Smith did all he was morally obliged to do as an employee of an asbestos firm? What about Lanza's suppression of data in his report?

7. It has been shown that spouses of asbestos workers can develop lung damage and cancer simply by breathing the fibers carried home on work clothes and that people living near asbestos plants experience higher rates of cancer than the general population does. Would it be possible to assign responsibility for these effects to individual members of asbestos companies? Should the companies themselves by held responsible?

APPENDIX 1A

The Language of Finance: Accounting Statements

As we set the stage for gaining a better understanding of financial management, it is imperative that we know the "language" of finance in describing a company's financial position. To a large extent, the language of finance is contained in the firm's financial or accounting statements. Most of us have been exposed to a basic financial accounting course, where this information is presented; however, let's refresh our memory of these basic statements.

In this appendix, we will:

1. Look at the format of basic financial statements.

2. Review some of the more important accounting principles used in reporting a firm's financial activities.

3. Describe briefly some of the significant relationships in the accounting data from the perspective of a financial manager.

4. Offer a brief caveat about the appropriate use of accounting information, and introduce the free cash flow concept.

Basic Financial Statements

Three financial statements generally serve to depict the financial status of a firm: the balance sheet, the income statement, and the statement of cash flows. The first two statements are described in this appendix, and the last one, the statement of cash flows, is presented in Chapter 12, where we develop in detail a framework for analyzing a company's financial strengths and weaknesses.

Assets

Current assets

Cash	$ 1,400	
Marketable securities—at cost (market value. $320)	300	
Accounts receivable	10,000	
Inventories	12,000	
Prepaid expenses	300	
Total current assets		$24,000

Fixed assets

Land		2,000	
Plant and equipment	$12,300		
Less: Accumulated depreciation	7,300		
Net plant and equipment		5,000	
Total fixed assets			7,000
Total assets			$31,000

Liabilities and Owners' Equity

Current liabilities

Accounts payable	$3,000	
Notes payable, 9%, due March 1, 1993	3,400	
Accrued salaries, wages, and other expenses	3,100	
Current portion of long-term debt	500	
Total current liabilities		$10,000

Long-term liabilities

Deferred income taxes	1,500	
First mortgage bonds, 7%, due January 1, 1999	6,300	
Debentures, 8½%, due June 30, 1999	2,900	
Total long-term liabilities		10,700

Owners' equity

Common stock (par value $1.00)	100	
Additional paid-in capital	2,000	
Retained earnings	8,200	
Total owners' equity		10,300
Total liabilities and owners' equity		$31,000

Balance Sheet

The **balance sheet** represents a statement of the financial position of the firm on a given date, including its asset holdings, liabilities, and owner-supplied capital. Assets represent the resources owned by the firm, whereas liabilities and owners' equity indicate how those resources were financed. Table 1A–1 gives a sample balance sheet for Jimco, Inc., as of December 31, 1992. Jimco had $31 million in assets, which it financed with $10 million in current (short-term) liabilities that must be repaid within the current year, $10,700,000 in noncurrent (long-term) liabilities, and $10,300,000 in owner-supplied funds. (Each term used in the balance sheet is defined in Appendix 1B).

Limitations of the Balance Sheet

A firm's balance sheet is typically prepared within the guidelines of "generally accepted accounting practice."[3] However, we must be aware of certain limitations of the statement. Some of the more notable are listed here.

1. The balance sheet does not reflect current value, because accountants have adopted historical cost as the basis for valuing and reporting assets and liabilities.
2. Estimates must be used to determine the level of several accounts according to different criteria. Examples include accounts receivable estimated in terms of collectibility, inventories based on salability, and fixed (noncurrent) assets based on useful life.[4]
3. The depreciation of long-term assets is accepted practice; however, appreciation or enhancement in asset values is generally ignored.[5] This is particularly crucial to firms holding large investments in appreciable assets such as land, timberlands, and mining properties.
4. Many items that have financial value are omitted from the balance sheet because they involve extreme problems of objective evaluation. The most obvious example consists of the human resources of the firm.[6]

In most cases little can be done to alleviate these shortcomings; however, we should at least be aware of their existence so that we can temper our analysis accordingly.

Income Statement

The **income statement** represents an attempt to measure the net results of the firm's operations over a specified interval, such as one quarter or one year. The income statement (sometimes referred to as a **profit and loss statement**) is compiled on an *accrual basis* rather than a *cash basis*. This means that an attempt is made to match the firm's revenues from the period's operations with the expenses incurred in generating those revenues. A condensed income statement for the year ended December 31, 1992, is provided in Table 1A–2 for Jimco, Inc. (The terms used in the income statement are defined in Appendix 1B.)

In looking at the income statement, it is helpful to think of it as comprising three types of activities: (1) the cost of producing or acquiring

---

[3]The sources of accounting principles are many; however, the main contributors certainly have been the Opinions of the Accounting Principles Board (APB), which was created by the American Institute of Certified Public Accountants (AICPA); and since 1973 the Financial Accounting Standards of the Financial Accounting Standards Board (FASB).

[4]In "Opinion 20" the Accounting Principles Board states that preparing financial statements requires estimating the effects of future events. Examples of items for which estimates are necessary include uncollectible receivables, inventory obsolescence, service lives and salvage values of depreciable assets, warranty costs, periods benefited by a defined cost, and recoverable mineral reserves. Since future events cannot be perceived with certainty, estimating requires the exercise of judgment. The implication here is that no reference guidelines can be constructed regarding these estimates; thus subjectivity enters into determining the affected accounts.

[5]The Tax Act of 1981 created the Accelerated Cost Recovery System (ACRS). This system greatly simplified the determination of asset useful life for cases in which accelerated depreciation (cost recovery) was elected. The ACRS was modified slightly by the TEFRA in 1982. See Chapter 2 for a description of ACRS.

[6]The subject of human resource accounting has received increased attention in recent years. For an overview of the subject, see Edwin H. Caplan and Stephen Landeckich, *Human Resource Accounting: Past, Present, and Future* (New York: National Association of Accountants, 1974); and Eric Flamholtz, *Human Resource Accounting* (Encino, CA: Dickinson, 1974).

Net sales		$51,000
Cost of goods sold		(38,000)
Gross profit		$13,000
Operating expenses		
Selling expenses	$3,100	
Depreciation expense	500	
General and administrative expense	5,400	(9,000)
Net operating income (NOI) or		$ 4,000
Earnings before interest and taxes (EBIT)		
Interest expense		(1,000)
Earnings before taxes (EBT)		$ 3,000
Income taxes[a]		(1,200)
Net income (NI)		$ 1,800
Disposition of net income		
Common stock dividends		$ 300
Change in retained earnings		1,500
Per share data (dollars)		
Number of shares of common stock		100,000 shares
Earnings per common share ($1,800,000 ÷ 100,000 shares)		$ 18
Dividends per common share ($ 300,000 ÷ 100,000 shares)		$ 3

TABLE 1A–2
Jimco, Inc., Statement
of Income for the Year Ended
December 31, 1992
($000 except per share data)

[a]A tax rate of 40% on all income is assumed here for simplicity.

the goods or services sold; (2) the expenses incurred in marketing and distributing the product or service to the customer, along with administrative operating expenses; and (3) the financing costs of doing business, for example, interest expense and dividend payments to the preferred stockholders. These three "income-statement activities" are shown graphically in Figure 1A–1.

Net Income and Cash Flow

As already suggested, the reported revenues and expenses need not represent actual cash flows for the period, so that the computed net earnings for the period do not equal the actual cash provided by the firm's operations. There are two basic reasons why the firm's net income does not equal net cash flow for the period. First, revenues and expenses are included in the income statement even though no cash flow might have occurred. For example, sales revenues consist of credit as well as cash sales. Furthermore, cash collections from prior period credit sales are not reflected in the current period's sales revenues. In addition, the expenses for the period represent all those expenditures made in the process of generating the period's revenues. Thus, wages, salaries, utilities, and other expenses may not be paid during the period in which they are *recognized* in the income statement. Second, certain expenses included within the income statement are not cash expenses at all. For example, depreciation expense does not involve a cash outflow to the firm, yet it is deducted from revenues for the period in computing net income. Other examples of noncash expenses include the amortization of goodwill, patent rights, and bond discounts. Finally, some cash outflows will not be shown as "expenses" in the income statement but will be recorded on the balance sheet as investments, such as plant and equipment. We will elaborate often on the difference between cash flow and net income; however, our focus will be on cash flows, because they form the basis for valuation. We will examine cash flows, also, when we prepare the cash budget in Chapter 13 and when we prepare a statement of cash flows in Chapter 12.

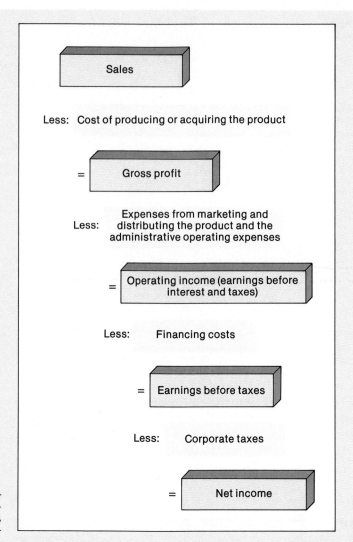

Basic Accounting Principles

A vast number of "generally acceptable accounting principles (GAAP)" have been developed by the accounting profession over the years. These guidelines cover almost every imaginable situation for reporting financially related transactions of the firm. Some of the more important ones for the study of finance include: (1) the historical cost principle; (2) the accrual or matching principle; (3) accounting for inventories and cost of goods sold; and (4) depreciation of fixed assets.

Historical Cost Principle

The **historical cost principle** provides the basis for determining the book values of the firm's balance sheet accounts. The primary advantage of historical cost is its objectivity. Its primary disadvantage is that the asset balances do not correspond to market values or replacement costs. Furthermore, since asset book values are not equal to market values, the book value of owners' equity does not equal its market value. In analyzing the firm's financial statements, the analyst must keep in mind that asset balances reflect historical costs of the related assets and not current market values.

Accrual or Matching Principle

To compute net income for a given year's operations, accountants must identify all revenue and expense items that belong within that year. The **accrual basis of accounting** attempts to allocate revenue and expense properly among the years that an enterprise is in operation. This method utilizes the **revenue realization principle** to assure that revenue is recognized in the period in which it is earned, and it uses the **matching principle** to determine the amount of expenses necessary during the period for the revenue to be generated. These expenses are thus *matched* against revenue for the period. The basic principle, therefore, is "Let the expense follow the revenue." Thus, wage expense is not recognized when it is paid nor necessarily when work is performed, but when the work performed actually contributes to revenues.

An example of the potential difficulties posed for the analyst by the matching principle can be found in the depreciation policies followed by different firms for like assets. For example, one major U.S. airline, airline A, depreciates its planes over 10 years. Another major U.S. airline, airline B, depreciates over as long as 16 years. Other things being equal, airline A would report higher expenses and lower profits from its operations than would airline B. Depreciation methods are discussed in Chapter 2.

Accounting for Inventories and Cost of Goods Sold

Several methods can be used to determine a firm's cost of goods sold. Each relates to the basis used in valuing the firm's inventory, since the firm's purchases that are *not* passed through the income statement as cost of goods sold remain in the firm's inventory account. We will discuss two common methods for determining the cost of goods sold and consequently the value of the inventory account. The first involves assigning to the period's cost of goods sold the prices paid for the oldest items of inventory held by the firm at the beginning of the period. This is commonly referred to as the **first-in, first-out, or FIFO,** method. The second assigns the cost of the most recently purchased inventory items to the period's cost of goods sold. This is called the **last-in, first-out, or LIFO,** method. The method selected can have a material effect on the firm's computed net earnings during a period in which the prices of its purchases consistently rose or fell. For example, in a period when prices have been rising, the use of the FIFO method results in a lower cost of goods sold, a larger gross profit, a higher tax liability, a higher inventory amount, and a higher net earnings figure than LIFO. LIFO, which costs the firm's sale items using the most recent prices paid by the firm, will result in a lower inventory amount, a higher cost of goods sold figure, and, consequently, lower gross profits, lower taxes, and lower net earnings. The opposite result would follow should prices have fallen during the period.

What importance should be attached to the choice of methods for determining cost of goods sold? Under either method the cash flows that result from sales will be the same, for the actual cost of the items sold does not vary with the method chosen for computing cost of goods sold. However, a very real cash flow effect can result in terms of the amount of taxes that the firm must pay. During a period of rising prices LIFO results in lower profits and, consequently, lower taxes being paid than does

FIFO, while during a period of falling prices the opposite is true.[7] Further-more, it should be noted that the reported inventory amounts may vary considerably with the application of one method as compared with the other—but the physical quantity and composition of the goods are not affected.

Depreciation of Fixed Assets

Depreciation expense represents an allocation of the cost of a fixed asset over its useful life. The objective is to match such costs with the revenues that result from their utilization in the enterprise. Furthermore, depreciation expense is used to reduce the balance sheet book value of the firm's fixed assets. Thus, the method used to determine depreciation expense also serves as the basis for determining the book value of fixed assets. The methods commonly used for computing depreciation are straight-line, double-declining balance, and the accelerated cost recovery system. These depreciation methods will be discussed in Chapter 2, when we look at depreciation as a tax-deductible expense.

Important Relationships in Accounting Data

As previously noted, the financial manager makes extensive use of the firm's accounting information. Chapter 12 outlines in detail how the firm uses such information. It will be helpful, however, to look briefly at some of the more important accounting relationships as a basis for understanding capital budgeting, working capital management, and other key areas.

An almost unlimited number of relationships could be considered. However, there are at least three relationships that might have the most important effect on firm and shareholder value. These are:

1. *The amount of operating profits per dollar of sales.*[8] This relationship indicates management's ability to control both cost of goods sold and operating expenses (such as selling and administrative expenses) relative to sales. This relationship is vitally important to a firm's financial well-being and bears upon the value investors are willing to place on the company.

2. *The amount of the firm's assets compared to its sales.* This relationship tells us how efficiently management is using the firm's assets to create sales. All companies must make an investment in assets so that they can generate sales. You cannot have any significant amount of sales without investing in assets, such as accounts receivables, inventories, equipment, and possibly real estate. However, your preference is to invest less rather than more.

3. *Debt to equity.* We shall see later that the use of debt increases the

---

[7]The Internal Revenue Service does not allow frequent changes in inventory policy. Once a policy has been adopted, it may not be changed without the Commissioner's consent. Furthermore, changing the inventory costing method solely for the purpose of reducing taxes is not accepted by the Internal Revenue Service. Instead, the taxpayer must show that the new method more closely matches revenues with cost of goods sold. See Regulation 1.471–2 of the Internal Revenue Code for a more detailed discussion.

[8]The term *profits* is used interchangeably with earnings or income.

risk exposure for the company's investors. The increased risk then affects the investors' required rate of return on their investments, and may thereby alter the firm's value.[9] Thus, the ratio of debt to equity is an important relationship for the financial manager.

A Word of Caution

While accounting information is vital in our study of a company's finances, a large body of evidence suggests that investors (stockholders) look behind accounting numbers to discover the underlying economic reality of a firm's performance. Thus, the economic reality of a firm's operations is ultimately reflected in the cash flow it provides to its investors, not in its reported earnings. Specifically, we will identify the firm's **free cash flow** to be the amount of cash that is available for distributing to its investors not only after operating expenses have been paid but after any investments have been made that will generate future cash flow. Free cash flow can be formulated as follows:

$$\text{Free cash flow} = \text{Operating profits} - \text{Income taxes} - \text{Additional investment in assets}$$

Throughout our study, we will refer to the firm's free cash flow. It is a basic concept in financial management.

---

[9]The relationship between a firm's use of debt and the value of the firm is a complex one, which will be studied in depth in later chapters.

Glossary of Accounting Terms

accelerated depreciation A term encompassing any method for computing depreciation expense wherein the charges decrease with time. Examples of accelerated methods include sum-of-the-years' digits and double-declining balance, as contrasted with straight-line.

accounts payable A current liability representing the total amount owed by a firm from its past (unpaid) credit purchases.

accounts receivable A current asset including all monies owed to a firm from past (uncollected) credit sales.

accrual basis of accounting The method of recognizing revenues when the earning process is virtually complete and when an exchange transaction has occurred, and recognizing expenses as they are incurred in generating those revenues. Thus, revenues and expenses recognized under the accrual basis of accounting are independent of the time when cash is received or expenditures are made. This contrasts with the cash basis of accounting.

accrued salaries and wages Salary and wage expense the firm owes but has not yet paid (a current liability).

accumulated depreciation The sum of depreciation charges on an asset since its acquisition. This total is deducted from gross fixed assets to compute net fixed assets. This balance sheet entry is sometimes referred to as the reserve for depreciation, accrued depreciation, or the allowance for depreciation.

ACRS Accelerated Cost Recovery System. (See Chapter 2, Appendix 2A.)

administrative expense An expense category used to report expenses incurred by the firm but not reflected in specific activities such as manufacturing or selling.

amortizing The procedure followed in allocating the cost of long-lived assets to the periods in which their benefits are derived. For fixed assets the amortization is called depreciation expense, whereas for wasting assets (natural resources) it is called depletion expense.

asset Anything of commercial value that is owned by a firm or individual.

authorized capital stock The total number of shares of stock the firm can issue, it is specified in the articles of incorporation.

bad debt expense An adjustment to income and accounts receivable reflecting the value of uncollectible accounts.

balance sheet A statement of financial position on a particular date. The balance sheet equation is as follows: total assets = total liabilities + owners' equity.

bond Long-term debt instrument carried on the balance sheet at its face amount or par value (usually $1,000 per bond), which is payable at maturity. The coupon rate on the bond is the percentage of the bond's face value payable in interest each year. Bonds usually pay interest semiannually.

book value The net amount of an asset shown in the accounts of a firm. When referring to an entire firm, it relates the excess of total assets over total liabilities (also referred to as owners' equity and net worth).

capital Sometimes, the total assets of a firm; at other times, the owners' equity alone.

capital stock All shares of outstanding common and preferred stock.

capitalization Stockholders' equity plus the par value of outstanding bonds.

cash basis of accounting An accounting system that recognizes income and expenses on a cash (when received and paid) rather than accrual basis.

cash flow The excess (deficiency) of cash receipts over cash disbursements for a given period.

common stock The stock interest of the residual owners of the firm. These owners have claim to earnings and asset values remaining after the claims of all creditors and preferred stockholders are satisfied.

cost of goods sold The total cost allocated to the production of a completed product for the period.

current assets Assets that are normally converted into cash within the operating cycle of the firm (normally a period of one year or less). Such items as cash, accounts receivable, marketable securities, prepaid expenses, and inventories are frequently found among a firm's current assets.

current liabilities Liabilities or debts of the firm that must be paid within the firm's normal operating cycle (usually one year or less), such as accounts and notes payable, income taxes payable, and wages and salaries payable.

debentures Long-term debt (bonds) that are secured only by the integrity of the issuer (that is, no specific assets are pledged as collateral).

deferred income taxes Income taxes that a firm recognizes as being owed based on its earnings but that are not payable until a later date.

depreciable life The period over which an asset is depreciated.

depreciation expense Amortization of plant, property, and equipment cost during an accounting period.

dividend A distribution of earnings to the owners of a corporation in the form of cash (cash dividend) or share of stock (stock dividend).

double-declining balance depreciation A method for computing declining balance depreciation expense in which the constant percentage is equal to $2/N$, where N represents the depreciable life of the asset.

earnings A synonym for net income or net profit after taxes. Owing to the ambiguity that arises in using the general term earnings, it is usually avoided in favor of more specific terms such as net operating earnings or earnings after taxes.

earnings after taxes (EAT) Other terms often used synonymously are net income and net profit after taxes.

earnings before interest and taxes (EBIT) A commonly used synonym for net operating income. Note that where other income exists, EBIT equals net operating income plus other income.

earnings before taxes (EBT) Total net earnings after the deduction of all tax-deductible expenses.

earnings per share (EPS) Net income after taxes available to the common stockholders (after preferred dividends) divided by the number of outstanding common shares.

equity financing The raising of funds through the sale of common or preferred stock.

extraordinary item A revenue or expense that is both unusual in nature and infrequent in occurrence. Such items and their tax effects are separated from ordinary income in the income statement.

FIFO A method for determining the inventory cost assigned to cost of goods sold wherein the cost of the oldest items in inventory is charged to the period's cost of goods sold (first in, first out). Ending inventories therefore will reflect the prices paid for the most recent purchases. See also the discussion in Appendix 1A.

fixed assets These assets share the characteristic that they are not converted into cash within a single operating cycle of the firm; they include buildings, equipment, and land.

historical cost principle The principle that assets and activities in the balance sheet and income statement and recorded at their historical purchase cost rather than current market value.

general and administrative expenses Expenses associated with the managerial and policy-making aspects of a business.

goodwill Included as an asset entry in the balance sheet to reflect the excess over fair market value paid for the assets of an acquired firm.

gross profit The excess of net sales over cost of goods sold.

income statement The statement of profit or loss for the period comprised of net revenues less expenses for the period. (See **accrual basis of accounting.**)

income tax An annual expense incurred by the firm. This is based on income and paid to a governmental entity.

intangible asset An asset that lacks physical substance, such as goodwill or a patent.

interest expense The price paid for borrowed money over some specified period of time.

inventory The balance in an asset account such as raw materials, work in process, or finished goods. (See **LIFO** and **FIFO.**)

lease A contract requiring payments by the user (lessee) to its owner (lessor) for the use of an asset. In accordance with FASB Statement 13 most financial lease agreements entered into after January 1, 1977, must be included in the assets and liabilities of the lessee's balance sheet. The right of the lessee to use the asset is represented by an asset called a lease-hold.

liability An obligation to pay a specified amount to a creditor in return for some current benefit.

LIFO A method for determining the inventory cost assigned to cost of goods sold whereby the cost of the most recent purchases of inventory is assigned to the period's cost of goods sold (last-in, first-out). Ending inventories thus contain the cost of the oldest items of inventory.

liquid assets Those assets of the firm that can easily be converted into cash with little or no loss in value. Generally included are cash, marketable securities, and sometimes accounts receivable.

long-term debt All liabilities of the firm that are not due and payable within one year. Examples include installment notes, equipment loans, and bonds payable.

marketable securities The securities (bonds and stocks) of other firms and governments held by a firm.

net income See **earnings after taxes (EAT).**

net operating income (NOI) Income earned by a firm in the course of its normal operations. Calculated as net sales less the sum of cost of goods sold and operating expenses.

net plant and equipment Gross plant and equipment less accumulated depreciation.

net sales Gross sales less returns, allowances, and cash discounts taken by customers.

notes payable A liability (normally short term) of the firm, representing a monetary indebtedness.

operating expense Any expense incurred in the normal operation of a firm.

owners' equity Total assets minus total liabilities, sometimes referred to as net worth.

paid-in capital The excess of total capital paid in over the stock's par or stated value. For example, if a share of stock with a $1 par value is sold by a firm for $10, the common stock account will be increased by $1 and paid-in capital will rise by $9.

par value The face value of a security.

patent The rights to the benefits of one's invention granted to the inventor by the government. These rights are extended for a maximum of 17 years.

preferred stock The capital stock of the owners of the firm whose claim on assets and income is secondary to that of bondholders but preferred as to that of the common stockholders.

profit and loss statement Another name for the income statement.

retained earnings The sum of a firm's net income over its life less all dividends paid.

selling expense An expense incurred in the selling of a firm's product. Examples include salespeople's commissions and advertising expenditures.

sinking fund Assets and their earnings set aside to retire long-term debt obligations of the firm. Payments into sinking funds are made after taxes and are usually described in the bond indenture (contract between the borrowing firm and the bond holders).

stock dividend A dividend that results in a transfer of retained earnings to the capital stock and paid-in capital accounts. This contrasts with a cash dividend. (See **dividend.**)

CHAPTER 2

Financial Markets, Business Organization, and the Tax Environment

An Introduction to Financial Markets ● Legal Forms of Business Organization
● Federal Income Taxation ● Appendix 2B: Methods of Depreciation

During the 1980s the business environment changed dramatically. Perhaps at no time since the Great Depression of the 1930s has corporate America undergone such a restructuring. Continuous and rapid change is now the norm as competition worldwide increases rapidly in the product markets as well as in the financial markets. It is essential in this volatile setting that the financial manager have a good grasp of the basic elements of the business environment. In this chapter, we will examine three of these elements:

1. The **financial markets,** where firms seek financing for their investments. We will review three basic concepts: the role of opportunity costs in determining interest rates, the impact of inflation on interest rates, and the relationship between interest rates and the length of time until a security matures, which we call the *term-to-maturity*. In Chapter 4, we will discuss the relationship between risk and rate of return, and in Chapter 18 we will consider the institutional setting in which firms buy and sell securities.

2. The basic legal forms of **business organization** that firms use to shape and support their activities. We will focus our attention on the sole proprietorship, the partnership, and the corporation.

3. Key elements of the corporate **tax environment,** or tax code. These elements are important influences on business behavior.

An Introduction to Financial Markets

Financial markets are made up of the institutions and procedures that nonfinancial companies use to raise funds for investments. Financial markets bring together net savers and net users of funds. For example, life insurance companies are net savers when their premium income exceeds the claims they must pay on policies they have sold. On the other hand, growing companies are frequently net users of funds because their expenditures often exceed their income. A growth company might borrow funds (i.e., sell debt securities) from the insurance company. This act is a typical financial market transaction. Chapter 18, on raising funds in the capital markets, details such investment banking transactions. Here, however, we will focus on how rates of return are determined in the financial markets.

Net users of funds must compete with one another for the funds supplied by net savers. Consequently, to obtain financing a firm must offer the supplier a rate of return competitive with the next best investment alternative. We refer to the rate of return on this next best investment alternative as the supplier's **opportunity cost of funds.** The opportunity cost concept is crucial in financial management, and we will refer to it often.

Perspective in Finance

Opportunity cost is the single most important concept in financial management. It matters not that your firm's debt has a cost of 12 percent; the more important issue in making financial decisions is what it would cost the firm to issue the debt today. Put another way, would you loan a firm money at 13 percent if you could earn 15 percent on a similar investment? Not if you have any "smarts."

Observing Rates of Return in the Financial Markets

History can tell us a great deal about the returns that investors earn in the financial markets. A primary source for a historical perspective comes from Ibbotson and Sinquefield's *Stocks, Bonds, Bills, and Inflation,* which examines the realized rates of return for a wide variety of securities spanning the period from 1926 through 1990.[1] As part of their study, Ibbotson and Sinquefield calculated the average annual rates of return investors earned over the preceding 64 years, along with the average inflation rate for the same time period. They also calculated the standard deviations of the returns for each type of security. The concept of standard deviation comes from our statistical colleagues, who use this measurement to indicate quantitatively how much dispersion or variability there is around the mean, or average, value of the item being measured—in this case, the rates of return in the financial markets.

Ibbotson and Sinquefield's results are summarized in Figure 2–1. These returns represent the average inflation rate and the average observed rates of return for different types of securities. The average inflation rate was 3.2 percent for the period covered by the study. We will refer to this rate as the "inflation-risk premium." The investor who earns only the rate of inflation has earned no "real return." That is, the *real return* is the return earned above the rate of increase in the general price level for goods and services in the economy, which is the inflation rate. In addition to the danger of not earning above the inflation rate, investors are concerned about the risk of the borrower defaulting or failing to repay the loan when due. Thus, we would expect a default-risk premium for long-term corporate bonds over long-term government bonds. The premium for 1926 to 1990 as shown in Figure 2–1, was 0.6 percent, or what is called 60 basis points (5.5 percent on long-term corporate bonds − 4.9 percent on long-term government bonds). We would also expect an even greater risk premium for common stocks vis-à-vis long-term corporate bonds, since the variability in average returns is greater for common stocks. The Ibbotson and Sinquefield study verifies such a risk premium, with common stocks (all firms) earning 6.6

[1]Roger G. Ibbotson and Rex A. Sinquefield, *Stocks, Bonds, Bills, and Inflation: Historical Returns* (Chicago: Dow Jones–Irwin, 1991).

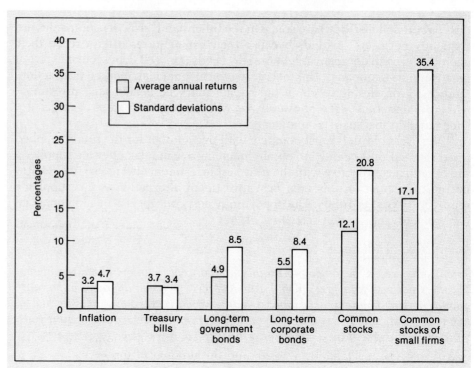

FIGURE 2–1.
Average Annual Returns and
Standard Deviations of Returns

Source: Roger G. Ibbotson and Rex
A. Singuefield, *Stocks, Bonds, Bills,
and Inflation: Historical Returns* (Chicago: Dow Jones–Irwin, 1991. © Ibbotson Associates.)

percent more than the rate earned on long-term corporate bonds (12.1 percent for common stocks − 5.5 percent for long-term coporate bonds). Finally, there is even a greater risk premium associated with the common stock of small firms (5 percent) when compared with all common stocks. This small firm or "size" risk premium probably reflects the lack of information available for small firms.

Remember that these returns are "averages" across many securities and over an extended period of time. However, these averages reflect the conventional wisdom regarding risk premiums—the greater the risk, the greater will be the expected returns. Such a relationship is shown in Figure 2–2, where the average returns are plotted against their standard deviations; note that higher average returns have historically been associated with higher dispersion in these returns.

FIGURE 2–2.
Rates of Return 1926–90

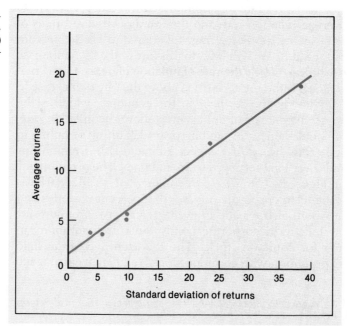

The Effects of Inflation on Rates of Return

When a rate of interest is quoted, it is generally the nominal, or observed rate. The **real rate of interest,** on the other hand, represents the rate of increase in actual purchasing power, after adjusting for inflation. For example, if you have $100 today and loan it to someone for a year at a nominal rate of interest of 11.3 percent, you will get back $111.30 in one year. But if during the year prices of goods and services rise by 5 percent, it will take $105 at year end to purchase the same goods and services that $100 purchased at the beginning of the year. What was your increase in purchasing power over the year? The quick and dirty answer is found by subtracting the inflation rate from the nominal rate, 11.3% − 5% = 6.3%, but this is not exactly correct. To be more precise, let the nominal rate of interest be represented by r, the anticipated rate of inflation by i, and the real rate of interest by R. Using these notations, we can express the relationship between the nominal interest rate, the rate of inflation, and the real rate of interest as follows:

$$1 + r = (1 + R)(1 + i) \tag{2-1}$$

or
$$r = R + i + iR$$

Consequently, the nominal rate of interest *(r)* is equal to the sum of the real rate of interest *(R)*, the inflation rate *(i)*, and the product of the real rate and the inflation rate. This relationship between nominal rates, real rates, and the rate of inflation has come to be called the **Fisher effect.**[2] It means that the observed nominal rate of interest includes both the real rate and an *inflation premium*.

Substituting into equation (2–1) using a nominal rate of 11.3 percent and an inflation rate of 5 percent, we can calculate the real rate of interest, R, as follows:

$$r = R + i + iR$$
$$.113 = R + .05 + .05R$$
$$R = .06 = 6\%$$

Thus, at the new higher prices, your purchasing power will have increased by only 6 percent, although you have $11.30 more than you had at the start of the year. To see why, let's assume that at the outset of the year one unit of the market basket of goods and services costs $1, so you could purchase 100 units with your $100. At the end of the year you have $11.30 more, but each unit now costs $1.05 (remember the 5 percent rate of inflation). How many units can you buy at the end of the year? The answer is $111.30 ÷ $1.05 = $106, which represents a 6 percent increase in real purchasing power.[3]

The Term Structure of Interest Rates

The·relationship between a debt security's rate of return and the length of time until the debt matures is known as the **term structure of interest rates** or the **yield to maturity.** For the relationship to be meaningful to us, all the factors other than maturity, meaning factors such as the chance of the bond defaulting, must be held constant. Thus, the term structure reflects observed rates or yields on similar securities, except for the length of time until maturity, at a particular moment in time.

Figure 2–3 shows an example of the term structure of interest rates. The curve is upward sloping, indicating that longer terms to maturity command higher returns, or yields. In this hypothetical term structure, the rate of interest on a 5-year note or bond is 11.5 percent, whereas the comparable rate on a 20-year bond is 13 percent.

---

[2]This relationship was analyzed many years ago by Irving Fisher.
[3]In Chapter 3 we will study more about the time value of money.

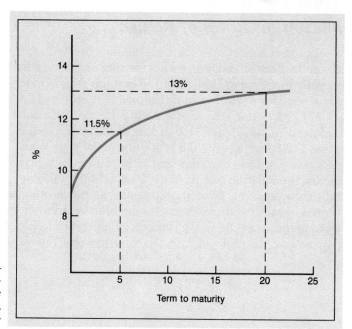

FIGURE 2–3.
The Term Structure
of Interest Rates

Observing Historical Term Structures of Interest Rates

As we might expect, the term structure of interest rates changes over time, depending on the environment. The particular term structure observed today may be quite different from the term structure a month ago and different still from the term structure one month from now.[4] A perfect example of the changing term structure, or yield curve, was witnessed during the early days of the Persian Gulf crisis in August 1990. Figure 2–4 shows the yield curves one day prior to the Iraqi invasion of Kuwait and then again just three weeks later. The change is noticeable, particularly for long-term interest rates. Investors quickly developed new fears about the prospect of increased inflation to be caused by the crisis and consequently increased their required rates of return.

Although the upward sloping term structure curves in Figures 2–3 and 2–4 are the ones most commonly observed, yield curves can assume several

[4]For a discussion of the problems involved in actually estimating the term structure at any point in time, see Willard T. Carleton and Ian A. Cooper, "Estimation and Uses of the Term Structure of Interest Rates," *Journal of Finance* 31 (September 1976), 1067–1084.

FIGURE 2–4.
Changes in the Term Structure
of Interest Rates for
Government Securities at the
Outbreak of the Persian Gulf
Crisis

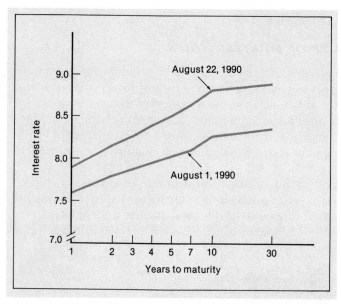

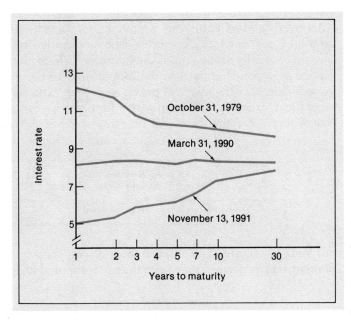

FIGURE 2–5.
Historical Term Structures of Interest Rates for Government Securities

shapes. Sometimes the term structure is downward sloping; at other times it rises and then falls (hump-backed); and at still other times it may be relatively flat. Figure 2–5 shows some yield curves at different points in time.

Trying to Explain the Shape of the Term Structure

A number of theories may explain the shape of the term structure of interest rates at any point in time. Three possible explanations are prominent: (1) the unbiased expectations theory, (2) the liquidity preference theory, and (3) the market segmentation theory.[5] Let's look at each in turn.

The Unbiased Expectations Theory

The **unbiased expectations theory** says that the term structure is determined by an investor's expectations about future interest rates.[6] To see how this works, consider the following investment problem faced by Mary Maxell. Mary has $10,000 that she wants to invest for two years, at which time she plans to use her savings to make a downpayment on a new home. Wanting not to take any risk of losing her savings, she decides to invest in U.S. government securities. She has two choices. First, she can purchase a government security that matures in two years, which offers her an interest rate of nine percent per year.[7] If she does this, she will have $11,881 in two years, calculated as follows:[8]

Principal amount	$10,000
Plus: Year 1 interest (.09 × $10,000)	900
Principal plus interest at the end of year 1	$10,900
Plus: Year 2 interest (.09 × $10,900)	981
Principal plus interest at the end of year 2	$11,881

[5]See Richard Roll, *The Behavior of Interest Rates: An Application of the Efficient Market Model to U.S. Treasury Bills* (New York: Basic Books, 1970).

[6]Irving Fisher thought of this idea in 1896. The theory was later refined by J. R. Hicks in *Value and Capital* (London: Oxford University Press, 1946) and F. A. Lutz and V. C. Lutz in *The Theory of Investment in the Firm* (Princeton, NJ: Princeton University Press, 1951).

[7]When the U.S. government, and other governments as well, issue securities to help finance government expenses, they issue these securities with different times to maturity, depending on the government's funding needs.

[8]We could also calculate the principal plus interest for Mary's investment using the following compound interest equation: $10,000(1 + .09)^2 = $11,881$. We will study the mathematics of compound interest in Chapter 3.

Alternatively, Mary could buy a government security maturing in one year that pays an 8 percent rate of interest. She would then need to purchase another one-year security at the end of the first year. Which alternative Mary will prefer obviously depends in part on the rate of interest she expects to receive on the government security she will purchase a year from now. We cannot tell Mary what the interest rate will be in a year; however, we can at least calculate the rate that will give her the same two-year total savings she would get from her first choice, or $11,881. The interest rate can be calculated as follows:

Savings needed in two years	$11,881
Savings at the end of the first year	
$10,000(1 + .08)	10,800
Interest needed in year two	$ 1,081

For Mary to receive $1,081 in the second year, she would have to earn about 10 percent on her second-year investment, computed as follows:

$$\frac{\text{interest received in year 2}}{\text{investment made at beginning of year 2}} = \frac{\$1,081}{\$10,800} = 10\%$$

So the term structure of interest rates for our example consists of the one-year interest rate of 8 percent and the two-year rate of 9 percent, which is shown in Figure 2–6. This exercise also gives us information about the *expected* one-year rate for investments made one year hence. In a sense, the term structure contains implications about investor expectations of future interest rates; thus, this explains the unbiased expectations theory of the term structure of interest rates.

Although we can see a relationship between current interest rates with different maturities and the investor's expectations about future interest rates, is this the whole story? Are there influences other than the investor's expectations about future interest rates? Probably, so let's continue to think about Mary's dilemma.

Liquidity Preference Theory

In presenting Mary's choices, we have suggested that she would be indifferent to a choice between the two-year government security offering a 9 percent return and two consecutive one-year investments offering 8 and 10 percent, respectively. However, that would be so only if she is unconcerned about the risk

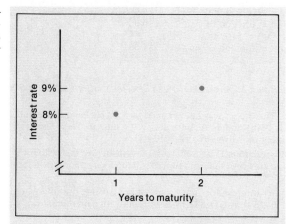

FIGURE 2–6.
Term Structure of Interest Rates

associated with not knowing the rate of interest on the second security as of today. If Mary is risk averse (that is, she dislikes risk), she might not be satisfied with expectations of a 10 percent return on the second one-year government security. She might require some additional expected return to be truly indifferent. Mary might in fact decide that she will expose herself to the uncertainty of future interest rates only if she can reasonably *expect* to earn an additional .5 percent in interest, or 10.5 percent, on the second one-year investment. This *risk premium* (additional required interest rate) to compensate for the risk of changing future interest rates is known as a **liquidity premium;** and this concept underlies the liquidity preference theory of the term structure. In the **liquidity preference theory,** investors require liquidity premiums to compensate them for buying securities that expose them to the risks of fluctuating interest rates.

Market Segmentation Theory

The **market segmentation theory** is the third popular theory of the term structure of interest rates.[9] This concept is built on the notion that legal restrictions and personal preferences limit choices for investors to certain ranges of maturities. For example, commercial banks prefer short- to medium-term maturities as a result of the short-term nature of their deposit liabilities.

---

[9]An early advocate of this theory was J. M. Culbertson, "The Term Structure of Interest Rates," *Quarterly Journal of Economics* 71 (November 1957), 489–504.

They prefer not to invest in long-term securities. Life insurance companies, on the other hand, have longer-term liabilities, so they prefer longer maturities in investments. At the extreme, the market segmentation theory implies that the rate of interest for a particular maturity is determined solely by demand and supply for a given maturity and that it is independent of the demand and supply for securities having different maturities. A more moderate version of the theory allows investors strong maturity preferences, but it also allows them to modify their feelings and preferences if significant yield inducements occur.[10]

This brief explanation of the financial markets will meet our needs until later, when we look closely at the process of issuing stocks and bonds in the financial markets. For now, we have introduced the importance of the financial markets as a basis for much that will come later.

Legal Forms of Business Organization

Legal forms of business organization are diverse and numerous. However, there are three basic categories: the sole proprietorship, the partnership, and the corporation. We will look at the relative importance of each form in the economy, then examine the nature of each and how to judge the best form for a particular company.

The Economic Significance of Organizational Forms

The economic significance of each type of business organization (sole proprietorship, partnership, and corporation) can be assessed in several ways. The most simple way is the number and dollar activity of each form. Table 2–1 offers us some insights for the period from 1970 through 1987, the most recent year for which data are available, and Figure 2–7 provides an overview of these statistics for 1987.[11] The information lets us weigh the significance of each type of organization, from which we can make the following observations:

1. The predominant form of business organization in the United States in pure numbers is by far the sole proprietorship, which comprised 71

---

[10]See, for example, Franco Modigliani and Richard Sutch, "Innovations in Interest Rate Policy," *American Economic Review* (May 1966), 178–97.
[11]U.S. Internal Revenue Service, *Statistics of Income, Corporation Income Tax Returns*, and *Statistics of Income Bulletin*, 1990.

TABLE 2–1. Proprietorships, Partnerships, and Corporations 1970–87

Year	Number and Percentage of Business			Dollar Amount (Billions) and Percentage of Sales			Dollar Amount (Billions) and Percentage of Profits		
	Proprietorship	Partnership	Corporation	Proprietorship	Partnership	Corporation	Proprietorship	Partnership	Corporation
1970	9,400	936	1,665	238	93	1,751	33	10	66
	78.33%	7.80%	13.87%	11.43%	4.47%	84.10%	30.28%	9.17%	60.55%
1975	10,882	1,073	2,024	339	147	3,199	45	8	143
	77.85%	7.68%	14.48%	9.2%	3.99%	86.81%	22.96%	4.08%	72.96%
1980	12,702	1,380	2,711	506	292	6,361	55	8	239
	75.64%	8.22%	16.14%	7.07%	4.08%	88.85%	18.21%	2.65%	79.14%
1985	11,929	1,714	3,277	540	368	8,398	79	−9	240
	70.50%	10.13%	19.37%	5.80%	3.95%	90.24%	25.48%	−2.90%	77.42%
1986	12,394	1,703	3,429	559	397	8,669	90	−17	270
	70.72%	9.72%	19.57%	5.81%	4.12%	90.07%	26.24%	−4.96%	78.72%
1987	13,091	1,650	3,612	611	474	9,581	105	−5	328
	71.33%	8.99%	19.68%	5.73%	4.44%	89.83%	24.53%	−1.17%	76.64%

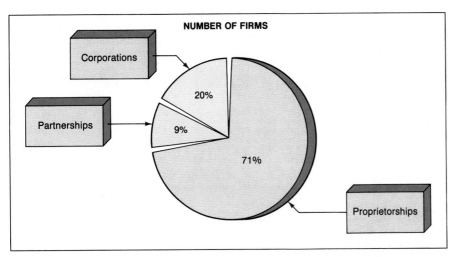

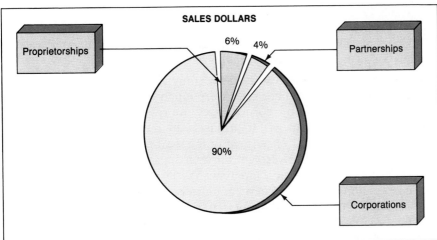

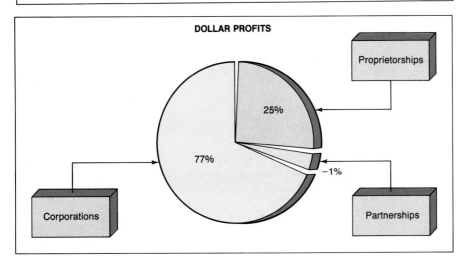

FIGURE 2–7.
Organizational Forms by
Number, Sales, and Profits

percent of the three forms in 1987. A distant second was the corporation at slightly above 19 percent, and last, the partnership at 9 percent.

2. From 1970 to 1987 the number of corporations more than doubled, which represents a 4.7 percent annual increase. The number of sole proprietorships, on the other hand, increased only 2 percent per annum. The lackluster growth in sole proprietorships can be attributed to the large reduction in these organizational forms in the single year of 1981 (not shown in the table), when the number of proprietorships fell 25 percent. The fallout probably came as a result of the recession, which affects the

TABLE 2–2. Organizational Forms by Industry in 1987

Industry	Percentage of Businesses			Dollar Amount of Sales		
	Proprietorship	Partnership	Corporation	Proprietorship	Partnership	Corporation
Agriculture	57.58%	23.76%	18.66%	15.57%	7.30%	77.12%
Mining	60.92	22.99	16.09	6.12	14.19	79.68
Construction	79.07	3.00	17.93	16.00	4.71	79.29
Manufacturing	52.25	5.08	42.67	0.63	1.08	98.29
Transport., & Pub. Util.	78.45	3.63	17.92	3.78	2.52	93.70
Wholesale & Retail	67.18	5.25	27.57	7.26	2.37	90.37
Fin, Insur., & Real Est.	47.59	32.17	20.24	4.27	12.53	83.20
Services	80.90	3.94	15.16	20.02	12.70	67.27

survival of smaller firms (sole proprietorships) more than larger businesses (corporations). Finally, the number of partnerships increased 3.4 percent per year.

3. From 1970 to 1987, sales activities of proprietorships declined from 11.4 percent to 5.7 percent. At the same time, corporations increased their share of sales from 84 percent to 90 percent. Partnership sales as a percentage of all sales essentially remained unchanged.

4. Although proprietorships garnered only about 6 percent of all sales in 1987, the profits on these sales were much larger on a relative basis than those experienced by corporations. More specifically, proprietorships captured 25 percent of all profits from only 6 percent of total sales; corporations earned 77 percent of the total profits from 90 percent of all sales. Stated differently, sole proprietorships in 1987 earned about $.17 on each dollar of sales or 17 percent ($105 billion/$611 billion), whereas corporations earned 3.4 percent on sales ($328 billion/$9,581 billion)—a surprising finding from any perspective.

5. In 1987, partnerships on average lost about $.01 per $1 in sales. However, a year earlier (1986), the loss was $.05 per $1 in sales. The losses relate to the use of partnerships in recent years in ventures that were largely motivated to provide wealthy investors large tax losses. The 1986 change in the tax code basically removed such incentives, and this fact probably accounts for the change from 1986 to 1987.

It is also beneficial for us to see the role of each form of business entity as it relates to basic industries. Table 2–2 classifies the number of business forms and the dollar sales activity according to industry. We can observe the following:

1. In terms of number of entities, corporations are particularly prevalent in manufacturing and are least predominant in services. Partnerships are especially noticeable in agriculture, mining, and finance, including real estate.

2. Proprietorships generate above-average sales in services, construction, and agriculture. Partnerships are stronger in mining, finance, and services. Corporations stand out in the manufacturing, transportation, public utilities, and wholesale and retailing industries.

The Nature of the Organizational Forms

To understand the basic differences between each legal form of business, we need to define each form and outline the procedures necessary for originating it; and we also need to be able to understand the advantages and disadvantages of each form.

Sole Proprietorship

The **sole proprietorship** is a business owned by a single individual. The owner maintains title to the assets and is personally responsible, generally without limitation, for the liabilities incurred. The proprietor is entitled to the profits from the business but must also absorb any losses. This form of business is initiated by the mere act of beginning business operations. Typically, no legal requirement must be met in starting the operation, particularly if the proprietor is conducting the business in his or her own name. If a special name is used, an assumed-name certificate should be filed, requiring a small registration fee. Some states require a periodic review of the certificate; otherwise the sole proprietorship has no time limit on its existence. Termination occurs on the owner's death or by the owner's choice. If the owner voluntarily terminates the business, the assumed-name certificate should be canceled. Briefly stated, the sole proprietorship is for all practical purposes the absence of any formal *legal* business structure.

Partnership

The primary difference between a **partnership** and a sole proprietorship is that the partnership has more than one owner. A partnership is an association of two or more persons coming together as co-owners for the purpose of operating a business for profit. Partnerships fall into two types: (1) general partnership and (2) limited partnership.

General partnership ■ In a **general partnership** each partner is fully responsible for the liabilities incurred by the partnership. Also, any partner's ill conduct even having the appearance of relating to the firm's business renders the remaining partners liable as well. The relationship between partners is dictated entirely by the partnership agreement, which may be an oral commitment or a formal document. Generally the partners should draft a written agreement that explicitly sets forth the basic relationships within the firm. At a minimum, the agreement should include the nature and amount of capital to be invested by each partner, the authority of the individual partners, the means for determining how profits and losses are to be shared, the duration of the partnership, the procedures for admitting a new partner, and the method for reformulating the partnership in the event of a partner's death or withdrawal from the partnership. It is essential to include any important terms in the agreement to minimize later misunderstandings. In addition, if a dispute arises and court action becomes necessary to resolve the problem, the court may be required to act in a manner conflicting with the partners' original intent. For example, if no agreement is evident, the law stipulates that each partner is to share in the profits and losses equally.

Limited partnership ■ In addition to the general partnership, in which all partners are jointly liable without limitation, many states provide for a **limited partnership.** The state statutes permit one or more of the partners to have limited liability, restricted to the amount of capital invested in the partnership. Several conditions must be met to qualify as a limited partner. First, at least one general partner must remain in the association for whom the privilege of limited liability does not apply. Second, the names of the limited partners may not appear in the name of the firm. Third, the limited partners may not participate in the management of the business. If one of these restrictions is violated, all partners forfeit their right to limited liability. In essence, the intent of the statutes creating the limited partnership is to provide limited liability for a person whose interest in the partnership is purely as an investor. That individual may not assume a management function within the organization.

A somewhat unique limited partnership, called a **master limited partnership (MLP),** was developed in the 1980s. The partnership units of the MLP are frequently traded on the major stock exchanges. The MLP has usually resulted from a corporation "spinning off" a part of the firm, oftentimes a productive asset, such as oil and gas production held by an oil company. By creating the MLP, the cash generated by the asset flows directly to the owners, which may reduce taxes and avoid possible conflicts of interest between shareholders and management.

Corporation

The **corporation** has been a significant factor in the economic development of the United States. As early as 1819 Chief Justice John Marshall set forth the legal definition of a corporation as "an artificial being, invisible, intangible, and existing only in the contemplation of law."[12] This entity *legally* functions separate and apart from its owners. As such, the corporation can individually sue and be sued, and purchase, sell, or own property; and its personnel are subject to criminal punishment for crimes. However, despite this legal separation, the corporation is composed of owners who dictate its direction and policies. The owners elect a board of directors, whose members in turn select individuals to serve as the corporate officers, including the president, the vice-president, the secretary, and the treasurer. Ownership is reflected by common stock certificates, designating the number of shares owned by its holder. The number of shares owned relative to the total number of shares outstanding determines the stockholder's proportionate ownership in the business. Since the shares are transferable, ownership in a corporation may be changed by a shareholder simply remitting the shares to the new shareholder. The investor's liability is confined to the amount of the investment in the company, thereby preventing creditors from confiscating the stockholders'

---

[12]*The Trustees of Dartmouth College v. Woodward,* 4 Wheaton 636 (1819).

TABLE 2–3.
Selection of Legal Form of Organization

Form of Organization	Organization Requirements and Costs	Liability of the Owners	Continuity of the Business
Sole proprietorship	Minimum requirements: Generally no registration or filing fee.	Unlimited liability.	Dissolved upon proprietor's death.
General partnership	Minimum requirements: Generally no registration or filing fee. Partnership agreement not legally required but is strongly suggested.	Unlimited liability.	Unless partnership agreement specifies differently, dissolved upon withdrawal or death of partner.
Limited partnership	Moderate requirements: Written agreement often required, including identification of general and limited partners.	General partners: Unlimited liability. Limited partners: Liability limited to investment in company.	General partners: Same as general partnership. Limited partners: Withdrawal or death does not affect continuity of business.
Corporation	Most expensive and greatest requirements: Filing fees; compliance with state regulations for corporations.	Liability limited to investment in company.	Continuity of business unaffected by shareholder withdrawal or death.
Form of organization normally favored	Proprietorship or general partnership	Limited partnership or corporation	Corporation

personal assets in settlement of unresolved claims. Finally, the life of a corporation is not dependent on the status of the investors. The death or withdrawal of an investor does not affect the continuity of the corporation.

Comparison of Organizational Forms

Owners of new businesses have some important decisions to make in choosing an organizational form. Not only must they consider a number of different factors, they might find that the variables they examine to make their decision may be in conflict. One consideration might suggest that a partnership is the best route, whereas another might indicate that a corporation is best. Table 2–3 provides an overview of the most important criteria. The bottom line in the table suggests a favored form of business organization given the particular list of factors above.

Perspective in Finance

The decision regarding which organizational form is most suitable should be based on an evaluation of the relative costs involved in carrying out the firm's business affairs; that is, minimizing organizational costs is the firm's goal.

Organization Requirements and Costs

In every instance, the sole proprietorship is the "cheapest" organization to organize. Generally no legal requirement must be satisfied; the owner simply begins operating. (Exceptions do exist, depending on the nature of the product or service.) The general partnership may possibly be as inexpensive to create as the proprietorship, in that no legal criterion must be met. However, if a partnership is to be functional in the long term, a written agreement is usually advisable. The importance of this contract cannot be overemphasized. This document, if properly prepared, may serve to avoid personal misunderstandings and may even minimize several disadvantages usually associated with the

Transferability of Ownership	Management Control and Regulations	Attractiveness for Raising Capital	Income Taxes
May transfer ownership in company name and assets.	Absolute management freedom, negligible formal requirements.	Limited to proprietor's personal capital.	Income from the business is taxed as personal income to the proprietor.
Requires the consent of all partners.	Majority vote of partners required for control; negligible formal requirements.	Limited to partners' ability and desire to contribute capital.	Income from the business is taxed as personal income to the partners.
General partners: Same as general partnership. Limited partners: May sell interest in the company.	General partners: Same as general partnership. Limited partners: Not permitted any involvement in management.	General partners: Same as general partnership. Limited partners: Limited liability provides a stronger inducement in raising capital.	General partners: Same as general partnership. Limited partners: Same as general partnership.
Easily transferred by transferring shares of stock.	Shareholders have final control, but usually board of directors controls company policies.	Usually the most attractive form for raising capital.	The corporation is taxed on its income and the stockholder is taxed when dividends are paid.
Depends upon the circumstances.	Control: Depends upon the circumstances. Regulation: Proprietorship and general partnership.	Corporation.	Depends upon circumstances.

partnership form of organization. The limited partnership is more expensive, owing to statutory requirements. The partners must provide a certification of the general partners and the limited partners and indicate the rights and responsibilities of each. Also, a written agreement is compulsory. The corporation is typically the most expensive form of business. As stated earlier, compliance with numerous statutory provisions is required. The legal costs and the time involved in creating a corporation exceed those for the other legal types of organization. In short, the organizational requirements increase as the formality of the organization increases, and in turn are more expensive. However, this consideration is of minimum importance, and to forgo a choice because of its initial cost may prove to be expensive in the long run.

Liability of the Owners

The sole proprietorship and the general partnership have an inherent disadvantage: the feature of unlimited liability. For these organizations there is no distinction between business assets and personal assets. The creditors lending money to the business can require the owners to sell personal assets if the firm is financially unable to repay its loans. The limited partnership alleviates this problem for the limited partner. However, a limited partner must be careful to maintain this protection. Failure to give *due notice* or to refrain from actively participating in management may result in the loss of this privilege. The corporation has a definite advantage in terms of limited liability, since creditors are able only to look at corporate assets in resolving claims. However, this advantage for the corporation may not always be realized. If a firm is small, its president may be required to guarantee a loan personally. Also, if the corporate form is being used to defraud creditors, the courts may "pierce the corporate veil" and hold the owners personally liable. Nevertheless, the limitation of liability is usually an important concern in the selection of the legal organization.

Continuity of the Business

The continuity of the business is largely a function of the legal form of organization. The sole proprietorship is immediately dissolved upon the owner's death. Likewise, the general partnership is terminated upon the death or withdrawal of a partner. This weakness can be minimized in the partnership through the written agreement by specifying what is to occur if a partner dies or desires to withdraw. Failure to incorporate such a provision into the agreement may result in a forced liquidation of the firm, possibly at an inopportune time. Finally, the corporation offers the greatest degree of continuity. The status of the investor simply does not affect the corporation's existence. The corporate business organization has a distinct advantage in its perpetual nature.

Transferability of Ownership

Transferability of ownership is intrinsically neither good nor bad; its desirability depends largely on the owners' preferences. In certain businesses the owners may want the option to evaluate any prospective new investors. In other circumstances, unrestricted transferability may be preferred. The sole proprietor has complete freedom to sell any interest in the business. At the other extreme, members of a general partnership may not sell or assign their interest without the prior consent of the remaining partners. However, this limitation may be removed by providing otherwise in the partnership agreement. The limited partnership has a twofold nature: The assignment of interest by general partners requires the prior consent of the other partners, whereas the limited partners have unrestricted transferability. The corporation affords the investors complete flexibility in transferring their interest.

Management Control and Regulations

The sole proprietor has absolute control of the firm and is not restrained by government regulation. With the few exceptions relating to assumed or fictitious names and special licensing, the sole proprietorship may operate in any state without complying with registration and qualification requirements. The general partnership is likewise not impeded by any significant government regulations. However, since control within this legal form of business is normally based on the majority vote, an increase in the number of partners reduces each partner's voice in management. The limited partnership is characterized by a restricted separation of ownership from control; there is no such separation in the sole proprietorship and the general partnership. As to government regulation, the limited partnership requires detailed registration to inform the public of the authority of the individual partners. Within the corporation, the control factor has two dimensions: (1) the **formal control** vested in the stockholders having the majority of the voting common shares and (2) the **functional control** exercised by the corporate officers in conducting the daily operations. For the small corporation, these two controls usually rest in the same individuals. However, as the size of the corporation increases, the two facets distinctly separate. Finally, the corporation is encumbered with substantial government regulation in terms of registrations as well as compliance with statutory requirements.

Attractiveness for Raising Capital

As a result of the limited liability, the ease of transferring ownership through the sale of common shares, and the flexibility in dividing the shares, the corporation is the supreme business entity in terms of attracting new capital. In contrast, the unlimited liabilities of the sole proprietorship and the general partnership are deterrents to raising equity capital. Between these extremes, the limited partnership does provide limited liability for the limited partners, which has a tendency to attract wealthy investors. However, the impracticality of having a large number of partners and the restricted marketability of an interest in a partnership prevent this form of organization from competing effectively with the corporation.

Income Taxes

Income taxes frequently have a major impact on an owner's selection of a legal business form. In the remainder of this chapter we will examine the basic tax implications for the financial manager. However, there are a few guidelines to remember.

The sole proprietorship and the partnership organization are not taxed as separate entities; the owners report business profits on their personal tax returns. The earnings from the company are taxable to the owner, regardless of whether these profits have been distributed to the investors. This feature may place the owner in a cash squeeze if taxes are due but income has been retained within the company. On the other hand, the corporation is taxed as a separate and distinct entity. This same income is taxed again when distributed to the shareholder in the form of dividends. Determination of the best form of legal entity with respect to taxes should be based on the objective of maximizing the after-tax profits to the owners.[13] This decision depends partly on tax rates for individuals relative to rates for the corporation. Whether or not the profits are to be retained in the business or paid as dividends to the common stockholders is also important.

---

[13]The firm's objective is to maximize shareholder wealth. However, since no risk is involved in selecting the form of business, maximizing profits will also maximize wealth.

Federal Income Taxation

Objectives of Income Taxation

Originally, the sole objective of the federal government in taxing income was to generate financing for government expenditures. Although this purpose continues to be important, *social* and *economic* objectives have been added. For instance, a company may receive possible reductions in taxes if (1) it undertakes certain technological research, or (2) if it pays wages to certain economically disadvantaged groups. Other socially oriented stipulations in the tax laws include exemptions for dependents, old age, and blindness, and a reduction in taxes on retirement income. In addition, the government uses tax legislation to stabilize the economy. In recessionary periods taxes may be reduced, giving the public more discretionary income in the hope that that income will be spent to increase the demand for products and thereby generate new jobs.

In short, three objectives may be given for the taxation of revenues: (1) the provision of revenues for government expenditures, (2) the achievement of socially desirable goals, and (3) economic stabilization.

Flexibility of a Partnership

Of course, S corporations avoid double taxation—but they don't enjoy all the advantages of partnerships when it comes to juggling income and deductions. For example, the 20%-owner of an S corporation normally must pay taxes on 20% of any income. By contrast, partnership members are free to divvy up any income and tax liability as they see fit. Thus, equal partners might change the allocations of profit or loss year to year to fit their individual tax needs. LLCs offer the same freedom.

With LLCs, as with regular corporations, only the company's assets, and not the owner's personal assets, are at risk in business-related lawsuits. In partnerships, so-called limited partners enjoy such protection, but general partners don't. And limited partners face restrictions on how active they can be in the business. LLCs are designed to protect all partners while imposing no limits on their activity.

Not surprisingly, lawyers in a few states say LLCs are an easy sell. Since Colorado's LLC statute went into effect in April 1990, 250 LLCs have been organized there, an official says. Forming an LLC usually costs $1,000 to $5,000 in attorney and filing fees, depending on complexity, says Mr. Maxfield, the Denver lawyer.

But some state programs have drawbacks. Florida LLCs are exempt from federal corporate taxes but subject to the state's 5.5% corporate-income tax. Since Florida has no personal income tax affecting partnership income, "that 5.5% is enough to scare people off," says Jose M. Sariego, a Miami lawyer.

Moreover, the IRS has yet to give its imprimatur to any state LLC program except Wyoming's, though a few LLCs elsewhere have gotten favorable private-letter rulings. And lawyers say it's unclear how enterprises treated as LLCs in their home states will be treated in states without LLC laws. Of the states without LLCs, Indiana alone explicitly recognizes LLCs organized elsewhere. "There has been no litigation on LLCs," says Robert R. Keatinge, a Colorado lawyer who heads the other ABA panel on LLCs. "And nobody wants to be the test case."

Benefit for Foreigners

Still, proponents say the LLC raises little risk for enterprises operating only in their home state or outside the U.S. And it's ideal for foreign investors—normally barred from S corporations.

LLCs don't limit the number or type of owners, as S corporations do, except for a two-owner minimum. But because of other restrictions, only closely held enterprises are suited to be LLCs. For example, if any owner leaves, the others must all formally agree to keep the enterprise going. "If you have 200 members, it's hard to get everybody to sign off on anything," Mr. Keatinge says.

But even closely held companies face uncertainties on a number of technical and procedural issues, such as whether the conversion of a partnership into an LLC amounts to a "termination" under tax law, which might increase tax liability. IRS rulings are still awaited. In the meantime, warns Ms. Spudis, the Chicago lawyer, many LLC investors are entering uncharted territory.

Source: Jeffrey A. Tannenbaum, *Wall Street Journal*, May 14, 1991, p. B2.

Types of Taxpayers

To understand the tax system, we must first ask, "Who is the taxpayer?" For the most part, there are three basic types of taxable entities: individuals, corporations, and fiduciaries. Individuals include company employees, self-employed persons owning their own businesses, and members of a partnership. Income is reported by these individuals in their personal tax returns.[14] The corporation, as a separate legal entity, reports its income and pays any taxes related to these profits. The owners (stockholders) of the corporation need not report these earnings in their personal tax returns, except when all or a part of the profits are distributed in the form of dividends. Finally, fiduciaries, such as estates and trusts, file a tax return and pay taxes on the income generated by the estate or trust.

Although taxation of individual and fiduciary income is an important source of income to the government, neither is especially relevant to the financial manager. Since most firms of any size are corporations, we will restrict our discussion to the corporation. A caveat is necessary, however. Tax legislation

---

[14]Partnerships report only the income from the partnership. The income is then reported again by each individual partner, who pays any taxes owed.

can be quite complex, with numerous exceptions to most general rules. The laws can also change quickly, and certain details discussed here may no longer apply in the near future. It sometimes is true that "a little knowledge is a dangerous thing."

Computing Taxable Income

The taxable income for a corporation is based on the gross income from all sources, except for allowable exclusions, less any tax-deductible expenses. *Gross income* equals the firm's dollar sales from its product less the cost of producing or acquiring the product. Tax-deductible expenses include any operating expenses, such as marketing expenses and administrative expenses. Also, *interest expense* paid on the firm's outstanding debt is a tax-deductible expense. However, dividends paid to the firm's stockholders, either preferred or common stockholders, are *not* deductible expenses. Other taxable income includes interest income and dividend income.

To demonstrate how to compute a corporation's taxable income, consider the J and S Corporation, a manufacturer of home accessories. The firm originally established by Kelly Stites had sales of $500,000 for the year. The cost of producing the accessories totaled $230,000. Operating expenses were $100,000. The corporation has $125,000 in debt outstanding, with a 16 percent interest rate, which resulted in $20,000 interest expense ($125,000 × .16 = $20,000). Management paid $10,000 in dividends to the firm's common stockholders. No other income, such as interest or dividend income, was received. The taxable income for the J and S Corporation would be $150,000, as shown in Table 2–4.

Once we know the J and S Corporation's taxable income, we can next determine the amount of taxes the firm will owe.

Computing the Taxes Owed

The taxes to be paid by the corporation on its taxable income are based on the corporate tax rate structure. The specific rates effective for the corporation, as of 1991, are given in Table 2–5.

TABLE 2–4. J and S Corporation Taxable Income		
Sales		$500,000
Cost of goods sold		230,000
Gross profit		$270,000
Operating expenses		
Administrative expenses	$40,000	
Depreciation expenses	15,000	
Marketing expenses	45,000	
Total operating expenses		100,000
Operating income (earnings before interest and taxes)		$170,000
Other income		0
Interest expense		20,000
Taxable income		$150,000
Dividends paid to common stockholders ($10,000) are not tax-deductible expenses.		

TABLE 2–5. Corporate Tax Rates	
15%	$ 0–$50,000
25%	$50,001–$75,000
34%	over $75,000
An additional 5% tax is imposed on income between $100,000 and $335,000.	

For example, the tax liability for the J and S Corporation, which had $150,000 in taxable earnings, would be $41,750, calculated as follows:

Earnings	×	Marginal Tax Rate	=	Taxes
$ 50,000	×	15%		$ 7,500
25,000	×	25%		6,250
75,000	×	34%		25,500
$150,000				$39,250

Add 5% surtax for income
exceeding $100,000
(5% × [$150,000 − $100,000])   2,500
Total tax liability $41,750

The tax rates shown in Table 2–5 are defined as the *marginal* tax rates, or rates applicable to the next dollar of income. For instance, if a firm has earnings of $60,000 and is contemplating an investment that would yield $10,000 in additional profits, the tax rate to be used in calculating the taxes on this added income is 25 percent; that is, the marginal tax rate is 25 percent. However, if the corporation already expects $75,000 without the new investment, the extra $10,000 in earnings would be taxed at 34 percent, the marginal tax rate. In the example, where the J and S Corporation has taxable income of $150,000, its marginal tax rate is 39 percent; that is, any additional income from new investments will be taxed at a rate of 39 percent. However, after taxable income exceeds $335,000, the marginal tax rate declines to 34 percent, when the 5 percent surtax no longer applies.

In addition to the marginal tax rate, we may also compute the *average* tax rate. For the firm earning $150,000 and owing $41,750 in taxes, the average tax rate is 27.8 percent, calculated as follows:

$$\text{average tax rate} = \text{total tax liability} \div \text{taxable income}$$
$$= \$41,750 \div \$150,000$$
$$= 27.8\%$$

Although we can calculate the average tax rate, *the marginal tax rate is far more important in financial decisions.* As will become increasingly clear throughout the text, we always want to consider the tax consequences of any financial decision. The appropriate rate to be used in the analysis is the marginal tax rate, the rate that will be applicable for any changes in earnings as a result of the action being taken. Thus, *when making financial decisions involving taxes, always use the marginal tax rate in your calculations.*[15]

The tax rate structure used in computing the J and S Corporation's taxes assumes that the income occurs in the United States. Given the globalization of the economy, it may well be that some of the income originates in a foreign country. If so, the tax rates, and the method of taxing the firm, frequently vary. Table 2–6 sheds some light on the basic differences in tax rates in several industrialized countries. As financial manager, you would minimize the firm's taxes by reporting as much income in the low-tax-rate countries and as little as possible in the high-tax-rate countries. Of course, other factors, such as political risk, may discourage your efforts to minimize taxes across national borders.

---

[15]After the company's taxable income exceeds $335,000, both the marginal and average tax rates equal 34 percent, owing to the elimination of the 5 percent surtax that applies to taxable income between $100,000 and $335,000.

TABLE 2–6.
Comparison of Foreign Taxes

Country	Income Tax Rates	Value-Added Tax	Other Taxes
France	42%	5.5% on food items; up to 33.3% on luxury items	
Japan	42% on income not distributed to stockholders; 32% if distributed		Excise taxes on consumer goods; 13.2% local taxes
Korea	20%–33%	10% on goods and services	
United Kingdom	25%–35%	15% on goods and services	
West Germany	56% on income not distributed to stockholders; 36% if distributed	14% on goods and services	

Source: International Tax Summaries, Coopers & Lybrand *International Tax Network* (New York: Wiley, 1989).

Other Tax Considerations

In addition to the fundamental computation of taxes, several other aspects of the existing tax legislation have relevance for the financial manager. These are (1) the dividend income exclusion for corporations, (2) the effects of depreciation on the firm's taxes, (3) the tax treatment of operating losses, and (4) the recognition of capital gains. We also need to consider any additional taxes that may be imposed on a firm for the "excessive accumulation" of profits within the business in an effort to avoid double taxation. Finally, we should be familiar with the tax provision that allows a corporation to be taxed as a partnership, which became increasingly important with the Tax Reform Act of 1986. Let's look at each of these tax provisions in turn.

Dividend Exclusion

A corporation may normally exclude 70 percent of any dividends received from another corporation. For instance, if corporation A owns common stock in corporation B and receives dividends of $1,000 in a given year, only $300 will be subject to tax, and the remaining $700 (70 percent of $1,000) will be tax exempt. If the corporation receiving the dividend income is in a 34 percent tax bracket, only $102 in taxes (34 percent of $300) will result.[16]

Depreciation

The methods for computing depreciation expense are explained in Appendix 2A. Essentially, there are three methods: (1) straight-line depreciation, (2) double-declining balance method, and (3) the accelerated cost recovery system. Any one of the three methods results in the same depreciation expense over the life of the asset; however, the last two approaches allow the firm to take the depreciation earlier as opposed to later, which in turn defers taxes until later. Assuming a time value of money, there is an advantage to using the accelerated techniques (Chapter 3 fully explains the time value of money). Also, manage-

---

[16]If corporation A owns at least 20 percent of corporation B, but less than 80 percent, 80 percent of any dividends received may be excluded from taxable income. If 80 percent or more is owned, all the dividends received may be excluded.

ment may use straight-line depreciation for reporting income to the shareholders while still using an accelerated method for calculating taxable income.

Net Operating Loss Deduction

If a corporation has an operating loss (which is simply a loss from operating a business), that loss may be applied against income in other years. The tax laws provide for a **net operating loss carryback and carryforward.** A carryback permits the taxpayer to apply the loss against the profits for the three prior years. If the loss has not been completely absorbed by the profits in these three years, the loss may be carried forward to each of the fifteen following years (carryforward). At that time, any loss still remaining may no longer be used as a tax deduction. To illustrate, a 1994 operating loss may be used to recover, in whole or in part, the taxes paid during 1991, 1992, and 1993. If any part of the loss still remains, this amount may be used to reduce taxable income, if any, during the fifteen-year period of 1995 through 2009. A complete example of the net operating loss deduction is provided below and in Table 2–7.

Capital Gains and Losses

An important tax consideration prior to 1987 was the preferential tax treatment for capital gains; that is, gains from the sale of assets not bought or sold in the ordinary course of business. The Tax Reform Act of 1986 repealed any special treatment of capital gains. Currently, capital gains are treated as ordinary income in computing taxable income. However, if a corporation has capital losses that exceed capital gains in any year, these net capital losses may not be deducted from ordinary income. The net losses may, however, be carried back and applied against net capital gains in each of the three years before the current year. If the loss is not completely used in the three prior years, any remaining loss may be carried forward and applied against any net gains in each of the next five years. For example, if a corporation has an $80,000 net capital loss in 1993, it may apply this loss against any net gains in 1990, 1991, and 1992. If any loss remains, it may be carried forward and applied against any gains through 1998.

EXAMPLE

As an example of the net operating loss carryback and carryforward, assume the Sang Lee Corporation, a trucking operation, has had the following profits and losses reported from 1987 through 1994:

1987	$ 52,000
1988	76,000
1989	100,000
1990	(152,000)
1991	100,000
1992	(194,000)
1993	12,000
1994	94,000

In 1990 and 1992 the corporation incurred operating losses, which may be applied to reduce taxable income and taxes in other years. The tax payments and tax refunds for each year are calculated in Table 2–7 on page 50.

TABLE 2-7.
Sang Lee Corporation Tax
Payments and Refunds

Year	Taxable Income	Tax Consequence
1987	$ 52,000	TAX PAYMENT OF $8,000 15% of $50,000 plus 25% of $2000.
1988	76,000	TAX PAYMENT OF $14,090 15% of $50,000 plus 25% of $25,000 plus 34% of $1,000.
1989	100,000	TAX PAYMENT OF $22,250 15% of $50,000 plus 25% of $25,000 plus 34% of $25,000.
1990	(152,000)	TAX REFUND OF $30,250 $52,000 of the $152,000 loss is applied against 1987 income for a refund of $8000; $76,000 of the loss is applied against 1988 income for a refund of $14,090, leaving $24,000 to be applied against 1989 income of $100,000 for a refund of $8160—34% of $24,000.
1991	100,000	TAX PAYMENT OF $22,250 Same computation as 1989.
1992	(194,000)	TAX REFUND OF $36,340 AND $18,000 CARRYFORWARD $76,000 of the loss is applied against 1989 income ($24,000 had already been used in 1990) for a refund of $14,090; $100,000 of the loss is applied against 1991 income for a refund of $22,250. The remaining $18,000 loss ($194,000−$176,000) is to be carried to future years.
1993	12,000	NO TAX PAYMENT OR REFUND; $6000 CARRYFORWARD The $18,000 carryforward from 1992 is used to avoid having to pay any tax, leaving $6000 carryforward ($18,000−$12,000) for future years.
1994	94,000	TAX PAYMENT OF $18,170 Tax is calculated on $88,000 income ($94,000 income less the $6000 carryforward originating in 1992): 15% of $50,000 plus 25% of $25,000 plus 34% of $13,000.

Accumulated Earnings Tax

The earnings generated by a corporation are potentially subject to "double taxation," first at the corporate level and then at the stockholder level as the firm's profits are distributed in the form of dividends. If the shareholders had no immediate need for dividend income, the corporation could retain its profits and perhaps even employ the funds for the personal benefit of the company's owners. For example, management could retain the corporate profits but make a personal loan to the stockholders. Also, if the profits were accumulated within the firm, the price of the common stock should rise. Until the stock is sold, the investor would not be required to pay any tax.

To prevent such stratagems, a 28 percent surtax in addition to the regular income tax is assessed at the corporate level on any accumulation of earnings by a corporation for the purpose of avoiding taxes on its shareholders. The tax does not apply to the retention of profits for *reasonable business needs*. Nor must the money be reinvested immediately as long as there is evidence that future needs require the current accumulation of earnings. Although it is difficult to state exactly when the accumulation of profits is thought to be *reasonable*, several examples would include (1) providing for the replacement of plant and equipment, (2) retiring debt created in connection with the corporation's business, (3) extending more credit to customers, and (4) financing the acquisition of a new business.

Subchapter S Corporation

In deciding between the sole proprietorship or partnership and the corporation tax considerations are important. Owners attempt to select the form of business organization that maximizes their *after-tax* returns. To minimize the tax influence on the decision, Congress established the **Subchapter S Corporation**, which enables a corporation to be taxed as a partnership. This provision eliminates the "double taxation" effect on the corporation. The Subchapter S Corporation files a tax return for information purposes only and pays no taxes. The taxes from the business are paid by the stockholder, whether or not the earnings are distributed. However, to qualify as a Subchapter S Corporation, the following requirements must be met:

1. The firm must be a domestic corporation.
2. There may be no more than 35 shareholders at the beginning of the corporation's life. These shareholders must be individuals, estates, or certain trusts.
3. The corporation cannot be a member of an affiliated group eligible to file a consolidated tax return with another corporation.
4. There may be only one class of stock.
5. A nonresident alien cannot be a stockholder.

Only small to moderate-sized firms typically can satisfy the Subchapter S Corporation requirements. However, if the qualifications can be met, the company may potentially receive the benefits of a corporation while being taxed as a partnership.

The Subchapter S Corporation became even more important in 1987, when the changes in tax rates placed the individual rates below the corporate rates. Thus, not only does the Subchapter S Corporation avoid double taxation, it also allows the owners of the firm to be taxed at a lower rate.

Corporate Taxes: An Example

To illustrate certain portions of the tax laws for a corporation, assume that the Griggs Corporation had sales during the past year of $5 million; its cost of goods sold was $3 million; and it incurred operating expenses of $1 million. In addition, it received $185,000 in interest income and $100,000 in dividend income from another corporation. In turn, it paid $40,000 in interest and $75,000 in dividends. Also, it sold old machinery, which had originally cost $350,000, for $200,000. The equipment, purchased five years ago, was being depreciated (straight-line) over a 10-year life. Finally, the company sold a piece of land for $100,000 that had cost $50,000 six years ago. Given this information, the firm's taxable income is $1,250,000, as computed in Table 2-8 on page 52.

Based on the tax rates from Table 2–5, Griggs's tax liability is $425,000, as shown in Table 2–8. Note that the $75,000 Griggs paid in dividends is not tax deductible. Also, since the firm's taxable income exceeds $335,000, and the 5 percent surtax no longer applies, the marginal tax rate and the average tax rate both equal 34 percent; that is, we could have computed Griggs's tax liability as 34 percent of $1,250,000, or $425,000.

Perspective in Finance

Few financial managers know and understand complex tax law. You need not be a tax wizard to be a good financial manager. However, you do need to know how taxes relate to investment decisions, financing decisions, and dividend policies of the firm.

Implications of Taxes in Financial Decision Making

Taxes play an important role in financial decision making. Hardly a decision is made by the financial manager without considering the impact of taxes. Although a complete understanding of tax consequences can only follow an understanding of the underlying financial principles, a brief integration of taxes

TABLE 2–8.
Griggs Corporation Tax
Computations

Sales			$ 5,000,000
Cost of goods sold			(3,000,000)
Gross profit			$ 2,000,000
Operating expenses			(1,000,000)
Operating income			$ 1,000,000
Other taxable income and expenses:			
Interest income		$ 185,000	
Dividend income	$ 100,000		
Less 70% exclusion	70,000	30,000	
Interest expense		(40,000)	175,000
Gain on sale of equipment:			
Selling price		$ 200,000	
Book value		175,000	25,000
Gain on land sale:			
Selling price		$ 100,000	
Cost		(50,000)	$ 50,000
Total taxable income			$ 1,250,000

Tax computation:

15% × $	50,000	=	$	7,500
25% ×	25,000	=		6,250
34% ×	1,175,000	=		399,500
	$1,250,000			

Add 5% surtax for income between $100,000 and $335,000	$ 11,750
Tax liability	$ 425,000

into the three primary areas of decision making for the financial manager is helpful.

Taxes and Capital Investment Decisions

As will be explained in more depth later, income taxes are a significant element in how a firm evaluates its investment decisions. When the company is analyzing the possible acquisition of a plant or equipment, the returns from the investment should be measured on an after-tax basis. Otherwise the company will be omitting an important variable. For example, suppose management is considering the purchase of production equipment costing $1,000. If the $1,000 is spent, the financing of the expenditure must come from *after-tax dollars*. Stated differently, the firm may keep this $1,000 without having to be concerned about any tax consequences. However, if the capital is expended on a capital project (plant or equipment), a portion of the cash inflows to be received from the investment will be taxed. Ignoring the time value of money, assume the project, if accepted, is expected to generate $1,200 in *cash inflows before taxes,* which at first might appear to be satisfactory. However, this $1,200 is *before-tax dollars,* which simply means that the firm has not paid the taxes that will be owed as a result of receiving these funds. If the company eventually has to pay $300 in taxes, only $900 will be received in *after-tax cash flows,* which is the amount directly comparable with the $1,000 investment cost. Clearly, the project is undesirable, but the taxes had to be included in the analysis before this fact could be determined.

    In computing the taxes resulting from an investment decision, the method of depreciation affects the timing and the amount of cash flow after taxes. The depreciation method will have an impact on the timing of taxes. Although the *total amount* of taxes is not altered, the use of accelerated depreciation, as opposed to straight-line depreciation, does result in lower taxable profits in the earlier years of the project's life and larger taxable profits in later years. In this manner, less taxes are paid in the initial years, with counterbalancing higher taxes in later years. When the time value of money is considered, this shift in taxes to later time periods proves beneficial.

Taxes and the Firm's Capital Structure

The second major policy variable for the financial manager is to determine the appropriate mix between debt and equity financing. Extensive controversy on this issue has continued for well over three decades. However, regardless of the many different views, the tax laws do give debt financing a definite cost advantage over preferred stock and common stock.[17] As already noted, *interest payments are a tax-deductible expense, whereas dividend payments to preferred stockholders and to common stockholders may not be used as deductions in computing a corporation's taxable profits.*

Taxes and Corporate Dividend Policies

The importance of taxes with respect to the firm's dividend policy is found primarily at the level of the common stockholder rather than at the corporate level. However, since the financial manager's objective is to maximize the common stockholder's wealth, the impact of taxes on shareholders is important. Remember that corporate earnings are taxed, whether or not the earnings are paid out in dividends or retained to be reinvested. If the dividends are paid, the investor will be required to report this income. On the other hand, if the profits are retained and reinvested, the price of the company's stock should increase. However, until the stock is actually sold at a gain, the shareholder is not required to recognize the income. Hence, the opportunity for the firm's common investors to delay the tax payment might influence their preference between capital gains and dividend income. In turn, this preference may affect the corporation's dividend policy.

SUMMARY

Financial managers must be aware of the external influences that affect firms. This chapter examines three key elements: the financial markets, the legal forms of business organization, and the tax structure.

The Financial Markets

The financial markets are the avenue that brings together savers and borrowers. Equally important, the markets give management an indication of investors' opportunity costs, which in turn suggest the rates of return that the investors require.

Rates in the financial markets are based on the demand and supply of money in the economy, as reflected in the risk-free rate of return. Also, the investor is rewarded for the potential loss of purchasing power resulting from inflation. Rates are further influenced by an investment's level of risk and the length of time securities take to mature.

Legal Forms of Organization

The sole proprietorship is a business operation owned and managed by a single individual. Initiating this form of business is simple and generally does not

---

[17]The tax advantage of debt for the corporation is a tax disadvantage to the investor holding the firm's debt. This issue is addressed more fully in Chapter 10.

involve any substantial organizational costs. The proprietor has complete control of the firm but must be willing to assume full responsibility for its outcomes.

The general partnership, which is simply a coming together of two or more individuals, is similar to the sole proprietorship. The limited partnership is another form of partnership sanctioned by states to permit all but one of the partners to have limited liability if this is agreeable to all partners.

The corporation increases the flow of capital from the public investors to the business community. Although larger organizational costs and regulations are imposed on this legal entity, the corporation is more conducive to raising large amounts of capital. Limited liability, continuity of life, and ease of transfer in ownership, which increases the marketability of the investment, have contributed greatly in attracting large numbers of investors into the corporate environment. The formal control of the corporation is vested in the parties who own the greatest number of shares. However, day-to-day operations are managed by the corporate officers, who theoretically serve on behalf of the common stockholders.

Taxes

Three taxable entities exist: the individual, including partnerships; the corporation; and the fiduciary. Only information on the corporate tax environment is given here.

For the most part, taxable income for the corporation is equal to the firm's operating income plus capital gains less any interest expense. The corporation is allowed an income exclusion of 70 percent of the dividends received from another corporation. Also, if the Internal Revenue Service considers the corporation to be retaining unreasonable amounts of earnings within the business, an accumulated earnings tax may be imposed. To minimize the tax influence in selecting the form of legal organization, a corporation may choose to be a Subchapter S Corporation and be taxed as a partnership, provided certain qualifications can be satisfied.

Tax consequences have a direct bearing on the decisions of the financial manager. The relationships are grounded in the taxability of investment income and the difference in tax treatment for interest expense and dividend payments. Also, shareholders' tax status may influence their preference between gains from stock sale and dividends, which in turn may influence corporate dividend policy.

STUDY QUESTIONS

2–1. Explain the term opportunity cost with respect to the cost of funds to the firm.

2–2. Compare and explain the historical rates of return for different types of securities.

2–3. Explain the impact of inflation on rates of returns.

2–4. Define the term structure of interest rates.

2–5. Explain the popular theories for the rationale of the term structure of interest rates.

2–6. Define (a) sole proprietorship, (b) partnership, and (c) corporation.

2–7. Identify the primary characteristics of each form of legal organization.

2–8. Using the following criteria, specify the legal form of business that is favored: (a) organizational requirements and costs, (b) liability of the owners, (c) continuity of business, (d) transferability of ownership, (e) management control and regulations, (f) ability to raise capital, and (g) income taxes.

2–9. Does a partnership pay taxes on its income? Explain.

2-10. When a corporation receives a dividend from another corporation, how is it taxed?

2-11. What is the purpose of the net operating deduction?

2-12. What is the rationale for an accumulated earnings tax?

2-13. What is the purpose of the Subchapter S Corporation? In general, what type of firm would qualify as a Subchapter S Corporation?

SELF-TEST PROBLEMS

ST-1. *(Term Structure of Interest Rates)* If the expected inflation rate is 4 percent and the nominal interest rate is 10.24 percent, what is the real interest rate?

ST-2. *(Term Structure of Interest Rates)* You have a friend with $10,000 to invest for the next two years. She is considering two choices: (1) to purchase a one-year government security paying 8 percent interest. At the end of the first year, she would buy another one-year government security; or (2) to purchase a two-year government security that pays 12 percent in annual interest. (Interest compounds annually; that is, she is allowed to reinvest the interest earned in the first year in the second year—she will earn interest on interest.)
   a. If she invests in the one-year security, what interest rate would she have to earn on the security purchased in the second year to make her indifferent between the two alternatives?
   b. If she told you that she required a 17.5 percent return on the one-year security to be bought in year 2, what would that suggest?

ST-3. *(Corporate Income Tax)* The Dana Flatt Corporation had sales of $2 million this past year. Its cost of goods sold was $1.2 million, and its operating expenses were $400,000. Interest expenses on outstanding debts were $100,000, and the company paid $40,000 in preferred stock dividends. The corporation received $10,000 in preferred stock dividends and interest income of $12,000. The firm sold stock that had been owned for two years for $40,000; the original cost of the stock was $30,000. Determine the corporation's taxable income and its tax liability.

ST-4. *(Carryback–Carryforward)* Stocking, Inc., has a chain of fast-food restaurants. The firm has been operating for eight years, during which time the profits have fluctuated significantly. The taxable income for the past eight years is shown below. Compute the tax payments and refunds for each year.

1986	$ (50,000)	1990	$ 50,000
1987	25,000	1991	150,000
1988	150,000	1992	200,000
1989	(225,000)	1993	(50,000)

STUDY PROBLEMS (SET A)

2-1A. *(Inflation and Interest Rates)* What would you expect the nominal rate of interest to be if the real rate is 4 percent and the expected inflation rate is 7 percent?

2-2A. *(Inflation and Interest Rates)* Assume the expected inflation rate to be 4 percent. If the current real rate of interest is 6 percent, what ought the nominal rate of interest be?

2-3A. *(Inflation and Interest Rates)* Assume the expected inflation rate to be 5 percent. If the current real rate of interest is 7 percent, what would you expect the nominal rate of interest to be?

2-4A. *(Term Structure of Interest Rates)* You want to invest your savings of $20,000 in government securities for the next two years. At the present, you can invest either in a security that pays interest of 8 percent per year for the next two years or in a security that matures in one year but pays only 6 percent interest. If you make the latter choice, you would then reinvest your savings at the end of the first year for another year.

a. Why might you choose to make the investment in the one-year security that pays an interest rate of only 6 percent, as opposed to investing in the two-year security paying 8 percent? Provide numerical support for your answer. Which theory of term structure have you supported in your answer?

b. Assume your required rate of return on the second-year investment is 11 percent; otherwise, you will choose to go with the two-year security. What rationale could you offer for your preference?

2–5A. *(Corporate Income Tax)* The William B. Waugh Corporation is a regional Toyota dealer. The firm sells new and used trucks and is actively involved in the parts business. During the most recent year the company generated sales of $3 million. The combined cost of goods sold and the operating expenses were $2.1 million. Also, $400,000 in interest expense was paid during the year. The firm received $6,000 during the year in dividend income from 1,000 shares of common stock that had been purchased three years previously. However, the stock was sold toward the end of the year for $100 per share; its initial cost was $80 per share. The company also sold land that had been recently purchased and had been held for only four months. The selling price was $50,000; the cost was $45,000. Calculate the corporation's tax liability.

2–6A. *(Corporate Income Tax)* Sales for L. B. Menielle, Inc., during the past year amounted to $5 million. The firm provides parts and supplies for oil field service companies. Gross profits for the year were $3 million. Operating expenses totaled $1 million. The interest and dividend income from securities owned were $20,000 and $25,000, respectively. The firm's interest expense was $100,000. The firm sold securities on two occasions during the year, receiving a gain of $40,000 on the first sale but losing $50,000 on the second. The stock sold first had been owned for four years; the stock sold second had been purchased three months prior to the sale. Compute the corporation's tax liability.

2–7A. *(Corporate Income Tax)* Sandersen, Inc., sells minicomputers. During the past year the company's sales were $3 million. The cost of its merchandise sold came to $2 million, and cash operating expenses were $400,000; depreciation expense was $100,000, and the firm paid $150,000 in interest on bank loans. Also, the corporation received $50,000 in dividend income but paid $25,000 in the form of dividends to its own common stockholders. Calculate the corporation's tax liability.

2–8A. *(Corporate Income Tax)* A. Don Drennan, Inc., had sales of $6 million during the past year. The company's cost of goods sold was 70 percent of sales; operating expenses, including depreciation, amounted to $800,000. The firm sold a capital asset (stock) for $75,000, which had been purchased five months earlier at a cost of $80,000. Determine the company's tax liability.

2–9A. *(Corporate Income Tax)* The Robbins Corporation is an oil wholesaler. The company's sales last year were $1 million, with the cost of goods sold equal to $600,000. The firm paid interest of $200,000, and its cash operating expenses were $100,000. Also, the firm received $40,000 in dividend income while paying only $10,000 in dividends to its preferred stockholders. Depreciation expense was $150,000. Compute the firm's tax liability. Based on your answer, does management need to take any additional action?

2–10A. *(Corporate Income Tax)* The Fair Corporation had sales of $5 million this past year. The cost of goods sold was $4.3 million and operating expenses were $100,000. Dividend income totaled $5,000. The firm sold land for $150,000 that had cost $100,000 five months ago. The firm received $150 per share from the sale of 1,000 shares of stock. The stock was purchased for $100 per share three years ago. Determine the firm's tax liability.

2–11A. *(Corporate Income Tax)* Sales for J. P. Hulett, Inc., during the past year amounted to $4 million. The firm supplies statistical information to engineering companies. Gross profits totaled $1 million, operating and depreciation expenses were $500,000 and $350,000, respectively. Dividend income for the year was $12,000. Compute the corporation's tax liability.

2–12A. *(Corporate Income Tax)* Anderson & Dennis, Inc., sells computer software. The company's past year's sales were $5 million. The cost of its merchandise sold came to $3 million. Operating expenses were $175,000, plus depreciation expenses totaling $125,000. The firm paid $200,000 interest on loans. The firm sold stock during the year, receiving a $40,000 gain on a stock owned six years but losing $60,000 on stock held four months. Calculate the company's tax liability.

2–13A. *(Corporate Income Tax)* G. R. Edwin, Inc., had sales of $6 million during the past year. The cost of goods sold amounted to $3 million. Operating expenses totaled $2.6 million and interest expense was $30,000. Determine the firm's tax liability.

2–14A. *(Corporate Income Tax)* The Analtoly Corporation is an electronics dealer and distributor. Sales for the last year were $4.5 million, and cost of goods sold and operating expenses totaled $3.2 million. Analtoly also paid $150,000 in interest expense, and depreciation expense totaled $50,000. In addition, the company sold securities for $120,000 that it had purchased four years earlier at a price of $40,000. Compute the tax liability for Analtoly.

2–15A. *(Corporate Income Tax)* Utsumi Inc. supplies wholesale industrial chemicals. Last year the company had sales of $6.5 million. Cost of goods sold and operating expenses amounted to 70 percent of sales, and depreciation and interest expenses were $75,000 and $160,000, respectively. Furthermore, the corporation sold 40,000 shares of Sumitono Industries for $10 a share. These shares were purchased a year ago for $8 each. In addition, Utsumi received $60,000 in dividend income. Compute the corporation's tax liability.

2–16A. *(Carryback–Carryforward)* The taxable income for Mokita, Inc., for the past seven years is given below. From the information provided, determine the firm's tax payments and tax refunds in each year.

1988	$ 25,000	1992	$(125,000)
1989	(75,000)	1993	(20,000)
1990	100,000	1994	80,000
1991	50,000		

2–17A. *(Carryback–Carryforward)* Given the taxable income figures below for the A. O. Faubus Corporation, compute the tax payment or tax refund in each year.

1987	$ 40,000	1991	$ 60,000
1988	(60,000)	1992	(100,000)
1989	30,000	1993	50,000
1990	80,000	1994	(75,000)

STUDY PROBLEMS (SET B)

2–1B. *(Inflation and Interest Rates)* What would you expect the nominal rate of interest to be if the real rate is 5 percent and the expected inflation rate is 3 percent?

2–2B. *(Inflation and Interest Rates)* Assume the expected inflation rate to be 4 percent. If the current real rate of interest is 6 percent, what ought the nominal rate of interest be?

2–3B. *(Inflation and Interest Rates)* Assume the expected inflation rate to be 9 percent. If the current real rate of interest is 5 percent, what would you expect the nominal rate of interest to be?

2–4B. *(Term Structure of Interest Rates)* You want to invest your savings of $30,000 in government securities for the next two years. At the present, you can invest either in a security that pays interest of 8 percent per year for the next two years or in a security that matures in one year and pays 10 percent interest. If you make the latter choice, you would then reinvest your savings at the end of the first year for another year.
   a. Why might you choose to make the investment in the one-year security that pays an interest rate of 10 percent, as opposed to investing in the two-year security paying 8 percent? Provide numerical support for your answer. Which theory of term structure have you supported in your answer?
   b. Assume your required rate of return on the second-year investment is 7 percent; otherwise, you will choose to go with the two-year security. What rationale could you offer for your preference?

2–5B. *(Corporate Income Tax)* The M. M. Roscoe Corporation is a regional truck dealer. The firm sells new and used trucks and is actively involved in the parts business. During the most recent year the company generated sales of $4 million. The combined cost of goods sold and the operating expenses were $3.2 million. Also,

$300,000 in interest expense was paid during the year. The firm received $5,000 during the year in dividend income from 1,000 shares of common stock that had been purchased three years previously. However, the stock was sold toward the end of the year for $100 per share; its initial cost was $80 per share. The company also sold land that had been recently purchased and had been held for only four months. The selling price was $55,000; the cost was $45,000. Calculate the corporation's tax liability.

2–6B. *(Corporate Income Tax)* Sales for J. P. Enterprises during the past year amounted to $5 million. The firm provides parts and supplies for oil field service companies. Gross profits for the year were $2.5 million. Operating expenses totaled $900,000. The interest and dividend income from securities owned were $15,000 and $25,000, respectively. The firm's interest expense was $100,000. The firm sold securities on two occasions during the year, receiving a gain of $45,000 on the first sale but losing $60,000 on the second. The stock sold first had been owned for five years; the stock sold second had been purchased three months prior to the sale. Compute the corporation's tax liability.

2–7B. *(Corporate Income Tax)* Carter B. Daltan, Inc., sells minicomputers. During the past year the company's sales were $3.5 million. The cost of its merchandise sold came to $2 million, and cash operating expenses were $500,000; depreciation expense was $100,000, and the firm paid $165,000 in interest on bank loans. Also, the corporation received $55,000 in dividend income but paid $25,000 in the form of dividends to its own common stockholders. Calculate the corporation's tax liability.

2–8B. *(Corporate Income Tax)* Kate Menielle, Inc., had sales of $8 million during the past year. The company's cost of goods sold was 60 percent of sales; operating expenses, including depreciation, amounted to $900,000. The firm sold a capital asset (stock) for $75,000, which had been purchased five months earlier at a cost of $80,000. Determine the company's tax liability.

2–9B. *(Corporate Income Tax)* The Burgess Corporation is an oil wholesaler. The company's sales last year were $2.5 million, with the cost of goods sold equal to $700,000. The firm paid interest of $200,000, and its cash operating expenses were $150,000. Also, the firm received $50,000 in dividend income while paying only $15,000 in dividends to its preferred stockholders. Depreciation expense was $150,000. Compute the firm's tax liability.

2–10B. *(Corporate Income Tax)* The A.K.U. Corporation had sales of $5.5 million this past year. The cost of goods sold was $4.6 million and operating expenses were $125,000. Dividend income totaled $5,000. The firm sold land for $150,000 that had cost $100,000 five months ago. The firm received $140 per share from the sale of 1,000 shares of stock. The stock was purchased for $100 per share three years ago. Determine the firm's tax liability.

2–11B. *(Corporate Income Tax)* Sales for Phil Schubert, Inc., during the past year amounted to $5 million. The firm supplies statistical information to engineering companies. Gross profits totaled $1.2 million, and operating and depreciation expenses were $500,000 and $400,000, respectively. Dividend income for the year was $15,000. Compute the corporation's tax liability.

2–12B. *(Corporate Income Tax)* Williams & Crisp, Inc., sells computer software. The company's past year's sales were $4.5 million. The cost of its merchandise sold came to $2.2 million. Operating expenses were $175,000, plus depreciation expenses totaling $130,000. The firm paid $150,000 interest on loans. The firm sold stock during the year, receiving a $50,000 gain on a stock owned six years but losing $70,000 on stock held four months. Calculate the company's tax liability.

2–13B. *(Corporate Income Tax)* J. Johnson, Inc., had sales of $7 million during the past year. The cost of goods sold amounted to $4 million. Operating expenses totaled $2.6 million and interest expense was $40,000. Determine the firm's tax liability.

2–14B. *(Corporate Income Tax)* The Kusomoto Corporation is an electronics dealer and distributor. Sales for the last year were $6.9 million, and cost of goods sold and operating expenses totaled $4.3 million. Kusomoto also paid $180,000 in interest expense, and depreciation expense totaled $40,000. In addition, the company sold securities for $117,000 that it had purchased four years earlier at a price of $37,000. Compute the tax liability for Kusomoto.

2–15B. *(Corporate Income Tax)* Martinez, Inc., supplies wholesale industrial chemicals. Last year the company had sales of $8.3 million. Cost of goods sold and operating expenses amounted to 77 percent of sales, and depreciation and interest expense were $79,000 and $150,000, respectively. Furthermore, the company sold 50,000 shares of Rose Corporation for $7.50 a share. These shares were purchased a year ago for $5 each. In addition, Martinez received $72,000 in dividend income. Compute the corporation's tax liability.

2–16B. *(Carryback–Carryforward)* The taxable income for Maness, Inc., for the past seven years is given below. From the information provided, determine the firm's tax payments and tax refunds in each year.

1988	$ 35,000	1992	$(175,000)
1989	(85,000)	1993	(40,000)
1990	150,000	1994	120,000
1991	100,000		

2–17B. *(Carryback–Carryforward)* Given the income figures below for the Tetsua Corporation, compute the tax payment or tax refund in each year.

1987	$ 60,000	1991	$ 80,000
1988	(90,000)	1992	(150,000)
1989	80,000	1993	75,000
1990	110,000	1994	(100,000)

Suggested Application for *DISCLOSURE*®

a. Using the *Disclosure* database, obtain the annual income statement for Pepsico and for Coca-Cola. What is each firm's reported taxable income (income before taxes) and the tax liability (provision for income taxes), as shown by *Disclosure*?

b. Given Pepsi's and Coke's taxable income and, using Table 2-5 (Corporate Tax Rates), estimate each firm's tax liability.

c. Compare your answers in parts **a** and **b** for each company. Why might these numbers be different?

SELF-TEST SOLUTIONS

SS–1.

r = nominal rate
R = real rate
i = inflation rate

$$r = R + i + iR$$
$$.1024 = R + .04 + .04R$$
$$R = .06 = 6\%.$$

SS–2. a. If your friend invested in the two-year security, she would have saved $12,544 ($10,000 × 1.12 × 1.12) by the end of the second year. Investing in the one-year security, she would have saved $10,800 ($10,000 × 1.08) by the end of the first year. To do as well as she would with the first choice, she would have to earn $1,744 in interest in the second year ($12,544 − $10,800). That means she would have to earn 16.15 percent on the investment bought in the second year ($1,744 ÷ $10,800).

b. If she is demanding a 17.5 percent rate on the second one-year investment, then the expectations theory is not explaining fully the term structure of interest rates. (The expectations theory suggests she should accept 16.15 percent in year 2.) She may be requiring a liquidity premium on the second-year investment to compensate for the uncertainty of the future interest rates in year 2.

Sales		$2,000,000
Cost of goods sold		1,200,000
Gross profit		$ 800,000
Tax-deductible expenses:		
Operating expenses	$400,000	
Interest expenses	100,000	500,000
		$ 300,000
Other income:		
Interest income		$ 12,000
Preferred dividend income	$ 10,000	
Less 70% exclusion	7,000	3,000
Taxable ordinary income		$ 315,000
Gain on sale:		
Selling price	$ 40,000	
Cost	30,000	10,000
Taxable income		$ 325,000

Tax liability:

$$
\begin{array}{rll}
.15 \times \$\ 50,000 = & \$\ \ 7,500 \\
.25 \times\ \ \ \ 25,000 = & 6,250 \\
.34 \times\ 250,000 = & 85,000 \\
5\%\ \text{surtax} & 11,250 \\
\hline
& \$110,000
\end{array}
$$

Year	Taxable Income	Tax Payments	Carryback	Carryforward	Tax Refunds
1986	$ (50,000)				
1987	25,000			$25,000 from 1986	
1988	150,000	$32,000[a]	$125,000 from 1989	25,000 from 1986	
1989	(225,000)				$32,000[b]
1990	50,000			50,000 from 1989	
1991	150,000	22,250[c]	50,000 from 1993	50,000 from 1989	
1992	200,000	61,250			
1993	(50,000)				14.750[d]

[a]Taxes are based on $125,000 ($150,000 taxable income − $25,000 carryforward from 1986).

[b]The tax refund results from a $125,000 carryback to 1988 to recoup the taxes paid in 1988.

[c]Taxes are based on $100,000 ($150,000 taxable income − $50,000 carryforward).

[d]The tax refund results form a $50,000 carryback to 1991. The taxes in 1991 were originally $22,250, based on $100,000 income. With the $50,000 carryback from 1993, the taxes for 1991 are recomputed on $50,000, or $7,500. The difference between the amount originally paid in 1991, or $22,250, and the recalculated $7,500 in taxes is $14,750.

APPENDIX 2A

Methods of Depreciation

If an asset purchased has a limited life beyond one year but its usefulness gradually declines over time, the taxpayer is not permitted to show the cost of the asset as a tax deduction in the year it is acquired. However, if the property is used in a business or profession or in the production of income, a part of the original cost may be written off as a tax deduction in each year of the asset's anticipated economic life. Examples of assets that may be depreciated include machinery and buildings.

COMPUTING DEPRECIATION PRIOR TO 1987 □ Historically, there have been

TABLE 2A–1.
Computation of Double-Declining Balance Depreciation Expense

Year	Book Value of Asset (First of Year)	Depreciation Rate	Depreciation Expense	Accumulated Depreciation	Book Value (End of Year)
1	$12,000.00	.40	$4,800.00	$ 4,800.00	$7,200.00
2	7,200.00	.40	2,880.00	7,680.00	4,320.00
3	4,320.00	.40	1,728.00	9,408.00	2,592.00
4	2,592.00	—	1,296.00[a]	10,704.00	1,296.00
5	1,296.00	—	1,296.00	12,000.00	.00

[a] Switching to straight-line depreciation in year 4 produced a depreciation expense of $1,296 ($2,592/2) for each of the two remaining years in the useful life of the asset, which exceeds the depreciation expense in these years if the double-declining balance method had been used.

two commonly used methods for computing depreciation: **straight-line (SL)** and **double-declining balance (DDB).** Of the two, straight-line is the simplest to understand and to use. Consider the following example: A firm purchases a fixed asset for $12,000 that has a five-year expected life and a $2,000 anticipated salvage value at the end of that period. Straight-line depreciation on the asset would be $2,400 per year ($12,000 ÷ 5 years = $2,400). Although there is a $2,000 salvage value, this value is disregarded in computing annual depreciation expense for tax purposes.

The double-declining balance method (DDB) is referred to as an accelerated depreciation method, because it provides for a more rapid rate of expensing the asset cost than the straight-line method does. This method involves depreciating the *undepreciated* value of the asset at twice the rate of the straight-line method. This method is demonstrated in Table 2A–1. In terms of the preceding example, the straight-line rate was $2,400 ÷ $12,000, or .2. Thus, the double-declining rate is 2 × .2, or .4.

Under the DDB method the asset would never be fully depreciated. The Internal Revenue Code allows the firm to switch over from DDB to straight-line any time before the end of the asset's useful life. The optimal time to make the switch is in that year when straight-line depreciation exceeds that of the double-declining balance method. Note in Table 2A–1 that the switch occurs in year 4.

With regard to the two methods for computing depreciation, note that the double-declining balance method offers the very real advantage of deferring the payment of taxes. The larger amounts of depreciation in the earlier years decrease taxable income in these years; however, smaller amounts of depreciation in later years subsequently increase taxable income. Consequently, taxes are deferred until these later years.

COMPUTING DEPRECIATION AFTER 1986 □ For assets acquired in 1987 or later, the modified **accelerated cost recovery system (ACRS)** is to be used in computing annual depreciation. Initially established in 1981, the ACRS was modified by tax law, effective January 1, 1987, to include three key variables in computing depreciation: (1) the asset depreciation range, (2) the method of depreciation, and (3) the averaging convention.

Prior to 1981, a depreciable asset was depreciated over its economic useful life. Now the depreciation period is based on the **asset depreciation range (ADR)** system, which groups assets into classes by asset type and industry. Given the type of asset, both the method of depreciation and the actual number of years to be used in depreciating the asset may then be determined. These methods and lives (classes) are presented in Table 2A–2. The first column classifies depreciable property into eight groups. The second column designates whether the asset is to be depreciated using

TABLE 2A–2.
Depreciation Methods and Lives

Type of Asset	Method	Lives (Class)
Property with ADR of 4 years or less, excluding automobiles and light trucks.	Double-declining balance	3-year
Property with ADR of more than 4 years and less than 10 years. Automobiles, light trucks, and R&D property are to be included.	Double-declinging balance	5-year
Property with ADR of 10 years or more and less than 16 years, and property without and ADR that is not classified elsewhere are to be included.	Double-declining balance	7-year
Property with ADR of 16 years or more and less than 20 years.	Double-declining balance	10-year
Property with ADR of 20 years or more and less than 25 years.	150% declining balance	15-year
Property with ADR of 25 years or more, other than real property, such as buildings.	Straight-line	27.5-year
Real property (buildings) with ADR greater than 25 years.	Straight-line	31.5-year

TABLE 2A–3.
Depreciation Percentages for Personal Property[a]

Recovery Year	3-Year (200% DDB)	5-Year (200% DDB)	7-Year (200% DDB)	10-Year (200% DDB)	15-Year (150% DB)	20-Year (150% DB)
1	33.0%	20.0%	14.3%	10.0%	5.0%	3.8%
2	45.0	32.0	24.5	18.0	9.5	7.2
3	15.0	19.2	17.5	14.4	8.6	6.7
4	7.0	11.5[b]	12.5	11.5	7.7	6.2
5		11.5	8.9[b]	9.2	6.9	5.7
6		5.8	8.9	7.4	6.2	5.3
7			8.9	6.6[b]	5.9[b]	4.9
8			4.5	6.6	5.9	4.5[b]
9				6.5	5.9	4.5
10				6.5	5.9	4.5
11				3.3	5.9	4.5
12					5.9	4.5
13					5.9	4.5
14					5.9	4.5
15					5.9	4.5
16					3.0	4.5
17						4.5
18						4.5
19						4.5
20						4.5
21						1.7
Total	100.0	100.0	100.0	100.0	100.0	100.0

[a] Assumes half-year convention applies.
[b] Switch over to straight-line depreciation over remaining useful life.

double-declining balance (200 percent), 150 percent declining balance, or straight-line. The last column indicates the depreciation life (class), which designates the number of years to be used in calculating depreciation.

The last consideration in computing depreciation is that tax legislation restricts the amount of depreciation that may be taken in the year an acquired or sold. These limitations have been called **averaging conventions.** The two primary conventions, or limitations, may be stated as follows:

1. **Half-year Convention:** Personal property, such as machinery, is treated as having been placed in service or disposed of at the midpoint of the taxable year. Thus, a half-year of depreciation generally is allowed for the taxable year in which property is placed in service or is disposed of.

2. **Mid-Month Convention:** Real property, such as buildings, is treated as being placed in service or disposed of in the middle of the month. Accordingly, a half-month of depreciation is allowed for the month disposed of or placed in service.

Using the ACRS to compute the depreciation for assets other than buildings results in a different percentage of the asset being depreciated each year. These percentages are shown in Table 2A–3. For buildings, the straight-line depreciation method is used. In lieu of the double-declining-balance method, a firm may use straight-line depreciation for any asset, regardless of asset class. However, the number of years designated for the particular asset class must still be used.

To demonstrate the use of the ACRS, assume that a piece of equipment costs $12,000 and has been assigned to a five-year class. Using the percentages in Table 2A–3 for a five-year class asset, the depreciation deductions would be calculated as shown in Table 2A–4.

Note that the averaging convention that allows for the half-year of depreciation in the first year results in a half-year of depreciation beyond the fifth year, or in year 6.

TABLE 2A–4.
ACRS Demonstrated

Year	Annual Depreciation	Depreciation Percentage
1	2,400	20.0%
2	3,840	32.0
3	2,304	19.2
4	1,380	11.5
5	1,380	11.5
6	696	5.8
	$12,000	100.0%

STUDY PROBLEMS

2A–1. *(Depreciation)* Compute the annual depreciation for an asset that cost $250,000 and that has an ADR of 6 years. Use the ACRS in your calculations.

2A–2. *(Depreciation)* You acquired a depreciable asset this year, costing $500,000. Your accountant tells you it has a 12-year ADR.

    a. Using the ACRS, compute the annual depreciation.

    b. What assumption is being made about when within the year you bought the asset?

CHAPTER 3

Mathematics of Finance

Compound Interest ● Compound Interest with Nonannual Periods ● Present Value ● Annuities ● Amortized Loans ● Present Value of an Uneven Stream ● Perpetuities ● Bond Valuation: An Illustration of the Time Value of Money

In the next four chapters we will focus on determining the value of the firm and the desirability of investment proposals. A key concept that underlies this material is the *time value of money;* that is, a dollar today is worth more than a dollar received a year from now. Intuitively this idea is easy to understand. We are all familiar with the concept of interest. This concept illustrates what economists call an *opportunity cost* of passing up the earning potential of a dollar today. This opportunity cost is the time value of money.

In evaluating and comparing investment proposals, we need to examine how dollar values might accrue from accepting these proposals. To do this, all dollar values must first be comparable; since a dollar received today is worth more than a dollar received in the future, we must move all dollar flows back to the present or out to a common future date. An understanding of the time value of money is essential, therefore, to an understanding of financial management, whether basic or advanced.

Compound Interest

Most of us encounter the concept of compound interest at an early age. Anyone who has ever had a savings account or purchased a government savings bond has received compound interest. **Compound interest** occurs when interest paid on the investment during the first period is added to the principal, then, during the second period, interest is earned on this new sum.

For example, suppose we place $100 in a savings account that pays 6 percent interest, compounded annually. How will our savings grow? At the end of the first year we have earned 6 percent, or $6 on our initial deposit of $100, giving us a total of $106 in our savings account. The mathematical formula illustrating this phenomenon is

$$FV_1 = PV(1 + i) \qquad \textbf{(3-1)}$$

where FV_1 = the future value of the investment at the end of one year

i = the annual interest (or discount) rate

PV = the present value, or original amount invested at the beginning of the first year

In our example

$$
\begin{aligned}
FV_1 &= PV(1 + i) \qquad \textbf{(3-1)}\\
&= \$100(1 + .06)\\
&= \$100(1.06)\\
&= \$106
\end{aligned}
$$

Carrying these calculations one period further, we find that we now earn the 6 percent interest on a principal of $106, which means we earn $6.36 in interest during the second year. Why do we earn more interest during the second year than we did during the first? Simply because we now earn interest on the sum of the original principal, or present value, and the interest we earned in the first year. In effect we are now earning interest on interest; this is the concept of compound interest. Examining the mathematical formula illustrating the earning of interest in the second year, we find

$$FV_2 = FV_1(1 + i) \qquad \textbf{(3-2)}$$

which, for our example, gives

$$
\begin{aligned}
FV_2 &= \$106(1.06)\\
&= \$112.36
\end{aligned}
$$

Looking back at equation (3–1), we can see that FV_1, or $106, is actually equal to $PV(1 + i)$, or $100 (1 + .06)$. If we substitute these values into equation (3–2), we get

$$
\begin{aligned}
FV_2 &= PV(1 + i)(1 + i)\\
&= PV(1 + i)^2 \qquad \textbf{(3-3)}
\end{aligned}
$$

Carrying this forward into the third year, we find that we enter the year with $112.36 and we earn 6 percent, or $6.74 in interest, giving us a total of $119.10 in our savings account. Expressing this mathematically:

$$
\begin{aligned}
FV_3 &= FV_2(1 + i) \qquad \textbf{(3-4)}\\
&= \$112.36(1.06)\\
&= \$119.10
\end{aligned}
$$

If we substitute the value in equation (3–3) for FV_2 into equation (3–4), we find

$$
\begin{aligned}
FV_3 &= PV(1 + i)(1 + i)(1 + i)\\
&= PV(1 + i)^3 \qquad \textbf{(3-5)}
\end{aligned}
$$

TABLE 3–1.
Illustration of Compound
Interest Calculations

Year	Beginning Value	Interest Earned	Ending Value
1	$100.00	$ 6.00	$106.00
2	106.00	6.36	112.36
3	112.36	6.74	119.10
4	119.10	7.15	126.25
5	126.25	7.57	133.82
6	133.82	8.03	141.85
7	141.85	8.51	150.36
8	150.36	9.02	159.38
9	159.38	9.57	168.95
10	168.95	10.13	179.08

By now a pattern is beginning to be evident. We can generalize this formula to illustrate the value of our investment if it is compounded annually at a rate of i for n years to be

$$FV_n = PV(1 + i)^n \qquad\qquad \text{(3–6)}$$

where FV_n = the future value of the investment at the end of n years

       n = the number of years during which the compounding occurs

       i = the annual interest (or discount) rate

   PV = the present value or original amount invested at the beginning of the first year

Table 3–1 illustrates how this investment of $100 would continue to grow for the first 10 years at a compound interest rate of 6 percent. Notice how the amount of interest earned annually increases each year. Again, the reason is that each year interest is received on the sum of the original investment plus any interest earned in the past.

When we examine the relationship between the number of years an initial investment is compounded for and its future value graphically, as shown in Figure 3–1, we see that we can increase the future value of an investment by increasing the number of years we let it compound or by compounding it at a higher interest rate. We can also see this from equation (3–6), since an increase in either i or n while PV is held constant will result in an increase in FV_n.

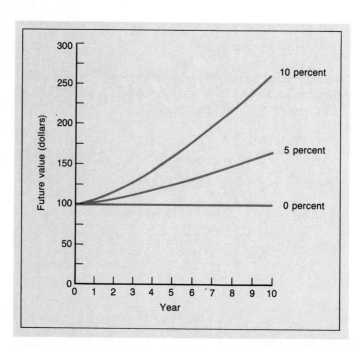

Perspective in Finance

Keep in mind that future cash flows are assumed to occur at the end of the time period during which they accrue. For example, if a cash flow of $100 occurs in time period 5, it is assumed to occur at the end of time period 5, which is also the beginning of time period 6. In addition, cash flows that occur in time t=0 occur right now; that is, they are already in present dollars.

If we place $1,000 in a savings account paying 5 percent interest compounded annually, how much will our account accrue to in ten years? Substituting $PV = \$1000$, $i = 5$ percent, and $n = 10$ years into equation (3–6), we get

$$FV_n = PV(1 + i)^n \tag{3-6}$$

$$= \$1000(1 + .05)^{10}$$

$$= \$1000(1.62889)$$

$$= \$1628.89$$

Thus at the end of ten years we will have $1,628.89 in our savings account.

As the determination of future value can be quite time consuming when an investment is held for a number of years, the **future-value interest factor** for i and n (**$FVIF_{i,n}$**), defined as $(1 + i)^n$, has been compiled in the back of the book for various values of i and n. An abbreviated compound interest or future-value interest factor table appears in Table 3–2, with a more comprehensive version of this table appearing in Appendix B at the back of this book. Alternatively, the $FVIF_{i,n}$ values could easily be determined using a calculator. Note that the compounding factors given in these tables represent the value of $1 compounded at rate i at the *end* of the nth year. Thus, to calculate the future value of an initial investment we need only determine the $FVIF_{i,n}$ using a calculator or the tables at the end of the text and multiply this times the initial investment. In effect, we can rewrite equation (3–6) as follows:

$$FV_n = PV(FVIF_{i,n}) \tag{3-6a}$$

n	1%	2%	3%	4%	5%	6%	7%	8%	9%	10%
1	1.010	1.020	1.030	1.040	1.050	1.060	1.070	1.080	1.090	1.100
2	1.020	1.040	1.061	1.082	1.102	1.124	1.145	1.166	1.188	1.210
3	1.030	1.061	1.093	1.125	1.158	1.191	1.225	1.260	1.295	1.331
4	1.041	1.082	1.126	1.170	1.216	1.262	1.311	1.360	1.412	1.464
5	1.051	1.104	1.159	1.217	1.276	1.338	1.403	1.469	1.539	1.611
6	1.062	1.126	1.194	1.265	1.340	1.419	1.501	1.587	1.677	1.772
7	1.072	1.149	1.230	1.316	1.407	1.504	1.606	1.714	1.828	1.949
8	1.083	1.172	1.267	1.369	1.477	1.594	1.718	1.851	1.993	2.144
9	1.094	1.195	1.305	1.423	1.551	1.689	1.838	1.999	2.172	2.358
10	1.105	1.219	1.344	1.480	1.629	1.791	1.967	2.159	2.367	2.594
11	1.116	1.243	1.384	1.539	1.710	1.898	2.105	2.332	2.580	2.853
12	1.127	1.268	1.426	1.601	1.796	2.012	2.252	2.518	2.813	3.138
13	1.138	1.294	1.469	1.665	1.886	2.133	2.410	2.720	3.066	3.452
14	1.149	1.319	1.513	1.732	1.980	2.261	2.579	2.937	3.342	3.797
15	1.161	1.346	1.558	1.801	2.079	2.397	2.759	3.172	3.642	4.177

TABLE 3–2.
$FVIF_{i,n}$ or the Compound Sum of $1

If we invest $500 in a bank where it will earn 8 percent compounded annually, how much will it be worth at the end of seven years? Looking at Table 3–2 in the row $n = 7$ and column $i = 8\%$, we find that $FVIF_{8\%,7yr}$ has a value of 1.714. Substituting this in equation (3–6a), we find

$$FV_n = PV \ (FVIF_{8\%,7yr}) \qquad \qquad \textbf{(3–6a)}$$
$$= \$500(1.714)$$
$$= \$857$$

Thus, we will have $857 at the end of seven years. ∎

In the future we will find several uses for equation (3–6); not only will we find the future value of an investment, but we can also solve for PV, i, or n. In any case, we will be given three of the four variables and will have to solve for the fourth.

Perspective in Finance

As you read through the chapter it is a good idea to solve the problems as they are presented. If you just read the problems, the principles behind them often do not sink in. The material presented in this chapter forms the basis for the rest of the course; therefore, a good command of the concepts underlying the time value of money is extremely important.

How many years will it take for an initial investment of $300 to grow to $774 if it is invested at 9 percent compounded annually? In this problem we know the initial investment, $PV = \$300$; the future value, $FV_n = \$774$; the compound growth rate, $i = 9$ percent, and we are solving for the number of years it must compound for, $n = ?$ Substituting the known values in equation (3–6), we find

$$FV_n = PV(1 + i)^n$$
$$\$774 = \$300(1 + .09)^n \qquad \qquad \textbf{(3–6)}$$
$$2.58 = (1 + .09)^n$$

Thus we are looking for a value of 2.58 in the $FVIF_{i,n}$ tables, and we know it must be in the 9% column. Looking down the 9% column for the value closest to 2.58, we find that it occurs in the $n = 11$ row. Thus, it will take eleven years for an initial investment of $300 to grow to $774 if it is invested at 9 percent compounded annually. ∎

At what rate must $100 be compounded annually for it to grow to $179.10 in ten years? In this case we know the initial investment, $PV = \$100$; the future value of this investment at the end of n years, $FV_n = \$179.10$; and the number of years that the initial investment will compound for, $n \doteq 10$ years. Substituting into equation (3–6), we get

$$FV_n = PV(1 + i)^n$$
$$\$179.10 = \$100(1 + i)^{10} \qquad \qquad \textbf{(3–6)}$$
$$1.791 = (1 + i)^{10}$$

We know we are looking in the $n = 10$ row of the $FVIF_{i,n}$ tables for a value of 1.791, and we find this in the $i = 6\%$ column. Thus, if we want our initial investment of $100 to accrue to $179.10 in 10 years, we must invest it at 6 percent. ∎

Moving Money Through Time with the Aid of a Financial Calculator

Time value of money calculations can be made simple with the aid of a **financial calculator.** In solving time value of money problems with a financial calculator you will be given three of four variables and will have to solve for the fourth. Before presenting any solutions using a financial calculator we will introduce the calculator's five most common keys. (In most time value of money problems, only four of these keys are relevant.) These keys are:

Menu Key	Description
N	Stores (or calculates) the total number of payments or compounding periods.
I%YR	Stores (or calculates) the interest or discount rate.
PV	Stores (or calculates) the present value of a cash flow or series of cash flows.
FV	Stores (or calculates) the future value, that is, the dollar amount of a final cash flow or the compound value of a single flow or series of cash flows.
PMT	Stores (or calculates) the dollar amount of each annuity payment deposited or received at the end of each year.

One thing you must keep in mind when using a financial calculator is that outflows generally have to be entered as negative numbers. In general, each problem will have two cash flows, one an outflow with a negative value and one an inflow with a positive value. The idea is that you deposit money in the bank at some point in time (an outflow), and at some other point in time you take money out of the bank (an inflow). Also, every calculator operates a bit differently with respect to entering variables. Needless to say, it is a good idea to familiarize yourself with exactly how your calculator functions.

As stated above, in any problem you will be given three of four variables. These four variables will always include *N* and *I%YR;* in addition, two out of the final three variables *PV, FV,* and *PMT* will also be included. To solve a time value of money problem using a financial calculator, all you need to do is enter the appropriate numbers for three of the four variables and then press the key of the final variable to calculate its value. It is also a good idea to enter zero for any of the five variables not included in the problem in order to clear that variable.

Now let's solve the previous example using a financial calculator. We were trying to find at what rate must $100 be compounded annually for it to grow to $179.10 in ten years. The solution using a financial calculator would be as follows:

Step 1: Input Values of Known Variables

Data Input	Function Key	Description
10	N	Stores *N* = 10 years
−100	PV	Stores *PV* = −$100
179.10	FV	Stores *FV* = $179.10
0	PMT	Clears *PMT* to = 0

Step 2: Calculate the Value of the Unknown Variable

Function Key	Answer	Description
I%YR	6.00%	Calculates *I%YR* = 6.00%

Any of the problems in this chapter can easily be solved using a financial calculator; and the solutions to many examples using an HP 17BII financial calculator are provided in the margins. If you are using the HP 17BII, make sure that you have selected both the "END MODE" and "one payment per year" *(1 P/YR)*. This sets the payment conditions to a maximum of one payment per period occurring at the end of the period. Also, to access the time value of money menu from the main menu on the HP 17BII, you must first press the *FIN* and *TVM* menu keys. One final point, you will notice that solutions using the present-value tables versus solutions using a calculator may vary slightly—a result of rounding errors in the tables.

For further explanation see Appendix A at the end of the book. It provides a tutorial on the use of other financial calculators, as well.

Perspective in Finance

The concepts of compound interest and present value will follow us through the remainder of this book. Not only will they allow us to determine the future value of any investment, but they will allow us to bring the benefits and costs from new investment proposals back to the present and thereby determine the value of the investment in today's dollars.

BASIC FINANCIAL MANAGEMENT IN PRACTICE

Andrew Tobias on the Power of Compounding

It was Homer who said that $1,000 invested at a mere 8 percent for 400 years would grow to $23 quadrillion—$5 million for every human on earth. (And you can't see any reason to save?) But, he said, the first 100 years are the hardest. (This was the late Sidney Homer, not Homer Homer—author of the classic *A History of Interest Rates*.)

What invariably happens is that long before the first 100 years are up, someone with access to the cache loses patience. The money burns a hole in his pocket. Or through his nose.

Doubtless that would have been true of the Corrêa fortune, too, had Domingos Faustino Corrêa not cut everyone out of his will for 100 years. That was in 1873, in Brazil. You could have gotten very tired waiting, but if you can establish that you are one of that misanthrope's 4,000-odd legitimate heirs, you may now have some money coming to you. Since 1873, Corrêa's estate has grown, by some estimates, to $12 billion.

Benjamin Franklin had much the same idea, only with higher purpose. Inventive to the end, he left £1,000 each to Boston and Philadelphia. The cities were to lend the money, at interest, to worthy apprentices. Then, after a century, they were to employ part of the fortune Franklin envisioned to construct some public work, while continuing to invest the rest.

One hundred ninety-two years later, when last I checked, Boston's funds exceeded $3 million, even after having been drained to build Franklin Union, and was being lent at interest to medical school students. Philadelphia's fund was smaller, but it, too, had been put to good use. All this from an initial stake of £2,000!

And then there was the king who held a chess tournament among the peasants—I may have this story a little wrong, but the point holds—and asked the winner what he wanted as his prize. The peasant, in apparent humility, asked only that a single kernel of wheat be placed for him on the first square of his chessboard, two kernels on the second, four on the third—and so forth. The king fell for it and had to import grain from Argentina for the next 700 years. Eighteen and a half million trillion kernels, or enough, if each kernel is a quarter-inch long (which it may not be; I've never seen wheat in its pre-English-muffin form), to stretch to the sun and back 391,320 times.

That was nothing more than one kernel's compounding at 100 percent per square for 64 squares. It is vaguely akin to the situation with our national debt.

Source: Andrew Tobias, *Money Angles* (New York: Linden Press, 1984), pp. 35–36. © 1984 by Andrew Tobias. Reprinted by permission of Andrew Tobias.

Compound Interest with Nonannual Periods

Until now we have assumed that the compounding period is always annual; however, it need not be, as evidenced by savings and loan associations and commercial banks that compound on a quarterly, daily, and in some cases continuous basis. Fortunately, this adjustment of the compounding period follows the same format as that used for annual compounding. If we invest our money for five years at 8 percent interest compounded semiannually, we are really investing our money for ten six-month periods during which we receive 4 percent interest each period. If it is compounded quarterly, we receive 2 percent interest per period for twenty three-month periods. This process can easily be generalized, giving us the following formula for finding the future value of an investment for which interest is compounded in nonannual periods:

$$FV_n = PV \left(1 + \frac{i}{m}\right)^{mn} \qquad (3\text{--}7)$$

where FV_n = the future value of the investment at the end of n years

n = the number of years during which the compounding occurs

i = annual interest (or discount) rate

PV = the present value or original amount invested at the beginning of the first year

m = the number of times compounding occurs during the year

In the case of continuous compounding, the value of m in equation (3–7) is allowed to approach infinity. In effect, with continuous compounding, interest begins to earn interest immediately. As this happens, the value of $[1 + (i/m)]^{mn}$ approaches e^{in}, with e being defined as follows and having a value of approximately 2.71828:

$$e = \lim_{m \to \infty} \left(1 + \frac{1}{m}\right)^m \qquad (3\text{--}8)$$

where ∞ indicates infinity. Thus the future value of an investment compounded continuously for n years can be determined from the following formula:

$$FV_n = PV \cdot e^{in} \qquad (3\text{--}9)$$

where FV_n = the future value of the investment at the end of n years

e = 2.71828

n = the number of years during which the compounding occurs

i = the annual interest (or discount) rate

PV = the present value or original amount invested at the beginning of the first year

Continuous compounding may appear complicated, but it is used frequently and is a valuable theoretical concept. Continuous compounding is important because it allows interest to be earned on interest more frequently than any other compounding method does. We can see the value of intrayear compounding by examining Table 3–3 on page 72. Since interest is earned on interest more frequently as the length of the compounding period declines, there is an inverse relationship between the length of the compounding period and the effective annual interest rate.

TABLE 3–3.
The Value of $100
Compounded at Various
Intervals

For One Year at i Percent				
i =	2%	5%	10%	15%
Compounded annually	$102.00	$105.00	$110.00	$115.00
Compounded semiannually	102.01	105.06	110.25	115.56
Compounded quarterly	102.02	105.09	110.38	115.87
Compounded monthly	102.02	105.12	110.47	116.08
Compounded weekly (52)	102.02	105.12	110.51	116.16
Compounded daily (365)	102.02	105.13	110.52	116.18
Compounded continuously	102.02	105.13	110.52	116.18

For 10 Years at i Percent				
i =	2%	5%	10%	15%
Compounded annually	$121.90	$162.89	$259.37	$404.56
Compounded semiannually	122.02	163.86	265.33	424.79
Compounded quarterly	122.08	164.36	268.51	436.04
Compounded monthly	122.12	164.70	270.70	444.02
Compounded weekly (52)	122.14	164.83	271.57	447.20
Compounded daily (365)	122.14	164.87	271.79	448.03
Compounded continuously	122.14	164.87	271.83	448.17

CALCULATOR SOLUTION

Data Input	Function Key
20	N
3	I%YR
100	PV
0	PMT

Function Key	Answer
FV	−180.61

EXAMPLE

If we place $100 in a savings account that yields 12 percent compounded quarterly, what will our investment grow to at the end of five years? Substituting $n = 5$, $m = 4$, $i = 12$ percent, and $PV = \$100$ into equation (3–7), we find

$$FV_5 = \$100 \left(1 + \frac{.12}{4}\right)^{4 \cdot 5}$$

$$= \$100(1 + .03)^{20}$$

$$= \$100(1.806)$$

$$= \$180.60$$

Thus, we will have $180.60 at the end of five years. Notice that the calculator solution is slightly different because of rounding errors in the tables, as explained in the previous section, and that it also takes on a negative value. ∎

EXAMPLE

How much money will we have at the end of twenty years if we deposit $1,000 in a savings account yielding 10 percent interest continuously compounded? Substituting $n = 20$, $i = 10$ percent, and $PV = \$1000$ into equation (3–9) yields

$$FV_{10} = \$1000(2.71828)^{.10 \cdot 20}$$

$$= \$1000(2.71828)^2$$

$$= \$1000(7.38905)$$

$$= \$7389.05$$

Thus, we will have $7389.05 at the end of twenty years. ∎

Present Value

Up until this point we have been moving money forward in time; that is, we know how much we have to begin with and are trying to determine how much that sum will grow in a certain number of years when compounded at a specific rate. We are now going to look at the reverse question: What is the value in today's dollars of a sum of money to be received in the future? The answer to this question will help us determine the desirability of investment projects in Chapters 6 and 7. In this case we are moving future money back to the present. We will be determining the **present value** of a lump sum, which in simple terms is the current value of a future payment. What we will be doing is, in fact, nothing other than inverse compounding. The differences in these techniques come about merely from the investor's point of view. In compounding we talked about the compound interest rate and the initial investment; in determining the present value we will talk about the discount rate and present value. Determination of the discount rate is the subject of Chapter 8 and can be defined as the rate of return available on an investment of equal risk to what is being discounted. Other than that, the technique and the terminology remain the same, and the mathematics are simply reversed. In equation (3–6) we were attempting to determine the future value of an initial investment. We now want to determine the initial investment or present value. By dividing both sides of equation (3–6) by $(1 + i)^n$, we get

$$PV = FV_n \left[\frac{1}{(1 + i)^n} \right] \qquad \textbf{(3–10)}$$

where FV_n = the future value of the investment at the end of n years

n = the number of years until the payment will be received

i = the annual discount (or interest) rate

PV = the present value of the future sum of money

Because the mathematical procedure for determining the present value is exactly the inverse of determining the future value, we also find that the relationships among n, i, and PV are just the opposite of those we observed in future value. The present value of a future sum of money is inversely related to both the number of years until the payment will be received and the discount rate. Graphically, this relationship can be seen in Figure 3–2.

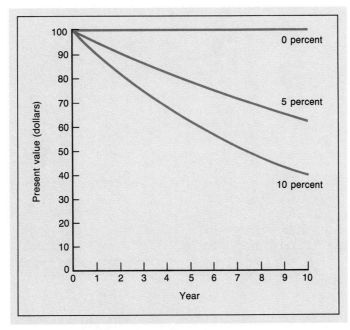

FIGURE 3–2.
Present Value of $100 to Be Received at a Future Date and Discounted Back to the Present at 0, 5, and 10 Percent

Perspective in Finance

While the present-value equation [equation (3–10)] will be used extensively in evaluating new investment proposals, it should be stressed that the present value equation is actually the same as the future value or compounding equation [equation (3–6)], where it is solved for **PV**.

EXAMPLE

CALCULATOR SOLUTION

Data Input	Function Key
10	N
6	I%YR
500	FV
0	PMT

Function Key	Answer
PV	−279.20

What is the present value of $500 to be received ten years from today if our discount rate is 6 percent? Substituting $FV_{10} = \$500$, $n = 10$, and $i = 6$ percent into equation (3–10), we find

$$PV = \$500 \left[\frac{1}{(1 + .06)^{10}} \right]$$

$$= \$500 \left(\frac{1}{1.791} \right)$$

$$= \$500(.558)$$

$$= \$279$$

Thus, the present value of the $500 to be received in ten years is $279. ■

To aid in the computation of present values, the **present-value interest factor** for i and n (**$PVIF_{i,n}$**), defined as $[1/(1 + i)^n]$, has been compiled for various combinations of i and n and appears in Appendix C at the back of this book. An abbreviated version of Appendix C appears in Table 3–4. A close examination shows that the values in Table 3–4 are merely the inverse of those found in Appendix B. This, of course, is as it should be, as the values in Appendix B are $(1 + i)^n$ and those in Appendix C are $[1/(1 + i)^n]$. Now, to determine the present value of a sum of money to be received at some future date, we need only determine the value of the appropriate $PVIF_{i,n}$, either by using a calculator or consulting the tables, and multiply it by the future value. In effect we can use our new notation and rewrite equation (3–10) as follows:

$$PV = FV_n(PVIF_{i,n}) \tag{3–10a}$$

TABLE 3–4.
$PVIF_{i,n}$ or the Present Value of $1

n	1%	2%	3%	4%	5%	6%	7%	8%	9%	10%
1	.990	.980	.971	.962	.952	.943	.935	.926	.917	.909
2	.980	.961	.943	.925	.907	.890	.873	.857	.842	.826
3	.971	.942	.915	.889	.864	.840	.816	.794	.772	.751
4	.961	.924	.888	.855	.823	.792	.763	.735	.708	.683
5	.951	.906	.863	.822	.784	.747	.713	.681	.650	.621
6	.942	.888	.837	.790	.746	.705	.666	.630	.596	.564
7	.933	.871	.813	.760	.711	.655	.623	.583	.547	.513
8	.923	.853	.789	.731	.677	.627	.582	.540	.502	.467
9	.914	.837	.766	.703	.645	.592	.544	.500	.460	.424
10	.905	.820	.744	.676	.614	.558	.508	.463	.422	.386
11	.896	.804	.722	.650	.585	.527	.475	.429	.388	.350
12	.887	.789	.701	.625	.557	.497	.444	.397	.356	.319
13	.879	.773	.681	.601	.530	.469	.415	.368	.326	.290
14	.870	.758	.661	.577	.505	.442	.388	.340	.299	.263
15	.861	.743	.642	.555	.481	.417	.362	.315	.275	.239

What is the present value of $1,500 to be received at the end of ten years if our discount rate is 8 percent? By looking at the $n = 10$ row and $i = 8\%$ column of Table 3–4, we find the $PVIF_{8\%, 10yr}$ is .463. Substituting this value into equation (3–10), we find

$$PV = \$1500(.463)$$

$$= \$694.50$$

Thus, the present value of this $1,500 payment is $694.50. ∎

Again, we only have one present-value–future-value equation; that is, equations (3–6) and (3–10) are identical. We have introduced them as separate equations to simplify our calculations; in one case we are determining the value in future dollars and in the other case the value in today's dollars. In either case the reason is the same: To compare values on alternative investments and to recognize that the value of a dollar received today is not the same as that of a dollar received at some future date, we must measure the dollar values in dollars of the same time period. Since all present values are comparable (they are all measured in dollars of the same time period) we can add and subtract the present value of inflows and outflows to determine the present value of an investment.

What is the present value of an investment that yields $500 to be received in five years and $1,000 to be received in ten years if the discount rate is 4 percent? Substituting the values of $n = 5$, $i = 4$ percent, and $FV_5 = \$500$; and $n = 10$, $i = 4$ percent, and $FV_{10} = \$1000$ into equation (3–10) and adding these values together, we find

$$PV = \$500 \left[\frac{1}{(1 + .04)^5} \right] + \$1000 \left[\frac{1}{(1 + .04)^{10}} \right]$$

$$= \$500 \, (PVIF_{4\%, 5yr}) + \$1000 \, (PVIF_{4\%, 10yr})$$

$$= \$500(.822) + \$1000(.676)$$

$$= \$411 + \$676$$

$$= \$1087$$

Again, present values are comparable because they are measured in the same time period's dollars. ∎

Annuities

An **annuity** is a series of equal dollar payments for a specified number of years. Because annuities occur frequently in finance—for example, as bond interest payments—we will treat them specially. Although compounding and determining the present value of an annuity can be dealt with using the methods we have just described, these processes can be time consuming, especially for larger annuities. Thus, we have modified the formulas to deal directly with annuities.

Compound Annuities

A **compound annuity** involves depositing or investing an equal sum of money at the end of each year for a certain number of years and allowing it to grow.

CALCULATOR SOLUTION

Data Input	Function Key
10	N
8	I%YR
1500	PV
0	PMT

Function Key	Answer
FV	−694.79

Year		0	1	2	3	4	5
Dollar deposits at end of year			500	500	500	500	500
							$ 500.00
							530.00
							562.00
							595.50
							631.00
Future value of the annuity							$2818.50

TABLE 3–5.
Illustration of a Five-Year
$500 Annuity Compounded
at 6 Percent

Perhaps we are saving money for education, a new car, or a vacation home. In any case we want to know how much our savings will have grown by some point in the future.

Actually, we can find the answer by using equation (3–6), our compounding equation, and compounding each of the individual deposits to its future value. For example, if to provide for a college education we are going to deposit $500 at the end of each year for the next five years in a bank where it will earn 6 percent interest, how much will we have at the end of five years? Compounding each of these values using equation (3–6), we find that we will have $2,818.50 at the end of five years.

$$FV_5 = \$500(1 + .06)^4 + \$500(1 + .06)^3 + \$500(1 + .06)^2$$
$$+ \$500(1 + .06) + \$500$$
$$= \$500(1.262) + \$500(1.191) + \$500(1.124) + \$500(1.060) + \$500$$
$$= \$631.00 + \$595.50 + \$562.00 + \$530.00 + \$500.00$$
$$= \$2818.50$$

From examining the mathematics involved and the graph of the movement of money through time in Table 3–5, we can see that this procedure can be generalized to

$$FV_n = PMT \left[\sum_{t=0}^{n-1} (1 + i)^t \right] \tag{3–11}$$

where FV_n = the future value of the annuity at the end of the nth year

   PMT = the annuity payment deposited or received at the end of each year

   i = the annual interest (or discount) rate

   n = the number of years for which the annuity will last

To aid in compounding annuities, the **future-value interest factor for an annuity** for i and n (**FVIFA$_{i,n}$**), defined as $\left[\sum_{t=0}^{n-1} (1 + i)^t \right]$, is provided in Appendix D for various combinations of n and i; an abbreviated version is shown in Table 3–6.

Using this new notation, we can rewrite equation (3–11) as follows:

$$FV_n = PMT(FVIFA_{i,n}) \tag{3–11a}$$

Reexamining the previous example, in which we determined the value after five years of $500 deposited at the end of each of the next five years in the bank at 6 percent, we would look in the $i = 6\%$ column and $n = 5$ year row and find the value of the $FVIFA_{6\%,5yr}$ to be 5.637. Substituting this value into equation (3–11a), we get

$$FV_5 = \$500(5.637)$$
$$= \$2818.50$$

**CALCULATOR
SOLUTION**

Data Input	Function Key
5	N
6	I%YR
500	PMT
0	PV

Function Key	Answer
FV	−2818.55

n	1%	2%	3%	4%	5%	6%	7%	8%	9%	10%
1	1.000	1.000	1.000	1.000	1.000	1.000	1.000	1.000	1.000	1.000
2	2.010	2.020	2.030	2.040	2.050	2.060	2.070	2.080	2.090	2.100
3	3.030	3.060	3.091	3.122	3.152	3.184	3.215	3.246	3.278	3.310
4	4.060	4.122	4.184	4.246	4.310	4.375	4.440	4.506	4.573	4.641
5	5.101	5.204	5.309	5.416	5.526	5.637	5.751	5.867	5.985	6.105
6	6.152	6.308	6.468	6.633	6.802	6.975	7.153	7.336	7.523	7.716
7	7.214	7.434	7.662	7.898	8.142	8.394	8.654	8.923	9.200	9.487
8	8.286	8.583	8.892	9.214	9.549	9.897	10.260	10.637	11.028	11.436
9	9.368	9.755	10.159	10.583	11.027	11.491	11.978	12.488	13.021	13.579
10	10.462	10.950	11.464	12.006	12.578	13.181	13.816	14.487	15.193	15.937
11	11.567	12.169	12.808	13.486	14.207	14.972	15.784	16.645	17.560	18.531
12	12.682	13.412	14.192	15.026	15.917	16.870	17.888	18.977	20.141	21.384
13	13.809	14.680	15.618	16.627	17.713	18.882	20.141	21.495	22.953	24.523
14	14.947	15.974	17.086	18.292	19.598	21.015	22.550	24.215	26.019	27.975
15	16.097	17.293	18.599	20.023	21.578	23.276	25.129	27.152	29.361	31.772

TABLE 3–6.
FVIFA$_{i,n}$, or the Sum of an Annuity of $1 for *n* Years

This is the same answer we obtained earlier.

Rather than asking how much we will accumulate if we deposit an equal sum in a savings account each year, a more common question is how much we must deposit each year to accumulate a certain amount of savings. This problem frequently occurs with respect to saving for large expenditures and pension funding obligations.

For example, we may know that we need $10,000 for education in eight years; how much must we deposit at the end of each year in the bank at 6 percent interest to have the college money ready? In this case we know the values of *n*, *i*, and *FV$_n$* in equation (3–11); what we do not know is the value of *PMT*. Substituting these example values in equation (3–11), we find

$$\$10,000 = PMT \left[\sum_{t=0}^{8-1} (1 + .06)^t \right]$$

$$\$10,000 = PMT\ (FVIFA_{6\%,8yr})$$

$$\$10,000 = A(9.897)$$

$$\frac{\$10,000}{9.897} = A$$

$$A = \$1010.41$$

Thus, we must deposit $1,010.41 in the bank at the end of each year for eight years at 6 percent interest to accumulate $10,000 at the end of eight years.

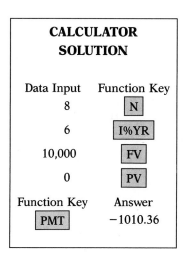

CALCULATOR SOLUTION

Data Input	Function Key
8	N
6	I%YR
10,000	FV
0	PV

Function Key	Answer
PMT	−1010.36

EXAMPLE

How much must we deposit in an 8 percent savings account at the end of each year to accumulate $5,000 at the end of ten years? Substituting the values $FV_{10} = \$5000$, $n = 10$, and $i = 8$ percent into equation (3–11), we find

$$\$5000 = PMT \left[\sum_{t=0}^{10-1} (1 + .08)^t \right] = PMT\ (FVIFA_{8\%,10yr})$$

$$\$5000 = PMT(14.487)$$

$$\frac{\$5000}{14.487} = PMT$$

$$PMT = \$345.14$$

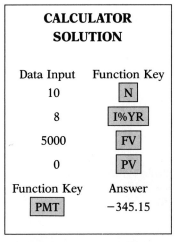

CALCULATOR SOLUTION

Data Input	Function Key
10	N
8	I%YR
5000	FV
0	PV

Function Key	Answer
PMT	−345.15

Thus, we must deposit $345.14 per year for ten years at 8 percent to accumulate $5,000.

Perspective in Finance

A timeline often makes it is easier to understand time value of money problems. By visually plotting the flow of money you can better determine which formula to use. Arrows placed above the line are inflows, whereas arrows below the line represent outflows. One thing is certain: Timelines reduce errors.

Present Value of an Annuity

Pension funds, insurance obligations, and interest received from bonds all involve annuities. To compare them, we need to know the present value of each. While we can find this by using the present-value table in Appendix C, this can be time consuming, particularly when the annuity lasts for several years. For example, if we wish to know what $500 received at the end of the next five years is worth to us given the appropriate discount rate of 6 percent, we can simply substitute the appropriate values into equation (3–10), such that

$$PV = \$500 \left[\frac{1}{(1 + .06)}\right] + \$500 \left[\frac{1}{(1 + .06)^2}\right] + \$500 \left[\frac{1}{(1 + .06)^3}\right]$$

$$+ \$500 \left[\frac{1}{(1 + .06)^4}\right] + \$500 \left[\frac{1}{(1 + .06)^5}\right]$$

$$= \$500(.943) + \$500(.890) + \$500(.840) + \$500(.792) + \$500(.747)$$

$$= \$2106$$

Thus, the present value of this annuity is $2,106.00. From examining the mathematics involved and the graph of the movement of these funds through time in Table 3–7, we see that this procedure can be generalized to

$$PV = PMT \left[\sum_{t=1}^{n} \frac{1}{(1 + i)^t}\right] \qquad (3–12)$$

where PMT = the annuity payment deposited or received at the end of each year

i = the annual discount (or interest) rate

PV = the present value of the future annuity

n = the number of years for which the annuity will last

To simplify the process of determining the present value of an annuity, the **present-value interest factor for an annuity** for i and n (**$PVIFA_{i,n}$**), defined as $\left[\sum_{t=1}^{n} \frac{1}{(1 + i)^t}\right]$, has been compiled for various combinations of i and n in Appendix E with an abbreviated version provided in Table 3–8.

TABLE 3–7.
Illustration of a Five-Year
$500 Annuity Discounted Back
to the Present at 6 Percent

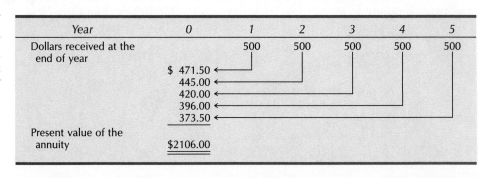

Year	0	1	2	3	4	5
Dollars received at the end of year		500	500	500	500	500
	$ 471.50 ←					
	445.00 ←					
	420.00 ←					
	396.00 ←					
	373.50 ←					
Present value of the annuity	$2106.00					

n	1%	2%	3%	4%	5%	6%	7%	8%	9%	10%
1	0.990	0.980	0.971	0.962	0.952	0.943	0.935	0.926	0.917	0.909
2	1.970	1.942	1.913	1.886	1.859	1.833	1.808	1.783	1.759	1.736
3	2.941	2.884	2.829	2.775	2.723	2.673	2.624	2.577	2.531	2.487
4	3.902	3.808	3.717	3.630	3.546	3.465	3.387	3.312	3.240	3.170
5	4.853	4.713	4.580	4.452	4.329	4.212	4.100	3.993	3.890	3.791
6	5.795	5.601	5.417	5.242	5.076	4.917	4.767	4.623	4.486	4.355
7	6.728	6.472	6.230	6.002	5.786	5.582	5.389	5.206	5.033	4.868
8	7.652	7.326	7.020	6.733	6.463	6.210	5.971	5.747	5.535	5.335
9	8.566	8.162	7.786	7.435	7.108	6.802	6.515	6.247	5.995	5.759
10	9.471	8.983	8.530	8.111	7.722	7.360	7.024	6.710	6.418	6.145
11	10.368	9.787	9.253	8.760	8.306	7.887	7.499	7.139	6.805	6.495
12	11.255	10.575	9.954	9.385	8.863	8.384	7.943	7.536	7.161	6.814
13	12.134	11.348	10.635	9.986	9.394	8.853	8.358	7.904	7.487	7.103
14	13.004	12.106	11.296	10.563	9.899	9.295	8.746	8.244	7.786	7.367
15	13.865	12.849	11.938	11.118	10.380	9.712	9.108	8.560	8.061	7.606

TABLE 3–8.
$PVIFA_{i,n}$, or the Present Value of an Annuity of $1

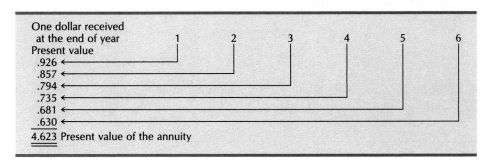

TABLE 3–9.
Present Value of a Six-Year Annuity Discounted at 8 Percent

Using this new notation we can rewrite equation (3–12) as follows:

$$PV = PMT\ (PVIFA_{i,n}) \qquad (3\text{–}12a)$$

Solving the previous example to find the present value of $500 received at the end of each of the next five years discounted back to the present at 6 percent, we look in the $i = 6\%$ column and $n = 5$ year row and find the $PVIFA_{6\%,5yr}$ to be 4.212. Substituting the appropriate values into equation (3–12a), we find

$$PV = \$500(4.212)$$
$$= \$2106$$

This, of course, is the same answer we calculated when we individually discounted each cash flow to the present. The reason is that we really only have *one* table; the Table 3–8 value for an *n*-year annuity for any discount rate *i* is merely the sum of the first *n* values in Table 3–4. We can see this by comparing the value in the present-value-of-an-annuity table (Table 3–8) for $i = 8$ percent and $n = 6$ years, which is 4.623, with the sum of the values in the $i = 8\%$ column and $n = 1, \ldots, 6$ rows of the present-value table (Table 3–4), which is equal to 4.623, as shown in Table 3–9.

EXAMPLE

What is the present value of a ten-year $1,000 annuity discounted back to the present at 5 percent? Substituting $n = 10$ years, $i = 5$ percent, and $PMT = \$1,000$ into equation (3–12), we find

$$PV = \$1000 \left[\sum_{t=1}^{10} \frac{1}{(1 + .05)^t} \right] = \$1000\ (PVIFA_{5\%,10yr})$$

Determining the value for the $PVIFA_{5\%,10yr}$ from Table 3–8, row $n = 10$, column i = 5%, and substituting it in, we get

$$PV = \$1000(7.722)$$
$$= \$7722$$

Thus, the present value of this annuity is $7,722. ■

As with our other compounding and present-value tables, given any three of the four unknowns in equation (3–12), we can solve for the fourth. In the case of the present-value-of-an-annuity table we may be interested in solving for PMT, if we know i, n, and PV. The financial interpretation of this action would be: How much can be withdrawn, perhaps as a pension or to make loan payments, from an account that earns i percent compounded annually for each of the next n years if we wish to have nothing left at the end of n years? For an example, if we have $5,000 in an account earning 8 percent interest, how large an annuity can we draw out each year if we want nothing left at the end of five years? In this case the present value, PV, of the annuity is $5000, $n = 5$ years, $i = 8$ percent, and PMT is unknown. Substituting this into equation (3–12), we find

$$\$5000 = PMT(3.993)$$
$$\$1252.19 = PMT$$

Thus, this account will fall to zero at the end of five years if we withdraw $1,252.19 at the end of each year.

Amortized Loans

This procedure of solving for PMT, the annuity payment value when i, n, and PV are known, is also used to determine what payments are associated with paying off a loan in equal installments over time. Loans that are paid off this way, in equal periodic payments, are called *amortized loans*. For example, suppose a firm wants to purchase a piece of machinery. To do this, it borrows $6,000 to be repaid in four equal payments at the end of each of the next four years, and the interest rate that is paid to the lender is 15 percent on the outstanding portion of the loan. To determine what the annual payments associated with the repayment of this debt will be, we simply use equation (3–12) and solve for the value of PMT, the annual annuity. Again we know three of the four values in that equation, PV, i, and n. PV, the present value of the future annuity, is $6,000; i, the annual interest rate, is 15 percent; and n, the number of years for which the annuity will last, is four years. PMT, the annuity payment received (by the lender and paid by the firm) at the end of each year, is unknown. Substituting these values into equation (3–12) we find

$$\$6000 = PMT\left[\sum_{t=1}^{4}\frac{1}{(1 + .15)^t}\right]$$
$$\$6000 = PMT\,(PVIFA_{15\%,4yr})$$
$$\$6000 = PMT(2.855)$$
$$\$2101.58 = PMT$$

To repay the principal and interest on the outstanding loan in four years the annual payments would be $2,101.58. The breakdown of interest and principal

Year	Annuity	Interest Portion of the Annuity[a]	Repayment of the Principal Portion of the Annuity[b]	Outstanding Loan Balance after the Annuity Payment
1	$2101.58	$900.00	$1201.58	$4798.42
2	2101.58	719.76	1381.82	3416.60
3	2101.58	512.49	1589.09	1827.51
4	2101.58	274.07	1827.51	

[a]The interest portion of the annuity is calculated by multiplying the outstanding loan balance at the beginning of the year by the interest rate of 15 percent. Thus, for year 1 it was $6000.00 × .15 = $900.00, for year 2 it was $4798.42 × .15 = $719.76, and so on.
[b]Repayment of the principal portion of the annuity was calculated by subtracting the interest portion of the annuity (column 2) from the annuity (column 1).

TABLE 3–10.
Loan Amortization Schedule Involving a $6,000 Loan at 15 Percent to Be Repaid in Four Years

payments is given in the *loan amortization schedule* in Table 3–10, with very minor rounding error. As you can see, the interest payment declines each year as the loan outstanding declines.

Present Value of an Uneven Stream

While some projects will involve a single cash flow and some annuities, many projects will involve uneven cash flows over several years. Chapter 6, which examines investments in fixed assets, presents this situation repeatedly. There we will be comparing not only the present value of cash flows between projects but also the cash inflows and outflows within a particular project, trying to determine that project's present value. However, this will not be difficult because the present value of any cash flow is measured in today's dollars and thus can be compared, through addition for inflows and subtraction for outflows, to the present value of any other cash flow also measured in today's dollars. For example, if we wished to find the present value of the following cash flows

Year	Cash Flow
1	$500
2	200
3	−400
4	500
5	500
6	500
7	500
8	500
9	500
10	500

given a 6 percent discount rate, we would merely discount the flows back to the present and total them by adding in the positive flows and subtracting the negative ones. However, this problem is complicated by the annuity of $500 that runs from years 4 through 10. To accommodate this, we can first discount the annuity back to the beginning of period 4 (or end of period 3) by multiplying it by the value of $PVIFA_{6\%,7yr}$ and get its present value at that point in time. We then multiply this value times the $PVIF_{6\%,3yr}$ in order to bring this single cash flow (which is the present value of the 7-year annuity) back to the present. In effect we discount twice, first back to the end of period 3, then back to the present. This is shown graphically in Table 3–11 and numerically in Table 3–12 on page 82. Thus, the present value of this uneven stream of cash flows is $2,657.94.

TABLE 3–11.
Illustration of an Example of Present Value of an Uneven Stream Involving One Annuity Discounted to Present at 6 Percent

Year	0	1	2	3	4	5	6	7	8	9	10
Dollars received at end of year		500	200	−400	500	500	500	500	500	500	500
	$ 471.50 ←										
	178.00 ←										
	−336.00 ←										
				$2791 ←							
	2344.44 ←										
Total present value	$2657.94										

TABLE 3–12.
Determination of Present Value of an Example with Uneven Stream Involving One Annuity Discounted to Present at 6 Percent

1. Present value of $500 received at the end of one year = $500(.943) = $ 471.50
2. Present value of $200 received at the end of two years = $200(.890) =   178.00
3. Present value of a $400 outflow at the end of three years = −$400(.840) =   −336.00
4. (a) Value at the end of year 3 of a $500 annuity, years 4 through 10 = $500(5.582) = $2791.00
   (b) Present value of $2791.00 received at the end of year 3 = $2,791(.840) =   2344.44
5. Total present value = $2657.94

[handwritten margin note: SINGLE YEAR IS PRESENT VALUE. MULTIPLE YEARS ARE Present Values for ANNUITY]

What is the present value of an investment involving $200 received at the end of years 1 through 5, a $300 cash outflow at the end of year 6, and $500 received at the end of years 7 through 10, given a 5 percent discount rate? Here we have two annuities, one that can be discounted directly back to the present by multiplying it by the value of the $PVIFA_{5\%, 5yr}$ and one that must be discounted twice to bring it back to the present. This second annuity, which is a four-year annuity, must first be discounted back to the beginning of period 7 (or end of period 6) by multiplying it by the value of the $PVIFA_{5\%, 4yr}$. Then the present value of this annuity at the end of period 6 (which can be viewed as a single cash flow) must be discounted back to the present by multiplying it by the value of the $PVIF_{5\%, 6yr}$.

To arrive at the total present value of this investment, we subtract the present value of the $300 cash outflow at the end of year 6 from the sum of the present value of the two annuities. Table 3–13 shows this graphically; Table 3–14 gives the calculations. Thus, the present value of this series of cash flows is $1,964.66.

TABLE 3–13.
Illustration of an Example of Present Value of an Uneven Stream Involving Two Annuities Discounted to Present at 5 Percent

Year	0	1	2	3	4	5	6	7	8	9	10
Dollars received at end of year		200	200	200	200	200	−300	500	500	500	500
	$ 865.80 ←										
	−223.80 ←										
							$1773 ←				
	1322.66 ←										
Total present value	$1964.66										

TABLE 3–14.
Determination of Present Value of an Example with Uneven Stream Involving Two Annuities Discounted to Present at 5 Percent

1. Present value of first annuity, years 1 through 5 = $200(4.329) = $ 865.80
2. Present value of $300 cash outflow = −$300(.746) =   −223.80
3. (a) Value at end of year 6 of second annuity, years 7 through 10 = $500(3.546) = $1773.00
   (b) Present value of $1773.00 received at the end of year 6 = $1773.00(.746) =   1322.66
4. Total present value = $1964.66

Perpetuities

A **perpetuity** is an annuity that continues forever; that is, every year from its establishment this investment pays the same dollar amount. An example of a perpetuity is preferred stock that yields a constant dollar dividend infinitely. Determining the present value of a perpetuity is delightfully simple; we merely need to divide the constant flow by the discount rate.[1] For example, the present value of a \$100 perpetuity discounted back to the present at 5 percent is \$100/.05 = \$2000. Thus, the equation representing the present value of a perpetuity is

$$PV = \frac{PP}{i} \qquad\qquad (3-13)$$

where PV = the present value of the perpetuity

PP = the constant dollar amount provided by the perpetuity

i = the annual interest (or discount) rate

EXAMPLE

What is the present value of a \$500 perpetuity discounted back to the present at 8 percent? Substituting PP = \$500 and i = .08 into equation (3–13), we find

$$PV = \frac{\$500}{.08} = \$6250$$

Thus, the present value of this perpetuity is \$6,250.

___
[1]See Chapter 5 for a mathematical derivation.

INTERNATIONAL FINANCIAL MANAGEMENT

Bringing Australs Back to the Present

In the previous chapter we looked at the Fisher effect and the effects of inflation on rates of return. We found that investors demand a return for delaying consumption, the risk-free rate, as well as an additional return for taking on added risk. The discount rate that we use to move money through time should reflect this return for delaying consumption; and as the Fisher effect showed, this discount rate should reflect anticipated inflation. In the United States anticipated inflation is quite low, although it does tend to fluctuate over time. Elsewhere in the world, however, the inflation rate is difficult to predict because it can be dramatically high and undergo huge fluctuations.

Let's look at Argentina, keeping in mind that similar examples abound in Central and South America and Eastern Europe. At the beginning of 1992, Argentina introduced its fifth currency in 22 years, the new peso. The austral, the currency that was replaced, was introduced in June of 1985 and was initially equal in value to \$1.25 in U.S. currency. Five and a half years later it took 100,000 australs to equal one dollar. Inflation had reached the point where the stack of money needed to buy a candy bar was bigger and weighed more than the candy bar itself, and many workers received their week's wages in grocery bags. Needless to say, if we were to move australs through time, we would have to use an extremely high interest or discount rate. Unfortunately, in countries suffering from hyperinflation, inflation rates tend to fluctuate dramatically, and this makes estimating the expected inflation rate even more difficult. For example, in 1989 the inflation rate in Argentina was 4,924 percent, then in 1990 it dropped to 1,344 percent, and in 1991 it was only 84 percent.

Bond Valuation: An Illustration of the Time Value of Money[2]

Bond valuation illustrates a combination of several discounting techniques and procedures, including an annuity, a single cash flow, and the use of semiannual compounding periods. Thus, as we will see, the present value of a bond can change dramatically as the discount rate changes. When a bond is purchased, the owner receives two things: (1) interest payments, which are generally made semiannually; and (2) repayment at maturity, of the full principal, regardless of the price the investor pays for the bond. For example, let us look at a bond that pays $45 semiannually and comes due in twenty years; that is, at the end of twenty years the bondholder will receive $1,000, the return of the principal, and the bond will terminate. What is this bond worth? It is worth the present value of the cash flows it provides. Thus, as the corresponding market discount or interest rate changes, the value of the bond changes. Let us examine the value of this bond, assuming medium, low, and high market discount rates—say, 10, 6, and 14 percent, respectively.

Bond Value at 10 Percent

The bond value is the sum of the present value of the interest payment annuity that the bondholder receives and the present value of the return of bond principal at maturity computed at the market discount rate of 10 percent paid semiannually; that is,

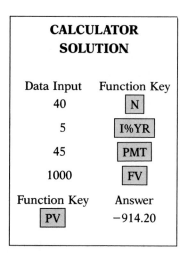

$$\begin{pmatrix} \text{bond value} \\ \text{at 10\%} \\ \text{compounded} \\ \text{semiannually} \end{pmatrix} = \begin{pmatrix} \text{present value} \\ \text{of interest} \\ \text{payments} \end{pmatrix} + \begin{pmatrix} \text{present value of} \\ \text{the return of} \\ \text{the principal} \end{pmatrix}$$

$$= PMT \left[\sum_{t=1}^{mn} \frac{1}{(1 + i/m)^t} \right] + FV_{nm} \left[\frac{1}{(1 + i/m)^{nm}} \right] \quad \textbf{(3-14)}$$

$$= \$45 \left[\sum_{t=1}^{40} \frac{1}{(1 + .05)^t} \right] + \$1000 \left[\frac{1}{(1 + .05)^{40}} \right]$$

$$= \$45(17.159) + \$1000(.142)$$

$$= \$772.16 + \$142$$

$$= \$914.16$$

Thus, the value of this bond that pays $45 semiannually, given a market discount rate of 10 percent, is $914.16.

Bond Value at 6 Percent

If the market discount rate drops to 6 percent paid semiannually, the procedure for determining the bond value remains the same, and the only change is that i now equals 6 percent. Logically, since the value of i appears only in the denominators of the present value of interest payments and the return of principal, the bond value should increase as i drops. Intuitively this makes sense; the cash flows to the bondholder all occur in the future, and they are now discounted back to the present at a lower discount rate, so their present value

---

[2]This section is also covered in Chapter 5 and can be omitted without loss of continuity.

should increase. The value of this bond at a 6 percent market discount rate becomes

$$\begin{array}{c}\text{bond value}\\\text{at 6\% compounded}\\\text{semiannually}\end{array} = \$45 \left[\sum_{t=1}^{40} \frac{1}{(1 + .03)^t} \right] + \$1000 \left[\frac{1}{(1 + .03)^{40}} \right]$$

$$= \$45(23.115) + \$1000(.307)$$

$$= \$1040.18 + \$307$$

$$= \$1347.18$$

If the market discount rate drops from 10 percent to 6 percent, the value of this bond will climb from $914.16 to $1,374.18.

Bond Value at 14 Percent

If the market discount rate climbs to 14 percent paid semiannually, the bond value will drop, as the future cash flows to the bondholder are now discounted back to the present at a higher discount rate

$$\begin{array}{c}\text{bond value}\\\text{at 14\% compounded}\\\text{semiannually}\end{array} = \$45 \left[\sum_{t=1}^{40} \frac{1}{(1 + .07)^t} \right] + \$1000 \left[\frac{1}{(1 + .07)^{40}} \right]$$

$$= \$45(13.332) + \$1000(.067)$$

$$= \$599.94 + \$67$$

$$= \$666.94$$

If the market discount rate climbs from 10 percent to 14 percent, the value of this bond will drop from $914.16 to $666.94. This illustrates the inverse relationship between interest rates or the market discount rate and bond prices. When the market discount rate goes up, bond values go down, and vice versa.

CALCULATOR SOLUTION	
Data Input	Function Key
40	N
3	I%YR
45	PMT
1000	FV
Function Key	Answer
PV	−1346.72

CALCULATOR SOLUTION	
Data Input	Function Key
40	N
7	I%YR
45	PMT
1000	FV
Function Key	Answer
PV	−666.71

SUMMARY

To make decisions, financial managers must compare the costs and benefits of alternatives that do not occur during the same time period. Whether to make profitable investments or to take advantage of favorable interest rates, financial decision making requires an understanding of the time value of money. Managers who use the time value of money in all of their financial calculations assure themselves of more logical decisions. The time value process first makes all dollar values comparable; since money has a time value, it moves all dollar flows either back to the present or out to a common future date. All time value formulas presented in this chapter actually stem from the single compounding formula $FV_n = PV(1 + i)^n$. The formulas are used to deal simply with common financial situations, for example, discounting single flows, compounding annuities, and discounting annuities. Table 3–15 provides a summary of these calculations.

Calculation	Equation
Future value of a single payment	$FV_n = PV(1 + i)^n = PV(FVIF_{i,n})$
Future value of a single payment with nonannual compounding	$FV_n = PV\left(1 + \dfrac{i}{m}\right)^{mn}$
Present value of a single payment	$PV = FV_n\left[\dfrac{1}{(1 + i)^n}\right] = FV_n\,(PVIF_{i,n})$
Future value of an annuity	$FV_n = PMT\left[\displaystyle\sum_{t=0}^{n-1}(1 + i)^t\right] = PMT\,(FVIFA_{i,n})$
Present value of an annuity	$PV = PMT\left[\displaystyle\sum_{t=1}^{n}\dfrac{1}{(1 + i)^t}\right] = PMT\,(PVIFA_{i,n})$
Present value of a perpetuity	$PV = \dfrac{PP}{i}$

TABLE 3–15.
Summary of Time Value of Money Equations*

Notation: FV_n = the future value of the investment at the end of n years
n = the number of years until payment will be received or during which compounding occurs
i = the annual interest or discount rate
PV = the present value of the future sum of money
m = the number of times compounding occurs during the year
PMT = the annuity payment deposited or received at the end of each year
PP = the constant dollar amount provided by the perpetuity

*Related tables appear in Appendixes B through E at the end of the book.

STUDY QUESTIONS

3–1. What is the time value of money? Why is it so important?

3–2. The processes of discounting and compounding are related. Explain this relationship.

3–3. How would an increase in the interest rate (i) or a decrease in the holding period (n) affect the future value (FV_n) of a sum of money? Explain why.

3–4. Suppose you were considering depositing your savings in one of three banks, all of which pay 5 percent interest; bank A compounds annually, bank B compounds semiannually, and bank C compounds continuously. Which bank would you choose? Why?

3–5. What is the relationship between the $PVIF_{i,n}$ (Table 3–4) and the $PVIFA_{i,n}$ (Table 3–8)? What is the $PVIFA_{10\%,\,10\text{ yr}}$? Add up the values of the $PVIF_{10\%,\,n}$ for $n = 1, \ldots,$ 10. What is this value? Why do these values have the relationship they do?

3–6. What is an annuity? Give some examples of annuities. Distinguish between an annuity and a perpetuity.

3–7. What does continuous compounding mean?

SELF-TEST PROBLEMS

ST–1. You place $25,000 in a savings account paying annual compound interest of 8 percent for three years and then move it into a savings account that pays 10 percent interest compounded annually. How much will your money have grown at the end of six years?

ST–2. You purchase a boat for $35,000 and pay $5,000 down and agree to pay the rest over the next 10 years in 10 equal annual payments that include principal payments plus 13 percent compound interest on the unpaid balance. What will be the amount of each payment?

ST–3. For an investment to grow eightfold in nine years, at what rate would it have to grow?

ST–4. You have the opportunity to buy a bond for $1,000 that will pay no interest during its ten-year life and have a value of $3,106 at maturity. What rate of return or yield does this bond pay?

STUDY PROBLEMS (SET A)

3–1A. (*Compound Interest*) To what amount will the following investments accumulate?
  a. $5,000 invested for 10 years at 10 percent compounded annually
  b. $8,000 invested for 7 years at 8 percent compounded annually
  c. $775 invested for 12 years at 12 percent compounded annually
  d. $21,000 invested for 5 years at 5 percent compounded annually

3–2A. (*Compound Value Solving for* n) How many years will the following take?
  a. $500 to grow to $1,039.50 if invested at 5 percent compounded annually
  b. $35 to grow to $53.87 if invested at 9 percent compounded annually
  c. $100 to grow to $298.60 if invested at 20 percent compounded annually
  d. $53 to grow to $78.76 if invested at 2 percent compounded annually

3–3A. (*Compound Value Solving for* i) At what annual rate would the following have to be invested?
  a. $500 to grow to $1,948.00 in 12 years
  b. $300 to grow to $422.10 in 7 years
  c. $50 to grow to $280.20 in 20 years
  d. $200 to grow to $497.60 in 5 years

3–4A. (*Present.Value*) What is the present value of the following future amounts?
  a. $800 to be received 10 years from now discounted back to present at 10 percent
  b. $300 to be received 5 years from now discounted back to present at 5 percent
  c. $1,000 to be received 8 years from now discounted back to present at 3 percent
  d. $1,000 to be received 8 years from now discounted back to present at 20 percent

3–5A. (*Compound Annuity*) What is the accumulated sum of each of the following streams of payments?
  a. $500 a year for 10 years compounded annually at 5 percent
  b. $100 a year for 5 years compounded annually at 10 percent
  c. $35 a year for 7 years compounded annually at 7 percent
  d. $25 a year for 3 years compounded annually at 2 percent

3–6A. (*Present Value of an Annuity*) What is the present value of the following annuities?
  a. $2,500 a year for 10 years discounted back to the present at 7 percent
  b. $70 a year for 3 years discounted back to the present at 3 percent
  c. $280 a year for 7 years discounted back to the present at 6 percent
  d. $500 a year for 10 years discounted back to the present at 10 percent

3–7A. (*Compound Value*) Brian Mosallam, who recently sold his Porsche, placed $10,000 in a savings account paying annual compound interest of 6 percent.
  a. Calculate the amount of money that will have accrued if he leaves the money in the bank for 1, 5, and 15 years.
  b. If he moves his money into an account that pays 8 percent or one that pays 10 percent, rework part (a) using these new interest rates.
  c. What conclusions can you draw about the relationship between interest rates, time, and future sums from the calculations you have done above?

3–8A. (*Compound Interest with Nonannual Periods*) Calculate the amount of money that will be in each of the following accounts at the end of the given deposit period:

Account	Amount Deposited	Annual Interest Rate	Compounding Period (Compounded Every ___ Months)	Deposit Period (Years)
Theodore Logan III	$ 1,000	10%	12	10
Vernell Coles	95,000	12	1	1
Thomas Elliott	8,000	12	2	2
Wayne Robinson	120,000	8	3	2
Eugene Chung	30,000	10	6	4
Kelly Cravens	15,000	12	4	3

3–9A. (*Compound Interest with Nonannual Periods*)
  a. Calculate the future sum of $5,000, given that it will be held in the bank five years at an annual interest rate of 6 percent.
  b. Recalculate part (a) using a compounding period that is (1) semiannual and (2) bimonthly.
  c. Recalculate parts (a) and (b) for a 12 percent annual interest rate.
  d. Recalculate part (a) using a time horizon of 12 years (annual interest rate is still 6 percent).
  e. With respect to the effect of changes in the stated interest rate and holding periods on future sums in parts (c) and (d), what conclusions do you draw when you compare these figures with the answers found in parts (a) and (b)?

3–10A. (*Solving for* i *in Annuities*) Nicki Johnson, a sophomore mechanical engineering student, receives a call from an insurance agent, who believes that Nicki is an older woman ready to retire from teaching. He talks to her about several annuities that she could buy that would guarantee her an annual fixed income. The annuities are as follows:

Annuity	Initial Payment into Annuity (at t = 0)	Amount of Money Received per Year	Duration of Annuity (Years)
A	$50,000	$8,500	12
B	$60,000	$7,000	25
C	$70,000	$8,000	20

If Nicki could earn 11 percent on her money by placing it in a savings account, should she place it instead in any of the annuities? Which ones, if any? Why?

3–11A. (*Future Value*) Sales of a new finance book were 15,000 copies this year and were expected to increase by 20 percent per year. What are expected sales during each of the next three years? Graph this sales trend and explain.

3–12A. (*Future Value*) Reggie Jackson, formerly of the New York Yankees, hit 41 home runs in 1980. If his home-run output grew at a rate of 10 percent per year, what would it have been over the following five years?

3–13A. (*Loan Amortization*) Mr. Bill S. Preston, Esq., purchased a new house for $80,000. He paid $20,000 down and agreed to pay the rest over the next 25 years in 25 equal annual payments that include principal payments plus 9 percent compound interest on the unpaid balance. What will these equal payments be?

3–14A. (*Solving for* PMT *in an Annuity*) To pay for your child's education you wish to have accumulated $15,000 at the end of 15 years. To do this you plan on depositing an equal amount into the bank at the end of each year. If the bank is willing to pay 6 percent compounded annually, how much must you deposit each year to obtain your goal?

3–15A. (*Solving for* i *in Compound Interest*) If you were offered $1,079.50 ten years from now in return for an investment of $500 currently, what annual rate of interest would you earn if you took the offer?

3–16A. (*Present Value and Future Value of an Annuity*) In 10 years you are planning on retiring and buying a house in Oviedo, Florida. The house you are looking at currently costs $100,000 and is expected to increase in value each year at a rate of 5 percent. Assuming you can earn 10 percent annually on your investments, how much must you invest at the end of each of the next 10 years to be able to buy your dream home when you retire?

3–17A. (*Compound Value*) The Aggarwal Corporation needs to save $10 million to retire a $10 million mortgage that matures on December 31, 2002. To retire this mortgage, the company plans to put a fixed amount into an account at the end of each year for 10 years, with the first payment occurring on December 31, 1993. The Aggarwal Corporation expects to earn 9 percent annually on the money in this account. What equal annual contribution must it make to this account to accumulate the $10 million by December 31, 2002?

3–18A. (*Compound Interest with Nonannual Periods*) After examining the various personal loan rates available to you, you find that you can borrow funds from a finance company at 12 percent compounded monthly or from a bank at 13 percent compounded annually. Which alternative is the most attractive?

3–19A. (*Present Value of an Uneven Stream of Payments*) You are given three investment alternatives to analyze. The cash flows from these three investments are as follows:

End of Year	Investment A	Investment B	Investment C
1	$10,000		$10,000
2	10,000		
3	10,000		
4	10,000		
5	10,000	$10,000	
6		10,000	50,000
7		10,000	
8		10,000	
9		10,000	
10		10,000	10,000

Assuming a 20 percent discount rate, find the present value of each investment.

3–20A. (*Present Value*) The Kumar Corporation is planning on issuing bonds that pay no interest but can be converted into $1,000 at maturity, seven years from their purchase. To price these bonds competitively with other bonds of equal risk, it is determined that they should yield 10 percent, compounded annually. At what price should the Kumar Corporation sell these bonds?

3–21A. (*Perpetuities*) What is the present value of the following?
  a. A $300 perpetuity discounted back to the present at 8 percent
  b. A $1,000 perpetuity discounted back to the present at 12 percent
  c. A $100 perpetuity discounted back to the present at 9 percent
  d. A $95 perpetuity discounted back to the present at 5 percent

3–22A. (*Continuous Compounding*) What is the value of $500 after five years if it is invested at 10 percent compounded continuously? (If you don't have a calculator capable of solving this problem, simply set it up.)

3–23A. (*Solving for* n *with Nonannual Periods*) About how many years would it take for your investment to grow fourfold if it were invested at 16 percent compounded semiannually?

3–24A. (*Bond Values*) You are examining three bonds with par value of $1,000 (you receive $1,000 at maturity) and are concerned with what would happen to their market value if interest rates (or the market discount rate) changed. The three bonds are

  Bond A—A bond with 3 years left to maturity that pays 10 percent per year compounded semiannually

  Bond B—A bond with 7 years left to maturity that pays 10 percent per year compounded semiannually

  Bond C—A bond with twenty years left to maturity that pays 10 percent per year compounded semiannually

What would be the value of these bonds if the market discount rate were
  a. 10 percent per year compounded semiannually?
  b. 4 percent per year compounded semiannually?
  c. 16 percent per year compounded semiannually?
  d. What observations can you make about these results?

3–25A. (*Complex Present Value*) How much do you have to deposit today so that beginning eleven years from now you can withdraw $10,000 a year for the next five years (periods 11 through 15) plus an *additional* amount of $20,000 in that last year (period 15)? Assume an interest rate of 6 percent.

3–26A. (*Loan Amortization*) On December 31, Beth Klemkosky bought a yacht for $50,000, paying $10,000 down and agreeing to pay the balance in 10 equal annual installments that include both the principal and 10 percent interest on the declining balance. How big would the annual payments be?

3–27A. (*Solving for* i *in an Annuity*) You lend a friend $30,000, which your friend will repay in five equal annual payments of $10,000, with the first payment to be received one year from now. What rate of return does your loan receive?

3–28A. (*Solving for* i *in Compound Interest*) You lend a friend $10,000, for which your friend will repay you $27,027 at the end of five years. What interest rate are you charging your "friend"?

3–29A. (*Loan Amortization*) A firm borrows $25,000 from the bank at 12 percent compounded annually to purchase some new machinery. This loan is to be repaid in equal annual installments at the end of each year over the next five years. How much will each annual payment be?

3–30A. (*Present Value Comparison*) You are offered $1,000 today, $10,000 in 12 years, or $25,000 in twenty-five years. Assuming that you can earn 11 percent on your money, which should you choose?

3–31A. (*Compound Annuity*) You plan on buying some property in Florida five years from today. To do this you estimate that you will need $20,000 at that time for the purchase. You would like to accumulate these funds by making equal annual deposits in your savings account, which pays 12 percent annually. If you make your first deposit at the end of this year and you would like your account to reach $20,000 when the final deposit is made, what will be the amount of your deposits?

3–32A. (*Complex Present Value*) You would like to have $50,000 in 15 years. To accumulate this amount you plan to deposit each year an equal sum in the bank, which will earn 7 percent interest compounded annually. Your first payment will be made at the end of the year.

    a. How much must you deposit annually to accumulate this amount?

    b. If you decide to make a large lump-sum deposit today instead of the annual deposits, how large should this lump-sum deposit be? (Assume you can earn 7 percent on this deposit.)

    c. At the end of five years you will receive $10,000 and deposit this in the bank toward your goal of $50,000 at the end of 15 years. In addition to this deposit, how much must you deposit in equal annual deposits to reach your goal? (Again assume you can earn 7 percent on this deposit.)

3–33A. (*Comprehensive Present Value*) You are trying to plan for retirement in 10 years, and currently you have $100,000 in a savings account and $300,000 in stocks. In addition you plan on adding to your savings by depositing $10,000 per year in your *savings account* at the end of each of the next five years and then $20,000 per year at the end of each year for the final five years until retirement.

    a. Assuming your savings account returns 7 percent compounded annually while your investment in stocks will return 12 percent compounded annually, how much will you have at the end of 10 years? (Ignore taxes.)

    b. If you expect to live for 20 years after you retire, and at retirement you deposit all of your savings in a bank account paying 10 percent, how much can you withdraw each year after retirement (20 equal withdrawals beginning one year after you retire) to end up with a zero balance at death?

3–34A. (*Loan Amortization*) On December 31, Son-Nan Chen borrowed $100,000, agreeing to repay this sum in 20 equal annual installments that include both the principal and 15 percent interest on the declining balance. How large will the annual payments be?

3–35A. (*Loan Amortization*) To buy a new house you must borrow $150,000. To do this you take out a $150,000, 30-year, 10 percent mortgage. Your mortgage payments, which are made at the end of each year (one payment each year), include both principal and 10 percent interest on the declining balance. How large will your annual payments be?

3–36A. (*Present Value*) The state lottery's million-dollar payout provides for one million dollars to be paid over 19 years in $50,000 amounts. The first $50,000 payment is made immediately and the 19 remaining $ 50,000 payments occur at the end of each of the next 19 years. If 10 percent is the appropriate discount rate, what is the present value of this stream of cash flows? If 20 percent is the appropriate discount rate, what is the present value of the cash flows?

3–37A. (*Solving for i in Compound Interest—Financial Calculator Needed*) In September 1963 the first issue of the comic book *X-MEN* was issued. The original price for that issue was 12 cents. By September 1992, 29 years later, the value of this comic book had risen to $990. What annual rate of interest would you have earned if you had bought the comic in 1963 and sold it in 1992?

3–38A. (*Comprehensive Present Value*) You have just inherited a large sum of money and you are trying to determine how much you should save for retirement and how much you can spend now. For retirement you will deposit today (January 1, 1993) a lump sum in a bank account paying 10 percent compounded annually. You don't plan on touching this deposit until you retire in five years (January 1, 1998), and you plan on living for 20 additional years and then dropping dead on December 31, 2017. During your retirement you would like to receive income of $50,000 per year to be received the first day of each year, with the first payment on January 1, 1998, and the last payment on January 1, 2017. Complicating this objective is your desire to have one final three-year fling during which time you'd like to track down all the original members of "Leave It to Beaver" and "The Brady Bunch" and get their autographs. To finance this you want to receive $250,000 on January 1, 2013, and *nothing* on January 1, 2014 and January 1, 2015, as you will be on the road. In

addition, after you pass on (January 1, 2018), you would like to have a total of $100,000 to leave to your children.
  a. How much must you deposit in the bank at 10 percent on January 1, 1993, to achieve your goal? (Use a timeline to answer this question.)
  b. What kinds of problems are associated with this analysis and its assumptions?

STUDY PROBLEMS (SET B)

3-1B. (*Compound Interest*) To what amount will the following investments accumulate?
  a. $4,000 invested for 11 years at 9 percent compounded annually
  b. $8,000 invested for 10 years at 8 percent compounded annually
  c. $800 invested for 12 years at 12 percent compounded annually
  d. $21,000 invested for 6 years at 5 percent compounded annually

3-2B. (*Compound Value Solving for* n) How many years will the following take?
  a. $550 to grow to $1,043.90 if invested at 6 percent compounded annually
  b. $40 to grow to $88.44 if invested at 12 percent compounded annually
  c. $110 to grow to $614.79 if invested at 24 percent compounded annually
  d. $60 to grow to $78.30 if invested at 3 percent compounded annually

3-3B. (*Compound Value Solving for* i) At what annual rate would the following have to be invested?
  a. $550 to grow to $1,898.60 in 13 years
  b. $275 to grow to $406.18 in 8 years
  c. $60 to grow to $279.66 in 20 years
  d. $180 to grow to $486.00 in 6 years

3-4B. (*Present Value*) What is the present value of the following future amounts?
  a. $800 to be received 10 years from now discounted back to present at 10 percent
  b. $400 to be received 6 years from now discounted back to present at 6 percent
  c. $1,000 to be received 8 years from now discounted back to present at 5 percent
  d. $900 to be received 9 years from now discounted back to present at 20 percent

3-5B. (*Compound Annuity*) What is the accumulated sum of each of the following streams of payments?
  a. $500 a year for 10 years compounded annually at 6 percent
  b. $150 a year for 5 years compounded annually at 11 percent
  c. $35 a year for 8 years compounded annually at 7 percent
  d. $25 a year for 3 years compounded annually at 2 percent

3-6B. (*Present Value of an Annuity*) What is the present value of the following annuities?
  a. $3,000 a year for 10 years discounted back to the present at 8 percent
  b. $50 a year for 3 years discounted back to the present at 3 percent
  c. $280 a year for 8 years discounted back to the present at 7 percent
  d. $600 a year for 10 years discounted back to the present at 10 percent

3-7B. (*Compound Value*) Trish Nealon, who recently sold her Porsche, placed $20,000 in a savings account paying annual compound interest of 7 percent.
  a. Calculate the amount of money that will have accrued if she leaves the money in the bank for 1, 5, and 15 years.
  b. If she moves her money into an account that pays 9 percent or one that pays 11 percent, rework part (a) using these new interest rates.
  c. What conclusions can you draw about the relationship between interest rates, time, and future sums from the calculations you have done above?

3-8B. (*Compound Interest with Nonannual Periods*) Calculate the amount of money that will be in each of the following accounts at the end of the given deposit period:

Account	Amount Deposited	Annual Interest Rate	Compounding Period (Compounded Every ___ Months)	Deposit Period (Years)
Korey Stringer	$ 2,000	12%	2	2
Eric Moss	50,000	12	1	1
Ty Howard	7,000	18	2	2
Rob Kelly	130,000	12	3	2
Matt Christopher	20,000	14	6	4
Juan Porter	15,000	15	4	3

3–9B. (*Compound Interest with Nonannual Periods*)
  a. Calculate the future sum of $6,000, given that it will be held in the bank five years at an annual interest rate of 6 percent.
  b. Recalculate part (a) using a compounding period that is (1) semiannual and (2) bimonthly.
  c. Recalculate parts (a) and (b) for a 12 percent annual interest rate.
  d. Recalculate part (a) using a time horizon of 12 years (annual interest rate is still 6 percent).
  e. With respect to the effect of changes in the stated interest rate and holding periods on future sums in parts (c) and (d), what conclusions do you draw when you compare these figures with the answers found in parts (a) and (b)?

3–10B. (*Solving for* i *in Annuities*) Ellen Denis, a sophomore mechanical engineering student, receives a call from an insurance agent, who believes that Ellen is an older woman ready to retire from teaching. He talks to her about several annuities that she could buy that would guarantee her an annual fixed income. The annuities are as follows:

Annuity	Initial Payment into Annuity (at t = 0)	Amount of Money Received per year	Duration of Annuity (Years)
A	$50,000	$8500	12
B	$60,000	$7000	25
C	$70,000	$8000	20

If Ellen could earn 12 percent on her money by placing it in a savings account, should she place it instead in any of the annuities? Which ones, if any? Why?

3–11B. (*Future Value*) Sales of a new marketing book were 10,000 copies this year and were expected to increase by 15 percent per year. What are expected sales during each of the next three years? Graph this sales trend and explain.

3–12B. (*Future Value*) Reggie Jackson, formerly of the New York Yankees, hit 41 home runs in 1980. If his home-run output grew at a rate of 12 percent per year, what would it have been over the following five years?

3–13B. (*Loan Amortization*) Stefani Moore purchased a new house for $150,000. She paid $30,000 down and agreed to pay the rest over the next 25 years in 25 equal annual payments that include principal payments plus 10 percent compound interest on the unpaid balance. What will these equal payments be?

3–14B. (*Solving for* PMT *in an Annuity*) To pay for your child's education you wish to have accumulated $25,000 at the end of 15 years. To do this you plan on depositing an equal amount into the bank at the end of each year. If the bank is willing to pay 7 percent compounded annually, how much must you deposit each year to obtain your goal?

3–15B. (*Solving for* i *in Compound Interest*) If you were offered $2,376.50 ten years from now in return for an investment of $700 currently, what annual rate of interest would you earn if you took the offer?

3–16B. (*Present Value and Future Value of an Annuity*) In 10 years you are planning on retiring and buying a house in Marco Island, Florida. The house you are looking at currently costs $125,000 and is expected to increase in value each year at a rate of 5 percent. Assuming you can earn 10 percent annually on your investments, how much must you invest at the end of each of the next 10 years to be able to buy your dream home when you retire?

3–17B. (*Compound Value*) The Knutson Corporation needs to save $15 million to retire a $15 million mortgage that matures on December 31, 2002. To retire this mortgage, the company plans to put a fixed amount into an account at the end of each year for 10 years, with the first payment occurring on December 31, 1993. The Knutson Corporation expects to earn 10 percent annually on the money in this account. What equal annual contribution must it make to this account to accumulate the $15 million by December 31, 2002?

3–18B. (*Compound Interest with Nonannual Periods*) After examining the various personal loan rates available to you, you find that you can borrow funds from a finance company at 24 percent compounded monthly or from a bank at 26 percent compounded annually. Which alternative is the most attractive?

3–19B. (*Present Value of an Uneven Stream of Payments*) You are given three investment alternatives to analyze. The cash flows from these three investments are as follows:

End of Year	Investment		
	A	B	C
1	$15,000		$20,000
2	15,000		
3	15,000		
4	15,000		
5	15,000	$15,000	
6		15,000	60,000
7		15,000	
8		15,000	
9		15,000	
10		15,000	20,000

Assuming a 20 percent discount rate, find the present value of each investment.

3–20B. (*Present Value*) The Shin Corporation is planning on issuing bonds that pay no interest but can be converted into $1,000 at maturity, eight years from their purchase. To price these bonds competitively with other bonds of equal risk, it is determined that they should yield 9 percent, compounded annually. At what price should the Shin Corporation sell these bonds?

3–21B. (*Perpetuities*) What is the present value of the following?
  a. A $400 perpetuity discounted back to the present at 9 percent
  b. A $1,500 perpetuity discounted back to the present at 13 percent
  c. A $150 perpetuity discounted back to the present at 10 percent
  d. A $100 perpetuity discounted back to the present at 6 percent

3–22B. (*Continuous Compounding*) What is the value of $600 after five years if it is invested at 10 percent compounded continuously? (If you don't have a calculator capable of solving this problem, simply set it up.)

3–23B. (*Solving for* n *with Nonannual Periods*) About how many years would it take for your investment to grow sevenfold if it were invested at 10 percent compounded semiannually?

3–24B. (*Bond Values*) You are examining three bonds with par value of $1,000 (you receive $1,000 at maturity) and are concerned with what would happen to their market value if interest rates (or the market discount rate) changed. The three bonds are

  Bond A—A bond with 7 years left to maturity that pays 10 percent per year compounded semiannually
  Bond B—A bond with 3 years left to maturity that pays 10 percent per year compounded semiannually
  Bond C—A bond with 20 years left to maturity that pays 10 percent per year compounded semiannually

What would be the value of these bonds if the market discount rate were
  a. 10 percent per year compounded semiannually?
  b. 4 percent per year compounded semiannually?
  c. 16 percent per year compounded semiannually?
  d. What observations can you make about these results?

3–25B. (*Complex Present Value*) How much do you have to deposit today so that beginning 11 years from now you can withdraw $10,000 a year for the next five years (periods 11 through 15) plus an *additional* amount of $15,000 in that last year (period 15)? Assume an interest rate of 7 percent.

3–26B. (*Loan Amortization*) On December 31, Loren Billingsley bought a yacht for $60,000, paying $15,000 down and agreeing to pay the balance in 10 equal annual installments that include both the principal and 9 percent interest on the declining balance. How big would the annual payments be?

3–27B. (*Solving for* i *in an Annuity*) You lend a friend $45,000, which your friend will repay in five equal annual payments of $9,000 with the first payment to be received one year from now. What rate of return does your loan receive?

3–28B. (*Solving for* i *in Compound Interest*) You lend a friend $15,000, for which your friend will repay you $37,313 at the end of five years. What interest rate are you charging your "friend"?

3–29B. (*Loan Amortization*) A firm borrows $30,000 from the bank at 13 percent compounded annually to purchase some new machinery. This loan is to be repaid in equal annual installments at the end of each year over the next four years. How much will each annual payment be?

3–30B. (*Present Value Comparison*) You are offered $1,000 today, $10,000 in 12 years, or $25,000 in 25 years. Assuming that you can earn 11 percent on your money, which should you choose?

3–31B. (*Compound Annuity*) You plan on buying some property in Florida five years from today. To do this you estimate that you will need $30,000 at that time for the purchase. You would like to accumulate these funds by making equal annual deposits in your savings account, which pays 10 percent annually. If you make your first deposit at the end of this year and you would like your account to reach $30,000 when the final deposit is made, what will be the amount of your deposits?

3–32B. (*Complex Present Value*) You would like to have $75,000 in 15 years. To accumulate this amount you plan to deposit each year an equal sum in the bank, which will earn 8 percent interest compounded annually. Your first payment will be made at the end of the year.
  a. How much must you deposit annually to accumulate this amount?
  b. If you decide to make a large lump-sum deposit today instead of the annual deposits, how large should this lump-sum deposit be? (Assume you can earn 8 percent on this deposit.)
  c. At the end of five years you will receive $20,000 and deposit this in the bank toward your goal of $75,000 at the end of 15 years. In addition to this deposit, how much must you deposit in equal annual deposits to reach your goal? (Again assume you can earn 8 percent on this deposit.)

3–33B. (*Comprehensive Present Value*) You are trying to plan for retirement in 10 years, and currently you have $150,000 in a savings account and $250,000 in stocks. In addition you plan on adding to your savings by depositing $8,000 per year in your *savings account* at the end of each of the next five years and then $10,000 per year at the end of each year for the final five years until retirement.
  a. Assuming your savings account returns 8 percent compounded annually while your investment in stocks will return 12 percent compounded annually, how much will you have at the end of 10 years? (Ignore taxes.)
  b. If you expect to live for 20 years after you retire, and at retirement you deposit all of your savings in a bank account paying 11 percent, how much can you withdraw each year after retirement (20 equal withdrawals beginning one year after you retire) to end up with a zero balance at death?

3–34B. (*Loan Amortization*) On December 31, Eugene Chung borrowed $200,000, agreeing to repay this sum in 20 equal annual installments that include both the principal and 10 percent interest on the declining balance. How large will the annual payments be?

3–35B. (*Loan Amortization*) To buy a new house you must borrow $250,000. To do this you take out a $250,000, 30-year, 9 percent mortgage. Your mortgage payments, which are made at the end of each year (one payment each year), include both principal and 9 percent interest on the declining balance. How large will your annual payments be?

3–36B. (*Present Value*) The state lottery's million-dollar payout provides for one million dollars to be paid over 24 years in $40,000 amounts. The first $40,000 payment is made immediately with the 24 remaining $40,000 payments occurring at the end of each of the next 24 years. If 10 percent is the appropriate discount rate, what is the present value of this stream of cash flows? If 20 percent is the appropriate discount rate, what is the present value of the cash flows?

3–37B. (*Solving for* i *in Compound Interest—Financial Calculator Needed*) In March 1963 issue number 39 of *Tales of Suspense* was issued. The original price for that issue was 12 cents. By March of 1992, 29 years later, the value of this comic book had risen to $875. What annual rate of interest would you have earned if you had bought the comic in 1963 and sold it in 1992?

3–38B. (*Comprehensive Present Value*) You have just inherited a large sum of money and you are trying to determine how much you should save for retirement and how much you can spend now. For retirement you will deposit today (January 1, 1993) a lump sum in a bank account paying 10 percent compounded annually. You don't plan on touching this deposit until you retire in 5 years (January 1, 1998), and you plan on living for 20 additional years and then dropping dead on December 31, 2017. During your retirement you would like to receive income of $60,000 per year to be received the first day of each year, with the first payment on January 1, 1998, and the last payment on January 1, 2017. Complicating this objective is your desire to have one final three-year fling during which time you'd like to track down all the original members of "The Mr. Ed Show" and "The Monkees" and get their autographs. To finance this you want to receive $300,000 on January 1, 2013, and *nothing* on January 1, 2014, and January 1, 2015, as you will be on the road. In addition, after you pass on (January 1, 2018), you would like to have a total of $100,000 to leave to your children.

a. How much must you deposit in the bank at 10 percent on January 1, 1993, in order to achieve your goal? (Use a time line in order to answer this question.)

b. What kinds of problems are associated with this analysis and its assumptions?

Suggested Application for *DISCLOSURE*®

Drawing from *Disclosure*, obtain the annual balance sheet for Marriott. Assume the corporation is able to renegotiate the amount listed as long-term debt as follows: 12 percent annual interest with the amount to be repaid in equal annual installments at the end of each year over the next 20 years. How much will each annual payment be?

SELF-TEST SOLUTIONS

SS-1. This is a compound interest problem in which you must first find the future value of $25,000 growing at 8 percent compounded annually for 3 years and then allow that future value to grow for an additional three years at 10 percent. First, the value of the $25,000 after three years growing at 8 percent is

$$FV_3 = PV(1 + i)^n$$

$$FV_3 = \$25,000(1 + .08)^3$$

$$FV_3 = \$25,000(1.260)$$

$$FV_3 = \$31,500$$

Thus, after three years you have $31,500. Now this amount is allowed to grow for three years at 10 percent. Plugging this into equation (3–6), with $PV = \$31,500$, $i = 10$ percent, $n = 3$ years, we solve for FV_3:

$$FV_3 = \$31,500(1 + .10)^3$$

$$FV_3 = \$31,500(1.331)$$

$$FV_3 = \$41,926.50$$

Thus, after six years the $25,000 will have grown to $41,926.50.

SS-2. This loan amortization problem is actually just a present-value-of-an-annuity problem in which we know the values of i, n, and PV and are solving for PMT. In this case the value of i is 13 percent, n is 10 years, and PV is $30,000. Substituting these values into equation (3–12) we find

$$\$30,000 = PMT \left[\sum_{t=1}^{10} \frac{1}{(1 + .13)^t} \right]$$

$$\$30,000 = PMT(5.426)$$

$$\$5528.93 = PMT$$

SS-3. This is a simple compound interest problem in which FV_9 is eight times larger than PV. Here again three of the four variables are known: $n = 9$ years, $FV_9 = 8$, and $PV = 1$, and we are solving for i. Substituting these values into equation (3–6) we find

$$FV_9 = PV(1 + i)^n$$

$$FV_9 = PV\ (FVIF_{i,n})$$

$$8 = 1(FVIF_{i,\ 9\ yr})$$

$$8.00 = FVIF_{i,\ 9yr}$$

Thus we are looking for an $FVIF_{i,\ 9\ yr}$ with a value of 8 in Appendix B, which occurs in the 9-year row. If we look in the 9-year row for a value of 8.00, we find it in the 26% column (8.004). Thus, the answer is 26 percent.

SS-4.
$$FV_n = PV(1 + i)^n$$

$$FV_n = PV(FVIF_{i,n})$$

$$\$3106 = \$1000(FVIF_{i,\ 10\ yr})$$

$$3.106 = FVIF_{i,\ 10\ yr}$$

Looking in the $n = 10$ row of Appendix B, we find a value of 3.106 in the 12% column. Therefore, $i = 12$ percent.

CONCLUSION

VIDEO CASE 1

CEO Compensation: Corporate Governance in Inaction?

from ABC News, *Nightline*, May 20, 1991

When we introduced this case, we asked many pertinent questions. See the Video Case Introduction on page 3.

Although it may be difficult to say whether a CEO deserves a specific level of pay, most people would agree that when a firm performs poorly the CEO should not get a raise or large bonus. Low profits imply that employees will receive small raises, at best, and may be laid off as the firm tries to cut costs. The idea that executives should thrive while their employees are losing jobs is unacceptable to most people. Similarly, if a firm provides little or no return to its shareholders, then most people would agree that the CEO should not be rewarded.

Although pay for performance makes sense, designing an appropriate compensation plan is difficult. Most pay packages include a salary, a bonus, and stock options, with stock options playing an increasingly large role. The prevalence of stock options is due, in part, to their accounting treatment. No costs or expenses are incurred when stock options are granted to executives, so profits are not affected. At first glance stock options appear to align the interests of shareholders and managers—if the stock price rises, both groups prosper. The problem with options is that if the firm does not perform, the manager does not feel the same pain as shareholders. As stock prices fall shareholders are hurt, but the options create only an opportunity loss for the managers and not a real cash loss. Therefore, stock options are an imperfect means of creating incentives for CEOs.

Executive compensation is determined by the board of directors. The board is elected by shareholders and charged with protecting and promoting the interests of shareholders, as well as evaluating and rewarding the firm's top managers. The large salaries of some CEOs, and the fact that pay and performance generally are not linked, suggest that boards may not protect the interests of shareholders very well. In fact, it would be very surprising if boards did control CEO compensation. More than 60 percent of outside directors are CEOs themselves, and so have no incentive to limit CEO pay.

If the board of directors fails to constrain managers from pursuing their own ends at the expense of shareholders, what can shareholders do? In the past almost the only recourse available to shareholders was to sell their stock. Occasionally an investor with large shareholdings in a firm would mount a proxy contest. For many reasons, proxy contests rarely result in the incumbent board being displaced. Recently institutional investors, such as pension funds, have begun sponsoring proposals requesting shareholder input regarding CEO salaries. To date, few of these proposals have passed, but they have certainly alerted the management of some firms that their days of unlimited discretion may be numbered.

Discussion questions

1. Does the enormous difference in pay between executives and employees affect morale?
2. How would you design a CEO pay package? How does your plan create the proper incentives? Would a rational manager accept your pay package?

Suggested readings

COLVIN, GEOFFREY. "How to Pay the CEO Right," *Fortune*, April 6, 1992.
WALLICH, PAUL, AND ELIZABETH CORCORAN. "Compensation Beyond the Call of Duty," *Scientific American* (April 1992).

VALUATION AND MANAGEMENT OF LONG-TERM INVESTMENTS

In Part 1 we described how present value is calculated and discussed how accounting data can be modified to represent cash flows. In Part 2 we combine these two concepts to *value* various types of investments. The basic method of valuation we will learn is equally applicable to an individual investor examining an investment in securities, a homeowner considering a mortgage refinancing, or a corporate financial manager deciding to finance the development of a new plant or product. Quite simply, the value of a long-term investment depends on the cash flows it generates for investors. The price someone is willing to pay for an investment—a share of stock, a corporate bond, a parcel of real estate—is the present value of those future cash flows. These cash flows are discounted at the investor's *required rate of return*. This rate varies depending on the risk of the investment under consideration; investors demand a higher rate of return from riskier investments. How risk is measured and how a particular required rate of return is assigned to a specific level of risk is a topic financial economists have been studying for years. Several approaches to these problems are discussed in Chapter 4, including the *capital asset pricing model (CAPM)*. Chapter 5 covers the process of valuing for bonds and stocks.

Determining which investments will enhance shareholders' wealth (the objective of the financial manager) is termed *capital budgeting*. The most useful capital budgeting technique is *net present value (NPV) analysis,* which compares the present value of the after-tax cash flows from an investment to the cost of making the investment (Chapter 6). Risk must be considered when performing an NPV analysis. When the firm chooses its investments it must pay attention to how the projects affect the riskiness of the firm (Chapters 7 and 8), because investors demand a higher rate of return from risky investments. The rate of return required by investors to buy a firm's securities depends on how much risk (or variability) the security adds to the investor's entire investment portfolio. Holding a portfolio composed of many securities helps reduce risk through *diversification*—the financial term for "not putting all your eggs in one basket."

INTRODUCTION

VIDEO CASE 2

Investing in Employee Productivity: An Application of Capital Budgeting

from ABC News, *Business World*, October 14, 1990

Chapters 6 and 7 of the text focus on methods used to evaluate the investment opportunities available to the firm. The *capital-budgeting* problems included in most financial management texts typically involve analyses of investments in new product lines or the process of replacing an old machine with a new, more efficient machine. It is fairly clear how one might estimate the sales of the new products, the savings from more efficient production, and the costs of acquiring the new machines. However, many situations faced by managers are not so straightforward. In this video case we examine a slightly different type of investment—investing in employee morale and commitment. The managers of Fel-Pro, a small manufacturer of gaskets in the Midwest, have decided that making investments in employee morale is good business. Employees receive cash bonuses on special occasions such as marriage, graduation, and birthdays; the firm provides day care for employees' children, a vacation ranch, and profit sharing.

- What does the firm expect as a return on its investment?
- How should costs and benefits be measured to evaluate this type of investment?
- Can discounted cash flow or net present value (NPV) techniques be applied to this investment?
- If this investment cannot be shown to have value for shareholders, should it be carried out?
- Does a firm have objectives to satisfy other than maximizing shareholder value?

At the end of this section of the book we will return to this case and discuss it further. In the meantime, as you read Chapters 5 through 8 think about how the techniques introduced in the chapters might be applied to the video case situation.

CHAPTER *4*

Risk and Rates of Return

Expected Return ● Risk ● The Investor's Required Rate of Return ● Rates of Return: The Investor's Experience ● Appendix 4a: Measuring a Stock's Return and Risk Using a Calculator ● Appendix 4B: Measuring the Required Rate of Return

Because we live in a world of uncertainty, how we see risk is vitally important in almost all dimensions of our life; certainly risk must be considered in financial decision making. The Greek poet and statesman Solon, writing in the sixth century B.C., stated:

> There is risk in everything that one does, and no one knows where he will make his landfall when his enterprise is at its beginning. One man, trying to act effectively, fails to foresee something and falls into great and grim ruination, but to another man, one who is acting ineffectively, a god gives good fortune in everything and escape from his folly.[1]

While Solon would have given more of the credit to Zeus than we might for the outcomes of our ventures, his insight reminds us that little is new in this world, including the need to acknowledge and compensate as best we can for the risks we encounter.

Without intending to be trite, risk means different things to different people, depending on the context and on how they feel about taking chances. For the student, risk is the possibility of failing an exam, or the chance of not making his or her best grades. For the coal miner or the oil field worker, risk is the chance of an explosion in the mine or at the well site. For the retired person, risk means perhaps not being able to live comfortably on a fixed income. For the entrepreneur, risk is the chance that a new venture will fail. In a financial context, we want to understand risk so that we can assess the level of risk inherent in an investment.

In addition to an understanding of risk, we want to get a grasp of the relationship between risk and the rates of return that we might expect to earn on an investment. In Chapter 2, we referred to the discount rate or the interest rate

---

[1]Translated by Arthur W. H. Adkins from the Greek text of Solon's poem "Prosperity, Justice and the Hazards of Life," in M. L. West, ed., *Iambi et Elegi Gracci ante Alexandrum Canttati*, vol. 2 (Oxford: Clarendon Press, 1972).

as the opportunity cost of funds, but we did not look at the causes for why that rate might be high or low. For example, in early 1992 you could buy bonds issued by DuPont that promised to pay an 8.4 percent rate of return. You could, on the other hand, buy bonds issued by Chrysler that would give you a 16 percent rate of return, provided that Chrysler makes the payments to the investors as promised. Why the difference?

In this chapter, we will examine the factors that determine rates of return (discount rates) in the capital markets and show how risk is an integral force underlying these returns. We will answer some important questions about risk and rates of return, including the following:

■ What do we mean by expected rates of return? How do we measure the expected return on an investment?

■ What is risk? How can it be measured?

■ How does diversification of investments affect the risk and expected returns of a portfolio of assets?

■ What determines the investor's required rates of return for securities with different levels of risk?

■ What can we learn from history about the relationship between risk and investor returns?

Expected Return

The expected benefits or returns that an investment generates come in the form of cash flows. *Cash flows*, not accounting profits, are the relevant variable the financial manager uses to measure returns. This principle holds true regardless of the type of security, whether it is a debt instrument, preferred stock, common stock, or any mixture of these (such as convertible bonds).

In an uncertain world, an accurate measurement of expected future cash flows is not easy for an investor to ascertain. To illustrate: Assume you are considering an investment costing $10,000, where the future cash flows from owning the security depend on the state of the economy, as estimated in Table 4-1.

Perspective in Finance

Continue to remember that future cash flows, not the reported earnings figure, determine the investor's rate of return.

State of the Economy	Probability of the States[a]	Cash Flows from the Investment	Percentage Returns (Cash Flow ÷ Investment Cost)
Economic recession	20%	$1000	10% ($1000 ÷ $10,000)
Moderate economic growth	30%	1200	12% ($1200 ÷ $10,000)
Strong economic growth	50%	1400	14% ($1400 ÷ $10,000)

TABLE 4-1.
Measuring the Expected Return

[a]The probabilities assigned to the three possible economic conditions have to be determined subjectively, which requires management to have a thorough understanding of both the investment cash flows and the general economy.

In any given year, the investment could produce any one of three possible cash flows depending on the particular state of the economy. With this information, how should we select the cash flow estimate that means the most for measuring the investment's expected rate of return? One approach is to calculate an *expected* cash flow. The expected cash flow is simply the weighted average of the *possible* cash flow outcomes such that the weights are the probabilities of the occurrence of the various states of the economy. Let X_i designate the ith possible cash flow, n reflect the number of possible states of the economy, and $P(X_i)$ indicate the probability that the ith cash flow or state of economy will occur. The expected cash flow, $\overline{X}$, may then be calculated as follows:

$$\overline{X} = X_1 P(X_1) + X_2 P(X_2) + \cdots + X_n P(X_n)$$

or
$$\overline{X} = \sum_{i=1}^{N} X_i P(X_i)$$

(4–1)

For the present illustration

$$\overline{X} = (.5)(\$1400) + (.3)(\$1200) + (.2)(\$1000) = \$1260$$

In addition to computing an expected dollar return from an investment, we can also calculate an expected percentage rate of return earned on the $10,000 investment. As the last column in Table 4–1 shows, the $1,400 cash inflow, assuming strong economic growth, represents a 14 percent return ($1,400 ÷ $10,000). Similarly, the $1,200 and $1,000 cash flows result in 12 percent and 10 percent returns, respectively. Using these percentage returns in place of the dollar amounts, the expected rate of return, $\overline{R}$, may be expressed as follows:

$$\overline{R} = R_1 P(R_1) + R_2 P(R_2) + \cdots + R_n P(R_n)$$

or
$$\overline{R} = \sum_{i=1}^{n} R_i P(R_i)$$

(4–2)

In our example:

$$\overline{R} = (.5)(14\%) + (.3)(12\%) + (.2)(10\%) = 12.6\%$$

With our concept and measurement of expected returns, let's consider the other side of the investment coin: risk.

Risk

To gain a basic understanding of investment risk, there are at least three fundamental questions that we must ask:

1. What is risk?
2. How do we know the amount of risk associated with a given investment; that is, how do we measure risk?
3. If we choose to diversify our investments by owning more than one asset, as most of us do, will such diversification reduce the riskiness of our combined portfolio of investments?[2]

[2]The logic in this section is the same as that used in Chapter 7 for capital budgeting under uncertainty.

What Is Risk?

Perspective in Finance

Risk is the potential variability in future cash flows. The wider the range of possible events that can occur, the greater the risk. If we think about it, this is a relatively intuitive concept.

To help us grasp the fundamental meaning of risk, consider two possible investments:

1. The first investment is a U.S. Treasury bill, a government security that matures in 90 days and promises to pay an annual return of 8 percent. If we purchase and hold this security for 90 days, we are virtually assured of receiving no more and no less than 8 percent. For all practical purposes, the risk of loss is nonexistent.

2. The second investment involves the purchase of the stock of a local publishing company. Looking at the past returns of the firm's stock, we have made the following estimate of the annual returns from the investment:

Chance of Occurrence	Rate of Return on Investment
1 chance in 10 (10%)	0%
2 chances in 10 (20%)	5%
4 chances in 10 (40%)	15%
2 chances in 10 (20%)	25%
1 chance in 10 (10%)	30%

Investing in the publishing company could conceivably provide a return as high as 30 percent if all goes well or no return (zero percent) if everything goes against the firm. However, in future years, both good and bad, we could expect a 15 percent return on average.[3]

$$\overline{R} = (.10)(0\%) + (.20)(5\%) + (.40)(15\%) + (.20)(25\%) + (.10)(30\%)$$

$$= 15\%$$

Comparing the Treasury bill investment with the publishing company investment, we see that the Treasury bills offer an expected 8 percent rate of return, while the publishing company has an expected rate of return of 15 percent. However, our investment in the publishing firm is clearly more "risky"—that is, there is greater uncertainty about the final outcome. Stated somewhat differently, there is a greater variation or dispersion of possible returns, which in turn implies greater risk.[4] Figure 4–1 shows these differences graphically in the form of discrete probability distributions.

Although the return from investing in the publishing firm is clearly less certain than for Treasury bills, quantitative measures of risk are useful when the

---

[3]We assume that the particular outcome or return earned in one year does *not* affect the return earned in the subsequent year. Technically speaking, the distribution of returns in any year is assumed to be independent of the outcome in any prior year.

[4]How can we possibly view variations above the expected return as risk? Should we not be concerned only with the negative deviations? Some would agree and view risk as only the negative variability in returns from a predetermined minimum acceptable rate of return. However, as long as the distribution of returns is symmetrical, the same conclusions will be reached.

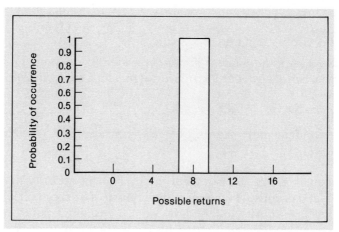

a.

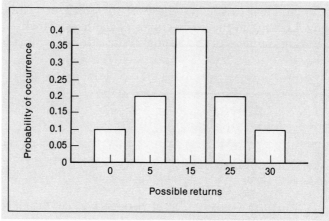

FIGURE 4–1.
Probability Distribution of
Returns for a Treasury Bill

b.

difference between two investments is not so evident. The standard deviation (σ) is such a measure. The **standard deviation** is simply the square root of the *average squared deviation of each possible return from the expected return;* that is

$$\sigma = \sqrt{\sum_{i=1}^{n} (R_i - \overline{R})^2 \, P(R_i)}$$

(4–3)

where n = the number of possible outcomes or different rates of return on the investment

R_i = the value of the ith possible rate of return

$\overline{R}$ = the expected value of the rates of return

$P(R_i)$ = the chance or probability that the ith outcome or return will occur.

For the publishing company, the standard deviation would be 9.22 percent, determined as follows:

$$\sigma = \left[\begin{array}{l} (\ 0\% - 15\%)^2(.10) + (\ 5\% - 15\%)^2(.20) \\ + (15\% - 15\%)^2(.40) + (25\% - 15\%)^2(.20) \\ + (30\% - 15\%)^2(.10) \end{array} \right]^{\frac{1}{2}}$$

$$= \sqrt{85\%} = 9.22\%$$

Although the standard deviation of returns provides us with a quantitative measure of an asset's riskiness, how should we interpret the result? What does it mean? Is the 9.22 percent standard deviation for the publishing company investment good or bad? First, we should remember that statisticians tell us that two-thirds of the time an event will fall within one standard deviation of the expected value (assuming the distribution is normally distributed; that is, it is shaped like a bell). Thus, given a 15 percent expected return and a standard deviation of 9.22 percent for the publishing company investment, we may reasonably anticipate that the actual returns will fall between 5.78 percent and 24.22 percent (15% ± 9.22%) two-thirds of the time—not much certainty with this investment.

A second way of answering the question of meaning about the standard deviation comes by comparing the investment in the publishing firm against other investments. The attractiveness of a security with respect to its return and risk cannot be determined in isolation. Only by examining other available alternatives can we reach a conclusion about a particular investment's risk. For example, if another investment, say an investment in a firm that owns a local radio station, has the same expected return as the publishing company, 15 percent, but with a standard deviation of 7 percent, we would consider the risk associated with the publishing firm, 9.22 percent, to be excessive. In the technical jargon of modern portfolio theory, the radio company investment is said to "dominate" the publishing firm investment. In common sense terms, this means that the radio company investment has the same expected return as the publishing company investment but is less risky.

What if we compare the investment in the publishing company with one in a quick oil-change franchise, an investment in which the expected rate of return is an attractive 24 percent but in which the standard deviation is estimated at 13 percent. Now what should we do? Clearly, the oil-change franchise has a higher expected rate of return, but it also has a larger standard deviation. In this example, we see that the real challenge in selecting the better investment comes when one investment has a higher expected rate of return but also exhibits greater risk. *Here the final choice is determined by our attitude toward risk, and there is no single right answer.* You might select the publishing company, while I might choose the oil-change investment, and neither of us would be wrong. We would simply be expressing our tastes and preferences about risk and return.

Perspective in Finance

The first Chinese symbol represents danger, the second stands for opportunity. The Chinese define risk as the combination of danger and opportunity. Greater risk, according to the Chinese, means we have greater opportunity to do well, but also greater danger to do badly.

Risk and Diversification

From the preceding discussion, we can define **risk** as the variability of anticipated returns as measured by the standard deviation. Let's consider for the moment how risk is affected if we diversify our investment by holding a variety of securities. You may or may not recall the disaster at the Union Carbide plant in Bhopal, India, that occurred in summer 1984. Thousands of individuals were killed or injured. While the financial considerations cannot compare to the loss of life, if you had invested your life saving of $400,000 in Union Carbide shortly before the Bhopal tragedy, the value of your savings would have declined by 40 percent to $240,000 almost overnight.[5] Or what if you had been fortunate enough to buy some Pennzoil stock in November 1985 immediately before Pennzoil was awarded $10.5 billion by the courts against Texaco for alleged misconduct in "tortuously" outbidding Pennzoil in Texaco's acquisition of Getty Oil Company? Based on this single event, Pennzoil stock almost doubled from $46 per share to $90 per share in a matter of days. Texaco stock, on the other hand, declined from $38 to $25.[6]

The events affecting Union Carbide, Texaco, and Pennzoil were unique to those firms; they had little, if any, impact on other companies. Other examples of events that are unique to a single company include labor strikes, the discovery of a new product or the sudden obsolescence of an old one, errors in judgment by a firm's management regarding a large capital investment, and the resignation or death of a key executive.

How do you feel about these unique events? Obviously, if you had been a stockholder in Pennzoil you would have felt great, but you might have decided to invest in Texaco (not a bad company), or even worse, Union Carbide. Most of us would like to avoid such fluctuations; that is, we are risk averse. Wouldn't it be great if we could reduce the risk associated with our portfolio, without having to accept a lower expected return? Good news—it is possible!

Partitioning the Risk

If we diversify our investments across different securities rather than invest in only one stock, the variability in the returns of our portfolio should decline. The reduction in risk will occur if the stock returns within our portfolio do not move precisely together over time—that is, if they are not perfectly correlated. Figure 4–2 shows graphically what we may expect to happen to the variability of returns as we add additional stocks to the portfolio. The reduction occurs because some of the volatility in returns of a stock are unique to that security. The unique variability of a single stock tends to be countered by the uniqueness of another security. However, we should not expect to eliminate all risk from our portfolio. In practice, it would be rather difficult to cancel all the variations in returns of a portfolio, because stock prices have some tendency to move together. Thus, we can divide the total risk (total variability) of our portfolio into two types of risk: (1) **firm-specific** or **company-unique risk** and (2) **market-related risk.** Company-unique risk might also be called **diversifiable risk,** since it can be diversified away. Market risk is **nondiversifiable risk;** it cannot be eliminated, no matter how much we diversify. These two types of risk are shown graphically in Figure 4–2. Total risk declines until we have approximately 20 securities, and then the decline becomes very slight.[7] The remaining risk, which would typically be about 40 percent of the total risk, is the portfolio's market risk. At this point, our portfolio is highly correlated with all securities in the marketplace. Events that affect our portfolio now are not so much unique events

[5]See "Union Carbide Shares Acquired by Bass Group," *Wall Street Journal* January 21, 1985, pp. 2–3. We must add that the price of the stock recovered in about six months.

[6]See "Pennzoil Rejects Texaco Offer," *Wall Street Journal* January 8, 1986, p. 3. The final settlement after Texaco filed for bankruptcy was $3 billion.

[7]A number of studies have noted that portfolios consisting of approximately 20 randomly selected common stocks have virtually no company-unique or diversifiable risk. See Robert C. Klemkosky and John D. Martin, "The Effect of Market Risk on Portfolio Diversification," *Journal of Finance* (March 1975), 147–154.

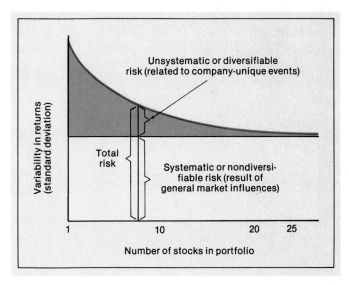

FIGURE 4-2.
Variability of Returns
Compared with Size
of Portfolio

but changes in the general economy, major political events, and sociological changes. Examples include changes in general interest rates, changes in tax legislation that affects companies, or increasing public concern about the effect of business practices on the environment.

Since we can remove the company-unique, or unsystematic risk, there is no reason to believe that the market will reward us with additional returns for assuming risk that could be avoided by simply diversifying. Our new measure of risk should therefore measure how responsive a stock or portfolio is to changes in a *market portfolio*, such as the New York Stock Exchange or the S&P 500 Index.[8] This relationship could be determined by plotting past returns, say on a monthly basis, of a particular stock or a portfolio of stocks against the returns of the *market portfolio* for the same period.

Measuring Market Risk: An Example

To help clarify the idea of systematic risk, let's examine the relationship between the common stock returns of Waste Management and the returns of the S&P 500 Index. The monthly returns for Waste Management and for the S&P 500 Index for the 24 months ending November 1991 are presented in Table 4–2, and in Figure 4–3. These monthly returns, or **holding-period returns,** as they are often called, are calculated as follows:[9]

$$R_t = \frac{P_t}{P_{t-1}} - 1 \qquad (4\text{–}4)$$

where R_t = the holding-period return in month t for Waste Management (or for the S&P Index)

P_t = the price of Waste Management's stock (or the S&P Index) at the end of month t

[8]The New York Stock Exchange Index is an index that reflects the performance of all stocks listed on the New York Stock Exchange. The Standard & Poor (S&P) 500 Index is similarly an index that measures the combined performance of the companies that constitute the largest 500 companies in the United States, as designated by Standard & Poor.

[9]For simplicity's sake, we are ignoring the dividend that the investor receives from the stock as part of the total return. In other words, letting D_t equal the dividend received by the investor in month t, the holding-period return would more accurately be measured as:

$$R_t = \frac{P_t + D_t}{P_{t-1}} - 1 \qquad (4\text{–}5)$$

TABLE 4–2.
Monthly Holding-Period
Returns, Waste Management,
and the S&P 500 Index
December 1989–
November 1991

Month and Year	Waste Management		S&P 500 Index	
	Prices	Returns	Prices	Returns
1989				
November	$32.44		$345.99	
December	35.00	7.90%	353.40	2.14%
1990				
January	30.75	−12.14%	329.08	−6.88%
February	31.63	2.85	331.89	0.85
March	34.13	7.91	339.94	2.43
April	36.13	5.86	330.80	−2.69
May	40.00	10.73	361.23	9.20
June	41.38	3.44	358.02	−0.89
July	41.38	0.00	356.15	−0.52
August	42.25	2.11	322.56	−9.43
September	33.75	−20.12	306.05	−5.12
October	33.75	0.00	304.00	−0.67
November	32.75	−2.96	322.22	5.99
December	35.00	6.87	328.72	2.02
1991				
January	39.38	12.50%	336.07	2.24%
February	42.25	7.30	365.65	8.80
March	39.50	−6.51	367.48	0.50
April	39.00	−1.27	379.02	3.14
May	40.88	4.81	389.83	2.85
June	36.50	−10.70	371.16	−4.79
July	37.75	3.42	380.93	2.63
August	39.50	4.64	395.43	3.81
September	37.13	−6.01	387.86	−1.91
October	37.13	0.00	384.20	−0.94
November	36.63	−1.35	376.55	−1.99
Average monthly return		0.80%		0.45%
Standard deviation		7.67%		4.45%

For instance, the holding-period return for Waste Management and the S&P Index for December 1989 is computed as follows:

$$\text{Waste Management return} = \frac{\text{stock price end of December 89}}{\text{stock price end of November 89}} - 1$$

$$= \frac{\$35.00}{\$32.44} - 1 = 7.90\%$$

$$\text{S\&P 500 Index return} = \frac{\text{index value end of December 89}}{\text{index value end of November 89}} - 1$$

$$= \frac{\$353.40}{\$345.99} - 1 = 2.14\%$$

At the bottom of Table 4–2, we have also computed the averages of the returns for the 24 months, both for Waste Management and for the S&P 500, and the standard deviation for these returns. Because we are using historical return data we assume each observation has an equal probability of occurrence. Thus the average return, $\bar{R}$, is found by summing the returns and dividing by the number of months; that is,

$$\text{average return} = \frac{\sum_{t=1}^{n} \text{return in month } t}{\text{number of months}} = \frac{\sum_{t=1}^{n} (R_t)}{n} \qquad \text{(4–6)}$$

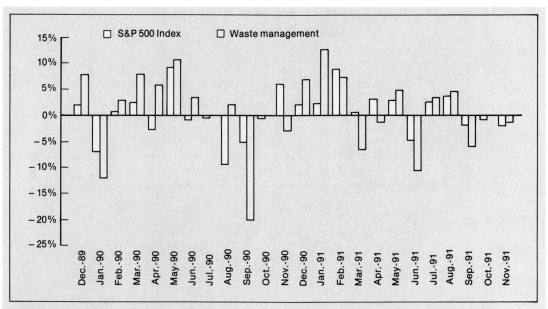

FIGURE 4-3.
Monthly Holding-Period Returns: Waste Management and the S&P 500 Index December 1989–November 1991

and the standard deviation is computed as:

$$\text{standard deviation} = \sqrt{\frac{\sum_{t=1}^{n} (\text{return in month } t - \text{average return})^2}{\text{number of months} - 1}} \quad \textbf{(4-7)}$$

$$= \sqrt{\frac{\sum_{t=1}^{n} = (R_t - \bar{R})^2}{n - 1}}$$

The average monthly return for Waste Management and the S&P 500 Index are found to be .80 percent and .45 percent, respectively. We also see that Waste Management has experienced greater volatility of returns over the two years, or a standard deviation of 7.67 percent compared to 4.45 percent for the S&P 500 Index. As explained earlier, we could avoid some of this risk (reduce the standard deviation) by diversifying our portfolio and owning other stocks as well. More will be said about this shortly.

It is also helpful to plot Waste Management's returns against the S&P 500 Index returns, which we have done in Figure 4–4. When we then draw a line of "best fit" through the plotted points, the slope of the line is 1.02.[10] The slope of this line of best fit, which we will call the **characteristic line,** tells us the average movement in the stock price of Waste Management in response to a movement in the general market (S&P 500 Index). The slope of the characteristic line, which is also called **beta,** is a measure of a stock's systematic or market risk. As indicated in Figure 4–4, the slope of the line is merely the ratio of the rise of the line relative to the run of the line.[11]

---

[10]Linear regression analysis is the statistical technique used to determine the slope of the line of best fit.

[11]To review: A line's rise is its vertical aspect, and its run is its horizontal aspect. For our purposes we are primarily interested in understanding the concept of beta. However, if you are interested in knowing how to compute a firm's beta, see Appendix 4A. Also, you should know that an estimate for the beta for many stocks is provided by investment services, such as Value Line or Merrill, Lynch, Pierce, Fenner & Smith.

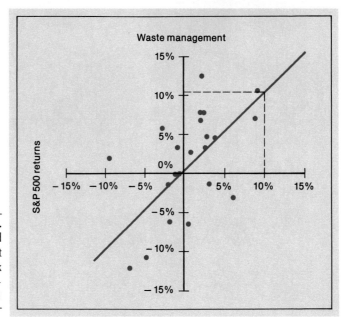

FIGURE 4–4.
Monthly Holding-Period
Returns: Waste Management
and the S&P 500 Index
December 1989–
November 1991

Perspective in Finance

*Let's say it again for emphasis: The slope of the characteristic line is called **beta**, and it is a measure of a stock's systematic or market risk.*

Measuring a Portfolio's Beta

From Figure 4–4, we see that the stock price of Waste Management on average moves almost one-for-one with the market (1.02 to 1). However, we also see a lot of fluctuation around this characteristic line. If we were, however, to diversify our holdings and own 20 stocks with betas of about 1, like that of Waste Management, we could essentially eliminate the variation around the line; that is, we would remove almost all the volatility in returns, except for what is caused by the general market, represented by the slope of the line. If we plotted the returns of our 20-stock portfolio against the S&P 500 Index, the points in our new graph would fit nicely along a straight line with a slope of 1.02. The new graph would look something like the one shown in Figure 4–5.

FIGURE 4–5.
Holding-Period Returns:
Hypothetical Portfolio and the
S&P 500 Index

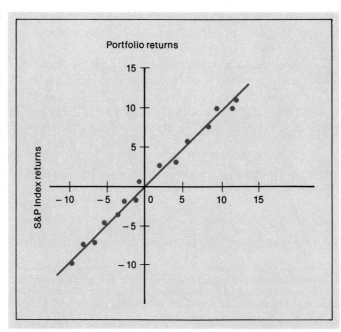

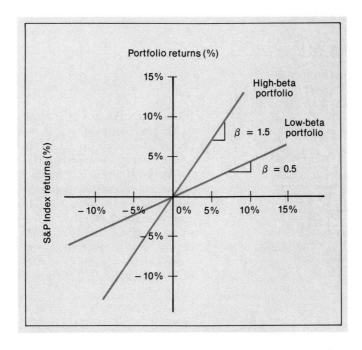

FIGURE 4-6.
Holding-Period Returns: High-
and Low-Beta Portfolios and the
S&P 500 Index

One remaining question needs to be addressed. Assume we were to diversify our portfolio, as we have just suggested, but instead of acquiring stocks with the same beta as Waste Management (1.02) we buy 8 stocks with betas of 1 and 12 stocks with betas of 1.5. What would the beta of our portfolio become? As it works out, the **portfolio beta** is merely the average of the individual stock betas. Actually, the portfolio beta is a weighted average of the individual security's betas, the weights being equal to the proportion of the portfolio invested in each security. Thus, the beta (β) of a portfolio consisting of n stocks is equal to:

$$\beta_{\text{portfolio}} = \sum_{j=1}^{n} (\text{percentage invested in stock } j) \times (\beta \text{ of stock } j) \qquad \textbf{(4-8)}$$

So, assuming we bought equal amounts of each stock in our new 20-stock portfolio, the beta would simply be 1.3, calculated as follows:

$$\text{portfolio beta} = \left(\frac{8}{20} \times 1.0\right) + \left(\frac{12}{20} \times 1.50\right)$$
$$= 1.3$$

Thus, whenever the general market increases or decreases one percent our new portfolio's returns would on average change 1.3 percent, which says that our new portfolio has more systematic or market risk than has the market as a whole.

We can conclude that the beta of a portfolio is determined by the betas of the individual stocks. If we have a portfolio consisting of stocks with low betas, then our portfolio will have a low beta. The reverse is true as well. Figure 4-6 presents these situations graphically.

The concept of beta is an underlying basis for measuring a security's or a portfolio's risk. It also proves useful when we attempt to specify what the relationship should be between an investor's required rate of return and the stock's or portfolio's risk—market risk, that is.

Perspective in Finance

We can reduce risk through diversifying our portfolio, but only to a point. What we remove is company-unique or specific risk (also known as diversifiable or

INTERNATIONAL FINANCIAL MANAGEMENT

Investing in Bonds in Different Countries

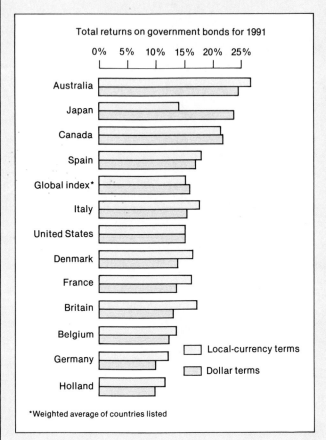

Total returns on government bonds for 1991

0% 5% 10% 15% 20% 25%

Australia
Japan
Canada
Spain
Global index*
Italy
United States
Denmark
France
Britain
Belgium
Germany
Holland

Local-currency terms

Dollar terms

*Weighted average of countries listed

If you had invested in government bonds in 1991, you would have done quite well, whether you lived in the United States and invested abroad or lived in another country where you invested. The figure to the left shows the rates of return you would have earned by buying government bonds in different countries and the average return, as estimated by J. P. Morgan's Global Index of government bonds. (The "dollar-term" returns assume you converted U.S. dollars into the local currency at the beginning of the year, made your investment, and then converted back to dollars at year end. Thus, your return was affected by the currency rates at the time of conversion.)

The high returns, which consisted of the interest received and the price increases in the bonds during the year, were attributable to decreasing interest rates and declining inflation rates. Australia, Japan, and Canada clearly had the highest returns, whereas European countries, with the exception of Spain, produced lower returns.

---

unsystematic risk). Systematic risk or market risk (also termed nondiversifiable risk) cannot be eliminated.

The Investor's Required Rate of Return

In this section we examine the concept of the investor's required rate of return, especially as it relates to the riskiness of the asset, and then we see how the required rate of return is measured.

The Required Rate of Return Concept

The **investor's required rate of return** can be defined as the minimum rate of return necessary to attract an investor to purchase or hold a security. This definition considers the investor's opportunity cost of making an investment; that is, if an investment is made, the investor must forgo the return available from the next best investment. This forgone return is an opportunity cost of undertaking the investment and consequently is the investor's required rate of return. In other words, we invest with the intention of achieving a rate of return sufficient to warrant making the investment. The investment will be made only if the purchase price is low enough relative to expected future cash flows to provide a rate of return greater than or equal to our required rate of return.

To help us better understand the nature of an investor's required rate of return, we can separate the return into its basic components: the *risk-free rate of return* plus a *risk premium*. Expressed as an equation:

$$R = R_f + RP$$

where R = the investor's required rate of return

        R_f = the risk-free return   **(4–9)**

      RP = the risk premium

The risk-free rate of return rewards us for deferring consumption, and not for assuming risk; that is, the risk-free return reflects the basic fact that we invest today so that we can consume more later. By itself, the risk-free rate should be used only as the required rate of return, or discount rate, for *riskless* investments. Typically, our measure for the risk-free rate of return is the U.S. Treasury bill rate.

     The risk premium, *RP*, is the additional return we must expect to receive for assuming risk. As the level of risk increases, we will demand additional expected returns. Even though we may or may not actually receive this incremental return, we must have reason to expect it; otherwise, why expose ourselves to the chance of losing all or part of our money?

EXAMPLE

To demonstrate the required rate of return concept, let us take Southwestern Bell, which has bonds that mature in 2007. Based on the market price of these bonds at year end 1991, we can determine that investors were expecting an 8.6 percent return. Later we will explain how we computed the 8.6 percent. The 90-day Treasury bill rate at that time was about 6 percent, which means that Southwestern Bell bondholders were requiring a risk premium of 2.6 percent.[12] Stated as an equation, we have

required rate (R)	=	risk-free rate (R_f)	+	risk premium (RP)
	=	6%	+	2.6%
	=	8.6%		

CH.7

                                                      ■

Measuring the Required Rate of Return

We have seen that (1) systematic risk is the only relevant risk—the rest can be diversified away, and (2) the required rate of return, *R*, equals the risk-free rate, R_f, plus a risk premium, *RP*. We may now examine how we actually estimate investors' required rates of return. Looking at equation (4–9), we see that the really tough task is how to estimate the risk premium.

     Although the finance profession has had difficulty in developing a practical approach to measure the investor's required rates of return, financial managers most often use a method called the **capital asset pricing model (CAPM)**. Although certainly not without its critics, the **CAPM** provides an intuitive approach for thinking about the return that an investor should require on an investment, given the asset's *systematic* or *market* risk.

     Equation (4–9) provides the natural starting point for measuring the

---

[12]The risk premium here can be thought of as a composite of a "default risk premium" (reflected in the difference in the bond's rate of return and the rate on a similar maturity government bond) and "term structure" premium (reflected in the difference in the 90-day Treasury bill rate and the long-term government bond rate).

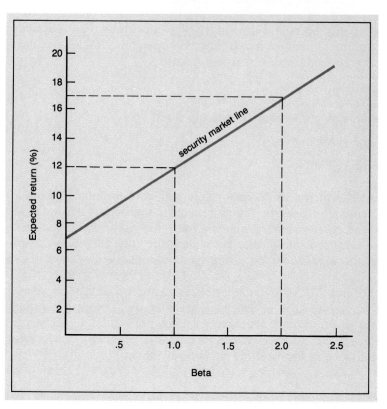

FIGURE 4-7.
Security Market Line

investors' required rate of return and sets us up for using the CAPM. Rearranging this equation to solve for the risk premium (*RP*), we have

$$RP = R - R_f \qquad (4\text{-}10)$$

which simply says that the risk premium for a security, *RP*, equals the security's expected return, *R*, less the risk-free rate existing in the market, R_f. For example, if the expected return for a security is 15 percent and the risk-free rate is 7 percent, the risk premium is 8 percent. Also, if the expected return for the market, R_m, is 12 percent, and the risk-free rate, R_f, is 7 percent, the risk premium, *RP*, for the general market would be 5 percent. This 5 percent risk premium would apply to any security having systematic (nondiversifiable) risk equivalent to the general market, or a beta of 1.

In this same market, a security with a beta of 2 should provide a risk premium of 10 percent, or twice the 5 percent risk premium existing for the market as a whole. Hence, in general, the appropriate required rate of return for the *j*th security, R_j, should be determined by

$$R_j = R_f + \beta_j(R_m - R_f) \qquad (4\text{-}11)$$

Equation (4-11) is the CAPM. This equation designates the risk–return tradeoff existing in the market, where risk is defined in terms of beta. Figure 4-7 graphs the CAPM as the **security market line.**[13] As presented in this figure,

---

[13] Two key assumptions are made in using the security market line. First, we assume that the marketplace where securities are bought and sold is highly efficient. Market efficiency indicates that the price of an asset responds quickly to new information, thereby suggesting that the price of a security reflects all available information. As a result, the current price of a security is considered to represent the best estimate of its future price. Second, the model assumes that a perfect market exists. A perfect market is one in which information is readily available to all investors at a nominal cost. Also, securities are assumed to be infinitely divisible, with any transaction costs incurred in purchasing or selling a security being negligible. Furthermore, investors are assumed to be single-period wealth maximizers who agree on the meaning and the significance of the available information. Finally, within the perfect market, all investors are *price takers*, which simply means that a single investor's actions cannot affect the price of a security. These assumptions are obviously not descriptive of reality. However, from the perspective of positive economics, the mark of a good theory is the accuracy of its predictions, not the validity of the simplifying assumptions that underlie its development.

securities with betas equal to 0, 1, and 2 should have required rates of return as follows:

$$\text{If } \beta_j = 0: R_j = 7\% + 0(12\% - 7\%) = 7\%$$

$$\text{If } \beta_j = 1: R_j = 7\% + 1(12\% - 7\%) = 12\%$$

$$\text{If } \beta_j = 2: R_j = 7\% + 2(12\% - 7\%) = 17\%$$

If $\beta = 1$, $R_j = R_m$

where the risk-free rate, R_f, is 7 percent and the expected market return, R_m, is 12 percent.[14]

Criticisms of CAPM

For several years, the CAPM was touted as the "new investment technology" and received the blessings of the vast majority of professional investors and finance professors. The CAPM was attractive largely because of its ability to present important theoretical insights (which professors loved) in simple and practical terms that could be applied in practice (which professional investors loved). In more recent years, however, researchers have questioned whether the model really works.[15]

The CAPM, like any abstract theory, has weaknesses. For example, we might question whether the risk of an asset can be totally captured in a single dimension of sensitivity to the market, as the CAPM proposes. There is some evidence that such things as the firm's size and even the time of year may affect risk-return relationships.[16] Also, we could become discouraged in our efforts to measure a security's beta if we find that different computation methods and different periods of measurement (e.g., using three years of data versus five years) give noticeably different results. An even more basic issue is our ability to test the model empirically. Some argue that we cannot verify the accuracy of the model because we cannot know with certainty that we are using the "true market portfolio" in comparing returns and systematic risk.[17]

Although the critics of CAPM have been vocal, the model is still widely used. Only one alternative theory has been offered as a complement, and even as a substitute, for the CAPM. This newer theory, the **arbitrage pricing model (APM)**, considers multiple economic factors when explaining required rates of return rather than looking at systematic risk or general market returns as the single determinant of an investor's required rate of return. However, despite having some desirable features and potential for the future, the arbitrage pricing model has yet to be of much practical use. We have, nevertheless, provided a brief treatment of the model in Appendix 4B.

Whichever model is used, one key point remains. To formulate a complete concept or understanding of security valuation, the topic of the next chapter, we must understand the nature of the investor's required rate of return. The required rate of return, which serves as the discount rate in the valuation process, is the investor's minimum acceptable return that would induce him or her to purchase or hold a security. The next chapter demonstrates this link by evaluating different types of securities.

---

[14]For a more in-depth explanation of the CAPM, see B. Rosenberg, "The Capital Asset Pricing Model and the Market Model," *Journal of Portfolio Management* (Winter 1981), 5–16.

[15]See Anise Wallace, "Is Beta Dead?" *Institutional Investor* (July 1980), 23–30; and Eugene Fama and Kenneth French, "The Cross-Section of Expected Stock Returns," University of Chicago Center for Research in Security Prices, 1991.

[16]See C. Barry and S. Brown, "Differential Information and the Small Firm Effect," *Journal of Financial Economics* (June 1984), 283–94; N. Chen and D. Hsieh, "An Exploratory Investigation of the Firm Size Effect," *Journal of Financial Economics* (September 1985), 451–71; and J. Jaffe and R. Westerfield, "The Week-End Effect in Common Stock Returns: The International Evidence," *Journal of Finance* (June 1985), 433–54.

[17]See, for example, Richard Roll, "A Critique of the Asset Pricing Theory's Tests," *Journal of Financial Economics* (March 1977), 129–76.

BASIC FINANCIAL MANAGEMENT IN PRACTICE

Beta Beaten

A battle between some of the top names in financial economics is attracting attention on Wall Street. Under attack is the famous capital-asset pricing model (CAPM), widely used to assess risk and return. A new paper by two Chicago economists, Eugene Fama and Kenneth French, explodes that model by showing that its key analytical tool does not explain why returns on shares differ.*

According to the CAPM, returns reflect risk. The model uses a measure called beta—shorthand for relative volatility—to compare the riskiness of one share with that of the whole market, on the basis of past price changes. A share with a beta of one is just as risky as the market; one with a beta of 0.5 is less risky. Because investors need to earn more on riskier investments, share prices will reflect the requirement for higher-than-average returns on shares with higher betas.

Whether beta does predict returns has long been debated. Studies have found that market capitalization, price/earnings ratios, leverage and book-to-market ratios do just as well. Messrs. Fama and French are clear: Beta is not a good guide.

The two economists look at all non-financial shares traded on the NYSE, AMEX and NASDAQ between 1963 and 1990. The shares were grouped into portfolios. When grouped solely on the basis of size (that is, market capitalization), the CAPM worked—but each portfolio contained a wide range of betas. So the authors grouped shares of similar beta and size. Betas now were a bad guide to returns.

Instead of beta, say Messrs. Fama and French, differences in firm size and in the ratio of book value to market value explain differences in returns—especially the latter. When shares were grouped by book-to-market ratios, the gap in returns between the portfolio with the lowest ratio and that with the highest was far wider than when shares were grouped by size.

So should analysts stop using the CAPM? Probably not. Although Mr. Fama and Mr. French have produced intriguing results, they lack a theory to explain them. Their best hope is that size and book-to-market ratios are proxies for other fundamentals. For instance, a high book-to-market ratio may indicate a firm in trouble; its earnings prospects might thus be especially sensitive to economic conditions, so its shares would need to earn a higher return than its beta suggested.

Advocates of CAPM—including Fischer Black, of Goldman Sachs, an investment bank, and William Sharpe of Stanford University, who won the Nobel prize for economics in 1990—reckon the results of the new study can be explained without discarding beta. Investors may irrationally favor big firms. Or they may lack the cash to buy enough shares to spread risk completely, so that risk and return are not perfectly matched in the market.

Those looking for a theoretical alternative to CAPM will find little satisfaction, however. Voguish rivals, such as the "arbitrage-pricing theory," are no better than CAPM and betas at explaining actual share returns. Which leaves Wall Street with an awkward choice: Believe the Fama-French evidence, despite its theoretical vacuum, and use size and the book-to-market ratios as a guide to returns; or stick with a theory that, despite the data, is built on impeccable logic.

---

*"The Cross-Section of Expected Stock Returns" by Eugene Fama and Kenneth French. University of Chicago Centre for Research in Security Prices, 1991.

Source: "Beta Beaten," *The Economist*, March 7, 1992, p. 87. Used by permission.

Rates of Return: The Investor's Experience

In speaking of expected rates of return, we have used a number of hypothetical examples; however, it is also interesting to look at returns that investors have actually received. Such information is readily available. For example, Ibbotson and Sinquefield have provided annual rates of return as far back as 1926.[18] In their results, they summarize, among other things, the annual returns for six portfolios of securities made up of:

1. Common stocks of large companies
2. Common stocks of small firms

---

[18]Roger G. Ibbotson and Rex A. Sinquefield, *Stocks, Bonds, Bills, and Inflation: Historical Return* (1926–1990) (Chicago, IL: Dow Jones-Irwin, 1991).

3. Long-term corporate bonds

4. Long-term U.S. government bonds

5. Intermediate-term U.S. government bonds

6. U.S. Treasury bills

Before comparing these returns, we should first think about what to expect. First, we would intuitively expect a Treasury bill to be the least risky of the six portfolios. Since a Treasury bill has a short-term maturity date, the price is less volatile (less risky) than the price of an intermediate- or long-term government security.[19] In turn, since there is a chance of default on a corporate bond, which is essentially nonexistent for government securities, a long-term government bond is less risky than a long-term corporate bond. Finally, common stock of large companies is more risky than a corporate bond, with small-company stocks being more risky than the portfolio of large-firm stocks.

With this in mind, we could reasonably expect different rates of return to the holders of these varied securities. If the market rewards an investor for assuming risk, the average annual rates of return should increase as risk increases.

A comparison of the annual rates of return for the six respective portfolios for the years 1926–1990 is provided in Figure 4–8. Four aspects of these returns

---

[19]For an explanation of the greater volatility for long-term bonds relative to short-term bonds see Appendix 5A.

FIGURE 4–8.
Annual Rates of Return 1926–90
Source: R. G. Ibbotson and R. A. Sinquefield, *Stocks, Bonds, Bills and Inflation: Historical Return* (Chicago, IL: Dow Jones–Irwin, 1991), p. 32.

Securities	Nominal Average Annual Returns	Standard Deviation of Returns	Real Average Annual Returns[a]	Risk Premiums[b]	Frequency of Returns Distributions
Common Stocks	12.1%	20.8%	9.0%	8.4%	
Small Company Stocks	17.1	35.4	14.0	13.4	
Long-Term Corporate Bonds	5.5	8.4	2.4	1.8	
Long-Term Government Bonds	4.9	8.5	1.8	1.2	
Intermediate-Term Government Bonds	5.1	5.5	2.0	1.4	
U.S. Treasury Bills	3.7	3.4	0.6	0	

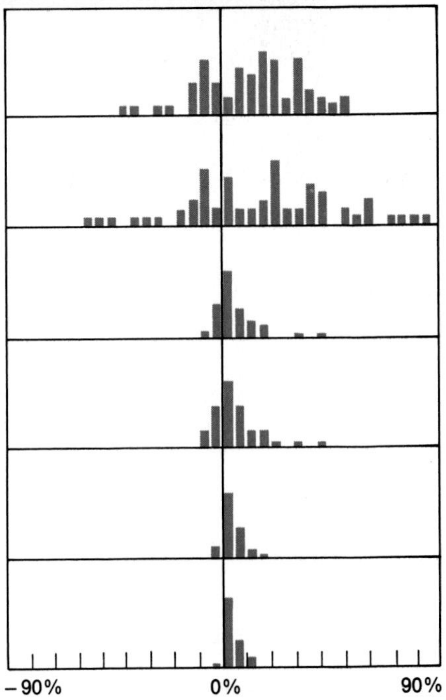

−90%　　　　0%　　　　90%

[a]Real return equals the nominal return less the average inflation rate from 1926 through 1990 0f 3.1 percent.
[b]Risk premium equals the nominal security return less the average risk-free rate (Treasury bills) of 3.7 percent.

are included: (1) the *nominal* average annual rate of return; (2) the standard deviation of the returns, which measures the volatility or riskiness of the portfolios; (3) the *real* average annual rate of return, which is the nominal return less the inflation rate; and (4) the risk premium, which represents the additional return received beyond the risk-free rate (Treasury bill rate) for assuming risk. Also, a frequency distribution of returns is provided. Looking first at the two columns of average annual returns and standard deviations, we gain a good overview of the risk–return relationships that have existed over the 65 years ending in 1990. For the most part, there has been a positive relationship between risk and return, with Treasury bills being least risky and common stocks being most risky. However, long-term government bonds have been as risky as corporate bonds. This aberration has largely been the result of the five years from 1977 through 1981, a period when interest rates rose to all-time highs, which had a significantly negative impact on bond prices.

The return information in Figure 4–8 clearly demonstrates that only common stock has in the long run served as an inflation hedge and provided any substantial risk premium. However, it is equally apparent that the common stockholder is exposed to sizable risk, as demonstrated by a 20.8 percent standard deviation for large-company stocks and a 35.4 percent standard deviation for small-company stocks. In fact, in the 1926–1990 time frame, common shareholders received negative returns in 18 of the 65 years, compared with only 1 in 65 for Treasury bills.

SUMMARY

In Chapter 2, the discount rate was defined as the interest rate of the opportunity cost of funds. At that point, we considered a number of important factors that influence interest rates, including (1) the price of deferring consumption, which determines the real rate of interest; (2) the expected or anticipated inflation rate, which produces an inflation-risk premium; (3) term to maturity, which produces a maturity or liquidity premium; and (4) the variability of future returns, which produces a risk premium.

This chapter returns to the study of rates of return, carefully examining the relationship between risk and rates of return. The variability of returns is the factor that defines risk for investors and financial managers. There is no simple way to measure risk, and individuals' attitudes toward risk taking vary. There is an important distinction between nondiversifiable risk and diversifiable risk. The only relevant risk, given an investor's opportunity to diversify a portfolio, is a security's nondiversifiable risk, which is also referred to as systematic or market risk.

The capital asset pricing model (CAPM) is useful in determining an appropriate required rate of return given an asset's systematic risk, as measured by its *beta*, or the way the stock responds to changes in the market's returns. Although the model offers the advantage of being relatively intuitive it is not definitive. Its assumptions and limitations suggest that critics will continue to look carefully for a more complete explanation for how rates are determined in the capital markets. Nevertheless, our observations do suggest that in general there is a relationship between risk and return in the capital markets. Thus, we can confidently say that as a general rule investors determine an appropriate required rate of return, depending on the amount of systematic risk inherent in a security. This minimum acceptable rate of return is equal to the risk-free rate plus a return premium for assuming the risk associated with the investment.

4–1. a. What is meant by the investor's required rate of return?
  b. How do we measure the riskiness of an asset?
  c. How should the proposed measurement of risk be interpreted?

4–2. What is (a) unsystematic risk (company-unique or diversifiable risk) and (b) systematic risk (market or nondiversifiable risk)?

4–3. What is the meaning of beta? How is it used to calculate R, the investor's required rate of return?

4–4. Define the security market line. What does it represent?

4–5. How do we measure the beta for a portfolio?

4–6. If we were to graph the returns of a stock against the returns of the S&P 500 Index, and the points did not follow a very ordered pattern, what could we say about that stock? If the stock's returns tracked the S&P 500 returns very closely, then what could we say?

4–7. Over the past six decades, we have had the opportunity to observe the rates of return and variability of these returns for different types of securities. Summarize these observations.

SELF-TEST PROBLEMS

ST–1. (*Expected Return and Risk*) Universal Corporation is planning to invest in a security that has several possible rates of return. Given the following probability distribution of returns, what is the expected rate of return on the investment? Also compute the standard deviation of the returns. What do the resulting numbers represent?

Probability	Return
.10	−10%
.20	5%
.30	10%
.40	25%

ST–2. (*Capital Asset Pricing Model*) Using the CAPM, estimate the appropriate required rate of return for the three stocks listed below, given that the risk-free rate is 5 percent, and the expected return for the market is 17 percent.

Stock	Beta
A	.75
B	.90
C	1.40

ST–3. (*Expected Return and Risk*) Given the holding-period returns shown below, calculate the average returns and the standard deviations for the Kaifu Corporation and for the market.

Month	Kaifu Corp.	Market
1	4%	2%
2	6	3
3	0	1
4	2	−1

ST–4. (*Holding-Period Returns*) From the price data that follow, compute the holding-period returns.

Time	Stock Price
1	$10
2	13
3	11
4	15

ST–5. **a.** (*Security Market Line*) Determine the expected return and beta for the following portfolio:

Stock	Percentage of Portfolio	Beta	Expected Return
1	40%	1.00	12%
2	25	0.75	11
3	35	1.30	15

b. Given the information above, draw the security market line and show where the securities fit on the graph. Assume that the risk-free rate is 8 percent and that the expected return on the market portfolio is 12 percent. How would you interpret these findings?

STUDY PROBLEMS (SET A)

4–1A. (*Expected Rate of Return and Risk*) Pritchard Press, Inc., is evaluating a security. One-year Treasury bills are currently paying 9.1 percent. Calculate the investment's expected return and its standard deviation. Should Pritchard invest in this security?

Probability	Return
.15	5%
.30	7%
.40	10%
.15	15%

4–2A. (*Expected Rate of Return and Risk*) Syntex, Inc., is considering an investment in one of two common stocks. Given the information that follows, which investment is better, based on risk (as measured by the standard deviation) and return?

Common Stock A		Common Stock B	
Probability	Return	Probability	Return
		.20	−5%
.30	11%	.30	6%
.40	15%	.30	14%
.30	19%	.20	22%

4–3A. (*Expected Rate of Return and Risk*) Friedman Manufacturing, Inc., has prepared the following information regarding two investments under consideration. Which investment should be accepted?

Common Stock A		Common Stock B	
Probability	Return	Probability	Return
.2	−2%	.10	4%
.5	18%	.30	6%
.3	27%	.40	10%
		.20	15%

4–4A. **a.** (*Required Rate of Return Using CAPM*) Compute a fair rate of return for Intel common stock, which has a 1.2 beta. The risk-free rate is 6 percent and the market portfolio (New York Stock Exchange stocks) has an expected return of 16 percent.

b. Why is the rate you computed a fair rate?

4–5A. (*Estimating Beta*) From the graph below relating the holding-period returns for Aram, Inc., to the S&P 500 Index, estimate the firm's beta.

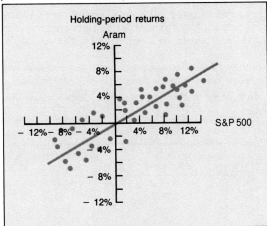

4–6A. (*Capital Asset Pricing Model*) Johnson Manufacturing, Inc., is considering several investments. The rate on Treasury bills is currently 6.75 percent, and the expected return for the market is 12 percent. What should be the required rates of return for each investment (using the CAPM)?

Security	Beta
A	1.50
B	.82
C	.60
D	1.15

4–7A. (*Capital Asset Pricing Model*) CSB, Inc., has a beta of .765. If the expected market return is 11.5 percent and the risk-free rate is 7.5 percent, what is the appropriate required return of CSB (using the CAPM)?

4–8A. (*Capital Asset Pricing Model*) The expected return for the general market is 12.8 percent, and the risk premium in the market is 4.3 percent. Tasaco, LBM, and Exxos have betas of .864, .693, and .575, respectively. What are the corresponding required rates of return for the three securities?

4–9A. (*Computing Holding-Period Returns*) From the price data below, compute the holding-period returns for Asman and Salinas.

Time	Asman	Salinas
1	$10	$30
2	12	28
3	11	32
4	13	35

How would you interpret the meaning of a holding-period return?

4–10A. *(Measuring Risk and Rates of Return)*

    a. Given the holding-period returns shown below, compute the average returns and the standard deviations for the Zemin Corporation and for the market.

Month	Zemin Corp.	Market
1	6%	4%
2	3	2
3	−1	1
4	−3	−2
5	5	2
6	0	2

    b. If Zemin's beta is 1.54 and the risk-free rate is 8 percent, what would be an appropriate required return for an investor owning Zemin? (*Note:* Because the above returns are based on monthly data, you will need to annualize the returns to make them compatible with the risk-free rate. For simplicity, you can convert from monthly to yearly returns by multiplying the average monthly returns by 12.)

    c. How does Zemin's historical average return compare with the return you believe to be a fair return, given the firm's systematic risk?

4–11A. *(Portfolio Beta and Security Market Line)* You own a portfolio consisting of the following stocks:

Stock	Percentage of Portfolio	Beta	Expected Return
1	20%	1.00	16%
2	30%	0.85	14%
3	15%	1.20	20%
4	25%	0.60	12%
5	10%	1.60	24%

The risk-free rate is 7 percent. Also, the expected return on the market portfolio is 15.5 percent.

    a. Calculate the expected return of your portfolio. (*Hint:* The expected return of a portfolio equals the weighted average of the individual stock's expected return, where the weights are the percentage invested in each stock.)

    b. Calculate the portfolio beta.

    c. Given the information above, plot the security market line on paper. Plot the stocks from your portfolio on your graph.

    d. From your plot in part (c), which stocks *appear* to be your winners and which ones appear to be losers?

    e. Why should you consider your conclusion in part (d) to be less than certain?

STUDY PROBLEMS (SET B)

4–1B. *(Expected Rate of Return and Risk)* B. J. Gautney Enterprises is evaluating a security. One-year Treasury bills are currently paying 8.9 percent. Calculate the investment's expected return and its standard deviation. Should Gautney invest in this security?

Probability	Return
.15	6%
.30	5%
.40	11%
.15	14%

4–2B. (*Expected Rate of Return and Risk*) Kelly B. Stites, Inc., is considering an investment in one of two common stocks. Given the information that follows, which investment is better, based on risk (as measured by the standard deviation) and return?

Common Stock A		Common Stock B	
Probability	Return	Probability	Return
		.15	6%
.20	10%	.30	8%
.60	13%	.40	15%
.20	20%	.15	19%

4–3B. (*Expected Rate of Return and Risk*) Clevenger Manufacturing, Inc., has prepared the following information regarding two investments under consideration. Which investment should be accepted?

Security A		Security B	
Probability	Return	Probability	Return
.20	−2%	.10	5%
.50	19%	.30	7%
.30	25%	.40	12%
		.20	14%

4–4B. a. (*Required Rate of Return Using CAPM*) Compute a *fair* rate of return for Apple common stock, which has a 1.5 beta. The risk-free rate is 8 percent and the market portfolio (New York Stock Exchange stocks) has an expected return of 16 percent.
b. Why is the rate you computed a *fair* rate?

4–5B. (*Estimating Beta*) From the graph below relating the holding-period returns for Bram, Inc. to the S&P 500 Index, estimate the firm's beta.

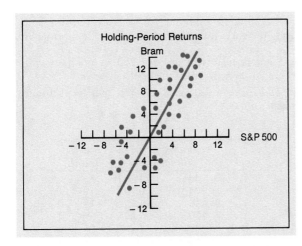

4–6B. (*Capital Asset Pricing Model*) Bobbi Manufacturing, Inc., is considering several investments. The rate on Treasury bills is currently 6.75 percent, and the expected return for the market is 12 percent. What should be the required rates of return for each investment (using the CAPM)?

Security	Beta
A	1.40
B	.75
C	.80
D	1.20

4–7B. (*Capital Asset Pricing Model*) Breckenridge, Inc., has a beta of .85. If the expected market return is 10.5 percent and the risk-free rate is 7.5 percent, what is the appropriate required return of Breckenridge (using the CAPM)?

4–8B. (*Capital Asset Pricing Model*) The expected return for the general market is 12.8 percent, and the risk premium in the market is 4.3 percent. Dupree, Yofota, and MacGrill have betas of .82, .570, and .680, respectively. What are the corresponding required rates of return for the three securities?

4–9B. (*Computing Holding-Period Returns*) From the price data below, compute the holding-period returns for O'Toole and Baltimore.

Time	O'Toole	Baltimore
1	$22	$45
2	24	50
3	20	48
4	25	52

How would you interpret the meaning of a holding-period return?

4–10B. (*Measuring Risk and Rates of Return*)
   a. Given the holding-period returns shown below, compute the average returns and the standard deviations for the Sugita Corporation and for the market.

Month	Sugita Corp.	Market
1	1.8%	1.5%
2	−0.5	1.0
3	2.0	0.0
4	−2.0	−2.0
5	5.0	4.0
6	5.0	3.0

   b. If Sugita's beta is 1.18 and the risk-free rate is 8 percent, what would be an appropriate required return for an investor owning Sugita? (Note: Because the above returns are based on monthly data, you will need to annualize the returns to make them compatible with the risk-free rate. For simplicity, you can convert from monthly to yearly returns by multiplying the average monthly returns by 12.)
   c. How does Sugita's historical average return compare with the return you believe to be a fair return, given the firm's systematic risk?

4–11B. (*Portfolio Beta and Security Market Line*) You own a portfolio consisting of the following stocks:

Stock	Percentage of Portfolio	Beta	Expected Return
1	10%	1.00	12%
2	25	0.75	11
3	15	1.30	15
4	30	0.60	9
5	20	1.20	14

The risk-free rate is 8 percent. Also, the expected return on the market portfolio is 11.6 percent.
   a. Calculate the expected return of your portfolio. (*Hint:* The expected return of a portfolio equals the weighted average of the individual stock's expected return, where the weights are the percentage invested in each stock.)
   b. Calculate the portfolio beta.
   c. Given the information above, plot the security market line on paper. Plot the stocks from your portfolio on your graph.
   d. From your plot in part (c), which stocks *appear* to be your winners and which ones appear to be losers?
   e. Why should you consider your conclusion in part (d) to be less than certain?

SS–1.

(A) Probability $P(R_i)$	(B) Return (R_i)	Expected Return $(\overline{R})$ $(A) \times (B)$	Weighted Deviation $(R_i - \overline{R})^2 P(R_k)$
.10	−10%	− 1%	52.9%
.20	5%	1%	12.8%
.30	10%	3%	2.7%
.40	25%	10%	57.6%
		$\overline{X} = 13\%$	$\sigma^2 = 126.0\%$
			$\sigma = 11.22\%$

From our studies in statistics, we know that if the distribution of returns were normal, then Universal could expect a return of 13 percent with a 67 percent possibility that this return would vary up or down by 11.22 percent between 1.78 percent (13% − 11.22%) and 24.22 percent (13% + 11.22%). However, it is apparent from the probabilities that the distribution is not normal.

SS–2.

Stock A	5% + .75(17% − 5%) = 14%
Stock B	5% + .90(17% − 5%) = 15.8%
Stock C	5% + 1.40(17% − 5%) = 21.8%

SS–3. *Kaifu*

Average return:

$$\frac{4\% + 6\% + 0\% + 2\%}{4} = 3\%$$

Standard deviation:

$$\sqrt{\frac{(4\% - 3\%)^2 + (6\% - 3\%)^2 + (0\% - 3\%)^2 + (2\% - 3\%)^2}{4 - 1}} = 2.58\%$$

Market

Average return:

$$\frac{2\% + 3\% + 1\% - 1\%}{4} = 1.25\%$$

Standard deviation:

$$\sqrt{\frac{(2\% - 1.25\%)^2 + (3\% - 1.25\%)^2 + (1\% - 1.25\%)^2 + (-1\% - 1.25\%)^2}{4 - 1}} = 1.71\%$$

SS–4.

Time	Stock Price	Holding-Period Return	
1	$10		
2	13	($13 ÷ $10) − 1 =	30.0%
3	11	($11 ÷ $13) − 1 =	−15.4%
4	15	($15 ÷ $11) − 1 =	36.4%

SS–5. a. Portfolio expected return:

$$(.4 \times 12\%) + (.25 \times 11\%) + (.35 \times 15\%) = 12.8\%$$

Portfolio beta:

$$(.4 \times 1) + (.25 \times .75) + (.35 \times 1.3) = 1.04$$

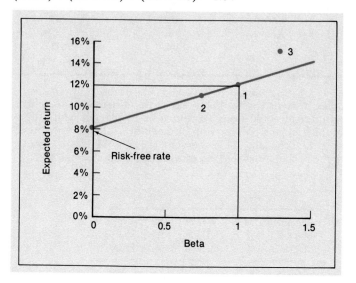

b. Stocks 1 and 2 seem to be right in line with the security market line, which suggests that they are earning a fair return, given their systematic risk. Stock 3, on the other hand, is earning more than a fair return (above the security market line). We might be tempted to conclude that security 3 is undervalued. However, we may be seeing an illusion; it is possible to misspecify the security market line by using bad estimates in our data.

APPENDIX 4A

Measuring a Stock's Return and Risk Using a Calculator (Average Return, Standard Deviation, Alpha, and Beta)

The capital asset pricing model (CAPM) draws heavily on our ability to measure a stock's return statistics, such as its beta. We must determine an accurate beta for the CAPM to yield good results. An estimate of the appropriate required rate of return is only as accurate as the data used to achieve it.

As noted in the chapter, there are some real difficulties in using the CAPM, most of which relate to empirical problems. Specifically, from where do we draw our data in making our estimates? Simply put, for us to use the model correctly, we need to know the *expectations* of the investors about *future* returns. However, only historical rates of return are available to us. Nevertheless, our best hope at seeing the future is by looking at the past. Essentially we use the historical return data and hope that the past will fairly reflect the investor's expectations about the future. Thus, when we compute the beta for a stock or a portfolio, as we did with Waste Management's stock in the chapter, we rely on the historical returns.

To compute the return statistics, professional analysts typically use five years of monthly return data, or 60 months, and make certain adjustments in their computations. For instance, we know that betas over time tend to move toward a value of 1. If the beta is at present substantially greater than 1, it will gradually decline over time, and betas that are substantially below 1 will tend to increase in future periods. So forecasters adjust for this observed tendency.

If we want to know the beta for asset j, be it a stock or a portfolio, we regress its returns on the market returns. The regression equation is as follows:

$$R_{jt} = a_j + b_j(R_{mt}) + e_{jt} \qquad \text{(4A–1)}$$

where
R_{jt} = the monthly holding-period return for asset j in month t

a_j = the alpha for asset j, the point where the regression line intercepts the vertical axis

b_j = the beta for asset j; the slope of the regression line

R_{mt} = the return on the market portfolio in month t

e_{jt} = the error term; the difference between the actual return in month t and the expected return given the market's return, that is, the distance the actual return lies away from the regression line

The objective is to find the alpha and beta values that minimize the sum of the square of the error terms. To do so, find the line that best fits the data; that is, that best describes the average relationship between asset j's returns and the market's returns. There are three ways for determining alpha and beta:

1. We can plot the return data on graph paper and then "eyeball" the regression line, trying to get what appears to be the best fit to the data. The point where the line crosses the vertical axis indicates our estimate for the alpha value. We would then estimate the beta by measuring how steeply the line increases vertically (asset j's return) relative to a change on the horizontal axis (market's return); that is, we would find:

$$\text{beta} = \frac{\text{rise}}{\text{run}} = \frac{\Delta R_{jt}}{\Delta R_{mt}} \qquad \text{(4A–2)}$$

The obvious limitation with this approach is its potential for error; accuracy depends in part on the sharpness of the eye. Your estimate would most likely be somewhat different from another person's, especially if the data did not have a tight fit.

2. We can use a statistical package or a computer spreadsheet to determine alpha and beta. This option is preferred, because of the easy calculations and the option to view the original return data to

check for accuracy in data entry. Also, we can quickly plot the data along with the fitted regression line.

3. We can use a calculator for the computation.

To demonstrate the use of the calculator in measuring the return statistics for a stock, let's use Coca-Cola's historical returns for the 12 months ending November 1991. These returns, along with the corresponding returns for the S&P 500 Index, are shown in Table 4A–1. We will use the HP 17BII to make our calculations.

Table 4A–1
Coca-Cola and S&P 500 Index Monthly Holding-Period Returns

Month and Year	Coca-Cola Monthly Returns	S&P 500 Index Monthly Returns
Dec. 90	0.54%	2.02%
Jan. 91	4.84	2.24
Feb. 91	7.44	8.80
Mar. 91	3.58	0.50
Apr. 91	−2.76	3.14
May 91	8.53	2.85
Jun. 91	−4.80	−4.79
Jul. 91	10.32	2.63
Aug. 91	9.36	3.81
Sept. 91	−1.90	−1.91
Oct. 91	3.29	−0.94
Nov. 91	4.13	−1.99

Keystroke	Display	Explanation
1. Enter data		
SUM		
▨ CLEAR DATA	CLEAR THE LIST?	Clears memory.
YES	ITEM(1)=?	
Enter the return data for the S&P Index.		
2.02 INPUT		Stores holding-period returns for the S&P 500. Index (x variables) into a SUM list.
2.24 INPUT		
8.80 INPUT		
.50 INPUT		
3.14 INPUT		
2.85 INPUT		
4.79 +/− INPUT		
2.63 INPUT		
3.81 INPUT		
1.91 +/− INPUT		
.94 +/− INPUT		
1.99 +/− INPUT	ITEM(13)=?	
	TOTAL=16.36	

Give the S&P Index return data (x-list) a name.

EXIT NAME	TYPE A NAME;[INPUT][a]	
SP INPUT	ITEM(13)=?	

Now enter the return data for Coca-Cola.

GET *NEW	ITEM(1)=?	Gets a new, empty list.
.54 INPUT		
4.84 INPUT		
7.44 INPUT		
3.58 INPUT		
2.76 +/− INPUT		
8.53 INPUT		
4.80 +/− INPUT		
10.32 INPUT		
9.36 INPUT		
1.90 +/− INPUT		
3.29 INPUT		
4.13 INPUT	ITEM(13)=?	
	TOTAL=42.57	

Give the Coca-Cola return data (y-list) a name.

EXIT NAME	TYPE NAME; [INPUT][a]	
COKE INPUT	ITEM(13)=?	
CALC MORE		
FRCST	SELECT X VARIABLE	
SP	SELECT Y VARIABLE	Selects S&P Index.

2. Calculate the alpha and beta values for the regression or characteristic line

COKE	LINEAR	Selects Coca-Cola as the y-list and indicates we are using linear regression.
M	M=0.85	Computes Coca-Cola's beta.
B	B=2.39	Y intercept of the characteristic line.

[a]See the HP 17BII Owner's Manual for an explanation of how to name a data list.

3. Compute the average holding-period returns and the standard deviations of the returns for Coca-Cola, and then the S&P 500 Index

| EXIT | EXIT | EXIT | MORE | ITEM(13)=? | Access the calculator's menu to compute the average return and standard deviation. |

Compute the mean or average return and the standard deviation for Coca-Cola.

| MEAN | MEAN=3.55 |
| STDEV | STDEV=4.95 |

Compute the mean or average return and the standard deviation for the S&P 500 Index.

EXIT	GET	SELECT A NAME
SP		ITEM(13)=?
CALC	MEAN	MEAN=1.36
STDEV		STDEV=3.51

STUDY PROBLEMS

4A–1. (*Computing Return Statistics for a Stock*) Using a calculator compute the following statistics for Arka stock: (1) alpha, (2) beta, (3) average return, and (4) standard deviation of return.

Yearly Holding-Period Returns		
Year	Arka	S&P
1991	10%	12%
1992	6	7
1993	18	24
1994	15	18

4A–2. (*Computing Return Statistics for a Stock*) Using a calculator calculate the following statistics for Son Sen, Inc., stock: (1) alpha, (2) beta, (3) average return, and (4) standard deviation of return.

Monthly Holding-Period Returns		
Month	Son Sen	S&P
January	0.6%	0.9%
February	0.3	1.0
March	−1.5	−1.0
April	−0.7	0.0
May	1.9	3.0
June	0.5	−1.5
July	2.5	3.0
August	0.8	1.2
September	−2.5	−4.0
October	3.0	4.5
November	0.4	1.4
December	0.1	0.2

APPENDIX 4B

Measuring the Required Rate of Return: The Arbitrage Pricing Model

The basic theme of the arbitrage pricing model (APM) may be summarized as follows:[20]

1. Actual security returns vary from their expected amounts because of *unanticipated* changes in a *number* of basic economic forces, such as industrial production, inflation rates, the term structure of interest rates, and the difference in interest rates between high- and low-risk bonds.[21].

2. Just as the CAPM defined a portfolio's systematic risk to be its sensitivity to the general-market returns (i.e., its beta coefficient), APM suggests that the risk of a security is reflected in its sensitivity to the unexpected changes in important economic forces.

3. Any two stocks or portfolios that have the same sensitivity to meaningful economic forces (that is, the same relevant or systematic risk) must have the same expected return. Otherwise, we could replace some of the stocks in our portfolio with other stocks having the same sensitivities but higher expected returns and earn riskless profits.

4. We would expect portfolios that are highly sensitive to unexpected changes in macroeconomic forces to offer investors high expected returns. This relationship may be represented quantitatively as follows:

---

[20]The following description of the APM is taken in part from Dorothy H. Bower, Richard S. Bower, and Dennis E. Logue, "A Primer on Arbitrage Pricing Theory," in Joel M. Stern and Donald H. Chew, Jr., eds., *The Revolution in Corporate Finance* (New York: Basil Blackwell, 1986), pp. 69–77.

[21]See R. Roll and S. Ross, "The Arbitrage Pricing Theory Approach to Strategic Portfolio Planning," *Financial Analysts Journal* (May–June 1984), 14–26.

$$E(R_i) = R_f + (S_{i1})(RP_1) + (S_{i2})(RP_2) + \ldots$$
$$+ (S_{ij})(RP_j) + \ldots + (S_{in})(RP_n) \quad \textbf{(4B-1)}$$

where $E(R_i)$ = the expected return for stock or portfolio i

R_f = the risk-free rate

S_{ij} = the sensitivity of stock i returns to unexpected changes in economic force j

RP_j = the market risk premium associated with an unexpected change in the jth economic force

n = the number of relevant economic forces

To help understand the APM model, we will draw from the actual research of Bower, Bower, and Logue, (BBL).[22] After computing monthly returns for 815 stocks from 1970 through 1979, BBL used a technique called factor analysis to study the general movement of monthly returns for the 815 stocks. The technique identified four factors that help explain the movement of the returns, and also used equation (4B–1) to represent the risk–return relationship in an APM format. The actual model appears as follows:

$$\text{expected return for stock } i = 6.2\% - 185.5\%(S_{i1})$$
$$+ 144.5\%(S_{i2})$$
$$+ 12.4\%\,(S_{i3}) - 274.4\%(S_{i4})$$

The value 6.2% in the equation is an estimate of the risk-free rate, as determined by the model; the remaining values, $-185.5\%, \ldots, -274.4\%$, signify the market risk premiums for each of the four factors; and the $S_{i1}, \ldots, S_{i4}$ represent the sensitivities of stock i to the four factors.

The BBL factors are determined statistically from past return data and were not intuitively or economically identified; that is, the technique provides *factors* that tell us more about the movement in the returns than would any other factors. Each factor could conceivably relate to a single economic variable; however, it is more likely that each factor represents the influence of several economic variables.[23]

Having specified the APM risk–return relationship, BBL then used the model to estimate the expected (required) rates of return for 17 stocks. This estimation required BBL to use regression analysis to study the relationships of the returns of the 17 stocks to the four factors. From this regression analysis, they were able to measure the sensitivity of each security's return to a particular factor. These *sensitivity coefficients* for a particular stock may then be combined with the APM model in equation (4B–1) to estimate the investors' required rate of return.

Using 3 of the 17 stocks to demonstrate the calculation, the regres-

---

[22]Dorothy A. Bower, Richard S. Bower, and Dennis E. Logue, "Equity Screening Rates Using Arbitrage Pricing Theory," in C. F. Lee, ed., *Advances in Financial Planning* (Greenwich, CT: JAI Press, 1984).

[23]As noted earlier in the chapter, work is under way to determine the economic factors that most influence security returns. See R. Roll and S. Ross, "The Arbitrage Pricing Theory Approach to Strategic Portfolio Planning," *Financial Analysts Journal* (May–June 1984), 14–26.

sion coefficients (sensitivity coefficients) for American Hospital Supply, CBS, and Western Union are shown here:

	Stock Sensitivity Coefficients (S)			
	Factor 1	Factor 2	Factor 3	Factor 4
American Hospital Supply	−0.050	0.010	0.040	0.020
CBS	−0.050	0.002	0.005	0.010
Western Union	−0.050	−0.020	−0.010	0.009

Using these stock sensitivity coefficients and the APM model, as developed by BBL, we can estimate the investors' expected (required) rate of return for each stock as follows:

American
Hospital Supply = 6.2% − 185.5%(−0.050) + 144.5%(0.010)
     +12.4%(0.040) − 274.4%(.020)
   = 11.93%

   CBS = 6.2% − 185.5%(−0.050) + 144.5%(0.002)
     +12.4%(0.005) − 274.4%(0.010)
   = 13.08%

Western Union = 6.2% − 185.5%(−0.050) + 144.5%(−0.020)
     +12.4%(−0.010) − 274.4%(0.009)
   = 9.99%

STUDY PROBLEMS

4B–1. (*Arbitrage Pricing Model*) Using the APM along with the results of the Bower, Bower, and Logue research just discussed, estimate the appropriate required rates of return for the following three stocks:

	Sensitivity Factor			
Stock	Factor 1	Factor 2	Factor 3	Factor 4
A	−0.070	−0.020	0.010	0.003
B	−0.070	0.030	0.005	0.010
C	−0.070	−0.010	0.006	0.009

4B–2. a. (*Required Rate of Return Using APM*) If we use the arbitrage pricing model to measure investors' required rate of return, what is our concept of risk?

b. Using the results of the Bower, Bower, and Logue study of return variability, as captured in equation (4B–1), calculate the investors' required rate of return for the following stocks:

Stock	Sensitivity Factor 1	2	3	4
A	−0.070	0.030	0.005	0.010
B	−0.070	−0.010	0.006	0.009
C	−0.050	0.004	−0.010	−0.007
D	−0.060	−0.007	−0.006	0.006

(b)

Stock	Beta
A	1.40
B	1.70
C	1.20
D	1.10

(c)

c. Assuming (i) a risk-free rate of 6.1 percent and (ii) an expected market return of 17.25 percent, estimate the investors' required rate of return for the four stocks in part (b), using the CAPM.

d. What might explain the differences in your answers to parts (b) and (c)?

CHAPTER 5

Bond and Stock Valuation

Definitions of Value • Valuation: An Overview • Valuation: The Basic Process • Bond Valuation •
Preferred Stock Valuation • Common Stock Valuation • Expected Rates of Return • Appendix 5A: More on
Bond Valuation • Appendix 5B: The Relationship Between Value and Earnings

What determines the real or intrinsic value of an asset, such as stocks and
bonds, land, or capital goods? Why does the value of an asset change so radically
at times? Why did Compaq common stock sell for about $78 in early 1991 and
then fall to $22 by the end of the same year? Coca-Cola common stock, on the
other hand, went from about $42 to $73 in the same period. Why the change?

An extreme situation, involving commercial land sales, existed in Dallas,
Texas, between 1982 and 1984. A speculator could purchase land for $1 million
and resell it within a matter of months for $2 million. The new purchaser could
frequently "flip" the land again for $3 million or even $4 million within less than
another year. By 1985, however, the financial institutions that had been
providing the credit to the speculators became concerned about the dizzying
rates of increase in land values. Government regulators of these institutions also
began discouraging further financing of commercial land. Without the support
of the financial markets, prospective buyers left the marketplace, setting in
motion a sharp decline in values. The end result for many investors, even today,
continues to be foreclosure and financial insolvency, if not bankruptcy.

These examples highlight the difficulty, as well as the importance, of the
valuation of assets—and particularly the need to predict future values in
financial management. The *Maxims* of the French writer La Rouchefoucauld,
written over three centuries ago, still speak to us: "The greatest of all gifts is the
power to estimate things at their true worth."

In this chapter we examine the concepts of and procedures for valuing
assets, especially **financial assets** (securities), such as bonds, preferred stock,
and common stock.[1] Since the financial manager's objective is to maximize the
value of the firm's common stock, we need to understand the constructs that
underlie value. The cost of capital, one integral concept, which will also be used
in capital budgeting in Chapters 6 and 7, is based on the rates of return used to

---

[1]We describe the functioning of the capital markets and the attributes of bonds, preferred stock, and
common stock in Chapter 20.

value the firm's financial securities. Thus, there are at least two reasons for studying the **valuation** of financial assets:

1. Understanding how to value financial securities is essential if managers are to meet the objective of maximizing the value of the firm's common stock.
2. The cost of capital used in making capital budgeting decisions is computed from the required rates of return investors use to value the firm's securities. Thus, our understanding of security valuation lays the foundation for estimating the firm's cost of capital, discussed in Chapter 8.

What we especially try to do in this chapter is the following:

1. Examine the variety of definitions given for the term *value,* including book value, liquidation value, market value, and intrinsic value.
2. Explain the basic concept of *valuing an asset.*
3. Look specifically at the valuation of bonds, preferred stock, and common stock.
4. Examine the concept of the *investor's expected rate of return,* particularly as it relates to bonds, preferred stock, and common stock.
5. Cover bond valuation, including the important concept of *duration,* more intensely (see Appendix 5A).
6. Examine the nature of the connection between a firm's common stock value and its earnings (see Appendix 5B). (In stock valuation, investors often use this relationship as a guide.)

Definitions of Value

The term *value* is often used in different contexts, depending on its application.[2] Examples of different uses of this term include book value, liquidation value, market value, and intrinsic value.

Book value is the value of an asset as shown on a firm's balance sheet. It represents a historical value rather than a current worth. For example, the book value for common stock is the sum of the stock's par value, the paid-in capital, and the retained earnings. The par value and the paid-in capital equal the amount the company received when the securities were originally issued. Retained earnings are the amount of net income retained within the firm as opposed to being paid out as dividends to common shareholders. The retention of earnings is an indirect way for the stockholders to invest more money in the firm. If we want to know the book value *per common share,* we simply divide the total book value of the stock by the number of shares outstanding. For example, the book value for PepsiCo's common stock on December 28, 1991, was $7.03, computed as follows:

Par value ($ millions)	$ 14.4
Paid-in capital ($ millions)	476.6
Retained earnings ($ millions)	5800.3
Less treasury stock ($ millions)	(745.9)
Total book value ($ millions)	$5545.4
Number of shares outstanding (millions)	789.1
Book value per share ($5545.4 ÷ 789.1 shares)	$ 7.03

[2]We are using the word *value* here as a noun. It is often used as a verb, such as when we say that we *value* an asset.

Liquidation value is the dollar sum that could be realized if an asset were sold individually and not as a part of a going concern. For example, if a product line is discontinued, the machinery used in its production might be sold. The sale price would be its liquidation value and would be determined independently of the firm's value. Similarly, if the firm's operations were discontinued and its assets were sold as a separate collection, the sales price would represent the firm's liquidation value.

The **market value** of an asset is the observed value for the asset in the marketplace. This value is determined by supply and demand forces working together in the marketplace, where buyers and sellers negotiate a mutually acceptable price for the asset. For instance, the market price for Ford common stock on December 13, 1991, was $31. This price was reached by a large number of buyers and sellers working through the New York Stock Exchange. In theory, a market price exists for all assets. However, many assets have no readily observable market price because trading seldom occurs. For instance, the market price for the common stock of Blanks Engraving, a Dallas-based family-owned firm, would be more difficult to establish than the market value of J. C. Penney's common stock.

The **intrinsic value** of an asset can be defined as the present value of the asset's expected future cash flows. This value is also called the **fair value,** as perceived by the investor, given the amount, timing, and riskiness of future cash flows. In essence, intrinsic value is like the value in the eyes of the investor. Given the risk, the investor determines the appropriate discount rate to use in computing the present or intrinsic value of the asset. Once the investor has estimated the intrinsic value of a security, this value can be compared with its market value. If the intrinsic value is greater than the market value, then the security is undervalued in the eyes of the investor. Should the market value exceed the investor's intrinsic value, then the security is overvalued.

We hasten to add that if the securities market is working efficiently, the market value and the intrinsic value of a security will be equal. Whenever a security's intrinsic value differs from its current market price, the competition among investors seeking opportunities to make a profit will quickly drive the market price back into equilibrium with intrinsic value. Thus, we may define an **efficient market** as one in which the values of all securities at any instant in time fully reflect all available information, which results in the market value and the intrinsic value being the same. If the markets are truly efficient, it is extremely difficult for an investor to make extra profits from an ability to predict prices.

The idea of market efficiency has been the backdrop for an intense battle between professional investors and university professors. The academic community has contended that a blindfolded monkey throwing darts at the list of securities in the *Wall Street Journal* could do as well as a professional money manager. Market professionals, on the other hand, retort that academicians are so immersed in research they could not recognize potential profits if these profits were delivered to their offices. The war has been intense but also one that the student of finance should find intriguing.

Perspective in Finance

Intrinsic value is the present value of expected future cash flows. This statement is true regardless of what type of asset we are valuing. If you remember only one thing from this chapter, remember that intrinsic value is the present value of expected future cash flows.

Valuation: An Overview

For our purposes, *the value of an asset is its intrinsic value, which is the present value of its expected future cash flows,* where these cash flows are discounted

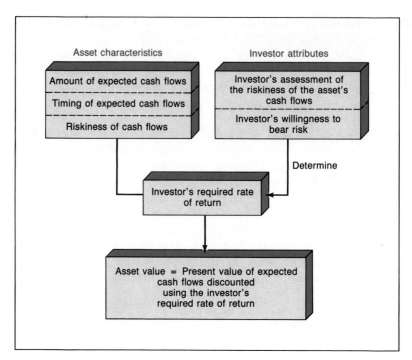

FIGURE 5–1.
Basic Factors Determining
an Asset's Value

back to the present using the investor's required rate of return. This statement is true for valuing all assets. It is the basis of almost all that we do in finance. Thus, value is affected by three elements:

1. The amount and timing of the asset's expected cash flows
2. The riskiness of these cash flows
3. The investor's required rate of return for undertaking the investment

The first two factors are characteristics of the asset, and the third one is a need of the investor. The required rate of return, studied in Chapter 4, is the minimum rate necessary to attract an investor to purchase or hold a security. This rate must be high enough to compensate the investor for the risk perceived in the asset's future cash flows. Figure 5–1 depicts the basic factors involved in valuation. As the figure shows, finding the value of an asset involves (1) assessing the asset's characteristics, which include the amount and timing of the expected cash flows and the riskiness of these cash flows; (2) determining the investor's required rate of return, which embodies the investor's attitude about assuming risk and perception of the riskiness of the asset; and (3) discounting the expected cash flows back to the present, using the investor's required rate of return.

Perspective in Finance

Intrinsic value is a function of the cash flows yet to be received, the riskiness of these cash flows, and the investor's required rate of return.

Valuation: The Basic Process

The valuation process can be described as follows: It is assigning value to an asset by calculating the present value of its expected future cash flows using the investor's required rate of return as the discount rate. The investor's required rate of return, R, is determined by the level of the risk-free rate of interest and the risk premium that the investor feels is necessary to compensate for the risks assumed in owning the asset. Therefore, the basic security valuation model can be defined mathematically as follows:

$$V = \frac{C_1}{(1 + R)^1} + \frac{C_2}{(1 + R)^2} + \cdots + \frac{C_n}{(1 + R)^n}$$

or   **(5-1)**   VALUATION
                                                                                                    FORMULA

$$V = \sum_{t=1}^{n} \frac{C_t}{(1 + R)^t}$$

where C_t = cash flow to be received in year t.

V = the intrinsic value or present value of an asset producing expected future cash flows, C_t, in years 1 through n

R = the investor's required rate of return

Using equation (5–1), there are three basic steps in the valuation process:

Step 1: Estimate the C_t in equation (5–1), which is the amount and timing of the future cash flows the security is expected to provide.

Step 2: Determine R, the investor's required rate of return. As explained in Chapter 4, we do this by evaluating the riskiness of the security's future cash flows and determining an appropriate risk premium, *RP*. We then observe the risk-free rate (such as the rate of interest on 90-day Treasury bills) and add the two together for the required rate of return.

Step 3: Calculate the intrinsic value, V, as the present value of expected future cash flows discounted at the investor's required rate of return.

Perspective in Finance

Equation (5–1), which measures the present value of future cash flows, is the basis of the valuation proces.. It is the most important equation in this chapter, because all the remaining equations are merely reformulations of this one equation. If we understand equation (5–1), all the valuation work we do, and a host of other topics as well, will be much clearer in our minds. It may be said that valuation is the foundation of much of what we do in our study of financial management.

With these brief, but important, principles of valuation as our foundation, we will now investigate the procedures for valuing particular types of securities. Specifically, we will learn how to value a bond, preferred stock, and common stock.

Bond Valuation

The process for valuing a bond requires first that we understand the terminology and institutional characteristics of a bond. More extensive coverage of the contractual provisions of a bond is provided in Chapter 20.

Perspective in Finance

The value of a bond is the present value both of future interest to be received and the par or maturity value of the bond. Simply list these cash flows, use your discount rate of return, and find the value.

Terminology

When a firm, or nonprofit institution needs financing, one source is **bonds.** This type of financing instrument is simply a long-term promissory note, issued by the borrower, promising to pay its holder a predetermined and fixed amount of interest each year. As a form of debt, a contract between the borrower and lender is executed, frequently called an **indenture.** Although the terms of the contract generally are extensive, incorporating detailed protective provisions for the creditor, only three items *directly* affect the cash flows from owning a bond: the bond's par value, maturity date, and the coupon rate of interest.

1. **Par value.** The amount the firm is to pay on the maturity date stated on the face of the bond. This amount, defined as the par value or face value, cannot be altered after the bond has been issued. Typically, the par value is set at $1,000. Hence, the issuing company contractually agrees to pay the investor this amount when the debt matures. The *par value* is essentially independent of the *intrinsic value* of the bond. Thus, although the price of the bond fluctuates in response to changing economic and market conditions, the par value remains constant.

2. **Maturity date.** As already suggested, a bond normally has a maturity date, at which time the borrowing organization is committed to repay the loan. At this time the holder of the security, assuming the company does not default on the obligation, is to receive cash in the amount of the par value.

3. **Coupon interest rate.** Besides paying the owner of the bond the par value at the maturity date, the borrower promises to pay a specified amount of interest each year. This annual amount is stated either in terms of dollars, such as $90, or as a percent of the par value. In either instance *the interest to be paid is inflexible.* When the contractual agreement specifies the interest as a percent of par value, this percentage is known as the coupon interest rate or the **contractual interest rate.** For instance, if the terms of a $1,000 par value bond set the annual interest at $90, the coupon rate is 9 percent, or $90 divided by $1,000. Furthermore, this rate should not be confused with the required rate of return.

Valuation Procedure

The valuation process for a bond, as depicted in Figure 5–2, requires knowledge of three essential elements: (1) the amount of the cash flows to be received by

---

FIGURE 5–2.
Data Requirements for Bond Valuation

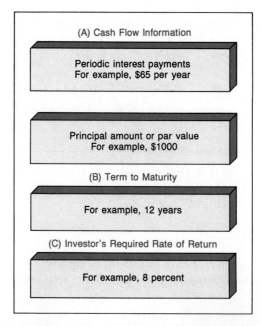

(A) Cash Flow Information

Periodic interest payments
For example, $65 per year

Principal amount or par value
For example, $1000

(B) Term to Maturity

For example, 12 years

(C) Investor's Required Rate of Return

For example, 8 percent

the investor, (2) the maturity date of the loan, and (3) the investor's required rate of return. The amount of cash flows is dictated by the periodic interest to be received and by the par value to be paid at maturity. Given these elements, we can compute the value of the bond, or the present value.

Consider a bond issued by CitiCorp, with a maturity date of 2007 and a stated coupon rate of 8.45 percent.[3] The group of bonds was originally issued at a price of $1,000. By late 1991, however, the investors' required rate of return had changed, and the bond value was less than $1,000. In fact, in 1991 investors were requiring a return of approximately 10 percent for this security. At this time the value of the security was approximately $880, which can be calculated using the following three-step valuation procedure:

Step 1: Estimate the amount and timing of the expected future cash flows. Two types of cash flows are received by the bondholder:

  1. Annual interest payments equal to the coupon rate of interest times the face value of the bond. In this example the interest payments equal $84.50 = .0845 × $1,000. Assuming that 1991 interest payments have already been made, these cash flows will be received by the bondholder in each of the 16 years before the bond matures (1992 through 2007 = 16 years).
  2. The face value of the bond of $1,000 to be received in 2007.
     To summarize, the cash flows received by the bondholder are as follows:

0	1	2	3	4	15	16
	$84.50	$84.50	$84.50	$84.50	$84.50	$84.50
						+$1000.00
						$1084.50

Step 2: Determine the investor's required rate of return by evaluating the riskiness of the bond's future cash flows. A 10 percent required rate of return for the CitiCorp bondholders is given.

Step 3: Calculate the intrinsic value of the bond as the present value of the expected future interest and principal payments discounted at the investor's required rate of return.

The present value of CitiCorp's bonds is found as follows:

$$\text{bond value} = V_b = \frac{\$ \text{ interest in year 1}}{(1 + \text{required rate of return})^1}$$

$$+ \frac{\$ \text{ interest in year 2}}{(1 + \text{required rate of return})^2}$$

$$+ \ldots + \frac{\$ \text{ interest in year 16}}{(1 + \text{required rate of return})^{16}}$$

$$+ \frac{\$ \text{ par value of bond}}{(1 + \text{required rate of return})^{16}}$$

or, summing over the interest payments,

$$V_b = \underbrace{\sum_{t=1}^{16} \frac{\$ \text{ interest in year } t}{(1 + \text{required rate of return})^t}}_{\text{present value of interest}} + \underbrace{\frac{\$ \text{ par value of bond}}{(1 + \text{required rate of return})^{16}}}_{\text{present value of par value}}$$

---

[3]CitiCorp remits the interest to its bondholders on a semiannual basis on January 15 and July 15. However, for the moment assume the interest is to be received annually. The effect of semiannual payments will be examined later.

Perspective in Finance

The foregoing equation is a restatement in a slightly different form of equation (5–1). Recall that equation (5–1) states that the value of an asset is the present value of future cash flows to be received by the investor.

Using I_t to represent the interest payment in year t, M to represent the bond's maturity (or par) value, and R_b to equal the bondholder's required rate of return, we may express the value of a bond maturing in year n as follows:

$$V_b = \sum_{t=1}^{n} \frac{\$I_t}{(1 + R_b)^t} + \frac{\$M}{(1 + R_b)^n} \qquad \textbf{(5–2a)}$$

Solving for the value of CitiCorp bonds. Since the interest payments I_t are an annuity for n years, and the maturity value is a one-time amount in year n, we can use the present-value factors in Appendixes C ($PVIF_{i,n}$) and E ($PVIFA_{i,n}$) to solve for the present value of the bond as follows:

$$V_b = \$I_t \, (PVIFA_{i,n}) + \$M \, (PVIF_{i,n}) \qquad \textbf{(5–2b)}$$

For CitiCorp,

$$V_b = \$I_t \, (PVIFA_{10\%,16}) + \$M(PVIF_{10\%,16})$$
$$= \$84.50 \, (7.824) + \$1000 \, (.218)$$
$$= \$661.13 + \$218.00$$
$$= \$879.13$$

Thus, if investors consider 10 percent to be an appropriate required rate of return in view of the risk level associated with CitiCorp's bonds, paying a price of $879.13 would satisfy their return requirement. ■

CALCULATOR SOLUTION[4]

Data Input	Function Key
16	N
10	I%YR
84.5	PMT
1000	FV

Function key	Answer[5]
PV	−878.73

And, to present the foregoing process of finding the present value graphically:

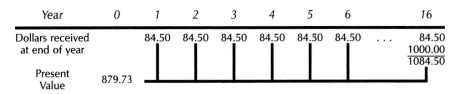

Year	0	1	2	3	4	5	6		16
Dollars received at end of year		84.50	84.50	84.50	84.50	84.50	84.50	...	84.50 1000.00 1084.50
Present Value	879.73								

Semiannual Interest Payments

In the preceding illustration, the interest payments were assumed to be paid annually. However, companies typically forward an interest check to bondholders semiannually. For example, rather than disbursing $84.50 in interest at the conclusion of each year, CitiCorp pays $42.25 (half of $84.50) on January 15 and July 15.

Several steps are involved in adapting equation (5–2a) for semiannual

---

[4]As noted in Chapter 3, we are using the HP 17BII in the margin notes. You may want to return to the Chapter 3 section, *Moving Through Time with the Aid of a Financial Calculator*, to see a more complete explanation of using the HP 17BII, or see Appendix A at the end of the text for a tutorial. For an explanation of other calculators, see the study guide that accompanies this text.

[5]A slightly different answer results because of small rounding errors that occur when using the interest factors from the present-value tables. Also, if the interest payments and par value are entered as positive numbers, the value will always be a negative number.

interest payments.[6] First, thinking in terms of *periods* instead of years, a bond with a life of n years paying interest semiannually has a life of $2n$ periods. In other words, a five-year bond ($n = 5$) that remits its interest on a semiannual basis actually makes 10 payments. Yet although the number of periods has doubled, the *dollar* amount of interest being sent to the investors for each period and the bondholders' required rate of return are half of the equivalent annual figures. I_t becomes $I_t/2$ and R_b is changed to $R_b/2$; thus, for semiannual compounding, equation (5–2a) becomes

$$V_b = \sum_{t=1}^{2n} \frac{\$I_t/2}{\left(1 + \dfrac{R_b}{2}\right)^t} + \frac{\$M}{\left(1 + \dfrac{R_b}{2}\right)^{2n}} \qquad \textbf{(5–3a)}$$

However, if the present-value tables are used, V_b is calculated as

$$V_b = \frac{\$I_t}{2} \left[PVIFA_{R_b/2,\, 2n}\right] + \$M \left[PVIF_{R_b/2,\, 2n}\right] \qquad \textbf{(5–3b)}$$

<hr>

EXAMPLE

To see the effect of semiannual interest payments on the value of a bond, assume the Garrett Corporation has issued a 9 percent, $1,000 bond. The debt is to mature in six years, and the investor's required rate of return is currently 8 percent. If interest is paid semiannually, the number of periods is 12 (6 years × 2); the dollar interest to be received by the investor at the end of each six-month period is $45 ($90 ÷ 2); and the required rate of return for six months is 4 percent (8% ÷ 2). Therefore, the valuation equation is

$$V_b = \sum_{t=1}^{12} \frac{\$45}{(1 + .04)^t} + \frac{\$1000}{(1 + .04)^{12}}$$

$$V_b = \$45 \left[PVIFA_{4\%,12}\right] + \$1000 \left[PVIF_{4\%,12}\right]$$

$$= \$45(9.385) + \$1000(.625)$$

$$= \$422.33 + \$625.00$$

$$= \$1047.33$$

CALCULATOR SOLUTION	
Data Input	Function Key
12	N
4	I%YR
45	PMT
1000	FV
Function Key	Answer
PV	−1046.93

Thus, the value (present value) of a bond paying $45 semiannually, and $1,000 at maturity (six years), is $1,047.33 (calculator solution $1,046.93) provided the investor's required rate of return is 8 percent compounded semiannually.[7]

The foregoing explanations of bond valuation represent only the basic issue of finding value. For those interested, more of the important relationships that affect bond values are explained in Appendix 5A. ■

<hr>

Preferred Stock Valuation

Like a bondholder, the owner of preferred stock should receive a *constant income* from the investment in each period. However, the return from preferred stock comes in the form of *dividends* rather than *interest*. In addition, while bonds generally have a specific maturity date, most preferred stocks are perpetuities (nonmaturing). In this instance, finding the value (present value) of

<hr>

[6]The logic for calculating the value of a bond that pays interest semiannually is similar to the material presented in Chapter 3, where compound interest with nonannual periods was discussed.
[7]A slightly different answer again results from differences in rounding.

preferred stock, V_p, with a level cash flow stream continuing indefinitely, may best be explained by an example.

To illustrate the valuation of a preferred stock, consider AT&T's preferred stock issue. Once again we use the three-step valuation procedure.

Step 1: Estimate the amount and timing of the receipt of the future cash flows the preferred stock is expected to provide.

AT&T's preferred stock pays an annual dividend of $3.64. The shares do not have a maturity date; that is, they go to perpetuity.

Step 2: Evaluate the riskiness of the preferred stock's future dividends and determine the investor's required rate of return.

The investor's required rate of return is assumed to equal 7.28 percent.

Step 3: Calculate the intrinsic value of the share of preferred stock, which is the present value of the expected dividends discounted at the investor's required rate of return.

The valuation model for a share of preferred stock, V_p, is defined as follows:

$$
\begin{aligned}
V_p &= \frac{\text{dividend in year 1}}{(1 + \text{required rate of return})^1} \\
&+ \frac{\text{dividend in year 2}}{(1 + \text{required rate of return})^2} \\
&+ \cdots + \frac{\text{dividend in infinity}}{(1 + \text{required rate of return})^\infty} \\
&= \frac{D_1}{(1 + R_p)^1} + \frac{D_2}{(1 + R_p)^2} + \cdots + \frac{D_\infty}{(1 + R_p)^\infty} \\
V_p &= \sum_{t=1}^{\infty} \frac{D_t}{(1 + R_p)^t}
\end{aligned}
\tag{5-4}
$$

Perspective in Finance

Equation (5–4) is a restatement in a slightly different form of equation (5–1). Recall that equation (5–1) states that the value of an asset is the present value of future cash flows to be received by the investor.

Since the dividends in each period are equal for preferred stock, equation (5–4) can be reduced to the following relationship:[8]

$$
V_p = \frac{\text{annual dividend}}{\text{required rate of return}} = \frac{D}{R_p}
\tag{5-5}
$$

Equation (5–5) represents the present value of an infinite stream of cash flows, where the cash flows are the same each year. We can determine the value of the AT&T preferred stock, using equation (5–5), as follows:

Preferred Stock

---

[8]To verify this result, consider the following equation:

(i)
$$
V_p = \frac{D_1}{(1 + R_p)} + \frac{D_2}{(1 + R_p)^2} + \cdots + \frac{D_n}{(1 + R_p)^n}
$$

If we multiply both sides of this equation by $(1 + R_p)$, we have

(ii)
$$
V_p(1 + R_p) = D_1 + \frac{D_2}{(1 + R_p)} + \cdots + \frac{D_n}{(1 + R_p)^{n-1}}
$$

[*cont. next pg.*]

$$V_p = \frac{D}{R_p} = \frac{\$3.64}{.0728} = \$50$$

Perspective in Finance

The value of a preferred stock is the present value of all future dividends. But because most preferred stocks are nonmaturing—the dividends continue to infinity—we have therefore to come up with a shortcut for finding value.

Common Stock Valuation

The third and last security we will learn to value is common stock. *Like both bonds and preferred stock, a common stock's value is equal to the present value of all future cash flows expected to be received by the stockholder.* However, in contrast to bonds, common stock does not promise its owners interest income or a maturity payment at some specified time in the future. Nor does common stock entitle the holder to a predetermined constant dividend, as does preferred stock. For common stock, the dividend is based on the profitability of the firm and on management's decision to pay dividends or to retain the profits for reinvestment purposes. As a consequence, dividend streams tend to increase with the growth in corporate earnings. Thus, the growth of future dividends is a prime distinguishing feature of common stock.

The Growth Factor in Valuing Common Stock

What is meant by the term *growth* when used in the context of valuing common stock? A company can grow in a variety of ways. It can become larger by borrowing money to invest in new projects. Likewise, it can issue new stock for expansion. Management could also acquire another company to merge with the existing firm, which would increase the firm's assets. In all these cases, the firm is growing through the use of new financing, by issuing debt or common stock. Although management could accurately say that the firm has grown, the original stockholders may or may not participate in this growth. Growth is realized through the infusion of new capital. The firm size has clearly increased, but unless the original investors increase their investment in the firm, they will own a smaller portion of the expanded business.

Another means of growing is internal growth, which requires that management retain some or all of the firm's profits for reinvestment in the firm, resulting in the growth of future earnings and hopefully the value of the common stock. This process underlies the essence of potential growth for the firm's current stockholders, and what we can call *the only relevant growth, for our purposes in valuing a firm's common shares.*[9]

Subtracting (i) from (ii) yields

$$V_p(1 + R_p - 1) = D_1 - \frac{D_n}{(1 + R_p)^n}$$

As n approaches infinity, $D_n/(1 + R_p)^n$ approaches zero. Consequently,

$$V_p R_p = D_1 \quad \text{and} \quad V_p = \frac{D_1}{R_p}$$

Since $D_1 = D_2 = \cdots = D_n$, we need not designate the year. Therefore,

(iii)
$$V_p = \frac{D}{R_p}$$

[9]We are not arguing that the existing common stockholders never benefit from the use of external financing; however, such benefit is more evasive when dealing with efficient capital markets.

EXAMPLE

To illustrate the nature of internal growth, assume that the return on equity for PepsiCo is 16 percent.[10] If PepsiCo's management decides to pay all the profits out in dividends to its stockholders, the firm will experience no growth internally. It might become larger by borrowing more money or issuing new stock, but internal growth will come only through the retention of profits. If, on the other hand, PepsiCo retained all the profits the stockholders' investment in the firm would grow by the amount of profits retained, or by 16 percent. If, however, management kept only 50 percent of the profits for reinvestment, the common shareholders' investment would increase only by half of the 16 percent return on equity, or by 8 percent. Generalizing this relationship, we have

$$g = ROE \times r, \tag{5-6}$$

where
g = the growth rate of future earnings and the growth in the common stockholders' investment in the firm

ROE = the return on equity (net income/common book value)

r = the company's percentage of profits retained, called the profit-retention rate[11]

Therefore, if only 25 percent of the profits were retained by PepsiCo, we would expect the common stockholders' investment in the firm and the value of the stock price to increase or grow by 4 percent; that is,

$$g = 16\% \times .25 = 4\% \qquad \blacksquare$$

In summary, common stockholders frequently rely on an increase in the stock price as a source of return. If the company is retaining a portion of its earnings for reinvestment, future profits and dividends should grow. This growth should be reflected in an increased market price of the common stock in future periods, provided that the return on the funds reinvested exceeds the

---

[10]The return on equity is the percentage return on the common shareholder's investment in the company and is computed as follows:

$$\text{return on equity} = \frac{\text{net income}}{(\text{par value} + \text{paid-in capital} + \text{retained earnings})}$$

[11]The retention rate is also equal to (1 − the percentage of profits paid out in dividends). The percentage of profits paid out in dividends is often called the **dividend-payout** ratio.

investor's required rate of return. Therefore, both types of return (dividends and price appreciation) are necessary in the development of a valuation model for common stock.

To explain this process, let us begin by examining how an investor might value a common stock that is to be held for only one year.

Common Stock Valuation— Single Holding Period

For an investor holding a common stock for only one year, the value of the stock should equal the present value of both the expected dividend to be received in one year, D_1, and the anticipated market price of the share at year end, P_1. If R_c represents a common stockholder's required rate of return, the value of the security, V_c, would be

$$V_c = \text{present value of dividend } (D_1)$$
$$+ \text{ present value of market price } (P_1)$$
$$= \frac{D_1}{(1 + R_c)} + \frac{P_1}{(1 + R_c)}$$

EXAMPLE

Suppose an investor is contemplating the purchase of RMI common stock at the beginning of this year. The dividend at year end is expected to be $1.64, and the market price by the end of the year is projected to be $22. If the investor's required rate of return is 18 percent, the value of the security would be

$$V_c = \frac{\$1.64}{1 + .18} + \frac{\$22}{1 + .18}$$
$$= \$1.39 + \$18.64$$
$$= \$20.03$$

Once again we see that valuation is the same three-step process. First we estimate the expected future cash flows from common stock ownership (a $1.64 dividend and a $22 end-of-year expected share price). Second, we estimate the investor's required rate of return after assessing the riskiness of the expected cash flows (assumed to be 18 percent). Finally, we discount the expected dividend and end-of-year share price back to the present at the investor's required rate of return.

Perspective in Finance

The intrinsic value of a common stock, like preferred stock, is the present value of all future dividends. And we have the same problem we had with preferred stock—it is hard to value cash flows that continue in perpetuity. So we must make some assumptions about the expected growth of future dividends. If, for example, we assume that dividends grow at a constant rate forever, we can then calculate the present value of the stock.

Common Stock Valuation— Multiple Holding Periods

Since common stock has no maturity date and is frequently held for many years, a *multiple-holding-period valuation model* is needed. The general common stock valuation model can be defined as follows:

$$V_c = \frac{D_1}{(1 + R_c)^1} + \frac{D_2}{(1 + R_c)^2} + \cdots$$
$$+ \frac{D_n}{(1 + R_c)^n} + \cdots + \frac{D_\infty}{(1 + R_c)^\infty}$$

(5–7)

Perspective in Finance

Equation (5–7) is a restatement in a slightly different form of equation (5–1). Recall that equation (5–1) states that the value of an asset is the present value of future cash flows to be received by the investor.

This equation simply indicates that we are discounting the dividend at the end of the first year, D_1, back one year, the dividend in the second year, D_2, back two years, . . . , the dividend in the nth year back n years, . . . , and the dividend in infinity back an infinite number of years. The required rate of return is R_c. In using equation (5–7), note that the value of the stock is established at the beginning of the year, say January 1, 1994. The most recent past dividend D_0 would have been paid the previous day, December 31, 1993. Thus, if we purchased the stock on January 1, the first dividend would be received in 12 months, on December 31, 1994, which is represented by D_1.

Fortunately, equation (5–7) can be reduced to a much more manageable form if dividends grow each year at a constant rate, g. The *constant growth* common stock valuation model is defined as follows:[12]

$$\text{common stock value} = \frac{\text{dividend in year 1}}{\text{required rate of return} - \text{growth rate}} \qquad (5\text{–}8)$$

$$V_c = \frac{D_1}{R_c - g}$$

Consequently, the intrinsic value (present value) of a share of common stock whose dividends grow at a constant annual rate can be calculated using equation (5–8). Although the interpretation of this equation may not be intuitively obvious, we should remember that it solves for the present value of the future dividend stream growing at a rate, g, to infinity, assuming that R_c is greater than g.

EXAMPLE

Consider the valuation of a share of common stock that paid a $2 dividend at the end of the last year and is expected to pay a cash dividend every year from now to

---

[12]Where common stock dividends grow at a constant rate of g every year, we can express the dividend in any year in terms of the dividend paid at the end of the previous year, D_0. For example, the expected dividend one year hence is simply $D_0(1 + g)$. Likewise, the dividend at the end of t years is $D_0(1 + g)^t$. Using this notation, the common stock valuation equation in (5–8) can be rewritten as follows:

$$V_c = \frac{D_0(1 + g)^1}{(1 + R_c)^1} + \frac{D_0(1 + g)^2}{(1 + R_c)^2} + \cdots + \frac{D_0(1 + g)^n}{(1 + R_c)^n} + \cdots + \frac{D_0(1 + g)^\infty}{(1 + R_c)^\infty} \qquad (5\text{–}9)$$

If both sides of equation (5–9) are multiplied by $(1 + R_c)/(1 + g)$ and then equation (5–10) is subtracted from the product, the result is

$$\frac{V_c(1 + R_c)}{1 + g} - V_c = D_0 - \frac{D_0(1 + g)^\infty}{(1 + R_c)^\infty} \qquad (5\text{–}10)$$

If $R_c > g$, which normally should hold, $[D_0(1 + g)^\infty/(1 + R_c)^\infty]$ approaches zero. As a result,

$$\frac{V_c(1 + R_c)}{1 + g} - V_c = D_0$$

$$V_c\left(\frac{1 + R_c}{1 + g}\right) - V_c\left(\frac{1 + g}{1 + g}\right) = D_0$$

$$V_c\left[\frac{(1 + R_c) - (1 + g)}{1 + g}\right] = D_0$$

$$V_c(R_c - g) = D_0(1 + g)$$

$$V_c = \frac{D_1}{R_c - g}$$

infinity. Each year the dividends are expected to grow at a rate of 10 percent. Based on an assessment of the riskiness of the common stock, the investor's required rate of return is 15 percent. Using this information, we would compute the value of the common stock as follows:

1. Since the $2 dividend was paid last year (actually yesterday), we must compute the next dividend to be received, that is, D_1, where

$$D_1 = D_0(1 + g)$$
$$= \$2(1 + .10)$$
$$= \$2.20$$

2. Now, using equation (5–8),

$$V_c = \frac{D_1}{R_c - g}$$
$$= \frac{\$2.20}{.15 - .10}$$
$$= \$44 \qquad \blacksquare$$

We have argued that the value of a common stock is equal to the present value of all future dividends, which is without question a fundamental premise of finance. In practice, however, managers, along with many security analysts, often talk about the relationship between stock value and earnings, rather than dividends. Appendix 5B provides some insights into the rationale and propriety of using earnings to value a firm's stock. We encourage you to be very cautious in using earnings to value a stock. Even though it may be a popular practice, the fact remains that investors look to the cash flows generated by the firm, not the earnings, for value. A firm's value truly is the present value of the cash flows it produces.

We now turn to our last issue in bond and stock valuation, that of the investor's expected returns, a matter of key importance to the financial manager.

Expected Rates of Return

Conceptually, each investor can have a different required rate of return for each individual security. However, the financial manager is interested in the required rate of return for the firm's securities that is implied by the market prices of those securities. The consensus of a firm's investors in their expected rate of return is reflected in the market price of the stock.

For example, the Alpha Co. has a bond with a current market price of $1,000 that is maturing in one year; the bond's face, or par, value is $1,000 and it pays $100 per year in interest. Using the bond valuation model in equation (5–2a):

$$V_b = \frac{\$I_1}{(1 + R_b)^1} + \frac{\$M}{(1 + R_b)^1} \qquad \textbf{(5–2a)}$$

we can solve for the investor's required rate of return implicit in the $1,000 market price of the bond; that is,

$$\$1000 = \frac{\$100}{(1 + R_b)^1} + \frac{\$1000}{(1 + R_b)^1}$$

Solving for R_b, we find that the $1,000 market price *implies* a required rate of return of 10 percent for investors at the margin—investors who are just willing to purchase the bond for $1,000 but will not pay a higher price for it. For these investors, the required rate of return equals the expected rate of return reflected in the bond's current market price. In this instance, both equal 10 percent.[13]

Bondholder's Expected Rate of Return (Yield to Maturity)

The expected rate of return implicit in the current bond price is the discount rate that equates the present value of the future cash flows with the current

_____

[13]This 10 percent required return for the investor at the margin is used in Chapter 8 to measure the cost of new debt capital to the firm; that is, if the firm sells a bond for $1,000 and plans to repay the $1,000 plus $100 interest one year later, then the cost of borrowing equals 10 percent. This 10 percent cost of borrowing is also the required rate of return of the investor at the margin.

THE TOP FIVE[a]
Added Value as a Percentage of Sales 1981–90

Country and Company Name	Industry	Percentage
United States		
1. Autodesk	computer services	33.9
2. UST	tobacco	33.7
3. King World	TV, radio	33.0
4. Community Psychiatric	health care	29.5
5. St. Jude Medical equipment	medical	29.3
Japan		
1. Fuji Photo Film	photographics	15.5
2. Murata Manufacturing	electronics	14.4
3. Kyocera	electronics	13.9
4. Matsushita Electric	electronics	7.8
5. Pioneer Electronics	electronics	7.5
Germany		
1. Harpener	conglomerate	20.9
2. Contigas	utilities	19.7
3. Leifheit	household	14.4
4. Boss (Hugo)	clothing	11.9
5. Nordcement	cement	11.5
France		
1. LVMH Moet/Vuitton	luxury goods	18.6
2. Legris	construction materials	12.7
3. Legrand	electricals	12.6
4. CGI Informatique	computer services	11.8
5. Salomon	sports goods	11.7
Britain		
1. Glaxo	pharmaceut	27.8
2. Alexander Proudfoot	fin services	26.7
3. Tiphook	transport	25.2
4. Cable and Wireless	telecoms	23.1
5. McCarthy and Stone	construction	22.7

[a]Only firms that met certain size criteria were considered.

market price of the bond.[14] The expected rate of return for a bond is also the rate of return the investor will earn if the bond is held to maturity, or the **yield to maturity.** Thus, when referring to bonds, the terms *expected rate of return* and *yield to maturity* are often used interchangeably.

EXAMPLE

To illustrate, consider the Brister Corporation's bonds, which are selling for $1,100. The bonds carry a coupon interest rate of 9 percent and mature in 10 years. (Remember the coupon rate determines the interest payment—coupon rate × par value.)

---

[14]When we speak of computing an expected rate of return, we are not describing the situation very accurately. Expected rates of return are ex ante (before the fact) and are based on "expected and unobservable future cash flows" and therefore can only be "estimated."

In determining the **expected rate** of return implicit in the current market price, we need to find the rate that discounts the anticipated cash flows back to a present value of $1,100, the existing market price for the bond.

Finding the expected rate of return for a bond using the present value tables is trial and error. We have to keep trying new rates until we find the discount rate that results in the present value of the future interest and maturity value of the bond just equaling the current market value of the bond. If the expected rate is somewhere between rates in the present value tables, we then must interpolate between the rates.

For our example, if we try 7 percent, the bond's present value is $1,140.16. Since the present value of $1,140.16 is greater than the market price of $1,100, we should try a higher rate. Increasing the discount rate say to 8 percent gives a present value of $1,066.90. Now the present value is less than the market price; thus, we know that the investor's expected rate of return is between 7 and 8 percent. These computations may be shown as follows:

		7 percent		8 percent	
Years	Cash flow	Present value factors	Present value	Present value factors	Present value
1–10	$ 90 per year	7.024	$ 632.16	6.710	$ 603.90
10	$1000 in year 10	0.508	508.00	0.463	$ 463.00
		Present value at 7 percent:	$1,140.16	Present value at 8 percent:	$1,066.90

Because we now know the rate is between 7 and 8 percent, we may interpolate to find the expected return. The process is as follows:

Rate	Value	Differences in Value	
7%	$1,140.16	} $40.16	} $73.26
R_b	1,100.00		
8%	1,066.90		

Solving for R_b by interpolation, we have:

$$R_b = 7\% + \left(\frac{\$40.16}{\$73.26}\right)(8\% - 7\%) = 7.55\%$$

Thus, the expected rate of return on the Brister Corporation's bonds for an investor who purchases the bonds for $1,100 is approximately 7.55 percent.

Rather than using the present value tables to compute the expected return for the Brister Corporation's bonds, which is cumbersome, it is much easier to use a calculator. The solution (using an HP-17B II) is shown in the adjacent margin. ■

The Preferred Stockholder's Expected Rate of Return

In computing the preferred stockholder's expected rate we use the valuation equation for preferred stock. Earlier, equation (5–5) specified the value of a preferred stock, V_p, as

$$V_p = \frac{\text{annual dividend}}{\text{required rate of return}} = \frac{D}{R_p} \qquad (5\text{–}5)$$

Solving (5–5) for R_p,

$$R_p = \frac{\text{annual dividend}}{\text{value}} = \frac{D}{V_p} \qquad \textbf{(5–11)}$$

which simply indicates that the expected rate of return of a preferred security equals the dividend yield (dividend/price). For example, if the present market price of preferred stock is \$50 and it pays a \$3.64 annual dividend, the expected rate of return implicit in the present market price is

$$R_p = \frac{D}{V_p} = \frac{\$3.64}{\$50} = 7.28\%$$

Therefore, investors at the margin (who pay \$50 per share for a preferred security that is paying \$3.64 in annual dividends) are expecting a 7.28 percent rate of return.

The Common Stockholder's Expected Rate of Return

The valuation equation for common stock was defined earlier as

$$\text{value} = \frac{\text{dividend in year 1}}{(1 + \text{required rate of return})^1}$$
$$+ \frac{\text{dividend in year 2}}{(1 + \text{required rate of return})^2}$$
$$+ \cdots + \frac{\text{dividend in year infinity}}{(1 + \text{required rate of return})^\infty} \qquad \textbf{(5–7)}$$

$$V_c = \frac{D_1}{(1 + R_c)^1} + \frac{D_2}{(1 + R_c)^2} + \cdots + \frac{D_\infty}{(1 + R_c)^\infty}$$

$$V_c = \sum_{t=1}^{\infty} \frac{D_t}{(1 + R_c)^t}$$

Owing to the difficulty of discounting to infinity, we made the key assumption that the dividends, D_t, increase at a constant annual compound growth rate of g. If this assumption is valid, equation (5–7) was shown to be equivalent to

$$\text{value} = \frac{\text{dividend in year 1}}{\text{required rate of return} - \text{growth rate}} \qquad \textbf{(5–8)}$$

$$V_c = \frac{D_1}{R_c - g}$$

Thus, V_c represents the maximum value that an investor having a required rate of return of R_c would pay for a security having an anticipated dividend in year 1 of D_1 that is expected to grow in future years at rate g.[15] Solving equation (5–8)

---

[15]At times the expected dividend at year end (D_1) is not given. Instead we might only know the most recent dividend (paid yesterday), that is, D_0. If so, equation (5–8) must be restated as follows:

$$V_0 = \frac{D_1}{(R_c - g)} = \frac{D_0(1 + g)}{(R_c - g)}$$

for R_c, we can compute the expected rate of return for common stock implicit in its current market price as follows:

$$R_c = \left(\frac{D_1}{V_c}\right) + g$$

↑   ↑
dividend   annual
yield   growth
rate

(5–12)

From this equation, the common stockholder's expected rate of return is equal to the dividend yield plus a growth factor. Although the growth rate, g, applies to the growth in the company's dividends, the firm's earnings per share and the stock prices may also be expected to increase at the same rate. For this reason, g represents the annual percentage growth in the stock price. In other words, the investors' expected rate of return is satisfied by receiving dividends, expressed as a percentage of the price of the stock (dividend yield), and capital gains, as reflected by the percentage growth rate. Be careful, however, not to assume from our discussion that the stock price moves exactly with the firm's earnings. As shown in Appendix 5B, earnings growth may or may not cause the share value to increase.

EXAMPLE

As an example of computing the expected rate of return for a common stock, where dividends are anticipated to grow at a constant rate to infinity, assume that a firm's common stock has a current market price of $44. If the expected dividend at the conclusion of this year is $2.20 and dividends and earnings are growing at a 10 percent annual rate (last year's dividend was $2), the expected rate of return implicit in the $44 stock price is as follows:

$$R_c = \frac{\$2.20}{\$44} + 10\% = 15\%$$

In summary, the expected rate of return implied by a given market price equals the required rate of return for investors at the margin. For these investors, the expected rate of return is just equal to their required rate of return, and therefore they are willing to pay the current market price for the security. These investors' required rate of return is of particular significance to the financial manager, because it represents the cost of new financing to the firm.

SUMMARY

Valuation is an important process in financial management. An understanding of the concepts and computational procedures in valuing a security underlies sound decision making. Valuation supports the financial officer's objective of maximizing the *value* of the firm's common stock.

For our purposes, *value is the present value of future cash flows expected to be received from an investment discounted at the investor's required rate of return*. In this context, the value of a security is a function of (1) the *expected cash inflows* from the asset, (2) the *riskiness* of the investment, and (3) the investor's *required rate of return*. In a world of uncertainty, returns are measured in terms of the *expected cash flows* anticipated from the security; a derivation of expected value takes into account possible future events and their probability.

Although the valuation of any security entails the same basic principles, the procedures used in each situation vary. For example, valuing a finite stream of cash flows involves computing the present value of the individual cash receipts for each period. An example of this type of valuation problem would be a bond that is scheduled to mature on a designated date. A second category of cash flow patterns involves an *infinite* cash flow stream, such as those from preferred stock and common stock. Although the underlying premise of valuation does not change—that is, value equals the present value of future cash flows—valuing such an asset requires a modification in the procedure. For securities with cash flows that are constant in each year, such as preferred stock, the present value equals the dollar amount of the annual dividend divided by the investor's required rate of return. Furthermore, for common stock where the future dividends are expected to increase at a constant growth rate, value may be given by the following equation:

$$\text{value} = \frac{\text{dividend in year one}}{\text{required rate of return} - \text{growth rate}} \qquad (5\text{--}8)$$

The *expected rate of return* on a security is the required rate of return of investors who are willing to pay the present market price for the security, but no higher price. This rate of return is important to the financial manager because it equals the required rate of return of the firm's investors. This rate is reached at the point where the present value of future cash flows to be received by the investor is just equal to the present market price of the security.

STUDY QUESTIONS

5–1. What are the basic differences between book value, liquidation value, market value, and intrinsic value?

5–2. Explain the three factors that determine the value of an asset.

5–3. Explain the relationship between an investor's required rate of return and the value of a security.

5–4. What is a general definition of the intrinsic value of a security?

5–5. a. How does a bond's par value differ from its market value?
b. Explain the difference between the coupon interest rate and a bondholder's required rate.

5–6. The common stockholders receive two types of return from their investment. What are they?

5–7. State how the investor's required rate of return is computed.

5–8. Define the investor's *expected* rate of return.

SELF-TEST PROBLEMS

ST–1. (*Bond Valuation*) Trico bonds have a coupon rate of 8 percent, a par value of $1,000, and will mature in 20 years. If you require a return of 7 percent, what price would you be willing to pay for the bond? What happens if you pay *more* for the bond? What happens if you pay *less* for the bond?

ST–2. (*Bond Valuation*) Sunn Co.'s bonds, maturing in seven years, pay 8 percent interest on a $1,000 face value. However, interest is paid semiannually. If your required rate of return is 10 percent, what is the value of the bond? How would your answer change if the interest were paid annually?

ST–3. (*Bond-holder's Expected Rate of Return*) Sharp Co. bonds are selling in the market for $1,045. These 15-year bonds pay 7 percent interest annually on a $1,000 par value. If they are purchased at the market price, what is the expected rate of return?

ST–4. (*Preferred Stock Valuation*) The preferred stock of Armlo pays a $2.75 dividend. What is the value of the stock if your required return is 9 percent?

ST–5. (*Common Stock Valuation*) Crosby Corporation's common stock paid $1.32 in dividends last year and is expected to grow indefinitely at an annual 7 percent rate. What is the value of the stock if you require an 11 percent return?

STUDY PROBLEMS (SET A)

5–1A. (*Bond Valuation*) Calculate the value of a bond that expects to mature in 12 years and has a $1,000 face value. The coupon interest rate is 8 percent and the investors' required rate of return is 12 percent.

5–2A. (*Preferred Stock Valuation*) What is the value of a preferred stock where the dividend rate is 14 percent on a $100 par value? The appropriate discount rate for a stock of this risk level is 12 percent.

5–3A. (*Bond Valuation*) Enterprise, Inc., bonds have a 9 percent coupon rate. The interest is paid semiannually and the bonds mature in eight years. Their par value is $1,000. If your required rate of return is 8 percent, what is the value of the bond? What is its value if the interest is paid annually?

5–4A. (*Bondholder Expected Return*) You are willing to pay $900 for a 10-year bond ($1,000 par value) that pays 8 percent interest (4 percent semiannually). What is your expected rate of return?

5–5A. (*Preferred Stockholder Expected Return*) Solitron's preferred stock is selling for $42.16 and pays $1.95 in dividends. What is your expected rate of return if you purchase the security at the market price?

5–6A. (*Preferred Stockholder Expected Return*) You own 200 shares of Somner Resources' preferred stock, which currently sells for $40 per share and pays annual dividends of $3.40 per share.
   a. What is your expected return?
   b. If you require an 8 percent return, given the current price should you sell or buy more stock?

5–7A. (*Common Stock Valuation*) You intend to purchase Marigo common stock at $50 per share, hold it one year, and sell after a dividend of $6 is paid. How much will the stock price have to appreciate if your required rate of return is 15 percent?

5–8A. (*Common Stockholder Expected Return*) Made-It's common stock currently sells for $22.50 per share. The company's executives anticipate a constant growth rate of 10 percent and an end-of-year dividend of $2.
   a. What is your expected rate of return?
   b. If you require a 17 percent return, should you purchase the stock?

5–9A. (*Common Stock Valuation*) Header Motor, Inc., paid a $3.50 dividend last year. At a growth rate of 5 percent, what is the value of the common stock if the investors require a 20 percent rate of return?

5–10A. (*Measuring Growth*) Given that a firm's return on equity is 18 percent and management plans to retain 40 percent of earnings for investment purposes, what will be the firm's growth rate?

5–11A. (*Capital Asset Pricing Model and Common Stock Valuation*) You are considering the purchase of 100 shares of Slick-Tex, Inc.'s common stock. The beta on the security is 1.65, and the current market premium is 5.6 percent.
   a. If the riskless rate of interest is currently 12 percent, what will your required rate of return be? (The solution requires you to use what you learned in Chapter 4.)
   b. Given the rate of return computed in part (a), an expected dividend of $8.50 and a 5 percent growth rate, what value do you place on the stock?

5–12A. (*Common Stockholder Expected Return*) The common stock of Zaldi Co. is selling for $32.84. The stock recently paid dividends of $2.94 per share and has a projected growth rate of 9.5 percent. If you purchase the stock at the market price, what is your expected rate of return?

5–13A. (*Common Stock Valuation*) Honeywag common stock is expected to pay $1.85 in dividends next year, and the market price is projected to be $42.50 by year end. If the investor's required rate of return is 11 percent, what is the current value of the stock?

5–14A. (*Common Stock Valuation*) The market price for Hobart common stock is $43. The price at the end of one year is expected to be $48, and dividends for next year should be $2.84. What is the expected rate of return?

5–15A. (*Bond Valuation*) Exxon 20-year bonds pay 9 percent interest annually on a $1,000 par value. If you buy the bonds at $945, what is your expected rate of return?

5–16A. (*Bondholder Expected Return*) Zenith Co.'s bonds mature in 12 years and pay 7 percent interest annually. If you purchase the bonds for $1,150, what is your expected rate of return?

5–17A. (*Bond Valuation*) National Steel 15-year, $1,000 par value bonds pay 8 percent interest annually. The market price of the bonds is $1,085, and your required rate of return is 10 percent.
  a. Compute the bond's expected rate of return.
  b. Determine the value of the bond to you, given your required rate of return.
  c. Should you purchase the bond?

5–18A. (*Preferred Stock Valuation*) Pioneer's preferred stock is selling for $33 in the market and pays a $3.60 annual dividend.
  a. What is the expected rate of return on the stock?
  b. If an investor's required rate of return is 10 percent, what is the value of the stock for that investor?
  c. Should the investor acquire the stock?

5–19A. (*Common Stock Valuation*) The common stock of NCP paid $1.32 in dividends last year. Dividends are expected to grow at an 8 percent annual rate for an indefinite number of years.
  a. If NCP's current market price is $23.50, what is the stock's expected rate of return?
  b. If your required rate of return is 10.5 percent, what is the value of the stock for you?
  c. Should you make the investment?

5–20A. (*A Comprehensive Problem in Valuing Securities*) You are considering three investments. The first is a bond that is selling in the market at $1,100. The bond has a $1,000 par value, pays interest at 13 percent, and is scheduled to mature in 15 years. For bonds of this risk class you believe that a 14 percent rate of return should be required. The second investment that you are analyzing is a preferred stock ($100 par value) that sells for $90 and pays an annual dividend of $13. Your required rate of return for this stock is 15 percent. The last investment is a common stock ($25 par value) that recently paid a $2 dividend. The firm's earnings per share have increased from $3 to $6 in 10 years, which also reflects the expected growth in dividends per share for the indefinite future. The stock is selling for $20, and you think a reasonable required rate of return for the stock is 20 percent.
  a. Calculate the value of each security based on your required rate of return.
  b. Which investment(s) should you accept? Why?
  c. 1. If your required rates of return changed to 12 percent for the bond, 14 percent for the preferred stock, and 18 percent for the common stock, how would your answers change to parts (a) and (b)?
  2. Assuming again that your required rate of return for the common stock is 20 percent, but the anticipated growth rate changes to 12 percent, would your answers to parts (a) and (b) be different?

STUDY PROBLEMS (SET B)

5–1B. (*Bond Valuation*) Calculate the value of a bond that expects to mature in 10 years and has a $1,000 face value. The coupon interest rate is 9 percent and the investors' required rate of return is 15 percent.

5–2B. (*Preferred Stock Valuation*) What is the value of a preferred stock where the dividend rate is 16 percent on a $100 par value? The appropriate discount rate for a stock of this risk level is 12 percent.

5–3B. (*Bond Valuation*) Pybus, Inc., bonds have a 10 percent coupon rate. The interest is paid semiannually and the bonds mature in 11 years. Their par value is $1,000. If your required rate of return is 9 percent, what is the value of the bond? What is its value if the interest is paid annually?

5–4B. (*Bondholder Expected Return*) You are willing to pay $950 for an 8-year bond ($1,000 par value) that pays 9 percent interest (4.5 percent semiannually). What is your expected rate of return?

5–5B. (*Preferred Stockholder Expected Return*) Shewmaker's preferred stock is selling for $55.16 and pays $2.35 in dividends. What is your expected rate of return if you purchase the security at the market price?

5–6B. (*Preferred Stockholder Expected Return*) You own 250 shares of McCormick Resources' preferred stock, which currently sells for $38.50 per share and pays annual dividends of $3.25 per share.
  a. What is your expected return?
  b. If you require an 8 percent return, given the current price, should you sell or buy more stock?

5–7B. (*Common Stock Valuation*) You intend to purchase Bama, Inc., common stock at $52.75 per share, hold it one year, and sell after a dividend of $6.50 is paid. How much will the stock price have to appreciate if your required rate of return is 16 percent?

5–8B. (*Common Stockholder Expected Return*) Blackburn & Smith's common stock currently sells for $23 per share. The company's executives anticipate a constant growth rate of 10.5 percent and an end-of-year dividend of $2.50.
  a. What is your expected rate of return?
  b. If you require a 17 percent return, should you purchase the stock?

5–9B. (*Common Stock Valuation*) Gilliland Motor, Inc., paid a $3.75 dividend last year. At a growth rate of 6 percent, what is the value of the common stock if the investors require a 20 percent rate of return?

5–10B. (*Measuring Growth*) Given that a firm's return on equity is 24 percent and management plans to retain 60 percent of earnings for investment purposes, what will be the firm's growth rate?

5–11B. (*Capital Asset Pricing Model and Common Stock Valuation*) You are considering the purchase of 125 shares of Happy-Hounts Inc.'s common stock. The beta on the security is 1.5, and the current market premium is 5.5 percent.
  a. If the riskless rate of interest is currently 13 percent, what will your required rate of return be? (The solution requires that you use what you learned in Chapter 4.)
  b. Given the rate of return computed in part (a), an expected dividend of $7.50, and a 5 percent growth rate, what value do you place on the stock?

5–12B. (*Common Stockholder Expected Return*) The common stock of Bouncy-Bob Moore Co. is selling for $33.84. The stock recently paid dividends of $3 per share and has a projected growth rate of 8.5 percent. If you purchase the stock at the market price, what is your expected rate of return?

5–13B. (*Common Stock Valuation*) Honeybee common stock is expected to pay $1.85 in dividends next year, and the market price is projected to be $40 by year end. If the investors' required rate of return is 12 percent, what is the current value of the stock?

5–14B. (*Common Stock Valuation*) The market price for M. Simpson & Co.'s common stock is $44. The price at the end of one year is expected to be $47, and dividends for next year should be $2. What is the expected rate of return?

5–15B. (*Bond Valuation*) Doisneau 20-year bonds pay 10 percent interest annually on a $1,000 par value. If you buy the bonds at $975, what is your expected rate of return?

5–16B. (*Bondholder Expected Return*) Hoyden Co.'s bonds mature in 15 years and pay 8 percent interest annually. If you purchase the bonds for $1,175, what is your expected rate of return?

5–17B. (*Bond Valuation*) Fingen 14-year, $1,000 par value bonds pay 9 percent interest annually. The market price of the bonds is $1,100 and your required rate of return is 10 percent.
  a. Compute the bond's expected rate of return.
  b. Determine the value of the bond to you, given your required rate of return.
  c. Should you purchase the bond?

5–18B. (*Preferred Stock Valuation*) Gree's preferred stock is selling for $35 in the market and pays a $4 annual dividend.
  a. What is the expected rate of return on the stock?

b. If an investor's required rate of return is 10 percent, what is the value of the stock for that investor?

c. Should the investor acquire the stock?

5-19B. (*Common Stock Valuation*) The common stock of KPD paid $1 in dividends last year. Dividends are expected to grow at an 8 percent annual rate for an indefinite number of years.

a. If KPD's current market price is $25, what is the stock's expected rate of return?

b. If your required rate of return is 11 percent, what is the value of the stock for you?

c. Should you make the investment?

5-20B. (*Comprehensive Problem in Valuing Securities*) You are considering three investments. The first is a bond that is selling in the market at $1,200. The bond has a $1,000 par value, pays interest at 14 percent, and is scheduled to mature in 12 years. For bonds of this risk class you believe that a 12 percent rate of return should be required. The second investment that you are analyzing is a preferred stock ($100 par value) that sells for $80 and pays an annual dividend of $12. Your required rate of return for this stock is 14 percent. The last investment is a common stock ($35 par value) that recently paid a $3 dividend. The firm's earnings per share have increased from $4 to $8 in 10 years, which also reflects the expected growth in dividends per share for the indefinite future. The stock is selling for $25, and you think a reasonable required rate of return for the stock is 20 percent.

a. Calculate the value of each security based on your required rate of return.

b. Which investment(s) should you accept? Why?

c. 1. If your required rates of return changed to 14 percent for the bond, 16 percent for the preferred stock, and 18 percent for the common stock, how would your answers change to parts (a) and (b)?

2. Assuming again that your required rate of return for the common stock is 20 percent, but the anticipated growth rate changes to 12 percent, would your answers to parts (a) and (b) be different?

Suggested Application for *DISCLOSURE*®

Using *Disclosure*, obtain the following information for the most recent year available for Johnson & Johnson:

a. Outstanding shares of common stock (Listed at the bottom of the annual income statement.)

b. The dividends and other distributions (See the Cash Flow Provided by Financing Activity section of the Cash Flow Statement.)

c. The firm's total common equity value.

d. The dividend per share.

e. The stock's dividend yield (dividend per share ÷ market price of stock).

f. The expected growth rate in earnings per share over the next five years (Zack's earnings estimates).

g. Assuming the growth rate in earnings per share is a reasonable estimate of the firm's growth rate in share price for the indefinite future, which it may not be, estimate your expected rate of return if you had purchased the stock at the time of the *Disclosure* report.

SELF-TEST SOLUTIONS

SS-1.

$$\text{price } (P_0) = \sum_{t=1}^{20} \frac{\$80}{(1.07)^t} + \frac{\$1000}{(1.07)^{20}}$$

Thus,

Present value of interest: $80(10.594) = \$ 847.52$

Present value of par value: $1000(0.258) = \underline{258.00}$

price $(P_0) = \underline{\underline{\$1105.52}}$

If you pay more for the bond, your required rate of return will not be satisfied. In other words, by paying an amount for the bond that exceeds $1,105.52, the expected rate of return for the bond is less than the required rate of return. If you have the opportunity to pay less for the bond, the expected rate of return exceeds the 7 percent required rate of return.

SS–2. If interest is paid semiannually:

$$\text{price } (P_0) = \sum_{t=1}^{14} \frac{\$40}{(1 + 0.05)^t} + \frac{\$1000}{(1 + 0.05)^{14}}$$

Thus,

$$
\begin{aligned}
\$\ \ 40(9.899) &= \$395.96 \\
\$1000(0.505) &= \ \underline{505.00} \\
\text{price } (P_0) &= \underline{\underline{\$900.96}}
\end{aligned}
$$

If interest is paid annually:

$$\text{price } (P_0) = \sum_{t=1}^{7} \frac{\$80}{(1.10)^t} + \frac{\$1000}{(1.10)^7}$$

$$P_0 = \$80\,(4.868) + \$1000\,(0.513)$$

$$P_0 = \$902.44$$

SS–3.

$$\$1045 = \sum_{t=1}^{15} \frac{\$70}{(1 + R_b)^t} + \frac{\$1000}{(1 + R_b)^{15}}$$

At 6%: $\$70(9.712) + \$1000(0.417) = \$1096.84$

At 7%: $\$70(9.108) + \$1000(0.362) = \$1000.00$

Interpolation:

$$\text{Expected rate of return: } R_b = 6\% + \frac{\$51.84}{\$96.84}\,(1\%) = 6.54\%$$

SS–4.

$$\text{price } (P_0) = \frac{\text{dividend}}{\text{required rate of return}} = \frac{\$2.75}{0.09} = \$30.56$$

SS–5.

$$\text{price } (P_0) = \left(\frac{\text{last year dividend } (1 + \text{growth rate})}{\text{required rate of return} - \text{growth rate}} \right)$$

$$= \frac{\$1.32(1.07)}{0.11 - 0.07}$$

$$= \$35.31$$

FINANCIAL CALCULATOR SOLUTION

Data input	Function key
15	N
70	+/− PMT
1000	+/− FV
1045	PV

Function key	Answer
I%YR	6.52

APPENDIX 5A

More on Bond Valuation: Understanding Key Relationships

In the chapter we learned to find the value of a bond (V_b), given (1) the amount of interest payments (I_t), (2) the maturity value (M), (3) the length of time to maturity (n years), and (4) the investor's required rate of return, R_b. We also learned how to compute the expected rate of return, which also happens to be the current interest rate on the bond, given (1) the current market value (V_b), (2) the amount of interest payments (I_t), (3) the maturity value (M), and (4) the length of time to maturity (n years). These computations represent the basics of bond valuation; however, a more complete understanding of bond valuation requires that we examine five additional key relationships.

First Relationship

The value of a bond is inversely related to changes in the investor's present required rate of return (the current interest rate). In other words, as interest rates increase (decrease), the value of the bond decreases (increases).

To illustrate, assume that an investor's required rate of return for a given bond is 12 percent. The bond has a par value of $1,000 and annual interest payments of $120, indicating a 12 percent coupon interest rate ($120 \div $1,000 = 12\%$). Assuming a five-year maturity date, the bond would be worth $1,000, computed as follows:

$$V_b = \frac{I_1}{(1 + R_b)^1} + \cdots + \frac{I_n}{(1 + R_b)^n} + \frac{M}{(1 + R)^n}$$

$$= \sum_{t=1}^{n} \frac{I_t}{(1 + R_b)^t} + \frac{M}{(1 + R_b)^n} \qquad \text{(5–2a)}$$

$$= \sum_{t=1}^{5} \frac{\$120}{(1 + .12)^t} + \frac{\$1000}{(1 + .12)^5}$$

$$V_b = \$120 \, (PVIFA_{12\%,5}) + \$1000 \, (PVIF_{12\%,5}) \qquad \text{(5–2b)}$$

$$V_b = \$120(3.605) + \$1000(.567)$$

$$= \$432.60 + \$567.00$$

$$= \$999.60 \cong \$1000.00$$

If, however, the investor's required rate of return (going interest rate) increases from 12 to 15 percent, the value of the bond would decrease to $899.24:

$$V_b = \$120 \, (PVIFA_{15\%,5}) + \$1000 \, (PVIF_{15\%,5})$$

$$V_b = \$120(3.352) + \$1000(.497) \qquad \text{(5–2b)}$$

$$= \$402.24 + \$497.00$$

$$= \$899.24$$

On the other hand, if the investor's required rate of return decreases to 9 percent, the bond would increase in value to $1,116.80:

$$V_b = \$120 \, (PVIFA_{9\%,5}) + \$1000 \, (PVIF_{9\%,5})$$

$$V_b = \$120(3.890) + \$1000(.650) \qquad \text{(5–2b)}$$

$$= \$466.80 + \$650.00$$

$$= \$1116.80$$

This inverse relationship between the investor's required rate of return and the value of a bond is presented in Figure 5A–1. Clearly, as an investor demands a higher rate of return, the value of the bond decreases. The higher rate of return the investor desires can be achieved only by paying less for the bond. Conversely, a lower required rate of return yields a higher market value for the bond.

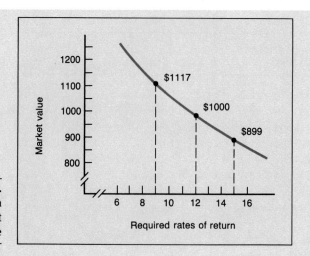

FIGURE 5A–1.
Value and Required Rates for a
5-Year Bond at 12 Percent
Coupon Rate

Changes in bond prices represent an element of uncertainty for the bond investor. If the current interest rate (required rate of return) changes, the price of the bond also fluctuates. An increase in interest rates causes the bondholder to incur a loss in market value. Since future interest rates and the resulting bond value cannot be predicted with certainty, a bond investor is exposed to the risk of changing values as interest rates vary. This risk has come to be known as **interest-rate risk.**

Second Relationship

The market value of a bond will be less than the par value if the investor's required rate is above the coupon interest rate; but it will be valued above par value if the investor's required rate of return is below the coupon interest rate.
Using the previous example, we observed that:

1. The bond has a *market* value of $1,000, equal to the par or maturity value, when the investor's required rate of return equals the 12 percent coupon interest rate. In other words, if

    required rate = coupon rate, then *market value = par value*
      12%   =   12% , then $1000   = $1000

2. When the required rate is 15 percent, which exceeds the 12 percent coupon rate, the market value falls below par value to $899.24; that is, if

    required rate > coupon rate, then *market value < par value*
      15%   >   12% , then · $899.24 < $1000

    In this case the bond sells at a discount below par value; thus it is called a **discount bond.**

3. When the required rate is 9 percent, or less than the 12 percent coupon rate, the market value, $1,116.80, exceeds the bond's par value. In this instance, if

    required rate < coupon rate, then *market value > par value*
      9%   <   12% , then $1116.80 > $1000

    The bond is now selling at a premium above par value; thus, it is a **premium bond.**

Third Relationship

As the maturity date approaches, the market value of a bond approaches its par value.

Continuing to draw from our example, the bond has five years remaining until the maturity date. At that time, the bond sells at a discount below par value ($899.24), when the required rate is 15 percent; and it sells at a premium above par value ($1,116.80), when the required rate is only 9 percent.

In addition to knowing value today, an investor would also be interested in knowing how these values would change over time, assuming no change in the current interest rates. For example, how will these values change when only two years remain until maturity rather than five years? Table 5A–1 shows the values with five years remaining to maturity, the values as recomputed with only two years left until the bonds mature, along with the changes in values between the five-year bonds and the two-year bonds. The following conclusions can be drawn from these results:

1. The premium bond sells for less as maturity approaches. The price decreases from $1,116.80 to $1,053.08 over the three years.

2. The discount bond sells for more as maturity approaches. The price increases from $899.24 to $951.12 over the three years.

Required Rate	Market Value If Maturity Is:		Change in Value
	5 Years	2 Years	
9%	$1116.80	$1053.08	−$63.72
12	1000.00	1000.00	.00
15	899.24	951.12	51.88

TABLE 5A–1.
Values Relative to Maturity Dates

The change in prices over the entire life of the bond is shown in Figure 5A–2. The graph clearly demonstrates that the value of a bond, either a

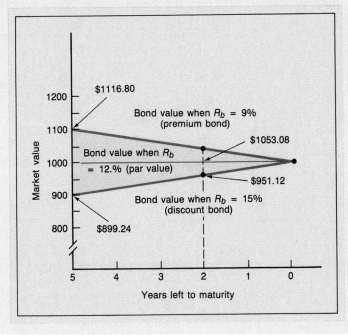

FIGURE 5A–2.
Value of a 12-Percent Coupon Bond During the Life of the Bond

premium or a discount bond, approaches par value as the maturity date becomes closer in time.

Fourth Relationship

Long-term bonds have greater interest rate risk than do short-term bonds.

As already noted, a change in current interest rates (required rate of return) causes a change in the market value of a bond. However, the impact on value is greater for long-term bonds than it is for short-term bonds.

In Figure 5A–1 we observed the effect of interest rate changes on a five-year bond paying a 12 percent coupon interest rate. What if the bond did not mature until 10 years from today instead of 5 years? Would the changes in market value be the same? Absolutely not. The changes in value would be more significant for the 10-year bond. For example, if we vary the current interest rates (the bondholder's required rate of return) from 9 percent to 12 percent and then to 15 percent, as we did earlier with the 5-year bond, the values for both the 5-year and the 10-year bonds would be as follows:

	Market Value for a 12% Coupon Rate Bond Maturing in	
Required Rate	5 Years	10 Years
9%	$1116.80	$1192.16
12	1000.00	1000.00
15	899.24	849.28

Using these values and the required rates, we can graph the changes in values for the two bonds relative to different interest rates. These comparisons are provided in Figure 5A–3. The figure clearly illustrates that the price of a long-term bond (say 10 years) is more responsive or sensitive to interest rate changes than the price of a short-term bond (say 5 years).

The reason long-term bond prices fluctuate more than short-term bond prices in response to interest rate changes is simple. Assume an investor bought a 10-year bond yielding a 12 percent interest rate. If the

FIGURE 5A–3.
Market Values of a 5-Year and a 10-Year Bond at Different Required Rates

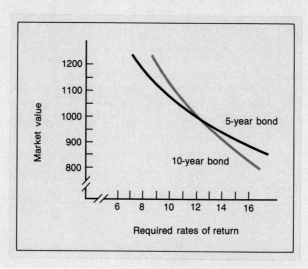

current interest rate for bonds of similar risk increased to 15 percent, the investor would be locked into the lower rate for 10 years. If, on the other hand, a shorter-term bond had been purchased, say one maturing in 2 years, the investor would have to accept the lower return for only 2 years and not the full 10 years. At the end of year 2, the investor would receive the maturity value of $1,000 and could buy a bond offering the higher 15 percent rate for the remaining 8 years. Thus, interest rate risk is determined, at least in part, by the length of time an investor is required to commit to an investment. However, the holder of a long-term bond may take some comfort from the fact that long-term interest rates are usually not as volatile as short-term rates. If the short-term rate changed one percentage point, for example, it would not be unusual for the long-term rate to change only .3 percentage points.

Fifth Relationship

The sensitivity of a bond's value to changing interest rates depends not only on the length of time to maturity but also on the pattern of cash flows provided by the bond.

It is not at all unusual for two bonds with the same maturity to react differently to a change in interest rates. Consider two bonds, A and B, both with 10-year maturities and the same 10 percent interest rate. Although the bonds are similar in terms of maturity date and the contractual interest rate, the structure of the interest payments is different for each bond. Bond A pays $100 interest annually, with the $1,000 principal being repaid at the end of the tenth year. Bond B is called a zero-coupon bond; it pays no interest until the bond matures. At that time the bondholder receives $1,593.70 in interest plus $1,000 in principal. The value of both bonds, assuming a market interest rate (required rate of return) of 10 percent, is $1,000. However, if interest rates fell to 6 percent, bond A's market value would be $1,294, compared with $1,447 for bond B. Why the difference? Both bonds have the same maturity, and each promises the same 10 percent rate of return. The answer lies in the differences in their cash flow patterns. Bond B's cash flows are received in the more distant future on average than are the cash flows for bond A. Since a change in interest rates always has a greater impact on the present value of later cash flows than on earlier cash flows (due to the effects of compounding), bonds with cash flows coming later, on average, will be more sensitive to interest rate changes than will bonds with earlier cash flows. This phenomenon was recognized in 1938 by Macaulay, who devised the concept of duration.

The **duration** of a bond is simply a measure of the responsiveness of its price to a change in interest rates. The greater the relative percentage change in a bond price in response to a given precentage change in the interest rate, the longer the duration. In computing duration, we consider not only the maturity or term over which cash flows are received but also the time pattern of interim cash flows. Specifically, duration is a weighted average time to maturity in which the weight attached to each year is the present value of the cash flow for that year. A measurement of duration may be represented as follows:

$$\text{duration} = \frac{\sum_{t=1}^{n} \dfrac{tC_t}{(1 + R_b)^t}}{P_0} \tag{5A-1}$$

where t = the year the cash flow is to be received

n = the number of years to maturity

C_t = the cash flow to be received in year t

R_b = the bondholder's required rate of return

P_0 = the bond's present value

For our two bonds, A and B, duration would be calculated as follows:

$$\text{duration bond A} = \frac{\left[\left((1)\frac{\$100}{(1.1)^1}+(2)\frac{\$100}{(1.1)^2}+(3)\frac{\$100}{(1.1)^3}\right.\right.}{\$1000}$$

$$+\cdots+\left.\left.(9)\frac{\$100}{(1.1)^9}+(10)\frac{\$1100}{(1.1)^{10}}\right)\right]$$

$$= 6.759$$

$$\text{duration bond B} = \frac{\left[\left((1)\frac{0}{(1.1)^1}+(2)\frac{0}{(1.1)^2}+(3)\frac{0}{(1.1)^3}\right.\right.}{\$1000}$$

$$+\cdots+\left.\left.(9)\frac{0}{(1.1)^9}+(10)\frac{\$2593.70}{(1.1)^{10}}\right)\right]$$

$$= 10$$

Thus, although both bonds have the same maturity, 10 years, the zero-coupon bond (bond B) is more sensitive to interest rate changes, as suggested by its higher duration, which in this instance equals its maturity.[16] The lesson learned: In assessing a bond's sensitivity to changing interest rates, the bond's duration is the appropriate measure, not the term to maturity.

SUMMARY

Certain key relationships exist in bond valuation. A brief summary of these factors includes the following:

1. A decrease in interest rates (required rates of return) will cause the value of a bond to increase; an interest rate increase will cause a

---

[16]Maturity and duration are the same only for zero-coupon bonds or securities that pay only one cash flow, and it occurs at maturity.

decrease in value. The change in value caused by changing interest rates is called *interest rate risk*.

2. If the bondholder's required rate of return (current interest rate) equals the coupon interest rate, the bond will sell at par, or maturity value.

3. If the current interest rate exceeds the bond's coupon rate, the bond will sell below par value, or at a *discount*.

4. If the current interest rate is less than the bond's coupon rate, the bond will sell above par value, or at a *premium*.

5. Regardless of whether a bond is selling below or above par value the value of the bond will gradually approach par value as the bond matures.

6. A bondholder owning a long-term bond is exposed to greater interest rate risk than one owning a short-term bond.

7. In understanding a bond's sensitivity to interest rate changes, we must consider not only the time to maturity, but also the time pattern of interim cash flows.

STUDY PROBLEMS

5A–1. (*Bond Valuation*) You own a bond that pays $100 in annual interest, with a $1,000 par value. It matures in 15 years. Your required rate of return is 12 percent.
  a. Calculate the value of the bond.
  b. How does the value change if your required rate of return (i) increases to 15 percent or (ii) decreases to 8 percent?
  c. Explain the implications of your answers in part (b) as they relate to interest rate risk, premium bonds, and discount bonds.
  d. Assume that the bond matures in 5 years instead of 15 years. Recompute your answers in part (b).
  e. Explain the implications of your answers in part (d) as they relate to interest rate risk, premium bonds, and discount bonds.

5A–2. (*Duration*) Calculate the value and the duration for the following bonds:

Bond	Years to Maturity	Annual Interest	Maturity Value
P	5	$100	$1000
Q	5	70	1000
R	10	120	1000
S	10	80	1000
T	15	65	1000

Your required rate of return is 8 percent.

The Relationship Between Value and Earnings

In understanding the relationship between a firm's earnings and the market price of its stock, it is helpful to look first at the relationship for a nongrowth firm and then expand our view to include the growth firm.

The Relationship Between Earnings and Value for the Nongrowth Company

When we speak of a nongrowth firm, we mean one that retains no profits for the purpose of reinvestment. The only investments made are for the purpose of maintaining status quo—that is, investing the amount of the depreciation taken on fixed assets so that the firm does not lose its current earnings capacity. The result is both constant earnings and a constant dividends stream to the common stockholder, since the firm is paying all earnings out in the form of dividends (i.e., dividend in year t equals earnings in year t). This type of common stock is essentially no different from a preferred stock. Recalling from our earlier discussion about valuing a preferred stock, we may value the nongrowth common stock similarly, expressing our valuation in one of two ways:

$$\text{value of a} \atop \text{nongrowth firm} = \frac{\text{earnings per share}_1}{\text{required rate of return}} \qquad \textbf{(5B–1)}$$

$$= \frac{\text{dividend per share}_1}{\text{required rate of return}} \qquad \textbf{(5B–2)}$$

or

$$V_{cng} = \frac{EPS_1}{R_c} = \frac{D_1}{R_c}$$

EXAMPLE

The Reeves Corporation expects its earnings per share this year to be $12, which is to be paid out in total to the investors in the form of dividends. If the investors have a required rate of return of 14 percent, the value of the stock would be $85.71:

$$V_{cng} = \frac{\$12}{.14} = \$85.71$$

In this instance, the relationship between value and earnings per share is direct and unmistakable. If earnings per share increases (decreases) 10 percent, then the value of the share should increase (decrease) 10 percent; that is, the ratio of price to earnings will be a constant, as will the ratio of earnings to price. A departure from the constant relationship would occur only if the investors change their required rate of return, owing to a change in their perception about such things as risk or anticipated inflation. Thus, there is good reason to perceive a relationship between next year's earnings and share price for the nongrowth company.

The Relationship Between Earnings and Value for the Growth Firm

Turning our attention now to the growth firm, one that does reinvest its profits back into the business, we will recall that our valuation model depended on dividends and earnings increasing at a constant growth rate. Returning to equation (5–8), we valued a common stock where dividends were expected to increase at a constant growth rate as follows:

$$\text{value} = \frac{\text{dividend}_1}{\text{required rate of return} - \text{growth rate}}$$

or

$$V_c = \frac{D_1}{R_c - g} \tag{5-8}$$

While equation (5–8) is certainly the conventional way of expressing value of the growth stock, it is not the only means. We could also describe the value of a stock as the present value of the dividend stream provided from the firm's existing assets plus the present value of any future growth resulting from the reinvestment of future earnings. We could represent this concept notationally as follows:

$$V_c = \frac{EPS_1}{R_c} + PVDG \tag{5B-3}$$

where EPS_1/R_c is the present value of the cash flow stream provided by the existing assets
$PVDG$ is the net present value of any dividend growth resulting from the reinvestment of future earnings

The first term, EPS_1/R_c, is immediately understandable given our earlier rationale about nongrowth stocks. The second term, the present value of future dividend growth ($PVDG$), needs some clarification.

To begin our explanation of $PVDG$, let r equal the fraction of a firm's earnings that are retained in the business, which implies that the dividend in year 1 (D_1) would equal $(1 - r) \times EPS_1$. Next, assume that any earnings that are reinvested yield a rate of ROE (return on equity). Thus, from the earnings generated in year 1, we would be investing the percentage of earnings retained, r, times the firm's earnings per share, EPS_1, or $r \times EPS_1$. In return, we should expect to receive a cash flow in all future years equal to the expected return on our investment, ROE, times the amount of our investment, or $r \times EPS_1 \times ROE$. Since the cash inflows represent an annuity continuing in perpetuity, the net present value from reinvesting a part of the firm's earnings in year 1 (NPV_1) would be equal to the present value of the new cash flows less the cost of the investment:

$$NPV_1 = \underbrace{\left(\frac{rEPS_1 ROE}{R_c}\right)}_{\substack{\text{present value} \\ \text{of increased} \\ \text{cash flows}}} - \underbrace{rEPS_1}_{\substack{\text{amount} \\ \text{of cash} \\ \text{retained and} \\ \text{reinvested}}} \tag{5B-4}$$

If we continued to reinvest a fixed percentage of earnings each year and earned *ROE* on these investments, there would also be a net present value in all the following years; that is, we would have a NPV_2, NPV_3, NPV_4, . . . NPV_∞. Also, since r and *ROE* are both constant, the series of *NPV*s will increase at a constant growth rate of $r \times ROE$. We may therefore use the *constant-growth valuation model* to value *PVDG* as follows:

$$PVDG = \frac{NPV_1}{R_c - g} \qquad \text{(5B–5)}$$

Thus, we may now establish the value of a common stock as the sum of (1) a present value of a constant stream of earnings generated from the firm's assets already in place and (2) the present value of an increasing dividend stream coming from the retention of profits; that is,

$$V_c = \frac{EPS_1}{R_c} + \frac{NPV_1}{R_c - g} \qquad \text{(5B–6)}$$

The Upp Corporation should earn $8 per share this year, of which 40 percent will be retained within the firm for reinvestment and 60 percent paid in the form of dividends to the stockholders. Management expects to earn an 18 percent return on any funds retained. Let us use both the constant-growth dividend model and the *PVDG* model to compute Upp's stock value.

Constant-Growth Dividend Model

Since we are assuming that the firm's ROE will be constant and that management faithfully intends to retain 40 percent of earnings each year to be used for new investments, the dividend stream flowing to the investor should increase by 7.2 percent each year, which we know by solving for $r \times ROE$, or $(.4)(18\%)$. The dividend for this year will be $4.80, which is the dividend-payout ratio of $(1 - r)$ times the expected earnings per share of $8 $(.60 \times \$8 = \$4.80)$. Given a 12 percent required rate of return for the investors, the value of the security may be shown to be $100.

$$V_c = \frac{D_1}{R_c - g}$$

$$= \frac{\$4.80}{.12 - .072} \qquad \text{(5–8)}$$

$$= \$100$$

PVDG Model

Restructuring the problem to compute separately the present value of the no-growth stream and the present value of future growth opportunities, we may again determine the value of the stock to be $100. Solving first for value assuming a no-growth scenario,

$$V_{cng} = \frac{EPS_1}{R_c}$$

$$= \frac{\$8}{.12} \tag{5B-7}$$

$$= \$66.67$$

We next estimate the value of the future growth opportunities coming from reinvesting corporate profits each year, which is

$$PVDG = \frac{NPV_1}{R_c - g} \tag{5B-8}$$

Knowing R_c to be 12 percent and the growth rate to be 7.2 percent, we lack knowing only NPV_1, which can easily be determined using equation (5B-4):

$$NPV_1 = \left(\frac{rEPS_1ROE}{R_c}\right) - rEPS_1$$

$$= \left(\frac{(.4)(\$8)(.18)}{.12}\right) - (.4)(\$8) \tag{5B-4}$$

$$= \$4.80 - \$3.20$$

$$= \$1.60$$

The *PVDG* may now be computed:

$$PVDG = \frac{\$1.60}{.12 - .072}$$

$$= \$33.33$$

Thus, the value of the combined streams is $100:

$$V_c = \$66.67 + \$33.33 = \$100$$

From the preceding example, we see that the value of the growth opportunities represents a significant portion of the total value, 33 percent to be exact. Furthermore, in looking at the *PVDG* model, we observe that value is influenced by the following: (1) the size of the firm's beginning earnings per share, (2) the percentage of profits retained, and (3) the spread between the return generated on new investments and the investor's required rate of return. The first factor relates to firm size; the second to management's decision about the firm's earnings retention rate. While the first two factors are not unimportant, the last one is the key to wealth creation by management. *Simply because management retains profits does not mean that wealth is created for the stockholders.* Wealth comes only if the return on equity from the investments, *ROE*, is greater than the investor's required rate of return, R_c. Thus, we should expect the market to assign value not only to the reported earnings per share for the current year but also to the anticipated growth opportunities that have a marginal rate of return that exceed the required rate of return of the firm's investors.

STUDY PROBLEMS

5B–1. (*Valuation of Common Stock–PVDG Model*) The Burgon Co. management expects the firm's earning per share to be $5 this forthcoming year. The firm's policy is to pay out 35 percent of its earnings in the form of dividends. In looking at the investment opportunities available to the firm, the return on equity should be 20 percent for the foreseeable future. Use the *PVDG* model to find the value of the company's stock. The stockholders' required rate of return is 16 percent. Verify your results with the constant-growth dividend model.

5B–2. (*Valuation of Common Stock–PVDG Model*) You want to know the impact of retaining earnings on the value of your firm's stock. Given the information below, calculate the value of the stock under the different scenarios.

a. Earnings per share on existing assets should be about $7 this forthcoming year.

b. The stockholder's required rate of return is 18 percent.

c. The expected return on equity may be as low as 16 percent or as high as 24 percent, with an expected return of 18 percent.

d. You are considering three earnings-retention policies on a long-term basis: (1) retain no earnings, instead distributing all earnings to stockholders in the form of dividends; (2) retain 30 percent of earnings; or (3) retain 60 percent of earnings.

CHAPTER 6

Capital Budgeting

Guidelines for Capital Budgeting ● Measuring a Project's Benefits and Costs ● Competitive Markets and Profitable Projects—Where Do Profitable Projects Come From? ● Nondiscounted Cash Flow Criteria for Capital-Budgeting Decisions ● Discounted Cash Flow Criteria for Capital-Budgeting Decisions ● A Glance at Actual Capital-Budgeting Practices

In Chapter 3 we developed tools for comparing cash flows that occur in different periods. This chapter uses these techniques in conjunction with additional decision rules to determine when to invest money in long-term assets, a process called **capital budgeting.** In evaluating capital investment proposals, we compare the costs and benefits of each in a number of ways. Some of these methods take into account the time value of money, others do not; however, each of these methods is used frequently in the real world. As you will see, our preferred method of analysis will be the net present value (NPV) method that compares the present value of inflows and outflows.

Capital budgeting is a decision-making process for investment in fixed assets; specifically, it involves measuring the incremental cash flows associated with investment proposals and evaluating the attractiveness of these cash flows relative to the project's cost. Typically these investments involve rather large cash outlays at the outset and commit the firm to a particular course of action over a relatively long period. Thus, if a capital-budgeting decision is incorrect, reversing it tends to be costly.

For example, about 35 years ago the Ford Motor Company's decision to produce the Edsel entailed an outlay of $250 million to bring the car to market and losses of approximately $200 million during the 2½ years it was produced—in all, a $450 million mistake.[1] This type of decision is costly to reverse. Fortunately for Ford, it was able to convert Edsel production facilities to produce the Mustang, thereby avoiding an even larger loss. In the 1980s General Motors made a major capital-budgeting decision by investing $3.5 billion to construct its Saturn automobile plant. As of 1992 sales looked good, but only time will tell if this decision proves to be profitable in the long run.

We look first at the purpose and importance of capital budgeting. Next, because capital-budgeting techniques rely on cash flows as inputs, we study how to determine these cash flows. Five capital-budgeting criteria are then provided

---

[1]"The Edsel Dies, and Ford Regroups Survivors," *Business Week* November 28, 1959, p. 27.

for evaluating capital investments, followed by a look at capital budgeting in practice.

Perspective in Finance

This chapter deals with decision rules for deciding when to invest in new projects. Before we can develop these rules we must be able to measure the benefits and costs of the new project by calculating cash flows. In reading over the upcoming section try not to look upon calculating cash flows as going down a checklist of possible sources of cash flows, but instead try to think about what cash flows are and what creates them.

Guidelines for Capital Budgeting

To evaluate investment proposals, we must first set guidelines by which we measure the value of each proposal.

Use Cash Flows Rather than Accounting Profits

We will use cash flows, not accounting profits, as our measurement tool. The firm receives and is able to reinvest cash flows, whereas accounting profits are shown when they are earned rather than when the money is actually in hand. Unfortunately, a firm's accounting profits and cash flows may not be timed to occur together. For example, capital expenses, such as vehicles and plant and equipment, are depreciated over several years, with their annual depreciation subtracted from profit. Cash flows correctly reflect the timing of benefits and costs, that is, when the money is received, when it can be reinvested, and when it must be paid out.

Think Incrementally

Unfortunately, calculating cash flows from a project may not be enough. Decision makers must ask: What new cash flows will the company as a whole receive if the company takes on a given project? What if the company does not take on the project? Interestingly, we may find that not all cash flows a firm expects from an investment proposal are incremental in nature. In measuring cash flows, however, the trick is to *think* incrementally. In doing so, we will see that only *incremental after-tax cash flows* matter. As such, our guiding rule in deciding if a cash flow is incremental will be to look at the company with, versus without, the new product. As you will see in the upcoming sections, this may be easier said than done.

Beware of Cash Flows Diverted from Existing Products

Assume for a moment that we are managers of a firm considering a new product line that might compete with one of our existing products and possibly reduce its sales. In determining the cash flows associated with the proposed project, we should consider only the incremental sales brought to the company as a whole. New-product sales achieved at the cost of losing sales of other products in our line are not considered a benefit of adopting the new product. For example, when General Foods' Post Cereal Division introduced its Dino Pebbles in 1991, the product competed directly with the company's Fruity Pebbles (in fact, the two were the same product with an addition to the former of dinosaur-shaped marshmallows). Post meant to target the market niche held by Kellogg's Marshmallow Krispies, but there was no question that sales recorded by Dino Pebbles bit into—literally cannibalized—Post's existing product line.

Remember that we are only interested in the sales dollars to the firm if this project is accepted, as opposed to what the sales dollars would be if the project is rejected. Just moving sales from one product line to a new product line does not bring anything new into the company, but if sales are captured from our competitors or if sales that would have been lost to new competing products are retained then these are relevant incremental cash flows. In each case these are the incremental cash flows to the firm—looking at the firm as a whole with the new product versus without the new product.

Look for Incidental or Synergistic Effects

Although in some cases a new project may take sales away from a firm's current projects, in other cases a new effort may actually bring new sales to the existing line. For example, in September 1991 USAir introduced service to Sioux City, Iowa. The new routes connecting this addition to the USAir system not only brought about new ticket sales on those routes, they also fed passengers to connecting routes. If managers were to look at only the revenue from ticket sales on the Sioux City routes, they would miss the incremental cash flow to the firm as a whole that results from taking on the new route. This is called an incidental, or *synergistic,* effect. The cash flow comes from *any* USAir flight that would not have occurred if service to Sioux City had not been available. The bottom line: Any cash flow to any part of the company that may result from the decision at hand must be considered when making that decision.

Work in Working Capital Requirements

Many times a new project will involve additional investment in working capital. This may take the form of new inventory to stock a sales outlet, additional investment in accounts receivable resulting from additional credit sales, or increased investment in cash to operate cash registers, and more. Working capital requirements are considered a cash flow even though they do not leave the company. How can investment in inventory be considered a cash outflow when the goods are still in the store? Because the firm does not have access to the inventory's cash value, the firm cannot use the money for other investments. Generally, working capital requirements are tied up over the life of the project. When the project terminates there is usually an offsetting cash inflow as the working capital is recovered.

Consider Incremental Expenses

Just as cash inflows from a new project are measured on an incremental basis, expenses should also be measured on an incremental basis. For example, if introducing a new-product line necessitates training the sales staff, the after-tax cash flow associated with the training program must be considered a cash outflow and charged against the project. If accepting a new project dictates that a production facility be reengineered, the after-tax cash flows associated with that capital investment should be charged against the project. Again, any incremental after-tax cash flow affecting the company as a whole is a relevant cash flow—whether it is flowing in or flowing out.

Remember That Sunk Costs Are Not Incremental Cash Flows

Only cash flows that are affected by the decision making at the moment are relevant in capital budgeting. The manager asks two questions: (1) Will this cash flow occur if the project is accepted? (2) Will this cash flow occur if the project is rejected? *Yes* to the first question and *no* to the second equals an incremental cash flow. For example, let's assume you are considering introducing a new taste treat called Puddin' in a Shoe. You would like to do some test marketing before production. If you are considering the decision to test market and have not yet done so, the costs associated with the test marketing are relevant cash flows. Conversely, if you have already test marketed, the cash flows involved in test marketing are no longer relevant in project evaluation. It's a matter of timing. Regardless of what you might decide about future production, the cash flows allocated to marketing have already occurred. As a rule, any cash flows that are not part of the accept–reject decision should not be included in capital-budgeting analysis.

Account for Opportunity Costs

Now we will focus on the cash flows that are lost because a given project consumes scarce resources that would have produced cash flows if that project had been rejected. This is the opportunity cost of doing business. For example, a product may use valuable floor space in a production facility. Although the cash flow is not obvious, the real question remains: What else could be done with this space? The space could have been rented out, or another product could have been stored there. The key point is that opportunity cost cash flows should reflect net cash flows that would have been received if the project under consideration was rejected. Again, we are analyzing the cash flows to the company as a whole—with or without the project.

Decide if Overhead Costs Are Truly Incremental Cash Flows

Although we certainly want to include any incremental cash flows resulting in changes from overhead expenses such as utilities and salaries, we also want to make sure that these are truly incremental cash flows. Many times, overhead expenses—heat, light, rent—would occur whether or not a given project were accepted or rejected. There is often simply not a single specific project to which these expenses can be allocated. Thus, the question is not whether or not the project benefits from overhead items, but whether or not the overhead costs are incremental cash flows associated with the project—and relevant to capital budgeting.

Ignore Interest Payments and Financing Flows

In evaluating new projects and determining cash flows, we must separate the investment decision from the financing decision. Interest payments and other financing cash flows that might result from raising funds to finance a project should not be considered incremental cash flows. If accepting a project means we have to raise new funds by issuing bonds, the interest charges associated with raising funds are not a relevant cash outflow. When we discount the incremental cash flows back to the present at the required rate of return, we are implicitly accounting for the cost of raising funds to finance the new project. In essence, the required rate of return reflects the cost of the funds needed to support the project. Managers first determine the desirability of the project and then determine how best to finance it.

Measuring a Project's Benefits and Costs

In measuring cash flows, we will be interested only in the **incremental,** or differential, **after-tax cash flows** that can be attributed to the proposal being evaluated. That is, we will focus our attention on the difference in the firm's after-tax cash flows *with* versus *without* the project. The worth of our decision depends on the accuracy of our cash flow estimates. For this reason we first examined the question of what cash flows are relevant. Now we will see that, in general, a project's cash flows will fall into one of three categories: (1) the initial outlay, (2) the differential flows over the project's life, (3) the terminal cash flow. *[handwritten: beginning / End of project]* After introducing these cash flow categories, we will examine several capital-budgeting criteria that will use these cash flows as inputs. *[handwritten: during middle of project]*

Initial Outlay

The **initial outlay** involves the immediate cash outflow necessary to purchase the asset and put it in operating order. This amount includes the cost of installing the asset (the asset's purchase price plus any expenses associated with shipping or installation) and any nonexpense cash outlays, such as increased working capital requirements. If we are considering a new sales outlet, there might be additional cash flows associated with investment in working capital in the form of increased inventory and cash necessary to operate the sales outlet. Although these cash flows are not included in the cost of the asset or even expensed on the books, they must be included in our analysis. The after-tax cost of expense items incurred as a result of new investment must also be included as cash outflows—for example, any training expenses or special engineering expenses that would not have been incurred otherwise. Finally, if the investment decision is a replacement decision, the cash inflow associated with the selling price of the old asset, in addition to any tax effects resulting from its sale, must be included.

Determining the initial outlay is a complex calculation. Table 6–1 summarizes some of the more common calculations involved in determining the initial outlay. This list is by no means exhaustive, but it should help simplify the calculations involved in the example that follows.

1. Installed cost of asset
2. Additional nonexpense outlays incurred (for example, working capital investments)
3. Additional expenses on an after-tax basis (for example, training expenses)
4. In a replacement decision, the *after-tax* cash flow associated with the sale of the old machine

TABLE 6–1.
Summary of Calculation of Initial Outlay Incremental After-Tax Cash Flow

Perspective in Finance

At this point we should note that the incremental nature of the cash flow is of great importance. In many cases if the project is not accepted, then "status quo" for the firm will simply not continue. In calculating incremental cash flows we must be realistic in estimating what the cash flows to the company would be if the new project is not accepted. The Financial Management in Practice, *"Using the Right Base Case," deals with precisely this question.*

Tax Effects—Sale of Old Machine

One of the most potentially confusing initial outlay calculations is for a replacement project involving the incremental tax payment associated with the sale of an old machine. Although these calculations were examined in Chapter 2, a review is appropriate here: There are three possible tax situations dealing with the sale of an old asset:

1. The old asset is sold for a price above the depreciated value. Here the difference between the old machine's selling price and its depreciated value is considered recapture of depreciation and taxed at the marginal corporate tax rate. If, for example, the old machine was originally purchased for $15,000, had a book value of $10,000, and was sold for $17,000, assuming the firm's marginal corporate tax rate is 34 percent, the taxes due from recapture of depreciation would be ($17,000 − $10,000)(.34), or $2,380.

FINANCIAL MANAGEMENT IN PRACTICE

Using the Right Base Case

Finance theory assumes that a project will be evaluated against its base case, that is, what will happen if the project is not carried out. Managers tend to explore fully the implications of adopting the project but usually spend less time considering the likely outcome of not making the investment. Yet unless the base case is realistic, the incremental cash flows—the difference between the "with" and the "without" scenarios—will mislead.

Often companies implicitly assume that the base case is simply a continuation of the status quo, but this assumption ignores market trends and competitor behavior. It also neglects the impact of changes the company might make anyway, like improving operations management.

Using the wrong base case is typical of product launches in which the new product will likely erode the market for the company's existing product line. Take Apple Computer's introduction of the Macintosh SE. The new PC had obvious implications for sales of earlier generation Macintoshes. To analyze the incremental cash flows arising from the new product, Apple would have needed to count the lost contribution from sales of its existing products as a cost of the launch.

Wrongly applied, however, this approach would equate the without case to the status quo: it would assume that without the SE, sales of existing Macintoshes would continue at their current level. In the competitive PC market, however, nothing stands still. Competitors like IBM would likely innovate and take market share away from the earlier generation Macintoshes—which a more realistic base case would have reflected. Sales of existing products would decline even in the base case.

Consider investments in the marketing of existing brands through promotions, media budgets, and the like. They are often sold as if they were likely to lead to ever-increasing market share. But competitors will also be promoting their brands, and market shares across the board still have to add up to 100%. Still, such an investment is not necessarily wasted. It may just need a more realistic justification: although the investment is unlikely to increase sales above existing levels, it may prevent sales from falling. Marketers who like positive thinking may not like this defensive argument, but it is the only argument that makes economic sense in a mature market.

In situations like this, when the investment is needed just to maintain market share, the returns may be high in comparison with the base case, but the company's reported profits may still go down. Senior managers are naturally puzzled at apparently netting only 5% on a project that had promised a 35% return.[2] Without the investment, however, the profit picture would have looked even worse, especially in the longer term.

Some projects disappoint for other reasons. Sometimes the original proposals are overoptimistic, partly because the base case is implicit or defined incorrectly. That is, if managers are convinced that the investment is sound and are frustrated because the figures fail to confirm their intuition, they may over-inflate projections of sales or earnings. But misstating the base case and then having to make unrealistic projections are unlikely to cancel each other out; they merely cloud the analysis.

2. The old asset is sold for its depreciated value. In this case no taxes result, as there is neither a gain nor a loss in the asset's sale.

3. The old asset is sold for less than its depreciated value. In this case the difference between the depreciated book value and the salvage value of the asset is used to offset ordinary income and thus results in tax savings. For example, if the depreciated book value of the asset is $10,000 and it is sold for $7,000, assuming the firm's marginal corporate tax rate is 34 percent, the cash inflow from tax savings is ($10,000 − $7,000)(.34), or $1,020.

EXAMPLE

To clarify the calculation of the initial outlay, consider an example of a company in the 34 percent marginal tax bracket. This company is considering the purchase of a new machine to be used in oil and gas drilling for $30,000 it has

---

[2]Joseph L. Bower, *Managing the Resource Allocation Process* (Boston: Harvard Business School Press, 1986), p. 13.

a five-year life (according to IRS guidelines) and will be depreciated using the *simplified straight-line method* (this depreciation method will be explained later). The useful life of this new machine is also five years. The new machine will replace an existing machine originally purchased for $30,000, 10 years ago, which currently has five more years of expected useful life. The existing machine will generate $2,000 of depreciation expenses for each of the next five years, at which time the book value will be equal to zero. To put the new machine in running order, it is necessary to pay shipping charges of $2,000 and installation charges of $3,000. Because the new machine will work faster than the old one, it will require an increase in goods-in-process inventory of $5,000. Finally, the old machine can be sold to a scrap dealer for $15,000.

The installed cost of the new machine would be the $30,000 cost plus $2,000 shipping and $3,000 installation fees, for a total of $35,000. Additional outflows are associated with taxes incurred on the sale of the old machine and with increased investment in inventory. Although the old machine has a book value of $10,000, it could be sold for $15,000. The increased taxes from recapture of depreciation will be equal to the selling price of the old machine less its depreciated book value times the firm's marginal tax rate, or ($15,000 − $10,000)(.34), or $1,700. The increase in goods-in-process inventory of $5,000 must also be considered part of the initial outlay, with an offsetting inflow of $5,000 corresponding to the recapture of this inventory occurring at the termination of the project. In effect, the firm invests $5,000 in inventory now, resulting in an initial cash outlay, and liquidates this inventory in five years, resulting in a cash inflow at the end of the project. The total outlays associated with the new machine are $35,000 for its installed cost, $1,700 in increased taxes, and $5,000 in investment in inventory, for a total of $41,700. This is somewhat offset by the sale of the old machine for $15,000. Thus, the net initial outlay associated with this project is $26,700. These calculations are summarized in Table 6–2.

Outflows:		
Purchase price	$30,000	
Shipping fee	2,000	
Installation fee	3,000	
Installed cost of machine		$35,000
Increased taxes from sale of old machine ($15,000–$10,000)(.34)		1,700
Increased investment in inventory		5,000
Total outflows		$41,700
Inflows:		
Salvage value of old machine		15,000
Net initial outlay		$26,700

TABLE 6–2.
Calculation of Initial Outlay for Example Problem

Differential Flows over Project's Life

The differential cash flows over the project's life involve the incremental after-tax cash flows resulting from increased revenues, plus labor or material savings, and reductions in selling expenses. Overhead items, such as utilities, heat, light, and executive salaries, are generally not affected. However, any resultant change in any of these categories must be included. Any increase in interest payments incurred as a result of issuing bonds to finance the project should *not* be included, as the costs of funds needed to support the project are implicitly accounted for by discounting the project back to the present using the required rate of return. Finally, an adjustment for the incremental change in taxes should be made, including any increase in taxes that might result from increased profits or any tax savings from an increase in depreciation expenses. Increased depreciation expenses affect tax-related cash flows by reducing

1. Added revenue offset by increased expenses
2. Labor and material savings
3. Increases in overhead incurred
4. Depreciation tax shield on an incremental basis in a replacement decision
5. Do *not* include interest expenses if the project is financed by issuing debt, as this is accounted for in the required rate of return

taxable income and thus lowering taxes. Table 6–3 lists some of the factors that might be involved in determining a project's differential cash flows. Before looking at an example, we will briefly examine the calculation of depreciation.

Perspective in Finance

Depreciation plays an important role in the calculation of cash flows. Although it is not a cash flow item, it lowers profits, which in turn lowers taxes. As a student, in developing a foundation in corporate finance, it is the concept of depreciation, not the calculation of it, that is important. The reason the calculation of depreciation is deemphasized is that it is extremely complicated and its calculation changes every few years as Congress enacts new tax laws. Through all this bear in mind that although depreciation is not a cash flow item, it does affect cash flows by lowering the level of profits on which taxes are calculated.

Depreciation and the Tax Reform Act of 1986

The Tax Reform Act of 1986 not only changed the tax rates corporations pay on their income, but also affected the calculation of their income. Although this was examined in Chapter 2, a review is appropriate here. This act introduced a modified version of the old Accelerated Cost Recovery System (ACRS) to be used for most tangible depreciable property placed in service beginning in 1987. Under this method, the life of the asset is determined according to the asset's class life, which is assigned by the IRS; for example, most computer equipment has a five-year asset life. It also allows for only a half year's deduction in the first year and a half year's deduction in the year after the recovery period. The asset is then depreciated using the 200 percent declining balance method or on an optional straight-line method. With respect to its treatment of depreciation, the Tax Reform Act of 1986 had both good and bad news for businesses. The bad news was that, in general, the depreciable lives of most assets increased; whereas the good news was that most depreciable business assets may now be written off using the 200 percent declining balance method rather than the 150 percent declining balance method.

Depreciation Calculation—Simplified Straight-Line Depreciation Method

Depreciation is calculated using a simplified straight-line method. This simplified process ignores the half-year convention that allows only a half-year's deduction in the year the project is placed in service and a half-year's deduction in the first year after the recovery period. By ignoring the half-year convention we are able to calculate annual depreciation by taking the project's initial depreciable value and dividing by its class or depreciable life as follows:

$$\text{annual depreciation using the simplified straight-line method} = \frac{\text{initial depreciable value}}{\text{depreciable life}}$$

The initial depreciable value is equal to the cost of the asset plus any expenses necessary to get the new asset into operating order.

This is not how depreciation would actually be calculated. The reason we have simplified the calculation is to allow you to focus directly on what should and should not be included in the cash flow calculations. Moreover, because the tax laws change rather frequently, we are more interested in recognizing the tax implications of depreciation rather than understanding the specific depreciation provisions of the current tax laws.

Our concern with depreciation is to highlight its importance in generating cash flow estimates and to indicate that the financial manager must be aware of the current tax provisions when evaluating capital-budgeting proposals.

Differential Flows over Project's Life

Extending the earlier example, which illustrated the calculations of the initial outlay, suppose that purchasing the machine is expected to reduce salaries by $10,000 per year and fringe benefits by $1,000 annually, because it will take only one man to operate, whereas the old machine requires two operators. In addition, the cost of defects will fall from $8,000 per year to $3,000. However, maintenance expenses will increase by $4,000 annually. The annual depreciation on this new machine is $7,000 per year, whereas the depreciation expense lost with the sale of the old machine is $2,000 for each of the next five years. Annual depreciation on the new machine is calculated using the simplified straight-line method just described—that is, taking the cost of the new machine plus any expenses necessary to put it in operating order and dividing by its depreciable life. For the new machine these calculations are reflected in Table 6–4.

Because the depreciation on the old machine is $2,000 per year, the increased depreciation will be from $2,000 per year to $7,000 per year, or an increase of $5,000 per year. Although this increase in depreciation expenses is not a cash flow item, it does affect cash flows by reducing book profits, which in turn reduces taxes.

To determine the annual net cash flows resulting from the acceptance of this project, the net savings *before* taxes using both book profit and cash flows must be found. The additional taxes are then calculated based on the before-tax book profit. For this example, Table 6–5 shows the determination of the differential cash flows on an after-tax basis. Thus, the differential cash flows over the project's life are $9,620.

New machine purchase price	$30,000
Shipping fee	2,000
Installation fee	3,000
Total depreciable value	$35,000
Divided by depreciable life	$35,000/5
Equals: Annual depreciation	$ 7,000

TABLE 6–4.
Calculation of Depreciation for New Machine Using Simplified Straight-Line Method

		Book Profit	Cash Flow
Savings:	Reduced salary	$10,000	$10,000
	Reduced fringe benefits	1,000	1,000
	Reduced defects ($8,000–$3,000)	5,000	5,000
Costs:	Increased maintenance expense	−4,000	−4,000
	Increased depreciation expense ($7,000–$2,000)	−5,000	
Net savings before taxes		$ 7,000	$12,000
Taxes (34%)		−2,380 →	−2,380
Net cash flow after taxes			$ 9,620

TABLE 6–5.
Calculation of Differential Cash Flows for Example Problem

Terminal Cash Flow

The calculation of the terminal cash flow is in general quite a bit simpler than the preceding two calculations. Flows associated with the project's termination

$$\Delta ATCF = \Delta BTCF(1 - t) + \Delta Depr.(t)$$

where $\Delta ATCF$ = the incremental change in the after-tax cash flows to the company as a whole

$\Delta BTCF$ = the incremental change in the before-tax cash flows to the firm as a whole

t = the marginal corporate tax rate

$\Delta Depr.$ = the incremental change in depreciation

generally include the salvage value of the project plus or minus any taxable gains or losses associated with its sales.

Under the current tax laws, in most cases there will be a forecasted taxable gain (resulting in a negative cash flow) associated with the salvage value at termination. This is because the current laws allow all projects to be depreciated to zero, and if a project has a book value of zero at termination and a positive salvage value, then that salvage value will be taxed. The tax effects associated with the salvage value of the project at termination are determined exactly like the tax effects on the sale of the old machine associated with the initial outlay. The salvage value proceeds are compared with the depreciated value, in this case zero, to determine the tax.

In addition to the salvage value, there may be a cash outlay associated with the project termination. For example, at the close of a strip-mining operation, the mine must be refilled in an ecologically acceptable manner. Finally, any working capital outlay required at the initiation of the project—for example, increased inventory needed for the operation of a new plant—will be recaptured at the termination of the project. In effect the increased inventory required by the project can be liquidated when the project expires. Table 6–6 provides a sample list of some of the factors that might affect a project's terminal cash flow.

TABLE 6–6.
Summary of Calculation of Terminal Cash Flow on After-Tax Basis

1. The after-tax salvage value of the project
2. Cash outlays associated with the project's termination
3. Recapture of nonexpense outlays that occurred at the project's initiation (for example, working capital investments)

Extending the example to termination, the depreciated book value and salvage value of the machine at the termination date will be equal to zero. However, there will be a cash flow associated with the recapture of the initial outlay of work-in-process inventory of $5,000. This flow is generated from the liquidation of the $5,000 investment in work-in-process inventory. Therefore, the expected total terminal cash flow equals $5,000.

If we were to construct a cash flow diagram from this example (Figure 6–1), it would have an initial outlay of $26,700, differential cash flows during years 1 through 5 of $9,620, and an additional terminal cash flow at the end of year 5 of $5,000. The cash flow occurring in year 5 is $14,620, the sum of the differential cash flow in year 5 of $9,620, and the terminal cash flow of $5,000.

Cash flow diagrams similar to Figure 6–1 will be used through the remainder of this chapter with arrows above the time line indicating cash inflows and arrows below the time line denoting outflows.

Although the preceding calculations for determining the incremental, after-tax, net cash flows do not cover all possible cash flows, they do set up a framework in which almost any situation can be handled. To simplify this framework, and to provide an overview of the calculations, Table 6–7 summarizes the rules in Tables 6–1, 6–3, and 6–6.

FIGURE 6–1.
Example Cash Flow Diagram

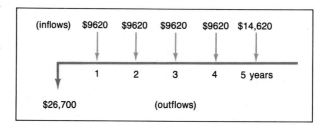

A. Initial Outlay
1. Installed cost of asset
2. Additional nonexpense outlays incurred (for example, working-capital investments)
3. Additional expenses, on an after-tax basis (for example, training expenses)
4. In a replacement decision, the *after-tax* flow associated with the sale of the old machine

B. Differential Cash Flows over the Project's Life
1. Added revenue offset by increased expenses
2. Labor and material savings
3. Increases in overhead incurred
4. Depreciation tax shield on an incremental basis in a replacement decision
5. Do *not* include interest expenses if the project is financed by issuing debt, as this is accounted for in the required rate of return

C. Terminal Cash Flow
1. The after-tax salvage value of the project
2. Cash outlays associated with the project's termination
3. Recapture of nonexpense outlays that occurred at the project's initiation (for example, working capital investments)

Perspective in Finance

In this chapter it is easy to get caught up in the calculations and forget that before the calculations can be made someone has to come up with the idea for the project. In some of the example problems you may see projects that appear to be extremely profitable. Unfortunately, it is unusual to have projects with dramatically high returns because of the very competitive nature of business. In the upcoming section we will explain why this is the case and point out where a company should look for profitable new projects.

Competitive Markets and Profitable Projects— Where Do Profitable Projects Come From?

At this point we are going to step back a bit and take a broad look at the capital-budgeting process. It is very easy to get caught up in the mechanics of capital budgeting without analyzing the process itself. Before moving on and examining the intricacies of capital budgeting we will examine where profitable projects come from.

In reality it is much easier evaluating profitable projects than it is finding them. If, for example, an industry is generating large profits, then new entrants are usually attracted. The additional competition and added capacity then can result in profits being driven down to the required rate of return. Conversely, if an industry is returning profits below the required rate of return, then some participants in the market drop out, reducing capacity and competition; in turn, prices are driven back up. This is precisely what happened in the VCR video rental market in the mid-1980s. This market developed suddenly with the opportunity for extremely large profits. As a result, because there were no barriers to entry, this market was flooded with new entries in short time. By 1987 the resultant competition and price cutting produced losses for many firms in this industry, forcing them to flee the market. As the competition lessened with firms moving out of the video rental industry profits again were able to rise to the point where the required rate of return could be earned on invested capital.

The point to all this is that in competitive markets extremely large profits simply cannot exist for very long. Given that somewhat bleak scenario, how can we find the good projects—that is, the ones that return more than the required rate of return? The answer is that as long as the markets are competitive they will be difficult to find. What we have to do is look to markets that are not perfectly competitive. The two most common ways of making the markets less competitive are to differentiate the product in some key way or to achieve a cost advantage that competitors cannot match, which in turn discourages new entrants into the market.

Successful investments involve those that reduce competition by creating barriers to entry either through product differentiation or cost advantages. If products are differentiated, consumer choice is no longer made by price alone. As such, capital budgeting projects that involve product differentiation allow for the possibility of extremely large profits.

Product differentiation has long been used as a means of insulating a product from competition, thereby allowing prices to stay sufficiently high to support large profits. For example, in the pharmaceutical industry patents have traditionally created competitive barriers. Products like SmithKline Beckman's Tagamet, used in the treatment of ulcers, and Hoffmann-La Roche's Valium, a tranquilizer, can protect themselves from direct competition.

Patents are one way of differentiating products. Service and quality have also been used successfully. For example, Caterpillar Tractor has long prided

---

INTERNATIONAL FINANCIAL MANAGEMENT

Equal Partners: GE's Factory Automation Joint Venture with Fanuc, Ltd. of Japan

Many times a firm may not have the ability to take on a profitable project alone; perhaps it needs marketing or technical expertise. If the firm can find another with the ability to fill that void, it could form a joint venture with that firm. In this way a capital budgeting project that would otherwise be rejected can now be profitably accepted.

In the future, when the history of General Electric's globalization efforts is written, the company's joint venture with FANUC, Ltd., of Japan may serve as the prologue. GE Fanuc Automation Corporation was formed in December 1986 to meld the strengths of each company. By the end of 1988, GE Fanuc had become the premier company serving American industry with industrial robots and computer numerical control (CNC) devices.

This strategic move was inspired by conditions at both companies. During the early 1980s, GE had become overextended in its ability to provide service and technology to U.S. automakers. The company tried to guarantee factory overhauls but it did not have the expertise or the technology to support an active marketing plan. Demand outpaced supply, and GE stretched itself too far to compete with the domestic leader, Allen-Bradley, which was outgunning GE in its own markets. During the same period, FANUC had gained world recognition as the best manufacturer of CNCs and robotic controls, but the company lacked the marketing capabilities of GE in American industry circles. The two companies contracted for a joint venture, and by 1987, a new automation plant opened in Charlottesville, Virginia, bringing together the power of GE's marketing and FANUC's quality engineering. By the end of 1988, GE Fanuc had captured an equal market share in U.S. sales with its competitors, Westinghouse and Allen-Bradley, and the company was positioning itself to market globally in both Europe and Asia by the early 1990s. During the three-year start-up period, managers discovered they were in a planning transition none of them had previously experienced. On the manufacturing floor, engineers had to develop plans that coincided with the Japanese approach to efficient, high-quality production. This meant that U.S. managers no longer produced "to stock" or could get away with "some rejects." Production objectives were 100 percent quality, on-time delivery, and no excess inventory or waste. Incremental planning each year, coupled with new processes and involvement of all employees in planning, helped create a GE Fanuc system in which customers received iron-clad guarantees of 100 percent quality and the lowest CNC and robotic machinery costs in the industry. Today the company is the low-cost producer with defect rates of less than 1 percent.

Source: "World Games," Monogram, 66, no. 1 (1988), pp. 1–9. Adapted by permission from David H. Holt, Management, 2nd ed. Copyright © 1990 by Prentice Hall, Inc. p. 231.

BASIC FINANCIAL MANAGEMENT IN PRACTICE

Finding Profitable Projects in Competitive Markets—Creating Them by Developing a Cost Advantage

Iowa Beef Packers and Federal Express have been able to win strong competitive positions by restructuring the traditional production-cost chains in their industries. In beef packing the traditional production sequence involved raising cattle on scattered farms and ranches, shipping them live to labor-intensive unionized slaughtering plants, and then transporting whole sides of beef to grocery retailers, whose butcher departments cut them into smaller pieces and packaged them for sale to grocery shoppers. Iowa Beef Packers revamped the traditional chain with a radically different strategy— large automated plants employing nonunion labor were built near economically transportable supplies of cattle, and the meat was partially butchered at the processing plant into smaller high-yield cuts (sometimes sealed in plastic casing ready for purchase), boxed, and shipped to retailers. IBP's inbound cattle transportation expenses, traditionally a major cost item, were cut significantly by avoiding the weight losses that occurred when live animals were shipped long distances; major outbound shipping cost savings were achieved by not having to ship whole sides of beef with their high waste factor. Iowa Beef's strategy was so successful that it was, in 1985, the largest U.S. meatpacker, surpassing the former industry leaders, Swift, Wilson, and Armour.

Federal Express innovatively redefined the production-cost chain for rapid delivery of small parcels.

Traditional firms like Emery and Airborne Express operated by collecting freight packages of varying sizes, shipping them to their destination points via air freight and commercial airlines, and then delivering them to the addressee. Federal Express opted to focus only on the market for overnight delivery of small packages and documents. These were collected at local drop points during the late afternoon hours, flown on company-owned planes during early evening hours to a central hub in Memphis, where—from 11 P.M. to 3 A.M. each night—all parcels were sorted and then reloaded on company planes and flown during the early morning hours to their destination points, where they were delivered the next morning by company personnel using company trucks. The cost structure so achieved by Federal Express was low enough to permit it to guarantee overnight delivery of a small parcel anywhere in the United States for a price as low as $11. In 1986 Federal Express had a 58 percent market share of the air-express package-delivery market versus a 15 percent share for UPS, 11 percent for Airborne Express, and 10 percent for Emery/Purolator.

Source: Arthur A. Thompson, Jr., *Economics of the Firm: Theory and Practice* (Englewood Cliffs, NJ: Prentice Hall, 1989), p. 451. Based on information in Michael E. Porter, *Competitive Advantage* (New York: Free Press, 1985), p. 109.

itself on the quality of its construction and earth-moving machinery. As a result, it has been able to securely hold on to its market. Similarly, some of the brand loyalty built up in recent years by Toyota and Honda Motors has been based on quality.

The quality of service can also create product differentiation as witnessed by Domino's Pizza and McDonald's. At McDonald's fast service, cleanliness, and consistency of product bring customers back. Regardless of how product differentiation occurs (focusing on service, advertising, the development of patents through research and development expenditures, or quality) the more the product is differentiated from competing products, the less competition that it will have to face and thus the greater the possibility of extremely large profits.

Economies of scale and the ability to produce at a cost below competition can effectively detour new entrants to the market and thereby reduce competition. The retail hardware industry is one in which this is the case. In the hardware industry there are several fixed costs that are independent of the store's size or annual sales. For example, inventory costs, advertising expenses, and managerial salaries are essentially the same regardless of annual sales. As a result, the more sales can be built up, the lower the per sales dollar cost of inventory, advertising, and management. Restocking from warehouses also becomes more efficient as delivery trucks can now be used to full potential.

Regardless of how the cost advantage is created—by economies of scale, proprietary technology, or monopolistic control of raw materials—the cost advantage deters new entrants from the market while allowing production at below industry cost. Thus, investments aimed at creating a significant cost advantage have the potential to be accompanied by large profits.

Thus, the key to locating profitable investment projects is first to understand how and where they exist in competitive markets. Once this is done the corporate philosophy must be directly aimed at creating or taking advantage of some imperfection in these markets—either through product differentiation or creation of a cost advantage—rather than looking to new markets or industries that appear to provide large profits. In effect, any perfectly competitive industry that looks too good to be true, won't be for long.

Nondiscounted Cash Flow Criteria for Capital-Budgeting Decisions

We are now ready to consider the interpretation of cash flows. Cash flows represent the benefits generated from accepting a capital-budgeting proposal. In the remainder of this chapter we will assume a given cash flow is generated by a project and work on determining whether or not that project should be accepted.

We will consider five commonly used criteria for determining acceptability of investment proposals. The first two are the least sophisticated, in that they do not incorporate the time value of money into their calculations; the final three do take it into account.

Nondiscounted Cash Flow Criterion 1: Payback Period

The **payback period** is the number of years needed to recover the initial cash outlay. As this criterion measures how quickly the project will return its original investment, it deals with cash flows rather than accounting profits. It also ignores the time value of money and does not discount these cash flows back to present. The accept–reject criterion involves whether or not the project's payback period is less than or equal to the firm's maximum desired payback period. For example, if a firm's maximum desired payback period is three years and an investment proposal requires an initial cash outlay of $10,000 and yields the following set of annual cash flows, what is its payback period? Should the project be accepted?

Year	After-Tax Cash Flow
1	$2000
2	4000
3	3000
4	3000
5	1000

In this case, after three years the firm will have recaptured $9,000 on an initial investment of $10,000, leaving $1,000 of the initial investment to be recouped. During the fourth year a total of $3,000 will be returned from this investment, and, assuming it will flow into the firm at a constant rate over the year, it will take one-third of the year ($1,000/$3,000) to recapture the remaining $1,000. Thus, the payback period on this project is three and a third years, which is more than the desired payback period. Using the payback period criterion, the firm would reject this project.

Although the payback period is used frequently, it does have some rather obvious drawbacks, which can best be demonstrated through the use of an example. Consider two investment projects, A and B, which involve an initial cash outlay of $10,000 each and produce the annual cash flows shown in Table 6–8. Both projects have a payback period of two years; therefore, in terms of the payback period criterion both are equally acceptable. However, if we had our choice, it is clear we would select A over B—for at least two reasons. First, regardless of what happens after the payback period, project A returns our initial investment to us earlier within the payback period. Thus, if there is a time value of money, the cash flows occurring within the payback period should not be weighted equally, as they are. In addition, all cash flows that occur after the payback period are ignored. This violates the principle that investors desire more in the way of benefits rather than less—a principle that is difficult to deny, especially when we are talking about money.

	A	B
Initial cash outlay	–$10,000	–$10,000
Annual net cash inflows:		
Year 1	6,000	5,000
2	4,000	5,000
3	3,000	0
4	2,000	0
5	1,000	0

TABLE 6–8.
Payback Period Example Projects

Although these deficiencies limit the value of the payback period as a tool for investment evaluation, the payback period method does have several positive features. First, it deals with cash flows, as opposed to accounting profits, and therefore focuses on the true timing of the project's benefits and costs, even though these cash flows are not adjusted for the time value of money. Second, it is easy to visualize, quickly understood, and easy to calculate. Finally, while the payback period method does have serious deficiencies, it is often used as a rough screening device to eliminate projects whose returns do not materialize until later years. This approach emphasizes the earliest returns, which in all likelihood are less uncertain and provides for the liquidity needs of the firm. Although these advantages of the payback period are certainly significant, its disadvantages severely limit its value as a discriminating capital-budgeting criterion.

Nondiscounted Cash Flow Criterion 2: Accounting Rate of Return

The **accounting rate of return (AROR)** compares the average after-tax profits with the average dollar size of the investment. The average profits figure is determined by adding up the after-tax profits generated by the investment over its life and dividing by the number of years. The average investment is determined by adding the initial outlay and the project's actual expected salvage value and dividing by two. This computation attempts to calculate the average value of an investment by simply averaging the initial and liquidation values. Thus, the accounting rate of return for an investment with an expected life of n years can be calculated as follows:

$$AROR = \frac{\sum_{t=1}^{n} (\text{accounting profit after tax}_t)/n}{(\text{initial outlay} + \text{expected salvage value})/2} \qquad (6-1)$$

The accept–reject criterion associated with the accounting rate of return compares the calculated return with a minimum acceptable AROR level. If the AROR is greater than this minimum acceptable level, the project is accepted; otherwise it is rejected.

Consider an investment in new machinery that requires an initial outlay of $20,000 and has an expected salvage value of zero after five years. Assume that this machine, if acquired, will result in an increase in after-tax profits of $800 each year for five years. In this case the average accounting profit is $800, whereas the average investment is ($20,000 + 0)/2, or $10,000. For this example, the AROR would be $800/$10,000, or 8 percent.

This technique seems straightforward enough, but its limitations detract significantly from its value as a discriminating capital-budgeting criterion. To examine these limitations, let us first determine the AROR of three proposals, each with an expected life of five years. Assume that the initial outlay associated with each project is $10,000 and it will have an expected salvage value of zero in five years. The minimum acceptable AROR for this firm is 8 percent, and the annual accounting profits from the three proposals are given in Table 6-9. In each case, the average annual accounting profit is $500, and the average investment is $5,000—that is, ($10,000 + 0)/2. Therefore, the AROR is 10 percent for each project, which indicates that the AROR method does not do an adequate job of discriminating among these projects.

TABLE 6-9.
Annual Accounting Profits
After Tax

Year	A	B	C
1	$ 0	$500	$ 0
2	1000	500	0
3	500	500	0
4	500	500	0
5	500	500	2500

A casual examination leads us to the conclusion that project B is the best, as it yields its returns earlier than either project A or C. However, the AROR technique gives equal weight to all returns within the project's life without any regard for the time value of money. The second major disadvantage associated with the AROR method is that it deals with accounting profit figures rather than cash flows. For this reason it does not truly reflect the proper timing of the benefits.

Despite the criticisms, the accounting rate of return has been a relatively popular tool for capital-budgeting analysis, primarily because it involves familiar terms that are easily accessible. Also it is easily understood. The AROR provides a measure of accounting profits per average dollar invested, and the intuitive appeal of this measurement has kept the method alive over the years. For our purposes, the AROR is inadequate, as it does not treat cash flows and does not take into account the time value of money.

Discounted Cash Flow Criteria for Capital-Budgeting Decisions

The final three capital-budgeting criteria to be examined base decisions on the investment's cash flows after adjusting for the time value of money. For the time being, the problem of incorporating risk into the capital-budgeting decision is ignored. This issue will be examined in Chapter 7. In addition, we will assume that the appropriate discount rate, required rate of return, or cost of capital is given. The determination of this rate is the topic of Chapter 8.

We will examine three discounted cash flow capital-budgeting techniques —net present value, profitability index, and internal rate of return.

Net Present Value

The **net present value (NPV)** of an investment proposal is equal to the present value of its annual net cash flows after tax less the investment's initial outlay. The net present value can be expressed as follows:

$$NPV = \sum_{t=1}^{n} \frac{ACF_t}{(1 + k)^t} - IO \qquad\qquad (6\text{--}2)$$

where ACF_t = the annual after-tax cash flow in time period t (this can take on either positive or negative values)

k = the appropriate discount rate, that is, the required rate of return or cost of capital[3]

IO = the initial cash outlay

n = the project's expected life

The project's net present value gives a measurement of the *net value* of an investment proposal in terms of today's dollars. Because all cash flows are discounted back to the present, comparing the difference between the present value of the annual cash flows and the investment outlay does not violate the time value of money assumption. The difference between the present value of the annual cash flows and the initial outlay determines the net value of accepting the investment proposal in terms of today's dollars. Whenever the project's NPV is greater than or equal to zero, we will accept the project; and whenever there is a negative value associated with the acceptance of a project, we will reject the project. If the project's net present value is zero, then it returns the required rate of return and should be accepted. This accept–reject criterion is illustrated below:

$$NPV \geq 0.0 \quad \text{Accept}$$
$$NPV < 0.0 \quad \text{Reject}$$

The following example illustrates the use of the net present value capital-budgeting criterion.

EXAMPLE

A firm is considering new machinery, for which the after-tax cash flows are shown in Table 6–10. If the firm has a 12 percent required rate of return, the present value of the after-tax cash flows is $47,678, as calculated in Table 6–11.

	After-Tax Cash Flow
Initial outlay	−$40,000
Inflow year 1	15,000
Inflow year 2	14,000
Inflow year 3	13,000
Inflow year 4	12,000
Inflow year 5	11,000

TABLE 6–10.
NPV Illustration of Investment in New Machinery

---

[3]The required rate of return or cost of capital is the rate of return necessary to justify raising funds to finance the project or, alternatively, the rate of return necessary to maintain the firm's current market price per share. These terms will be defined in greater detail in Chapter 8.

Furthermore, the net present value of the new machinery is $7,678. Because this value is greater than zero, the net present value criterion indicates that the project should be accepted.

TABLE 6–11.
Calculation for NPV Illustration of Investment in New Machinery

	After-Tax Cash Flow	Present Value Factor at 12 Percent	Present Value
Inflow year 1	$15,000	.893	$13,395
Inflow year 2	14,000	.797	11,158
Inflow year 3	13,000	.712	9,256
Inflow year 4	12,000	.636	7,632
Inflow year 5	11,000	.567	6,237
Present value of cash flows			$47,678
Investment initial outlay			40,000
Net present value			$ 7,678

CALCULATOR SOLUTION[4]

Data Input	Function Key
40,000	+/− INPUT
15,000	INPUT
14,000	INPUT
13,000	INPUT
12,000	INPUT
11,000	INPUT
	EXIT CALC
12	I%

Function Key	Answer
NPV	7674.63

[4]If you are using an HP 17BII, first get to the CPLO menu, and be certain that you have already cleared all prior data entries, selected both the "END MODE" and "one payment per year" (1P/YR), and turned the # times prompting (#T?) off. For further explanation see Appendix A.

Note that the worth of the net present value calculation is a function of the accuracy of cash flow predictions. Before the NPV criterion can be reasonably applied, incremental costs and benefits must first be estimated, including the initial outlay, the differential flows over the project's life, and the terminal cash flow.

In comparing the NPV criterion with those that we have already examined, we find it far superior. First of all, it deals with cash flows rather than accounting profits. In this regard it is sensitive to the true timing of the benefits resulting from the project. Moreover, recognizing the time value of money allows comparison of the benefits and costs in a logical manner. Finally, because projects are accepted only if a positive net present value is associated with them, the acceptance of a project using this criterion will increase the value of the firm, which is consistent with the goal of maximizing the shareholders' wealth.

The disadvantage of the NPV method stems from the need for detailed, long-term forecasts of the incremental cash flows accruing from the project's acceptance. Despite this drawback, the net present value is the most theoretically correct criterion that we will examine. The following example provides an additional illustration of its application.

EXAMPLE

A firm is considering the purchase of a new computer system, which will cost $30,000 initially, to aid in credit billing and inventory management. The incremental after-tax cash flows resulting from this project are provided in Table 6–12. The required rate of return demanded by the firm is 10 percent. To determine the system's net present value, the three-year $15,000 cash flow annuity is first discounted back to present at 10 percent. From Appendix E in the back of this book, we find that PVIFA $_{10\%, 3\,yr}$ is 2.487. Thus, the present value of this $15,000 annuity is $37,305.

Because the cash inflows have been discounted back to the present, they can now be compared with the initial outlay. This is because both of the flows are now stated in terms of today's dollars. Subtracting the initial outlay

TABLE 6–12.
NPV Example Problem of Computer System

	After-Tax Cash Flow
Initial outlay	−$30,000
Year 1	15,000
Year 2	15,000
Year 3	15,000

($30,000) from the present value of the cash inflows ($37,305), we find that the system's net present value is $7,305. Because the NPV on this project is positive, the project should be accepted. ∎

Profitability Index (Benefit/Cost Ratio)

The **profitability index (PI)**, or **benefit/cost ratio**, is the ratio of the present value of the future net cash flows to the initial outlay. Although the net present value investment criterion gives a measure of the absolute dollar desirability of a project, the profitability index provides a relative measure of an investment proposal's desirability—that is, the ratio of the present value of its future net benefits to its initial cost. The profitability index can be expressed as follows:

$$PI = \frac{\sum_{t=1}^{n} \frac{ACF_t}{(1 + k)^t}}{IO} \qquad\qquad (6\text{--}3)$$

where ACF_t = the annual after-tax cash flow in time period t (this can take on either positive or negative values)

   k = the appropriate discount rate; that is, the required rate of return or the cost of capital

   IO = the initial cash outlay

   n = the project's expected life

The decision criterion with respect to the profitability index is to accept the project if the PI is greater than or equal to 1.00, and to reject the project if the PI is less than 1.00.

$$PI \geqslant 1.0 \quad \text{Accept}$$
$$PI < 1.0 \quad \text{Reject}$$

Looking closely at this criterion, we see that it yields the same accept–reject decision as does the net present value criterion. Whenever the present value of the project's net cash flows is greater than its initial cash outlay, the project's net present value will be positive, signaling a decision to accept. When this is true, then the project's profitability index will also be greater than 1, as the present value of the net cash flows (the PI's numerator) is greater than its initial outlay (the PI's denominator). Although these two decision criteria will always yield the same decision, they will not necessarily rank acceptable projects in the same order. This problem of conflicting ranking will be dealt with at a later point.

Because the net present value and profitability index criteria are essentially the same, they have the same advantages over the other criteria examined. Both employ cash flows, recognize the timing of the cash flows, and are consistent with the goal of maximization of shareholders' wealth. The major disadvantage of this criterion, similar to the net present value criterion, is that it requires long, detailed cash flow forecasts.

EXAMPLE

A firm with a 10 percent required rate of return is considering investing in a new machine with an expected life of six years. The after-tax cash flows resulting from this investment are given in Table 6–13. Discounting the project's future

TABLE 6–13.
PI Illustration of Investment in New Machinery

	After-Tax Cash Flow
Initial outlay	−$50,000
Inflow year 1	15,000
Inflow year 2	8,000
Inflow year 3	10,000
Inflow year 4	12,000
Inflow year 5	14,000
Inflow year 6	16,000

TABLE 6–14.
Calculation for PI Illustration of Investment in New Machinery

	After-Tax Cash Flow	Present Value Factor at 10 Percent	Present Value
Initial outlay	−$50,000	1.0	−$50,000
Inflow year 1	15,000	0.909	13,635
Inflow year 2	8,000	0.826	6,608
Inflow year 3	10,000	0.751	7,510
Inflow year 4	12,000	0.683	8,196
Inflow year 5	14,000	0.621	8,694
Inflow year 6	16,000	0.564	9,024

$$PI = \frac{\sum_{t=1}^{n} \frac{ACF_t}{(1+k)^t}}{IO}$$

$$= \frac{\$13,635 + \$6,608 + \$7,510 + \$8,196 + \$8,694 + \$9,024}{\$50,000}$$

$$= \frac{\$53,667}{\$50,000}$$

$$= 1.0733$$

net cash flows back to the present yields a present value of $53,667; dividing this value by the initial outlay of $50,000 gives a profitability index of 1.0733, as shown in Table 6–14. This tells us that the present value of the future benefits accruing from this project is 1.0733 times the level of the initial outlay. Because the profitability index is greater than 1.0, the project should be accepted. ■

Internal Rate of Return

The **internal rate of return (IRR)** attempts to answer this question: What rate of return does this project earn? For computational purposes, the internal rate of return is defined as the discount rate that equates the present value of the project's future net cash flows with the project's initial cash outlay. Mathematically, the internal rate of return is defined as the value *IRR* in the following equation:

$$IO = \sum_{t=1}^{n} \frac{ACF_t}{(1 + IRR)^t} \qquad (6\text{–}4)$$

where ACF_t = the annual after-tax cash flow in period t (this can take on either a positive or negative value)

IO = the initial cash outlay

n = the project's expected life

IRR = the project's internal rate of return

In effect, the IRR is analogous to the concept of the yield to maturity for bonds, which was examined in Chapter 5. In other words, a project's internal rate of return is simply the rate of return that the project earns.

The decision criterion associated with the internal rate of return is to accept the project if the internal rate of return is greater than or equal to the required rate of return. We reject the project if its internal rate of return is less than this required rate of return. This accept–reject criterion is illustrated below:

$$IRR \geq \text{required rate of return} \quad \text{Accept}$$
$$IRR < \text{required rate of return} \quad \text{Reject}$$

If the internal rate of return on a project is equal to the shareholders' required rate of return, then the project should be accepted. This is because the firm is earning the rate that its shareholders are requiring. However, the acceptance of a project with an internal rate of return below the investors' required rate of return will decrease the firm's stock price.

If the NPV is positive, then the IRR must be greater than the required rate of return, k. Thus, all the discounted cash flow criteria are consistent and will give similar accept–reject decisions. In addition, because the internal rate of return is another discounted cash flow criterion, it exhibits the same general advantages and disadvantages as both the net present value and profitability index, and has an additional disadvantage of being tedious to calculate if a financial calculator is not available.

Computing the IRR with a Financial Calculator

With today's calculators, the determination of an internal rate of return is merely a matter of a few keystrokes. In Chapter 3, whenever we were solving time value of money problems for i, we were really solving for the internal rate of return. For instance, in the example on page 68, when we solved for the rate that $100 must be compounded annually for it to grow to $179.10 in 10 years, we were actually solving for that problem's internal rate of return. Thus, with financial calculators we need only input the initial outlay, the cash flows and their timing, and then input the function key **I** or the **IRR** button to calculate the internal rate of return.

Computing the IRR for Even Cash Flows

In this section we are going to put our calculators aside and examine the mathematical process of calculating internal rates of return for a better understanding of the IRR.

The calculation of a project's internal rate of return can be either very simple or relatively complicated. As an example of straightforward solution, assume that a firm with a required rate of return of 10 percent is considering a project that involves an initial outlay of $45,555. If the investment is taken, the after-tax cash flows are expected to be $15,000 per annum over the project's four-year life. In this case, the internal rate of return is equal to *IRR* in the following equation:

$$\$45,555 = \frac{\$15,000}{(1 + IRR)^1} + \frac{\$15,000}{(1 + IRR)^2} + \frac{\$15,000}{(1 + IRR)^3} + \frac{\$15,000}{(1 + IRR)^4}$$

From our discussion of the present value of an annuity in Chapter 3, we know that this equation can be reduced to

$$\$45,555 = \$15,000 \left[\sum_{t=1}^{4} \frac{1}{(1 + IRR)^t} \right]$$

CALCULATOR SOLUTION[5]		
Data Input	Function Key	
45,555	+/−	INPUT
15,000		INPUT
15,000		INPUT
15,000		INPUT
15,000		INPUT
	EXIT	CALC

Function Key	Answer
IRR%	12.01

<hr/>

[5]If you are using an HP 17BII, first get to the CFLO menu and be certain that you have already cleared all prior data entries, selected both the "END MODE" and "one payment per year" (1P/YR), and turned the # times prompting (#T?) off. For further explanation see Appendix A.

Appendix E gives values for the $PVIFA_{i,n}$ for various combinations of i and n, which further reduces this equation to

$$\$45,555 = \$15,000 \ (PVIFA_{i, \ 4 \ yr})$$

Dividing both sides by $15,000, this becomes

$$3.037 = PVIFA_{i, \ 4 \ yr}$$

Hence, we are looking for $PVIFA_{i, \ 4 \ yr}$ of 3.037 in the four-year row of Appendix E. This value occurs when i equals 12 percent, which means that 12 percent is the internal rate of return for the investment. Therefore, since 12 percent is greater than the 10 percent required return, the project should be accepted.

Computing the IRR for Uneven Cash Flows

Unfortunately, while solving for the IRR is quite easy when using a financial calculator or spreadsheet, it can be solved directly in the tables only when the future after-tax net cash flows are in the form of an annuity or a single payment. With a calculator the process is simple, one need only key in the initial cash outlay, the cash flows and their timing, and press the *I* or *IRR* button. When a financial calculator is not available and these flows are in the form of an uneven series of flows, a trial-and-error approach is necessary. To do this, we first determine the present value of the future after-tax net cash flows using an arbitrary discount rate. If the present value of the future cash flows at this discount rate is larger than the initial outlay, the rate is increased; if it is smaller than the initial outlay, the discount rate is lowered; and the process begins again. This search routine is continued until the present value of the future after-tax cash flows is equal to the initial outlay. The interest rate that creates this situation is the internal rate of return. This is the same basic process that a financial calculator uses to calculate an IRR.

To illustrate the procedure, consider an investment proposal that requires an initial outlay of $3,817 and returns $1,000 at the end of year 1, $2,000 at the end of year 2, and $3,000 at the end of year 3. In this case, the internal rate of return must be determined using trial and error. This process is presented in Table 6–15, in which an arbitrarily selected discount rate of 15 percent was chosen to begin the process. The trial-and-error technique slowly centers in on the project's internal rate of return of 22 percent. The project's internal rate of return is then compared with the firm's required rate of return, and if the *IRR* is the larger, the project is accepted.

TABLE 6–15.
Computing IRR for Uneven Cash Flows Without a Financial Calculator

Initial outlay	−$3817
Flow year 1	1000
Flow year 2	2000
Flow year 3	3000

Solution:
  Step 1: Pick an arbitrary discount rate, and use it to determine the present value of the inflows.
  Step 2: Compare the present value of the inflows with the initial outlay; if they are equal you have determined the IRR.
  Step 3: If the present value of the inflows is larger (less than) than the initial outlay raise (lower) the discount rate.
  Step 4: Determine the present value of the inflows, and repeat Step 2.

TABLE 6–15. (cont.)

1. Try i = 15 percent:

	Net Cash Flows	Present Value Factor at 15 Percent	Present Value
Inflow year 1	$1000	.870	$ 870
Inflow year 2	2000	.756	1512
Inflow year 3	3000	.658	1974
Present value of inflows			$4356
Initial outlay			−$3817

2. Try i = 20 percent:

	Net Cash Flows	Present Value Factor at 20 Percent	Present Value
Inflow year 1	$1000	.833	$ 833
Inflow year 2	2000	.694	1388
Inflow year 3	3000	.579	1737
Present value of inflows			$3958
Initial outlay			−$3817

3. Try i = 22 percent:

	Net Cash Flows	Present Value Factor at 22 Percent	Present Value
Inflow year 1	$1000	.820	$ 820
Inflow year 2	2000	.672	1344
Inflow year 3	3000	.551	1653
Present value of inflows			$3817
Initial outlay			−$3817

CALCULATOR SOLUTION[6]

Data Input	Function Key
3817	+/− INPUT
1000	INPUT
2000	INPUT
3000	INPUT
	EXIT CALC

Function Key	Answer
IRR%	21.98

[6]If you are using an HP 17BII, first get to the CFLO menu and be certain that you have already cleared all prior data entries, selected both the "END MODE" and "one payment per year" (1P/YR), and turned the # times prompting (#T?) off. For further explanation see Appendix A.

EXAMPLE

A firm with a required rate of return of 10 percent is considering three investment proposals. Given the information in Table 6–16, management plans to calculate the internal rate of return for each project and determine which projects should be accepted.

	A	B	C
Initial outlay	$10,000	$10,000	$10,000
Inflow year 1	3,362	0	1,000
Inflow year 2	3,362	0	3,000
Inflow year 3	3,362	0	6,000
Inflow year 4	3,362	13,605	7,000
	13.00	8.00	19.04

TABLE 6–16.
Three IRR Investment Proposal Examples

Because project A is an annuity, we can easily calculate its internal rate of return by determining the $PVIFA_{i,\,4\,yr}$ necessary to equate the present value of the future cash flows with the initial outlay. This computation is done as follows:

$$IO = ACF_t\left[\sum_{t=1}^{n}\frac{1}{(1 + IRR)^t}\right]$$

$$\$10,000 = \$3362\left[\sum_{t=1}^{4}\frac{1}{(1 + IRR)^t}\right]$$

$$\$10,000 = \$3362\,(PVIFA_{i,\,4\,yr})$$

$$2.974 = (PVIFA_{i,\,4\,yr})$$

We are looking for a $PVIFA_{i, 4\ yr}$ of 2.974, in the four-year row of Appendix E, which occurs in the $i = 13$ percent column. Thus, 13 percent is the internal rate of return. Because this rate is greater than the firm's required rate of return of 10 percent, the project should be accepted.

Project B involves a single future cash flow of $13,605, resulting from an initial outlay of $10,000; thus, its internal rate of return can be determined directly from the present-value table in Appendix C as follows:

$$IO = ACF_t\left[\frac{1}{(1 + IRR)^t}\right]$$

$$\$10,000 = \$13,605\left[\frac{1}{(1 + IRR)^4}\right]$$

$$\$10,000 = \$13,605(PVIF_{i, 4\ yr})$$

$$.735 = (PVIF_{i, 4\ yr})$$

This tells us that we should look for a $PVIF_{i, 4\ yr}$ of .735 in the four-year row of Appendix C, which occurs in the $i = 8$ percent column. We may therefore conclude that 8 percent is the internal rate of return. Because this rate is less than the firm's required rate of return of 10 percent, project B should be rejected.

TABLE 6–17.
Computing the IRR
for Project C

1. Try $i = 15$ percent:

	Net Cash Flows	Present Value Factor at 15 Percent	Present Value
Inflow year 1	$1,000	.870	$ 870
Inflow year 2	3,000	.756	2,268
Inflow year 3	6,000	.658	3,948
Inflow year 4	7,000	.572	4,004
Present value of inflows			$11,090
Initial outlay			$10,000

2. Try $i = 20$ percent:

	Net Cash Flows	Present Value Factor at 20 Percent	Present Value
Inflow year 1	$1,000	.833	$ 833
Inflow year 2	3,000	.694	2,082
Inflow year 3	6,000	.579	3,474
Inflow year 4	7,000	.482	3,374
Present value of inflows			$ 9,763
Initial outlay			$10,000

3. Try $i = 19$ percent:

	Net Cash Flows	Present Value Factor at 19 Percent	Present Value
Inflow year 1	$1,000	.840	$ 840
Inflow year 2	3,000	.706	2,118
Inflow year 3	6,000	.593	3,558
Inflow year 4	7,000	.499	3,493
Present value of inflows			$10,009
Initial outlay			$10,000

The uneven nature of the future cash flows associated with project C necessitates the use of the trial-and-error method. The internal rate of return for project C is equal to the value of IRR in the following equation:

$$\$10{,}000 = \frac{\$1000}{(1 + IRR)^1} + \frac{\$3000}{(1 + IRR)^2} + \frac{\$6000}{(1 + IRR)^3} + \frac{\$7000}{(1 + IRR)^4} \quad \textbf{(6-5)}$$

Arbitrarily selecting a discount rate of 15 percent and substituting it into equation (6–5) for IRR reduces the right-hand side of the equation to $11,090, as shown in Table 6–17. Therefore, because the present value of the future cash flows is larger than the initial outlay, we must raise the discount rate to find the project's internal rate of return. Substituting 20 percent for the discount rate, the right-hand side of equation (6–5) now becomes $9,763. As this is less than the initial outlay of $10,000, we must now decrease the discount rate. In other words, we know that the internal rate of return for this project is between 15 and 20 percent. Because the present value of the future flows discounted back to present at 20 percent was only $237 too low, a discount rate of 19 percent is selected. As shown in Table 6–17, a discount rate of 19 percent reduces the present value of the future inflows down to $10,009, which is approximately the same as the initial outlay. Consequently, project C's internal rate of return is approximately 19 percent.[8] Because the internal rate of return is greater than the firm's required rate of return of 10 percent, this investment should be accepted. ■

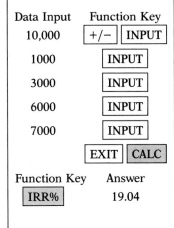

CALCULATOR SOLUTION[7]

Data Input	Function Key
10,000	+/– INPUT
1000	INPUT
3000	INPUT
6000	INPUT
7000	INPUT
	EXIT CALC

Function Key	Answer
IRR%	19.04

[7]If you are using an HP 17BII, first get to the CFLO menu and be certain that you have already cleared all prior data entries, selected both the "END MODE" and "one payment per year" (1P/YR), and turned the # times prompting (#T?) off. For further explanation see Appendix A.

Complications with IRR: Multiple Rates of Return

Although any project can have only one NPV and one PI, a single project under certain circumstances can have more than one IRR. The reason for this can be traced to the calculations involved in determining the IRR. Equation (6–4) states that the IRR is the discount rate that equates the present value of the project's future net cash flows with the project's initial outlay:

$$IO = \sum_{t=1}^{n} \frac{ACF_t}{(1 + IRR)^t} \quad \textbf{(6-4)}$$

However, because equation (6–4) is a polynomial of a degree n, it has n solutions. Now if the initial outlay (IO) is the only negative cash flow and all the annual after-tax cash flows (ACF_t) are positive, then all but one of these n solutions is either a negative or imaginary number and there is no problem. But problems occur when there are sign reversals in the cash flow stream; in fact there can be as many solutions as there are sign reversals. Thus, a normal pattern with a negative initial outlay and positive annual after-tax cash flows (−, +, +, +, . . . , +) after that has only one sign reversal, hence only one positive IRR. However, a pattern with more than one sign reversal can have more than one IRR. Consider, for example, the following pattern of cash flows.[9]

---

[8]If desired, the actual rate can be more precisely approximated through interpolation as follows:

		Discount Rate	Present Value
		19%	$10,009
		20	9,763
	Difference	1%	$ 246

Proportion $9 is $= \frac{\$9}{\$246} = .0366\%$
of $246

$19\% + .0366\% = 19.0366\%$

---

[9]This example is taken from James H. Lorie and Leonard J. Savage, "Three Problems in Rationing Capital," *Journal of Business* 28 (October 1955), pp. 229–39.

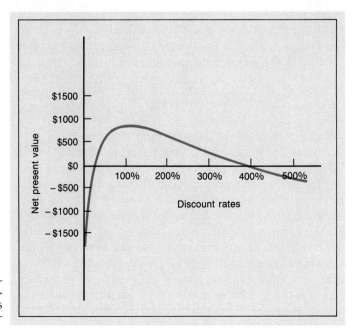

FIGURE 6–2.
Multiple IRRs

	After-Tax Cash Flow
Initial outlay	−$ 1,600
Year 1	+$10,000
Year 2	−$10,000

In this pattern of cash flows there are two sign reversals, from −$1,600 to + $10,000 and then from + $10,000 to −$10,000, so there can be as many as two positive IRRs that will make the present value of the future cash flows equal to the initial outlay. In fact two internal rates of return solve this problem, 25 and 400 percent. Graphically what we are solving for is the discount rate that makes the project's NPV equal to zero; as Figure 6–2 illustrates, this occurs twice.

Which solution is correct? The answer is that neither solution is valid. Although each fits the definition of IRR, neither provides any insight into the true project returns. In summary, when there is more than one sign reversal in the cash flow stream, the possibility of multiple IRRs exists, and the normal interpretation of the IRR loses its meaning.

Discounted Cash Flow Criteria: Comprehensive Example

To demonstrate further the computations for the discounted cash flow techniques, assume that a manufacturing firm in the electronic components field is in the 34 percent marginal tax bracket with a 15 percent required rate of return or cost of capital. Management is considering replacing a hand-operated assembly machine with a fully automated assembly operation. Given the information in Table 6–18, we want to determine the cash flows associated with this proposal, the project's net present value, profitability index, and internal rate of return, and then to apply the appropriate decision criteria.

First, the initial outlay is determined to be $44,680, as reflected in Table 6–19. Next, the differential cash flows over the project's life are calculated as shown in Table 6–20, yielding an estimated $15,008 cash flow per annum. In making these computations, the incremental change in depreciation was determined by first calculating the original depreciable value, which is equal to

TABLE 6–18.
Comprehensive Capital
Budgeting Example

Existing situation:	One part-time operator—salary $12,000
	Variable overtime—$1000 per year
	Fringe benefits—$1000 per year
	Cost of defects—$6000 per year
	Current book value—$10,000
	Expected life—15 years
	Expected salvage value—$0
	Age—10 years
	Annual depreciation—$2000 per year
	Current salvage value of old machine—$12,000
	Annual maintenance—$0
	Marginal tax rate—34 percent
	Required rate of return—15 percent
Proposed situation:	Fully automated operation—no operator necessary
	Cost of machine—$50,000
	Shipping fee—$1000
	Installation costs—$5000
	Expected economic life—5 years
	Depreciation method—simplified straight line over 5 years
	Salvage value after 5 years—$0
	Annual maintenance—$1000
	Cost of defects—$1000

TABLE 6–19.
Calculation of Initial Outlay
for Comprehensive Example

Outflows:	
Cost of new machine	$50,000
Shipping fee	1,000
Installation cost	5,000
Increased taxes on sale of old machine ($12,000 − $10,000) (.34)	680
Inflows:	
Salvage value—old machine	−12,000
Net initial outlay	$44,680

	Book Profit	Cash Flow
Savings: Reduced salary	$12,000	$12,000
Reduced variable overtime	1,000	1,000
Reduced fringe benefits	1,000	1,000
Reduced defects ($6,000–$1,000)	5,000	5,000
Costs: Increased maintenance expense	−1,000	−1,000
Increased depreciation expense ($11,200–$2,000)	−9,200	
Net savings before taxes	$ 8,800	$18,000
Taxes (34%)	−2,992 ⟶	−2,992
Net cash flow after taxes		$15,008

the cost of the new machine ($50,000) plus any expense charges necessary to get the new machine in operating order (shipping fee of $1,000 plus the installation fee of $5,000). This depreciable amount was then divided by five years. The annual depreciation lost with the sale of the old machine was then subtracted out ($10,000/5 = $2,000 per year for the old machine's remaining five years of life). Once the change in taxes is determined from the incremental change in book profit, it is subtracted from the net cash flow savings before taxes, yielding the $15,008 net cash flow after taxes.

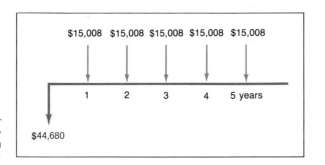

FIGURE 6–3.
Cash Flow Diagram

Finally, the terminal cash flow associated with the project has to be determined. In this case, since the new machine is expected to have a zero salvage value, there will be no terminal cash flow. The cash flow diagram associated with this project is shown in Figure 6–3.

The net present value for this project is calculated below:

$$NPV = \sum_{t=1}^{n} \frac{ACF_t}{(1+k)^t} - IO \tag{6-2}$$

$$= \sum_{t=1}^{5} \frac{\$15,008}{(1+.15)^t} - \$44,680$$

$$= \$15,008 \, (PVIFA_{15\%,\,5\,yr}) - \$44,680$$

$$= \$15,008 \, (3.352) - \$44,680$$

$$= \$50,307 - \$44,680$$

$$= \$5627$$

Because its net present value is greater than zero, the project should be accepted. The profitability index, which gives a measure of relative desirability of a project, is calculated as follows:

$$PI = \frac{\displaystyle\sum_{t=1}^{n} \frac{ACF_t}{(1+k)^t}}{IO} \tag{6-3}$$

$$= \frac{\$50,307}{\$44,680}$$

$$= 1.13$$

Because the project's PI is greater than 1, the project should be accepted.

The internal rate of return can be determined directly from the present-value-of-an-annuity table, as follows:

$$IO = \sum_{t=1}^{n} \frac{ACF_t}{(1+IRR)^t} \tag{6-4}$$

$$\$44,680 = \$15,008 \, (PVIFA_{i,\,5\,yr})$$

$$2.977 = PVIFA_{i,\,5\,yr}$$

Looking for the value of the $PVIFA_{i,\,5\,yr}$ in the 5-year row of the table in Appendix D, we find that the value of 2.977 occurs between the 20 percent column (2.991) and the 21 percent column (2.926). As a result, the project's internal rate of return is between 20 and 21 percent, and the project should be accepted.

Applying the decision criteria to this example, we find that each of them indicates the project should be accepted, as the net present value is positive, the

ETHICS IN FINANCIAL MANAGEMENT

Bad Apple for Baby

It's a widely held, but hard to prove belief that a company gains because it is perceived as more socially responsive than its competitors. Over the years, the three major manufacturers of baby food—Gerber Products, Beech-Nut Nutrition and H. J. Heinz—had, with almost equal success, gone out of their way to build an image of respectability.

Theirs is an almost perfect zero-sum business. They know, at any given time, how many babies are being born. They all pay roughly the same price for their commodities, and their manufacturing and distribution costs are almost identical. So how does one company gain a market share edge over another, especially in a stagnant or declining market?

The answer for Beech-Nut was to sell a cheaper, adulterated product. Beginning in 1977, the company began buying a chemical concoction, made up mostly of sugar and water, and labeling it as apple juice. Sales of that product brought Beech-Nut an estimated $60 million between 1977 and 1982, while reducing material costs about $250,000 annually.

When various investigators tried to do something about it, the company stonewalled. Among other things, they shipped the bogus juice out of a plant in New York to Puerto Rico, to put it beyond the jurisdiction of federal investigators, and they even offered the juice as a give-away to reduce their stocks after they were finally forced to discontinue selling it.

In the end, the company pleaded guilty to 215 counts of introducing adulterated food into commerce and violating the Federal Food Drug and Cosmetic Act. The FDA fined Beech-Nut $2 million.

In addition, Beech-Nut's president, Neils Hoyvald, and its vice president of operations, John Lavery, were found guilty of similar charges. Each faces a year and one day in jail and a $100,000 fine. Both are now out on appeal on a jurisdiction technicality.

Why did they do it? The Fort Washington, Pa.-based company will not comment. But perhaps some portion of motive can be inferred from a report Hoyvald wrote to Nestle, the company which had acquired Beech-Nut in the midst of his coverup. "It is our feeling that we can report safely now that the apple juice recall has been completed. If the recall had been effectuated in early June [when the FDA had first ordered it], over 700,000 cases in inventory would have been affected . . . due to our many delays, we were only faced with having to destroy 20,000 cases."

One thing is clear: Two executives of a company with an excellent reputation breached a trust and did their company harm.

Since 1987, when the case was brought to a close, Beech-Nut's share of the overall baby food market has fallen from 19.1% to 15.8%. So what was gained in the past has been lost in the present, and perhaps for the future as well.

Source: Stephen Kindel, "Bad Apple for Baby," *Financial World* June 27, 1989, p. 48.

profitability index is greater than 1.0, and the internal rate of return is greater than the firm's required rate of return of 15 percent.

Ethics in Capital Budgeting

Although it may not seem obvious, ethics has a role in capital budgeting. Beech-Nut provides an example of how these rules have been violated in the past and what the consequences can be. No doubt this project appeared to have a positive net present value associated with it, but in fact, it cost Beech-Nut tremendously. The *Ethics in Financial Management* insert, "Bad Apple for Baby," provides a narrative of what occurred.

A Glance at Actual Capital-Budgeting Practices

During the past 35 years the popularity of each of the capital budgeting methods has shifted rather dramatically. In the 1950s the payback period and AROR methods dominated capital budgeting, but through the 1960s and 1970s the discounted cash flow decision techniques slowly displaced the nondiscounted

TABLE 6–21.
Past Surveys of Capital-Budgeting Practices—Percent of Respondents Using Each Technique

Capital-Budgeting Technique	Klammer, 1959	Klammer, 1964	Klammer, 1970	Petty et al., 1972	Kim and Farragher, 1975	Gitman and Forrester, 1977	Kim and Farragher, 1979	Kim, Crick, and Kim, 1986
Primary method:								
NPV	5%	15%	27%	15%	26%	13%	19%	21%
IRR	8	17	30	41	37	53	49	49
Payback	34	24	12	11	15	9	12	19
AROR	34	30	26	31	10	25	8	8
Secondary method:								
NPV	2%	3%	7%	14%	7%	28%	8%	24%
IRR	1	2	6	19	7	14	8	15
Payback	18	21	32	37	33	44	39	35
AROR	4	9	11	24	3	14	3	19

Sources:
Thomas Klammer, "Empirical Evidence of the Adoption of Sophisticated Capital Budgeting Techniques," *Journal of Business* (July 1972), pp. 387–397; J. William Petty, David F. Scott, Jr., and Monroe M. Bird, "The Capital Expenditure Decision-Making Process of Large Corporations," *Engineering Economist* (Spring 1975), pp. 159–172; S. H. Kim and E. J. Farragher, "Capital Budgeting Practices in Large Industrial Firms," *Baylor Business Studies* (November 1976), pp. 19–25; Lawrence J. Gitman and John R. Forrester, Jr., "Forecasting and Evaluation Practices and Performance: A Survey of Capital Budgeting," *Financial Management* (Fall 1977), pp. 66–71; S. H. Kim and E. J. Farragher, "Current Capital Budgeting Practices," *Management Accounting* (June 1981), pp. 26–30; Suk H. Kim, T. Crick, and Sesung H. Kim, "Do Executives Practice What Academics Preach?" *Management Accounting* (November 1986), pp. 49–52.

techniques. This movement from the payback period and AROR to net present value and the internal rate of return is shown in Table 6–21, which indicates the growth in popularity of these techniques as reflected in surveys of practices over the years. Interestingly, although most firms use the NPV and IRR as their primary techniques, most firms also use the payback period as a secondary decision method for capital budgeting. In a sense they are using the payback period to control for risk. The logic behind this is that because the payback period dramatically emphasizes early cash flows, which are presumably more certain—that is, have less risk—than cash flows that occur later in a project's life, its use will lead to projects with more certain cash flows.

A reliance on the payback period came out even more dramatically in a recent study of the capital-budgeting practices of 12 large manufacturing firms.[11] Information for this study was gathered from interviews over one to three days in addition to an examination of the records of about 400 projects. This study revealed several points of interest. First, firms were typically found to categorize capital investments as mandatory (regulations and contracts, capitalized maintenance, replacement of antiquated equipment, product quality) or discretionary (expanded markets, new businesses, cost cutting), with the decision-making process being different for mandatory and discretionary projects. Second, it was found that the decision-making process was different for projects of differing size. In fact, approval authority tended to rest in different locations, depending upon the size of the project. Table 6–22 provides the typical levels of approval authority.

The study also showed that while the discounted cash flow methods are used at most firms, the simple payback criterion was the measure relied on primarily in one-third of the firms examined. The use of the payback period seemed to be even more common for smaller projects, with firms severely simplifying the discounted cash flow analysis or relying primarily on the

[11]Marc Ross, "Capital Budgeting Practices of Twelve Large Manufacturers," *Financial Management*, 15 (Winter 1986), pp. 15–22.

Project Size	Typical Boundaries	*Primary Decision Site*
Very small	Up to $100,000	Plant
Small	$100,000 to $1,000,000	Division
Medium	$1 million to $10 million	Corporate investment committee
Large	Over $10 million	CEO & board

TABLE 6–22.
Project Size and
Decision-Making Authority

payback period. Thus, although discounted cash flow decision techniques have become more widely accepted, their use depends to an extent on the size of the project and where within the firm the decision is being made.

SUMMARY

The process of capital budgeting involves decision making with respect to investment in fixed assets. Specifically, we examine the measurement of incremental cash flows associated with a firm's investment proposals and the evaluation of those proposals. In measuring cash flows we focus on the **incremental** or differential **after-tax cash flows** attributed to the investment proposal. In general, a project's cash flows fall into one of three categories: (1) the initial outlay, (2) the differential flows over the project's life, (3) the terminal cash flow. A summary of the typical entries in each of these categories appears in Table 6–7.

We examine five commonly used criteria for determining the acceptance or rejection of capital-budgeting proposals. The first two methods, the payback period and accounting rate of return, are nondiscounted and do not incorporate the time value of money into their calculations. The discounted methods, the net present value, profitability index, and internal rate of return, do account for the time value of money. These methods are summarized in Table 6–23.

Nondiscounted Cash Flow Methods

1. Payback period = number of years required to recapture the initial investment

Accept if payback < maximum acceptable payback period
Reject if payback > maximum acceptable payback period

Advantages:
1. Uses cash flows.
2. Is easy to calculate and understand.
3. May be used as rough screening device.

Disadvantages:
1. Ignores the time value of money.
2. Ignores cash flows occurring after the payback period.

2. $$\text{Accounting rate of return} = \frac{\sum_{t=1}^{n} (\text{accounting profit after tax}_t)/n}{(\text{initial investment} + \text{expected salvage value})/2}$$

where n = project's expected life

Accept if AROR > minimum acceptable rate of return
Reject if AROR < minimum acceptable rate of return

Advantages:
1. Involves familiar, easily accessible terms.
2. Is easy to calculate and understand.

Disadvantages:
1. Ignores the time value of money.
2. Uses accounting profits rather than cash flows.

TABLE 6–23.
Capital-Budgeting Criteria

TABLE 6–23.
(Cont.)

Discounted Cash Flow Methods

3. Net present value = present value of the annual cash flows after tax less the investment's initial outlay

$$NPV = \sum_{t=1}^{n} \frac{ACF_t}{(1 + k)^t} - IO$$

where ACF_t = the annual after-tax cash flow in time period t (this can take on either positive or negative values)

k = the appropriate discount rate, that is, the required rate of return or the cost of capital[a]

IO = the initial cash outlay

n = the project's expected life

Accept if $NPV \geq 0.0$
Reject if $NPV < 0.0$

Advantages:
1. Uses cash flows.
2. Recognizes the time value of money.
3. Is consistent with the firm goal of shareholder wealth maximization.

Disadvantages:
1. Requires detailed long-term forecasts of the incremental benefits and costs.

4. Profitability index = the ratio of the present value of the future net cash flows to the initial outlay

$$PI = \frac{\sum_{t=1}^{n} \frac{ACF_t}{(1 + k)^t}}{IO}$$

Accept if $PI \geq 1.0$
Reject if $PI < 1.0$

Advantages:
1. Uses cash flows.
2. Recognizes the time value of money.
3. Is consistent with the firm goal of shareholder wealth maximization.

Disadvantages:
1. Requires detailed long-term forecasts of the incremental benefits and costs.

5. Internal rate of return = the discount rate that equates the present value of the project's future net cash flows with the project's initial outlay

$$IO = \sum_{t=1}^{n} \frac{ACF_t}{(1 + IRR)^t}$$

where IRR = the project's internal rate of return

Accept if $IRR \geq$ required rate of return
Reject if $IRR <$ required rate of return

Advantages:
1. Uses cash flows.
2. Recognizes the time value of money.

Disadvantages:
1. Requires detailed long-term forecasts of the incremental benefits and costs.
2. Can involve tedious calculations.
3. Possibility of multiple IRRs.

[a]The cost of capital is discussed in Chapter 8.

STUDY QUESTIONS

6-1. Why is the capital-budgeting decision such an important process? Why are capital-budgeting errors so costly?

6-2. Why do we focus on cash flows rather than accounting profits in making our capital-budgeting decisions? Why are we interested only in incremental cash flows rather than total cash flows?

6-3. If depreciation is not a cash flow expense, does it affect the level of cash flows from a project in any way?

6-4. If a project requires additional investment in working capital, how should this be treated in calculating cash flows?

6-5. How do sunk costs affect the determination of cash flows associated with an investment proposal?

6-6. What are the criticisms of the use of the payback period as a capital-budgeting technique? What are its advantages? Why is it so frequently used?

6-7. In some countries, expropriation of foreign investments is a common practice. If you were considering an investment in one of those countries, would the use of the payback period criterion seem more reasonable than it otherwise might? Why?

6-8. What are the criticisms of the use of the accounting rate of return as a capital-budgeting technique? What are its advantages?

6-9. Briefly compare and contrast the three discounted cash flow criteria. What are the advantages and disadvantages of the use of each of these methods?

SELF-TEST PROBLEMS

ST-1. The Scotty Gator Corporation of Meadville, Pa., maker of Scotty's electronic components, is considering replacing one of its current hand-operated assembly machines with a new fully automated machine. This replacement would mean the elimination of one employee, generating salary and benefit savings. Given the following information, determine the cash flows associated with this replacement.

Existing situation: One full-time machine operator—salary and benefits, $25,000 per year
Cost of maintenance—$2000 per year
Cost of defects—$6000
Original depreciable value of old machine—$50,000
Annual depreciation—$5000 per year
Expected life—10 years
Age—five years old
Expected salvage value in five years—$0
Current salvage value—$5000
Marginal tax rate—34 percent

Proposed situation: Fully automated machine
Cost of machine—$60,000
Installation fee—$3000
Shipping fee—$3000
Cost of maintenance—$3000 per year
Cost of defects—$3000 per year
Expected life—five years
Salvage value—$20,000
Depreciation method—simplified straight-line method over five years

ST-2. Given the cash flow information in problem ST-1 and a required rate of return of 15 percent, complete the following for the new, fully automated machine:
a. Payback period
b. Net present value
c. Profitability index
d. Internal rate of return
Should this project be accepted?

STUDY PROBLEMS (SET A)

6-1A. (*Capital Gains Tax*) The J. Harris Corporation is considering selling one of its old assembly machines. The machine, purchased for $30,000 five years ago, had an expected life of 10 years and an expected salvage value of zero. Assume Harris uses simplified straight-line depreciation, creating depreciation of $3,000 per year, and could sell this old machine for $35,000. Also assume a 34 percent marginal tax rate.

a. What would be the taxes associated with this sale?

b. If the old machine were sold for $25,000, what would be the taxes associated with this sale?

c. If the old machine were sold for $15,000, what would be the taxes associated with this sale?

d. If the old machine were sold for $12,000, what would be the taxes associated with this sale?

6–2A. (*Cash Flow Calculations*) The Winky Corporation, maker of electronic components, is considering replacing a hand-operated machine used in the manufacture of electronic components with a new fully automated machine. Given the following information, determine the cash flows associated with this replacement.

Existing situation:	Two full-time machine operators—salaries $10,000 each per year
	Cost of maintenance—$5000 per year
	Cost of defects—$5000
	Original cost of old machine—$30,000
	Expected life—10 years
	Age—five years old
	Expected salvage value—$0
	Depreciation method—simplified straight-line over 10 years, $3000 per year
	Current salvage value—$10,000
	Marginal tax rate—34 percent
Proposed situation:	Fully automated machine
	Cost of machine—$55,000
	Installation fee—$5000
	Cost of maintenance—$6000 per year
	Cost of defects—$2000 per year
	Expected life—five years
	Salvage value—$0
	Depreciation method—simplified straight-line method over five years

6–3A. (*Capital-Budgeting Calculation*) Given the cash flow information in problem 6–2A and a required rate of return of 15 percent, compute the following for the automated machine:

a. Payback period

b. Net present value

c. Profitability index

d. Internal rate of return

Should this project be accepted?

6–4A. (*AROR Calculation*) Two mutually exclusive projects are being evaluated using the accounting rate of return. Each project has an initial cost of $20,000 and a salvage value of $4,000 after six years. Given the following information:

	Annual Accounting Profits after Tax	
Year	Project A	Project B
1	$ 2,000	$10,000
2	2,000	10,000
3	2,000	10,000
4	13,000	5,000
5	13,000	5,000
6	14,000	5,000

a. Determine each project's AROR.

b. Which project should be selected, using this criterion? Would you support that recommendation? Why or why not?

6–5A. (*IRR Calculation*) Determine the internal rate of return on the following projects:

a. An initial outlay of $10,000 resulting in a single cash flow of $17,182 after 8 years

b. An initial outlay of $10,000 resulting in a single cash flow of $48,077 after 10 years

    c. An initial outlay of $10,000 resulting in a single cash flow of $114,943 after 20 years

    d. An initial outlay of $10,000 resulting in a single cash flow of $13,680 after 3 years

6–6A. (*IRR Calculation*) Determine the internal rate of return on the following projects:

    a. An initial outlay of $10,000 resulting in a cash flow of $1,993 at the end of each year for the next 10 years

    b. An initial outlay of $10,000 resulting in a cash flow of $2,054 at the end of each year for the next 20 years

    c. An initial outlay of $10,000 resulting in a cash flow of $1,193 at the end of each year for the next 12 years

    d. An initial outlay of $10,000 resulting in a cash flow of $2,843 at the end of each year for the next 5 years

6–7A. (*IRR Calculation*) Determine the internal rate of return to the nearest percent on the following projects:

    a. An initial outlay of $10,000 resulting in a cash flow of $2,000 at the end of year 1, $5,000 at the end of year 2, and $8,000 at the end of year 3

    b. An initial outlay of $10,000 resulting in a cash flow of $8,000 at the end of year 1, $5,000 at the end of year 2, and $2,000 at the end of year 3

    c. An initial outlay of $10,000 resulting in a cash flow of $2,000 at the end of years 1 through 5 and $5,000 at the end of year 6

6–8A. (*New Project Analysis*) The Chung Chemical Corporation is considering the purchase of a chemical analysis machine. Although the machine being considered will not produce any increase in sales revenues, it will result in before-tax the reduction of labor costs by $35,000 per year. The machine has a purchase price of $100,000, and it would cost an additional $5,000 to properly install this machine. In addition, to properly operate this machine, inventory must be increased by $5,000. This machine has an expected life of 10 years, after which it will have no salvage value. Also, assume simplified straight-line depreciation and that this machine is being depreciated down to zero, a 34 percent marginal tax rate, and a required rate of return of 15 percent.

    a. What is the initial outlay associated with this project?

    b. What are the annual after-tax cash flows associated with this project, for years 1 through 9?

    c. What is the terminal cash flow in year 10 (i.e., what is the annual after-tax cash flow in year 10 plus any additional cash flows associated with termination of the project)?

    d. Should this machine be purchased?

6–9A. (*New Project Analysis*) Raymobile Motors is considering the purchase of a new production machine for $500,000. Although the purchase of this machine will not produce any increase in sales revenues, it will result in a before-tax reduction of labor costs by $150,000 per year. To operate this machine properly, workers would have to go through a brief training session that would cost $25,000. In addition, it would cost $5,000 to install this machine properly. Also, because this machine is extremely efficient, its purchase would necessitate an increase in inventory of $30,000. This machine has an expected life of 10 years, after which it will have no salvage value. Assume simplified straight-line depreciation and that this machine is being depreciated down to zero, a 34 percent marginal tax rate, and a required rate of return of 15 percent.

    a. What is the initial outlay associated with this project?

    b. What are the annual after-tax cash flows associated with this project, for years 1 through 9?

    c. What is the terminal cash flow in year 10 (i.e., what is the annual after-tax cash flow in year 10 plus any additional cash flows associated with termination of the project)?

    d. Should this machine be purchased?

6–10A. (*New Project Analysis*) Garcia's Truckin' Inc. is considering the purchase of a new production machine for $200,000. Although the purchase of this machine will not produce any increase in sales revenues, it will result in a reduction before-tax of labor costs by $50,000 per year. To operate this machine properly, workers would have to go through a brief training session that would cost $5,000. In addition, it would cost $5,000 to install this machine properly. Also, because this machine is extremely efficient, its purchase would necessitate an increase in inventory of $20,000. This machine has an expected life of 10 years, after which it will have no salvage value. Finally, to purchase the new machine, it appears that the firm would have to borrow $100,000 at 8 percent interest from its local bank, resulting in additional interest payments of $8,000 per year. Assume simplified straight-line depreciation and that this machine is being depreciated down to zero, a 34 percent marginal tax rate, and a required rate of return of 10 percent.

   a. What is the initial outlay associated with this project?
   b. What are the annual after-tax cash flows associated with this project, for years 1 through 9?
   c. What is the terminal cash flow in year 10 (i.e., what is the annual after-tax cash flow in year 10 plus any additional cash flows associated with termination of the project)?
   d. Should this machine be purchased?

6-11A. (*Cash Flow—Capital-Budgeting Calculation*) The C. Duncan Chemical Corporation is considering replacing one of its machines with a new, more efficient machine. The old machine presently has a book value of $100,000 and could be sold for $60,000. The old machine is being depreciated on a simplified straight-line basis down to a salvage value of zero over the next five years, generating depreciation of $20,000 per year. The replacement machine would cost $300,000, and have an expected life of five years, after which it could be sold for $50,000. Because of reductions in defects and material savings, the new machine would produce cash benefits of $90,000 per year before depreciation and taxes. Assuming simplified straight-line depreciation and the replacement machine is being depreciated down to zero for tax purposes even though it can be sold at termination for $50,000, a 34 percent marginal tax rate, and a required rate of return of 15 percent, find:
   a. The payback period
   b. The net present value
   c. The profitability index
   d. The internal rate of return

6-12A. (*Cash Flow—Capital-Budgeting Calculation*) The Sumitomo Chemical Corporation is considering replacing a five-year-old machine that originally cost $50,000, presently has a book value of $25,000, and could be sold for $60,000. This machine is currently being depreciated using the simplified straight-line method down to a terminal value of zero over the next five years, generating depreciation of $5,000 per year. The replacement machine would cost $125,000, and have a five-year expected life over which it would be depreciated down using the simplified straight-line method and have no salvage value at the end of five years. The new machine would produce savings before depreciation and taxes of $45,000 per year. Assuming a 34 percent marginal tax rate and a required rate of return of 10 percent, calculate
   a. The payback period
   b. The net present value
   c. The profitability index
   d. The internal rate of return

6-13A. (*Cash Flow—Capital-Budgeting Calculation*) The Mad Dog Hansen Electronic Components Corporation is considering replacing a 10-year-old machine that originally cost $30,000, has a current book value of $10,000 with five years of expected life left, and is being depreciated using the simplified straight-line method over its 15-year expected life down to a terminal value of zero in five years, generating depreciation of $2,000 per year. The replacement machine being considered would cost $80,000 and have a five-year expected life over which it would be depreciated using the simplified straight-line method down to zero. At termination in five years the new machine would have a salvage value of $40,000. Material efficiencies resulting from the replacement would result in savings of $30,000 per year before depreciation and taxes. Currently, the old machine could be sold for $15,000. Assuming simplified straight-line depreciation, a 34 percent marginal tax rate, and a required rate of return of 20 percent, calculate
   a. The payback period
   b. The net present value
   c. The profitability index
   d. The internal rate of return

6-14A. (*NPV PI and IRR Calculations*) Fijisawa, Inc., is considering a major expansion of its product line and has estimated the following cash flows associated with such an expansion. The initial outlay associated with the expansion would be $1,950,000 and the project would generate incremental after-tax cash flows of $450,000 per year for six years. The appropriate required rate of return is 9 percent.
   a. Calculate the net present value.
   b. Calculate the profitability index.
   c. Calculate the internal rate of return.
   d. Should this project be accepted?

6–15A. (*Internal Rate of Return Calculations*) Given the following cash flows, determine the internal rate of return for projects A, B, and C.

	Project A	Project B	Project C
Initial Investment:	$50,000	$100,000	$450,000
Cash Inflows:			
Year 1	$10,000	25,000	200,000
Year 2	15,000	25,000	200,000
Year 3	20,000	25,000	200,000
Year 4	25,000	25,000	—
Year 5	30,000	25,000	—

6–16A. (*NPV with Varying Required Rates of Return*) Big Steve's, makers of swizzle sticks, is considering the purchase of a new plastic stamping machine. This investment requires an initial outlay of $100,000 and will generate after-tax cash inflows of $18,000 per year for 10 years. For each of the listed required rates of return, determine the project's net present value.
  a. The required rate of return is 10 percent.
  b. The required rate of return is 15 percent.
  c. Would the project be accepted under part (a) or (b)?
  d. What is this project's internal rate of return?

6–17A. (*Comprehensive Cash Flow—Capital-Budgeting Calculation*) The L. Knutson Company, a manufacturer of electronic components in the 34 percent marginal tax bracket, is considering the purchase of a new fully automated machine to replace an older, manually operated one. The machine being replaced, now five years old, originally had an expected life of 10 years, was being depreciated using the simplified straight-line method from $20,000 down to zero, thus generating $2,000 in depreciation per year, and could be sold for $25,000. The old machine took one operator who earned $15,000 per year in salary and $2,000 per year in fringe benefits. The annual costs of maintenance and defects associated with the old machine were $7,000 and $3,000, respectively. The replacement machine being considered had a purchase price of $50,000, a salvage value after five years of $10,000, and would be depreciated over five years using the simplified straight-line depreciation method down to zero. To get the automated machine in running order, there would be a $3,000 shipping fee and a $2,000 installation charge. In addition, because the new machine would work faster than the old one, investment in raw materials and goods-in-process inventories would need to be increased by a total of $5,000. The annual costs of maintenance and defects on the new machine would be $2,000 and $4,000, respectively. The new machine also requires maintenance workers to be specially trained; fortunately, a similar machine was purchased three months ago, and at that time the maintenance workers went through the $5,000 training program needed to familiarize themselves with the new equipment. The firm's management is uncertain whether or not to charge half of this $5,000 training fee toward the new project. Finally, to purchase the new machine, it appears the firm would have to borrow an additional $20,000 at 10 percent interest from its local bank, resulting in additional interest payments of $2,000 per year. The required rate of return on projects of this kind is 20 percent.
  a. What is the project's initial outlay?
  b. What are the differential cash flows over the project's life?
  c. What is the terminal cash flow?
  d. Draw a cash flow diagram for this project.
  e. If the firm requires a minimum payback period on projects of this type of three years, should this project be accepted?
  f. Calculate the project's AROR.
  g. What is its net present value?
  h. What is its profitability index?
  i. What is its internal rate of return?
  j. Should the project be accepted? Why or why not?

6–18A. (*Cash Flow—Capital-Budgeting Calculation*) The Beamer Corp. is considering expanding its highly technical construction facilities. The construction will take a total of four years until it is completed and ready for operation. The following data and assumptions describe the proposed expansion:
  a. To make this expansion feasible, R&D expenditures of $200,000 must be made

immediately to ensure that the construction facilities are competitively efficient ($t = 0$).

b. At the end of the first year the land will be purchased and construction on stage 1 of the facilities will begin, involving a cash outflow of $150,000 for the land and $300,000 for the construction facilities.

c. Stage 2 of the construction will involve a $300,000 cash outflow at the end of year 2.

d. At the end of year 3, when production begins, inventory will be increased by $50,000.

e. The first sales from operation of the new plant will occur at the end of year 4 and be $800,000 and continue at that level for 10 years (with the final flow from sales occurring at the end of year 13).

f. Operating costs on these sales are composed of $100,000 fixed operating costs per year and variable operating costs equal to 40 percent of sales.

g. The construction facilities will be depreciated using the simplified straight-line method over their 10-year life down to zero. When the plant is closed it will be sold for $50,000. (*Note:* Assume the investment in plant is depreciated using the simplified straight-line method from $600,000 down to zero over its 10-year life during years $t = 4$ through 13.) Do not depreciate the land.

h. When the plant is closed, the land will be sold for $200,000 ($t = 13$).

i. The company is in the 34 percent marginal tax bracket. Given a 12 percent required rate of return, what is the NPV of this project? Should it be accepted?

6–19A. (*Cash Flow—Capital-Budgeting Calculation*) The Steel Mill Corporation of Asbury Park, N.J., must replace its executive jet and is considering two mutually exclusive planes as replacements. As far as it is concerned, both planes are identical and each will provide annual benefits, before maintenance, taxes, and depreciation, of $40,000 per year for the life of the plane; however, the costs on each are decidedly different. The first is a Point Blank Jet and costs $94,000. It has an expected life of seven years, will be depreciated using the simplified straight-line method down to zero, and will require major maintenance at the end of year 4. The annual maintenance costs are $8,000 for the first three years, $25,000 in year 4, and $10,000 for years 5 through 7. Its salvage value at the end of year 7 is $24,000.

The other plane is a Honeybilt Jet costing $100,000 and also having an expected life of seven years, over which it will be depreciated using the simplified straight-line method down to zero. Its maintenance expenses are expected to be $9,000 the first four years, rising to $18,000 annually for years 5 through 7. In years 3 and 5 the jet engine must be overhauled at an expense of $15,000 each time; this overhaul expense is in excess of the maintenance expenses. Finally, at the end of year 7 this jet will have a salvage value of $30,000. Given a 34 percent marginal tax rate and a 10 percent required rate of return, what is the NPV on each jet? Which should be taken?

STUDY PROBLEMS (SET B)

6–1B. (*Capital Gains Tax*) The R. T. Kleinman Corporation is considering selling one of its old assembly machines. The machine, purchased for $40,000 five years ago, had an expected life of 10 years and an expected salvage value of zero. Assume Kleinman uses simplified straight-line depreciation, creating depreciation of $4,000 per year, and could sell this old machine for $45,000. Also assume a 34 percent marginal tax rate.

a. What would be the taxes associated with this sale?

b. If the old machine were sold for $40,000, what would be the taxes associated with this sale?

c. If the old machine were sold for $20,000, what would be the taxes associated with this sale?

d. If the old machine were sold for $17,000, what would be the taxes associated with this sale?

6–2B. (*Cash Flow Calculations*) The Yonan Componants Corporation, maker of electronic components, is considering replacing a hand-operated machine used in the manufacture of electronic components with a new fully automated machine. Given the following information, determine the cash flows associated with this replacement.

Existing situation:	Two full-time machine operator—salaries $12,000 per year
	Cost of maintenance—$6000 per year
	Cost of defects—$5000 per year
	Original cost of old machine—$40,000
	Expected life—10 years
	Age—five years old
	Expected salvage value—$0
	Depreciation method—simplified straight-line over 10 years, $4000 per year
	Current salvage value—$10,000
	Marginal tax rate—34 percent
Proposed situation:	Fully automated machine
	Cost of machine—$55,000
	Installation fee—$6000
	Cost of maintenance—$6000 per year
	Cost of defects—$2500 per year
	Expected life—five years
	Salvage value—$0
	Depreciation method—simplified straight-line over five years

6-3B. (*Capital-Budgeting Calculation*) Given the cash flow information in problem 6–2B and a required rate of return of 17 percent, compute the following for the automated machine:
   a. Payback period
   b. Net present value
   c. Profitability index
   d. Internal rate of return
   Should this project be accepted?

6-4B. (*AROR Calculation*) Two mutually exclusive projects are being evaluated using the accounting rate of return. Each project has an initial cost of $35,000 and a salvage value of $7,000 after six years. Given the following information:

Annual Accounting Profits after Tax		
Year	Project A	Project B
1	$ 2,500	$10,500
2	2,500	10,500
3	2,500	10,500
4	13,000	5,000
5	13,000	5,000
6	14,000	5,000

   a. Determine each project's AROR.
   b. Which project should be selected, using this criterion? Would you support that recommendation? Why or why not?

6-5B. (*IRR Calculation*) Determine the internal rate of return on the following projects:
   a. An initial outlay of $10,000 resulting in a single cash flow of $19,926 after 8 years
   b. An initial outlay of $10,000 resulting in a single cash flow of $20,122 after 12 years
   c. An initial outlay of $10,000 resulting in a single cash flow of $121,000 after 22 years
   d. An initial outlay of $10,000 resulting in a single cash flow of $19,254 after 5 years

6-6B. (*IRR Calculation*) Determine the internal rate of return on the following projects:
   a. An initial outlay of $10,000 resulting in a cash flow of $2,146 at the end of each year for the next 10 years
   b. An initial outlay of $10,000 resulting in a cash flow of $1,960 at the end of each year for the next 20 years
   c. An initial outlay of $10,000 resulting in a cash flow of $1,396 at the end of each year for the next 12 years
   d. An initial outlay of $10,000 resulting in a cash flow of $3,197 at the end of each year for the next 5 years

6–7B. (*IRR Calculation*) Determine the internal rate of return to the nearest percent on the following projects:

    a. An initial outlay of $10,000 resulting in a cash flow of $3,000 at the end of year 1, $5,000 at the end of year 2, and $7,500 at the end of year 3

    b. An initial outlay of $12,000 resulting in a cash flow of $9,000 at the end of year 1, $6,000 at the end of year 2, and $2,000 at the end of year 3

    c. An initial outlay of $8,000 resulting in a cash flow of $2,000 at the end of years 1 through 5 and $5,000 at the end of year 6

6–8B. (*New Project Analysis*) The Guo Chemical Corporation is considering the purchase of a chemical analysis machine. Although the machine being considered will not produce any increase in sales revenues, it will result in the before-tax reduction of labor costs by $70,000 per year. The machine has a purchase price of $250,000, and it would cost an additional $10,000 to install this machine properly. In addition, to operate this machine properly, inventory must be increased by $15,000. This machine has an expected life of 10 years, after which it will have no salvage value. Also, assume simplified straight-line depreciation and that this machine is being depreciated down to zero, a 34 percent marginal tax rate, and a required rate of return of 15 percent.

    a. What is the initial outlay associated with this project?

    b. What are the annual after-tax cash flows associated with this project, for years 1 through 9?

    c. What is the terminal cash flow in year 10 (i.e., what is the annual after-tax cash flow in year 10 plus any additional cash flows associated with termination of the project)?

    d. Should this machine be purchased?

6–9B. (*New Project Analysis*) El Gato's Motors is considering the purchase of a new production machine for $1,000,000. Although the purchase of this machine will not produce any increase in sales revenues, it will result in a before-tax reduction of labor costs by $400,000 per year. To operate this machine properly, workers would have to go through a brief training session that would cost $100,000. In addition, it would cost $50,000 to install this machine properly. Also, because this machine is extremely efficient, its purchase would necessitate an increase in inventory of $150,000. This machine has an expected life of 10 years, after which it will have no salvage value. Assume simplified straight-line depreciation and that this machine is being depreciated down to zero, a 34 percent marginal tax rate, and a required rate of return of 12 percent.

    a. What is the initial outlay associated with this project?

    b. What are the annual after-tax cash flows associated with this project, for years 1 through 9?

    c. What is the terminal cash flow in year 10 (i.e., what is the annual after-tax cash flow in year 10 plus any additional cash flows associated with termination of the project)?

    d. Should this machine be purchased?

6–10B. (*New Project Analysis*) Weir's Truckin' Inc. is considering the purchase of a new production machine for $100,000. Although the purchase of this machine will not produce any increase in sales revenues, it will result in a before-tax reduction of labor costs by $25,000 per year. To operate this machine properly, workers would have to go through a brief training session that would cost $5,000. In addition, it would cost $5,000 to install this machine properly. Also, because this machine is extremely efficient, its purchase would necessitate an increase in inventory of $25,000. This machine has an expected life of 10 years, after which it will have no salvage value. Finally, to purchase the new machine, it appears that the firm would have to borrow $80,000 at 10 percent interest from its local bank, resulting in additional interest payments of $8,000 per year. Assume simplified straight-line depreciation and that this machine is being depreciated down to zero, a 34 percent marginal tax rate, and a required rate of return of 12 percent.

    a. What is the initial outlay associated with this project?

    b. What are the annual after-tax cash flows associated with this project, for years 1 through 9?

    c. What is the terminal cash flow in year 10 (i.e., what is the annual after-tax cash flow in year 10 plus any additional cash flows associated with termination of the project)?

    d. Should this machine be purchased?

6–11B. (*Cash Flow—Capital-Budgeting Calculation*) The Kensinger Corporation is considering replacing one of its machines with a new, more efficient machine. The old machine presently has a book value of $100,000 and could be sold for $60,000. The old machine is being depreciated on a simplified straight-line basis down to a salvage value of zero over the next five years, generating depreciation of $20,000 per year. The replacement machine would cost $350,000, and have an expected life of five years, after which it could be sold for $50,000. Because of reductions in defects and material savings, the new machine would produce cash benefits of $100,000 per year before depreciation and taxes. Assuming simplified straight-line depreciation, a 34 percent marginal tax rate, and a required rate of return of 15 percent, find

   a. The payback period
   b. The net present value
   c. The profitability index
   d. The internal rate of return

6–12B. (*Cash Flow—Capital-Budgeting Calculation*) The Taiheiyo Chemical Corporation is considering replacing a five-year-old machine that originally cost $50,000, presently has a book value of $25,000, and could be sold for $60,000. This machine is currently being depreciated using the simplified straight-line method down to a terminal value of zero over the next five years, generating depreciation of $5,000 per year. The replacement machine would cost $100,000 and have a five-year expected life over which it would be depreciated down using the simplified straight-line method and have no salvage value at the end of five years. The new machine would produce savings before depreciation and taxes of $35,000 per year. Assuming a 34 percent marginal tax rate and a required rate of return of 10 percent, calculate

   a. The payback period
   b. The net present value
   c. The profitability index
   d. The internal rate of return

6–13B. (*Cash Flow—Capital-Budgeting Calculation*) The G. Rod Electronic Components Corporation is considering replacing a 10-year-old machine that originally cost $37,500, has a current book value of $12,500 with five years of expected life left, and is being depreciated using the simplified straight-line method over its 15-year expected life down to a terminal value of zero in five years, generating depreciation of $2,500 per year. The replacement machine being considered would cost $100,000 and have a five-year expected life over which it would be depreciated using the simplified straight-line method down to zero. At termination in five years the new machine would have a salvage value of $35,000. Material efficiencies resulting from the replacement would result in savings of $30,000 per year before depreciation and taxes. Currently, the old machine could be sold for $17,000. Assuming simplified straight-line depreciation, a 34 percent marginal tax rate, and a required rate of return of 20 percent, calculate

   a. The payback period
   b. The net present value
   c. The profitability index
   d. The internal rate of return

6–14B. (*NPV PI and IRR Calculations*) Gecewich, Inc., is considering a major expansion of its product line and has estimated the following cash flows associated with such an expansion. The initial outlay associated with the expansion would be $2,500,000 and the project would generate incremental after-tax cash flows of $750,000 per year for six years. The appropriate required rate of return is 11 percent.

   a. Calculate the net present value.
   b. Calculate the profitability index.
   c. Calculate the internal rate of return.
   d. Should this project be accepted?

6–15B. (*Internal Rate of Return Calculations*) Given the following cash flows, determine the internal rate of return for projects A, B, and C.

	Project A	Project B	Project C
Initial Investment:	$75,000	$95,000	$395,000
Cash Inflows:			
Year 1	$10,000	25,000	150,000
Year 2	10,000	25,000	150,000
Year 3	30,000	25,000	150,000
Year 4	25,000	25,000	—
Year 5	30,000	25,000	—

6–16B. (*NPV with Varying Required Rates of Return*) Bert's, makers of gourmet corn dogs, is considering the purchase of a new plastic stamping machine. This investment requires an initial outlay of $150,000 and will generate after-tax cash inflows of $25,000 per year for 10 years. For each of the listed required rates of return, determine the project's net present value.

a. The required rate of return is 9 percent.

b. The required rate of return is 15 percent.

c. Would the project be accepted under part (a) or (b)?

d. What is this project's internal rate of return?

6–17B. (*Comprehensive Cash Flow—Capital-Budgeting Calculation*) The L. Bellich Company, a manufacturer of electronic components in the 34 percent marginal tax bracket, is considering the purchase of a new fully automated machine to replace an older, manually operated one. The machine being replaced, now five years old, originally had an expected life of 10 years, was being depreciated using the simplified straight-line method from $20,000 down to zero, thus generating $2,000 in depreciation per year, and could be sold for $25,000. The old machine took one operator who earned $18,000 per year in salary and $3,000 per year in fringe benefits. The annual costs of maintenance and defects associated with the old machine were $6,000 and $3,500, respectively. The replacement machine under consideration had a purchase price of $45,000, a salvage value after five years of $10,000, and would be depreciated over five years using the simplified straight-line depreciation method down to zero. To get the automated machine in running order, there would be a $3,000 shipping fee and a $2,000 installation charge. In addition, because the new machine would work faster than the old one, investment in raw materials and goods-in-process inventories would need to be increased by a total of $4,000. The annual costs of maintenance and defects on the new machine would be $1,500 and $4,000, respectively. The new machine also requires maintenance workers to be specially trained; fortunately, a similar machine was purchased three months prior, and at that time the maintenance workers went through the $5,000 training program needed to familiarize themselves with the new equipment. The firm's management is uncertain whether or not to charge half of this $5,000 training fee toward the new project. Finally, to purchase the new machine, it appears the firm would have to borrow an additional $20,000 at 10 percent interest from its local bank, resulting in additional interest payments of $2,000 per year. The required rate of return on projects of this kind is 20 percent.

a. What is the project's initial outlay?

b. What are the differential cash flows over the project's life?

c. What is the terminal cash flow?

d. Draw a cash flow diagram for this project.

e. If the firm requires a minimum payback period on projects of this type of three years, should this project be accepted?

f. Calculate the project's AROR.

g. What is its net present value?

h. What is its profitability index?

i. What is its internal rate of return? (only attempt if you have a calculator that does IRRs)

j. Should the project be accepted? Why or why not?

6–18B. (*Cash Flow—Capital-Budgeting Calculation*) The Hokie Tech Corp. is considering expanding its highly technical construction facilities. The construction will take a total of four years until it is completed and ready for operation. The following data and assumptions describe the proposed expansion:

a. To make this expansion feasible, R&D expenditures of $175,000 must be made immediately to ensure that the construction facilities are competitively efficient (*t* = 0).

b. At the end of the first year the land will be purchased and construction on stage 1 of the facilities will begin, involving a cash outflow of $100,000 for the land and $300,000 for the construction facilities.

c. Stage 2 of the construction will involve a $250,000 cash outflow at the end of year 2.

d. At the end of year 3, when production begins, inventory will be increased by $50,000.

e. The first sales from operation of the new plant will occur at the end of year 4 and be $850,000 and continue at that level for 10 years (with the final flow from sales occurring at the end of year 13).

f. Operating costs on these sales are composed of $100,000 fixed operating costs per year and variable operating costs equal to 45 percent of sales.

g. The construction facilities will be depreciated using the simplified straight-line method over their 10-year life down to zero. When the plant is closed it will be sold for $50,000. (*Note:* Assume the investment in plant is depreciated using the simplified straight-line method from $550,000 down to zero over its 10-year life during years $t = 4$ through 13.) Do not depreciate the land.

h. When the plant is closed, the land will be sold for $225,000 ($t = 13$).

i. The company is in the 34 percent marginal tax bracket.

Given a 12 percent required rate of return, what is the NPV of this project? Should it be accepted?

6–19B. (*Cash Flow—Capital-Budgeting Calculation*) The M. Jose Corporation of Akron, Ohio, must replace its executive jet and is considering two mutually exclusive planes as replacements. As far as it is concerned, both planes are identical and each will provide annual benefits, before maintenance, taxes, and depreciation, of $50,000 per year for the life of the plane; however, the costs on each are decidedly different. The first is a Zips Jet and costs $94,000. It has an expected life of seven years, will be depreciated using the simplified straight-line method down to zero, and will require major maintenance at the end of year 4. The annual maintenance costs are $7,500 for the first three years, $25,000 in year 4, and $10,000 for years 5 through 7. Its salvage value at the end of year 7 is $24,000.

The other plane is a Hokie Jet costing $100,000 and also having an expected life of seven years, over which it will be depreciated using the simplified straight-line method down to zero. Its maintenance expenses are expected to be $9,000 the first four years, rising to $18,000 annually for years 5 through 7. In years 3 and 5 the jet engine must be overhauled at an expense of $13,000 each time; this overhaul expense is in excess of the maintenance expenses. Finally, at the end of year 7 this jet will have a salvage value of $30,000. Given a 34 percent marginal tax rate and a 10 percent required rate of return, what is the NPV on each jet? Which should be taken?

CASE PROBLEMS

DANFORTH & DONNALLEY LAUNDRY PRODUCTS COMPANY

CAPITAL BUDGETING: RELEVANT CASH FLOWS

On April 14, 1993, at 3:00 P.M., James Danforth, president of Danforth & Donnalley (D&D) Laundry Products Company, called to order a meeting of the financial directors. The purpose of the meeting was to make a capital-budgeting decision with respect to the introduction and production of a new product, a liquid detergent called Blast.

D&D was formed in 1968 with the merger of Danforth Chemical Company, headquartered in Seattle, Washington, producers of Lift-Off detergent, the leading laundry detergent on the West Coast, and Donnalley Home Products Company, headquartered in Detroit, Michigan, makers of Wave detergent, a major midwestern laundry product. As a result of the merger, D&D was producing and marketing two major product lines. Although these products were in direct competition, they were not without product differentiation: Lift-Off was a low-suds, concentrated powder, and Wave was a more traditional powder detergent. Each line brought with it considerable brand loyalty, and by 1993, sales from the two detergent lines had increased tenfold from 1968 levels, with both products now being sold nationally.

In the face of increased competition and technological innovation, D&D spent large amounts of time and money over the past four years researching and developing a new, highly concentrated liquid laundry detergent. D&D's new detergent, which they called Blast, had many obvious advantages over the conventional powdered products. It was felt that with Blast the consumer would benefit in three major areas. Blast was so highly concentrated that only 2 ounces was needed to do an average load of laundry as compared with 8 to 12 ounces of powdered detergent. Moreover, being a liquid, it was possible to pour Blast directly on stains and hard-to-wash spots, eliminating the need for a pre-soak and giving it cleaning abilities that powders could not possibly match. And, finally, it would be packaged in a lightweight, unbreakable plastic bottle with a sure-grip handle, making it much easier to use and more convenient to store than the bulky boxes of powdered detergents with which it would compete.

The meeting was attended by James Danforth, president of D&D; Jim Donnalley, director of the board; Guy Rainey, vice-president in charge of new products; Urban McDonald, controller; and Steve Gasper, a newcomer to D&D's financial staff, who was invited by McDonald to sit in on the meeting. Danforth called the meeting to order, gave a brief statement of its purpose, and immediately gave the floor to Guy Rainey.

Rainey opened with a presentation of the cost and cash flow analysis for the new product. To keep things clear, he passed out copies of the projected cash flows to those present (see Exhibits 1 and 2). In support of this information, he provided some insight as to how these calculations were determined. Rainey proposed that the initial cost for Blast included $500,000 for the test marketing, which was conducted in the Detroit area and completed in the previous June, and $2 million for new specialized equipment and packaging facilities. The estimated life for the facilities was 15 years, after which they would have no salvage value. This 15-year estimated life assumption coincides with company policy set by Donnalley not to consider cash flows occurring more than 15 years into the future, as estimates that far ahead "tend to become little more than blind guesses."

Rainey cautioned against taking the annual cash flows (as shown in Exhibit 1) at face value because portions of these cash flows actually are a result of sales that had been diverted from Lift-Off and Wave. For this reason, Rainey also produced the annual cash flows that had been adjusted to include only those cash flows incremental to the company as a whole (as shown in Exhibit 2).

At this point, discussion opened between Donnalley and McDonald, and it was concluded that the opportunity cost on funds is 10 percent. Gasper then questioned the fact that no costs were included in the proposed cash budget for plant facilities, which would be needed to produce the new product.

EXHIBIT 1.
D&D Laundry Products Company *Annual Cash Flows from the Acceptance of Blast (Including flows resulting from sales diverted from the existing product lines)*

Year	Cash Flows	Year	Cash Flows
1	$280,000	9	350,000
2	280,000	10	350,000
3	280,000	11	250,000
4	280,000	12	250,000
5	280,000	13	250,000
6	350,000	14	250,000
7	350,000	15	250,000
8	350,000		

EXHIBIT 2.
D&D Laundry Products Company *Annual Cash Flows from the Acceptance of Blast (Not including those flows resulting from sales diverted from the existing product lines)*

Year	Cash Flows	Year	Cash Flows
1	$250,000	9	315,000
2	250,000	10	315,000
3	250,000	11	225,000
4	250,000	12	225,000
5	250,000	13	225,000
6	315,000	14	225,000
7	315,000	15	225,000
8	315,000		

Rainey replied that, at the present time, Lift-Off's production facilities were being used at only 55 percent of capacity, and because these facilities were suitable for use in the production of Blast, no new plant facilities other than the specialized equipment and packaging facilities previously mentioned need be acquired for the production of the new product line. It was estimated that full production of Blast would only require 10 percent of the plant capacity.

McDonald then asked if there had been any consideration of increased working capital needs to operate the investment project. Rainey answered that there had and that this project would require $200,000 of additional working capital; however, as this money would never leave the firm and always would be in liquid form it was not considered an outflow and hence was not included in the calculations.

Donnalley argued that this project should be charged something for its use of the current excess plant facilities. His reasoning was that, if an outside firm tried to rent this space from D&D, it would be charged somewhere in the neighborhood of $2 million, and since this project would compete with the current projects, it should be treated as an outside project and charged as such; however, he went on to acknowledge that D&D has a strict policy that forbids the renting or leasing out of any of its production facilities. If they didn't charge for facilities, he concluded, the firm might end up accepting projects that under normal circumstances would be rejected.

From here, the discussion continued, centering on the questions of what to do about the "lost contribution from other projects," the test marketing costs, and the working capital.

QUESTIONS

1. If you were put in the place of Steve Gasper, would you argue for the cost from market testing to be included as a cash outflow?

2. What would your opinion be as to how to deal with the question of working capital?

3. Would you suggest that the product be charged for the use of excess production facilities and building?

4. Would you suggest that the cash flows resulting from erosion of sales from current laundry detergent products be included as a cash inflow? If there were a chance of competition introducing a similar product if you do not introduce Blast, would this affect your answer?

5. If debt is used to finance this project, should the interest payments associated with this new debt be considered cash flows?

6. What are the NPV, IRR, and PI of this project, including cash flows resulting from lost sales from existing product lines? What are the NPV, IRR, and PI of this project excluding these flows? Under the assumption that there is a good chance that competition will introduce a similar product if you don't, would you accept or reject this project?

FORD'S PINTO

ETHICS CASE: THE VALUE OF LIFE

There was a time when the "made in Japan" label brought a predictable smirk of superiority to the face of most Americans. The quality of most Japanese products usually was as low as their price. In fact, few imports could match their domestic counterparts, the proud products of "Yankee know-how." But by the late 1960s, an invasion of foreign-made goods chiseled a few worry lines into the countenance of American industry. And in Detroit, worry was fast fading to panic as the Japanese, not to mention the Germans, began to gobble up more and more of the subcompact auto market.

Never one to take a back seat to the competition, Ford Motor Company decided to meet the threat from abroad head-on. In 1968, Ford executives decided to produce the Pinto. Known inside the company as "Lee's car," after Ford president Lee Iacocca, the Pinto was to weigh no more than 2,000 pounds and cost no more than $2,000.

Eager to have its subcompact ready for the 1971 model year, Ford decided to compress the normal drafting-board-to-showroom time of about three-and-a-half years into two. The compressed schedule meant that any design changes typically made before production-line tooling would have to be made during it.

Before producing the Pinto, Ford crash-tested eleven of them, in part to learn if they met the National Highway Traffic Safety Administration (NHTSA) proposed safety standard that all autos be able to withstand a fixed-barrier impact of 20 miles per hour without fuel loss. Eight standard-design Pintos failed the tests. The three cars that passed the test all had some kind of gas-tank modification. One had a plastic baffle between the front of the tank and the differential housing; the second had a piece of steel between the tank and the rear bumper; and the third had a rubber-lined gas tank.

Ford officials faced a tough decision. Should they go ahead with the standard design, thereby meeting the production time table but possibly jeopardizing consumer safety? Or should they delay production of the Pinto by redesigning the gas tank to make it safer and thus concede another year of subcompact dominance to foreign companies?

To determine whether to proceed with the original design of the Pinto fuel tank, Ford decided to use a capital budgeting approach, examining the expected costs and the social benefits of making the change. Would the social benefits of a new tank design outweigh design costs, or would they not?

To find the answer, Ford had to assign specific values to the variables involved. For some factors in the equation, this posed no problem. The costs of design improvement, for example, could be estimated at eleven dollars per vehicle. But what about human life? Could a dollar-and-cents figure be assigned to a human being?

NHTSA thought it could. It had estimated that society loses $200,725 every time a person is killed in an auto accident. It broke down the costs as follows:

Future productivity losses	
Direct	$132,000
Indirect	41,300
Medical costs	
Hospital	700
Other	425
Property damage	1,500
Insurance administration	4,700
Legal and court expenses	3,000
Employer losses	1,000
Victim's pain and suffering	10,000
Funeral	900
Assets (lost consumption)	5,000
Miscellaneous accident costs	200
Total per fatality	$200,725[1]

Ford used NHTSA and other statistical studies in its cost-benefit analysis, which yielded the following estimates:

Benefits	
Savings:	180 burn deaths, 180 serious burn injuries, 2,100 burned vehicles
Unit cost:	$200,000 per death, $67,000 per injury, $700 per vehicle
Total benefit:	(180 × $200,000) + (180 × $67,000) + (2,100 × $700) = $49.5 million
Costs	
Sales:	11 million cars, 1.5 million light trucks
Unit cost:	$11 per car, $11 per truck
Total cost:	12.5 million × $11 = $137.5 million[2]

Since the costs of the safety improvement outweighed its benefits, Ford decided to push ahead with the original design.

Here is what happened after Ford made this decision:

Between 700 and 2,500 persons died in accidents involving Pinto fires between 1971 and 1978. According to sworn testimony of Ford engineer Harley Copp, 95 percent of them would have survived if Ford had located the fuel tank over the axle (as it had done on its Capri automobiles).

NHTSA's standard was adopted in 1977. The Pinto then acquired a rupture-proof fuel tank. The following year Ford was obliged to recall all 1971–1976 Pintos for fuel-tank modifications.

Between 1971 and 1978, approximately fifty lawsuits were brought against Ford in connection with rear-end accidents in the Pinto. In the Richard Grimshaw case, in addition to awarding over $3 million in compensatory damages to the victims of a Pinto crash, the jury awarded a landmark $125 million in punitive damages against Ford. The judge reduced punitive damages to $3.5 million.

On August 10, 1978, eighteen-year-old Judy Ulrich, her sixteen-year-old sister Lynn, and their eighteen-year-old cousin Donna, in their 1973 Ford Pinto, were struck from the rear by a van near Elkhart, Indiana. The gas tank of the Pinto exploded on impact. In the fire that resulted, the three teenagers were burned to death. Ford was charged with criminal homicide. The judge presiding over the twenty-week trial advised jurors that Ford should be convicted if it had clearly disregarded the harm that might result from its actions and that disregard represented a substantial deviation from accepta-

[1]Ralph Drayton, "One Manufacturer's Approach to Automobile Safety Standards," *CTLA News* 8 (February 1968), p. 11.

[2]Mark Dowie, "Pinto Madness," *Mother Jones*, September–October 1977, p. 20. See also Russell Mokhiber, *Corporate Crime and Violence* (San Francisco: Sierra Club Books, 1988), pp. 373–382, and Francis T. Cullen, William J. Maakestad, and Gray Cavender, *Corporate Crime Under Attack: The Ford Pinto Case and Beyond* (Cincinnati: Anderson Publishing, 1987).

ble standards of conduct. On March 13, 1980, the jury found Ford not guilty of criminal homicide.

For its part, Ford has always denied that the Pinto is unsafe compared with other cars of its type and era. The company also points out that in every model year the Pinto met or surpassed the government's own standards. But what the company doesn't say is that successful lobbying by it and its industry associates was responsible for delaying for nine years the adoption of NHTSA's 20 miles per hour crash standard. And Ford critics claim that there were more than forty European and Japanese models in the Pinto price and weight range with safer gas-tank position. "Ford made an extremely irresponsible decision," concludes auto safety expert Byron Bloch, "when they placed such a weak tank in such a ridiculous location in such a soft rear end."

QUESTIONS

1. Do you think Ford approached this question properly?

2. What responsibilities to its customers do you think Ford had? Were their actions ethically appropriate?

3. Would it have made a moral or ethical difference if the $11 savings had been passed on to Ford's customers? Could a rational customer have chosen to save $11 and risk the more dangerous gas tank? Would that have been similar to making air bags optional? What if Ford had told potential customers about its decision?

4. Should Ford have been found guilty of criminal homicide in the Ulrich case?

5. If you, as a financial manager at Ford, found out about what had been done, what would you do?

Adapted by permission from William Shaw and Vincent Barry, *Moral Issues in Business*, 5th ed., pp. 86–88. © 1992 by Wadsworth, Inc.

SELF-TEST SOLUTIONS

SS–1: **STEP 1:** First calculate the initial outlay.

Initial outlay	
Outflows:	
Cost of machine	$60,000
Installation fee	3,000
Shipping fee	3,000
Inflows:	
Salvage value—old machine	− 5,000
Tax savings on sale of old machine ($25,000—$5,000) (.34)	− 6,800
	$54,200

STEP 2: Calculate the differential cash flows over the project's life.

		Book Profit	Cash Flow
Savings:	Reduced salary	$25,000	$25,000
	Reduced defects	3,000	3,000
Costs:	Increased maintenance	− 1,000	− 1,000
	Increased depreciation ($13,200—$5000)[a]	− 8,200	
Net savings before taxes		$18,800	$27,000
Taxes (.34)		− 6,392	− 6,392
Annual net cash flow after taxes			$20,608

[a]Annual depreciation on the new machine is equal to the cost of the new machine ($60,000) plus any expenses necessary to get it in operating order (the shipping fee of $3,000 plus the installation fee of $3,000) divided by the depreciable life (five years).

STEP 3: Calculate the terminal cash flow.

Salvage value—new machine	$20,000
Less: Taxes—recapture of depreciation ($20,000 × .34)	6,800
	$13,200

Thus, the cash flow in the final year will be equal to the annual net cash flow in that year of $20,608 plus the terminal cash flow of $13,200 for a total of $33,808.

SS–2:

a. Payback period $= \dfrac{\$54,200}{\$20,608} = 2.630$ years

b. $NPV = \sum\limits_{t=1}^{n} \dfrac{ACF_t}{(1 + k)^t} - IO$

$= \sum\limits_{t=1}^{4} \dfrac{\$20,608}{(1 + .15)^t} + \dfrac{\$33,808}{(1 + .15)^5} - \$54,200$

$= \$20,608\,(2.855) + \$33,808\,(.497) - \$54,200$

$= \$58,836 + \$16,803 - \$54,200$

$= \$21,439$

c. $PI = \dfrac{\sum\limits_{t=1}^{n} \dfrac{ACF_t}{(1 + k)^t}}{IO}$

$= \dfrac{\$75,639}{\$54,200}$

$= 1.396$

d. $IO = \sum\limits_{t=1}^{n} \dfrac{ACF_t}{(1 + IRR)^t}$

$\$54,200 = \$20,608\,(PVIFA_{IRR\%,\,4\,yr}) + \$33,808\,(PVIF_{IRR\%,\,5\,yr})$

Try 29 percent:

$\$54,200 = \$20,608\,(2.203) + \$33,808\,(.280)$

$= \$45,399 + 9,466$

$= \$54,865$

Try 30 percent:

$\$45,200 = \$20,608\,(2.166) + \$33,808\,(.269)$

$= \$44,637 + 9.094$

$= \$53,731$

Thus, the IRR is just below 30 percent and the project should be accepted because the NPV is positive, the PI is greater than 1.0, and the IRR is greater than the required rate of return of 15 percent.

CHAPTER 7

Advanced Topics in Capital Budgeting

In the previous chapter we focused solely on the decision-making process in capital budgeting for a single project. Sometimes, however, we must choose among several acceptable projects. At other times the number of projects that can be accepted or the total budget is limited; that is, capital rationing is imposed. In these cases managers may assign different rankings depending on the discounted cash flow criterion being used. In this chapter we examine the reasons for these differences. We also explore the rationale behind capital rationing and project ranking and the ways in which they affect capital-budgeting decisions. We then turn our attention to the problem of capital budgeting under uncertainty. In discussing capital-budgeting techniques in the preceding chapter, we implicitly assumed the level of risk associated with each investment proposal was the same. In this chapter we lift that assumption and examine various ways in which risk can be incorporated into the capital-budgeting decision.

Capital Rationing

The use of our capital-budgeting decision rules developed in Chapter 6, implies that the size of the capital budget is determined by the availability of acceptable investment proposals. However, a firm may place a limit on the dollar size of the capital budget. This situation is called **capital rationing.**

Using the internal rate of return as the firm's decision rule, a firm accepts all projects with an internal rate of return greater than the firm's required rate of return. This rule is illustrated in Figure 7–1, where projects A through E would be chosen. However, when capital rationing is imposed, the dollar size of the total investment is limited by the budget constraint. In Figure 7–1 the budget constraint of $X precludes the acceptance of an attractive investment, project E. This situation obviously contradicts prior decision rules. Moreover,

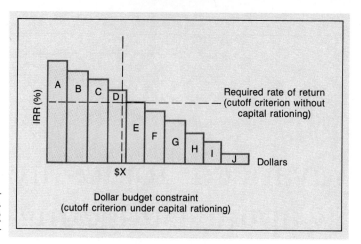

FIGURE 7-1.
Projects Ranked by IRR

the solution of choosing the projects with the highest internal rate of return is complicated by the fact that some projects may be indivisible; for example, it is meaningless to recommend that half a computer be acquired.

Perspective in Finance

It is always somewhat uncomfortable to deal with problems associated with capital rationing because, under capital rationing, projects with positive net present values are rejected. This is a situation that violates the goal of the firm of shareholder wealth maximization. However, in the real world capital rationing does exist, and managers must deal with it. Actually, often when firms impose capital constraints they are recognizing that they do not have the ability to profitably handle more than a certain number or dollar value of new projects.

Rationale for Capital Rationing

We will first ask why capital rationing exists and whether or not it is rational. In general, three principal reasons are given for imposing a capital-rationing constraint. First, management may think that market conditions are temporarily adverse. In the period surrounding the stock market crash of 1987 this reason was frequently given. At that time interest rates were high, and stock prices were depressed. Second, there may be a shortage of qualified managers to direct new projects; this can happen when projects are of a highly technical nature. Third, there may be intangible considerations. For example, the management may simply fear debt, wishing to avoid interest payments at any cost. Or perhaps issuance of common stock may be limited to maintain a stable dividend policy.

Despite strong evidence that capital rationing exists in practice, the question remains as to its effect on the firm. In brief, the effect is negative, and its degree depends on the severity of the rationing. If the rationing is minor and short-lived, then the firm's share price will not suffer to any great extent. In this case capital rationing can probably be excused, although it should be noted that any capital rationing that rejects projects with positive net present values is contrary to the firm's goal of maximization of shareholders' wealth. If the capital rationing is a result of the firm's decision to limit dramatically the number of new projects or to limit total investment to internally generated funds, then this policy will eventually have a significantly negative effect on the firm's share price. For example, a lower share price will eventually result from lost competitive advantage if, owing to a decision to limit arbitrarily its capital budget, a firm fails to upgrade its products and manufacturing process.

Project	Initial Outlay	Profitability Index	Net Present Value
A	$200,000	2.4	$280,000
B	200,000	2.3	260,000
C	800,000	1.7	560,000
D	300,000	1.3	90,000
E	300,000	1.2	60,000

TABLE 7–1.
Capital-Rationing Example of Five Indivisible Projects

Capital Rationing and Project Selection

If the firm decides to impose a capital constraint on investment projects, the appropriate decision criterion is to select the set of projects with the highest net present value subject to the capital constraint. This guideline may preclude merely taking the highest-ranked projects in terms of the profitability index or the internal rate of return. If the projects shown in Figure 7–1 are divisible, the last project accepted may be only partially accepted. Although partial accept-ances may be possible in some cases, the indivisibility of most capital invest-ments prevents it. If a project is a sales outlet or a truck, it may be meaningless to purchase half a sales outlet or half a truck.

To illustrate this procedure, consider a firm with a budget constraint of $1 million and five indivisible projects available to it, as given in Table 7–1. If the highest-ranked projects were taken, projects A and B would be taken first. At that point there would not be enough funds available to take project C; hence, projects D and E would be taken. However, a higher total net present value is provided by the combination of projects A and C. Thus projects A and C should be selected from the set of projects available. This illustrates our guideline: to select the set of projects that maximizes the firm's net present value.

Project Ranking

In the past, we have proposed that all projects with a positive net present value, a profitability index greater than 1.0, or an internal rate of return greater than the required rate of return be accepted, assuming there is no capital rationing. However, this acceptance is not always possible. In some cases, when two projects are judged acceptable by the discounted cash flow criteria, it may be necessary to select only one of them, as they are mutually exclusive. **Mutually exclusive projects** occur when a set of investment proposals perform essential-ly the same task; acceptance of one will necessarily mean rejection of the others. For example, a company considering the installation of a computer system may evaluate three or four systems, all of which may have positive net present values; however, the acceptance of one system will automatically mean rejection of the others. In general, to deal with mutually exclusive projects, we will simply rank them by means of the discounted cash flow criteria and select the project with the highest ranking. On occasion, however, problems of conflicting ranking may arise.

Problems in Project Ranking

There are three general types of ranking problems—the size disparity problem, the time disparity problem, and the unequal lives problem. Each involves the possibility of conflict in the ranks yielded by the various discounted cash flow capital-budgeting criteria. As noted in the previous chapter, when one discount-ed cash flow criterion gives an accept signal, they will all give an accept signal, but they will not necessarily rank all projects in the same order. In most cases this disparity is not critical; however, for mutually exclusive projects the ranking order is important.

Size Disparity

NPV SIZE

The *size disparity problem* occurs when mutually exclusive projects of unequal size are examined. This problem is most easily illustrated with the use of an example.

Suppose that a firm with a cost of capital of 10 percent is considering two mutually exclusive projects, A and B. Project A involves a $200 initial outlay and cash inflow of $300 at the end of one year, whereas project B involves an initial outlay of $1,500 and a cash inflow of $1,900 at the end of one year. The net present value, profitability index, and internal rate of return for these projects are given in Table 7–2.

TABLE 7–2.
Size Disparity Ranking Problem

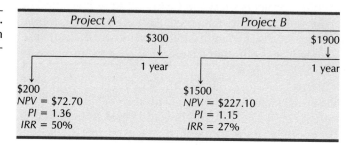

In this case, if the net present value criterion is used, project B should be accepted, whereas if the profitability index or the internal rate of return criterion is used, project A should be chosen. The question now becomes: Which project is better? The answer depends on whether or not capital rationing exists. Without capital rationing, project B is better because it provides the largest increase in shareholders' wealth; that is, it has a larger net present value. If there is a capital constraint, the problem then focuses on what can be done with the additional $1,300 that is freed if project A is chosen (costing $200, as opposed to $1,500). If the firm can earn more on project A plus the project financed with the additional $1,300 than it can on project B, then project A and the marginal project should be accepted. In effect, we are attempting to select the set of projects that maximize the firm's NPV. Thus, if the marginal project has a net present value greater than $154.40, selecting it plus project A with a net present value of $72.70 will provide a net present value greater than $227.10, the net present value for project B. ■

In summary, whenever the size disparity problem results in conflicting rankings, between mutually exclusive projects, the project with the largest net present value will be selected, provided there is no capital rationing. When capital rationing exists, the firm should select the set of projects with the largest net present value.

Time Disparity

difference in when Receiving funds

The *time disparity problem* and the conflicting rankings that accompany it result from the differing reinvestment assumptions made by the net present value and internal rate of return decision criteria. The NPV criterion assumes that cash flows over the life of the project can be reinvested at the required rate of return or cost of capital, whereas the IRR criterion implicitly assumes that the cash flows over the life of the project can be reinvested at the internal rate of return. Again, this problem may be illustrated through the use of an example.

Suppose a firm with a required rate of return or cost of capital of 10 percent and with no capital constraint is considering the two mutually exclusive projects illustrated in Table 7–3. The net present value and profitability index indicate that project A is the better of the two, whereas the internal rate of return indicates that project B is the better. Project B receives its cash flows earlier than project A, and the different assumptions made as to how these flows can be reinvested result in the difference in rankings. Which criterion should be followed depends on which reinvestment assumption is used. The net present value criterion is preferred in this case because it makes the most acceptable assumption for the wealth-maximizing firm. It is certainly the most conservative assumption that can be made, because the required rate of return is the lowest possible reinvestment rate. Moreover, as we have already noted, the net present value method maximizes the value of the firm and the shareholders' wealth.

	Project A			Project B		
	$100	$200	$2000	$650	$650	$650
	↓	↓	↓	↓	↓	↓
	1	2	3 years	1	2	3 years

$1000
NPV = $758.10
PI = 1.758
IRR = 35%

$1000
NPV = $616.55
PI = 1.617
IRR = 42 to 43%

TABLE 7–3.
Time Disparity Ranking Problem

Unequal Lives

The final ranking problem to be examined centers on the question of whether or not it is appropriate to compare mutually exclusive projects with different life spans.

– Life SPAN

Suppose a firm with a 10 percent required rate of return is faced with the problem of replacing an aging machine and is considering two replacement machines, one with a three-year life and one with a six-year life. The relevant cash flow information for these projects is given in Table 7–4.

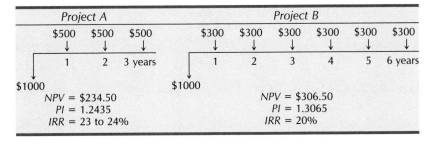

	Project A			Project B					
	$500	$500	$500	$300	$300	$300	$300	$300	$300
	↓	↓	↓	↓	↓	↓	↓	↓	↓
	1	2	3 years	1	2	3	4	5	6 years

$1000
NPV = $234.50
PI = 1.2435
IRR = 23 to 24%

$1000
NPV = $306.50
PI = 1.3065
IRR = 20%

TABLE 7–4.
Unequal Lives Ranking Problem

Examining the discounted cash flow criteria, we find that the net present value and profitability index criteria indicate that project B is the better project, whereas the internal rate of return favors project A. This ranking inconsistency is caused by the different life spans of the projects being compared. In this case the decision is a difficult one because the projects are not comparable.

The problem of incomparability of projects with different lives arises because future profitable investment proposals may be rejected without being included in the analysis. This can easily be seen in a replacement problem such as the present example, in which two mutually exclusive machines with different lives are being considered. In this case a comparison of the net present values alone on each of these projects would be misleading. If the project with the shorter life were taken, at its termination the firm could replace the machine and receive additional benefits, whereas acceptance of the project with the longer life would exclude this possibility, a possibility that is not included in the analysis. The key question thus becomes Does today's investment decision include all future profitable investment proposals in its analysis? If not, the projects are not comparable. In this case, if project B is taken, then the project that could have been taken after three years when project A terminates is automatically rejected without being included in the analysis. Thus, acceptance of project B not only forces rejection of project A, but also forces rejection of any replacement machine that might have been considered for years 4 through 6 without including this replacement machine in the analysis.

There are several methods to deal with this situation. The first option is to assume that the cash inflows from the shorter-lived investment will be reinvested at the cost of capital until the termination of the longer-lived asset. Although this approach is the simplest, merely calculating the net present value, it actually ignores the problem at hand—that of allowing for participation in another replacement opportunity with a positive net present value. The proper solution thus becomes the projection of reinvestment opportunities into the future—that is, making assumptions about possible future investment opportunities. Unfortunately, while the first method is too simplistic to be of any value, the second is extremely difficult, requiring extensive cash flow forecasts. The final technique for confronting the problem is to assume that reinvestment opportunities in the future will be similar to the current ones. The two most common ways of doing this are by creating a replacement chain to equalize life spans or calculating the project's Equivalent Annual Annuity (EAA). Using a replacement chain, the present example would call for the creation of a two-chain cycle for project A—that is, we assume that project A can be replaced with a similar investment at the end of three years. Thus, project A would be viewed as two A projects occurring back to back, as illustrated in Figure 7–2. The net present value on this replacement chain is $426.50, which is comparable with project B's net present value. Therefore, project A should be accepted because the net present value of its replacement chain is greater than the net present value of project B.

FIGURE 7–2. Replacement Chain Illustration: Two A Projects

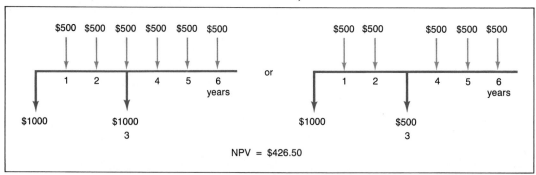

NPV = $426.50

The equivalent annual annuity (EAA) approach ■ One problem with replacement chains is that depending on the life of each project, it can be quite difficult to come up with equivalent lives. For example, if the two projects had 7– and 13–year lives, a 91-year replacement chain would be needed to establish equivalent lives. In this case it is easier to determine the project's **equivalent**

PART 2: VALUATION AND
MANAGEMENT OF LONG & TERM
INVESTMENTS
226

annual annuity (EAA). A project's EAA is simply an annuity cash flow that yields the same present value as the project's NPV. To calculate a project's EAA we need only calculate a project's NPV and then divide that number by the $PVIFA_{i,n}$ to determine the dollar value of an n-year annuity that would produce the same NPV as the project. This can be done in two steps as follows:

Step: 1: *Calculate the project's NPV.* In Table 7–4 we determined that project A had an NPV of $234.50, whereas project B had an NPV of $306.50.

Step: 2: *Calculate the EAA.* The EAA is determined by dividing each project's NPV by the $PVIFA_{i,n}$, where i is the required rate of return and n is the project's life. This determines the level of an annuity cash flow that would produce the same NPV as the project. For project A the $PVIFA_{10\%, 3\,yr}$ is equal to 2.487, whereas the $PVIFA_{10\%, 6\,yr}$ for project B is equal to 4.355. Dividing each project's NPV by the appropriate $PVIFA_{i,n}$ we determine the EAA for each project:

$$EAA_A = NPV/PVIFA_{i,n}$$
$$= \$234.50/2.487$$
$$= \$94.29$$
$$EAA_B = \$306.29/4.355$$
$$= \$70.38$$

How do we interpret the EAA? For a project with an n-year life, it tells us what the dollar value is of an n-year annual annuity that would provide the same NPV as the project. Thus, for project A it means that a three-year annuity of $94.29 given a discount rate of 10 percent would produce a net present value the same as project A's net present value, which is $234.50. We can now compare the equivalent annual annuities directly to determine which project is better. We can do this because we now have found the level of annual annuity that produces an NPV equivalent to the project's NPV. Thus, because they are both annual annuities they are comparable. An easy way to see this is to use the EAA's to create infinite life replacement chains. To do this we need only calculate the present value of an infinite stream or perpetuity of equivalent annual annuities. This is done by using the present value of an annuity formula, that is, simply dividing the equivalent annual annuity by the appropriate discount rate. In this case we find:

$$NPV_{\infty, A} = \$94.29/.10$$
$$= \$942.90$$
$$NPV_{\infty, B} = \$70.38/.10$$
$$= \$703.80$$

Here we have calculated the present value of an infinite life replacement chain. Because the EAA method provides the same results as the infinite-life replacement chain it really doesn't matter which method you prefer to use.

Inflation and Capital-Budgeting Decisions

It is always important to consider the effect of inflation in capital-budgeting decisions. Although every project is affected a little differently by inflation, there are four general ways in which inflation can affect capital-budgeting decisions:

1. Increased inflation will cause the required rate of return on the project to rise. As cash flows received in the future will buy less with increased

inflation, investors will demand a higher required rate of return on funds invested. This is called the Fisher Effect and was referred to in Chapter 2. It states that the required rate of return on a project is

$$R_j = R_j^* + \rho$$

where R_j is the required rate of return in nominal terms, R_j^* is the required rate of return in real terms, and ρ is the weighted average anticipated inflation rate over the life of the project.[1]

2. Both anticipated cash inflows and outflows could be affected by inflation. Inflation may well affect materials, wages, sales, and administrative expenses while also affecting the selling price of the item being produced. It is obviously impossible to generalize on exactly how it will affect these items for all projects, but it is safe to assume it could have a significant impact on both cash inflows and outflows.

3. The salvage value of the project could also be affected by inflation. Again, it is impossible to generalize on exactly what the relationship will be on all capital-budgeting projects.

4. The fact that depreciation charges do not change with inflation also distorts capital-budgeting decisions. Because depreciation charges are based on original costs rather than replacement costs, they are not affected by inflation. As such, if inflation increases while depreciation remains constant, a smaller percentage of the cash inflows is sheltered by depreciation and thus a larger percentage is taxed. The end result of this is that the real after-tax cash flows decline over time as taxes increase faster than inflation because everything but depreciation is free to rise with inflation.

How can financial managers adjust capital-budgeting decisions for inflation? They must anticipate and include any effects of expected inflation in the cash flow estimates and also include it in the estimate of the required rate of return. Because it does affect the magnitude of the cash flows, it must be allowed for to produce an appropriate capital-budgeting decision.

Risk and the Investment Decision

Up to this point we have ignored risk in capital budgeting; that is, we have discounted expected cash flows back to present and ignored any uncertainty that there might be surrounding that estimate. In reality the future cash flows associated with the introduction of a new sales outlet or a new product are estimates of what is expected to happen in the future, not necessarily what will happen in the future. For example, when the Ford Motor Company made its decision to introduce the Edsel, you can bet that the expected cash flows it based its decision on were nothing like the cash flows it realized. In effect, the cash flows we have discounted back to the present have only been our best estimate of the expected future cash flows. A cash flow diagram based on the possible outcomes of an investment proposal rather than the expected values of these outcomes appears in Figure 7–3.

In this section we will assume that under conditions of risk we do not know beforehand what cash flows will actually result from a new project. However, we do have expectations concerning the possible outcomes and are able to assign probabilities to these outcomes. Stated another way, although we do not know the cash flows resulting from the acceptance of a new project will be, we can formulate the probability distributions from which the flows will be drawn.

[1]Actually $(1 + R_j) = (1 + R_j^*)(1 + \rho)$; thus, $R_j = R_j^* + \rho + R_j^*\rho$. However, because $R_j^*\rho$ is assumed to be extremely small and inconsequential, it is generally dropped from consideration.

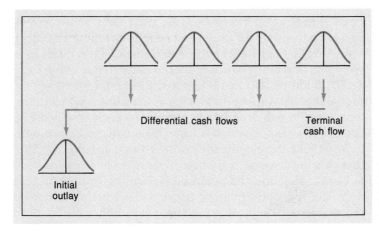

FIGURE 7-3.
Cash Flow Diagram Based
on Possible Outcomes

As we learned in Chapter 4, risk occurs when there is some question as to the future outcome of an event. We will now proceed with an examination of the logic behind this definition. Again, risk is defined as the potential variability in future cash flows.

The fact that variability reflects risk can easily be shown with a coin toss. Consider the possibility of flipping a coin—heads you win, tails you lose—for 25

INTERNATIONAL FINANCIAL MANAGEMENT

The Pursuit of Global Strategies

One way that an international project's risk can be lessened is through joint ventures and strategic alliances. This is one way a firm can eliminate an area of concern that it might be facing with the introduction of a new product. For example a firm with an excellent product but marketing expertise only in the U.S. might combine with another firm with direct access to marketing channels in Europe. Jointly the two can introduce their product into the European markets.

The Ford automobile that a customer buys in the United Kingdom was probably designed in West Germany and built in Spain. In the United States, Inland Steel and Japan's Nippon Steel are jointly building the world's most advanced continuous cold steel mill at New Carlisle, Indiana. Inland's motivation is to get to use Nippon's technology, while Nippon will be able to bypass import quotas.

These are examples of global strategies. These firms are seeking competitive advantages outside their domestic borders.[2] Through global strategies, firms can exploit economies of scale through global volume and taking preemptive positions through large investments in other countries. Interdependent companies may achieve synergies by carefully combining different activities. Don't be surprised if your photocopying machine that was designed in Toronto, incorporates microprocessing chips made in Taiwan and a physical case manufactured in Japan, was assembled in South Korea, and was sold out of warehouses in Melbourne, London, and Los Angeles. Each of these locations was strategically chosen to gain a competitive advantage.

One of the most popular techniques for achieving a global strategy is to develop strategic alliances by finding partners in another country with whom strengths can be shared.[3] Inland Steel has done that with Nippon Steel in Indiana. Boeing and Europe's Airbus are currently doing research jointly in order to spread the risk in developing the next generation of commercial aircraft. As the cost of "going it alone" to reach global markets becomes prohibitively expensive, you can expect to see an increasing number of strategic alliances, some of which will even be among former rivals. For instance, Texas Instruments sued Hitachi of Japan in 1986 for patent infringement. The two have since teamed up to develop the next generation of memory chips.

[2]See, for example, James Leontiades, "Going Global—Global Strategies vs. National Strategies," *Long Range Planning*, December 1986, pp. 96–104; Sumantra Ghoshal, "Global Strategy: An Organizing Framework," *Strategic Management Journal*, September–October 1987, pp. 425–40; Richard I. Kirkland, Jr., "Entering a New Age of Boundless Competition," *Fortune*, March 14, 1988, pp. 40–48; and Jeremy Main, "How to Go Global—And Why," *Fortune*, August 28, 1989, pp. 70–76.

[3]See, for example, Kathryn Rudie Harrigan, "Strategic Alliances: Their New Role in Global Competition," *Columbia Journal of World Business*, Summer 1987, pp. 67–69; Louis Kraar, "Your Rivals Can Be Your Allies," *Fortune*, March 27, 1989, pp. 66–76; and Bryan Borys and David B. Jemison, "Hybrid Arrangements as Strategic Alliances: Theoretical Issues in Organizational Combinations," *Academy of Management Review*, April 1989, pp. 234–49.

cents with your finance professor. Most likely you would be willing to take on this game, because the utility gained from winning 25 cents is about equal to the utility lost if you lose 25 cents. Conversely, if the flip is for $1,000, you may be willing to play only if you are offered more than $1,000 if you win—say, you win $1,500 if it turns out heads and lose $1,000 if it turns out tails. In each case the probability of winning and losing is the same; that is, there is an equal chance that the coin will land heads or tails. In each case, however, the width of the dispersion changes, which is why the second coin toss is more risky and why you may not take the chance unless the payoffs are altered. The key here is the fact that only the dispersion changes; the probability of winning or losing is the same in each case. Thus, the potential variability in future returns reflects the risk.

The final question to be addressed is whether or not individuals are in fact risk averse. Although we do see people gambling where the odds of winning are against them, it should be stressed that monetary return is not the only possible return they may receive. A nonmonetary, psychic reward accrues to some gamblers, allowing them to fantasize that they will break the bank, never have to work again, and retire to some offshore island. Actually, the heart of the question is how wealth is measured. Although gamblers appear to be acting as risk seekers, they actually attach an additional nonmonetary return to gambling; the risk is in effect its own reward. When this is considered, their actions seem totally rational. It should also be noted that although gamblers appear to be pursuing risk on one hand, on the other hand they are also eliminating some risk by purchasing insurance and diversifying their investments.

In the remainder of this chapter we assume that although future cash flows are not known with certainty, the probability distribution from which they come is known. Also, because we have illustrated that the dispersion of possible outcomes reflects risk, we are prepared to use a measure of dispersion or variability later in the chapter when we quantify risk.

In the pages that follow, remember that there are only two basic issues that we address: (1) How should risk be incorporated into capital-budgeting analysis? (2) What is risk in terms of capital-budgeting decisions, and how should it be measured?

What Measure of Risk Is Relevant in Capital Budgeting

Before we begin our discussion of how to adjust for risk it is important to determine just what type of risk we are to adjust for. In capital budgeting, a project's risk can be looked at in three levels. First, there is _total project risk_, which is a project's risk ignoring the fact that much of this risk will be diversified away as the project is combined with the firm's other projects and assets. Second, we have the project's _contribution-to-firm risk,_ which is the amount of risk that the project contributes to the firm as a whole; this measure considers the fact that some of the project's risk will be diversified away as the project is combined with the firm's other projects and assets, but ignores the effects of diversification of the firm's shareholders. Finally, there is _systematic risk,_ which is the risk of the project from the viewpoint of a well-diversified shareholder; this measure considers the fact that some of a project's risk will be diversified away as the project is combined with the firm's other projects, and, in addition, some of the remaining risk will be diversified away by shareholders as they combine this stock with other stocks in their portfolio. Graphically, this is shown in Figure 7–4.

Should we be interested in total project risk? The answer is no. Perhaps the easiest way to understand why not is to look at an example. Let's take the case of research and design projects at Johnson & Johnson. Each year Johnson & Johnson takes on hundreds of new R & D projects, knowing that they only have about a 10 percent probability of being successful. If they are successful, the

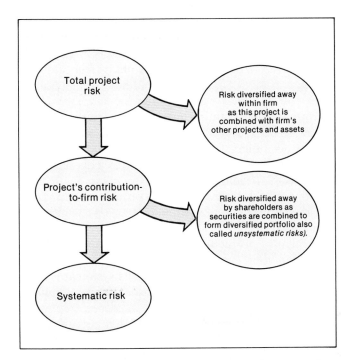

FIGURE 7–4.
Looking at Three Measures of a
Project's Risk

profits can be enormous; if they fail, the investment is lost. If the company has only one project, and it is an R&D project, the company would have a 90 percent chance of failure. Thus, if we look at these R & D projects individually and measure their total project risk, we would have to judge them to be enormously risky. However, if we consider the effect of the diversification that comes about from taking on several hundred independent R & D projects a year, all with a 10 percent chance of success, we can see that these R & D projects do not add much in the way of risk to Johnson & Johnson. In short, because much of a project's risk is diversified away within the firm, total project risk is an inappropriate measure of the meaningful level of risk of a capital budgeting project.

Should we be interested in the project's contribution-to-firm risk? Once again, the answer is no, provided investors are well diversified, and there is no chance of bankruptcy. From our earlier discussion of risk in Chapter 4 we saw that as shareholders, if we combined our security with other securities to form a diversified portfolio much of the risk of our security would be diversified away. Thus, all that affects the shareholders is the systematic risk of the project, and as such is all that is theoretically relevant for capital budgeting.

Measuring Risk for Capital-Budgeting Purposes and a Dose of Reality—Is Systematic Risk All There Is?

According to the CAPM, systematic risk is the only relevant risk for capital budgeting purposes; however, reality complicates this somewhat. In many instances a firm will have undiversified shareholders including owners of small corporations. Because they are not diversified, for those shareholders the relevant measure of risk is the project's contribution-to-firm risk.

The possibility of bankruptcy also affects our view of what measure of risk is relevant. Because the project's contribution-to-firm risk can affect the possibility of bankruptcy, this may be an appropriate measure of risk if there are costs associated with bankruptcy. Quite obviously, in the real world there is a cost associated with bankruptcy. First, if a firm fails, its assets, in general, cannot be sold for their true economic value. Moreover, the amount of money actually available for distribution to stockholders is further reduced by liquidation and legal fees that must be paid. Finally, the opportunity cost associated with the delays related to the legal process further reduces the funds available to the shareholder. Therefore, because costs are associated with bankruptcy, reduction of the chance of bankruptcy has a very real value associated with it.

Indirect costs of bankruptcy also affect other areas of the firm including production, sales, and the quality and efficiency of management. For example, firms with a higher probability of bankruptcy may have a more difficult time recruiting and retaining quality managers because jobs with that firm are viewed as being less secure. Suppliers also may be less willing to sell on credit. Finally, customers may lose confidence and fear that the firm may not be around to honor the warranty or to supply spare parts for the product in the future. As a result, as the probability of bankruptcy increases, the eventual bankruptcy may become self-fulfilling as potential customers and suppliers flee. The end result is that the project's contribution-to-firm risk is also a relevant risk measure for capital budgeting.

Finally, problems in measuring a project's systematic risk make its implementation extremely difficult. As we will see later on in this chapter, it is much easier talking about a project's systematic risk than it is measuring it.

Given all this, what do we use? The answer is that we will give consideration to both measures. We know in theory systematic risk is correct. We also know that bankruptcy costs and undiversified shareholders violate the assumptions of the theory, which brings us back to the concept of a project's contribution-to-firm risk. Still, the concept of systematic risk holds value for capital budgeting decisions, because that is the risk that shareholders are compensated for assuming. As such, we will concern ourselves with both the project's contribution-to-firm risk and the project's systematic risk, and not try to make any specific allocation of importance between the two for capital-budgeting purposes.

Methods for Incorporating Risk into Capital Budgeting

In the preceding chapter we ignored any risk differences between projects. This assumption is simple but not valid; different investment projects do in fact contain different levels of risk. We will now look at several methods for incorporating risk into the analysis. The first technique, the *certainty equivalent approach*, attempts to incorporate the manager's utility function into the analysis. The second technique, the *risk-adjusted discount rate*, is based on the notion that investors require higher rates of return on more risky projects.

Certainty Equivalent Approach

The **certainty equivalent approach** involves a direct attempt to allow the decision maker to incorporate his or her utility function into the analysis. The financial manager is allowed to substitute the certain dollar amount that he or she feels is equivalent to the expected but risky cash flow offered by the investment for that risky cash flow in the capital-budgeting analysis. In effect, a set of riskless cash flows is substituted for the original risky cash flows, between both of which the financial manager is indifferent. To a certain extent this process is like the old television program "Let's Make a Deal." On that show Monty Hall asked contestants to trade certain outcomes for uncertain outcomes. In some cases contestants were willing to make a trade, and in some cases they were not; it all depended upon how risk averse they were. The main difference between what we are doing and what was done on "Let's Make a Deal" is that on the TV show contestants were in general not indifferent with the respect to certain outcome and the risky outcome, whereas in the certainty equivalent approach managers are indifferent.

To illustrate the concept of a certainty equivalent, let us look at a simple coin toss. Assume you can play the game only once and if it comes out heads, you win $10,000, and if it comes out tails you win nothing. Obviously, you have a 50 percent chance of winning $10,000 and a 50 percent chance of winning nothing, with an expected value of $5,000. Thus, $5,000 is your uncertain expected value outcome. The certainty equivalent then becomes the amount you would demand to make you indifferent with regard to playing and not playing the game. If you are indifferent with respect to receiving $3,000 for certain and not playing the game, then $3,000 is the certainty equivalent.

To simplify future calculations and problems, let us define certainty equivalent coefficients (α_t) that represent the ratio of the certain outcome to the risky outcome, between which the financial manager is indifferent. In equation form, α_t can be represented as follows:

$$\alpha_t = \frac{\text{certain cash flow}_t}{\text{risky cash flow}_t} \qquad (7\text{--}1)$$

Thus, the alphas can vary between 0, in the case of extreme risk, and 1, in the case of certainty. To obtain the value of the equivalent certain cash flow, we need only multiply the risky cash flow and the α_t. When this is done, we are indifferent with respect to this certain cash flow and the risky cash flow. In the preceding example of the simple coin toss, the certain cash flow was $3,000, while the risky cash flow was $5,000, the expected value of the coin toss; thus, the certainty equivalent coefficient is 3000/5000 = .6. In summary, by multiplying the certainty equivalent coefficient (α_t) times the expected but risky cash flow, we can determine an equivalent certain cash flow.

Once this risk is taken out of the project's cash flows, those cash flows are discounted back to present at the risk-free rate of interest, and the project's net present value or profitability index is determined. If the internal rate of return is calculated, it is then compared with the risk-free rate of interest rather than the firm's required rate of return in determining whether or not it should be accepted or rejected. The certainty equivalent method can be summarized as follows:

$$NPV = \sum_{t=1}^{n} \frac{\alpha_t ACF_t}{(1 + i_F)^t} - IO \qquad (7\text{--}2)$$

where α_t = the certainty equivalent coefficient in period t

ACF_t = the annual after-tax expected cash flow in period t

IO = the initial cash outlay

n = the project's expected life

i_F = the risk-free interest rate

The certainty equivalent approach can be summarized as follows:

Step 1:   Risk is removed from the cash flows by substituting equivalent certain cash flows for the risky cash flows. If the certainty equivalent coefficient (α_t) is given, this is done by multiplying each risky cash flow by the appropriate α_t value.

Step 2:   These riskless cash flows are then discounted back to the present at the riskless rate of interest.

Step 3:   The normal capital-budgeting criteria are then applied, except in the case of the internal rate of return criterion, where the project's internal rate of return is compared with the risk-free rate of interest rather than the firm's required rate of return.

A firm with a 10 percent required rate of return is considering building new research facilities with an expected life of five years. The initial outlay associated with this project involves a certain cash outflow of $120,000. The expected cash inflows and certainty equivalent coefficients, α_t, are as follows:

Year	Expected Cash Flow	Certainty Equivalent Coefficient, α_t
1	$10,000	.95
2	20,000	.90
3	40,000	.85
4	80,000	.75
5	80,000	.65

The risk-free rate of interest is 6 percent. What is the project's net present value?

To determine the net present value of this project using the certainty equivalent approach, we must first remove the risk from the future cash flows. We do so by multiplying each expected cash flow by the corresponding certainty equivalent coefficient, α_t.

Expected Cash Flow	Certainty Equivalent Coefficient, α_t	$\alpha_t \times$ (Expected Cash Flow) = Equivalent Riskless Cash Flow
$10,000	.95	$ 9,500
20,000	.90	18,000
40,000	.85	34,000
80,000	.75	60,000
80,000	.65	52,000

The equivalent riskless cash flows are then discounted back to the present at the riskless interest rate, not the firm's required rate of return. The required rate of return would be used if this project had the same level of risk as a typical project for this firm. However, these equivalent cash flows have no risk at all; hence, the appropriate discount rate is the riskless rate of interest. The equivalent riskless cash flows can be discounted back to present at the riskless rate of interest, 6 percent, as follows:

Year	Equivalent Riskless Cash Flow	Present Value Factor at 6 Percent	Present Value
1	$ 9,500	.943	$ 8,958.50
2	18,000	.890	16,020.00
3	34,000	.840	28,560.00
4	60,000	.792	47,520.00
5	52,000	.747	38,844.00

$$NPV = -\$120,000 + \$8958.50 + \$16,020 + \$28,560 + \$47,520$$
$$+ \$38,844$$
$$= \$19,902.50$$

Applying the normal capital-budgeting decision criteria, we find that the project should be accepted, as its net present value is greater than zero. ∎

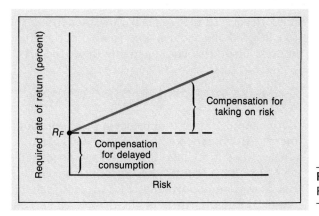

FIGURE 7–5.
Risk–Return Relationship

Risk-Adjusted Discount Rates

The use of risk-adjusted discount rates is based on the concept that investors demand higher returns for more risky projects. This is the basic principle behind the CAPM, and the relationship between risk and return is illustrated graphically in Figure 7–5.

The required rate of return on any investment should include compensation for delaying consumption equal to the risk-free rate of return, plus compensation for any risk taken on. If the risk associated with the investment is greater than the risk involved in a typical endeavor, the discount rate is adjusted upward to compensate for this added risk. Once the firm determines the appropriate required rate of return for a project with a given level of risk, the cash flows are discounted back to present at the risk-adjusted discount rate. Then the normal capital-budgeting criteria are applied, except in the case of the internal rate of return. For the IRR, the hurdle rate with which the project's internal rate of return is compared now becomes the risk-adjusted discount rate. Expressed mathematically, the net present value using the risk-adjusted discount rate becomes

$$NPV = \sum_{t=1}^{n} \frac{ACF_t}{(1 + i^*)^t} - IO \qquad \textbf{(7–3)}$$

where ACF_t = the annual after-tax expected cash flow in time period t

IO = the initial cash outlay

i^* = the risk-adjusted discount rate

n = the project's expected life

The logic behind the risk-adjusted discount rate stems from the idea that if the level of risk in a project is different from that in the typical firm project, then management must incorporate the shareholders' probable reaction to this new endeavor into the decision-making process. If the project has more risk than a typical project, then a higher required rate of return should apply. Otherwise, marginal projects will lower the firm's share price—that is, reduce shareholders' wealth. This will occur as the market raises its required rate of return on the firm to reflect the addition of a more risky project, whereas the incremental cash flows resulting from the acceptance of the new project are not large enough to offset this change fully. By the same logic, if the project has less than normal risk, a reduction in the required rate of return is appropriate. Thus, the risk-adjusted discount method attempts to apply more stringent standards— that is, require a higher rate of return—to projects that will increase the firm's risk level. This is because these projects will lead shareholders to demand a higher required rate of return to compensate them for the higher risk level of the firm. If this adjustment is not made, the marginal projects containing above-average risk could actually lower the firm's share price.

EXAMPLE

A toy manufacturer is considering the introduction of a line of fishing equipment with an expected life of five years. In the past, this firm has been quite conservative in its investment in new products, sticking primarily to standard toys. In this context, the introduction of a line of fishing equipment is considered an abnormally risky project. Management thinks that the normal required rate of return for the firm of 10 percent is not sufficient. Instead, the minimally acceptable rate of return on this project should be 15 percent. The initial outlay would be $110,000, and the expected cash flows from this project are as given below:

Year	Expected Cash Flow
1	$30,000
2	30,000
3	30,000
4	30,000
5	30,000

Discounting this annuity back to the present at 15 percent yields a present value of the future cash flows of $100,560. Because the initial outlay on this project is $110,000, the net present value becomes −$9,440, and the project should be rejected. If the normal required rate of return of 10 percent had been used as the discount rate, the project would have been accepted with a net present value of $3,730. ∎

In practice, when the risk-adjusted discount rate is used, projects are generally grouped according to purpose, or risk class; then the discount rate preassigned to that purpose or risk class is used. For example, a firm with a required rate of return of 12 percent might use the following rate-of-return categorization:

Project	Required Rate of Return
Replacement decision	12%
Modification or expansion of existing product line	15
Project unrelated to current operations	18
Research and development operations	25

The purpose of this categorization of projects is to make their evaluation easier, but it also introduces a sense of the arbitrary into the calculations that makes the evaluation less meaningful. The tradeoffs involved in the classification above are obvious; time and effort are minimized, but only at the cost of precision.

Certainty Equivalent Versus Risk-Adjusted Discount Rate Methods

The primary difference between the certainty equivalent approach and the risk-adjusted discount rate approach involves the point at which the adjustment for risk is incorporated into the calculations. The certainty equivalent penalizes

TABLE 7–5.
Computational Steps in Certainty Equivalent
and Risk-Adjusted Discount Rate Methods

Certainty Equivalent	Risk-Adjusted Discount Rate
STEP 1: Adjust the expected cash flows, ACF_t, downward for risk by multiplying them by the corresponding certainty equivalent, risk coefficient, α_t.	STEP 1: Adjust the discount rate upward for risk.
STEP 2: Discount the certainty equivalent, riskless, cash flows back to the present using the *risk-free rate of interest.*	STEP 2: Discount the expected cash flows back to present using the risk-adjusted discount rate.
STEP 3: Apply the normal decision criteria, except in the case of the internal rate of return, where the risk-free rate of interest replaces the required rate of return as the hurdle rate.	STEP 3: Apply the normal decision criteria, except in the case of the internal rate of return, where the risk-adjusted discount rate replaces the required rate of return as the hurdle rate.

or adjusts downward the value of the expected annual after-tax cash flows, ACF_t, which results in a lower net present value for a risky project. The risk-adjusted discount rate, conversely, leaves the cash flows at their expected value and adjusts the required rate of return, i, upward to compensate for added risk. In either case the project's net present value is being adjusted downward to compensate for additional risk. The computational differences are illustrated in Table 7–5.

In addition to the difference in point of adjustment for risk, the risk-adjusted discount rate makes the implicit assumption that risk becomes greater as we move further out in time. Although this is not necessarily a good or bad assumption, we should be aware of it and understand it. Let's look at an example in which the risk-adjusted discount rate is used and then determine what certainty equivalent coefficients, α_t, would be necessary to arrive at the same solution.

EXAMPLE

Assume that a firm with a required rate of return of 10 percent is considering introducing a new product. This product has an initial outlay of $800,000, an expected life of 15 years, and after-tax cash flows of $100,000 each year during its life. Because of the increased risk associated with this project, management is requiring a 15 percent rate of return. Let us also assume that the risk-free rate of return is 6 percent.

If the firm chose to use the certainty equivalent method, the certainty equivalent cash flows would be discounted back to the present at 6 percent, the risk-free rate of interest. The present value of the $100,000 cash flow occurring at the end of the first year discounted back to present at 15 percent is $87,000. The present value of this $100,000 flow discounted back to present at the risk-free rate of 6 percent is $94,300. Thus, if the certainty equivalent approach were used, a certainty equivalent coefficient, α_1, of .9226 would be necessary to produce a present value of $87,000. In other words, the same results can be obtained in the first year by using the risk-adjusted discount rate and adjusting the discount rate up to 15 percent or by using the certainty equivalent approach and adjusting the expected cash flows by a certainty equivalent coefficient of .9226.

Under the risk-adjusted discount rate, the present value of the $100,000 cash flow occurring at the end of the second year becomes $75,600, and to produce an identical present value under the certainty equivalent approach, a certainty equivalent coefficient of .8494 would be needed. Following this through for the life of the project yields the certainty equivalent coefficients given in Table 7–6.

TABLE 7-6.
Certainty Equivalent Coefficients Yielding Same Results as Risk-Adjusted Discount Rate of 15 Percent in Illustrative Example

Year	1	2	3	4	5	6	7	8	9	10
α_t:	.9226	.8494	.7833	.7222	.6653	.6128	.5654	.5215	.4797	.4427

What does this analysis suggest? It indicates that if the risk-adjusted discount rate method is used, we are adjusting downward the value of future cash flows that occur further in the future more severely than earlier cash flows.

In summary, the use of the risk-adjusted discount rate assumes that risk increases over time and that cash flows occurring further in the future should be more severely penalized.

Perspective in Finance

If performed properly, either of these methods can do a good job of adjusting for risk. However, by far, the most popular method of risk adjustment is the risk-adjusted discount rate. The reason for the popularity of the risk-adjusted discount rate over the certainty equivalent approach is purely and simply its ease of implementation.

Risk-Adjusted Discount Rate and Measurement of a Project's Systematic Risk

When we initially talked about systematic risk or the beta, we were talking about measuring it for the entire firm. As you recall, although we could estimate a firm's beta using historical data, we did not have complete confidence in our results. As we will see, estimating the appropriate level of systematic risk for a single project is even more fraught with difficulties. To truly understand what it is that we are trying to do and the difficulties that we will encounter let us step back a bit and examine systematic risk and the risk adjustment for a project.

What we are trying to do is to use the CAPM to determine the level of risk and the appropriate risk–return tradeoffs for a particular project. We will then take the expected return on this project and compare it to the risk–return tradeoffs suggested by the CAPM to determine whether or not the project should be accepted. If the project appears to be a typical one for the firm, using the CAPM to determine the appropriate risk–return tradeoffs and then judging the project against them may be a warranted approach. But if the project is not a typical project, what do we do? Historical data generally do not exist for a new project. In fact, for some capital investments, for example, a truck or a new building, historical data would not have much meaning. What we need to do is make the best out of a bad situation. We either (1) fake it—that is, use historical accounting data, if available, to substitute for historical price data in estimating systematic risk, or (2) we attempt to find a substitute firm in the same industry as the capital-budgeting project and use the substitute firm's estimated systematic risk as a proxy for the project's systematic risk.

Beta Estimation Using Accounting Data

When we are dealing with a project that is identical to the firm's other projects, we need only estimate the level of systematic risk for the firm and use that estimate as a proxy for the project's risk. Unfortunately, when projects are not typical of the firm this approach does not work. For example, when R. J. Reynolds introduces a new food through one of its food products divisions, this new product most likely carries with it a different level of systematic risk than is typical for Reynolds as a whole.

To get a better approximation of the systematic risk level on this project we will estimate the level of systematic risk for the food division and use that as a proxy for the project's systematic risk. Unfortunately, historical stock price data are available only for the company as a whole, and as you recall historical stock return data are generally used to estimate a firm's beta. Thus, we are forced to use *accounting return data* rather than historical stock return data for the division to estimate the division's systematic risk. To estimate a project's beta using accounting data we need only run a time series regression of the division's return on assets (net income/total assets) on the market index (the S&P 500). The regression coefficient from this equation would be the project's accounting beta and would serve as an approximation for the project's true beta or measure of systematic risk. Alternatively, a multiple regression model based on accounting data could be developed to explain betas. The results of this model could then be applied to firms which are not publicly traded to estimate their betas.

How good is the accounting beta technique? It certainly is not as good as a direct calculation of the beta. In fact, the correlation between the accounting beta and the beta calculated on historical stock return data is only about 0.6; however, better luck has been experienced with multiple regression models used to predict betas. Unfortunately, in many cases there may not be any realistic alternative to the calculation of the accounting beta. Owing to the importance of adjusting for a project's risk, the accounting beta method is much preferred to doing nothing.

The Pure Play Method for Estimating a Project's Beta

Whereas the accounting beta method attempts to directly estimate a project or division's beta, the *pure play method* attempts to identify publicly traded firms that are engaged solely in the same business as the project or division. Once the

---

FINANCIAL MANAGEMENT IN PRACTICE

Taking Risks at Johnson & Johnson

Taking risks is not always risky, in some cases it is simply the prudent thing to do. Although one isolated R & D project may be risky by itself, an R & D program may not have much risk at all. Although most R & D projects are doomed to failure, enough of them make it and produce profits at a high enough level to make the entire R & D program profitable.

During the 1980s, James Burke has quintupled research spending at Johnson & Johnson, encouraged the introduction of more than 200 new products during a five-year period, and instituted a philosophy of innovation that allows managers to fail. As J & J's chief executive, Burke has spent thirty years nurturing innovation through new products.

His first stay at J & J lasted only one year. In 1953, he left, feeling stifled and bored. Before his departure, Burke suggested that J & J create a new-products division. In less than three weeks, he was back to head this division. After accepting, Burke set about developing new ideas, until he was summoned to the office of the chairman, General Robert Wood Johnson. It seems that one of Burke's first innovations, a children's chest rub, had failed dismally.

General Johnson asked, "Are you the one who cost us all that money?" Burke nodded. The General said, "Well, I just want to congratulate you. If you are making mistakes, that means you are making decisions and taking risks. And we don't grow unless you take risks."

Today Burke is still spreading the gospel of innovation. "Any successful growth company is riddled with failures, and there's just not any other way to do it," he explains. "We love to win, but we also have to lose in order to grow." Burke believes that innovation can be nurtured through creative conflict, by encouraging an entrepreneurial urge and open debate on new ideas among his people.

Sources: Kenneth Labich, "The Innovators," *Fortune*, June 6, 1988, pp. 50–64; and Laura L. Nash, "Johnson & Johnson's Credo," in *Corporate Ethics: A Prime Business Asset* (New York: Business Roundtable, 1988), pp. 77–104. Adapted by permission from David H. Holt, *Management*, 2nd ed., p. 25. Copyright © 1990 by Prentice Hall, Inc.

proxy or pure play firm is identified, its systematic risk is determined and then used as a proxy for the project or division's level of systematic risk. What we are doing is looking for a publicly traded firm on the outside that looks like our project and using that firm's required rate of return to judge our project. In doing so we are presuming that the systematic risk and the capital structure of the proxy firm are identical to those of the project.

In using the pure play method it should be noted that a firm's capital structure is reflected in its beta. When the capital structure of the proxy firm is different from that of the project's firm, some adjustment must be made for this difference. Although not a perfect approach, it does provide some insights as to the level of systematic risk a project might have.

FIGURE 7–6.
Capital-Budgeting Simulation

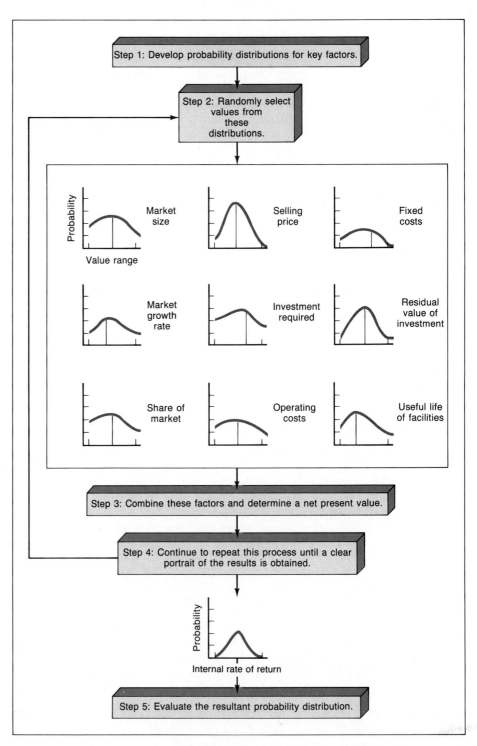

Other Approaches to Evaluating Risk in Capital Budgeting

Simulation

Another method for evaluating risk in the investment decision is through the use of **simulation.** The certainty equivalent and risk-adjusted discount rate approaches provided us with a single value for the risk-adjusted net present value, whereas a simulation approach gives us a probability distribution for the investment's net present value or internal rate of return. Simulation imitates the performance of the project under evaluation. This is done by randomly selecting observations from each of the distributions that affect the outcome of the project, combining those observations to determine the final output of the project, and continuing with this process until a representative record of the project's probable outcome is assembled.

The easiest way to develop an understanding of the computer simulation process is to follow through an example simulation for an investment project evaluation. Suppose a chemical producer is considering an extension to its processing plant. The simulation process is portrayed in Figure 7–6. First the probability distributions are determined for all the factors that affect the project's returns; in this case, let us assume there are nine such variables:

1. Market size
2. Selling price
3. Market growth rate
4. Share of market (which results in physical sales volume)
5. Investment required
6. Residual value of investment
7. Operating costs
8. Fixed costs
9. Useful life of facilities

Then the computer randomly selects one observation from each of the probability distributions, according to its chance of actually occurring in the future. These nine observations are combined, and a net present value or internal rate of return figure is calculated. This process is repeated as many times as desired, until a representative distribution of possible future outcomes is assembled. Thus, the inputs to a simulation include all the principal factors affecting the project's profitability, and the simulation output is a probability distribution of net present values or internal rates of return for the project. The decision maker bases the decision on the full range of possible outcomes. The project is accepted if the decision maker feels that enough of the distribution lies above the normal cutoff criteria ($NPV \geq 0$, $IRR \geq$ required rate of return).

Suppose that the output from the simulation of a chemical producer's project is as given in Figure 7–7 on page 242. This output provides the decision maker with the probability of different outcomes occurring in addition to the range of possible outcomes. Sometimes called *scenario analysis*, this examination identifies the range of possible outcomes under the worst, best, and most likely case. The firm's management will examine the distribution to determine the project's level of risk and then make the appropriate adjustment.

You'll notice that although the simulation approach helps us to determine the amount of total risk that a project has, it does not differentiate between systematic and unsystematic risk. Because systematic risk cannot be diversified

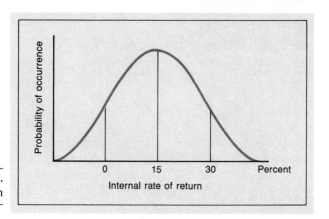

FIGURE 7-7.
Output from Simulation

away for free, the simulation approach does not provide a complete method of risk assessment. However, it does provide important insights as to the total risk level of a given investment project. Now we will look briefly at how the simulation approach can be used to perform sensitivity analysis.

Sensitivity Analysis Through Simulation Approach

Sensitivity analysis involves determining how the distribution of possible net present values or internal rates of return for a particular project is affected by a change in one particular input variable. This is done by changing the value of one input variable while holding all other input variables constant. The distribution of possible net present values or internal rates of return that is generated is then compared with the distribution of possible returns generated before the change was made to determine the effect of the change. For this reason sensitivity analysis is commonly called *"What if?" Analysis*.

For example, the chemical producer that was considering a possible expansion to its plant may wish to determine the effect of a more pessimistic forecast of the anticipated market growth rate. After the more pessimistic forecast replaces the original forecast in the model, the simulation is rerun. The two outputs are then compared to determine how sensitive the results are to the revised estimate of the market growth rate.

By modifying assumptions made about the values and ranges of the input factors and rerunning the simulation, management can determine how sensitive the outcome of the project is to these changes. If the output appears to be highly sensitive to one or two of the input factors, the financial managers may then wish to spend additional time refining those input estimates to make sure they are accurate.

Probability Trees

A *probability tree* is a graphic exposition of the sequence of possible outcomes; it presents the decision maker with a schematic representation of the problem in which all possible outcomes are pictured. Moreover, the computations and results of the computations are shown directly on the tree, so that the information can be easily understood.

To illustrate the use of a probability tree, suppose a firm is considering an investment proposal that requires an initial outlay of $1 million and will yield resultant cash flows for the next two years. During the first year let us assume there are three possible outcomes, as shown in Table 7-7. Graphically, each of these three possible alternatives is represented on the probability tree in Figure 7-8 as one of the three possible branches. The second step in the probability tree is to continue drawing branches in

TABLE 7–7.
Possible Outcomes in Year 1

	Probability		
	.5 Outcome 1	.3 Outcome 2	.2 Outcome 3
Cash flow	$600,00	$700,000	$800,000

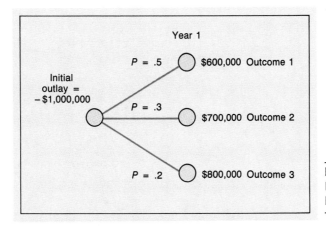

FIGURE 7–8.
First Stage of a Probability-Tree
Diagram

a similar manner so that each of the possible outcomes during the second year is represented by a new branch. For example, if outcome 1 occurs in year 1, a 20 percent chance of a $300,000 cash flow and an 80 percent chance of a $600,000 cash flow in year 2 have been projected. Two branches would be sent out from the outcome 1 node, reflecting these two possible outcomes. The cash flows that occur if outcome 1 takes place and the probabilities associated with them are called **conditional outcomes** and **conditional probabilities** because they can occur only if outcome 1 occurs during the first year. Finally, to determine the probability of the sequence of a $600,000 flow in year 1 and a $300,000 outcome in year 2, the probability of the $600,000 flow (.5) is multiplied by the conditional probability of the second flow (.2), telling us that this sequence has a 10 percent chance of occurring; this is called its **joint probability.** Letting the values in Table 7–8 represent the conditional outcomes and their respective conditional probabilities, we can complete the probability tree, as shown in Figure 7–9 on page 244.

The financial manager, by examining the probability tree, is provided with the expected internal rate of return for the investment, the range of possible outcomes, and a listing of each possible outcome with the probability associated with it. In this case, the expected internal rate of return is 14.74 percent, and there is a 10 percent chance of incurring the worst possible outcome with an internal rate of return of −7.55 percent. There is a 2 percent probability of achieving the most favorable outcome, an internal rate of return of 37.98 percent.

Decision making with probability trees does not mean simply the acceptance of any project with an internal rate of return greater than the firm's required rate of return, because the project's required rate of return has not yet been adjusted for risk. As a result, the financial decision maker must examine

TABLE 7–8.
Conditional Outcomes
and Probabilities for Year 2

Year 1	If Outcome 1 $ACF_1 = \$600,000$		If Outcome 2 $ACF_1 = \$700,000$		If Outcome 3 $ACF_1 = \$800,000$	
Year 2	Then ACF_2	Probability	Then ACF_2	Probability	Then ACF_2	Probability
	$300,000	.2	$300,000	.2	$400,000	.2
	600,000	.8	500,000	.3	600,000	.7
			700,000	.5	800,000	.1

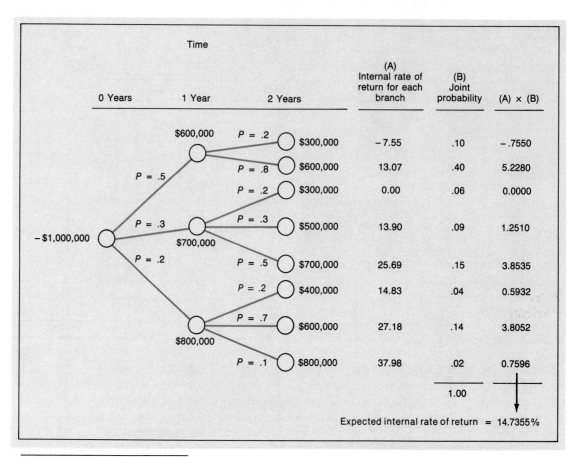

FIGURE 7-9.
Probability Tree

the entire distribution of possible internal rates of return and then, based on that examination, decide, given her or his aversion to risk, if enough of this distribution is above the appropriate (risk-adjusted) required rate of return to warrant acceptance of the project. Thus, the probability tree allows the manager to quickly visualize the possible future events, their probabilities, and their outcomes. In addition, the calculation of the expected internal rate of return and enumeration of the distribution should aid the financial manager in determining the risk level of the project.

Other Sources and Measures of Risk

Time Dependence of Cash Flows

Up to this point, in all approaches other than the probability tree we have assumed that the cash flow in one period is independent of the cash flow in the previous period. Although this assumption is appealing because it is simple, in many cases it is also invalid. For example, if a new product is introduced and the initial public reaction is poor, resulting in low initial cash flows, then cash flows in future periods are likely to be low. An extreme example of this is Ford's experience with the Edsel. Poor consumer acceptance and sales in the first year were followed by even poorer results in the second year. If the Edsel had been received favorably during its first year, it quite likely would have done well in the second year. The end effect of time dependence of cash flows is to increase the risk of the project over time. That is, because large cash flows in the first period lead to large cash flows in the second period, and low cash flows in the first period lead to low cash flows in the second period, the probability distribution of possible net present values tends to be wider than if the cash flows were not dependent over time. The greater the degree of correlation between flows over time, the greater will be the dispersion of the probability distribution.

Skewness

In all previous approaches other than simulation and probability trees, we have assumed that the distributions of net present values for projects being evaluated are normally distributed. This assumption is not always valid. When it is true, the standard deviation provides an adequate measure of the distribution's dispersion; however, when the distribution is not normally distributed, reliance on the standard deviation can be misleading.

A distribution that is not symmetric is said to be skewed. A **skewed distribution** has either a longer "tail" to the right or to the left. For example, if a distribution is skewed to the right, most values will be clustered around the left end, and the distribution will appear to have a long tail on the right end of the range of values. Graphic illustrations of skewed distributions are presented in Figure 7–10.

The difficulty associated with skewed distributions arises from the fact that the use of the expected value and standard deviation alone may not be enough to differentiate properly between two distributions. For example, the two distributions shown in Figure 7–11 have the same expected value and the same standard deviation; however, distribution A is skewed to the left while B is skewed to the right. If a financial manager were given a choice between these two distributions, assuming they are mutually exclusive, he or she would most likely choose distribution B, because it involves less chance of a negative net present value. Thus, skewness can affect the level of risk and the desirability of a distribution.

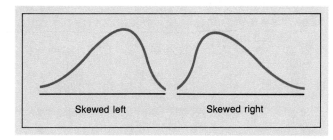

Skewed left   Skewed right

FIGURE 7–10.
Examples of Skewed Distributions

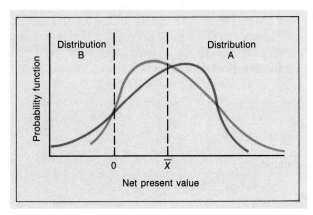

FIGURE 7–11.
Two Distributions with Identical Expected Values and Standard Deviations but Different Skewness

SUMMARY

This chapter introduces several complications into the capital-budgeting process. First, we examine capital rationing and the problems it can create by imposing a limit on the dollar size of the capital budget. Although capital rationing does not, in general, lead to the goal of maximization of shareholders' wealth, it does exist in practice. We also discuss problems associated with the evaluation of mutually exclusive projects. Mutually exclusive projects occur when a set of investment proposals perform essentially the same task. In general, to deal with mutually exclusive projects we rank them by means of the discounted cash flow criteria and select the project with the highest ranking. Conflicting rankings may arise because of the size disparity problem, the time disparity problem, and unequal lives. The problem of incomparability of projects with different lives is not simply a result of the different lives; rather, it arises because future profitable investment proposals may be rejected without being included in the analysis. Replacement chains and equivalent annual annuities are presented as possible solutions to this problem.

We also cover the problem of incorporating risk into the capital-budgeting decision. First we explore just what type of risk to adjust for: total project risk, the project's contribution-to-firm risk, or the project's systematic risk. In theory, systematic risk is the appropriate risk measure, but bankruptcy costs and the issue of undiversified shareholders also give weight to considering a project's contribution-to-firm risk as the appropriate risk measure. Both measures of risk are valid, and we avoid making any specific allocation of importance between the two in capital budgeting.

Several commonly used methods for incorporating risk into capital budgeting are (1) the certainty equivalent method, (2) risk-adjusted discount rates, (3) simulation, and (4) probability trees. The certainty equivalent approach involves a direct attempt to incorporate the decision maker's utility function into the analysis. Under this method, cash flows are adjusted downward by multiplying them by certainty equivalent coefficients, α_t, which transform the risky cash flows into equivalent certain cash flows in terms of desirability. A project's net present value using the certainty equivalent method for adjusting for risk becomes

$$NPV = \sum_{t=1}^{n} \frac{\alpha_t ACF_t}{(1 + i_F)^t} - IO$$

The risk-adjusted discount rate involves an upward adjustment of the discount rate to compensate for risk. This method is based on the concept that investors demand higher returns for riskier projects.

The simulation and probability-tree methods are used to provide information as to the location and shape of the distribution of possible outcomes. Decisions could be based directly on these methods, or they could be used to determine input into either certainty equivalent or risk-adjusted discount method approaches.

STUDY QUESTIONS

7-1. What are mutually exclusive projects? Why might the existence of mutually exclusive projects cause problems in the implementation of the discounted cash flow capital-budgeting criteria?

7-2. What are common reasons for capital rationing? Is capital rationing rational?

7-3. How should managers compare two mutually exclusive projects of unequal size? Would your approach change if capital rationing existed?

7–4. What causes the time disparity ranking problem? What reinvestment rate assumptions are associated with the net present value and internal rate of return capital-budgeting criteria?

7–5. When might two mutually exclusive projects having unequal lives be incomparable? How should managers deal with this problem?

7–6. In the preceding chapter we examined the payback period capital-budgeting criterion. Often this capital-budgeting criterion is used as a risk-screening device. Explain the rationale behind its use.

7–7. The use of the risk-adjusted discount rate assumes that risk increases over time. Justify this assumption.

7–8. What are the similarities and differences between the risk-adjusted discount rate and certainty equivalent methods for incorporating risk into the capital-budgeting decision?

7–9. What is the value of using the probability-tree technique for evaluating capital-budgeting projects?

7–10. Explain how simulation works. What is the value in using a simulation approach?

7–11. What does time dependence of cash flows mean? Why might cash flows be time *p. 244* dependent? Give some examples.

7–12. What does skewness mean? If a distribution is skewed, how does this affect the *p. 245* significance of its standard deviation and mean?

SELF-TEST PROBLEMS

ST–1. The J. Serrano Corporation is considering signing a one-year contract with one of two computer-based marketing firms. Although one is more expensive, it offers a more extensive program and thus will provide higher after-tax net cash flows. Assume these two options are mutually exclusive and that the required rate of return is 12 percent. Given the following after-tax net cash flows:

Year	Option A	Option B
0	−$50,000	−$100,000
1	70,000	130,000

a. Calculate the net present value
b. Calculate the profitability index
c. Calculate the internal rate of return
d. If there is no capital-rationing constraint, which project should be selected? If there is a capital-rationing constraint, how should the decision be made?

ST–2. The N. Sen Corp. is considering two mutually exclusive projects. Both require an initial outlay of $25,000 and will operate for five years. The probability distributions associated with each project for years 1 through 5 are given below:

Cash Flow Years 1–5

Project A		Project B	
Probability	Cash Flow	Probability	Cash Flow
.20	$10,000	.20	$ 6,000
.60	15,000	.60	18,000
.20	20,000	.20	30,000

Because project B is the riskier of the two projects, the management of N. Sen has decided to apply a required rate of return of 18 percent to its evaluation, but only a 12 percent required rate of return to project A.
a. Determine the expected value of each project's cash flows.
b. Determine each project's risk-adjusted net present value.

ST–3. G. Norohna and Co. is considering two mutually exclusive projects. The expected values for each project's cash flows are given below.

Year	Project A	Project B
0	−$300,000	−$300,000
1	100,000	200,000
2	200,000	200,000
3	200,000	200,000
4	300,000	300,000
5	300,000	400,000

The company has decided to evaluate these projects using the certainty equivalent method. The certainty equivalent coefficients for each project's cash flows are given below.

Year	Project A	Project B
0	1.00	1.00
1	.95	.90
2	.90	.80
3	.85	.70
4	.80	.60
5	.75	.50

Given that this company's normal required rate of return is 15 percent and the after-tax risk-free rate is 8 percent, which project should be selected?

STUDY PROBLEMS (SET A)

7–1A. (*Size Disparity Ranking Problem*) The D. Dorner Farms Corporation is considering purchasing one of two fertilizer-herbicides for the upcoming year. The more expensive of the two is the better and will produce a higher yield. Assume these projects are mutually exclusive and that the required rate of return is 10 percent. Given the following after-tax net cash flows:

Year	Project A	Project B
0	−$500	−$5000
1	700	6000

a. Calculate the net present value.
b. Calculate the profitability index.
c. Calculate the internal rate of return.
d. If there is no capital-rationing constraint, which project should be selected? If there is a capital-rationing constraint, how should the decision be made?

7–2A. (*Time Disparity Ranking Problem*) The State Spartan Corporation is considering two mutually exclusive projects. The cash flows associated with those projects are as follows:

Year	Project A	Project B
0	−$50,000	−$ 50,000
1	15,625	0
2	15,625	0
3	15,625	0
4	15,625	0
5	15,625	$100,000

The required rate of return on these projects is 10 percent.
a. What is each project's payback period?
b. What is each project's net present value?
c. What is each project's internal rate of return?

d. What has caused the ranking conflict?

e. Which project should be accepted? Why?

7-3A. (*Unequal Lives Ranking Problem*) The B. T. Knight Corporation is considering two mutually exclusive pieces of machinery that perform the same task. The two alternatives available provide the following set of after-tax net cash flows:

Year	Equipment A	Equipment B
0	−$20,000	−$20,000
1	12,590	6,625
2	12,590	6,625
3	12,590	6,625
4		6,625
5		6,625
6		6,625
7		6,625
8		6,625
9		6,625

Equipment A has an expected life of three years, whereas equipment B has an expected life of nine years. Assume a required rate of return of 15 percent.

a. Calculate each project's payback period.

b. Calculate each project's net present value.

c. Calculate each project's internal rate of return.

d. Are these projects comparable?

e. Compare these projects using replacement chains and EAA. Which project should be selected? Support your recommendation.

7-4A. (*EAAs*) The Andrzejewski Corporation is considering two mutually exclusive projects, one with a 3-year life and one with a 7-year life. The after-tax cash flows from the two projects are as follows:

Year	Project A	Project B
0	−$50,000	−$50,000
1	20,000	36,000
2	20,000	36,000
3	20,000	36,000
4	20,000	
5	20,000	
6	20,000	
7	20,000	

a. Assuming a 10 percent required rate of return on both projects, calculate each project's EAA. Which project should be selected?

b. Calculate the present value of an infinite-life replacement chain for each project.

7-5A. (*Capital Rationing*) The Cowboy Hat Company of Stillwater, Okla., is considering seven capital investment proposals, for which the funds available are limited to a maximum of $12 million. The projects are independent and have the following costs and profitability indexes associated with them:

Project	Cost	Profitability Index
A	$4,000,000	1.18
B	3,000,000	1.08
C	5,000,000	1.33
D	6,000,000	1.31
E	4,000,000	1.19
F	6,000,000	1.20
G	4,000,000	1.18

a. Under strict capital rationing, which projects should be selected?

b. What problems are there with capital rationing?

7–6A. (*Risk-Adjusted NPV*) The Hokie Corporation is considering two mutually exclusive projects. Both require an initial outlay of $10,000 and will operate for five years. The probability distributions associated with each project for years 1 through 5 are given as follows:

Cash Flow Years 1–5

Project A		Project B	
Probability	Cash Flow	Probability	Cash Flow
.15	$4,000	.15	$ 2,000
.70	5,000	.70	6,000
.15	6,000	.15	10,000

Because project B is the riskier of the two projects, the management of Hokie Corporation has decided to apply a required rate of return of 15 percent to its evaluation but only a 12 percent required rate of return to project A.
a. Determine the expected value of each project's cash flows.
b. Determine each project's risk-adjusted net present value.
c. What other factors might be considered in deciding between these two projects?

7–7A. (*Risk-Adjusted NPV*) The Goblu Corporation is evaluating two mutually exclusive projects, both of which require an initial outlay of $100,000. Each project has an expected life of five years. The probability distributions associated with the annual cash flows from each project are given below:

Cash Flow Years 1–5

Project A		Project B	
Probability	Cash Flow	Probability	Cash Flow
.10	$35,000	.10	$10,000
.40	40,000	.20	30,000
.40	45,000	.40	45,000
.10	50,000	.20	60,000
		.10	80,000

The normal required rate of return for Goblu is 10 percent, but because these projects are riskier than most, they are requiring a higher-than-normal rate of return on them. On project A they are requiring a 12 percent and on project B a 13 percent rate of return.
a. Determine the expected value for each project's cash flows.
b. Determine each project's risk-adjusted net present value.
c. What other factors might be considered in deciding between these projects?

7–8A. (*Certainty Equivalents*) The V. Coles Corp. is considering two mutually exclusive projects. The expected values for each project's cash flows are given below:

Year	Project A	Project B
0	−$1,000,000	−$1,000,000
1	500,000	500,000
2	700,000	600,000
3	600,000	700,000
4	500,000	800,000

The management has decided to evaluate these projects using the certainty equivalent method. The certainty equivalent coefficients for each project's cash flows are given below:

Year	Project A	Project B
0	1.00	1.00
1	.95	.90
2	.90	.70
3	.80	.60
4	.70	.50

Given that this company's normal required rate of return is 15 percent and the after-tax risk-free rate is 5 percent, which project should be selected?

7-9A. (*Certainty Equivalents*) Neustal, Inc., has decided to use the certainty equivalent method in determining whether or not a new investment should be made. The expected cash flows associated with this investment and the estimated certainty equivalent coefficients are as follows:

Year	Expected Values for Cash Flows	Certainty Equivalent Coefficients
0	−$90,000	1.00
1	25,000	0.95
2	30,000	0.90
3	30,000	0.83
4	25,000	0.75
5	20,000	0.65

Given that Neustal's normal required rate of return is 18 percent and that the after-tax risk free rate is 7 percent, should this project be accepted?

7-10A. (*Risk-Adjusted Discount Rates and Risk Classes*) The G. Wolfe Corporation is examining two capital-budgeting projects with five-year lives. The first, project A, is a replacement project; the second, project B, is a project unrelated to current operations. The G. Wolfe Corporation uses the risk-adjusted discount rate method and groups projects according to purpose and then uses a required rate of return or discount rate that has been preassigned to that purpose or risk class. The expected cash flows for these projects are given below:

	Project A	Project B
Initial Investment:	$250,000	$400,000
Cash Inflows:		
Year 1	$ 30,000	$135,000
Year 2	40,000	135,000
Year 3	50,000	135,000
Year 4	90,000	135,000
Year 5	130,000	135,000

The purpose/risk classes and preassigned required rates of return are as follows:

Purpose	Required Rate of Return
Replacement decision	12%
Modification or expansion of existing product line	15
Project unrelated to current operations	18
Research and development operations	20

Determine the project's risk-adjusted net present value.

7-11A. (*Certainty Equivalents*) Nacho Nachtmann Company uses the certainty equivalent approach when it evaluates risky investments. The company presently has two mutually exclusive investment proposals, with an expected life of four years each, to choose from with money it received from the sale of part of its toy division to another company. The expected net cash flows are given below:

Year	Project A	Project B
0	−$50,000	−$50,000
1	15,000	20,000
2	15,000	25,000
3	15,000	25,000
4	45,000	30,000

The certainty equivalent coefficients for the net cash flows are as follows:

Year	Project A	Project B
0	1.00	1.00
1	.95	.90
2	.85	.85
3	.80	.80
4	.70	.75

Which of the two investment proposals should be chosen, given that the after-tax risk-free rate of return is 6 percent?

7–12A. (*Probability Trees*) The M. Solt Corporation is evaluating an investment proposal with an expected life of two years. This project will require an initial outlay of $1,200,000. The resultant possible cash flows are given below:

Possible Outcomes in Year 1

	Probability		
	.6	.3	.1
	Outcome 1	Outcome 2	Outcome 3
Cash flow =	$700,00	$850,000	$1,000,000

Conditional Outcomes and Probabilities for Year 2

If $ACF_1 = \$700,000$		If $ACF_1 = \$850,000$		If $ACF_1 = \$1,000,000$	
ACF_2	Probability	ACF_2	Probability	ACF_2	Probability
$ 300,000	.3	$ 400,000	.2	$ 600,000	.1
700,000	.6	700,000	.5	900,000	.5
1,100,000	.1	1,000,000	.2	1,100,000	.4
		1,300,000	.1		

a. Construct a probability tree representing the possible outcomes.
b. Determine the joint probability of each possible sequence of events taking place.
c. What is the expected IRR of this project?
d. What is the range of possible IRRs for this project?

7–13A. (*Probability Trees*) The E. Swank Corporation is considering an investment project with an expected life of two years. The initial outlay on this project would be $600,000, and the resultant possible cash flows are given below:

Possible Outcomes in Year 1

	Probability		
0	.4	.4	.3
	Outcome 1	Outcome 2	Outcome 3
Cash flow =	$300,000	$350,000	$450,000

Conditional Outcomes and Probabilities for Year 2

If $ACF_1 = \$300,000$		If $ACF_1 = \$350,000$		If $ACF_1 = \$450,000$	
ACF_2	Probability	ACF_2	Probability	ACF_2	Probability
$200,000	.3	$250,000	.2	$ 300,000	.2
300,000	.7	450,000	.5	500,000	.5
		650,000	.3	700,000	.2
				1,000,000	.1

a. Construct a probability tree representing the possible outcomes.

b. Determine the joint probability of each possible sequence of events taking place.

c. What is the expected IRR of this project?

d. What is the range of possible IRRs for this project?

7-14A. (*Probability Trees*) V. Janjigian, Inc., is considering expanding its operations into computer-based basketball games. Janjigian feels that there is a three-year life associated with this project, and it will initially involve an investment of $100,000. It also believes there is a 60 percent chance of success and a cash flow of $100,000 in year 1 and a 40 percent chance of failure and a $10,000 cash flow in year 1. If the project fails in year 1, there is a 60 percent chance that it will produce cash flows of only $10,000 in years 2 and 3. There is also a 40 percent chance that it will *really* fail and Janjigian will earn nothing in year 2 and get out of this line of business, with the project terminating and no cash flow occurring in year 3. If, conversely, this project succeeds in the first year, then cash flows in the second year are expected to be $200,000, $175,000, or $150,000 with probabilities of .30, .50, and .20, respectively. Finally, if the project succeeds in the third and final year of operation, the cash flows are expected to be either $30,000 more or $20,000 less than they were in year 2, with an equal chance of occurrence.

a. Construct a probability tree representing the possible outcomes.

b. Determine the joint probability of each possible sequence of events.

c. What is the expected IRR?

d. What is the range of possible IRRs for this project?

STUDY PROBLEMS (SET B)

7-1B. (*Size Disparity Ranking Problem*) The Unk's Farms Corporation is considering purchasing one of two fertilizer-herbicides for the upcoming year. The more expensive of the two is the better and will produce a higher yield. Assume these projects are mutually exclusive and that the required rate of return is 10 percent. Given the following after-tax net cash flows:

Year	Project A	Project B
0	-$650	-$4,000
1	800	5,500

a. Calculate the net present value.

b. Calculate the profitability index.

c. Calculate the internal rate of return.

d. If there is no capital-rationing constraint, which project should be selected? If there is a capital-rationing constraint, how should the decision be made?

7-2B. (*Time Disparity Ranking Problem*) The Z. Bello Corporation is considering two mutually exclusive projects. The cash flows associated with those projects are as follows:

Year	Project A	Project B
0	-$50,000	-$ 50,000
1	16,000	0
2	16,000	0
3	16,000	0
4	16,000	0
5	16,000	$100,000

The required rate of return on these projects is 11 percent.

a. What is each project's payback period?

b. What is each project's net present value?

c. What is each project's internal rate of return?

d. What has caused the ranking conflict?

e. Which project should be accepted? Why?

7-3B. (*Unequal Lives Ranking Problem*) The Battling Bishops Corporation is considering two mutually exclusive pieces of machinery that perform the same task. The two alternatives available provide the following set of after-tax net cash flows:

Year	Equipment A	Equipment B
0	-$20,000	-$20,000
1	13,000	6,500
2	13,000	6,500
3	13,000	6,500
4		6,500
5		6,500
6		6,500
7		6,500
8		6,500
9		6,500

Equipment A has an expected life of three years, whereas equipment B has an expected life of nine years. Assume a required rate of return of 14 percent.
a. Calculate each project's payback period.
b. Calculate each project's net present value.
c. Calculate each project's internal rate of return.
d. Are these projects comparable?
e. Compare these projects using replacement chains and EAAs. Which project should be selected? Support your recommendation.

7-4B. (*EAAs*) The Anduski Corporation is considering two mutually exclusive projects, one with a 5-year life and one with a 7-year life. The after-tax cash flows from the two projects are as follows:

Year	Project A	Project B
0	-$40,000	-$40,000
1	20,000	25,000
2	20,000	25,000
3	20,000	25,000
4	20,000	25,000
5	20,000	25,000
6	20,000	
7	20,000	

a. Assuming a 10 percent required rate of return on both projects, calculate each project's EAA. Which project should be selected?

b. Calculate the present value of an infinite-life replacement chain for each project.

7-5B. (*Capital Rationing*) The Taco Toast Company is considering seven capital investment proposals, for which the funds available are limited to a maximum of $12 million. The projects are independent and have the following costs and profitability indexes associated with them:

Project	Cost	Profitability Index
A	$4,000,000	1.18
B	3,000,000	1.08
C	5,000,000	1.33
D	6,000,000	1.31
E	4,000,000	1.19
F	6,000,000	1.20
G	4,000,000	1.18

a. Under strict capital rationing, which projects should be selected?
b. What problems are associated with imposing capital rationing?

7-6B. (*Risk-Adjusted NPV*) The Cake-O-Las Corporation is considering two mutually exclusive projects. Each of these projects requires an initial outlay of $10,000 and will operate for five years. The probability distributions associated with each project for years 1 through 5 are given as follows:

Cash Flow Years 1–5

Project A		Project B	
Probability	Cash Flow	Probability	Cash Flow
.20	$5,000	.20	$ 3,000
.60	6,000	.60	7,000
.20	7,000	.20	11,000

Because project B is the riskier of the two projects, the management of Cake-O-Las Corporation has decided to apply a required rate of return of 18 percent to its evaluation but only a 13 percent required rate of return to project A.
a. Determine the expected value of each project's cash flows.
b. Determine each project's risk-adjusted net present value.
c. What other factors might be considered in deciding between these two projects?

7-7B. (*Risk-Adjusted NPV*) The Dorf Corporation is evaluating two mutually exclusive projects, both of which require an initial outlay of $125,000. Each project has an expected life of five years. The probability distributions associated with the annual cash flows from each project are given below:

Cash Flow Years 1–5

Project A		Project B	
Probability	Cash Flow	Probability	Cash Flow
.10	$40,000	.10	$ 20,000
.40	45,000	.20	40,000
.40	50,000	.40	55,000
.10	55,000	.20	70,000
		.10	90,000

The normal required rate of return for Dorf is 10 percent, but because these projects are riskier than most, Dorf is requiring a higher-than-normal rate of return on them. On project A it is requiring an 11 percent and on project B a 13 percent rate of return.
a. Determine the expected value for each project's cash flows.
b. Determine each project's risk-adjusted net present value.
c. What other factors might be considered in deciding between these projects?

7-8B. (*Certainty Equivalents*) The Temco Corp. is considering two mutually exclusive projects. The expected values for each project's cash flows are given below:

Year	Project A	Project B
0	−$1,000,000	−$1,000,000
1	600,000	600,000
2	750,000	650,000
3	600,000	700,000
4	550,000	750,000

Temco has decided to evaluate these projects using the certainty equivalent method. The certainty equivalent coefficients for each project's cash flows are given below:

Year	Project A	Project B
0	1.00	1.00
1	.90	.95
2	.90	.75
3	.75	.60
4	.65	.60

Given that this company's normal required rate of return is 15 percent and the after-tax risk-free rate is 5 percent, which project should be selected?

7-9B. (*Certainty Equivalents*) Perumperal, Inc., has decided to use the certainty equivalent method in determining whether or not a new investment should be made. The expected cash flows associated with this investment and the estimated certainty equivalent coefficients are as follows:

Year	Expected Values for Cash Flows	Certainty Equivalent Coefficients
0	−$100,000	1.00
1	30,000	0.95
2	25,000	0.90
3	30,000	0.83
4	20,000	0.75
5	25,000	0.65

Given that Perumperal's normal required rate of return is 18 percent and that the after-tax risk free rate is 8 percent, should this project be accepted?

7-10B. (*Risk-Adjusted Discount Rates and Risk Classes*) The Kick 'n' MacDonald Corporation is examining two capital-budgeting projects with five-year lives. The first, project A, is a replacement project; the second, project B, is a project unrelated to current operations. The Kick 'n' MacDonald Corporation uses the risk-adjusted discount rate method and groups projects according to purpose and then uses a required rate of return or discount rate that has been preassigned to that purpose or risk class. The expected cash flows for these projects are given below:

	Project A	Project B
Initial Investment:	$300,000	$450,000
Cash Inflows:		
Year 1	$ 30,000	$130,000
Year 2	40,000	130,000
Year 3	50,000	130,000
Year 4	80,000	130,000
Year 5	120,000	130,000

The purpose-risk classes and preassigned required rates of return are as follows:

Purpose	Required Rate of Return
Replacement decision	13%
Modification or expansion of existing product line	16
Project unrelated to current operations	18
Research and development operations	20

Determine the project's risk-adjusted net present value.

7-11B. (*Certainty Equivalents*) The M. Jose Company uses the certainty equivalent approach when it evaluates risky investments. The company presently has two mutually exclusive investment proposals, with an expected life of four years each, to choose from with money it received from the sale of part of its toy division to another company. The expected net cash flows are given below:

Year	Project A	Project B
0	−$75,000	−$75,000
1	20,000	25,000
2	20,000	30,000
3	15,000	30,000
4	50,000	25,000

The certainty equivalent coefficients for the net cash flows are as follows:

Year	Project A	Project B
0	1.00	1.00
1	.90	.95
2	.85	.85
3	.80	.80
4	.70	.75

Which of the two investment proposals should be chosen, given that the after-tax risk-free rate of return is 7 percent?

7–12B. (*Probability Trees*) The Buckeye Corporation is evaluating an investment proposal with an expected life of two years. This project will require an initial outlay of $1,300,000. The resultant possible cash flows are given below:

Possible Outcomes in Year 1

	Probability		
	.6	.3	.1
	Outcome 1	Outcome 2	Outcome 3
Cash flow =	$750,000	$900,000	$1,500,000

Conditional Outcomes and Probabilities for Year 2

If $ACF_1 = \$750,000$		If $ACF_1 = \$900,000$		If $ACF_1 = \$1,500,000$	
ACF_2	Probability	ACF_2	Probability	ACF_2	Probability
$ 300,000	.10	$ 400,000	.2	$ 600,000	.3
700,000	.50	700,000	.5	900,000	.6
1,100,000	.40	900,000	.2	1,100,000	.1
		1,300,000	.1		

a. Construct a probability tree representing the possible outcomes.
b. Determine the joint probability of each possible sequence of events taking place.
c. What is the expected IRR of this project?
d. What is the range of possible IRRs for this project?

7–13B. (*Probability Trees*) The OSUCOWBOYS Corporation is considering an investment project with an expected life of two years. The initial outlay on this project would be $700,000, and the resultant possible cash flows are given below:

Possible Outcomes in Year 1

	Probability		
	.4	.4	.2
	Outcome 1	Outcome 2	Outcome 3
Cash flow =	$325,000	$350,000	$475,000

Conditional Outcomes and Probabilities for Year 2

If $ACF_1 = \$325,000$		If $ACF_1 = \$350,000$		If $ACF_1 = \$475,000$	
ACF_2	Probability	ACF_2	Probability	ACF_2	Probability
$ 200,000	.3	$ 250,000	.2	$ 300,000	.2
350,000	.7	400,000	.5	550,000	.5
		650,000	.3	600,000	.2
				1,000,000	.1

a. Construct a probability tree representing the possible outcomes.
b. Determine the joint probability of each possible sequence of events taking place.
c. What is the expected IRR of this project?
d. What is the range of possible IRRs for this project?

7–14B. (*Probability Trees*) Mac's Buffaloes, Inc., is considering expanding its operations into computer-based basketball games. Mac's Buffaloes feels that there is a three-year life associated with this project, and it will initially involve an investment of $120,000. It also feels there is a 70 percent chance of success and a cash flow of $100,000 in year 1 and a 30 percent chance of "failure" and a $10,000 cash flow in year 1. If the project "fails" in year 1, there is a 60 percent chance that it will produce cash flows of only $10,000 in years 2 and 3. There is also a 40 percent chance that it will really fail and Mac's Buffaloes earn nothing in year 2 and get out of this line of business, with the project terminating and no cash flow occurring in year 3. If, on the other hand, this project succeeds in the first year, then cash flows in the second year are expected to be $225,000, $180,000, or $140,000 with probabilities of .30, .50, and .20, respectively. Finally, if the project succeeds in the third and final year of operation, the cash flows are expected to be either $30,000 more or $20,000 less than they were in year 2, with an equal chance of occurrence.
a. Construct a probability tree representing the possible outcomes.
b. Determine the joint probability of each possible sequence of events.
c. What is the expected IRR?
d. What is the range of possible IRRs for this project?

CASE PROBLEMS

HARDING PLASTIC MOLDING COMPANY

CAPITAL BUDGETING: RANKING PROBLEMS

On January 11, 1993, the finance committee of Harding Plastic Molding Company (HPMC) met to consider eight capital-budgeting projects. Present at the meeting were Robert L. Harding, president and founder, Susan Jorgensen, comptroller, and Chris Woelk, head of research and development. Over the past five years, this committee has met every month to consider and make final judgment on all proposed capital outlays brought up for review during the period.

Harding Plastic Molding Company was founded in 1965 by Robert L. Harding to produce plastic parts and molding for the Detroit automakers. For the first 10 years of operations, HPMC worked solely as a subcontractor for the automakers, but since then has made strong efforts to diversify in an attempt to avoid the cyclical problems faced by the auto industry. By 1993, this diversification attempt had led HPMC into the production of over 1,000 different items, including kitchen utensils, camera housings, and phonographic and recording equipment. It also led to an increase in sales of 800 percent during the 1975–1993 period. As this dramatic increase in sales was paralleled by a corresponding increase in production volume, HPMC was forced, in late 1991, to expand production facilities. This plant and equipment expansion involved capital expenditures of approximately $10.5 million and resulted in an increase of production capacity of about 40 percent. Because of this increased production capacity, HPMC has made a concerted effort to attract new business and consequently has recently entered into contracts with a large toy firm and a major discount department store chain. While non-auto-related business has grown significantly, it still only represents 32 percent of HPMC's overall business. Thus, HPMC has continued to solicit nonautomotive business, and as a result of this effort and its internal research and development, the firm has four sets of mutually exclusive projects to consider at this month's finance committee meeting.

Over the past 10 years, HPMC's capital-budgeting approach has evolved into a somewhat elaborate procedure in which new proposals are categorized into three areas: profit, research and development, and safety. Projects falling into the profit or research and development areas are evaluated using present value techniques, assuming a 10 percent opportunity rate; those falling into the safety classification are evaluated in a more subjective framework. Although research and development projects have to receive favorable results from the present value criteria, there is also a total dollar limit assigned to projects of this category, typically running about $750,000 per year. This limitation was imposed by Harding primarily because of the limited availability of quality researchers in the plastics industry. Harding felt that if more funds than this were allocated, "we simply couldn't find the manpower to administer them properly." The benefits derived from safety projects, on the other hand, are not in terms of cash flows; hence, present value methods are not used at all in their evaluation. The subjective approach used to evaluate safety projects is a result of the pragmatically difficult task of quantifying the benefits from these projects into dollar terms. Thus, these projects are subjectively evaluated by a management–worker committee with a limited budget. All eight projects to be evaluated in January are classified as profit projects.

The first set of projects listed on the meeting's agenda for examination involve the utilization of HPMC's precision equipment. Project A calls for the production of vacuum containers for thermos bottles produced for a large discount hardware chain. The containers would be manufactured in five different size and color combinations. This project would be carried out over a three-year period, for which HPMC would be guaranteed a minimum return plus a percentage of the sales. Project B involves the manufacture of inexpensive photographic equipment for a national photography outlet. Although HPMC currently has excess plant capacity, each of these projects would utilize precision equipment of which the excess capacity is limited. Thus, adopting either project would tie up all precision facilities. In addition, the purchase of new equipment would be both prohibitively expensive and involve a time delay of approximately two years, thus making these projects mutually exclusive. (The cash flows associated with these two projects are given in Exhibit 1.)

The second set of projects involves the renting of computer facilities over a one-year period to aid in customer billing and perhaps inventory control. Project C entails the evaluation of a customer billing system proposed by Advanced Computer Corporation. Under this system all the bookkeeping and billing presently being done by HPMC's accounting department would be done by Advanced. In addition to saving costs involved in bookkeeping, Advanced would provide a more efficient billing system and do a credit analysis of delinquent customers, which could be used in the future for in-depth credit analysis. Project D is proposed by International Computer Corporation and includes a billing system similar to that offered by Advanced and, in addition, an inventory control system that will keep track of all raw materials and parts in stock and reorder when necessary, thereby reducing the likelihood of material stockouts, which has become more and more frequent over the past three years. (The cash flows for these projects are given in Exhibit 2.)

<table>
<tr><td colspan="3">

EXHIBIT 1.
Harding Plastic Molding
Company
</td><td colspan="3">

EXHIBIT 2.
Harding Plastic Molding
Company
</td></tr>
<tr><td colspan="3">*Cash Flows*</td><td colspan="3">*Cash Flows*</td></tr>
<tr><td>*Year*</td><td>*Project A*</td><td>*Project B*</td><td>*Year*</td><td>*Project C*</td><td>*Project D*</td></tr>
<tr><td>0</td><td>$−75,000</td><td>$−75,000</td><td>0</td><td>$−8,000</td><td>$−20,000</td></tr>
<tr><td>1</td><td>10,000</td><td>43,000</td><td>1</td><td>11,000</td><td>25,000</td></tr>
<tr><td>2</td><td>30,000</td><td>43,000</td><td></td><td></td><td></td></tr>
<tr><td>3</td><td>100,000</td><td>43,000</td><td></td><td></td><td></td></tr>
</table>

The third decision that faces the financial directors of HPMC involves a newly developed and patented process for molding hard plastics. HPMC can either manufacture and market the equipment necessary to mold such plastics or it can sell the patent rights to Polyplastics Incorporated, the world's largest producer of plastics products. (The cash flows for projects E and F are shown in Exhibit 3.) At present, the process has not been fully tested, and if HPMC is going to market it itself, it will be necessary to complete this testing and begin production of plant facilities immediately. On the other hand, the selling of these patent rights to Polyplastics would involve only minor testing and refinements, which could be completed within the year. Thus, a decision as to the proper course of action is necessary immediately.

The final set of projects up for consideration revolve around the replacement of some of the machinery. HPMC can go in one of two directions. Project G suggests the purchase and installation of moderately priced, extremely efficient equipment with an expected life of five years; project H advocates the purchase of a similarly priced, although less efficient, machine with life expectancy of 10 years. (The cash flows for these alternatives are shown in Exhibit 4.)

As the meeting opened, debate immediately centered on the most appropriate method for evaluating all the projects. Harding suggested that as the projects to be considered were mutually exclusive, perhaps their usual capital-budgeting criteria of net present value was inappropriate. He felt that, in examining these projects, perhaps they

EXHIBIT 3.
Harding Plastic Molding
Company

EXHIBIT 4.
Harding Plastic Molding
Company

	Cash Flows	
Year	Project E	Project F
0	$-30,000	$-271,500
1	210,000	100,000
2		100,000
3		100,000
4		100,000
5		100,000
6		100,000
7		100,000
8		100,000
9		100,000
10		100,000

	Cash Flows	
Year	Project G	Project H
0	$-500,000	$-500,000
1	225,000	150,000
2	225,000	150,000
3	225,000	150,000
4	225,000	150,000
5	225,000	150,000
6		150,000
7		150,000
8		150,000
9		150,000
10		150,000

should be more concerned with relative profitability or some measure of yield. Both Jorgensen and Woelk agreed with Harding's point of view, with Jorgensen advocating a profitability index approach and Woelk preferring the use of the internal rate of return. Jorgensen argued that the use of the profitability index would provide a benefit–cost ratio, directly implying relative profitability. Thus, they merely need to rank these projects and select those with the highest profitability index. Woelk agreed with Jorgensen's point of view, but suggested that the calculation of an internal rate of return would also give a measure of profitability and perhaps be somewhat easier to interpret. To settle the issue, Harding suggested that they calculate all three measures, as they would undoubtedly yield the same ranking.

From here the discussion turned to an appropriate approach to the problem of differing lives among mutually exclusive projects E and F, and G and H. Woelk argued that there really was not a problem here at all, that as all the cash flows from these projects can be determined, any of the discounted cash flow methods of capital budgeting will work well. Jorgensen argued that although this was true, some compensation should be made for the fact that the projects being considered did not have equal lives.

QUESTIONS

1. Was Harding correct in stating that the NPV, PI, and IRR necessarily will yield the same ranking order? Under what situations might the NPV, PI, and IRR methods provide different rankings? Why is it possible?

2. What are the NPV, PI, and IRR for projects A and B? What has caused the ranking conflicts? Should project A or B be chosen? Might your answer change if project B is a typical project in the plastic molding industry? For example, if projects for HPMC generally yield approximately 12 percent, is it logical to assume that the IRR for project B of approximately 33 percent is a correct calculation for ranking purposes? (*Hint:* Examine the reinvestment rate assumption.)

3. What are the NPV, PI, and IRR for projects C and D? Should project C or D be chosen? Does your answer change if these projects are considered under a capital constraint? What return on the marginal $12,000 not employed in project C is necessary to make one indifferent to choosing one project over the other under a capital-rationing situation?

4. What are the NPV, PI, and IRR for projects E and F? Are these projects comparable even though they have unequal lives? Why? Which project should be chosen? Assume that these projects are not considered under a capital constraint.

5. What are the NPV, PI, and IRR for projects G and H? Are these projects comparable even though they have unequal lives? Why? Which project should be chosen? Assume that these projects are not considered under a capital constraint.

MADE IN THE U.S.A.: DUMPED IN BRAZIL, AFRICA . . .

ETHICS IN DEALING WITH UNCERTAINTY IN CAPITAL BUDGETING, OR WHAT HAPPENS WHEN A PROJECT IS NO LONGER SELLABLE

In an uncertain world, capital budgeting attempts to determine what the future of a new product will bring and how then to act on that forecast. We never know for certain what the future will bring, but we do arrive at some idea of what the distribution of possible outcomes looks like. Unfortunately, when there is uncertainty, the outcome is not always a good one. For example, what happens if the government rules that our product is not safe. The answer is that we must abandon the product. The question then becomes what to do with the inventory we currently have on hand. We certainly want to deal with it in a way that is in the best interests of our shareholders. We also want to obey the law and act ethically. As with most ethical questions, there isn't necessarily a right or wrong answer.

When it comes to the safety of young children, fire is a parent's nightmare. Just the thought of their young ones trapped in their cribs and beds by a raging nocturnal blaze is enough to make most mothers and fathers take every precaution to ensure their children's safety. Little wonder that when fire-retardant children's pajamas hit the market in the mid-1970s, they proved an overnight success. Within a few short years more than 200 million pairs were sold, and the sales of millions more were all but guaranteed. For their manufacturers, the future could not have been been brighter. Then, like a bolt from the blue, came word that the pajamas were killers.

In June 1977, the U.S. Consumer Product Safety Commission (CPSC) banned the sale of these pajamas and ordered the recall of millions of pairs. Reason: The pajamas contained the flame-retardant chemical Tris (2,3-dibromoprophyl), which had been found to cause kidney cancer in children.

Whereas just months earlier the 100 medium- and small-garment manufacturers of the Tris-impregnated pajamas couldn't fill orders fast enough, suddenly they were worrying about how to get rid of the millions of pairs now sitting in warehouses. Because of its toxicity, the sleepwear couldn't even be thrown away, let alone sold. Indeed, the CPSC left no doubt about how the pajamas were to be disposed of—buried or burned or used as industrial wiping cloths. All meant millions of dollars in losses for manufacturers.

The companies affected—mostly small, family-run operations employing fewer than 100 workers—immediately attempted to shift blame to the mills that made the cloth. When that attempt failed, they tried to get the big department stores that sold the pajamas and the chemical companies that produced Tris to share the financial losses. Again, no sale. Finally, in desperation, the companies lobbied in Washington for a bill making the federal government partially responsible for the losses. It was the government, they argued, that originally had required the companies to add Tris to pajamas and then had prohibited their sale. Congress was sympathetic; it passed a bill granting companies relief. But President Carter vetoed it.

While the small firms were waging their political battle in the halls of Congress, ads began appearing in the classified pages of *Women's Wear Daily*. "Tris-Tris-Tris . . . We will buy any fabric containing Tris," read one. Another said, "Tris—we will purchase any large quantities of garments containing Tris."[1] The ads had been placed by exporters, who began buying up the pajamas, usually at 10 to 30 percent of the normal wholesale price. Their intent was clear: to dump* the carcinogenic pajamas on overseas markets.[2]

Tris is not the only example of dumping. In 1972, 400 Iraqis died and 5,000 were hospitalized after eating wheat and barley treated with a U.S.-banned organic mercury fungicide. Winstrol, a synthetic male hormone that had been found to stunt the growth of American children, was made available in Brazil as an appetite stimulant for children. Depo-Provera, an injectable contraceptive known to cause malignant tumors in animals, was shipped overseas to seventy countries where it was used in U.S.-sponsored population control programs. And 450,000 baby pacifiers, of the type known to have caused choking deaths, were exported for sale overseas.

---

[1]Mark Hosenball, "Karl Marx and the Pajama Game," *Mother Jones*, November 1979, p. 47.

*"Dumping" is a term apparently coined by *Mother Jones* magazine to refer to the practice of exporting to overseas countries products that have been banned or declared hazardous in the United States.

[2]Unless otherwise noted, the facts and quotations reported in this case are based on Mark Dowie, "The Corporate Crime of the Century," *Mother Jones*, November 1979, and Russell Mokhiber, *Corporate Crime and Violence* (San Francisco: Sierra Club Books, 1988), pp. 181–195. See also Jane Kay, "Global Dumping of U.S. Toxics Is Big Business," *San Francisco Examiner*, September 23, 1990, p. A2.

Manufacturers that dump products abroad clearly are motivated by profit or at least by the hope of avoiding financial losses resulting from having to withdraw a product from the market. For government and health agencies that cooperate in the exporting of dangerous products, the motives are more complex.

For example, as early as 1971 the dangers of the Dalkon Shield intrauterine device were well documented.[3] Among the adverse reactions were pelvic inflammation, blood poisoning, pregnancies resulting in spontaneous abortions, tubal pregnancies, and uterine perforations. A number of deaths were even attributed to the device. Faced with losing its domestic market, A. H. Robins Co., manufacturer of the Dalkon Shield, worked out a deal with the Office of Population within the U. S. Agency for International Development (AID), whereby AID bought thousands of the devices at a reduced price for use in population-control programs in forty-two countries.

Why do governmental and population-control agencies approve for sale and use overseas birth control devices proved dangerous in the United States? They say their motives are humanitarian. Since the rate of dying in childbirth is high in Third World countries, almost any birth control device is preferable to none. Third World scientists and government officials frequently support this argument. They insist that denying their countries access to the contraceptives of their choice is tantamount to violating their countries' national sovereignty.

Apparently this argument has found a sympathetic ear in Washington, for it turns up in the "notification" system that regulates the export of banned or dangerous products overseas. Based on the principles of national sovereignty, self-determination, and free trade, the notification system requires that foreign governments be notified whenever a product is banned, deregulated, suspended, or canceled by an American regulatory agency. The State Department, which implements the system, has a policy statement on the subject that reads in part: "No country should establish itself as the arbiter of others' health and safety standards. Individual governments are generally in the best position to establish standards of public health and safety."

Critics of the system claim that notifying foreign health officials is virtually useless. For one thing, other governments rarely can establish health standards or even control imports into their countries. Indeed, most of the Third World countries where banned or dangerous products are dumped lack regulatory agencies, adequate testing facilities, and well-staffed customs departments.

Then there's the problem of getting the word out about hazardous products. In theory, when a government agency such as the Environmental Protection Agency or the Food and Drug Administration (FDA) finds a product hazardous, it is supposed to inform the State Department, which is to notify local health officials. But agencies often fail to inform the State Department of the product they have banned or found harmful. And when it is notified, its communiqués typically go no further than the U.S. embassies abroad. One embassy official even told the General Accounting Office that he "did not routinely forward notification of chemicals not registered in the host country because it may adversely affect U.S. exporting." When foreign officials are notified by U.S. embassies, they sometimes find the communiqués vague or ambiguous or too technical to understand.

In an effort to remedy these problems, at the end of his term in office, President Jimmy Carter issued an executive order that (1) improved export notice procedures; (2) called for publishing an annual summary of substances banned or severely restricted for domestic use in the United States; (3) directed the State Department and other federal agencies to participate in the development of international hazards alert systems; and (4) established procedures for placing formal export licensing controls on a limited number of extremely hazardous substances. In one of his first acts as president, however, Ronald Reagan rescinded the order. Later in his administration, the law that formerly prohibited U.S. pharmaceutical companies from exporting drugs that are banned or not registered in this country was weakened to allow the export to twenty-one countries of drugs not yet approved for use in the United States.

But even if communication procedures were improved or the export of dangerous products forbidden, there are ways that companies can circumvent these threats to their profits—for example, by simply changing the name of the product or by exporting the individual ingredients of a product to a plant in a foreign country. Once there, the ingredients can be reassembled and the product dumped.[4] Upjohn, for example, through its Belgian subsidiary, continues to produce Depo-Provera, which the FDA has consistently refused to approve for use in this country. And the prohibition on the export of dangerous drugs is not that hard to sidestep. "Unless the package bursts open on the dock," one drug company executive observes, "you have no chance of being caught."

[3]See Mark Dowie and Tracy Johnston, "A Case of Corporate Malpractice," *Mother Jones*, November 1976.

[4]Mark Dowie, "A Dumper's Guide to Tricks of the Trade," *Mother Jones*, November 1979, p. 25.

Unfortunately for us, in the case of pesticides the effects of overseas dumping are now coming home. The Environmental Protection Agency bans from the United States all crop uses of DDT and Dieldrin, which kill fish, cause tumors in animals, and build up in the fatty tissue of humans. It also bans heptachlor, chlordane, leptophos, endrin, and many other pesticides, including 2,4,5-T (which contains the deadly poison dioxin, the active ingredient in Agent Orange, the notorious defoliant used in Vietnam) because they are dangerous to human beings. No law, however, prohibits the sale of DDT and these other U.S.-banned pesticides overseas, where thanks to corporate dumping they are routinely used in agriculture. The FDA now estimates, through spot checks, that 10 percent of our imported food is contaminated with illegal residues of banned pesticides. And the FDA's most commonly used testing procedure does not even check for 70 percent of the pesticides known to cause cancer.

QUESTIONS

1. Was the dumping in this case ethical? Those involved in the dumping might have argued that the people receiving the pajamas would not have otherwise had access to such clothing and were notified of the health and safety hazards. Does this affect your feelings about the case? What do you think about the exportation of the Dalkon Shield? Can it be justified because the rate of dying during childbirth in Third World countries is extremely high, and, as such, any effective birth control device is better than none?

2. What obligations did the financial managers have to their shareholders to do whatever is possible to avoid major financial losses associated with these products?

3. Is it still immoral or unethical to dump goods when doing so does not violate any U.S. laws? How about when those receiving the goods know the dangers? Why do you think dumpers dump? Do you think they believe what they are doing is ethically acceptable?

Adapted by permission from William Shaw and Vincent Barry, *Moral Issues in Business*, 5th ed., pp. 28–31. Copyright © 1992 by Wadsworth, Inc.

SELF-TEST SOLUTIONS

SS–1. a. $NPV_A = \$70,000 \left[\dfrac{1}{(1 + .12)^1} \right] - \$50,000$

$\qquad = \$70,000\,(.893) - \$50,000$

$\qquad = \$62,510 - \$50,000$

$\qquad = \$12,510$

$\quad NPV_B = \$130,000 \left[\dfrac{1}{(1 + .12)^1} \right] - \$100,000$

$\qquad = \$130,000\,(.893) - \$100,000$

$\qquad = \$116,090 - \$100,000$

$\qquad = \$16,090$

b. $PI_A = \dfrac{\$62,510}{\$50,000}$

$\qquad = 1.2502$

$\quad PI_B = \dfrac{\$116,090}{\$100,000}$

$\qquad = 1.1609$

c. $\$50,000 = \$70,000\,(FVIF_{i,\,1\,yr})$

$\quad .7143 = FVIF_{i,\,1\,yr}$

Looking for a value of $FVIF_{i,\,1\,yr}$ in Appendix C, a value of .714 is found in the 40 percent column. Thus, the IRR is 40 percent.

$\$100,000 = \$130,000\,(FVIF_{i,\,1\,yr})$

$\quad .7692 = FVIF_{i,\,1\,yr}$

Looking for a value of $\text{FVIF}_{i,\,1\,\text{yr}}$ in Appendix C a value of .769 is found in the 30 percent column. Thus, the IRR is 30 percent.

d. If there is no capital rationing, project B should be accepted because it has a larger net present value. If there is a capital constraint, the problem focuses on what can be done with the additional $50,000 (the additional money that could be invested if project A with an initial outlay of $50,000 were selected over project B with an initial outlay of $100,000). In the capital constraint case, if Serrano can earn more on project A plus the marginal project financed with the additional $50,000 than it can on project B, then project A and the marginal project should be accepted.

SS-2. a. $\bar{X} = \sum\limits_{t=1}^{N} X_i P(X_i)$

$\begin{aligned}
\bar{X}_A &= 0.20(\$10,000) + 0.60(\$15,000) + 0.20(\$20,000) \\
&= \$2,000 + \$9,000 + \$4,000 \\
&= \$15,000 \\
\bar{X}_B &= 0.20(\$6,000) + 0.60(\$18,000) + 0.20(\$30,000) \\
&= \$1,200 + \$10,800 + \$6,000 \\
&= \$18,000
\end{aligned}$

b. $NPV = \sum\limits_{t=1}^{n} \dfrac{ACF_t}{(1 + i^*)^t} - IO$

$\begin{aligned}
NPV_A &= \$15,000(3.605) - \$25,000 \\
&= \$54,075 - \$25,000 \\
&= \$29,075 \\
NPV_B &= \$18,000(3.127) - \$25,000 \\
&= \$56,286 - \$25,000 \\
&= \$31,286
\end{aligned}$

SS-3. Project A:

Year	(A) Expected Cash Flow	(B) α_t	(A · B) (Expected Cash Flow) × (α_t)	Present Value Factor at 8%	Present Value
0	−$300,000	1.00	−$300,000	1.000	−$300,000
1	100,000	.95	95,000	0.926	87,970
2	200,000	.90	180,000	0.857	154,260
3	200,000	.85	170,000	0.794	134,980
4	300,000	.80	240,000	0.735	176,400
5	300,000	.75	225,000	0.681	153,225
				$NPV_A =$	$406,835

Project B:

Year	(A) Expected Cash Flow	(B) α_t	(A · B) (Expected Cash Flow) × (α_t)	Present Value Factor at 8%	Present Value
0	−$300,000	1.00	−$300,000	1.000	−$300,000
1	200,000	.90	180,000	0.926	166,680
2	200,000	.80	160,000	0.857	137,120
3	200,000	.70	140,000	0.794	111,160
4	300,000	.60	180,000	0.735	132,300
5	400,000	.50	200,000	0.681	136,200
				$NPV_B =$	$383,460

Thus, project A should be selected since it has the higher NPV.

CHAPTER 8

Cost of Capital

The Concept of the Cost of Capital • Factors Determining the Weighted Cost of Capital • Assumptions of the Weighted Cost of Capital Model • Computing the Weighted Cost of Capital • Marginal Cost of Capital: A Comprehensive Example • Required Rate of Return for Individual Projects: An Alternative Approach • A Firm's Cost of Capital: Some Recent Evidence

Having studied risk and rates of return (Chapter 4), the valuation of financial securities (Chapter 5), and capital budgeting (Chapters 6 and 7) we are now ready to connect the firm's investment decisions with its financing decisions. The cost of capital provides this fundamental connecting link.[1] The interrelationships are visualized in Figure 8–1.

How a firm finances its assets affects its cost of capital, which in turn affects which investments it will accept. Also, the investments that are selected, depending on their riskiness, may affect the firm's cost of capital and determine in part what financing options are available.

This chapter details the concepts behind the cost of capital, as well as the procedures for estimating the firm's cost of capital. For the time being, how the

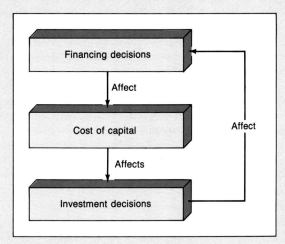

FIGURE 8–1.
Cost of Capital.
Connecting Investment
and Financing Decisions

---

[1]The term "cost of capital" may be used interchangeably with the firm's required rate of return, the hurdle rate, the discount rate, and the opportunity cost.

firm finances its investments, is held constant; that is, we assume a constant debt–equity mix. This assumption will be relaxed in Chapter 10 when we study the relationship between the firm's cost of capital and its financing decisions. In this chapter, we look at the following topics:

1. The basic concept underlying the cost of capital
2. The key factors influencing a corporation's cost of capital
3. The assumptions generally required in measuring and using a firm's overall or companywide cost of capital
4. The calculation of a corporation's overall cost of capital
5. An approach to measuring a project-specific required rate of return as an alternative to the firm's weighted cost of capital
6. An empirical study of the cost of capital of large firms, as estimated by the firm's managers

Perspective in Finance

The cost of capital is the rate that the firm must earn on its investments if it wants to keep the investors satisfied. The way the firm does that is by seeing that the investors earn their required rate of return.

The Concept of the Cost of Capital

A firm's **cost of capital** is the rate that must be earned in order to satisfy the firm's investors for a given level of risk.

If the firm earned exactly its cost of capital on an investment project, then we would expect the price of its common stock to remain unchanged following acceptance of the project. However, if a rate different from the cost of capital was attained, we would expect the price of the stock to change. For example, in Figure 8–2 the internal rates of return for projects A, B, and C exceed the firm's cost of capital, so accepting these projects would increase the value of the firm's common stock. In contrast, investing in projects D and E would lower the stock value, which says that the best level of capital expenditures equals $17 million. *Therefore, the cost of capital is the rate of return on investments that leaves the price*

FIGURE 8–2.
Investment and Financing
Schedules

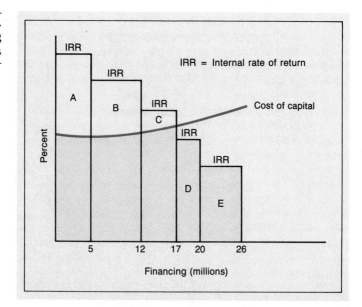

of the firm's common stock unchanged. (As we will see later, we must assume that all the projects in Figure 8–2 are similar in terms of risk.)

While we are trying to find the rate of return on an investment that leaves the common stock price unchanged, we must also consider the other sources of capital, such as debt and preferred stock. To illustrate, the Salinas Corporation's capital structure is presented in Table 8–1. The company is using three sources of capital: debt, preferred stock, and common stock. Management is considering a $200,000 investment opportunity with an expected internal rate of return of 14 percent. Assume that we know that the current cost of the firm's capital (required rate of return) for each source of financing has been determined to be

Cost of debt capital	10%
Cost of preferred stock	12
Cost of common stock	16

Given this information, should the firm make the investment? The creditors and preferred stockholders would probably encourage us to undertake the project. However, because the 14 percent internal rate of return on the investment is less than the common stockholders' required rate of return, shareholders might argue that the investment should be forgone. What decision should the financial manager make?

To answer this question, we must know what percentage of the $200,000 is to be provided by each type of investor. If we intend to maintain the same capital structure mix as reflected in Table 8–1 (30 percent debt, 10 percent preferred stock, and 60 percent common stock), we could compute a *weighted cost of capital,* where the weights equal the percentage of capital to be financed by each source. For our example, the weighted cost of the individual sources of capital as computed in Table 8–2 is 13.8 percent. From this calculation we would conclude that an investment offering at least a 13.8 percent return would be acceptable to the company's investors. The investment should be undertaken, because the 14 percent rate of return more than satisfies all investors, as indicated by a 13.8 percent weighted cost of capital. Again, the **weighted cost of capital** for a firm is equal to the cost of each source of financing (debt, preferred stock, and common stock) multiplied by the percentage of the financing provided by that source. Thus, when we are speaking of a company's cost of capital, we mean its weighted cost of capital.

	Amount	Percentage of Capital Structure
Bonds	$ 600,000	30%
Preferred stock	200,000	10
Common stock	1,200,000	60
Total liabilities and equity	$2,000,000	100%

TABLE 8–1.
Salinas Corporation Capital Structure

	Weights (Percentage of Financing)	Cost of Individual Sources	Weighted Cost
Debt	30%	10%	3.0%
Preferred stock	10	12	1.2
Common stock	60	16	9.6
	100%	Weighted cost of capital:	13.8%

TABLE 8–2.
Salinas Corporation Weighted Cost of Capital

But What If?

The weighted cost of capital may be fine in theory, but what if a company could borrow the entire amount needed for an investment in a new product line? Is it really necessary to use the weighted cost of capital, or would it be all right to make the decision based on simply the cost of the debt providing the funding?

Consider the Poling Corporation. Management believes it could earn 14 percent from purchasing $500,000 in new equipment, which would allow it to expand the business. Although the firm works to maintain a capital structure with equal amounts of debt and equity, the bank is willing to loan the firm the entire $500,000 at an interest rate of 12 percent. Without our even having to compute it, we know the firm's earnings per share would increase if the firm earned a rate exceeding the cost of the financing, in this case 12 percent. (We will see later in Chapter 10 that a firm's earnings will increase from using debt any time the return on the investment is greater than the cost of the debt financing.)

Poling's financial officer has also estimated the firm's cost of equity (common stock) at 18 percent. Because the firm can finance the purchase fully by debt, however, management has decided to make the investment and finance it by borrowing the money from the bank at the 12 percent. The investment is made, and all seems well.

The following year, management finds another investment opportunity costing $500,000 but with an expected internal rate of return this time of 17 percent—better than the previous year's 14 percent. When management approaches the bankers for financing, however, they find them unwilling to lend any more money to Poling. In the words of one banker, "Poling has used up all of its debt capacity." The firm must now issue new common stock before the bank will be agreeable to fund any more loans. Because the investment does not earn the cost of equity of 18 percent, however, management believes there to be no other option than to reject the investment.

What is the moral of the story for Poling? Intuitively, we can see that Poling's management has made a mistake. Making the investment in the first year has denied the firm the opportunity to make a better decision in the second year.

As a more general statement, we can conclude that a firm should never use a single cost of financing as the hurdle rate (discount rate) for making capital budgeting decisions. Particularly when we use debt, we have implicitly used up some of our *debt capacity* for future investments, and only until we complement the use of debt with equity may we be able to continue to use more debt in the future.[2] Thus, we ought always to use the weighted cost of capital, and not an individual cost of funds, as our discount rate for investment decisions. So, let's look more carefully at the weighted cost of capital.

Perspective in Finance

When we compute a firm's weighted cost of capital, we are simply calculating the average of its costs of money from all investors, those being creditors and stockholders.

Factors Determining the Weighted Cost of Capital

To gain further insight into the meaning of the firm's cost of capital, we need to consider the elements in the business environment that cause a company's weighted cost of capital to be high or low. Looking at Figure 8–3, we see four

[2]The issue of debt capacity will be discussed more completely in Chapters 9 and 10.

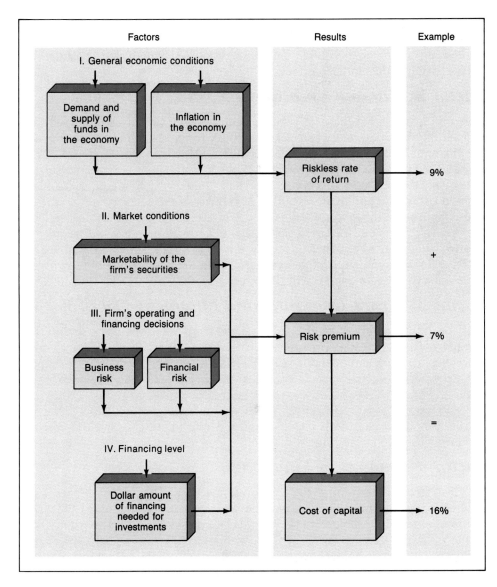

FIGURE 8–3.
Primary Factors Influencing
the Cost of
Particular Sources of Capital

primary factors: general economic conditions, the marketability of the firm's securities (market conditions), operating and financing conditions within the company, and the amount of financing needed for new investments. These four variables also relate to our discussion in Chapter 4, where we separated an investor's required rate of return into the riskless or *risk-free rate* of return and the *risk premium*. These two aspects of risk are also key ingredients in the firm's cost of capital.

Perspective in Finance

The cost of capital for a firm is driven by the demand for and supply of money in the economy and the riskiness of the firm.

Factor 1: General Economic Conditions

As briefly noted in Chapter 2, general economic conditions determine the demand for and supply of capital within the economy, as well as the level of expected inflation. This economic variable is reflected in the riskless rate of return. This rate represents the rate of return on risk-free investments, such as the interest rate on short-term U.S. government securities. In principle, as the demand for money in the economy changes relative to the supply, investors alter their required rate of return. For example, if the demand for money increases without an equivalent increase in the supply, lenders will raise their required interest rate. At the same time, if inflation is expected to deteriorate the purchasing power of the dollar, investors require a higher rate of return to compensate for this anticipated loss.[3]

Factor 2: Market Conditions

When an investor purchases a security with a significant investment risk, an opportunity for additional returns is necessary to make the investment attractive. Essentially, as risk increases, the investor requires a higher rate of return. This increase is called a **risk premium.** When investors increase their required rate of return, the cost of capital rises simultaneously. Remember we have defined risk as the potential variability of returns. If the security is not readily marketable when the investor wants to sell, or even if a continuous demand for the security exists but the price varies significantly, an investor will require a relatively high rate of return. Conversely, if a security is readily marketable and its price is reasonably stable, the investor will require a lower rate of return and the company's cost of capital will be lower.

Factor 3: Firm's Operating and Financing Decisions

Risk, or the variability of returns, also results from decisions made within the company. Risk resulting from these decisions is generally divided into two types: business risk and financial risk. **Business risk** is the variability in returns on assets and is affected by the company's investment decisions. **Financial risk** is the increased variability in returns to common stockholders as a result of financing with debt or preferred stock. As business risk and financial risk increase or decrease, the investor's required rate of return (and the cost of capital) will move in the same direction.[4]

Factor 4: Amount of Financing

The last factor determining the corporation's cost of funds is the level of financing that the firm requires. As the financing requirements of the firm become larger, the weighted cost of capital increases for several reasons. For instance, as more securities are issued, additional **flotation costs,** or the cost incurred by the firm from issuing securities, will affect the percentage cost of the funds to the firm. Also, as management approaches the market for large amounts of capital relative to the firm's size, the investors' required rate of return may rise. Suppliers of capital become hesitant to grant relatively large sums without evidence of management's capability to absorb this capital into the business. This is typically "too much too soon." Also, as the size of the issue increases, there is greater difficulty in placing it in the market without reducing the price of the security, which also increases the firm's cost of capital.

A Summary Illustration

To summarize, the important variables influencing a corporation's cost of capital include the following:

1. **General economic conditions.** This factor determines the risk-free rate or riskless rate of return.
2. **Marketability of a company's securities.** As the marketability of a security increases, investors' required rates of return decrease, lowering the corporation's cost of capital.
3. **Operating and financial decisions made by management.** If management accepts investments with high levels of risk or if it uses debt or preferred stock extensively, the firm's risk increases. Investors then

[3]This effect was referenced earlier in Chapter 2 as the Fisher Effect.
[4]Both forms of risk, business and financial, are explained and illustrated in Chapter 9.

ETHICS IN FINANCIAL MANAGEMENT

How Do Managers Resolve Ethical Decisions?

What makes a managerial choice an ethical one? Brief et al. (1991) suggest that if the decision entails reflection on the moral significance of the choice, then the choice is an ethical one. How do managers resolve ethical dilemmas? There is some evidence suggesting that two factors come to bear on ethical choices: values and accountability.

We will consider two social value systems that are present in Western society, which are particularly relevant to the study of finance. These are the Smithian and Humanitarian value systems. The Smithian system is derived from the writings of the 18th-century moral philosopher and political economist Adam Smith. This value system is reflected in the current-day teachings of economists such as Milton Friedman (1962). Briefly, this system holds that when individuals pursue their own self-interest in the market place, they contribute to the good of society. At the firm level this system provides the underlying basis for the market system and is used as the basis for corporate self-interest. In contrast, the Humanitarian system is based on the fundamental premise of the equality of individuals in society. This system seeks to protect individuals from the harshness of the market system and to promote equality of opportunity.

Personal value systems are not all that impact managerial decisions having ethical implications. Managers are influenced by their perception of the value systems of the individuals to whom they are held accountable. That is, ethical choices made by managers are influenced by the values they believe are held by the person to whom they are accountable. Arendt (1951, 1977) provides evidence that suggests that the effects of accountability may be more profound than those of the individual manager's values. Consequently, the poten-

tially overpowering effects of hierarchical accountability may lead individual managers not to construe the moral significance attached to the choices they make. They may see no choice but to comply to the higher authority. Brief et al. (1991) provide empirical evidence bearing on the question of the relative importance of personal values versus accountability in the choices made by individuals. Using a set of experiments involving 135 M.B.A. students, they concluded that personal values may not be related to how an individual chooses to resolve ethical dilemmas when the choices (values) of the higher authority are known explicitly.

Note that we have not addressed the normative issue: How should ethical dilemmas be resolved? Instead we have addressed the positive question: How do managers actually deal with ethical choices? The principal finding of the studies we have reviewed is that the *perceived values of one's superiors* have a profound impact on the way in which subordinates resolve ethical dilemmas. So choose your superior carefully.

Sources: H. Arendt, *The Origins of Totalitarianism* (New York: Harcourt Brace, 1951); H. Arendt, *Eichmann in Jerusalem* (New York: Penguin Books, 1977); Arthur Brief, Janet M. Dukerich, and Lucinda I. Doran, "Resolving Ethical Dilemmas in Management: Experimental Investigations of Values, Accountability, and Choice," *Journal of Applied Social Psychology* 21 (1991), pp. 380–96; M. Friedman, *Capitalism and Freedom* (Chicago: University of Chicago Press, 1962); C. S. McCoy, *Management of Values: The Ethical Differences in Corporate Policy and Performance* (Boston: Pitman, 1985); P. E. Tetlock, "Accountability and Complexity of Thought," *Journal of Personality and Social Psychology* 45 (1983), pp. 74–83; P. E. Tetlock, "Accountability: The Neglected Social Context of Judgement and Choice," *Research in Organizational Behavior* 7 (1985), pp. 297–332.

require a higher rate of return, which causes a higher cost of capital to the company.

4. **Amount of financing needed.** Requests for larger amounts of capital increase the firm's cost of capital.

The right-hand margin of Figure 8–3 presents an illustration of the cost of capital for a particular source. The risk-free rate, determined by the general economic conditions, is 9 percent. However, owing to the additional risks associated with the security, the firm has to earn an additional 7 percent to satisfy the investors' required rate of return of 16 percent.

Assumptions of the Weighted Cost of Capital Model

In a complex business world, difficulties quickly arise in computing a corporation's cost of capital. For this reason, we make several simplifying assumptions.

Constant Business Risk

Business risk is defined as the potential variability of returns on an investment, and the level of business risk within a firm is determined by management's investment policies. An investor's required rate of return for a company's securities—and therefore the firm's cost of capital—is a function of the firm's current business risk. If this risk level is altered, the corporation's investors will naturally change their required rates of return, which in turn modifies the cost of capital. However, the amount of change in the cost of capital resulting from a given increase or decrease in business risk is difficult to assess. For this reason, the cost of capital calculation assumes that any investment under consideration will not significantly change the firm's business risk. In other words, *the cost of capital is an appropriate investment criterion only for an investment having a business risk level similar to that of existing assets.*

Constant Financial Risk

Financial risk has been defined as the increased variability in returns on common stock resulting from the increased use of debt and preferred stock financing.[5] Also, financial risk relates to the threat of bankruptcy. As the percentage of debt in the capital structure increases, the possibility that the firm will be unable to pay interest and the principal balance is also increased. As a result, the level of financial risk in a company has an impact upon the investors' required rate of return. As the amount of debt rises, the common stockholders will increase their required rate of return. *In other words, the costs of individual sources of capital are a function of the current financial structure.* For this reason, the data used in computing the cost of capital are appropriate only if management continues to use the same financial mix. If the present capital structure consists of 40 percent debt, 10 percent preferred stock, and 50 percent common stock, this capital structure is assumed to be maintained in the financing of future investments.

Constant Dividend Policy

A third assumption required in estimating the cost of capital relates to the corporation's dividend policy. For ease of computation, we generally assume that a firm's dividends are increasing at a constant annual growth rate. Also, we assume this growth to be a function of the firm's earning capabilities and not merely the result of paying out a larger percentage of the company's earnings. Thus, it is implicitly assumed that the dividend payout ratio (dividends/net income) is constant.

The assumptions of the weighted cost of capital model are quite restrictive. In a practical investment analysis, the financial executive may need a range of possible cost of capital values rather than a single-point estimate. For example, it may be more appropriate to talk in terms of a 10 to 12 percent range as an estimate of the firm's cost of capital, rather than assuming that a precise number can be determined. In this chapter, however, our principal concern will be with calculating a single cost of capital figure.

Perspective in Finance

To compute a firm's weighted cost of capital, we must assume that the firm's financial mix will not change, that we will continue to invest in projects of about the same risk as we have done in the past, and that we will not change the percentage of earnings paid out in dividends to the stockholders.

[5]This concept is further explained in Chapter 9.

Computing the Weighted Cost of Capital

A firm's weighted cost of capital is a composite of the individual costs of financing, weighted by the percentage of financing provided by each source. Therefore, a firm's weighted cost of capital is a function of (1) the individual costs of capital and (2) the makeup of the capital structure—the percentage of funds provided by debt, preferred stock, and common stock. Also, as we noted earlier, the amount of funds needed affects the cost of capital. We will discuss this last consideration, the level of financing, later.

As we explain the procedures for computing a company's cost of capital, it is helpful to remember three basic steps.

1. Calculate the costs of capital for each individual source of financing used by the firm; those generally include debt, preferred stock, and common stock.

2. Determine the percentage of debt, preferred stock, and common stock to be used in financing future investments.

3. Using the individual costs and the capital structure percentages in the first two steps, compute an overall or weighted cost of capital for the various amounts of financing that might be needed.

The computations are not difficult if we understand our purpose: We want to calculate the firm's overall cost of capital. For a simple exercise, calculate the average age of students in a course where 40 percent are 19 years old, 50 percent are 20 years old, and 10 percent are 21 years old. We can easily find the average age to be 19.7 years by weighting each age by the percentage in each age category [(40%)(19) + (50%)(20) + (10%)(21)]. In a similar way, the weighted cost of capital is estimated by weighting the cost of each individual source by the percentage of financing it provides. If we finance an investment by 40 percent debt at a 10 percent cost and 60 percent common equity at a cost of 18 percent, the weighted cost of capital is 14.8 percent (.40 × 10% + .60 × 18% = 14.8%). Thus, although the details become somewhat involved, the basic approach, which is summarized in Figure 8–4, is relatively simple. As we move through the steps, try not to lose sight of this objective.

Determining Individual Costs of Capital

Companies attempting to attract new investors have created a large variety of financing instruments. However, we will examine only three basic types of securities: debt, preferred stock, and common stock. In calculating their respective costs, the objective is to determine *the rate of return the company must earn on its investments to satisfy investors' required rates of return after allowing for any flotation costs incurred in raising new funds.* Also, because the cash flows

---

FIGURE 8–4.
Computing the Weighted Cost of Capital: Basic Steps

Remember: To compute a firm's weighted cost of capital requires us to do three things:

1. Compute the cost of capital for each and every source of financing (i.e., each source of debt, preferred stock, and common stock).

2. Determine the percentage of debt, preferred stock, and common stock to be used in the financing of future investments.

3. Calculate the firm's weighted average cost of capital using the percentage of financing as the weights.

used in capital-budgeting analysis (net present value, profitability index, and internal rate of return) are on an after-tax basis, the required rates of return should also be expressed on an after-tax basis.

Cost of Debt — *ie BONDS + SECURITIES*

The cost of debt may be defined as the rate that must be received from an investment *to achieve the required rate of return for the creditors.* In Chapter 5 the required rate of return for debt capital was found by a trial-and-error process or with the use of a financial calculator, where we solved for R_d in the following equation:

$$P_0 = \frac{\$I_1}{(1 + R_d)^1} + \frac{\$I_2}{(1 + R_d)^2} + \ldots + \frac{\$I_n}{(1 + R_d)^n} + \frac{\$M}{(1 + R_d)^n} \qquad (8-1)$$

$$P_0 = \$I_t(PVIFA_{R_d,\ n}) + \$M(PVIF_{R_d,\ n})$$

where P_0 = the market price of the debt

   $\$I_t$ = the annual dollar interest paid to the investor

   $\$M$ = the maturity value of the debt

   R_d = the required rate of return of the debt holder

   n = the number of years to maturity

If we use the interest factors in the present value tables, the equation would be restated as follows:

EXAMPLE

Assume that an investor is willing to pay \$908.32 for a bond. The security has a \$1,000 par value, pays 8 percent in annual interest, and matures in 20 years. According to either a calculator or table values, the investor's required rate of return is found to be 9 percent, which is the rate that sets the present value of the future interest payments and the maturity value equal to the price of the bond, or

$$\$908.32 = \sum_{t=1}^{20} \frac{\$80}{(1 + .09)^t} + \frac{\$1000}{(1 + .09)^{20}}$$

$$\$908.32 = \$908.32$$

However, if brokerage commissions and legal and accounting fees are incurred in issuing the security, the company will not receive the full \$908.24 market price. As a result, the effective cost of these funds is larger than the investor's 9 percent required rate of return. To adjust for this difference, we would simply use the *net price* after flotation costs in place of the market price in equation (8-1). Thus, the equation becomes

$$NP_0 = \sum_{t=1}^{n} \frac{\$I_t}{(1 + k_d)^t} + \frac{\$M}{(1 + k_d)^N} \qquad (8-2)$$

where NP_0 represents the net amount received by the company from issuing the debt, k_d equals the *before-tax* cost of debt, and the remaining variables retain their meaning from equation (8-1). If in the present example the company nets \$850 after issuance costs, the equation should read

$$\$850 = \sum_{t=1}^{20} \frac{\$80}{(1 + k_d)^t} + \frac{\$1000}{(1 + k_d)^{20}}$$

$$= \$80(PVIFA_{kd,\ 20}) + \$1000(PVIF_{kd,\ 20})$$

Solving for k_d in equation (8–2) may be achieved by trial and error by using the present value tables. We know that the rate is above 9 percent because a 9 percent rate had already given us a $908.32 value. We need the discount rate that gives us an $850 value. If *10 percent* is selected as a trial discount rate, a present value of $830.12 results. With this information, we may conclude that the before-tax cost of the debt capital is between 9 and 10 percent; therefore, we may approximate it by interpolating between these two rates. The computation is shown as follows:

Rate	Value	Differences in Values	
9%	$908.32		
k_d	850.00 net proceeds	} $58.32	} $78.20
10%	830.12		

Solving for k_d by interpolation,

$$k_d = .09 + \left(\frac{\$58.32}{\$78.20}\right)(.10 - .09) = .0975 = 9.75\%$$

The same answer may be found by using a financial calculator, as shown in the margin. Thus, the company's cost of debt, before recognizing the tax deductibility of interest expense, is 9.73 percent.[6] We want to know the *after-tax* cost of the debt, however, not the before-tax cost. Because interest is a tax-deductible expense, for every $1 we pay in interest, we lower the firm's tax liability by $1 times the tax rate. If our company has an effective tax rate, including all federal and state taxes, of 40 percent, then a dollar in interest means that we save $.40 in taxes. That is, the after-tax cost is only $.60, or $1 (1 − .40 tax rate). Applying the same logic to our cost of debt, we may correctly conclude that the after-tax cost of debt is found by multiplying the before-tax interest rate by [1 − (tax rate)]. If T is the company's marginal tax rate and k_d is the before-tax cost of debt, the after-tax cost of new debt financing, K_d, is found as follows:

$$K_d = k_d(1 - T) \tag{8–3}$$

If in the present example the corporation's tax rate is 40 percent, then the after-tax cost of debt is 5.84 percent:

$$K_d = 9.73\%(1 - .40) = 5.84\%$$

In summary, the firm must earn 5.84 percent on its borrowed capital *after the payment of taxes*. In doing so, the investors will earn a 9 percent rate of return (their required rate) on their $908.32 investment (market price of the bond).

Cost of Preferred Stock

Determining the cost of preferred stock follows the same logic as the cost of debt computations. *The objective is to find the rate of return that must be earned on the preferred stockholders' investment to satisfy their required rate of return.*

In Chapter 5 the value of a preferred stock, P_0, that is nonmaturing and promising a constant dividend per year was defined as follows:

$$P_0 = \frac{dividend}{required\ rate\ of\ return\ for\ a\ preferred\ stockholder} = \frac{D}{R_p} \tag{8–4}$$

CALCULATOR SOLUTION

Data Input	Function Key
20	N
850	+/− PV
80	PMT
1000	FV
Function Key	Answer
I% YR	9.73*

---

*The difference between 9.75 percent and 9.73 percent is simply the result of rounding.
[6]For simplicity, we have ignored the fact that flotation costs may be amortized off as a tax-deductible expense over the life of the bond. The difference in the answer is relatively small.

From this equation, the required rate of return, R_p, is defined as

$$R_p = \frac{\text{dividend}}{\text{market price}} = \frac{D}{P_0} \qquad (8-5)$$

If, for example, a preferred stock pays $1.50 in annual dividends and sells for $15, the investors' required rate of return is 10 percent:

$$R_p = \frac{\$1.50}{\$15} = 10\%$$

Yet even if these preferred stockholders have a 10 percent required rate of return, the effective cost of this capital will be greater owing to the flotation costs incurred in issuing the security. If a firm were to net $13.50 per share after issuance costs, rather than the full $15 market price, the cost of preferred stock, K_p, should be calculated using the net price received by the company. Therefore

$$K_p = \frac{\text{dividend}}{\text{net price}} = \frac{D}{NP_0} \quad \text{— after flotation costs} \qquad (8-6)$$

For the preceding example, the cost would be

$$K_p = \frac{\$1.50}{\$13.50} = 11.11\%$$

No adjustment for taxes is required, since preferred stock dividends are not tax deductible. Thus, the firm must earn the cost of preferred capital after taxes have been paid, which for the preceding example was 11.1 percent.

Cost of Common Stock

Although debt and preferred stock must be issued to receive any new money from these sources, common stockholders can provide additional capital in one of two ways. First, new common stock may be issued. Second, the earnings available to common stockholders can be retained, in whole or in part, within the company and used to finance future investments. Retained earnings represent the largest source of capital for most U.S. corporations. As much as 70 percent of a company's financing in any year may come from the profits retained within the business. To distinguish between these two sources, we will use the term **internal common equity** to designate the profits retained within the business for investment purposes, and **external common equity** to represent a new issue of common stock.

Cost of internal common equity ■ When managers are considering the retention of earnings as a means for financing an investment, they are serving in a *fiduciary* capacity. That is, the stockholders have entrusted the company assets to management. If the company's objective is to maximize the wealth of its common stockholders, management should retain the profits *only if* the company's investments within the firm are at least as attractive as the stockholders' next best investment opportunity.[7] Otherwise the profits should be paid out in dividends, permitting the investor to invest more profitably elsewhere.

How can management know the stockholders' alternative investment opportunities? Certainly identifying those specific investments is not feasible. However, the investors' required rate of return should be a function of competing investment opportunities. If the only other investment alternative of similar risk has a 12 percent return, one would expect a rational investor to set a

[7]Other factors may justify management's not adhering completely to this principle. We will cover these issues in the discussion on dividend policy in Chapter 11.

minimum acceptable return on investment at 12 percent. In other words, *the investors' required rate of return should be equal to the expected rate of the best competing investment available.* Thus, if the common stockholders' required rate of return is used as a minimum return for investments financed by common stock investors, management may be assured that its investment policies are acceptable to the common stockholder.

To measure the common stockholders' required rate of return, we will suggest three alternative approaches: (1) the dividend-growth model, (2) the capital asset pricing model, and (3) the risk-premium approach.

DIVIDEND-GROWTH MODEL □ In Chapter 5, the value of a common stock was found to be equal to the present value of the expected future dividends, discounted at the common stockholders' *required rate of return.* Since the stock has no maturity date, these dividends extend to infinity. For an investor with a required rate of return of R_c, the value of a common stock, P_0, promising dividends of D_t in year t would be

$$P_0 = \frac{D_1}{(1 + R_c)^1} + \frac{D_2}{(1 + R_c)^2} + \cdots + \frac{D_n}{(1 + R_c)^n} + \cdots + \frac{D_\infty}{(1 + R_c)^\infty} \quad (8\text{--}7)$$

Because the market price of the security, P_0, is known, the required rate of return of an investor purchasing the security at this price can be determined by estimating future dividends, D_t, and solving for R_c using equation (8–7). Furthermore, if the dividends are increasing at a constant annual rate of growth (g), that is less than R_c (the required rate), then R_c may be measured as follows:[8]

$$R_c = \left(\frac{\text{dividend in year 1}}{\text{market price}}\right) + \left(\begin{array}{c}\text{annual growth rate}\\ \text{in dividends}\end{array}\right) = \frac{D_1}{P_0} + g \quad (8\text{--}8)$$

To convert from the common investor's required rate of return in equation (8–8) to the cost of internal common funds, no adjustment is required for taxes. Dividends paid to the firm's common stockholders are *not* tax deductible; therefore, the cost is already on an after-tax basis. Also, flotation costs are not involved in computing the cost of internal common, because the funds are already within the business. Thus, the investor's required rate of return, R_c, is the same as the cost of internal common equity, K_c.

EXAMPLE

To demonstrate the computation, the Talbot Corporation's common stockholders recently received a $2 dividend per share, and they expect dividends to grow at an annual rate of 10 percent. If the market price of the security is $50, the investor's required rate of return is

$$R_c = K_c = \frac{D_1}{P_0} + g$$

$$= \frac{\$2(1 + .10)}{\$50} + .10 \quad\quad (8\text{--}8)$$

$$= \frac{\$2.20}{\$50} + .10 = .144$$

$$= 14.4\%$$

Note that the forthcoming dividend, D_1, is estimated by taking the past dividend, $2, and increasing it by 10 percent, the expected growth rate. That is, $D_1 = D_0 (1.10) = \$2(1.10) = \$2.20$. ∎

---

[8]For additional explanation, see Chapter 5.

The dividend-growth model has been a relatively popular approach for calculating the cost of equity. The primary difficulty, as you might expect, is estimating the expected growth rate in future dividends. One possible source of such expectations are investment advisory services such as Merrill Lynch and Value Line. There are even services that collect and publish the forecasts of a large number of analysts. For instance, Institutional Broker's Estimate System (IBES) publishes earnings per share forecasts made by about 2,000 analysts on a like number of stocks. Although these forecasts are helpful in reducing the problems of the dividend-growth model, they cannot be considered completely accurate. Growth estimates are generally available only for about five years, and not for the indefinite future, as required by the constant-growth model. Also, analysts usually state their forecasts in terms of earnings rather than dividends, which does not meet the strict requirements of the dividend-growth model. Even so, the earnings information is helpful, because dividend growth in the long run is dependent on earnings. Also, the analysts' forecasts are helpful because they provide direct measures of the expectations that determine values in the market.

The use of analysts' forecasts in conjunction with the dividend-growth model to compute required rates of return for the Standard and Poor's 500 stocks has been studied by Harris.[9] Computing an average of the analysts' forecasts of five-year growth rates in EPS, Harris used this average as a proxy for the growth rate in dividends. Then, using the dividend-growth model (equation 8–8), he estimated an average cost of equity for the S&P 500 stocks. He next compared these required rates with the yields on U.S. Treasury bonds to see how much risk premium common stockholders were expecting. The analysis was conducted for each quarter from 1982 through 1984. Results of the Harris study are presented in Table 8–3. The findings suggest that common stockholders have required a return of between 17.26 and 20.08 percent on average each year for 1982 through 1984. For the three-year period, the average required rate of return was 18.41 percent. The average risk premiums of common stockhold-

TABLE 8–3.
Required Rates of Return and Risk Premiums

	Government Bond Yield	S&P 500 Required Return	S&P 500 Risk Premium
1982			
Quarter 1	14.27	20.81	6.54
Quarter 2	13.74	20.68	6.94
Quarter 3	12.94	20.23	7.29
Quarter 4	10.72	18.58	7.86
Average	12.92	20.08	7.16
1983			
Quarter 1	10.87	18.07	7.20
Quarter 2	10.80	17.76	6.96
Quarter 3	11.79	17.90	6.11
Quarter 4	11.90	17.81	5.91
Average	11.34	17.88	6.54
1984			
Quarter 1	12.09	17.22	5.13
Quarter 2	13.21	17.42	4.21
Quarter 3	12.83	17.34	4.51
Quarter 4	11.78	17.05	5.27
Average	12.48	17.26	4.78
Average 1982–1984	12.25	18.41	6.16

Source: Robert Harris, "Using Analysts' Forecasts to Estimate Shareholder Required Returns," *Financial Management* (Spring 1986), 62. Used by permission.

[9]Robert Harris, "Using Analysts' Forecasts to Estimate Shareholder Required Returns," *Financial Management* (Spring 1986), pp. 58–67.

ers each year, which are shown in the last column of Table 8–3, ranged from 4.78 percent to 7.16 percent, for an average of 6.16 percent. However, we should remember that these returns apply only for equity investments of average riskiness. As we well know, the risk of individual securities will differ from the average, as will the stockholders' required returns.

Although the results in Table 8–3 look reasonable, the same computations for individual stocks may not be as plausible, largely because of measurement errors that occur when only one or a few stocks are analyzed. Moreover, the constant growth assumption of the model may be inconsistent with reality.

THE CAPM APPROACH ▫ Drawing from Chapter 4, we can estimate the cost of equity using the capital asset pricing model (CAPM). Remember that investors should require a rate of return that at least equals the risk-free rate plus a risk premium appropriate for the level of systematic risk associated with the particular security. Using the CAPM, we may represent the equity required rate of return (cost of internal equity) as follows:

$$R_c = K_c = R_f + \beta (R_m - R_f) \qquad (8-9)$$

where R_c, K_c = the required rate of return of the equity shareholders, and also the cost of internal equity capital

R_f = the risk-free rate

β = beta, or the measure of a stock's systematic risk

R_m = the expected rate of return for the market as a whole— that is, the expected return for the "average security"

For example, assume the risk-free rate is 7 percent, the expected return in the market is 16 percent, and the beta for Talbot Corporation's common stock is .82. Then the cost of internal equity would be estimated as follows:

$$K_c = R_f + \beta (R_m - R_f)$$
$$= 7\% + .82 (16\% - 7\%)$$
$$= 14.4\%$$

Although using the CAPM appears relatively easy, its application is not entirely straightforward, particularly in the corporate setting. In estimating the risk-free rate, the market rate, and the security's beta, our goal is to describe the expectations in the minds of the investors, because it is these expectations that determine how assets are valued. Such a task is difficult. However, as indicated earlier, financial service companies now help provide limited information about investor expectations.

Perspective in Finance

The CAPM says that an investor's required rate of return is equal to the risk-free rate plus a risk premium, where the only risk of any importance is systematic risk. Systematic risk is measured by beta, which tells us how our stock responds to changes in the general market.

RISK-PREMIUM APPROACH ▫ Because we know that common stockholders will demand a return premium above the bondholder's required rate of return, we may state the cost of equity as follows:

$$K_c = K_d + RP_c \qquad (8-10)$$

where, as before, K_c and K_d represent the cost of common and debt, respectively. RP_c is the additional return premium common stockholders expect for assuming greater risk than bondholders. Because we can compute the cost of debt with some degree of confidence, the key to estimating the cost of equity is in knowing RP_c, the risk premium.

We again are in some difficulty, because we have no direct means of computing RP_c. We can only draw from our experience, which tells us that the risk premium of a firm's common stocks relative to its own bonds has for the most part been between 3 and 5 percent. In times when interest rates are historically high, the premium is usually low. In years when interest rates are at historical lows, the premium has been higher. Using an average premium of 4 percent, we would approximate the cost of equity capital as follows:

$$K_c = K_d + 4\%$$

For a firm with Aaa-rated bonds that have a cost of 9 percent, the cost of equity would be estimated to be 13 percent (9 percent cost of debt plus the 4 percent average premium); a more risky company, with bonds that are rated Baa with a 13 percent cost, could expect its cost of equity to approximate 17 percent (13 percent + 4 percent).

The risk-premium approach is somewhat similar in concept to CAPM in that both recognize that common stockholders require a risk premium. The differences between the two approaches come from using different beginning points (CAPM uses the risk-free rate and the risk-premium approach uses the firm's cost of debt) and in how the risk premium is estimated. Both estimates of the risk premium involve subjectivity; however, CAPM has a more developed conceptual basis. Even so, the risk-premium approach is at times the best we can do, especially when the dividend-growth model and the CAPM give unreasonable estimates. Even if the dividend-growth and CAPM approaches are thought to fit the situation, the risk-premium technique gives us a good way to verify the reasonableness of our results.

Cost of new common stock ■ If internal common equity does not provide all the equity capital needed for new investments, the firm may need to issue new common stock. Again, this capital should not be acquired from the investors unless the expected returns on the prospective investments exceed a rate sufficient to satisfy the stockholders' required rate of return. Because the required rate of return of common stockholders was measured using equation (8–10), the only adjustment necessary is to consider the potential flotation costs incurred from issuing the stock. The effect of the flotation costs on the cost of common stock may be found by reducing the market price of the stock by the amount of these costs.[10] Thus, the cost of new common stock, K_{nc}, is

$$K_{nc} = \frac{D_1}{NP_0} + g \qquad \text{(8–11)}$$

where NP_0 equals the net proceeds per share received by the company. If, in the preceding example, flotation costs are 15 percent of the market price, the cost of capital for the new common stock, or external common, would be 15.18 percent, calculated as follows:

$$K_{nc} = \frac{\$2.20}{\$50 - .15(\$50)} + .10$$

$$= \frac{\$2.20}{\$42.50} + .10 = .1518$$

$$= 15.18\%$$

[10]For another approach to adjusting for flotation costs, see John R. Ezzell and R. Burr Porter, "Flotation Costs and the Weighted Average Cost of Capital," *Journal of Financial and Quantitative Analysis* 11 (September 1976), pp. 403–13.

In this example, if management achieves a 15.18 percent return on the net capital received from common stockholders, it will satisfy the investors' required rate of return of 14.4 percent, as determined earlier by equation (8–8).

Selection of Capital Structure Weights

The individual costs of capital will be different for each source of capital in the firm's capital structure. To use these costs of capital in our investment analyses, we must compute a composite or overall cost of capital. *The weights for computing this overall cost should reflect the corporation's financing mix.* For instance, if creditors are expected to finance 30 percent of the new investments and common stockholders are to provide the remaining 70 percent, the weighted cost should reflect this mix.

Several choices for selecting the financing weights for a composite cost of capital are available. Theoretically, the actual mix to be used in financing the proposed investments should be used as the weights. This approach, however, presents a problem. The costs of capital for individual sources depend on the firm's financial risk, which in turn is affected by its financial mix. If management alters the present financial structure, the individual costs will change, making it more difficult to compute the cost of capital. Thus, we will assume that the company's financial mix is relatively stable and that these weights will closely approximate future financing. Although this assumption may not be strictly met in any particular year, firms frequently have a **target capital structure** (desired debt–equity mix), which is maintained over the long term. The target financing mix provides the appropriate weights to be used in calculating the firm's weighted cost of capital. Consider the following:

EXAMPLE

The Ash Company's current financing mix is contained in Table 8–4. The firm's chief financial officer, Tony Ash, does not want to alter the firm's financial risk, instead he chooses to maintain the same relative mix of capital in financing future investments. Thus, given our assumption of a constant financial mix, we will use these percentages as the weights in computing Ash's weighted cost of capital. ■

Computing the Weighted Cost of Capital

Let's now compute the weighted cost of capital for a firm, which is simply the weighted average of the individual costs, given the firm's financial mix. This calculation is best demonstrated with an example. So let's return to Ash, Inc.

In Table 8–4, we estimated Ash's financial mix for the purpose of computing the firm's weighted or overall cost of capital. Let's further assume that management has computed the individual costs of capital for the firm, shown in Table 8–5. For the time being, we will restrict equity financing to the

Investor Group	Amount of Funds Raised ($)	Percentage of Total
Bonds	$1,750,000	35%
Preferred stock	250,000	5
Common stock	3,000,000	60
Total new financing	$5,000,000	100%

TABLE 8–4.
Ash, Inc., Capital Structure

Investor Group	Component Costs
Bonds	7%
Preferred stock	13
Common stock (internal only)	16

TABLE 8–5.
Component Costs of Capital for Ash, Inc.

(1) Investor Group	(2) Weight[a]	(3) Individual Costs[b]	(4) Weighted Costs (2 × 3)
Bonds	35%	7%	2.45%
Preferred stock	5	13	0.65
Common stock (internal only)	60	16	9.60
		Weighted cost of capital (K_0):	12.70%

[a]Taken from the desired financing mix presented in Table 8–4.
[b]Taken from Table 8–5.

retained earnings available for reinvestment, or internally generated common equity. We are assuming Ash will not issue any new common stock. Therefore, the cost of new common stock is not relevant. Table 8–6 combines the weights from Table 8–4 and the individual cost for each security from Table 8–5 into a single weighted cost of capital. Given that the assumptions of the weighted cost of capital concept are met and that common equity requirements can be satisfied internally, the company's weighted cost of capital is 12.7 percent. This rate is the firm's minimum acceptable rate of return for new investments. It therefore is the appropriate discount rate for capital-budgeting analysis for Ash, Inc., and a very important number in the process of determining the net present value of prospective capital investments for the firm.

We have now observed the process for measuring a company's weighted cost of capital. We cannot overstate the importance of this calculation; so much of what we do depends on our measuring the firm's weighted cost of capital with some degree of accuracy. Again, however, we must take care not to place too much confidence in our measurement techniques. We cannot say with any real conviction that we can figure precisely a firm's cost of capital. Remember the limiting effects of our assumptions, especially about constant business risk and financial risk. At best, we will only have an approximation of the firm's weighted cost of capital, but an approximation certainly beats assigning an arbitrary rate. Nevertheless, given the difficulties in measuring the cost, we must test the sensitivity of our results, that is, the value of the net present value, according to a reasonable range of values for the cost of capital rather than using a single-point estimate.

We now need to consider the effects of the level of financing on the firm's cost of capital. That is, as the firm continues to raise more capital for investment purposes, how is the cost of capital affected?

Level of Financing and the Weighted Cost of Capital

Impact of a New Common Stock Issue

In the previous illustration, we assumed that no new common stock was to be issued. If new common stock is issued, the firm's weighted cost of capital will increase, because external equity capital has a higher cost than internal equity owing to the flotation costs.

Generally the firm should use its cheapest sources of funds first while maintaining its desired debt–equity mix. In other words, because internally generated common stock costs less, it should be blended with debt until fully exhausted. Beyond this point, the weighted cost of capital increases, because the firm has to rely on new common stock for its equity financing. This basic concept is best explained through an example.[11]

[11]Although we assume a constant debt–equity mix, we have no reason or need to assume a constant mix between internally generated equity and new common stock. Rather, we assume that we first use internal equity funds until exhausted, and then, if more equity is needed, we issue common stock.

The Crisp Corporation, an independent oil company, is contemplating three major capital investments in 1993. The first proposal is the acquisition of equipment used to examine geological formations. This new equipment should improve the success ratio in discovering productive oil and gas reserves. The second proposal is investing in water flooding equipment. This process would involve injecting large amounts of water into underground oil reserves, which permits a more efficient recovery of the minerals. Third, new and advanced drilling equipment appears to offer significant cost savings in drilling for oil and gas. The costs and expected returns for these three possible investments are shown in Table 8–7. Management must decide which of these projects should be accepted.

If any of the proposed projects are accepted, the financing will consist of 50 percent debt and 50 percent common. Based on the anticipated profits during 1994, the company should have $1,500,000 in profits available for reinvestment (internal common). The costs of capital for each source of financing have been computed and are presented in Table 8–8.

	Investment Cost	Expected Internal Rate of Return
Geological equipment	$1,500,000	14%
Water flooding equipment	2,000,000	18
Drilling equipment	2,500,000	11

TABLE 8–7.
Crisp Corporation's Investment Opportunities

Source	Cost
Debt (after-tax cost)	6%
Internally generated common ($1,500,000)	14
New common stock	18

TABLE 8–8.
Crisp Corporation's Individual Costs of Capital

The weighted cost of capital, K_0, would be calculated as follows:

$$K_0 = \left[\left(\begin{array}{c} \text{percentage of} \\ \text{debt financing} \end{array} \right) \times \left(\begin{array}{c} \text{cost of} \\ \text{debt} \end{array} \right) \right] \qquad \textbf{(8–12)}$$
$$+ \left[\left(\begin{array}{c} \text{percentage of} \\ \text{common financing} \end{array} \right) \times \left(\begin{array}{c} \text{cost of} \\ \text{common} \end{array} \right) \right]$$

If only internally generated common is utilized, the weighted cost of capital is 10 percent:

$$K_0 = [50\% \times 6\%] + [50\% \times 14\%] = 10 \text{ percent}$$

When new common stock is used rather than internally generated common, however, the weighted cost of capital is 12 percent:

$$K_0 = [50\% \times 6\%] + [50\% \times 18\%] = 12 \text{ percent}$$

Which weighted cost of capital should be used in evaluating the three investments?

To answer this question, we must first rank the projects in descending order by their respective internal rates of return. Second, we must calculate the level of *total* financing at which point our internal equity is expended. In the Crisp Corporation illustration, $3 million in total new investments may be financed with internal common and debt, without having to change the present financial mix of 50 percent debt and 50 percent common, and without having to issue common stock. The $3 million is determined by solving the following equation:

$$\begin{pmatrix} \text{internally generated} \\ \text{common financing} \\ \text{available} \end{pmatrix} = \begin{pmatrix} \text{percentage of} \\ \text{common financing} \end{pmatrix} \times \begin{pmatrix} \text{total financing} \\ \text{from all sources} \end{pmatrix} \quad (8\text{--}13)$$

For the Crisp Corporation,

$$\$1,500,000 = (50\%) \times (\text{total financing})$$

which indicates that if Crisp has $1,500,000 in internally generated common and management maintains a 50 percent debt ratio, it will be able to finance $3 million of total investments without issuing new common stock. Equation (8–13) may be changed to solve directly for the amount of total financing; this is

$$\begin{aligned} \frac{\text{total financing}}{\text{from all sources}} &= \frac{\text{internally generated common}}{\text{percentage of common financing}} \\ &= \frac{\$1,500,000}{.50} \quad\quad (8\text{--}14) \\ &= \$3,000,000 \end{aligned}$$

Therefore, for a total investment level of $3 million or less, the firm's weighted cost of capital is expected to be 10 percent. Beyond this level of total financing our internal common is totally exhausted, and the weighted cost of capital increases to 12 percent. This reflects the increased cost of new common beyond the $3 million in total financing from both debt and common.

The relationship between the weighted costs of capital and the amount of financing being sought is portrayed graphically by Figure 8–5. The graph depicts the firm's **weighted marginal cost of capital.** The term *marginal* is used because the computed cost of capital shows the weighted cost of each additional dollar of financing. This marginal cost of capital represents the appropriate criterion for making investment decisions. Thus, the firm should continue to invest up to the point where the marginal rate of return earned on new investment (IRR) equals the marginal cost of new capital. This comparison is reflected in Figure 8–6, where the firm's optimal capital budget is found to be $3,500,000. The company should invest in water flooding machinery and the geological equipment. However, because the weighted marginal cost of capital is greater than the expected internal rate of return of the drilling equipment, this investment should be rejected. ■

FIGURE 8–5.
Crisp Corporation's Weighted
Marginal Cost of Capital

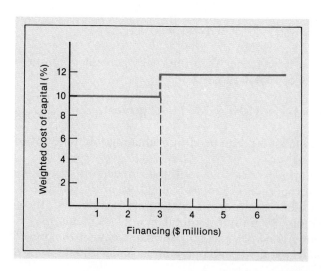

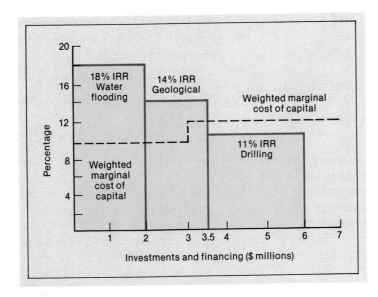

FIGURE 8–6.
Crisp Corporation: Comparison of Investment Returns and the Weighted Marginal Cost of Capital

General Effect of New Financing on the Marginal Cost of Capital

Thus far, we have considered only the effect of increases in the cost of common stock on the firm's weighted marginal cost of capital. Similar effects will occur as the cost of any source of financing increases. If the 6 percent cost of debt capital for Crisp Corporation increased to 8 percent after the firm issued $2 million in bonds, an increase in the weighted marginal cost of capital would have occurred at the $4 million financing level from all sources. This **break** in the marginal cost of capital curve is determined as

$$\frac{\text{total financing}}{\text{from all sources}} = \frac{\text{maximum amount of lower-cost debt}}{\text{percentage of debt financing}}$$

$$= \frac{\$2,000,000}{.50} \tag{8-15}$$

$$= \$4,000,000$$

As a general rule, *changes in the weighted marginal cost of capital will occur when the cost of an individual source increases.* The break in the marginal cost of capital curve will occur at the dollar financing level where

$$\frac{\text{total financing}}{\text{from all sources}} = \frac{\begin{array}{c}\text{maximum amount of a}\\ \text{lower-cost source of capital}\end{array}}{\begin{array}{c}\text{percentage financing}\\ \text{provided by the source}\end{array}} \tag{8-16}$$

Summary of Computations

The steps that have been described in calculating a firm's weighted *marginal* cost of capital may be summarized as follows:

1. Determine the percentage of financing to be used from each source of capital (debt, preferred stock, and common equity).

2. Compute the points on the marginal cost of capital curve where the weighted cost will increase.

3. Calculate the costs of each individual source of capital.

4. Compute the weighted cost of capital for the company, which will be different as the amount of financing increases.

5. Construct a graph that compares the internal rates of return with the weighted cost of capital, which will indicate which investments should be accepted.

Marginal Cost of Capital: A Comprehensive Example

To help bring together the principles for computing a firm's weighted cost of capital, consider J. M. Williams, Inc., a manufacturer of medical and surgical instruments. The firm's desired financing mix is presented in Table 8–9. Management attempts to maintain a relatively constant capital structure mix from year to year.

The most recent earnings per share (1992) was $8, which was twice the earnings per share in 1986, and this represents a growth rate of about 12 percent.[12] Dividends and the market price of the firm's common stock have grown at the same rate. The dividend payout ratio, which equals the ratio of common dividends to earnings available to common, has been 50 percent, and J. McDonald Williams, president, intends to hold to this dividend policy in the future.[13] Five investments are being examined by the company for 1993. The costs and the expected internal rates of return for these projects are provided in Table 8–10. To finance these investments, Williams expects to have $500,000 from 1993 retained earnings available for reinvestment, and new security issues can be sold. The firm's current financing mix will be maintained and the firm's business risk should not change. The following information is available regarding the individual costs of capital:

1. **Bonds.** An amount not exceeding $240,000 could be issued in new bonds. The issue, after considering the effect of flotation costs, would have an effective before-tax cost of 13 percent. If additional debt is required, the effective yield would have to be increased to 16 percent. The firm's marginal tax rate is 34 percent.

TABLE 8–9.
J. M. Williams, Inc.,
December 31, 1992

Total Liabilities and Equity	Capital Structure Mix (%)
Bonds	30.0%
Preferred stock	7.5
Common stock	62.5
Total liabilities and equity	100.0%

TABLE 8–10.
J. M. Williams, Inc.,
1993 Investment Opportunities

Investment	Estimated Cost	Projected Internal Rates of Return
A	$ 450,000	22%
B	500,000	19
C	300,000	17
D	250,000	14
E	500,000	12
Total proposed budget	$2,000,000	

[12]This growth rate is computed by dividing the 1992 earnings per share by the 1986 earnings per share, $8/$4 = 2, which represents the compound interest factor for 6 years at 12 percent. That is, [EPS 1986 $(1 + g)^6$ = EPS 1992], or $4(1 + g)^6$ = $8; thus, $(1 + g)^6$ = $8/$4 = 2. Looking up a compound interest factor of two for six years in Appendix B, we find it corresponds to a growth rate of about 12 percent. The same solution could be found by using the present value equation. Also, the solution could be found using a financial calculator. (For the HP 17B II: *FIN; TVM;* 4 +/− *PV;* 8 *FV;* 6 *N; I% YR*—which gives an answer of 12.2 percent.)

[13]Dividend policy is discussed in Chapter 11.

2. **Preferred stock.** New preferred stock could be issued by Williams with a par value of $50, paying $6 in annual dividends. The market price of the security is $45, but $1.80 per share in flotation costs would be incurred for an issue size of $105,000 or less. Additional preferred stock could be sold at $45; however, the flotation costs would be $3.33 per share.

3. **Common stock.** Common stock can be sold at the existing $75 market price. If the issue size is not greater than $375,000, a 15 percent flotation cost would result. For any additional common stock, the flotation costs would increase to 20 percent of the market price. As already noted, last year's dividend per share was $4 and dividends are expected to grow at 12 percent per year. As already noted, last year's dividend per share was $4 and dividends are expected to grow at 12 percent per year.

With the foregoing information and by using the following five steps, we can construct a weighted marginal cost of capital curve as follows:

Step 1: *Determine the financial mix.* In Table 8–9, the desired financial mix for Williams was shown to be 30 percent in debt, 7.5 percent in preferred stocks, and 62.5 percent in common equity. For Step 1, we assume that future financing will be made in the same proportions.

Step 2: *Compute when costs will increase.* With the preceding weights and knowing the amount of capital available at each cost, we can compute the points at which breaks in the marginal cost curve will occur. Remember that an increase in the weighted cost of capital occurs when one of the individual costs increases. For example, if the cost of debt rises, the weighted cost must also be higher. We need to know where these increases in the weighted cost will occur. For Williams, Inc., we know that the cost of the bonds increases if we issue more than $240,000 in new bonds. If debt represents 30 percent of all sources, how much in total financing will be possible before this increase in debt financing (bonds) affects the weighted marginal cost of capital? Using equation (8–16), we see that the weighted cost will increase when $800,000 in total capital has been raised, which is computed as follows:

$$\text{total financing available with} \atop \text{the lower-cost debt} = \frac{\text{total debt available at} \atop \text{a lower cost}}{\text{percentage of debt financing}}$$

$$= \frac{\$240,000}{.30}$$

$$= \$800,000$$

In other words, when we raise $800,000 in total financing and 30 percent is from debt, we will have used $240,000 in bonds (30 percent of $800,000). This same procedure must be followed for increases in the cost of preferred stock and for common equity, both for internally generated common and a new common stock. These calculations are shown in Table 8–11, and the results indicate two breaks in

TABLE 8–11.
J. M. Williams, Inc., Dollar Breaks in Marginal Cost of Capital Curve

I. *Debt*

$$\text{total financing available with} \atop \text{the lower-cost debt} = \frac{\text{total debt available at lower cost}}{\text{percentage of debt financing}}$$

$$= \frac{\$240,000}{.30}$$

$$= \$800,000$$

II. *Preferred Stock*

$$\text{total financing available with} \atop \text{cheaper preferred stock} = \frac{\text{total preferred stock available at lower cost}}{\text{percentage of preferred stock financing}}$$

$$= \frac{\$105,000}{.075}$$

$$= \$1,400,000$$

TABLE 8-11.
(cont.)

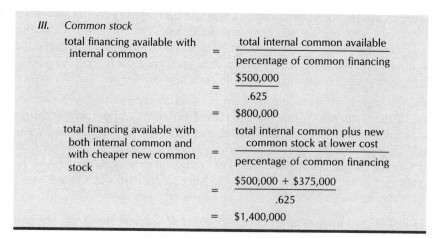

III. *Common stock*

$$\text{total financing available with internal common} = \frac{\text{total internal common available}}{\text{percentage of common financing}}$$

$$= \frac{\$500,000}{.625}$$

$$= \$800,000$$

$$\text{total financing available with both internal common and with cheaper new common stock} = \frac{\text{total internal common plus new common stock at lower cost}}{\text{percentage of common financing}}$$

$$= \frac{\$500,000 + \$375,000}{.625}$$

$$= \$1,400,000$$

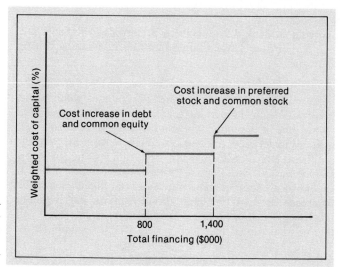

FIGURE 8-7.
J. M. Williams, Inc., Breaks in the Weighted Cost of Capital

the curve. Increases in the marginal cost of capital occur as the amount of total financing reaches (1) $800,000 (cost of debt and common equity simultaneously increase), and (2) $1,400,000 (cost of preferred stock increases and cost of common equity increases). This result is presented in Figure 8-7.

Step 3:   Calculate the cost of individual sources. The next step requires computing the individual costs of capital, which is presented in Table 8-12, where the amount of capital and the costs for these funds are provided. For debt the costs need only to be adjusted by Williams' marginal income tax rate. For a 34 percent income tax rate, the 13 percent and 16 percent costs of debt have an effective after-tax cost of 8.6 percent and 10.6 percent, respectively. The cost of preferred stock, which equals the dollar dividend relative to the net price per share received by the company, equals 13.9 percent for the first $105,000 and 14.4 percent for any greater amounts. The cost of internally generated common equals the dividend yield (the forthcoming dividend per share/price) plus the expected growth in dividends. The dividend yield is 6 percent ($4.48/$75). An annual compound growth rate of 12 percent is estimated from the past growth in earnings per share. The dividend yield of 6 percent plus the 12 percent growth rate produces an 18 percent cost of internally generated common. The costs of new common stock are easily determined by adjusting the required rate of return of the common stockholders by the flotation costs in issuing the stock. These calculations yield a cost of new common up to $375,000 of 19 percent and 19.5 percent for an amount exceeding $375,000.

Step 4:   Solve for the weighted marginal cost of capital. With the preceding information, the weighted marginal costs of capital relative to the funds raised may be determined. Because the weighted cost of capital does not change for the first $800,000 in total financing, the weighted marginal cost of capital is determined by using the lowest costs of the individual sources. The weighted costs of financing up

TABLE 8-12.
J. M. Williams, Inc., Amount and Costs of Individual Sources, December 1988

Source	Amount Available	Cost Calculations
I. Debt		$\left(\begin{array}{c}\text{after-tax}\\ \text{cost of bonds}\end{array}\right) = \left(\begin{array}{c}\text{before-tax}\\ \text{cost}\end{array}\right)(1 - \text{tax rate})$
	(a) $0–240,000	$K_d = 13\%\,(1 - .34) = 8.6\%$
	(b) Over $240,000	$K_d = 16\%\,(1 - .34) = 10.6\%$
II. Preferred stock		$\left(\begin{array}{c}\text{cost of}\\ \text{preferred}\end{array}\right) = \left(\dfrac{\text{dividend per share}}{\begin{array}{c}\text{market price less}\\ \text{flotation costs}\end{array}}\right)$
	(a) $0–105,000	$K_p = \dfrac{\$6}{\$45 - \$1.80} = 13.9\%$
	(b) Over $105,000	$K_p = \dfrac{\$6}{\$45 - \$3.33} = 14.4\%$
III. Common financing A. Internal common		$\left(\begin{array}{c}\text{cost of}\\ \text{internal common}\end{array}\right) = \left(\dfrac{\text{dividend in one year}}{\text{market price}}\right) + \text{growth}$
	$0–$500,000	$K_c = \dfrac{\$4(1 + .12)}{\$75} + .12 = 18.0\%$
B. New common stock		$\left(\begin{array}{c}\text{cost of new}\\ \text{common}\\ \text{stock}\end{array}\right) = \left(\dfrac{\text{dividend per share}}{\begin{array}{c}\text{market price less}\\ \text{flotation costs}\end{array}}\right) + \text{growth}$
	(a) $0–$375,000	$K_c = \dfrac{\$4(1 + .12)}{\$75 - \$11.25} + .12 = 19.0\%$
	(b) Over $375,000	$K_{nc} = \dfrac{\$4(1 + .12)}{\$75 - \$15} + .12 = 19.5\%$

Calculations

(1) Source	(2) Proportions	(3) Cost of Capital	(4) Weighted Cost of Capital (2 × 3)
Bonds	30.0%	8.6%	2.58%
Preferred stock	7.5	13.9	1.04
Common equity	62.5	18.0	11.25
	100.0%	Weighted cost of capital:	14.87%

TABLE 8-13.
J. M. Williams, Inc., Weighted Marginal Cost of Capital for $0–$800,000 Funds Raised

to $800,000 are calculated in Table 8–13. The percentage of capital that would be provided by each source is presented in column 2, and the cost of each individual source of capital appears in column 3 (taken from Table 8–12). Multiplying the weights (column 2) times the individual costs (column 3) and summing the results produce a weighted cost of 14.87 percent. This cost applies to any amount of financing (including debt, preferred stock, and common equity) up to but not exceeding $800,000.

After the first $800,000 has been used to finance new investments, the costs of debt and common equity will increase. The costs increase because we will have exceeded $240,000 in debt and $500,000 in common equity. Taking the increased costs from Table 8–12 for these two sources (preferred stock cost has not changed), we calculate a weighted marginal cost of capital for an amount greater than $800,000 but not exceeding $1,400,000. This weighted cost is now 16.10 percent and is given in Table 8–14, where the new costs for debt and

(1) Source	(2) Proportions	(3) Cost of Capital	(4) Weighted Cost of Capital (2 × 3)
Bonds	30.0%	10.6%	3.18%
Preferred stock	7.5	13.9	1.04
Common equity	62.5	19.0	11.88
	100.0%	Weighted cost of capital:	16.10%

(1) Source	(2) Proportions	(3) Cost of Capital	(4) Weighted Cost of Capital (2 × 3)
Bonds	30.0%	10.6%	3.18%
Preferred stock	7.5	14.4	1.08
Common equity	62.5	19.5	12.19
	100.0%	Weighted cost of capital:	16.45%

common equity are shown in the boxes. Otherwise the calculation is no different from the weighted cost of capital for less than $800,000.

Should the firm finance over $1,400,000, the weighted marginal cost of capital will again rise. Because we now need over $105,000 in preferred stock and $875,000 in common equity to raise more than $1,400,000 in total financing, the costs of preferred stock and common equity will increase. These new costs are presented in Table 8–15. They result in a final weighted cost of capital of 16.45 percent.

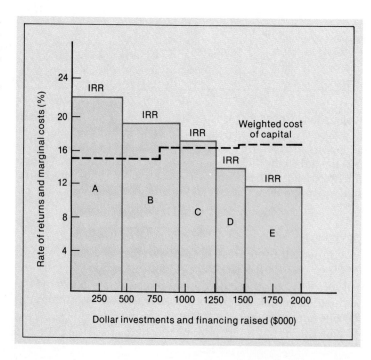

BASIC FINANCIAL MANAGEMENT IN PRACTICE

Management Myopia: Limited Evidence on the Matter

American managers are often accused of short-termism. Corporate near-sightedness, the indictment reads, is the reason American companies invest less than their main foreign competitors, and American productivity has grown so slowly in recent years. Is the charge true? Evidence is largely anecdotal. In a new study, James Poterba of MIT and Lawrence Summers of the World Bank have bothered to ask managers for their opinion.* The findings are hardly conclusive, but they might lead to a better class of anecdote.

Messrs Poterba and Summers sent a questionnaire to the chief executives of Fortune 1,000 firms, with a covering letter from John Young, chairman of Hewlett-Packard, and John MacArthur, dean of Harvard Business School, asking for help. They received 228 replies, 97 of them from identifiable manufacturers—the sort of companies most often said to be short-termist. This pretty unimpressive response, together with the possibility of bias (the chief executives who answered may be untypically concerned about short-termism), means the results have to be handled with care.

The survey asked chief executives what proportion of their investment in R&D was devoted to projects that would generate no income during the next five years. Answers varied widely, but averaged 21% overall and 23% for manufacturers. The survey then asked what proportion of investment was of that far-sighted sort ten years ago. The answers were 19% overall and 22% for manufacturers. On this measure, it seems, the firms are slightly less short-sighted than they used to be.

Chief executives were asked to state their "hurdle rates"—the smallest return expected of a project if the company is to go ahead with it. Two-thirds of the answers were given in the form of nominal rates. The authors converted nominal to real by deducting five percentage points, representing long-term expected inflation. The resulting average real rates, shown in the table, are surprisingly high. Since the 1920s the real return on American corporate bonds has averaged 2%; the real

CORPORATE TIME HORIZONS

	All	Manufacturing
Fraction of R&D in long-term projects (%)	21.1	22.6
Real hurdle rate (%)	12.2	11.6
Increase in investment if stock market correctly valued long-term investments (%)	20.7	19.0
Time horizon of the companies relative to: (1 =longer, 5 =shorter)		
U.S. competitors	2.5	2.4
European competitors	3.2	3.1
Asian competitors	3.8	3.8

Source: Poterba and Summers.

return on equities 7%. Average hurdle rates of 12% seem unduly demanding.

Corporate near-sightedness is often blamed on Wall Street. Unsurprisingly, three-quarters of the bosses thought their firms undervalued. Asked how much more they would invest if financial markets valued long-term investment correctly, the average answer was 21%.

Next, the survey asked each company to judge its time horizon against (a) other American firms, (b) European firms and (c) Asian firms. Answers were given on a scale of one (less short-sighted) to five (more short-sighted). Interestingly, the chief executives thought themselves less short-sighted than their counterparts at home. But they believed they were more short-sighted than their European competitors, and even more so than Asians.

*James Poterba and Lawrence Summers, Time Horizons of American Firms: New Evidence from a Survey of CEOs. Unpublished manuscript.
Source: *The Economist*, December 14, 1991, p. 73. Used by permission.

In summary, the weighted cost of capital for J. M. Williams, Inc., increases as the amount of money needed becomes larger, with the costs being as follows:

Total Financing	Weighted Cost
$0–$800,000	14.87%
$800,001–$1,400,000	16.10
Over $1,400,000	16.45

Step 5: *Compare investment returns with weighted costs.* The weighted marginal costs of capital are to be used in determining whether to accept any or all of the investment prospects being reviewed by Williams. A ranking of the projects, taken from Table 8–10, and a comparison of the returns against the weighted costs of capital are given in Figure 8–8. As is evident from the figure, Williams' optimal capital budget

for 1993 is $1,250,000. The particular investments that should be included in the budget are projects A, B, and C, with the returns for projects D and E falling short of the weighted cost of capital hurdle rate.

Required Rate of Return for Individual Projects: An Alternative Approach

Two basic assumptions were made in the preceding sections in computing the firm's weighted cost of capital as a cutoff rate for new capital investments. First, the riskiness of the project being evaluated is assumed to be similar to the riskiness of the company's existing assets. That is, acceptance of the investment will not alter the firm's overall business risk. Second, future investments are assumed to be financed in the same proportions of debt, preferred stock, and common stock as past investments. Frequently these two assumptions are not met in practice. Firms often do make investments that have risk characteristics different from the firm's existing assets. They may also finance a given project with all debt, and then rely solely on equity for the next investment. Also, given the nature of an investment, they may be able to use more debt than what was possible for prior investments.

Regarding constant business risk, Figure 8–9 illustrates the problem that occurs from using the weighted cost of capital for projects having different levels of risk. In the figure, the orange line represents the firm's weighted cost of capital, K_0. This cost of capital, computed earlier in the chapter, does not allow for the varying levels of project risk but is appropriate only for projects having a level of risk shown at point RL_0 in the figure. The return–risk line in the figure more correctly gives the message that a higher cost of capital should be used as the level of risk increases. That is, we should use different costs of capital (required rates of return) for investments having different levels of risk.

Investment A and B in the figure may be used to illustrate any incorrect decisions that might result from the use of the firm's cost of capital as the cutoff

FIGURE 8–9.
Return–Risk Relationship

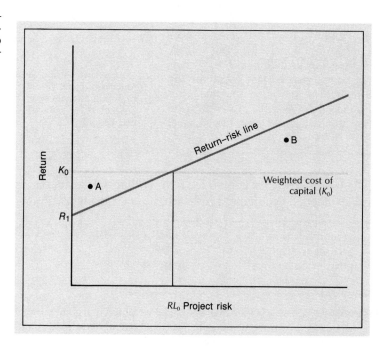

rate for project acceptance where the risk inherent in A is below the firm's risk level of RL_0 and project B's risk exceeds RL_0. Investment A would be rejected and investment B accepted if the required rate being used were the weighted marginal cost of capital. However, if the return–risk line accurately measures the market return–risk relationship, investment A should be accepted and investment B rejected. Although the expected return for investment A is below the firm's weighted marginal cost of capital, the reduction in risk sufficiently justifies accepting the investment's lower expected return.

In determining a fair or appropriate rate of return for a project given its level of risk, remember our discussion in Chapter 4 on the types of risk. We could think of risk as the total variability in returns for the investment, without any regard for how it relates to the firm's other investments. That is, we could look at *project risk,* or risk in isolation. We could think alternatively of the riskiness of the project in terms of its contribution to the riskiness of the firm's portfolio of assets. Taking this contribution-to-firm approach, we would measure risk as the standard deviation of the returns for all the firm's assets taken together including the new project. A third option, and the one we choose to take, is to see risk in terms of *risk to shareholders.* We assume that the firm's investors hold a diversified portfolio of investments and that we want our measure of risk to indicate the incremental risk the project adds to the investors' (not the firm's) diversified portfolio. In this situation, the CAPM gives us a way to evaluate a project. Using the CAPM, the required rate of return for the *j*th project may be expressed as follows:[14]

$$K_j = R_f + \beta_j(R_m - R_f) \tag{8-17}$$

where β_j (beta) identifies the volatility of the *j*th project returns relative to the investor's widely diversified portfolio. Thus, β_j represents the effect of the *j*th project on the riskiness of the investor's portfolio, which is also the relevant risk used in the market to value the asset. As in Chapter 4, R_m and R_f represent the expected return for the diversified portfolio and for a risk-free asset, respectively.[15]

EXAMPLE

To illustrate the use of the capital asset pricing model for determining the required rate of return for a project, suppose a firm is considering a capital investment with an expected return of 16 percent. Management believes that the riskiness of the project should be analyzed in terms of its contribution to the risk of a diversified investor's portfolio. The expected return for a diversified portfolio of assets, R_m, is 14 percent, and the risk-free rate, R_f, is 6 percent. Management has estimated the beta for the project to be 1.12, which indicates

[14]For further explanation, see Ezra Solomon, "Measuring a Company's Cost of Capital," *Journal of Business* (October 1955), pp. 95–117; Steward C. Myers, "Interactions of Corporate Financing and Investment Decision—Implications for Capital Budgeting," *Journal of Finance* (March 1974), pp. 1–25; Richard S. Bower and Jeffery M. Jenks, "Divisional Screening Rates," *Financial Management* (Autumn 1975), pp. 42–49; Donald I. Tuttle and Robert H. Litzenberger, "Leverage Diversification and Capital Market Effects on a Risk-Adjusted Capital Budgeting Framework," *Journal of Finance* (June 1968), pp. 427–43; and John D. Martin and David F. Scott, Jr., "Debt Capacity and the Capital Budgeting Decision," *Financial Management* (Summer 1976), pp. 7–14.
[15]For our purposes, we shall assume that the firm finances all its investments with equity. Thus, we need not be concerned with the problems that arise from having to adjust for different financing mixes. This issue is simply beyond the scope of our studies; however, to see how it is done, look at Thomas Conine and Maurry Tamarkin, "Divisional Cost of Capital Estimation: Adjusting for Financial Leverage," *Financial Management* (Spring 1985), pp. 54–58.

that a 1 percent change in the market portfolio's risk premium (that is, $R_m - R_f$) will produce an expected 1.12 percent change in the investment's risk premium $(K_j - R_f)$. We may therefore estimate the appropriate required rate of return for the project as follows:

$$K_j = R_f + \beta_j(R_m - R_f)$$
$$= .06 + 1.12(.14 - .06) = .1496 \qquad (8-17)$$
$$= 14.96\%$$

Because the 16 percent expected return for the investment exceeds the required rate of return of 14.96 percent, the investment should be made. ■

Although conceptually attractive, the use of the capital asset pricing model in calculating a project required rate of return is difficult, owing to measurement problems. The primary difficulty lies in measuring the project's beta, that is, the systematic risk of the project. About the only practical way to circumvent this problem, as was suggested in Chapter 7, is to use the beta of a "pure-play" firm as the project's beta or alternatively by using selected accounting data for this purpose. Also, the model maintains that the relevant risk is limited to the portion of the risk that the *investor* cannot eliminate through diversification. For this premise to hold, bankruptcy costs are assumed to equal zero if the firm fails. In reality, bankruptcy costs are generally significant. Therefore, if a project increases significantly the probability of firm bankruptcy, total variability of project returns is the appropriate risk measure.

A Firm's Cost of Capital: Some Recent Evidence

An interesting survey of the 100 largest corporations listed on the New York Stock Exchange was conducted by Blume, Friend, and Westerfield. In this survey, managers were asked to indicate various cost of capital figures.[16] The results are reported in Table 8–16.

Of the 30 companies that responded to the survey, 10 were public utilities and 20 were nonfinancial corporations from a variety of industries. From the results, we can see that higher costs of capital prevailed when public utilities were excluded, which implies that public utilities are less risky. Even more

TABLE 8–16.
Average Costs of Capital and Investment: Cutoff Rates for Plant and Equipment

Industries	Before-Tax Cost-of-Debt(%)	After-Tax Cost (%) New Common Equity	Retained Earnings	Debt	Weighted Cost	After-tax Cutoff Rate for Plant and Equipment Investments Least Risky	Most Risky
All industries	12.5%	17.2%	16.6%	6.4%	12.4%	12.9%	19.6%
All industries except public utilities	12.5	17.8	17.0	6.3	13.1	13.1	20.3

Source: Marshall E. Blume, Irwin Friend, and Randolph Westerfield, "Impediments to Capital Formation: Summary Report of a Survey of Nonfinancial Corporations," Working Paper (Philadelphia: Wharton School, University of Pennsylvania, 1980), 6.

[16]Marshall E. Blume, Irwin Friend, and Randolph Westerfield, "Impediments to Capital Formation: Summary Report of a Survey of Nonfinancial Corporations," Working Paper (Philadelphia: Wharton School, University of Pennsylvania, 1980), p. 6.

significantly, the results suggest that new common stock is slightly more expensive than internal common (retained earnings) and that internal common is four to five percentage points more costly than the *before-tax* cost of debt. We should also note that the weighted cost of capital, which falls around 12 to 13 percent, is at the bottom range of the cutoff or hurdle rate used to evaluate investments in plant and equipment. Thus, either new investments were considered more risky than existing investment or management is imposing capital rationing.

In addition to the results summarized in Table 8–16, the authors found that

1. The dividend-growth model is the most frequently used method for estimating the cost of equity. However, the CAPM is also coming to be used with the dividend-growth model.
2. If management perceives the cost of a particular source to be excessive, it will rely more heavily on other sources. That is, how a firm finances its investments is affected by management's perception of the relative costs of each source of capital.

SUMMARY

Cost of capital is an important concept within financial management. In making an investment, the cost of capital is the rate of return that must be achieved on the company's projects in order to satisfy the investor's required rate of return. If the rate of return from the corporation's investments equals the cost of capital, the price of the stock should remain unchanged. In other words, the firm's cost of capital may be defined as the rate of return from an investment that will leave the company's stock price unchanged. Therefore, the cost of capital, if certain assumptions are met, represents the minimum acceptable rate of return for new corporate investments.

The factors that affect a firm's cost of capital consist of four components. First, general economic conditions (as reflected in the demand and supply of funds in the economy), as well as inflationary pressures, affect the general level of interest rates. Second, the marketability of the firm's securities has an impact on the cost of capital. Any change in the marketability of a firm's stock will affect investors' required rate of return. These changes directly influence the firm's cost of capital. Third, the firm's operating and financial risks are reflected in its cost of capital. Finally, a relationship exists between a firm's cost of capital and the dollar amount of financing needed for future investments.

Cost of Individual Sources of Financing

The cost of debt is equal to the effective interest rate on new debt adjusted for the tax deductibility of the interest expense. The cost of preferred stock is equal to the effective dividend yield on new preferred stock. In making this computation, we should use the net price received by the company from the new issue. Thus,

$$\text{cost of preferred stock} = \frac{\text{annual dividend}}{\text{net price of preferred stock}} \qquad (8\text{--}6)$$

In calculating the cost of common equity, we distinguish between the costs of internally generated funds and the costs of new common stock. If historical data reasonably reflect the expectations of investors, the cost of internally generated capital is equal to the dividend yield on the common stock plus the anticipated percentage increase in dividends (and in the price of the stock) during the forthcoming year. If, however, the common equity is to be acquired by issuing new common stock, the cost of common should recognize the effect of flotation costs. This alteration results in the following equation for the cost of new common stock:

$$\left(\begin{array}{c}\text{cost of new}\\\text{common}\end{array}\right) = \left(\frac{\text{dividend in year 1}}{\text{market price} - \text{flotation cost}}\right) + \left(\begin{array}{c}\text{annual growth rate}\\\text{in dividends}\end{array}\right) \tag{8-11}$$

where (market price − flotation cost) is equivalent to the net market price.

We may also compute the cost of equity by using the CAPM or the risk-premium technique.

Weighted Cost of Capital

A firm's weighted cost of capital is a composite of the individual costs of financing weighted by the percentage of financing provided by each source. In this chapter we assume that the firm is to finance future investments in the same manner as past investments. The problem of defining the best set of weights is addressed in Chapter 10. Hence, the existing capital structure was used for developing the weighting scheme.

Marginal Cost of Capital

Because the amount of financing has an effect upon the firm's weighted cost of effect capital, the expected return from an investment must be compared with the marginal cost of financing the project. If the cost of capital rises as the level of financing increases, we should use the marginal cost of capital, and not the average cost of all funds raised. Following the basic economic principle of marginal analysis, investments should be made to the point where marginal revenue (internal rate of return) equals the marginal cost of capital.

Measuring the Cost of Capital for Individual Projects

Owing to the limiting assumptions associated with an overall cost of capital for the firm, a single hurdle rate is not generally appropriate for all the investments a firm will analyze. In particular, if the risk associated with a specific investment is significantly different from the firm's existing assets, the weighted cost of capital should not be employed. In this context, a minimum acceptable rate of return that recognizes the different risk levels has to be used. To implement such an approach, financial managers must identify the appropriate measure of risk; generally an analysis of systematic risk through the CAPM model is the best choice.

STUDY QUESTIONS

8–1. Define the term *cost of capital*.

8–2. Why do we calculate a firm's cost of capital?

8–3. In computing the cost of capital, which sources of capital do we consider?

8–4. In general, what factors determine a firm's cost of capital? In answering this question, identify the factors that are within management's control and those that are not.

8–5. What limitations exist in using the firm's cost of capital as an investment hurdle rate?

8-6. How does a firm's tax rate affect its cost of capital? What is the effect of the flotation costs associated with a new security issue?

8-7. a. Distinguish between internal common equity and new common stock.
b. Why is a cost associated with internal common equity?
c. Compare approaches that could be used in computing the cost of common equity.

8-8. Define the expression *marginal cost of capital*. Why is the marginal cost of capital an appropriate investment criterion?

8-9. How may we avoid the limitation of the weighted cost of capital approach when it requires that we assume business risk is constant?

8-10. What might we expect to see in practice in the relative costs of different sources of capital?

SELF-TEST PROBLEMS

ST-1. (*Individual Costs of Capital*) Compute the cost for the following sources of financing:
a. A $1,000 par value bond with a market price of $970 and a coupon interest rate of 10 percent. Flotation costs for a new issue would be approximately 5 percent. The bonds mature in 10 years and the corporate tax rate is 34 percent.
b. A preferred stock selling for $100 with an annual dividend payment of $8. If the company sells a new issue, the flotation cost will be $9 per share. The company's marginal tax rate is 30 percent.
c. Internally generated common totaling $4.8 million. The price of the common stock is $75 per share, and the dividends per share were $9.80 last year. These dividends are not expected to increase.
d. New common stock where the most recent dividend was $2.80. The company's dividends per share should continue to increase at an 8 percent growth rate into the indefinite future. The market price of the stock is currently $53; however, flotation costs of $6 per share are expected if the new stock is issued.

ST-2. (*Level of Financing*) The Argue Company has the following capital structure mix:

Debt	30%
Preferred stock	15
Common stock	55
	100%

Assuming that management intends to maintain the above financial structure, what amount of *total* investments may be financed if the firm uses (a) $100,000 of debt, (b) $150,000 of debt, (c) $40,000 of preferred stock, (d) $90,000 of preferred stock, (e) $200,000 of internally generated common equity, (f) $200,000 of internally generated common equity plus $300,000 in new common stock?

ST-3. (*Marginal Cost-of-Capital Curve*) The Zenor Corporation is considering three investments. The costs and expected returns of these projects are shown below:

Investment	Investment Cost	Internal Rate of Return
A	$165,000	17%
B	200,000	13
C	125,000	12

The firm would finance the projects by 40 percent debt and 60 percent common equity. The after-tax cost of debt is 7 percent for the first $120,000, after which the cost will be 11 percent. Internally generated common totaling $180,000 is available, and the common stockholders' required rate of return is 19 percent. If new stock is issued, the cost will be 22 percent.
a. Construct a weighted marginal cost of capital curve.
b. Which projects should be accepted?

ST-4. (*Weighted Cost of Capital*) Todd Owens is the new vice-president–finance for Brister, Inc. He is preparing his recommendations for the firm's capital budget. With the information provided below, prepare a graph comparing the company's weighted cost of capital and the prospective investment returns. Which investments should be made?

Investment	Investment Cost	Rate of Return
A	$200,000	18%
B	125,000	16
C	150,000	12
D	275,000	10

The firm's capital structure consists of $2 million in debt, $500,000 in preferred stock, and $2.5 million in common equity. This capital mix is to be maintained for future investments.

The cost of debt (before-tax) is 12 percent for the first $120,000; thereafter, the cost will be 15 percent.

The company's preferred stock sells for $95 and pays a 14 percent dividend rate on a par value of $100. A new offering of this stock would entail underwriting costs and a price discount of 8 percent of the present market price. If the issue exceeded $50,000, the flotation costs would increase to 11 percent.

The common equity portion of the investments will be financed first by profits retained within the company of $150,000. If additional common financing is needed, new common stock can be issued at the $30 current price less flotation costs of $3 per share. Management expects to pay a dividend at the end of this year of $2.50, and dividends should increase at an annual rate of 9 percent thereafter. The firm's marginal tax rate is 34 percent.

ST–5. (*Individual Project—Required Return*) Scudder Corporation is evaluating three investments that have the expected returns and betas listed below. Managers want to determine the required rates of return of the projects using the capital asset pricing model. The expected return of a diversified portfolio is 15 percent. The rate on U.S. government securities is 8 percent. Which investments should they make?

Investment	Expected Return	Beta
A	18.8%	1.10
B	13.5	.90
C	15.0	.80

STUDY PROBLEMS (SET A)

8–1A. (*Individual or Component Costs of Capital*) Compute the cost for the following sources of financing:

a. A bond that has a $1,000 par value (face value) and a contract or coupon interest rate of 11 percent. A new issue would have a flotation cost of 5 percent of the $1,125 market value. The bonds mature in 10 years. The firm's average tax rate is 30 percent and its marginal tax rate is 34 percent.

b. A new common stock issue that paid a $1.80 dividend last year. The par value of the stock is $15, and earnings per share have grown at a rate of 7 percent per year. This growth rate is expected to continue into the foreseeable future. The company maintains a constant dividend/earnings ratio of 30 percent. The price of this stock is now $27.50, but 5 percent flotation costs are anticipated.

c. Internal common equity where the current market price of the common stock is $43. The expected dividend this coming year should be $3.50, increasing thereafter at a 7 percent annual growth rate. The corporation's tax rate is 34 percent.

d. A preferred stock paying a 9 percent dividend on a $150 par value. If a new issue is offered, flotation costs will be 12 percent of the current price of $175.

e. A bond selling to yield 12 percent after flotation costs, but prior to adjusting for the marginal corporate tax rate of 34 percent. In other words, 12 percent is the rate that equates the net proceeds from the bond with the present value of the future cash flows (principal and interest).

8-2A. (*Level of Financing*) The Mathews Company has the following capital structure mix:

Debt	$525,000
Preferred stock	225,000
Common stock	450,000

Using that capital structure mix, compute the total investment amount if the company uses
a. $700,000 of debt
b. $67,500 of preferred stock
c. $300,000 of retained earnings only, or
d. $100,000 of retained earnings plus $600,000 of new common stock

8-3A. (*Individual or Component Costs of Capital*) Compute the cost for the following sources of financing:
a. A bond selling to yield 8 percent after flotation cost, but prior to adjusting for the marginal corporate tax rate of 34 percent. In other words, 8 percent is the rate that equates the net proceeds from the bond with the present value of the future cash flows (principal and interest).
b. A new common stock issue that paid a $1.05 dividend last year. The par value of the stock is $2, and the earnings per share have grown at a rate of 5 percent per year. This growth rate is expected to continue into the foreseeable future. The company maintains a constant dividend/earnings ratio of 40 percent. The price of this stock is now $25, but 9 percent flotation costs are anticipated.
c. A bond that has a $1,000 par value (face value) and a contract or coupon interest rate of 12 percent. A new issue would net the company 90 percent of the $1,150 market value. The bonds mature in 20 years, and the firm's average tax rate is 30 percent and its marginal tax rate is 34 percent.
d. A preferred stock paying a 7 percent dividend on a $100 par value. If a new issue is offered, the company can expect to net $85 per share.
e. Internal common equity where the current market price of the common stock is $38. The expected dividend this forthcoming year should be $3, increasing thereafter at a 4 percent annual growth rate. The corporation's tax rate is 34 percent.

8-4A. (*Cost of Equity*) Salte Corporation is issuing new common stock at a market price of $27. Dividends last year were $1.45 and are expected to grow at an annual rate of 6 percent forever. Flotation costs will be 6 percent of market price. What is Salte's cost of equity?

8-5A. (*Cost of Debt*) Belton is issuing a $1,000 par value bond that pays 7 percent annual interest and matures in 15 years. Investors are willing to pay $958 for the bond. Flotation costs will be 11 percent of market value. The company is in an 18 percent tax bracket. What will be the firm's after-tax cost of debt on the bond?

8-6A. (*Cost of Preferred Stock*) The preferred stock of Walter Industries sells for $36 and pays $2.50 in dividends. The net price of the security after issuance costs is $32.50. What is the cost of capital for the preferred stock?

8-7A. (*Cost of Debt*) The Zephyr Corporation is contemplating a new investment to be financed 33 percent from debt. The firm could sell new $1,000 par value bonds at a net price of $945. The coupon interest rate is 12 percent, and the bonds would mature in 15 years. If the company is in a 34 percent tax bracket, what is the after-tax cost of capital to Zephyr for bonds?

8-8A. (*Cost of Preferred Stock*) Your firm is planning to issue preferred stock. The stock sells for $115; however, if new stock is issued, the company would receive only $98. The par value of the stock is $100 and the dividend rate is 14 percent. What is the cost of capital for the stock to your firm?

8-9A. (*Cost of Internal Equity*) Pathos Co.'s common stock is currently selling for $21.50. Dividends paid last year were $.70. Flotation costs on issuing stock will be 10 percent of market price. The dividends and earnings per share are projected to have an annual growth rate of 15 percent. What is the cost of internal common equity for Pathos?

8-10A. (*Cost of Equity*) The common stock for the Bestsold Corporation sells for $58. If a new issue is sold, the flotation cost is estimated to be 8 percent. The company pays 50 percent of its earnings in dividends, and a $4 dividend was recently paid. Earnings per share five years ago were $5. Earnings are expected to continue to grow at the same annual rate in the future as during the past five years. The firm's marginal tax rate is 34 percent. Calculate the cost of (a) internal common and (b) external common.

8–11A. (*Cost of Debt*) Sincere Stationery Corporation needs to raise $500,000 to improve its manufacturing plant. It has decided to issue a $1,000 par value bond with a 14 percent annual coupon rate and a 10-year maturity. If the investors require a 9 percent rate of return

  a. Compute the market value of the bonds.
  b. What will the net price be if flotation costs are 10.5 percent of the market price?
  c. How many bonds will the firm have to issue to receive the needed funds?
  d. What is the firm's after-tax cost of debt if its average tax rate is 25 percent and its marginal tax rate is 34 percent?

8–12A. (*Cost of Debt*)

  a. Rework problem 8–11A assuming a 10 percent coupon rate. What effect does changing the coupon rate have on the firm's after-tax cost of capital?
  b. Why is there a change?

8–13A. (*Weighted Cost of Capital*) The capital structure for the Carion Corporation is provided below. The company plans to maintain its debt structure in the future. If the firm has a 5.5 percent cost of debt, a 13.5 percent cost of preferred stock, and an 18 percent cost of common stock, what is the firm's weighted cost of capital?

Capital Structure ($000)	
Bonds	$1083
Preferred stock	268
Common stock	3681
	$5032

8–14A. (*Level of Financing*) Using the same capital structure mix as problem 8–13A, what would the total investment amount be if the firm used the following?

  a. $200,000 of debt
  b. $40,000 of preferred stock
  c. $100,000 of retained earnings
  d. $100,000 of retained earnings plus $50,000 of new common stock

8–15A. (*Weighted Cost of Capital*) The capital structure for Nealon, Inc., is provided below. Flotation costs would be (a) 15 percent of market value for a new bond issue, (b) $1.21 per share for common stock, and (c) $2.01 per share for preferred stock. The dividends for common stock were $2.50 last year and are projected to have an annual growth rate of 6 percent. The firm is in a 34 percent tax bracket. What is the weighted cost of capital if the firm finances in the proportions shown below? Market prices are $1,035 for bonds, $19 for preferred stock, and $35 for common stock. There will be $500,000 of internal common available.

Nealon, Inc., Balance Sheet

Type of Financing	Percentage of Future Financing
Bonds (8%, $1000 par, 16-year maturity)	38%
Preferred stock (5000 shares outstanding, $50 par, $1.50 dividend)	15
Common stock	47
Total	100%

8–16A. (*Weighted Cost of Capital*) The Bach's Candy Corporation has determined the company's marginal costs of capital for debt, preferred stock, and common equity as follows:

Source	Amount of Capital	Cost
Debt	$0–$175,000	4.8%
	$175,001–$300,000	5.5
	over $300,000	6.0
Preferred stock	$0–$50,000	10.0
	$50,001–$75,000	12.0
	over $75,000	13.0
Common stock	$0–$400,000[a]	15.0
	$400,001–$750,000	18.0
	over $750,000	22.0

[a]$400,000 is available from internally generated common equity.

The firm maintains a capital mix of 45 percent debt, 5 percent preferred stock, and 50 percent common stock. Construct Bach's weighted marginal cost of capital curve.

8–17A. (*Marginal Cost of Capital*) Mary Basett, Inc., a national advertising firm, is analyzing the following investment opportunities.

Investment	Investment Cost	Internal Rate of Return
A	$ 50,000	14.5%
B	200,000	17.9
C	325,000	15.6
D	125,000	12.4
E	400,000	10.9
F	75,000	13.8

The information needed to calculate the firm's weighted marginal cost of capital curve is presented below. Construct Basett's weighted marginal cost of capital curve and decide which investments should be accepted.

Source	Percentage	Amount of Capital	After-Tax Cost
Debt	40%	$0–$300,000	4.5%
		over $300,000	6.0
Preferred stock	8	$0–$ 50,000	9.5
		$50,001–$100,000	10.5
		over $100,000	11.0
Common stock	52	$0–$520,000	16.0
		over $520,000	18.0

8–18A. (*Weighted Cost of Capital*) Blacktop Chemical Co. is considering five investments. The cost of each is shown below. Retained earnings of $650,000 will be available for investment purposes, and management can issue the following securities:

1. **Bonds.** $270,000 can be issued at an after-flotation, before-tax cost of 8.5 percent. Above $270,000 the cost will be 9.75 percent.
2. **Preferred stock.** The stock can be issued at the prevailing market price. Issuance will cost $1.55 per share up to an issue size of $90,000; thereafter costs will be $2.80 per share.
3. **Common stock.** The stock will be issued at the market price. For an issue of $250,000, flotation costs will be $1 per share. For any additional common, the flotation costs should then be $1.75 per share.

The tax rate for the firm is 34 percent. Common dividends last year were $1.80 and are expected to grow at an annual rate of 9 percent. Market prices are $975 for bonds, $39 for preferred stock, and $23 for common stock. Determine which projects should be accepted, based upon a comparison of the IRR of the investments and the weighted marginal cost of capital. The firm's capital structure is shown below, and the same mix is to be used for future investments.

Investment	Cost	IRR
A	$ 200,000	16%
B	650,000	12
C	115,000	9
D	875,000	10
E	180,000	15
Total	$2,020,000	

Capital Structure	Amount of Capital	Percentages of Financing
Bonds (9%, $1000 par, 18-year maturity)	$3,000,000	43%
Preferred stock (10%, $45 par, 30,000 shares outstanding)	1,350,000	20
Common stock	2,600,000	37
Total	$6,950,000	100%

8–19A. (*Weighted Cost of Capital*) Heard Ski, Inc., is a regional manufacturer of ski equipment. The firm's target financing mix appears as follows:

	Percentage
Debt	30%
Preferred stock	10
Common stock	60
Total	100%

The corporation's management is currently involved in evaluating the capital budget. Six investments are under consideration. The costs and the expected internal rates of return for these projects are given as follows:

Investment	Cost	Internal Rate of Return
A	$175,000	16%
B	100,000	14
C	125,000	12
D	200,000	10
E	250,000	9
F	150,000	8

As the accept-reject criterion, Paul Heard, president of the firm, has compiled the necessary data for computing the firm's weighted marginal cost of capital. The cost information indicates the following:

1. Debt can be raised at the following before-tax costs:

Amount	Cost
$0–150,000	8.0%
$150,001–$225,000	9.0
over $225,000	10.5

2. Preferred stock can be issued paying an annual dividend of $8.50. The par value of the stock is $100. Also, the market price of the stock is $100. If new stock were issued, the company would receive a net price of $80 on the first $75,000. Thereafter, the net amount received would be reduced to $75.

3. Common equity is provided first by internally generated funds. Profits for the year that should be available for reinvestment purposes are projected at $150,000. Additional common stock can be issued at the current $72 market price less 15 percent in flotation costs. However, if more than $225,000 in new common stock is required, a 20 percent flotation cost is expected. The dividend per share was $2.75 last year, and the long-term growth rate for dividends is 9 percent.

a. Given that the firm's marginal tax rate is 34 percent, compute the company's weighted marginal cost of capital at a financing level up to $1 million.

b. Construct a graph that presents the firm's weighted marginal cost of capital relative to the amount of financing.

c. What is the appropriate size of the capital budget, and which projects should be accepted?

8–20A. (*Individual Project—Required Return*) The Welton Corporation is examining two capital investments. Management wants to analyze the riskiness of the projects in terms of their effect on the riskiness of an investor's diversified portfolio. The beta for project A is 1.05 and .80 for B. The expected return for a diversified portfolio is 16 percent. The risk-free rate is 7 percent. Project A is expected to return 15.7 percent; project B, 17.5 percent. Which investment(s) should the company accept?

8–21A. (*Individual Project—Required Return*) Hastings, Inc., is analyzing several investments. The expected returns and betas of each project are given below. The firm's cost of capital is 16.5 percent. The current rate on long-term U.S. government securities is 8.5 percent. The expected return for a well-diversified portfolio is 15 percent. Which investments should the firm accept?

Project	Investment's Expected Return	Beta
A	18.0%	1.2
B	13.8	0.9
C	15.3	1.0
D	11.4	0.7

STUDY PROBLEMS (SET B)

8–1B. (*Individual or Component Costs of Capital*) Compute the cost for the following sources of financing:
   a. A bond that has a $1,000 par value (face value) and a contract or coupon interest rate of 12 percent. A new issue would have a flotation cost of 6 percent of the $1,125 market value. The bonds mature in 10 years. The firm's average tax rate is 30 percent and its marginal tax rate is 34 percent.
   b. A new common stock issue that paid a $1.75 dividend last year. The par value of the stock is $15, and earnings per share have grown at a rate of 8 percent per year. This growth rate is expected to continue into the foreseeable future. The company maintains a constant dividend/earnings ratio of 30 percent. The price of this stock is now $28, but 5 percent flotation costs are anticipated.
   c. Internal common equity where the current market price of the common stock is $43.50. The expected dividend this coming year should be $3.25, increasing thereafter at a 7 percent annual growth rate. The corporation's tax rate is 34 percent.
   d. A preferred stock paying a 10 percent dividend on a $125 par value. If a new issue is offered, flotation costs will be 12 percent of the current price of $150.
   e. A bond selling to yield 13 percent after flotation costs, but prior to adjusting for the marginal corporate tax rate of 34 percent. In other words, 13 percent is the rate that equates the net proceeds from the bond with the present value of the future cash flows (principal and interest).

8–2B. (*Level of Financing*) The Dave Collier Company has the following capital structure mix:

Debt	$600,000
Preferred stock	200,000
Common stock	400,000

Using the same capital structure mix, compute the total investment amount if the company uses
   a. $500,000 of debt.
   b. $50,000 of preferred stock.
   c. $275,000 of retained earnings only, or
   d. $125,000 of retained earnings plus $600,000 of new common stock

8–3B. (*Individual or Component Costs of Capital*) Compute the cost for the following sources of financing:
   a. A bond selling to yield 9 percent after flotation cost, but prior to adjusting for the marginal corporate tax rate of 34 percent. In other words, 9 percent is the rate that equates the net proceeds from the bond with the present value of the future cash flows (principal and interest).
   b. A new common stock issue that paid a $1.25 dividend last year. The par value of the stock is $2, and the earnings per share have grown at a rate of 6 percent per year. This growth rate is expected to continue into the foreseeable future. The company maintains a constant dividend/earnings ratio of 40 percent. The price of this stock is now $30, but 9 percent flotation costs are anticipated.
   c. A bond that has a $1,000 par value (face value) and a contract or coupon interest rate of 13 percent. A new issue would net the company 90 percent of the $1,125 market value. The bonds mature in 20 years, and the firm's average tax rate is 30 percent and its marginal tax rate is 34 percent.
   d. A preferred stock paying a 7 percent dividend on a $125 par value. If a new issue is offered, the company can expect to net $90 per share.
   e. Internal common equity where the current market price of the common stock

is $38. The expected dividend this forthcoming year should be $4, increasing thereafter at a 5 percent annual growth rate. The corporation's tax rate is 34 percent.

8–4B. (*Cost of Equity*) Falon Corporation is issuing new common stock at a market price of $28. Dividends last year were $1.30 and are expected to grow at an annual rate of 7 percent forever. Flotation costs will be 6 percent of market price. What is Falon's cost of equity?

8–5B. (*Cost of Debt*) Temple is issuing a $1,000 par value bond that pays 8 percent annual interest and matures in 15 years. Investors are willing to pay $950 for the bond. Flotation costs will be 11 percent of market value. The company is in a 19 percent tax bracket. What will be the firm's after-tax cost of debt on the bond?

8–6B. (*Cost of Preferred Stock*) The preferred stock of Gator Industries sells for $35 and pays $2.75 in dividends. The net price of the security after issuance costs is $32.50. What is the cost of capital for the preferred stock?

8–7B. (*Cost of Debt*) The Walgren Corporation is contemplating a new investment to be financed 33 percent from debt. The firm could sell new $1,000 par value bonds at a net price of $950. The coupon interest rate is 13 percent, and the bonds would mature in 15 years. If the company is in a 34 percent tax bracket, what is the after-tax cost of capital to Walgren for bonds?

8–8B. (*Cost of Preferred Stock*) Your firm is planning to issue preferred stock. The stock sells for $120; however, if new stock is issued, the company would receive only $97. The par value of the stock is $100 and the dividend rate is 13 percent. What is the cost of capital for the stock to your firm?

8–9B. (*Cost of Internal Equity*) The common stock for Oxford, Inc., is currently selling for $22.50. Dividends paid last year were $.80. Flotation costs on issuing stock will be 10 percent of market price. The dividends and earnings per share are projected to have an annual growth rate of 16 percent. What is the cost of internal common equity for Oxford?

8–10B. (*Cost of Equity*) The common stock for the Hetterbrand Corporation sells for $60. If a new issue is sold, the flotation cost is estimated to be 9 percent. The company pays 50 percent of its earnings in dividends, and a $4.50 dividend was recently paid. Earnings per share five years ago were $5. Earnings are expected to continue to grow at the same annual rate in the future as during the past five years. The firm's marginal tax rate is 35 percent. Calculate the cost of (a) internal common and (b) external common.

8–11B. (*Cost of Debt*) Gillian Stationery Corporation needs to raise $600,000 to improve its manufacturing plant. It has decided to issue a $1,000 par value bond with a 15 percent annual coupon rate and a 10-year maturity. If the investors require a 10 percent rate of return
a. Compute the market value of the bonds.
b. What will the net price be if flotation costs are 11.5 percent of the market price?
c. How many bonds will the firm have to issue to receive the needed funds?
d. What is the firm's after-tax cost of debt if its average tax rate is 25 percent and its marginal tax rate is 34 percent?

8–12B. (*Cost of Debt*)
a. Rework problem 8–11B assuming a 10 percent coupon rate. What effect does changing the coupon rate have on the firm's after-tax cost of capital?
b. Why is there a change?

8–13B. (*Weighted Cost of Capital*) The capital structure for the Bias Corporation is provided below. The company plans to maintain its debt structure in the future. If the firm has a 6 percent cost of debt, a 13.5 percent cost of preferred stock, and a 19 percent cost of common stock, what is the firm's weighted cost of capital?

Capital Structure ($000)	
Bonds	$1100
Preferred stock	250
Common stock	3700
	$5050

8–14B. (*Level of Financing*) Using the same capital structure mix as problem 8–13B, what would the total investment amount be if the firm used the following?
a. $150,000 of debt
b. $60,000 of preferred stock

c. $120,000 of retained earnings

d. $120,000 of retained earnings plus $60,000 of new common stock

8–15B. (*Weighted Cost of Capital*) R. Stewart, Inc.'s capital structure is provided below. Flotation costs would be (a) 13 percent of market value for a new bond issue, (b) $1.25 per share for common stock, and (c) $2.50 per share for preferred stock. The dividends for common stock were $3.25 last year and are projected to have an annual growth rate of 6 percent. The firm is in a 34 percent tax bracket. What is the weighted cost of capital if the firm finances in the proportions shown below? Market prices are $1,040 for bonds, $18 for preferred stock, and $30 for common stock. There will be $250,000 of internal common.

R. Stewart, Inc., Balance Sheet

Type of Financing	Percentage of Future Financing
Bonds (8%, $1000 par, 16-year maturity)	38%
Preferred stock (5000 shares outstanding, $50 par, $1.50 dividend)	15
Common stock	47
Total	100%

8–16B. (*Weighted Cost of Capital*) The Hun Sen Corporation has determined the company's marginal costs of capital for debt, preferred stock, and common equity as follows:

Source	Amount of Capital	Cost
Debt	$0–$200,000	6.0%
	$200,001–$350,000	7.5
	over $350,000	9.0
Preferred stock	$0–$70,000	11.0
	$70,001–$100,000	13.0
	over $100,000	14.0
Common stock	$0–$500,000[a]	16.0
	$500,001–$750,000	20.0
	over $750,000	22.0

[a]$500,000 is available from internally generated common equity.

The firm maintains a capital mix of 50 percent debt, 10 percent preferred stock, and 40 percent common stock. Construct Hun Sen's weighted marginal cost of capital curve.

8–17B. (*Marginal Cost of Capital*) Itoh, Inc., a national advertising firm, is analyzing the following investment opportunities:

Investment	Investment Cost	Internal Rate of Return
A	$ 100,000	17.0%
B	150,000	16.0
C	325,000	15.0
D	175,000	19.0
E	425,000	14.0
F	100,000	12.0

The information needed to calculate the firm's weighted marginal cost of capital curve is presented below. Construct Itoh's weighted marginal cost of capital curve and decide which investments should be accepted.

Source	Percentage	Amount of Capital	After-Tax Cost
Debt	45%	$0–$300,000	7.0%
		over $300,000	8.0
Preferred stock	10	$0–$ 50,000	10.0
		$50,001–$100,000	11.0
		over $100,000	13.0
Common stock	45	$0–$520,000	18.0
		over $520,000	20.0

8–18B. (*Weighted Cost of Capital*) Hannitin Co. is considering five investments. The cost of each is shown below. Retained earnings of $850,000 will be available for investment purposes, and management can issue the following securities:

1. **Bonds.** $350,000 can be issued at an after-flotation, before-tax cost of 9 percent. Above $350,000 the cost will be 10.75 percent.
2. **Preferred stock.** The stock can be issued at the prevailing market price. Issuance will cost $1.75 per share up to an issue size of $100,000; thereafter costs will be $2.40 per share.
3. **Common stock.** The stock will be issued at the market price. For an issue of $300,000, flotation costs will be $2 per share. For any additional common, the flotation costs should then be $2.75 per share.

The tax rate for the firm is 40 percent. Common dividends last year were $2.50 and are expected to grow at an annual rate of 10 percent. Market prices are $975 for bonds, $49 for preferred stock, and $43 for common stock. Determine which projects should be accepted, based upon a comparison of the IRR of the investments and the weighted marginal cost of capital. The firm's capital structure is shown below, and the same mix is to be used for future investments.

Investment	Cost	IRR
A	$ 250,000	21%
B	700,000	17
C	100,000	12
D	500,000	13
E	250,000	17
Total	1,800,000	

Capital Structure	Amount of Capital	Percentages of Financing
Bonds (9%, $1000 par, 18-year maturity)	$2,800,000	35%
Preferred stock (10%, $45 par, 30,000 shares outstanding)	1,200,000	15
Common stock	4,000,000	50
Total	$8,000,000	100%

8–19B. (*Weighted Cost of Capital*) Dalton Ski, Inc., is a regional manufacturer of ski equipment. The firm's target financing mix appears as follows:

	Percentage
Debt	30%
Preferred stock	10
Common stock	60
Total	100%

The corporation's management is currently involved in evaluating the capital budget. Six investments are under consideration. The costs and the expected internal rates of return for these projects are given as follows:

Investment	Cost	Internal Rate of Return
A	$175,000	19%
B	100,000	16
C	125,000	15
D	200,000	13
E	250,000	12
F	150,000	10

As the accept-reject criterion, Carter Dalton, president of the firm, has compiled the necessary data for computing the firm's weighted marginal cost of capital. The cost information indicates the following:

1. Debt can be raised at the following before-tax costs:

Amount	Cost
$0–$200,000	9%
$200,001–$300,000	10
over $300,000	11

2. Preferred stock can be issued paying an annual dividend of $10. The par value of the stock is $100. Also, the market price of the stock is $100. If new stock were issued, the company would receive a net price of $90 on the first $100,000. Thereafter, the net amount received would be reduced to $85.

3. Common equity is provided first by internally generated funds. Profits for the year that should be available for reinvestment purposes are projected at $200,000. Additional common stock can be issued at the current $80 market price less 15 percent in flotation costs. However, if more than $250,000 in new common stock is required, a 20 percent flotation cost is expected. The dividend per share was $4 last year, and the long-term growth rate for dividends is 12 percent.

   a. Given that the firm's marginal tax rate is 40 percent, compute the company's weighted marginal cost of capital at a financing level up to $1 million.

   b. Construct a graph that presents the firm's weighted marginal cost of capital relative to the amount of financing.

   c. What is the appropriate size of the capital budget, and which projects should be accepted?

8–20B. (*Individual Project—Required Return*) Dellington, Inc., is examining two capital investments. Management wants to analyze the riskiness of the projects in terms of their effect on the riskiness of an investor's diversified portfolio. The beta for project A is 1.10 and 1.25 for B. The expected return for a diversified portfolio is 13 percent. The risk-free rate is 7 percent. Project A is expected to return 16.8 percent; project B, 20.5 percent. Which investment(s) should the company accept?

8–21B. (*Individual Project—Required Return*) Badger, Inc., is analyzing several investments. The expected returns and beta of each project are given below. The firm's cost of capital is 16.5 percent. The current rate on long-term U.S. government securities is 8.5 percent. The expected return for a well-diversified portfolio is 16 percent. Which investments should the firm accept?

Project	Investment's Expected Return	Beta
A	20.0%	1.25
B	16.2	1.10
C	15.0	0.90
D	11.2	0.75

Suggested Application for *DISCLOSURE*®

Using *Disclosure*, obtain the following information about AT&T:

1. Latest closing stock price
2. The expected growth rate in earnings per share over the next five years (Zack's earnings estimates).
3. The indicated annual dividend
4. The dividend payout ratio (dividend/earnings)

Assume that (a) the par value of the stock is $15, (b) earnings per share growth rate will continue indefinitely, (c) the company maintains a constant dividend/earnings ratio, and (d) 5 percent flotation costs are anticipated for any new stock issue.

a. Estimate the cost of equity of internally generated common.

b. Estimate the cost of equity for newly issued shares.

The following notations are used in this group of problems:

k_d = the before-tax cost of debt

K_d = the after-tax cost of debt

K_p = the after-tax cost of preferred stock

K_c = the after-tax cost of internal common stock

K_{nc} = the after-tax cost of new common stock

T = the marginal tax rate

D_t = the dollar dividend per share, where D_0 is the most recently paid dividend and D_1 is the forthcoming dividend

P_0 = the value (present value) of a security

NP_0 = the value of a security less any flotation costs incurred in issuing the security

SS–1. a.

$$\$921.50 = \sum_{t=1}^{10} \frac{\$100}{(1 + k_d)^t} + \frac{\$1000}{(1 + k_d)^{10}}$$

Rate	Value
11%	$940.90
k_d%	$921.50
12%	$887.00

$\}$ $19.40

$\}$ $53.90

$$k_d = 0.11 + \left(\frac{\$19.40}{\$53.90}\right) 0.01 = 11.36\%$$

$$K_d = 11.36\% (1 - 0.34) = 7.50\%$$

b.

$$K_p = \frac{D}{NP_0}$$

$$K_p = \frac{\$8}{\$100 - \$9} = 8.79\%$$

c.

$$K_c = \frac{D_1}{P_0} + g$$

$$K_c = \frac{\$9.80}{\$75} + 0\% = 13.07\%$$

d.

$$K_{nc} = \frac{D_1}{NP_0} + g$$

$$K_{nc} = \frac{\$2.80(1 + 0.08)}{\$53 - \$6} + 0.08 = 14.43\%$$

SS–2.

$$\text{dollar breaks} = \frac{\text{amount of financing at a given cost}}{\text{percentage of funds provided by the specific source}}$$

a. $\dfrac{\$100,000}{0.30} = \$333,333.33$

b. $\dfrac{\$150,000}{0.30} = \$500,000$

c. $\dfrac{\$40,000}{0.15} = \$266,666.67$

d. $\dfrac{\$90,000}{0.15} = \$600,000$

e. $\dfrac{\$200,000}{0.55} = \$363,636.36$

f. $\dfrac{\$500,000}{0.55} = \$909,090.91$

SS–3. a. Increases (breaks) in the weighted marginal cost of capital curve will occur as follows:

Increase from the cost of debt:

$$\frac{\$120,000}{.40} = \$300,000$$

Increase from the cost of common:

$$\frac{\$180,000}{.60} = \$300,000$$

Weighted cost of capital (K_0) for

	$0–$300,000 Total Financing				Over $300,000 Total Financing		
	Weights	Costs	Weighted costs		Weights	Costs	Weighted costs
Debt	40%	7%	2.80%	Debt	40%	11%	4.4%
Common stock	60	19	11.40	Common stock	60	22	13.2
			$K_0 = \underline{\underline{14.20\%}}$				$K_0 = \underline{\underline{17.6\%}}$

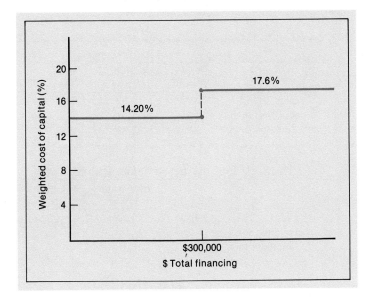

b. Only project A should be accepted.

SS–4. (1) Compute weights

	Capital Structure	Capital Mix (Weights)
Debt	$2,000,000	40%
Preferred stock	500,000	10
Common stock	2,500,000	50
	$5,000,000	100%

(2) Compute individual costs

Debt

$0–$120,000: 12% (1 − .34) = 7.92%
over $120,000: 15% (1 − .34) = 9.90%

Preferred Stock

$0–$50,000: $\dfrac{\$14}{\$95(1-.08)} = \dfrac{\$14}{\$87.40} = 16.02\%$

over $50,000: $\dfrac{\$14}{\$95(1-.11)} = \dfrac{\$14}{\$84.55} = 16.56\%$

Common Stock

$0–$150,000: $\left(\dfrac{\$2.50}{\$30}\right) + .09 = .1733 = 17.33\%$

over $150,000: $\left(\dfrac{\$2.50}{\$27}\right) + .09 = .1826 = 18.26\%$

(3) Calculate increases (breaks) in the weighted marginal cost of capital curve caused by increases in the cost of

Debt	Preferred Stock	Common Stock
$\dfrac{\$120,000}{.40} = \$300,000$	$\dfrac{\$50,000}{.10} = \$500,000$	$\dfrac{\$150,000}{.50} = \$300,000$

(4) Construct the weighted cost of capital curve

$0–$300,000 Total Financing

	Weights	Individual costs	Weighted costs
Debt	40%	7.92%	3.17
Preferred stock	10	16.02	1.60
Common stock	50	17.33	8.67
		$K_0 =$	13.44%

At Least $300,001 but Not More Than $500,000

	Weights	Individual costs	Weighted costs
Debt	40%	9.90%	3.96%
Preferred stock	10	16.02	1.60
Common stock	50	18.26	9.13
		$K_0 =$	14.69%

Over $500,000

	Weights	Individual costs	Weighted costs
Debt	40%	9.90%	3.96%
Preferred stock	10	16.56	1.66
Common stock	50	18.26	9.13
		$K_0 =$	14.75%

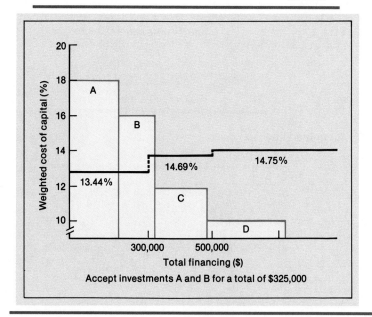

Accept investments A and B for a total of $325,000

SS–5.

Project	Required Rate of Return	Expected Return	Decision
A $0.08 + (0.15 - 0.08)(1.10) =$	15.7%	18.8%	Accept
B $0.08 + (0.15 - 0.08)(.90) =$	14.3	13.5	Reject
C $0.08 + (0.15 - 0.08)(.80) =$	13.6	15.0	Accept

VIDEO CASE 2

Investing in Employee Productivity: An Application of Capital Budgeting

from ABC News, *Business World*, October 14, 1990

In the introduction to this video case we asked a list of pertinent questions. See Video Case 2 Introduction on page 99.

If the programs Fel-Pro implemented increase employee satisfaction, the firm could benefit in many ways. Lower employee turnover, lower absenteeism, and fewer job-related accidents and illnesses (which translate into lower health insurance claims) all reduce costs and thereby increase profits. If the firm ever comes on hard times, the loyalty built by these programs might allow the firm to ask for help from its employees in the form of lower raises, unpaid leaves, and so on.

Program costs are fairly easy to estimate. One problem with cost estimation in programs with volunteer participation is uncertainty about the number of employees who will participate. Once the program is opened to all employees, the firm must either be prepared to make sufficient opportunities available for all interested employees or explain how the resources will be rationed.

Arriving at quantitative estimates for the programs' benefits can be very difficult. One approach would be to estimate how much absenteeism and employee turnover costs the firm, then estimate how absenteeism and turnover are affected by the programs. The value of loyalty and commitment are much more difficult to measure.

In theory NPV analysis could be used to evaluate investments such as this, but the inability to quantify all future benefits makes applying NPV nearly impossible. Because the benefits are more difficult to value than the costs, strict application of NPV analysis may produce results that are biased against acceptance.

Managers' primary commitment is to shareholders. If there are no benefits from implementing the employee incentive programs, they should not be implemented. Implementing costly programs that produce no benefits will eventually harm more groups than shareholders alone. If the firm becomes less competive because of these extra costs, then employees may lose their jobs, and communities may lose factories. Although the objective of maximization of shareholder wealth appears, at first glance, to ignore the many other constituencies associated with a firm—employees, suppliers, customers, and the community—it is the only objective that assures the firm's long-term viability, and thereby the firm's continued support of its various constituents.

Discussion questions

1. Like employee morale, the benefits of adding personal computers to the workplace are difficult to estimate. What are some of the benefits from providing computers to employees and how might those benefits be estimated?

2. One form of employee benefit is training. However, as employees improve their skills or learn new skills, they become more attractive to competitors and may be hired away. Firms that provide training but experience high turnover bear costs but receive no benefits. How would you address this potential problem? Examples to consider are the extensive training programs offered by many banks. After 10 to 16 months of training, during which the employees-in-training have not been particularly productive for the bank, they are attractive to other banks or many corporations.

Suggested readings

FISHER, ANNE. "The Morale Crisis," *Fortune*, November 18, 1991.
KIRKPATRICK, DAVID. "Here Comes the Payoff from PCs," *Fortune*, November 18, 1991.

PART 3

FINANCIAL STRUCTURE AND DIVIDEND POLICY

In Part 2 we examined how corporate managers go about identifying profitable investment opportunities using NPV analysis. Besides investing in productive assets, financial managers face two purely financial decisions that may affect the well-being of shareholders: choosing the optimal mix of debt and equity, or the *capital structure decision,* and deciding how much cash to distribute to shareholders, or the *dividend policy decision.*

During the 1980s firms drastically changed how they financed their assets. Corporate managers increasingly relied on debt financing, or *financial leverage.* Did this change benefit the shareholders these managers serve? Or did it jeopardize the financial security of the shareholders and other stakeholders of the firm? In Chapters 9 and 10 we examine more carefully how debt financing affects firm value and thereby the wealth of shareholders. These chapters also set the stage for our discussion later in the text of the wild world of corporate finance in the 1980s with its hostile takeovers, management buyouts, leveraged buyouts, junk bonds, and bankruptcies.

Some of the questions we will address, but not resolve entirely, regard the advantages and risks inherent in debt financing. For example: • How does debt increase or decrease firm cash flows? • How much debt can a firm safely support, and what characteristics determine this level? • Is it costly for a firm to have too much or too little debt? • Do managerial incentives change as debt levels increase?

A less dramatic but equally puzzling problem for the financial manager is how dividends affect share price (Chapter 11). Because we have already defined share value as the present value of the firm's future dividends, how can this be puzzling? Also, most successful firms pay dividends, which seems like strong evidence of their value. Nonetheless, there are questions to ask about how shareholders perceive dividend payments, what type of firms should refrain from paying dividends, and how firms actually pay dividends. We are also interested in comparing the payment of cash dividends to stock splits and other methods of distributing cash to shareholders.

INTRODUCTION

VIDEO CASE 3

RJR Nabisco Bondholder Lawsuits: A Leverage Related Agency Problem

from ABC News, *Business World*, November 20, 1988

Chapters 9 and 10 of the text introduce the concept of financial leverage, describe the costs and benefits associated with debt financing, and discuss how firms might choose an *optimal* mix of debt and equity. Financial leverage, or using "other people's money," generates both costs and benefits for shareholders. The advantages of debt financing include the tax deductibility of interest payments and some potentially valuable changes in managerial behavior. The disadvantages of debt are the increased probability of financial distress or bankruptcy, and the costs of covenants demanded by bondholders before they will lend the firm funds. The *optimal* capital structure uses debt until the advantages of leverage are just offset by the disadvantages. Figure 10–7 of the text diagrams this tradeoff between the costs and benefits of leverage. As you can see from Figure 10–7, as debt is increased beyond the optimum mix the value of the firm falls. The accompanying video case provides a real-world example of some of the factors involved in leverage increases.

The video case describes how the announcement of the RJR management buyout proposal has sparked the wrath of several investors who own RJR Nabisco bonds. These bondholders suddenly own bonds worth 20 percent less than they were yesterday. For some bondholders that amounts to a lot of money. For example, Metropolitan Life Insurance suffered a $40 million loss on the value of their investment in RJR bonds.

For the management buyout to proceed, RJR will have to borrow an enormous amount of money—possibly $12 to $16 *billion*. The borrowed funds will be used to repurchase all the firm's outstanding stock and *take the firm private* (see Chapter 23 for more on leveraged buyouts). By adding this new debt to the existing bonds, such as those owned by MetLife and other insurance companies, the risk of the existing bonds increases dramatically. As you know from earlier chapters, as risk increases security prices fall. Bondholders have a contractual agreement to accept a fixed-interest payment or coupon rate. This coupon rate was determined when there was no suspicion that a leveraged buyout might occur. Risk has increased with the proposed buyout, but bondholders are stuck with the agreed-on coupon rate—a coupon rate that no longer reflects the risk of the firm.

- If the total market value of the firm (the sum of the market value of the firm's debt and equity) falls, can the transaction be good for shareholders?
- Why do bondholders appear to be forgotten in management buyouts or LBO transactions?
- What can bondholders do to protect themselves from being damaged in situations such as this?

Consider these questions as you read Chapters 9 and 10. We will continue our discussion of this video case at the end of the section.

CHAPTER 9

Analysis and Impact of Leverage

Business and Financial Risk • Breakeven Analysis • Operating Leverage • Financial Leverage • Combination of Operating and Financial Leverage

Our work in Chapters 4, 5, and 8 allowed us to develop an understanding of how financial assets are valued in the marketplace. Drawing on the tenets of valuation theory, we presented various approaches to measuring the cost of funds to the business organization. This chapter presents concepts that relate to the valuation process and the cost of capital; it also discusses the crucial problem of planning the firm's financing mix.

The cost of capital provides a direct link between the formulation of the firm's asset structure and its financial structure. This is illustrated in Figure 9–1. Recall that the cost of capital is a basic input to the time-adjusted capital-budgeting models. It therefore affects the capital budgeting, or asset selection, process. The cost of capital is affected, in turn, by the composition of the right-hand side of the firm's balance sheet—that is, its financial structure.

This chapter examines tools that can be useful aids to the financial manager in determining the firm's proper financial structure. First, we review the technique of breakeven analysis. This provides the foundation for the relationships to be highlighted in the remainder of the chapter. We then examine the concept of operating leverage, some consequences of the firm's use of financial leverage, and the impact on the firm's earnings stream when operating and financial leverage are combined in various patterns. Our immediate tasks are to distinguish two types of risk that confront the firm and to clarify some key terminology that will be used throughout this and the subsequent chapter.

Perspective in Finance

In this chapter we become more precise in assessing the causes of variability in the firm's expected revenue streams. It is useful to think of business risk as induced by the firm's investment decisions. That is, the composition of the firm's assets determines its exposure to business risk. In this way, business risk is a direct function of what appears on the left-hand side of the company's balance sheet. Financial risk is properly attributed to the manner in which the firm's

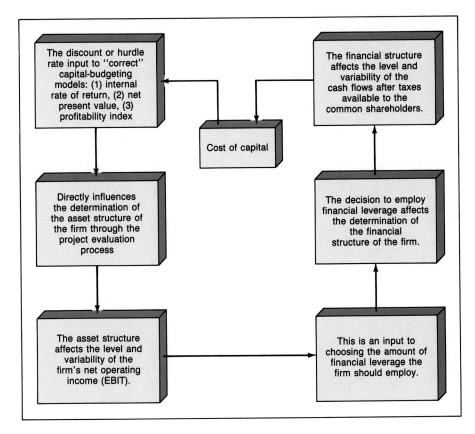

FIGURE 9-1.
Cost of Capital as a Link between Firm's Asset Structure and Financial Structure

managers have decided to arrange the right-hand side of the company's balance sheet. The choice to use more financial leverage means that the firm will experience greater exposure to financial risk. The tools developed here will help you quantify the firm's business and financial risk. A solid understanding of these tools will make you a better financial manager.

Business and Financial Risk

In studying capital-budgeting techniques we referred to **risk** as the likely variability associated with expected revenue or income streams. As our attention is now focused on the firm's financing decision rather than its investment decision, it is useful to separate the income stream variations attributable to (1) the company's exposure to business risk and (2) its decision to incur financial risk.

Business risk refers to the relative dispersion (variability) in the firm's expected earnings before interest and taxes (EBIT).[1] Figure 9-2 shows a subjectively estimated probability distribution of next year's EBIT for the Pierce Grain Company and the same type of projection for Pierce's larger competitor, the Blackburn Seed Company. The expected value of EBIT for Pierce is $100,000, with an associated standard deviation of $20,000. If next year's EBIT for Pierce fell one standard deviation short of the expected $100,000, the actual EBIT would equal $80,000. Blackburn's expected EBIT is $200,000, and the size of the associated standard deviation is $20,000. The standard deviation for the expected level of EBIT is the same for both firms. We would say that Pierce's

---

[1] If what the accountants call "other income" and "other expenses" are equal to zero, then EBIT is equal to net operating income. These terms will be used interchangeably.

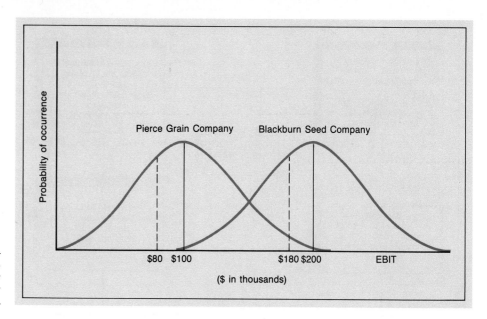

FIGURE 9–2.
Subjective Probability
Distribution of Next Year's EBIT

degree of business risk exceeds Blackburn's because of its larger coefficient of variation of expected EBIT, as follows:

$$\text{Pierce's coefficient of}\atop\text{variation of expected EBIT} = \frac{\$20,000}{\$100,000} = .20$$

$$\text{Blackburn's coefficient of}\atop\text{variation of expected EBIT} = \frac{\$20,000}{\$200,000} = .10$$

The relative dispersion in the firm's EBIT stream, measured here by its expected coefficient of variation, is the *residual* effect of several causal influences. Dispersion in operating income does not *cause* business risk; rather, this dispersion, which we call business risk, is the *result* of several influences. Some of these are listed in Table 9–1, along with an example of each particular attribute. Notice that the company's cost structure, product demand characteristics, and intraindustry competitive position all affect its business risk exposure. Such business risk is a direct result of the firm's investment decision. It is the firm's asset structure, after all, that gives rise to both the level and variability of its operating profits.

TABLE 9–1.
Concept of Business Risk

Business Risk Attribute	Example[a]
1. Sensitivity of the firm's product demand to general economic conditions	If GNP declines, does the firm's sales level decline by a greater percentage?
2. Degree of competition	Is the firm's market share small in comparison with other firms that produce and distribute the same product(s)?
3. Product diversification	Is a large proportion of the firm's sales revenue derived from a single major product or product line?
4. Operating leverage	Does the firm utilize a high level of operating leverage resulting in a high level of fixed costs?
5. Growth prospects	Are the firm's product markets expanding and (or) changing, making income estimates and prospects highly volatile?
6. Size	Does the firm suffer a competitive disadvantage due to lack of size in assets, sales, or profits that translates into (among other things) difficulty in tapping the capital market for funds?

[a]Affirmative responses indicate greater business risk exposure.

Financial risk, conversely, is a direct result of the firm's financing decision. In the context of selecting a proper financing mix, this risk applies to (1) the additional variability in earnings available to the firm's common shareholders and (2) the additional chance of insolvency borne by the common shareholder caused by the use of financial leverage.[2] **Financial leverage** means financing a portion of the firm's assets with securities bearing a fixed (limited) rate of return in hopes of increasing the ultimate return to the common stockholders. The decision to use debt or preferred stock in the financial structure of the corporation means that those who own the common shares of the firm are exposed to financial risk. Any given level of variability in EBIT will be *magnified* by the firm's use of financial leverage, and such additional variability will be embodied in the variability of earnings available to the common stockholder and earnings per share. If these magnifications are negative, the common stockholder has a higher chance of insolvency than would have existed had the use of fixed charge securities (debt and preferred stock) been avoided.

The closely related concepts of business and financial risk are crucial to the problem of financial structure design. This follows from the impact of these types of risk on the variability of the earnings stream flowing to the company's shareholders. In the rest of this chapter we study techniques that permit a precise assessment of the earnings stream variability caused by (1) operating leverage and (2) financial leverage. We have already defined financial leverage. Table 9–1 shows that the business risk of the enterprise is influenced by the use of what is called operating leverage. **Operating leverage** refers to the incurrence of fixed operating costs in the firm's income stream. To understand the nature and importance of operating leverage, we need to draw upon the basics of cost-volume-profit analysis, or *breakeven analysis*.

Perspective in Finance

The breakeven analysis concepts presented in the next section are often covered in many of your other classes such as basic accounting principles and managerial economics. This just shows you how important and accepted this tool is within the realm of business decision making. The "Objective and Uses" section below identifies five typical uses of the breakeven model. You can probably add an application or two of your own. Hotels and motels, for instance, know exactly what their breakeven occupancy rate is. This breakeven occupancy rate gives them an operating target. This operating target, in turn, often becomes a crucial input to the hotel's advertising strategy. You may not want to become a financial manager—but you do want to understand how to compute breakeven points.

Breakeven Analysis

The technique of breakeven analysis is familiar to legions of businesspeople. It is usefully applied in a wide array of business settings, including both small and large organizations. This tool is widely accepted by the business community for two reasons: It is based on straightforward assumptions, and companies have found that the information gained from the breakeven model is beneficial in decision-making situations.

Objective and Uses

The objective of *breakeven analysis* is to determine the *breakeven quantity of output* by studying the relationships among the firm's cost structure, volume of

---

[2]Note that the concept of financial risk used here differs from that used in our examination of cash and marketable securities management in Chapter 15.

output, and profit. Alternatively, the firm ascertains the breakeven level of sales dollars that corresponds to the breakeven quantity of output. We will develop the fundamental relationships by concentrating on units of output and then extend the procedure to permit direct calculation of the breakeven sales level.

What is meant by the breakeven quantity of output? It is that quantity of output, denominated in units, that results in an EBIT level equal to zero. Use of the breakeven model, therefore, enables the financial officer (1) to determine the quantity of output that must be sold to cover all operating costs, as distinct from financial costs, and (2) to calculate the EBIT that will be achieved at various output levels.

There are many actual and potential applications of the breakeven approach. Some of these include

1. **Capital expenditure analysis.** As a *complementary* technique to discounted cash flow evaluation models, the breakeven model locates in a rough way the sales volume needed to make a project economically beneficial to the firm. It should *not* be used to replace the time-adjusted evaluation techniques.

2. **Pricing policy.** The sales price of a new product can be set to achieve a target EBIT level. Furthermore, should market penetration be a prime objective, a price could be set that would cover slightly more than the variable costs of production and provide only a partial contribution to the recovery of fixed costs. The negative EBIT at several possible sales prices can then be studied.

3. **Labor contract negotiations.** The effect of increased variable costs resulting from higher wages on the breakeven quantity of output can be analyzed.

4. **Cost structure.** The choice of reducing variable costs at the expense of incurring higher fixed costs can be evaluated. Management might decide to become more capital-intensive by performing tasks in the production process through use of equipment rather than labor. Application of the breakeven model can indicate what the effects of this tradeoff will be on the breakeven point for the given product.

5. **Financing decisions.** Analysis of the firm's cost structure will reveal the proportion that fixed operating costs bear to sales. If this proportion is high, the firm might reasonably decide not to add any fixed financing costs on top of the high fixed operating costs.

Essential Elements of the Breakeven Model

To implement the breakeven model, we must separate the production costs of the company into two mutually exclusive categories: fixed costs and variable costs. You will recall from your study of basic economics that in the long run all costs are variable. Breakeven analysis, therefore, is a short-run concept.

Assumed Behavior of Costs

Fixed costs ■ Fixed costs, also referred to as **indirect costs,** do not vary in total amount as sales volume or the quantity of output changes over some *relevant* range of output. Total fixed costs are independent of the quantity of product produced and equal some constant dollar amount. As production volume increases, fixed cost per unit of product falls, as fixed costs are spread over larger and larger quantities of output. Figure 9–3 graphs the behavior of total fixed costs with respect to the company's relevant range of output. This total is shown to be unaffected by the quantity of product that is manufactured and sold. Over some other relevant output range, the amount of total fixed costs might be higher or lower for the same company.

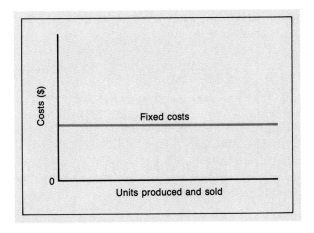

FIGURE 9–3.
Fixed-Cost Behavior over
Relevant Range of Output

In a manufacturing setting, some specific examples of fixed costs are

1. Administrative salaries
2. Depreciation
3. Insurance
4. Lump sums spent on intermittent advertising programs
5. Property taxes
6. Rent

Variable costs ▪ Variable costs are sometimes referred to as **direct costs.** Variable costs are fixed per unit of output but vary in total as output changes. Total variable costs are computed by taking the variable cost per unit and multiplying it by the quantity produced and sold. The breakeven model assumes proportionality between total variable costs and sales. Thus, if sales rise by 10 percent, it is assumed that variable costs will rise by 10 percent. Figure 9–4 graphs the behavior of total variable costs with respect to the company's relevant range of output. Total variable costs are seen to depend on the quantity of product that is manufactured and sold. Notice that if zero units of the product are manufactured, then variable costs are zero, but fixed costs are greater than zero. This implies that some contribution to the coverage of fixed costs occurs as long as the selling price per unit exceeds the variable cost per unit. This helps explain why some firms will operate a plant even when sales are *temporarily* depressed—that is, to provide some increment of revenue toward the coverage of fixed costs.

For a manufacturing operation, some examples of variable costs include

1. Direct labor
2. Direct materials

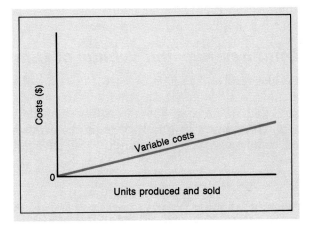

FIGURE 9–4.
Variable-Cost Behavior over
Relevant Range of Output

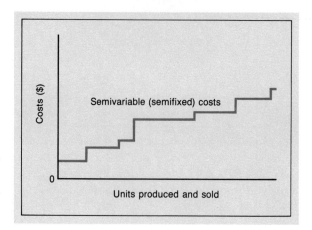

FIGURE 9–5.
Semivariable Cost Behavior over the Relevant Range of Output

3. Energy costs (fuel, electricity, natural gas) associated with the production area

4. Freight costs for products leaving the plant

5. Packaging

6. Sales commissions

More on behavior of costs ■ No one really believes that *all* costs behave as neatly as we have illustrated the fixed and variable costs in Figures 9–3 and 9–4. Nor does any law or accounting principle dictate that a certain element of the firm's total costs always be classified as fixed or variable. This will depend on each firm's specific circumstances. In one firm energy costs may be predominantly fixed, whereas in another they may vary with output.[3]

Furthermore, some costs may be fixed for a while, then rise sharply to a higher level as a higher output is reached, remain fixed, and then rise again with further increases in production. Such costs may be termed either (1) **semivariable** or (2) **semifixed.** The label is your choice, because both are used in industrial practice. An example might be the salaries paid production supervisors. Should output be cut back by 15 percent for a short period, the management of the organization is not likely to lay off 15 percent of the supervisors. Similarly, commissions paid to salespeople often follow a stepwise pattern over wide ranges of success. This sort of cost behavior is shown in Figure 9–5.

To implement the breakeven model and deal with such a complex cost structure, the financial manager must (1) identify the most relevant output range for planning purposes and then (2) approximate the cost effect of semivariable items over this range by segregating a portion of them to fixed costs and a portion to variable costs. In the actual business setting this procedure is not fun. It is not unusual for the analyst who deals with the figures to spend considerably more time allocating costs to fixed and variable categories than in carrying out the actual breakeven calculations.

Total Revenue and Volume of Output

Besides fixed and variable costs, the essential elements of the breakeven model include total revenue from sales and volume of output. **Total revenue** means sales dollars and is equal to the selling price per unit multiplied by the quantity sold. The **volume of output** refers to the firm's level of operations and may be indicated either as a unit quantity or as sales dollars.

[3]In a greenhouse operation, where plants are grown (manufactured) under strictly controlled temperatures, heat costs will tend to be fixed whether the building is full or only half full of seedlings. In a metal stamping operation, where levers are being produced, there is no need to heat the plant to as high a temperature when the machines are stopped and the workers are not there. In this latter case, the heat costs will tend to be variable.

Finding the Breakeven Point

Finding the breakeven point in terms of units of production can be accomplished in several ways. All approaches require the essential elements of the breakeven model just described. The breakeven model is a simple adaptation of the firm's income statement expressed in the following analytical format:

$$\text{sales} - (\text{total variable cost} + \text{total fixed cost}) = \text{profit} \qquad (9\text{–}1)$$

On a units of production basis, it is necessary to introduce (1) the price at which each unit is sold and (2) the variable cost per unit of output. Because the profit item studied in breakeven analysis is EBIT, we will use that acronym instead of the word "profit." In terms of units, the income statement shown in equation (9–1) becomes the breakeven model by setting EBIT equal to zero:

$$\left(\begin{array}{c}\text{sales price} \\ \text{per unit}\end{array}\right)\left(\begin{array}{c}\text{units} \\ \text{sold}\end{array}\right) - \left[\left(\begin{array}{c}\text{variable cost} \\ \text{per unit}\end{array}\right)\left(\begin{array}{c}\text{units} \\ \text{sold}\end{array}\right)\right.$$
$$\left. + \left(\begin{array}{c}\text{total fixed} \\ \text{cost}\end{array}\right)\right] = \text{EBIT} = \$0 \qquad (9\text{–}2)$$

Our task now becomes finding the number of units that must be produced and sold in order to satisfy equation (9–2)—that is, to arrive at an EBIT = \$0. This can be done by (1) trial-and-error analysis, (2) contribution-margin analysis, or (3) algebraic analysis. Each approach will be illustrated using the same set of circumstances.

Problem Situation

Even though the Pierce Grain Company manufactures several different products, it has observed over a lengthy period that its product mix is rather constant. This allows management to conduct its financial planning by use of a "normal" sales price per unit and "normal" variable cost per unit. The "normal" sales price and variable cost per unit are calculated from the constant product mix. It is like assuming that the product mix is one big product. The selling price is \$10 and the variable cost is \$6. Total fixed costs for the firm are \$100,000 per year. What is the breakeven point in units produced and sold for the company during the coming year?

Trial-and-Error Analysis

The most cumbersome approach to determining the firm's breakeven point is to employ the trial-and-error technique illustrated in Table 9–2. The process

TABLE 9–2.
Pierce Grain Company Sales, Cost, and Profit Schedule

(1) Units Sold	(2) Unit Sales Price	(3)=(1)×(2) Sales	(4) Unit Variable Cost	(5)=(1)×(4) Total Variable Cost	(6) Total Fixed Cost	(7)=(5)+(6) Total Cost	(8)=(3)−(7) EBIT
1. 10,000	\$10	\$100,000	\$6	\$ 60,000	\$100,000	\$160,000	\$−60,000 1.
2. 15,000	10	150,000	6	90,000	100,000	190,000	−40,000 2.
3. 20,000	10	200,000	6	120,000	100,000	220,000	−20,000 3.
4. 25,000	10	250,000	6	150,000	100,000	250,000	0 4.
5. 30,000	10	300,000	6	180,000	100,000	280,000	20,000 5.
6. 35,000	10	350,000	6	210,000	100,000	310,000	40,000 6.

Input Data
Unit sales price = \$10
Unit variable cost = \$6
Total fixed cost = \$100,000

Output Data
Breakeven point in units = 25,000 units produced and sold
Breakeven point in sales = \$250,000

simply involves the arbitrary selection of an output level and the calculation of a corresponding EBIT amount. When the level of output is found that results in an EBIT = $0, the breakeven point has been located. Notice that Table 9–2 is just equation (9–2) in worksheet form. For the Pierce Grain Company, total operating costs will be covered when 25,000 units are manufactured and sold. This tells us that if sales equal $250,000, the firm's EBIT will equal $0.

Contribution-Margin Analysis

Unlike trial and error, use of the contribution margin technique permits direct computation of the breakeven quantity of output. The **contribution margin** is the difference between the unit selling price and unit variable costs, as follows:

$$\begin{array}{l} \text{Unit sales price} \\ -\ \underline{\text{Unit variable cost}} \\ =\ \underline{\text{Unit contribution margin}} \end{array}$$

The use of the word "contribution" in the present context means contribution to the coverage of fixed operating costs. For the Pierce Grain Company, the unit contribution margin is

Unit sales price	$10
Unit variable cost	−6
Unit contribution margin	$ 4

If the annual fixed costs of $100,000 are divided by the unit contribution margin of $4, we find the breakeven quantity of output for Pierce Grain is 25,000 units. With much less effort, we have arrived at the identical result found by trial and error. Figure 9–6 portrays the contribution-margin technique for finding the breakeven point.

Algebraic Analysis

To explain the algebraic method for finding the breakeven output level, we need to adopt some notation. Let

$$Q = \text{the number of units sold}$$

$$Q_B = \text{the breakeven level of } Q$$

$$P = \text{the unit sales price}$$

$$F = \text{total fixed costs anticipated over the planning period}$$

$$V = \text{the unit variable cost}$$

FIGURE 9–6.
Contribution-Margin Approach
to Breakeven Analysis

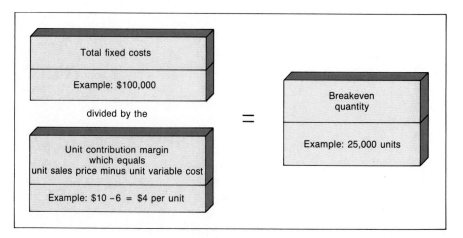

Equation (9–2), the breakeven model, is repeated below as equation (9–2a) with the model symbols used in place of words. The breakeven model is then solved for Q, the number of units that must be sold in order that EBIT will equal $0. We label the breakeven point quantity Q_B.

$$(P \cdot Q) - [(V \cdot Q) + (F)] = \text{EBIT} = \$0$$
$$(P \cdot Q) - (V \cdot Q) - F = \$0 \qquad \text{(9–2a)}$$
$$Q(P - V) = F$$
$$Q_B = \frac{F}{P - V} \qquad \text{(9–3)}$$

Observe that equation (9–3) says: divide total fixed operating costs, F, by the unit contribution margin, $P - V$, and the breakeven level of output, Q_B, will be obtained. The contribution margin analysis is nothing more than equation (9–3) in different garb.

Application of equation (9–3) permits direct calculation of Pierce Grain's breakeven point, as follows:

$$Q_B = \frac{F}{P - V} = \frac{\$100,000}{\$10 - \$6} = 25,000 \text{ units}$$

Breakeven Point in Sales Dollars

In dealing with the multiproduct firm, it is convenient to compute the breakeven point in terms of sales dollars rather than units of output. Sales, in effect, become a common denominator associated with a particular product mix. Furthermore, an outside analyst may not have access to internal unit cost data. He or she may, however, be able to obtain annual reports for the firm. If the analyst can separate the firm's total costs as identified from its annual reports into their fixed and variable components, he or she can calculate a general breakeven point in sales dollars.

We will illustrate the procedure using the Pierce Grain Company's cost structure, contained in Table 9–2. Suppose that the information on line 5 of Table 9–2 is arranged in the format shown in Table 9–3. We will refer to this type of financial statement as an **analytical income statement.** This distinguishes it from audited income statements published, for example, in the annual reports of public corporations. If we are aware of the simple mathematical relationships on which cost-volume-profit analysis is based, we can use Table 9–3 to find the breakeven point in sales dollars for the Pierce Grain Company.

First, let us explore the logic of the process. Recall from equation (9–1) that

$$\text{sales} - (\text{total variable cost} + \text{total fixed cost}) = \text{EBIT}$$

If we let total sales = S, total variable cost = VC, and total fixed cost = F, the preceding relationship becomes

$$S - (VC + F) = \text{EBIT}$$

Sales	$300,000
Less: Total variable costs	180,000
Revenue before fixed costs	$120,000
Less: Total fixed costs	100,000
EBIT	$ 20,000

TABLE 9–3.
Pierce Grain Company
Analytical Income Statement

Because variable cost per unit of output and selling price per unit are *assumed* constant over the relevant output range in breakeven analysis, the ratio of total sales to total variable cost, *VC/S*, is a constant for any level of sales. This permits us to rewrite the previous expression as

$$S - \left[\left(\frac{VC}{S}\right)S\right] - F = \text{EBIT}$$

and

$$S\left(1 - \frac{VC}{S}\right) - F = \text{EBIT}$$

At the breakeven point, however, EBIT = 0, and the corresponding breakeven level of sales can be represented as *S**. At the breakeven level of sales, we have

$$S^*\left(1 - \frac{VC}{S}\right) - F = 0$$

or

$$S^*\left(1 - \frac{VC}{S}\right) = F$$

Therefore,

for SALES IN $

$$S^* = \frac{F}{1 - \frac{VC}{S}} \qquad\qquad (9\text{–}4)$$

The application of equation (9–4) to Pierce Grain's analytical income statement in Table 9–3 permits the breakeven sales level for the firm to be directly computed, as follows:

$$S^* = \frac{\$100,000}{1 - \frac{\$180,000}{\$300,000}}$$

$$= \frac{\$100,000}{1 - .60} = \$250,000$$

Notice that this is indeed the same breakeven sales level for Pierce Grain that is indicated on line 4 of Table 9–2.

Graphic Representation, Analysis of Input Changes, and Cash Breakeven Point

In making a presentation to management, it is often effective to display the firm's cost-volume-profit relationships in the form of a chart. Even those individuals who truly enjoy analyzing financial problems find figures and equations dry material at times. Furthermore, by quickly scanning the basic breakeven chart, the manager can approximate the EBIT amount that will prevail at different sales levels.

Such a chart has been prepared for the Pierce Grain Company. Figure 9–7 has been constructed for this firm using the input data contained in Table 9–2. Total fixed costs of $100,000 are added to the total variable costs associated with each production level to form the total costs line. When 25,000 units of product are manufactured and sold, the sales line and total costs line intersect. This means, of course, that the EBIT that would exist at that volume of output is zero.

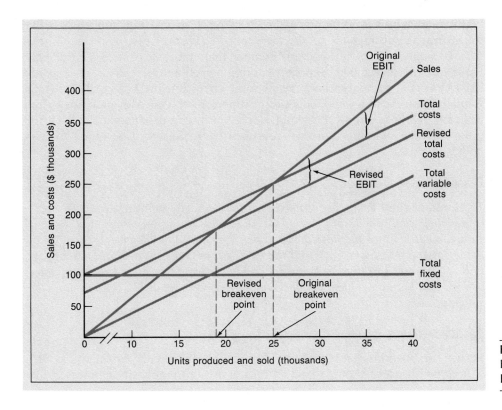

FIGURE 9–7.
Pierce Grain Company's
Breakeven Chart

Beyond 25,000 units of output, notice that sales revenues exceed the total costs line. This causes a positive EBIT. This positive EBIT, or profits, is labeled "original EBIT" in Figure 9–7.

The unencumbered nature of the breakeven model makes it possible to quickly incorporate changes in the requisite input data and generate the revised output. Suppose a favorable combination of events causes Pierce Grain's fixed costs to decrease by $25,000. This would put total fixed costs for the planning period at a level of $75,000 rather than the $100,000 originally forecast. Total costs, being the sum of fixed and variable costs, would be lower by $25,000 at all output levels. The revised total costs line in Figure 9–7 reflects Pierce Grain's reduction in fixed costs. Under these revised conditions, the new breakeven point in units would be as follows:

$$Q_B = \frac{\$75,000}{\$10 - \$6} = 18,750 \text{ units}$$

The revised breakeven point of 18,750 units is identified in Figure 9–7, along with the revised EBIT amounts that would prevail at differing output and sales levels. The chart clearly indicates that at any specific production and sales level, the revised EBIT would exceed the original EBIT. This must be the case, as the revised total costs line lies below the original total costs line over the entire relevant output range. The effect on the breakeven point caused by other changes in (1) the cost structure or (2) the pricing policy can be analyzed in a similar fashion.

The data in Figure 9–7 can be used to demonstrate another version of basic cost-volume-profit analysis. This can be called **cash breakeven analysis.** If the company's fixed- or variable-cost estimates allow for any noncash expenses, then the resultant breakeven point is higher on an accounting profit basis than on a cash basis. This means the firm's production and sales levels do not have to be as great to cover the cash costs of manufacturing the product.

What are these noncash expenses? The largest and most significant is depreciation expense. Another category is prepaid expenses. Insurance policies are at times paid to cover a three-year cycle. Thus, the time period for which the breakeven analysis is being performed might *not* involve an actual cash outlay for insurance coverage.

For purposes of illustration, assume that noncash expenses for Pierce Grain amount to $25,000 over the planning period and that all these costs are fixed. We can compare the revised total costs line in Figure 9–7, which implicitly assumes a lower fixed *cash* cost line, with the sales revenue line to find the cash breakeven point. Provided Pierce Grain can produce and sell 18,750 units over the planning horizon, revenues from sales will be equal to cash operating costs.

Perspective in Finance

The limitations of the breakeven models that we have examined are really the underlying assumptions of the models. All models rest upon some set of assumptions and knowing those assumptions is requisite to effective application of the technique. This does not mean the tool is of no value in decision making; it only means that you need to be aware of exactly what you are doing when you use the tool to make a business decision. If you can explain the assumptions to someone else, you can effectively use the technique.

Limitations of Breakeven Analysis

Earlier we identified some of the applications of breakeven analysis. This technique is a useful tool in many settings. It must be emphasized, however, that breakeven analysis provides a *beneficial guide* to managerial action, not the final answer. The use of cost-volume-profit analysis has limitations, which should be kept in mind. These include the following:

1. The cost-volume-profit relationship is assumed to be linear. This is realistic only over narrow ranges of output.

2. The total revenue curve (sales curve) is presumed to increase linearly with the volume of output. This implies *any* quantity can be sold over the relevant output range at that *single* price. To be more realistic, it is necessary in many situations to compute *several* sales curves and corresponding breakeven points at differing prices.

3. A constant production and sales mix is assumed. Should the company decide to produce more of one product and less of another, a new breakeven point would have to be found. Only if the variable cost-to-sales ratios were identical for products involved would the new calculation be unnecessary.

4. The breakeven chart and the breakeven computation are static forms of analysis. Any alteration in the firm's cost or price structure dictates that a new breakeven point be calculated. Breakeven analysis is more helpful, therefore, in stable industries than in dynamic ones.

Operating Leverage

If *fixed* operating costs are present in the firm's cost structure, so is *operating leverage*. Fixed operating costs do *not* include interest charges incurred from the firm's use of debt financing. Those costs will be incorporated into the analysis when financial leverage is discussed.

So operating leverage *arises* from the firm's use of fixed operating costs. But what is operating leverage? **Operating leverage** is the responsiveness of the firm's EBIT to fluctuations in sales. By continuing to draw on our data for the Pierce Grain Company, we can illustrate the concept of operating leverage. Table 9–4 contains data for a study of a possible fluctuation in the firm's sales

Item	Base Sales Level, t	Forecast Sales Level, t + 1
Sales	$300,000	$360,000
Less: Total variable costs	180,000	216,000
Revenue before fixed costs	$120,000	$144,000
Less: Total fixed costs	100,000	100,000
EBIT	$ 20,000	$ 44,000

level. It is assumed that Pierce Grain is currently operating at an annual sales level of $300,000. This is referred to in the tabulation as the base sales level at t (time period zero). The question is: How will Pierce Grain's EBIT level respond to a positive 20 percent change in sales? A sales volume of $360,000, referred to as the forecast sales level at $t + 1$, reflects the 20 percent sales rise anticipated over the planning period. Assume that the planning period is one year.

Operating leverage relationships are derived within the mathematical assumptions of cost-volume-profit analysis. In the present example, this means that Pierce Grain's variable cost-to-sales ratio of .6 will continue to hold during time period $t + 1$, and the fixed costs will hold steady at $100,000.

Given the forecasted sales level for Pierce Grain and its cost structure, we can measure the responsiveness of EBIT to the upswing in volume. Notice in Table 9–4 that EBIT is expected to be $44,000 at the end of the planning period. The percentage change in EBIT from t to $t + 1$ can be measured as follows:

$$\text{percentage change in EBIT} = \frac{\$44,000_{t+1} - \$20,000_t}{\$20,000_t}$$

$$= \frac{\$24,000}{\$20,000}$$

$$= 120\%$$

We know that the projected fluctuation in sales amounts to 20 percent of the base period, t, sales level. This is verified below:

$$\text{percentage change in sales} = \frac{\$360,000_{t+1} - \$300,000_t}{\$300,000_t}$$

$$= \frac{\$60,000}{\$300,000}$$

$$= 20\%$$

By relating the percentage fluctuation in EBIT to the percentage fluctuation in sales, we can calculate a specific measure of operating leverage. Thus, we have

$$\begin{array}{l}\text{degree of operating leverage} \\ \text{from the base sales level(s)}\end{array} = \text{DOL}_s = \frac{\text{percentage change in EBIT}}{\text{percentage change in sales}} \quad (9\text{–}5)$$

Applying equation (9–5) to our Pierce Grain data gives

$$\text{DOL}_{\$300,000} = \frac{120\%}{20\%} = 6 \text{ times}$$

Unless we understand what the specific measure of operating leverage tells us, the fact that we may know it is equal to 6 times is nothing more than sterile information. For Pierce Grain, the inference is that for *any* percentage fluctuation in sales from the base level, the percentage fluctuation in EBIT will be six

Item	Base Sales Level, t	Forecast Sales Level, t + 1
Sales	$300,000	$240,000
Less: Total variable costs	180,000	144,000
Revenue before fixed costs	$120,000	$ 96,000
Less: Total fixed costs	100,000	100,000
EBIT	$ 20,000	$ −4,000

times as great. If Pierce Grain expected only a 5 percent rise in sales over the coming period, a 30 percent rise in EBIT would be anticipated as follows:

$$\text{(percentage change in sales)} \times (\text{DOL}_s) = \text{percentage change in EBIT}$$

$$(5\%) \times (6) = 30\%$$

We will now return to the postulated 20 percent change in sales. What if the direction of the fluctuation is expected to be negative rather than positive? What is in store for Pierce Grain? Unfortunately for Pierce Grain, but fortunately for the analytical process, we will see that the operating leverage measure holds in the negative direction as well. This situation is displayed in Table 9–5.

At the $240,000 sales level, which represents the 20 percent decrease from the base period, Pierce Grain's EBIT is expected to be −$4,000. How sensitive is EBIT to this sales change? The magnitude of the EBIT fluctuation is calculated as[4]

$$\text{percentage change in EBIT} = \frac{-\$4,000_{t+1} - \$20,000_t}{\$20,000_t}$$

$$= \frac{-\$24,000}{\$20,000}$$

$$= -120\%$$

Making use of our knowledge that the sales change was equal to −20 percent permits us to compute the specific measure of operating leverage as

$$\text{DOL}_{\$300,000} = \frac{-120\%}{-20\%} = 6 \text{ times}$$

What we have seen, then, is that the degree of operating leverage measure works in the positive or negative direction. A negative change in production volume and sales can be magnified severalfold when the effect on EBIT is calculated.

To this point our calculations of the degree of operating leverage have required two analytical income statements: one for the base period and a second for the subsequent period that incorporates the possible sales alteration. This cumbersome process can be simplified. If unit cost data are available to the financial manager, the relationship can be expressed directly in the following manner:

$$\text{DOL}_s = \frac{Q(P - V)}{Q(P - V) - F} \tag{9–6}$$

Observe in equation (9–6) that the variables were all previously defined in our algebraic analysis of the breakeven model. Recall that Pierce sells its product at $10 per unit, the unit variable cost is $6, and total fixed costs over the planning horizon are $100,000. Still assuming that Pierce is operating at a

[4]Some students have conceptual difficulty in computing these percentage changes when negative amounts are involved. Notice by inspection in Table 9–5 that the *difference* between an EBIT amount of +$20,000 at t and −$4,000 at t + 1 is −$24,000.

$300,000 sales volume, which means output (Q) is 30,000 units, we can find the degree of operating leverage by application of equation (9–6):

$$DOL_{\$300,000} = \frac{30,000(\$10 - \$6)}{30,000(\$10 - \$6) - \$100,000} = \frac{\$120,000}{\$20,000} = 6 \text{ times}$$

Whereas equation (9–6) requires us to know unit cost data to carry out the computations, the next formulation we examine does not. If we have an analytical income statement for the base period, then equation (9–7) can be employed to find the firm's degree of operating leverage:

$$DOL_s = \frac{\text{revenue before fixed costs}}{\text{EBIT}} = \frac{S - VC}{S - VC - F} \qquad (9\text{–}7)$$

Use of equation (9–7) in conjunction with the base period data for Pierce Grain shown in either Table 9–4 or 9–5 gives

$$DOL_{\$300,000} = \frac{\$120,000}{\$20,000} = 6 \text{ times}$$

The three versions of the operating leverage measure all produce the same result. Data availability will sometimes dictate which formulation can be applied. The crucial consideration, though, is that you grasp what the measurement tells you. For Pierce Grain, a 1 percent change in sales will produce a 6 percent change in EBIT.

Perspective in Finance

Before we complete our discussion of operating leverage and move on to the subject of financial leverage, ask yourself "which type of leverage is more under the control of management?" You will probably (and correctly) come to the conclusion that the firm's managers have less control over its operating cost structure and almost complete control over its financial structure. What the firm actually produces, for example, will determine to a significant degree the division between fixed and variable costs. There is more room for substitution among the various sources of financial capital than there is among the labor and real capital inputs that enable the firm to meet its production requirements. Thus, you can anticipate more arguments over the choice to use a given degree of financial leverage than the corresponding choice over operating leverage use.

Implications

As the firm's scale of operations moves in a favorable manner above the breakeven point, the degree of operating leverage at each subsequent (higher) sales base will decline. In short, the greater the sales level, the lower the degree of operating leverage. This is demonstrated in Table 9–6 for the Pierce Grain

Units Produced and Sold	Sales Dollars	DOL_s
25,000	$ 250,000	Undefined
30,000	300,000	6.00
35,000	350,000	3.50
40,000	400,000	2.67
45,000	450,000	2.25
50,000	500,000	2.00
75,000	750,000	1.50
100,000	1,000,000	1.33

TABLE 9–6.
Pierce Grain Company Degree of Operating Leverage Relative to Different Sales Bases

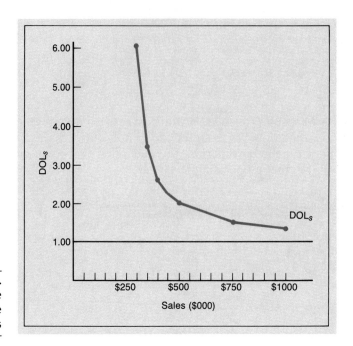

FIGURE 9–8.
Pierce Grain Company Degree
of Operating Leverage Relative
to Different Sales Bases

Company. At the breakeven sales level for Pierce Grain, the degree of operating leverage is *undefined,* because the denominator in any of the computational formulas is zero. Notice that beyond the breakeven point of 25,000 units, the degree of operating leverage declines. It will decline at a decreasing rate and asymptotically approach a value of 1.00. As long as some fixed operating costs are present in the firm's cost structure, however, operating leverage exists, and the degree of operating leverage (DOL$_s$) will exceed 1.00. Operating leverage is present, then, whenever the firm faces the following situation:

$$\frac{\text{percentage change in EBIT}}{\text{percentage change in sales}} > 1.00$$

The data in Table 9–6 are presented in graphic form in Figure 9–8.

The greater the firm's degree of operating leverage, the more its profits will vary with a given percentage change in sales. Thus, operating leverage is definitely an attribute of the business risk that confronts the company. From Table 9–6 and Figure 9–8 we have seen that the degree of operating leverage falls as sales increase past the firm's breakeven point. The sheer size and operating profitability of the firm, therefore, affect and can lessen its business-risk exposure.

The manager considering an alteration in the firm's cost structure will benefit from an understanding of the operating leverage concept. It might be possible to replace part of the labor force with capital equipment (machinery). A possible result is an increase in fixed costs associated with the new machinery and a reduction in variable costs attributable to a lower labor bill. This conceivably could raise the firm's degree of operating leverage at a specific sales base. If the prospects for future sales increases are high, then increasing the degree of operating leverage might be a prudent decision. The opposite conclusion will be reached if sales prospects are unattractive.

Perspective in Finance

As you are introduced to the topic of financial leverage *remember that this is one of the most crucial policy areas on which a financial executive spends his or her time. We describe and measure here what happens to the firm's earnings per share when financial risk is assumed. Try to understand this effect. We demonstrate how actually to measure this effect in the next section. By now you should be realizing that variability of all types—be it in an earnings stream or in stock returns—is a central element of financial thought* and *the practice of financial management.*

Financial Leverage

We have defined *financial leverage* as the practice of financing a portion of the firm's assets with securities bearing a fixed rate of return in hope of increasing the ultimate return to the common shareholders. In the present discussion we focus on the responsiveness of the company's earnings per share to changes in its EBIT. For the time being, then, the return to the common stockholder being concentrated upon is earnings per share. We are *not* saying that earnings per share is the appropriate criterion for all financing decisions. In fact, the weakness of such a contention will be examined in the next chapter. Rather, the use of financial leverage produces a certain type of *effect*. This effect can be illustrated clearly by concentrating on an earnings-per-share criterion.

Let us assume that the Pierce Grain Company is in the process of getting started as a going concern. The firm's potential owners have calculated that $200,000 is needed to purchase the necessary assets to conduct the business. Three possible financing plans have been identified for raising the $200,000; they are presented in Table 9–7. In plan A no financial risk is assumed: the entire $200,000 is raised by selling 2,000 common shares, each with a $100 par value. In plan B a moderate amount of financial risk is assumed: 25 percent of the assets are financed with a debt issue that carries an 8 percent annual interest rate. Plan C would use the most financial leverage: 40 percent of the assets would be financed with a debt issue costing 8 percent.[5]

Table 9–8 presents the impact of financial leverage on earnings per share associated with each fund-raising alternative. If EBIT should increase from

[handwritten annotation: NO DEBT]

---

[5]In actual practice moving from a 25 to a 40 percent debt ratio would probably result in a higher interest rate on the additional bonds. That effect is ignored here to let us concentrate on the ramifications of using different proportions of debt in the financial structure.

TABLE 9–7.
Pierce Grain Company Possible
Financial Structures

Plan A: 0% debt

		Total debt	$ 0
		Common equity	200,000[a]
Total assets	$200,000	Total liabilities and equity	$200,000

Plan B: 25% debt at 8% interest rate

		Total debt	$ 50,000
		Common equity	150,000[b]
Total assets	$200,000	Total liabilities and equity	$200,000

Plan C: 40% debt at 8% interest rate

		Total debt	$ 80,000
		Common equity	120,000[c]
Total assets	$200,000	Total liabilities and equity	$200,000

[a]2,000 common shares outstanding
[b]1,500 common shares outstanding
[c]1,200 common shares outstanding

(1) EBIT	(2) Interest	(3)=(1)−(2) EBT	(4)=(3)×.5 Taxes	(5)=(3)−(4) Net Income to Common	(6) Earnings per Share	
Plan A: 0% debt; $200,000 common equity; 2000 shares						
$ 0	$ 0	$ 0	$ 0	$ 0	$ 0	
20,000	0	20,000	10,000	10,000	5.00 ⎫	100%
40,000	0	40,000	20,000	20,000	10.00 ⎭	
60,000	0	60,000	30,000	30,000	15.00	
80,000	0	80,000	40,000	40,000	20.00	
Plan B: 25% debt; 8% interest rate; $150,000 common equity; 1500 shares						
$ 0	$4,000	$ (4,000)	$ (2,000)[a]	$ (2,000)	$ (1.33)	
20,000	4,000	16,000	8,000	8,000	5.33 ⎫	125%
40,000	4,000	36,000	18,000	18,000	12.00 ⎭	
60,000	4,000	56,000	28,000	28,000	18.67	
80,000	4,000	76,000	38,000	38,000	25.33	
Plan C: 40% debt; 8% interest rate; $120,000 common equity; 1200 shares						
$ 0	$6,400	$ (6,400)	$ (3,200)[a]	$ (3,200)	$ (2.67)	
20,000	6,400	13,600	6,800	6,800	5.67 ⎫	147%
40,000	6,400	33,600	16,800	16,800	14.00 ⎭	
60,000	6,400	53,600	26,800	26,800	22.33	
80,000	6,400	73,600	36,800	36,800	30.67	

[a]The negative tax bill recognizes the credit arising from the carryback and carryforward provision of the tax code. See Chapter 2.

$20,000 to $40,000, then earnings per share would rise by 100 percent under plan A. The same positive fluctuation in EBIT would occasion an earnings per share rise of 125 percent under plan B, and 147 percent under plan C. In plans B and C the 100 percent increase in EBIT (from $20,000 to $40,000) is magnified to a greater than 100 percent increase in earnings per share. The firm is employing financial leverage, and exposing its owners to financial risk, when the following situation exists:

$$\frac{\text{percentage change in earnings per share}}{\text{percentage change in EBIT}} > 1.00$$

By following the same general procedures that allowed us to analyze the firm's use of operating leverage, we can lay out a precise measure of financial leverage. Such a measure deals with the sensitivity of earnings per share to EBIT fluctuations. The relationship can be expressed as

$$\begin{array}{l} \text{degree of financial} \\ \text{leverage (DFL) from} = \text{DFL}_{EBIT} = \dfrac{\text{percentage change in}}{\text{percentage change in EBIT}} \quad \textbf{(9-8)} \\ \text{base EBIT level} \end{array}$$

Use of equation (9–8) with each of the financing choices outlined for Pierce Grain is shown subsequently. The base EBIT level is $20,000 in each case.

$$\text{Plan A:} \quad \text{DFL}_{\$20,000} = \frac{100\%}{100\%} = 1.00 \text{ time}$$

$$\text{Plan B:} \quad \text{DFL}_{\$20,000} = \frac{125\%}{100\%} = 1.25 \text{ times}$$

$$\text{Plan C:} \quad \text{DFL}_{\$20,000} = \frac{147\%}{100\%} = 1.47 \text{ times}$$

Like operating leverage, the *degree of financial leverage* concept performs in the negative direction as well as the positive. Should EBIT fall by 10 percent, the Pierce Grain Company would suffer a 12.5 percent decline in earnings per share under plan B. If plan C were chosen to raise the necessary financial capital, the decline in earnings would be 14.7 percent. Observe that the greater the DFL, the greater the fluctuations (positive or negative) in earnings per share. The common stockholder is required to endure greater variations in returns when the firm's management chooses to use more financial leverage rather than less. The DFL measure allows the variation to be quantified.

greater risk

Rather than taking the time to compute percentage changes in EBIT and earnings per share, the DFL can be found directly, as follows:

$$\text{DFL}_{EBIT} = \frac{\text{EBIT}}{\text{EBIT} - I} \quad \textbf{(9-9)}$$

In equation (9–9) the variable, I, represents the total interest expense incurred on *all* the firm's contractual debt obligations. If six bonds are outstanding, I is the sum of the interest expense on all six bonds. If the firm has preferred stock in its financial structure, the dividend on such issues must be inflated to a before-tax basis and included in the computation of I.[6] In this latter instance, I is in reality the sum of all fixed financing costs.

Equation (9–9) has been applied to each of Pierce Grain's financing plans (Table 9–8) at a base EBIT level of $20,000. The results are as follows:

$$\text{Plan A:} \quad \text{DFL}_{\$20,000} = \frac{\$20,000}{\$20,000 - 0} = 1.00 \text{ time}$$

$$\text{Plan B:} \quad \text{DFL}_{\$20,000} = \frac{\$20,000}{\$20,000 - \$4000} = 1.25 \text{ times}$$

$$\text{Plan C:} \quad \text{DFL}_{\$20,000} = \frac{\$20,000}{\$20,000 - \$6400} = 1.47 \text{ times}$$

---

[6]Suppose (1) preferred dividends of $4,000 are paid annually by the firm and (2) it faces a 40 percent marginal tax rate. How much must the firm earn *before taxes* to make the $4,000 payment out of after-tax earnings? Because preferred dividends are not tax deductible to the paying company, we have $4000/(1 − .40) = $6666.67. Recall from Chapter 2 that the Tax Reform Act of 1986 provided for the taxation of corporate incomes at a maximum rate of 34 percent for tax years beginning *after* June 30, 1987. This maximum rate applies to taxable incomes over $75,000. Under this new tax provision, the firm would need to earn only $6,060.61 before taxes to make the $4,000 preferred dividend payment. That is, $4000/(1 − .34) = $6060.61. Note that from a financial policy viewpoint, the 1986 tax act reduced *somewhat* the tax shield advantages of corporate debt financing and simultaneously reduced the tax bias against preferred stock and common stock financing.

As you probably suspected, the measures of financial leverage shown previously are identical to those obtained by use of equation (9–8). This will always be the case.

Perspective in Finance

The effect on the earnings stream available to the firm's common stockholders from combining operating and financial leverage in large degrees is dramatic. When the use of both leverage types is indeed heavy, a large sales increase will result in a very large rise in earnings per share. Be aware, though, that the very same thing happens in the opposite direction should the sales change be negative! Piling heavy financial leverage use on a high degree of operating leverage, then, is a very risky way to do business. This is why you will find leveraged buyouts are not concentrated in heavy, durable goods industries. The firms in such industries have major (real) capital spending requirements. Rather, the firms favored in leveraged buyouts will be those with comparatively low levels of operating leverage; retail operations are good examples. As a result, many national retail chains and department stores have been involved in leveraged buyouts during the past few years. The leveraged buyout, by its very nature, translates into a high degree of financial leverage use.

Combination of Operating and Financial Leverage

Changes in sales revenues cause greater changes in EBIT. Additionally, changes in EBIT translate into larger variations in both earnings per share (EPS) and total earnings available to the common shareholders (EAC), if the firm chooses to use financial leverage. It should be no surprise, then, to find out that combining operating and financial leverage causes rather large variations in earnings per share. This entire process is visually displayed in Figure 9-9.

Because the risk associated with possible earnings per share is affected by the use of combined or total leverage, it is useful to quantify the effect. For an illustration, we refer once more to the Pierce Grain Company. The cost structure identified for Pierce Grain in our discussion of breakeven analysis still holds. Furthermore, assume that plan B, which carried a 25 percent debt ratio, was chosen to finance the company's assets. Turn your attention to Table 9-9.

In Table 9-9 an increase in output for Pierce Grain from 30,000 to 36,000 units is analyzed. This increase represents a 20 percent rise in sales revenues. From our earlier discussion of operating leverage and the data in Table 9-9, we can see that this 20 percent increase in sales is magnified into a 120 percent rise

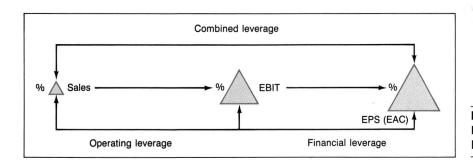

FIGURE 9-9.
Leverage and Earnings Fluctuations

TABLE 9-9.
Pierce Grain Company
Combined Leverage Analysis

Item	Base Sales Level, t	Forecast Sales Level, t + 1	Selected Percentage Changes
Sales	$300,000	$360,000	+20
Less: Total variable costs	180,000	216,000	
Revenue before fixed costs	$120,000	$144,000	
Less: Total fixed costs	100,000	100,000	
EBIT	$ 20,000	$ 44,000	+120
Less: Interest expense	4,000	4,000	
Earnings before taxes (EBT)	$ 16,000	$ 40,000	
Less: Taxes at 50%	8,000	20,000	
Net income	$ 8,000	$ 20,000	+150
Less: Preferred dividends	0	0	
Earnings available to common (EAC)	$ 8,000	$ 20,000	+150
Number of common shares	1,500	1,500	
Earnings per share (EPS)	$ 5.33	$ 13.33	+150

$$\text{Degree of operating leverage} = \text{DOL}_{\$300,000} = \frac{120\%}{20\%} = 6 \text{ times}$$

$$\text{Degree of financial leverage} = \text{DFL}_{\$20,000} = \frac{150\%}{120\%} = 1.25 \text{ times}$$

$$\text{Degree of combined leverage} = \text{DCL}_{\$300,000} = \frac{150\%}{20\%} = 7.50 \text{ times}$$

in EBIT. From this base sales level of $300,000 the degree of operating leverage is 6 times.

The 120 percent rise in EBIT induces a change in earnings per share and earnings available to the common shareholders of 150 percent. The degree of financial leverage is therefore 1.25 times.

The upshot of the analysis is that the 20 percent rise in sales has been magnified to 150 percent, as reflected by the percentage change in earnings per share. The formal measure of combined leverage can be expressed as follows:

$$\begin{pmatrix} \text{degree of combined} \\ \text{leverage from the} \\ \text{base sales level} \end{pmatrix} = DCL_s = \left(\frac{\text{percentage change in earnings per share}}{\text{percentage change in sales}} \right) \quad (9\text{--}10)$$

This equation was used in the bottom portion of Table 9–9 to determine that the degree of combined leverage from the base sales level of $300,000 is 7.50 times. Pierce Grain's use of both operating and financial leverage will cause any percentage change in sales (from the specific base level) to be magnified by a factor of 7.50 when the effect on earnings per share is computed. A 1 percent change in sales, for example, will result in a 7.50 percent change in earnings per share.

Notice that the degree of combined leverage is actually the *product* (not the simple sum) of the two independent leverage measures. Thus, we have

$$(DOL_s) \times (DFL_{EBIT}) = DCL_s$$
$$\text{or} \qquad (6) \times (1.25) = 7.50 \text{ times} \qquad (9\text{--}11)$$

It is possible to ascertain the degree of combined leverage in a direct fashion, without determining any percentage fluctuations or the separate leverage values. We need only substitute the appropriate values into equation (9–12):[7]

$$DCL_s = \frac{Q(P - V)}{Q(P - V) - F - I} \qquad (9\text{--}12)$$

The variable definitions in equation (9–12) are the same ones that have been employed throughout this chapter. Use of equation (9–12) with the information in Table 9–9 gives

$$DCL_{\$300,000} = \frac{\$30,000(\$10 - \$6)}{\$30,000(\$10 - \$6) - \$100,000 - \$4000}$$
$$= \frac{\$120,000}{\$16,000}$$
$$= 7.5 \text{ times}$$

Implications

The total risk exposure the firm assumes can be managed by combining operating and financial leverage in different degrees. Knowledge of the various leverage measures aids the financial officer in determining the proper level of overall risk that should be accepted. If a high degree of business risk is inherent to the specific line of commercial activity, then a low posture regarding financial risk would minimize *additional* earnings fluctuations stemming from sales changes. Conversely, the firm that by its very nature incurs a low level of fixed operating costs might choose to use a high degree of financial leverage in the hope of increasing earnings per share and the rate of return on the common equity investment.

[7]As was the case with the degree of financial leverage metric, the variable, I, in the combined leverage measure must include the before-tax equivalent of any preferred dividend payments when preferred stock is in the financial structure.

BASIC FINANCIAL MANAGEMENT IN PRACTICE

Taxes and Debt

In the next chapter we will explore in more detail the theory and practice of financial structure determination. All this means, really, is deciding how to arrange the funds' sources that accountants place on the right-hand side of the balance sheet. This is both a controversial and fascinating area of research and financial policy making. Of course, arranging those sources of financial capital should be done with the best interests of the firm's shareholders in mind.

Mr. Frederick T. Furlong, a research officer with the Federal Reserve Bank of San Francisco, discusses the tendency present in our financial system for firms to favor debt financing over common equity financing. Notice his emphasis on the U.S. tax system.

In recent years, nonfinancial corporations have expanded debt and retired equity. This trend towards increased debt has raised concerns that U.S. firms are becoming more vulnerable to an economic downturn. The well-publicized problems of specific high-leveraged corporations have added to this concern, and have led to increases in interest rates on speculative-grade, or junk bonds, which should limit issuance of this type of debt. For most corporations, however, the trend in debt issuance could continue, given the way U.S. tax laws favor debt over equity.

U.S. tax policy generally favors the use of debt over equity financing by corporations. Owners of corporate stock in effect pay taxes on profits twice, once when the corporation pays taxes on its earnings and again when individuals pay taxes on dividends or capital gains. In contrast, interest on debt is a tax-deductible expense for businesses, and so, is taxed only once, as ordinary income to debt holders.

Tax considerations are not the only factors affecting a firm's leverage, or debt/equity mix. For example, the higher risk associated with heavy reliance on debt (relative to equity) tends to limit corporate leverage. By increasing the probability that a firm will not be able to meet promised payments, increased reliance on debt raises expected bankruptcy costs. Because debt holders require compensation for this increased risk, the cost of issuing debt should rise and offset tax benefits (and other factors) favoring debt financing.

In the long run, corporations can be expected to operate with a debt/equity mix that balances these and many other influences. Changes in the tax code that increase the tax advantage of debt financing, then, alter this balance and encourage corporations to increase leverage and realign their debt/equity mix.

It is clear that U.S. tax policy has contributed to higher corporate leverage. It is equally clear that changes in tax policy aimed at reducing the bias toward debt could greatly reduce leverage. Significant changes in the tax laws that would eliminate or reduce taxes on dividends and/or capital gains, however, are not likely in the near future. Without such measures, U.S. tax policy will continue to foster a market environment that is favorable to high corporate leverage.

Source: "Corporate Debt," *Federal Reserve Bank of San Francisco Weekly Letter*, November 24, 1989, pp. 1, 3.

SUMMARY

In this chapter we begin to study the process of arriving at an appropriate financial structure for the firm. We examine tools that can assist the financial manager in this task. We are mainly concerned with assessing the variability in the firm's residual earnings stream (either earnings per share or earnings available to the common shareholders) induced by the use of operating and financial leverage. This assessment builds on the tenets of breakeven analysis.

Breakeven Analysis

Breakeven analysis permits the financial manager to determine the quantity of output or the level of sales that will result in an EBIT level of zero. This means the firm has neither a profit nor a loss before any tax considerations. The effect of price changes, cost structure changes, or volume changes on profits (EBIT) can be studied. To make the technique operational, it is necessary that the firm's costs be classified as fixed or variable. Not all costs fit neatly into one of these two categories. Over short planning horizons, though, the preponderance of costs can be assigned to either the fixed or variable classification. Once the cost structure has been identified, the breakeven point can be found by use of (1) trial-and-error analysis, (2) contribution-margin analysis, or (3) algebraic analysis.

$$Q = \frac{F}{P-V}$$

Operating Leverage

Operating leverage is the responsiveness of the firm's EBIT to changes in sales revenues. It arises from the firm's use of fixed operating costs. When fixed operating costs are present in the company's cost structure, changes in sales are magnified into even greater changes in EBIT. The firm's degree of operating leverage from a base sales level is the percentage change in EBIT divided by the percentage change in sales. All types of leverage are two-edged swords. When sales decrease by some percentage, the negative impact upon EBIT will be even larger.

Financial Leverage

A firm employs financial leverage when it finances a portion of its assets with securities bearing a fixed rate of return. The presence of debt and/or preferred stock in the company's financial structure means that it is using financial leverage. When financial leverage is used, changes in EBIT translate into larger changes in earnings per share. The concept of the degree of financial leverage dwells on the sensitivity of earnings per share to changes in EBIT. The DFL from a base EBIT level is defined as the percentage change in earnings per share divided by the percentage change in EBIT. All other things equal, the more fixed-charge securities the firm employs in its financial structure, the greater its degree of financial leverage. Clearly, EBIT can rise or fall. If it falls, and financial leverage is used, the firm's shareholders endure negative changes in earnings per share that are larger than the relative decline in EBIT. Again, leverage is a two-edged sword.

TABLE 9–10.
Summary of Leverage Concepts and Calculations

Technique	Description or Concept	Calculation	Text Reference
Breakeven Analysis			
1. Breakeven point quantity	Total fixed costs divided by the unit contribution margin	$Q_B = \dfrac{F}{P - V}$	(9–3)
2. Breakeven sales level	Total fixed costs divided by 1 minus the ratio of total variable costs to the associated level of sales	$S^* = \dfrac{F}{1 - \dfrac{VC}{S}}$	(9–4)
Operating Leverage			
3. Degree of operating leverage	Percentage change in EBIT divided by the percentage change in sales; or revenue before fixed costs divided by revenue after fixed costs	$DOL_s = \dfrac{Q(P - V)}{Q(P - V) - F}$	(9–6)
Financial Leverage			
4. Degree of financial leverage	Percentage change in earnings per share divided by the percentage change in EBIT; or EBIT divided by EBT.[a]	$DFL_{EBIT} = \dfrac{EBIT}{EBIT - I}$	(9–9)
Combined Leverage			
5. Degree of combined leverage	Percentage change in earnings per share divided by the percentage change in sales; or revenue before fixed costs divided by EBT.[a]	$DCL_s = \dfrac{Q(P - V)}{Q(P - V) - F - I}$	(9–12)

[a]The use of EBT here presumes no preferred dividend payments. In the presence of preferred dividend payments replace EBT with earnings available to common stock (EAC).

Combining Operating and Financial Leverage

Firms use operating and financial leverage in various degrees. The joint use of operating and financial leverage can be measured by computing the degree of combined leverage, defined as the percentage change in earnings per share divided by the percentage change in sales. This measure allows the financial manager to ascertain the effect on total leverage caused by adding financial leverage on top of operating leverage. Effects can be dramatic, because the degree of combined leverage is the product of the degrees of operating and financial leverage. Table 9–10 summarizes the salient concepts and calculation formats discussed in this chapter.

STUDY QUESTIONS

9–1. Distinguish between business risk and financial risk. What gives rise to, or causes, each type of risk?

9–2. Define the term *financial leverage*. Does the firm use financial leverage if preferred stock is present in the capital structure?

9–3. Define the term *operating leverage*. What type of effect occurs when the firm uses operating leverage?

9–4. What is the difference between the (ordinary) breakeven point and the cash breakeven point? Which will be the greater?

9–5. A manager in your firm decides to employ breakeven analysis. Of what shortcomings should this manager be aware?

9–6. What is meant by total risk exposure? How may a firm move to reduce its total risk exposure?

9–7. If a firm has a degree of combined leverage of 3.0 times, what does a negative sales fluctuation of 15 percent portend for the earnings available to the firm's common stock investors?

9–8. Breakeven analysis assumes linear revenue and cost functions. In reality these linear functions over large output and sales levels are highly improbable. Why?

SELF-TEST PROBLEMS

ST–1. (*Breakeven Point*) You are a hard-working analyst in the office of financial operations for a manufacturing firm that produces a single product. You have developed the following cost structure information for this company. All of it pertains to an output level of 10 million units. Using this information, find the breakeven point in units of output for the firm.

Return on operating assets	= 30%
Operating asset turnover	= 6 times
Operating assets	= $20 million
Degree of operating leverage	= 4.5 times

ST–2. (*Leverage Analysis*) You have developed the following analytical income statement for your corporation. (See page 340.) It represents the most recent year's operations, which ended yesterday. Your supervisor in the financial studies office has just handed you a memorandum that asked for written responses to the following questions:

a. At this level of output, what is the degree of operating leverage?
b. What is the degree of financial leverage?
c. What is the degree of combined leverage?
d. What is the firm's breakeven point in sales dollars?
e. If sales should increase by 30 percent, by what percent would earnings before taxes (and net income) increase?

Sales	$20,000,000
Variable costs	12,000,000
Revenue before fixed costs	$ 8,000,000
Fixed costs	5,000,000
EBIT	$ 3,000,000
Interest expense	1,000,000
Earnings before taxes	$ 2,000,000
Taxes (0.50)	1,000,000
Net income	$ 1,000,000

    f. Prepare an analytical income statement that verifies the calculations from part (e) above.

ST–3. (*Fixed Costs and the Breakeven Point*) Bonaventure Manufacturing expects to earn $210,000 next year after taxes. Sales will be $4 million. The firm's single plant is located on the outskirts of Olean, N.Y. The firm manufactures a combined bookshelf and desk unit used extensively in college dormitories. These units sell for $200 each and have a variable cost per unit of $150. Bonaventure experiences a 30 percent tax rate.
    a. What are the firm's fixed costs expected to be next year?
    b. Calculate the firm's breakeven point in both units and dollars.

STUDY PROBLEMS (SET A)

9–1A. (*Breakeven Point and Operating Leverage*) Some financial data for each of three firms are given below:

	Jake's Lawn Chairs	Sarasota Sky Lights	Jefferson Wholesale
Average selling price per unit	$32.00	$875.00	$97.77
Average variable cost per unit	$17.38	$400.00	$87.00
Units sold	18,770	2,800	11,000
Fixed costs	$120,350	$850,000	$89,500

    a. What is the profit for each company at the indicated sales volume?
    b. What is the breakeven point in units for each company?
    c. What is the degree of operating leverage for each company at the indicated sales volume?
    d. If sales were to decline, which firm would suffer the largest relative decline in profitability?

9–2A. (*Leverage Analysis*) You have developed the following analytical income statement for your corporation. It represents the most recent year's operations, which ended yesterday.

Sales	$45,750,000
Variable costs	22,800,000
Revenue before fixed costs	$22,950,000
Fixed costs	9,200,000
EBIT	13,750,000
Interest expense	1,350,000
Earnings before taxes	$12,400,000
Taxes (.50)	6,200,000
Net income	$ 6,200,000

Your supervisor in the controller's office has just handed you a memorandum asking for written responses to the following questions:
    a. At this level of output, what is the degree of operating leverage?
    b. What is the degree of financial leverage?

c. What is the degree of combined leverage?

d. What is the firm's breakeven point in sales dollars?

e. If sales should increase by 25 percent, by what percent would earnings before taxes (and net income) increase?

9–3A. (*Breakeven Point and Operating Leverage*) Footwear, Inc., manufactures a complete line of men's and women's dress shoes for independent merchants. The average selling price of its finished product is $85 per pair. The variable cost for this same pair of shoes is $58. Footwear, Inc., incurs fixed costs of $170,000 per year.

a. What is the breakeven point in pairs of shoes for the company?

b. What is the dollar sales volume the firm must achieve to reach the breakeven point?

c. What would be the firm's profit or loss at the following units of production sold: 7,000 pairs of shoes? 9,000 pairs of shoes? 15,000 pairs of shoes?

d. Find the degree of operating leverage for the production and sales levels given in part (c) above.

9–4A. (*Breakeven Point and Operating Leverage*) Zeylog Corporation manufactures a line of computer memory expansion boards used in microcomputers. The average selling price of its finished product is $180 per unit. The variable cost for these same units is $110. Zeylog incurs fixed costs of $630,000 per year.

a. What is the breakeven point in units for the company?

b. What is the dollar sales volume the firm must achieve to reach the breakeven point?

c. What would be the firm's profit or loss at the following units of production sold: 12,000 units? 15,000 units? 20,000 units?

d. Find the degree of operating leverage for the production and sales levels given in part (c) above.

9–5A. (*Breakeven Point and Operating Leverage*) Some financial data for each of three firms are shown below:

	Blacksburg Furniture	Lexington Cabinets	Williamsburg Colonials
Average selling price per unit	$15.00	$400.00	$40.00
Average variable cost per unit	$12.35	$220.00	$14.50
Units sold	75,000	4,000	13,000
Fixed costs	$35,000	$100,000	$70,000

a. What is the profit for each company at the indicated sales volume?

b. What is the breakeven point in units for each company?

c. What is the degree of operating leverage for each company at the indicated sales volume?

d. If sales were to decline, which firm would suffer the largest relative decline in profitability?

9–6A. (*Fixed Costs and the Breakeven Point*) A & B Beverages expects to earn $50,000 next year after taxes. Sales will be $375,000. The store is located near the shopping district surrounding Blowing Rock University. Its average product sells for $27 a unit. The variable cost per unit is $14.85. The store experiences a 40 percent tax rate.

a. What are the store's fixed costs expected to be next year?

b. Calculate the store's breakeven point in both units and dollars.

9–7A. (*Breakeven Point and Profit Margin*) Mary Clark, a recent graduate of Clarion South University, is planning to open a new wholesaling operation. Her target operating profit margin is 26 percent. Her unit contribution margin will be 50 percent of sales. Average annual sales are forecast to be $3,250,000.

a. How large can fixed costs be for the wholesaling operation and still allow the 26 percent operating profit margin to be achieved?

b. What is the breakeven point in dollars for the firm?

9–8A. (*Leverage Analysis*) You have developed the following analytical income statement for your corporation. (See page 342.) It represents the most recent year's operations, which ended yesterday. Your supervisor in the controller's office has just handed you a memorandum asking for written responses to the following questions:

a. At this level of output, what is the degree of operating leverage?

b. What is the degree of financial leverage?

Sales	$30,000,000
Variable costs	13,500,000
Revenue before fixed costs	$16,500,000
Fixed costs	8,000,000
EBIT	$ 8,500,000
Interest expense	1,000,000
Earnings before taxes	$ 7,500,000
Taxes (.50)	3,750,000
Net income	$ 3,750,000

c. What is the degree of combined leverage?
d. What is the firm's breakeven point in sales dollars?
e. If sales should increase by 25 percent, by what percent would earnings before taxes (and net income) increase?

9–9A. (*Breakeven Point*) You are a hard-working analyst in the office of financial operations for a manufacturing firm that produces a single product. You have developed the following cost structure information for this company. All of it pertains to an output level of 10 million units. Using this information, find the breakeven point in units of output for the firm.

Return on operating assets	= 25%
Operating asset turnover	= 5 times
Operating assets	= $20 million
Degree of operating leverage	= 4 times

9–10A. (*Breakeven Point and Operating Leverage*) Allison Radios manufactures a complete line of radio and communication equipment for law enforcement agencies. The average selling price of its finished product is $180 per unit. The variable cost for these same units is $126. Allison Radios incurs fixed costs of $540,000 per year.
a. What is the breakeven point in units for the company?
b. What is the dollar sales volume the firm must achieve in order to reach the breakeven point?
c. What would be the firm's profit or loss at the following units of production sold: 12,000 units? 15,000 units? 20,000 units?
d. Find the degree of operating leverage for the production and sales levels given in part (c) above.

9–11A. (*Breakeven Point and Operating Leverage*) Some financial data for each of three firms are given below:

	Oviedo Seeds	Gainesville Sod	Athens Peaches
Average selling price per unit	$ 14.00	$200.00	$25.00
Average variable cost per unit	$ 11.20	$130.00	$17.50
Units sold	100,000	10,000	48,000
Fixed costs	$ 25,000	$100,000	$35,000

a. What is the profit for each company at the indicated sales volume?
b. What is the breakeven point in units for each company?
c. What is the degree of operating leverage for each company at the indicated sales volume?
d. If sales were to *decline*, which firm would suffer the largest relative decline in profitability?

9–12A. (*Fixed Costs and the Breakeven Point*) Dot's Quik-Stop Party Store expects to earn $40,000 next year after taxes. Sales will be $400,000. The store is located near the fraternity-row district of Cambridge Springs State University and sells only kegs of beer for $20 a keg. The variable cost per keg is $8. The store experiences a 40 percent tax rate.
a. What are the Party Store's fixed costs expected to be next year?
b. Calculate the firm's breakeven point in both units and dollars.

9–13A. (*Fixed Costs and the Breakeven Point*) Albert's Cooling Equipment hopes to earn $80,000 next year after taxes. Sales will be $2 million. The firm's single plant is located on the edge of Slippery Rock, Pa., and manufactures only small refrigerators. These are used in many of the dormitories found on college campuses. The refrigerators sell for $80 per unit and have a variable cost of $56. Albert's experiences a 40 percent tax rate.

    a. What are the firm's fixed costs expected to be next year?

    b. Calculate the firm's breakeven point both in units and dollars.

9–14A. (*Breakeven Point and Selling Price*) Gerry's Tool and Die Company will produce 200,000 units next year. All of this production will be sold as finished goods. Fixed costs will total $300,000. Variable costs for this firm are relatively predictable at 75 percent of sales.

    a. If Gerry's Tool and Die wants to achieve an earnings before interest and taxes level of $240,000 next year, at what price per unit must it sell its product?

    b. Based on your answer to part (a), set up an analytical income statement that will verify your solution.

9–15A. (*Breakeven Point and Selling Price*) Parks Castings, Inc., will manufacture and sell 200,000 units next year. Fixed costs will total $300,000, and variable costs will be 60 percent of sales.

    a. The firm wants to achieve an earnings before interest and taxes level of $250,000. What selling price per unit is necessary to achieve this result?

    b. Set up an analytical income statement to verify your solution to part (a).

9–16A. (*Breakeven Point and Profit Margin*) A recent business graduate of Midwestern State University is planning to open a new wholesaling operation. His target operating profit margin is 28 percent. His unit contribution margin will be 50 percent of sales. Average annual sales are forecast to be $3,750,000.

    a. How large can fixed costs be for the wholesaling operation and still allow the 28 percent operating profit margin to be achieved?

    b. What is the breakeven point in dollars for the firm?

9–17A. (*Operating Leverage*) Rocky Mount Metals Company manufactures an assortment of woodburning stoves. The average selling price for the various units is $500. The associated variable cost is $350 per unit. Fixed costs for the firm average $180,000 annually.

    a. What is the breakeven point in units for the company?

    b. What is the dollar sales volume the firm must achieve to reach the breakeven point?

    c. What is the degree of operating leverage for a production and sales level of 5,000 units for the firm? (Calculate to three decimal places.)

    d. What will be the projected effect upon earnings before interest and taxes if the firm's sales level should increase by 20 percent from the volume noted in part (c) above?

9–18A. (*Breakeven Point and Operating Leverage*) The Portland Recreation Company manufactures a full line of lawn furniture. The average selling price of a finished unit is $25. The associated variable cost is $15 per unit. Fixed costs for Portland average $50,000 per year.

    a. What is the breakeven point in units for the company?

    b. What is the dollar sales volume the firm must achieve to reach the breakeven point?

    c. What would be the company's profit or loss at the following units of production sold: 4,000 units? 6,000 units? 8,000 units?

    d. Find the degree of operating leverage for the production and sales levels given in part (c) above.

    e. What is the effect on the degree of operating leverage as sales rise above the breakeven point?

9–19A. (*Fixed Costs*) Detroit Heat Treating projects that next year its fixed costs will total $120,000. Its only product sells for $12 per unit, of which $7 is a variable cost. The management of Detroit is considering the purchase of a new machine that will lower the variable cost per unit to $5. The new machine, however, will add to fixed costs through an increase in depreciation expense. How large can the *addition* to fixed costs be to keep the firm's breakeven point in units produced and sold unchanged?

9–20A. (*Operating Leverage*) The management of Detroit Heat Treating did not purchase the new piece of equipment (see problem 9–19A). Using the existing cost structure, calculate the degree of operating leverage at 30,000 units of output. Comment on the meaning of your answer.

9–21A. (*Leverage Analysis*) An analytical income statement for Detroit Heat Treating is shown below. It is based upon an output (sales) level of 40,000 units. You may refer to the original cost structure data in problem (9–19A).

Sales	$480,000
Variable costs	280,000
Revenue before fixed costs	$200,000
Fixed costs	120,000
EBIT	$ 80,000
Interest expense	30,000
Earnings before taxes	$ 50,000
Taxes	25,000
Net income	$ 25,000

a. Calculate the degree of operating leverage at this output level.
b. Calculate the degree of financial leverage at this level of EBIT.
c. Determine the combined leverage effect at this output level.

9–22A. (*Breakeven Point*) You are employed as a financial analyst for a single-product manufacturing firm. Your supervisor has made the following cost structure information available to you, all of which pertains to an output level of 1,600,000 units.

Return on operating assets	= 15% percent
Operating asset turnover	= 5 times
Operating assets	= $3 million
Degree of operating leverage	= 8 times

Your task is to find the breakeven point in units of output for the firm.

9–23A. (*Fixed Costs*) Des Moines Printing Services is forecasting fixed costs next year of $300,000. The firm's single product sells for $20 per unit and incurs a variable cost per unit of $14. The firm may acquire some new binding equipment that would lower variable cost per unit to $12. The new equipment, however, would add to fixed costs through the price of an annual maintenance agreement on the new equipment. How large can this increase in fixed costs be and still keep the firm's present breakeven point in units produced and sold unchanged?

9–24A. (*Leverage Analysis*) Your firm's cost analysis supervisor supplies you with the following analytical income statement and requests answers to the four questions listed below the statement.

Sales	$12,000,000
Variable costs	9,000,000
Revenue before fixed costs	$ 3,000,000
Fixed costs	2,000,000
EBIT	$ 1,000,000
Interest expense	200,000
Earnings before taxes	$ 800,000
Taxes	400,000
Net income	$ 400,000

a. At this level of output, what is the degree of operating leverage?
b. What is the degree of financial leverage?
c. What is the degree of combined leverage?
d. What is the firm's breakeven point in sales dollars?

9–25A. (*Leverage Analysis*) You are supplied with the following analytical income statement for your firm. It reflects last year's operations.

a. At this level of output, what is the degree of operating leverage?
b. What is the degree of financial leverage?
c. What is the degree of combined leverage?
d. If sales should increase by 20 percent, by what percent would earnings before taxes (and net income) increase?
e. What is your firm's breakeven point in sales dollars?

Sales	$16,000,000
Variable costs	8,000,000
Revenue before fixed costs	$ 8,000,000
Fixed costs	4,000,000
EBIT	$ 4,000,000
Interest expense	1,500,000
Earnings before taxes	$ 2,500,000
Taxes	1,250,000
Net income	$ 1,250,000

9–26A. (*Sales Mix and Breakeven Point*) Toledo Components produces four lines of auto accessories for the major Detroit automobile manufacturers. The lines are known by the code letters A, B, C, and D. The current sales mix for Toledo and the contribution margin ratio (unit contribution margin divided by unit sales price) for these product lines are as follows:

Product Line	Percent of Total Sales	Contribution Margin Ratio
A	33⅓%	40%
B	41⅔	32
C	16⅔	20
D	8⅓	60

Total sales for next year are forecast to be $120,000. Total fixed costs will be $29,400.
  a. Prepare a table showing (1) sales, (2) total variable costs, and (3) the total contribution margin associated with each product line.
  b. What is the aggregate contribution margin ratio indicative of this sales mix?
  c. At this sales mix, what is the breakeven point in dollars?

9–27A. (*Sales Mix and Breakeven Point*) Because of production constraints, Toledo Components (see problem 9–26A) may have to adhere to a different sales mix for next year. The alternative plan is outlined below:

Product Line	Percent of Total Sales
A	25%
B	36⅔
C	33⅓
D	5

  a. Assuming all other facts in problem 9–26A remain the same, what effect will this different sales mix have on Toledo's breakeven point in dollars?
  b. Which sales mix will Toledo's management prefer?

STUDY PROBLEMS (SET B)

9–1B. (*Breakeven Point and Operating Leverage*) Avitar Corporation manufactures a line of computer memory expansion boards used in microcomputers. The average selling price of its finished product is $175 per unit. The variable cost for these same units is $115. Avitar incurs fixed costs of $650,000 per year.
  a. What is the breakeven point in units for the company?
  b. What is the dollar sales volume the firm must achieve to reach the breakeven point?
  c. What would be the firm's profit or loss at the following units of production sold: 10,000 units? 16,000 units? 20,000 units?
  d. Find the degree of operating leverage for the production and sales levels given in part (c) above.

9–2B. (*Breakeven Point and Operating Leverage*) Some financial data for each of three firms are given below:

	Durham Furniture	Raleigh Cabinets	Charlotte Colonials
Average selling price per unit	$20.00	$435.00	$35.00
Average variable cost per unit	$13.75	$240.00	$15.75
Units sold	80,000	4,500	15,000
Fixed costs	$40,000	$150,000	$60,000

    a. What is the profit for each company at the indicated sales volume?
    b. What is the breakeven point in units for each company?
    c. What is the degree of operating leverage for each company at the indicated sales volume?
    d. If sales were to decline, which firm would suffer the largest relative decline in profitability?

9–3B. (*Fixed Costs and the Breakeven Point*) Cypress Books expects to earn $55,000 next year after taxes. Sales will be $400,008. The store is located near the shopping district surrounding Sheffield University. Its average product sells for $28 a unit. The variable cost per unit is $18. The store experiences a 45 percent tax rate.
    a. What are the store's fixed costs expected to be next year?
    b. Calculate the store's breakeven point in both units and dollars.

9–4B. (*Breakeven Point and Profit Margin*) A recent graduate of Neeley University is planning to open a new wholesaling operation. Her target operating profit margin is 28 percent. Her unit contribution margin will be 45 percent of sales. Average annual sales are forecast to be $3,750,000.
    a. How large can fixed costs be for the wholesaling operation and still allow the 28 percent operating profit margin to be achieved?
    b. What is the breakeven point in dollars for the firm?

9–5B. (*Leverage Analysis*) You have developed the following analytical income statement for your corporation. It represents the most recent year's operations, which ended yesterday.

Sales	$40,000,000
Variable costs	16,000,000
Revenue before fixed costs	$24,000,000
Fixed costs	10,000,000
EBIT	$14,000,000
Interest expense	1,150,000
Earnings before taxes	$12,850,000
Taxes	3,750,000
Net income	$ 9,100,000

Your supervisor in the controller's office has just handed you a memorandum asking for written responses to the following questions:
    a. At this level of output, what is the degree of operating leverage?
    b. What is the degree of financial leverage?
    c. What is the degree of combined leverage?
    d. What is the firm's breakeven point in sales dollars?
    e. If sales should increase by 20 percent, by what percent would earnings before taxes (and net income) increase?

9–6B. (*Breakeven Point*) You are a hard-working analyst in the office of financial operations for a manufacturing firm that produces a single product. You have developed the following cost structure information for this company. All of it pertains to an output level of 7 million units. Using this information, find the breakeven point in units of output for the firm.

Return on operating assets	= 25%
Operating asset turnover	= 5 times
Operating assets	= $18 million
Degree of operating leverage	= 6 times

9–7B. (*Breakeven Point and Operating Leverage*) Matthew Electronics manufactures a complete line of radio and communication equipment for law enforcement agencies. The average selling price of its finished product is $175 per unit. The variable cost for these same units is $140. Matthew's incurs fixed costs of $550,000 per year.

    a. What is the breakeven point in units for the company?

    b. What is the dollar sales volume the firm must achieve to reach the breakeven point?

    c. What would be the firm's profit or loss at the following units of production sold: 12,000 units? 15,000 units? 20,000 units?

    d. Find the degree of operating leverage for the production and sales levels given in part (c) above.

9–8B. (*Breakeven Point and Operating Leverage*) Some financial data for each of three firms are given below:

	Farm City Seeds	Empire Sod	Golden Peaches
Average selling price per unit	$ 15.00	$190.00	$28.00
Average variable cost per unit	$ 11.75	$145.00	$19.00
Units sold	120,000	9,000	50,000
Fixed costs	$ 30,000	$110,000	$33,000

    a. What is the profit for each company at the indicated sales volume?

    b. What is the breakeven point in units for each company?

    c. What is the degree of operating leverage for each company at the indicated sales volume?

    d. If sales were to *decline*, which firm would suffer the largest relative decline in profitability?

9–9B. (*Fixed Costs and the Breakeven Point*) Keller's Keg expects to earn $38,000 next year after taxes. Sales will be $420,002. The store is located near the fraternity-row district of Blue Springs State University and sells only kegs of beer for $17 a keg. The variable cost per keg is $9. The store experiences a 35 percent tax rate.

    a. What are Keller Keg's fixed costs expected to be next year?

    b. Calculate the firm's breakeven point in both units and dollars.

9–10B. (*Fixed Costs and the Breakeven Point*) Mini-Kool hopes to earn $70,000 next year after taxes. Sales will be $2,500,050. The firm's single plant manufactures only small refrigerators. These are used in many recreational campers. The refrigerators sell for $75 per unit and have a variable cost of $58. Albert's experiences a 45 percent tax rate.

    a. What are the firm's fixed costs expected to be next year?

    b. Calculate the firm's breakeven point both in units and dollars.

9–11B. (*Breakeven Point and Selling Price*) Heritage Chain Company will produce 175,000 units next year. All of this production will be sold as finished goods. Fixed costs will total $335,000. Variable costs for this firm are relatively predictable at 80 percent of sales.

    a. If Heritage Chain wants to achieve an earnings before interest and taxes level of $270,000 next year, at what price per unit must it sell its product?

    b. Based on your answer to part (a), set up an analytical income statement that will verify your solution.

9–12B. (*Breakeven Point and Selling Price*) Thomas Appliances, will manufacture and sell 190,000 units next year. Fixed costs will total $300,000, and variable costs will be 75 percent of sales.

    a. The firm wants to achieve an earnings before interest and taxes level of $250,000. What selling price per unit is necessary to achieve this result?

    b. Set up an analytical income statement to verify your solution to part (a).

9–13B. (*Breakeven Point and Profit Margin*) A recent business graduate of Dewey University is planning to open a new wholesaling operation. His target operating profit margin is 25 percent. His unit contribution margin will be 60 percent of sales. Average annual sales are forecast to be $4,250,000.

    a. How large can fixed costs be for the wholesaling operation and still allow the 25 percent operating profit margin to be achieved?

    b. What is the breakeven point in dollars for the firm?

9–14B. (*Operating Leverage*) The B. H. Williams Company manufactures an assortment of woodburning stoves. The average selling price for the various units is $475. The associated variable cost is $350 per unit. Fixed costs for the firm average $200,000 annually.

    a. What is the breakeven point in units for the company?

    b. What is the dollar sales volume the firm must achieve to reach the breakeven point?

    c. What is the degree of operating leverage for a production and sales level of 6,000 units for the firm? (Calculate to three decimal places.)

    d. What will be the projected effect on earnings before interest and taxes if the firm's sales level should increase by 13 percent from the volume noted in part (c) above?

9–15B. (*Breakeven Point and Operating Leverage*) The Palm Patio Company manufactures a full line of lawn furniture. The average selling price of a finished unit is $28. The associated variable cost is $17 per unit. Fixed costs for Palm Patio average $55,000 per year.

    a. What is the breakeven point in units for the company?

    b. What is the dollar sales volume the firm must achieve to reach the breakeven point?

    c. What would be the company's profit or loss at the following units of production sold: 4,000 units? 6,000 units? 8,000 units?

    d. Find the degree of operating leverage for the production and sales levels given in part (c) above.

    e. What is the effect on the degree of operating leverage as sales rise above the breakeven point?

9–16B. (*Fixed Costs*) Tropical Sun projects that next year its fixed costs will total $135,000. Its only product sells for $13 per unit, of which $6 is a variable cost. The management of Tropical is considering the purchase of a new machine that will lower the variable cost per unit to $5. The new machine, however, will add to fixed costs through an increase in depreciation expense. How large can the *addition* to fixed costs be to keep the firm's breakeven point in units produced and sold unchanged?

9–17B. (*Operating Leverage*) The management of Tropical Sun did not purchase the new piece of equipment (see problem 9–16B). Using the existing cost structure, calculate the degree of operating leverage at 40,000 units of output. Comment on the meaning of your answer.

9–18B. (*Leverage Analysis*) An analytical income statement for Tropical Sun is shown below. It is based on an output (sales) level of 50,000 units. You may refer to the original cost structure data in problem (9–16B).

Sales	$650,000
Variable costs	300,000
Revenue before fixed costs	$350,000
Fixed costs	135,000
EBIT	$215,000
Interest expense	60,000
Earnings before taxes	$155,000
Taxes	70,000
Net income	$ 85,000

    a. Calculate the degree of operating leverage at this output level.

    b. Calculate the degree of financial leverage at this level of EBIT.

    c. Determine the combined leverage effect at this output level.

9–19B. (*Breakeven Point*) You are employed as a financial analyst for a single-product manufacturing firm. Your supervisor has made the following cost structure information available to you, all of which pertains to an output level of 1,700,000 units.

Return on operating assets	= 16 percent
Operating asset turnover	= 6 times
Operating assets	= $3.25 million
Degree of operating leverage	= 9 times

Your task is to find the breakeven point in units of output for the firm.

9-20B. (*Fixed Costs*) Sausalito Silkscreen is forecasting fixed costs next year of $375,000. The firm's single product sells for $25 per unit and incurs a variable cost per unit of $13. The firm may acquire some new binding equipment that would lower variable cost per unit to $11. The new equipment, however, would add to fixed costs through the price of an annual maintenance agreement on the new equipment. How large can this increase in fixed costs be and still keep the firm's present breakeven point in units produced and sold unchanged?

9-21B. (*Leverage Analysis*) Your firm's cost analysis supervisor supplies you with the following analytical income statement and requests answers to the four questions listed below the statement.

Sales	$13,750,000
Variable costs	9,500,000
Revenue before fixed costs	$ 4,250,000
Fixed costs	3,000,000
EBIT	$ 1,250,000
Interest expense	250,000
Earnings before taxes	$ 1,000,000
Taxes	430,000
Net income	$ 570,000

a. At this level of output, what is the degree of operating leverage?
b. What is the degree of financial leverage?
c. What is the degree of combined leverage?
d. What is the firm's breakeven point in sales dollars?

9-22B. (*Leverage Analysis*) You are supplied with the following analytical income statement for your firm. It reflects last year's operations.

Sales	$18,000,000
Variable costs	7,000,000
Revenue before fixed costs	$11,000,000
Fixed costs	6,000,000
EBIT	$ 5,000,000
Interest expense	1,750,000
Earnings before taxes	$ 3,250,000
Taxes	1,250,000
Net income	$ 2,000,000

a. At this level of output, what is the degree of operating leverage?
b. What is the degree of financial leverage?
c. What is the degree of combined leverage?
d. If sales should increase by 15 percent, by what percent would earnings before taxes (and net income) increase?
e. What is your firm's breakeven point in sales dollars?

9-23B. (*Sales Mix and the Breakeven Point*) Wayne Automotive produces four lines of auto accessories for the major Detroit automobile manufacturers. The lines are known by the code letters A, B, C, and D. The current sales mix for Wayne and the contribution margin ratio (unit contribution margin divided by unit sales price) for these product lines are as follows:

Product Line	Percent of Total Sales	Contribution Margin Ratio
A	25⅔%	40%
B	41⅓	32
C	19⅔	20
D	13⅓	60

Total sales for next year are forecast to be $150,000. Total fixed costs will be $35,000.

a. Prepare a table showing (1) sales, (2) total variable costs, and (3) the total contribution margin associated with each product line.

b. What is the aggregate contribution margin ratio indicative of this sales mix?

c. At this sales mix, what is the breakeven point in dollars?

9–24B. (*Sales Mix and the Breakeven Point*) Because of production constraints, Wayne Automotive (see problem 9–23B) may have to adhere to a different sales mix for next year. The alternative plan is outlined below:

Product Line	Percent of Total Sales
A	33⅓%
B	41⅔
C	16⅔
D	8⅓

a. Assuming all other facts in problem 9–23B remain the same, what effect will this different sales mix have on Wayne's breakeven point in dollars?

b. Which sales mix will Wayne's management prefer?

Suggested Application for DISCLOSURE®

Access the *Disclosure* database and review the financial statements for J. C. Penney Co. For the most recent two years, identify the firm's (a) sales, (b) operating profits, and (c) net income. Calculate the percentage change for each item. Use this information to estimate the firm's (a) degree of operating leverage, (b) degree of financial leverage, and (c) degree of combined leverage. Interpret your answers.

CASE PROBLEM

ERIE GENERAL PRODUCERS

BREAKEVEN ANALYSIS, OPERATING LEVERAGE, FINANCIAL LEVERAGE

Erie General Producers (EGP) is a medium-size public corporation that until recently consisted of two divisions. The Retail Furniture Group (RFG) has eight locations in the northeastern Ohio area, mostly concentrated around Cleveland. These retail outlets generate sales of contemporary, traditional, and early American furniture. In addition, casual and leisure furniture lines are carried by the stores. The other (old) division of EGP is its Concrete Group (CG). The CG operates three plants in the North Tonawanda area of western New York. These plants produce precast concrete wall panels and concrete stave farm silos. The company headquarters of EGP is located in Erie, Pa. This community touches Lake Erie in northwestern Pennsylvania and is about 140 miles north of Pittsburgh. Because Erie is almost equidistant from Cleveland and North Tonawanda and is a connecting hub for several interstate highways, it makes a sensible spot for the firm's home offices.

EGP was started 10 years ago as Erie Producers by its current president and board chairman, Anthony Toscano. During the firm's existence it has enjoyed periods of both moderate and strong growth in sales, assets, and earnings. Key managerial decisions have always been dominated by Toscano, who openly boasts of the fact that his company has never suffered through a year of negative earnings despite the often cyclical nature of both the retail furniture (RFG) and concrete (CG) divisions.

Recently Mr. Toscano decided to acquire a third division for his firm. The division manufactures special machinery for the seafood processing industry and is appropriately called the Seafood Industry Group (SIG). The financial settlement for the acquisition took place yesterday. Currently, the SIG consists of one manufacturing plant in Erie. A single product is to be manufactured, assembled, and shipped from the facility. That product, however, represents a design breakthrough and carries with it a projected contribution margin ratio of .4000. This is greater than that enjoyed by either of EGP's other two divisions.

EGP's manufacturing operation in Erie will produce a new machine called "The Picker." The Picker was invented and successfully tested by Ben Pinkerton, the major stockholder and manager of a small seafood processing firm in Morattico, Va. Pinkerton plans and supervises all operations at Eastern Shore Processors. Eastern Shore specializes in freezing and pasteurizing crab meat. Freezing and pasteurizing procedures have been a boon to the seafood industry, for they permit the processor to retain a product without spoilage in hopes of higher prices at a later date. In comparing his industry to that of agriculture, Pinkerton aptly states: "The freezer is our grain elevator."

The seafood processing industry is characterized by a notable lack of capital equipment and a corresponding heavy use of human labor. Pinkerton will tell you that at Eastern Shore Processors a skilled crab meat picker will produce about 30 pounds of meat per day. No matter how skilled the human picker, however, he will leave about 10 pounds of meat per day in the top piece of the crab shell. This past year, after five years of trying, Pinkerton perfected a machine that would recover about 30 percent of this otherwise lost meat. In exchange for cash, Eastern Shore Processors sold all rights to The Picker to EGP. Thus, Toscano established the SIG and immediately made plans to manufacture The Picker.

Recent income statements for the older divisions of EGP are contained in Exhibits 1 and 2. Toscano has now decided to assess more fully the probable impact of the decision to establish the SIG on the financial condition of EGP. Toscano knew that such figures should have been generated prior to the decision to enter this special field, but his seasoned judgment led him to a quick choice. He has requested several pieces of information, detailed below, from his chief financial officer.

		EXHIBIT 1.
Sales	$12,000,000	Erie General Producers
Less: total variable costs	7,920,000	Retail Furniture Group
Revenue before fixed costs	$ 4,080,000	Income Statement,
Less: total fixed costs	2,544,000	December 31, Last Year
EBIT	$ 1,536,000	
Less: interest expense	192,000	
Earnings before taxes	$ 1,344,000	
Less: taxes @ 50%	672,000	
Net profit	$ 672,000	

		EXHIBIT 2.
Sales	$8,000,000	Erie General Producers
Less: total variable costs	5,920,000	Concrete Group
Revenue before fixed costs	$2,080,000	Income Statement,
Less: total fixed costs	640,000	December 31, Last Year
EBIT	$1,440,000	
Less: interest expense	80,000	
Earnings before taxes	$1,360,000	
Less: taxes @ 50%	680,000	
Net profit	$ 680,000	

QUESTIONS AND PROBLEMS

1. Using last year's results, determine the breakeven point in dollars for EGP (i.e., before investing in the new SIG). The breakeven point is defined here in the traditional manner where EBIT = $0. (*Hint:* Use an aggregate contribution-margin ratio in your analysis.)

2. Using last year's results, determine what volume of sales must be reached to cover *all* before-tax costs.

3. Next year's sales for the SIG are projected to be $4,000,000. Total fixed costs will be $640,000. This division will have no outstanding debt on its balance sheet. EGP uses a 50 percent tax rate in all its financial projections. Using the format of Exhibits 1 and 2, construct a pro forma income statement for the SIG.

4. After the SIG begins operations, what will be EGP's breakeven point in dollars (a) as traditionally defined and (b) reflecting the coverage of *all* before-tax costs? Base the

new sales mix on last year's sales performance for the older divisions plus that anticipated next year for the SIG. Using your answer to part (b) of this question, construct an analytical income statement demonstrating that earnings before taxes = $0.

5. Using next year's anticipated sales volume for EGP (including the SIG), compute (a) the degree of operating leverage, (b) the degree of financial leverage, and (c) the degree of combined leverage. Comment on the meaning of each of these statistics.

6. Using projected figures, determine whether acquisition of the SIG will increase or decrease the vulnerability of EGP's earnings before interest and taxes (EBIT) to cyclical swings in sales. Show your work.

7. Review the key assumptions of cost-volume-profit analysis.

SELF-TEST SOLUTIONS

SS-1. *Step 1: Compute the operating profit margin:*

$$(\text{margin}) \times (\text{turnover}) = \text{return on operating assets}$$
$$(M) \quad \times \quad (6) \quad = 0.30$$
$$M = 0.30/6 = 0.05$$

Step 2: Compute the sales level associated with the given output level:

$$\frac{\text{sales}}{\$20,000,000} = 6$$
$$\text{sales} = \$120,000,000$$

Step 3: Compute EBIT:

$$(.05) (\$120,000,000) = \$6,000,000 = \text{EBIT}$$

Step 4: Compute revenue before fixed costs. Because the degree of operating leverage is 4.5 times, revenue before fixed costs (RBF) is 4.5 times EBIT, as follows:

$$\text{RBF} = (4.5) (\$6,000,000) = \$27,000,000$$

Step 5: Compute total variable costs:

$$(\text{sales}) - (\text{total variable costs}) = \$27,000,000$$
$$\$120,000,000 - (\text{total variable costs}) = \$27,000,000$$
$$\text{total variable costs} = \$93,000,000$$

Step 6: Compute total fixed costs:

$$\text{RBF} - \text{fixed costs} = \text{EBIT}$$
$$\$27,000,000 - \text{fixed costs} = \$6,000,000$$
$$\text{Fixed costs} = \$21,000,000$$

Step 7: Find the selling price per unit (P), and the variable cost per unit (V):

$$P = \frac{\text{sales}}{\text{output in units}} = \frac{\$120,000,000}{10,000,000} = \$12.00$$

$$V = \frac{\text{total variable costs}}{\text{output in units}} = \frac{\$93,000,000}{10,000,000} = \$9.30$$

Step 8: Compute the breakeven point:

$$Q_B = \frac{F}{P - V} = \frac{\$21,000,000}{\$12.00 - \$9.30}$$

$$= \frac{\$21,000,000}{\$2.70} = \underline{\$7,777,778 \text{ units}}$$

The firm will break even when it produces and sells 7,777,778 units.

SS–2: **a.** $\dfrac{\text{Revenue before fixed costs}}{\text{EBIT}} = \dfrac{\$8,000,000}{\$3,000,000} = \underline{2.67 \text{ times}}$

b. $\dfrac{\text{EBIT}}{\text{EBIT} - I} = \dfrac{\$3,000,000}{\$2,000,000} = \underline{1.50 \text{ times}}$

c. $\text{DCL}_{\$20,000,000} = (2.67)(1.50) = \underline{4.00 \text{ times}}$

d. $S^* = \dfrac{F}{1 - \dfrac{VC}{S}} = \dfrac{\$5,000,000}{1 - \dfrac{\$12\,M}{\$20\,M}} = \dfrac{\$5,000,000}{1 - 0.60} = \dfrac{\$5,000,000}{0.40} = \underline{\$12,500,000}$

e. $(30\%)(4.00) = \underline{120\%}$

f.

Sales	$26,000,000
Variable costs	15,600,000
Revenue before fixed costs	$10,400,000
Fixed costs	5,000,000
EBIT	$ 5,400,000
Interest expense	1,000,000
Earnings before taxes	$ 4,400,000
Taxes (0.50)	2,200,000
Net income	$ 2,200,000

We know that sales have increased by 30 percent to $26 million from the base sales level of $20 million.

Let us focus now on the change in earnings before taxes. We can compute that change as follows:

$$\frac{\$4,400,000 - \$2,000,000}{\$2,000,000} = \frac{\$2,400,000}{\$2,000,000} = 120\%$$

Because the tax rate was held constant, the percentage change in net income will also equal 120 percent. The fluctuations implied by the degree of combined leverage measure are therefore accurately reflected in this analytical income statement.

SS–3. **a.** $\{(P \cdot Q) - [V \cdot Q + (F)]\}\,(1 - T) = \$210,000$

$[(\$4,000,000) - (\$3,000,000) - F]\,(.7) = \$210,000$

$(\$1,000,000 - F)\,(.7) = \$210,000$

$\$700,000 - .7F = \$210,000$

$.7F = \$490,000$

$F = \underline{\$700,000}$

Fixed costs next year, then, are expected to be $700,000.

b. $Q_B = \dfrac{F}{P - V} = \dfrac{\$700,000}{\$50} = \underline{14,000 \text{ units}}$

$S^* = \dfrac{F}{1 - \dfrac{VC}{S}} = \dfrac{\$700,000}{1 - .75} = \dfrac{\$700,000}{.25} = \underline{\$2,800,000}$

The firm will breakeven (EBIT = 0) when it sells 14,000 units. With a selling price of $200 per unit, the breakeven sales level is $2,800,000.

CHAPTER *10*

Planning the Firm's Financing Mix

A Glance at Capital Structure Theory • Basic Tools of Capital Structure Management • A Glance at Actual Capital Structure Management • International Perspective

In this chapter we direct our attention to the determination of an appropriate financing mix for the firm. First, we must distinguish between financial structure and capital structure. **Financial structure** is the mix of all items that appear on the right-hand side of the company's balance sheet. **Capital structure** is the mix of the *long-term* sources of funds used by the firm. The relationship between financial and capital structure can be expressed in equation form:

$$\text{(financial structure)} - \text{(current liabilities)} = \text{capital structure} \quad \textbf{(10–1)}$$

Prudent **financial structure design** requires answers to the following two questions:

1. What should be the maturity composition of the firm's sources of funds; in other words, how should a firm best divide its total fund sources between short- and long-term components?

2. In what proportions relative to the total should the various forms of *permanent* financing be utilized?

The major influence on the maturity structure of the financing plan is the nature of the assets owned by the firm. A company heavily committed to real capital investment, represented primarily by fixed assets on its balance sheet, *should* finance those assets with permanent (long-term) types of financial capital. Furthermore, the permanent portion of the firm's investment in current assets should likewise be financed with permanent capital. Alternatively, assets held on a temporary basis are to be financed with temporary sources. The present discussion assumes that the bulk of the company's current liabilities are comprised of temporary capital.

This **hedging concept** is discussed in both Chapters 14 and 17. Accordingly, our focus in this chapter is an answer to the second of the two questions noted previously—this process is usually called *capital-structure management*.

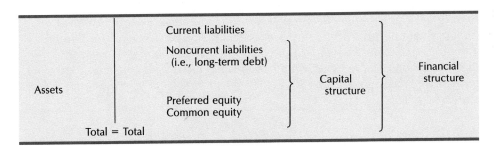

TABLE 10–1.
Balance Sheet

The *objective* of capital-structure management is to mix the permanent sources of funds used by the firm in a manner that will maximize the company's common stock price. Alternatively, this objective may be viewed as a search for the funds mix that will minimize the firm's composite cost of capital. We can call this proper mix of funds sources the **optimal capital structure.**

Table 10–1 looks at equation (10–1) in terms of a simplified balance sheet format. It helps us visualize the overriding problem of capital structure management. The sources of funds that give rise to financing fixed costs (long-term debt and preferred equity) must be combined with common equity in the proportions most suitable to the investing marketplace. If that mix can be found, then holding all other factors constant, the firm's common stock price will be maximized.

While equation (10–1) quite accurately indicates that the corporate capital structure may be viewed as an absolute dollar *amount*, the *real* capital structure problem is one of balancing the array of funds sources in a proper manner. Our use of the term *capital structure* emphasizes this latter problem of relative magnitude, or proportions.

The rest of this chapter will cover three main areas. First, we discuss the theory of capital structure to provide a perspective. Second, we examine the basic tools of capital structure management. We conclude with a real-world look at actual capital structure management.

Perspective in Finance

It pays to understand the essential components of capital structure theory. The assumption of excessive financial risk can put the firm into bankruptcy proceed-

---

BASIC FINANCIAL MANAGEMENT IN PRACTICE

Financing Mix and Corporate Strategy

It is important to understand the basics of capital structure theory because the choice of an appropriate *financing mix* is a central component of overall business strategy. The theory, then, affects strategy.

This is illustrated in the following excerpt from the 1985 annual report published by the Coca-Cola Company. Notice how the concepts of *financial leverage* and *debt capacity* are woven into the discussion.

In the financial arena, the Coca-Cola Company is pursuing a more aggressive policy. We are using greater financial leverage whenever strategic investment opportunities are available. We are reinvesting a larger portion of our earnings by increasing dividends at a lesser rate than earnings per share growth. We are maintaining our

effective income tax rate at a level well below our historical rate. And, we are continuing to repurchase our common shares when excess cash or debt capacity exceed near-term investment requirements.

Another principle in our strategy requires us to consider divesting assets when they no longer generate acceptable returns and earnings growth or are inconsistent with our focus on consumer products. Accordingly, over the last five years we have sold a wine business, a private-label instant coffee and tea unit, a boiler and industrial water purification subsidiary, a regional pasta operation and private-label plastic products businesses.

Source: The Coca-Cola Company, *Annual Report*, 1985, p. 6.

ings. Some argue that the decision to use little financial leverage results in an undervaluation of the firm's shares in the marketplace. The effective financial manager must know how to find the area of optimum financial leverage use—this will enhance share value, all other considerations held constant. Thus, grasping the theory will make you better able to formulate a sound financial structure policy.

A Glance at Capital Structure Theory

An enduring controversy within financial theory concerns the effect of financial leverage on the overall cost of capital to the enterprise. The heart of the argument may be stated in the form of a question:

Can the firm affect its overall cost of funds, either favorably or unfavorably, by varying the mixture of financing sources used?

This controversy has taken many elegant forms in the finance literature. Most of these presentations appeal more to academics than financial management practitioners. To emphasize the ingredients of capital structure theory that have practical applications for business financial management, we will pursue an intuitive, or nonmathematical, approach to reach a better understanding of the underpinnings of this *cost of capital–capital structure argument*.

The Importance of Capital Structure

It makes economic sense for the firm to strive to minimize the cost of using financial capital. Both capital costs and other costs, such as manufacturing costs, share a common characteristic in that they potentially reduce the size of the cash dividend that could be paid to common stockholders.

We saw in Chapters 5 and 8 that the ultimate value of a share of common stock depends in part on the returns investors expect to receive from holding the stock. Cash dividends comprise all (in the case of an infinite holding period) or part (in the case of a holding period less than infinity) of these expected returns. Now, hold constant all factors that could affect share price except capital costs. If these capital costs could be kept at a minimum, the dividend stream flowing to the common stockholders would be maximized. This, in turn, would maximize the firm's common stock price.

If the firm's cost of capital can be affected by its capital structure, then capital structure management is clearly an important subset of business financial management.

Analytical Setting

The essentials of the capital structure controversy are best highlighted within a framework that economists would call a "partial equilibrium analysis." In a partial equilibrium analysis changes that *do* occur in several factors and have an impact on a certain key item are ignored to study the effect of changes in a main factor on that same item of interest. Here, two items are simultaneously of interest: (1) K_0, the firm's composite cost of capital, and (2) P_0, the market price of the firm's common stock. The firm's use of financial leverage is the main factor that is allowed to vary in the analysis. This means that important financial decisions, such as investing policy and dividend policy, are held constant throughout the discussion. We are concerned with the effect of changes in the financing mix on share price and capital costs.

Our analysis will be facilitated if we adopt a *simplified* version of the basic dividend valuation model presented in Chapter 5 in our study of valuation principles and in Chapter 8 in our assessment of the cost of capital. That model is shown below as equation (10–2):

$$P_0 = \sum_{t=1}^{\infty} \frac{D_t}{(1 + K_c)^t} \qquad (10\text{–}2)$$

where P_0 = the current price of the firm's common stock

D_t = the cash dividend per share expected by investors during period t

K_c = the cost of common equity capital

We can strip away some complications by making the following assumptions concerning the valuation process implicit in equation (10–2):

1. Cash dividends paid will not change over the infinite holding period. Thus, $D_1 = D_2 = D_3 = \ldots = D_\infty$. There is no expected growth by investors in the dividend stream.
2. The firm retains none of its current earnings. This means that *all* of each period's per-share earnings are paid to stockholders in the form of cash dividends. The firm's dividend payout ratio is 100 percent. Cash dividends per share in equation (10–2), then, also equal earnings per share for the same period.

ASSUMPTIONS

Under these assumptions, the cash dividend flowing to investors can be viewed as a level payment over an infinite holding period. The payment stream is perpetual, and according to the mathematics of perpetuities, equation (10–2) reduces to equation (10–3), where E_t represents earnings per share during period t.

$$P_0 = \frac{D_t}{K_c} = \frac{E_t}{K_c} \qquad (10\text{–}3)$$

In addition to the suppositions noted above, the analytical setting for the discussion of capital structure theory includes the following assumptions:

1. Corporate income is not subject to any taxation. The major implication of removing this assumption is discussed later.
2. Capital structures consist of only stocks and bonds. Furthermore, the degree of financial leverage used by the firm is altered by the issuance of

common stock with the proceeds used to retire existing debt, or the issuance of debt with the proceeds used to repurchase stock. This permits leverage use to vary but maintains constancy of the total book value of the firm's capital structure.

3. The expected values of all investors' forecasts of the future levels of net operating income (EBIT) for each firm are identical. Say that you forecast the average level of EBIT to be achieved by General Motors over a very long period ($n \rightarrow \infty$). Your forecast will be the same as our forecast, and both will be equal to the forecasts of all other investors interested in General Motors common stock. In addition, we do not expect General Motors' EBIT to grow over time. Each year's forecast is the same as any other year's. This is consistent with our assumption underlying equation (10–3), where the firm's dividend stream is not expected to grow.

4. Securities are traded in perfect or efficient financial markets. This means that transaction costs and legal restrictions do not impede any investors' incentives to execute portfolio changes that they expect will increase their wealth. Information is freely available. Moreover, corporations and individuals that are equal credit risks can borrow funds at the same rates of interest.

This completes our description of the analytical setting. We now discuss three differing views on the relationship between use of financial leverage and common stock value.

Perspective in Finance

The discussion and illustrations of the two extreme positions on the importance of capital structure that follow are meant to highlight the critical differences between differing viewpoints. This is not to say that the markets really behave in strict accordance with either position—they don't. The point is to identify polar positions on how things might *work. Then by* relaxing *various restrictive assumptions, a more useful theory of how financing decisions are actually made becomes possible. That results in the third, or moderate, view.*

Extreme Position 1: Independence Hypothesis (NOI Theory)[1]

The crux of this position is that the firm's composite cost of capital, K_0, and common stock price, P_0, are both *independent* of the degree to which the company chooses to use financial leverage. In other words, no matter how *modest* or *excessive* the firm's use of debt financing, its common stock price will not be affected. Let us illustrate the mechanics of this point of view.

Suppose that Rix Camper Manufacturing Company has the following financial characteristics:

> Shares of common stock outstanding = 2,000,000 shares
> Common stock price, P_0 = \$10 per share
> Expected level of net operating income (EBIT) = \$2,000,000
> Dividend payout ratio = 100 percent

---

[1]The net operating income and net income capitalization methods, which are referred to here as "extreme positions 1 and 2," were first presented in comprehensible form by Durand. See David Durand, "Costs of Debt and Equity Funds for Business: Trends and Problems of Measurement," *Conference on Research in Business Finance* (New York: National Bureau of Economic Research, 1952), reprinted in Ezra Solomon, ed., *The Management of Corporate Capital* (New York: Free Press, 1959), pp. 91–116. The leading proponents of the independence hypothesis in its various forms are Professors Modigliani and Miller. See Franco Modigliani and Merton H. Miller, "The Cost of Capital, Corporation Finance and the Theory of Investment," *American Economic Review* 48 (June 1958), pp. 261–97; Franco Modigliani and Merton H. Miller, "Corporate Income Taxes and the Cost of Capital: A Correction," *American Economic Review* 53 (June 1963), pp. 433–43; and Merton H. Miller, "Debt and Taxes," *Journal of Finance* 32 (May 1977), pp. 261–75.

Capital Structure Information	
Shares of common stock outstanding = 1,200,000	
Bonds at 6 percent = $8,000,000	
Earnings Information	
Expected level of net operating income (EBIT) =	$2,000,000
Less: Interest expense	480,000
Earnings available to common stockholders	$1,520,000
Earnings per share (E_t)	$1.267
Dividends per share (D_t)	$1.267
Percentage change in both earnings per share and dividends per share relative to the unlevered capital structure	26.7 percent

Currently the firm uses no financial leverage; its capital structure consists entirely of common equity. Earnings per share and dividends per share equal $1 each. When the capital structure is all common equity, the cost of common equity, K_c, and the weighted cost of capital, K_0, are equal. If equation (10–3) is restated in terms of the cost of common equity, we have for Rix Camper

$$K_c = \frac{D_t}{P_0} = \frac{\$1}{\$10} = 10\%$$

Now, the management of Rix Camper decides to use some debt capital in its financing mix. The firm sells $8 million worth of long-term debt at an interest rate of 6 percent. With no taxation of corporate income, this 6 percent interest rate is the cost of debt capital, K_d. The firm uses the proceeds from the sale of the bonds to repurchase 40 percent of its outstanding common shares. After the capital-structure change has been accomplished, Rix Camper Manufacturing Company has the financial characteristics displayed in Table 10–2.

Based on the preceding data we notice that the recapitalization (capital structure change) of Rix Camper will result in a dividend paid to owners that is 26.7 percent higher than it was when the firm used no debt in its capital structure. Will this higher dividend result in a lower composite cost of capital to Rix and a higher common stock price? According to the principles of the independence hypothesis, the answer is "No."

The independence hypothesis suggests that the total market value of the firm's outstanding securities is *unaffected* by the manner in which the right-hand side of the balance sheet is arranged. That is, the sum of the market value of outstanding debt plus the sum of the market value of outstanding common equity will always be the *same* regardless of how much or little debt is actually used by the company. If capital structure has no impact on the total market value of the company, then that value is arrived at by the marketplace's capitalizing (discounting) the firm's expected net operating income stream. Therefore, the independence hypothesis rests upon what is called the **net operating income (NOI) approach to valuation.**

The format is a very simple one, and the market value of the firm's common stock turns out to be a residual of the valuation process. Recall that before Rix Camper's recapitalization, the total market value of the firm was $20 million (2 million common shares times $10 per share). The firm's cost of common equity, K_c, and its weighted cost of capital, K_0, were each equal to 10 percent. The composite discount rate, K_0, is used to arrive at the market value of the firm's securities. After the recapitalization, we have for Rix Camper

	Expected level of net operating income Capitalized at K_O = 10 percent	$ 2,000,000
=	Market value of debt and equity	$20,000,000
−	Market value of the new debt	8,000,000
=	Market value of the common stock	$12,000,000

With this valuation format, what is the market price of each share of common stock? Because we know that 1.2 million shares of stock are outstanding after the capital structure change, the market price per share is $10 ($12 million/1.2 million). This is exactly the market value per share, P_0, that existed *before* the change.

Now, if the firm is using some debt that has an *explicit cost* of 6 percent, K_d, and the weighted (composite) cost of capital, K_0, is still 10 percent, it stands to reason that the cost of common equity, K_c, has risen above its previous level of 10 percent. What will the cost of common equity be in this situation? As we did previously, we can take equation (10–3) and restate it in terms of K_c, the cost of common equity. After the recapitalization, the cost of common equity for Rix Camper is shown to *rise* to 12.67 percent:

$$K_c = \frac{D_t}{P_0} = \frac{\$1.267}{\$10} = 12.67\%$$

The cost of common equity for Rix Camper is 26.7 percent higher than it was before the capital structure shift. Notice in Table 10–2 that this is *exactly* equal to the percentage increase in earnings and dividends per share that accompanies the same capital structure adjustment. This highlights a fundamental relationship that is an integral part of the independence hypothesis. It concerns the perceived behavior in the firm's cost of common equity as expected dividends (earnings) increase relative to a financing mix change:

$$\text{percentage change in } K_c = \text{percentage change in } D_t$$

In this framework the use of a greater degree of financial leverage may result in greater earnings and dividends, but the firm's cost of common equity will rise at precisely the same rate as the earnings and dividends do. Thus, the inevitable tradeoff between the higher expected return in dividends and earnings (D_t and E_t) and increased risk that accompanies the use of debt financing manifests itself in a linear relationship between the cost of common equity (K_c) and financial leverage use. This view of the relationship between the firm's cost of funds and its financing mix is shown graphically in Figure 10–1. Figure 10–2 relates the firm's stock price to its financing mix under the same set of assumptions.

In Figure 10–1 the firm's overall cost of capital, K_0, is shown to be unaffected by an increased use of financial leverage. If more debt is used in the

FIGURE 10–1.
Capital Costs and Financial Leverage: No Taxes — Independence Hypothesis (NOI Theory)

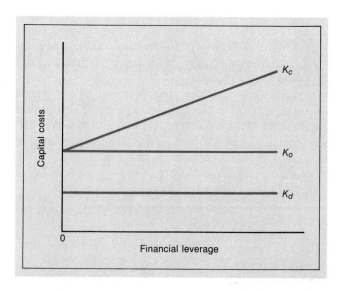

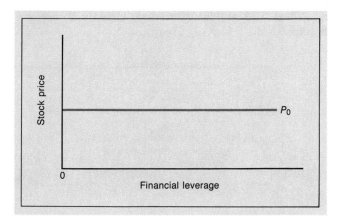

capital structure, the cost of common equity will rise at the same rate additional earnings are generated. This will keep the composite cost of capital to the corporation unchanged. Figure 10-2 shows that because the cost of capital will not change with the leverage use, neither will the firm's stock price.

Debt financing, then, has two costs—its **explicit cost of capital**, K_d, calculated according to the formats outlined in Chapter 8, and an implicit cost. The **implicit cost of debt** is the change in the cost of common equity brought on by using financial leverage (additional debt). The real cost of debt is the sum of these explicit and implicit costs. In general, the real cost of *any* source of capital is its explicit cost, plus the change that it induces in the cost of any other source of funds.

Followers of the independence hypothesis argue that the use of financial leverage brings a change in the cost of common equity large enough to offset the benefits of higher dividends to investors. Debt financing is not as cheap as it first appears to be. This will keep the composite cost of funds constant. The implication for management is that one capital structure is as good as any other; financial officers should not waste time searching for an optimal capital structure. One capital structure, after all, is as beneficial as any other, because all result in the same weighted cost of capital.

Extreme Position 2: Dependence Hypothesis (NI Theory)

The dependence hypothesis is at the opposite pole from the independence hypothesis. It suggests that both the weighted cost of capital, K_0, and common stock price, P_0, *are affected* by the firm's use of financial leverage. No matter how modest or excessive the firm's use of debt financing, both its cost of debt capital, K_d, and cost of equity capital, K_c, will not be affected by capital structure management. Because the cost of debt is less than the cost of equity, greater financial leverage will lower the firm's composite cost of capital indefinitely. Greater use of debt financing will thereby have a favorable effect on the company's common stock price. By returning to the Rix Camper situation, we can illustrate this point of view.

The same capital structure shift is being evaluated. That is, management will market $8 million of new debt at a 6 percent interest rate and use the proceeds to purchase its own common shares. Under this approach the market is assumed to capitalize (discount) the expected earnings available to the common stockholders to arrive at the aggregate market value of the common stock. The market value of the firm's common equity is *not* a residual of the valuation process. After the recapitalization, the firm's cost of common equity,

K_c, will still be equal to 10 percent. Thus, a 10 percent cost of common equity is applied in the following format:

	Expected level of net operating income	$ 2,000,000
−	Interest expense	480,000
=	Earnings available to common stockholders capitalized at K_C = 10 percent	$ 1,520,000
=	Market value of the common stock	$15,200,000
+	Market value of the new debt	8,000,000
=	Market value of debt and equity	$23,200,000

When we assume that the firm's capital structure consists only of debt and common equity, earnings available to the common stockholders is synonymous with net income. In the valuation process outlined above, it is net income that is actually capitalized to arrive at the market value of the common equity. Because of this, the dependence hypothesis is also called the **net income approach to valuation.**

Notice that the total market value of the firm's securities has risen to $23.2 million from the $20 million level that existed before the firm moved from the unlevered to the levered capital structure. The per-share value of the common stock is also shown to rise under this valuation format. With 1.2 million shares of stock outstanding, the market price per share is $12.67 ($15.2 million/1.2 million).

This increase in the stock price to $12.67 represents a 26.7 percent rise over the previous level of $10 per share. This is exactly equal to the percentage change in earnings per share and dividends per share calculated in Table 10–1. This permits us to characterize the dependence hypothesis in a very succinct fashion:

percentage change in K_c = 0 percent < percentage change in D_t (over all degrees of leverage)

percentage change in P_0 = percentage change in D_t

The dependence hypothesis suggests that the *explicit* and *implicit* costs of debt are one and the same. The use of more debt does *not* change the firm's cost of common equity. Using more debt, which is explicitly cheaper than common equity, will lower the firm's composite cost of capital, K_0. If you take the market value of Rix Camper's common stock according to the net income theory of $15.2 million and express it as a percent of the total market value of the firm's securities, you get a market value weight of .655 ($15.2 million/$23.2 million). In a similar fashion, the market value weight of Rix Camper's debt is found to be .345 ($8 million/$23.2 million). After the capital structure adjustment, the firm's weighted cost of capital becomes

$$K_0 = (.345)(6.00\%) + (.655)(10.00\%) = 8.62\%$$

So, changing the financing mix from all equity to a structure including both debt and equity lowered the composite cost of capital from 10 percent to 8.62 percent. The ingredients of the dependence hypothesis are illustrated in Figures 10–3 and 10–4.

The implication for management from Figures 10–3 and 10–4 is that the firm's cost of capital, K_0, will decline as the debt-to-equity ratio increases. This also implies that the company's common stock price will rise with increased leverage use. Because the cost of capital decreases continuously with leverage, the firm should use as much leverage as is possible. Next, we will move toward

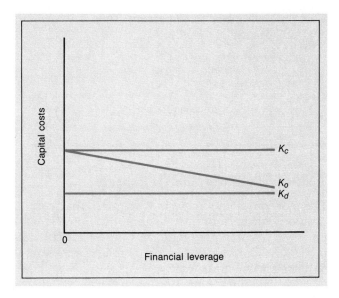

FIGURE 10–3.
Capital Costs and Financial Leverage: No Taxes— Dependence Hypothesis (NI Theory)

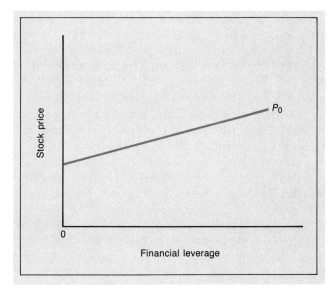

FIGURE 10–4.
Stock Price and Financial Leverage: No Taxes— Dependence Hypothesis (NI Theory)

reality in the analytical setting of our capital structure discussion. This is accomplished by relaxing some of the major assumptions that surrounded the independence and dependence hypotheses.

Moderate Position: Corporate Income Is Taxed — *CLOSER TO REALITY* *and Firms May Fail*

In general, an analysis of extreme positions may be useful in that you are forced to sharpen your thinking not only about the poles, but also the situations that span the poles. In microeconomics the study of perfect competition and monopoly provides a better understanding of the business activity that occurs in the wide area between these two model markets. In a similar fashion, the study of the independence and dependence hypotheses of the importance of capital structure helps us formulate a more informed view of the possible situations between those polar positions.

We turn now to a description of the cost of capital–capital structure relationship that has rather wide appeal to both business practitioners and academics. This moderate view (1) admits to the fact that interest expense is tax deductible and (2) acknowledges that the probability of the firm's suffering bankruptcy costs is directly related to the company's use of financial leverage.

	Unlevered Capital Structure	Levered Capital Structure
Expected level of net operating income	$2,000,000	$2,000,000
Less: Interest expense	0	480,000
Earnings before taxes	$2,000,000	$1,520,000
Less: Taxes at 50%	1,000,000	760,000
Earnings available to common stockholders	$1,000,000	$ 760,000
Expected payments to *all* security holders	$1,000,000	$1,240,000

Tax Deductibility of Interest Expense

This portion of the analysis recognizes that corporate income is subject to taxation. Furthermore, we assume that interest expense is tax deductible for purposes of computing the firm's tax bill. In this environment the use of debt financing should result in a higher total market value for the firm's outstanding securities. We will see why subsequently.

We continue with our Rix Camper Manufacturing Company example. First, consider the total cash payments made to all security holders (holders of common stock plus holders of bonds). In the no-tax case, the sum of cash dividends paid to common shareholders plus interest expense amounted to $2 million both (1) when financing was all by common equity and (2) after the proposed capital structure adjustment to a levered situation was accomplished. The *sum* of the cash flows that Rix Camper could pay to its contributors of debt and equity capital was not affected by its financing mix.

When corporate income is taxed by the government, however, the sum of the cash flows made to all contributors of financial capital *is affected* by the firm's financing mix. Table 10–3 illustrates this point.

If Rix Camper makes the capital structure adjustment identified in the preceding sections of this chapter, the total payments to equity and debt holders will be $240,000 *greater* than under the all-common-equity capitalization. Where does this $240,000 come from? The government's take, through taxes collected, is lower by that amount. This difference, which flows to the Rix Camper security holders, is called the **tax shield** on interest. In general, it may be calculated by equation (10–4), where r_d is the interest rate paid on the debt, M is the principal amount of the debt, and t is the firm's marginal tax rate:

$$\text{tax shield} = r_d(M)(t) \tag{10–4}$$

The moderate position on the importance of capital structure presumes that the tax shield must have value in the marketplace. Accordingly, this tax benefit will increase the total market value of the firm's outstanding securities relative to the all-equity capitalization. Financial leverage does affect firm value. Because the cost of capital is just the other side of the valuation coin, financial leverage also affects the firm's composite cost of capital. Can the firm increase firm value indefinitely and lower its cost of capital continuously by using more and more financial leverage? Common sense would tell us "No!" So would most financial managers and academicians. The acknowledgment of bankruptcy costs provides one possible rationale.

The Likelihood of Firm Failure

The probability that the firm will be unable to meet the financial obligations identified in its debt contracts increases as more debt is employed. The highest costs would be incurred if the firm actually went into bankruptcy proceedings. Here, assets would be liquidated. If we admit that these assets might sell for something less than their perceived market values, equity investors and debt holders could both suffer losses. Other problems accompany bankruptcy proceedings. Lawyers and accountants have to be hired and paid. Managers must spend time preparing lengthy reports for those involved in the legal action.

Milder forms of financial distress also have their costs. As their firm's financial condition weakens, creditors may take action to restrict normal business activity. Suppliers may not deliver materials on credit. Profitable capital investments may have to be forgone, and dividend payments may even be interrupted. At some point the expected cost of default will be large enough to outweigh the tax shield advantage of debt financing.[2] The firm will turn to other sources of financing, mainly common equity. At this point the real cost of debt is thought to be higher than the real cost of common equity.

Moderate View: Saucer-Shaped Cost of Capital Curve

This moderate view of the relationship between financing mix and the firm's cost of capital is depicted in Figure 10–5. The result is a saucer-shaped (or U-shaped) average cost of capital curve, K_0. The firm's average cost of equity, K_c, is seen to rise over all positive degrees of financial leverage use. For a while the firm can borrow funds at a relatively low cost of debt, K_d. Even though the cost of equity is rising, it does not rise at a fast enough rate to offset the use of the less expensive debt financing. Thus, between points 0 and A on the financial-leverage axis, the average cost of capital declines and stock price rises.

Eventually, the threat of financial distress causes the cost of debt to rise. In Figure 10–5 this increase in the cost of debt shows up in the average cost of debt curve, K_d, at point A. Between points A and B, mixing debt and equity funds produces an average cost of capital that is (relatively) flat. The firm's **optimal range of financial leverage** lies between points A and B. All capital structures between these two points are *optimal* because they produce the lowest composite cost of capital. As we said in the introduction to this chapter, finding this optimal range of financing mixes is the *objective of capital structure management*.

Point B signifies the firm's debt capacity. **Debt capacity** is the maximum

---

[2]Even this argument that the tradeoff between bankruptcy costs and the tax shield benefit of debt financing can lead to an optimal structure has its detractors. See Robert A. Haugen and Lemma W. Senbet, "The Insignificance of Bankruptcy Costs to the Theory of Optimal Capital Structure," *Journal of Finance* 33 (May 1978), pp. 383–93.

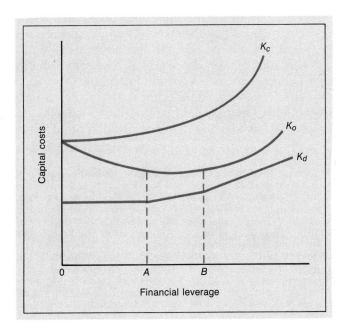

FIGURE 10–5.
Capital Costs and Financial Leverage: The Moderate View, Considering Taxes and Financial Distress

proportion of debt the firm can include in its capital structure and still maintain its lowest composite cost of capital. Beyond point B, additional fixed-charge capital can be attracted only at very costly interest rates. At the same time, this excessive use of financial leverage would cause the firm's cost of equity to rise at a faster rate than previously. The composite cost of capital would then rise quite rapidly, and the firm's stock price would decline.

This version of the moderate view as it relates to the firm's stock price is characterized subsequently. The notation is the same as that found in our discussion of the independence and dependence hypotheses.

1. Between points 0 and A:
   $0 <$ percentage change in $P_0 <$ percentage change in D_t

2. Between points A and B:
   percentage change in $P_0 = 0$

3. Beyond point B:
   percentage change in $P_0 < 0$

Perspective in Finance

Given the same task or assignment, it is quite likely that you will do it better for yourself than for someone else. If you are paid well enough, you might do the job about as effectively for that other person. Once you receive compensation, your work will be evaluated by someone. This process of evaluation is called "monitoring" within most discussions on agency costs.

This describes the heart of what is called the "agency problem." As American businesses have grown in size, the owners and managers have become (for the most part) separate groups of individuals. An inherent conflict exists, therefore, between managers and shareholders for whom managers act as agents in carrying out their objectives (for example, corporate goals). The following discussion relates the agency problem to the financial decision-making process of the firm.

Firm Value and Agency Costs

In Chapter 1 of this text we mentioned *the agency problem*. Recall that the agency problem gives rise to *agency costs*, which tend to occur in business organizations because ownership and management control are often separate. Thus, the firm's managers can be properly thought of as agents for the firm's stockholders.[3] To ensure that agent-managers act in the stockholders' best interests requires that they have (1) proper incentives to do so and (2) that their decisions are monitored. The incentives usually take the form of executive compensation plans and perquisites. The perquisites might be a bloated support staff, country club memberships, luxurious corporate planes, or other amenities of a similar nature. Monitoring requires that certain costs be borne by the stockholders, such as (1) bonding the managers, (2) auditing financial statements, (3) structuring the organization in unique ways that limit useful

---

[3]Economists have studied the problems associated with control of the corporation for decades. An early, classic work on this topic was A. A. Berle, Jr., and G. C. Means, *The Modern Corporation and Private Property* (New York: Macmillan, 1932). The recent emphasis in corporate finance and financial economics stems from the important contribution of Michael C. Jensen and William H. Meckling, "Theory of the Firm: Managerial Behavior, Agency Costs and Ownership Structure," *Journal of Financial Economics* 3 (October 1976), pp. 305–60. Professors Jensen and Smith have analyzed the bondholder–stockholder conflict in a very clear style. See Michael C. Jensen and Clifford W. Smith, Jr., "Stockholder, Manager, and Creditor Interests: Applications of Agency Theory," in Edward I. Altman and Marti G. Subrahmanyam, eds., *Recent Advances in Corporate Finance* (Homewood, IL: Richard D. Irwin, 1985), pp. 93–131. An entire volume dealing with agency problems, including those of capital-structure management, is Amir Barnea, Robert A. Haugen, and Lemma W. Senbet, *Agency Problems and Financial Contracting* (Englewood Cliffs, NJ: Prentice Hall, 1985).

managerial decisions, and (4) reviewing the costs and benefits of management perquisites. This list is indicative, not exhaustive. The main point is that monitoring costs are ultimately covered by the owners of the company—its common stockholders.

Capital structure management *also* gives rise to agency costs. Agency problems stem from conflicts of interest, and capital structure management encompasses a natural conflict between stockholders and bondholders. Acting in the stockholders' best interests might cause management to invest in extremely risky projects. Existing investors in the firm's bonds could logically take a dim view of such an investment policy. A change in the risk structure of the firm's assets would change the business risk exposure of the firm. This could lead to a downward revision of the bond rating the firm currently enjoys. A lowered bond rating in turn would lower the current market value of the firm's bonds. Clearly, bondholders would be unhappy with this result.

To reduce this conflict of interest, the creditors (bond investors) and stockholders may agree to include several protective covenants in the bond contract. These bond covenants are discussed in more detail in Chapter 20, but essentially they may be thought of as restrictions on managerial decision making. Typical covenants restrict payment of cash dividends on common stock, limit the acquisition or sale of assets, or limit further debt financing. To make sure that the protective covenants are complied with by management means that monitoring costs are incurred. Like all monitoring costs, they are borne by common stockholders. Further, like many costs, they involve the analysis of an important tradeoff.

Figure 10–6 displays some of the tradeoffs involved with the use of protective bond covenants. Note (in the left panel of Figure 10–6) that the firm might be able to sell bonds that carry no protective covenants only by incurring very high interest rates. With no protective covenants, there are no associated monitoring costs. Also, there are no lost operating efficiencies, such as being able to move quickly to acquire a particular company in the acquisitions market. Conversely, the willingness to submit to several covenants could reduce the explicit cost of the debt contract, but would involve incurring significant monitoring costs and losing some operating efficiencies (which also translates into higher costs). When the debt issue is first sold, then, a tradeoff will be arrived at between incurring monitoring costs, losing operating efficiencies, and enjoying a lower explicit interest cost.

Next, we have to consider the presence of monitoring costs at low levels of leverage and at higher levels of leverage. When the firm operates at a low debt-to-equity ratio, there is little need for creditors to insist on a long list of bond covenants. The financial risk is just not there to require that type of activity. The firm will likewise benefit from low explicit interest rates when leverage is low. When the debt-to-equity ratio is high, however, it is logical for creditors to demand a great deal of monitoring. This increase in agency costs will raise the implicit cost (the true total cost) of debt financing. It seems logical,

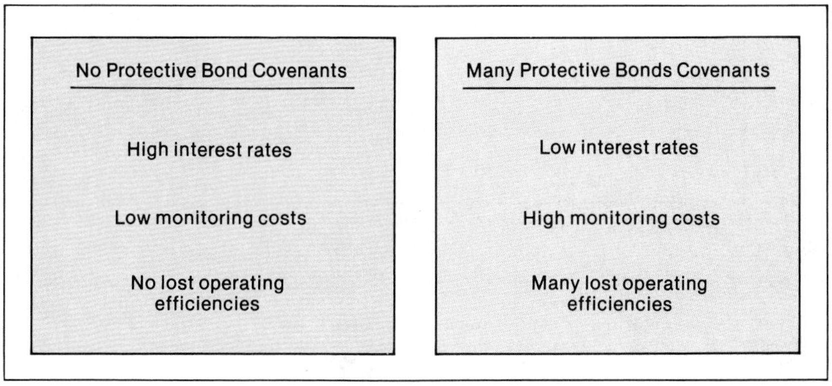

No Protective Bond Covenants	Many Protective Bonds Covenants
High interest rates	Low interest rates
Low monitoring costs	High monitoring costs
No lost operating efficiencies	Many lost operating efficiencies

FIGURE 10–6.
Agency Costs of Debt: Tradeoffs

then, to suggest that monitoring costs will rise as the firm's use of financial leverage increases. Just as the likelihood of firm failure (financial distress) raises a company's overall cost of capital (K_0), so do agency costs. On the other side of the coin, this means that total firm value (the total market value of the firm's securities) will be *lower* owing to the presence of agency costs. Taken together, the presence of agency costs and the costs associated with financial distress argue in favor of the concept of an *optimal* capital structure for the individual firm.

This discussion can be summarized by introducing equation (10–5) for the market value of the levered firm.

$$\begin{array}{l} \text{market value of} \\ \text{levered firm} \end{array} = \begin{array}{l} \text{market value of} \\ \text{unlevered firm} \end{array} + \begin{array}{l} \text{present value} \\ \text{of tax shields} \end{array} \qquad \textbf{(10–5)}$$

$$- \left(\begin{array}{l} \text{present value} \\ \text{of financial} \\ \text{distress costs} \end{array} + \begin{array}{l} \text{present value} \\ \text{of agency} \\ \text{costs} \end{array} \right)$$

The relationship expressed in equation (10–5) is presented graphically in Figure 10–7. There we see that the tax shield effect is dominant until point A is reached. After point A, the rising costs of the likelihood of firm failure (financial distress) and agency costs cause the market value of the levered firm to decline. The *objective* for the financial manager here is to find point B by using all of his or her analytical skill; this must also include a good dose of seasoned judgment. At point B the actual market value of the levered firm is maximized, and its composite cost of capital (K_0) is at a minimum. The implementation problem is that the precise costs of financial distress and monitoring can only be estimated by subjective means; a definite mathematical solution is not available. Thus, planning the firm's financing mix always requires good decision making and management judgment.

FIGURE 10–7.
Firm Value Considering Taxes, Agency Costs, and Financial Distress Costs

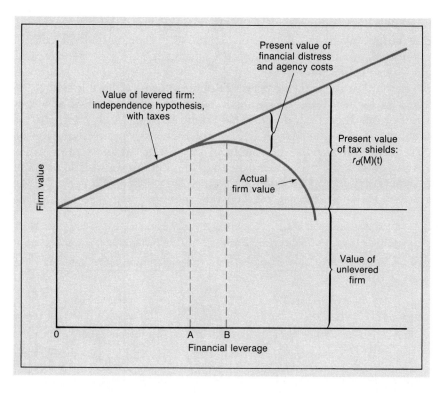

Agency Costs, Free Cash Flow, and Capital Structure

In 1986, Professor Michael C. Jensen further extended the concept of agency costs into the area of capital structure management. The contribution revolves around a concept that Jensen labels "free cash flow."

Professor Jensen defines free cash flow as follows:[4]

> Free cash flow is cash flow in excess of that required to fund all projects that have positive net present values when discounted at the relevant cost of capital.

Jensen then puts forth that substantial free cash flow can lead to misbehavior by managers and poor decisions that are *not* in the best interests of the firm's common stockholders. In other words, managers have an incentive to hold on to the free cash flow and have "fun" with it, rather than "disgorging" it, say, in the form of higher cash dividend payments.

But, all is not lost. This leads to what Jensen calls his "control hypothesis" for debt creation. This means that by levering up, the firm's shareholders will enjoy increased control over their management team. For example, if the firm issues new debt and uses the proceeds to retire outstanding common stock, then management is obligated to pay out cash to service the debt—this simultaneously reduces the amount of free cash flow available to management with which to have fun.

We can also refer to this motive for financial leverage use as the "threat hypothesis." Management works under the threat of financial failure—therefore, according to the "free cash flow theory of capital structure," it works more efficiently. This is supposed to reduce the agency costs of free cash flow—which will in turn be recognized by the marketplace in the form of greater returns on the common stock.

Note that the *free cash flow theory of capital structure* does not give a theoretical solution to the question of just how much financial leverage is enough. Nor does it suggest how much leverage is too much leverage. It is a way of thinking about why shareholders and their boards of directors might use more debt to control management behavior and decisions. The basic decision tools of capital structure management still have to be utilized. They will be presented later in this chapter.

In the *Basic Financial Management in Practice* that follows by Professor Ben Bernanke, observe that not all analysts totally buy into the control hypothesis for debt creation. Bernanke reviews Jensen's free cash flow theory and also comments on the buildup in corporate leverage that has occurred in recent years—especially in the 1980s.

Managerial Implications

Where does our examination of capital structure theory leave us? The upshot is that the determination of the firm's financing mix is centrally important to the financial manager. The firm's stockholders are affected by capital structure decisions.

At the very least, and before bankruptcy costs and agency costs become detrimental, the tax shield effect will cause the shares of a levered firm to sell at a higher price than they would if the company had avoided debt financing. Owing to both the risk of failure and agency costs that accompany the excessive

---

[4]Michael C. Jensen, "Agency Costs of Free Cash Flow, Corporate Finance, and Takeovers," *American Economic Review* 76 (May 1986), pp. 323–29.

BASIC FINANCIAL MANAGEMENT IN PRACTICE

Ben Bernanke on the Free Cash Flow Theory of Capital Structure
and the Buildup in Corporate Debt

INTRODUCTION

The idea is that the financial structure of firms influences the incentives of "insiders" (managers, directors, and large shareholders with some operational interest in the business) and that, in particular, high levels of debt may increase the willingness of insiders to work hard and make profit-maximizing decisions. This incentive-based approach makes a valuable contribution to our understanding of a firm's capital structure. But while this theory might explain why firms like to use debt in general, does it explain why the use of debt has increased so much in recent years?

Michael Jensen, a founder and leading proponent of the incentive-based approach to capital structure, argues that it can. Jensen focuses on a recent worsening of what he calls the "free cash flow" problem. Free cash flow is defined as the portion of a corporation's cash flow that it is unable to invest profitably within the firm. Companies in industries that are profitable but no longer have much potential for expansion—the U.S. oil industry, for example—have a lot of free cash flow.

Why is free cash flow a problem? Jensen argues that managers are often tempted to use free cash flow to expand the size of the company, even if the expansion is not profitable. This is because managers feel that their power and job satisfaction are enhanced by a growing company; so given that most managers' compensation is at best weakly tied to the firm's profitability, Jensen argues that managers will find it personally worthwhile to expand even into money-losing operations. In principle, the board of directors and shareholders should be able to block these unprofitable investments; however, in practice, the fact that the management typically has far more information about potential investments than do outside directors and shareholders makes it difficult to second-guess the managers' recommendations.

HOW MORE LEVERAGE CAN HELP

The company manager with lots of free cash flow may attempt to use that cash to increase his power and perquisites, at the expense of the shareholders. Jensen argues that the solution to the free-cash-flow problem is more leverage. For example, suppose that management uses the free cash flow of the company, plus the proceeds of new debt issues, to repurchase stock from the outside shareholders—that is, to do a management buyout. This helps solve the free-cash-flow problem in several ways. The personal returns of the managers are now much more closely tied to the profits of the firm, which gives them incentives to be more efficient. Second, the re-leveraging process removes the existing free cash from the firm, so that any future investment projects will have to be financed externally; thus, future projects will have to meet the market test of being acceptable to outside bankers or bond purchasers. Finally, the high interest payments implied by re-leveraging impose a permanent discipline on the managers; in order to meet these payments, they will have to ruthlessly cut money-losing operations, avoid questionable investments, and take other efficiency-promoting actions.

According to Jensen, a substantial increase in free-cash-flow problems—resulting from deregulation, the maturing of some large industries, and other factors—is a major source of the recent debt expansion. Jensen also points to a number of institutional factors that have promoted increased leverage. These include relaxed restrictions on mergers, which have lowered the barriers to corporate takeovers created by the antitrust laws, and increased financial sophistication, such as the greatly expanded operations of takeover specialists like Drexel Burnham Lambert Inc. and the development of the market for "junk bonds." Jensen's diagnosis is not controversial: it's quite plausible that these factors, plus changing norms about what constitutes an "acceptable" level of debt, explain at least part of the trend toward increased corporate debt. One important piece of evidence in favor of this explanation is that net equity issues have been substantially negative since 1983. This suggests that much of the proceeds of the new debt issues is being used to repurchase outstanding shares. This is what we would expect if corporations are attempting to re-leverage their existing assets, rather than using debt to expand their asset holdings. However, the implied conclusion—that the debt buildup is beneficial overall to the economy—is considerably more controversial.

CRITICISMS OF THE INCENTIVE-BASED RATIONALE FOR INCREASED DEBT

Jensen and other advocates of the incentive-based approach to capital structure have made a cogent theoretical case for the beneficial effects of debt finance, and many architects of large-scale restructurings have given improved incentives and the promise of greater efficiency as a large part of the rationale for increased leverage. The idea that leverage is beneficial has certainly been embraced by the stock market: even unsubstantiated rumors of a potential leveraged buy-out (LBO) have been sufficient to send the stock price of the targeted company soaring, often by 40 percent or more. At a minimum, this indicates that stock market participants *believe* that higher leverage increases profitability. Proponents of restructuring interpret this as evidence that debt is good for the economy.

There are, however, criticisms of this conclusion. First, the fact that the stock market's expectations of company profitability rise when there is a buy-out is not proof that profits *will* rise in actuality. It is still too soon to judge whether the increased leverage of the 1980s will lead to a sustained increase in profitability. One might think of looking to historical data for an answer to this question. But buy-outs in the 1960s and 1970s were somewhat different in character from more recent restructurings, and, in any case, the profitability evidence on the earlier episodes is mixed.

Even if the higher profits expected by the stock market do materialize, there is contention over where they are likely to come from. The incentive-based theory of capital structure says they will come from improved efficiency. But some opponents have argued that the higher profits will primarily reflect transfers to the shareholders from other claimants on the corporation —its employees, customers, suppliers, bondholders, and the government. Customers may be hurt if takeovers are associated with increased monopolization of markets. Bondholders have been big losers in some buyouts, as higher leverage has increased bankruptcy risk and thus reduced the value of outstanding bonds. The government may have lost tax revenue, as companies, by increasing leverage, have increased their interest deductions (although there are offsetting effects here, such as the taxes paid by bought-out shareholders on their capital gains). The perception that much of the profits associated with releveraging and buyouts comes from "squeezing" existing beneficiaries of the corporation explains much of the recent political agitation to limit these activities.

The debt buildup can also be criticized from the perspective of incentive-based theories themselves. Two points are worth noting: first, the principal problem that higher leverage is supposed to address is the relatively weak connection between firms' profits and managers' personal returns, which reduces managers' incentives to take profit-maximizing actions. But if this is truly the problem, it could be addressed more directly—without subjecting the company to serious bankruptcy risk— simply by changing managerial compensation schemes to include more profit-based incentives.

THE DOWNSIDE OF DEBT FINANCING

Increased debt is not the optimal solution to all incentive problems. For example, it has been shown, as a theoretical proposition, that managers of debt-financed firms have an incentive to choose riskier projects over safe ones; this is because firms with fixed-debt obligations enjoy all of the upside potential of high-risk projects but share the downside losses with the debt holders, who are not fully repaid if bad investment outcomes cause the firm to fail.

That high leverage does not always promote efficiency can be seen when highly leveraged firms suffer losses and find themselves in financial distress. When financial problems hit, the need to meet interest payments may force management to take a very short-run perspective, leading them to cut back production and employment, cancel even potentially profitable expansion projects, and sell assets at fire-sale prices. Because the risk of bankruptcy is so great, firms in financial distress cannot make long-term agreements; they lose customers and suppliers who are afraid they cannot count on an ongoing relationship, and they must pay wage premiums to hire workers.

These efficiency losses, plus the direct costs of bankruptcy (such as legal fees), are the potential downside of high leverage.

Source: Ben Bernanke, "Is There Too Much Corporate Debt?" *Business Review*, Federal Reserve Bank of Philadelphia (September–October 1989), pp. 5–8.

use of leverage, the financial manager must exercise caution in the use of fixed-charge capital. This problem of searching for the optimal range of use of financial leverage is our next task.[5]

Perspective in Finance

You have now developed a workable knowledge of capital structure theory. This makes you better equipped to search for your firm's optimal capital structure. Several tools are available to help you in this search process and simultaneously help you make prudent financing choices. These tools are decision oriented. They assist us in answering this question: "The next time we need $20 million, should we issue common stock or sell long-term bonds?"

Basic Tools of Capital Structure Management

Recall from Chapter 9 that the use of financial leverage has two effects on the earnings stream flowing to the firm's common stockholders. For clarity of exposition Tables 9-7 and 9-8 are repeated here as Tables 10-4 and 10-5. Three possible financing mixes for the Pierce Grain Company are contained in Table 10-4, and an analysis of the corresponding financial leverage effects is displayed in Table 10-5.

---

[5]The relationship between capital structure and enterprise valuation by the marketplace continues to stimulate considerable research output. The complexity of the topic is reviewed in Stewart C. Myers, "The Capital Structure Puzzle," *Journal of Finance* 39 (July 1984), pp. 575–92. Ten useful papers are contained in Benjamin M. Friedman, ed., *Corporate Capital Structures in the United States* (Chicago: National Bureau of Economic Research and The University of Chicago Press, 1985).

TABLE 10–4.
Pierce Grain Company Possible
Capital Structures

Plan A: 0% debt

		Total debt	$ 0
		Common equity	200,000[a]
Total assets	$200,000	Total liabilities and equity	$200,000

Plan B: 25% debt at 8% Interest rate

		Total debt	$ 50,000
		Common equity	150,000[b]
Total assets	$200,000	Total liabilities and equity	$200,000

Plan C: 40% debt at 8% Interest rate

		Total debt	$ 80,000
		Common equity	120,000[c]
Total assets	$200,000	Total liabilities and equity	$200,000

[a]2,000 common shares outstanding
[b]1,500 common shares outstanding
[c]1,200 common shares outstanding

(1)	(2)	(3) = (1) − (2)	(4) = (3) × .5	(5) = (3) − (4)	(6)
				Net Income	Earnings
EBIT	Interest	EBT	Taxes	to Common	per Share

Plan A: 0% debt; $200,000 common equity; 2000 shares

$ 0	$ 0	$ 0	$ 0	$ 0	$ 0
20,000	0	20,000	10,000	10,000	5.00 } 100%
40,000	0	40,000	20,000	20,000	10.00
60,000	0	60,000	30,000	30,000	15.00
80,000	0	80,000	40,000	40,000	20.00

Plan B: 25% debt; 8% Interest rate; $150,000 common equity; 1500 shares

$ 0	$4,000	$ (4,000)	$ (2,000)[a]	$ (2,000)	$ (1.33)
20,000	4,000	16,000	8,000	8,000	5.33 } 125%
40,000	4,000	36,000	18,000	18,000	12.00
60,000	4,000	56,000	28,000	28,000	18.67
80,000	4,000	76,000	38,000	38,000	25.33

Plan C: 40% debt; 8% Interest rate; $120,000 common equity; 1200 shares

$ 0	$6,400	$ (6,400)	$ (3,200)[a]	$ (3,200)	$ (2.67)
20,000	6,400	13,600	6,800	6,800	5.67 } 147%
40,000	6,400	33,600	16,800	16,800	14.00
60,000	6,400	53,600	26,800	26,800	22.33
80,000	6,400	73,600	36,800	36,800	30.67

[a]The negative tax bill recognizes the credit arising from the carryback and carryforward
provision of the tax code. See Chapter 2.

The *first financial leverage effect* is the added variability in the earnings-per-share stream that accompanies the use of fixed-charge securities in the company's capital structure. By means of the degree-of-financial-leverage measure (DFL_{EBIT}) we explained how this variability can be quantified. The firm that uses more financial leverage (rather than less) will experience larger relative changes in its earnings per share (rather than smaller) following EBIT fluctuations. Assume that Pierce Grain elected financing plan C rather than plan A. Plan C is highly levered and plan A is unlevered. A 100 percent increase in EBIT from $20,000 to $40,000 would cause earnings per share to rise by 147 percent under plan C, but only 100 percent under plan A. Unfortunately, the effect would operate in the negative direction as well. A given change in EBIT is *magnified* by the use of financial leverage. This magnification is reflected in the variability of the firm's earnings per share.

The *second financial leverage effect* concerns the level of earnings per share at a given EBIT under a given capital structure. Refer to Table 10–5. At the EBIT level of $20,000, earnings per share would be $5, $5.33, and $5.67 under financing arrangements A, B, and C, respectively. Above a critical level of EBIT, the firm's earnings per share will be higher if greater degrees of financial leverage are employed. Conversely, below some critical level of EBIT, earnings per share will suffer at greater degrees of financial leverage. Whereas the first financial-leverage effect is quantified by the degree-of-financial-leverage measure (DFL_{EBIT}), the second is quantified by what is generally referred to as EBIT–EPS analysis. EPS refers, of course, to earnings per share. The rationale underlying this sort of analysis is simple. Earnings is one of the key variables that influences the market value of the firm's common stock. The effect of a financing decision on EPS, then, should be understood because the decision will probably affect the value of the stockholders' investment.

EBIT–EPS Analysis

Example Assume that plan B in Table 10–5 is the existing capital structure for the Pierce Grain Company. Furthermore, the asset structure of the firm is such that EBIT is expected to be $20,000 per year for a very long time. A capital investment is available to Pierce Grain that will cost $50,000. Acquisition of this asset is expected to raise the projected EBIT level to $30,000, permanently. The firm can raise the needed cash by (1) selling 500 shares of common stock at $100 each or (2) selling new bonds that will net the firm $50,000 and carry an interest rate of 8.5 percent. These capital structures and corresponding EPS amounts are summarized in Table 10–6.

At the projected EBIT level of $30,000, the EPS for the common stock and debt alternatives are $6.50 and $7.25, respectively. Both are considerably above the $5.33 that would occur if the new project were rejected and the additional financial capital were not raised. Based on a criterion of selecting the financing plan that will provide the highest EPS, the bond alternative is favored. But what if the basic business risk to which the firm is exposed causes the EBIT level to vary over a considerable range? Can we be sure that the bond alternative will *always* have the higher EPS associated with it? The answer, of course, is "No." When the EBIT level is subject to uncertainty, a graphic analysis of the proposed financing plans can provide useful information to the financial manager.

TABLE 10–6.
Pierce Grain Company Analysis of Financing Choices

Part A: Capital Structures

Existing Capital Structure		With New Common Stock Financing		With New Debt Financing	
Long-term debt at 8%	$ 50,000	Long-term debt at 8%	$ 50,000	Long-term debt at 8%	$ 50,000
Common stock	150,000	Common stock	200,000	Long-term debt at 8.5%	50,000
				Common stock	150,000
Total liabilities and equity	$200,000	Total liabilities and equity	$250,000	Total liabilities and equity	$250,000
Common shares outstanding	1,500	Common shares outstanding	2,000	Common shares outstanding	1,500

Part B: Projected EPS Levels

	Existing Capital Structure	With New Common Stock Financing	With New Debt Financing
EBIT	$20,000	$30,000	$30,000
Less: Interest expense	4,000	4,000	8,250
Earnings before taxes (EBIT)	$16,000	$26,000	$21,750
Less: Taxes at 50%	8,000	13,000	10,875
Net Income	$ 8,000	$13,000	$10,875
Less: Preferred dividends	0	0	0
Earnings available to common	$ 8,000	$13,000	$10,875
EPS	$5.33	$6.50	$7.25

Graphic Analysis

The EBIT–EPS analysis chart allows the decision maker to visualize the impact of different financing plans on EPS over a range of EBIT levels. The relationship between EPS and EBIT is linear. All we need, therefore, to construct the chart is two points for each alternative. Part B of Table 10–6 already provides us with one of these points. The answer to the following question for each choice gives us the second point: At what EBIT level will the EPS for the plan be exactly zero? If the EBIT level *just covers* the plan's financing costs (on a before-tax basis), then EPS will be zero. For the stock plan, an EPS of zero is associated with an EBIT of $4,000. The $4,000 is the interest expense incurred under the existing capital structure. If the bond plan is elected, the interest costs will be the present $4,000 plus $4,250 per year arising from the new debt issue. An EBIT level of $8,250, then, is necessary to provide a zero EPS with the bond plan.

The EBIT–EPS analysis chart representing the financing choices available to the Pierce Grain Company is shown as Figure 10–8. EBIT is charted on the horizontal axis and EPS on the vertical axis. The intercepts on the horizontal axis represent the before-tax equivalent financing charges related to each plan. The straight lines for each plan tell us the EPS amounts that will occur at different EBIT amounts.

Notice that the bond-plan line has a *steeper slope* than the stock-plan line. This ensures that the lines for each financing choice will *intersect*. Above the intersection point, EPS for the plan with greater leverage will exceed that for the plan with lesser leverage. The intersection point, encircled in Figure 10–8, occurs at an EBIT level of $21,000 and produces EPS of $4.25 for each plan. When EBIT is $30,000, notice that the bond plan produces EPS of $7.25 and the

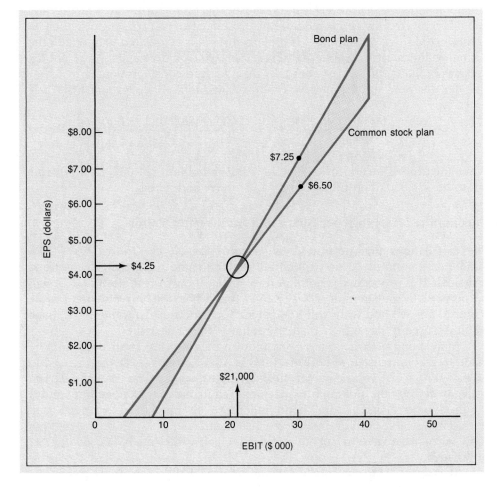

FIGURE 10–8.
EBIT–EPS Analysis Chart

stock plan, $6.50. Below the intersection point, EPS with the stock plan will *exceed* that with the more highly levered bond plan. The steeper slope of the bond-plan line indicates that with greater leverage, EPS is more sensitive to EBIT changes. This same concept was discussed in Chapter 9 when we derived the degree of financial leverage measure.

Computing Indifference Points

The point of intersection in Figure 10–8 is called the **EBIT–EPS indifference point.** It identifies the EBIT level at which the EPS will be the same regardless of the financing plan chosen by the financial manager. This indifference point, sometimes called the breakeven point, has major implications for financial planning. At EBIT amounts in excess of the EBIT indifference level, the more heavily levered financing plan will generate a higher EPS. At EBIT amounts below the EBIT indifference level, the financing plan involving less leverage will generate a higher EPS. It is important, then, to know the EBIT indifference level.

We can find it graphically, as in Figure 10–8. At times it may be more efficient, though, to calculate the indifference point directly. This can be done by using the following equation:

$$\overset{\textit{EPS: Stock Plan}}{\underbrace{\frac{(\text{EBIT} - I)(1 - t) - P}{S_s}}} = \overset{\textit{EPS: Bond Plan}}{\underbrace{\frac{(\text{EBIT} - I)(1 - t) - P}{S_b}}} \qquad \textbf{(10–6)}$$

where S_s and S_b are the number of common shares outstanding under the stock and bond plans, respectively, I is interest expense, t is the firm's income tax rate, and P is preferred dividends paid. In the present case P is zero, because there is no preferred stock outstanding. If preferred stock is associated with one of the financing alternatives, keep in mind that the preferred dividends, P, are not tax deductible. Equation (10–6) *does* take this fact into consideration.

For the present example, we calculate the indifference level of EBIT as

$$\frac{(\text{EBIT} - \$4000)(1 - 0.5) - 0}{2000} = \frac{(\text{EBIT} - \$8250)(1 - 0.5) - 0}{1500}$$

When the expression above is solved for EBIT, we obtain $21,000. If EBIT turns out to be $21,000, then EPS will be $4.25 under both plans.

Uncommitted Earnings per Share and Indifference Points

The calculations that permitted us to solve for Pierce Grain's EBIT–EPS indifference point made no explicit allowance for the repayment of the bond principal. This procedure is not that unrealistic. It only presumes the debt will be perpetually outstanding. This means that when the current bond issue matures, a new bond issue will be floated. The proceeds from the newer issue would be used to pay off the maturity value of the older issue.

Many bond contracts, however, require that **sinking fund payments** be made to a bond trustee. **A sinking fund** is a real cash reserve that is used to provide for the orderly and early retirement of the principal amount of the bond issue. Most often the sinking fund payment is a mandatory fixed amount and is required by a clause in the bond indenture. Sinking fund payments can represent a sizable cash drain on the firm's liquid resources. Moreover, sinking fund payments are a return of borrowed principal, so they are *not* tax deductible to the firm.

Because of the potentially serious nature of the cash drain caused by sinking fund requirements, the financial manager might be concerned with the uncommitted earnings per share (UEPS) related to each financing plan. The calculation of UEPS recognizes that sinking fund commitments have been honored. UEPS can be used, then, for discretionary spending—such as the payment of cash dividends to common stockholders or investment in capital facilities.

If we let SF be the sinking fund payment required in a given year, the EBIT–UEPS indifference point can be calculated as

$$\underset{\text{UEPS: Stock Plan}}{\frac{(\text{EBIT} - I)(1 - t) - P - SF}{S_s}} = \underset{\text{UEPS: Bond Plan}}{\frac{(\text{EBIT} - I)(1 - t) - P - SF}{S_b}} \quad \textbf{(10-7)}$$

If several bond issues are already outstanding, then I in equations (10–6) and (10–7) for the stock plan consists of the sum of their related interest payments. For the bond plan, I would be the *sum of existing plus new interest charges*. In equation (10–7) the same logic applies to the sinking fund variable, SF. The indifference level of EBIT based on UEPS will always exceed that based on EPS.

Word of Caution

Above the EBIT–EPS indifference point, a more heavily levered financial plan promises to deliver a larger EPS. Strict application of the criterion of selecting the financing plan that produces the highest EPS might have the firm issuing debt most of the time it raised external capital. Our discussion of capital-structure theory taught us the dangers of that sort of action.

The primary weakness of EBIT–EPS analysis is that it disregards the implicit costs of debt financing. The effect of the specific financing decision on the firm's cost of common equity capital is totally ignored. Investors should be concerned with both the *level* and *variability* of the firm's expected earnings stream. EBIT–EPS analysis considers only the level of the earnings stream and ignores the variability (riskiness) inherent in it. Thus, this type of analysis must be used in conjunction with other basic tools in reaching the objective of capital-structure management.

Comparative Leverage Ratios

In Chapter 12 we will explore the overall usefulness of financial ratio analysis. Leverage ratios are one of the categories of financial ratios identified in that chapter. We emphasize here that the computation of leverage ratios is one of the basic tools of capital structure management.

Two types of leverage ratios must be computed when a financing decision faces the firm. We call these *balance sheet leverage ratios* and *coverage ratios*. The firm's balance sheet supplies inputs for computing the balance sheet leverage ratios. In various forms these balance sheet metrics compare the firm's use of funds supplied by creditors with those supplied by owners.

Inputs to the coverage ratios *generally* come from the firm's income statement. At times the external analyst may have to consult balance sheet information to construct some of these needed estimates. On a privately placed debt issue, for example, some fraction of the current portion of the firm's long-term debt might have to be used as an estimate of that issue's sinking fund. Coverage ratios provide estimates of the firm's ability to service its financing contracts. High coverage ratios, compared with a standard, imply unused debt capacity.

TABLE 10–7.
Comparative Leverage Ratios: Worksheet for Analyzing Financing Plans

Ratios	Computation Method	Existing Ratio	Ratio with New Common Stock Financing	Ratio with New Debt Financing
Balance sheet leverage ratios				
1. Debt ratio	$\dfrac{\text{total liabilities}}{\text{total assets}}$	———— %	———— %	———— %
2. Long-term debt to total capitalization	$\dfrac{\text{long-term debt}}{\text{long-term debt + net worth}}$	———— %	———— %	———— %
3. Total liabilities to net worth	$\dfrac{\text{total liabilities}}{\text{net worth}}$	———— %	———— %	———— %
4. Common equity ratio	$\dfrac{\text{common equity}}{\text{total assets}}$	———— %	———— %	———— %
Coverage ratios				
1. Times interest earned	$\dfrac{\text{EBIT}}{\text{annual interest expense}}$	———— times	———— times	———— times
2. Times burden covered	$\dfrac{\text{EBIT}}{\text{interest} + \dfrac{\text{sinking fund}}{1-t}}$	———— times	———— times	———— times
3. Cash flow overall coverage ratio	$\dfrac{\text{EBIT + lease expense + depreciation}}{\text{interest + lease expense}}$ $+ \dfrac{\text{preferred dividends}}{1-t}$ $+ \dfrac{\text{principal payments}}{1-t}$	———— times	———— times	———— times

A Worksheet

Table 10–7 is a sample worksheet used to analyze financing choices. The objective of the analysis is to determine the effect each financing plan will have on key financial ratios. The financial officer can compare the existing level of each ratio with its projected level, taking into consideration the contractual commitments of each alternative.

In reality we know that EBIT might be expected to vary over a considerable range of outcomes. For this reason the coverage ratios should be calculated several times, each at a different level of EBIT. If this is accomplished over all possible values of EBIT, a probability distribution for each coverage ratio can be constructed. This provides the financial manager with much more information than simply calculating the coverage ratios based on the expected value of EBIT.

Industry Norms

The comparative leverage ratios calculated according to the format laid out in Table 10–7, or in a similar format, have additional utility to the decision maker if they can be compared with some standard. Generally, corporate financial analysts, investment bankers, commercial bank loan officers, and bond-rating agencies rely on industry classes from which to compute "normal" ratios. Although industry groupings may actually contain firms whose basic business risk exposure differs widely, the practice is entrenched in American business behavior.[6] At the very least, then, the financial officer must be interested in *industry standards* because almost everybody else is.

[6]An approach to grouping firms based on several component measures of business risk, as opposed to ordinary industry classes, is reported in John D. Martin, David F. Scott, Jr., and Robert F. Vandell, "Equivalent Risk Classes: A Multidimensional Examination," *Journal of Financial and Quantitative Analysis* 14 (March 1979), pp. 101–18.

Several published studies indicate that capital structure ratios vary in a significant manner among industry classes.[7] For example, random samplings of the common equity ratios of large retail firms seem to differ statistically from those of major steel producers. The major steel producers use financial leverage to a lesser degree than do the large retail organizations. On the whole, firms operating in the *same* industry tend to exhibit capital structure ratios that cluster around a central value, which we call a norm. Business risk will vary from industry to industry. As a consequence, the capital structure norms will vary from industry to industry.

This is not to say that all companies in the industry will maintain leverage ratios "close" to the norm. For instance, firms that are very profitable may display *high* coverage ratios and *high* balance sheet leverage ratios. The moderately profitable firm, though, might find such a posture unduly risky. Here the usefulness of industry normal leverage ratios is clear. If the firm chooses to deviate in a material manner from the accepted values for the key ratios, it must have a sound reason.

Companywide Cash Flows: What Is the Worst that Could Happen?

In Chapter 12 we will note that liquidity ratios are designed to measure the ability of the firm to pay its bills on time. Financing charges are just another type of bill that eventually comes due for payment. Interest charges, preferred dividends, lease charges, and principal payments all must be paid on time, or the company risks being caught in bankruptcy proceedings. To a lesser extent, dispensing with financing charges on an other than timely basis can result in severely restricted business operations. We have just seen that coverage ratios provide a measure of the safety of one general class of payment—financing charges. Coverage ratios, then, and liquidity ratios are very close in concept.

A more comprehensive method is available for studying the impact of capital structure decisions on corporate cash flows. The method is simple but nonetheless very valuable. It involves the preparation of a series of cash budgets under (1) different economic conditions and (2) different capital structures.[8] The net cash flows under these different situations can be examined to determine if the financing requirements expose the firm to a degree of default risk too high to bear.

In work that has been highly acclaimed, Donaldson has suggested that the firm's debt-carrying capacity (defined in the broad sense here to include preferred dividend payments and lease payments) ought to depend on the net cash flows the firm could expect to receive during a recessionary period.[9] In other words, *target capital structure proportions* could be set by planning for the "worst that could happen." An example will be of help.

Suppose that a recession is expected to last for one year.[10] Moreover, the end of the year represents the bottoming-out, or worst portion of the recession.

[7]See, for example, Eli Schwartz and J. Richard Aronson, "Some Surrogate Evidence in Support of the Concept of Optimal Financial Structure," *Journal of Finance* 22 (March 1967), pp. 10–18; David F. Scott, Jr., "Evidence on the Importance of Financial Structure," *Financial Management* 1 (Summer 1972), pp. 45–50; and David F. Scott, Jr., and John D. Martin, "Industry Influence on Financial Structure," *Financial Management* 4 (Spring 1975), pp. 67–73.

[8]Cash budget preparation is discussed in Chapter 13.

[9]Refer to Gordon Donaldson, "New Framework for Corporate Debt Policy," *Harvard Business Review* 40 (March–April 1962), pp. 117–31; Gordon Donaldson, *Corporate Debt Capacity* (Boston: Division of Research, Graduate School of Business Administration, Harvard University, 1961), Chap. 7; and Gordon Donaldson, "Strategy for Financial Emergencies," *Harvard Business Review* 47 (November–December 1969), pp. 67–79.

[10]The analysis can readily be extended to cover a recessionary period of several years. All that is necessary is to calculate the cash budgets over a similar period.

Equation (10–8) defines the cash balance, CB_r, the firm could expect to have at the end of the recession period.[11]

$$CB_r = C_0 + (C_s + OR) - (P_a + RM + \cdots + E_n) - FC \qquad (10\text{–}8)$$

where C_0 = the cash balance at the beginning
of the recession

C_s = collection from sales

OR = other cash receipts

P_a = payroll expenditures

RM = raw material payments

E_n = the last of a long series of expenditures
over which management has little control
(nondiscretionary expenditures)

FC = fixed financial charges associated with
a specific capital structure

If we let the net of total cash receipts and nondiscretionary expenditures be represented by NCF_r, then equation (10–8) can be simplified to

$$CB_r = C_0 + NCF_r - FC \qquad (10\text{–}9)$$

The inputs to equation (10–9) come from a detailed cash budget. The variable representing financing costs, FC, can be changed in accordance with several alternative financing plans to ascertain if the net cash balance during the recession, CB_r, might fall below zero.

Suppose that some firm typically maintains $500,000 in cash and marketable securities. This amount would be on hand at the start of the recession period. During the economic decline, the firm projects that its net cash flows from operations, NCF_r, will be $2 million. If the firm currently finances its assets with an unlevered capital structure, its cash balance at the worst point of the recession would be

$$CB_r = \$500{,}000 + \$2{,}000{,}000 - \$0 = \$2{,}500{,}000$$

This procedure allows us to study many different situations.[12] Assume that the same firm is considering a shift in its capitalization such that annual interest and sinking fund payments will be $2,300,000. If a recession occurred, the firm's cash balance at the end of the adverse economic period would be

$$CB_r = \$500{,}000 + \$2{,}000{,}000 - \$2{,}300{,}000 = \$200{,}000$$

The firm ordinarily maintains a liquid asset balance of $500,000. Thus, the effect of the proposed capital structure on the firm's cash balance during adverse circumstances might seem too risky for management to accept. When the chance of being out of cash is too high for management to bear, the use of financial leverage has been pushed beyond a reasonable level. According to this tool, the appropriate level of financial leverage is reached when the chance of being out of cash is exactly equal to that which management will assume.

---

[11]For the most part, the present notation follows that of Donaldson.

[12]It is not difficult to improve the usefulness of this sort of analysis by applying the technique of simulation to the generation of the various cash budgets. This facilitates the construction of probability distributions of net cash flows under differing circumstances. Simulation was discussed in Chapter 7.

A Glance at Actual Capital Structure Management

In this chapter we have discussed (1) the concept of an optimal capital structure, (2) the search for an appropriate range of financial leverage, and (3) the fundamental tools of capital structure management. Now we will examine some opinions and practices of financial executives that support our emphasis on the importance of capital structure management.

The Conference Board has surveyed 170 senior financial officers with respect to their capital structure practices.[13] Of these 170 executives, 102, or 60 percent, stated that they *do* believe there is an optimum capital structure for the corporation. Sixty-five percent of the responding practitioners worked for firms

---

[13]Francis J. Walsh, Jr., *Planning Corporate Capital Structures* (New York: The Conference Board, 1972).

with annual sales in excess of $200 million. One executive who subscribed to the optimal capital structure concept stated:

> In my opinion, there is an optimum capital structure for companies. However, this optimum capital structure will vary by individual companies, industries, and then is subject to changing economies, by money markets, earnings trends, and prospects . . . the circumstances and the lenders will determine an optimum at different points in time.[14]

This survey and others consistently point out that (1) financial officers set target debt ratios for their companies, and (2) the values for those ratios are influenced by a conscious evaluation of the basic business risk to which the firm is exposed.

Target Debt Ratios

Selected comments from financial executives point to the widespread use of target debt ratios. A vice-president and treasurer of the American Telephone and Telegraph Company (AT&T) described his firm's debt ratio policy in terms of a range:

> All of the foregoing considerations led us to conclude, and reaffirm for a period of many years, that the proper range of our debt was 30% to 40% of total capital. Reasonable success in meeting financial needs under the diverse market and economic conditions that we have faced attests to the appropriateness of this conclusion.[15]

In a similar fashion the president of Fibreboard Corporation identified his firm's target debt ratio and noted how it is related to the uncertain nature of the company's business:

> Our objective is a 30% ratio of debt to capitalization. We need that kind of flexibility to operate in the cyclical business we are in.[16]

In the Conference Board survey mentioned earlier, 84 of the 102 financial officers who subscribed to the optimal capital structure concept stated that their firm *has* a target debt ratio.[17] The most frequently mentioned influence on the level of the target debt ratio was ability to meet financing charges. Other factors identified as affecting the target were (1) maintaining a desired bond rating, (2) providing an adequate borrowing reserve, and (3) exploiting the advantages of financial leverage.

Who Sets Target Debt Ratios?

From the preceding discussion, we know that firms *do* use target debt ratios in arriving at financing decisions. But who sets or influences these target ratios? This and other questions concerning corporate financing policy were investigated in one study published in 1982.[18] This survey of the 1,000 largest industrial firms in the United States (as ranked by total sales dollars) involved responses from 212 financial executives.

In one portion of this study the participants were asked to rank several

---

[14]Ibid., p. 14.

[15]John J. Scanlon, "Bell System Financial Policies," *Financial Management* 1 (Summer 1972), pp. 16–26.

[16]*Business Week*, December 6, 1976, p. 30.

[17]Walsh, *Planning Corporate Capital Structures*, p. 17.

[18]David F. Scott, Jr., and Dana J. Johnson, "Financing Policies and Practices in Large Corporations," *Financial Management* 11 (Summer 1982), pp. 51–59.

TABLE 10–8.
Setting Target Financial
Structure Ratios

Type of Influence	Rank	
	1	2
Internal management and staff analysts	85%	7%
Investment bankers	3	39
Commercial bankers	0	9
Trade creditors	1	0
Security analysts	1	4
Comparative industry ratios	3	23
Other	7	18
Total	100%	100%

Source: David F. Scott, Jr., and Dana J. Johnson, "Financing Policies and Practices in Large Corporations," *Financial Management* 11 (Summer 1982), p. 53.

possible influences on their target leverage (debt) ratios. Table 10–8 displays the percentage of responses ranked either number one or number two in importance. Ranks past the second are omitted in that they were not very significant. Notice that the most important influence is the firm's own management group and staff of analysts. This item accounted for 85 percent of the responses ranked number one. Of the responses ranked number two in importance, investment bankers dominated the outcomes and accounted for 39 percent of such replies. The role of investment bankers in the country's capital market system is explored in some detail in Chapter 18. Also notice that comparisons with ratios of industry competitors and commercial bankers have some impact on the determination of leverage targets.

Debt Capacity

Previously in this chapter we noted that the firm's debt capacity is the maximum proportion of debt that it can include in its capital structure and still maintain its lowest composite cost of capital. But how do financial executives make the concept of debt capacity operational? Table 10–9 is derived from the same 1982 survey, involving 212 executives, mentioned above. These executives defined debt capacity in a wide variety of ways. The most popular approach was as a target percentage of total capitalization. Twenty-seven percent of the respondents thought of debt capacity in this manner. Forty-three percent of the participating executives remarked that debt capacity is defined in terms of some balance-sheet-based financial ratio (see the first three items in Table 10–9). Maintaining a specific bond rating was also indicated to be a popular approach to implementing the debt capacity concept.

TABLE 10–9.
Definitions of Debt Capacity
in Practice

Standard or Method	1,000 Largest Corporations (Percent Using)
Target percent of total capitalization (long-term debt to total capitalization)	27%
Long-term debt to net worth ratio (or its inverse)	14
Long-term debt to total assets	2
Interest (or fixed charge) coverage ratio	6
Maintain bond ratings	14
Restrictive debt covenants	4
Most adverse cash flow	4
Industry standard	3
Other	10
No response	16
Total	100%

Source: Derived from David F. Scott, Jr., and Dana J. Johnson, "Financing Polices and Practices in Large Corporations," *Financial Mangement* 11 (Summer 1982), pp. 51-59.

Increased Leverage

Corporate financing policies change over time. Are U.S. companies more heavily levered than in past periods? The data seem to substantiate such a tendency.

It is true, however, that *not* all leverage measures indicate notable rises in fixed-income financing. This means, confusingly enough, that the significance of the rise in debt use depends on how the financial structure relationships are measured.

Aggregate relationships generally point to more leverage use. For instance, between 1983 and 1988, the debt of nonfinancial corporations grew at about 1.7 times the rate of growth in nominal gross national product. On the other hand, debt-to-equity ratios measured at market value for what is called the "nonfinancial corporate sector" are higher than they were in 1970, but have remained reasonably steady since 1980.

One measure of financial leverage, though, *has* displayed a significant deterioration since around 1970. Further, most studies *agree* on this particular finding. In Table 10–7 under the heading called "coverage ratios" you will observe a metric called the "times interest earned" ratio. Let's just call it the interest coverage ratio for the rest of this discussion.

Studies usually measure the coverage ratio just as it is displayed in Table 10–7. Table 10–7 also contains another metric called the "long-term debt to total capitalization" ratio. This is the same ratio listed at the top of Table 10–9—which indicates its popularity with practicing financial executives.

Table 10–10 presents some results from a study of financial structure tendencies over the 1970–86 period. The 100 largest nonfinancial corporations were studied in selected years with regard to several financial leverage measures.

Size was based on the book value of total assets. Two of those measures are shown in Table 10–10. Part A of the table shows the coverage and long-term debt to total capitalization ratios for all 100 firms for the selected years. Part B of the table shows the results for *only* those firms that existed across *all* years of the study. This means 47 firms from the 1970 list *also* existed in identifiable form in 1986. The second ratio in each panel was measured at *book* value.

Two main points can be made. First, there is a definite, observed weakening in interest coverage ratios since 1970. We can offer, then, that the likelihood of firm failure has increased over the past two decades for the sample firms. Second, the long-term debt to total capitalization ratios are rather stable over the period. Other researchers have noted this same set of relationships. They are not contradictory—it merely emphasizes that more than one approach has to be taken to assess leverage use. The debt and stock metrics have grown at about the same rates over time—but earnings available to service the interest payments on the debt have lagged.

TABLE 10–10.
Indicators of Financial Leverage Use

Part A: 100 Largest (by total assets) Nonfinancial Corporations				
Year/Ratio	1986	1980	1975	1970
Coverage ratio (times)	4.98	8.64	7.85	9.09
Long-term debt to total capitalization (%)	31.9	26.3	30.9	31.2

Part B: 47 "Survivors" of the 100 Largest Nonfinancial Corporations				
Year/Ratio	1986	1980	1975	1970
Coverage ratio (times)	3.91	8.91	9.97	13.22
Long-term debt to total capitalization (%)	30.4	26.0	27.8	26.1

Source: Derived from David F. Scott, Jr., and Nancy Jay, "Leverage Use in Corporate America," *Working Paper 9011*, Orlando, FL: Dr. Phillips Institute for the Study of American Business Activity, University of Central Florida, January 1990.

The most-recent U.S. recession began in July 1990. Most analysts agree that this recession will be a real (tough) test of recent capital structure policies. One study estimated that about 10 percent of nonfinancial firms will have serious financial difficulties, if any recession is roughly as troubling as the one experienced during 1981–82. You can see how crucial the analysis of financial risk is both to the firm *and* to the aggregate economy.[19] This is expanded on subsequently.

Business Cycles

Effective financial managers—those who assist in creating value for the firm's common shareholders—are perceptive about and in constant communication with the financial marketplace. When market conditions change abruptly, company financial policies and decisions must adapt to the new conditions. Some firms, however, do a better job of adjusting than others. Companies that are slow to adapt to changes in the aggregate, or overall, business environment face a lower level of cash flow generation and increased risk of financial distress.

Changes in the aggregate business environment are often referred to as *business cycles*. There are many useful definitions of such cycles. For example, Dr. Fischer Black, a former finance professor and later an executive with the well-known investment banking firm of Goldman, Sachs & Co., defined business cycles as follows:[20]

> Business cycles are fluctuations in economic activity. Business cycles show up in virtually all measures of economic activity—output, income, employment, unemployment, retail sales, new orders by manufacturers, even housing starts. When times are good, they tend to be good all over; and when times are bad, they tend to be bad all over.

A slightly different but compatible definition of business cycles that we will use is: **Business cycles** are a series of commercial adjustments to unanticipated, new information accentuated by *both* public policy decisions and private-sector decisions. When the decisions, on balance, are correct the economy expands. When the decisions, on balance, are incorrect, the economy contracts.

Since the end of World War II, the U.S. has endured nine recessions. Recessions are the contractionary or negative phase of the entire business cycle. Those nine recessions are documented in Table 10–11.

Typically, different stages of the business cycle induce a different set of relationships in the financial markets. These different relationships are reflected in the different capital structure decisions managers make. For example, relationships between interest rates and equity prices may differ sharply over different phases of the cycle. Some phases of the cycle favor the issuance of debt securities over equity instruments, and vice versa. Complicating the decision-making setting for the manager is the fact that financial relationships will be *dissimilar* over each cycle.[21]

The recession that began in July 1990 has produced its own set of unique financial characteristics. Accordingly, financial managers altered their firms' capital structures in response to new information that included capital cost relationships in the financial markets. Managers began to reverse some of the

---

[19]Ben Bernanke, "Is There Too Much Corporate Debt?" *Business Review*, Federal Reserve Bank of Philadelphia (September–October 1989), p. 10. Similar findings on increased leverage use are found in Margaret Mendenhall Blair, "A Surprising Culprit Behind the Rush to Leverage," *The Brookings Review* (Winter 1989–90), 19–26.

[20]Fischer Black, "The ABCs of Business Cycles," *Financial Analysts Journal* 37 (November–December 1981), pp. 75–80. Dr. Black touched on similar and other far-reaching points in his compelling presidential address to the American Finance Association; see Fischer Black, "Noise," *Journal of Finance* 41 (July 1986), pp. 529–43.

[21]Available discussions and studies on the relationship between business cycles and corporate financing patterns are not plentiful. One such study is Robert A. Taggart, Jr., "Corporate Financing: Too Much Debt?" *Financial Analysts Journal* 42 (May–June 1986), pp. 35–42.

TABLE 10–11.
Post–World War II U.S.
Business Cycles

Start of Recession (Peaks)	End (Troughs)	Length (Months)
November 1948	October 1949	11
July 1953	May 1954	10
August 1957	April 1958	8
April 1960	February 1961	10
December 1969	November 1970	11
November 1973	March 1975	16
January 1980	July 1980	6
July 1981	November 1982	16
July 1990	Not yet dated[a]	—

Source: National Bureau of Economic Research (NBER).
[a]Note the Business Cycle Dating Committee of the NBER will establish the technical end to this recession.

financial leverage buildup that occurred in the 1980s. Specifically, by early 1991, corporations began to take advantage of an improved market for common equities and brought to the marketplace substantial amounts of new common stock issues.

The *Basic Financial Management in Practice* that follows discusses the reactions of financial managers to the special characteristics of the 1990

BASIC FINANCIAL MANAGEMENT IN PRACTICE

Cycles and Trends in Financing Practices

Encouraged by the stock market's gains this year and a desire to strengthen their financial condition, American companies are issuing new stock at the fastest pace since before the "Black Monday" crash in October 1987.

The surge of equity offerings has been fueled both by small, young companies selling stock publicly for the first time and by big, established corporations seeking extra cash to reduce debt or to get an edge over weaker competitors.

If the trend continues, as many experts expect, it will have a favorable impact on the U.S. economy by raising fresh capital to nourish companies' growth and by helping to reverse some of the excessive borrowing undertaken during the 1980s.

On the other hand, a flood of new issues pouring into the market also eventually could tend to depress stock prices, simply because there may not be enough demand to absorb the growing supply. Some Wall Street professionals already see some "indigestion" developing for new issues, particularly for high-flying, newly issued stocks in some biotechnology and medical companies.

So far, however, the market's appetite for new stock has been more than sufficient. Both institutional and individual investors have bid eagerly for newly issued shares and sent prices up sharply in many cases. Some traders have reaped gains of more than 30 percent in a few hours as prices soar for newly available stock in companies that seem to have outstanding prospects for growth.

The thriving market in new stock appears to herald an important shift in sentiment in the financial markets. It marks the first time since the 1987 crash that companies are finding it easy to raise substantial amounts of money through the relatively cheap means of selling equity, or stock, in themselves.

Previously, because of skepticism about the stock market after the crash and general worries about America's financial condition, companies had to resort more often to issuing debt, on which they must make regular interest payments.

"The equity markets for several years had not been a place for companies to raise much capital, and that has reversed, and that's good," says Steven G. Einhorn, a partner and co-chairman of investment policy at Goldman, Sachs & Co., a New York investment bank.

Einhorn estimates that U.S. companies will issue between $40 billion and $50 billion of new stock this year and about the same amount again in 1992. Not since 1987 has the annual total exceeded $40 billion, and it has averaged only $24 billion a year from 1988 through 1990.

Source: "Wall Street Returns to a Capital Idea," by Robert J. McCartney, *The Washington Post* National Weekly Edition, May 27–June 2, 1991, pp. 21, 22.

recession. It emphasizes the point that managers know about business cycles and react to them.

Business Risk

The single most important factor that should affect the firm's financing mix is the underlying nature of the business in which it operates. In Chapter 9 we defined business risk as the relative dispersion in the firm's expected stream of EBIT. If the nature of the firm's business is such that the variability inherent in its EBIT stream is high, then it would be unwise to impose a high degree of financial risk on top of this already uncertain earnings stream.

Corporate executives are likely to point this out in discussions of capital-structure management. A financial officer in a large steel firm related:

> The nature of the industry, the marketplace, and the firm tend to establish debt limits that any prudent management would prefer not to exceed. Our industry is capital intensive and our markets tend to be cyclical. . . . The capability to service debt while operating in the environment described dictates a conservative financial structure.[22]

Notice how that executive was concerned with both his firm's business risk exposure and its cash flow capability for meeting any financing costs. The AT&T financial officer referred to earlier also has commented on the relationship between business and financial risk:

> In determining how much debt a firm can safely carry, it is necessary to consider the basic risks inherent in that business. This varies considerably among industries and is related essentially to the nature and demand for an industry's product, the operating characteristics of the industry, and its ability to earn an adequate return in an unknown future.[23]

It appears clear that the firm's capital structure cannot be properly designed without a thorough understanding of its commercial strategy.

Financial Managers and Theory

Earlier in this chapter we discussed a *moderate view* of capital structure theory. The saucer-shaped cost of capital curve implied by this theory (Figure 10–9)

[22]Walsh, *Planning Corporate Capital Structures*, p. 18.
[23]Scanlon, "Bell System Financial Policies," p. 19.

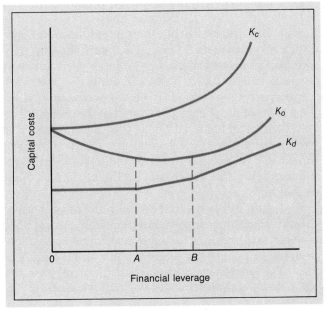

FIGURE 10–9.
Capital Costs: The Moderate View

predicts that managers will add debt to the firm's capital structure when current leverage use is *below* the firm's optimal range of leverage use at the base of the overall cost of capital curve. Conversely, managers will add equity when leverage use is above this optimal range. Under these conditions above *both* financing activities lower the cost of capital to the firm and increase shareholder wealth.

A recent survey of chief financial officers of the top (largest) nonfinancial, nonregulated U.S. firms addressed these predicted activities. Of the 800 firms surveyed, 117 responded, for a response rate of 14.6 percent. These decision makers were asked how their firms would respond if confronted with certain, specific financing situations.

It should be noted that the moderate view does not distinguish between internal equity (retained earnings and depreciation) and external equity (the sale of common stock). The questions posed to the financial managers, however, *do* make this distinction. Based on our financial asset valuation models, common equity is generally considered the most *expensive* source of funds, exceeding the costs of both debt and preferred stock. The cost of external equity exceeds internal equity by the addition of flotation costs. (Recall our discussion in Chapter 8 on these relationships.)

Addressing the downward-sloping portion of the cost of capital curve, managers were asked what their financing choice would be if (1) the firm has internal funds *sufficient* for investment requirements (capital budgeting needs), but (2) the debt ratio is *below* the level preferred by the firm. The moderate theory predicts that managers will add debt to the firm's capital structure in this situation. However, 81 percent of the respondents said they would use *internal equity* to finance their investments. Only 17 percent suggested they would use long-term debt, and 11 percent selected short-term debt. In this situation, most managers indicated they would choose to use the more expensive internal equity rather than the (seemingly) less expensive debt for investments.

Similarly, when internal funds are sufficient for new investment and the debt level *exceeds* the firm's optimum range of leverage use, managers again chose to use internal equity in 81 percent of the responses. Seventeen percent would issue new equity if market conditions were favorable. Because the debt level is currently *excessive*, the moderate theory would predict that external equity would be added to minimize the cost of capital. Instead, most firms preferred to fund investment with the internal funds. This is a prevalent tendency in American industry.

Responses to the preceding questions imply that, if managers follow the financing activity prescribed by the moderate view, it is *only* after internal funds have been *exhausted*. Because these internal funds are relatively expensive (compared with new debt), their use as the *initial* financing option indicates that either: (1) managers do not view their financing goal to be the minimization of the firm's cost of capital, or (2) the explicit and implicit costs of new security issues are *understated*. If this is actually the case, internal funds may be the *least* expensive source of funds from the perspective of financial managers. This may be a form of the agency problem that we previously discussed in this chapter.

The chief financial officers were also asked what their financing decision would be under these conditions: (1) the firm requires external funds, (2) financial leverage use *exceeds* the desired level, and (3) equity markets are underpricing the firm's stock. Table 10–12 contains the responses to this question.

In this difficult situation, 68 percent of the managers indicated that they would *reduce* their investment plans. That is, capital budgets would shrink. The primary explanations for such investment restriction were (1) that it was in the best interest of current shareholders, and (2) that it controlled risk.

The next-favored choice (28 percent) was the use of short-term debt, sometimes combined with investment reduction. This suggests that managers

TABLE 10–12.
Managers and Theory: Some
Responses

Question	
Your firm requires external funds to finance the next period's capital investments. Financial leverage use exceeds that preferred by the firm. Equity markets are underpricing your securities. Would your firm:	
Choices	Responses
Reduce your investment plans?	68%
Obtain short-term debt?	28
Attempt to provide the market with adequate information to correctly price your securities before issuing equity?	13
Issue long-term debt?	13
Issue equity anyway?	4
Reduce your dividend payout?	4

Source: Adapted from David F. Scott, Jr., and Nancy Jay, "Financial Managers and Capital Structure Theories," *Working Paper 9203*, Orlando, FL: Dr. Phillips Institute for the Study of American Business Activity, University of Central Florida, March 1992.

attempt to wait out difficult market conditions by adopting short-term solutions. The *timing* of security issues with favorable market conditions is a *major* objective of financial managers and entirely consistent with the optimal capital structure range defined under the moderate theory (Figure 10–9).

Only 4 percent of the respondents indicated that they would issue equity despite the underpricing of the firm's stock. Thirteen percent of the firms indicated that they would attempt to correct the adverse pricing by providing the market with adequate information before attempting to issue equity.

Another 13 percent of the respondents indicated that they would add long-term debt, moving leverage use further beyond the optimal range.

Only 4 percent of the executives responding to this situation stated they would obtain needed funds by *reducing* the cash dividend payout. To managers, the shareholders' cash dividends are quite important. Firms prefer to forgo profitable projects rather than to reallocate the shareholders' *expected* cash dividends to investment. Dividend policies are discussed extensively in Chapter 11.

You can see that our ability as analysts to *predict* financing choices, as opposed to *prescribing* them, is far from perfect. In many instances managers appear to react as popular capital structure theories suggest. In other instances, though, managers either are rejecting some aspects of the theories, or the theories need more work. Understanding these aberrations is useful to the analyst.

A thorough grounding in both the *theory* of financing decisions and in the *tools* of capital structure management will assist you in making sound choices that maximize shareholder wealth. This combination of theory and practical tools also permits you to ask some very perceptive questions when faced with a decision-making situation.

International Perspective

Capital Costs

From our work in Chapter 8 we understand how to estimate the firm's cost of financial capital. From our work here in Chapter 10 we understand the problems associated with designing the firm's overall financing mix. The cost tradeoffs and differing risk exposures have been illustrated.

Because of the globalization of the world's financial markets and intercountry acquisitions, we must be aware of differences in capital costs among

INTERNATIONAL FINANCIAL MANAGEMENT

Comparative Costs

Figuring the true cost of capital is complicated. Most capital is raised by borrowings—bond issues and bank loans—or by the sale of stock. The cost of borrowed money is, of course, the monthly interest payments, but the cost of selling stock or equity in a company is more than the quarterly dividend payments. Total profit must be high enough to persuade investors to buy and hold stock.

Borrowing money does not put American companies at a disadvantage. Although interest rates are higher in the United States than in West Germany and Japan, the differential almost disappears once allowance is made for inflation and tax breaks, according to a study by Robert N. McCauley and Steven A. Zimmer, of the Federal Reserve Bank of New York.

Adjusted in this fashion, the average borrowing costs from 1983 through 1988 were 1.8 percent in the United States, 1.7 percent in Japan and zero in Germany, the two economists found.

But American companies have greater difficulty talking potential equity investors into paying a high price for stock in a company whose current earnings are low. To lure investors, American companies had to earn 10.8 cents each year for every dollar invested in stock in the 1983–88 period, compared with 6.4 cents in West Germany and only 4.9 cents in Japan, the Fed study found.

American companies have not yet sold a big percentage of their shares to foreigners—so the demands of American shareholders determine the cost of capital, even though many companies borrow abroad. The total capital costs, through stock sales and borrowing, averaged 6.4 cents annually for each dollar raised by an American company in the 1983–88 period. The comparable figure for Japanese companies was 2.7 cents and for German companies 1.6 cents, the Fed economists said.

Their much-cited study helps to support several contentions. One is that Americans should save more, thus making more funds available for investment. Another is that the investment tax credit should be restored to lower investment costs. A third is that American companies are being forced to raise more capital through debt than new stock.

Japanese capital costs are rising—partly because equity capital is perhaps costlier than the Japanese acknowledge, but also because Japanese companies have recently increased the equity portion of their capital. Eventually, the process might bring capital costs in Japan and the United States close to each other.

The Entrepreneur's View

The acceleration of Japanese purchases of American corporate icons like Rockefeller Center, Columbia Pictures and CBS Records should come as no surprise, given the huge advantage that the Japanese enjoy in capital costs. Recent studies have found that America's capital is between 2½ and 4 times as expensive as Japan's. Inexpensive capital has given the Japanese a booming manufacturing sector and ample cash with which to purchase foreign assets.

Why is Japan's capital so much cheaper? According to George Hatsopoulos, an expert on the cost of capital, the differential results from three factors:

First, Japanese companies are able to obtain more of their financing in low-cost debt or debt-like instruments, while the structure of the American financial system dictates that American companies rely on expensive equity financing. Japanese debt-to-equity ratios are roughly 3-to-1, while ours are 1-to-3.

Second, the Japanese save more than three times as much of their incomes as Americans, thereby creating a greater pool of capital for investment within their country.

Third, tax policy in Japan helps reduce the cost of capital by encouraging savings and investment.

The general perception about Japan's advantage in the cost of capital is that it is the result of interest rate subsidies. But subsidies are not as critical as the differences in debt-equity ratios. Tradition in the United States requires that balance sheets be heavily weighted toward equity and that corporations be debt-adverse. In Japan, debt and debt-like instruments are common. It is becoming increasingly clear that in the 1990's, American companies will be reducing their debt while they increase their reliance on equity financing.

The problem with America's reliance on equity financing is that it is extremely expensive. It is expensive because entrepreneurs must give away a piece of the company.

Sources: Louis Uchitelle, "Theory of Decline Fails to Hold Up," *New York Times*, December 18, 1989, p. 26Y; William Farley, "The Cost of Capital: How to Make Raising Money Cheaper," *New York Times*, December 24, 1989, p. 2F.

nations. The present economic strength of Japan makes it a good country for comparison.

The two pieces on page 390 deal with international comparisons of capital costs and debt-to-equity ratios in the United States, Japan, and West Germany. Notice that while leverage ratios in the United States have risen over the past 10 years or so, the Japanese financial system supports significantly higher debt levels. Some analysts think that high capital costs in the United States put this country at a competitive disadvantage with its overseas trading partners. The initial piece is by a business writer for the *New York Times*. The second is by an American entrepreneur.

SUMMARY

This chapter deals with the design of the firm's financing mix, particularly emphasizing management of the firm's permanent sources of funds—that is, its capital structure. The objective of capital structure management is to arrange the company's sources of funds so that its common stock price will be maximized, all other factors held constant.

Capital Structure Theory

Can the firm affect its composite cost of capital by altering its financing mix? Attempts to answer this question have comprised a significant portion of capital structure theory for over three decades. Extreme positions show that the firm's stock price is either unaffected or continually affected as the firm increases its reliance on leverage-inducing funds. In the real world, an operating environment where interest expense is tax deductible and market imperfections operate to restrict the amount of fixed-income obligations a firm can issue, most financial officers and financial academics subscribe to the concept of an optimal capital structure. The optimal capital structure minimizes the firm's composite cost of capital. Searching for a proper range of financial leverage, then, is an important financial management activity.

Complicating the manager's search for an optimal capital structure are conflicts that lead to agency costs. A natural conflict exists between stockholders and bondholders (the agency costs of debt). To reduce excessive risk taking by management on behalf of stockholders, it may be necessary to include several protective covenants in bond contracts that serve to restrict managerial decision making.

Another type of agency cost is related to "free cash flow." Managers, for example, have an incentive to hold on to free cash flow and enjoy it, rather than paying it out in the form of higher cash-dividend payments. This conflict between managers and stockholders leads to the concept of the *free cash flow theory of capital structure*. This same theory is also known as the *control hypothesis* and the *threat hypothesis*. The ultimate resolution of these agency costs affects the specific form of the firm's capital structure.

Tools of Capital Structure Management

The decision to use senior securities in the firm's capitalization causes two types of financial leverage effects. The first is the added variability in the earnings per share stream that accompanies the use of fixed-charge securities. We explained in Chapter 9 how this could be quantified by use of the degree of financial leverage metric. The second financial leverage effect relates to the level of earnings per share (EPS) at a given EBIT under a specific capital structure. We rely on EBIT–EPS analysis to measure this second effect. Through EBIT–EPS analysis the decision maker can inspect the impact of alternative financing plans on EPS over a full range of EBIT levels.

A second tool of capital structure management is the calculation of comparative leverage ratios. Balance sheet leverage ratios and coverage ratios can be computed according to the contractual stipulations of the proposed financing plans. Comparison of these ratios with industry standards enables the financial officer to determine if the firm's key ratios are materially out of line with accepted practice.

A third tool is the analysis of corporate cash flows. This process involves the preparation of a series of cash budgets that consider different economic conditions and different capital structures. Useful insight into the identification of proper target capital structure ratios can be obtained by analyzing projected cash flow statements that assume adverse operating circumstances.

Capital Structure Practices

Surveys indicate that most financial officers in large firms believe in the concept of an optimal capital structure. The optimal capital structure is approximated by the identification of target debt ratios. The targets reflect the firm's ability to service fixed financing costs and also consider the business risk to which the firm is exposed.

Survey studies have provided information on who sets or influences the firm's target leverage ratios. The firm's own management group and staff of analysts are the major influence, followed in importance by investment bankers. Studies also show that executives operationalize the concept of debt capacity in many ways. The most popular approach is to define debt capacity in terms of a target long-term debt to total capitalization ratio. Maintaining a specific bond rating (such as Aa or A) is also a popular approach to implementing the debt capacity concept.

Financing policies change in significant ways over time. During the 1980s, for example, most studies confirm that U.S. companies "levered up" when compared with past decades. Specifically, interest coverage ratios deteriorated during the 1980s when compared with the 1970s.

The early 1990s are displaying a reversal of this trend. Effective financial managers have a sound understanding of business cycles. The recession that started in July 1990 produced a unique set of financial characteristics that led to relatively high common stock prices. Accordingly, financial managers reversed some of the leverage buildup incurred during the 1980s by bringing substantial amounts of new common stock to the marketplace.

Other studies of managers' financing tendencies suggest that (1) a tremendous preference for the use of internally generated equity to finance investments exists, (2) firms prefer to forgo seemingly profitable projects rather than reduce shareholders' expected cash dividends to finance a greater part of the capital budget, and (3) that security issues are timed with favorable market conditions.

STUDY QUESTIONS

10-1. Define the following terms:
  a. Financial structure
  b. Capital structure
  c. Optimal capital structure
  d. Debt capacity

10-2. What is the primary weakness of EBIT–EPS analysis as a financing decision tool?

10-3. What is the objective of capital structure management?

10-4. Distinguish between (a) balance sheet leverage ratios and (b) coverage ratios. Give two examples of each and indicate how they would be computed.

10-5. Why might firms whose sales levels change drastically over time choose to use debt only sparingly in their capital structures?

10-6. What condition would cause capital structure management to be a meaningless activity?

10-7. What does the term *independence hypothesis* mean as it applies to capital structure theory?

10-8. Who have been the foremost advocates of the independence hypothesis?

10-9. A financial manager might say that the firm's composite cost of capital is saucer-shaped or U-shaped. What does this mean?

10-10. Define the EBIT–EPS indifference point.

10-11. What is UEPS?

10-12. Explain how industry norms might be used by the financial manager in the design of the company's financing mix.

10-13. Define the term *free cash flow*.

10-14. What is meant by the *free cash flow theory of capital structure?*

10-15. Briefly describe the trend in corporate use of financial leverage during the 1980s.

10-16. Why should the financial manager be familiar with the business cycle?

10-17. In almost every instance what funds source do managers use first in the financing of their capital budgets?

SELF-TEST PROBLEMS

ST-1. (*Analysis of Recessionary Cash Flows*) The management of Story Enterprises is considering an increase in its use of financial leverage. The proposal on the table is to sell $6 million of bonds that would mature in 20 years. The interest rate on these bonds would be 12 percent. The bond issue would have a sinking fund attached to it requiring that one-twentieth of the principal be retired each year. Most business economists are forecasting a recession that will affect the entire company in the coming year. Story's management has been saying, "If we can make it through this, we can make it through anything." The firm prefers to carry an operating cash balance of $750,000. Cash collections from sales next year will total $3 million. Miscellaneous cash receipts will be $400,000. Raw material payments will be $700,000. Wage and salary costs will be $1,200,000 on a cash basis. On top of this, Story will experience nondiscretionary cash outlays of $1.2 million, *including* all tax payments. The firm faces a 34 percent tax rate.

a. At present, Story is unlevered. What will be the total fixed financial charges the firm must pay next year?

b. If the bonds are issued, what is your forecast for the firm's expected cash balance at the end of the recessionary year (next year)?

c. As Story's financial consultant, do you recommend that it issue the bonds?

ST-2. (*Assessing Leverage Use*) Some financial data and the appropriate industry norm for three companies are shown in the following table:

Measure	Firm X	Firm Y	Firm Z	Industry Norm
Total debt to total assets	20%	30%	10%	30%
Times interest and preferred dividend coverage	8 times	16 times	19 times	8 times
Price/earnings ratio	9 times	11 times	9 times	9 times

a. Which firm appears to be employing financial leverage to the most appropriate degree?

b. In this situation, which "financial leverage effect" appears to dominate the market valuation process?

ST-3. (*EBIT–EPS Analysis*) Four engineers from Martin-Bowing Company are leaving that firm in order to form their own corporation. The new firm will produce and distribute computer software on a national basis. The software will be aimed at scientific markets and at businesses desiring to install comprehensive information systems. Private investors have been lined up to finance the new company. Two financing proposals are being studied. Both of these plans involve the use of some financial leverage; however, one is much more highly levered than the other. Plan A requires the firm to sell bonds with an effective interest rate of 14 percent. One million dollars would be raised in this manner. In addition, under plan A, $5 million would be raised by selling stock at $50 per common share. Plan B also involves raising $6 million. This would be accomplished by selling $3 million of bonds at an interest rate of 16 percent. The other $3 million would come from selling common stock at $50 per share. In both cases the use of financial leverage is considered to be a permanent part of the firm's capital structure, so no fixed maturity date is used in the analysis. The firm considers a 50 percent tax rate appropriate for planning purposes.

a. Find the EBIT indifference level associated with the two financing plans, and prepare an EBIT–EPS analysis chart.

b. Prepare an analytical income statement that demonstrates that EPS will be the same regardless of the plan selected. Use the EBIT level found in part (a) above.

c. A detailed financial analysis of the firm's prospects suggests that long-term EBIT will be above $1,188,000 annually. Taking this into consideration, which plan will generate the higher EPS?

d. Suppose that long-term EBIT is forecast to be $1,188,000 per year. Under plan A, a price/earnings ratio of 13 would apply. Under plan B, a price/earnings ratio of 11 would apply. If this set of financial relationships does hold, which financing plan would you recommend be implemented?

e. Again, assume an EBIT level of $1,188,000. What price/earnings ratio applied to the EPS of plan B would provide the same stock price as that projected for plan A? Refer to your data from part (d) above.

STUDY PROBLEMS (SET A)

10–1A. (*EBIT–EPS Analysis*) A group of retired college professors has decided to form a small manufacturing corporation. The company will produce a full line of traditional office furniture. Two financing plans have been proposed by the investors. Plan A is an all-common-equity alternative. Under this agreement, 1 million common shares will be sold to net the firm $20 per share. Plan B involves the use of financial leverage. A debt issue with a 20-year maturity period will be privately placed. The debt issue will carry an interest rate of 10 percent, and the principal borrowed will amount to $6 million. The corporate tax rate is 50 percent.

a. Find the EBIT indifference level associated with the two financing proposals.

b. Prepare an analytical income statement that proves EPS will be the same regardless of the plan chosen at the EBIT level found in part (a).

c. Prepare an EBIT–EPS analysis chart for this situation.

d. If a detailed financial analysis projects that long-term EBIT will always be close to $2.4 million annually, which plan will provide for the higher EPS?

10–2A. (*Capital Structure Theory*) Deep End Pools & Supplies has an all common equity capital structure. Some financial data for the company are shown below:

> Shares of common stock outstanding = 900,000
> Common stock price, P_o = $30 per share
> Expected level of EBIT = $5,400,000
> Dividend payout ratio = 100 percent

In answering the following questions, assume that corporate income is not taxed.

a. Under the present capital structure, what is the total value of the firm?

b. What is the cost of common equity capital, K_c? What is the composite cost of capital, K_o?

c. Now, suppose Deep End sells $1.5 million of long-term debt with an interest rate of 8 percent. The proceeds are used to retire the outstanding common stock. According to the net operating income theory (the independence hypothesis), what will be the firm's cost of common equity after the capital structure change?

  1. What will be the dividend per share flowing to the firm's common shareholders?

  2. By what percentage has the dividend per share changed owing to the capital structure change?

  3. By what percentage has the cost of common equity changed owing to the capital structure change?

  4. What will be the composite cost of capital after the capital structure change?

10-3A. (*EBIT–EPS Analysis*) Four recent liberal arts graduates have interested a group of venture capitalists in backing a new business enterprise. The proposed operation would consist of a series of retail outlets to distribute and service a full line of vacuum cleaners and accessories. These stores would be located in Dallas, Houston, and San Antonio. Two financing plans have been proposed by the graduates. Plan A is an all-common-equity structure. Two million dollars would be raised by selling 80,000 shares of common stock. Plan B would involve the use of long-term debt financing. One million dollars would be raised by marketing bonds with an effective interest rate of 12 percent. Under this alternative, another million dollars would be raised by selling 40,000 shares of common stock. With both plans, then, $2 million is needed to launch the new firm's operations. The debt funds raised under Plan B are considered to have no fixed maturity date, in that this portion of financial leverage is thought to be a permanent part of the company's capital structure. The fledgling executives have decided to use a 40 percent tax rate in their analysis, and they have hired you on a consulting basis to do the following:

    a. Find the EBIT indifference level associated with the two financing proposals.

    b. Prepare an analytical income statement that proves EPS will be the same regardless of the plan chosen at the EBIT level found in part (a) above.

10-4A. (*EBIT–EPS Analysis*) Three recent graduates of the computer science program at Southern Tennessee Tech are forming a company to write and distribute software for various personal computers. Initially, the corporation will operate in the southern region of Tennessee, Georgia, North Carolina, and South Carolina. Twelve serious prospects for retail outlets have already been identified and committed to the firm. The firm's software products have been tested and displayed at several trade shows and computer fairs in the perceived operating region. All that is lacking is adequate financing to continue with the project. A small group of private investors in the Atlanta, Georgia, area is interested in financing the new company. Two financing proposals are being evaluated. The first (plan A) is an all common equity capital structure. Two million dollars would be raised by selling common stock at $20 per common share. Plan B would involve the use of financial leverage. One million dollars would be raised selling bonds with an effective interest rate of 11 percent (per annum). Under this second plan, the remaining $1 million would be raised by selling common stock at the $20 price per share. The use of financial leverage is considered to be a permanent part of the firm's capitalization, so no fixed maturity date is needed for the analysis. A 34 percent tax rate is appropriate for the analysis.

    a. Find the EBIT indifference level associated with the two financing plans.

    b. A detailed financial analysis of the firm's prospects suggests that the long-term EBIT will be above $300,000 annually. Taking this into consideration, which plan will generate the higher EPS?

    c. Suppose long-term EBIT is forecast to be $300,000 per year. Under plan A, a price/earnings ratio of 19 would apply. Under plan B, a price/earnings ratio of 15 would apply. If this set of financial relationships does hold, which financing plan would you recommend?

10-5A. (*EBIT–EPS Analysis*) Three recent liberal arts graduates have interested a group of venture capitalists in backing a new business enterprise. The proposed operation would consist of a series of retail outlets to distribute and service a full line of personal computer equipment. These stores would be located in southern New Jersey, New York, and Pennsylvania. Two financing plans have been proposed by the graduates. Plan A is an all common equity structure. Three million dollars would be raised by selling 75,000 shares of common stock. Plan B would involve the use of long-term debt financing. One million dollars would be raised by marketing bonds with an effective interest rate of 15 percent. Under this alternative, another $2 million would be raised by selling 50,000 shares of common stock. With both plans, then, $3 million is needed to launch the new firm's operations. The debt funds raised under plan B are considered to have no fixed maturity date, in that this proportion of financial leverage is thought to be a permanent part of the company's capital structure. The fledgling executives have decided to use a 34 percent tax rate in their analysis, and they have hired you on a consulting basis to do the following:

    a. Find the EBIT indifference level associated with the two financing proposals.

    b. Prepare an analytical income statement that proves EPS will be the same regardless of the plan chosen at the EBIT level found in part (a) above.

10-6A. (*EBIT–EPS Analysis*) Two recent graduates of the computer science program at Ohio Tech are forming a company to write, market, and distribute software for various personal computers. Initially, the corporation will operate in the Midwest area of Illinois, Indiana, Michigan, and Ohio. Twelve serious prospects for retail outlets in these different states have already been identified and committed to the firm. The firm's software products have been tested and displayed at several trade shows and computer fairs in the perceived operating region. All that is lacking is adequate financing to continue the project. A small group of private investors in the Columbus, Ohio, area are interested in financing the new company. Two financing proposals are being evaluated. The first (plan A) is an all common equity capital structure. Four million dollars would be raised by selling stock at $40 per common share. Plan B would involve the use of financial leverage. Two million dollars would be raised by selling bonds with an effective interest rate of 16 percent (per annum). Under this second plan, the remaining $2 million would be raised by selling common stock at the $40 price per share. This use of financial leverage is considered to be a permanent part of the firm's capitalization, so no fixed maturity date is needed for the analysis. A 50 percent tax rate is appropriate for the analysis.

a. Find the EBIT indifference level associated with the two financing plans.

b. Prepare an analytical income statement that proves EPS will be the same regardless of the plan chosen at the EBIT level found in part (a) above.

c. A detailed financial analysis of the firm's prospects suggests that long-term EBIT will be above $800,000 annually. Taking this into consideration, which plan will generate the higher EPS?

d. Suppose that long-term EBIT is forecast to be $800,000 per year. Under plan A, a price/earnings ratio of 12 would apply. Under plan B, a price/earnings ratio of 10 would apply. If this set of financial relationships does hold, which financing plan would you recommend be implemented?

10–7A. (*Analysis of Recessionary Cash Flows*) The management of Idaho Produce is considering an increase in its use of financial leverage. The proposal on the table is to sell $10 million of bonds that would mature in 20 years. The interest rate on these bonds would be 15 percent. The bond issue would have a sinking fund attached to it requiring that one-twentieth of the principal be retired each year. Most business economists are forecasting a recession that will affect the entire economy in the coming year. Idaho's management has been saying, "If we can make it through this, we can make it through anything." The firm prefers to carry an operating cash balance of $1 million. Cash collections from sales next year will total $4 million. Miscellaneous cash receipts will be $300,000. Raw material payments will be $800,000. Wage and salary costs will total $1.4 million on a cash basis. On top of this, Idaho will experience nondiscretionary cash outflows of $1.2 million *including* all tax payments. The firm faces a 50 percent tax rate.

a. At present, Idaho is unlevered. What will be the total fixed financial charges the firm must pay next year?

b. If the bonds are issued, what is your forecast for the firm's expected cash balance at the end of the recessionary year (next year)?

c. As Idaho's financial consultant, do you recommend that it issue the bonds?

10–8A. (*EBIT–EPS Analysis*) Four recent business school graduates have interested a group of venture capitalists in backing a small business enterprise. The proposed operation would consist of a series of retail outlets that would distribute and service a full line of energy-conservation equipment. These stores would be located in northern Virginia, western Pennsylvania, and throughout West Virginia. Two financing plans have been proposed by the graduates. Plan A is an all-common-equity capital structure. Three million dollars would be raised by selling 60,000 shares of common stock. Plan B would involve the use of long-term debt financing. One million dollars would be raised by marketing bonds with an interest rate of 10 percent. Under this alternative another $2 million would be raised by selling 40,000 shares of common stock. With both plans, then, $3 million is needed to launch the new firm's operations. The debt funds raised under plan B are considered to have no fixed maturity date, in that this proportion of financial leverage is thought to be a permanent part of the company's capital structure. The fledgling executives have decided to use a 40 percent tax rate in their analysis.

a. Find the EBIT indifference level associated with the two financing proposals.

b. Prepare an analytical income statement that proves EPS will be the same regardless of the plan chosen at the EBIT level found in part (a).

10–9A. (*EBIT–EPS Analysis*) A group of college professors have decided to form a small manufacturing corporation. The company will produce a full line of contemporary furniture. Two financing plans have been proposed by the investors. Plan A is an all-common-equity alternative. Under this arrangement 1,400,000 common shares will be sold to net the firm $10 per share. Plan B involves the use of financial leverage. A debt issue with a 20-year maturity period will be privately placed. The debt issue will carry an interest rate of 8 percent and the principal borrowed will amount to $4 million. The corporate tax rate is 50 percent.

a. Find the EBIT indifference level associated with the two financing proposals.

b. Prepare an analytical income statement that proves EPS will be the same regardless of the plan chosen at the EBIT level found in part (a).

c. Prepare an EBIT–EPS analysis chart for this situation.

d. If a detailed financial analysis projects that long-term EBIT will always be close to $1,800,000 annually, which plan will provide for the higher EPS?

10–10A. (*EBIT–EPS Analysis*) The professors in problem 10–9A contacted a financial consultant to provide them with some additional information. They felt that in a few years the stock of the firm would be publicly traded over the counter, so they were interested in the consultant's opinion as to what the stock price would be under the financing plan outlined in problem 10–9A. The consultant agreed that the projected long-term EBIT level of $1,800,000 was reasonable. He also felt that if plan A were selected, the marketplace would apply a price/earnings ratio of 12 times to the company's stock; for plan B he estimated a price/earnings ratio of 10 times.

a. According to this information, which financing alternative would offer a higher stock price?

b. What price/earnings ratio applied to the EPS related to plan B would provide the same stock price as that projected for plan A?

c. Comment upon the results of your analysis of problems 10–9A and 10–10A.

10–11A. (*Analysis of Recessionary Cash Flows*) Cavalier Agriculture Supplies is undertaking a thorough cash flow analysis. It has been proposed by management that the firm expand by raising $5 million in the long-term debt markets. All of this would be immediately invested in new fixed assets. The proposed bond issue would carry an 8 percent interest rate and have a maturity period of 20 years. The bond issue would have a sinking fund provision that one-twentieth of the principal would be retired annually. Next year is expected to be a poor one for Cavalier. The firm's management feels, therefore, that the upcoming year would serve well as a model for the worst possible operating conditions that the firm can be expected to encounter. Cavalier ordinarily carries a $500,000 cash balance. Next year sales collections are forecast to be $3 million. Miscellaneous cash receipts will total $200,000. Wages and salaries will amount to $1 million. Payments for raw materials used in the production process will be $1,400,000. In addition, the firm will pay $500,000 in nondiscretionary expenditures including taxes. The firm faces a 50 percent tax rate.

a. Cavalier currently has no debt or preferred stock outstanding. What will be the total fixed financial charges that the firm must meet next year?

b. What is the expected cash balance at the end of the recessionary period (next year), assuming the debt is issued?

c. Based on this information, should Cavalier issue the proposed bonds?

10–12A. (*Assessing Leverage Use*) Some financial data for three corporations are displayed below:

Measure	Firm A	Firm B	Firm C	Industry Norm
Debt ratio	20%	25%	40%	20%
Times burden covered	8 times	10 times	7 times	9 times
Price/earnings ratio	9 times	11 times	6 times	10 times

a. Which firm appears to be excessively levered?

b. Which firm appears to be employing financial leverage to the most appropriate degree?

c. What explanation can you provide for the higher price/earnings ratio enjoyed by firm B as compared with firm A?

10–13A. (*Assessing Leverage Use*) Some financial data and the appropriate industry norm are shown in the following table:

Measure	Firm X	Firm Y	Firm Z	Industry Norm
Total debt to total assets	35%	30%	10%	35%
Times interest and preferred dividend coverage	7 times	14 times	16 times	7 times
Price/earnings ratio	8 times	10 times	8 times	8 times

a. Which firm appears to be using financial leverage to the most appropriate degree?

b. In this situation which "financial leverage effect" appears to dominate the market's valuation process?

10–14A. (*Capital Structure Theory*) Boston Textiles has an all common equity capital structure. Pertinent financial characteristics for the company are shown below:

Shares of common stock outstanding = 1,000,000
Common stock price, P_0 = $20 per share
Expected level of EBIT = $5,000,000
Dividend payout ratio = 100 percent

In answering the following questions, assume that corporate income is not taxed.

a. Under the present capital structure, what is the total value of the firm?

b. What is the cost of common equity capital, K_c? What is the composite cost of capital, K_0?

c. Now, suppose that Boston Textiles sells $1 million of long-term debt with an interest rate of 8 percent. The proceeds are used to retire outstanding common stock. According to NOI theory (the independence hypothesis), what will be the firm's cost of common equity *after* the capital structure change?

    1. What will be the dividend per share flowing to the firm's common shareholders?

    2. By what percent has the dividend per share changed owing to the capital structure change?

    3. By what percent has the cost of common equity changed owing to the capital structure change?

    4. What will be the composite cost of capital after the capital structure change?

10–15A. (*Capital Structure Theory*) South Bend Auto Parts has an all common equity capital structure. Some financial data for the company are shown below:

Shares of common stock outstanding = 600,000
Common stock price, P_0 = $40 per share
Expected level of EBIT = $4,200,000
Dividend payout ratio = 100 percent

In answering the following questions, assume that corporate income is not taxed.

a. Under the present capital structure, what is the total value of the firm?

b. What is the cost of common equity capital, K_c? What is the composite cost of capital, K_0?

c. Now, suppose South Bend sells $1 million of long-term debt with an interest rate of 10 percent. The proceeds are used to retire outstanding common stock. According to the net operating income theory (the independence hypothesis), what will be the firm's cost of common equity after the capital structure change?

    1. What will be the dividend per share flowing to the firm's common shareholders?

    2. By what percentage has the dividend per share changed owing to the capital structure change?

    3. By what percentage has the cost of common equity changed owing to the capital structure change?

    4. What will be the composite cost of capital after the capital structure change?

10–16A. (*EBIT–EPS Analysis*) Albany Golf Equipment is analyzing three different financing plans for a newly formed subsidiary. The plans are described below:

Plan A	*Plan B*		*Plan C*	
Common stock: $100,000	Bonds at 9%:	$20,000	Preferred stock at 9%:	$20,000
	Common stock:	80,000	Common stock:	80,000

In all cases the common stock will be sold to net Albany $10 per share. The subsidiary is expected to generate an average EBIT per year of $22,000. The management of Albany places great emphasis on EPS performance. Income is taxed at a 50 percent rate.

a. Where feasible, find the EBIT indifference levels between the alternatives.

b. Which financing plan do you recommend that Albany pursue?

10–1B. (*EBIT–EPS Analysis*) Three recent graduates of the computer science program at Midstate University are forming a company to write and distribute software for various personal computers. Initially, the corporation will operate in the southern region of Michigan, Illinois, Indiana, and Ohio. Twelve serious prospects for retail outlets have already been identified and committed to the firm. The firm's software products have been tested and displayed at several trade shows and computer fairs in the perceived operating region. All that is lacking is adequate financing to continue with the project. A small group of private investors in the Chicago, Illinois, area is interested in financing the new company. Two financing proposals are being evaluated. The first (plan A) is an all common equity capital structure. Three million dollars would be raised by selling common stock at $20 per common share. Plan B would involve the use of financial leverage. Two million dollars would be raised selling bonds with an effective interest rate of 11 percent (per annum). Under this second plan, the remaining $1 million would be raised by selling common stock at the $20 price per share. The use of financial leverage is considered to be a permanent part of the firm's capitalization, so no fixed maturity date is needed for the analysis. A 34 percent tax rate is appropriate for the analysis.

  a. Find the EBIT indifference level associated with the two financing plans.

  b. A detailed financial analysis of the firm's prospects suggests that the long-term EBIT will be above $450,000 annually. Taking this into consideration, which plan will generate the higher EPS?

  c. Suppose long-term EBIT is forecast to be $450,000 per year. Under plan A, a price/earnings ratio of 19 would apply. Under plan B, a price/earnings ratio of 12.39 would apply. If this set of financial relationships does hold, which financing plan would you recommend?

10–2B. (*EBIT–EPS Analysis*) Three recent liberal arts graduates have interested a group of venture capitalists in backing a new business enterprise. The proposed operation would consist of a series of retail outlets to distribute and service a full line of personal computer equipment. These stores would be located in Texas, Arizona, and New Mexico. Two financing plans have been proposed by the graduates. Plan A is an all common equity structure. Four million dollars would be raised by selling 80,000 shares of common stock. Plan B would involve the use of long-term debt financing. Two million dollars would be raised by marketing bonds with an effective interest rate of 16 percent. Under this alternative, another $2 million would be raised by selling 50,000 shares of common stock. With both plans, then, $4 million is needed to launch the new firm's operations. The debt funds raised under plan B are considered to have no fixed maturity date, in that this proportion of financial leverage is thought to be a permanent part of the company's capital structure. The fledgling executives have decided to use a 34 percent tax rate in their analysis, and they have hired you on a consulting basis to do the following:

  a. Find the EBIT indifference level associated with the two financing proposals.

  b. Prepare an analytical income statement that proves EPS will be the same regardless of the plan chosen at the EBIT level found in part (a) above.

10–3B. (*EBIT–EPS Analysis*) Two recent graduates of the computer science program at Ohio Tech are forming a company to write, market, and distribute software for various personal computers. Initially, the corporation will operate in the Midwest area of Missouri, Iowa, Nebraska, and Kansas. Eight prospects for retail outlets in these different states have already been identified and committed to the firm. The firm's software products have been tested. All that is lacking is adequate financing to continue the project. A small group of private investors are interested in financing the new company. Two financing proposals are being evaluated. The first (plan A) is an all common equity capital structure. Three million dollars would be raised by selling stock at $40 per common share. Plan B would involve the use of financial leverage. One million dollars would be raised by selling bonds with an effective interest rate of 14 percent (per annum). Under this second plan, the remaining $2 million would be raised by selling common stock at the $40 price per share. This use of financial leverage is considered to be a permanent part of the firm's capitalization, so no fixed maturity date is needed for the analysis. A 50 percent tax rate is appropriate for the analysis.

  a. Find the EBIT indifference level associated with the two financing plans.

  b. Prepare an analytical income statement that proves EPS will be the same regardless of the plan chosen at the EBIT level found in part (a) above.

  c. A detailed financial analysis of the firm's prospects suggests that long-term EBIT will be above \$750,000 annually. Taking this into consideration, which plan will generate the higher EPS?

 d. Suppose that long-term EBIT is forecast to be \$750,000 per year. Under plan A, a price/earnings ratio of 12 would apply. Under plan B, a price/earnings ratio of 9.836 would apply. If this set of financial relationships does hold, which financing plan would you recommend be implemented?

10–4B. (*Analysis of Recessionary Cash Flows*) The management of Cincinnati Collectibles (CC) is considering an increase in its use of financial leverage. The proposal on the table is to sell \$11 million of bonds that would mature in 20 years. The interest rate on these bonds would be 16 percent. The bond issue would have a sinking fund attached to it requiring that one-twentieth of the principal be retired each year. Most business economists are forecasting a recession that will affect the entire economy in the coming year. CC's management has been saying, "If we can make it through this, we can make it through anything." The firm prefers to carry an operating cash balance of \$500,000. Cash collections from sales next year will total \$3.5 million. Miscellaneous cash receipts will be \$300,000. Raw material payments will be \$800,000. Wage and salary costs will total \$1.5 million on a cash basis. On top of this, CC will experience nondiscretionary cash outflows of \$1.3 million *including* all tax payments. The firm faces a 50 percent tax rate.

 a. At present, CC is unlevered. What will be the total fixed financial charges the firm must pay next year?

 b. If the bonds are issued, what is your forecast for the firm's expected cash balance at the end of the recessionary year (next year)?

 c. As CC's financial consultant, do you recommend that it issue the bonds?

10–5B. (*EBIT–EPS Analysis*) Four recent business school graduates have interested a group of venture capitalists in backing a small business enterprise. The proposed operation would consist of a series of retail outlets that would distribute and service a full line of energy-conservation equipment. These stores would be located in northern California, western Nevada, and throughout Oregon. Two financing plans have been proposed by the graduates. Plan A is an all common equity capital structure. Five million dollars would be raised by selling 75,000 shares of common stock. Plan B would involve the use of long-term debt financing. Two million dollars would be raised by marketing bonds with an interest rate of 12 percent. Under this alternative another \$3 million would be raised by selling 55,000 shares of common stock. With both plans, then, \$5 million is needed to launch the new firm's operations. The debt funds raised under plan B are considered to have no fixed maturity date, in that this proportion of financial leverage is thought to be a permanent part of the company's capital structure. The fledgling executives have decided to use a 40 percent tax rate in their analysis.

 a. Find the EBIT indifference level associated with the two financing proposals.

 b. Prepare an analytical income statement that proves EPS will be the same regardless of the plan chosen at the EBIT level found in part (a).

10–6B. (*EBIT–EPS Analysis*) A group of college professors have decided to form a small manufacturing corporation. The company will produce a full line of contemporary furniture. Two financing plans have been proposed by the investors. Plan A is an all-common-equity alternative. Under this arrangement 1,200,000 common shares will be sold to net the firm \$10 per share. Plan B involves the use of financial leverage. A debt issue with a 20-year maturity period will be privately placed. The debt issue will carry an interest rate of 9 percent and the principal borrowed will amount to \$3.5 million. The corporate tax rate is 50 percent.

 a. Find the EBIT indifference level associated with the two financing proposals.

 b. Prepare an analytical income statement that proves EPS will be the same regardless of the plan chosen at the EBIT level found in part (a).

 c. Prepare an EBIT–EPS analysis chart for this situation.

 d. If a detailed financial analysis projects that long-term EBIT will always be close to \$1,500,000 annually, which plan will provide for the higher EPS?

10–7B. (*EBIT–EPS Analysis*) The professors in problem 10–6B contacted a financial consultant to provide them with some additional information. They felt that in a few years the stock of the firm would be publicly traded over the counter, so they were interested in the consultant's opinion as to what the stock price would be under the financing plan outlined in problem 10–6B. The consultant agreed that the projected long-term EBIT level of \$1,500,000 was reasonable. He also felt that if plan A were selected, the marketplace would apply a price/earnings ratio of 13 times to the company's stock; for plan B he estimated a price earnings ratio of 11 times.

 a. According to this information, which financing alternative would offer a higher stock price?

b. What price/earnings ratio applied to the EPS related to plan B would provide the same stock price as that projected for plan A?

c. Comment upon the results of your analysis of problems 10–6B and 10–7B.

10–8B. (*Analysis of Recessionary Cash Flows*) Seville Cranes, Inc., is undertaking a thorough cash flow analysis. It has been proposed by management that the firm expand by raising $6 million in the long-term debt markets. All of this would be immediately invested in new fixed assets. The proposed bond issue would carry a 10 percent interest rate and have a maturity period of 20 years. The bond issue would have a sinking fund provision that one-twentieth of the principal would be retired annually. Next year is expected to be a poor one for Seville. The firm's management feels, therefore, that the upcoming year would serve well as a model for the worst possible operating conditions that the firm can be expected to encounter. Seville ordinarily carries a $750,000 cash balance. Next year sales collections are forecast to be $3.5 million. Miscellaneous cash receipts will total $200,000. Wages and salaries will amount to $1.2 million. Payments for raw materials used in the production process will be $1,500,000. In addition, the firm will pay $500,000 in nondiscretionary expenditures including taxes. The firm faces a 50 percent tax rate.

a. Seville currently has no debt or preferred stock outstanding. What will be the total fixed financial charges that the firm must meet next year?

b. What is the expected cash balance at the end of the recessionary period (next year), assuming the debt is issued?

c. Based on this information, should Seville issue the proposed bonds?

10–9B. (*Assessing Leverage Use*) Some financial data for three corporations are displayed below:

Measure	Firm A	Firm B	Firm C	Industry Norm
Debt ratio	15%	20%	35%	25%
Times burden covered	9 times	11 times	6 times	9 times
Price/earnings ratio	10 times	12 times	5 times	10 times

a. Which firm appears to be excessively levered?

b. Which firm appears to be employing financial leverage to the most appropriate degree?

c. What explanation can you provide for the higher price/earnings ratio enjoyed by firm B as compared with firm A?

10–10B. (*Assessing Leverage Use*) Some financial data and the appropriate industry norm are shown in the following table:

Measure	Firm X	Firm Y	Firm Z	Industry Norm
Total debt to total assets	40%	35%	10%	35%
Times interest and preferred dividend coverage	8 times	13 times	16 times	7 times
Price/earnings ratio	8 times	11 times	8 times	8 times

a. Which firm appears to be using financial leverage to the most appropriate degree?

b. In this situation which "financial leverage effect" appears to dominate the market's valuation process?

10–11B. (*Capital Structure Theory*) Whittier Optical Labs has an all common equity capital structure. Pertinent financial characteristics for the company are shown below:

Shares of common stock outstanding = 1,000,000
Common stock price, P_0 = $22 per share
Expected level of EBIT = $4,750,000
Dividend payout ratio = 100 percent

In answering the following questions, assume that corporate income is not taxed.

a. Under the present capital structure, what is the total value of the firm?

b. What is the cost of common equity capital, K_c? What is the composite cost of capital, K_0?

c. Now, suppose that Whittier sells $1 million of long-term debt with an interest rate of 9 percent. The proceeds are used to retire outstanding common stock. According to NOI theory (the independence hypothesis), what will be the firm's cost of common equity *after* the capital-structure change?

   1. What will be the dividend per share flowing to the firm's common shareholders?

   2. By what percentage has the dividend per share changed owing to the capital structure change?

   3. By what percentage has the cost of common equity changed owing to the capital structure change?

   4. What will be the composite cost of capital after the capital structure change?

10–12B. (*Capital Structure Theory*) Fernando Hotels has an all common equity capital structure. Some financial data for the company are shown below:

Shares of common stock outstanding = 575,000
Common stock price, P_0 = $38 per share
Expected level of EBIT = $4,500,000
Dividend payout ratio = 100 percent

In answering the following questions, assume that corporate income is not taxed.

a. Under the present capital structure, what is the total value of the firm?

b. What is the cost of common equity capital, K_c? What is the composite cost of capital, K_0?

c. Now, suppose Fernando sells $1.5 million of long-term debt with an interest rate of 11 percent. The proceeds are used to retire outstanding common stock. According to the net operating income theory (the independence hypothesis), what will be the firm's cost of common equity after the capital structure change?

   1. What will be the dividend per share flowing to the firm's common shareholders?

   2. By what percent has the dividend per share changed owing to the capital structure change?

   3. By what percent has the cost of common equity changed owing to the capital structure change?

   4. What will be the composite cost of capital after the capital structure change?

10–13B. (*EBIT–EPS Analysis*) Mount Rosemead Health Services, Inc., is analyzing three different financing plans for a newly formed subsidiary. The plans are described below:

Plan A	Plan B	Plan C
Common stock: $150,000	Bonds at 10%: $50,000 Common stock: $100,000	Preferred stock at 10%: $50,000 Common stock: $100,000

In all cases the common stock will be sold to net Mount Rosemead $10 per share. The subsidiary is expected to generate an average EBIT per year of $36,000. The management of Mount Rosemead places great emphasis on EPS performance. Income is taxed at a 50 percent rate.

a. Where feasible, find the EBIT indifference levels between the alternatives.

b. Which financing plan do you recommend that Mount Rosemead pursue?

Suggested Application for *DISCLOSURE* ®

a. Using *Disclosure*, find the following information for the Proctor & Gamble Company for the most recent year: (1) number of shares of common stock outstanding, (2) common stock share price, (3) earnings before interest and taxes (income before tax + interest expense), (4) the company's total debt, and (5) the firm's debt-to-equity mix

b. What is the total equity value of the company?

c. Assume that the company's dividend payout ratio is 100 percent; that corporate income is not taxed; and that the required rate of return for the firm if it were all equity is 12 percent. Then: (1) Use the net operating income approach to estimate the firm's total equity value. (2) Use the net income approach to value the company's equity value. (3) Explain why there are differences in the values found above.

SPECIALTY AUTO PARTS:

FINANCIAL-LEVERAGE ANALYSIS

Specialty Auto Parts (SAP) is located in Toledo, Ohio. The firm was founded in 1919 by C. K. Blackburn, who served as president and chairman of the board until his death in early 1976. Both positions are now filled by Ken Blackburn, C. K.'s eldest son, who is carrying on his father's dogmatic tradition of "high quality products for a quality industry." Mark Dennis, vice-president of finance, often argued formally and informally against the total emphasis contained in the latter four words of that phrase, which trademarked all of SAP's advertisements. Dennis simply felt that by concentrating upon supplying component parts only to the auto industry, an undue exposure to basic business risk was assumed.

SAP manufactures a very wide range of component parts, subassemblies, and final assemblies for sale to the major automobile producers, who are largely concentrated 61 miles north, in Detroit. Standard items in the product line include hubs, rims, brakes, antiskid units, and mirrors. C. K. Blackburn had taken immense pride in all facets of SAP's activities, ranging from the early decision to locate in Toledo to the firm's solid reputation within key offices in Detroit's Fisher Building. In retrospect, the location decision was a fine one. An expressway connects Toledo with Detroit, making truck transportation extremely swift. Further, Toledo is located on the west end of Lake Erie, with a good port facility, enabling the firm to receive raw materials via marine transportation and to ship finished goods to other key automotive centers, such as Cleveland across the lake.

Blackburn family interests own 51 percent of the common stock of SAP. Over the years outside financing has been almost completely shunned by the organization. The SAP annual report of four years past contains this statement: "We will continue to finance corporate growth primarily through the internal generation of funds." Recent auto industry trends, however, have necessitated a shift by SAP management away from strict adherence to that policy. A national recession saw last year's motor vehicle factory sales of passenger cars drop 24 percent from the previous annual period. This, in turn, adversely affected the profitability and funds-generating capacity of SAP. On top of this, the officials of SAP have decided upon a major product mix shift. The firm underestimated the demand for disc brakes, which have been installed on about 84 to 86 percent of passenger cars in recent years (see Exhibit 1). SAP's capacity to produce in this area will be increased during the next year. The volume achieved on the sale of antiskid units has proved to be a disappointment. Accordingly, some factory space and equipment devoted to this product line will be redeployed into other more profitable activities.

Noting the public's acceptance of rear window defoggers, the firm has developed the technology necessary to be competitive in this product. To effect this expertise, however, substantial equipment purchases will be required within the next six months. The end result is that SAP must raise $6 million in the capital markets through either the sale of new common stock or the issuance of bonds. The new common shares could be sold to net the firm $48 per share. The common stock price of SAP shares in the marketplace is now $54. Allen Winthrop, who is a partner in the investment banking house long used by SAP, has assured Mark Dennis that the new bond issue could be placed with an 8 percent interest rate. Winthrop's counsel always has been highly valued by Dennis and other members of the SAP top management team.

Factory Installations of Selected Equipment (Percent of Total Units Installed Upon)		
Automobile equipment	Most recent year	One year earlier
Power brakes, 4-wheel drum	2.4	1.0
Power brakes, 2 or 4-wheel disc	64.8	74.5
Disc brakes manual	19.2	11.2
Skid control device	0.9	1.9
Rear window defogger	21.5	16.4

EXHIBIT 1
Specialty Auto Parts

A preliminary meeting took place one week ago with Dennis Winthrop, and Ken Blackburn in attendance. The only topic discussed was the $6 million financing choice facing SAP. Exhibits 2, 3, and 4 were analyzed at length. Dennis felt that the firm's owners would benefit if the asset expansion were financed with debt capital. Also, Blackburn liked having total control over the firm's operations. With 51 percent of the common shares family owned, Blackburn knew that he could personally choose a course of action when a tough situation faced SAP. Incidentally, the corporate charter of SAP does not provide for the election of directors via a cumulative voting procedure.

EXHIBIT 2
Specialty Auto Parts

Abbreviated Balance Sheet, December 31, Last Year

Assets	
Current assets	$14,750,000
Net plant and equipment	19,000,000
Other	2,250,000
Total assets	$36,000,000
Liabilities and Equity	
Current liabilities	$ 4,920,000
Long-term debt	
First mortgage bonds, 20 years to maturity, at 7%	2,950,000
Common stock, $5 par	5,000,000
Capital surplus	10,000,000
Retained earnings	13,130,000
Total liabilities and equity	$36,000,000

Dennis pointed out to Blackburn that apart from the family, no "public" investor controlled as much as 5 percent of the outstanding common shares. Thus, Dennis noted effective control of the firm's operations would remain with the Blackburn family should the new common stock alternative be elected. Dennis did not think it would be prudent to elect the debt alternative *only* because it would ensure Blackburn family control over SAP in the strictest sense.

Both Dennis and Blackburn were concerned with the effect of additional financial leverage upon the firm's price/earnings ratio. To deal partially with this question, Winthrop's staff prepared Exhibit 4. Winthrop suggested to Blackburn that his firm prepare for the "worst that could happen." He stated that SAP's price/earnings ratio might remain unchanged from its present level of 9.59 times if the debt alternative were

EXHIBIT 3
Specialty Auto Parts

Income Statement, December 31, Last Year

Sales	$112,000,000
Variable costs	88,476,520
Fixed costs (excluding interest)	12,064,980
Interest expense	206,500
Earnings before taxes	$ 11,252,000
Taxes (at 50%)	5,626,000
Net profit	$ 5,626,000

chosen. He did not, however, believe such an occurrence to be highly likely. Winthrop offered his best guess that SAP's price/earnings ratio will fall to 9.3 times if bonds are sold and will rise to 10 times if the common stock alternative is selected.

EXHIBIT 4
Specialty Auto Parts

Main Competitors' Selected Financial Relationships

Firm	Debt ratio[a]	Tier[b]	P/E ratio[c]
Atlas Auto Components	32.7%	7	7.5
Autonite	20.1%	38	9.5
Kalsey-Ways, Ltd.	24.2%	14	9.0
L-G Parts	26.8%	14	9.0
Morgan-Wells, Inc.	19.0%	29	11.0
Simple average	24.6%	20.4	9.2

[a]Total debt divided by total assets.
[b]Times interest earned ratio.
[c]Price to earnings ratio.

Prior to taking the question before the entire board, Ken Blackburn wanted to review a more substantial body of analysis with Dennis and Winthrop. He gave Dennis a week to prepare the information requested below.

QUESTIONS AND PROBLEMS

1. Dennis has projected that the firm's variable cost to sales ratio will be .79 after the $6 million expansion is effected. In addition, fixed costs apart from interest will rise to an annual level of $13 million. Calculate the level of sales that will equate earnings per share regardless of whether the subject $6 million is financed with bonds or common stock.

2. Set up income statements for bond financing and common stock financing using the sales volume determined earlier, and demonstrate that earnings per share will indeed be the same under the assumed conditions.

3. Use last year's results as the base period. Compute earnings per share under each financing alternative for sales levels equal to (a) 70 percent, (b) 85 percent, (c) 100 percent, (d) 110 percent, and (e) 120 percent of the base period results.

4. Employing the price/earnings ratios suggested by Winthrop, project the common stock prices for each financing choice at the sales levels just analyzed.

5. Again taking Winthrop's "best guess" price/earnings ratios, determine the sales level that will equate market price per share regardless of the financing source chosen.

6. After reviewing recent marketing department forecasts of sales levels, Ken Blackburn concluded, "Rarely will SAP experience revenues below the $120 million mark." If Blackburn is correct, which financing alternative do you recommend?

SELF-TEST SOLUTIONS

SS–1. a. FC = interest + sinking fund

$FC = (\$6,000,000) \, (.12) + (\$6,000,000/20)$

$FC = \$720,000 + \$300,000 = \underline{\underline{\$1,020,000}}$

b. $CB_r = C_0 + NCF_r - FC$

where $C_0 = \$750,000$
$FC = \$1,020,000$

and

$$NCF_r = \$3,400,000 - \$3,100,000 = \$300,000$$

so

$$CB_r = \$750,000 + \$300,000 - \$1,020,000$$

$$CB_r = \underline{\underline{\$30,000}}$$

c. We know that the firm has a preference for maintaining a cash balance of $750,000. The joint impact of the recessionary economic environment and the proposed issue of bonds would put the firm's recessionary cash balance (CB_r) at $30,000. Because the firm desires a minimum cash balance of $750,000 ($C_0$), the data suggest that the proposed bond issue should be postponed.

SS–2. a. Firm Y seems to be using financial leverage to the most appropriate degree. Notice that its price/earnings ratio of 16 times exceeds that of firm X (at 9 times) and firm Z (also at 9 times).

b. The first financial leverage effect refers to the added variability in the earnings per share stream caused by the use of leverage-inducing financial instruments. The second financial leverage effect concerns the level of earnings per share at a specific EBIT associated with a specific capital structure.

Beyond some critical EBIT level, earnings per share will be higher if more leverage is used. Based on the company data provided, the marketplace for financial instruments is weighing the second leverage effect more heavily. Firm Z, therefore, seems to be underlevered (is operating *below* its theoretical leverage capacity).

SS–3 b.

Plan A		Plan B
EPS: Less-Levered Plan		**EPS: More-Levered Plan**
$\dfrac{(EBIT - I)\,(1 - t) - P}{S_A}$	$=$	$\dfrac{(EBIT - I)\,(1 - t) - P}{S_B}$
$\dfrac{(EBIT - \$140{,}000)\,(1 - 0.5)}{100{,}000\ (shares)}$	$=$	$\dfrac{(EBIT - \$480{,}000)\,(1 - 0.5)}{60{,}000\ (shares)}$
$\dfrac{0.5\ EBIT - \$70{,}000}{10}$	$=$	$\dfrac{0.5\ EBIT - \$240{,}000}{6}$
$EBIT = \$990{,}000$		

b. The EBIT–EPS analysis chart for Martin-Bowing is presented in Figure 10–10.

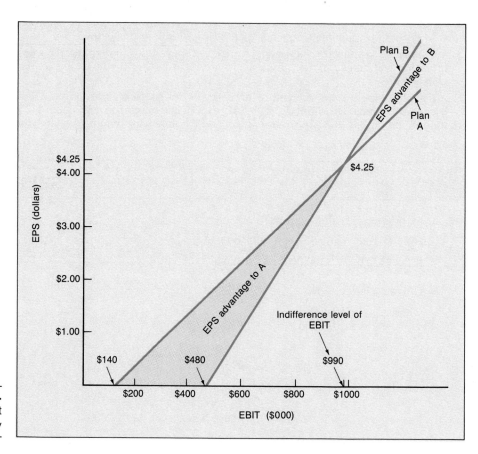

FIGURE 10–10.
EBIT–EPS Analysis Chart
for Martin-Bowing Company

	Plan A	Plan B
EBIT	$990,000	$990,000
I	140,000	480,000
EBT	$850,000	$510,000
T (.5)	425,000	255,000
NI	$425,000	$255,000
P	0	0
EAC	$425,000	$255,000
÷ No. of common shares	100,000	60,000
EPS	$ 4.25	$ 4.25

c. Because $1,188,000 exceeds the calculated indifference level of $990,000, the more highly levered plan (plan B) will produce the higher EPS.

d. At this stage of the problem it is necessary to compute EPS under each financing alternative. Then the relevant price/earnings ratio for each plan can be applied to project the common stock price for the plan at a specific EBIT level.

	Plan A	Plan B
EBIT	$1,188,000	$1,188,000
I	140,000	480,000
EBT	$1,048,000	$ 708,000
T (.5)	524,000	354,000
NI	$ 524,000	$ 354,000
P	0	0
EAC	$ 524,000	$ 354,000
÷ No. of common shares	100,000	60,000
EPS	$ 5.24	$ 5.90
× P/E ratio	13	11
= Projected stock price	$ 68.12	$ 64.90

Notice that the greater riskiness of plan B results in the market applying a lower price/earnings multiple to the expected EPS. Therefore, the investors would actually enjoy a higher stock price under plan A ($68.12) than they would under plan B ($64.90).

e. Here, we want to find the price/earnings ratio that would equate the common stock prices for both plans at an EBIT level of $1,188,000. All we have to do is take plan B's EPS and relate it to plan A's stock price. Thus:

$$\$5.90 \ (P/E) = \$68.12$$
$$(P/E) = \$68.12/\$5.90 = \underline{11.546.}$$

A price/earnings ratio of 11.546 when applied to plan B's EPS would give the same stock price as that of plan A ($68.12).

CHAPTER *11*

Dividend Policy and Internal Financing

Key Terms • Does Dividend Policy Affect Stock Price? • The Dividend Decision in Practice • Dividend Payment Procedures • Stock Dividends and Stock Splits • Stock Repurchases

We know that maximizing the value, or price, of the firm's common stock is the primary goal in financial decision making. The success or failure of a management decision is determined by its impact on the common stock price. We observed that the company's investment (Chapters 6, 7, and 8) and financing decisions (Chapters 9 and 10) can increase the value of the firm. As we look at the firm's *dividend* and *internal financing* policies, we return to the same basic question: Can management influence the price of the firm's stock, in this case through its dividend policies? Toward that end, we have six specific objectives for this chapter.

1. Study the relationship between a corporation's dividend policy and the market price of its common stock.
2. Present practical considerations that may be important to the firm's dividend policy.
3. Review the types of dividend policy corporations frequently use.
4. Study the procedures a company follows in administering the dividend payment.
5. Examine the use of noncash dividends (stock dividends and stock splits).
6. Explain the use of stock repurchases.

Perspective in Finance

We have a problem: None of us can say for certain that a firm's dividend policy matters. By matters, we mean that it affects the firm's stock price. We can't explain why firms act the way they do when it comes to paying dividends. Conversely, chief financial officers, since the beginning of time, have acted like dividend policy is important. Perhaps we cannot resolve this important issue. We can only try, and we shall try in this chapter.

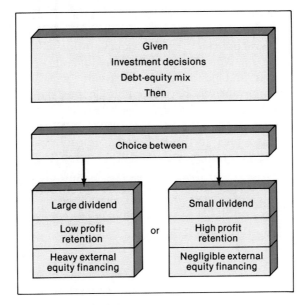

FIGURE 11–1.
Dividend-Retention-Financing
Tradeoffs

Key Terms

Before taking up the particular issues relating to dividend policy, we must understand several key terms and interrelationships.

A firm's dividend policy includes two basic components. First, the **dividend payout ratio** indicates the amount of dividends paid relative to the company's earnings. For instance, if the dividend per share is $2 and the earnings per share is $4, the payout ratio is 50 percent ($2 ÷ $4). The second component is the *stability* of the dividends over time. As will be observed later in the chapter, dividend stability may be almost as important to the investor as the amount of dividends received.

In formulating a dividend policy, the financial manager faces tradeoffs. Assuming that management has already decided how much to invest and chosen its debt–equity mix for financing these investments, the decision to pay a large dividend means simultaneously deciding to retain little, if any, profits; this in turn results in a greater reliance on external equity financing. Conversely, given the firm's investment and financing decisions, a small dividend payment corresponds to high profit retention with less need for externally generated equity funds. These tradeoffs, which are fundamental to our discussion, are illustrated in Figure 11–1.

Does Dividend Policy Affect Stock Price?[1]

The fundamental question to be resolved in our study of the firm's dividend policy may be stated simply: What is a sound rationale or motivation for dividend payments? If we believe our objective should be to maximize the value

---

[1]The concepts of this section draw heavily from Donald H. Chew, Jr., ed., "Do Dividends Matter? A Discussion of Corporate Dividend Policy," in *Six Roundtable Discussions of Corporate Finance with Joel Stern* (New York: Quorum Books, 1986), pp. 67–101; and a book of readings edited by Joel M. Stern and Donald H. Chew, Jr., *The Revolution in Corporate Finance* (New York: Basil Blackwell, 1986). Specific readings included Merton Miller, "Can Management Use Dividends to Influence the Value of the Firm?" pp. 299–303; Richard Brealey, "Does Dividend Policy Matter?" pp. 304–9; and Michael Rozeff, "How Companies Set Their Dividend Payout Ratios," 320–26.

of the common stock, we may restate the question as follows: Given the firm's capital-budgeting and borrowing decisions, what is the effect of the firm's dividend policies on the stock price? *Does a high dividend payment decrease stock value, increase it, or make no real difference?*

At first glance, we might reasonably conclude that a firm's dividend policy is important. We have already (Chapter 5) defined the value of a stock to be equal to the present value of future dividends. How can we now suggest that dividends are not important? Why do so many companies pay dividends, and why is a page in the *Wall Street Journal* devoted to dividend announcements? Based on intuition, we could quickly conclude that dividend policy is important. However, we might be surprised to learn that the dividend question has been a controversial issue for well over three decades. It has even been called the "dividend puzzle."[2]

Three Basic Views

Some would argue that the amount of the dividend is irrelevant, and any time spent on the decision is a waste of energy. Others contend that a high dividend will result in a high stock price. Still others take the view that dividends actually hurt the stock value. Let us look at these three views in turn.

View 1: Dividend Policy Is Irrelevant

Much of the controversy about the dividend issue is based in the time-honored disagreements between the academic and professional communities. Experienced practitioners perceive stock price changes as resulting from dividend announcement and therefore see dividends as important. Professors who argue that dividends are irrelevant see a failure to carefully define dividend policy and argue that the relationship between dividends and stock price may be an illusion.[3]

The position that dividends are not important rests on two preconditions. First, we assume that investment and borrowing decisions have already been made, and that these decisions will not be altered by the amount of any dividend payments. Second, "perfect" capital markets are assumed to exist, which means that (1) investors can buy and sell stocks without incurring any transaction costs, such as brokerage commissions; (2) companies can issue stocks without any cost of doing so; (3) there are no corporate or personal taxes; (4) complete information about the firm is readily available; and (5) there are no conflicts of interest between managements and stockholders.

The first assumption—that we have already made the investment and financing decisions—simply keeps us from confusing the issues. We want to know the effect of dividend decisions on a stand-alone basis, without mixing in other decisions. The second assumption, that of perfect markets, also allows us to study the effect of dividend decisions in isolation, much like a physicist studies motion in a vacuum to avoid the influence of friction.

Given these assumptions, the effect of a dividend decision on share price may be stated unequivocally: There is no relationship between dividend policy and stock value. One dividend policy is as good as another one. In the aggregate, investors are concerned only with *total* returns from investment decisions; they are indifferent whether these returns come from capital gains or dividend income. They also recognize that the dividend decision, given the investment policy, is really a choice of financing strategy. Chapter 8 discussed the principles underlying growth. To finance growth, the firm (a) may choose to issue stock,

---

[2]See Fischer Black, "The Dividend Puzzle," *Journal of Portfolio Management* 2 (Winter 1976), pp. 5–8.

[3]For an excellent presentation of this issue, see Merton Miller, "Can Management Use Dividends to Influence the Value of the Firm?" in Joel M. Stern and Donald H. Chew, Jr., eds., *The Revolution in Corporate Finance* (New York: Basil Blackwell, 1986), pp. 299–305.

allowing internally generated funds (profits) to be used to pay dividends; or (b) it may use internally generated funds to finance its growth, while paying less in dividends, but not having to issue stock. In the first case, shareholders receive dividend income; in the second case, the value of their stock should increase, providing capital gains. The nature of the return is the only difference; total returns should be about the same. Thus, to argue that paying dividends can make shareholders better off is to argue that paying out cash with one hand and taking it back with the other hand is a worthwhile activity for management.

The firm's dividend payout could affect stock price if the shareholder has no other way to receive income from the investment. However, assuming the capital markets are relatively efficient, a stockholder who needs current income could always sell shares. If the firm pays a dividend, the investor could eliminate any dividend received, in whole or in part, by using the dividend to purchase stock. The investor can thus personally create any desired dividend stream, no matter what dividend policy is in effect.

An example of dividend irrelevance ■ To demonstrate the argument that dividends may not matter, come to the Land of Ez (pronounced "ease"), where the environment is quite simple. First, the king, being a kind soul, has imposed *no income taxes* on his subjects. Second, investors can buy and sell securities without paying any *sales commissions*. In addition, when a company issues new securities (stocks or bonds), there are *no flotation costs*. Furthermore, the Land of Ez is completely computerized, so that all information about firms is *instantaneously available* to the public at *no cost*. Next, all investors realize that the value of a company is a function of its investment opportunities and its financing decisions. Therefore, the dividend policy offers *no new information* about either the firm's ability to generate earnings or the riskiness of its earnings. Finally, all firms are owned and managed by the same parties; thus, we have no potential conflict between owners and managers.

Within this financial utopia, would a change in a corporation's dividend stream have any effect on the price of the firm's stock? The answer is *no*. To illustrate, consider Dowell Venture, Inc., a corporation that received a charter at the end of 1993 to conduct business in the Land of Ez. The firm is to be financed by common stock only. Its life is to extend for only two years (1994 and 1995), at which time it will be liquidated.

Table 11-1 presents Dowell Venture's balance sheet at the time of its formation, as well as the projected cash flows from the short-term venture. The anticipated cash flows are based on an expected return on investment of 20 percent, which is exactly what the common shareholders require as a rate of return on their investment in the firm's stock.

At the end of 1994 an additional investment of $300,000 will be required, which may be financed by (1) retaining $300,000 of the 1994 profits, or (2) issuing new common stock, or (3) some combination of both of these. In fact, two dividend plans for 1994 are under consideration. The investors would receive either $100,000 or $250,000 in dividends. If $250,000 is paid out of 1994's $400,000 in earnings, the company would be required to issue $150,000

	December 31, 1993
Total assets	$2,000,000
Common stock (100,000 shares)	$2,000,000

	1994	1995
Projected cash available from operations for paying dividends or for reinvesting	$400,000	$460,000

TABLE 11-1.
Dowell Venture, Inc.,
Financial Data

TABLE 11–2.
Dowell Venture, Inc.,
1994 Proposed Dividend Plans

	Plan 1	Plan 2
Internally generated cash flow	$400,000	$400,000
Dividend for 1994	100,000	250,000
Cash available for reinvestment	$300,000	$150,000
Amount of investment in 1994	300,000	300,000
Additional external financing required	$ 0	$150,000

in new stock to make up the difference in the total amount of funds needed of $300,000 and the $150,000 that is retained. Table 11–2 depicts these two dividend plans and the corresponding new stock issue. Our objective in analyzing the data is to answer this question: Which dividend plan is preferable to the investors? In answering this question, we must take three steps: (1) Calculate the amount and timing of the dividend stream for the *original* investors. (2) Determine the present value of the dividend stream for each dividend plan. (3) Select the dividend alternative providing the higher value to the investors.

Step 1: *Computing the Dividend Streams.* The first step in this process is presented in Table 11–3. The dividends in 1994 (line 1, Table 11–3) are readily apparent from the data in Table 11–2. However, the amount of the dividend to be paid to the present shareholders in 1995 has to be calculated. To do so, we assume that investors receive (1) their original investments (line 2, Table 11–3), (2) any funds retained within the business in 1994 (line 3, Table 11–3), and (3) the profits for 1995 (line 4, Table 11–3). However, if additional stockholders invest in the company, as with plan 2, the dividends to be paid to these investors must be subtracted from the total available dividends (line 6, Table 11–3). The remaining dividends (line 7, Table 11–3) represent the amount current stockholders will receive in 1995. Therefore, the amounts of the dividend may be summarized as follows:

Dividend Plan	1994	1995
1	$1.00	$27.60
2	2.50	25.80

	Plan 1		Plan 2	
	Total Amount	Amount Per Share[a]	Total Amount	Amount Per Share[a]
Year 1 (1994)				
(1) Dividend	$ 100,000	$1.00	$ 250,000	$2.50
Year 2 (1995)				
Total dividend consisting of:				
(2) Original investment:				
(a) Old investors	$2,000,000		$2,000,000	
(b) New investors	0		150,000	
(3) Retained earnings from 1994	300,000		150,000	
(4) Profits for 1995	460,000		460,000	
(5) Total dividend to all investors in 1995	$2,760,000		$2,760,000	
(6)				
Less dividends to new investors:				
(a) Original investment	0		(150,000)	
(b) Profits for new investors (20% of $150,000 investment)	0		(30,000)	
(7) Liquidating dividends available to original investors in 1995	$2,760,000	$27.60	$2,580,000	$25.80

[a]Number of original shares outstanding equals 100,000.

Step 2: *Determining the Present Value of the Cash Flow Streams.* For each of the dividend payment streams the resulting common stock value is

$$\text{stock price (plan 1)} = \frac{\$1.00}{(1 + .20)} + \frac{\$27.60}{(1 + .20)^2} = \$20$$

$$\text{stock price (plan 2)} = \frac{\$2.50}{(1 + .20)} + \frac{\$25.80}{(1 + .20)^2} = \$20$$

Therefore, the two approaches provide the same end product; that is, the market price of Dowell Venture's common stock is $20 regardless of the dividend policy chosen.

Step 3: *Select the Best Dividend Plan.* If the objective is to maximize the shareholders' wealth, either plan is equally acceptable. Alternatively, shifting the dividend payments between years by changing the dividend policy does not affect the value of the security. Thus, only if investments are made with expected returns exceeding 20 percent will the value of the stock increase. In other words, the only wealth-creating activity in the Land of Ez, where companies are financed entirely by equity, is management's investment decisions.

View 2: High Dividends Increase Stock Value

The belief that a firm's dividend policy is unimportant implicitly assumes that an investor should use the same required rate of return whether income comes through capital gains or through dividends. However, dividends are more predictable than capital gains; management can control dividends, but it cannot dictate the price of the stock. Investors are less certain of receiving income from capital gains than from dividends. The incremental risk associated with capital gains relative to dividend income implies a higher required rate for discounting a dollar of capital gains than for discounting a dollar of dividends. In other words, we would value a dollar of expected dividends more highly than a dollar of expected capital gains. We might, for example, require a 14 percent rate of return for a stock that pays its entire return from dividends, but a 20 percent return for a high-growth stock that pays no dividend. In so doing, we would give a higher value to the dividend income than we would to the capital gains. This view, which says dividends are more certain than capital gains, has been called the "bird-in-the-hand" theory.

The position that dividends are less risky than capital gains, and should therefore be valued differently, is not without its critics. If we hold to our basic decision not to let the firm's dividend policy influence its investment and capital-mix decisions, the company's operating cash flows, both in expected amount and variability, are unaffected by its dividend policy. Because the dividend policy has no impact on the volatility of the company's overall cash flows, it has no impact on the riskiness of the firm.

Increasing a firm's dividend does not reduce the basic riskiness of the stock; rather, if a dividend payment requires management to issue new stock, it only transfers risk *and* ownership from the current owners to new owners. We would have to acknowledge that the current investors who receive the dividend trade an uncertain capital gain for a "safe" asset (the cash dividend). However, if risk reduction is the only goal, the investor could have kept the money in the bank and not bought the stock in the first place.

We might find fault with this "bird-in-the-hand" theory, but there is still a strong perception among many investors and professional investment advisors that dividends are important. They frequently argue their case based on their own personal experience. As expressed by one investment advisor:

> In advising companies on dividend policy, we're absolutely sure on one side that the investors in companies like the utilities and the suburban banks want dividends. We're absolutely sure on the other side that . . . the high-technology companies should have no dividends. For the high earners—the ones that have a high rate of return like 20 percent, or more than their cost of capital—we think

they should have a low payout ratio. We think a typical industrial company which earns its cost of capital—just earns its cost of capital—probably should be in the average [dividend payout] range of 40 to 50 percent.[4]

View 3: Low Dividends Increase Stock Value

The third view of how dividends affect stock price proposes that dividends actually hurt the investor. This argument has largely been based on the difference in tax treatment for dividend income and capital gains. Unlike the investors in the great Land of Ez, most other investors do pay income taxes. For these taxpayers, the objective is to maximize the after-tax return on investment relative to the risk assumed. This objective is realized by *minimizing* the effective tax rate on the income and, whenever possible, by *deferring* the payment of taxes.

Until 1987, the effective tax rate on the gain from the sale of stock was usually only 40 percent of the tax on dividend income, assuming the investor was subject to taxes. Effective January 1, 1987, federal tax law eliminated the special tax treatment given capital gains so that such gains are now taxed at the same rates as dividend income.

While the relative tax rate advantage available for capital gains no longer exists, a distinct benefit still remains for capital gains vis-à-vis dividend income. Taxes on dividend income are paid when the dividend is received, while taxes on price appreciation (capital gains) are deferred until the stock is actually sold. Thus, when it comes to tax considerations, most investors still prefer the retention of a firm's earnings as opposed to the payment of cash dividends. If earnings are retained within the firm, the stock price increases, but the increase is not taxed until the stock is sold.

Although the majority of investors are subject to taxes, certain investment companies, trusts, and pension plans are exempt on their dividend income. Also, for tax purposes a corporation may exclude 70 percent of the dividend income received from another corporation. In these cases, investors may prefer dividends over capital gains.

To summarize, when it comes to taxes, we want to maximize our *after*-tax return, as opposed to the *before*-tax return. Investors try to defer taxes whenever possible. Stocks that allow tax deferral (low dividends—high capital gains) will possibly sell at a premium relative to stocks that require current taxation (high dividends—low capital gains). In this way, the two stocks may provide comparable *after-tax* returns. This suggests that a policy of paying low dividends will result in a higher stock price. That is, high dividends hurt investors, while low dividends and high retention help investors. This is the logic of advocates of the low-dividend policy.

Improving Our Thinking

We have now looked at three views on dividend policy. Which is right? The argument that dividends are irrelevant is difficult to refute, given the perfect market assumptions. However, in the real world, it is not always easy to feel comfortable with such an argument. Conversely, the high-dividend philosophy, which measures risk by how we split the firm's cash flows between dividends and retention, is not particularly appealing when studied carefully. The third view, which is essentially a tax argument against high dividends, is persuasive. Even today, although the preferential tax rate for capital gains no longer exists, its "deferral advantage" is still alive and well. However, if low dividends are so advantageous and generous dividends are so hurtful, why do companies

[4]From a discussion by John Childs, an investment adviser at Kidder Peabody, in Donald H. Chew, Jr., ed., "Do Dividends Matter? A Discussion of Corporate Dividend Policy," in *Six Roundtable Discussions of Corporate Finance with Joel Stern* (New York: Quorum Books, 1986), pp. 83–84.

BASIC FINANCIAL MANAGEMENT IN PRACTICE

Excerpts from "Do Dividends Matter? A Discussion of Corporate Dividend Policy"

January 6, 1982

Joseph T. Willett, Moderator: I would like to welcome the participants and guests to this discussion, the subject of which is Corporate Dividend Policy. The general questions we want to address are these: Does dividend policy matter? And if so, why and how does it matter? Certain people argue that the theory of finance, combined with the treatment of dividends under U.S. tax law, would suggest that low dividends benefit investors. Others argue that because of the demand by some investors for current income, high dividends benefit investors. In the presence of these widely held views, I think it is fair to say that most carefully executed research has revealed no consistent relationship between dividends and share prices. From these studies, the market collectively appears to be "dividend neutral." That is, while individual investors may have preferences between dividends and capital gains, the results suggest neither a preference for nor an aversion to dividends. Which, of course, doesn't satisfy either the pro-dividend or anti-dividend group. Amid all this confusion, one observation stands out: nearly all successful firms pay dividends. And, furthermore, dividend policy is an important concern of most chief financial officers and financial managers generally. These facts of corporate practice, in light of all the evidence on the subject, present us with a puzzle—one which has continued to baffle the academic finance profession. In a paper written in 1976, entitled "The Dividend Puzzle," Fischer Black of MIT—one of the most widely respected researchers in the field—posed the question: "What should the individual investor do about dividends in his portfolio? What should the corporation do about dividend policy?"

Joel Stern: I'd like to point out that the major reason why people like Fischer Black believe they don't know the answer to the question of the appropriate dividend policy is this: the evidence that has been accumulated in the academic community by serious researchers—by people that we have a lot of respect for, who are on the faculties of the premiere business schools—almost without exception, these academics find that there is no evidence to suggest that investors at the margin, where prices are set, have any preference for dividends over capital gains. This supports the point of view that the price-setting, marginal investor is "dividend-neutral,"

which means that a dollar of dividends gained is equal to a dollar of capital gains returned, while being indifferent how that return was divided between dividends and price appreciation. There is a second point of view, that has been expressed recently in research, which shows that investors who receive dividends cannot undo the harmful tax consequences of receiving that dividend. And, as a result, the market is actually "dividend averse," marking down prices of shares that pay cash dividends, so that the pretax returns that investors earn are high enough such that, post-tax, the returns are what they would have been had the company not paid cash dividends in the first place. But there is no creditable evidence that I am aware of—none that has been accepted by the academic finance community—that shows that investors prefer dividends over capital gains.

If the evidence that has been published to date says that investors are dividend neutral or dividend averse, then how is it that somebody with the esteem of Fischer Black can come along and say: "We don't know what the right dividend policy is." The problem is that he is what we call a "positive economist." That doesn't mean that he is an economist who is positive about things. It means that he says the job of the economist is to account for what we see around us. He believes that markets behave in a sensible fashion at the margin; that under the guidance of the dominant price-setting investors, the market behaves in a rational manner, making the right choices for itself. Therefore, he is saying that there must be a reason why almost all companies for all time have been paying cash dividends. If a few companies paid dividends for all time, or almost all companies paid dividends only occasionally, then one could make the case that it is possible dividends are really not important. But, if we find that almost all companies pay dividends for almost all time, there must be a good reason why they are paying the dividends. Therefore, who are we, as financial advisors, to say to a company, "No, don't pay cash dividends. After all, it won't harm you very much despite the fact that almost all companies are paying cash dividends"? That wouldn't make very much sense.

Source: Donald H. Chew, Jr., ed., "Do Dividends Matter? A Discussion of Corporate Dividend Policy," in *Six Roundtable Discussions of Corporate Finance with Joel Stern* (New York: Quorum Books, 1986), p. 67–101.

continue to pay dividends? It is difficult to believe that managers would forgo such an easy opportunity to benefit their stockholders. What are we missing?

The need to find the missing elements in our "dividend puzzle" has not been ignored. When we need to understand better an issue or phenomenon, we have two options: improving our thinking or gathering more evidence about the topic. Scholars and practitioners have taken both approaches. Although no single definitive answer has yet been found that is acceptable to all, several plausible extensions have been developed. Some of the more popular additions include (1) the residual dividend theory, (2) the clientele effect, (3) information effects, (4) agency costs, and (5) expectations theory.

The Residual Dividend Theory

Within the Land of Ez, companies were blessed with professional consultants who were essentially charitable in nature; they did not seek any compensation when they helped a firm through the process of issuing stock. (Even in the Land of Ez, managers needed help from investment bankers, accountants, and attorneys to sell a new issue.) However, in reality the process is quite expensive, and may cost as much as 20 percent of the dollar issue size.[5]

If a company incurs flotation costs, that may have a direct bearing on the dividend decision. Because of these costs, a firm must issue a larger amount of securities in order to receive the amount required for investment. For example, if $300,000 is needed to finance proposed investments, an amount exceeding the $300,000 will have to be issued to offset flotation costs incurred in the sale of the new stock issue. This means, very simply, that new equity capital raised through the sale of common stock will be more expensive than capital raised through the retention of earnings. (Remember what we learned in Chapter 8?)

In effect, flotation costs eliminate our indifference between financing by internal capital and by new common stock. Earlier, the company could pay dividends and issue common stock or retain profits. However, when flotation costs exist, internal financing is preferred. Dividends are paid only if profits are not completely used for investment purposes; that is, only when there are "residual earnings" after the financing of new investments. This policy is called the **residual dividend theory**.[6]

With the assumption of no flotation costs removed, the firm's dividend policy would be as follows:

1. Maintain the optimum debt ratio in financing future investments.
2. Accept an investment if the net present value is positive. That is, the expected rate of return exceeds the cost of capital.
3. Finance the equity portion of new investments *first* by internally generated funds. Only after this capital is fully utilized should the firm issue new common shares.
4. If any internally generated funds still remain after making all investments, pay dividends to the investors. However, if all internal capital is needed for financing the equity portion of proposed investments, pay no dividend.

EXAMPLE

Assume that the Krista Corporation finances 40 percent of its investments with debt and the remaining 60 percent with common equity. Two million dollars have been generated from operations and may be used to finance the common equity portion of new investments or to pay common dividends. The firm's

[5]We discuss the costs of issuing securities in Chapter 18.
[6]The residual dividend theory is consistent with the "pecking order" theory of finance as described by Stewart Myers, "The Capital Structure Puzzle," *The Journal of Finance* (July 1984), pp. 575–92.

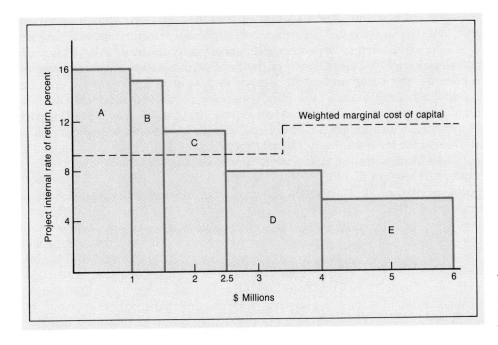

FIGURE 11–2.
Krista Corporation Investment Schedule

management is considering five investment opportunities. Figure 11–2 graphs the expected rate of return for these investments, along with the firm's weighted marginal cost of capital curve. From the information contained in the figure, we would accept projects A, B, and C, requiring $2.5 million in total financing. Therefore, $1 million in new debt (40% of $2.5 million) would be needed, with common equity providing $1.5 million (60% of $2.5 million). In this instance the dividend payment decision would be to pay $500,000 in dividends, which is the *residual*, or remainder, of the $2 million internally generated capital.

To illustrate further, consider the dividend decision if project D had also been acceptable. If this investment were added to the firm's portfolio of proposed capital expenditures, then $4 million in new financing would be needed. Debt financing would constitute $1.6 million (40% × $4 million) and common equity would provide the additional $2.4 million (60% × $4 million). Because only $2 million is available internally, $400,000 in new common stock would be issued. The residual available for dividends would be zero, and no dividend would be paid. ■

In summary, dividend policy is influenced by (1) the company's investment opportunities, (2) the capital structure mix, and (3) the availability of internally generated capital. In the Krista Corporation example, dividends were paid *only* after all acceptable investments had been financed. This logic, called the residual dividend theory, implies that the dividends to be paid should equal the equity capital *remaining* after financing investments. According to this theory, dividend policy is a passive influence, having by itself no direct influence on the market price of the common stock.

The Clientele Effect

What if the investors living in the Land of Ez did not like the dividend policy chosen by Dowell's management? No problem. They could simply satisfy their personal income preferences by purchasing or selling securities when the dividends received did not satisfy their current needs for income. If an investor did not view the dividends received in any given year to be sufficient, he or she could simply sell a portion of stock, thereby "creating a dividend." In addition, if the dividend were larger than the investor desired, he or she could purchase stock with the "excess cash" created by the dividend. However, once we leave the Land of Ez, we find that such adjustments in stock ownership are not cost free. When an investor buys or sells stock, brokerage fees are incurred, ranging from approximately 1 to 10 percent. Even more costly, the investor who buys the stock with cash received from a dividend will have to pay taxes before reinvesting the cash. And when a stock is bought or sold, it must first be reevaluated. Acquisition of the information for decision making also may be time consuming and costly. Finally, aside from the cost of buying or selling part of the stock, some institutional investors, such as university endowment funds, are precluded from selling stock and "spending" the proceeds.

As a result of these considerations, investors may not be too inclined to buy stocks that require them to "create" a dividend stream more suitable to their purposes. Rather, if investors do in fact have a preference between dividends and capital gains, we could expect them to seek firms that have a dividend policy consistent with these preferences. They would, in essence, "sort themselves out" by buying stocks that satisfy their preferences for dividends and capital gains. Individuals and institutions that need current income would be drawn to companies that have high dividend payouts. Other investors, such as wealthy individuals, would much prefer to avoid taxes by holding securities that offer no or small dividend income but large capital gains. In other words, there would be a **clientele effect:** Firms draw a given clientele, given their stated dividend policy.

The possibility that clienteles of investors exist might lead us to believe that the firm's dividend policy matters. However, unless there is a greater aggregate demand for a particular policy than the market can satisfy, dividend policy is still unimportant; one policy is as good as the other. The clientele effect only warns firms to avoid making capricious changes in their dividend policy. Given that the firm's investment decisions are already made, the level of the dividend is still unimportant. The change in the policy matters only when it requires clientele to shift to another company.

The Information Effect

The investor in the Land of Ez would argue with considerable persuasion that a firm's value is determined strictly by its investment and financing decisions, and that the dividend policy has no impact on value. Yet we know from experience that a large, unexpected change in dividends can have a significant impact on the stock price. For instance, in November 1990 Occidental Petroleum cut its dividend from $2 to $1. In response, the firm's stock price went from about $32 to $17. How can we suggest that dividend policy matters little, when we can cite numerous such examples of a change in dividend affecting the stock price, especially when the change is negative?

Despite such "evidence," we are not looking at the real cause and effect. It may be that investors use a change in dividend policy as a *signal* about the firm's financial condition, especially its earning power. Thus, a dividend increase that is larger than expected might signal to investors that management expects significantly higher earnings in the future. Conversely, a dividend decrease, or even a less than expected increase, might signal that management is forecasting less favorable future earnings.

Some would argue that management frequently has inside information about the firm that it cannot make available to investors. This difference in accessibility to information between management and investors, called **information asymmetry,** may result in a lower stock price than would occur under conditions of certainty. This reasoning says that, by regularly increasing dividends, management is making a commitment to continue these cash flows to the stockholders for the foreseeable future. So in a risky marketplace, dividends become a means to minimize any "drag" on the stock price that might come from differences in the level of information available to managers and investors.

Dividends may therefore be important only as a communication tool; management may have no other credible way to inform investors about future earnings, or at least no convincing way that is less costly.

Agency Costs

Let us return again to the Land of Ez. We had avoided any potential conflict between the firm's investors and managers by assuming them to be one and the same. With only a cursory look at the real marketplace, we can see that managers and investors are typically not the same people, and as noted in the preceding section, these two groups do not have the same access to information about the firm. If the two groups are not the same, we must then assume that management is dedicated to maximizing shareholder wealth.[7] That is, we are making a presupposition that the market values of companies with separate owners and managers will not differ from those of owner-managed firms.

Two possibilities should help managers see things as the equity investors see them: (1) Low market values may attract takeover bids; and (2) a competitive labor market may allow investors to replace uncooperative managers. That is, if management is not sensitive to the need to maximize shareholder wealth, new investors may buy the stock, take control of the firm, and remove management.[8] If current management is being less than supportive of the owners, these owners can always seek other managers who will work in the investors' best interest. If these two market mechanisms worked perfectly without any cost, the potential conflict would be nonexistent. In reality, however, conflicts may still exist, and the stock price of a company owned by investors who are separate from management may be less than the stock value of a closely held firm. The difference in price is the cost of the conflict to the owners, which has come to be called **agency costs**.[9]

Recognizing the possible problem, management, acting independently or at the insistence of the board of directors, frequently takes action to minimize the cost associated with the separation of ownership and management control. Such action, which in itself is costly, includes auditing by independent accountants, assigning supervisory functions to the company's board of directors, creating covenants in lending agreements that restrict management's powers, and providing incentive compensation plans for management that help "bond" the management with the owners.

A firm's dividend policy may be perceived by owners as a tool to minimize agency costs. Assuming that the payment of a dividend requires management to issue stock to finance new investments, new investors may be attracted to the company only if management provides convincing information that the capital will be used profitably. Thus, the payment of dividends indirectly results in a closer monitoring of management's investment activities. In this case, dividends may make a meaningful contribution to the value of the firm.

Expectations Theory[10]

A common thread throughout much of our discussion of dividend policy, particularly as it relates to information effects, is the word *expected*. We should not overlook the significance of this word when we are making any financial decision within the firm. No matter what the decision area, how the market

[7]This issue was addressed briefly in Chapter 1.

[8]The "corporate control hypothesis," especially as it relates to companies merging or being acquired, has generated a great amount of interest in recent years. For example, see the April 1983 issue of *Journal of Financial Economics*.

[9]See M. C. Jenson, and W. H. Meckling, "Theory of the Firm: Managerial Behavior, Agency Costs, and Ownership Structure," *Journal of Financial Economics* (October 1976), pp. 305–60.

[10]Much of the thoughts in this section came from Merton Miller, "Can Management Use Dividends to Influence the Value of the Firm?" in *The Revolution in Corporate Finance*, ed., Joel M. Stern, and Donald H. Chew, Jr. (New York: Basil Blackwell, 1986), pp. 299–303.

price responds to management's actions is not determined entirely by the action itself; it is also affected by investors' expectations about the ultimate decision to be made by management.

As the time approaches for management to announce the amount of the next dividend, investors form expectations as to how much that dividend will be. These expectations are based on several factors internal to the firm, such as past dividend decisions, current and expected earnings, investment strategies, and financing decisions. They also consider such things as the condition of the general economy, the strength or weakness of the industry at the time, and possible changes in government policies.

When the actual dividend decision is announced, the investor compares the actual decision with the expected decision. If the amount of the dividend is as expected, even if it represents an increase from prior years, the market price of the stock will remain unchanged. However, if the dividend is higher or lower than expected, investors will reassess their perceptions about the firm. They will question the meaning of the *unexpected* change in the dividend. They may use the unexpected dividend decision as a clue about unexpected changes in earnings; that is, the unexpected dividend change has information content about the firm's earnings and other important factors. In short, management's actual decision about the firm's dividend policy may not be terribly significant, unless it departs from investors' expectations. If there is a difference between actual and expected dividends, we will more than likely see a movement in the stock price.

The Empirical Evidence

Our search for an answer to the question of dividend relevance has been less than successful. We have given it our best thinking, but still no single definitive position has emerged. Maybe we could gather evidence to show the relationship between dividend practices and security prices. We might also inquire into the perceptions of financial managers who make decisions about dividend policies, with the idea that their beliefs affect their decision making. Then we could truly know that dividend policy is important or that it does not matter.

To test the relationship between dividend payments and security prices, we could compare a firm's dividend yield (dividend/stock price) and the stock's total return. The question is: Do stocks that pay high dividends provide higher or lower returns to investors? Such tests have been conducted with the use of highly sophisticated statistical techniques. Despite the use of these extremely powerful analytical tools, which involve intricate and complicated procedures, the results have been mixed.[11] However, over long periods, the results have given a slight advantage to the low-dividend stocks; that is, stocks that pay lower dividends appear to have higher prices. The findings are far from conclusive, however, owing to the relatively large standard errors of the estimates. (The apparent differences may be the result of random sampling error and not real differences.) We simply have been unable to disentangle the effect of dividend policy from other influences.

Several reasons may be given for our inability to arrive at conclusive results. First, to be accurate, we would need to know the amount of dividends investors *expected* to receive. Because these expectations cannot be observed, we can only use historical data, which may or may not relate to current expectations. Second, most empirical studies have assumed a linear relationship

---

[11]See F. Black and M. Scholes, "The Effects of Dividend Yield and Dividend Policy on Common Stock Prices and Returns," *Journal of Financial Economics* 1 (May 1974), pp. 1–22; P. Hess, "The Ex-Dividend Behavior of Stock Returns: Further Evidence on Tax Effects," *Journal of Finance* 37 (May 1982), pp. 445–56; R. H. Litzenberger and K. Ramaswamy, "The Effect of Personal Taxes and Dividends on Capital Asset Prices: Theory and Empirical Evidence," *Journal of Financial Economics* 7 (June 1979), pp. 163–95; and M. H. Miller and M. Scholes, "Dividends and Taxes: Some Empirical Evidence," *Journal of Political Economy* 90 (1982), pp. 1118–41.

between dividend payments and stock prices. The actual relationship may be nonlinear, possibly even discontinuous. Whatever the reasons, the evidence to date is inconclusive and the vote is still out.

Because our statistical prowess does not provide any conclusive evidence, let's turn to our last hope. What do the financial managers of the world believe about the relevance of dividend policy? While we may not conclude that a manager's opinion is necessarily the "final word on the matter," having these insights is helpful. If financial managers believe that dividends matter and act consistently in accordance with that conviction, they could influence the relationship between stock value and dividend policy.

To help us gain some understanding of managements' perceptions, let's turn to a study by Baker, Farrelly, and Edelman, which surveyed financial executives at 318 firms listed on the New York Stock Exchange.[12] The study, conducted in 1983, is summarized in Table 11–4. In looking at the Baker, Farrelly, and Edelman results, the evidence favors the relevance of dividend policy, but not overwhelmingly so. For the most part, managers are divided between believing that dividends are important and having no opinion in the matter.

Regarding the question about the price–dividend relationship, Baker et al. asked the financial managers straight up, "Does the firm's dividend policy affect the price of the common stock?" Slightly more than 60 percent of the responses were affirmative, which is significant, but there were still almost 40 percent who had no opinion or disagreed. Thus, we could conclude that most managers think that dividends matter, but they have no mandate. Similarly, when asked if dividends provide informational content about the firm's future (Questions 2 and 3), the managers are basically split between "no opinion" and "agreement." When asked about the tradeoff between dividends and capital gains (Questions 4 and 5), almost two-thirds of the managers thought stockholders have a preference for dividend or capital gains, with a lesser number (56 percent) believing that investors perceive the relative riskiness of capital gains and dividends to be different. Interestingly enough, though, almost half of the managers felt no clear responsibility to be responsive to stockholders' preferences. Specifically, 56 percent of the financial executives either had no opinion or did not believe that stockholders are attracted to firms that have dividend policies appropriate to the

Statement of Managerial Beliefs	Level of Managers' Agreement		
	Agree-ment	No Opinion	Disagree-ment
1. A firm's dividend payout ratio affects the price of the common stock.	61	33	6
2. Dividend payments provide a signaling device of future prospects.	52	41	7
3. The market uses dividend announcements as information for assessing security value.	43	51	6
4. Investors have different perceptions of the relative riskiness of dividends and retained earnings.	56	42	2
5. Investors are basically indifferent with regard to returns from dividends versus those from capital gains.	6	30	64
6. A stockholder is attracted to firms that have dividend policies appropriate to the stockholder's particular tax environment.	44	49	7
7. Management should be responsive to its shareholders' preferences regarding dividends.	41	49	10

TABLE 11–4
Management Opinion Survey on Dividends

Source: Adapted from H. Kent Baker, Gail E. Farrelly, and Richard B. Edelman, "A Survey of Management Views on Dividend Policy," *Financial Management* (Autumn 1985), p. 81.

[12]H. Kent Baker, Gail E. Farrelly, and Richard B. Edelman, "A Survey of Management Views on Dividend Policy," *Financial Management* (Autumn 1985), pp. 78–84.

stockholder's particular tax environment. Finally, Statement 7 suggests that the majority of managers are not true believers in the concept of a clientele effect.

What Are We to Conclude?

We have now looked carefully at the importance of a firm's dividend policy as management seeks to increase the shareholders' wealth. We have gone to great lengths to gain insight and understanding from our best thinking. We have even drawn from the empirical evidence on hand to see what the findings suggest.

A reasonable person cannot reach a definitive conclusion; nevertheless, management is left with no choice. A firm must develop a dividend policy, it is hoped, based on the best available knowledge. Although we can give advice only with some reservation, the following conclusions would appear reasonable:

1. As a firm's investment opportunities increase, the dividend payout ratio should decrease. In other words, an inverse relationship should exist between the amount of investments with an expected rate of return that exceeds the cost of capital and the dividends remitted to investors. Because of flotation costs associated with raising external capital, the retention of internally generated equity financing is preferable to selling stock (in terms of the wealth of the current common shareholders).

2. The firm's dividend policy appears to be important; however, appearances may be deceptive. The real issue may be the firm's *expected* earning power and the riskiness of these earnings. Investors may be using the dividend payment as a source of information about the company's *expected* earnings. Management's actions regarding dividends may carry greater weight than a statement by management that earnings will be increasing.

3. If dividends influence stock price, this is probably based on the investor's desire to minimize and defer taxes, and from the role of dividends in minimizing agency costs.

4. If the expectations theory has merit, which we believe it does, management should avoid surprising investors when it comes to the firm's dividend decision. The firm's dividend policy might effectively be treated as a *long-term residual*. Rather than projecting investment requirements for a single year, management could anticipate financing needs for several years. Based upon the expected investment opportunities during the planning horizon, the firm's debt–equity mix, and the funds generated from operations, a *target* dividend payout ratio could be established. If internal funds remained after projection of the necessary equity financing, dividends would be paid. However, the planned dividend stream should distribute residual capital evenly to investors over the planning period. Conversely, if over the long term the entire amount of internally generated capital is needed for reinvestment in the company, then no dividend should be paid.

The Dividend Decision in Practice

In setting a firm's dividend policy, financial managers must work in the world of reality with the concepts we have set forth so far in this chapter. Again, although these concepts do not provide an equation that explains the key relationships, they certainly give us a more complete view of the finance world, which can only help us make better decisions. Other considerations of a more practical nature also appear as part of the firm's decision making about its dividend policy.

Other Practical Considerations

Many considerations may influence a firm's decision about its dividends, some of them unique to that company. Some of the more general considerations are given subsequently.

Legal Restrictions

Certain legal restrictions may limit the amount of dividends a firm may pay. These legal constraints fall into two categories. First, *statutory restrictions* may prevent a company from paying dividends. While specific limitations vary by state, generally a corporation may not pay a dividend (1) if the firm's liabilities exceed its assets, (2) if the amount of the dividend exceeds the accumulated profits (retained earnings), and (3) if the dividend is being paid from capital invested in the firm.

The second type of legal restriction is unique to each firm and results from restrictions in debt and preferred stock contracts. To minimize their risk, investors frequently impose restrictive provisions upon management as a condition to their investment in the company. These constraints may include the provision that dividends may not be declared prior to the debt being repaid. Also, the corporation may be required to maintain a given amount of working capital. Preferred stockholders may stipulate that common dividends may not be paid when any preferred dividends are delinquent.

Liquidity Position

Contrary to common opinion, the mere fact that a company shows a large amount of retained earnings in the balance sheet does not indicate that cash is available for the payment of dividends. The firm's current position in liquid assets, including cash, is basically independent of the retained earnings account. Historically, a company with sizable retained earnings has been successful in generating cash from operations. Yet these funds are typically either reinvested in the company within a short period or used to pay maturing debt. Thus, a firm may be extremely profitable and still be *cash poor*. Because dividends are paid with cash, *and not with retained earnings*, the firm must have cash available for dividends to be paid. Hence, the firm's liquidity position has a direct bearing on its ability to pay dividends.

Absence or Lack of Other Sources of Financing

As already noted, a firm may (1) retain profits for investment purposes, or (2) pay dividends and issue new debt or equity securities to finance investments. For many small or new companies, this second option is not realistic. These firms do not have access to the capital markets, so they must rely more heavily upon internally generated funds. As a consequence, the dividend payout ratio is generally much lower for a small or newly established firm than for a large, publicly owned corporation.

Earnings Predictability

A company's dividend payout ratio depends to some extent on the predictability of a firm's profits over time. If earnings fluctuate significantly, management cannot rely on internally generated funds to meet future needs. When profits are realized, the firm may retain larger amounts to ensure that money is available when needed. Conversely, a firm with a stable earnings trend will typically pay a larger portion of its earnings out in dividends. This company has less concern about the availability of profits to meet future capital requirements.

BASIC FINANCIAL MANAGEMENT IN PRACTICE

By the Throat

An Irishman raised in England and educated at Oxford and Harvard Business School is going to end up a firm favourite with management academics. Dermot Dunphy, who runs Sealed Air, America's leading specialty-packaging company, has made a high-debt strategy work where so many others (including Beazer in the previous story) have failed.

Sealed Air produces the sheets of plastic bubble wrap that are so tempting to pop. By the mid-1980s the 25-year-old firm had changed packaging worldwide with proprietary light-weight materials such as padded "Jiffy" envelopes and the polystyrene foam that encloses most things packed in boxes. The company dominated its domestic market and was successful abroad, even in such tough markets as Japan. But it had also become complacent. The business was such a cash-cow that Sealed Air's managers just milked its sales and grew lazy at manufacturing.

This was dangerous. Its bubble-wrap patents were starting to run out, and rivals were appearing on the horizon. After buying several other packaging firms to expand its product line, there were few companies in the industry left to buy. In 1989 Mr. Dunphy decided to shake his colleagues' complacency by abruptly handing $328m back to shareholders in the form of a $40-a-share special dividend, at a time when the shares were trading at $45.

This was, indeed, quite a jolt. The biggest annual dividend Sealed Air had ever paid shareholders was 58 cents. The payout was equivalent to 87% of the company's market capitalisation—and 94% of the cash had to be borrowed. Mr Dunphy borrowed 70% of the dividend-money from his banks, after some arm-twisting. He raised the rest by selling junk bonds. The dividend transformed Sealed Air into a company with negative net worth of $177.5m.

This created what Mr Dunphy calls a "controlled crisis." But high debt-repayments have concentrated managers' minds wonderfully. Delivery lead times have been halved and operating margins improved by one-third compared with levels before the debt was taken on. Earnings per share (calculated after tax) soared 56% last year and are likely to rise 27% this year. Pre-tax profits are set to rise 20%, to around $30m, on sales up 4% to about $430m compared with a year earlier. This is despite the fact that many of the company's customers, especially in America, are suffering from recession.

Source: "Sealed Air," *The Economist*, September 14, 1991. Used by permission.

Ownership Control

For many large corporations, control through the ownership of common stock is not an issue. However, for many small and medium-sized companies, maintaining voting control takes a high priority. If the present common shareholders are unable to participate in a new offering, issuing new stock is unattractive, in that the control of the current stockholders is diluted. The owners might prefer that management finance new investments with debt and through profits rather than by issuing new common stock. This firm's growth is then constrained by the amount of debt capital available and by the company's ability to generate profits.

Inflation

Before the late 1970s, inflationary pressures had not been a significant problem for either consumers or businesses. However during much of the 1980s, the deterioration of the dollar's purchasing power had a direct impact on the replacement of fixed assets. In a period of inflation, ideally, as fixed assets become worn and obsolete, the funds generated from depreciation are used to finance the replacements. As the cost of equivalent equipment continues to increase, the depreciation funds are insufficient. This requires a greater retention of profits, which implies that dividends have to be adversely affected. In the 1990s, inflation may not be a primary concern—only time will tell.

Alternate Dividend Policies

Regardless of a firm's long-term dividend policy, most firms choose one of several year-to-year dividend payment patterns:

1. **Constant dividend payout ratio.** In this policy, the percentage of earnings paid out in dividends is held constant. Although the dividend-to-earnings ratio is stable, the dollar amount of the dividend naturally fluctuates from year to year as profits vary.

2. **Stable dollar dividend per share.** This policy maintains a relatively stable dollar dividend over time. An increase in the dollar dividend usually does not occur until management is convinced that the higher dividend level can be maintained in the future. Management also will not reduce the dollar dividend until the evidence clearly indicates that a continuation of the present dividend cannot be supported.

3. **Small, regular dividend plus a year-end extra.** A corporation following this policy pays a small regular dollar dividend plus a year-end *extra dividend* in prosperous years. The extra dividend is declared toward the end of the fiscal year, when the company's profits for the period can be estimated. Management's objective is to avoid the connotation of a permanent dividend. However, this purpose may be defeated if *recurring* extra dividends come to be expected by investors. General Motors is an example of a firm that employs the low stable dividend plus an extra dividend at the end of the year.

Of the three dividend policies, the stable dollar dividend is by far the most common. Figure 11–3 graphs the general tendency of companies to pay stable, but increasing, dividends, even though the profits fluctuate significantly. In a study by Lintner, corporate managers were found to be reluctant to change the dollar amount of the dividend in response to temporary fluctuations in earnings from year to year. This aversion was particularly evident when it came to decreasing the amount of the dividend from the previous level.[13] Smith explained the stable dividend in terms of his "increasing-stream hypothesis of dividend policy."[14] He proposed that dividend stability is essentially a smoothing

---

[13]John Lintner, "Distribution of Income of Corporations Among Dividends, Retained Earnings, and Taxes," *American Economic Review* 46 (May 1956), pp. 97–113.

[14]Keith V. Smith, "Increasing-Stream Hypothesis of Corporate Dividend Policy," *California Management Review* 15 (Fall 1971), pp. 56–64.

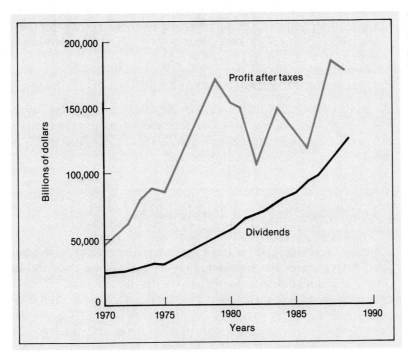

FIGURE 11–3.
Corporate Earnings
and Dividends

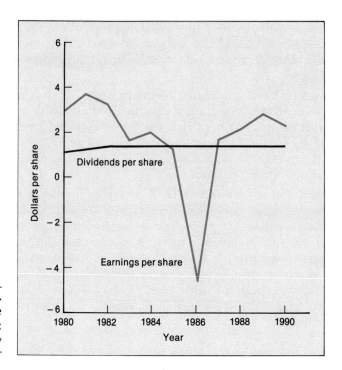

FIGURE 11–4.
Earnings per Share
and Dividends per Share:
W. R. Grace & Company

of the dividend stream to minimize the effect of other types of company reversals. Thus, corporate managers make every effort to avoid a dividend cut, attempting instead to develop a gradually increasing dividend series over the long-term future. However, if a dividend reduction is absolutely necessary, the cut should be large enough to reduce the probability of future cuts.

As an example of a stable dividend policy, Figure 11–4 compares W. R. Grace & Co.'s earnings per share and dividends per share for 1980 through 1990. Ignoring 1985 and 1986, when earnings were exceptionally low, the firm has, on average, paid approximately 54 percent of its earnings out in dividends. This percentage, however, has varied from 36 percent in 1980 to 88 percent in 1983. The historical dividends and earnings patterns for the firm clearly demonstrate management's hesitancy to change dividends in response to short-term fluctuations in earnings. Profits have been highly volatile since 1981; however, the dollar dividends have been held constant or even increased. Conversely, when profits rose sharply in 1981, dividends were increased only slightly.

Perspective in Finance

We don't know much with certitude about dividend policy and its effect on the firm's stock price, but we do know quite alot about dividend practices, including the fact that managers fear the thought of cutting the dividend. It usually will be done only as a last resort. Count on it.

Dividend Payment Procedures

After the firm's dividend policy has been structured, several procedural details must be arranged. For instance, how frequently are dividend payments to be made? If a stockholder sells the shares during the year, who is entitled to the dividend? To answer these questions, we need to understand dividend payment procedures.

Generally, companies pay dividends on a quarterly basis. To illustrate, IBM pays $4.40 per share in annual dividends. However, the firm actually issues a $1.10 quarterly dividend for a total yearly dividend of $4.40 ($1.10 × 4 quarters).

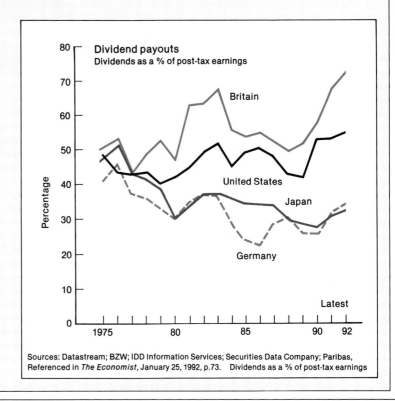
The final approval of a dividend payment comes from the board of directors. As an example, Delta Airlines, on January 26, 1992, announced that holders of record as of February 5 would receive a $.30 dividend. The dividend payment was to be made on March 1. January 26 is the **declaration date**—the date when the dividend is formally declared by the board of directors. The **date of record,** February 5, designates when the stock transfer books are to be closed. Investors shown to own the stock on this date receive the dividend. If a notification of a transfer is recorded subsequent to February 5, the new owner is not entitled to the dividend. However, a problem could develop if the stock were sold on February 4, one day prior to the record date. Time would not permit the sale to be reflected on the stockholder list by the February 5 date of record. To avoid this problem, stock brokerage companies have uniformly decided to terminate the right of ownership to the dividend four working days prior to the record date. This prior date is the **ex-dividend date.** Therefore, any acquirer of Delta stock on February 2, or thereafter does not receive the dividend. Finally, the company mails the dividend check to each investor on March 1, the **payment date.** These events may be diagramed as follows:

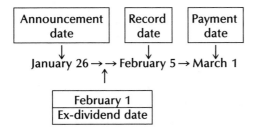

Stock Dividends and Stock Splits

An integral part of dividend policy is the use of **stock dividends** and **stock splits.** Both involve issuing new shares of stock on a pro rata basis to the current shareholders, while the firm's assets, its earnings, and the risk assumed and the investor's percentage of ownership in the company remain unchanged. The only *definite* result from either a stock dividend or stock split is the increase in the number of shares of stock outstanding.

To illustrate the effect of a stock dividend, assume that the Katie Corporation has 100,000 shares outstanding.[15] The firm's after-tax profits are $500,000, or $5 in earnings per share. At present, the company's stock is selling at a price/earnings multiple of 10, or $50 per share. Management is planning to issue a 20 percent stock dividend, so that a stockholder owning 10 shares would receive two additional shares. We might immediately conclude that this investor is being given an asset (two shares of stock) worth $100; consequently, his or her personal worth should increase by $100. This conclusion is erroneous. The firm will be issuing 20,000 new shares (100,000 shares × 20 percent). Since the $500,000 in after-tax profits does not change, the new earnings per share will be $4.167 ($500,000 ÷ 120,000 shares). If the price/earnings multiple remains at 10, the market price of the stock after the dividend should fall to $41.67 ($4.167 earnings per share × 10). The investor now owns 12 shares worth $41.67, which provides a $500 total value; thus he or she is neither better nor worse off than before the stock dividend.

This example may make us wonder why a corporation would even bother with a stock dividend or stock split if no one benefits. However, before we study the rationale for such distributions, we should understand the differences between a stock split and a stock dividend.

Stock Dividend versus Split

The only difference between a stock dividend and a stock split relates to their respective accounting treatment. Stated differently, *there is absolutely no difference on an economic basis between a stock dividend and a stock split.* Both represent a proportionate distribution of additional shares to the present stockholders. However, *for accounting purposes* the stock split has been defined as a stock dividend exceeding 25 percent.[16] Thus, a stock dividend is arbitrarily defined as a distribution of shares up to 25 percent of the number of shares currently outstanding.

The accounting treatment for a stock dividend requires the issuing firm to capitalize the "market value" of the dividend. In other words, the dollar amount of the dividend is transferred from retained earnings to the capital accounts (par and paid-in capital). This procedure may best be explained by an example. Assume that the L. Bernard Corporation is preparing to issue a 15 percent stock dividend. Table 11–5 presents the equity portion of the firm's balance sheet prior to the distribution. The market price for the stock has been $14. Thus, the 15 percent stock dividend increases the number of shares by 150,000 (1,000,000 shares × 15 percent). The "market value" of this increase is $2,100,000 (150,000 shares × $14 market price). To record this transaction, $2,100,000 would be transferred from retained earnings, resulting in a $300,000 increase in total par value (150,000 shares × $2 par value) and a $1,800,000 increment to paid-in capital. The $1,800,000 is the residual difference between $2,100,000 and $300,000. Table 11–6 shows the revised balance sheet.

---

[15]The logic of this illustration is equally applicable to a *stock split.*

[16]The 25 percent standard applies only to corporations listed on the New York Stock Exchange. The American Institute of Certified Public Accountants states that a stock dividend greater than 20 or 25 percent is for all practical purposes a stock split.

Common stock	
Par value (1,000,000 shares outstanding; $2 par value)	$ 2,000,000
Paid-in capital	8,000,000
Retained earnings	15,000,000
Total equity	$25,000,000

TABLE 11–6.
L. Bernard Corporation Balance
Sheet After Stock Dividend

Common stock	
Par value (1,150,000 shares outstanding; $2 par value)	$ 2,300,000
Paid-in capital	9,800,000
Retained earnings	12,900,000
Total equity	$25,000,000

TABLE 11–7.
L. Bernard Corporation Balance
Sheet After Stock Split

Common stock	
Par value (2,000,000 shares outstanding; $1 par value)	$ 2,000,000
Paid-in capital	8,000,000
Retained earnings	15,000,000
Total equity	$25,000,000

What if the management of L. Bernard Corporation changed the plan and decided to split the stock two for one? In other words, a *100 percent increase* in the number of shares would result. In accounting for the split, the changes to be recorded are (1) the increase in the number of shares and (2) the decrease in the per-share par value from $2 to $1. The dollar amounts of each account do not change. Table 11–7 reveals the new balance sheet.

Thus, for a stock dividend, an amount equal to the market value of the stock dividend is transferred from retained earnings to the capital stock accounts. When stock is split, only the number of shares changes, and the par value of each share is decreased proportionately. Despite this dissimilarity in accounting treatment, remember that no real economic difference exists between a split and a dividend.

Rationale for a Stock Dividend or Split

Although *stock* dividends and splits occur far less frequently than *cash* dividends, a significant number of companies choose to use these share distributions either with or in lieu of cash dividends. Since no economic benefit results, how do corporations justify these distributions?

Proponents of stock dividends and splits frequently maintain that stockholders receive a key benefit because the price of the stock will not fall precisely in proportion to the share increase. For a two-for-one split, the price of the stock might not decrease a full 50 percent, and the stockholder is left with a higher total value. There are two reasons for this disequilibrium. First, many financial executives believe that an optimal price range exists. Within this range the total market value of the common stockholders is thought to be maximized. As the price exceeds this range, fewer investors can purchase the stock, thereby restraining the demand. Consequently, downward pressure is placed on its price. The second explanation relates to the *informational content* of the dividend-split announcement. Stock dividends and splits have generally been associated with companies with growing earnings. The announcement of a stock dividend or split has therefore been perceived as favorable news. The empirical evidence, however, fails to verify these conclusions. Most studies indicate that investors are perceptive in identifying the true meaning of a share distribution. If the stock dividend or split is not accompanied by a positive trend in earnings and increases in cash dividends, price increases surrounding the stock dividend or split are insignificant.[17] Therefore, we should be suspicious of the assertion that a stock dividend or split can help increase the investors' worth.

A second reason for stock dividends or splits is the conservation of corporate cash. If a company is encountering cash problems, it may substitute a stock dividend for a cash dividend. However, as before, investors will probably look beyond the dividend to ascertain the underlying reason for conserving cash. If the stock dividend is an effort to conserve cash for attractive investment opportunities, the shareholder may bid up the stock price. If the move to conserve cash relates to financial difficulties within the firm, the market price will most likely react adversely.

Stock Repurchases

For well over three decades, corporate managements have been active in repurchasing their own equity securities. Several reasons have been given for repurchasing stock. Examples of such benefits include

1. Means for providing an internal investment opportunity
2. Approach for modifying the firm's capital structure
3. Favorable impact on earnings per share
4. Elimination of a minority ownership group of stockholders
5. Minimization of dilution in earnings per share associated with mergers and options
6. Reduction in the firm's costs associated with servicing small stockholders

Also, from the shareholders' perspective, a stock repurchase, as opposed to a cash dividend, has a potential tax advantage.

Share Repurchase as a Dividend Decision

Clearly, the payment of a common stock dividend is the conventional method for distributing a firm's profits to its owners. However, it need not be the only way. Another approach is to repurchase the firm's stock. The concept may best be explained by an example.

EXAMPLE

Telink, Inc., is planning to pay $4 million ($4 per share) in dividends to its common stockholders. The following earnings and market price information is provided for Telink:

Net income	$7,500,000
Number of shares	1,000,000
Earnings per share	$7.50
Price/earnings ratio	8
Expected market price per share after dividend payment	$60

In a recent meeting several board members, who are also major stockholders, questioned the need for a dividend payment. They maintain that they do not

[17]See James A. Millar and Bruce D. Fielitz, "Stock Split and Stock-Dividend Decisions," *Financial Management* (Winter 1973), pp. 35–45; and Eugene Fama, Lawrence Fisher, Michael Jensen, and Richard Roll, "The Adjustment of Stock Prices to New Information," *International Economic Review* (February 1969), pp. 1–21.

need the income, so why not allow the firm to retain the funds for future investments? In response, management contends that the available investments are not sufficiently profitable to justify retention of the income. That is, the investors' required rates of return exceed the expected rates of return that could be earned with the additional $4 million in investments.

Because management opposes the idea of retaining the profits for investment purposes, one of the firm's directors has suggested that the $4 million be used to repurchase the company's stock. In this way, the value of the stock should increase. This result may be demonstrated as follows:

1. Assume that shares are repurchased by the firm at the $60 market price (ex-dividend price) plus the contemplated $4 dividend per share, or for $64 per share.

2. Given a $64 price, 62,500 shares would be repurchased ($4 million ÷ $64 price).

3. If net income is not reduced, but the number of shares declines as a result of the share repurchase, earnings per share would increase from $7.50 to $8, computed as follows:

$$\text{earnings per share} = \text{net income/outstanding shares}$$

$$(\text{before repurchase}) = \$7,500,000/1,000,000$$

$$= \$7.50$$

$$(\text{after repurchase}) = \$7,500,000/(1,000,000 - 62,500)$$

$$= \$8$$

4. Assuming that the price/earnings ratio remains at 8, the new price after the repurchase would be $64, up from $60, where the increase exactly equals the amount of the dividend forgone. ■

In this example, Telink's stockholders are essentially provided the same value, whether a dividend is paid or stock is repurchased. If management pays a dividend, the investor will have a stock valued at $60 plus $4 received from the dividend. Conversely, if stock is repurchased in lieu of the dividend, the stock will be worth $64. These results were based upon assuming (1) the stock is being repurchased at the exact $64 price, (2) the $7,500,000 net income is unaffected by the repurchase, and (3) the price/earnings ratio of 8 does not change after the repurchase. Given these assumptions, however, the stock repurchase serves as a perfect substitute for the dividend payment to the stockholders.

The Investor's Choice

Given the choice between a stock repurchase and a dividend payment, which would an investor prefer? In perfect markets, where there are no taxes, no commissions when buying and selling stock, and no informational content assigned to a dividend, the investor would be indifferent with regard to the choices. The investor could create a dividend stream by selling stock when income is needed.

If market imperfections exist, the investor may have a preference for one of the two methods of distributing the corporate income. First, the firm may have to pay too high a price for the repurchased stock, which is to the detriment of the remaining stockholders. If a relatively large number of shares are being bought, the price may be bid up too high, only to fall after the repurchase operation. Second, as a result of the repurchase the market may perceive the riskiness of the corporation as increasing, which would lower the price/earnings ratio and the value of the stock.

Financing or Investment Decision

Repurchasing stock when the firm has excess cash may be regarded as a dividend decision. However, a stock repurchase may also be viewed as a financing decision. By issuing debt and then repurchasing stock, a firm can immediately alter its debt–equity mix toward a higher proportion of debt. Rather than choosing how to distribute cash to the stockholders, management is using a stock repurchase as a means to change the corporation's capital structure.

In addition to dividend and financing decisions, many managers consider a stock repurchase an investment decision. When equity prices are depressed in the marketplace, management may view the firm's own stock as being materially undervalued and representing a good investment opportunity. While the firm's management may be wise to repurchase stock at unusually low prices, this decision cannot and should not be viewed in the context of an investment decision. Buying its own stock cannot provide expected returns as other investments do. No company can survive, much less prosper, by investing only in its own stock.

The Repurchase Procedure

If management intends to repurchase a block of the firm's outstanding shares, it should make this information public. All investors should be given the opportunity to work with complete information. They should be told the purpose of the repurchase, as well as the method to be used to acquire the stock.

Three methods for stock repurchase are available. First, the shares could be bought in the *open market*. Here the firm acquires the stock through a stockbroker at the going market price. This approach may place an upward pressure on the stock price until the stock is acquired. Also, commissions must be paid to the stockbrokers as a fee for their services.

The second method is to make a tender offer to the firm's shareholders. A **tender offer** is a formal offer by the company to buy a specified number of shares at a predetermined and stated price. The tender price is set above the current market price in order to attract sellers. A tender offer is best when a relatively large number of shares are to be bought, since the company's intentions are clearly known and each shareholder has the opportunity to sell the stock at the tendered price.

The third and final method for repurchasing stock entails the purchase of the stock from one or more major stockholders. These purchases are made on a *negotiated basis*. Care should be taken to ensure a fair and equitable price. Otherwise the remaining stockholders may be hurt as a result of the sale.

SUMMARY

In determining the firm's dividend policy, the key issue is the dividend payout ratio (the percentage of the earnings paid out in dividends). This decision has an immediate impact upon the firm's financial mix. As the dividend payment is increased, less funds are available internally for financing investments. Consequently, if additional equity capital is needed, the company has to issue new common stock. Keeping this interaction between the level of dividends and financing in mind, management has to determine the *best* dividend policy for the company's investors. However, selection of the most beneficial dividend payment is not easily accomplished. Management cannot apply an equation to resolve the question. We simply have been unable to disentangle the relationship between dividend policy and share price.

In its simplest form, the dividend payment is a *residual* factor. In this context, the dividend equals the remaining internal capital after financing the equity portion of investments. However, this single criterion fails to recognize (1) the tax benefit of capital gains, (2) agency costs, (3) the clientele effect, and (4) the informational content of a given policy. Furthermore, other considerable factors include the firm's liquidity position, the accessibility to capital markets, inflation, legal restrictions, the stability of earnings, and the desire of investors to maintain control of the company.

Given the firm's investment opportunities, and the imperfections in the market, the financial manager should probably apply the residual dividend theory over the long term. In essence, the firm's investment opportunities are projected throughout a multiple-year planning horizon. Given these investment needs, the target debt mix, and the anticipated earnings, then the amount of money available to pay dividends for the planning period may be determined. The dividend payments should then be made so that large and unexpected changes in the dividend per share are avoided.

Stock dividends and stock splits have been used by corporations either in lieu of or to supplement cash dividends. At the present, no empirical evidence identifies a relationship between stock dividends and splits and the market price of the stock. Yet a stock dividend or split could conceivably be used to keep the stock price within an optimal trading range. Also, if investors perceive that the stock dividend contained favorable information about the firm's operations, the price of the stock could increase.

As an alternative to paying a dividend, management can repurchase stock. However, investors may still prefer dividends to a stock repurchase.

STUDY QUESTIONS

11-1. What is meant by the term *dividend payout ratio?*

11-2. Explain the tradeoff between retaining internally generated funds and paying cash dividends.

11-3. a. What are the assumptions of a perfect market?
b. What effect does dividend policy have on the share price in a perfect market?

11-4. What is the impact of flotation costs on the financing decision?

11-5. a. What is the *residual dividend theory?*
b. Why is this theory operational only in the long term?

11-6. Why might investors prefer capital gains to the same amount of dividend income?

11-7. What legal restrictions may limit the amount of dividends to be paid?

11-8. How does a firm's liquidity position affect the payment of dividends?

11-9. How can ownership control constrain the growth of a firm?

11-10. a. Why is a stable dollar dividend policy popular from the viewpoint of the corporation?
b. Is it also popular with investors? Why?

11-11. Explain declaration date, date of record, and ex-dividend date.

11-12. What are the advantages of a stock split or dividend over a cash dividend?

11-13. Why would a firm repurchase its own stock?

SELF-TEST PROBLEMS

ST-1. (*Dividend Growth Rate*) Schulz, Inc., maintains a constant dividend payout ratio of 35 percent. Earnings per share last year were $8.20 and are expected to grow indefinitely at a rate of 12 percent. What will be the dividend per share this year? In five years?

ST–2. (*Residual Dividend Theory*) Britton Corporation is considering four investment opportunities. The required investment outlays and expected rates of return for these investments are shown below. The firm's cost of capital is 14 percent. The investments are to be financed by 40 percent debt and 60 percent common equity. Internally generated funds totaling $750,000 are available for reinvestment.

  a. Which investments should be accepted? According to the residual dividend theory, what amount should be paid out in dividends?

  b. How would your answer change if the cost of capital were 10 percent?

Investment	Investment Cost	Internal Rates of Return
A	$275,000	17.50%
B	325,000	15.72
C	550,000	14.25
D	400,000	11.65

ST–3. (*Stock Split*) The debt and equity section of the Robson Corporation balance sheet is shown below. The current market price of the common shares is $20. Reconstruct the financial statement assuming that (a) a 15 percent stock dividend is issued and (b) a two-for-one stock split is declared.

Robson Corporation

Debt	$1,800,000
Common	
Par ($2; 100,000 shares)	200,000
Paid-in capital	400,000
Retained earnings	900,000
	$3,300,000

STUDY PROBLEMS (SET A)

11–1A. (*Flotation Costs and Issue Size*) Your firm needs to raise $10 million. Assuming that flotation costs are expected to be $15 per share and that the market price of the stock is $120, how many shares would have to be issued? What is the dollar size of the issue?

11–2A. (*Flotation Costs and Issue Size*) If flotation costs for a common stock issue are 18 percent, how large must the issue be so that the firm will net $5,800,000? If the stock sells for $85 per share, how many shares must be issued?

11–3A. (*Residual Dividend Theory*) Terra Cotta finances new investments by 40 percent debt and 60 percent equity. The firm needs $640,000 for financing new investments. If retained earnings available for reinvestment equal $400,000, how much money will be available for dividends in accordance with the residual dividend theory?

11–4A. (*Stock Dividend*) RCB has 2 million shares of common stock outstanding. Net income is $550,000, and the P/E ratio for the stock is 10. Management is planning a 20 percent stock dividend. What will be the price of the stock after the stock dividend? If an investor owns 100 shares prior to the stock dividend, does the total value of his or her shares change? Explain.

11–5A. (*Dividends in Perfect Markets*) The management of Harris, Inc., is considering two dividend policies for the years 1993 and 1994, one and two years away. In 1995 the management is planning to liquidate the firm. One plan would pay a dividend of $2.50 in 1993 and 1994 and a liquidating dividend of $45.75 in 1995. The alternative would be to pay out $4.25 in dividends in 1993, $4.75 in dividends in 1994, and a final dividend of $40.66 in 1995. The required rate of return for the common stockholders is 18 percent. Management is concerned about the effect of the two dividend streams on the value of the common stock.

  a. Assuming perfect markets, what would be the effect?

  b. What factors in the real world might change your conclusion reached in part (a)?

11–6A. (*Long-Term Residual Dividend Policy*) Stetson Manufacturing, Inc., has projected its investment opportunities over a five-year planning horizon. The cost of each year's investment and the amount of internal funds available for reinvestment for that year are given below. The firm's debt–equity mix is 35 percent debt and 65 percent equity. There are currently 100,000 shares of common stock outstanding.

a. What would be the dividend each year if the residual dividend theory were used on a year-to-year basis?

b. What target stable dividend can Stetson establish by using the long-term residual dividend theory over the future planning horizon?

c. Why might a residual dividend policy applied to the five years as opposed to individual years be preferable?

Year	Cost of Investments	Internal Funds Available for Reinvestment or for Dividends
1	$350,000	$250,000
2	475,000	450,000
3	200,000	600,000
4	980,000	650,000
5	600,000	390,000

11–7A. (*Stock Split*) You own 5 percent of the Trexco Corporation's common stock, which most recently sold for $98 prior to a planned two-for-one stock split announcement. Before the split there are 25,000 shares of common stock outstanding.

a. Relative to now, what will be your financial position after the stock split? (Assume the stock price falls proportionately.)

b. The executive vice-president in charge of finance believes the price will only fall 40 percent after the split because she feels the price is above the optimal price range. If she is correct, what will be your net gain?

11–8A. (*Dividend Policies*) The earnings for Crystal Cargo, Inc., have been predicted for the next five years and are listed below. There are 1 million shares outstanding. Determine the yearly dividend per share to be paid if the following policies are enacted:

a. Constant dividend payout ratio of 50 percent.

b. Stable dollar dividend targeted at 50 percent of the earnings over the five-year period.

c. Small, regular dividend of $.50 per share plus a year-end extra when the profits in any year exceed $1,500,000. The year-end extra dividend will equal 50 percent of profits exceeding $1,500,000.

Year	Profits After Taxes
1	$1,400,000
2	2,000,000
3	1,860,000
4	900,000
5	2,800,000

11–9A. (*Repurchase of Stock*) The Dunn Corporation is planning to pay dividends of $500,000. There are 250,000 shares outstanding, with an earnings per share of $5. The stock should sell for $50 after the ex-dividend date. If instead of paying a dividend, management decides to repurchase stock

a. What should be the repurchase price?

b. How many shares should be repurchased?

c. What if the repurchase price is set below or above your suggested price in part (a)?

d. If you own 100 shares, would you prefer that the company pay the dividend or repurchase stock?

11–10A. (*Flotation Costs and Issue Size*) D. Butler, Inc., needs to raise $14 million. Assuming that the market price of the firm's stock is $95 and flotation costs are 10 percent of the market price, how many shares would have to be issued? What is the dollar size of the issue?

11–11A. (*Residual Dividend Theory*) Martinez, Inc., finances new acquisitions with 70 percent debt and the rest in equity. The firm needs $1.2 million for a new acquisition. If retained earnings available for reinvestment are $450,000, how much money will be available for dividends according to the residual dividend theory?

11–12A. (*Stock Split*) You own 20 percent of Rainy Corp., which recently sold for $86 before a planned two-for-one stock split announcement. Before the split there are 80,000 shares of common stock outstanding.

a. What is your financial position before the split, and what will it be after the stock split? (Assume the stock falls proportionately.)

b. Your stockbroker believes the market will react positively to the split and that the price will fall only 45 percent after the split. If she is correct, what will be your net gain?

STUDY PROBLEMS (SET B)

11–1B. (*Flotation Costs and Issue Size*) Your firm needs to raise $12 million. Assuming that flotation costs are expected to be $17 per share and that the market price of the stock is $115, how many shares would have to be issued? What is the dollar size of the issue?

11–2B. (*Flotation Costs and Issue Size*) If flotation costs for a common stock issue are 14 percent, how large must the issue be so that the firm will net $6,100,000? If the stock sells for $76 per share, how many shares must be issued?

11–3B. (*Residual Dividend Theory*) Steven Miller finances new investments by 35 percent debt and 65 percent equity. The firm needs $650,000 for financing new investments. If retained earnings available for reinvestment equal $375,000, how much money will be available for dividends in accordance with the residual dividend theory?

11–4B. (*Stock Dividend*) DCA has 2.5 million shares of common stock outstanding. Net income is $600,000, and the P/E ratio for the stock is 10. Management is planning an 18 percent stock dividend. What will be the price of the stock after the stock dividend? If an investor owns 120 shares before the stock dividend, does the total value of his or her shares change? Explain.

11–5B. (*Dividends in Perfect Markets*) The management of Montford, Inc., is considering two dividend policies for the years 1993 and 1994, one and two years away. In 1995 the management is planning to liquidate the firm. One plan would pay a dividend of $2.55 in 1993 and 1994 and a liquidating dividend of $45.60 in 1995. The alternative would be to pay out $4.35 in dividends in 1993, $4.70 in dividends in 1994, and a final dividend of $40.62 in 1995. The required rate of return for the common stockholders is 17 percent. Management is concerned about the effect of the two dividend streams on the value of the common stock.

a. Assuming perfect markets, what would be the effect?

b. What factors in the real world might change your conclusion reached in part (a)?

11–6B. (*Long-Term Residual Dividend Policy*) Wells Manufacturing, Inc., has projected its investment opportunities over a five-year planning horizon. The cost of each year's investment and the amount of internal funds available for reinvestment for that year are given below. The firm's debt–equity mix is 40 percent debt and 60 percent equity. There are currently 125,000 shares of common stock outstanding.

a. What would be the dividend each year if the residual dividend theory were used on a year-to-year basis?

b. What target stable dividend can Wells establish by using the long-term residual dividend theory over the future planning horizon?

c. Why might a residual dividend policy applied to the five years as opposed to individual years be preferable?

Year	Cost of Investments	Internal Funds Available for Reinvestment or for Dividends
1	$360,000	$225,000
2	450,000	440,000
3	230,000	600,000
4	890,000	650,000
5	600,000	400,000

11–7B. (*Stock Split*) You own 8 percent of the Standlee Corporation's common stock, which most recently sold for $98 before a planned two-for-one stock split announcement. Before the split there are 30,000 shares of common stock outstanding.

a. Relative to now, what will be your financial position after the stock split? (Assume the stock price falls proportionately.)

b. The executive vice-president in charge of finance believes the price will only fall 45 percent after the split because she thinks the price is above the optimal price range. If she is correct, what will be your net gain?

11–8B. (*Dividend Policies*) The earnings for Carlson Cargo, Inc., have been predicted for the next five years and are listed below. There are 1 million shares outstanding. Determine the yearly dividend per share to be paid if the following policies are enacted:

a. Constant dividend payout ratio of 40 percent.

b. Stable dollar dividend targeted at 40 percent of the earnings over the five-year period.

c. Small, regular dividend of $.50 per share plus a year-end extra when the profits in any year exceed $1,500,000. The year-end extra dividend will equal 50 percent of profits exceeding $1,500,000.

Year	Profits After Taxes
1	$1,500,000
2	2,000,000
3	1,750,000
4	950,000
5	2,500,000

11–9B. (*Repurchase of Stock*) The B. Phillips Corporation is planning to pay dividends of $550,000. There are 275,000 shares outstanding, with an earnings per share of $6. The stock should sell for $45 after the ex-dividend date. If instead of paying a dividend, management decides to repurchase stock

a. What should be the repurchase price?

b. How many shares should be repurchased?

c. What if the repurchase price is set below or above your suggested price in part (a)?

d. If you own 100 shares, would you prefer that the company pay the dividend or repurchase stock?

11–10B. (*Flotation Costs and Issue Size*) D. B. Fool, Inc., needs to raise $16 million. Assuming that the market price of the firm's stock is $100 and flotation costs are 12 percent of the market price, how many shares would have to be issued? What is the dollar size of the issue?

11–11B. (*Residual Dividend Theory*) Maness, Inc., finances new acquisitions with 35 percent in equity and the rest in debt. The firm needs $1.5 million for a new acquisition. If retained earnings available for reinvestment are $525,000, how much money will be available for dividends according to the residual dividend theory?

11–12B. (*Stock Split*) You own 25 percent of The Star Corporation, which recently sold for $90 before a planned two-for-one stock split announcement. Before the split there are 90,000 shares of common stock outstanding.

a. What is your financial position before the split, and what will it be after the stock split? (Assume the stock falls proportionately.)

b. Your stock broker believes the market will react positively to the split and that the price will fall only 45 percent after the split. If she is correct, what will be your net gain?

Suggested Application for *DISCLOSURE*®

Compare the dividend practices for the companies listed below, using the *Disclosure* database as your source of information. Make your comparisons in terms of (a) the percentage of earnings paid out in dividends each year, and (b) the stability of dividends over time. What do you believe accounts for the differences?

Boeing   WalMart

Exxon   Phillip Morris Companies, Inc.

SELF-TEST SOLUTIONS

SS–1. Dividend per share = 35% × $8.20

$$= \$2.87$$

Dividends:

1 year = $2.87 (1 + 0.12)

$$= \$3.21$$

5 years = $2.87 $(1 + 0.12)^5$

$$= \$2.87 \ (1.762)$$

$$= \$5.06$$

SS–2. a. Investments A, B, and C will be accepted, requiring $1,150,000 in total financing. Therefore, 40 percent of $1,150,000 or $460,000 in new debt will be needed, and common equity will have to provide $690,000. The remainder of the $750,000 internal funds will be $60,000, which will be paid out in dividends.

b. Assuming a 10 percent cost of capital, all four investments would be accepted, requiring total financing of $1,550,000. Equity would provide 60 percent, or $930,000 of the total, which would not leave any funds to be paid out in dividends. New common would have to be issued.

SS–3. a. If a 15 percent stock dividend is issued, the financial statement would appear as follows:

Robson Corporation

Debt	$1,800,000
Common	
Par ($2 par, 115,000 shares)	230,000
Paid-in capital	670,000
Retained earnings	600,000
	$3,300,000

b. A two-for-one split would result in a 100 percent increase in the number of shares. Because the total par value remains at $200,000, the new par value per share is $1 ($200,000 ÷ 200,000 shares). The new financial statement would be as follows:

Robson Corporation

Debt	$1,800,000
Common	
Par ($1 par, 200,000 shares)	200,000
Paid-in capital	400,000
Retained earnings	900,000
	$3,300,000

CONCLUSION

VIDEO CASE 3

RJR Nabisco Bondholder Lawsuits: A Leverage Related Agency Problem

from ABC News, *Business World*, November 20, 1988

In the introduction to Video Case 3 on page 313 we asked several important questions that you should now refer to.

Although the announcement of the RJR Nabisco management buyout proposal caused the market value of RJR bonds to fall by 20 percent, the transaction could be valuable to shareholders. If the transaction shifts value from bondholders to shareholders then the transaction might be very attractive to shareholders, despite (or possibly because of) the losses suffered by bondholders. The *static tradeoff theory* suggests that managers should search for the amount of leverage that maximizes firm value, but the theory does not recognize that the interests of shareholders and bondholders may differ. Once bondholders commit funds and agree to a coupon rate, they are at the mercy of shareholders. Shareholders have an incentive, once bonds have been issued, to change the riskiness of the firm. Increased risk provides shareholders with an opportunity for high returns. Moreover, they won't have to share those returns with bondholders because the bondholders have agreed to accept a fixed coupon rate as payment for the use of their funds. This is where the agency conflict between bondholders and shareholders arises. Because managers work for shareholders, we would expect managers to make decisions that maximize share value with little concern about bondholders. In the RJR case, shareholders will be offered a large premium for their shares, so they will benefit; whereas bondholders suffer the affects of increased risk.

Bondholders are not stupid and do recognize the incentives shareholders have to pull such bait-and-switch tricks on them. How can they avoid such problems? Bond covenants provide some protection by restricting the ways managers, on behalf of shareholders, can enhance share value by reducing the value of the bondholders' claim on the firm. Before the early 1980s bondholders could not have foreseen the emergence of leveraged buyouts, so they did not include protective covenants for such transactions. Since then, however, rating agencies evaluate bonds for *event risk,* the possibility of a takeover or other type of restructuring.

In later chapters we will reconsider the value of leveraged buyouts or leveraged management buyouts. This video has introduced just one dimension of a complex transaction that although fraught with potential conflicts of interest may also produce enormous benefits for shareholders and the buyout teams.

Discussion questions

1. What is the opposite of event risk? This situation occurs when a firm becomes safer than it was when bonds were originally issued. As a manager would this concern you? If so, what would you do? (*Hint*: See Frank Easterbrook, "Two Agency Cost Explanations for Dividends," *American Economic Review*, 1984.)
2. Why do you think that bondholders did not demand more complete contractual protection? Can you imagine a contract that protects one of the contracting parties from every eventuality? Why are such contracts unlikely to exist?

Suggested reading

CRABBE, LELAND. "Event Risk: An Analysis of Losses to Bondholders," and "Super Poison Put," *Bond Covenants, Federal Reserve Board Discussion Paper #111,* February 1990.

PART 4

FINANCIAL ANALYSIS, PLANNING, AND CONTROL

All managers need to be able to evaluate performance, plan for the future, and figure out whether objectives are or are not being met. Financial analysis, particularly ratio analysis, is an important tool for determining how a business is performing (Chapter 12). Careful examination of a firm's financial ratios can uncover potential trouble spots or help identify strengths. Ratio analysis may seem tedious or mechanical. In fact, if done properly the opposite is true: Ratio analysis requires artful judgment and serious detective work. Well-executed financial analysis brings a firm's ratios to life—it tells a story about how the firm has performed and is likely to perform in the near future. Financial analysts play an important role in financial markets. They determine bond ratings, recommend stocks to clients, and may even determine when firms are in default of credit agreements. Financial analysis is a tool every student of finance needs in his or her tool kit.

We have already discussed how future cash flows determine the value of assets: Expected dividends help determine stock prices, and expected cash flows are instrumental in capital-budgeting analysis. Now we learn some tools for forecasting those future cash flows (Chapter 13). Financial planning, or *pro forma analysis*, allows managers to prepare for the future by projecting future financial statements. These *pro forma financial statements* help managers estimate future loan needs, plan how to invest surplus cash, or even test different financial strategies such as changes in credit terms, or the effect of higher or lower sales growth rates. Investment bankers use these tools to analyze multibillion dollar takeovers, whereas small business owners use them to construct documents to take to their local bank for a seasonal loan. Like ratio analysis, pro forma analysis is an important tool for future financial managers.

INTRODUCTION

VIDEO CASE 4

Bond-Rating Agencies: Using Financial Analysis to Forecast the Riskiness of Bonds

from ABC News, *Business World*, June 23, 1991

Part 4 introduces the topics of financial analysis and forecasting. An important use of financial analysis is the evaluation of investments. Bond-rating agencies such as Moody's and Standard and Poor's apply these techniques in evaluating the riskiness of corporate and municipal bonds. Using past financial data and forecasts of economic trends, these agencies give borrowers a letter rating, such as AA (double A) or BBB (triple B), which indicates the overall quality of the bond being sold to investors. The higher the rating (AAA is the highest), the more certain the rating agency is that the interest and principal payments of a bond will be paid in a timely manner. Some investors, such as pension funds, are allowed to invest only in high-rated (or investment-quality) bonds. Rating agencies periodically review the rating of bonds.

- If you were asked to give a rating to a municipal bond, what information would you examine?
- Is evaluating a city's ability to service debt analogous to analyzing a firm? What are the similarities, and what are the differences?
- Do you think the rating agencies decisions matter to state and local governments?

As you read Chapters 12 and 13, consider these questions. The video case describes some of the factors that Moody's and Standard and Poor's consider when assigning or revising a city's bond rating. At the end of this section we will return to this video case and discuss some of the issues it raises.

CHAPTER *12*

Evaluating Financial Performance

Basic Financial Statements • Financial Ratios • Integrated Form of Financial Analysis Based on Earning Power

Financial analysis is the assessment of a firm's past, present, and anticipated future financial condition. Its objectives are to determine the firm's financial strengths and to identify its weaknesses. For example, a firm's staff may perform an internal financial analysis to assess the firm's liquidity or measure its past performance. Alternatively, financial analysis may come from outside the firm in an effort to determine the firm's creditworthiness or investment potential. Regardless of origin of the analysis, the tools used in financial analysis are basically the same.

Financial ratios are the principal tools of financial analysis, because they can be used to answer a variety of questions regarding a firm's financial well-being. For example, a commercial bank loan officer considering an application for a six-month loan might want to know whether the applicant firm is solvent or liquid; a potential investor in the firm's common stock might want to know how profitable the firm has been; and an internal financial analyst might want to know whether the firm can reasonably afford to borrow all or part of the funds needed to finance a planned expansion. Answers to these questions can be obtained through the use of financial ratios.

We begin our discussion of financial analysis with an overview of the firm's basic financial statements. These include the balance sheet, income statement, statement of changes in financial condition (source and use of funds statement), and statement of cash flow. Then we will provide a survey of key financial ratios that can be used to assess the firm's financial condition.

Perspective in Finance

Financial statement analysis has probably been introduced in your basic accounting courses. However, the evaluation of financial performance is so important to the financial manager that a review is appropriate here.

Basic Financial Statements

In Chapter 2 we discussed the fact that corporate and noncorporate business enterprises report their financial position and performance through the use of three basic financial statements: the **balance sheet,** the **income statement** and the **statement of cash flow.**

The balance sheet and income statement for Jimco, Inc., are found in Tables 12–1 and 12–2, respectively. We will use the information contained in these statements to derive the statement of changes in financial position and then the statement of cash flow. Appendix 1A contains a discussion of the balance sheet and income statement.

Perspective in Finance

The double-entry system of accounting used in this country dates back to about 3600 B.C., with the first published work describing the system by Luca Pacioli of Venice in 1494. Although the details of the double-entry system can be overwhelming to the novice, the mathematical content of these financial statements is straightforward.

> *1. Balance sheet or statement of financial position*

$$liabilities + owners' \ equity = assets$$

TABLE 12–1.
Jimco, Inc., Balance Sheet
December 31, 1992 ($000)

Assets		
Current assets		
Cash		$ 1,400
Marketable securities—at cost (market value, $320)		300
Accounts receivable		10,000
Inventories		12,000
Prepaid expenses		300
Total current assets		$24,000
Fixed assets		
Land		2,000
Plant and equipment	$12,300	
Less: accumulated depreciation	7,300	
Net plant and equipment		5,000
Total fixed assets		7,000
Total assets		$31,000

Liabilities and Owners' Equity		
Current liabilities		
Accounts payable	$3,000	
Notes payable, 9%, due March 1, 1993	3,400	
Accrued salaries, wages, and other expenses	3,100	
Current portion of long-term debt	500	
Total current liabilities		$10,000
Long-term liabilities		
Deferred income taxes	1,500	
First mortgage bonds, 7%, due January 1, 1993	6,300	
Debentures, 8½%, due June 30, 1999	2,900	
Total long-term liabilities		10,700
Owners' equity		
Common stock (par value $1.00)	100	
Additional paid-in capital	2,000	
Retained earnings	8,200	
Total owners' equity		10,300
Total liabilities and owners' equity		$31,000

Net sales		$51,000
Cost of goods sold		(38,000)
Gross profit		$13,000
Operating expenses		
Selling expenses	$3,100	
Depreciation expense	500	
General and administrative expense	5,400	(9,000)
Net operating income (NOI)		$ 4,000
Interest expense		(1,000)
Earnings before taxes (EBT)		$ 3,000
Income taxes[a]		(1,200)
Net income (NI)		$ 1,800
Disposition of net income		
Common stock dividends		$ 300
Change in retained earnings		1,500
Per-share data (dollars)		
Number of shares of common stock		100,000 shares
Earnings per common share ($1,800,000 ÷ 100,000 shares)		$ 18
Dividends per common share ($300,000 ÷ 100,000 shares)		$ 3

[a]A tax rate of 40 percent on all income is assumed here for simplicity.

2. *Income statement or statement of results from operations*

$$revenues + gains - expenses - losses = income$$

3. *Cash flow statement*

$$cash\ inflow - cash\ outflow = change\ in\ cash$$

Statement of Cash Flows and Statement of Changes in Financial Position

In 1971 the Accounting Principles Board made the statement of changes in financial position a required component of the firm's published corporate reports. However, this statement of generally accepted accounting practice (sometimes referred to simply as GAAP) was superseded by Financial Accounting Standards Board (FASB) Standard 95 in November 1987. This standard states that for fiscal years ending after July 15, 1988, a firm's financial statements will include a statement of cash flows. We will discuss both the source and use of funds statement and the statement of cash flows to assess the similarities in the two statements.

Statement of Changes in Financial Position

The **statement of changes in financial position** (often referred to as a *source and use of funds statement*) provides an accounting of the resources allocated during a specific period and their uses. Specifically, the source and use statement provides the basis for answering such questions as the following:

1. Where did the profits go?
2. Why were the dividends not larger?
3. Why was money borrowed during the period?
4. How was expansion in plant and equipment financed?
5. How was retirement of debt accomplished?
6. What became of the proceeds of the bond issue?

The source and use statement has become a standard tool of financial analysis because it contains extremely useful information. No single format is universally adopted for the source and use of funds statement. The form we have chosen to use is

Cash: Beginning balance
Plus: Sources of cash for the period
Minus: Uses of cash for the period
Cash: Ending balance

The source and use statement explains the changes that took place in the firm's cash balance over the period of interest. Note that *funds* are defined as *cash*, such that the two terms can be used interchangeably.

Sources of funds ■ The firm can obtain funds (cash) from one of four principal sources.

1. From its operations (commonly referred to as funds provided by operations)
2. By borrowing (by means of a short-term note payable or long-term debt in the form of a bond issue)
3. By the sale of assets
4. By issuing common or preferred stock

The firm's sources of funds (with the exception of funds provided by operations) can be identified by observing changes in the balance sheet between the beginning and ending of the statement period. For example, a decrease in accounts receivable over the period would signal that the firm collected more dollars from its credit accounts than it created through new credit sales; hence, this was a source of funds. In general, a decrease in an asset balance denotes a source of funds. Furthermore, an increase in a liability account signals that net additional borrowing took place during the period, thus providing a source of funds to the firm. An increase in the common and preferred stock accounts also indicates sources of funds to the firm. Finally, funds provided by operations are found by summing net income for the period and any noncash expenses (such as depreciation and amortizations of goodwill or bond discount). Note that noncash expenses are deducted from the firm's revenues, because they are tax deductible. However, because no cash changes hands for these noncash expenses, to measure the funds provided by the firm's operations, they must be added back to net income. For example, if net income for the period was $40,000 and noncash expenses were $8,000, then funds provided by operations would equal $48,000.

Uses of funds ■ A firm uses funds (cash) to purchase assets, repay loans, repurchase outstanding shares of its common and preferred stock, and pay cash dividends to preferred and common stockholders. Thus, uses of funds are just the opposite of the sources discussed earlier. For example, issuing or selling bonds is a source of funds, whereas repaying a loan is a use.

Example: Preparing the source and use statement for Jimco, Inc. ■ Jimco's comparative balance sheets for 1991 and 1992 are given in Table 12–3. These statements, along with Jimco's 1992 income statement (Table 12–2), provide all the information needed to prepare the firm's statement of sources and uses of funds for the year ended December 31, 1992.

The column entitled *changes* in Table 12–3 provides the basis for determining Jimco's sources and uses of funds. Note that cash decreased by $100,000 during the year. Because this change in cash is *explained* by the statement of sources and uses of funds, we will ignore it for the time being. Marketable securities did not change; thus no source or use of funds was provided. The accounts receivable balance increased by $1,500,000, indicating that more

TABLE 12–3.
Jimco, Inc.,
Comparative Balance Sheets
December 31, 1991
and 1992 ($000)

Assets			
	1991	1992	Changes
Current assets			
Cash	$ 1,500	$ 1,400	$ (100)
Marketable securities	300	300	—
Accounts receivable	8,500	10,000	1,500
Inventories	11,300	12,000	700
Prepaid expenses	200	300	100
Total current assets	$21,800	$24,000	$2,200
Fixed assets			
Land	$ 2,000	$ 2,000	$ —
Plant and equipment	11,200	12,300	1,100
Less: Accumulated depreciation	(6,800)	(7,300)	(500)
Net plant and equipment	4,400	5,000	600
Total fixed assets	6,400	7,000	600
Total assets	$28,200	$31,000	$2,800

Liabilities and Owners' Equity			
	1991	1992	Changes
Current liabilities			
Accounts payable	$ 3,200	$ 3,000	$ (200)
Notes payable	900	3,400	2,500
Accrued salaries, wages, and other expenses	3,800	3,100	(700)
Current portion of long-term debt	500	500	—
Total current liabilities	$ 8,400	$10,000	$1,600
Long-term liabilities			
Deferred income taxes	$ 1,400	$ 1,500	$ 100
First mortgage bonds	6,600	6,300	(300)
Debenture bonds	3,000	2,900	(100)
Total long-term liabilities	$11,000	$10,700	$ (300)
Owners' equity			
Common stock (par value $1.00)	$ 100	$ 100	—
Additional paid-in capital	2,000	2,000	—
Retained earnings	6,700	8,200	1,500
Total owners' equity	$ 8,800	$10,300	$1,500
Total liabilities and owners' equity	$28,200	$31,000	$2,800

credit sales were made during the period than were collected. Hence, the firm *used* funds to invest in accounts receivable. Inventories and prepaid expenses increased by $700,000 and $100,000, respectively, also indicating uses of funds. In addition, Jimco increased plant and equipment by $1,100,000, which constitutes still another use of funds.[1] Note that the increase in accumulated depreciation of $500,000 equals depreciation expense for the period. Because depreciation expense will be considered in the source and use statement in conjunction with our analysis of the firm's income statement, we will explain this item later.

Looking at the changes in the firm's liabilities, we note first that accounts payable decreased by $200,000. This indicates that the firm paid off more accounts payable than it created during the year. This constitutes a use of funds. Notes payable increased by $2,500,000, signaling a source of funds from short-term borrowing. The accrued salaries, wages, and other expense accounts

---

[1] The use of funds attributed to the purchase of plant and equipment can also be obtained from an analysis of the change in the net plant and equipment account. For Jimco, Inc., this can be accomplished as follows:

Net plant and equipment (1992)	$5000
Plus: depreciation expense for the period	500
	5500
Less: Net plant and equipment (1991)	(4400)
Net purchase (sale) of plant and equipment	$1100

TABLE 12–4.
Jimco, Inc.,
Statement of Sources and Uses
of Funds for Year Ended
December 31, 1992 ($000)

Cash balance (December 31, 1991)		$1500	
Sources of funds			
Funds provided by operations:			
Net income	$1800		
Depreciation	500	2300	47%
Increase in deferred income taxes		100	2
Increase in notes payable		2500	51
Total funds provided		$4900	100%
Uses of funds			
Common stock dividends		$ 300	6%
Purchase of plant and equipment		1100	22
Increase in accounts receivable		1500	30
Increase in inventories		700	14
Increase in prepaid expenses		100	2
Decrease in accounts payable		200	4
Decrease in accrued salaries, wages, and other expenses		700	14
Decrease in mortgage bonds		300	6
Decrease in debenture bonds		100	2
Total uses of funds		$5000	100%
Cash balance (December 31, 1992)		$1400	

decreased by $700,000 during the period, which indicates a use of funds. Deferred income taxes increased by $100,000 (source). Both the first mortgage bonds and the debenture bonds decreased for the period by $300,000 and $100,000, respectively. Both decreases constitute uses of funds for the period.

The common stock accounts (common stock at par and paid-in capital) did not change for the period, indicating no new stock was issued and none was repurchased. Jimco's retained earnings increased by $1,500,000. This represents the net income for 1992 of $1,800,000 less common stock dividends of $300,000. Because net income is included as a source of funds (as a part of funds provided by operations) and dividends are counted as a use of funds, the change in the retained earnings account is not used directly in preparing the source and use of funds statement.

To summarize, we determine sources and uses by analyzing the changes in the balance sheet accounts between two points in time (for example, between December 31, 1991, and December 31, 1992). However, we disregard the change in accumulated depreciation in the balance sheet. In place of this change, we show the depreciation expense for the year as a source of funds. Also, the change in retained earnings is not included directly in the statement. Because the change in retained earnings equals net income less dividends paid, we prefer to list these latter items separately instead.

Table 12–4 contains Jimco's statement of sources and uses of funds for the year ended December 31, 1992. Note that Jimco's sources of funds were from operations (47 percent), deferred taxes (2 percent), and notes payable (51 percent). The firm's principal uses of funds related to the purchase of plant and equipment (22 percent); increases in accounts receivable (30 percent) and inventories (14 percent); and reductions in accounts payable (4 percent) and accrued expenses (14 percent). Thus, the source and use of funds statement provides the analyst with a useful tool for determining *where the firm obtained cash* during a prior period and *how that cash was spent.*

Statement of Cash Flows

In defining the format for the statement of cash flow the Financial Accounting Standards Board sought to resolve some of the confusion that often arises out of the use of cash flow terminology in corporate practice. Specifically, this statement explains the changes in cash plus cash equivalents rather than in ambiguous terms such as *funds.*[2]

---

[2]Cash equivalents are defined as short-term, highly liquid investments that are readily convertible into known amounts of cash and are so near to their maturity that they pose an insignificant risk of changes in value because of changes in interest rates.

Cash flows from operating activities		
Net income (from the statement of income)	$1800	
Add (deduct) to reconcile net income to net cash flow		
Increase in accounts receivable	(1500)	
Increase in inventories	(700)	
Increase in prepaid expenses	(100)	
Depreciation expense	500	
Decrease in accounts payable	(200)	
Decrease in accrued wages	(700)	
Increase in deferred income taxes	100	
Net cash inflow from operating activities		($800)
Cash flows from investing activities		
Cash inflows		
Cash outflows		
Purchase of plant and equipment	($1100)	
Net cash outflow from investment activities		($1100)
Cash flows from financing activities		
Cash inflows		
Increase in notes payable	$2500	
Cash outflows		
Decrease in mortgage bonds	(300)	
Decrease in debenture bonds	(100)	
Common dividends	(300)	
Net cash inflow from financing activities		$1800
Effect of foreign exchange rates		-0-
Net increase (decrease) in cash during the period		($100)
Cash balance at the beginning of the period	$1500	
Cash balance at the end of the period	$1400	

The basic form of the statement of cash flow for Jimco, Inc., is illustrated in Table 12–5. Because cash is the basis, the content of this statement is equivalent to the statement of sources and uses of funds statement. The differences are that the format of the cash flow statement separates sources and uses of cash into four categories (operating activities, investment activities, and financing activities, and foreign exchange effects) and the focus of the statement is on cash plus cash equivalents. Technically, FASB 95 provided for the construction of the cash flow statement using either a direct or indirect method. The only difference in the two methods relates to the first section (cash flow from operating activities). The example in Table 12–5 uses the indirect method. We also illustrate the direct method.

A review of Jimco's Statement of Cash Flows for 1992 indicates that the firm realized a $1,800 positive cash flow from its financing activities, which was $100 less than the cash outflow realized from the sum of the firm's operating activities ($800), and its investments in plant, machinery, and equipment.

Accountants generally prefer the direct method of the cash flow format. The direct method is illustrated below for Jimco, Inc. Once again the income statement is restated to reflect its cash flow equivalent. We first adjust reported

Cash flows from *operating* activities	
Cash inflows from operating activities	
From customers (sales + beginning AR − ending AR)	$49,500
Cash outflows from operating activities	
Cash paid to suppliers (cost of goods sold + beginning inventory − ending inventory + beginning AP − ending AP)	(38,900)
Cash paid for remaining expenses (selling expense + general and administrative expense + beginning accrued expenses − ending accrued expenses + ending prepaid expenses − beginning prepaid expenses)	(9,300)
Cash paid for interest expense (interest expense + beginning accrued interest expense − ending accrued interest expense)	(1,000)
Cash paid for income tax (income tax liability + beginning deferred taxes − ending deferred taxes)	(1,100)
Net cash inflow (outflow) from operating activities	($800)

sales to reflect only cash received by subtracting (adding) any increase (decrease) in accounts receivable (AR). *Cash paid to suppliers* is calculated by adjusting cost of goods sold for any decrease in inventories and any increase in accounts payable (AP). Next, *cash paid for remaining expenses* is found by adjusting the sum of all remaining expenses from the income statement (selling plus general and administrative expense) and adjusting for any changes in accruals and prepaid expenses.

Cash paid for interest expense is calculated by adjusting reported interest expense for any change in accrued interest for the period. Finally, *cash paid for income tax* is found by adjusting the reported tax liability for any change in deferred taxes over the period.

Note that the indirect method begins with net income and then adds back all expenses that did not result in a cash outflow for the period. The direct method begins with operating sales revenues (adjusted for credit sales) and then deducts only those expenses that actually resulted in a cash outflow. So, in a sense, the two methods for arriving at cash flow from operations differ in terms of whether we start at the top (direct method) or the bottom (indirect method) of the income statement. Both methods simply convert the firm's statement of net income to its cash flow equivalent.

Financial Ratios

Financial ratios give the analyst a way of making meaningful comparisons of a firm's financial data at different points in time and with other firms. For example, the inventories for a firm with $10 million in annual sales would be expected to be larger than those for a comparable firm with sales of only $5 million. However, the ratio of sales to inventory might be similar for the two firms. *Financial ratios represent an attempt to standardize financial information to facilitate meaningful comparisons.*

Financial ratios provide the basis for answering some very important questions concerning the financial *well-being* of the firm. Examples include the following:

1. *How liquid is the firm?* Liquidity refers to the firm's ability to meet maturing

obligations and to convert assets into cash. This factor is obviously very important to the firm's creditors.

2. *Is management generating sufficient profits from the firm's assets?* Because the primary purpose for purchasing an asset is to produce profits, the analyst often seeks an indication of the adequacy of the profits being realized. If the level of profits appears insufficient in relation to the investment, an investigation into the reasons for the inferior returns is in order.

3. *How does the firm's management finance its investments?* These decisions have a direct impact on the returns provided to the common stockholders.

4. *Are the common stockholders receiving sufficient returns on their investment?* The objective of the financial manager is to maximize the value of the firm's common stock, and the level of returns for investors relative to their investment is a key factor in determining that value.

The mathematics underlying ratio analysis are quite simple. However, using and interpreting financial ratios to answer questions and make decisions requires a great deal of skill and a thorough understanding of the tools of financial analysis. The balance of this chapter is devoted to a discussion of financial ratios and their use in financial analysis.

Perspective in Finance

Mathematically a financial ratio is nothing more than a ratio whose numerator and denominator are comprised of financial data. Sound simple? Well, in concept it is. The objective in using a ratio when analyzing financial information is simply to standardize the information being analyzed so that comparisons can be made between ratios of different firms or possibly the same firm at different points in time. So try to keep this in mind as you read through the discussion of financial ratios. All we are doing is trying to standardize financial data so that we can make comparisons with industry norms or other standards.

Using Financial Ratios

Financial ratios provide useful tools for analysis when compared against a standard or norm. Two such norms are commonly used. The first consists of similar ratios for the same firm from previous financial statements. An analysis based on comparisons of this type is commonly referred to as a **trend analysis.** A second norm comes from the ratios of other firms that are considered comparable in their general characteristics to the subject firm—generally this involves the use of published industry average ratios.

There are two widely used sources of industry average ratios. Dun and Bradstreet annually publishes a set of 14 key ratios for each of the 125 lines of business. Robert Morris Associates, the association of bank loan and credit officers, publishes a set of 16 key ratios for over 350 lines of business. Table 12–6 gives an example of Robert Morris standard ratios for the farm machinery and equipment manufacturing industry.

The ratio norms in Table 12–6 are classified by firm size to provide the basis for more meaningful comparisons. Thus, a firm with total assets of less than $500,000 would not be compared with firms having a much larger asset base. Note also that **common size financial statements** are reported as well as the 16 key ratios. The common size balance sheet simply represents each asset, liability, and owner's equity account as a percent of total assets, whereas each entry in the income statement is given as a percent of sales. Thus, ratios are effectively related to each of the 19 entries in the balance sheet and 6 entries in the income statement. Furthermore, three levels are reported for each of the 16

Manufacturers Farm Machinery & Equipment	46(4/1–9/30/90)		65(10/1/90)–3/31/91	
Asset Size	0-500M[a]	500M-2MM	2-10MM	10-50MM
Number of Statements[b]	14	28	41	21
Assets	%	%	%	%
Cash and equivalents	8.5	6.0	4.4	6.4
Trade receivables—(net)	22.5	17.4	19.0	30.3
Inventory	44.4	48.2	44.4	34.9
All other current	.2	2.1	1.6	1.6
Total current	75.5	73.7	69.4	73.2
Fixed assets (net)	22.9	21.3	22.9	17.7
Intangibles (net)	.9	.5	.7	1.0
All other noncurrent	.7	4.5	7.0	8.1
Total assets	100.0	100.0	100.0	100.0
Liabilities				
Notes payable–short term	11.1	14.0	14.5	13.8
Current maturity–LTD	2.8	4.0	3.3	3.0
Trade payables	20.7	14.7	11.5	9.1
Income taxes payable	1.0	.5	1.0	.4
All other current	8.2	8.9	8.2	10.6
Total current	44.0	42.2	38.4	36.9
Long-term debt	17.8	15.4	17.9	14.4
Deferred taxes	.0	.1	.9	.8
All other noncurrent	4.8	3.0	2.1	2.8
Net worth	33.4	39.3	40.7	45.1
Total liabilities and net worth	100.0	100.0	100.0	100.0
Income data				
Net sales	100.0	100.0	100.0	100.0
Gross profit	29.2	31.1	28.9	26.7
Operating expenses	24.7	24.8	22.0	17.9
Operating profit	4.5	6.3	6.9	8.9
All other expenses (net)	1.6	2.7	2.6	2.0
Profit before taxes	2.9	3.6	4.3	6.9
Ratios[c]				
Current	2.3	2.8	2.5	3.2
	1.7	2.0	1.8	2.0
	1.6	1.1	1.4	1.7
Quick	.9	1.0	1.1	1.6
	.6	.5	.5	1.1
	.4	.3	.4	.6
Sales/receivables[d]	13 27.2	12 30.3	24 15.1	41 8.8
	26 13.9	22 16.4	37 10.0	63 5.8
	35 10.5	43 8.5	49 7.5	111 3.3
Cost of sales/Inventory[e]	47 7.7	73 5.0	76 4.8	69 5.3
	61 6.0	126 2.9	126 2.9	101 3.6
	96 3.8	174 2.1	183 2.0	159 2.3
Cost of sales/Payables	6 56.5	11 33.2	17 21.7	20 18.5
	27 13.3	24 15.3	26 13.9	28 12.9
	62 5.9	51 7.1	46 7.9	37 10.0
Sales/Working capital	5.4	4.5	3.7	2.4
	9.6	7.6	6.1	4.6
	16.2	67.4	9.6	7.0
Ratios[c]				
EBIT/Interest	7.5	5.0	4.3	9.5
	(13) 3.8	(26) 3.0	(40) 2.3	(20) 2.4
	1.4	1.5	1.3	1.7
Net profit + Depr., Dep., Amort./Cur. mat. LTD		5.1	3.6	49.0
		(16) 1.9	(34) 2.5	(13) 4.4
		.7	1.0	1.8
Fixed/Worth	.3	.2	.3	.2
	.5	.6	.6	.3
	1.5	1.1	.9	.6

TABLE 12-6.
Robert Morris Associates
Industry Average Ratios, 1991

TABLE 12-6.
(Cont.)

Debt/Worth	1.0 1.7 3.5	.7 1.8 4.0	.8 1.5 2.8	.7 1.0 3.6
% Profit before taxes/ Tangible net worth	55.6 (13) 33.1 8.1	50.7 (27) 21.2 8.3	30.7 (40) 17.5 3.6	34.5 21.0 10.5
% Profit before taxes/Total assets	22.4 7.2 3.3	15.3 9.2 1.9	11.7 7.7 1.4	15.3 8.7 3.9
Sales/Net fixed assets	43.2 14.1 6.9	28.4 10.7 6.6	16.0 9.4 5.0	19.6 9.8 7.1
Sales/Total assets	4.4 3.4 1.8	2.7 2.2 1.6	2.4 1.6 1.3	2.0 1.4 1.1
% Depreciation, Depletion, Amortization/Sales	1.1 (12) 1.6 3.1	.9 (26) 1.3 3.1	.9 (40) 1.7 2.6	1.0 (20) 1.6 2.6
% Officers' compensation/Sales	1.3 (13) 5.9 11.9			
Net sales ($) Total assets ($)	12032M 4235M	66780M 30715M	347880M 189788M	809740M 517151M

Reprinted with permission, copyright Robert Morris Associates 1991, One Liberty Place, Philadelphia, PA 19103.
[a] M = $ thousand; MM = $ million.
[b] When there are fewer than 10 financial statements for a particular size category, the composite data are not shown in that category because such a small sample is usually not representative and could be misleading.
[c] Three ratio values are reported. The middle value is the median and represents the ratio falling halfway between the strongest ratio and the weakest ratio. The figure that falls halfway between the median and the strongest ratio is the upper quartile and the figure that falls halfway between the median and the weakest ratio is the lower quartile.
[d] The columns in bold type are "days' receivables" or average collection period.
[e] The columns in bold type are "days' inventory" or the average number of days that a dollar is held in inventory.

key ratios. These refer to the first, second, and third quartiles. Thus, the analyst is given some idea as to how much variation exists within the industry in regard to each ratio.

Categories of Financial Ratios

There are four basic categories of financial ratios. Each represents an important aspect of the firm's financial condition. The categories consist of liquidity, efficiency, leverage, and profitability ratios. Each category is explained by using an example set of financial ratios computed using the 1992 financial statements of Jimco, Inc. (Jimco's balance sheet and income statement were presented in Tables 12-1 and 12-2.)

Jimco, Inc., manufactures and sells light-duty garden tractors and implements. The firm has been in business for more than 20 years and is considered by its competitors to be well managed.

Liquidity Ratios

Liquidity ratios provide the basis for answering the question: *Does the firm have sufficient cash and near cash assets to pay its bills on time?*

Current liabilities represent the firm's maturing financial obligations. The firm's ability to repay these obligations when due depends largely on whether it has sufficient cash together with other assets that can be converted into cash before the current liabilities mature. The firm's current assets are the primary sources of funds needed to repay current and maturing financial obligations. Thus, the *current ratio* is a logical measure of liquidity.

Current ratio ■ The **current ratio** is computed as follows:

$$\text{current ratio} = \frac{\text{current assets}}{\text{current liabilities}}$$

$$= \frac{\$24,000,000}{\$10,000,000} \qquad (12-1)$$

$$= 2.40 \text{ times}$$

$$\text{industry average} = 2.0 \text{ times}$$

For 1992 Jimco's current assets were 2.40 times larger than its current liabilities. Although no firm plans to liquidate a major portion of its current assets to meet its matching current liabilities, this ratio does indicate the margin of safety (the liquidity) of the firm.

Using the industry norms provided in Table 12–6, Jimco's current ratio is higher than the median industry ratio of 2.0.[3] Note that Jimco has between $10 million and $50 million in total assets; thus the fourth-column figures are appropriate. In addition, Jimco's 2.40 current ratio falls well within range of the first and third quartile of 1.7 to 3.2 observed for its industry. Thus, Jimco's current ratio is not *out of line* with the current ratios of many of the firms in its industry.

Acid test or quick ratio ■ Because inventories are generally the least liquid of the firm's assets, it may be desirable to remove them from the numerator of the current ratio, thus obtaining a more refined liquidity measure. For Jimco, the **acid test ratio** is computed as follows:

$$\text{acid test ratio} = \frac{\text{current assets} - \text{inventories}}{\text{current liabilities}}$$

$$= \frac{\$12,000,000}{\$10,000,000} \qquad (12-2)$$

$$= 1.20 \text{ times}$$

$$\text{industry average} = 1.1$$

Once again Jimco's acid test ratio is higher than the median ratio for its industry of 1.1. Thus, on the basis of its current and acid test ratios, Jimco offers no visible evidence of a liquidity problem.

Efficiency Ratios

Efficiency ratios provide the basis for assessing how effectively the firm is using its resources to generate sales. For example, a firm that produces $8 million in sales using $4 million in assets is certainly using its resources more efficiently than a similar firm that has $6 million invested in assets.

Efficiency ratios can be defined for each asset category in which a firm invests. Our discussion will include a limited number of key efficiency ratios, related to accounts receivable, inventories, net fixed assets, and total assets.

---

[3]Note that 1991 industry ratios are used in the analysis, because more recent information was not available at the time of writing. The analyst will find that published industry averages are generally a year behind, owing to the time required to collect and publish them.

Average collection period ■ The **average collection period ratio** serves as the basis for determining how rapidly the firm's credit accounts are being collected. The lower this number is, other things being the same, the more efficient the firm is in managing its investment in accounts receivable. We can also think of this ratio in terms of the number of daily credit sales contained in accounts receivable. That is, the average collection period is equal to the accounts receivable balance divided by the firm's average daily credit sales. Computing the ratio for Jimco, we find

$$\text{average collection period} = \frac{\text{accounts receivable}}{\text{annual credit sales}/360}$$

$$= \frac{\$10,000,000}{\$(51,000,000/360)} = 70.6 \quad \textbf{(12-3)}$$

$$\text{industry average} = 63 \text{ days}$$

Therefore, on average, Jimco collects its credit sales every 70.6 days.

The **accounts receivable turnover ratio** is often used in the place of the average collection period ratio, because it contains the same information. For Jimco this ratio would equal

$$\text{accounts receivable turnover} = \frac{\text{credit sales}}{\text{accounts receivable}}$$

$$= \frac{\$51,000,000}{\$10,000,000} = 5.10 \text{ times} \quad \textbf{(12-4)}$$

$$\text{industry average} = 5.8 \text{ times}$$

Thus, Jimco is turning its accounts receivable over at a rate of 5.10 times per year. This easily translates into an average collection period of 70.6 days. That is, if Jimco's receivables turnover is 5.10 times in a 360-day year, then its average collection period must be 365/5.10 = 71.6 days.

The industry norm for the receivables turnover ratio is 5.8 times, which translates into an average collection period of 365/5.8 = 63 days. Jimco's ratio's are well within the first and third quartiles for its industry. Thus there is no evidence of slow-paying accounts, which would call for added analysis.[4]

Inventory turnover ■ The effectiveness or efficiency with which a firm is managing its investment in inventories is reflected in the number of times that its inventories are turned over (replaced) during the year. The **inventory turnover ratio** is defined as follows:

$$\text{inventory turnover} = \frac{\text{cost of goods sold}}{\text{inventories}}$$

$$= \frac{\$38,000,000}{\$12,000,000} \quad \textbf{(12-5)}$$

$$= 3.17 \text{ times}$$

$$\text{industry average} = 3.6 \text{ times}$$

---

[4]Although it will not be discussed here, one tool for further assessing the liquidity of a firm's receivables is an **aging of accounts receivable schedule.** Such a schedule identifies the number and dollar value of accounts outstanding for various periods. For example, accounts that are less than 10 days old, 11 to 20 days, and so forth might be examined. Still another way to construct the schedule would involve analyzing the length of time to eventual collection of accounts over a past period. For example, how many accounts were outstanding less than 10 days when collected, between 10 and 20 days, and so forth.

Thus, Jimco turns over its inventories 3.17 times per year.[5] When quarterly or monthly information is available, an average inventory figure should be used in order to eliminate the influence of any seasonality in inventory levels.

Jimco's inventory turnover ratio of 3.17 compares favorably with the industry norm of 3.6 times. Therefore, Jimco invests slightly more in inventories per dollar of sales than does the average firm in its industry.

Fixed asset turnover ■ To measure the efficiency with which the firm uses its investment in fixed assets, we calculate the **fixed asset turnover ratio** as follows:

$$\text{fixed asset turnover} = \frac{\text{sales}}{\text{net fixed assets}}$$

$$= \frac{\$51,000,000}{\$7,000,000} \qquad \textbf{(12–6)}$$

$$= 7.286 \text{ times}$$

$$\text{industry average} = 9.8 \text{ times}$$

Thus, Jimco has a larger investment in fixed assets relative to its sales volume than is the case for the industry norm.

Total asset turnover ■ The **total asset turnover ratio** indicates how many dollars in sales the firm squeezes out of each dollar it has invested in assets. For Jimco, we calculate this ratio as follows:

$$\text{total asset turnover} = \frac{\text{sales}}{\text{total assets}}$$

$$= \frac{\$51,000,000}{\$31,000,000} \qquad \textbf{(12–7)}$$

$$= 1.645 \text{ times}$$

$$\text{industry average} = 1.4 \text{ times}$$

Jimco's total asset turnover ratio compares satisfactorily with the industry norm of 1.4. This ratio indicates that, compared to other firms in its industry, Jimco's management has efficiently utilized its resources in generating sales.

Because total assets equals the sum of fixed and current assets, we can use our turnover ratios for both total and fixed assets to analyze the efficiency with which the firm manages its investment in current assets. For example, because Jimco's total asset turnover ratio was higher than the industry norm, the lower than average fixed asset turnover indicates that Jimco's investment in current assets must be smaller, in relation to sales, than the industry norm.

Leverage Ratios

Leverage ratios provide the basis for answering two questions: *How has the firm financed its assets?* and *Can the firm afford the level of fixed charges associated with its use of non-owner-supplied funds such as bond interest and principal repayments?* The first question is answered through the use of *balance sheet leverage ratios*, the second by using income statement based on ratios, or simply *coverage ratios*.

It will be useful at this point to review the concept of leverage, or in this

---

[5]Some analysts prefer the use of sales in the numerator of the inventory turnover ratio. However, cost of goods sold is used here, because inventories are stated at cost, and to use sales in the numerator would add a potential source of distortion to the ratio when comparisons are made across firms that have different "markups" on their cost of goods sold.

case financial leverage.[6] Financial leverage results when a firm obtains financing for its investments from sources other than the firm's owners. For a corporation, this means funds from any source other than the common stockholders. Thus, **financial leverage** is leverage that results from the firm's use of debt financing, financial leases, and preferred stock. These sources of financing share a common characteristic: They all require a fixed cash payment or return for their use. That is, debt requires contractually set interest and principal payments, leases require fixed rental payments, and preferred stock usually requires a fixed cash dividend. This requirement provides the basis for the *leverage* in financial leverage. If the firm earns a return higher than the rate required by the suppliers of leverage funds, then the excess goes to the common stockholders. However, should the return earned fall below the required return, then the common stockholders must make up the difference out of the returns on their invested funds. This, in a nutshell, is the concept of financial leverage.

Balance sheet leverage ratios ■ These ratios provide the basis for answering the question: *Where did the firm obtain the financing for its investments?* The label **balance sheet leverage ratios** is used to indicate that these ratios are computed using information from the balance sheet alone.

DEBT RATIO □ The **debt ratio** measures the extent to which the total assets of the firm have been financed using borrowed funds. For Jimco, the ratio is computed as follows:

$$\text{debt ratio} = \frac{\text{total liabilities}}{\text{total assets}} \text{ or}$$

$$\frac{\text{current liabilities} + \text{noncurrent liabilities}}{\text{total assets}}$$

$$= \frac{\$(10,000,000 + 10,700,000)}{\$31,000,000} \tag{12-8}$$

$$= .668, \text{ or } 66.8\%$$
$$\text{industry average} = 54.9\%$$

Thus, Jimco has financed approximately 67 percent of its assets with borrowed funds. This compares with only 54.9 percent for the industry. Note that this ratio is found by using the common size balance sheet in Table 12–6. Simply sum the percent of total assets financed by current liabilities, long-term debt, and all other noncurrent liabilities. Jimco has relied on the use of nonowner financing to a far greater extent than the average firm in its industry. This, in turn, means that Jimco may have difficulty trying to borrow additional funds in the future.

LONG-TERM DEBT TO TOTAL CAPITALIZATION □ The **long-term debt** to **total capitalization ratio** indicates the extent to which the firm has used long-term debt in its permanent financing. **Total capitalization** represents the sum of all the permanent sources of financing used by the firm, including long-term debt, preferred stock, and common equity. For Jimco, the ratio is computed as follows:

$$\begin{array}{c} \text{long-term debt} \\ \text{to total capitalization} \end{array} = \frac{\text{long-term (noncurrent) liabilities}}{\begin{array}{c} \text{long-term debt} + \text{preferred stock} + \\ \text{common equity} \end{array}}$$

$$= \frac{\$10,700,000}{(\$10,700,000 + 10,300,000)} \tag{12-9}$$

---

[6]The concept of leverage was discussed more fully in Chapter 9.

$$= .509, \text{ or } 50.9\%$$

$$\text{industry average} = 22.8\%$$

Therefore, Jimco has obtained a little more than half its permanent financing from debt sources.

Once again referring to the common size balance sheet in Table 12–6 for an industry norm, note that current liabilities account for 36.9 percent of total assets; thus permanent financing is equal to $(1 - .369)$, or 63.1 percent of total assets. Furthermore, long-term debt accounts for 14.4 percent of total assets; thus it accounts for $14.4/63.1 = 22.8$ percent of the firm's total capitalization. It is evident that Jimco uses far more long-term debt in its total capitalization than is characteristic of its industry.

One point about lease financing should be made concerning balance sheet leverage ratios. Because most firms must include the present value of long-term financial lease agreements in the assets and liabilities of the balance sheet, it is now possible to assess their impact on the firm's balance sheet leverage ratios.[7] Annual lease payments generally are contained in footnotes to the firm's financial statements; thus, their effect on the firm's coverage ratios, which are discussed next, can be assessed.

Coverage ratios ■ These ratios are a second category of leverage ratios, and they are used to measure the firm's ability to cover the finance charges associated with its use of financial leverage. They provide the basis for answering the question of whether the firm has used too much financial leverage?

TIMES INTEREST EARNED RATIO □ The **times interest earned ratio** indicates the firm's ability to meet its interest payments out of its annual operating earnings. The ratio measures the number of times the firm is covering its interest. Jimco's ratio is computed as follows:[8]

$$\begin{aligned} \text{times interest earned} &= \frac{\text{net operating income (NOI) or earnings before interest and taxes (EBIT)}}{\text{annual interest expense}} \\ &= \frac{\$4,000,000}{\$1,000,000} \\ &= 4.00 \text{ times} \end{aligned} \tag{12-10}$$

$$\text{industry average} = 2.4 \text{ times}$$

This ratio is much higher than the industry norm of 2.4 times, which is somewhat surprising in light of Jimco's higher than average use of financial leverage. However, it appears that Jimco's earnings are such that it can reasonably *afford* the higher use of financial leverage.

CASH FLOW OVERALL COVERAGE RATIO □ This ratio compares the cash flow (from net operating income) available to meet fixed financial commitments against the cash flow requirements of these obligations. The financial commitments are interest, lease payments, preferred dividends, and debt principal repayments. The cash available to pay these obligations equals net operating income plus

---

[7]The Financial Accounting Standards Board in late 1976 issued Statement No. 13, which established that a lease that transfers substantially all of the benefits and risks incident to the ownership of property should be accounted for as an acquisition of an asset and the incurrence of an obligation by the lessee. As a result, many firms are now forced to include the value of their lease agreements directly in the balance sheet rather than treat them as operating leases which are reported in footnotes to the balance sheet. Chapter 19 discusses lease accounting further.

[8]The interchangeable use of EBIT and NOI presumes there was no "other" income earned by the firm. If the presence of other nonoperating income is thought to be transitory, then NOI should be used; if not, then EBIT is appropriate.

depreciation. We also add lease payments to operating income plus depreciation, because lease payments have been deducted from revenues to calculate net operating income. We adjust debt principal repayment and preferred stock dividends that are not tax deductible on a before-tax basis, because we need to compute the amount of before-tax cash flows that are required to make these payments. For instance, we might assume that Jimco's current portion of long-term debt ($500,000) equals the principal repayment for the period. However, to pay $500,000 using after-tax income, we would have to earn $833,333 before taxes. That is, $833,333 income less taxes at a 40 percent rate ($333,333 = .40 × $833,333) leaves $500,000 after taxes to make the principal repayment. For preferred stock dividends and debt principal repayment, we have to make the following adjustments:

$$\text{before-tax cost of preferred stock dividends} = \frac{\text{preferred stock dividend}}{(1 - \text{marginal tax rate})}$$

$$\text{before-tax debt principal repayment requirement} = \frac{\text{principal repayment}}{(1 - \text{marginal tax rate})}$$

We can now compute Jimco's cash flow coverage ratio, as follows:

$$\text{cash flow overall coverage ratio} = \frac{\begin{array}{c}\text{net operating income + lease} \\ \text{expense + depreciation}\end{array}}{\begin{array}{c}\text{interest + lease expense +} \\ \text{preferred dividends/} \\ (1 - \text{marginal tax rate}) + \\ \text{principal payments/} \\ (1 - \text{marginal tax rate})\end{array}} \quad \textbf{(12–11)}$$

$$= \frac{\$(4,000,000 + 500,000)}{\$(1,000,000 + 500,000/(1 - .40))}$$

$$= \frac{\$4,500,000}{\$1,833,333} = 2.45 \text{ times}$$

Thus, Jimco's operating earnings were 4.00 times its interest expense, whereas the firm's operating cash flows were only 2.45 times its total finance charges.

One further refinement may be desirable in the cash flow overall coverage ratio. This relates to the coverage of any common dividends the firm wishes to pay. For example, should Jimco desire to pay dividends to common stockholders totaling $300,000, then the firm must earn $300,000/(1 − .40) = $500,000 on a before-tax basis. Adding this figure for common dividends to the firm's existing finance charges reduces the coverage ratio to 1.93 times. This second version of the coverage ratio is particularly useful when the firm analyzes alternative sources of long-term financing and wishes to maintain a stable dividend payment to its common stockholders.

Summarizing the results of Jimco's leverage ratios, we have made two basic observations: First, Jimco has used more nonowner financing than is characteristic of its industry. Second, Jimco's earnings are such that it can apparently afford the higher use of financial leverage.

Profitability Ratios

As we have discussed, financial ratios help us answer some very important questions about the effectiveness of the firm's management of its resources to produce profits. Specifically, **profitability ratios** can be used to answer such questions as these: *How much of each sales dollar was management able to convert into profits? How much profit did the firm earn on each dollar of assets under its control?* For discussion purposes we will divide profitability ratios into two groups: profitability in relation to sales and profitability in relation to investment.

Profitability in relation to sales ■ These ratios can be used to assess the ability of the firm's management to control the various expenses involved in generating sales. The profit ratios discussed here are commonly referred to as **profit margins** and include the gross profit margin, operating profit margin, and net profit margin.

GROSS PROFIT MARGIN □ The **gross profit margin** is calculated as follows:

$$\text{gross profit margin} = \frac{\text{gross profit}}{\text{net sales}}$$

$$= \frac{\$13,000,000}{\$51,000,000} \qquad \textbf{(12-12)}$$

$$= .255, \text{ or } 25.5\%$$

$$\text{industry average} = 26.7\%$$

Thus Jimco's gross profit constitutes 25.5 percent of firm sales. This margin reflects the firm's markup on its cost of goods sold as well as the ability of management to minimize the firm's cost of goods sold in relation to sales (and the method for determining that cost).

The common size income statement found in Table 12–6 provides an industry norm of 26.7 percent. Thus, Jimco's gross profit margin does not appear to be out of line. Note that the gross profit margin reflects both the level of Jimco's cost of goods sold and the size of the firm's markup on those costs, or its pricing policy.

OPERATING PROFIT MARGIN □ Moving down the income statement, the next profit figure encountered is net operating income (or EBIT). This profit figure serves as the basis for computing the **operating profit margin.** For Jimco this profit margin is found as follows:

$$\text{operating profit margin} = \frac{\text{net operating income}}{\text{sales}}$$

$$= \frac{\$4,000,000}{\$51,000,000} \qquad \textbf{(12-13)}$$

$$= .0784, \text{ or } 7.84\%$$

$$\text{industry average} = 8.9\%$$

The operating profit margin reflects the firm's operating expenses as well as its cost of goods sold. Therefore, this ratio serves as an overall measure of operating effectiveness.

Again, the industry norm is obtained from the common size income statement in Table 12–6. Jimco's operating profit margin is slightly lower than the industry norm of 8.9 percent. Thus, Jimco's operating expenses per dollar of sales were slightly higher than the industry norm.

NET PROFIT MARGIN □ The final profit margin considered involves the net after-tax profits of the firm as a percent of sales. For Jimco the **net profit margin** is computed as follows:

$$\text{net profit margin} = \frac{\text{net income}}{\text{sales}} = \frac{\$1,800,000}{\$51,000,000} = .035, \text{ or } 3.5\% \qquad \textbf{(12-14)}$$

$$\text{industry average} = 4.14\%$$

Therefore, $.035 of each sales dollar is converted into profits after taxes. Note that this profit margin reflects the firm's cost of goods sold, operating expenses, finance charges (interest expense), and taxes. For the industry, profits before taxes are 6.9 percent of sales. Assuming that firms on the average pay approximately 40 percent of their taxable earnings in taxes, this produces a net profit margin of .069 (1 − .40) = .0414, or 4.14% percent. Hence, Jimco's net profit margin is slightly below par for its industry. In the next category of profitability ratios we investigate the return on the firm's total investment, and the return on the investment of the common stockholders.

Profitability in relation to investment ■ This category of profitability ratios attempts to measure firm profits in relation to the invested funds used to generate those profits. Thus, these ratios are very useful in assessing the overall effectiveness of the firm's management.

OPERATING INCOME RETURN ON INVESTMENT □ The **operating income return on investment** reflects the rate of return on the firm's total investment before interest and taxes. For Jimco, this return measure is computed as follows:

$$\text{operating income return on investment} = \frac{\text{net operating income}}{\text{total assets}}$$

$$= \frac{\$4,000,000}{\$31,000,000} \qquad (12\text{–}15)$$

$$= .129, \text{ or } 12.9\%$$

$$\text{industry average} = 12.5\%$$

Jimco's management produced a 12.9 percent return on its total assets before interest and taxes have been paid.[9] It is this 12.9 percent rate of return that should be compared with the cost of borrowed funds to determine whether leverage is *favorable* or *unfavorable*. If the firm is borrowing at a cost less than 12.9 percent, then leverage is favorable and will result in higher after-tax earnings to its stockholders.[10]

This rate of return is useful in assessing operating effectiveness of the firm's management. The operating return on investment does not reflect the influence of the firm's use of financial leverage. Neither the numerator (operating income) nor the denominator (total assets) is affected by the way in which the firm has financed its assets. Thus it provides a measure of management's effectiveness in making operating decisions as opposed to financing decisions.

An industry norm for this ratio is not readily available in Table 12–6. However, we can calculate one, using the information given there. Sales divided by total assets equals 1.4; and the operating profit margin is 8.9 percent of sales for the industry. Using the following relationship, we derive an industry norm of 12.5 percent. Thus, Jimco's operating rate of return compares favorably with the industry norm.

---

[9]Intangible assets are often subtracted from total assets in an effort to measure the firm's return on invested capital. The lack of physical qualities of intangible assets makes evidence of their existence elusive, their value often difficult to estimate, and their useful lives indeterminable. The Accounting Principles Board gives this subject attention in Opinion 17. However, because Jimco has no intangible assets, no adjustment is necessary.

[10]The concept of leverage was fully developed earlier in Chapter 9. Very simply, when a firm borrows money that requires a fixed return, then the return to the common shareholders will be enhanced only if the return the firm earns on these borrowed funds exceeds their cost. For the firm as a whole the operating income rate of return measures the before-tax-and-interest rate of return on the firm's investment. This rate must exceed the cost of borrowed funds for the firm as a whole to experience *favorable* financial leverage. The favorableness of financial leverage is determined by the effect of its use on earnings per share to the firm's common stockholders.

$$\frac{\text{operating income}}{\text{sales}} \times \frac{\text{sales}}{\text{total assets}} = \frac{\text{operating income}}{\text{total assets}}$$

$$.089 \quad \times \quad 1.4 \quad = \quad .125, \text{ or } 12.5\%$$

(12–16)

In deriving the industry norm for the operating income return on investment ratio, we have identified a very useful relationship between operating profit margin and the ratio of sales divided by total assets (which we earlier referred to as total asset turnover). That is, *a firm's rate of return on investment is a function of (1) how much profit it squeezes out of each dollar of sales (as reflected in its operating profit margin), and (2) how much it has invested in assets to produce those sales (as reflected in the total asset turnover ratio).* Jimco's below-average operating profit margin, combined with its higher than average turnover of total investment in assets, produce an operating income return on investment that is above its industry norm.

RETURN ON TOTAL ASSETS OR RETURN ON INVESTMENT □ The **return on total assets** or **return on investment ratio** relates after-tax income to the firm's total investment in assets. For Jimco, this ratio is found as follows:

$$\text{return on total assets} = \frac{\text{net income}}{\text{total assets}}$$

$$= \frac{\$1,800,000}{\$31,000,000}$$

(12–17)

$$= .058, \text{ or } 5.8\%$$

$$\text{industry average} = 5.80\%$$

Again total assets are used in an attempt to measure total investment. An industry norm can be obtained from Table 12–6 in a manner similar to that used with the operating rate of return. That is

$$\text{return on total assets} = \frac{\text{net income}}{\text{sales}} \times \frac{\text{sales}}{\text{total assets}}$$

(12–18)

Earlier the net income to sales ratio for the industry was estimated to be 4.14 percent. Using the industry's sales to total assets ratio of 1.4 produces an industry norm for return on total assets of .0414 × 1.4 = .058, or 5.80% percent. Thus, Jimco provides the same return on its total investment as the average for other firms in its industry.

RETURN ON COMMON EQUITY □ The **return on common equity ratio** measures the rate of return earned on the common stockholder's investment. Jimco earned the following rate of return for its common stockholders:

$$\text{return on common equity} = \frac{\text{net income available to common}}{\text{common equity}}$$

$$= \frac{\$1,800,000}{\$10,300,000}$$

(12–19)

$$= .175, \text{ or } 17.5\%$$

$$\text{industry average} = 9.32\%$$

Net income available to common equity is simply net income less any preferred dividends the firm might have to pay. This earnings figure is sometimes referred to as **net common stock earnings (NCSE).**

Table 12–6 does not contain an industry norm for this ratio. However, the following relation can be used to derive an industry norm from the return on total assets ratio and the debt ratio:

$$\text{return on common equity} = \frac{\text{return on total assets}}{(1 - \text{debt ratio})} \qquad (12\text{--}20)$$

Recall that the debt ratio is simply total liabilities divided by total assets. The industry norm for the return on common equity ratio is found as follows:

$$\frac{.058}{(1 - .549)} = .0932, \text{ or } 9.32\%$$

Thus, Jimco's 17.5 percent return compares *very* favorably with that of the industry. This higher than average return reflects both the firm's above-average asset turnover and its above-average use of financial leverage (as reflected in its debt ratio).

In summary, Jimco has slightly below-average profits in relation to its sales; however, the firm has an above-average return on common equity. This factor results from the firm's above-average asset turnover and the fact that Jimco used more leverage than the norm for its industry.

Trend Analysis

We noted earlier that a firm's financial ratios can be compared with two types of standards, and we have discussed industry norms as the basis for comparison. Now we demonstrate the use of trend comparisons. Figure 12–1 graphs Jimco's current ratio, acid test ratio, debt ratio, and return on total asset ratio for the past five years.

Surveying the trend in Jimco's liquidity ratios reveals a gradual deterioration. This deterioration in liquidity does not, at least for the present, represent a

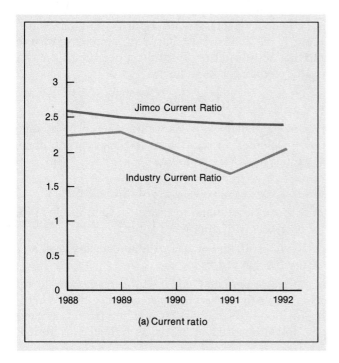

(a) Current ratio

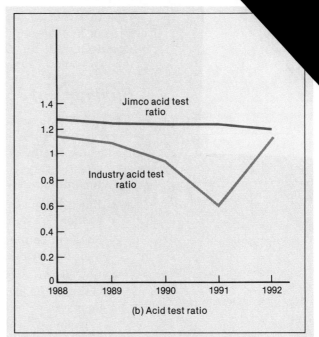

(b) Acid test ratio

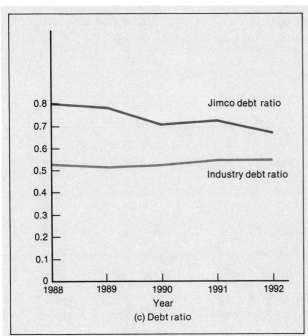

(c) Debt ratio

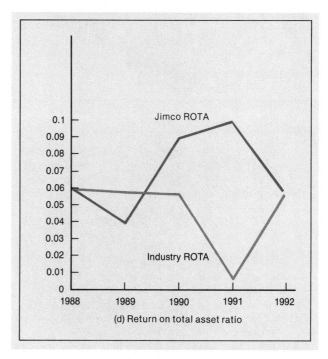

(d) Return on total asset ratio

FIGURE 12–1.
Trend Analysis Illustration

problem, as Jimco's current and acid test ratios compared very favorably with their respective industry norms. However, any increase or continuation of the trend could pose a problem for Jimco and the trend should be monitored closely.

Jimco's debt ratio appears to have declined slightly over the past five years, with moderate interim fluctuations. However, no material change in the ratio appears to have occurred over the period. In light of Jimco's current use of leverage, any further increases in this ratio may be unwarranted, however.

Finally, the return on total assets ratio for the past five years depicts the

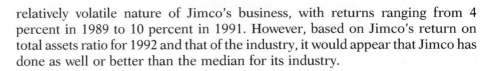

relatively volatile nature of Jimco's business, with returns ranging from 4 percent in 1989 to 10 percent in 1991. However, based on Jimco's return on total assets ratio for 1992 and that of the industry, it would appear that Jimco has done as well or better than the median for its industry.

Summary of Jimco's Financial Ratios

Table 12–7 summarizes Jimco's financial ratios, as well as the corresponding industry norms. Each ratio is evaluated in relation to the appropriate norm. Briefly, the results of those comparisons are as follows:

1. Jimco's liquidity position is very closely in line with the industry.
2. Jimco has made extensive use of financial leverage. In fact, the firm has financed 67 percent of its assets with nonowner funds.
3. The firm can apparently *afford* its higher use of financial leverage, as is indicated by the times interest earned ratio.
4. Jimco's profit margins are approximately equal to the respective norms; however, the firm has been able to convert these profit margins into better than average rates of return on investment. This resulted from the higher than average sales per dollar invested in assets as reflected in Jimco's efficiency ratios.
5. Finally, Jimco has benefited from the favorable use of financial leverage. The firm earned a very favorable 17.5 percent return on the investment of its common stockholders, compared with 9.32 percent for the industry.

TABLE 12–7.
Summary of Ratios for Jimco, Inc.

Ratio	Formula	Calculation	Industry Average	Evaluation
Liquidity ratios				
1. Current ratio	Current assets/current liabilities	$24,000,000/10,000,000 = 2.40 times	2.0 times	Good
2. Acid test ratio	(Current assets − inventories)/ current liabilities	$12,000,000/10,000,000 = 1.20 times	1.1 times	Good
Efficiency ratios				
3. Average collection period	Average accounts receivable/ (annual credit sales/360)	$10,000,000/(51,000,000/365) = 71.6 days	63 days	Satisfactory
4. Inventory turnover	Cost of goods sold/ending inventory	$38,000,000/12,000,000 = 3.17 times	3.6 times	Satisfactory
5. Fixed asset turnover	Sales/fixed assets	$51,000,000/7,000,000 = 7.286 times	9.8 times	Poor
6. Total asset turnover	Sales/total assets	$51,000,000/31,000,000 = 1.645 times	1.4 times	Good
Leverage ratios				
7. Debt ratio	Total liabilities/total assets	$20,700,000/31,000,000 = 66.8%	54.9%	Poor
8. Long-term debt to total capitalization	Long-term debt/total capitalization	$10,700,000/21,000,000 = 50.9%	22.8%	Poor
9. Times interest earned	Net operating income/annual interest expense	$4,000,000/1,000,000 = 4.00 times	2.4 times	Excellent
10. Cash flow overall coverage ratio	(NOI + lease expense + depreciation/interest + lease expense + principal payments/ (1 − tax rate)	$4,500,000/1,833,333 = 2.45 times	N.A.[a]	—
Profitability ratios				
11. Gross profit margin	Gross profit/sales	$13,000,000/51,000,000 = 25.5%	26.7%	Satisfactory
12. Operating profit margin	Net operating income/sales	$4,000,000/51,000,000 = 7.84%	8.9%	Satisfactory
13. Net profit margin	Net income/sales	$1,800,000/51,000,000 = 3.5%	4.14%	Satisfactory
14. Operating income return on investment	Net operating income/total assets	$4,000,000/31,000,000 = 12.9%	12.5%	Satisfactory
15. Return on total assets	Net income/total assets	$1,800,000/31,000,000 = 5.8%	5.8%	Satisfactory
16. Return on common equity	Net income available to common/common equity	$1,800,000/10,300,000 = 17.5%	9.32%	Excellent

[a]Norm was not available.

RETURN ON SALES NET INCOME/Gross Profit

Integrated Form of Financial Analysis Based on Earning Power

Table 12-7 presents an alternative format for analyzing financial ratios. This approach focuses on the firm's earning power as measured by two of the firm's profitability ratios: the operating income return on investment and the return on common equity. This methodology is particularly well suited to internal analyses carried out by the firm's management. The reason is that the analysis focuses directly on firm profitability, which in turn reflects how well the firm is being managed. In addition, the analysis of earning power is a valuable guide to analyzing a firm's financial management from the common shareholder's perspective.

The analysis of a firm's earning power involves a two-stage procedure designed to answer two basic questions:

Stage 1: How effective has the firm's management been in generating sales using the total assets of the firm and converting those sales into operating profits?

Stage 2: How effective has the firm's management been in forming a financial structure that increases the returns to the common shareholders? Here we analyze the effect of the firm's financing decisions (that is, the mixture of debt and owner financing used by the firm) on the rate of return earned on the common stockholder's investment.

Figure 12-2 on page 466 provides a template for carrying out the first stage of the analysis of Jimco's earning power. Note first that the focus of this stage is on the operating income return on investment. This ratio reflects the return earned on the firm's investment in assets from operations and before giving any consideration to how the firm's investments were financed. Note that the operating income return on investment can be broken down into the product of two ratios,

$$\frac{\text{operating income}}{\text{return on investment}} = \frac{\text{operating}}{\text{profit}} \times \frac{\text{total asset}}{\text{turnover}}$$
$$\text{margin}$$

$$\text{or} = \frac{\text{operating income}}{\text{sales}} \times \frac{\text{sales}}{\text{total assets}} = \frac{\text{operating income}}{\text{total assets}}$$

Figure 12-2 simply lays out the relationships that underlie the operating profit margin and total asset turnover ratios. The left-hand branch of Figure 12-2 shows the determinants of the operating profit margin, and the right-hand branch details the determinants of the total asset turnover ratio.

A total of seven ratios are calculated in the first stage of the analysis of Jimco's earning power. The first is the operating income return on investment (Step 1). Step 2 involves calculating the operating profit margin, which, along with the total asset turnover (Step 4), determines the operating income return on investment. Step 3 involves calculation of the gross profit margin, which provides the basis for assessing the impact of cost of goods sold on the operating profit margin calculated in Step 2. Steps 5 to 7 involve the calculation of the fixed asset turnover, accounts receivable turnover, and inventory turnover ratios, which provide the basis for a detailed analysis of the determinants of the total asset turnover ratio (calculated in Step 4).

Note that by following the steps in Figure 12-2, the analyst is led through a detailed analysis of the determinants of the operating income return on investment. Each successive step provides the basis for understanding more about the determinants of this rate of return. For example, the total asset turnover ratio is

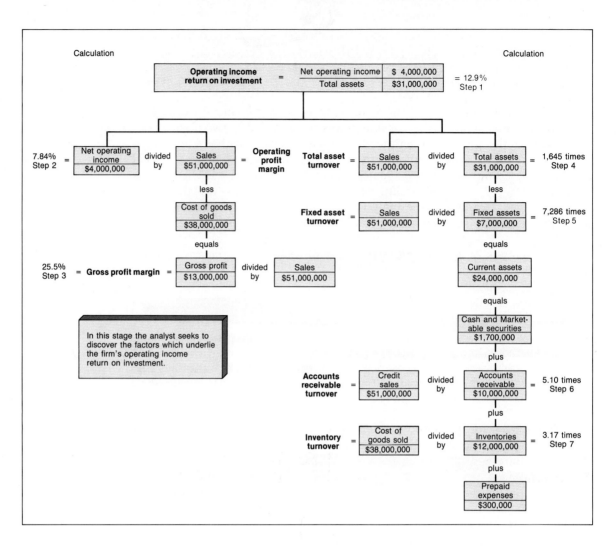

Step	Ratio	Formula	Calculation	Industry[a]	Evaluation
1	Operating income return on investment	$\dfrac{\text{Net operating income}}{\text{Total assets}}$	$\dfrac{\$\,4{,}000{,}000}{\$31{,}000{,}000} = 12.9\%$	12.5%	Satisfactory
2	Operating profit margin	$\dfrac{\text{Net operating income}}{\text{Sales}}$	$\dfrac{\$\,4{,}000{,}000}{\$51{,}000{,}000} = 7.84\%$	8.9%	Satisfactory
3	Gross profit margin	$\dfrac{\text{Gross profit}}{\text{Sales}}$	$\dfrac{\$13{,}000{,}000}{\$51{,}000{,}000} = 25.5\%$	26.7%	Satisfactory
4	Total asset turnover	$\dfrac{\text{Sales}}{\text{Total assets}}$	$\dfrac{\$51{,}000{,}000}{\$31{,}000{,}000} = 1.645 \text{ times}$	1.4 times	Good
5	Fixed asset turnover	$\dfrac{\text{Sales}}{\text{Fixed assets}}$	$\dfrac{\$51{,}000{,}000}{\$\,7{,}000{,}000} = 7.286 \text{ times}$	9.8 times	Poor
6	Accounts receivable turnover	$\dfrac{\text{Credit sales}}{\text{Accounts receivable}}$	$\dfrac{\$51{,}000{,}000}{\$10{,}000{,}000} = 5.10 \text{ times}$	5.8 times	Satisfactory
7	Inventory turnover	$\dfrac{\text{Cost of goods sold}}{\text{Inventories}}$	$\dfrac{\$38{,}000{,}000}{\$12{,}000{,}000} = 3.17 \text{ times}$	3.6 times	Satisfactory

[a]Based on Robert Morris Associates figures from Table 12.6.

FIGURE 12–2.
Analyzing Earning Power: Stage 1 (Analyzing the Operating
Income Return on Investment)

one of the two basic determinants of the operating income return on investment (the other is the operating profit margin). By analyzing the fixed asset turnover ratio in conjunction with the total asset turnover, the analyst can determine whether fixed or current assets caused the total asset turnover ratio to deviate from the industry average. Furthermore, the accounts receivable turnover and inventory turnover ratios can be analyzed to determine the effect of the level of investment in these assets on total asset turnover, and, consequently, the observed operating income return on investment.

Figure 12–3 provides a template for use in analyzing the effect of the firm's financing decisions on the return earned on the common stockholder's invest-

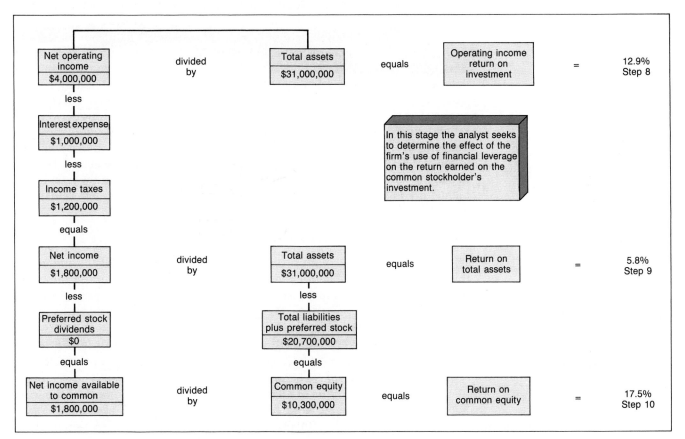

Step	Ratio	Formula	Calculation	Industry[a]	Evaluation
8	Operating income return on investment	Net operating income / Total assets	$\frac{\$4,000,000}{\$31,000,000} = 12.9\%$	12.5%	Satisfactory
9	Return on total assets	Net income / Total assets	$\frac{\$1,800,000}{\$31,000,000} = 5.8\%$	5.8%	Satisfactory
10	Return on common equity	Net income available to common / Common equity	$\frac{\$1,800,000}{\$10,300,000} = 17.5\%$	9.32%	Excellent

[a]Based on Robert Morris Associates figures from Table 12.6.

FIGURE 12–3.
Analyzing Earning Power: Stage 2
(Return Earned on Common Stockholder's Investment)

ment. The analysis presented in Figure 12–3 depends on the following basic relationship:

$$\frac{\text{return on}}{\text{common equity}} = \frac{\text{net income available to common}}{\text{common equity}}$$

This figure leads us through an analysis of the determinants of this ratio. Note that we begin the analysis with the operating income return on investment ratio, which was the subject of the analysis in Figure 12–2. Next, Step 9 involves calculation of the return on total assets. This ratio is then adjusted for the influence of the firm's use of financial leverage in order to calculate the return on common equity. In Step 10 we measure the rate of return earned on the common stockholders' investment in the firm, which reflects both the firm's operating and financing decisions.

The 10-step procedure outlined in Figures 12–2 and 12–3 connects the return earned on common equity to the firm's use of financial leverage and operating profitability. The operating rate of return ratio was shown to be determined by the firm's profit margins on sales (Steps 2 and 3) and the sales to asset relationship (Steps 4 through 7). The real value of this approach to financial analysis is its ability to demonstrate the interrelationships between the return earned on the owners' investment in the firm and a wide variety of financial attributes of the firm. The analyst is provided with a "roadmap" to follow in determining how successful the firm's management has been in managing its resources to maximize the return earned on the owners' investment. In addition, the analyst can determine why that particular return was earned.

Limitations of Ratio Analysis

The analyst who works with financial ratios must be aware of the limitations involved in their use. The following list includes some of the more important pitfalls that may be encountered in computing and interpreting financial ratios:

1. **It is sometimes difficult to identify the industry category to which a firm belongs when the firm engages in multiple lines of business.**

2. **Published industry averages are only approximations and provide the user with *general guidelines* rather than scientifically determined averages of the ratios of all or even a representative sample of the firms within the industry.** Note, for example, the cautionary statement (Figure 12–4) prepared by Robert Morris Associates in conjunction with its published industry ratios (as contained in Table 12–6).

3. **Accounting practices differ widely among firms and can lead to differences in computed ratios.** For example, the use of last-in, first-out (LIFO) in inventory valuation can, in a period of rising prices, lower the firm's inventory account and increase its inventory turnover ratio as compared with that of a firm that uses first-in, first-out (FIFO). In addition, firms may choose different methods of depreciating their fixed assets.

4. **Financial ratios can be too high or too low.** For example, a current ratio that exceeds the industry norm may signal the presence of excess liquidity, which results in a lowering of overall profits in relation to the firm's investment in assets. On the other hand, a current ratio that falls below the norm indicates the possibility that the firm has inadequate liquidity and may at some future date be unable to pay its bills on time.

5. **An industry average may not provide a desirable target ratio or norm.** At best an industry average provides a guide to the financial position of the average firm in the industry. We might note here that the industry norms

RMA recommends that Statement Studies data be regarded only as general guidelines and not as absolute industry norms. There are several reasons why the data may not be fully representative of a given industry:

(1) The financial statements used in the *Statement Studies* are not selected by any random or statistically reliable method. RMA member banks voluntarily submit the raw data they have available each year provided that the companies' total assets are less than $250 million, except for the contractors' statements which have no upper size limit.

(2) Many companies have varied product lines; however, the *Statement Studies* categorize them by their primary product Standard Industrial Classification (SIC) number only.

(3) Some of our industry samples are rather small in relation to the total number of firms in a given industry. A relatively small sample can increase the changes that some of our composites do not fully represent an industry.

(4) There is the chance that an extreme statement can be present in a sample, causing a disproportionate influence on the industry composite. This is particularly true in a relatively small sample.

(5) Companies within the same industry may differ in their method of operations which in turn can directly influence their financial statements. Since they are included in our sample, too, these statements can significantly affect our composite calculations.

(6) Other considerations that can result in variations among different companies engaged in the same general line of business are different labor markets; geographical location; different accounting methods; quality of products handled; sources and methods of financing; and terms of sale.

For these reasons, RMA does not recommend the Statement Studies *figures be considered as absolute norms for a given industry. Rather the figures should be used only as general guidelines and in addition to the other methods of financial analysis. RMA makes no claim as to the representativeness of the figures printed in this book.*

Reprinted with permission, Robert Morris Associates, 1991.

FIGURE 12–4.
Interpretation of Statement Studies Figures

provided in Table 12–5 contain both the average ratio and the upper and lower quartiles for the firms used in preparing the average. Thus, the greater the difference in the upper and lower quartiles, the less meaningful is the industry average in terms of its ability to represent that ratio for the industry.[11]

6. **Many firms experience seasonality in their operations.** Thus, balance sheet entries and their corresponding ratios will vary with the time of year when the statements are prepared. To avoid this problem, an average account balance should be used (for several months or quarters during the year) rather than the year-end total. For example, an average of month-end

---

[11]Rose and Cunningham (1991) compare the industry financial ratios from Robert Morris and Associates with those of Dun & Bradstreet and find that they differ significantly within the same industry classifications. This finding points out the need to carefully consider the choice of an industry norm. In fact, your analysis may require that you construct your own norm from, say, a list of the four or five firms in a particular industry that might provide the most appropriate standard of comparison for the firm being analyzed.

inventory balance might be used to compute a firm's inventory turnover ratio when the firm is subject to a significant seasonality in its sales (and correspondingly in its investment in inventories).

Given their limitations, financial ratios provide the analyst with a very useful tool for assessing a firm's financial condition. The analyst should, however, be aware of these potential weaknesses when performing a ratio analysis. In many cases the real value derived from analyzing financial ratios is that they tell us what questions to ask.

SUMMARY

Basic Financial Statements

Three basic financial statements are commonly used to describe the financial condition and performance of the firm: the balance sheet, the income statement, and the statement of cash flows. The balance sheet provides a picture of the firm's assets, liabilities, and owners' equity on a particular date, whereas the income statement reflects the net revenues from the firm's operations over a given period. The statement of cash flows combines information from both the balance sheet and income statement to describe sources and uses of cash for a given period in the firm's history.

Financial Ratios

Financial ratios are the principal tool of financial analysis. Sometimes referred to simply as benchmarks, ratios standardize financial information so that comparisons can be made between firms of varying sizes. Two broad groups of analysts find financial ratios useful. The first is comprised of internal financial analysts who use them to measure and track company performance through time. The focus of their analysis is frequently related to various measures of profitability used to evaluate the performance of the firm from the perspective of the owners. The second group of users of financial ratios include analysts external to the firm who, for one reason or another, have an interest in the firm's economic well-being. An example of this group would be a loan officer of a commercial bank who wishes to determine the credit worthiness of a loan applicant. Here the focus of the analysis is on the firm's previous use of financial leverage, and its ability to pay the interest and principal associated with the loan request.

Financial ratios are of four main kinds: (1) liquidity, (2) efficiency, (3) leverage, and (4) profitability ratios. The financial statements of Jimco, Inc., demonstrate the computation of a sample listing of ratios from each category. Those discussed here represent only one possible listing that can be used in performing a financial analysis.

Analysis of Financial Ratios

Two methods are demonstrated for analyzing financial ratios. The first involves trend analysis for the firm over time; the second involves making ratio comparisons with industry norms. A set of industry norms from Robert Morris Associates is presented and used in the analysis of an example company, Jimco, Inc. In addition, an integrated form of financial analysis based on earning power focuses the user's attention on the underlying determinants of a firm's profitability.

12-1. The basic financial statements of an organization consist of the balance sheet, income statement, and cash flow statement. Describe the nature of each and explain how their functions differ.

12-2. Why is it that the preferred stockholders' equity section of the balance sheet changes only when new shares are sold, whereas the common equity section changes from year to year regardless of whether new shares are bought or sold?

~ APPENDIX 1A p. 21

12-3. Discuss two reasons why net income for a particular period does not necessarily reflect a firm's cash flow during that period.

12-4. The four basic groups of financial ratios are liquidity, efficiency, leverage, and profitability ratios. Discuss the nature of each group and list two example ratios that you would use to measure that aspect of a firm's financial condition.

12-5. Discuss briefly the two sources of standards or norms that can be used in performing ratio analyses.

12-6. Where can the analyst obtain industry norms? What are the limitations of industry average ratios? Discuss briefly.

SELF-TEST PROBLEMS

ST-1. (*Ratio Analysis and Short-Term Liquidity*) Ray's Tool and Supply Company of Austin, Texas has been expanding its level of operations for the past two years. The firm's sales have grown rapidly as a result of the expansion in the Austin economy. However, Ray's is a privately held company, and the only source of available funds it has is a line of credit with the firm's bank. The company needs to expand its inventories to meet the needs of its growing customer base but also wishes to maintain a current ratio of at least 3 to 1. If Ray's current assets are $6,000,000, and its current ratio is now 4 to 1, how much can it expand its inventories (financing the expansion with its line of credit) before the target current ratio is violated?

ST-2. (*Ratio Analysis of Loan Request*) On February 3, 1993, Mr. Jerry Simmons, chief financial officer for **M & G Industries**, contacted the firm's bank regarding a loan. The loan was to be used to repay notes payable and to finance current assets. Mr. Simmons wanted to repay the loan plus interest in one year. On receiving the loan request, the bank asked that the firm supply it with complete financial statements for the past two years. These statements are presented below:

	1991	1992
Cash	$ 9,000	$ 500
Accounts receivable	12,500	16,000
Inventories	29,000	45,500
Total current assets	$ 50,500	$ 62,000
Land	20,000	26,000
Buildings and equipment	70,000	100,000
Less: allowance for depreciation	28,000	38,000
Total fixed assets	$ 62,000	$ 88,000
	$112,500	$150,000
Accounts payable	$ 10,500	$ 22,000
Bank notes	17,000	47,000
Total current liabilities	$ 27,500	$ 69,000
Long-term debt	28,750	22,950
Common stock	31,500	31,500
Retained earnings	24,750	26,550
	$112,500	$150,000

M & G Industries Balance Sheets at End of Calendar Year

M & G Industries Income Statements for Years Ending December 31		1991	1992
Sales		$125,000	$160,000
Cost of goods sold		75,000	96,000
Gross profit		$ 50,000	$ 64,000
Operating expense			
Fixed cash operating expense		21,000	21,000
Variable operating expense		12,500	16,000
Depreciation		4,500	10,000
Total operating expense		38,000	47,000
Earnings before interest and taxes		$ 12,000	$ 17,000
Interest		3,000	6,100
Earnings before taxes		$ 9,000	$ 10,900
Taxes		4,500	5,450
Net income		$ 4,500	$ 5,450

a. Based on the preceding statements, complete the following table:

M & G Industries Ratio Analysis

	Industry Averages	Actual 1991	Actual 1992
Current ratio	1.80		
Acid test ratio	.70		
Average collection period[a]	37 days		
Inventory turnover[a]	2.50 times		
Debt to total assets	58%		
Long-term debt to total capitalization	33%		
Times interest earned	3.8 times		
Gross profit margin	38%		
Operating profit margin	10%		
Net profit margin	3.5%		
Total asset turnover	1.14 times		
Fixed asset turnover	1.40 times		
Operating income return on investment	11.4%		
Return on total assets	4.0%		
Return on common equity	9.5%		

[a]Based on a 360-day year and on end-of-year figures.

b. Analyze Mr. Simmons's loan request. Would you grant the loan? Explain.

ST–3. (*Cash Flow Statement*)
a. Prepare a cash flow statement for M & G Industries for 1992, using information given in Self-Test Problem ST–1.
b. How does this statement supplement your ratio analysis from Self-Test Problem ST–1? Explain.

STUDY PROBLEMS (SET A)

12–1A. (*Ratio Analysis*) The Mitchem Marble Company has a target current ratio of 2 to 1 but has experienced some difficulties financing its expanding sales in the past few months. At present the current ratio of 2.5 to 1 is based on current assets of $2.5 million. If Mitchem expands its receivables and inventories using its short-term line of credit, how much additional funding can it borrow before its current ratio standard is reached?

12–2A. (*Ratio Analysis*) The balance sheet and income statement for the J. P. Robard Mfg. Company are as follows:

Balance Sheet ($000)	
Cash	$ 500
Accounts receivable	2000
Inventories	1000
Current assets	$3500
Net fixed assets	$4500
Total assets	$8000
Accounts payable	$1100
Accrued expenses	600
Short-term notes payable	300
Current liabilities	$2000
Long-term debt	$2000
Owners' equity	$4000
	$8000

Income Statement ($000)	
Net sales (all credit)	$8000
Cost of goods sold	(3300)
Gross profit	$4700
Operating expenses[a]	(3000)
Net operating income	$1700
Interest expense	(367)
Earnings before taxes	$1333
Income taxes (40%)	(533)
Net income	$ 800

[a]Including depreciation expense of $500 for the year.

Calculate the following ratios:

Current ratio	Average collection period
Debt ratio	Inventory turnover
Times interest earned	Fixed asset turnover
Total asset turnover	Operating return on investment
Gross profit margin	Return on total assets
Operating profit margin	Return on common equity
Net profit margin	

12-3A. (*Analyzing Profitability*) The R. M. Smithers Corporation earned a net profit margin of 5 percent based on sales of $10 million and total assets of $5 million last year.
   a. What was Smithers' rate of return on total assets?
   b. During the coming year the company president has set a goal of attaining a 12 percent return on total assets. How much must firm sales rise, other things being the same, for the goal to be achieved? (State your answer as an annual growth rate in sales.)
   c. If Smithers finances 30 percent of its assets by borrowing, what was its return on common equity for last year? What will it be next year if the return on total asset goal is achieved?

12-4A. (*Using Financial Ratios*) The Brenmar Sales Company had a gross profit margin of 30 percent and sales of $9 million last year. Seventy-five percent of the firm's sales are on credit while the remainder are cash sales. Brenmar's current assets equal $1,500,000, its current liabilities equal $300,000, and it has $100,000 in cash plus marketable securities.
   a. If Brenmar's accounts receivable are $562,500, what is its average collection period?
   b. If Brenmar reduces its average collection period to 20 days, what will be its new level of accounts receivable?
   c. Brenmar's inventory turnover ratio is 9 times. What is the level of Brenmar's inventories?

12–5A. (*Ratio Analysis of Loan Request*) Pamplin, Inc., has recently applied for a loan from the Second National Bank to be used to expand the firm's inventory of soil pipe used in construction and agriculture. This expansion is predicted on expanded sales predicted for the coming year. Pamplin's financial statements for the two most recent years are as follows:

Pamplin, Inc., Balance Sheet
at 12/31/91 and 12/31/92

Assets		
	1991	1992
Cash	$ 200	$ 150
Accounts receivable	450	425
Inventory	550	625
Current assets	1200	1200
Plant and equipment	2200	2600
Less: accumulated depreciation	(1000)	(1200)
Net plant and equipment	1200	1400
Total assets	$2400	$2600

Liabilities and Owners' Equity		
	1991	1992
Accounts payable	$ 200	$ 150
Notes payable—current (9%)	0	150
Current liabilities	200	300
Bonds	600	600
Owners' equity		
Common stock	300	300
Paid-in capital	600	600
Retained earnings	700	800
Total owners' equity	1600	1700
Total liabilities and owners' equity	$2400	$2600

Income Statement	1991	1992
Sales	$1200	$1450
Cost of goods sold	700	850
Gross profit	$ 500	$ 600
Operating expenses	30	40
Depreciation	220	200
Net operating income	$ 250	$ 360
Interest expense	50	60
Net income before taxes	$ 200	$ 300
Taxes (40%)	80	120
Net income	$ 120	$ 180

a. Compute the following ratios for Pamplin, Inc., from the financial statements provided above:

	1991	1992	Industry Norm
Current ratio			5.0 ×
Acid test (quick) ratio			3.0 ×
Inventory turnover			2.2 ×
Average collection period			90 days
Debt ratio			.33
Times interest earned			7.0 ×
Total asset turnover			.75 ×
Fixed asset turnover			1.0 ×
Operating profit margin			.20
Net profit margin			.12
Return on total assets			.09

b. Based on your answer in (a) above, what are Pamplin's financial strengths and weaknesses?

c. Would you make the loan? Why or why not?

12–6A. (*Cash Flow Statement*) Prepare a cash flow statement for Pamplin, Inc., for the year ended December 31, 1992 (problem 12–5A).

12–7A. (*Cash Flow Statement*) (a) Prepare a statement of cash flow for the Waterhouse Co. in the year 1992. (b) What were the firm's primary sources and uses of cash?

	1991	1992
Cash	$ 75,000	$ 82,500
Receivables	102,000	90,000
Inventory	168,000	165,000
Prepaid expenses	12,000	13,500
Fixed assets	325,500	468,000
Accumulated depreciation	94,500	129,000
Patents	61,500	52,500
	$649,500	$742,500
Accounts payable	$124,500	$112,500
Taxes payable	97,500	105,000
Mortgage payable	150,000	—
Preferred stock	—	225,000
Additional paid-in capital—preferred	—	6,000
Common stock	225,000	225,000
Retained earnings	52,500	69,000
	$649,500	$742,500

Additional Information:

1. The only entry in the accumulated depreciation account is the depreciation expense for the period.

2. The only entries in the retained earnings account are for dividends paid in the amount of $18,000 and for the net income for the year.

3. The income statement for 1992 is as follows:

Sales	$187,500
Cost of sales[a]	141,000
Gross profit	46,500
Operating expenses	12,000
Net income	$ 34,500

[a]Includes depreciation expense of $34,500.

12–8A. (*Review of Financial Statements*) Prepare a balance sheet and income statement at December 31, 1992, for the Sharpe Mfg. Co. from the scrambled list of items below. Ignore income taxes and interest expense.

Accounts receivable	$120,000
Machinery and equipment	700,000
Accumulated depreciation	236,000
Notes payable—current	100,000
Net sales	800,000
Inventory	110,000
Accounts payable	90,000
Long-term debt	160,000
Cost of goods sold	500,000
Operating expenses	280,000
Common stock	320,000
Cash	96,000
Retained earnings—prior year	?
Retained earnings—current year	?

12–9A. (*Financial Ratios—Investment Analysis*) The annual sales for Salco, Inc., were $4.5 million last year. The firm's end-of-year balance sheet appeared as follows:

Current assets	$ 500,000	Liabilities	$1,000,000
Net fixed assets	$1,500,000	Owners' equity	$1,000,000
	$2,000,000		$2,000,000

The firm's income statement for the year was as follows:

Sales	$4,500,000
Less: cost of goods sold	(3,500,000)
Gross profit	1,000,000
Less: operating expenses	(500,000)
Net operating income	500,000
Less: interest expense	(100,000)
Earnings before taxes	400,000
Less: taxes	(200,000)
Net income	$ 200,000

a. Calculate Salco's total asset turnover, operating profit margin, and operating income return on investment.
b. Salco plans to renovate one of its plants, which will require an added investment in plant and equipment of $1 million. The firm will maintain its present debt ratio of .5 when financing the new investment and expects sales to remain constant, while the operating profit margin will rise to 13 percent. What will be the new operating income return on investment for Salco after the plant renovation?
c. Given that the plant renovation in part (b) occurs and Salco's interest expense rises by $50,000 per year, what will be the return earned on the common stockholders' investment? Compare this rate of return with that earned before the renovation.

12–10A. (*Statement of Cash Flow*) The consolidated balance sheets of the TMU Processing Company are presented below for June 1, 1991, and May 31, 1992 (millions of dollars). TMU earned $14 million after taxes during the year ended May 31, 1992, and paid common dividends of $10 million.

	June 1, 1991	May 31, 1992
Cash	$ 10	$ 8
Accounts receivable	12	22
Inventories	8	14
Current assets	$ 30	$ 44
Gross fixed assets	100	110
Less: accumulated depreciation	(40)	(50)
Net fixed assets	$ 60	$ 60
Total assets	$ 90	$104
Accounts payable	$ 12	$ 9
Notes payable	7	7
Long-term debt	11	24
Common stock	20	20
Retained earnings	40	44
Total liabilities and owners' equity	$ 90	$104

a. Prepare a statement of cash flow for TMU Processing Company. (*Hint:* Use the indirect method.)
b. Summarize your findings.

12–11A. (*Comprehensive Financial Analysis Problem*) The T. P. Jarmon Company manufactures and sells a line of exclusive sportswear. The firm's sales were $600,000 for the year just ended, and its total assets exceed $400,000. The company was started by Mr. Jarmon just 10 years ago and has been profitable every year since its inception. The chief financial officer for the firm, Brent Vehlim, has decided to seek a line of credit from the firm's bank totaling $80,000. In the past the company has relied on its suppliers to finance a large part of its needs for inventory. However, in recent months tight money conditions have led the firm's suppliers to offer sizable cash discounts to speed up payments for purchases. Mr. Vehlim wants to use the line of credit to supplant a large portion of the firm's payables during the summer months, which are the firm's peak seasonal sales period.

The firm's two most recent balance sheets were presented to the bank in support of its loan request. In addition, the firm's income statement for the year just ended was provided to support the loan request. These statements are found below:

T. P. Jarmon Company Balance Sheets for 12/31/91 and 12/31/92

Assets	1991	1992
Cash	$ 15,000	$ 14,000
Marketable securities	6,000	6,200
Accounts receivable	42,000	33,000
Inventory	51,000	84,000
Prepaid rent	1,200	1,100
Total current assets	$115,200	$138,300
Net plant and equipment	286,000	270,000
Total assets	$401,200	$408,300

Liabilities and Stockholders' Equity	1991	1992
Accounts payable	$ 48,000	$ 57,000
Notes payable	15,000	13,000
Accruals	6,000	5,000
Total current liabilities	$ 69,000	$ 75,000
Long-term debt	$160,000	$150,000
Common stockholders' equity	$172,200	$183,300
Total liabilities and equity	$401,200	$408,300

T.P. Jarmon Company Income Statement for the Year Ended 12/31/92

Sales		$600,000
Less: cost of goods sold		460,000
Gross profits		$140,000
Less: expenses		
General and administrative	$30,000	
Interest	$10,000	
Depreciation	30,000	
Total		70,000
Profit before taxes		$ 70,000
Less: taxes		27,100
Profits after taxes		$42,900
Less: cash dividends		31,800
To retain earnings		$ 11,100

Jan Fama, associate credit analyst for the Merchants National Bank of Midland, Michigan, was assigned the task of analyzing Jarmon's loan request.

a. Calculate the financial ratios for 1992 corresponding to the industry norms provided below:

Ratio	Norm	Jarmon's Ratio	Evaluation
Current ratio	1.8 times		
Acid test ratio	.9 times		
Debt ratio	.5		
Long-term debt to total capitalization	.7		
Times interest earned	10 times		
Average collection period	20 days		
Inventory turnover (based on cost of goods sold)	7 times		
Return on total assets	8.4%		
Gross profit margin	25%		
Net profit margin	7%		
Operating return on investment	16.8%		
Operating profit margin	14%		
Total asset turnover	1.2 times		
Fixed asset turnover	1.8 times		

b. Which of the ratios reported above in the industry norms do you feel should be most crucial in determining whether the bank should extend the line of credit? What strengths and weaknesses are apparent from your analysis of Jarmon's financial ratios?

c. Based on the ratio analysis you performed in part (b), would you recommend approval of the loan request? Discuss.

d. Prepare a cash flow statement for Jarmon covering the year ended December 31, 1992. How does this statement directly support your ratio analysis of Jarmon?

e. Perform an analysis of Jarmon's earning power using the procedure laid out in Figures 12–2 and 12–3.

12–12A. (*Preparing the Statement of Cash Flow*) Comparative balance sheets for December 31, 1991, and December 31, 1992, for the Abrams Mfg. Company are found below:

	1992	1991
Cash	$100,000.00	$ 89,000.00
Accounts receivable	70,000.00	64,000.00
Inventory	100,000.00	112,000.00
Prepaid expenses	10,000.00	10,000.00
Plant and equipment	311,000.00	238,000.00
Accumulated depreciation	−66,000.00	−40,000.00
	$525,000.00	$473,000.00
Accounts payable	$ 90,000.00	$ 85,000.00
Accrued liabilities	63,000.00	68,000.00
Mortgage payable		70,000.00
Preferred stock	100,000.00	
Additional paid-in capital—preferred stock	20,000.00	
Common stock	205,000.00	205,000.00
Retained earnings	47,000.00	45,000.00
	$525,000.00	$473,000.00

Abram's 1992 income statement is found below:

Sales	$184,000
Cost of sales	150,000
Gross profit	34,000
Operating expenses	10,000
Net income	$ 24,000

Additional information:

a. The only entry in the accumulated depreciation account is for 1992 depreciation.

b. The firm paid $22,000 in dividends during 1992.

Prepare a 1992 statement of cash flow for Abrams using the indirect method.

12–13A. (*Analyzing the Statement of Cash Flow*) Identify any financial weaknesses revealed in the statement of cash flow for the Westlake Manufacturing Co.

Westlake Manufacturing Co. Statement of Cash Flow for Current Year

Cash flow from operating activities		
Net income	$540,000	
Add (deduct) to reconcile net income to net cash flow		
Decrease in accounts receivable	40,000	
Increase in inventories	(240,000)	
Increase in prepaid expenses	(10,000)	
Depreciation expense	60,000	
Decrease in accrued wages	(50,000)	
Net cash flow from operating activities		$340,000
Cash flow from investing activities		
Sale (purchase) of plant and equipment		2,400,000
Cash flow from financing activities		
Issuance of bonds payable	1,000,000	
Repayment of short-term debt	(3,000,000)	
Payment of long-term debt	(500,000)	
Payment of dividends	(1,000,000)	
Net cash from financing activities		(3,500,000)
Net increase (decrease) in cash for the period		(760,000)

CASE PROBLEM

L. M. MYERS, INC.

FINANCIAL ANALYSIS

L. M. Myers, Inc., is one of the three largest grain exporters in the United States. The firm also engages in soybean processing and several other related activities. During fiscal 1991–1992 Myers derived 72.1 percent of its sales from its exporting activities, 14.8 percent from agriproducts, and the remainder from chemical and consumer products. Myers' nonexport sales are derived almost completely from soybean processing activities, including the production and sale of a number of food ingredients. One of the most promising soybean derivatives produced by the company is a newly developed meat substitute called "Prosoy." At present Prosoy is marketed almost strictly as a ground beef substitute; however, plans are under way to market the product in a number of other forms resembling familiar cuts of meat, such as bacon and even roasts. The success that the company has enjoyed with Prosoy in its initial three years of production promises to make soybean processing an even more important segment of the firm's overall sales. Other soybean-related products produced by the firm include a number of derivatives used in animal and poultry feeds. Myers' export business primarily involves corn, wheat, and some soybeans. The principal investment made by the firm related to its exporting operations involves a chain of grain elevators at strategic locations along the Mississippi River. These elevators are used to store grain and load it onto ships, which deliver it all over the world.

For the fiscal year just ended Myers experienced an overall sales growth of 10 percent. This increase represented a mere 5 percent increase in export-related activities and a whopping 20 percent increase in sales related to soybean processing. This and other factors have led the company to make a commitment to expand its processing capacity by $20 million during the next three years. The firm plans to finance the expansion through an $11 million bond issue and through the retention of earnings.

Owing to the seasonal nature of its export business, Myers has had to borrow heavily during the harvest months to finance seasonal inventory buildups and then repay the loans as sales are made throughout the year. In the past the company has arranged with a group of banks for a line of credit (discussed in Chapter 16) sufficient to meet its credit needs; however, in recent years this arrangement has become increasingly more cumbersome as the firm's total needs for funds have grown. This and cost considerations have led Myers' financial vice-president, James Graham, to consider the possibility of raising all or at least a part of the firm's credit needs through a commercial paper issue (also discussed in Chapter 17). Mr. Graham is somewhat concerned about his firm's creditworthiness in light of the industry norms generally used by banks and other creditors. His concern relates to the fact that Myers has never issued commercial paper and the belief that only the most creditworthy of borrowers can successfully use the commercial paper market to raise funds.

QUESTIONS

1. Using the financial statements for Myers presented below, what is the calculation of the financial ratios contained in Exhibit 1?
2. Based on your calculated ratios and the associated industry norms, what is your financial analysis of Myers?

L. M. Myers, Inc., Balance Sheets
for Years Ended December 31 ($000)

Assets	1991	1992
Cash	$ 11,451	$ 12,844
Accounts receivable	64,199	52,599
Marketable securities	—	33,995
Inventories	69,814	75,366
Deferred income taxes	2,948	2,750
Prepaid expenses	1,089	1,794
Total current assets	$149,501	$179,348
Investments and advances	11,681	12,012
Other assets	14,509	3,735
Net property and equipment	118,810	153,856
Total assets	$294,501	$348,951

Liabilities and Stockholders' Equity	1991	1992
Accounts payable	$ 34,327	$ 35,099
Notes payable	14,544	20,907
Accrued income and other taxes	28,526	40,112
Other accrued expenses	19,854	22,299
Total current liabilities	$ 97,251	$118,417
Long-term debt	75,817	67,006
Cumulative preferred stock	582	565
Common stock	26,596	26,812
Capital surplus	2,030	2,606
Retained earnings	92,683	133,559
Less common stock held in treasury	(458)	(14)
Total stockholders' equity	121,433	163,528
Total liabilities and stockholders' equity	$294,501	$348,951

L. M. Myers, Inc., Income Statements
for Years Ended December 31 ($000)

	1991	1992
Sales (net)	$706,457	$777,104
Less: cost of goods sold	(637,224)	(662,093)
Gross profit	$ 69,233	$115,011
Operating expenses		
Selling and administrative expenses	(17,612)	(17,804)
Labor expense	(9,418)	(15,263)
Depreciation	(6,976)	(7,428)
Miscellaneous operating expenses	(1,887)	(2,011)
Total	($ 35,893)	($ 42,506)

	1991	1992
Net operating income	$ 33,340	$ 72,505
Interest income	512	2,012
	33,852	74,517
Less: interest expense	(9,127)	(8,408)
Earnings before taxes	$ 24,725	$ 66,109
Less: taxes payable	(5,440)	(25,232)
Net income	$ 19,285	$ 40,877
Less: Preferred dividends	(58)	(56)
Net earnings available to common	$ 19,227	$ 40,821

EXHIBIT 1.
Financial Ratios for L. M. Myers, Inc.

Ratio	1991	1992	Industry Norm[a]
Acid test ratio			1.00 ×
Current ratio			1.61 ×
Average collection period[b]			30.00 days
Inventory turnover[b]			10.1 ×
Debt ration			49.1%
Long-term debt to total capitalization			31.0%
Times interest earned			5.87 ×
Cash flow overall coverage ratio			7.42 ×
Total asset turnover			2.1 ×
Gross profit margin			11.7%
Operating profit margin			7.6%
Operating income return on investment			14.75%
Return on total assets			8.45%
Return on common equity			21.39%

[a]These industry norms pertain to Myers' grain export operations, which comprised over 70 percent of the firm's sales for 1991. Also, the industry averages are applicable to both 1991 and 1992.
[b]Compute using end-of-year figures and assuming all sales are credit sales.

STUDY PROBLEMS (SET B)

12–1B. (*Ratio Analysis*) The Allandale Office Supply Company has a target current ratio of 2 to 1 but has experienced some difficulties financing its expanding sales in the past few months. At present the current ratio of 2.75 to 1 is based upon current assets of $3.0 million. If Allandale expands its receivables and inventories using its short-term line of credit, how much additional funding can it borrow before its current ratio standard is reached?

12–2B. (*Ratio Analysis*) The balance sheet and income statement for the Simsboro Paper Company are as follows:

Balance Sheet ($000)	
Cash	$1000
Accounts receivable	1500
Inventories	1000
Current assets	$3500
Net fixed assets	$4500
Total assets	$8000

Balance Sheet (cont.)	
Accounts payable	$1000
Accrued expenses	600
Short-term notes payable	200
Current liabilities	$1800
Long-term debt	2100
Owners' equity	$4100
	$8000

Income Statement ($000)	
Net sales (all credit)	$7500
Cost of goods sold	(3000)
Gross profit	$4500
Operating expenses[a]	(3000)
Net operating income	$1500
Interest expense	(367)
Earnings before taxes	$1133
Income taxes (40%)	(453)
Net income	$ 680

[a]Including depreciation expense of $500 for the year.

Calculate the following ratios:

Current ratio	Gross profit margin
Debt ratio	Operating profit margin
Times interest earned	Net profit margin
Average collection period	Operating return on investment
Inventory turnover	Return on total assets
Fixed asset turnover	Return on common equity
Total asset turnover	

12–3B. (*Analyzing Profitability*) The R. M. Senchack Corporation earned a net profit margin of 6 percent based on sales of $11 million and total assets of $6 million last year.

  a. What was Senchack's rate of return on total assets?

  b. During the coming year the company president has set a goal of attaining a 13 percent return on total assets. How much must firm sales rise, other things being the same, for the goal to be achieved? (State your answer as an annual growth rate in sales.)

  c. If Senchack finances 25 percent of its assets by borrowing, what was its return on common equity for last year? What will it be next year if the return on total asset goal is achieved?

12–4B. (*Using Financial Ratios*) Brenda Smith, Inc., had a gross profit margin of 25 percent and sales of $9.75 million last year. Seventy-five percent of the firm's sales are on credit while the remainder are cash sales. The company's current assets equal $1,550,000, its current liabilities $300,000, and it has $150,000 in cash plus marketable securities.

  a. If Smith's accounts receivable are $562,500, what is its average collection period?

  b. If Smith reduces its average collection period to 20 days, what will be its new level of accounts receivable?

  c. Smith's inventory turnover ratio is 8 times. What is the level of the firm's inventories?

12–5B. (*Ratio Analysis of Loan Request*) The J. B. Chavez Corporation has experienced two consecutive years of improved sales and foresees the need to increase its investment in inventories and receivables to meet yet a third year of increased sales. Chavez's President, J. B. Chavez, Jr., recently approached the company's bank (First State Bank) to discuss the possibility of extending the firm's line of credit to cover the firm's projected future funds requirements. The financial statements for the firm are found below:

J. B. Chavez Corporation, Balance Sheet at 12/31/91 and 12/31/92 ($000)

Assets

	12/31/91	12/31/92
Cash	$ 225	$ 175
Accounts receivable	450	430
Inventory	575	625
Current assets	1250	1230
Plant and equipment	2200	2500
Less: Accumulated depreciation	(1000)	(1200)
Net plant and equipment	1200	1300
Total assets	$2450	$2530

Liabilities and Owners' Equity

	1991	1992
Accounts payable	$ 250	$ 115
Notes payable—current (9%)	0	115
Current liabilities	250	230
Bonds	600	600
Owners' equity		
Common stock	300	300
Paid-in capital	600	600
Retained earnings	700	800
Total owners' equity	1600	1700
Total liabilities and owners' equity	$2450	$2530

J. B. Chavez Corporation
Income Statement Year Ended
12/31/91 and 12/31/92

	1991	1992
Sales	$1250	$1450
Cost of goods sold	700	875
Gross profit	$ 550	$ 575
Operating expenses	30	45
Depreciation	220	200
Net operating income	$ 300	$ 330
Interest expense	50	60
Net income before taxes	$ 250	$ 270
Taxes (40%)	100	108
Net income	$ 150	$ 162

a. Compute the following ratios for Chavez from the financial statements provided above:

	1991	1992	Industry Norm
Current ratio			5.0
Acid test (quick) ratio			3.0
Inventory turnover			2.2
Average collection period			90 days
Debt ratio			.33%
Times interest earned			7.0 ×
Total asset turnover			.75 ×
Fixed asset turnover			1.0 ×
Operating profit margin			20%
Net profit margin			12%
Return on total assets			9%

b. Based on your answer in (a) above, what are Chavez's financial strengths and weaknesses?

c. Would you make the loan? Why or why not?

12–6B. (*Cash Flow Statement*) Prepare a cash flow statement for Chavez for the year ended December 31, 1992 (problem 12–5B).

12–7B. (*Cash Flow Statement*) (a) Prepare a cash flow statement for Cramer, Inc., for 1992. (b) What were the firm's primary sources and uses of cash?

Cramer, Inc., for 1992

	1991	1992
Cash	$ 76,000	$ 82,500
Receivables	100,000	91,000
Inventory	168,000	163,000
Prepaid expenses	11,500	13,500
Fixed assets	325,500	450,000
Accumulated depreciation	94,500	129,000
Patents	61,500	52,500
	$648,000	$723,500

	1991	1992
Accounts payable	$123,000	$ 93,500
Taxes payable	97,500	105,000
Mortgage payable	150,000	—
Preferred stock	—	225,000
Additional paid-in capital —preferred	—	6,000
Common stock	225,000	225,000
Retained earnings	52,500	69,000
	$648,000	$723,500

Additional Information:

1. The only entry in the accumulated depreciation account is the depreciation expense for the period.

2. The only entries in the retained earnings account are for dividends paid in the amount of $20,000 and for the net income for the year.

3. The income statement for 1992 is as follows:

Sales	$190,000
Cost of sales[a]	140,000
Gross profit	50,000
Operating expenses	13,500
Net income	$ 36,500

[a]Includes depreciation of $34,500.

12–8B. (Basic Financial Statements) Prepare a balance sheet and income statement at December 31, 1992, for the Sabine Mfg. Co. from the scrambled list of items below. Ignore income taxes and interest expense.

Accounts receivable	$150,000
Machinery and equipment	700,000
Accumulated depreciation	236,000
Notes payable—current	90,000
Net sales	900,000
Inventory	110,000
Accounts payable	90,000
Long-term debt	160,000
Cost of goods sold	550,000
Operating expenses	280,000
Common stock	320,000
Cash	90,000
Retained earnings—prior year	?
Retained earnings—current year	?

12–9B. (*Financial Ratios—Investment Analysis*) The annual sales for Salco, Inc., were $5,000,000 last year. The firm's end-of-year balance sheet appeared as follows:

Current assets	$ 500,000	Liabilities	$1,000,000
Net fixed assets	$1,500,000	Owners' equity	$1,000,000
	$2,000,000		$2,000,000

The firm's income statement for the year was as follows:

Sales	$5,000,000
Less: Cost of goods sold	(3,000,000)
Gross profit	2,000,000
Less: Operating expenses	(1,500,000)
Net operating income	500,000
Less: Interest expense	(100,000)
Earnings before taxes	400,000
Less: Taxes	(160,000)
Net income	$ 240,000

a. Calculate Salco's total asset turnover, operating profit margin, and operating income return on investment.

b. Salco plans to renovate one of its plants, which will require an added investment in plant and equipment of $1 million. The firm will maintain its present debt ratio of .5 when financing the new investment and expects sales to remain constant, whereas the operating profit margin will rise to 13 percent. What will be the new operating income return on investment for Salco after the plant renovation?

c. Given that the plant renovation in part (b) occurs and Salco's interest expense rises by $40,000 per year, what will be the return earned on the common stockholders' investment? Compare this rate of return with that earned before the renovation.

12–10B. (*Cash Flow Statement*) The consolidated balance sheets of the SMU Processing Company are presented below for June 1, 1991, and May 31, 1992 (millions of dollars). SMU earned $14 million after taxes during the year ended May 31, 1992, and paid common dividends of $10 million.

	June 1, 1991	May 31, 1992
Cash	$ 10	$ 8
Accounts receivable	12	22
Inventories	8	14
Current assets	$ 30	$ 44
Gross fixed assets	100	110
Less: Accumulated depreciation	(40)	(50)
Net fixed assets	$ 60	$ 60
Total assets	$ 90	$104
Accounts payable	$ 12	$ 9
Notes payable	7	7
Long-term debt	11	24
Common stock	20	20
Retained earnings	40	44
Total liabilities and owners' equity	$ 90	$104

a. Prepare a cash flow statement for SMU Processing Company. (Hint: Use the indirect method.)

b. Summarize your findings.

12–11B. (*Comprehensive Financial Analysis Problem*) RPI Inc. is a manufacturer and retailer of high-quality sports clothing and gear. The firm was started several years ago by a group of serious outdoors enthusiasts who felt there was a need for a firm that could provide quality products at reasonable prices. The result was RPI Inc. Since its inception the firm has been profitable with sales that last year totaled $700,000 and assets in excess of $400,000. The firm now finds its growing sales outstrip its ability to finance its inventory needs. The firm now estimates that it will need a line of credit of $100,000 during the coming year. To finance this funding requirement the management plans to seek a line of credit with its bank.

The firm's most recent financial statements were provided to its bank as support for the firm's loan request. Joanne Peebie, a loan analyst trainee for the Morristown Bank and Trust, has been assigned the task of analyzing the firm's loan request.

RPI Inc. Balance Sheets for 12/31/91 and 12/31/92

Assets		
	1991	1992
Cash	$ 16,000	$ 17,000
Marketable securities	7,000	7,200
Accounts receivable	42,000	38,000
Inventory	50,000	93,000
Prepaid rent	1,200	1,100
Total current assets	$116,200	$156,300
Net plant and equipment	286,000	290,000
Total assets	$402,200	$446,300

Liabilities and Stockholders' Equity		
	1991	1992
Accounts payable	$ 48,000	$ 55,000
Notes payable	16,000	13,000
Accruals	6,000	5,000
Total current liabilities	$ 70,000	$ 73,000
Long-term debt	$160,000	$150,000
Common stockholders' equity	$172,200	$223,300
Total liabilities and equity	$402,200	$446,300

RPI Inc. Income Statement for Year Ended 12/31/92

Sales		$700,000
Less: Cost of goods sold		500,000
Gross profits		$200,000
Less: Expenses		
General and administrative	$50,000	
Interest	10,000	
Depreciation	30,000	
Total		90,000
Profit before taxes		$110,000
Less: Taxes (38%)		27,100
Profits after taxes		$82,900
Less: Cash dividends		31,800
To retained earnings		$ 51,100

a. Calculate the financial ratios for 1992 corresponding to the industry norms provided below:

Ratio	Norm	RPI Ratio	Evaluation
Current ratio	1.8 times		
Acid test ratio	.9 times		
Debt ratio	.5		
Long-term debt to total capitalization	.7		

Ratio	Norm	RPI Ratio	Evaluation
Times interest earned	10 times		
Average collection period	20 days		
Inventory turnover (based on COGS)	7 times		
Return on total assets	8.4%		
Gross profit margin	25%		
Net profit margin	7%		
Operating return on investment	16.8%		
Operating profit margin	14%		
Total asset turnover	1.2 times		
Fixed asset turnover	1.8 times		

b. Which of the ratios reported above in the industry norms do you think should be most crucial in determining whether the bank should extend the line of credit? What strengths and weaknesses are apparent from your analysis of RPI's financial ratios?

c. Based upon the ratio analysis you performed in part (b), would you recommend approval of the loan request? Discuss.

d. Prepare a statement of cash flow for RPI covering the year ended December 31, 1992. How does this statement directly support your ratio analysis of RPI?

e. Perform an analysis of RPI's earning power using the procedure laid out in Figures 12–2 and 12–3.

12–12B. (*Preparation Statement of Cash Flow*) Comparative balance sheets for December 31, 1991, and December 31, 1992, for the Barron Mfg. Company are found below:

	1991	1992
Cash	$ 70,000.00	$ 89,000.00
Accounts receivable	70,000.00	64,000.00
Inventory	80,000.00	102,000.00
Prepaid expenses	10,000.00	10,000.00
Plant and equipment	301,000.00	238,000.00
Accumulated depreciation	– 66,000.00	– 40,000.00
	$465,000.00	$463,000.00
Accounts payable	$ 80,000.00	$ 85,000.00
Accrued liabilities	63,000.00	68,000.00
Mortgage payable		60,000.00
Preferred stock	60,000.00	
Additional paid-in capital— preferred stock	10,000.00	
Common stock	205,000.00	205,000.00
Retained earnings	47,000.00	45,000.00
	$465,000.00	$463,000.00
Sales	$204,000.00	
Cost of sales	160,000.00	
Gross profit	44,000.00	
Operating expenses	10,000.00	
Net income	$34,000.00	

Additional Information:

a. The only entry in the accumulated depreciation account is for 1992 depreciation.

b. The firm paid $32,000 in dividends during 1992.

Prepare a 1992 statement of cash flow for Abrams using the indirect method.

12–13B. (*Analyzing the Statement of Cash Flow*) Identify any financial weaknesses revealed in the statement of cash flow for the Simsboro Pulpwood Mill, Inc.

Simsboro Pulpwood Mill, Inc., Statement of Cash Flow for Current Year

Cash flow from operating activities		
Net income	$500,000	
Add (deduct) to reconcile net income to net cash flow		
Decrease in accounts receivable	200,000	
Increase in inventories	(400,000)	
Increase in prepaid expenses	(100,000)	
Depreciation expense	600,000	
Decrease in accrued wages	(50,000)	
Net cash flow from operating activities		$750,000
Cash flow from investing activities		
Purchase (sale) of plant and equipment		(2,250,000)
Cash flow from financing activities		
Issuance of bonds payable	5,000,000	
Repayment of short-term debt	(3,000,000)	
Payment of long-term debt	(500,000)	
Payment of dividends	(1,000,000)	
Net cash from financing activities		500,000
Net increase (decrease) in cash for the period		(1,000,000)

Suggested Application for *DISCLOSURE*®

a. Access the *Disclosure* database to obtain the last three annual financial statements for the Chrysler Corporation and Ford Motor Company. Calculate the following financial ratios for each firm for each of the last three years:

Current Ratio
Quick Ratio
Accounts receivable turnover (assuming all reported sales are credit sales)
Inventory turnover
Operating return on investment
Operating profit margin
Gross profit margin
Total asset turnover
Debt ratio
Times interest earned
Return on equity

What differences do you see in the two firm's ratios that you consider to be important.

b. Perform an Earning Power analysis for Nike Inc.'s using data from Disclosure for the most recent three years. Perform a similar analysis for Reebok. How are the two firms different?

SELF-TEST SOLUTIONS

SS–1. Note that Ray's current ratio before the inventory expansion is as follows:

$$\text{current ratio} = \$6,000,000/\text{current liabilities} = 4$$

Thus, the firm's present level of current liabilities is $1,500,000. If the expansion in inventories is financed entirely with borrowed funds, then the change in inventories, ΔInv, is equal to the change in current liabilities and the firm's current ratio after the expansion can be defined as follows:

$$\text{current ratio} = (\$6,000,000 + \Delta\text{Inv})/(\$1,500,000 + \Delta\text{Inv}) = 3$$

Note that we set the new current ratio equal to the firm's target of 3 to 1. Solving for the value of ΔInv in the above equation, we determine that the firm can expand its inventories and finance the expansion with current liabilities by $750,000 and still maintain its target current ratio.

SS-2.   M & G Industries Ratio Analysis

	Industry Averages	1991	1992
Current ratio	1.80	1.84	0.90
Acid test ratio	0.70	0.78	0.24
Average collection period	37 days	36 days	36 days
Inventory turnover	2.50 ×	2.59 ×	2.11 ×
Debt ratio	58%	50%	61.3%
Long-term debt to total capitalization	33%	33.8%	28.3%
Times interest earned	3.8 ×	4.0 ×	2.79 ×
Gross profit margin	38%	40.0%	40.0%
Operating profit margin	10%	9.6%	10.6%
Net profit margin	3.5%	3.6%	3.4%
Total asset turnover	1.14 ×	1.11 ×	1.07 ×
Fixed asset turnover	1.40 ×	2.02 ×	1.82 ×
Operating income return on investment	11.4%	10.6%	11.3%
Return on total assets	4.0%	4.0%	3.6%
Return on common equity	9.5%	8.0%	9.4%

b. It appears that M & G is in a very weak position to request an additional loan. An examination of the ratios computed in part (a) shows that the liquidity of M & G has decreased considerably during the past year to a point well below the industry average. In addition, its debt ratio has risen to a point above the industry average, although the difference is not particularly large. However, an additional loan would increase this difference. The times interest earned ratio has decreased significantly over the preceding year to a point well below the industry norm of 3.8 ×. The firm's profit margins are very near the respective norms. The return on the owners' investment is good, but the firm's low liquidity and extensive use of financial leverage do not warrant approval of the loan.

SS-3.   M & G Industries Statement of Cashflow
for the Year Ended December 31, 1992

a. Cash flows from *operating* activities

Net income (from the statement of income)	$ 5,450	
Add (deduct) to reconcile net income to net cash flow		
Increase in accounts payable	$11,500	
Increase in inventories	($16,500)	
Depreciation expense	$10,000	
Increase in accounts receivable	($ 3,500)	
Net cash inflow from operating activities		$6,950
Cash flows from *investing* activities		
Cash inflows		
Cash outflows		
Purchase of land	($ 6,000)	
Purchase of plant and equipment	($30,000)	
Net cash outflow from investment activities		($36,000)
Cash flows from *financing* activities		
Cash inflows		
Increase in bank notes	$30,000	
Cash outflows		
Decrease in long-term debt	($ 5,800)	
Common dividends	($ 3,650)	
Net cash inflow from financing activities		$20,550
Effect of foreign exchange rates		-0-
Net increase (decrease) in cash during the period		($ 8,500)
Cash balance at the beginning of the period	$9,000	
Cash balance at the end of the period	$ 500	

b. The cash flow statement is an important supplement to ratio analysis. This statement directs the analysts' attention to where M & G Industries obtained financing during the period and how those funds were spent. For example, 52 percent of M & G's funds came from an increase in bank notes, whereas 20 percent came from an increase in AP. In addition, the largest uses of funds were additions to buildings and equipment and increases in inventories. Thus, M & G did little in the most recent operating period to alleviate the financial problems we noted earlier in our ratio analysis. In fact, M & G aggravated matters by purchasing fixed assets using short-term sources of financing. It would appear that another short-term loan at this time is *not* warranted.

CHAPTER 13

Financial Forecasting, Planning, and Budgeting

Financial Forecasting • Financial Planning and Budgeting • Computerized Financial Planning • Appendix 13A: Microcomputers and Spreadsheet Software in Financial Planning

The impact of computers and financial software on the practice of financial forecasting, planning, and budgeting has been dramatic. Financial spreadsheet programs allow the financial analyst to tabulate very large and cumbersome budgets, which, with the aid of a microcomputer, can then be easily modified to reflect any number of possible scenarios. This type of "trial-and-error" analysis can greatly enhance analysts' decision-making capability by allowing them quickly and easily to assess the importance of the projections and assumptions that go into any financial plan.

This chapter has two primary objectives: First, it will develop an appreciation for the role of forecasting in the firm's financial planning process. Basically, forecasts of future sales revenues and their associated expenses give the firm the information needed to project its future needs for financing. Second, the chapter will provide an overview of the firm's budgetary system, including the cash budget and the pro forma, or planned income, statement and balance sheet. Pro forma financial statements give the financial manager a useful tool for analyzing the effects of the firm's forecasts and planned activities on its financial performance, as well as its needs for financing. In addition, pro forma statements can be used as a benchmark or standard to compare against actual operating results. Used in this way, pro forma statements are an instrument for controlling or monitoring the firm's progress throughout the planning period.

Financial Forecasting

Forecasting in financial management is needed when the firm is ready to estimate its future financial needs. The basic steps involved in predicting those financing needs are the following: *Step 1:* Project the firm's sales revenues and expenses over the planning period. *Step 2:* Estimate the levels of investment in current and fixed assets that are necessary to support the projected sales. *Step 3:* Determine the firm's financing needs throughout the planning period.

The Cash Flow Cycle

The entire firm's operations can be visualized through the use of a **cash flow cycle diagram.** The diagram, as shown in Figure 13–1, depicts the firm's operations as a large pump that pushes cash through various reservoirs such as inventories and accounts receivable and dispenses cash for taxes, interest and principal payments on debt, and cash dividends to the shareholders. The problem in financial forecasting is one of predicting cash inflows and outflows and the corresponding financial needs of the firm. The firm's needs are related to the size of the various reservoirs that hold cash. The reservoirs represent the various assets in which the firm must make investments to produce the expected level of sales.

Tracing the Cash Flow Cycle

Since the firm's cash flow cycle is a continuous process, we will find it useful for illustrative purposes to consider the first cycle of a new firm. The process begins with the firm's cash reservoir, which consists initially of the owner's investment (funds raised through the issuance of stock) and funds borrowed from creditors. This cash is used to acquire plant and equipment, as well as supplies and materials. It is also used to pay wages and salaries, to pay for utilities such as heat and power, and to replace materials, plant, and equipment that are used or worn out in the process of making the firm's product. These expenditures represent payments for labor and capital used in producing the firm's salable product. Sales are then made either for cash or on credit (with some leakage for

FIGURE 13–1. Cash Flow Cycle Diagram

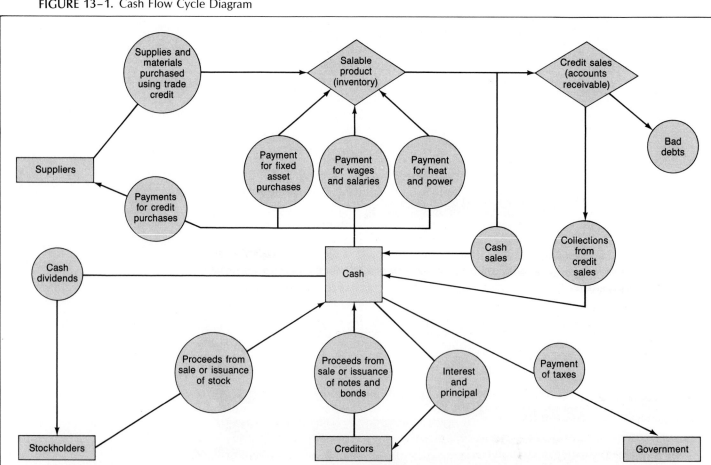

bad debt losses). To this cash flow stream are added cash inflows resulting from the sale of assets such as equipment, land, or securities. In the final phase of the cycle, cash is dispersed to pay obligations to suppliers for materials purchased on credit, income taxes to the government, interest and principal to the firm's creditors, and cash dividends to the firm's owners. Finally, any cash not paid in dividends is reinvested in the firm and becomes a part of the owners' investment.

Forecasting Cash Flows

The problem of financial forecasting, to summarize, consists of predicting future sales, which in turn provides the basis for predicting the level of investment in inventories, receivables, plant, and equipment required to support the firm's projected sales. Through the use of the cash budget the information from these projections is combined to provide an estimate of the firm's future financing needs.

Sales Forecast

The key ingredient in the firm's planning process is the **sales forecast.** This projection will generally be derived using information from a number of sources. At a minimum, the sales forecast for the coming year would reflect (1) any past trend in sales that is expected to carry through into the new year and (2) the influence of any events that might materially affect that trend.[1] An example of the latter would be the initiation of a major advertising campaign or a change in the firm's pricing policy.

Forecasting Financial Variables

Traditional financial forecasting takes the sales forecast as a given and makes projections of its impact on the firm's various expenses, assets, and liabilities. The most commonly used method for making these projections is the percent of sales method.

Percent of Sales Method of Financial Forecasting

The **percent of sales method** involves estimating the level of an expense, asset, or liability for a future period as a percent of the sales forecast. The percentage used can come from the most recent financial statement item as a percent of current sales, from an average computed over several years, from the judgment of the analyst, or from some combination of these sources.

Figure 13–2 presents a complete example of the use of the percent of sales method of financial forecasting. In this example each item in the firm's balance

FIGURE 13–2.
Using the Percent of Sales Method to Forecast Future Financing Requirements

Assets	Present (1992)	Percent of Sales (1992 Sales = $10 M)	Projected (Based on 1993 Sales = $12 M)
Current assets	$2 M	$\frac{\$2\ M}{\$10\ M} = 20\%$	$.2 \times \$12\ M = \$2.4\ M$
Net fixed assets	4 M	$\frac{\$4\ M}{\$10\ M} = 40\%$	$.4 \times \$12\ M =$ 4.8 M
Total	$6 M		$7.2 M
Liabilities and Owners' Equity			
Accounts payable	$1.0 M	$\frac{\$1\ M}{\$10\ M} = 10\%$	$.10 \times \$12\ M = \$1.2\ M$
Accrued expenses	1.0 M	$\frac{\$1\ M}{\$10\ M} = 10\%$	$.10 \times \$12\ M = \$1.2\ M$
Notes payable	.5 M	NA[a]	no change	.5 M
Long-term debt	$2.0 M	NA[a]	no change	2.0 M
Total liabilities	$4.5 M		$4.9 M
Common stock	$ .1 M	NA[a]	$ .1 M
Paid-in capital	.2 M	NA[a]	.2 M
Retained earnings	1.2 M		$1.2\ M + [.05 \times \$12\ M \times (1 - .5)] =$ 1.5 M[b]
Common equity	$1.5 M		$1.8 M
Total	$6.0 M		Total financing provided $6.7 M
			Discretionary financing needed .5 M[c]
			Total $7.2 M

[a]Not applicable. These account balances are assumed not to vary with sales.

[b]Projected retained earnings equals the beginning level ($1.2 M) plus projected net income less any dividends paid. In this case net income is projected to equal 5 percent of sales, and dividends are projected to equal half of net income: .05 × $12 M × (1 − .5) = $300,000.

[c]Discretionary financing needed equals projected total assets ($7.2 M) less projected total liabilities ($4.9 M) less projected common equity ($1.8), or $7.2 M − 4.9 M − 1.8 M = $500,000.

[1]A complete discussion of forecast methodologies is outside the scope of this book. The interested reader will find the following references helpful: F. Gerard Adams, *The Business Forecasting Revolution* (Oxford: Oxford University Press, 1986); C.W.J. Granger, *Forecasting in Business and Economics*, 2d ed. (Boston, MA: Academic Press, 1989); and Paul Newbold and Theodore Bos, *Introductory Business Forecasting* (Cincinnati, OH: Southwestern, 1990).

sheet that varies with sales is converted to a percentage of 1992 sales. The forecast of the new balance for each item is then calculated by multiplying this percentage times the $12 million in projected sales for the 1993 planning period. This method of forecasting future financing is not as precise or detailed as the method using a cash budget, which is presented later; however, it offers a relatively low-cost and easy-to-use first approximation of the firm's financing needs for a future period.

Note that in the example in Figure 13–2, both current and fixed assets are assumed to vary with the level of firm sales. This means that the firm does not have sufficient productive capacity to absorb a projected increase in sales. Thus, if sales were to rise by $1, fixed assets would rise by $.40, or 40 percent of the projected increase in sales. Note that if the fixed assets the firm presently owns were sufficient to support the projected level of new sales, these assets should not be allowed to vary with sales. If this were the case, then fixed assets would not be converted to a percent of sales and would be projected to remain unchanged for the period being forecast.

Also, we note that accounts payable and accrued expenses are the only liabilities allowed to vary with sales. Both these accounts might reasonably be expected to rise and fall with the level of firm sales; hence the use of the percent of sales forecast. Because these two categories of current liabilities normally vary directly with the level of sales, they are often referred to as **spontaneous sources of financing.** Chapter 14, which discusses working-capital management, has more to say about these forms of financing. Notes payable, long-term debt, common stock, and paid-in capital are *not* assumed to vary directly with the level of firm sales. These sources of financing are termed **discretionary,** in that the firm's management must make a conscious decision to seek additional financing using any one of them. Finally, we note that the level of retained earnings *does* vary with estimated sales. The predicted change in the level of retained earnings equals the difference in estimated after-tax profits (projected net income) of $600,000 and common stock dividends of $300,000.

Thus, using the example from Figure 13–2, we estimate that firm sales will increase from $10 M to $12 M, which will cause the firm's needs for total assets to rise to $7.2 M. These assets will then be financed by $4.9 M in existing liabilities plus spontaneous liabilities; $1.8 M in owner funds, including $300,000 in retained earnings from next year's sales; and, finally, $500,000 in discretionary financing, which can be raised by issuing notes payable, selling bonds, offering an issue of stock, or some combination of these sources.

In summary, we can estimate the firm's needs for discretionary financing, using the percent of sales method of financial forecasting, by following a four-step procedure:

Step 1: Convert each asset and liability account that varies directly with firm sales to a percent of current year's sales.

EXAMPLE

$$\frac{\text{current assets}}{\text{sales}} = \frac{\$2 \text{ M}}{\$10 \text{ M}} = .2 \text{ or } 20\%$$

Step 2: Project the level of each asset and liability account in the balance sheet using its percent of sales multiplied by projected sales or by leaving the account balance unchanged where the account does not vary with the level of sales.

EXAMPLE

$$\text{projected current assets} =$$
$$\text{projected sales} \times \frac{\text{current assets}}{\text{sales}} = \$12 \text{ M} \times .2 = 2.4 \text{ M}$$

Step 3: Project the level of new retained earnings available to help finance the firm's operations. This equals projected net income for the period less planned common stock dividends.

$$\text{projected addition to retained earnings} =$$
$$\text{projected sales} \times \frac{\text{net income}}{\text{sales}} \times \left(1 - \frac{\text{cash dividends}}{\text{net income}} \right)$$
$$= \$12 \text{ M} \times .05 \times [1 - .5] = \$300,000$$

Step 4: Project the firm's need for discretionary financing as the projected level of total assets less projected liabilities and owners' equity.

$$\text{discretionary financing needed} =$$
$$\text{projected total assets} - \text{projected total liabilities} - \text{projected owners' equity}$$
$$= \$7.2 \text{ M} - \$4.9 \text{ M} - \$1.8 \text{ M} = \$500,000$$

As we noted earlier, the principal virtue of the percent of sales method of financial forecasting is its simplicity. To obtain a more precise estimate of the amount and timing of the firm's future financing needs, we require a cash budget. The percent of sales method of financial forecasting does provide a very useful, low-cost forerunner to the development of the more detailed cash budget, which the firm will ultimately use to estimate its financing needs.

Perspective in Finance

Are you beginning to wonder exactly where finance *comes into financial forecasting? To this point financial forecasting looks for all the world like financial statement forecasting. The reason for this is the fact that we have adopted the accountant's model of the firm, the balance sheet, as the underlying structure of the financial forecast. The key to financial forecasting is the identification of the firm's anticipated future financing requirements, and these requirements can be identified as the "plug figure" or simply the number that balances a pro forma balance sheet.*

Financial Planning and Budgeting

Financial forecasts are put to use in constructing financial plans. These plans culminate in the preparation of a cash budget and a set of pro forma statements for a future period in the firm's operations.

Budget Functions

A **budget** is simply a forecast of future events. For example, students preparing for final exams make use of time budgets, which help them allocate their limited preparation time among their courses. Students also must budget their financial resources among competing uses, such as books, tuition, food, rent, clothes, and extracurricular activities.

Budgets perform three basic functions for a firm. First, they indicate the amount and timing of the firm's needs for future financing. Second, they provide the basis for taking corrective action in the event that budgeted figures do not match actual or realized figures. Third, budgets provide the basis for performance evaluation. Plans are carried out by people, and budgets provide benchmarks that management can use to evaluate the performance of those responsible for carrying out those plans and, in turn, controlling their actions. Thus, budgets are valuable aids in both planning and controlling aspects of the firm's financial management.

In the pages that follow, we will develop an example budgetary system for a retailing firm. The primary emphasis will be on the cash budget and pro forma financial statements. These statements provide the information needed for a detailed estimate of the firm's future financing requirements.

The Budgetary System

Although our interest in financial planning focuses on the cash budget, a number of other budgets provide the basis for its preparation. This system of budgets allows planning for each source of cash flow, both inflow and outflow, that will affect the firm throughout the planning period. In general, a business will utilize four types of budgets: physical budgets, cost budgets, profit budgets, and cash budgets. Figure 13–3 on page 498 presents an overview of the budgetary system.

Physical budgets include budgets for physical as opposed to financial items. Examples include budgets for unit sales, personnel, unit production, inventories, and physical facilities. These budgets are used as the basis for generating cost, cash, and profit budgets. **Cost budgets** are prepared for every major expense category of the firm. For example, a manufacturing firm would prepare cost budgets for manufacturing or production costs, selling costs, administrative costs, financing costs, and research and development costs. These cost budgets along with the sales budget provide the basis for preparing a **profit budget.** Finally, converting all the budget information to a cash basis provides the information required to prepare the cash budget.

The Cash Budget

The **cash budget** represents a detailed plan of future cash flows and is composed of four elements: cash receipts, cash disbursements, net change in cash for the period, and new financing needed.

Example. ■ To demonstrate the construction and use of the cash budget, consider Salco Furniture Company, Inc., a regional distributor of household

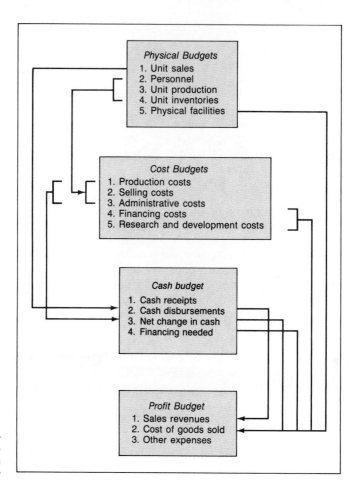

FIGURE 13–3.
The Budget System

furniture. Salco's sales are highly seasonal, peaking in the months of March through May. Roughly 30 percent of Salco's sales are collected one month after the sale, 50 percent two months after the sale, and the remainder during the third month following the sale.

Salco attempts to pace its purchases with its forecast of future sales. Purchases generally equal 75 percent of sales and are made two months in advance of anticipated sales. Payments are made in the month following purchases. For example, June sales are estimated at $100,000, thus April purchases are .75 × $100,000 = $75,000. Correspondingly, payments for purchases in May equal $75,000. Wages, salaries, rent, and other cash expenses are recorded in Table 13–1 on page 500, which gives Salco's cash budget for the six-month period ended in June 1993. Additional expenditures are recorded in the cash budget related to the purchase of equipment in the amount of $14,000 during February and the repayment of a $12,000 loan in May. In June Salco will pay $7,500 interest on its $150,000 in long-term debt for the period of January–June 1993. Interest on the $12,000 short-term note repaid in May for the period January through May equals $600 and is paid in May.

Salco presently has a cash balance of $20,000 and wants to maintain a minimum balance of $10,000. Additional borrowing necessary to maintain that minimum balance is estimated in the final section of Table 13–1. Borrowing takes place at the beginning of the month in which the funds are needed. Interest on borrowed funds equals 12 percent per annum, or 1 percent per month, and is paid in the month following the one in which funds are borrowed. Thus, interest on funds borrowed in January will be paid in February equal to 1 percent of the loan amount outstanding during January.

The financing-needed line on Salco's cash budget indicates that the firm will need to borrow $36,350 in February, $65,874 in March, $86,633 in April, and $97,599 in May. Only in June will the firm be able to reduce its borrowing to $79,875. Note that the cash budget indicates not only the amount of financing needed during the period but also when the funds will be needed.

Fixed Versus Flexible Budgets

The cash budget given in Table 13–1 for Salco, Inc., is an example of a **fixed budget.** Cash flow estimates are made for a single set of monthly sales estimates. Thus, the estimates of expenses and new financing needed are meaningful only for the level of sales for which they were computed. To avoid this limitation, several budgets corresponding to different sets of sales estimates can be prepared. Such a **flexible budget** fulfills two basic needs: First, it gives information regarding the range of the firm's possible financing needs, and second it provides a standard against which to measure the performance of subordinates who are responsible for the various cost and revenue items contained in the budget.

This second function deserves some additional comment. The obvious problem that arises relates to the fact that costs vary with the actual level of sales experienced by the firm. Thus, if the budget is to be used as a standard for performance evaluation or control, it must be constructed to match realized sales and production figures. This can involve much more than simply "adjusting cost figures up or down in proportion to the deviation of actual from planned sales"; that is, costs may not vary in strict proportion to sales, just as

Worksheet	Oct.	Nov.	Dec.
Sales	$55,000	$62,000	$50,000
Collections:			
First month (30%)			
Second month (50%)			
Third month (20%)			
Total			
Purchases			$56,250
Payments (one-month lag)			
Cash receipts:			
Collections			
Cash disbursements:			
Purchases			
Wages and salaries			
Rent			
Other expenses			
Interest expense on existing debt ($12,000 note and $150,000 in long-term debt)			
Taxes			
Purchase of equipment			
Loan repayment ($12,000 note due in May)			
Total disbursements:			
Net monthly charge			
Plus: Beginning cash balance			
Less: Interest on short-term borrowing			
Equals: Ending cash balance—no borrowing			
Financing needed[a]			
Ending cash balance			
Cumulative borrowing			

[a]The amount of financing that is required to raise the firm's ending cash balance up to its $10,000 desired cash balance.

inventory levels may not vary as a constant percent of sales. Thus, preparation of a flexible budget involves reestimating all the cash expenses that would be incurred at each of several possible sales levels. This process might utilize a variant of the percent of sales method discussed earlier.

Budget Period

There are no strict rules for determining the length of the budget period. However, as a general rule it should be long enough to show the effect of management policies yet short enough so that estimates can be made with reasonable accuracy. Applying this rule of thumb to the Salco example in Table 13–1, it appears that the six-month budget period is too short, in that whether the planned operations of the firm will be successful over the coming fiscal year is not known; that is, for most of the first six-month period the firm is operating with a cash flow deficit. If this does not reverse in the latter six months of the year, then a reevaluation of the firm's plans and policies is clearly in order.

Longer-range budgets are also prepared in the form of the **capital-expenditure budget.** This budget details the firm's plans for acquiring plant and equipment over a 5-year, 10-year, or even longer period. Furthermore, firms often develop comprehensive long-range plans extending up to 10 years into the future. These plans are generally not as detailed as the annual cash budget, but they do consider such major components as sales, capital expenditures, new-product development, capital funds acquisition, and employment needs.

Jan.	Feb.	Mar.	Apr.	May	June	July	Aug.
$60,000	$75,000	$88,000	$100,000	$110,000	$100,000	$80,000	$75,000
15,000	18,000	22,500	26,400	30,000	33,000		
31,000	25,000	30,000	37,500	44,000	50,000		
11,000	12,400	10,000	12,000	15,000	17,600		
$57,000	55,400	62,500	75,900	89,000	100,600		
66,000	75,000	82,500	75,000	60,000	56,250		
56,250	66,000	75,000	82,500	75,000	60,000		
$57,000	55,400	62,500	75,900	89,000	100,600		
$56,250	66,000	75,000	82,500	75,000	60,000		
3,000	10,000	7,000	8,000	6,000	4,000		
4,000	4,000	4,000	4,000	4,000	4,000		
1,000	500	1,200	1,500	1,500	1,200		
				600	7,500		
		4,460			5,200		
	14,000						
				12,000			
$64,250	94,500	91,660	96,000	99,100	81,900		
$(7,250)	(39,100)	(29,160)	(20,100)	(10,100)	18,700		
20,000	12,750	10,000	10,000	10,000	10,000		
—	—	(364)	(659)	(866)	(976)		
12,750	(26,350)	(19,524)	(10,759)	(966)	27,724		
—	36,350	29,524	20,759	10,966	(17,724)[b]		
$12,750	10,000	10,000	10,000	10,000	10,000		
—	36,350	65,874	86,633	97,599	79,875		

[b]Negative financing needed simply means the firm has excess cash that can be used to retire a part of its short-term borrowing from prior months.

Pro Forma Financial Statements

The final stage in the budgeting process involves construction of a set of **pro forma financial statements** depicting the end result of the planning period's operations. Financial information for Salco, Inc., is used to demonstrate the construction of the pro forma income statement and balance sheet. To do this, we need Salco's cash budget (found in Table 13–1) and its beginning balance sheet, which depicts the financial condition of the firm at the start of the planning period (see Table 13–2 on page 502).

The Pro Forma Income Statement

The **pro forma income statement** represents a statement of planned profit or loss for a future period. For Salco a six-month pro forma income statement is constructed from the information contained in the cash budget found in Table 13–1. The final statement is presented in Table 13–3 on page 502.

Net sales, found by summing the six monthly sales projections (January through June) from Table 13–1, total $533,000. Cost of goods sold is computed as 75 percent of sales, or $399,750. This figure could also have been found by summing purchases for November through April, which represent items sold from January through June. Recall that purchases are made two months in advance, so that items sold in January through June were purchased in November through April.

Assets		
Current assets		
Cash	$ 20,000	
Accounts receivable	104,400	
Inventories	101,250	
Total current assets		$225,650
Fixed assets		
Net plant and equipment		180,000
Total assets		$405,650

Liabilities and Owners' Equity		
Current liabilities		
Accounts payable	$ 56,250	
Notes payable (due in May 1991)	12,000	
Taxes payable	4,460	
Total current liabilities		$ 72,710
Noncurrent liabilities		
Long-term debt		150,000
Stockholders' equity		
Common stock ($1 per)	$ 20,000	
Paid-in capital	50,000	
Retained earnings	112,940	
Total owners' equity		182,940
Total liabilities and owners' equity		$405,650

TABLE 13–3.
Salco Furniture Co., Inc.,
Pro Forma Income Statement
for the Six-Month Period
Ended June 30, 1993

Sales	(from cash budget—Table 13–1)		$533,000
Cost of goods sold	(75% of sales)		(399,750)
Gross profit	(calculation)		$133,250
Operating Expenses			
Depreciation	[($17,200 ÷ 2) + $230]	$ 8,830	
Wages and salaries	(from cash budget—Table 13–1)	38,000	
Rent	(from cash budget—Table 13–1)	24,000	
Other expenses	(from cash budget—Table 13–1)	6,900	(77,730)
Net operating income	(calculation)		$ 55,520
Interest expense	(calculation—see text footnote 3)		(11,764)
Earnings before taxes	(calculation)		$ 43,756
Income taxes payable	(40%)		(17,502)
Net income	(calculation)		$ 26,254

Depreciation expense cannot be obtained from the cash budget, since it does not constitute a cash flow. Thus, this expense must be determined from the depreciation schedules of Salco's plant and equipment. On its existing fixed assets Salco has an annual depreciation expense of $17,200. In addition, the $14,000 piece of equipment purchased at the end of February will be depreciated over a 15-year life toward a $3,650 salvage value. Using straight-line depreciation and depreciating the asset for 4 months of the budget period, we find this amounts to roughly $230. Thus, total depreciation expense for the period is $8,830 [or ($17,200 ÷ 2) + $230].

Wages and salaries, rent, and other expenses are found by summing the relevant cash flow items from the cash budget for the months of January through June. This assumes, of course, that all these expenses are paid at the end of each month in which they are earned, rent is not paid in advance, and all other expenses are paid on a monthly basis except interest on short-term borrowing, which is paid in the month following its incurrence. Wages and salaries total $38,000, rent expense equals $24,000, and other expenses are expected to be $6,900.

Subtracting the above operating expenses from gross profit leaves a net operating income of $55,520. Interest expense of $11,764 is then deducted from net operating income to obtain earnings before taxes of $43,756.[2] Federal income taxes payable are found using a 40 percent corporate income tax rate. For Salco this equals a tax expense for the period of $17,502. Finally, subtracting the estimated taxes from earnings before taxes indicates net income for the period of $26,254.

Net Cash Flow Versus Net Income

The difference in the cash and accrual bases of accounting for corporate income is vividly demonstrated in the cash budget and pro forma income statements for the period. On a cash flow basis the firm has a substantial net negative cash flow, while on an accrual basis the firm earned $26,254. The difference, of course, relates to when revenues and expenses are accounted for or recognized in the two statements. In the cash budget, revenues and expenses are included in the months in which cash is actually received or disbursed. In the income statement revenues and expenses are included in the month in which the corresponding sale took place, which is usually not the same month in which cash is received. The income statement is therefore prepared on an accrual basis. See Appendix 1A for added discussion of the income statement.

The Pro Forma Balance Sheet

We can construct the **pro forma balance sheet** for Salco by using information from the cash budget (Table 13–1); the December 31, 1992, balance sheet (Table 13–2); and the pro forma income statement (Table 13–3). Salco's pro forma balance sheet for June 30, 1993, is presented in Table 13–4 on page 504. Estimates of the individual statement entries are provided below.

Ending cash from the cash budget, $10,000, becomes the cash entry in Salco's pro forma balance sheet. The accounts receivable balance is found as follows:

Accounts receivable (12/31/92) (from Table 13–2)	$104,400
+ Credit sales (from Table 13–1)	533,000
− Collections (from Table 13–1)	(440,400)
Accounts receivable (6/30/93) (calculation)	$197,000

The beginning balance for accounts receivable is taken from the December 31, 1992, balance sheet (Table 13–2), and credit sales and collections are obtained by summing across the relevant cash budget monthly totals. Inventories are determined in a similar manner:

Inventories (12/31/92) (from Table 13–2)	$101,250
+ Purchases (from Table 13–1)	414,750
− Cost of goods sold (from Table 13–3)	(399,750)
Inventories (6/30/93) (calculation)	$116,250

---

[2]Total interest expense *incurred* (but not necessarily paid) during the period equals $7,500 on long-term debt plus $600 on the $12,000 note repaid in May, plus the sum of all interest incurred during the budget period on short-term borrowing. Note that we include $364 for February, $659 for March, and so forth, plus $799 for June, which was incurred but not paid until July.

Assets		
Current assets		
Cash	$ 10,000	
Accounts receivable	197,000	
Inventories	116,250	
Total current assets		$323,250
Fixed assets		
Net plant and equipment		185,170
Total assets		$508,420

Liabilities and Owners' Equity		
Current liabilities		
Accounts payable	$ 56,250	
Interest payable	799	
Notes payable[a]	79,875	
Taxes payable	12,302	
Total current liabilities		$149,226
Noncurrent liabilities		
Long-term debt		150,000
Stockholders' equity		
Common stock	$ 20,000	
Paid-in capital	50,000	
Retained earnings	139,194	
Total owners' equity		$209,194
Total liabilities and owners' equity		$508,420

[a]Cumulative borrowing for the period was assumed to take the form of notes payable. This figure is taken from the cumulative borrowing row of cash budget contained in Table 13–1.

Purchases were found by summing relevant monthly figures from the cash budget for all six months of the budget period; and cost of goods sold was taken from the pro forma income statement in Table 13–3. The net plant and equipment figure is found as follows:

Net plant and equipment (12/31/92) (from Table 13–2)	$180,000
+ Purchases of plant and equipment (from Table 13–1)	14,000
− Depreciation expense (from Table 13–3)	(8,830)
Net plant and equipment (6/30/93) (calculation)	$185,170

Purchases of plant and equipment are reflected in the cash budget, and depreciation expense is taken from the pro forma income statement. The only changes that took place during the period involved the $14,000 purchase and depreciation expense of $8,830, leaving a net balance of $185,170. Total assets for Salco are therefore expected to be $508,420.

The liability accounts are estimated using the same basic methodology as that used in finding asset balances. Accounts payable is found as follows:

Accounts payable (12/31/92) (from Table 13–2)	$ 56,250
+ Purchases (from Table 13–1)	414,750
− Payments (from Table 13–1)	(414,750)
Accounts payable (6/30/93) (calculation)	$ 56,250

During June the firm had total borrowing of $77,875, on which it owes $799 in interest. However, since interest is not paid in the month in which the expense is incurred, this interest liability still exists at the end of June. We can analyze the ending balance for Interest payable as follows:

Interest payable (12/31/92)	$0
+ Interest expense (see text footnote 3)	11,764
− Interest paid	10,965
Interest payable (6/30/93)	$799

Again, purchases and payments were taken from the cash budget for each of the six months of the budget period. Notes payable are found as follows:

Notes payable (12/31/92) (from Table 13–2)	$12,000
+ Borrowing (6/30/93) (from Table 13–1)	79,875
− Repayments (from Table 13–1)	(12,000)
Notes payable (6/30/93) (calculation)	$79,875

Here it is assumed that the total new financing needed during the period ($79,875) would be raised through notes payable. Salco's use of short-term financing may or may not be desirable, as we shall see in Chapter 14 when we discuss working-capital management. An accrued interest expense item of $799 is created as a result of interest expense in that amount that was incurred during June on short-term borrowing but will not be paid until July. Next, compute taxes payable as follows:

Taxes payable (12/31/92) (from Table 13–2)	$ 4,460
+ Tax liability for the period (from Table 13–3)	17,502
− Tax payments made during the period (from Table 13–1)	(9,660)
Taxes payable (6/30/93) (calculation)	$12,302

Long-term debt, common stock, and paid-in capital remain unchanged for the period, as no new stock or long-term debt was issued nor was any repurchased or retired. Finally, the retained earnings balance is found as follows:

Retained earnings (12/31/92) (from Table 13–2)	$112,940
+ Net income for the period (from Table 13–3)	26,254
− Cash dividends (from Table 13–1)	0
Retained earnings (6/30/93) (calculation)	$139,194

Since no common dividends were paid (none were considered in the cash budget—Table 13–1), the new retained earnings figure is $139,194.

Salco's management may now wish to perform a financial analysis using the newly prepared pro forma statements. Such an analysis would provide the basis for evaluating the firm's planned financial performance over the next six months. It would entail use of a set of ratios such as those discussed in Chapter 12, which could be compared with prior-year figures and industry averages. If this analysis identified any potential weakness, the firm could take steps to correct it before it became reality.

Financial Control

The pro forma statements just prepared can be used to *monitor* or control the firm's financial performance. One approach involves preparing pro forma statements for each month during the planning period. Actual operating results for each month's operations can then be compared with the projected or pro forma figures. This type of analysis provides an early warning system to detect financial problems as they develop. In particular, by comparing actual monthly (or even weekly) operating results with projected revenue and expense items (from pro forma income statements), the financial manager can maintain a very close watch on the firm's overall profitability and take an active role in determining the firm's overall performance for the planning period.

Financial Planning and Budgeting: Closing Comments

Two aspects of pro forma statements should be emphasized. First, these figures represent single-point estimates of each of the items in the entire system of budgets and the resulting pro forma statements. Although these might be the *best estimates* of what the future will hold for Salco, drawing up at least two additional sets of estimates is desirable, corresponding to the very worst set of circumstances that the firm might face and the very best. These extremes provide the necessary input for formulating contingency financing plans should a deviation from the expected figures occur. Second, notes payable was used as a *plug* figure for additional financing needed. The actual source of financing selected will depend on a number of factors, including (1) the length of the period for which the financing will be needed, (2) the cost of alternative sources of funds, and (3) the preferences of the firm's management regarding the use of debt versus equity. These factors will be further investigated in Chapter 17, when we discuss short-term financing.

Computerized Financial Planning

In recent years a number of developments in both computer hardware (machines) and software (programs) have reduced the tedium of the planning and budgeting process immensely. These include the introduction of "user-friendly" or "easy-to-use" computer programs that are specialized for application to financial planning.

Financial planning software packages (sometimes referred to as electronic spreadsheets) were first made popular on large mainframe computers but quickly spread to personal computers in the early eighties. These packages allow even a computer novice to utilize a personal computer to construct budgets and forecasts. The real advantage of the computer is realized there is a need for different scenarios to be evaluated quickly and at a low cost in man-hours.

Another major development that has had a significant impact on the extent to which computers are used in the planning and budgeting process is the advent of the microcomputer. For mere hundreds of dollars the financial analyst's desk can contain the computing power it took hundreds of thousands of dollars to buy just a decade ago. The development of financial planning software has paralleled the development of microcomputer technology. The number of spreadsheet packages has mushroomed over the past five years. These packages generally sell for less than $500 and include graphics programs as well as elementary database management capabilities.[3] The Appendix to this chapter offers a sample spreadsheet exercise.

---

[3] The number and variety of financial spreadsheet programs has expanded dramatically since the introduction of the original Visi-Calc program. These include Lotus 1–2–3 and Excel, among others. In addition, there is a growing set of products referred to as "expert systems," which attempt to mimic the decisions of experts. To date these efforts have produced a limited number of financial applications software related to such things as the capital-budgeting decision (discussed earlier in Chapter 6), but they offer an opportunity to expand the capabilities of the financial manager of the future.

This chapter develops the role of forecasting within the context of the firm's financial planning efforts. Forecasts of the firm's sales revenues and related expenses provide the basis for projecting future financing needs. The most popular method for forecasting financial variables is the percent of sales method.

Forecasts of firm sales and expenses are used to develop the cash budget for the planning period, which is then used to estimate the firm's future financing needs. In this chapter all needed financing is supplied through short-term notes. However, in Chapters 17 and 20 we will look more closely at sources of financing. Chapter 17 deals with the choice between current or short-term financing versus long-term financing; Chapter 20 with the choice among long-term sources (bonds, preferred stock, and common stock).

Pro forma financial statements provide the user with the basis for (1) evaluating the results of the firm's financial plans and (2) controlling the firm's operations during the planning period.

STUDY QUESTIONS

13–1. Discuss the shortcomings of the percent of sales method of financial forecasting.

13–2. Explain how a fixed cash budget differs from a variable or flexible cash budget. p 499

13–3. What two basic needs does a flexible (variable) cash budget serve? p. 499

13–4. What would be the probable effect on a firm's cash position of the following events?
   a. Rapidly rising sales
   b. A delay in the payment of payables
   c. A more liberal credit policy on sales (to the firm's customers)
   d. Holding larger inventories

13–5. How long should the budget period be? Why would a firm not set a rule that all p.500 budgets be for a 12-month period?

13–6. A cash budget is usually thought of as a means of planning for future financing needs. Why would a cash budget also be important for a firm that had excess cash on hand?

13–7. Explain why a cash budget would be of particular importance to a firm that experiences seasonal fluctuations in its sales.

13–8. Is there a difference between estimated net profit after taxes for a period and the estimated net addition to the cash balance? Explain.

SELF-TEST PROBLEMS

ST–1. (*Financial Forecasting*) Use the percent of sales method to prepare a pro forma income statement for Calico Sales Co., Inc. Projected sales for next year equal $4 million. Cost of goods sold equals 70 percent of sales, administrative expense equals $500,000, and depreciation expense is $300,000. Interest expense equals $50,000 and income is taxed at a rate of 40 percent. The firm plans to spend $200,000 during the period to renovate its office facility and will retire $150,000 in notes payable. Finally, selling expense equals 5 percent of sales.

ST–2. (*Pro Forma Statements and Liquidity Analysis*) The balance sheet for Odom Manufacturing Company on December 31, 1992, is on page 508.

The Treasurer of Odom Manufacturing wishes to borrow $500,000, the funds from which would be applied in the following manner:
   1. $100,000 to reduce accounts payable
   2. $ 75,000 to retire current notes payable
   3. $175,000 to expand existing plant facilities
   4. $ 80,000 to increase inventories
   5. $ 70,000 to increase cash on hand

Odom Manufacturing Co. Balance Sheet, December 31, 1992

Cash	$ 250,000	Accounts payable	$ 850,000
Accounts receivable	760,000	Notes payable	550,000
Inventory	860,000	Current liabilities	$1,400,000
Current assets	$1,870,000	Long-term debt	800,000
Property, plant, and equipment	1,730,000	Common stock	600,000
		Retained earnings	800,000
		Total liabilities and	
Total assets	$3,600,000	stockholders' equity	$3,600,000

Repayment of the $500,000 will be in 20 years with interest paid annually.

a. Assuming that the loan is obtained, prepare a pro forma balance sheet for Odom Manufacturing that reflects the use of the loan proceeds.

b. Did the firm's liquidity improve after the loan was obtained and the proceeds were dispensed in the above manner? Why or why not?

ST-3. (*Cash Budget*) Stauffer, Inc., has estimated sales and purchase requirements for the last half of the coming year. Past experience indicates that it will collect 20 percent of its sales in the month of the sale, 50 percent of the remainder one month after the sale, and the balance in the second month following the sale. Stauffer prefers to pay for half its purchases in the month of the purchase and the other half the following month. Labor expense for each month is expected to equal 5 percent of that month's sales, with cash payment being made in the month in which the expense is incurred. Depreciation expense is $5,000 per month; miscellaneous cash expenses are $4,000 per month and are paid in the month incurred. General and administrative expenses of $50,000 are recognized and paid monthly. A $60,000 truck is to be purchased in August and is to be depreciated on a straight-line basis over 10 years with no expected salvage value. The company also plans to pay a $9,000 cash dividend to stockholders in July. The company feels that a minimum cash balance of $30,000 should be maintained. Any borrowing will cost 12 percent annually, with interest paid in the month following the month in which the funds are borrowed. Borrowing takes place at the beginning of the month in which the need for funds arises. For example, if during the month of July the firm should need to borrow $24,000 to maintain its $30,000 desired minimum balance, then $24,000 will be taken out on July 1 with interest owed for the entire month of July. Interest for the month of July would then be paid on August 1. Sales and purchase estimates are shown below. Prepare a cash budget for the months of July and August (cash on hand 6/30 was $30,000, while sales for May and June were $100,000 and purchases were $60,000 for each of these months).

Month	Sales	Purchases
July	$120,000	$50,000
August	150,000	40,000
September	110,000	30,000

STUDY PROBLEMS (SET A)

13-1A. (*Financial Forecasting*) Sambonoza Enterprises projects its sales next year to be $4 million and expects to earn 5 percent of that amount after taxes. The firm is currently in the process of projecting its financing needs and has made the following assumptions (projections):

1. Current assets will equal 20 percent of sales while fixed assets will remain at their current level of $1 million.
2. Common equity is presently $0.8 million, and the firm pays out half its after-tax earnings in dividends.
3. The firm has short-term payables and trade credit that normally equal 10 percent of sales and has no long-term debt outstanding.

What are Sambonoza's financing needs for the coming year?

13-2A. (*Financial Forecasting—Percent of Sales*) Tulley Appliances, Inc., projects next year's sales to be $20 million. Current sales are at $15 million based on current assets of $5 million and fixed assets of $5 million. The firm's net profit margin is 5 percent after taxes. Tulley forecasts that current assets will rise in direct proportion to the increase in sales, but fixed assets will increase by only $100,000. At present Tulley has $1.5 million in accounts payable plus $2 million in long-term debt (due in 10 years) outstanding and common equity (including $4 million in retained earnings) totaling $6.5 million. Tulley plans to pay $500,000 in common stock dividends next year.

a. What are Tulley's total financing needs (i.e., total assets) for the coming year?

b. Given the firm's projections and dividend payment plans, what are its discretionary financing needs?

c. Based on the projections given and assuming that the $100,000 expansion in fixed assets will occur, what is the largest increase in sales the firm can support without having to resort to the use of discretionary sources of financing?

13–3A. (*Pro Forma Balance Sheet Construction*) Use the following industry average ratios to construct a pro forma balance sheet for Carlos Menza Inc.

Total asset turnover	2	times
Average collection period (assume a 360-day year)	9	days
Fixed asset turnover	5	times
Inventory turnover (based on cost of goods sold)	3	times
Current ratio	2	times
Sales (all on credit)	$4.0 million	
Cost of goods sold	75% of sales	
Debt ratio	50%	

Cash		Current liabilities	
Accounts receivable		Long-term debt	
		Common stock plus	
Net fixed assets	$_____	retained earnings	_____
	$══════		$══════

13–4A. (*Cash Budget*) The Sharpe Corporation's projected sales for the first eight months of 1993 are as follows:

January	$ 90,000	May	$300,000
February	120,000	June	270,000
March	135,000	July	225,000
April	240,000	August	150,000

Of Sharpe's sales, 10 percent is for cash, another 60 percent is collected in the month following sale, and 30 percent is collected in the second month following sale. November and December sales for 1992 were $220,000 and $175,000, respectively.

Sharpe purchases its raw materials two months in advance of its sales equal to 60 percent of their final sales price. The supplier is paid one month after it makes delivery. For example, purchases for April sales are made in February and payment is made in March.

In addition, Sharpe pays $10,000 per month for rent and $20,000 each month for other expenditures. Tax prepayments of $22,500 are made each quarter, beginning in March.

The company's cash balance at December 31, 1992, was $22,000; a minimum balance of $15,000 must be maintained at all times. Assume that any short-term financing needed to maintain cash balance would be paid off in the month following the month of financing if sufficient funds are available. Interest on short-term loans (12 percent) is paid monthly. Borrowing to meet estimated monthly cash needs takes place at the beginning of the month. Thus, if in the month of April the firm expects to have a need for an additional $60,500, these funds would be borrowed at the beginning of April with interest of $605 (.12 × 1/12 × $60,500) owed for April and paid at the beginning of May.

a. Prepare a cash budget for Sharpe covering the first seven months of 1993.

b. Sharpe has $200,000 in notes payable due in July that must be repaid or renegotiated for an extension. Will the firm have ample cash to repay the notes?

13–5A. (*Financial Forecasting—Pro Forma Statements*) The Bell Retailing Company has been engaged in the process of forecasting its financing needs over the next quarter and has made the following forecasts of planned cash receipts and disbursements:

1. Historical and predicted sales:

	Historical		Predicted	
April	$ 80,000	July	$130,000
May	100,000	August	130,000
June	120,000	September	120,000
		October	100,000

2. The firm incurs and pays a monthly rent expense of $3,000.
3. Wages and salaries for the coming months are estimated as follows (with payments coinciding with the month in which the expense is incurred):

July	$18,000
August	18,000
September	16,000

4. Of the firm's sales, 40 percent is collected in the month of sale, 30 percent one month after sale, and the remaining 30 percent two months after sale.
5. Merchandise is purchased one month before the sales month and is paid for in the month it is sold. Purchases equal 80 percent of sales.
6. Tax prepayments are made on the calendar quarter, with a prepayment of $1,000 in July based on earnings for the quarter ended June 30.
7. Utilities for the firm average 2 percent of sales and are paid in the month of their incurrence.
8. Depreciation expense is $12,000 annually.
9. Interest on a $40,000 bank note (due in November) is payable at an 8 percent annual rate in September for the three-month period just ended.
10. The firm follows a policy of paying no cash dividends.

Based on the above, supply the following items:

a. Prepare a monthly cash budget for the three-month period ended September 30, 1993.
b. If the firm's beginning cash balance for the budget period is $5,000, and this is its minimum desired balance, determine when and how much the firm will need to borrow during the budget period. The firm has an $80,000 line of credit with its bank with interest (12 percent annual rate) paid monthly (for example, for a loan taken out at the end of December, interest would be paid at the end of January and every month thereafter so long as the loan was outstanding).
c. Prepare a pro forma income statement for Bell covering the three-month period ended September 30, 1993. Use a 40 percent tax rate.
d. Given the following balance sheet dated June 30, 1993, and the pro forma income statement from (c), prepare a pro forma balance sheet for September 30, 1993.

Bell Retailing Co. Balance Sheet, June 30, 1993

Cash	$ 5,000	Accounts payable	$104,000
Accounts receivable	102,000	Bank notes (8%)	40,000
Inventories	114,000	Accrued taxes	1,000
Current assets	221,000	Current liabilities	145,000
Net fixed assets	120,000	Common stock ($1 par)	100,000
		Paid-in capital	28,400
		Retained earnings	67,600
Total assets	$341,000	Total liabilities and capital	$341,000

13-6A. (*Forecasting Accounts Receivable*) Sampkin Mfg. is evaluating the effects of extending trade credit to its out-of-state customers. In the past Sampkin has given credit to local customers but has insisted on cash on delivery from customers in the bordering state of South Dakota. At present Sampkin's average collection period is

30 days based on total sales; that is, including both its $900,000 in-state credit sales and its $300,000 out-of-state cash sales, the firm's accounts receivable balance is 30 days.

$$\text{average collection period} = \frac{\text{accounts receivable}}{\text{sales}/360}$$

$$= \frac{\$100,000}{\$1,200,000/360} = 30 \text{ days}$$

a. Calculate Sampkin's average collection period based on credit sales alone.

b. If Sampkin extends credit to its out-of-state customers, it expects total credit sales to rise to $1,500,000. If the firm's average collection period remains the same as in part **a** above, what will be the new level of accounts receivable?

13–7A. (*Forecasting Accounts Receivable*) The Ace Traffic Company sells its merchandise on credit terms of 2/10, net 30 (2 percent discount if payment is made within 10 days or the net amount is due in 30 days). Only a part of the firm's customers take the trade discount, so that the firm's average collection period is 20 days.

a. Based on estimated sales of $400,000, project Ace's accounts receivable balance for the coming year.

b. If Ace changes its cash discount terms to 1/10, net 30, it expects its average collection period will rise to 28 days. Estimate Ace's accounts receivable balance based on the new credit terms and expected sales of $400,000.

13–8A. (*Percent of Sales Forecasting*) Which of the following accounts would most likely vary directly with the level of firm sales? Discuss each briefly.

	Yes	No
Cash	——	——
Marketable securities	——	——
Accounts payable	——	——
Notes payable	——	——
Plant and equipment	——	——
Inventories	——	——

13–9A. (*Financial Forecasting—Percent of Sales*) The balance sheet of the Thompson Trucking Company (TTC) follows:

Thompson Trucking Company Balance Sheet, January 31, 1992 ($ millions)

Current assets	$10	Accounts payable	$ 5
Net fixed assets	15	Notes payable	0
Total	$25	Bonds payable	10
		Common equity	10
		Total	$25

TTC had sales for the year ended 1/31/92 of $50 million. The firm follows a policy of paying all net earnings out to its common stockholders in cash dividends. Thus, TTC generates no funds from its earnings that can be used to expand its operations (assume that depreciation expense is just equal to the cost of replacing worn-out assets).

a. If TTC anticipates sales of $80 million during the coming year, develop a pro forma balance sheet for the firm for 1/31/93. Assume that current assets vary as a percent of sales, net fixed assets remain unchanged, accounts payable vary as a percent of sales, and use notes payable as a balancing entry.

b. How much "new" financing will TTC need next year?

c. What limitations does the percent of sales forecast method suffer from? Discuss briefly.

13–10A. (*Financial Forecasting—Discretionary Financing Needed*) The most recent balance sheet for the Armadillo Dog Biscuit Co. is shown in the table below. The company is about to embark on an advertising campaign, which is expected to raise sales from the present level of $5 million to $7 million by the end of next year. The firm is presently operating at full capacity and will have to increase its investment in both current and fixed assets to support the projected level of new sales. In fact, the firm estimates that both categories of assets will rise in direct proportion to the projected increase in sales.

      The firm's net profits were 6 percent of current year's sales but are expected to rise to 7 percent of next year's sales. To help support its anticipated growth in asset needs next year, the firm has suspended plans to pay cash dividends to its stockholders. In years past a $1.50 per share dividend has been paid annually.

Armadillo Dog Biscuit Co., Inc. ($ millions)

	Present Level	Percent of Sales	Projected Level
Current assets	$2.0		
Net fixed assets	3.0		
Total	$5.0		
Accounts payable	$0.5		
Accrued expenses	0.5		
Notes payable	—		
Current liabilities	$1.0		
Long-term debt	$2.0		
Common stock	0.5		
Retained earnings	1.5		
Common equity	$2.0		
Total	$5.0		

      Armadillo's payables and accrued expenses are expected to vary directly with sales. In addition, notes payable will be used to supply the funds needed to finance next year's operations and that are not forthcoming from other sources.

a. Fill in the table and project the firm's needs for discretionary financing. Use notes payable as the balancing entry for future discretionary financing needed.

b. Compare Armadillo's current ratio and debt ratio (total liabilities/total assets) before the growth in sales and after. What was the effect of the expanded sales on these two dimensions of Armadillo's financial condition?

c. What difference, if any, would have resulted if Armadillo's sales had risen to $6 million in one year and $7 million only after two years? Discuss only; no calculations required.

13–11A. (*Financial Forecasting—Changing Credit Policy*) Island Resorts, Inc., has $400,000 invested in receivables throughout much of the year. It has annual credit sales of $3,600,000 and a gross profit margin of 80 percent.

a. What is Island Resorts' average collection period? [*Hint:* Recall that average collection period = accounts receivable/(credit sales/360).]

b. By how much would Island Resorts be able to reduce its accounts receivable if it were to change its credit policies in a way that reduced its average collection period to 30 days without affecting annual credit sales?

13–12A. (*Forecasting Discretionary Financing Needs*) Fishing Charter, Inc., estimates that it invests 30 cents in assets for each dollar of new sales. However, 5 cents in profits are produced by each dollar of additional sales, of which 1 cent can be reinvested in the firm. If sales rise from their present level of $5 million by $500,000 next year, and the ratio of spontaneous liabilities of sales is .15, what will be the firm's need for discretionary financing? (*Hint:* In this situation you do not know what the firm's existing level of assets is, nor do you know how those assets have been financed. Thus, you must estimate the change in financing needs and match this change with the expected changes in spontaneous liabilities, retained earnings, and other sources of discretionary financing.)

13-13A. (*Preparation of a Cash Budget*) Harrison Printing has projected its sales for the first eight months of 1993 as follows:

January	$100,000	May	$275,000
February	120,000	June	200,000
March	150,000	July	200,000
April	300,000	August	180,000

Harrison collects 20 percent of its sales in the month of the sale, 50 percent in the month following the sale, and the remaining 30 percent two months following the sale. During November and December of 1992 Harrison's sales were $220,000 and $175,000, respectively.

Harrison purchases raw materials two months in advance of its sales equal to 65 percent of its final sales. The supplier is paid one month after delivery. Thus, purchases for April sales are made in February and payment is made in March.

In addition, Harrison pays $10,000 per month for rent and $20,000 each month for other expenditures. Tax prepayments of $22,500 are made each quarter beginning in March. The company's cash balance as of December 31, 1992, was $22,000; a minimum balance of $20,000 must be maintained at all times to satisfy the firm's bank line of credit agreement. Harrison has arranged with its bank for short-term credit at an interest rate of 12 percent per annum (1 percent per month) to be paid monthly. Borrowing to meet estimated monthly cash needs takes place at the beginning of the month, but interest is not paid until the end of the following month. Consequently, if the firm were to need to borrow $50,000 during the month of April, then it would pay $500 (= .01 × $50,000) in interest during May. Finally, Harrison follows a policy of repaying any outstanding short-term debt in any month in which its cash balance exceeds the minimum desired balance of $20,000.

a. Harrison needs to know what its cash requirements will be for the next six months so that it can renegotiate the terms of its short-term credit agreement with its bank, if necessary. To evaluate this problem the firm plans to evaluate the impact of a ±20 percent variation in its monthly sales efforts. Prepare a six-month cash budget for Harrison, and use it to evaluate the firm's cash needs.

b. Harrison has a $200,000 note due in June. Will the firm have sufficient cash to repay the loan?

CASE PROBLEM

LINCOLN PLYWOOD, INC.

FINANCIAL FORECASTING

Lincoln Plywood, Inc. (LPI), owns and operates a plywood fabricating plant in southern Georgia. LPI's primary product is 4-by-8-foot sheets of pine plywood used in the construction industry. The plywood is formed out of thin sheets of wood that are "peeled" from pine logs bought in the region. A number of varieties of thicknesses and grades of plywood can be made in LPI's plant, ranging from 1/4-inch sheets used as paneling in new homes to 3/4-inch sheets used in framing and heavy industrial applications. LPI's sales have grown rapidly over the past 10 years at an average of 10 percent per year. This growth has resulted from the housing boom that occurred during this period, and in particular the very rapid rate of regional growth in the Atlanta area.

The firm's management has been pleased with the growth in sales; however, during the past six months it has begun to experience some cash flow problems that appear to have gotten out of control (LPI's current balance sheet is shown below). The firm's controller, James Christian, is aware of the decline in the firm's cash position and plans to correct the problem as soon as an appropriate course of action can be identified. One factor that he feels is surely making the problem worse is the firm's credit and collections policy. In particular LPI recently "liberalized" its credit terms in an effort to stimulate demand in the face of stiffening competition. The full effect of the change is not known, but Christian plans to address that problem when he makes his projection of cash needs for the coming year.

Lincoln Plywood, Inc., Balance Sheet
for December 31, 19x1

Assets		
Cash		$ 125,000
Accounts receivable	$ 517,500	
Less: Allowance for bad debts	7,500	510,000
Inventories		725,000
Current assets		$1,360,000
Plant and equipment	$2,320,000	
Less: Accumulated depreciation	(1,280,000)	
Net plant and equipment		1,040,000
Total assets		$2,400,000

Lincoln Plywood, Inc., Balance Sheet
for December 31, 19x1 (cont.)

Liabilities and Owners' Equity	
Accounts payable	$ 30,000
Accrued taxes	50,000
Accrued expenses	270,000
Current liabilities	$ 350,000
Common stock	$ 400,000
Retained earnings	1,650,000
Common equity	$2,050,000
Total liabilities and owner's equity	$2,400,000

LPI's cash cycle is a relatively simple one. The firm purchases timber, processes that timber by turning it into various types of plywood products, sells the timber on credit, and collects its credit sales. The cash flow problem the firm currently faces is partly a result of its increasing the term over which credit sales can be repaid. In fact, following its recent liberalization of credit terms, the firm estimates that only 10 percent of its customers will pay within the month of the sale, 46 percent of the total will be collected in one month, and the remainder is collected in the second month following the sale.

Christian plans to make a monthly cash budget for LPI spanning the next six months (January through June) and has already projected firm sales as follows:

Month	Projected Sales
January	$500,000
February	300,000
March	250,000
April	525,000
May	800,000
June	250,000

The monthly sales estimates reflect a long-established seasonality in the firm's sales. However, the firm's purchases of timber are not closely matched to its sales. The harvest of timber is heavily seasonal due to the problems associated with getting the timber out of the woods during the rainy winter months. Since LPI contracts up to 8 months in advance for its timber purchases, it has a very good idea of what its expenditures for timber will be over the six-month planning horizon. Specifically, LPI has contracted to make the following timber purchases:

Month	Purchase Contracts
January	$120,000
February	120,000
March	200,000
April	300,000
May	550,000
June	600,000

LPI's standard purchase contract calls for cash payment 30 days following the delivery, and its purchases during December were only $20,000. Timber purchases are added to the firm's inventories at cost plus a processing cost equal to half the cost of the timber. Thus, for the month of December LPI increased its inventories by a total of $30,000, and this is the outstanding balance of accounts payable for December. This balance will be paid in full in January.

In addition to its timber purchases, LPI plans to acquire a new chipping machine used to convert waste resulting from its processing of the timber to chips of wood that are then sold to paper mills, which convert the chips to paper stock. The new machine will cost $400,000 and will be purchased and paid for in February. The firm also plans to acquire a new forklift truck in April, which will cost $60,000. The purchase will be paid for in May. LPI's monthly depreciation expense for January and February is $15,000 per month but will increase by $8,000 per month in March because of the purchase of the new chipping machine, and it will increase again in June by $1,000 per month because of the purchase of the forklift.

Christian estimates the firm's general and administrative expense to be $70,000 per month, with payment being made in the month of the expense's incurrence. The firm also has a category called miscellaneous cash expenses, which is estimated to be at $20,000 per month and paid monthly. Although LPI has no formal policy with regard to its minimum cash balance, Christian feels that a $100,000 balance is the minimum he would like to have over the planning horizon. Finally, LPI plans to make a cash dividend payment to stockholders at the end of March and June equal to $100,000 and will also make quarterly tax payments of $50,000 in the months of January and April. (For planning purposes, a 30 percent tax rate is used in estimating LPI's tax liability.)

QUESTIONS

1. Prepare a month-by-month cash budget for LPI for the next six months. You may assume that any borrowing that must be undertaken will cost 1 percent interest per month, with interest paid the month following the month in which borrowing takes place. Assume borrowing is at the beginning of the month. November and December sales for the current year were $350,000 and $400,000, respectively.

2. Prepare pro forma income statements for the three-month periods ended with March and June. You may assume that inventories consist of materials and related labor expense. Cost of goods sold equals 75 percent of sales and comprises materials and related labor.

3. Prepare a pro forma balance sheet for LPI for the end of March and June. You may assume that accrued expenses and common stock do not change over the 6-month planning period.

4. Given LPI's financing requirements for the period, what suggestions do you have for James Christian for raising the necessary funds? Discuss your reasons for the stated plans.

STUDY PROBLEMS (SET B)

13–1B. (*Financial Forecasting*) Simpson Inc. projects its sales next year to be $5 million and expects to earn 6 percent of that amount after taxes. The firm is currently in the process of projecting its financing needs and has made the following assumptions (projections):
   1. Current assets will equal 15 percent of sales while fixed assets will remain at their current level of $1 million.
   2. Common equity is presently $0.7 million, and the firm pays out half its after-tax earnings in dividends.
   3. The firm has short-term payables and trade credit that normally equal 11 percent of sales and has no long-term debt outstanding.
   What are Simpson's financing needs for the coming year?

13–2B. (*Financial Forecasting—Percent of Sales*) Carson Enterprises is in the midst of its annual planning exercise. Bud Carson, the owner, is a mechanical engineer by education and has only modest skills in financial planning. In fact, the firm has operated in the past on a "crisis" basis with little attention paid to the firm's financial affairs until a problem arose. This worked reasonably well for several years, until the firm's growth in sales created a serious cash flow shortage last year. Bud was able to convince the firm's bank to come up with the needed funds but an outgrowth of the agreement was that the firm would begin to make forecasts of its financing requirements annually. To support its first such effort Bud has made the following estimates for next year: Sales are currently $18 million with projected sales of $25 million for next year. The firm's current assets equal $7 million while its fixed assets are $6 million. The best estimate Bud can make is that current assets will equal the current proportion of sales while fixed assets will rise by $100,000. At the present time the firm has accounts payable of $1.5 million, $2 million in long-term debt, and common equity totaling $9.5 million (including $4 million in retained earnings). Finally, Carson Enterprises plans to continue paying its dividend of $600,000 next year and has a 5 percent profit margin.

   a. What are Carson's total financing needs (i.e., total assets) for the coming year?

   b. Given the firm's projections and dividend payment plans, what are its discretionary financing needs?

   c. Based on the projections given and assuming that the $100,000 expansion in fixed assets will occur, what is the largest increase in sales the firm can support without having to resort to the use of discretionary sources of financing?

13–3B. (*Pro Forma Balance Sheet Construction*) Use the following industry average ratios to construct a pro forma balance sheet for the V. M. Willet Co.

Total asset turnover	2.5 times
Average collection period (assume a 360-day year)	10 days
Fixed asset turnover	6 times
Inventory turnover (based on cost of goods sold)	4 times
Current ratio	3 times
Sales (all on credit)	$5 million
Cost of goods sold	80% of sales
Debt ratio	60%

Cash		Current liabilities	
Accounts receivable		Long-term debt	
Inventories		Common stock plus	
Net fixed assets	$_____	retained earnings	_____
	$_____		$_____

13–4B. (*Cash Budget*) The Carmel Corporation's projected sales for the first eight months of 1993 are as follows:

January	$100,000	May	$275,000
February	110,000	June	250,000
March	130,000	July	235,000
April	250,000	August	160,000

Of Carmel's sales, 20 percent is for cash, another 60 percent is collected in the month following sale, and 20 percent is collected in the second month following sale. November and December sales for 1992 were $220,000 and $175,000, respectively.

   Carmel purchases its raw materials two months in advance of its sales equal to 70 percent of their final sales price. The supplier is paid one month after it makes delivery. For example, purchases for April sales are made in February and payment is made in March.

   In addition, Carmel pays $10,000 per month for rent and $20,000 each month for other expenditures. Tax prepayments of $23,000 are made each quarter, beginning in March.

   The company's cash balance at December 31, 1992, was $22,000; a minimum balance of $20,000 must be maintained at all times. Assume that any short-term financing needed to maintain cash balance would be paid off in the month following the month of financing if sufficient funds are available. Interest on short-term loans (12 percent) is paid monthly. Borrowing to meet estimated monthly cash needs takes place at the beginning of the month. Thus, if in the month of April the firm expects to have a need for an additional $60,500, these funds would be borrowed at the beginning of April with interest of $605 (.12 × 1/12 × $60,500) owed for April and paid at the beginning of May.

a. Prepare a cash budget for Carmel covering the first seven months of 1993.

b. Carmel has $250,000 in notes payable due in July that must be repaid or renegotiated for an extension. Will the firm have ample cash to repay the notes?

13–5B. (*Financial Forecasting—Pro Forma Statements*) In the Spring of 1993, Juan Sanchez, the chief financial analyst for Jarrett Sales Company, found himself faced with a major financial forecasting exercise. He had joined the firm about three months before and was just beginning to feel comfortable with his new duties when he was called into his supervisor's office about 3:30

p.m. on a Friday afternoon. It seems that Margaret Simpson, the analyst who had been in charge of the firm's annual financial planning task, had taken a leave of absence and would not be available to help prepare the firm's projected financing needs for the coming quarter. The job fell in his lap and it needed to be completed by Monday at 2:00 P.M., when the company president met with the executive committee to work out their plans for requesting a limit for the firm's line of credit with its bank for the next quarter. After reviewing Ms. Simpson's files Juan found that the task might not be so difficult as he had first thought. In fact, the critical forecasts had been compiled and were contained in the file. In addition, Juan found some carefully documented assumptions that he could use to compile the necessary forecast. This information follows:

1. Historical and predicted sales:

	Historical		Predicted
April	$ 80,000	July	$140,000
May	110,000	August	120,000
June	120,000	September	120,000
		October	100,000

2. The firm incurs and pays a monthly rent expense of $2,500.
3. Wages and salaries for the coming months are estimated as follows (with payments coinciding with the month in which the expense is incurred):

July	$20,000
August	18,000
September	13,000

4. Of the firm's sales, 40 percent is collected in the month of sale, 30 percent one month after sale, and the remaining 30 percent two months after sale.
5. Merchandise is purchased one month before the sales month and is paid for in the month it is sold. Purchases equal 80 percent of sales.
6. Tax prepayments are made on the calendar quarter, with a prepayment of $1,000 in July based on earnings for the quarter ended June 30.
7. Utilities for the firm average 2 percent of sales and are paid in the month of their incurrence.
8. Depreciation expense is $12,000 annually.
9. Interest on a $40,000 bank note (due in November) is payable at an 8 percent annual rate in September for the three-month period just ended.
10. The firm follows a policy of paying no cash dividends.

Based on the above, supply the following items:

a. Prepare a monthly cash budget for the three-month period ended September 30, 1993.

b. If the firm's beginning cash balance for the budget period is $5,000 and this is its minimum desired balance, determine when and how much the firm will need to borrow during the budget period. The firm has an $80,000 line of credit with its bank with interest (12 percent annual rate) paid monthly (for example, for a loan taken out at the end of December, interest would be paid at the end of January and every month thereafter so long as the loan was outstanding).

c. Prepare a pro forma income statement for Jarrett covering the three-month period ended September 30, 1993. Use a 40 percent tax rate.

d. Given the following balance sheet dated June 30, 1993, and the pro forma income statement from (c), prepare a pro forma balance sheet for September 30, 1993.

Jarrett Sales Co. Balance Sheet, June 30, 1993

Cash	$ 5,000	Accounts payable	$104,000
Accounts receivable	102,000	Bank notes (8%)	40,000
Inventories	114,000	Accrued taxes	1,000
Current assets	221,000	Current liabilities	145,000
Net fixed assets	120,000	Common stock ($1 par)	100,000
		Paid-in capital	28,400
		Retained earnings	67,600
Total assets	$341,000	Total liabilities and capital	$341,000

13-6B. (*Forecasting Accounts Receivable*) Sam's Mfg. Co. is evaluating the effects of extending trade credit to its out-of-state customers. In the past Sam's has given credit to local customers but has insisted on cash on delivery from customers in the bordering state of South Dakota. At present Sam's average collection period is 30 days based on total sales; that is, including both its $700,000 in-state credit sales and its $500,000 out-of-state cash sales, the firm's accounts receivable balance is 30 days.

$$\text{average collection period} = \frac{\text{accounts receivable}}{\text{sales}/360}$$

$$= \frac{\$100,000}{\$1,200,000/360} = 30 \text{ days}$$

a. Calculate Sam's average collection period based on credit sales alone.
b. If Sam's extends credit to its out-of-state customers, it expects total credit sales to rise to $1,250,000. If the firm's average collection period remains the same, what will be the new level of accounts receivable?

13-7B. (*Forecasting Accounts Receivable*) The Wong Distribution Company sells its merchandise on credit terms of 2/10, net 30 (2 percent discount if payment is made within 10 days or the net amount is due in 30 days). Only a part of the firm's customers take the trade discount, so that the firm's average collection period is 20 days.
a. Based on estimated sales of $500,000, project Wong's accounts receivable balance for the coming year.
b. If Wong changes its cash discount terms to 1/10, net 30, it expects its average collection period will rise to 28 days. Estimate Wong's accounts receivable balance based on the new credit terms and expected sales of $500,000.

13-8B. (*Percent of Sales Forecasting*) Which of the following accounts would most likely vary directly with the level of firm sales? Discuss each briefly.

	Yes	No
Cash	____	____
Marketable securities	____	____
Accounts payable	____	____
Notes payable	____	____
Plant and equipment	____	____
Inventories	____	____

13-9B. (*Financial Forecasting—Percent of Sales*) The balance sheet of the Chavez Drilling Company (CDC) follows:

Chavez Drilling Company Balance Sheet for January 31, 1992 ($ millions)

Current assets	$15	Accounts payable	$10
Net fixed assets	15	Notes payable	0
Total	$30	Bonds payable	10
		Common equity	10
		Total	$30

CDC had sales for the year ended 1/31/92 of $60 million. The firm follows a policy of paying all net earnings out to its common stockholders in cash dividends. Thus, CDC generates no funds from its earnings that can be used to expand its operations (assume that depreciation expense is just equal to the cost of replacing worn-out assets).

a. If CDC anticipates sales of $80 million during the coming year, develop a pro forma balance sheet for the firm for 1/31/93. Assume that current assets vary as a percent of sales, net fixed assets remain unchanged, accounts payable vary as a percent of sales, and use notes payable as a balancing entry.

b. How much "new" financing will CDC need next year?

c. What limitations does the percent of sales forecast method suffer from? Discuss briefly.

13–10B. (*Financial Forecasting—Discretionary Financing Needed*) Symbolic Logic Corporation (SLC) is a technological leader in the application of surface mount technology in the manufacture of printed circuit boards used in the personal computer industry. The firm has recently patented an advanced version of its original path-breaking technology and expects sales to grow from their present level of $5 million to $8 million by the end of the coming year. Since the firm is at present operating at full capacity it expects to have to increase its investment in both current and fixed assets in proportion to the predicted increase in sales.

The firm's net profits were 7 percent of current year's sales but are expected to rise to 8 percent of next year's sales. To help support its anticipated growth in asset needs next year, the firm has suspended plans to pay cash dividends to its stockholders. In years past a $1.25 per share dividend has been paid annually.

Symbolic Logic Corporation ($ millions)

	Present Level	Percent of Sales	Projected Level
Current assets	$2.5		
Net fixed assets	3.0		
Total	$5.5		
Accounts payable	$1.0		
Accrued expenses	0.5		
Notes payable	—		
Current liabilities	$1.5		
Long-term debt	$2.0		
Common stock	0.5		
Retained earnings	1.5		
Common equity	$2.0		
Total	$5.5		

SLC's payables and accrued expenses are expected to vary directly with sales. In addition, notes payable will be used to supply the funds needed to finance next year's operations and that are not forthcoming from other sources.

a. Fill in the table and project the firm's needs for discretionary financing. Use notes payable as the balancing entry for future discretionary financing needed.

b. Compare SLC's current ratio and debt ratio (total liabilities/total assets) before the growth in sales and after. What was the effect of the expanded sales on these two dimensions of SLC's financial condition?

c. What difference, if any, would have resulted if SLC's sales had risen to $6 million in one year and $8 million only after two years? Discuss only; no calculations required.

13–11B. (*Financial Forecasting—Changing Credit Policy*) Carrier Pigeon Communications (CPC) has $400,000 invested in receivables throughout much of the year. It has annual credit sales of $3,500,000 and a gross profit margin of 75 percent.

a. What is CPC's average collection period? [*Hint:* Recall that average collection period = accounts receivable/(credit sales/360).]

b. By how much would CPC be able to reduce its accounts receivable if it were to change its credit policies in a way that reduced its average collection period to 30 days without affecting annual credit sales?

13–12B. (*Forecasting Discretionary Financing Needs*) Royal Charter, Inc., estimates that it invests 40 cents in assets for each dollar of new sales. However, 5 cents in profits are produced by each dollar of additional sales, of which 1 cent can be reinvested in the firm. If sales rise from their present level of $5 million by $500,000 next year, and the ratio of spontaneous liabilities of sales is .15, what will be the firm's need for discretionary financing? (*Hint:* In this situation you do not know what the firm's existing level of assets is, nor do you know how those assets have been financed. Thus, you must estimate the change in financing needs and match this change with the expected changes in spontaneous liabilities, retained earnings, and other sources of discretionary financing.)

13–13B. (*Preparation of a Cash Budget*) Halsey Enterprises has projected its sales for the first eight months of 1993 as follows:

January	$120,000	May	$225,000
February	160,000	June	250,000
March	140,000	July	210,000
April	190,000	August	220,000

Halsey collects 30 percent of its sales in the month of the sale, 30 percent in the month following the sale, and the remaining 40 percent two months following the sale. During November and December of 1992 Halsey's sales were $230,000 and $225,000, respectively.

Halsey purchases raw materials two months in advance of its sales equal to 75 percent of its final sales. The supplier is paid one month after delivery. Thus, purchases for April sales are made in February and payment is made in March.

In addition, Halsey pays $12,000 per month for rent and $20,000 each month for other expenditures. Tax prepayments of $26,500 are made each quarter beginning in March. The company's cash balance as of December 31, 1992, was $28,000; a minimum balance of $25,000 must be maintained at all times to satisfy the firm's bank line of credit agreement. Halsey has arranged with its bank for short-term credit at an interest rate of 12 percent per annum (1 percent per month) to be paid monthly. Borrowing to meet estimated monthly cash needs takes place at the beginning of the month, but interest is not paid until the end of the following month. Consequently, if the firm were to need to borrow $50,000 during the month of April, then it would pay $500 (= .01 × $50,000) in interest during May. Finally, Halsey follows a policy of repaying any outstanding short-term debt in any month in which its cash balance exceeds the minimum desired balance of $25,000.

a. Halsey needs to know what its cash requirements will be for the next six months so that it can renegotiate the terms of its short-term credit agreement with its bank, if necessary. To evaluate this problem the firm plans to evaluate the impact of a ±20 percent variation in its monthly sales efforts. Prepare a six-month cash budget for Halsey and use it to evaluate the firm's cash needs.

b. Halsey has a $200,000 note due in July. Will the firm have sufficient cash to repay the loan?

Suggested Application for *DISCLOSURE*®

Use the percentage-of-sales method to prepare a pro forma balance sheet three years from the date of the most recent balance sheet shown in *Disclosure* for Motorola.

In developing the balance sheet, make the following assumptions:

1. the firm's net profit margin (net income/net sales) will remain the same as in the most recent year's data;
2. accounts payable and acrued expenses will increase proportionately with sales;
3. sales are expected to increase at an annual rate of 12 percent per year over the next three years;
4. other current liabilities will not change over the period;
5. long-term debt will increase or decrease as needed for financing the firm's growth in sales (i.e., the is a plug figure to balance the pro forma balance sheet);
6. the ratio of dividends to net income will remain the same as in the most recent year; and
7. no new stock (common or preferred) will be issued.

Use the following format to prepare your pro forma balance sheet:

Current assets	$
Property, plant, and equipment	
Other assets	_____
Total assets	$_____

Accounts Payable	$
Accrued expenses	
Other current liabilities	_____
Total current liabilities	$_____
Long-term debt	$_____
Preferred stock	
Common stock	
Capital surplus	
Retained earnings	_____
Total liabilities and equity	$_____

SS-1. Calico Sales Co., Inc., Pro Forma Income Statement

Sales		$4,000,000
COGS (70%)		(2,800,000)
Gross profit		1,200,000
Operating expense		
Selling expense (5%)	$200,000	
Administrative expense	500,000	
Depreciation expense	300,000	(1,000,000)
Net operating income		200,000
Interest		(50,000)
Earnings before taxes		150.000
Taxes (40%)		(60,000)
Net income		$ 90,000

Although the office renovation expenditure and debt retirement are surely cash outflows, they do not enter the income statement directly. These expenditures affect expenses for the period's income statement only through their effect on depreciation and interest expense. A cash budget would indicate the full cash impact of the renovation and debt retirement expenditures.

SS-2. Odom Manufacturing Co. Pro Forma Balance Sheet

a.

Cash	$ 320,000	Accounts payable	$ 750,000
Accounts receivable	760,000	Notes payable	475,000
Inventory	940,000	Total current liabilities	$1,225,000
Total current assets	$2,020,000	Long-term debt	1,300,000
Property, plant, and		Common stock	600,000
equipment	$1,905,000	Retained earnings	800,000
		Total liabilities and	
Total assets	$3,925,000	shareholders' equity	$3,925,000

b. To assess whether or not the firm's liquidity position has improved with the securing of the $500,000 loan, its current financial position must be compared with its position before the loan was granted.

	Position Before Loan	Position After Loan
Current ratio	1.34	1.65
Acid test ratio	0.72	0.88

These two ratios indicate that there has been an improvement in Odom's liquidity position and that the firm was justified in seeking the loan and in allocating the funds as previously described.

SS-3.

	May	June	July	Aug.
Sales	$100,000	$100,000	$120,000	$150,000
Purchases	60,000	60,000	50,000	40,000
Cash Receipts:				
Collections from month of sale (20%)	20,000	20,000	24,000	30,000
1 month later (50% of uncollected amount)		40,000	48,000	48,000
2 months later (balance)			40,000	40,000
Total receipts			$104,000	$118,000
Cash Disbursements:				
Payments for purchases—				
From 1 month earlier			$ 30,000	$ 25,000
From current month			$ 25,000	20,000
Total			$ 55,000	$ 45,000
Miscellaneous cash expenses			4,000	4,000
Labor expense (5% of sales)			6,000	7,500
General and administrative expense ($50,000 per month)			50,000	50,000
Truck purchase			0	60,000
Cash dividends			9,000	—
Total disbursements			(124,000)	(166,500)
			(20,000)	(48,500)
Plus: Beginning cash balance			30,000	30,000
Less: Interest on short-term borrowing (1% of prior month's borrowing)				(200)
Equals: Ending cash balance—without borrowing			10,000	(18,700)
Financing needed to reach target cash balance			20,000	48,700
Cumulative borrowing			20,000	68,700

APPENDIX 13A

Microcomputers and Spreadsheet Software in Financial Planning

In the body of the chapter we briefly discussed the role of personal computers and spreadsheet software in financial planning. The purpose of this appendix is to illustrate how a computerized financial planning model can be constructed and used. Before we jump into that exercise, however, let's first talk about effective spreadsheet design.

How to Design an Effective Spreadsheet Model

Back in the dark ages of computing, when we had to program computers using languages such as Fortran, Cobol, and Pascal, we were told to always "flowchart" our programs. These flowcharts were like outlines, and they helped organize the programmer's work so that others could more easily follow it. A current equivalent of flowcharting can be of great use to spreadsheet users. The particular methodology was devised by Urschel [1987] and is summarized in the following box:[4]

[4]W. Urschel, "Worksheets by Design," *PC World* (September 1987).

The four blocks provide a useful structure for the person building the spreadsheet model. They also make it easy for others to interpret and use the model. We will illustrate this recommended structure in the development of the spreadsheet model for the cash budgeting exercise that follows.

Spreadsheet Modeling Exercise

Cramer Enterprises, Inc., has projected its sales for the first eight months of 1993 as follows:

January	$100,000	May	$275,000
February	140,000	June	250,000
March	150,000	July	200,000
April	250,000	August	120,000

Cramer collects 20 percent of its sales in the month of the sale, 50 percent in the month following the sale, and the remaining 30 percent two months following the sale. During November and December of 1992 Cramer's sales were $220,000 and $175,000, respectively.

Cramer purchases raw materials two months in advance of its sales equal to 65 percent of those sales. The supplier is paid one month after delivery. Thus, purchases for April sales are made in February and payment is made in March.

In addition, Cramer pays $10,000 per month for rent and $20,000 each month for other expenditures. Tax prepayments of $22,500 are made each quarter beginning in March. The company's cash balance as of December 31, 1992, was $22,000; a minimum balance of $20,000 must be maintained at all times to satisfy the firm's bank line of credit agreement. Cramer has arranged with its bank for short-term credit at an interest rate of 12 percent per annum (1 percent per month) to be paid monthly. Borrowing to meet estimated monthly cash needs takes place at the beginning of the month, but interest is not paid until the end of the following month. Consequently, if the firm were to need to borrow $50,000 during the month of April, then it would pay $500 (= .01 × $50,000) in interest during May. Finally, Cramer follows a policy of repaying any outstanding short-term debt in any month in which its cash balance exceeds the minimum desired balance of $20,000.

Cramer faces two related problems. First, the firm needs to know what its cash requirements will be for the next six months so that it can renegotiate the terms of its short-term credit agreement with its bank, if necessary. Second, Cramer has a $200,000 note due June 30 and needs to determine whether it will have sufficient cash to repay the loan.

Sample Spreadsheet Model

Table 13A–1 contains the the cash budget for Cramer spanning the first six months of 1993. The model is composed of four blocks, following the procedure discussed earlier. Note that the first block contains all those elements that the analyst might wish to use in performing a sensitivity analysis of the final outcome. The second contains raw data inputs, and the third consists of intermediate calculations necessary to support the bottom line results found in block 4.

A quick analysis of the results indicate the following: Cramer will not need to borrow until March, when it will need an additional $27,500, and then in April, when its total borrowing needs rise to $97,025. In May the firm will be able to retire $31,530 of its short-term borrowing, and by June it will be able to retire all the seasonal debt it borrowed over the planning period. However, the firm's projected cash balance for June is only $33,850, which is insufficient to retire the $200,000 note by June 30.

	A	B	C	D	E	F	G	H	I
1				TABLE 13A–1.					
2				Cramer Enterprises, Inc.					
3				Cash Budget: January–June 1993					
4									
5	Block 1: Assumptions								
6									
7	Minimum Cash Balance		20,000						
8	Beginning Cash Balance		22,000						
9									
10	Sales Expansion %		0.00%		Annual Interest				
11	Purchases as a % Sales		65%		Rate	12.00%			
12									
13	Collections:	Current Mo.	1 Mo. Later	2 Mo. Later					
14		20%	50%	30%					
15									
16	Block 2: Inputs								
17									
18	Historical Sales and Base Case Sales Predictions for Future Sales								
19	January	100,000		May	275,000				
20	February	140,000		June	250,000				
21	March	150,000		July	200,000				
22	April	250,000		August	120,000				

	A	B	C	D	E	F	G	H	I
23				(TABLE 13A–1 cont.)					
24	Block 3: Calculations								
25									
26									
27		November	December	January	February	March	April	May	June
28		220,000	175,000	100,000	140,000	150,000	250,000	275,000	250,000
29	Collections:								
30	Month of sales			20,000	28,000	30,000	50,000	55,000	50,000
31	First month			87,500	50,000	70,000	75,000	125,000	137,500
32	Second month			66,000	52,500	30,000	42,000	45,000	75,000
33	Total collections			173,500	130,500	130,000	167,000	225,000	262,500
34	Purchases	65,000	91,000	97,500	162,500	178,750	162,500	130,000	97,500
35	Payments		65,000	91,000	97,500	162,500	178,750	162,500	130,000
36									
37	*Cash Budget for January through June*			January	February	March	April	May	June
38									
39	*Cash Receipts*			173,500	130,500	130,000	167,000	225,000	262,500
40	(collections)								
41	Cash Disbursements								
42	Payments for Purchases			91,000	97,500	162,500	178,750	162,500	130,000
43	Rent			10,000	10,000	10,000	10,000	10,000	10,000
44	Other Expenditures			20,000	20,000	20,000	20,000	20,000	20,000
45	Tax Deposits					22,500			22,500
46	Interest on S-T						275	970	655
47	Borrowing								
48	*Total Disbursements*			121,000	127,500	215,000	209,025	193,470	183,155
49									
50	*Net Monthly Change*			52,500	3,000	−85,000	−42,025	31,530	79,345
51									
52	Block 4: Bottom Line								
53									
54	Beginning Cash Balance			22,000	74,500	77,500	−7,500	20,000	20,000
55	Ending Cash (No Borrowing)			74,500	77,500	−7,500	−49,525	51,530	99,345
56	Needed (No Borrowing)			0	0	27,500	69,525	0	0
57	Loan Repayment			0	0	0	0	31,530	65,495
58	Ending Cash Balance			74,500	77,500	20,000	20,000	20,000	33,850
59	Cumulative Borrowing			0	0	27,500	97,025	65,495	0
60									

At this point you might want to explore the sensitivity of the cash requirements of the firm to changes in projected levels of sales. In the assumptions block of the model you will see a variable called "Sales Expansion %." This variable allows the analyst to increase the January through September sales forecasts by an arbitrary percentage and then see the impact of the change on the firm's cash requirements. For example, decreasing sales by −20 percent or increasing them by +20 percent has the following impact on the firm's projected level of borrowing for the months of March, April, and May:

Sales Expansion %	Cumulative Borrowing Needs		
	March	April	May
−20	$ 2,900	$ 45,229	$ 25,681
−10	15,200	71,127	45,588
0	27,500	97,025	65,495
10	39,800	122,923	85,402
20	52,100	148,821	105,309

The effect of changes in projected sales on Cramer's cumulative borrowing needs is dramatic. A ±20 percent variation in sales estimates leads to an increase in the maximum level of borrowing from $45,229 to $148,821 for the planning period. This is but one type of sensitivity analysis that Cramer might want to perform. The real value of having a spreadsheet model of the financial forecasting problem is the ease with which the user can perform such analyses.

Cell Formulas in the Model

Table 13A–2 contains the model's cell formulas for blocks 3 and 4 and the month of January. Note that this spreadsheet was done using the Excel spreadsheet program; however, the cell formulas differ only slightly for Lotus 1–2–3. The principal difference is that Lotus formulas begin with a "+" or "−" rather than an "=". Of course, there are other differences in the two programs, and we will point out one of them in the following discussion.

Perhaps the most interesting cell formula in the spreadsheet model is found in block 4 of the model, where the debt repayment for the month is calculated. The cell formula for cell D57 is the following:

=IF((AND(C59>0,D55>$C$7)),MIN(C59,D55-$C$7),0)

This statement calculates the debt repayment. Note that the loan repayment is made *only* when two conditions are met. The first is that the cumulative borrowing be greater than zero (C59>0) and, second, that the firm have excess cash on hand that can be used to repay a portion of the debt (D55>$C$7). If both these conditions are satisfied, then the debt repayment is set equal to the *minimum* of the amount of short-term debt owed (cell C59) or the amount of excess cash over and above the desired

TABLE 13A–2.
Cell Formulas for the Cramer Cash Budget Problem
for November Through January

	A	B	C	D
23				
24	Block 3: Calculations			
25				
26				
27		November	December	January
28		220000	175000	=B19*(1+$C$10)
29	Collections:			
30	Month of Sales			=$B$14*D28
31	First month			=$C$14*C28
32	Second month			=$D$14*B28
33	Total collections			=$D$26+D31+D32
34	Purchases	=$C$11*D28	=$C$11*E28	=$C$11*F28
35	Payments		=B34	=C34
36				
37	*Cash Budget*			January
38				
39	*Cash Receipts*			=D33
40	(collections)			
41	Cash Disbursements			
42	Payments for Purchases			=D35
43	Rent			10000
44	Other Expenditures			20000
45	Tax Deposits			
46	Interest on S-T			
47	Borrowing			
48	*Total Disbursements*			=SUM(D42:D47)
49				
50	*Net Monthly Change*			=D39-D48
51				
52	Block 4: Bottom Line			
53				
54	Beginning Cash Balance			=$C$8
55	Ending Cash (No Borrowing)			=D50+D54
56	Needed (Borrowing)			=IF(D55-$C$7>0,0,$C$7-D55)
57	Loan Repayment			=IF((AND(C59>0,D55>$C$7)),MIN(C59,D55-$C$7),0)
58	Ending Cash Balance			=D50+D54+D56
59	Cumulative Borrowing			=D56

minimum balance (D55-$C$7). The corresponding cell formula using Lotus 1–2–3 is slightly different and appears as follows:

$$@IF((C59>0\#and\#D55>\$C\$5),@MIN(C59,D55-\$C\$5),0)$$

The result in both instances is the same, however. This example cell formula demonstrates the fact that you can incorporate fairly sophisticated logic into your spreadsheet model.

CONCLUSION

VIDEO CASE 4

Bond-Rating Agencies: Using Financial Analysis to Forecast the Riskiness of Bonds

from ABC News, *Business World*, June 23, 1991

When we introduced Video Case 4 on page 441, we asked some questions that you should now review.

The information required for any analysis depends on the question you are trying to answer. In the case of giving a quality rating to a municipal bond, you want to know if the city issuing the bond can pay it back. Moreover, you would like to know how easily the city can make the repayment; that is, how much safety is there in the city's ability to service the debt obligations. If repayment is certain, then you assign the bond a high rating (AAA or AA); however, if there are situations that might threaten repayment, a lower rating is assigned. Similar to analyzing a corporate bond, you want to examine items such as the *interest coverage ration, leverage ratio,* and *the stability of the revenue stream.* Cities and states differ from firms because they raise money through taxation, not the sale of goods. Therefore you need to examine the tax base to determine the revenue stream or the stability of the tax revenues. The tax revenues of states that rely on just a sales tax or just an income tax may be affected differently during economic downturns than states using both types of taxing mechanisms. Other outstanding debt, such as previously issued bonds, also affects a city or state's ability to service its debt.

The bond rating assigned to a city or state government matters very much. When the bond-rating agencies threatened to lower the rating on bonds about to be issued by the state of California from AAA to AA, the state treasurer estimated that it would cost the state of California (actually, taxpayers in California) an extra $8 million per year in higher interest expense over the life of the bonds, about 25 years (*New York Times,* December 14, 1991, I8, p. 4). Therefore, because the impact of a mistake is significant, bond-rating agencies have to do careful, thorough research.

Discussion question

1. A strategy that might work well for rating agencies is to underrate all bonds slightly but safely: *When in doubt, downgrade.* This would help assure that the rating agency is rarely embarrassed by a municipality (or corporation) that defaults after the agency gave the organization a good rating. Who is injured by such a strategy? Why is such a strategy unlikely to exist in the marketplace? As an investor, if you knew that rating agencies used such a strategy, what would you do?

Suggested reading

WAKEMAN, L. MACDONALD. "The Real Function of Bond Rating Agencies," in *The Revolution in Corporate Finance*, ed. Stern and Chew. New York: Blackwell, 1986.

PART 5

WORKING-CAPITAL MANAGEMENT

Working capital refers to a firm's current assets. Net working capital is the difference between the current assets and liabilities, and indicates the firm's liquidity position. Current assets include cash, marketable securities, accounts receivable, and inventories. These are the assets that allow the firm to operate from day to day—to pay employees, provide credit to customers, and assure that goods are available. Because current assets make up more than 40 percent of the average firm's total assets, proper management of current assets is important to a firm's long-term financial health. It is not surprising that financial managers spend much of their time on working-capital management. Chapter 14 introduces the general concepts used in working-capital management, and the remaining chapters in the section, Chapters 15 through 17, work through the more specific aspects of working-capital management.

Working-capital management decisions depend on the same logic as other financial decisions: How does the decision affect shareholder wealth? The working-capital management decisions facing the manager include the following: What minimum cash balance should the firm maintain? How should cash surpluses be invested? What type of credit policy should the firm adopt? Should there be a cash discount for early payment? How should the firm grant credit or increased credit to customers? What level of inventories should the firm maintain? What are the benefits and costs of holding too much or too little inventory? Should the firm try to take advantage of cash discounts offered by its suppliers? What type of short-term financing should the firm use? Bank loans? Supplier credit?

In these chapters a great deal of up-to-the-minute practical detail is provided to help answer these questions and other questions that the financial manager must struggle with on a daily basis.

INTRODUCTION

VIDEO CASE 5

The Campeau Bankruptcy: The Sudden Deterioration of Supplier Accounts Receivable

from ABC News, *Business World*, January 7, 1990

Most small firms are so strapped for cash that they live or die according to the management of their working capital. A few uncollectible credit accounts or some inventory that has to be written off can make the difference between profits and problems. This video case documents how the Campeau retailing empire bankruptcy has created serious problems for many of the small businesses supplying Campeau stores. As the video shows, when one link in the chain of credit sales snaps (or looks like it is about to snap) the effect is felt far down the line. Designers hire contractors to manufacture their designs and factors to collect their receivables. If the designers do not get paid, the contractors and factors get hurt too. As we discussed in the section opener, managing a firm's working capital—its cash, accounts receivable, credit policy, and inventory—is crucial to most firms' financial health. This video case shows how sensitive small firms are to sudden changes in the value of these accounts.

- If you were supplying the Campeau chain what could you have done to foresee the problems?
- Is there something special about the garment industry that might make it particularly prone to these types of problems?
- If suppliers choose not to deliver their garments to Campeau during the Christmas season, what other options do they have? And what happens to items left over after the Christmas season?
- Which suppliers do you think were hit hardest by Campeau's problems?

As you read Chapters 14 through 17, consider these questions. At the end of this section we will return to this case and discuss some issues it raises to address these questions.

CHAPTER 14

Introduction to Working-Capital Management

Managing Current Assets ● Managing Current Liabilities ● Appropriate Level of Working Capital

Traditionally, **working capital** has been defined as the firm's investment in current assets. **Current assets** comprise all assets that the firm expects to convert into cash within the year, including cash, marketable securities, accounts receivable, and inventories. Managing the firm's working capital, however, has come to mean more than simply managing the firm's investment in current assets. In fact, a more descriptive title for this chapter might be "Net Working-Capital Management," where **net working capital** refers to the difference in the firm's current assets and its current liabilities:

$$\text{net working capital} = \text{current assets} - \text{current liabilities} \qquad \textbf{14-1}$$

Thus, in managing the firm's net working capital, we are concerned with *managing the firm's liquidity*. This entails managing two related aspects of the firm's operations:

1. Investment in current assets
2. Use of short-term or current liabilities

Perspective in Finance

This chapter provides the basic principles underlying the analysis of each of these aspects. These principles are then applied in each of the following chapters in this section. Specifically, Chapter 15 discusses the management of the firm's investment in cash and marketable securities, while Chapter 16 addresses the problems associated with managing the firm's investments in accounts receivable and inventories. Finally, Chapter 17 presents a discussion of sources of short-term or current liabilities and their role in the sound financial management of the firm.

Managing Current Assets

Other things remaining the same, the greater the firm's investment in current assets, the greater its liquidity. As a means of increasing its liquidity, the firm may choose to invest additional funds in cash or marketable securities. Such action involves a tradeoff, however, since such assets earn little or no return. The firm thus finds that it can reduce its risk of illiquidity only by reducing its overall return on invested funds, and vice versa.

The Risk–Return Tradeoff from Investing in Current Assets

The **risk–return tradeoff** involved in managing the firm's liquidity via investing in marketable securities is illustrated in the following example. Firms A and B are identical in every respect but one: Firm B has invested $10,000 in marketable securities, which has been financed with common equity; that is, the firm sold shares of common stock and raised $10,000. The balance sheets and net incomes of the two firms are shown in Table 14–1. Note that Firm A has a current ratio of 2.5 (reflecting net working capital of $30,000) and earns a 10 percent return on its total assets. Firm B, with its larger investment in marketable securities, has a current ratio of 3 and has net working capital of $40,000. Since the marketable securities earn a return of only 6 percent before taxes (3 percent after taxes with a 50 percent tax rate), Firm B earns only 9.6 percent on its total investment. Thus, investing in current assets, and in particular in marketable securities, does have a favorable effect on liquidity, but it also has an unfavorable effect on the firm's rate of return earned on invested funds. The risk–return tradeoff involved in holding more cash and marketable securities, therefore, is one of added liquidity versus reduced profitability.

LIQUIDITY ↑ PROFITABILITY ↓

Balance Sheets		Firm A		Firm B
Cash		$ 1,000		$ 1,000
Marketable securities				10,000
Accounts receivable		19,000		19,000
Inventories		30,000		30,000
Current assets		$ 50,000		$ 60,000
Net fixed assets		100,000		100,000
Total		$150,000		$160,000
Current liabilities		$ 20,000		$ 20,000
Long-term debt		30,000		30,000
Common equity		100,000		110,000
Total		$150,000		$160,000
Net income		$ 15,000		$ 15,300[a]
Current ratio [current assets/current liabilities]	$\dfrac{\$50,000}{\$20,000} =$	2.5 times	$\dfrac{\$60,000}{\$20,000} =$	3.0 times
Net working capital [current assets – current liabilities]		$ 30,000		$ 40,000
Return on total assets [net income/total assets]	$\dfrac{\$15,000}{\$150,000} =$	10%	$\dfrac{\$15,300}{\$160,000} =$	9.6%

TABLE 14–1.
Effects of Investing in Current Assets on Liquidity and Profitability

[a]During the year firm B held $10,000 in marketable securities, which earned a 6 percent return or $600 for the year. After paying taxes at a rate of 50 percent, the firm netted a $300 return on this investment.

Managing Current Liabilities

The second and final determinant of the firm's net working capital relates to its use of current versus long-term debt. Here, too, the firm faces a risk–return tradeoff. *Other things remaining the same, the greater the firm's reliance on short-term debt or current liabilities in financing its asset investments, the lower will be its liquidity.* On the other hand, the use of current liabilities offers some very real advantages in that they can be less costly than long-term financing and they provide the firm with a flexible means of financing its fluctuating needs for assets. We will discuss each of the advantages and disadvantages associated with the use of current liabilities as a source of financing. In addition, we will give an example to demonstrate the risk–return tradeoff associated with the use of current versus long-term liabilities.

Advantages of Current Liabilities

Flexibility

Current liabilities offer the firm a flexible source of financing. They can be used to match the timing of a firm's needs for short-term financing. If, for example, a firm needs funds for a three-month period during each year to finance a seasonal expansion in inventories, then a three-month loan can provide substantial cost savings over a long-term loan (even if the interest rate on short-term financing should be higher). The use of long-term debt in this situation involves borrowing for the entire year rather than for the period when the funds are needed, which increases the amount of interest the firm must pay. This brings us to the second advantage generally associated with the use of short-term financing.

Interest Cost

In general, interest rates on short-term debt are lower than on long-term debt for a given borrower. This relationship was introduced earlier in Chapter 2 and is referred to as the **term structure of interest rates.** For a given firm, the term structure might appear as follows:

Loan Maturity	Interest Rate
3 months	9.00%
6 months	9.25
1 year	9.80
3 years	10.20
5 years	10.90
10 years	11.40
30 years	12.80

Note that this term structure reflects the rates of interest applicable to a given borrower at a particular point in time; it would not, for example, describe the rates of interest available to another borrower or even those applicable to the same borrower at a different point in time.

Disadvantages of Current Liabilities

The use of current liabilities or short-term debt as opposed to long-term debt subjects the firm to a greater risk of illiquidity for two reasons. First, short-term debt, due to its very nature, must be repaid or rolled over more often, and so it increases the possibility that the firm's financial condition might deteriorate to a point where the needed funds might not be available.[1]

A second disadvantage of short-term debt is the uncertainty of interest costs from year to year. For example, a firm borrowing during a six-month period each year to finance a seasonal expansion in current assets might incur a different rate of interest each year. This rate reflects the current rate of interest at the time of the loan, as well as the lender's perception of the firm's riskiness. If fixed rate long-term debt were used, the interest cost would be known for the entire period of the loan agreement.

The Risk–Return Tradeoff from Using Current Liabilities

Consider the risk–return characteristics of firm X and firm Y, whose balance sheets and income statements are given in Table 14–2 on the next page. Both firms had the same seasonal needs for financing throughout the past year. In

---

[1]The dangers of such a policy are readily apparent in the experiences of firms that have been forced into bankruptcy. Penn Central, for example, had $80 million in short-term debt that it was unable to refinance (roll over) when it became bankrupt.

BASIC FINANCIAL MANAGEMENT IN PRACTICE

How Firms Manage Their Working Capital

	Electronic Computers[a]		Book Publishing[b]		Air Transportation[c]		Oil and Gas Exploration[d]		Gasoline Stations[e]		Restaurants[f]	
Current Assets (%)	72	73	68	70	46	39	48	33	45	48	25	25
Current Liabilities (%)	40	38	43	53	37	43	40	31	38	39	36	38
Long-Term Debt (%)	12	11	17	14	23	26	27	28	27	22	32	33

The above table provides aggregate percent of assets numbers for six different industries and two time periods. The first column of percentages under each industry reflects the average for the corresponding industry for 1990–91, and the second column reflects the 1986–87 average.

Averaged across all industries for both years current assets were 49% of total assets, while current liabilities averaged 40% and long-term debt was only 23%. There is substantial variation in the relative importance of current assets across industries, with electronic computers and book publishing having the highest percent of assets invested in current assets, and restaurants having the lowest. Note also the relationship between current liabilities and long-term debt. With the exception of the restaurant industry, current liabilities are anywhere from two to four times as large as long-term debt.

So what can we conclude? First, current assets are a major component of a firm's investments and can constitute as much as 70 percent of firm assets. Second, most firms maintain current ratios (i.e., current assets/ current liabilities) greater than 1, although this relationship varies both across industries and over time. Finally, long-term debt is frequently a less important source of financing (measured in terms of its percent of assets) than are current liabilities. The message is this. Working-capital management is extremely important to the firm's financial well-being and deserves serious consideration!

Reprinted with permission, copyright Robert Morris Associates 1991 (Philadelphia, PA.).
[a]Manufacturers—Electronic Computers SIC #3571. [b]Manufacturers—Books: Publishing, or Publishing and Printing SIC #2731. [c]Services—Air Transportation, Scheduled SIC #4512. [d]Contractors—Oil and Gas Well Drilling SIC #1381. [e]Retailers—Gasoline Service Stations SIC #5541. [f]Retailers—Restaurants SIC #5812.

Balance Sheets		
	Firm X	Firm Y
Current assets	$ 60,000	$ 60,000
Net fixed assets	140,000	140,000
Total	$200,000	$200,000
Accounts payable	$ 20,000	$ 20,000
Notes payable	—	40,000
Current liabilities	$ 20,000	$ 60,000
Long-term debt	40,000	—
Common equity	140,000	140,000
Total	$200,000	$200,000

Income Statements		
Net operating income	$ 44,000	$ 44,000
Less: Interest expense	4,000[a]	900[b]
Earnings before taxes	40,000	43,100
Less: Taxes (50%)	20,000	21,550
Net income	$ 20,000	$ 21,550

Current ratio $\left[\dfrac{\text{current assets}}{\text{current liabilities}}\right]$ $\dfrac{\$60,000}{\$20,000} = 3$ times $\qquad \dfrac{\$60,000}{\$60,000} = 1$ time

Net working capital
[current assets − current liabilities] $\qquad$ $40,000 $\qquad$ $0

Return on total assets $\left[\dfrac{\text{net income}}{\text{total assets}}\right]$ $\dfrac{\$20,000}{\$200,000} = 10\%$ $\qquad \dfrac{\$21,550}{\$200,000} = 10.8\%$

[a]Firm X paid interest during the entire year on $40,000 in long-term debt at a rate of 10 percent. Its interest expense for the year was .10 × $40,000 = $4,000.
[b]Firm Y paid interest on $40,000 for one month and on $20,000 for four months at 9 percent interest during the year. Thus, Firm Y's interest expense for the year equals $40,000 × .09 × 1/12 plus $20,000 × .09 × 4/12, or $300 + $600 = $900.

December they each required $40,000 to finance a seasonal expansion in accounts receivable. In addition, during the four-month period beginning with August and extending through November both firms needed $20,000 to support a seasonal buildup in inventories. Firm X financed its seasonal financing requirements using $40,000 in long-term debt carrying an annual interest rate of 10 percent. Firm Y, on the other hand, satisfied its seasonal financing needs using short-term borrowing on which it paid 9 percent interest. Since firm Y borrowed only when it needed the funds and did so at the lower rate of interest on short-term debt, its interest expense for the year was only $900, whereas firm X incurred $4,000 in annual interest expense.[2]

The end result of the two firm's financing policies is evidenced in their current ratio, net working capital, and return on total assets, which appear at the bottom of Table 14–2. Firm X, using long-term rather than short-term debt, has a current ratio of 3 and $40,000 in net working capital, whereas firm Y's current ratio is only 1, which represents zero net working capital. However, owing to its lower interest expense, firm Y was able to earn 10.8 percent on its invested funds, whereas firm X produced a 10 percent return. Thus, a firm can reduce its risk of illiquidity through the use of long-term debt at the expense of a reduction in its return on invested funds. Once again we see that the risk–return tradeoff involves an increased risk of illiquidity versus increased profitability.

liquidity + profitability ↑

[2]Interest expense calculations are found in the footnotes to Table 14–2.

Appropriate Level of Working Capital

Managing the firm's net working capital (its liquidity) has been shown to involve simultaneous and interrelated decisions regarding investment in current assets and use of current liabilities. Fortunately, a guiding principle exists that can be used as a benchmark for the firm's working-capital policies: the **hedging principle,** or **principle of self-liquidating debt.** This principle provides a guide to the maintenance of a level of liquidity sufficient for the firm to meet its maturing obligations on time.[3]

Perspective in Finance

In Chapter 10 we discussed the firm's financing decision in terms of the choice between debt and equity sources of financing. There is, however, yet another critical dimension of the firm's financing decision. This relates to the maturity structure of the firm's debt. How should the decision be made as to whether to use short-term or current debt or longer-maturity debt? This is one of the fundamental questions addressed in this chapter and one that is critically important to the financial success of the firm. Basically, the hedging principle is one possible rule of thumb for guiding a firm's debt maturity financing decisions. This principle states that financing maturity should follow the cash-flow-producing characteristics of the asset being financed. For example, an asset that is expected to provide cash flows over an extended period of time such as five years should, in accordance with the hedging principle, be financed with debt with a pattern of similar cash flow requirements. Note that when the hedging principle is followed, the firm's debt will "self-liquidate" because the assets being financed will generate sufficient cash to retire the debt as it comes due.

Hedging Principle

Very simply, the *hedging principle* involves *matching* the cash-flow-generating characteristics of an asset with the maturity of the source of financing used to finance its acquisition. For example, a seasonal expansion in inventories, according to the hedging principle, should be financed with a short-term loan or current liability. The rationale underlying the rule is straightforward. Funds are needed for a limited period of time, and when that time has passed, the cash needed to repay the loan will be generated by the sale of the extra inventory items. Obtaining the needed funds from a long-term source (longer than one year) would mean that the firm would still have the funds after the inventories they helped finance had been sold. In this case the firm would have "excess" liquidity, which it either holds in cash or invests in low-yield marketable securities until the seasonal increase in inventories occurs again and the funds are needed. This would result in an overall lowering of firm profits, as we saw earlier in the example presented in Table 14–2.

Consider a second example in which a firm purchases a new conveyor belt system, which is expected to produce cash savings to the firm by eliminating the need for two laborers and, consequently, their salaries. This amounts to an

---

[3]A value-maximizing approach to the management of the firm's liquidity involves assessing the value of the benefits derived from increasing the firm's investment in liquid assets and weighing them against the added costs to the firm's owners resulting from investing in low-yield current assets. Unfortunately, the benefits derived from increased liquidity relate to the expected costs of bankruptcy to the firm's owners, and these costs are "unmeasurable" by existing technology. Thus, a "valuation" approach to liquidity management exists only in the theoretical realm.

annual savings of $14,000, while the conveyor belt costs $150,000 to install and will last 20 years. If the firm chooses to finance this asset with a 1-year note, then it will not be able to repay the loan from the cash flow generated by the asset. In accordance with the hedging principle, the firm should finance the asset with a source of financing that more nearly matches the expected life and cash-flow-generating characteristics of the asset. In this case, a 15- to 20-year loan would be more appropriate.

Permanent and Temporary Assets

The notion of *maturity matching* in the hedging principle can be most easily understood when we think in terms of the distinction between **permanent** and **temporary investments in assets** as opposed to the more traditional fixed and current asset categories. A permanent investment in an asset is an investment that the firm expects to hold for a period longer than one year. Note that we are referring to the period of time the firm plans to hold an investment, not the useful life of the asset. For example, permanent investments are made in the firm's minimum level of current assets, as well as in its fixed assets. Temporary asset investments, on the other hand, are composed of current assets that will be liquidated and *not* replaced within the current year. Thus, some part of the firm's current assets is permanent and the remainder is temporary. For example, a seasonal increase in level of inventories is a temporary investment; the buildup in inventories will be eliminated when it is no longer needed.

Spontaneous, Temporary, and Permanent Sources of Financing

Since total assets must always equal the sum of spontaneous, temporary, and permanent sources of financing, the hedging approach provides the financial manager with the basis for determining the sources of financing to use at any point in time.

Now, what constitutes a temporary, permanent, or spontaneous source of financing? Temporary sources of financing consist of current liabilities. Short-term notes payable (discussed in Chapter 17) constitute the most common example of a temporary source of financing. Examples of notes payable include unsecured bank loans, commercial paper, and loans secured by accounts receivable and inventories. Permanent sources of financing include inter-mediate-term loans (discussed in Chapter 19), long-term debt, preferred stock, and common equity (discussed in Chapter 20).

Spontaneous sources of financing consist of trade credit and other accounts payable that arise *spontaneously* in the firm's day-to-day operations. For example, as the firm acquires materials for its inventories, trade credit is often made available spontaneously or on *demand* from the firm's suppliers. Trade credit appears on the firm's balance sheet as accounts payable, and the size of the accounts payable balance varies directly with the firm's purchases of inventory items. In turn, inventory purchases are related to anticipated sales. Thus, part of the financing needed by the firm is spontaneously provided in the form of trade credit.

In addition to trade credit, wages and salaries payable, accrued interest, and accrued taxes also provide valuable sources of spontaneous financing. These expenses accrue throughout the period until they are paid. For example, if a firm has a wage expense of $10,000 a week and pays its employees monthly, then its employees effectively provide financing equal to $10,000 by the end of the first week following a payday, $20,000 by the end of the second week, and so forth. Since these expenses generally arise in direct conjunction with the firm's ongoing operations, they too are referred to as *spontaneous*.

Hedging Principle: Graphic Illustration

The hedging principle can now be stated very succinctly: *Asset needs of the firm not financed by spontaneous sources should be financed in accordance with this rule: Permanent asset investments are financed with permanent sources, and temporary investments are financed with temporary sources.*

The hedging principle is depicted in Figure 14–1. Total assets are broken down into temporary and permanent asset investment categories. The firm's permanent investment in assets is financed by the use of permanent sources of financing (intermediate- and long-term debt, preferred stock, and common equity) or spontaneous sources (trade credit and other accounts payable).[4] Its temporary investment in assets is financed with temporary (short-term) debt.

Modifications to the Hedging Principle

Figures 14–2 and 14–3 depict two modifications of the strict hedging approach to working-capital management. In Figure 14–2 the firm follows a more cautious plan, whereby permanent sources of financing exceed permanent assets in trough periods so that excess cash is available (which must be invested in marketable securities).[5] Note that the firm actually has excess liquidity during the low ebb of its asset cycle, and thus faces a lower risk of being caught short of cash than a firm that follows the pure hedging approach. However, the firm also increases its investment in relatively low-yield assets so that its return on investment is diminished (recall the example from Table 14–1).

---

[4]For illustration purposes spontaneous sources of financing are treated as if their amount were fixed. In practice, of course, spontaneous sources of financing fluctuate with the firm's purchases and its expenditures for wages, salaries, taxes, and other items that are paid on a delayed basis. In the appendix to this chapter we will discuss the more realistic case of fluctuating spontaneous sources of financing.

[5]Marketable securities and cash management are discussed in Chapter 15.

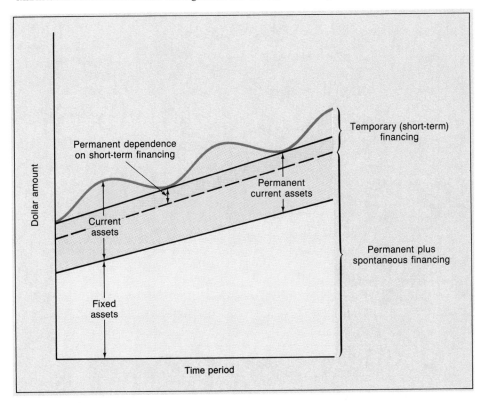

FIGURE 14–1.
Hedging Financing Strategy

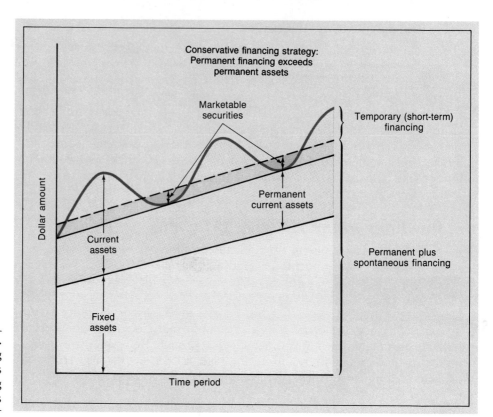

FIGURE 14–2.
Conservative Financing
Strategy: Spontaneous Plus
Permanent Sources of Financing
Exceed Permanent Assets

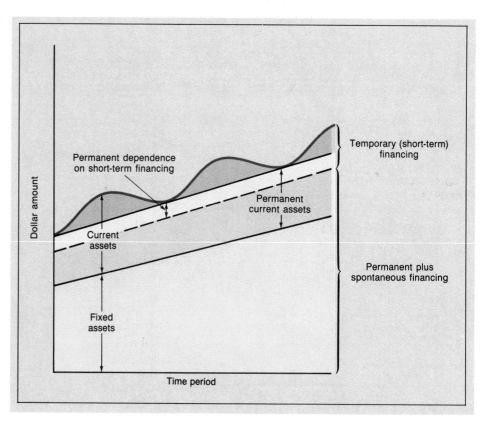

FIGURE 14–3.
Aggressive Financing Strategy:
Permanent Reliance on
Short-Term Financing

In contrast, Figure 14–3 depicts a firm that continually finances a part of its permanent asset needs with temporary or short-term funds and thus follows a more aggressive strategy in managing its working capital. Even when its investment in asset needs is lowest, the firm must still rely on short-term or temporary financing. Such a firm would be subject to increased risks of a cash shortfall in that it must depend on a continual rollover or replacement of its short-term debt with more short-term debt. The benefit derived from following such a policy relates to the possible savings resulting from the use of lower-cost short-term debt (as opposed to long-term debt—recall the example presented in Table 14–2).

Most firms will not exclusively follow any one of the three strategies outlined here in determining their reliance on short-term credit. Instead, a firm will at times find itself overly reliant on permanent financing and thus holding excess cash; at other times it may have to rely on short-term financing throughout an entire operating cycle. The hedging approach does, however, provide an important benchmark that can be used to guide decisions regarding the appropriate use of short-term credit.

SUMMARY

Working-capital management involves managing the firm's liquidity, which in turn involves managing (1) the firm's investment in current assets and (2) its use of current liabilities. Each of these problems involves risk–return tradeoffs. Investing in current assets reduces the firm's risk of illiquidity at the expense of lowering its overall rate of return on its investment in assets. Furthermore, the use of long-term sources of financing enhances the firm's liquidity while reducing its rate of return on assets.

The *hedging principle*, or *principle of self-liquidating debt*, is a benchmark for working-capital decisions. Basically, this principle involves matching the cash-flow-generating characteristics of an asset with the cash flow requirements of the source of funds used to finance its acquisition.

Chapters 15 and 16 discuss the problems involved in managing the firm's investment in current assets. This includes the management of cash, marketable securities, accounts receivable, and inventories. Chapter 17 discusses short-term financing. Two basic problems are encountered in attempting to manage the firm's use of short-term financing: (1) How much short-term financing should the firm use? (2) What specific sources should be selected? This chapter addressed the first of these questions with the hedging principle. The answer to the second question involves analyzing the relative costs of the available sources of short-term credit, an issue addressed at length in Chapter 17.

STUDY QUESTIONS

14-1. Define and contrast the terms *working capital* and *net working capital*.

14-2. Discuss the risk–return relationship involved in the firm's asset investment decisions as that relationship pertains to working-capital management.

14-3. What advantages and disadvantages are generally associated with the use of short-term debt? Discuss.

14-4. Explain what is meant by the statement "The use of current liabilities as opposed to long-term debt subjects the firm to a greater risk of illiquidity."

14-5. Define the hedging principle. How can this principle be used in the management of working capital?

14-6. Define the following terms:
  a. Permanent asset investments
  b. Temporary asset investments
  c. Permanent sources of financing
  d. Temporary sources of financing
  e. Spontaneous sources of financing

SELF-TEST PROBLEMS

ST-1. (*Investing in Current Assets and the Return on Common Equity*) Walker Enterprises is presently evaluating its investment in working capital for the coming year. Specifically, the firm is analyzing its level of investment in current assets. The firm projects that it will have sales of $4,000,000 next year, and its fixed assets are projected to total $1,500,000. The firm pays interest at a rate of 10 percent on its short- and long-term debt (which is managed by the firm so as to equal a target of 40 percent of assets). The firm projects its earnings before interest and taxes to be 15 percent of sales and faces a 30 percent tax rate.
  a. If Walker decides to follow a working-capital strategy calling for current assets equal to 40 percent of sales, what will be the firm's return on common equity?
  b. Answer (a) for a current asset to sales ratio of 60 percent.
  c. Throughout this analysis we have assumed that the rate of return earned by the firm on sales is independent of its investment in current assets. Is this a valid assumption?

ST-2. (*Using Marketable Securities to Increase Liquidity*) The balance sheet for the Simplex Mfg. Co. follows for the year ended December 31, 19X5:

Simplex Mfg. Co. Balance Sheet, December 31, 19X5

Cash	$10,000	
Accounts receivable	50,000	
Inventories	40,000	
Total current assets		$100,000
Net fixed assets		100,000
Total		$200,000
Current liabilities	$ 60,000	
Long-term liabilities	40,000	
Common equity	100,000	
Total		$200,000

During 19X5 the firm earned net income after taxes of $20,000 based on net sales of $400,000.
  a. Calculate Simplex's current ratio, net working-capital position, and return on total assets ratio (net income/total assets) using the above information.
  b. The vice-president of finance at Simplex is considering a plan for enhancing the firm's liquidity. The plan involves raising $20,000 in common equity and investing in marketable securities that will earn 8 percent before taxes and 4.8 percent after taxes. Calculate Simplex's current ratio, net working capital, and return on total asset ratio after the plan has been implemented. (**Hint:** Net income will now become $20,000, plus .048 × $20,000, or $20,960.)
  c. Will the plan proposed in (b) enhance firm liquidity? Explain.
  d. What effect does the plan proposed in (b) have on firm profitability? Explain.

ST-3. (*Using Long-Term Debt to Increase Liquidity*) On April 30, 19X5, the Jamax Sales Company had the following balance sheet and income statement for the year just ended:

Jamax Sales Company Balance Sheet, April 30, 19X5

Current assets		$100,000	
Net fixed assets		200,000	
Total			$300,000
Accounts payable	$30,000		
Notes payable (14%)[a]	40,000		
Total		$ 70,000	
Long-term debt (10%)		100,000	
Common equity		130,000	
Total			$300,000

Partial Income Statement for the year ended April 30, 19X5

Net operating income	$72,800
Less: Interest expense[b]	12,800
Earnings before taxes	$60,000
Less: Taxes (50%)	30,000
Net income	$30,000

[a]The short-term notes are outstanding during the latter half of the firm's fiscal year in response to the firm's seasonal need for funds.
[b]Total interest expense for the year consists of 14% interest on the firm's $40,000 note for a six-month period (.14 × $40,000 × 1/2), $2,800, plus 10% of the firm's $100,000 long-term note for a full year (.10 × $100,000), or $10,000. Thus, total interest expense for the year is $2,800, plus $10,000 or $12,800.

a. Calculate Jamax's current ratio, net working capital, and return on total assets.
b. The treasurer of Jamax was recently advised by the firm's investment banker that its current ratio was considered below par. In fact, a current ratio of 2 was considered to be a sign of a healthy liquidity position. In response to this news the treasurer devised a plan whereby the firm would issue $40,000 in 13 percent long-term debt and pay off its short-term notes payable. This long-term note would be outstanding all year long, and when the funds were not needed to finance the firm's seasonal asset needs, they would be invested in marketable securities earning 8 percent before taxes. If the plan had been in effect last year, other things being the same, what would have been the firm's current ratio, net working capital, and return on total assets ratio? (*Hint:* The firm's net income with the change would have been $29,600.)
c. With implementation of the plan put forth in (b) did Jamax's liquidity improve to the desired level (based on a desired current ratio of 2.)?
d. How was the firm's profitability in relation to total investment affected by the change in financial policy?

STUDY PROBLEMS (SET A)

14–1A. (*Investing in Current Assets and the Return on Common Equity*) In June the MacMinn Company began planning for the coming year. A primary concern is its working-capital management policy. In particular, the firm's management is considering the effects of its investment in current assets on the return earned on common shareholders' equity. The firm projects that it will have sales of $8,000,000 next year, and its fixed assets are projected to total $2,000,000. It pays interest at a rate of 12 percent on its short- and long-term debt (which is managed by the firm so as to equal a target of 30 percent of assets). Finally, the firm projects its earnings before interest and taxes to be 15 percent of sales and faces a 30 percent tax rate.
    a. If MacMinn decides to follow a working-capital strategy calling for current assets equal to 40 percent of sales, what will be the firm's return on common equity?
    b. Answer (a) for a current-asset-to-sales ratio of 60 percent.

c. Throughout this analysis we have assumed that the rate of return earned by the firm on sales is independent of its investment in current assets. Is this a valid assumption?

14–2A. (*Managing Firm Liquidity*) As of September 30, 19X5, the balance sheet and income statement for Trecor Mfg. Company appeared as follows:

Trecor Mfg. Company
Balance Sheet, September 30, 19X5

Current assets	$ 500,000
Net fixed assets	500,000
Total	$1,000,000
Accounts payable	$ 100,000
Notes payable (17%)[a]	400,000
Total	$ 500,000
Long-term debt (12%)	100,000
Common equity	400,000
Total	$1,000,000

[a]Short-term notes are used to finance a three-month seasonal expansion in Trecor's asset needs. This period is the same for every year and extends from July through September with the note being due October 1.

Trecor Mfg. Company
Income Statement, September 30, 19X5

Net operating income	$195,666
Less: Interest expense[b]	(29,000)
Earnings before taxes	166,666
Less: Taxes (40%)	(66,666)
Net income	$100,000

[b]Interest expense was calculated as follows: Notes payable (.17 × $400,000 × 1/4 year)

$$= \$17,000$$

Long-term debt (.12 × $100,000 × 1 year)

$$= \underline{12,000}$$
$$\text{Total} = \$29,000$$

a. Calculate the current ratio, net working capital, return on total assets, and return on common equity ratio for Trecor.

b. Assume that you have just been hired as financial vice-president of Trecor. One of your first duties is to assess the firm's liquidity. Based on your analysis, you plan to issue $400,000 in common stock and use the proceeds to retire the firm's notes payable. Recalculate the ratios from (a) and assess the change in the firm's liquidity.

c. Given your actions in (b), assume now that in the future you will finance your three-month seasonal need for $400,000 using a long-term bond issue that will carry an interest cost of 15 percent. (Note that during the time the funds are needed your current assets increase by $400,000 because of increased inventories and receivables.) In addition, you estimate that during the nine months you do not need the funds, they can be invested in marketable securities to earn a rate of 10 percent. Recalculate the financial ratios from (a) for 19X6 where all revenues and nonfinance expenses are expected to be the same as in 19X5. Analyze the results of your plan.

14–3A. (*Managing Firm Liquidity*) Reanalyze (c) of problem 14–2A assuming that a three-month short-term note is used as opposed to the bonds. The note carries a rate of 15 percent per annum.

14–4A. (*The Hedging Principle*) H. O. Hielregal, Inc., estimates that its current assets are about 25 percent of sales. The firm's current balance sheet is presented here:

H. O. Hielregal Balance Sheet
December 31, 19X5 ($ millions)

Current assets	$2.0	Trade credit and	
Fixed assets	2.8	accounts payable	$ .8
		Long-term debt	1.0
Total	$4.8	Common equity	3.0
		Total	$4.8

Hielregal pays out all of its net income in cash dividends to its stockholders. Trade credit and accounts payable equal 10 percent of the firm's sales.

a. Based on the following five-year sales forecast, prepare five end-of-year pro forma balance sheets that indicate "additional financing needed" for each year as a balancing account. Fixed assets are expected to increase by $.2 million each year.

Year	Predicted Sales ($ Millions)
19X6	10
19X7	11
19X8	13
19X9	14
19X0	15

b. Using your answer to (a) above develop a financing policy for Hielregal that is consistent with the following goals:
  1. A minimum current ratio of 2 and a maximum of 3.
  2. A debt-to-total-assets ratio of 35 to 45 percent. You may issue new common stock to raise equity funds.

STUDY PROBLEMS (SET B)

14–1B. (*Investing in Current Assets and the Return on Common Equity*) The managers of Tharp's Tarps, Inc., are considering a possible change in their working-capital management policy. Specifically, they are concerned with the effect of their investment in current assets on the return earned on common shareholders' equity. They expect sales of $7,000,000 next year and project that fixed assets will total $2,000,000. The firm pays 11 percent interest on both short- and long-term debt (which is managed by the firm so as to equal a target of 30 percent of assets) and faces a 30 percent tax rate. Finally, the firm projects its earnings before interest and taxes to be 15 percent of sales.
  a. If management follows a working-capital strategy calling for current assets equal to 50 percent of sales, what will be the firm's return on common equity?
  b. Answer (a) for a current-asset-to-sales ratio of 40 percent.
  c. Is it reasonable to assume, as we did, that the rate of return earned by the firm on sales is independent of its investment in current assets?

14–2B. (*Managing Firm Liquidity*) As of September 30, 19X1, the balance sheet and income statement of No-Soy Foods, Inc., appeared as follows:

No-Soy Foods, Inc.
Balance Sheet, September 30, 19X1

Current assets	$ 625,000
Net fixed assets	400,000
Total	$1,025,000
Accounts payable	$ 125,000
Notes payable (17%)[a]	400,000
Total	$ 525,000
Long-term debt (12%)	100,000
Common equity	400,000
Total	$1,025,000

No-Soy Foods, Inc.
Income Statement, September 30, 19X1

Net operating income	$195,666
Less: Interest expense[b]	(29,000)
Earnings before taxes	166,666
Less: Taxes (40%)	(66,666)
Net income	$100,000

[a]Short-term notes are used to finance a three-month seasonal expansion in No-Soy Foods' asset needs. This period is the same for every year and extends from July through September with the note being due October 1.

[b]Interest expense was calculated as follows:
Notes payable (.17 × $400,000 × 1/4 year) = $17,000
Long-term debt (.12 × $100,000 × 1 year) = 12,000
Total = $29,000

  a. Calculate the current ratio, net working capital, return on total assets, and return on common equity ratio for No-Soy.
  b. Assume that you have just been hired as financial vice-president of No-Soy. One of your first duties is to assess the firm's liquidity. Based on your analysis, you plan to issue $400,000 in common stock and use the proceeds to retire the firm's notes payable. Recalculate the ratios from (a) and assess the change in the firm's liquidity.

c. Given your actions in (b), assume now that in the future you will finance your three-month seasonal need for $400,000 using a long-term bond issue that will carry an interest cost of 15 percent. (Note that during the time the funds are needed your current assets increase by $400,000 because of increased inventories and receivables.) In addition, you estimate that during the nine months you do not need the funds, they can be invested in marketable securities to earn a rate of 10 percent. Recalculate the financial ratios from (a) for 19X2 where all revenues and nonfinance expenses are expected to be the same as in 19X1. Analyze the results of your plan.

14-3B. (*Managing Firm Liquidity*) Reanalyze (c) of problem 14–2B assuming that a three-month short-term note is used as opposed to the bonds. The note carries a rate of 15 percent per annum.

14-4B. (*The Hedging Principle*) B. A. Freeman, Inc., successfully sells bail bond franchises throughout the country. Its founder, Mr. Freeman, estimates current assets to be 30 percent of sales. The firm's current balance sheet is as follows:

B. A. Freeman Balance Sheet
December 31, 19X1 ($ millions)

Current assets	$2.0	Trade credit and	
Fixed assets	2.8	accounts payable	$ .8
		Long-term debt	1.0
Total	$4.8	Common equity	3.0
		Total	$4.8

Freeman pays out all of its net income in cash dividends to its stockholders. Trade credit and accounts payable equal 10 percent of the firm's sales.

a. Based on the following five-year sales forecast, prepare five end-of-year pro forma balance sheets that indicate "additional financing needed" for each year as a balancing account. Fixed assets are expected to increase by $.3 million each year.

Year	Predicted Sales ($ Millions)
19X2	10
19X3	11
19X4	13
19X5	14
19X6	15

b. Using your answer to (a) develop a financing policy for Freeman that is consistent with the following goals:
 1. A minimum current ratio of 2.5 and a maximum of 3.5.
 2. A debt-to-total-assets ratio of 35 to 45 percent. You may issue new common stock to raise equity funds.

SELF-TEST SOLUTIONS

SS-1. a. Walker's pro forma balance sheet for next year will appear as follows:

Current assets	$1,600,000	Debt (40% of assets)	$1,240,000
Fixed assets	1,500,000	Owner's equity	1,860,000
Total	$3,100,000	Total	$3,100,000

Projected earnings are calculated as follows:

Sales	$4,000,000
EBIT (15%)	$ 600,000
Interest	(124,000)
EBT	$ 476,000
Taxes (30%)	(142,800)
Net income	$ 333,200

Thus, the firm's return on common equity is

$$\$333,200/\$1,860,000 = 17.9\%$$

b. Under this scenario, Walker's pro forma balance sheet for next year will appear as follows:

Current assets	$2,400,000	Debt (40% of assets)	$1,560,000
Fixed assets	1,500,000	Owner's equity	2,340,000
Total	$3,900,000	Total	$3,900,000

Projected earnings are calculated as follows:

Sales	$4,000,000
EBIT (15%)	$ 600,000
Interest	(156,000)
EBT	$ 444,000
Taxes	(133,200)
Net income	$ 310,800

Thus, the firm's return on common equity is $310,800/2,340,000 = 13.3\%$.

c. One would expect that the firm would earn some positive return from investing in current assets. For example, the firm could hold some of its current assets in marketable securities earning some positive rate of return. Note, however, that as long as these current assets earn a rate of return less than the cost of financing the investment, the rate of return on the common shareholders' equity will decrease with increased investment in current assets.

SS–2. a.
$$\text{current ratio} = \frac{\text{current assets}}{\text{current liabilities}}$$

$$= \frac{\$100,000}{\$60,000} = \underline{1.67 \times}$$

$$\text{net working capital} = \text{current assets} - \text{current liabilities}$$

$$= \$100,000 - \$60,000 = \underline{\$40,000}$$

$$\text{return on total assets} = \frac{\text{net income}}{\text{total assets}}$$

$$= \frac{\$ \ 20,000}{\$200,000} = \underline{10\%}$$

b.
$$\text{current ratio} = \frac{\$120,000}{\$ \ 60,000} = \underline{2 \times}$$

$$\text{net working capital} = \$120,000 - \$60,000 = \underline{\$60,000}$$

$$\text{return on total assets} = \frac{\$ \ 20,960}{220,000} = \underline{9.52\%}$$

c. Yes, the firm's liquidity position as measured by the current ratio and the amount of net working capital has definitely improved. However, as we see in the answer to (b), profitability has been adversely affected.

d. Simplex's return on total assets declined from 10 percent to 9.52 percent as a result of the new financing plan. This occurred because it was earning 10 percent after taxes on its $200,000 investment and it invested $20,000 in marketable securities earning only 4.8 percent after taxes. The result was a decline in firm profitability in relation to assets.

SS–3. a.
$$\text{current ratio} = \frac{\text{current assets}}{\text{current liabilities}}$$

$$= \frac{\$100,000}{\$70,000} = \underline{1.43 \times}$$

$$\text{net working capital} = \text{current assets} - \text{current liabilities}$$

$$= \$100,000 - \$70,000$$

$$= \underline{\$ \ 30,000}$$

$$\text{return on total assets} = \frac{\text{net income}}{\text{total assets}}$$

$$= \frac{\$ \ 30,000}{\$300,000}$$

$$= \underline{10\%}$$

b.

$$\text{current ratio} = \frac{\$100,000}{\$\ 30,000} = \underline{3.33\ \times}$$

$$\text{net working capital} = \$100,000 - \$30,000 = \underline{\$70,000}$$

$$\text{return on total assets} = \frac{\$\ 29,600}{300,000} = \underline{9.87\%}$$

c. Yes, the current ratio of 3.33 is now well above the 2 standard when the funds are needed.

d. Firm profitability declined slightly because the firm used a permanent source of financing to replace a more flexible short-term source. The firm actually saves interest expense through the plan during the six-month period when the funds are needed (13 percent on long-term funds versus 14 percent on short-term notes); however, during the six months when the funds are not needed, the firm can earn a before-tax return of only 8 percent, while the funds cost 13 percent.

In this case, the added liquidity of the plan appears to overshadow the modest loss in expected profitability.

CHAPTER 15

Cash and Marketable Securities Management

Why a Company Holds Cash • Variations in Liquid Asset Holdings • Cash Management Objectives and Decisions • Collection and Disbursement Procedures • Electronic Funds Transfer • Evaluation of Costs of Cash-Management Services • Composition of Marketable Securities Portfolio • A Glance at Actual Cash-Management Practices • Appendix 15A: Cash Management Models

Chapter 14 introduced and overviewed the concept of working-capital management. Now we will consider the various elements of the firm's working capital in some depth. This chapter and Appendix 15A center on the formulation of financial policies for management of cash and marketable securities. We explore three major areas: (1) techniques available to management for favorably influencing cash receipts and disbursements patterns, (2) sensible investment possibilities that enable the company productively to employ excess cash balances, and (3) some straightforward models that can assist financial officers in deciding on how much cash to hold. Appendix 15A presents these models.

First it will be helpful to distinguish among some terms. **Cash** is the currency and coin the firm has on hand in petty cash drawers, in cash registers, or in checking accounts at the various commercial banks where its demand deposits are maintained. **Marketable securities** are those security investments the firm can quickly convert into cash balances. Most firms in the United States tend to hold marketable securities with very short maturity periods—less than one year. No law, of course, dictates that instruments with longer terms to maturity must be avoided. Rather, the decision to keep the average maturity quite short is based upon some sound business reasoning, which will be discussed later. Marketable securities are also referred to as **near cash** or **near-cash assets** because they can be turned into cash in a short period of time. Taken together, cash and near cash are known as **liquid assets.**

Perspective in Finance

It is useful to think of the firm's cash balance as a reservoir that rises with cash inflows and falls with cash outflows. Any nonfinancial firm (in other words, any company that manufactures products, such as Ford Motor Company) desires to minimize its cash balances consistent with meeting its financial obligations in a timely manner.

Holding too much cash—what analysts tend to call "excess cash"—results in a loss of profitability to the firm. The auto manufacturer, for example, is not in *business to build up its cash reservoir. Rather, it wants to manage its cash balance in order to maximize its financial returns—this will enhance shareholder wealth.*

Our emphasis in this chapter is to learn how to effectively manage the firm's cash and marketable securities investments. We begin with a review of the basic cash flow process and the motives that economic units have for holding cash balances. In recent years the financial function of cash management has grown in stature. Now, trade associations and professional certifications exist just for this function, and cash management is usually part of treasury management within the company.

Why a Company Holds Cash

A thorough understanding of why and how a firm holds cash requires an accurate conception of how cash flows into and through the enterprise. Figure 15–1 depicts the process of cash generation and disposition in a typical manufacturing setting. The arrows designate the direction of the flow—that is, whether the cash balance increases or decreases.

Cash Flow Process

The firm experiences irregular increases in its cash holdings from several external sources. Funds can be obtained in the financial markets from the sale of securities, such as bonds, preferred stock, and common stock, or the firm can enter into nonmarketable debt contracts with lenders such as commercial banks. These irregular cash inflows do not occur on a daily basis. They tend to be episodic; the financing arrangements that give rise to them are effected at wide intervals. The reason is that external financing contracts usually involve

FIGURE 15–1.
The Cash Generation and Disposition Process

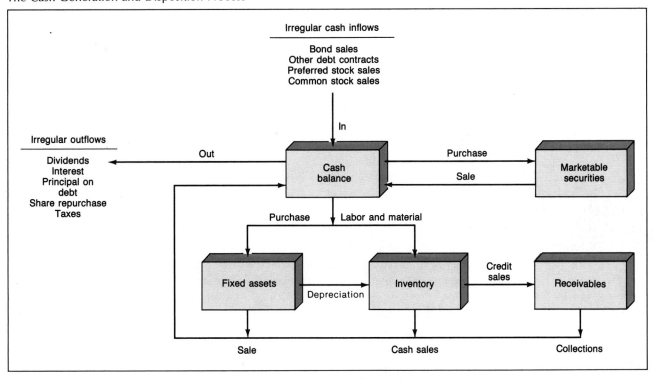

huge sums of money stemming from a major need identified by the company's management, and these needs do not occur every day. For example, a new product might be in the launching process, or a plant expansion might be required to provide added productive capacity.

In most organizations the financial officer responsible for cash management also controls the transactions that affect the firm's investment in marketable securities. As excess cash becomes temporarily available, marketable securities are purchased. When cash is in short supply, a portion of the marketable securities portfolio is liquidated.

Whereas the irregular cash inflows are from external sources, the other main sources of cash to the firm arise from internal operations and occur on a more regular basis. Over long periods, the largest receipts come from accounts receivable collections and to a lesser extent from direct cash sales of finished goods. Many manufacturing concerns also generate cash on a regular basis through the liquidation of scrap or obsolete inventory. In the automobile industry, large and costly machines called chip crushers grind waste metal into fine scrap, which brings considerable revenue to the major producers. At various times fixed assets may also be sold, thereby generating some cash inflow. This is not a large source of funds except in unusual situations where, for instance, a complete plant renovation may be taking place.

Apart from the investment of excess cash in near-cash assets, the cash balance experiences reductions for three key reasons. First, on an irregular basis, withdrawals are made to (1) pay cash dividends on preferred and common stock shares, (2) meet interest requirements on debt contracts, (3) repay the principal borrowed from creditors, (4) buy the firm's own shares in the financial markets for use in executive compensation plans or as an alternative to paying a cash dividend, and (5) pay tax bills. Again, by an *irregular basis* we mean items *not* occurring on a daily or frequent schedule. Second, the company's capital expenditure program designates that fixed assets be acquired at various intervals. Third, inventories are purchased on a regular basis to ensure a steady flow of finished goods off the production line. Note that the arrow linking the investment in fixed assets with the inventory account is labeled *depreciation*. This indicates that a portion of the cost of fixed assets is charged against the products coming off the assembly line. This cost is subsequently recovered through the sale of the finished goods inventory, since the product selling price will be set by management to cover all the costs of production, including depreciation.

The variety of influences that constantly affect the cash balance held by the firm can be synthesized in terms of the classic motives for holding cash, as identified in the literature of economic theory.

Motives for Holding Cash

In a classic economic treatise John Maynard Keynes segmented the firm's, or any economic unit's, demand for cash into three categories: (1) the transactions motive, (2) the precautionary motive, and (3) the speculative motive.[1]

Transactions Motive

Balances held for transactions purposes allow the firm to dispense with cash needs that arise in the ordinary course of doing business. In Figure 15–1, transactions balances would be used to meet the irregular outflows as well as the planned acquisition of fixed assets and inventories.

---

[1]John Maynard Keynes, *The General Theory of Employment, Interest, and Money* (New York: Harcourt Brace Jovanovich, 1936).

The relative amount of transactions cash held is significantly affected by the industry in which the firm operates. If revenues can be forecast to fall within a tight range of outcomes, then the ratio of cash and near cash to total assets will be less for the firm than if the prospective cash inflows might be expected to vary over a wide range. It is well known that utilities can forecast cash receipts quite accurately, because of stable demand for their services. This enables the firm to stagger its billings throughout the month and to time them to coincide with planned expenditures. Inflows and outflows of cash are thus synchronized. We would expect the cash holdings of utility firms relative to sales or assets to be less than those associated with a major retail chain that sells groceries. The grocery concern experiences many transactions each day, almost all of which involve an exchange of cash.

Firms competing in the *same* industry may experience notably different strains on their cash balances. Transactions balances in the railroad industry are simultaneously influenced by a seasonal factor and a geographic factor. Consider the seasonal factor. During the summer months, all the railroads that crisscross the North American continent pay out large amounts of cash for materials and labor necessary to upgrade track beds. Old ties are replaced, new rail is laid, switches are adjusted, signal systems are overhauled. Now, consider the geographic factor. The railroad companies that serve the northern routes, including Canada, also suffer sizable cash drains throughout the winter season because of harsh weather conditions. Snow must be swept out of switches, ice is actually burned off the rails, and derailments occur with far greater frequency than at any other time of the year. Cash balances for the railroads in the northern states and Canada can therefore be expected to be relatively higher during the winter season than for railroads operating in more southerly areas.

The Precautionary Motive

Precautionary balances are a buffer stock of liquid assets. This motive for holding cash relates to the maintenance of balances to be used to satisfy possible, but as yet indefinite, needs.

In our discussion of transactions balances we saw that cash flow predictability could affect a firm's cash holdings through synchronization of receipts and disbursements. Cash flow predictability also has a material influence on the firm's demand for cash through the precautionary motive. The airline industry provides a typical illustration. Air passenger carriers are plagued with a high degree of cash flow uncertainty. The weather, rising fuel costs, and continual strikes by operating personnel make cash forecasting difficult for any airline. The upshot of this problem is that because of all the things that *might* happen, the minimum cash balances desired by the management of the air carriers tend to be large.

In addition to cash flow predictability, the precautionary motive for holding cash is affected by access to external funds. Especially important are cash sources that can be tapped on short notice. Good banking relationships and established lines of credit can reduce the need to keep cash on hand. This unused borrowing power obviates somewhat the need to invest in precautionary balances.

In actual business practice, the precautionary motive is met to a large extent by the holding of a portfolio of *liquid assets*, not just cash. Notice in Figure 15–1 the two-way flow of funds between the company's holdings of cash and marketable securities. In large corporate organizations, funds may flow either into or out of the marketable securities portfolio on a daily basis. Because some actual rate of return can be earned on the near-cash assets, compared with a zero rate of return available on cash holdings, it is logical that investment in marketable securities will meet in part the firm's precautionary needs.

The Speculative Motive

Cash is held for speculative purposes in order to take advantage of potential profit-making situations. Construction firms that build private dwellings will at times accumulate cash in anticipation of a significant drop in lumber costs. If the price of building supplies does drop, the companies that built up their cash balances stand to profit by purchasing materials in large quantities. This will reduce their cost of goods sold and increase their net profit margin. Generally, the speculative motive is the least important component of a firm's preference for liquidity. The transactions and precautionary motives account for most of the reasons why a company holds cash balances.

Variations in Liquid Asset Holdings

Decisions that concern the amounts of liquid assets to hold rest with the financial officer responsible for cash management. Several factors that can be expected to influence the financial officer's investment in cash and near cash have just been reviewed. Not all these factors affect every firm. Moreover, factors that do affect many companies do so in differing degrees. Because the executives responsible for the ultimate cash management choices have different risk-bearing preferences, we might expect that liquid asset holdings among firms would exhibit considerable variation. Table 15–1 shows us that this is true.

Allegheny Power and American Electric Power are both utilities and operate in an environment where cash flows are highly predictable relative to other industries. We see that Allegheny Power holds a very small proportion of its total assets in the form of liquid assets—only 1.9 percent. American Electric Power invests more heavily in liquidity, but to the extent of only 2.2 percent of total assets.

Even firms that operate in a regulated setting can experience sudden shifts in liquidity. At the end of 1978, Allegheny Power had a liquid asset to total asset ratio of 0.5 percent. At the end of 1981, however, it stood at a much higher 3.1 percent. By the end of 1982, this ratio had decreased to 0.3 percent, but as we see in Table 15–1, it rose to 1.9 percent by year-end 1988. Companies continually adjust their liquid asset positions to meet operating needs and to respond to the real investment requirements of strategic plans.

Chrysler Corporation and Ford Motor Company compete in a more risky global arena than do electric utilities like Allegheny Power and American Electric Power. We expect, then, the overall cash management policies of firms in the automobile industry to be quite different from those of utilities. Chrysler is one of the great corporate rebuilding stories of recent decades. The firm required special relief in the form of the federal Chrysler Corporation Loan Guarantee Act of 1979. Without that act, it is unlikely that the firm would exist today.

Notice in Table 15–1 that Chrysler and Ford maintain stronger liquidity postures than either Allegheny or American Electric Power. At the end of 1988,

TABLE 15–1.
Liquid Asset Positions of
Selected Firms for 1988 (%)

Ratios	Allegheny Power System	American Electric Power	Chrysler Corp.	Ford Motor	Amoco Corp.	Chevron Corp.	Exxon Corp.
Cash to total assets	0.8	1.2	3.4	3.8	0.8	3.8	3.1
Marketable securities to total assets	1.1	1.0	3.3	2.6	1.0	1.5	0.1
Total liquid assets to total assets	1.9	2.2	6.7	6.4	1.8	5.3	3.2

Source: Annual Reports, 1988, for the respective companies.

Chrysler held 6.7 percent of its total assets in highly liquid form; Ford held 6.4 percent of its assets in liquid form. Chrysler held a greater proportion of its liquid assets in the form of marketable securities rather than cash. There is an important advantage to the type of liquid asset mix displayed by Chrysler. Marketable securities earn a positive rate of return, while the mere holding of cash earns a zero return.

The examples of Chrysler and Ford suggest that it takes *more* than a knowledge of the industry class in which a firm operates to understand its cash management policies. This is emphasized further by looking at the liquid asset structures of the three firms in the petroleum refining industry also displayed in Table 15–1. Notice that Amoco, Chevron, and Exxon had liquid asset to total asset ratios at the end of 1988 of 1.8 percent, 5.3 percent, and 3.2 percent, respectively. Amoco, in fact, had a liquid asset structure quite similar to that usually found in the electric utility industry. Chevron, conversely, invested more heavily in total liquidity—to a level similar to that found in the auto manufacturing industry. The executives of these three petroleum companies perceive their liquidity needs quite differently. Different corporate strategies and different risk-bearing preferences with respect to the chances of running out of cash cause variations in levels of liquidity investment.

These examples of the liquid asset holdings of some specific firms are only snapshots at a fixed point in time. We must remember that assets are acquired, wasted, and sold every day—the management of cash and near cash is a dynamic process. The flow of cash as depicted in Figure 15–1 never ceases. Cash inflows and outflows affecting the size of the firm's cash reservoir occur simultaneously. This ensures that the overall problem of cash and marketable securities management will remain complex. To cut through this complexity it is imperative that the firm's cash management system be designed to operate with clearly defined objectives.

Perspective in Finance

Any company can benefit from a properly designed cash-management system. If you identify what you believe to be a superbly run business organization, the odds are that firm has in place a sound cash-management system. Before we explore several cash-management techniques, it is necessary to introduce (1) the risk–return tradeoff, (2) the objectives, and (3) the decisions that comprise the center of the cash-management process. Keep in mind that the billion-dollar company will save millions each year by grasping these concepts—while the small and midsized organization may actually enhance its overall chances of survival. The following section provides the rationale and structure for knowing about all of the techniques and financial instruments discussed in the remainder of the chapter.

Cash Management Objectives and Decisions

The Risk–Return Tradeoff

A companywide cash management program must be concerned with minimizing the firm's risk of insolvency. In the context of cash management, the term **insolvency** describes the situation where the firm is unable to meet its maturing liabilities on time. In such a case the company is **technically insolvent** in that it lacks the necessary liquidity to make prompt payment on its current debt obligations. A firm could avoid this problem by carrying large cash balances to pay the bills that come due. Production, after all, would soon come to a halt should payments for raw material purchases be continually late or omitted entirely. The firm's suppliers would just cut off further shipments. In fact, fear of irritating a key supplier by being past due on the payment of a trade payable does cause some financial managers to invest in too much liquidity.

The management of the company's cash position, however, is one of those problem areas where you are criticized if you don't and criticized if you do. True, the production process will eventually be halted should too little cash be available to pay bills. Although if excessive cash balances are carried, the value of the enterprise in the financial marketplace will be suppressed because of the large cost of income forgone. The explicit return earned on idle cash balances is zero.

The financial manager must strike an acceptable balance between holding too much cash and too little cash. This is the focal point of the risk–return tradeoff. A large cash investment minimizes the chances of insolvency, but penalizes company profitability. A small cash investment frees excess balances for investment in both marketable securities and longer-lived assets; this enhances company profitability and the value of the firm's common shares, but increases the chances of running out of cash.

The Objectives

The risk–return tradeoff can be reduced to two prime objectives for the firm's cash-management system:

1. Enough cash must be on hand to meet the disbursal needs that arise in the course of doing business.
2. Investment in idle cash balances must be reduced to a minimum.

Evaluation of these operational objectives, and a conscious attempt on the part of management to meet them, gives rise to the need for some typical cash-management decisions.

The Decisions

Two conditions would allow the firm to operate for extended periods with cash balances near or at a level of zero: (1) a completely accurate forecast of net cash flows over the planning horizon and (2) perfect synchronization of cash receipts and disbursements.

Cash flow forecasting is the initial step in any effective cash-management program. This is usually accomplished by the finance function's evaluation of data supplied by the marketing and production functions in the company. The *cash budget* is a device used to forecast the cash flows over the planning period. (Cash-budgeting procedures were explained in Chapter 13.) Here we must emphasize, that the net cash flows pinpointed in the formal cash budget are only estimates, subject to considerable variation. A totally accurate cash flow projection is an ideal, not a reality.

Our discussion of the cash flow process depicted in Figure 15–1 showed that inflows and outflows are not synchronized. Some inflows and outflows are irregular; others are more continual. Some finished goods are sold directly for cash, but more likely the sales will be on account. The receivables, then, will have to be collected before a cash inflow is realized. Raw materials have to be purchased, but several suppliers are probably used, and each may have its own payment date. Further, no law of doing business fixes receivable collections to coincide with raw material payments dates. So the second criterion that would permit operation of the firm with extremely low cash balances is not met in actual practice either.

Given that the firm will, as a matter of necessity, invest in some cash balances, certain types of decisions related to the size of those balances dominate the cash-management process. These include decisions that answer the following questions:

1. What can be done to speed up cash collections and slow down or better control cash outflows?

2. What should be the composition of a marketable securities portfolio?

3. How should investment in liquid assets be split between actual cash holdings and marketable securities?

The remainder of this chapter dwells on the first two of these three questions. The third is explored in the appendix.

Perspective in Finance

Although the sheer number of cash collection and payment techniques is large, the concepts on which those techniques rest are quite simple. Controlling *the cash inflow and outflow is a major theme of treasury management. But, within the confines of ethical management, the cash manager is always thinking (1) "How can I speed up the firm's cash receipts?" and (2) "How can I slow down the firm's cash payments and not irritate too many important constituencies— such as suppliers?"*

The critical point is that cash saved becomes available for investment elsewhere in the company's operations, and at a positive rate of return this will increase total profitability. Grasping the elements of cash management requires that you understand the concept of cash float. *We address the concept of float and float reduction early in the discussion on collection and disbursement procedures.*

Collection and Disbursement Procedures

The efficiency of the firm's cash-management program can be enhanced by knowledge and use of various procedures aimed at (1) accelerating cash receipts and (2) improving the methods used to disburse cash. We will see that greater opportunity for corporate profit improvement lies with the cash receipts side of the funds flow process, although it would be unwise to ignore opportunities for favorably affecting cash-disbursement practices.

Managing the Cash Inflow[2]

The reduction of float lies at the center of the many approaches employed to speed up cash receipts. **Float** (or total float) has four elements as follows:

1. **Mail float** is caused by the time lapse from the moment a customer mails a remittance check until the firm begins to process it.

2. **Processing float** is caused by the time required for the firm to process remittance checks before they can be deposited in the bank.

3. **Transit float** is caused by the time necessary for a deposited check to clear through the commercial banking system and become usable funds to the company. Credit is deferred for a maximum of two business days on checks that are cleared through the Federal Reserve System.[3]

---

[2]The discussions on cash receipt and disbursement procedures draw heavily on materials that were generously provided by the managements of the Chase Manhattan Bank, Continental Bank, and First National Bank of Chicago.

[3]One of the things that the Federal Reserve System does is provide check-clearing facilities for depository institutions. This is referred to as the "clearing system," or the "clearing mechanism." These terms will be used several times in this chapter. Should the paying bank and collecting bank be located in the same Federal Reserve District, credit will be available to the collecting bank in one business day. Local clearinghouses exist apart from the Federal Reserve's clearing mechanism. These involve a consortium of local banks that meet each business day, through their representatives, in order to clear checks drawn on each other. Same-day funds availability is possible through the use of a local clearinghouse if published settlement times are met.

4. **Disbursing float** derives from the fact that funds are available in the company's bank account until its payment check has cleared through the banking system. Typically, funds available in the firm's banks *exceed* the balances indicated on its own books (ledgers).

We will use the term *float* to refer to the total of its four elements just described. Float reduction can yield considerable benefits in terms of usable funds that are released for company use and returns produced on such freed-up balances. As an example, for 1991 IBM reported total revenues of $64.8 billion. The amount of usable funds that would be released if IBM could achieve a one-day reduction in float can be approximated by dividing annual revenues (sales) by the number of days in a year.[4] In this case one day's freed-up balances would be

$$\frac{\text{annual revenues}}{\text{days in year}} = \frac{\$64,800,000,000}{365} = \$177,534,247$$

If these released funds, which represent one day's sales, of approximately $177.5 million could be invested to return 6 percent a year, then the annual value of the one-day float reduction would be

$$\text{(sales per day)} \times \text{(assumed yield)} = \$177,534,247 \times .06 = \$10,652,055$$

It is clear that effective cash management can yield impressive opportunities for profit improvement. Let us look now at specific techniques for reducing float.

The Lock-Box Arrangement

The lock-box system is the most widely used commercial banking service for expediting cash gathering. Banks have offered this service since 1946. Such a system speeds up the conversion of receipts into usable funds by reducing both mail and processing float. In addition, it is possible to reduce transit float if lock boxes are located near Federal Reserve Banks and their branches. For large corporations that receive checks from all parts of the country, float reductions of two to four days are not unusual.

Figure 15–2 illustrates an elementary, but typical, cash collection system for a hypothetical firm. It also shows the origin of mail float, processing float, and transit float. In this system the customer places his or her remittance check in the U.S. mail, which is then delivered to the firm's headquarters. This causes the mail float. On the check's arrival at the firm's headquarters (or local collection center), general accounting personnel must go through the book-keeping procedures needed to prepare them for local deposit. The checks are then deposited. This causes the processing float. The checks are then forwarded for payment through the commercial bank clearing mechanism. The checks will be charged against the customer's own bank account. At this point the checks are said to be "paid" and become "good" funds available for use by the company that received them. This bank clearing procedure represents transit float and, as we said earlier, can amount to a delay of up to two business days.[5]

The lock-box arrangement shown in Figure 15–3 is based on a simple procedure. The firm's customers are instructed to mail their remittance checks

---

[4]Frederick W. Searby, "Use Your Hidden Cash Resources," *Harvard Business Review* 46 (March–April 1968), pp. 71–80.

[5]A clear description of the Federal Reserve check-clearing mechanism can be found in Thomas A. Gittings, "Sinking Float," *Economic Perspectives*, Federal Reserve Bank of Chicago, 4 (May–June 1980), 19–23.

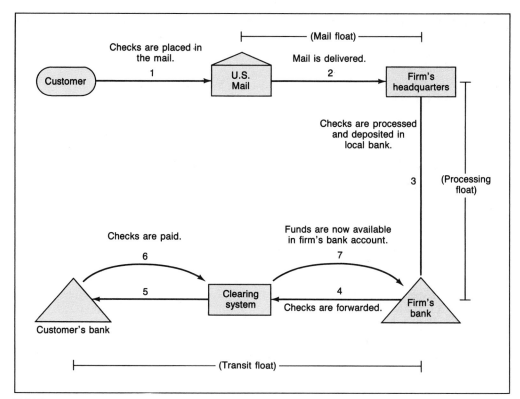

FIGURE 15–2.
Ordinary Cash-Gathering System

FIGURE 15–3.
Simple Lock-Box System

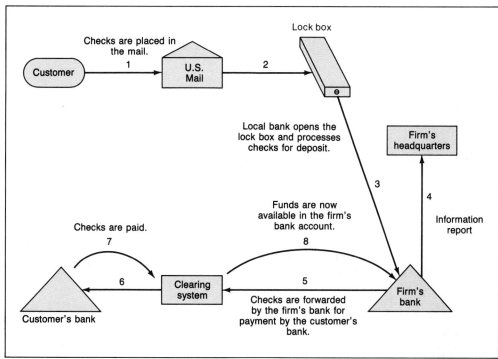

not to company headquarters or regional offices, but to a numbered Post Office box. The bank that is providing the lock-box service is authorized to open the box, collect the mail, process the checks, and deposit the checks directly into the company's account.

Commercial banks have gone to great lengths in refining their lock-box procedures in an attempt to gain an edge over their competitors. Major banks have their own zip codes to accelerate postal handling. Even helicopters are sometimes used to speed documents from the Post Office to the bank or from the bank to a local clearinghouse.

Typically a large bank will collect payments from the lock box at one- to two-hour intervals, 365 days of the year. During peak business hours, the bank may pick up mail every 30 minutes.

Once the mail is received at the bank, the checks will be examined, totaled, photocopied, and microfilmed. A deposit form is then prepared by the bank, and each batch of processed checks is forwarded to the collection department for clearance. Funds deposited in this manner are usually available for company use in one business day or less.

The bank can notify the firm via some type of telecommunications system the same day deposits are made as to their amount. At the conclusion of each day all check photocopies, invoices, deposit slips, and any other documents included with the remittances are mailed to the firm.

Note that the firm that receives checks from all over the country will have to use several lock boxes to take full advantage of a reduction in mail float. The firm's major bank should be able to offer as a service a detailed lock-box study, analyzing the company's receipt patterns to determine the proper number and location of lock-box receiving points.

The two systems described by Figures 15–2 and 15–3 are summarized in Table 15–2. There, the step numbers refer to those shown in Figure 15–2 (the

TABLE 15–2.
Comparison of Ordinary Cash-Gathering System with Simple Lock-Box System

Step Numbers	Ordinary System and Time		Advantage of Lock Box
1	Customer writes check and places it in the mail	1 Day	
2	Mail is delivered to firm's headquarters	2 Days	Mail will not have to travel as far. Result: save 1 day
3	Accounting personnel process the checks and deposit them in the firm's local bank	2 Days	Bank personnel prepare checks for deposit. Result: save 2 days
4 and 5	Checks are forwarded for payment through the clearing mechanism	1 Day	As the lock boxes are located near Federal Reserve Banks or branches, transit float can be reduced.
6 and 7	The firm receives notice from its bank that the checks have cleared and the funds are now "good"	1 Day	Result: save 1 day
	Total working days	7	Overall result: Save 4 working days

ordinary system). Furthermore, Table 15–2 assumes that the customer and the firm's headquarters or its collection center are located in different cities. This causes the lag of two working days before the firm actually receives the remittance check. We notice at the bottom of Table 15–2 that the installation of the lock-box system can result in funds being credited to the firm's bank account a full *four* working days *faster* than is possible under the ordinary collection system.

Previously in this chapter we calculated the 1991 sales per day for IBM to be $177.5 million and assumed that firm could invest its excess cash in marketable securities to yield 6 percent annually. If IBM could speed up its cash collections by four days, as the hypothetical firm did in Table 15–2, the results would be startling. The gross annual savings to IBM (apart from operating the lock-box system) would amount to $42.6 million, as follows:

$$(\text{sales per day}) \times (\text{days of float reduction}) \times (\text{assumed yield})$$
$$= \$177,534,247 \times (4) \times .06 = \$42,608,219$$

As you might guess, the prospects for generating revenues of this magnitude are important not only to the firms involved, but also to commercial banks that offer lock-box services.

In summary, the benefits of a lock-box arrangement are these:

1. **Increased working cash.** The time required for converting receivables into available funds is reduced. This frees up cash for use elsewhere in the enterprise.
2. **Elimination of clerical functions.** The bank takes over the tasks of receiving, endorsing, totaling, and depositing checks. With less handling of receipts by employees, better audit control is achieved and the chance of documents becoming lost is reduced.
3. **Early knowledge of dishonored checks.** Should a customer's check be uncollectible because of lack of funds, it is returned, usually by special handling, to the firm.

These benefits are not free. Usually, the bank levies a charge for each check processed through the system. The benefits derived from the acceleration of receipts must exceed the incremental costs of the lock-box system, or the firm would be better off without it. Companies that find the average size of their remittances to be quite small, for instance, might avoid a lock-box plan. One major Chicago bank has pointed out that for companies with less than $500,000 in average monthly sales or with customer remittance checks averaging less than $1,000, the lock-box approach would probably not yield a great enough benefit to offset its costs. Later in this chapter a straightforward method for assessing the desirability of a specific cash-management service, such as the lock-box arrangement, will be illustrated.

Preauthorized Checks (PACs)

Whereas the lock-box arrangement can often reduce total float by two to four days, for some firms the use of PACs can be an even more effective way of converting receipts into working cash. A PAC resembles the ordinary check, but it does not contain nor require the signature of the person on whose account it is being drawn. A PAC is created only with the individual's legal authorization.

The PAC system is advantageous when the firm regularly receives a large volume of payments of a fixed amount from the same customers. This type of cash-management service has proved useful to insurance companies, savings and loan associations, consumer credit firms, leasing enterprises, and charitable and religious organizations. The objective of this system is to reduce both

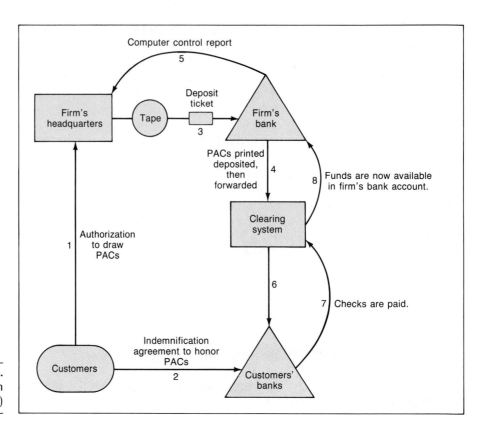

FIGURE 15–4.
Preauthorized Check System
(PAC)

mail and processing float. Notice, in relation to either the typical cash-gathering system (Figure 15–2) or the lock-box system (Figure 15–3), that the customer no longer (1) physically writes his or her own check or (2) deposits such check in the mail.

The operation of a PAC system is illustrated in Figure 15–4. It involves the following sequence of events:

1. The firm's customers authorize it to draw checks on their respective demand deposit accounts.
2. Indemnification agreements are signed by the customers and forwarded to the banks where they maintain their demand deposit accounts. These agreements authorize the banks to honor the PACs when they are presented for payment through the commercial bank clearing system.
3. The firm prepares a magnetic tape that contains all appropriate information about the regular payments.
4. At each processing cycle (monthly, weekly, semimonthly) the corporation retains a hard copy listing of all tape data for control purposes. Usually, the checks that are about to be printed will be deposited in the firm's demand deposit account, so a deposit ticket will also be forwarded to the bank.
5. Upon receipt of the tape the bank will produce the PACs, deposit them to the firm's account, forward them for clearing through the commercial banking system, and return a control report to the firm.

For firms that can take advantage of a PAC system, the benefits include the following:

1. **Highly predictable cash flows.**
2. **Reduced expenses.** Billing and postage costs are eliminated, and the clerical processing of customer payments is significantly reduced.
3. **Customer preference.** Many customers prefer not to be bothered with a regular billing. With a PAC system the check is actually written for the

customer and the payment made even if he or she is on vacation or otherwise out of town.

4. **Increased working cash.** Mail float and processing float can be dramatically reduced in comparison with other payment processing systems.

Depository Transfer Checks

Both depository transfer checks and wire transfers are used in conjunction with what is known as **concentration banking.** A concentration bank is one where the firm maintains a major disbursing account.

In an effort to accelerate collections, many companies have established multiple collection centers. Regional lock-box networks are one type of approach to strategically located collection points. Even without lock boxes, firms may have numerous sales outlets throughout the country and collect cash over the counter. This requires many local bank accounts to handle daily deposits. Rather than have funds sitting in these multiple bank accounts in different geographic regions of the country, most firms will regularly transfer the surplus balances to one or more concentration banks. Centralizing the firm's pool of cash provides the following benefits:

1. **Lower levels of excess cash.** Desired cash balance target levels are set for each regional bank. These target levels consider both compensating balance requirements and necessary working levels of cash. Cash in excess of the target levels can be transferred regularly to concentration banks for deployment by the firm's top-level management.

2. **Better control.** With more cash held in fewer accounts, stricter control over available cash is achieved. Quite simply, there are fewer problems. The concentration banks can prepare sophisticated reports that detail corporatewide movements of funds into and out of the central cash pool.

3. **More efficient investments in near-cash assets.** The coupling of information from the firm's cash forecast with data on available funds supplied by the concentration banks allows the firm quickly to transfer cash to the marketable securities portfolio.

Depository transfer checks provide a means for moving funds from local bank accounts to concentration accounts. The depository transfer check itself is an unsigned, nonnegotiable instrument. It is payable only to the bank of deposit (the concentration bank) for credit to the firm's specific account. The firm files an authorization form with each bank from which it might withdraw funds. This form instructs the bank to pay the depository transfer checks without any signature. The movement of cash through the use of depository transfer checks can operate with a conventional mail system or an automated system.

When the mail system is used, a company employee deposits the day's receipts in a local bank and fills out a preprinted depository transfer check for the exact amount of the deposit. The company then mails the depository transfer check to the firm's concentration bank. While this document is traveling in the mails, the checks just deposited at the local bank are being cleared. As soon as the concentration bank receives the depository transfer check, the firm's account is credited for the designated amount. The funds credited to the concentration account are not available for the firm's use, of course, until the document has been cleared with the local depository bank for payment.

If the firm's depository banks are geographically dispersed such that the mail will take several days in reaching the concentration bank, then *no* float reduction might be achieved through this system. In an attempt to reduce the mail float associated with conventional depository transfer check systems, some banks have initiated a type of special mail handling of these instruments that can cut as much as one full day off regular mail delivery schedules.

An innovation in speeding cash into concentration accounts is the **auto-**

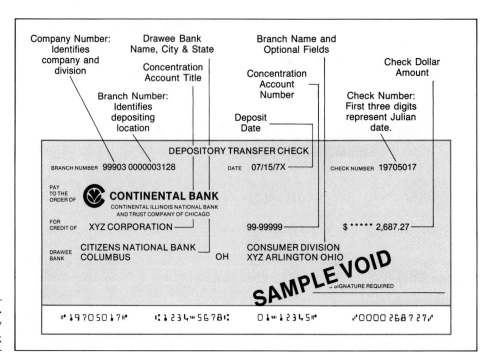

FIGURE 15–5.
Sample Depository
Transfer Check

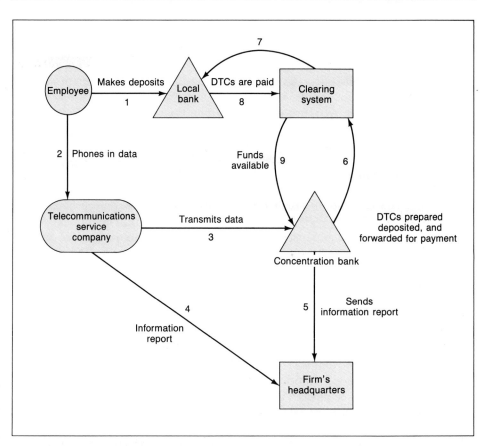

FIGURE 15–6.
Automated Depository
Transfer Check System (DTC)

mated depository transfer check system. In this system the mail float involved in moving the transfer document from the local bank to the concentration bank is *eliminated*. Here is how it works.

The local company employee makes the daily deposit as usual. This employee does *not*, however, manually fill out the preprinted depository transfer check; instead, he or she telephones the deposit information to a regional data collection center. Usually, the center is operated for a fee by a firm, such as National Data Corporation. Various data collection centers will accumulate information throughout the day on the firm's regional deposits. Then, at specified cutoff times the deposit information from all local offices is transmitted to the concentration bank.

At this point the concentration bank prepares the depository transfer check and credits it to the company's account. A sample depository transfer check prepared at a concentration bank is shown in Figure 15–5. The transfer checks are placed into the commercial bank check-clearing process and presented to the firm's local bank for payment. When paid by the local bank, the funds become available in the concentration account for company use. Major banks claim that funds transferred by use of the automated depository transfer check system can become available for company use in one business day or less. This system is depicted in Figure 15–6.

Wire Transfers

The fastest way to move cash between banks is by use of **wire transfers,** which eliminate transit float. Funds moved in this manner, then, immediately become usable funds or "good funds" to the firm at the receiving bank. The following two major communication facilities are used to accommodate wire transfers:

1. **Bank Wire.** Bank Wire is a private wire service used and supported by approximately 250 banks in the United States for transferring funds, exchanging credit information, or effecting securities transactions.
2. **Federal Reserve Wire System.** The Fed Wire is directly accessible to commercial banks that are members of the Federal Reserve System. A commercial bank that is not on the Bank Wire or is not a member of the Federal Reserve System can use the wire transfer through its correspondent bank.

Wire transfers are often initiated on a standing-order basis. By means of a written authorization from company headquarters, a local depository bank might be instructed to transfer funds regularly to the firm's concentration bank. For example, available funds in excess of $100,000 might be transferred to the concentration bank every Tuesday and Thursday.

As might be expected, wire transfers are a relatively expensive method of marshaling funds through a firm's money management system. A single wire transfer costs about $5. This is about fifteen times as costly as a conventional depository transfer check. Generally, the movement of small amounts does not justify the use of wire transfers.

Management of Cash Outflow

Significant techniques and systems for improving the firm's management of cash disbursements include (1) zero balance accounts, (2) payable-through drafts, and (3) remote disbursing. The first two offer markedly better control over companywide payments, and as a secondary benefit they *may* increase disbursement float. The last technique, remote disbursing, aims solely to increase disbursement float.

Zero Balance Accounts

Large corporations that operate multiple branches, divisions, or subsidiaries often maintain numerous bank accounts (in different banks) for the purpose of making timely operating disbursements. It does make good business sense for payments for purchased parts that go into, say, an automobile transmission to be made by the Transmission and Chassis Division of the auto manufacturer rather than its central office. The Transmission and Chassis Division originates such purchase orders, receives and inspects the shipment when it arrives at the plant, authorizes payment, and writes the appropriate check. To have the central office involved in these matters would be a waste of company time.

What tends to happen, however, is that with several divisions utilizing their own disbursal accounts, excess cash balances build up in outlying banks and rob the firm of earning assets. Zero balance accounts are used to alleviate this problem. The objectives of a zero balance account system are (1) for the firm to achieve better control over its cash payments, (2) to reduce excess cash balances held in regional banks for disbursing purposes, and (3) to increase disbursing float.

Zero balance accounts permit centralized control (at the headquarters level) over cash outflows while maintaining divisional disbursing authority. Under this system the firm's authorized employees, representing their various divisions, continue to write checks on their individual accounts. Note that the numerous individual disbursing accounts are now *all* located in the same concentration bank. Actually, these separate accounts contain no funds at all, thus their appropriate label, "zero balance." These accounts have all the characteristics of regular demand deposit accounts including separate titles, numbers, and statements.

Figure 15–7 presents a schematic of a zero balance account (ZBA) disbursing system. The firm is assumed to have three operating divisions—each with its own ZBA. The system works as follows. The firm's authorized agents write their payment checks as usual against their specific accounts (Step 1). These checks clear through the banking system in the usual way. On a daily basis checks will be presented to the firm's concentration bank (the drawee bank)

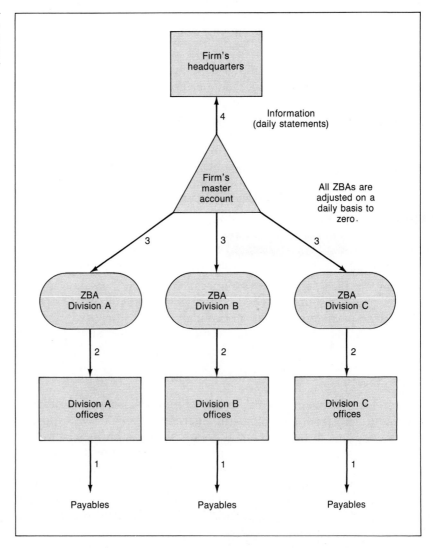

FIGURE 15–7.
Zero Balance Account Cash Disbursement System (ZBA)

bank (the drawee bank) for payment. As the checks are paid by the bank, negative (debit) balances will build in the proper disbursing accounts (Step 2). At the end of each day the negative balances will be restored to a zero level by means of credits to the zero balance accounts (Step 3); a corresponding reduction in funds is made against the firm's concentration (master) demand deposit account (also Step 3). Each morning a report is electronically forwarded to corporate headquarters reflecting the balance in the master account as well as the previous day's activity in each zero balance account (Step 4). Using the report, the financial officer in charge of near-cash investments is ready to initiate appropriate transactions.

Managing the cash outflow through use of a ZBA system offers the following benefits to the firm with many operating units:

1. Centralized control over disbursements is achieved, even though payment authority continues to rest with operating units.

2. Management time spent on superficial cash-management activities is reduced. Exercises such as observing the balances held in numerous bank accounts, transferring funds to those accounts short of cash, and reconciling the accounts demand less attention.

3. Excess balances held in outlying accounts can be reduced.

4. The costs of cash management can be reduced, as wire transfers to build up funds in outlying disbursement accounts are eliminated.

5. Funds may be made available for company use through an increase in disbursement float. When local bank accounts are used to pay nearby suppliers, the checks clear rapidly. The same checks, if drawn on a ZBA located in a more distant concentration bank, will take more time to clear against the disbursing firm's account.

Payable-Through Drafts

Payable-through drafts are legal instruments that have the physical appearance of ordinary checks (see Figure 15–8) but are *not* drawn on a bank. Instead, payable-through drafts are drawn on and payment is authorized by the issuing firm against its demand deposit account. Like checks, the drafts are cleared through the banking system and are presented to the issuing firm's bank. The bank serves as a collection point and passes the drafts on to the firm. The corporate issuer usually has to return by the following business day all drafts it does not wish to cover (pay). Those documents not returned to the bank are automatically paid. The firm inspects the drafts for validity by checking signatures, amounts, and dates. Stop-payment orders can be initiated by the company on any drafts considered inappropriate.

The main purpose of using a payable-through draft system is *to provide for effective control over field payments*. Central office control over payments begun

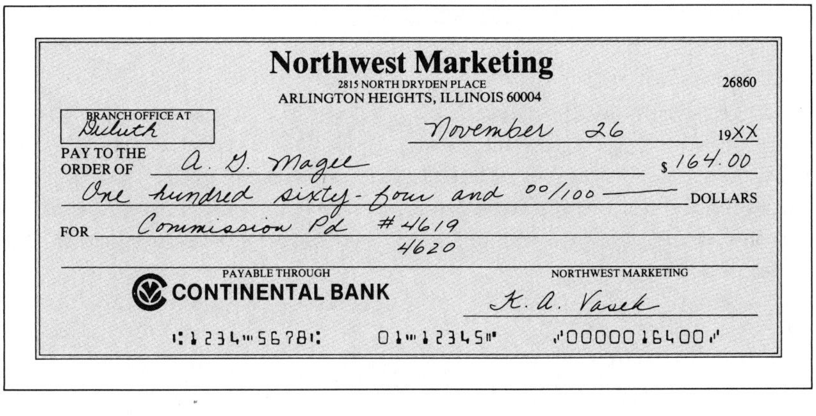

FIGURE 15–8.
Sample Payable-Through Draft

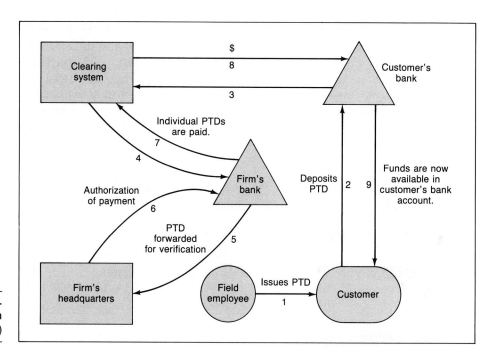

FIGURE 15–9.
Payable-Through Draft Cash
Disbursement System (PTD)

by regional units is provided as the drafts are reviewed in advance of final payment. Payable-through drafts, for example, are used extensively in the insurance industry. The claims agent does not typically have check-signing authority against a corporate disbursement account. This agent can issue a draft, however, for quick settlement of a claim.

The Federal Reserve System requires transfer of available or "good" funds upon presentation of drafts to the payable-through bank. The payable-through bank will cover drafts but will be reluctant to absorb the float that would occur until the issuing firm authorized payment the next business day. Therefore, the drafts that are presented for payment will usually be charged *in total* against the corporate master demand deposit account. This is for purposes of measuring usable funds available to the firm on that day. Legal payment of the *individual drafts* will still take place after their review and approval by the firm. Figure 15–9 illustrates a payable-through draft system.

Remote Disbursing

A few banks will provide the corporate customer with a cash-management service specifically designed to extend disbursing float. The firm's concentration bank may have a correspondent relationship with a smaller bank located in a distant city. In that remote city the Federal Reserve System is unable to maintain frequent clearings of checks drawn on local banks. For example, a firm that is located in Dallas and maintains its master account there may open an account with a bank situated in, say, Amarillo, Texas. The firm will write the bulk of its payment checks against the account in the Amarillo bank. The checks will probably take at least one business day longer to clear, so the firm can "play the float" to its advantage.

A firm must use this technique of remote disbursing with extreme care. If a key supplier of raw materials located in Dallas has to wait the extra day for funds drawn on the Amarillo account, the possibility of incurring ill will might outweigh the apparent gain from an increase in the disbursing float. The impact on the firm's reputation of using remote disbursing should be explicitly evaluated.

As you might guess, the practice of remote disbursing has come under criticism by bank regulatory authorities. In early 1979 the Federal Reserve Bank of Dallas noted:

> A policy discouraging remote disbursement—the use of remote banks by businesses, usually corporations, to delay payment of bills—has been adopted by the Board of Governors [of the Federal Reserve System]. The Board believes the banking industry has a public responsibility not to design, offer, promote or otherwise encourage the use of a service expressly intended to delay final settlement. The Board is calling on the nation's banks to join in the effort to eliminate remote disbursement practices.[6]

Electronic Funds Transfer

In the purest economic sense, "total" float should equal zero days and therefore should be worth zero dollars to any business firm or other economic unit in the society. Float is really a measure of inefficiency of the financial system in an economy. It is a friction of the business environment that stems from the fact that all information arising from business transactions cannot be instantaneously transferred among the parties involved.

Today the extensive use of electronic communication equipment is serving to reduce float. The central concept of electronic funds transfer (EFT) is simple. If firm A owes money to firm B, this situation ought to be immediately reflected on both the books and the bank accounts of these two companies. Instantaneous transfer of funds would eliminate float. Of course this ideal within the U.S. financial system has not been reached; the trend toward it, however, is readily observable.

Automated teller machines, like those imbedded in the wall of your supermarket or at the airline terminal, are familiar devices to most consumers. Businesses are now beginning to use even more advanced systems like terminal-based wire transfers to move funds within their cash-management systems.[7]

The heart of EFT is the elimination of the check as a method of transferring funds. The elimination of the check may never occur, but certainly a move toward a financial system that uses fewer checks will. Transit, mail, and processing float become less important as EFT becomes more important. Simultaneously, this also implies that disbursing float becomes trivial.

The process of EFT should provide for a more efficient economy. Funds tied up in accounts receivable, for example, will be released for more productive alternative uses. This does not mean that financial institutions will have no cash-management services to offer. It does mean that the nature of their cash-management services will change.

Perspective in Finance

Our previous work in Chapter 9 presented the popular breakeven model used by financial executives, accountants, and economists. The benefit to the firm of a given cash-management service can be assessed in a similar manner. Such a model follows. More complicated methods can be presented (some that involve use of an appropriate company discount rate), but the model below is used by managers and is easily explained to them. The important point is: Cash-management services are not free.

---

[6]"Remote Disbursement Policy Adopted," *Voice of the Federal Reserve Bank of Dallas* (February 1979), p. 10.

[7]See Christopher Huppert and Nina Henry, "Risks and Rewards of Terminal-Based Wire Transfers," *Cashflow* 4 (July–August 1983), pp. 24–27.

Evaluation of Costs of Cash-Management Services

A form of breakeven analysis can help the financial officer decide whether a particular collection or disbursement service will provide an economic benefit to the firm. The evaluation process involves a very basic relationship in microeconomics:

$$\text{added costs} = \text{added benefits} \qquad \textbf{(15–1)}$$

If equation (15–1) holds exactly, then the firm is no better or worse off for having adopted the given service. We will illustrate this procedure in terms of the desirability of installing an additional lock box. Equation (15–1) can be restated on a per-unit basis as follows:

$$P = (D)(S)(i) \qquad \textbf{(15–2)}$$

where P = increases in per-check processing cost if the new system is adopted

D = days saved in the collection process (float reduction)

S = average check size in dollars

i = the daily, before-tax opportunity cost (rate of return) of carrying cash

Assume now that check processing cost, P, will rise by $.18 a check if the lock box is used. The firm has determined that the average check size, S, that will be mailed to the lock-box location will be $900. If funds are freed by use of the lock box, they will be invested in marketable securities to yield an *annual* before-tax return of 6 percent. With these data it is possible to determine the reduction in check collection time, D, that is required to justify use of the lock box. That level of D is found to be

$$\$.18 = (D)(\$900)\left(\frac{.06}{365}\right)$$

$$1.217 \text{ days} = D$$

Thus, the lock box is justified if the firm can speed up its collections by *more* than 1.217 days. This same style of analysis can be adapted to analyze the other tools of cash management.

Before moving on to a discussion of the firm's marketable securities portfolio, it will be helpful to draw together the preceding material. Table 15–3 summarizes the salient features of the cash-collection and disbursal techniques we have considered here.

Perspective in Finance

Designing the marketable securities portfolio is one of the more pleasant tasks in financial management. This is because it is usually done with excess *cash that is available for short periods of time. The firm typically has excess cash when operations are going well; some firms never get the opportunity to design such a near-cash portfolio or to spend much time even thinking about it.*

We will review the major securities that make up the portfolios designed by cash managers. Note that the firm's main line of business activity will have a key impact on how much risk is assumed in the portfolio.

If the firm is in the business of manufacturing personal computers, it is likely management will feel that that business itself is risky enough. Thus, not much additional risk will be embedded in the marketable securities portfolio.

TABLE 15–3.
Features of Selected Cash-Collection and Disbursal Techniques: A Summary

Technique	Objective	How Accomplished
Cash-Collection Techniques		
1. Lock-box system	Reduce (1) mail float, (2) processing float, and (3) transit float.	Strategic location of lock boxes to reduce mail float and transit float. Firm's commercial bank has access to lock box to reduce processing float.
2. Preauthorized checks	Reduce (1) mail float and (2) processing float.	The firm writes the checks (the PACs) *for* its customers to be charged against their demand deposit accounts.
3. (Ordinary) Depository transfer checks	Eliminate excess funds in regional banks.	Used in conjunction with concentration banking whereby the firm maintains several collection centers. The transfer check authorizes movement of funds from a local bank to the concentration bank.
4. Automated depository transfer check	Eliminate the mail float associated with the ordinary transfer check.	Telecommunications company transmits deposit data to the firm's concentration bank.
5. Wire transfers	Move funds immediately between banks. This eliminates transit float in that only "good funds" are transferred.	Use of Bank Wire or the Federal Reserve Wire System.
Cash-Disbursal Techniques		
1. Zero balance accounts	(1) Achieve better control over cash payments, (2) reduce excess cash balances held in regional banks, and (3) possibly increase disbursing float.	Establish zero balance accounts for all of the firm's disbursing units. These accounts are all in the same concentration bank. Checks are drawn against these accounts, with the balance in each account never exceeding $0. Divisional disbursing authority is thereby maintained at the local level of management.
2. Payable-through drafts	Achieve effective central office control over field-authorized payments.	Field office issue drafts rather than checks to settle up payables.
3. Remote disbursing	Extend disbursing float.	Write checks against demand deposit accounts held in distant banks.

In addition, observe how critical the concept of liquidity *is to this aspect of cash management. Most large organizations will transfer funds into and out of the portfolio several times a day. Ready convertibility into cash, therefore, is a prime determinant of the final composition.*

Composition of Marketable Securities Portfolio

Once the design of the firm's cash receipts and payments system has been determined, the financial manager faces the task of selecting appropriate financial assets for inclusion in the firm's marketable securities portfolio.

General Selection Criteria

Certain criteria can provide the financial manager with a useful framework for selecting a proper marketable securities mix. These considerations include evaluation of the (1) financial risk, (2) interest rate risk, (3) liquidity, (4) taxability, and (5) yields among different financial assets. We will briefly delineate these criteria from the investor's viewpoint.

Financial Risk

Financial risk here refers to the uncertainty of expected returns from a security attributable to possible changes in the financial capacity of the security issuer to make future payments to the security owner. If the chance of default on the terms of the instrument is high (low), then the financial risk is said to be high

BASIC FINANCIAL MANAGEMENT IN PRACTICE

Float and the Clearing System

We have seen that understanding the concept of *float* is central to understanding efficient cash-management activities. The following discussion emphasizes the importance of float to the Federal Reserve System and also highlights the evolution of what we have called the "clearing system."

The Federal Reserve's check processing service began in 1916. It was free to member banks who would bundle up the checks they received each day and deposit them at the nearest Federal Reserve Bank or branch. The Fed would sort the checks according to the banks on which they were drawn and then send them right out to those banks for payment.

Member banks kept reserve accounts at the Fed which were used, among other things, to make and receive payments for checks. The Fed would credit the reserve accounts of banks that deposited checks for collection and charge the accounts of banks on which checks were drawn.

The Fed developed schedules of how long it normally took to process checks and present them in various locations around the country, and it gave credit to depositing banks according to those schedules rather than the actual collection time.

Thus banks that sent checks to a Federal Reserve Bank or branch for collection knew in advance exactly when they would receive credit in their reserve accounts, no matter what else happened.

The Fed's availability schedules went all the way up to eight days back in 1916, but now, thanks to computers and high-speed transportation, the maximum is two normal business days anywhere in the country.

Float and Monetary Policy

In addition to the expense and inefficiency, the Federal Reserve has other good reasons for being concerned about float. One is that it complicates the Fed's job of managing the money supply.

The Fed does this by trying to maintain appropriate levels of reserves in the banking system. As Federal Reserve credit, float is a part of bank reserves and is the most volatile and least predictable part.

Fluctuations in float mean that the banking system winds up with large variations in reserves for brief periods and the Fed must try to offset them. The less fluctuating float there is the more precise monetary policy can be.

For years the Federal Reserve has been taking steps to reduce float. In the 1970s, the Reserve Banks established dozens of new regional centers to process checks overnight, and made more effective use of air charter services.

Eliminate Float or Charge For It

In spite of these and other actions, Federal Reserve float reached a daily average of $6.7 billion in 1979, partly due to a tremendous increase in check volume. All this float was interfering with the Fed's efforts to stem inflation as well as costing billions to support.

In 1980, Congress passed the Monetary Control Act (MCA) which made sweeping changes in the Nation's financial system. The new law directed the Federal Reserve to begin charging for many of its services such as collecting checks, and to make them available to all depository institutions, not just banks which were members of the Federal Reserve System. The MCA also said the Federal Reserve must eliminate float or charge for it as a part of its check collection services. In effect, it was goodbye to loans without interest from the Fed.

Right off the Federal Reserve tried to reduce float with faster transportation and many other operational improvements. Success was dramatic and by 1982 total Federal Reserve float was at a daily average of $1.8 billion—down by almost $5 billion in three years. But even this was not good enough.

In early 1983, the Fed announced a major new program to squeeze Federal Reserve float out of the check stream. Among other things, the Fed pushed back the time of day when it could present checks to paying institutions. It offered institutions several new ways to get credit for deposits and it added the cost of all remaining holdover float to the price of its check services. By the end of the year when these new procedures were in full effect, Federal Reserve float was either eliminated or priced, just as the Monetary Control Act required.

Many depository institutions are not entirely happy about having to pay for something they used to get for free, but in the end the entire economy will be better off with float down and out. Check payments will be faster, monetary policy will be more precise, and much of the money the Federal Reserve formerly spent to support float will be available to the U.S. Treasury.

Source: L. C. Murdoch, Jr., "Float in the Check Stream," Federal Reserve Bank of Philadelphia (1984), pp. 7–8, 10–12.

(low). It is clear that the financial risk associated with holding commercial paper, which we will see shortly is nothing more than a corporate IOU, exceeds that of holding securities issued by the United States Treasury.

In both financial practice and research, when estimates of risk-free returns are desired, the yields available on Treasury securities are consulted and the safety of other financial instruments is weighed against them. Because the marketable securities portfolio is designed to provide a return on funds that would otherwise be tied up in idle cash held for transactions or precautionary purposes, the financial officer is not usually willing to assume much financial risk in the hope of greater return.

Interest Rate Risk[8]

Interest rate risk refers to the uncertainty of expected returns from a financial instrument attributable to changes in interest rates. Of particular concern to the corporate treasurer is the price volatility associated with instruments that have long, as opposed to short, terms to maturity. An illustration can help clarify this point.

Suppose the financial officer is weighing the merits of investing temporarily available corporate cash in a new offering of U.S. Treasury obligations that will mature in either (1) three years or (2) 20 years from the date of issue. The purchase price of the three-year notes or 20-year bonds is at their par value of $1,000 per security. The maturity value of either class of security is equal to par, $1,000, and the coupon rate (stated interest rate) is set at 7 percent, compounded annually.

If after one year from the date of purchase prevailing interest rates rise to 9 percent, the market prices of these currently outstanding Treasury securities will fall to bring their yields to maturity in line with what investors could obtain by buying a new issue of a given instrument. The market prices of *both* the 3-year and 20-year obligations will decline. The price of the 20-year instrument will decline by a greater dollar amount, however, than that of the three-year instrument.

One year from the date of issue the price obtainable in the marketplace for the original 20-year instrument, which now has 19 years to go to maturity, can be found by computing P as follows:

$$P = \sum_{T=1}^{19} \frac{\$70}{(1 + .09)^T} + \frac{\$1000}{(1 + .09)^{19}} = \$821.01$$

In the previous expression (1) T is the year in which the particular return, either interest or principal amount, is received; (2) $70 is the annual interest payment; and (3) $1,000 is the contractual maturity value of the bond. The rise in interest rates has forced the market price of the bond down to $821.01.

Now, what will happen to the price of the note that has two years remaining to maturity? In a similar manner, we can compute its price, P:

$$P = \sum_{T=1}^{2} \frac{\$70}{(1 + .09)^T} + \frac{\$1000}{(1 + .09)^2} = \$964.84$$

The market price of the shorter-term note will decline to $964.84. Table 15–4 shows that the market value of the shorter-term security was penalized much less by the given rise in the general level of interest rates.

If we extended the illustration, we would see that, in terms of market price, a one-year security would be affected less than a two-year security, a 91-day

---

[8]The computations in this discussion assume some knowledge of basic interest calculations. The concept can be grasped without the mathematical example, however. The "Mathematics of Finance" is covered in Chapter 3.

TABLE 15–4.
Market Price Effect of Rise
in Interest Rates

Item	Three-year Instrument	Twenty-year Instrument
Original price	$1000.00	$1000.00
Price after one year	964.84	821.01
Decline in price	$ 35.16	$ 178.99

security less than a 182-day security, and so on. Equity securities would exhibit the largest price changes because of their infinite maturity periods. To hedge against the price volatility caused by interest rate risk, the firm's marketable securities portfolio will tend to be composed of instruments that mature over short periods.

Liquidity

In the present context of managing the marketable securities portfolio, **liquidity** refers to ability to transform a security into cash. Should an unforeseen event require that a significant amount of cash be immediately available, then a sizable portion of the portfolio might have to be sold. The financial manager will want the cash *quickly* and will not want to accept a large *price concession* in order to convert the securities. Thus, in the formulation of preferences for the inclusion of particular instruments in the portfolio, the manager must consider (1) the period needed to sell the security and (2) the likelihood that the security can be sold at or near its prevailing market price. The latter element, here, means that "thin" markets, where relatively few transactions take place or where trades are accomplished only with large price changes between transactions, will be avoided.

Taxability

The tax treatment of the income a firm receives from its security investments does not affect the ultimate mix of the marketable securities portfolio as much as the criteria mentioned earlier. This is because the interest income from most instruments suitable for inclusion in the portfolio is taxable at the federal level. Still, some corporate treasurers seriously evaluate the taxability of interest income and capital gains.

The interest income from only one class of securities escapes the federal income tax. That class of securities is generally referred to as **municipal obligations,** or more simply as **municipals.** Because of the tax-exempt feature of interest income from state and local government securities, municipals sell at lower yields to maturity in the market than do securities that pay taxable interest. The after-tax yield on a municipal obligation, however, could be higher than the yield from a non-tax-exempt security. This would depend mainly on the purchasing firm's tax situation.

Consider Table 15–5. A firm is assumed to be analyzing whether to invest in a one-year tax-free debt issue yielding 6 percent on a $1,000 outlay or a one-year taxable issue that yields 8 percent on a $1,000 outlay. The firm pays federal taxes at the rate of 34 percent. The yields quoted in the financial press and in the prospectuses that describe debt issues are *before-tax* returns. The actual *after-tax* return enjoyed by the investor depends on his or her tax bracket. Notice that the actual after-tax yield received by the firm is only 5.28 percent on the taxable issue versus 6 percent on the tax-exempt obligation. The lower portion of Table 15–5 shows that the fully taxed bond must yield 9.091 percent to make it comparable with the tax-exempt issue.

At times in the history of corporate income taxation, capital gains have been taxed at a lower rate than ordinary income (such as interest income).

TABLE 15–5.
Comparison of After-Tax Yields

	Tax-exempt Debt Issue (6% Coupon)	Taxable Debt Issue (8% Coupon)
Interest income	$ 60.00	$ 80.00
Income tax (.34)	0.00	27.20
After-tax interest income	$ 60.00	$ 52.80
After-tax yield	$\dfrac{\$60.00}{\$1000.00} = 6\%$	$\dfrac{\$52.80}{\$1000.00} = 5.28\%$

Derivation of equivalent before-tax yield on a taxable debt issue:

$$r = \frac{r^*}{1 - T} = \frac{.06}{1 - .34} = 9.091\%$$

where r = equivalent before-tax yield,
r^* = after-tax yield on tax-exempt security,
T = firm's marginal income tax rate.

Proof: Interest income [$1000 × .09091]   = $90.91
Income tax (.34)   30.91
After-tax interest income $60.00

Under such circumstances, bonds selling at a discount from their face value may be attractive investments to tax-paying firms. Should a high level of interest rates currently exist, the market prices of debt issues that were issued in the past at low coupon rates will be depressed. This, as we said previously, brings their yield to maturity up to that obtainable on a new issue. Part of the yield to maturity on a bond selling at a discount is a *capital gain*, or the difference between the purchase price and the maturity value. Provided the firm held the fixed-income security for the requisite holding period, the return after tax could be higher than that derived from a comparable issue carrying a higher coupon but selling at par.[9] We say *could* be higher, as the marketplace is rather efficient and recognizes this feature of taxability; consequently, discount bonds will sell at lower yields than issues that have similar risk characteristics but larger coupons. For short periods, however, a firm *might* find a favorable yield advantage by purchasing discount bonds.

Yields

The final selection criterion that we mention is a significant one—the yields that are available on the different financial assets suitable for inclusion in the near-cash portfolio. By now it is probably obvious that the factors of (1) financial risk, (2) interest rate risk, (3) liquidity, and (4) taxability all influence the available yields on financial instruments. The yield criterion involves an evaluation of the risks and benefits inherent in all of these factors. If a given risk is assumed, such as lack of liquidity, a higher yield may be expected on the non-liquid instrument.

---

[9]Beginning in 1978 the holding period for long-term capital gain situations increased to 12 months. The Tax Reform Act of 1984 reduced the long-term capital-gain holding period for *individual investors* (not corporate investors) to six months. On October 22, 1986, the Tax Reform Act of 1986 became law. This sweeping revision of the tax code *eliminated* favorable tax rates for net capital gains effective January 1, 1987, for both corporations and individuals. As is obvious, tax laws change frequently. Congress and presidential administrations seem to have fun tinkering with the tax code. The important point is to understand the basic method of analysis and then use the proper tax rate in effect at the specific time. Chapter 2 discusses the tax constraints on businesses in more detail.

In early 1992, one of the public policy issues being debated in Congress and given considerable attention in the media was the possibility of reinstating some form of a favorable capital gains tax for both individuals and corporations. President Bush was totally in favor of such a tax code change. The actual form of the proposed change gained much scrutiny. The length of time the law would be in effect, the actual rate, or whether the rate might vary with respect to the holding period of the asset were all being hashed over.

Considerations	→	Influence	→	Focus Upon	→	Determine
Financial risk Interest rate risk Liquidity Taxability		Yields		Risk vs. return preferences		Marketable securities mix

FIGURE 15–10.
Designing the Marketable
Securities Portfolio

Figure 15–10 summarizes our framework for designing the firm's marketable securities portfolio. The four basic considerations are shown to influence the yields available on securities. The financial manager must focus on the risk–return tradeoffs identified through analysis. Coming to grips with these tradeoffs will enable the financial manager to determine the proper marketable securities mix for the company. Let us look now at the marketable securities prominent in firms' near-cash portfolios.

Marketable Security Alternatives

U.S. Treasury Bills

U.S. Treasury bills are the best-known and most popular short-term investment outlet among firms. A Treasury bill is a direct obligation of the United States government sold on a regular basis by the U.S. Treasury. New Treasury bills are issued in denominations of $10,000, $15,000, $50,000, $100,000, $500,000, and $1,000,000. In effect, therefore, one can buy bills in multiples of $5,000 above the smallest purchase price of $10,000 by combining $10,000 bills and $15,000 bills to reach the desired sum.

At present bills are regularly offered with maturities of 91, 182, and 365 days. A nine-month bill has been sold from time to time, but due to its lack of popularity among investors it is not now being issued. The three-month and six-month bills are auctioned weekly by the Treasury, and the one-year bills are offered every four weeks. Bids (orders to purchase) are accepted by the various Federal Reserve Banks and their branches, which perform the role of agents for the Treasury. Each Monday, bids are received until 1:30 P.M.; after that time they are opened, tabulated, and forwarded to the Treasury for allocation (filling the purchase orders).

Treasury bills are sold on a discount basis; for that reason the investor does not receive an actual interest payment. The return is the difference between the purchase price and the face (par) value of the bill.

The bills are marketed by the Treasury only in *bearer* form. They are purchased, therefore, without the investor's name on them. This attribute makes them easily transferable from one investor to the next. Of prime importance to the corporate treasurer is the fact that a very active secondary market exists for bills. After a bill has been acquired by the firm, should the need arise to turn it into cash, a group of securities dealers stand ready to purchase it. This highly developed secondary market for bills not only makes them extremely liquid, but also allows the firm to buy bills with maturities of a week or even less.

As bills have the full financial backing of the United States government, they are, for all practical purposes, risk free. This negligible financial risk and high degree of liquidity makes the yields lower than those obtainable on other marketable securities. The income from Treasury bills is subject to federal income taxes, but *not* to state and local government income taxes. An often neglected taxability feature of Treasury bills relates to their capital gains status. In the eyes of the Internal Revenue Service, bills are *not* capital assets. This means any financial gain on their sale prior to maturity is taxed as an *ordinary* gain. This would not be the case with other government securities, such as Treasury notes (original maturities of one to seven years) or Treasury bonds (generally with original maturities of over five years). As Treasury notes and bonds approach maturity, they can become attractive alternatives to Treasury bills in the firm's near-cash portfolio.

Federal Agency Securities

Federal agency securities are debt obligations of corporations and agencies that have been created to effect the various lending programs of the United States government. Five such government-sponsored corporations account for the majority of outstanding agency debt. The "big five" agencies are

1. **The Federal National Mortgage Association (FNMA).** FNMA renders supplementary assistance to the secondary market for mortgages. During periods of tight credit FNMA provides liquidity by purchasing mortgages from private financial institutions, such as savings and loan associations. When credit is easier to obtain, FNMA sells mortgages.

2. **The Federal Home Loan Banks (FHLB).** The 12 regional banks in the FHLB system operate as a credit reserve system under the supervision of the Federal Home Loan Bank Board. The credit reserve system is provided for the benefit of the system's members, all of which engage in home mortgage lending.

3. **The Federal Land Banks.** The 12 regional banks are owned by almost 300 local Federal Land Bank Associations. Federal Land Bank loans are arranged by the local associations. Loans are made to persons who are (or become) members of the associations and who are engaged in agriculture, provide agricultural services, or own rural homes.

4. **The Federal Intermediate Credit Banks.** These 12 banks make loans to and purchase notes originating from loans made to farmers by other financial institutions involved in agricultural lending.

5. **The Banks for Cooperatives.** The 12 district Banks for Cooperatives make loans to cooperative associations, owned and controlled by farmers, that market farm products, purchase farm supplies, or provide general farm business services.

It is not true that the "big five" federally sponsored agencies are owned by the United States government and that the securities they issue are fully guaranteed by the government. The "big five" agencies are now entirely owned by their member associations or the general public. In addition, it is the issuing agency that stands behind its promises to pay, not the federal government.

These agencies sell their securities in a variety of denominations. The entry barrier caused by the absolute dollar size of the smallest available Treasury bill—$10,000—is not as severe in the market for agencies. A wide range of maturities is also available. Obligations can at times be purchased with maturities as short as 30 days or as long as 15 years. Most outstanding agency debt, in excess of 80 percent, will mature in five years or less.

Agency debt usually sells on a coupon basis and pays interest to the owner on a semiannual schedule, although there are exceptions. Some issues have been sold on a discount basis, and some have paid interest only once a year.

If the likelihood is great that a marketable security will have to be liquidated before its contractual maturity date, then the financial officer must take care when making a selection of agency debt. The secondary market for the debt of the "big five" agencies is well developed in the shorter maturity categories—five years or less. It is not as strong in the longer maturity categories. To move such an issue, then, the financial officer may have to sell it at a depressed price.

The income from agency debt that the investor receives is subject to taxation at the federal level. Of the "big five" agencies, only the income from FNMA issues is taxed at the state and local level.

The yields available on agency obligations will always exceed those of Treasury securities of similar maturity. This yield differential is attributable to lesser marketability and greater default risk. The financial officer might keep in mind, however, that none of these agency issues has ever gone into default.

Bankers' Acceptances

Bankers' acceptances are one of the least understood instruments suitable for inclusion in the firm's marketable securities portfolio. Their part in United States commerce today is largely concentrated in the financing of foreign transactions. Generally, an acceptance is a draft (order to pay) drawn on a specific bank by an exporter in order to obtain payment for goods shipped to a customer, who maintains an account with that specific bank. An example of the sequence of events leading to the creation of a bankers' acceptance would go like this:

1. A retailer in San Francisco wants to import a shipment of stereo equipment from Tokyo. He goes to his commercial bank, which examines his credit standing and finds it satisfactory.

2. The importer's commercial bank sends the Tokyo exporter a letter of credit (a sophisticated reference letter) which authorizes the exporter to draw a draft on the San Francisco commercial bank. In the meantime, the importer has signed a contract with his bank agreeing to pay the bank the amount of the draft plus a commission in time for the bank to honor the draft at maturity.

3. Having received the letter of credit, the exporter draws a time draft on the San Francisco bank for the amount of the sale price and releases the stereo equipment for shipment. He retains possession of critical documents associated with the sale, such as the bill of lading, the transfer of title to the merchandise, and insurance papers.

4. The exporter will probably not want to wait several months for his funds, so he will obtain cash at once by selling (discounting) the draft with his bank in Tokyo at less than its face value. The shipping documents are turned over to the Tokyo bank.

5. The Tokyo bank will forward the draft and shipping documents to its correspondent bank in the United States. The correspondent bank will present the draft to the importer's San Francisco bank for acceptance.

6. The San Francisco bank (the drawee bank) will observe that the draft was authorized by its own letter of credit, will detach all shipping documents, and will stamp the draft "accepted." At this time, and not before, the bankers' acceptance is created. It is now a negotiable instrument, payable to the bearer.

7. The maturity period of the acceptance will be prearranged between the firm importing the stereo equipment and its San Francisco bank. When the draft is presented for acceptance, the maturity period begins, as most drafts are "sight drafts." This means, for instance, that if the maturity period is to be 90 days, the 90-day period begins *after* the drawee bank accepts the draft.

8. After accepting the draft, the San Francisco bank will notify its customer (the importer) that he can pick up the shipping documents, which will enable him to take possession of his stereo equipment. In exchange for the shipping documents, the drawee bank will obtain a signed document from the importer (a trust receipt) giving the bank a security interest in the goods. The importer can take title to the goods, sell them, and pay the San Francisco bank the face value of the acceptance (plus the stipulated service fee) shortly before its maturity.

9. The United States correspondent bank, which now holds the acceptance, will be instructed by the Tokyo bank to take either of two courses of action: (1) hold the acceptance until it matures as an investment or (2) immediately sell the acceptance in the market and credit its deposit account.

10. This latter course of action makes acceptances available to corporate treasurers for inclusion in near-cash portfolios.

Because acceptances are used to finance the acquisition of goods by one party, the document is not "issued" in specialized denominations; its dollar size is determined by the cost of the goods being purchased. Usual sizes, however, range from $25,000 to $1 million. The maturities on acceptances run from 30 to 180 days, although longer periods are available from time to time. The most common period is 90 days.

Acceptances, like Treasury bills, are sold on a discount basis and are payable to the bearer of the paper. A secondary market for the acceptances of large banks does exist. These transactions in acceptances are handled by only seven major dealers, all located in New York City. Included in this group are such well-known firms as the First Boston Corporation and Merrill Lynch, Pierce, Fenner & Smith, Inc.

The income generated from investing in acceptances is fully taxable at the federal, state, and local levels. Because of their greater financial risk and lesser liquidity, acceptances provide investors a yield advantage over Treasury bills and agency obligations. In fact, the acceptances of major banks are a very safe investment, making the yield advantage over Treasuries worth looking at from the firm's vantage point.

Negotiable Certificates of Deposit

A **negotiable certificate of deposit, CD,** is a marketable receipt for funds that have been deposited in a bank for a fixed time period. The deposited funds earn a fixed rate of interest. These are not to be confused with ordinary passbook savings accounts or nonmarketable time deposits offered by all commercial banks. CDs are offered by major money-center banks. We are talking here about "corporate" CDs—not those offered to individuals.

CDs are offered by key banks in a variety of denominations running from $25,000 to $10,000,000. The popular sizes are $100,000, $500,000, and $1,000,000.

The original maturities on CDs can range from 1 to 18 months. Periodic reporting surveys of commercial banks that are members of the Federal Reserve System consistently indicate that from 70 to 87 percent of outstanding CDs have maturity periods of four months or less.

CDs are offered by banks on a basis differing from Treasury bills; that is, they are not sold at a discount. Rather, when the certificate matures, the owner receives the full amount deposited plus the earned interest.

A secondary market for CDs does exist, the heart of which is found in New York City. While CDs may be issued in registered or bearer form, the latter facilitates transactions in the secondary market and thus is the most common.

Even though the secondary market for CDs of large banks is well organized, it does not operate as smoothly as the aftermarket in Treasuries. CDs are more heterogeneous than Treasury bills. Treasury bills have similar rates, maturity periods, and denominations; more variety is found in CDs. This makes it harder to liquidate large blocks of CDs, because a more specialized investor must be found. The securities dealers who "make" the secondary market in CDs mainly trade in $1 million units. Smaller denominations can be traded but will bring a relatively lower price. The First Boston Corporation and Salomon Brothers are two of the major dealers in CDs.

The income received from an investment in CDs is subject to taxation at all government levels. In recent years CD yields have been above those available on bankers' acceptances.

Commercial Paper

Commercial paper refers to short-term, unsecured promissory notes sold by large businesses to raise cash. These are sometimes described in the popular financial press as short-term corporate IOUs. Because they are unsecured, the issuing side of the market is dominated by large corporations, which typically maintain sound credit ratings. The issuing (borrowing) firm can sell the paper to a dealer who will in turn sell it to the investing public; if the firm's reputation is solid, the paper can be sold directly to the ultimate investor.

The denominations in which commercial paper can be bought vary over a wide range. At times paper can be obtained in sizes from $5,000 to $5 million, or even more. Sometimes dealers will sell notes in multiples as small as $1,000 or $5,000 above the initial $5,000 denomination. This depends on the dealer. The usual denominations are $25,000, $50,000, $100,000, $250,000, $500,000, and $1 million. Major dealers in the dealer-placed market include the First Boston Corporation; Goldman, Sachs & Co.; Merrill Lynch, Pierce, Fenner & Smith, Inc.; and Salomon Brothers.

Commercial paper can be purchased with maturities that range from 3 to 270 days. Notes with maturities exceeding 270 days are very rare, because they would have to be registered with the Securities and Exchange Commission—a task firms avoid, when possible, because it is time consuming and costly.

These notes are *generally* sold on a discount basis in bearer form, although sometimes paper that is interest bearing and can be made payable to the order of the investor is available.

The next point is of considerable interest to the financial officer responsible for management of the firm's near-cash portfolio. For practical purposes, there is *no* active trading in a secondary market for commercial paper. This distinguishes commercial paper from all the previously discussed short-term investment vehicles. On occasion, a dealer or finance company (the borrower) will redeem a note prior to its contract maturity date, but this is not a regular procedure. Thus, when the corporation evaluates commercial paper for possible inclusion in its marketable securities portfolio, it should plan to hold it to maturity.

The return on commercial paper is fully taxable to the investor at all levels of government. Because of its lack of marketability, commercial paper in past years consistently provided a yield advantage over other near-cash assets of comparable maturity. The lifting of interest rate ceilings in 1973 by the Federal Reserve Board on certain large CDs, however, allowed commercial banks to make CD rates fully competitive in the attempt to attract funds. Over any time period, then, CD yields *may* be slightly above the rates available on commercial paper.

Repurchase Agreements

Repurchase agreements (repos) are legal contracts that involve the actual sale of securities by a *borrower* to the *lender,* with a commitment on the part of the borrower to *repurchase* the securities at the contract price plus a stated interest charge. The securities sold to the lender are U.S. government issues or other instruments of the money market such as those described above. The borrower is either a major financial institution—most important, a commercial bank—or a dealer in U.S. government securities.

Why might the corporation with excess cash prefer to buy repurchase agreements rather than a given marketable security? There are two major reasons. First, the original maturities of the instruments being sold can, in effect, be adjusted to suit the particular needs of the investing corporation. Funds available for very short time periods, such as one or two days, can be productively employed. The second reason is closely related to the first. The firm could, of course, buy a Treasury bill and then resell it in the market in a few days when cash was required. The drawback here would be the risk involved in liquidating the bill at a price equal to its earlier cost to the firm. The purchase of a repo removes this risk. The contract price of the securities that make up the arrangement is *fixed* for the duration of the transaction. The corporation that buys a repurchase agreement, then, is protected against market price fluctuations throughout the contract period. This makes it a sound alternative investment for funds that are freed up for only very short periods.

These agreements are usually executed in sizes of $1 million or more.[10] The maturities may be for a specified time period or may have no fixed maturity date. In the latter case either lender or borrower may terminate the contract without advance notice.

The returns the lender receives on repurchase agreements are taxed at all governmental levels. Because the interest rates are set by direct negotiation between lender and borrower, no regular published series of yields is available for direct comparison with the other short-term investments. The rates available on repurchase agreements, however, are closely related to, but generally *less* than, Treasury bill rates of comparable maturities.

Money Market Mutual Funds

During the summer months of 1974, yields on three-month Treasury bills, three-month CDs, and four- to six-month commercial paper reached 9.37, 12.48, and 11.85 percent, respectively.[11] Before 1974 the opportunity for small firms, and small savers in general, to take advantage of attractive rates of return on short-term securities was extremely limited. The smallest Treasury bill requires a $10,000 investment. While commercial paper can at times be obtained in $5,000 denominations, it lacks the liquidity of Treasuries that is often preferable to financial managers.

The U.S. financial market system is an extraordinarily flexible vehicle of capitalism. This flexibility was demonstrated in 1974 and 1975. During that time over 25 money market mutual funds, also called liquid-asset funds, began to sell their shares to the public.

Money market funds typically invest in a diversified portfolio of short-term, high-grade debt instruments such as those described above. Some such funds, however, will accept more interest rate risk in their portfolios and acquire some corporate bonds and notes. The portfolio composition of 508 money market funds at the end of 1990 is shown in Table 15–6. We see that commercial paper, repurchase agreements, plus all CDs (both domestic plus Eurodollar) represented slightly in excess of 74 percent of money fund assets at this point in time. The

Type of Investment	Amount ($ billions)	Percent of Total
U.S. Treasury bills	25.5	6.15%
Other Treasury securities	20.0	4.82
Other U.S. securities (agencies)	36.9	8.90
Repurchase agreements	59.0	14.23
Commercial bank and other domestic CDs	20.9	5.04
Eurodollar CDs	27.1	6.53
Commercial paper	200.2	48.28
Bankers' acceptances	6.4	1.54
Cash reserves and other	18.7	4.51
Total net assets	414.7	100.0

Source: Investment Company Institute, 1991 *Mutual Fund Fact Book* (Washington, DC, 1991), p. 27.

TABLE 15–6.
Money Market Funds Asset Composition, Year-End 1990

---

[10]Occasionally, repurchase agreements smaller than $100,000 are transacted. See Norman N. Bowsher, "Repurchase Agreements," *Review*, Federal Reserve Bank of St. Louis, 61 (September 1979), pp. 17–22.

[11]Federal Reserve Bank of St. Louis, *U.S. Financial Data*, various issues, 1974.

average maturity period for these same 508 funds stood at 41 days at year-end 1990. The interest rate risk contained in this overall portfolio is, therefore, rather small.

The money market funds sell their shares to raise cash, and by pooling the funds of large numbers of small savers, they can build their liquid-asset portfolios. Many of these funds allow the investor to start an account with as little as $1,000. This small initial investment, coupled with the fact that some liquid-asset funds permit subsequent investments in amounts as small as $100, makes this type of outlet for excess cash suited to the small firm and even the individual. Furthermore, the management of a small enterprise may not be highly versed in the details of short-term investments. By purchasing shares in a liquid-asset fund, the investor is also buying managerial expertise.

Money market mutual funds offer the investing firm a high degree of liquidity. By redeeming (selling) shares, the investor can obtain cash quickly. Procedures for liquidation vary among the funds, but shares can usually be redeemed by means of (1) special redemption checks supplied by the fund, (2) telephone instructions, (3) wire instructions, or (4) a letter. When liquidation is ordered by telephone or wire, the mutual fund can remit to the investor by the next business day.

During the spring of 1980, yields on key money market instruments rose to near record levels. In March 1980, three-month Treasury bills, three-month CDs, and four-month commercial paper carried annual rates of return of 15.37, 16.87, and 16.17 percent, respectively. This made money market funds extraordinarily attractive to both corporations and individuals.

Actually, the flow of funds into the money market vehicles had already begun to accelerate by year-end 1979, as is substantiated by Table 15–7. Data for open-end investment companies are also presented for comparison purposes. Notice the fantastic jump in financial assets held by the money market funds from year-end 1978 to 1979. Then the U.S. economy suffered two recessions with little relief between them. The first began in January 1980 and ended seven months later in July. The second began in July 1981 and ended in November 1982, or 17 months after it began. The Federal Reserve System was trying to wring a very high rate of inflation out of the economy. It did this by keeping interest rates high. This made short-term debt instruments popular with investors.

As a result, the financial assets of money market mutual funds swelled to $219.8 billion by the end of 1982. The national economic recovery that began in late 1982 was foreshadowed by an upswing in common equity prices as early as August of that same year.[12] Through early 1987 the economy avoided another recession and stock prices in general moved upward. Simultaneously, interest rates decreased over this 1982–87 time frame. Investors, then, reduced their holdings of money funds and moved into equities. The data for 1983 in Table 15–7 reflect these portfolio shifts. Notice that despite low nominal interest rates, money fund assets rebounded strongly in 1984 and 1985. This trend has continued, with money fund assets standing at $533.1 billion at the end of 1991. The sustained growth and popularity of money market mutual funds was again punctuated after the onset of the national recession that began in July 1990. Confronting lower relative yields on money market instruments (e.g., Treasury bills), the financial assets held by money funds still continued to expand during 1991—albeit at a slower pace than the robust expansion enjoyed by equity-oriented mutual funds. Clearly, these money funds have been totally accepted as an investment outlet by the investing public.

---

[12]A fine article by A. L. Malabre, Jr., discusses the concept of stock market prices as a leading economic indicator and also touches upon the relationship among stock price changes, interest rate movements, and money supply changes. See "The Stock Market and the Business Cycle," *Wall Street Journal*, February 23, 1987, p. 1.

TABLE 15–7.
Investment Companies, Total Financial Assets Held, 1975–1991 ($ billions)

Type	Year								
	1975	1976	1977	1978	1979	1980	1981	1982	1983
Money market funds	3.7	3.7	3.9	10.8	45.2	76.4	186.2	219.8	179.4
pen-end investment companies	43.0	46.5	45.5	46.0	51.8	61.8	59.8	76.9	112.1

Type	Year							
	1984	1985	1986	1987	1988	1989	1990	1991
Money market funds	233.6	243.8	292.1	316.1	338.0	428.1	484.4	533.1
Open-end investment companies	136.7	240.2	413.5	460.1	478.3	555.1	547.3	764.0

Source: Flow of Funds Section, *Flow of Funds Accounts, Assets and Liabilities Outstanding*, 1965–88 and 1974–91 (Washington, DC: Board of Governors of the Federal Reserve System, September 1989 and January 1992), p. 30 in both issues.

The returns earned from owning shares in a money market fund are taxable at all governmental levels. The yields follow the returns the investor could receive by purchasing the marketable securities directly.

Money Market Deposit Accounts

The depressed economy of 1980–82 placed tremendous financial strain on the depository institutions in the United States. Both commercial banks and thrift institutions suffered. Congress reacted by passing the Depository Institutions Act in 1982. The objective of the act was to enable both banks and thrifts to compete with the fast-growing money market mutual funds. The result was that the Depository Institutions Deregulatory Committee authorized banks and thrifts to offer to investors a new type of account called the money market deposit account (MMDA).[13] The MMDAs became available to the public on December 14, 1982. These accounts differ from the money market fund accounts in significant ways:

1. They carry federal deposit insurance of up to $100,000 per account.

2. They require a minimum balance of $2,500. If the balance falls below the designated $2,500, it earns only the passbook savings rate.

3. Each account is limited to a maximum of six transactions per month, of which only three may be by check. In effect this means the other three transactions must be accomplished by use of preauthorized withdrawals.

The yield on the MMDAs is set individually by each offering bank or thrift institution. The maximum period for which the yield can be guaranteed by the financial institution is one month.

The third characteristic of the MMDAs renders them inappropriate for most businesses as a vehicle for the investment of excess cash. Firms do not want to be restricted on the number of times per month that they can tap their liquid asset reserves. On the other hand, the MMDAs have become very popular with *individual* investors. As was the intent of the Depository Institutions Act, a significant volume of funds has flowed from the money fund accounts to the MMDAs.

---

[13]The Depository Institutions Deregulatory Committee was established by the authority of the Depository Institutions Deregulation and Monetary Control Act of 1980. It includes representatives from the several federal agencies that oversee financial institutions. In January 1983 the Depository Institutions Deregulatory Committee permitted both banks and thrifts to offer what are called "super NOW accounts." These super NOW accounts differed from the MMDAs in that the number of transactions per month was *not* limited. The super NOW accounts, however, could be offered only to individuals and *not* to businesses. A good synopsis of the major banking acts that affect the U.S. economy (and other detailed information on the money market) can be found in Marcia Stigum, *The Money Market*, rev. ed. (Homewood, IL: Dow Jones–Irwin, 1983), pp. 124–27.

BASIC FINANCIAL MANAGEMENT IN PRACTICE

The Federal Reserve and Interest Rates

The following section, "Yield Structure of Marketable Securities," refers to the role of the Federal Reserve System—the nation's central bank—in affecting yields on money market instruments. The two pieces below expand our understanding of the Federal Reserve System. The first discussion deals with the basic organization of the system. The longer discussion focuses on the Fed's role in interest rate determination.

Organization

Many people are not aware that the Federal Reserve System is not part of the executive branch of the federal government, like the U.S. Treasury or Commerce Departments. Rather it is a blend of both public and private enterprise. The nation's central bank is an agency created by Congress, but the Fed's decentralized structure of 12 district banks and 25 branches gives each unit some aspects of privately owned businesses. The Fed's operational arms at the various bank and branches, for example, compete with one another—and with private sector organizations to provide quality financial services.

The Federal Reserve System is also similar to private businesses in that each bank and branch elects a board of directors. Contributing expertise gained from their own professions, the Fed directors play an integral role in the System's ability to formulate monetary policy and provide high-quality financial services to depository institutions and the U.S. Treasury.

The Fed and Interest Rates

It is often suggested that the Federal Reserve tightly controls all interest rates. Actually, the Federal Reserve sets only one interest rate, its discount rate. In addition, the Federal Reserve's open market operations in recent years have been aimed at holding another rate, the federal funds rate, close to levels indicated by the Federal Open Market Committee (FOMC), the Federal Reserve's primary monetary policymaking body.

This article explains how changes in the federal funds rate and the discount rate work through financial markets to affect other short-term interest rates such as those on Treasury bills and certificates of deposit. It also explains why the influence of changes in the funds rate and the discount rate on long-term rates, such as mortgage rates and corporate bond yields, is relatively weak.

Monetary Policy in Brief

The Federal Reserve's monetary policy can be defined as the Fed's use of its influence on reserves in the banking system to influence money and credit and, through them, the economy. The federal funds rate and the discount rate figure importantly in the conduct of monetary policy, and many observers regard these two rates as the principal indicators of the direction of policy. Declines in these rates are taken as signs that the Federal Reserve wants to encourage money and credit growth, or "ease" money and credit conditions, while increases in these rates are interpreted as Fed efforts to restrain money and credit growth, or "tighten" money and credit conditions.

Federal funds are reserves lent overnight by depository institutions with excess reserves to depository institutions with insufficient reserves. The *federal funds rate* is a market rate of interest determined by the supply and demand for reserves. The Fed directly affects the funds rate by buying and selling government securities in the "open market" to influence the supply of reserves, and, therefore, federal funds in the banking system. When the Federal Reserve wants to ease money and credit conditions through open market operations, for example, it supplies additional reserves to the banking system by purchasing additional short-term government securities.

When a depository institution is short on the reserves it needs to meet regulatory requirements, it may also borrow reserves from its regional Federal Reserve Bank at the discount rate. The *discount rate* is an "administered" rate, set at a certain level and held there by administrative decision. Changes in the discount rate are initiated by the boards of directors of the individual Reserve Banks, but the Federal Reserve's Board of Governors in Washington must approve all changes. This coordination generally results in roughly simultaneous changes at all Reserve Banks.

Effect of Changes in the Funds Rate on Short-Term Rates

The Federal Reserve exercises a strong influence on other short-term rates through its influence on the federal funds rate, because the funds rate is the base rate to which other money market rates are anchored. To see this, consider the rate on bank certificates of deposit (CDs), which are generally arranged for a few months. Banks can raise funds either through CDs or federal funds and therefore choose whichever option is expected to be cheaper. CD rates are roughly aligned with an average of expected future funds rates over the term of the CD. Hence if bankers see a rise in the federal funds rate, and expect it to persist, they will bid up the rate on CDs. Likewise, corporations considering a Treasury bill purchase have the option of lending their funds daily over the term of the bill at the overnight rate on repurchase agreements, which is closely tied to the federal funds rate. Hence, they will require a higher Treasury bill rate following an increase in the funds rate that they believe to be persistent.

As these examples illustrate, the arbitrage activities of money market participants will generally keep other short-term rates in line with the federal funds rate, abstracting from differences in default risk. Hence, persistent increases in the federal funds rate engineered by the Federal Reserve will generally lead to comparable increases in other short-term interest rates.

Changes in the Discount Rate

As indicated above, banks can borrow reserves at the discount window or they can acquire reserves in the federal funds market. (Of course, individual banks can also acquire reserves by selling off securities.) Under the operating procedures used by the Federal Reserve in the 1980s, increases in the discount rate that raise the cost of acquiring borrowed reserves also can lead quickly to an increase in the cost of acquiring reserves in the federal funds market. Hence, under these procedures the discount rate can have a strong direct effect on the funds rate and other market rates.

More generally, if changes in the discount rate are viewed by market participants as signaling a "tighter" monetary policy in the future, then they can influence the current level of market interest rates regardless of the Fed's operating procedures. The reason is that anticipation of a tighter policy will raise the expected future level of the funds rate. A higher expected funds rate will then raise current rates on CDs and Treasury bills as in the examples above. Such effects are usually labeled "announcement effects" by market participants.

Long-Term Rates

The ability of the Federal Reserve to directly influence the level of interest rates diminishes greatly at longer maturities. The reason is that longer-term interest rates, such as mortgage rates and corporate bond yields, are largely determined by the expected rate of inflation. To appreciate the influence of inflation expectations on longer-term rates, suppose that the long-term expected inflation rate were 5 percent. Lenders would be unwilling to lend at 5 percent because the interest income would be completely offset by the inflation loss. Lenders want to cover the expected inflation loss and earn some real rate of return, considered usually to be about 4 percent. Borrowers, for their part, are willing to pay the inflation premium because they expect to repay their debts with cheaper dollars. Therefore, one can reasonably expect long-term interest rates to be about 4 percentage points above the expected inflation rate. It follows that an important way to reduce long-term rates is to lower the expected rate of inflation. The historical data in Chart 1 show that long-term rates have come down only after inflation has declined.

Short- and Long-Term Rates: A Case Study

The relatively weak link between movements in the federal funds rate and movements in long-term rates can be illustrated by the behavior of rates over the last couple of years. From June 1989 through June 1991, the federal funds rate fell 4 percentage points, from about 9.75 percent to about 5.75 percent, and other short-term rates also declined about 4 percentage points. Long-term rates, however, fell only about 1 percentage point over this period, as illustrated in Chart 2.

How should these declines be interpreted in light of the previous discussion? Apparently, the public's inflation outlook did not change much from June 1989 through June 1991 because long-term rates did not move much over this period. Evidently, the public believed that the Fed's downward pressure on short-term rates were anti-recession moves that would not

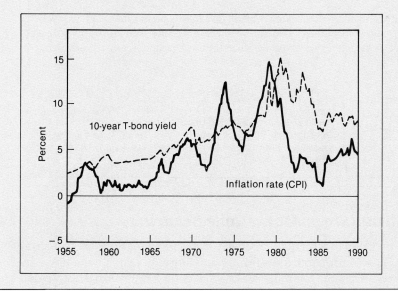

CHART 1.
Long-Term Rates Fall
After Inflation Falls

BASIC FINANCIAL MANAGEMENT IN PRACTICE (cont.)

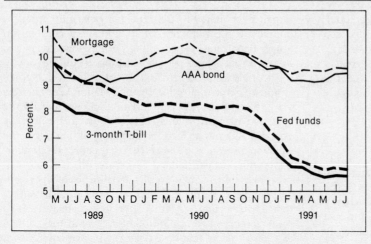

CHART 2.
Long-Term Rates Can Be
Stubborn

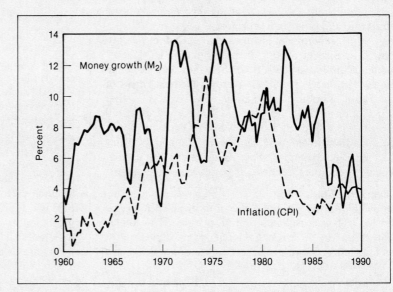

CHART 3.
Inflation Follows Excess
Money Growth
Four-Quarter Changes

significantly alter the inflation outlook. In July and August of 1991, however, declines in long-term rates suggested perceived progress in reducing expected inflation.

The Fed's Role
The historical data show that long-term interest rates decline when the expected rate of inflation declines. Further, empirical evidence strongly suggests that, over time, inflation results from excessive increases in the money supply (Chart 3). To prevent inflation and to concurrently bring down long-term rates, policymakers must ensure that, over time, the money supply grows only as fast as the economy's potential growth in output.

Sources: "Organization" is from "Board Member Finds Parallels between the Fed and His Own Business," *Financial Update*, Federal Reserve Bank of Atlanta, 3 (Fall 1990), p. 3; "The Fed and Interest Rates" is from Craig Carlock, "How the Federal Reserve Influences Interest Rates," *Cross Sections*, Federal Reserve Bank of Richmond, 8 (Fall 1991), pp. 12–14.

The Yield Structure of Marketable Securities

What type of return can the financial manager expect on a marketable securities portfolio? This is a reasonable question. Some insight can be obtained by looking at the past, although we must realize that future returns are not guided by past experience. It is also useful to have some understanding of how the returns on one type of instrument stack up against another. The behavior of

Year	T-Bills	Agencies	Acceptances	Commercial Paper	CDs
1965	3.93	4.14	4.19	4.25	4.31
1966	4.81	5.22	5.37	5.51	5.43
1967	4.30	4.60	4.81	5.11	4.99
1968	5.27	5.54	5.72	5.92	5.79
1969	6.54	7.12	7.51	7.76	7.66
1970	6.58	6.94	7.50	7.89	7.68
1971	4.39	4.56	4.94	5.12	5.07
1972	4.02	4.22	4.52	4.63	4.61
1973	6.87	7.40	8.03	8.11	8.21
1974	7.78	8.73	9.85	10.06	10.28
1975	5.85	6.03	6.28	6.41	6.61
1976	5.03	5.15	5.18	5.28	5.31
1977	5.17	5.38	5.45	5.45	5.55
1978	7.12	7.68	7.91	7.73	8.05
1979	9.84	10.53	10.76	10.72	11.02
1980	11.51	12.09	12.72	12.66	13.07
1981	14.03	15.28	15.32	15.32	15.91
1982	10.69	11.68	11.89	11.89	12.27
1983	8.61	8.95	8.90	8.88	9.07
1984	9.52	10.13	10.14	10.10	10.37
1985	7.48	8.00	7.92	7.95	8.05
1986	5.98	6.49	6.38	6.49	6.51
1987	5.82	6.47	6.75	6.82	6.87
1988	6.68	7.60	7.56	7.66	7.73
1989	8.12	8.75	8.87	8.99	9.09
1990	7.51	7.99	7.93	8.06	8.15
1991	5.42	5.81	5.70	5.87	5.83

Source: Salomon Brothers, "An Analytical Record of Yields and Yield Spreads," March 1980; and *Federal Reserve Bulletin* 69 (November 1983), p. A 26; 70 (August 1984), p. A 24; 73 (February 1987), p. A 24; 76 (January 1990), p. A 24; 78 (March 1992), p. A 24.

yields on short-term debt instruments over the 1965–89 period is shown in Table 15–8. An examination of the data in that table permits the following generalizations:

1. The returns from the various instruments are highly correlated in the positive direction over time. That is, the yields tend to rise and fall together.

2. The yields are quite volatile over time. For example, notice the large increases in returns from 1968 to 1969, 1972 to 1973, 1978 to 1979, 1980 to 1981, and 1988 to 1989. Further, notice the significant decline in yields that persisted during 1991. These low yields were associated with the 1990 recession and related loosening of monetary policy by Federal Reserve decision makers. Indeed, yields on short-term Treasury securities fell below 4 percent during the first quarter of 1992. Such abrupt alterations in the structure of yields suggest that financial managers should make an attempt to understand policy making by the Federal Reserve. This is important as most monetary policy actions by the Fed directly affect the rates of return that are available on money market instruments. The Fed has more influence on short-term instruments (such as three-month Treasury bills) than it does on long-term securities (such as 30-year Treasury bonds). The financial manager, then, cannot plan on any given level of returns prevailing over a long time period. Also, observe the relatively high yields during 1974 that led to the formation of a large number of money market mutual funds. High yields prevailed again in 1979–82 and aided their growth.

3. A basic change has occurred in the underlying structure of yields. Between 1966 and 1972, if we ranked the instruments in Table 15–8 from low to high yield, we would have

Treasury bills (low yield)
Federal agency securities
Bankers' acceptances

TABLE 15–9.
Features of Selected Money Market Instruments

Instrument	Denominations	Maturities	Basis	Form	Liquidity	Taxability
U.S. Treasury bills—direct obligations of the U.S. government	$ 10,000 15,000 50,000 100,000 500,000 1,000,000	91 days 182 days 365 days 9-month not presently issued	Discount	Bearer	Excellent secondary market	Exempt from state and local income
Federal agency securities—obligations of corporations and agencies created to effect the federal government's lending programs	Wide variation; from $1,000 to $1 million	5 days (Farm Credit consolidated systemwide discount notes) to more than 10 years	Discount or coupon; usually on coupon	Bearer or registered	Good for issues of "big five" agencies	Generally exempt at local level; FNMA issues are *not*
Bankers' acceptances—drafts accepted for future payment by commercial banks	No set size; typically range from $25,000 to $1 million	Predominantly from 30 to 180 days	Discount	Bearer	Good for acceptances of large "money market" banks	Taxed at all levels of government
Negotiable certificates of deposit—marketable receipts for funds deposited in a bank for a fixed time period	$25,000 to $10 million	1 to 18 months	Accrued interest	Bearer or registered; bearer is preferable from liquidity standpoint	Fair to good	Taxed at all levels of government
Commercial paper—short-term unsecured promissory notes	$5,000 to $5 million; $1,000 and $5,000 multiples above the initial offering size are sometimes available	3 to 270 days	Discount	Bearer	Poor; no active secondary market in usual sense	Taxed at all levels of government
Repurchase agreements—legal contracts between a borrower (security seller) and lender (security buyer). The borrower will repurchase at the contract price plus an interest charge.	Typical sizes are $500,000 or more	According to terms of contract	Not applicable	Not applicable	Fixed by the agreement; that is, borrower will repurchase	Taxed at all levels of government
Money market mutual funds—holders of diversified portfolios of short-term, high-grade debt instruments	Some require an initial investment as small as $1,000	Your shares can be sold at any time	Net asset value	Registered	Good; provided by the fund itself	Taxed at all levels of government

588

Certificates of deposit
Commercial paper (high yield)

Since 1973, for the most part, the annual yields available on negotiable certificates of deposit exceeded those of commercial paper. This phenomenon is the direct result of Federal Reserve Board action that removed interest rate limits on large certificates of deposit.

The discussion in this chapter on designing the firm's marketable securities portfolio touched upon the essential elements of several near-cash assets. At times it is difficult to sort out the distinguishing features among these short-term investments. To alleviate that problem, Table 15–9 draws together their principal characteristics.

A Glance at Actual Cash-Management Practices

We have dealt at length in this chapter with (1) the collection and disbursement procedures the firm can use to manage its cash balances more effectively and (2) the composition of the firm's marketable securities portfolio. Now let's relate our discussion to the findings of some studies that focus on corporate cash-management practices.

Surveys conducted by (1) Gitman, Moses, and White and (2) Mathur and

---

BASIC FINANCIAL MANAGEMENT IN PRACTICE

Investment Practices

A study published in 1987 by Frankle and Collins provided some new insights on the investment tendencies of cash managers. The results differ somewhat from those reported in earlier studies. The researchers sampled the *Fortune 1000* list of large industrial firms and achieved a response rate of about 22 percent.

In the Frankle and Collins study the respondents were asked to describe their own approach to cash management—from "aggressive" to "passive." Only those ultimately classified as aggressive or moderate are commented upon here.

One portion of the study asked the managers to identify the percentage of their short-term portfolios invested in the typical marketable securities. The five most popular instruments and the respective percentages are shown below.

Type of Security	Aggressive Manager	Moderate Manager
Treasury securities	5.55%	8.82%
Commercial paper	18.16	17.53
Domestic CDs	11.45	6.87
Eurodollar CDs	36.77	24.28
Repurchase agreements	11.27	18.99

Unlike earlier studies, this piece of research indicated that Eurodollar CDs are preferred by aggressive cash managers with commercial paper being ranked second and domestic CDs ranked third. The moderate managers also liked Eurodollar CDs, with repurchase agreements ranked second and commercial paper ranked third.

Another question in the study asked the managers to indicate which investment attributes shaped their ultimate investment decisions. The aggressive managers ranked *rate of return* first, *risk of default* second, and *maturity* third. The moderate managers ranked *risk of default* first in importance, *rate of return* second, and *maturity* third.

Compared to earlier work on cash-management practices, this study suggests that those responsible for the investment of excess corporate cash are assuming even a *bit* more risk in their portfolios in exchange for higher expected returns. This may be due to the increased emphasis placed by corporate management on the cash-management function and the growing sophistication of those who practice the trade.

Source: Based on Alan W. Frankle and J. Markham Collins, "Investment Practices of the Domestic Cash Manager," *Journal of Cash Management* 7 (May/June 1987), pp. 50–53.

Loy centered on both the cash-management services offered by commercial banks and the investment of excess cash in the marketable securities portfolio.[14] Gitman, Moses, and White surveyed 300 of the 1,000 largest industrial firms in the United States ranked by total sales dollars for 1975 (the *Fortune 1000* list). They received 98 responses to their questionnaire, for a response rate of 32.7 percent. With regard to speeding up the firm's cash receipts, it was found that 80 percent of the respondents used lock-box systems and 61 percent used selected disbursing points (remote disbursing) to slow down or better control cash payments.

The Mathur and Loy study centered on the 200 largest industrial firms from the *Fortune 500* list for 1979. Of these 200 firms, 160 were sampled. A response rate of 46 percent was achieved. This study showed that almost all of the respondents used lock-box services (96 percent). In addition, concentration banking was employed by 80 percent of the survey participants.

These same two studies touched upon the management of the marketable securities portfolio. Gitman, Moses, and White found that the most favored security for the investment of excess cash was commercial paper. It was followed in popularity by repurchase agreements, Treasury securities, and CDs. Mathur and Loy also found that commercial paper was the most favored marketable security investment. Furthermore, repurchase agreements and CDs ranked high on respondents' most favored lists. Mathur and Loy also reported that, on average, the firms invest in 3.6 different types of marketable securities.

We all know that commercial paper, CDs, and repurchase agreements are more risky investments than Treasury securities. It seems that those who are responsible for making marketable security investment decisions in large firms do not consider the risk differences among the traditional money market instruments to be very significant. They are willing to trade the greater riskiness inherent in the "non-Treasury" instruments for their higher expected yield.

SUMMARY

Firms hold cash to satisfy transactions, precautionary, and speculative needs for liquidity. Because cash balances provide no direct return, the precautionary motive for investing in cash is satisfied in part by holdings of marketable securities.

Cash-Management Objectives and Decisions

The financial manager must (1) make sure that enough cash is on hand to meet the payment needs that arise in the course of doing business and (2) attempt to reduce the firm's idle cash balances to a minimum.

Collection and Disbursement Procedures

To reduce float, the firm can benefit considerably through the use of (1) lock-box arrangements, (2) preauthorized checks, (3) special forms of depository transfer checks, and (4) wire transfers. Lock-box systems and preauthorized checks serve to reduce mail and processing float. Depository transfer checks and wire transfers move funds between banks; they are often used in conjunction with concentration banking. Both the lock-box and preauthorized check systems can be employed as part of the firm's concentration banking setup to speed receipts to regional collection centers.

---

[14]Lawrence J. Gitman, Edward A. Moses, and I. Thomas White, "An Assessment of Corporate Cash Management Practices," *Financial Management* 8 (Spring 1979), pp. 32–41; and Ike Mathur and David Loy, "Corporate-Banking Cash Management Relationships: Survey Results," *Journal of Cash Management* 3 (October–November 1983), pp. 35–46.

The firm can delay and favorably affect the control of its cash disbursements through the use of (1) zero balance accounts, (2) payable-through drafts, and (3) remote disbursing. Zero balance accounts allow the company to maintain central-office control over payments while permitting the firm's several divisions to maintain their own disbursing authority. Because key disbursing accounts are located in one major concentration bank, rather than in multiple banks across the country, excess cash balances that tend to build up in the outlying banks are avoided. Payable-through drafts are legal instruments that look like checks but are drawn on and paid by the issuing firm rather than its bank. The bank serves as a collection point for the drafts. Effective central-office control over field-authorized payments is the main reason such a system is used; it is not used as a major vehicle for extending disbursing float. Remote disbursing, however, is used to increase disbursing float. Remote disbursing refers to the process of writing payment checks on banks located in cities distant from the one where the check is originated.

Before any of these collection and disbursement procedures is initiated by the firm, a careful analysis should be undertaken to see if the expected benefits outweigh the expected costs.

Marketable Securities Portfolio

The factors of (1) financial risk, (2) interest rate risk, (3) liquidity, and (4) taxability affect the yields available on marketable securities. By considering these four factors simultaneously with returns desired from the portfolio, the financial manager can design the mix of near-cash assets most suitable for a firm.

The chapter evaluated the features of several marketable securities. Treasury bills and federal agency securities are extremely safe investments. Bankers' acceptances, CDs, and commercial paper provide higher yields in exchange for greater risk assumption. Unlike the other instruments, commercial paper enjoys no *developed* secondary market. The firm can hedge against price fluctuations through the use of repurchase agreements. Money market mutual funds, a recent phenomenon of our financial market system, are particularly well suited for the short-term investing needs of small firms.

STUDY QUESTIONS

15-1. What is meant by the cash flow process?

15-2. Identify the principal motives for holding cash and near-cash assets. Explain the purpose of each motive.

15-3. What is concentration banking and how may it be of value to the firm?

15-4. Distinguish between depository transfer checks and automated depository transfer checks (ADTC).

15-5. In general what type of firm would benefit from the use of a preauthorized check system? What specific types of companies have successfully used this device to accelerate cash receipts?

15-6. What are the two major objectives of the firm's cash-management system?

15-7. What three decisions dominate the cash-management process?

15-8. Within the context of cash management, what are the key elements of (total) float? Briefly define each element.

15-9. Distinguish between financial risk and interest rate risk as these terms are commonly used in discussions of cash management.

15-10. What is meant when we say, "A money market instrument is highly liquid"?

15-11. Which money market instrument is generally conceded to have no secondary market?

15-12. Your firm invests in only three different classes of marketable securities: commercial paper, Treasury bills, and federal agency securities. Recently, yields on these money market instruments of three months' maturity were quoted at 6.10, 6.25, and 5.90 percent. Match the available yields with the types of instruments your firm purchases.

15-13. What two major factors led to the inception of a large number of money market mutual funds during 1974 and 1975?

15-14. What two key factors might induce a firm to invest in repurchase agreements rather than a specific security of the money market?

SELF-TEST PROBLEMS

ST-1. (*Costs of Services*) Creative Fashion Designs is evaluating a lock-box system as a cash receipts acceleration device. In a typical year this firm receives remittances totaling $7 million by check. The firm will record and process 4,000 checks over the same time period. Ocala National Bank has informed the management of Creative Fashion Designs that it will process checks and associated documents through the lock-box system for a unit cost of $.25 per check. Creative Fashion Designs' financial manager has projected that cash freed by adoption of the system can be invested in a portfolio of near-cash assets that will yield an annual before-tax return of 8 percent. Creative Fashion Designs' financial analysts use a 365-day year in their procedures.

a. What reduction in check collection time is necessary for Creative Fashion Designs to be neither better nor worse off for having adopted the proposed system?

b. How would your solution to (a) be affected if Creative Fashion Designs could invest the freed balances only at an expected annual return of 5.5 percent?

c. What is the logical explanation for the differences in your answers to (a) and (b) above?

ST-2. (*Cash Receipts Acceleration System*) Artie Kay's Komputer Shops is a large, national distributor and retailer of microcomputers, personal computers, and related software. The company has its central offices in Dearborn, Michigan, not far from the Ford Motor Company executive offices and headquarters. Only recently has Artie Kay's begun to pay serious attention to its cash-management procedures. Last week the firm received a proposal from the Detroit National Bank. The objective of the proposal is to speed up the firm's cash collections.

Artie Kay's now uses a centralized billing procedure. All checks are mailed to the Dearborn headquarters office for processing and eventual deposit. Remittance checks now take an average of five business days to reach the Dearborn office. The in-house processing at Artie Kay's is quite slow. Once in Dearborn, another three days are needed to process the checks for deposit at Detroit National.

The daily cash remittances of Artie Kay's average $200,000. The average check size is $800. The firm currently earns 10.6 percent on its marketable securities portfolio and expects this rate to continue to be available.

The cash acceleration plan suggested by officers of Detroit National involves both a lock-box system and concentration banking. Detroit National would be the firm's only concentration bank. Lock boxes would be established in (1) Seattle, (2) San Antonio, (3) Chicago, and (4) Detroit. This would reduce mail float by 2.0 days. Processing float would be reduced to a level of 0.5 days. Funds would then be transferred twice each business day by means of automated depository transfer checks from local banks in Seattle, San Antonio, and Chicago to the Detroit National Bank. Each ADTC costs $20. These transfers will occur all 270 business days of the year. Each check processed through the lock-box system will cost Artie Kay's $.25.

a. What amount of cash balances will be freed if Artie Kay's adopts the system proposed by Detroit National?

b. What is the opportunity cost of maintaining the current banking arrangement?

c. What is the projected annual cost of operating the proposed system?

d. Should Artie Kay's adopt the new system? Compute the net annual gain or loss associated with adopting the system.

ST-3. (*Buying and Selling Marketable Securities*) Mountaineer Outfitters has $2 million in excess cash that it might invest in marketable securities. In order to buy and sell the securities, however, the firm must pay a transactions fee of $45,000.

a. Would you recommend purchasing the securities if they yield 12 percent annually and are held for
   1. One month?
   2. Two months?

3. Three months?

4. Six months?

5. One year?

b. What minimum required yield would the securities have to return for the firm to hold them for three months (what is the breakeven yield for a three-month holding period)?

STUDY PROBLEMS (SET A)

15–1A. (*Concentration Banking*) Byron Sporting Goods operates in Miami, Florida. The firm produces and distributes a full line of athletic equipment on a nationwide basis. The firm presently uses a centralized billing system. Byron Sporting Goods has annual credit sales of $362 million. Austin National Bank has presented an offer to operate a concentration banking system for the company. Byron already has an established line of credit with Austin. Austin says it will operate the system on a flat-fee basis of $175,000 per year. The analysis done by the bank's cash-management services division suggests that three days in mail float and one day in processing float can be eliminated.

Because Byron borrows almost continuously from Austin National, the value of the float reduction would be applied against the line of credit. The borrowing rate on the line of credit is set at an annual rate of 7 percent. Further, because of the reduction in clerical help, the new system will save the firm $57,500 in processing costs. Byron uses a 365-day year in analyses of this sort. Should Byron accept the bank's offer to install the new system?

15–2A. (*Lock-Box System*) The Marino Rug Co. is located on the outskirts of Miramar, Florida. The firm specializes in the manufacture of a wide variety of carpet and tile. All of the firm's output is shipped to 12 warehouses, which are located in the largest metropolitan areas nationwide. National Bank of Miami is Marino Rug's lead bank. National Bank has just completed a study of Marino's cash collection system. Overall, National estimates that it can reduce Marino's total float by three days with the installation of a lock-box arrangement in each of the firm's 12 regions. The lock-box arrangement would cost each region $325 per month. Any funds freed up would be added to the firm's marketable securities portfolio and would yield 9.75 percent on an annual basis. Annual sales average $6,232,375 for each regional office. The firm and the bank use a 365-day year in their analyses. Should Marion's management approve the use of the proposed system?

15–3A. (*Marketable Securities Portfolio*) Mac's Tennis Racket Manufacturing Company currently pays its employees on a weekly basis. The weekly wage bill is $675,000. This means that on the average the firm has accrued wages payable of ($675,000 + $0)/2 = $337,500.

Jimmy McEnroe works as the firm's senior financial analyst and reports directly to his uncle, who owns all of the firm's common stock. Jimmy McEnroe wants to move to a monthly wage payment system. Employees would be paid at the end of every fourth week. Jimmy is aware that the labor union representing the company's workers will not permit the monthly payments system to take effect unless the workers are given some type of fringe-benefit compensation.

A plan has been worked out whereby the firm will make a contribution to the cost of life insurance coverage for each employee. This will cost the firm $50,775 annually. Jimmy McEnroe expects the firm to earn 8.5 percent annually on its marketable securities portfolio.

a. Based on the projected information, should Mac's Tennis Racket Manufacturing Company move to the monthly wage payment system?

b. What annual rate of return on the marketable securities portfolio would enable the firm just to break even on this proposal?

15–4A. (*Buying and Selling Marketable Securities*) Miami Dice & Card Company has generated $800,000 in excess cash that it could invest in marketable securities. In order to buy and sell the securities, the firm will pay total transactions fees of $20,000.

a. Would you recommend purchasing the securities if they yield 10.5 percent annually and are held for

1. One month?

2. Two months?

3. Three months?

4. Six months?

5. One year?

b. What minimum required yield would the securities have to return for the firm to hold them for two months (what is the breakeven yield for a two-month holding period)?

15–5A. (*Cash Receipts Acceleration System*) James Waller Nail Corp. is a buyer and distributor of nails used in the home building industry. The firm has grown very quickly since it was established eight years ago. Waller Nail has managed to increase sales and profits at a rate of about 18 percent annually, despite moderate economic growth at the national level. Until recently, the company paid little attention to cash-management procedures. James Waller, the firm's president, said: "With our growth—who cares?" Bending to the suggestions of several analysts in the firm's finance group, Waller did agree to have a proposal prepared by the Second National Bank in Tampa, Florida. The objective of the proposal is to accelerate the firm's cash collections.

At present, Waller Nail uses a centralized billing procedure. All checks are mailed to the Tampa office headquarters for processing and eventual deposit. Under this arrangement, all customers' remittance checks take an average of five business days to reach the Tampa office. Once in Tampa, another two days are needed to process the checks for deposit at the Second National Bank.

Daily cash remittances at Waller Nail average $750,000. The average check size is $3,750. The firm currently earns 9.2 percent annually on its marketable securities portfolio.

The cash-acceleration plan presented by the officers of Second National Bank involves both a lock-box system and concentration banking. Second National would be the firm's only concentration bank. Lock boxes would be established in (1) Los Angeles, (2) Dallas, (3) Chicago, and (4) Tampa. This would reduce funds tied up in mail float to 3.5 days. Processing float would be totally eliminated. Funds would then be transferred twice each business day by means of automated depository transfer checks from local banks in Los Angeles, Dallas, and Chicago to the Second National Bank. Each ADTC costs $27. These transfers will occur all 270 business days of the year. Each check processed through the lock box will cost Waller Nail $.35.

a. What amount of cash balances will be freed if Waller Nail adopts the system proposed by Second National Bank?

b. What is the opportunity cost of maintaining the current banking arrangement?

c. What is the projected annual cost of operating the proposed system?

d. Should Waller Nail Corp. adopt the system? Compute the net annual gain or loss associated with adopting the system.

15–6A. (*Concentration Banking*) Walkin Chemicals operates in New Orleans. The firm produces and distributes industrial cleaning products on a nationwide basis. The firm presently uses a centralized billing system. Walkin Chemicals has annual credit sales of $438 million. Creole National Bank has presented an offer to operate a concentration banking system for the company. Walkin already has an established line of credit with Creole. Creole says it will operate the system on a flat fee basis of $250,000 per year. The analysis done by the bank's cash-management services division suggests that two days in mail float and one day in processing float can be eliminated.

Because Walkin borrows almost continuously from Creole National, the value of the float reduction would be applied against the line of credit. The borrowing rate on the line of credit is set at an annual rate of 11 percent. Further, because of a reduction in clerical help, the new system will save the firm $65,000 in processing costs. Walkin uses a 365-day year in analyses of this sort. Should Walkin accept the bank's offer to install the new system?

15–7A. (*Lock-Box System*) Advanced Electronics is located in Nashville, Tennessee. The firm manufactures components used in a variety of electrical devices. All the firm's finished goods are shipped to five regional warehouses across the United States.

First Volunteer Bank of Nashville is Advanced Electronics' lead bank. First Volunteer recently completed a study of Advanced Electronics' cash-collection system. First Volunteer estimates that it can reduce Advanced Electronics' total float by 2.5 days with the installation of a lock-box arrangement in each of the firm's five regions.

The lock-box arrangement would cost each region $500 per month. Any funds freed up would be added to the firm's marketable securities portfolio and would yield 11.75 percent on an annual basis. Annual sales average $10,950,000 for each regional office. The firm and the bank use a 365-day year in their analyses. Should Advance Electronics' management approve the use of the proposed system?

15–8A. (*Costs of Services*) The Mountain Furniture Company of Scranton, Pennsylvania, may install a lock-box system to speed up its cash receipts. On an annual basis, Mountain Furniture receives $40 million in remittances by check. The firm will record and process 15,000 checks over the year. The Third Bank of Scranton will administer the system at a cost of $.35 per check. Cash that is freed up by use of the system can be invested to yield 9 percent on an annual before-tax basis. A 365-day year is used for analysis purposes. What reduction in check collection time is necessary for Mountain Furniture to be neither better nor worse off for having adopted the proposed system?

15–9A. (*Cash Receipts Acceleration System*) Ronda Ball Kitchens Corp. is a medium-size manufacturer, buyer, and installer of quality kitchen equipment and apparatus. The firm, which was established five years ago, has grown very quickly. Despite some rough economic times that included two recessions in three years, Ball Kitchens has managed to increase sales and profits at an approximate rate of 20 percent annually. Until recently, the firm paid no attention to its cash-management procedures. Ronda Ball, the company's president, just said, "We are too busy growing to worry about those trivial things." Bending to the pleas of several analysts in the firm's finance group, Ball did agree to have a proposal prepared by the Pan-Atlantic Bank in Orlando, Florida. The objective of the proposal is to speed up the firm's cash collections.

At present, Ball Kitchens uses a centralized billing procedure. All checks are mailed to the Orlando headquarters office for processing and eventual deposit. Under this arrangement all of the customers' remittance checks take an average of four business days to reach the Orlando office. Once in Orlando, another two days are needed to process the checks for deposit at the Pan-Atlantic Bank.

The daily cash remittances of Ball Kitchens average $500,000. The average check size is $2,000. The firm currently earns 8.8 percent annually on its marketable securities portfolio.

The cash-acceleration plan of the officers of Pan-Atlantic involves both a lock-box system and concentration banking. Pan-Atlantic would be the firm's only concentration bank. Lock boxes would be established in (1) Los Angeles, (2) Houston, (3) Chicago, and (4) Orlando. This would reduce funds tied up by mail float to 2.5 days. Processing float would be eliminated. Funds would then be transferred twice each business day by means of automated depository transfer checks from local banks in Los Angeles, Houston, and Chicago to the Pan-Atlantic Bank. Each ADTC costs $22. These transfers will occur all 270 business days of the year. Each check processed through the lock-box system will cost Ball Kitchens $.20.

  a. What amount of cash balances will be freed if Ball Kitchens adopts the system proposed by Pan-Atlantic?

  b. What is the opportunity cost of maintaining the current banking arrangement?

  c. What is the projected annual cost of operating the proposed system?

  d. Should Ball Kitchens adopt the new system? Compute the net annual gain or loss associated with adopting the system.

15–10A. (*Buying and Selling Marketable Securities*) Saturday Knights Live Products, Inc., has $1 million in excess cash that it might invest in marketable securities. In order to buy and sell the securities, however, the firm must pay a transactions fee of $30,000.

  a. Would you recommend purchasing the securities if they yield 11 percent annually and are held for

    1. One month?

    2. Two months?

    3. Three months?

    4. Six months?

    5. One year?

  b. What minimum required yield would the securities have to return for the firm to hold them for three months (what is the breakeven yield for a three-month holding period?).

15–11A. (*Concentration Banking*) Columbia Textiles, located in South Carolina, manufactures and distributes textile products on a nationwide basis. The firm has always used a centralized billing system. Columbia Textiles has annual credit sales of $365 million. South Carolina National Bank has approached Columbia Textiles with an offer to establish and operate a concentration banking system for the company. Columbia already has an established line of credit with this same bank. South Carolina National says it will operate the system on a flat fee basis of $200,000 per year. A detailed analysis done by the bank's cash-management services division shows conclusively that two days in mail float and one day in processing float can be eliminated. Because Columbia borrows almost continuously from South Carolina National, the value of the float reduction would be applied against the line of credit. The borrowing rate on the line of credit is set at an annual rate of 15 percent. In addition, because of a reduction in clerical help, the new system will save the firm $50,000 per year in processing costs. Columbia uses a 365-day year in analyses of this sort. Should Columbia accept the bank's offer to install the new system?

15-12A. (*Lock-Box System*) Penn Foundry is located on the outskirts of State College, Pennsylvania. The firm specializes in the manufacture of aluminum and steel castings, which are used for numerous automobile parts. All of the firm's output is shipped to 10 warehouses near major auto assembly plants across the United States. First Quaker Bank of Philadelphia is Penn Foundry's lead bank. First Quaker has just completed a study of Penn's cash collection system. Overall, First Quaker estimates that it can reduce Penn's total float by 2.5 days with the installation of a lock-box arrangement in each of the firm's 10 regions. The lock-box arrangement would cost each region $300 per month. Any funds freed up would be added to the firm's marketable securities portfolio and would yield 10.5 percent on an annual basis. Annual sales average $5,475,000 for each regional office. The firm and the bank use a 365-day year in their analyses. Should Penn Foundry's management approve the use of the proposed system?

15-13A. (*Valuing Float Reduction*) Griffey Manufacturing Company is forecasting that next year's gross revenues from sales will be $890 million. The senior treasury analyst for the firm expects the marketable securities portfolio to earn 9.60 percent over this same time period. A 365-day year is used in all the firm's financial procedures. What is the value to the company of one day's float reduction?

15-14A. (*Costs of Services*) The Idaho Lumber Company may install a lock-box system in order to speed up its cash receipts. On an annual basis, Idaho receives $60 million of remittances by check. The firm will record and process 18,000 checks over the year. The Pocatello Fourth National Bank will administer the system for a unit cost of $.30 per check. Cash that is freed by the use of this system can be invested to yield 8 percent on an annual before-tax basis. A 365-day year is used for analysis purposes. What reduction in check collection time is necessary for Idaho Lumber to be neither better nor worse off for having adopted the proposed system?

15-15A. (*Costs of Services*) Mustang Ski-Wear, Inc., is investigating the possibility of adopting a lock-box system as a cash receipts acceleration device. In a typical year this firm receives remittances totaling $12 million by check. The firm will record and process 6,000 checks over this same time period. The Colorado Springs Second National Bank has informed the management of Mustang that it will expedite checks and associated documents through the lock-box system for a unit cost of $.20 per check. Mustang's financial manager has projected that cash freed by adoption of the system can be invested in a portfolio of near-cash assets that will yield an annual before-tax return of 7 percent. Mustang financial analysts use a 365-day year in their procedures.
   a. What reduction in check collection time is necessary for Mustang to be neither better nor worse off for having adopted the proposed system?
   b. How would your solution to (a) be affected if Mustang could invest the freed balances only at an expected annual return of 4.5 percent?
   c. What is the logical explanation for the difference in your answers to (a) and (b)?

15-16A. (*Valuing Float Reduction*) The Columbus Tool and Die Works will generate $18 million in credit sales next year. Collections occur at an even rate, and employees work a 270-day year. At the moment, the firm's general accounting department ties up five days' worth of remittance checks. An analysis undertaken by the firm's treasurer indicates that new internal procedures can reduce processing float by two days. If Columbus Tool invests the released funds to earn 8 percent, what will be the annual savings?

15-17A. (*Lock-Box System*) Penn Steelworks is a distributor of cold-rolled steel products to the automobile industry. All its sales are on a credit basis, net 30 days. Sales are evenly distributed over its 10 sales regions throughout the United States. Delinquent accounts are no problem. The company has recently undertaken an analysis aimed at improving its cash-management procedures. Penn determined that it takes an average of 3.2 days for customers' payments to reach the head office in Pittsburgh from the time they are mailed. It takes another full day in processing time prior to depositing the checks with a local bank. Annual sales average $4,800,000 for each regional office. Reasonable investment opportunities can be found yielding 7 percent per year. To alleviate the float problem confronting the firm, the use of a lock-box system in each of the 10 regions is being considered. This would reduce mail float by 1.2 days. One day in processing float would also be eliminated, plus a full day in transit float. The lock-box arrangement would cost each region $250 per month.
   a. What is the opportunity cost to Penn Steelworks of the funds tied up in mailing and processing? Use a 365-day year.
   b. What would the net cost or savings be from use of the proposed cash-acceleration technique? Should Penn adopt the system?

15–18A. (*Valuing Float Reduction*) Next year P. F. Anderson Motors expects its gross revenues from sales to be $80 million. The firm's treasurer has projected that its marketable securities portfolio will earn 6.50 percent over the coming budget year. What is the value of one day's float reduction to the company? Anderson Motors uses a 365-day year in all of its financial analysis procedures.

15–19A. (*Cash Receipts Acceleration System*) Peggy Pierce Designs, Inc., is a vertically integrated, national manufacturer and retailer of women's clothing. Currently, the firm has no coordinated cash-management system. A proposal, however, from the First Pennsylvania Bank aimed at speeding up cash collections is being examined by several of Pierce's corporate executives.

The firm currently uses a centralized billing procedure, which requires that all checks be mailed to the Philadelphia head office for processing and eventual deposit. Under this arrangement all the customers' remittance checks take an average of five business days to reach the head office. Once in Philadelphia another two days are required to process the checks for ultimate deposit at the First Pennsylvania Bank.

The firm's daily remittances average $1 million. The average check size is $2,000. Pierce Designs currently earns 6 percent annually on its marketable securities portfolio.

The cash acceleration plan proposed by officers of First Pennsylvania involves both a lock-box system and concentration banking. First Pennsylvania would be the firm's only concentration bank. Lock boxes would be established in (1) San Francisco, (2) Dallas, (3) Chicago, and (4) Philadelphia. This would reduce funds tied up by mail float to three days, and processing float will be eliminated. Funds would then be transferred twice each business day by means of automated depository transfer checks from local banks in San Francisco, Dallas, and Chicago to the First Pennsylvania Bank. Each ADTC costs $15. These transfers will occur all 270 business days of the year. Each check processed through the lock-box system will cost $.18.

  a. What amount of cash balances will be freed if Pierce Designs, Inc., adopts the system suggested by First Pennsylvania?
  b. What is the opportunity of maintaining the current banking setup?
  c. What is the projected annual cost of operating the proposed system?
  d. Should Pierce adopt the new system? Compute the net annual gain or loss associated with adopting the system.

15–20A. (*Marketable Securities Portfolio*) The Alex Daniel Shoe Manufacturing Company currently pays its employees on a weekly basis. The weekly wage bill is $500,000. This means that on the average the firm has accrued wages payable of ($500,000 + $0)/2 = $250,000.

Alex Daniel, Jr., works as the firm's senior financial analyst and reports directly to his father, who owns all of the firm's common stock. Alex Daniel, Jr., wants to move to a monthly wage payment system. Employees would be paid at the end of every fourth week. The younger Daniel is fully aware that the labor union representing the company's workers will not permit the monthly payments system to take effect unless the workers are given some type of fringe benefit compensation.

A plan has been worked out whereby the firm will make a contribution to the cost of life insurance coverage for each employee. This will cost the firm $35,000 annually. Alex Daniel, Jr., expects the firm to earn 7 percent annually on its marketable securities portfolio.

  a. Based on the projected information, should Daniel Shoe Manufacturing move to the monthly wage payment system?
  b. What annual rate of return on the marketable securities portfolio would enable the firm to just break even on this proposal?

15–21A. (*Valuing Float Reduction*) The Cowboy Bottling Company will generate $12 million in credit sales next year. Collections of these credit sales will occur evenly over this period. The firm's employees work 270 days a year. Currently, the firm's processing system ties up four days' worth of remittance checks. A recent report from a financial consultant indicated procedures that will enable Cowboy Bottling to reduce processing float by two full days. If Cowboy invests the released funds to earn 6 percent, what will be the annual savings?

15–22A. (*Valuing Float Reduction*) Montgomery Woodcraft is a large distributor of wood-working tools and accessories to hardware stores, lumber yards, and tradesmen. All its sales are on a credit basis, net 30 days. Sales are evenly distributed over its 12 sales regions throughout the United States. There is no problem with delinquent accounts. The firm is attempting to improve its cash-management procedures.

Montgomery recently determined that it took an average of 3.0 days for customers' payments to reach their office from the time they were mailed and another day for processing before payments could be deposited. Annual sales average $5,200,000 for each region, and investment opportunities can be found to return 9 percent per year. What is the opportunity cost to the firm of the funds tied up in mailing and processing? In your calculations use a 365-day year.

15–23A. (*Lock-Box System*) To mitigate the float problem discussed above, Montgomery Woodcraft is considering the use of a lock-box system in each of its regions. By so doing, it can reduce the mail float by 1.5 days and receive the *other* benefits of a lock-box system. It also estimates that transit float could be reduced to half its present duration of two days. Use of the lock-box arrangement in each of its regions will cost $300 per month. Should Montgomery Woodcraft adopt the system? What would the net cost or savings be?

15–24A. (*Accounts Payable Policy and Cash Management*) Bradford Construction Supply Company is suffering from a prolonged decline in new construction in its sales area. In an attempt to improve its cash position, the firm is considering changes in its accounts payable policy. After careful study it has determined that the only alternative available is to slow disbursements. Purchases for the coming year are expected to be $37.5 million. Sales will be $65 million, which represents about a 20 percent drop from the current year. Currently, Bradford discounts approximately 25 percent of its payments at 3 percent 10 days, net 30, and the balance of accounts are paid in 30 days. If Bradford adopts a policy of payment in 45 days or 60 days, how much can the firm gain if the annual opportunity cost of investment is 12 percent? What will be the result if this action causes Bradford Construction suppliers to increase their prices to the company by 0.5 percent to compensate for the 60-day extended term of payment? In your calculations use a 365-day year and ignore any compounding effects related to expected returns.

15–25A. (*Interest Rate Risk*) Two years ago your corporate treasurer purchased for the firm a 20-year bond at its par value of $1,000. The coupon rate on this security is 8 percent. Interest payments are made to bondholders once a year. Currently, bonds of this particular risk class are yielding investors 9 percent. A cash shortage has forced you to instruct your treasurer to liquidate his bond.
   a. At what price will your bond be sold? Assume annual compounding.
   b. What will be the amount of your gain or loss over the original purchase price?
   c. What would be the amount of your gain or loss had the treasurer originally purchased a bond with a four-year rather than a 20-year maturity? (Assume all characteristics of the bonds are identical except their maturity periods.)
   d. What do we call this type of risk assumed by your corporate treasurer?

15–26A. (*Marketable Securities Portfolio*) Red Raider Feedlots has $4 million in excess cash to invest in a marketable securities portfolio. Its broker will charge $10,000 to invest the entire $4 million. The president of Red Raider wants at least half of the $4 million invested at a maturity period of three months or less; the remainder can be invested in securities with maturities not to exceed six months. The relevant term structure of short-term yields follows:

Maturity	Available Yield (Annual)
One month	6.2%
Two months	6.4
Three months	6.5
Four months	6.7
Five months	6.9
Six months	7.0

   a. What should be the maturity periods of the securities purchased with the excess $4 million to maximize the before-tax income from the added investment? What will be the amount of the income from such an investment?
   b. Suppose that the president of Red Raider relaxes his constraint on the maturity structure of the added investment. What would be your profit-maximizing investment recommendation?
   c. If one-sixth of the excess cash is invested in each of the maturity categories shown above, what would be the before-tax income generated from such an action?

15–27A. (*Comparison of After-Tax Yields*) The corporate treasurer of Aggieland Fireworks is considering the purchase of a BBB-rated bond that carries a 9 percent coupon. The BBB-rated security is taxable, and the firm is in the 46 percent marginal tax bracket. The face value of this bond is $1,000. A financial analyst who reports to the corporate treasurer has alerted him to the fact that a municipal obligation is coming to the market with a 5½ percent coupon. The par value of this security is also $1,000.

    a. Which one of the two securities do you recommend the firm purchase? Why?

    b. What must the fully taxed bond yield before tax to make it comparable with the municipal offering?

15–28A. (*Comparison of Yields*) A large proportion of the marketable securities portfolio of Edwards Manufacturing is invested in Treasury bills yielding 6.52 percent before consideration of income taxes. Hoosierville Utilities is bringing a new issue of preferred stock to the marketplace. The new preferred issue will yield 9.30 percent before taxes. The corporate treasurer for Edwards wants to evaluate the possibility of shifting a portion of the funds tied up in Treasury bills to the preferred stock issue.

    a. Calculate the ultimate yields available to Edwards from investing in each type of security. Edwards is in the 46 percent tax bracket.

    b. What factors apart from the available yields should be analyzed in this situation?

15–29A. (*Forecasting Excess Cash*) The C. K. S. Stove Company manufactures wood-burning stoves in the Pacific Northwest. Despite the recent popularity of this product, the firm has experienced a very erratic sales pattern. Owing to volatile weather conditions and abrupt changes in new housing starts, it has been extremely difficult for the firm to forecast its cash balances. Still, the company president is disturbed by the fact that the firm has never invested in any marketable securities. Instead, the liquid asset portfolio has consisted entirely of cash. As a start toward reducing the firm's investment in cash and releasing some of it to near-cash assets, a historical record and projection of corporate cash holdings is needed. Over the past five years sales have been $10 million, $12 million, $11 million, $14 million, and $19 million, respectively. Sales forecasts for the next two years are $23 and $21 million. Total assets for the firm are 60 percent of sales. Fixed assets are the higher of 50 percent of total assets or $4 million. Inventory and receivables amount to 70 percent of current assets and are held in equal proportions.

    a. Prepare a worksheet that details the firm's balance sheets for each of the past five years and for the forecast periods.

    b. What amount of cash will the firm have on hand during each year for short-term investment purposes?

STUDY PROBLEMS (SET B)

15–1B. (*Buying and Selling Marketable Securities*) Universal Concrete Company has generated $700,000 in excess cash that it could invest in marketable securities. In order to buy and sell the securities, the firm will pay total transactions fees of $25,000.

    a. Would you recommend purchasing the securities if they yield 11.5 percent annually and are held for

        1. One month?

        2. Two months?

        3. Three months?

        4. Six months?

        5. One year?

    b. What minimum required yield would the securities have to return for the firm to hold them for two months (what is the breakeven yield for a two-month holding period)?

15–2B. (*Cash Receipts Acceleration System*) Kobrin Door & Glass, Inc., is a buyer and distributor of doors used in the home building industry. The firm has grown very quickly because it was established eight years ago. Kobrin Door has managed to increase sales and profits at a rate of about 18 percent annually, despite moderate economic growth at the national level. Until recently, the company paid little attention to cash-management procedures. Charles Kobrin, the firm's president, said: "With our growth—who cares?" Bending to the suggestions of several analysts in the firm's finance group. Kobrin did agree to have a proposal prepared by the First Citizens Bank in Tampa, Florida. The objective of the proposal is to accelerate the firm's cash collections.

    At present, Kobrin Door uses a centralized billing procedure. All checks are mailed to the Tampa office headquarters for processing and eventual deposit. Under this arrangement, all customers' remittance checks take an average of five business days to reach the Tampa office. Once in Tampa, another two days are needed to process the checks for deposit at the First Citizens Bank.

Daily cash remittances at Kobrin Door average $800,000. The average check size is $4,000. The firm currently earns 9.5 percent annually on its marketable securities portfolio.

The cash-acceleration plan presented by the officers of First Citizens Bank involves both a lock-box system and concentration banking. First Citizens would be the firm's only concentration bank. Lock boxes would be established in (1) Los Angeles, (2) Dallas, (3) Chicago, and (4) Tampa. This would reduce funds tied up in mail float to 3.5 days. Processing float would be totally eliminated. Funds would then be transferred twice each business day by means of automated depository transfer checks from local banks in Los Angeles, Dallas, and Chicago to the First Citizens Bank. Each depository transfer check (ADTC) costs $30. These transfers will occur all 270 business days of the year. Each check processed through the lock box will cost Kobrin Door $.40.

    a. What amount of cash balances will be freed if Kobrin Door adopts the system proposed by First Citizens Bank?

    b. What is the opportunity cost of maintaining the current banking arrangement?

    c. What is the projected annual cost of operating the proposed system?

    d. Should Kobrin Door & Glass adopt the system? Compute the net annual gain or loss associated with adopting the system.

15–3B. (*Concentration Banking*) Smith & Tucker (S&T) Enterprises operates in New Orleans. The firm manufactures and distributes quality furniture on a nationwide basis. The firm presently uses a centralized billing system. S&T has annual credit sales of $438 million. Bayou National Bank has presented an offer to operate a concentration banking system for the company. S&T already has an established line of credit with Bayou. Bayou says it will operate the system on a flat fee basis of $300,000 per year. The analysis done by the bank's cash-management services division suggests that two days in mail float and one day in processing float can be eliminated.

Because S&T borrows almost continuously from Bayou National, the value of the float reduction would be applied against the line of credit. The borrowing rate on the line of credit is set at an annual rate of 11 percent. Further, because of a reduction in clerical help, the new system will save the firm $68,000 in processing costs. S&T uses a 365-day year in analyses of this sort. Should S&T accept the bank's offer to install the new system?

15–4B. (*Lock-Box System*) Regency Components is located in Nashville, Tennessee. The firm manufactures components used in a variety of electrical devices. All the firm's finished goods are shipped to five regional warehouses across the United States.

Tennessee State Bank of Nashville is Regency Components' lead bank. Tennessee State recently completed a study of Regency's cash-collection system. Tennessee State estimates that it can reduce Regency's total float by 3.0 days with the installation of a lock-box arrangement in each of the firm's five regions.

The lock-box arrangement would cost each region $600 per month. Any funds freed up would be added to the firm's marketable securities portfolio and would yield 11.0 percent on an annual basis. Annual sales average $10,000,000 for each regional office. The firm and the bank use a 365-day year in their analyses. Should Regency Components' management approve the use of the proposed system?

15–5B. (*Costs of Services*) The Hallmark Technology Company of Scranton, Pennsylvania, may install a lock-box system in order to speed up its cash receipts. On an annual basis, Hallmark receives $50 million in remittances by check. The firm will record and process 20,000 checks over the year. The Third Bank of Scranton will administer the system at a cost of $.37 per check. Cash that is freed up by use of the system can be invested to yield 9 percent on an annual before-tax basis. A 365-day year is used for analysis purposes. What reduction in check collection time is necessary for Hallmark to be neither better nor worse off for having adopted the proposed system?

15–6B. (*Cash Receipts Acceleration System*) Lee Collins Woodcrafts Corp. is a medium-sized manufacturer, buyer, and installer of quality kitchen equipment and apparatus. The firm, which was established five years ago, has grown very quickly. Despite some rough economic times that included two recessions in three years, Collins Woodcrafts has managed to increase sales and profits at an approximate rate of 20 percent annually. Until recently, the firm paid no attention to its cash-management procedures. Lee Collins, the company's president, just said, "We are too busy growing to worry about those trivial things." Bending to the pleas of several analysts in the firm's finance group, Collins did agree to have a proposal prepared by the Pan-Atlantic Bank in Orlando, Florida. The objective of the proposal is to speed up the firm's cash collections.

At present, Collins Woodcrafts uses a centralized billing procedure. All checks are mailed to the Orlando headquarters office for processing and eventual deposit. Under this arrangement all of the customers' remittance checks take an average of four business days to reach the Orlando office. Once in Orlando, another two days are needed to process the checks for deposit at the Pan-Atlantic Bank.

The daily cash remittances of Collins Woodcrafts average $450,000. The average check size is $2,000. The firm currently earns 8.5 percent annually on its marketable securities portfolio.

The cash-acceleration plan presented by the officers of Pan-Atlantic involves both a lock-box system and concentration banking. Pan-Atlantic would be the firm's only concentration bank. Lock boxes would be established in (1) Los Angeles, (2) Houston, (3) Chicago, and (4) Orlando. This would reduce funds tied up by mail float to 2.5 days. Processing float would be eliminated. Funds would then be transferred twice each business day by means of automated depository transfer checks from local banks in Los Angeles, Houston, and Chicago to the Pan-Atlantic Bank. Each depository transfer check (ADTC) costs $25. These transfers will occur all 270 business days of the year. Each check processed through the lock-box system will cost Collins Woodcrafts $.25.

  a. What amount of cash balances will be freed if Collins Woodcrafts adopts the system proposed by Pan-Atlantic?
  b. What is the opportunity cost of maintaining the current banking arrangement?
  c. What is the projected annual cost of operating the proposed system?
  d. Should Collins Woodcrafts adopt the new system? Compute the net annual gain or loss associated with adopting the system.

15–7B. (*Buying and Selling Marketable Securities*) Western Photo Corp. has $1 million in excess cash that it might invest in marketable securities. In order to buy and sell the securities, however, the firm must pay a transactions fee of $35,000.
  a. Would you recommend purchasing the securities if they yield 10 percent annually and are held for
    1. One month?
    2. Two months?
    3. Three months?
    4. Six months?
    5. One year?
  b. What minimum required yield would the securities have to return for the firm to hold them for three months (what is the breakeven yield for a three-month holding period)?

15–8B. (*Concentration Banking*) Block Music Company, located in South Carolina, manufactures and distributes musical instruments on a nationwide basis. The firm has always used a centralized billing system. Block Music has annual credit sales of $375,000 million. South Carolina National Bank has approached Block Music with an offer to establish and operate a concentration banking system for the company. Block already has an established line of credit with this same bank. South Carolina National says it will operate the system on a flat fee basis of $150,000 per year. A detailed analysis done by the bank's cash-management services division shows conclusively that two days in mail float and one day in processing float can be eliminated. Because Block borrows almost continuously from South Carolina National, the value of the float reduction would be applied against the line of credit. The borrowing rate on the line of credit is set at an annual rate of 16 percent. In addition, because of a reduction in clerical help, the new system will save the firm $40,000 per year in processing costs. Block uses a 365-day year in analyses of this sort. Should Block Music accept the bank's offer to install the new system?

15–9B. (*Lock-Box System*) Metrocorp is located on the outskirts of State College, Pennsylvania. The firm specializes in the manufacture of aluminum and steel castings, which are used for numerous automobile parts. All of the firm's output is shipped to 10 warehouses near major auto assembly plants across the United States. First Quaker Bank of Philadelphia is Metrocorp's lead bank. First Quaker has just completed a study of Metrocorp's cash collection system. Overall, First Quaker estimates that it can reduce Metrocorp's total float by 2.5 days with the installation of a lock-box arrangement in each of the firm's 10 regions. The lock-box arrangement would cost each region $300 per month. Any funds freed up would be added to the firm's marketable securities portfolio and would yield 10.0 percent on an annual basis. Annual sales average $4,475,000 for each regional office. The firm and the bank use a 365-day year in their analyses. Should Metrocorp's management approve the use of the proposed system?

15–10B. (*Valuing Float Reduction*) Brady Consulting Services is forecasting that next year's gross revenues from sales will be $900 million. The senior treasury analyst for the firm expects the marketable securities portfolio to earn 9.5 percent over this same time period. A 365-day year is used in all the firm's financial procedures. What is the value to the company of one day's float reduction?

15-11B. (*Costs of Services*) The Discount Storage Co. may install a lock-box system to speed up its cash receipts. On an annual basis, Discount receives $55 million of remittances by check. The firm will record and process 20,000 checks over the year. The Pocatello Fourth National Bank will administer the system for a unit cost of $.30 per check. Cash that is freed by the use of this system can be invested to yield 8 percent on an annual before-tax basis. A 365-day year is used for analysis purposes. What reduction in check collection time is necessary for Discount Storage to be neither better nor worse off for having adopted the proposed system?

15-12B. (*Costs of Services*) Colorado Communications is investigating the possibility of adopting a lock-box system as a cash receipts acceleration device. In a typical year this firm receives remittances totaling $10 million by check. The firm will record and process 7,000 checks over this same time period. The Colorado Springs Second National Bank has informed the management of Colorado Comm that it will expedite checks and associated documents through the lock-box system for a unit cost of $.30 per check. Colorado Comm's financial manager has projected that cash freed by adoption of the system can be invested in a portfolio of near-cash assets that will yield an annual before-tax return of 7 percent. Colorado Comm's financial analysts use a 365-day year in their procedures.
   a. What reduction in check collection time is necessary for Colorado Comm to be neither better nor worse off for having adopted the proposed system?
   b. How would your solution to (a) be affected if Colorado Comm could invest the freed balances only at an expected annual return of 4.5 percent?
   c. What is the logical explanation for the difference in your answers to (a) and (b)?

15-13B. (*Valuing Float Reduction*) Campus Restaurants, Inc., will generate $17 million in credit sales next year. Collections occur at an even rate, and employees work a 270-day year. At the moment, the firm's general accounting department ties up four days' worth of remittance checks. An analysis undertaken by the firm's treasurer indicates that new internal procedures can reduce processing float by two days. If Campus invests the released funds to earn 9 percent, what will be the annual savings?

15-14B. (*Lock-Box System*) Alpine Systems is a distributor of refrigerated storage units to the meat products industry. All its sales are on a credit basis, net 30 days. Sales are evenly distributed over its 10 sales regions throughout the United States. Delinquent accounts are no problem. The company has recently undertaken an analysis aimed at improving its cash-management procedures. Alpine determined that it takes an average of 3.2 days for customers' payments to reach the head office in Pittsburgh from the time they are mailed. It takes another full day in processing time prior to depositing the checks with a local bank. Annual sales average $5,000,000 for each regional office. Reasonable investment opportunities can be found yielding 8 percent per year. To alleviate the float problem confronting the firm, the use of a lock-box system in each of the 10 regions is being considered. This would reduce mail float by 1.0 days. One day in processing float would also be eliminated, plus a full day in transit float. The lock-box arrangement would cost each region $225 per month.
   a. What is the opportunity cost to Alpine Systems of the funds tied up in mailing and processing? Use a 365-day year.
   b. What would the net cost or savings be from use of the proposed cash-acceleration technique? Should Alpine adopt the system?

15-15B. (*Valuing Float Reduction*) Next year Concept Realty expects its gross revenues from sales to be $90 million. The firm's treasurer has projected that its marketable securities portfolio will earn 6.50 percent over the coming budget year. What is the value of one day's float reduction to the company? Concept Realty uses a 360-day year in all of its financial analysis procedures.

15-16B. (*Cash Receipts Acceleration System*) Carter's Bicycles, Inc., is a vertically integrated, national manufacturer and retailer of racing bicycles. Currently, the firm has no coordinated cash-management system. A proposal, however, from the First Pennsylvania Bank aimed at speeding up cash collections is being examined by several of Carter's corporate executives.

   The firm currently uses a centralized billing procedure, which requires that all checks be mailed to the Philadelphia head office for processing and eventual deposit. Under this arrangement all the customers' remittance checks take an average of four business days to reach the head office. Once in Philadelphia another 1.5 days are required to process the checks for ultimate deposit at the First Pennsylvania Bank.

The firm's daily remittances average $1 million. The average check size is $2,000. Carter's currently earns 7 percent annually on its marketable securities portfolio.

The cash-acceleration plan proposed by officers of First Pennsylvania involves both a lock-box system and concentration banking. First Pennsylvania would be the firm's only concentration bank. Lock boxes would be established in (1) San Francisco, (2) Dallas, (3) Chicago, and (4) Philadelphia. This would reduce funds tied up by mail float to three days, and processing float will be eliminated. Funds would then be transferred twice each business day by means of automated depository transfer checks from local banks in San Francisco, Dallas, and Chicago to the First Pennsylvania Bank. Each ADTC costs $16. These transfers will occur all 270 business days of the year. Each check processed through the lock-box system will cost $.22.

a. What amount of cash balances will be freed if Carter's Bicycles adopts the system suggested by First Pennsylvania?

b. What is the opportunity of maintaining the current banking setup?

c. What is the projected annual cost of operating the proposed system?

d. Should Carter's adopt the new system? Compute the net annual gain or loss associated with adopting the system.

15–17B. (*Marketable Securities Portfolio*) Katz Jewelers currently pays its employees on a weekly basis. The weekly wage bill is $500,000. This means that on the average the firm has accrued wages payable of ($500,000 + $0)/2 = $250,000.

Harry Katz works as the firm's senior financial analyst and reports directly to his father, who owns all of the firm's common stock. Harry Katz wants to move to a monthly wage payment system. Employees would be paid at the end of every fourth week. The younger Katz is fully aware that the labor union representing the company's workers will not permit the monthly payments system to take effect unless the workers are given some type of fringe benefit compensation.

A plan has been worked out whereby the firm will make a contribution to the cost of life insurance coverage for each employee. This will cost the firm $40,000 annually. Harry Katz expects the firm to earn 8 percent annually on its marketable securities portfolio.

a. Based on the projected information, should Katz Jewelers move to the monthly wage payment system?

b. What annual rate of return on the marketable securities portfolio would enable the firm to just break even on this proposal?

15–18B. (*Valuing Float Reduction*) Magic Hardware Stores, Inc., will generate $12 million in credit sales next year. Collections of these credit sales will occur evenly over this period. The firm's employees work 270 days a year. Currently, the firm's processing system ties up 4.5 days' worth of remittance checks. A recent report from a financial consultant indicated procedures that will enable Magic Hardware to reduce processing float by two full days. If Magic invests the released funds to earn 7 percent, what will be the annual savings?

15–19B. (*Valuing Float Reduction*) True Locksmith is a large distributor of residential locks to hardware stores, lumber yards, and tradesmen. All its sales are on a credit basis, net 30 days. Sales are evenly distributed over its 10 sales regions throughout the United States. There is no problem with delinquent accounts. The firm is attempting to improve its cash-management procedures. True Locksmith recently determined that it took an average of 3.0 days for customers' payments to reach their office from the time they were mailed, and another day for processing before payments could be deposited. Annual sales average $5,000,000 for each region, and investment opportunities can be found to return 9 percent per year. What is the opportunity cost to the firm of the funds tied up in mailing and processing? In your calculations use a 365-day year.

15–20B. (*Lock-Box System*) To mitigate the float problem discussed above, True Locksmith is considering the use of a lock-box system in each of its regions. By so doing, it can reduce the mail float by 1.5 days and receive the *other* benefits of a lock-box system. It also estimates that transit float could be reduced to half its present duration of two days. Use of the lock-box arrangement in each of its regions will cost $350 per month. Should True Locksmith adopt the system? What would the net cost or savings be?

15–21B. (*Accounts Payable Policy and Cash Management*) Meadowbrook Paving Company is suffering from a prolonged decline in new development in its sales area. In an attempt to improve its cash position, the firm is considering changes in its accounts payable policy. After careful study it has determined that the only alternative available is to slow disbursements. Purchases for the coming year are expected to be $40 million. Sales will be $65 million, which represents about a 15 percent drop from the current year. Currently, Meadowbrook discounts approximately 25 percent of its payments at 3 percent 10 days, net 30, and the balance of accounts are paid in 30 days. If Meadowbrook adopts a policy of payment in 45 days or 60 days, how much can the firm gain if the annual opportunity cost of investment is 11 percent? What will be the result if this action causes Meadowbrook Paving suppliers to increase their prices to the company by 0.5 percent to compensate for the 60-day extended term of payment? In your calculations use a 365-day year and ignore any compounding effects related to expected returns.

15–22B. (*Interest Rate Risk*) Two years ago your corporate treasurer purchased for the firm a 20-year bond at its par value of $1,000. The coupon rate on this security is 8 percent. Interest payments are made to bondholders once a year. Currently, bonds of this particular risk class are yielding investors 9 percent. A cash shortage has forced you to instruct your treasurer to liquidate his bond.
  a. At what price will your bond be sold? Assume annual compounding.
  b. What will be the amount of your gain or loss over the original purchase price?
  c. What would be the amount of your gain or loss had the treasurer originally purchased a bond with a four-year rather than a 20-year maturity? (Assume all characteristics of the bonds are identical except their maturity periods.)
  d. What do we call this type of risk assumed by your corporate treasurer?

15–23B. (*Marketable Securities Portfolio*) Spencer Pianos has $3.5 million in excess cash to invest in a marketable securities portfolio. Its broker will charge $15,000 to invest the entire $3.5 million. The president of Spencer wants at least half of the $3.5 million invested at a maturity period of three months or less; the remainder can be invested in securities with maturities not to exceed six months. The relevant term structure of short-term yields follows:

Maturity Period	Available Yield (Annual)
One month	6.2%
Two months	6.4
Three months	6.5
Four months	6.7
Five months	6.9
Six months	7.0

  a. What should be the maturity periods of the securities purchased with the excess $3.5 million in order to maximize the before-tax income from the added investment? What will be the amount of the income from such an investment?
  b. Suppose that the president of Spencer relaxes his constraint on the maturity structure of the added investment. What would be your profit-maximizing investment recommendation?
  c. If one-sixth of the excess cash is invested in each of the maturity categories shown above, what would be the before-tax income generated from such an action?

15–24B. (*Comparison of After-Tax Yields*) The corporate treasurer of Ward Grocers is considering the purchase of a BBB-rated bond that carries an 8.0 percent coupon. The BBB-rated security is taxable, and the firm is in the 46 percent marginal tax bracket. The face value of this bond is $1,000. A financial analyst who reports to the corporate treasurer has alerted him to the fact that a municipal obligation is coming to the market with a 5½ percent coupon. The par value of this security is also $1,000.
  a. Which one of the two securities do you recommend the firm purchase? Why?
  b. What must the fully taxed bond yield before tax to make it comparable with the municipal offering?

15–25B. (*Comparison of Yields*) A large proportion of the marketable securities portfolio of Bentley Boats is invested in Treasury bills yielding 7.0 percent before consideration of income taxes. Hoosierville Utilities is bringing a new issue of preferred stock to the marketplace. The new preferred issue will yield 9.30 percent before taxes. The corporate treasurer for Bentley wants to evaluate the possibility of shifting a portion of the funds tied up in Treasury bills to the preferred stock issue.
  a. Calculate the ultimate yields available to Bentley from investing in each type of security. Bentley is in the 46 percent tax bracket.
  b. What factors apart from the available yields should be analyzed in this situation?

15–26B. (*Forecasting Excess Cash*) Fashionable Floors, Inc., manufactures carpet in the Pacific Northwest. Despite the popularity of this product, the firm has experienced a very erratic sales pattern. Owing to volatile weather conditions and abrupt changes in new housing starts, it has been extremely difficult for the firm to forecast its cash balances. Still, the company president is disturbed by the fact that the firm has never invested in any marketable securities. Instead, the liquid asset portfolio has consisted entirely of cash. As a start toward reducing the firm's investment in cash and releasing some of it to near-cash assets, a historical record and projection of corporate cash holdings is needed. Over the past five years sales have been $10 million, $12 million, $11 million, $14 million, and $19 million, respectively. Sales forecasts for the next two years are $24 and $20 million. Total assets for the firm are 65 percent of sales. Fixed assets are the higher of 50 percent of total assets or $4 million. Inventory and receivables amount to 70 percent of current assets and are held in equal proportions.

a. Prepare a worksheet that details the firm's balance sheets for each of the past five years and for the forecast periods.

b. What amount of cash will the firm have on hand during each year for short-term investment purposes?

CASE PROBLEM

CALIFORNIA TRANSISTOR

CASH MANAGEMENT

Michael Broski is the assistant treasurer for California Transistor (CalTrans). He has been with the firm for nine years. The first six were spent within the technology ranks of the company as an electronics engineer. Broski, in fact, took his bachelor's degree in electronics engineering from a famous California-located university noted for its excellent faculty in all phases of engineering. After two years as a senior engineer for the organization, Broski indicated an interest in the administrative management of the firm. He spent one year as an analyst in the treasury department and has just completed his second as the assistant treasurer. During the latter three years, he has steeped himself in literature that focuses on the finance function of the corporate enterprise. In addition, he attended short courses and seminars by national management and accounting associations that dealt with most phases of the financial conduct of the firm. Within CalTrans, other cost accountants, cost analysts, financial analysts, and treasury analysts viewed Broski's rapid grasp of finance concepts as nothing short of phenomenal.

CalTrans is located on the outskirts of San Diego, California. The firm began in the middle 1950s as a small manufacturer of radio and television components. By the late 1950s, it had expanded into the actual installation and service of complete communications systems on navigable vessels. Ships from the U.S. Navy and from the tuna industry use the San Diego port facilities as a major repair yard. During the early years of the firm's activity, defense contracts typically accounted for 80 to 90 percent of annual revenues. CalTrans' management felt, however, that excessive reliance on defense contracts could lead to some very lean years with regard to business receipts. The company expanded during the 1960s into several related fields. Today CalTrans is active in the home entertainment market as well as the defense market. Transistors and integrated circuits are produced for a wide range of final products including radios, televisions, pocket calculators, citizens band receivers, stereo equipment, and ship communications systems. Defense-related business now accounts for 25 to 30 percent of the company's annual sales. This transition to a more diversified enterprise has tended to reduce the inherent "lumpiness" of cash receipts that plagues many small firms relying on defense contracts. In the early years of CalTrans' existence, progress payments on major contracts would often be months apart as the jobs moved toward completion. Currently, the firm enjoys a reasonably stable sales pattern over its fiscal year.

Broski has been studying the behavior of the company's daily and monthly net cash balances. Over the most recent 24 months, he observed that CalTrans' ending cash balance (by month) ranged between $144,000 and $205,000. Only twice during the period that he investigated had the daily closing cash balance even been as low as $100,000. Broski also noted that the firm had no outstanding short-term borrowings throughout these two years. This led him to believe that CalTrans was carrying excessive cash balances; this was probably a tendency that had its roots in the period when defense contracts were the key revenue item for the company. This "first pass" analysis gained the attention of Donald Crawford, who is Broski's boss and CalTrans' treasurer. Crawford is 65 years old and due to retire on July 1 of this year. He has been CalTrans' only treasurer. Broski would like to move into Crawford's job upon his retirement and feels that the treasurer's recommendation might sew it up for him. He also knows that statements relating to excess cash balances being carried by the company will have to be made very tactfully and with Crawford's agreement. That bit of financial policymaking has always rested with the company treasurer. Broski decided that the best plan would be to present

Crawford with a solid analysis of the problem and convince him that a reduction in balances held for transactions purposes would be in the best interests of the firm. As all key officers own considerable stock options, potential increases in corporate profitability usually are well received by management.

Earlier this year Broski attended a cash-management seminar in Los Angeles, sponsored by the commercial bank with which CalTrans holds most of its deposits. The instructor spoke of the firm's cash balance as being "just another inventory." It was offered that the same principles that applied to the determination of an optimal stock of some raw material item also might be applied to the selection of an optimal average amount of transaction cash. Broski really liked that presentation. He walked away from it feeling that he could put it to work. He decided to adapt the basic economic order quantity model to his cash balance problem.

To make the model "workable," it is necessary to build an estimate of the fixed costs associated with adding to or subtracting from the company's inventory of cash. As CalTrans experienced no short-term borrowings within the past two years, Broski considered this element of the problem to be the fixed costs of liquidating a portion of the firm's portfolio of marketable securities.

In Exhibit 1, Broski has summarized the essential activities that occur whenever a liquidation of a part of the securities' portfolio takes place. In all of the firm's cost analysis procedures, it is assumed that a year consists of 264 working days. An eight-hour working day is also utilized in making wage and salary cost projections. Also, minutes of labor are converted into thousandths of an hour. The assistant treasurer felt that from the information in Exhibit 1, he could make a decent estimate of the fixed cost of a security transaction (addition to the firm's cash account).

CalTrans' marketable securities portfolio is usually concentrated in three major money market instruments: (1) Treasury bills, (2) bankers' acceptances, and (3) prime commercial paper. A young analyst who works directly for Michael Broski supplied him with some recent rates of return on these types of securities (Exhibit 2). Broski expressed his concern to the analyst about the possibilities of high rates, such as those experienced during 1973 and 1974, continuing. His intuition or feel for the market led him to believe that short-term interest rates would be closer to 1975 levels during this next year than any other levels identified in Exhibit 2. Thus, Broski decided to use a 6 percent annual yield in this study as a reasonable return to expect from his firm's marketable securities portfolio. Then a review of cash flow patterns over the last five years, including the detailed examination of the most recent 24 months, led to a projection of a typical monthly cash outflow (or demand for cash for transactions purposes) of $800,000.

EXHIBIT 1. California Transistor: Fixed Costs Associated with Securities Liquidation	

Activity	Details
1. Long-distance phone calls.	Cost: $2.75
2. Assistant treasurer's time: 22 minutes	Annual salary for this position is $27,000.
3. Typing of authorization letter, with three carbon copies, and careful proofreading: 17 minutes.	Annual salary for this position is $8000.
4. Carrying original authorization letter to treasurer, who reads and signs it: 2 minutes by same secretary as above, and 2 minutes by for the treasurer.	Annual salary the treasurer is $38,000.
5. Movement of authorization letter just signed by the treasurer to the controller's office, followed by the opening of a new account, recording of the transaction, and proofing of the transaction: 2 minutes by same secretary as above, 10 minutes for account opening by general accountant, and 8 minutes for recording and proofing by the same general accountant.	Annual salary for the general accountant is $12,000.
6. Fringe benefits incurred on above times.	Cost: $4.42
7. Brokerage fee on each transaction.	Cost $7.74

EXHIBIT 2. California Transistor: Selected Money Market Rates (Annual Yields)	

Year	Prime Commercial Paper: 90–119 Days	Bankers' Acceptances 90 Days	Three-Month Treasury Bills
1972	4.66%	4.47%	4.07%
1973	8.20	8.08	7.04
1974	10.05	9.92	7.89
1975	6.26	6.30	5.84
Simple Average	7.29	7.19	6.21

Source: *Federal Reserve Bulletin*, Board of Governors of the Federal Reserve System (January 1976), p. A27.

QUESTIONS

1. Determine the optimal cash withdrawal size from the CalTrans marketable securities portfolio during a typical month.

2. What is the total cost (in dollars) for the use of cash held for transactions purposes during the period of analysis?

3. What will be the firm's average cash balance during a typical month?

4. Assuming that fractional cash withdrawals or orders can be made, how often will an order be placed? The firm operates continually for 30 days each month.

5. If the company's cash balance at the start of a given month is $800,000, how much of that amount would initially be invested in securities?

6. Graph the behavior pattern of the $800,000 balance (mentioned above) over a 30-day month. In constructing your graph, round off the frequency of orders to the nearest whole day and disregard separation of the balance between cash and securities.

7. To understand the logic of the model further, provide a graph that identifies in general (1) the total cost function of holding the cash, (2) the fixed costs associated with cash transfers, and (3) the opportunity cost of earnings forgone by holding cash balances. Use dollar amounts to label the key points on the axes as they were previously computed in questions 1 and 2. Also, identify the major assumptions of this model in a cash-management setting.

SELF-TEST SOLUTIONS

SS–1. **a.** Initially, it is necessary to calculate Creative Fashions' average remittance check amount and the daily opportunity cost of carrying cash. The average check size is

$$\frac{\$7,000,000}{4,000} = \$1750 \text{ per check}$$

The daily opportunity cost of carrying cash is

$$\frac{0.08}{365} = 0.0002192 \text{ per day}$$

Next, the days saved in the collection process can be evaluated according to the general format (see equation 14–1 in the text of this chapter) of

$$\text{added costs} = \text{added benefits}$$

or

$$P = (D)\ (S)\ (i)\ [\text{see equation 14–2}]$$

$$\$0.25 = (D)\ (\$1750)\ (.0002192)$$

$$0.6517 \text{ days} = D$$

Creative Fashion Designs therefore will experience a financial gain if it implements the lock-box system and by doing so will speed up its collections by more than 0.6517 days.

b. Here the daily opportunity cost of carrying cash is

$$\frac{0.055}{365} = 0.0001507 \text{ per day}$$

For Creative Fashion Designs to break even, should it choose to install the lock-box system, cash collections must be accelerated by 0.9480 days, as follows:

$$\$0.25 = (D)\ (\$1750)\ (.0001507)$$

$$0.9480 \text{ days} = (D)$$

c. The breakeven cash-acceleration period of 0.9480 days is greater than the 0.6517 days found in (a). This is due to the lower yield available on near-cash assets of 5.5 percent annually, versus 8.0 percent. Since the alternative rate of return on the freed-up balances is lower in the second situation, more funds must be invested to cover the costs of operating the lock-box system. The greater cash-acceleration period generates this increased level of required funds.

SS–2. a. Reduction in mail float:

$$(2.0 \text{ days}) (\$200,000) = \$400,000$$

$$+ \text{ reduction in processing float:}$$

$$(2.5 \text{ days}) (\$200,000) = \underline{500,000}$$

$$= \text{total float reduction} = \underline{\underline{\$900,000}}$$

b. The opportunity of maintaing the present banking arrangement is

$$\left(\begin{array}{c}\text{forecast yield on marketable}\\ \text{securities portfolio}\end{array}\right) \cdot \left(\begin{array}{c}\text{total float}\\ \text{reduction}\end{array}\right)$$

$$(.106) (\$900,000) = \underline{\underline{\$95,400}}$$

c. The average number of checks to be processed each day through the lock-box arrangement is

$$\frac{\text{daily remittances}}{\text{average check size}} = \frac{\$200,000}{\$800} = 250 \text{ checks}$$

The resulting cost of the lock-box system on an annual basis is

$$(250 \text{ checks}) (\$0.25) (270 \text{ days}) = \$16,875$$

Next, we must calculate the estimated cost of the ADTC system. Detroit National Bank will *not* contribute to the cost of the ADTC arrangement because it is the lead concentration bank and thereby receives the transferred data. This means that Artie Kay's Komputer Shops will be charged for six ADTCs (three locations @ two checks each) each business day. Therefore, the ADTC system costs

$$(6 \text{ daily transfers}) (\$20 \text{ per transfer}) (270 \text{ days}) = \$32,400$$

We now have the total cost of the proposed system:

Lock-box cost	$16,875
ADTC cost	32,400
Total cost	$49,275

d. Our analysis suggests that Artie Kay's Komputer Shops should adopt the proposed cash receipts acceleration system. The projected net annual gain is $46,125 as follows:

Projected return on freed balances	$95,400
Less: Total cost of new system	49,275
Net annual gain	$46,125

SS–3. a. Here we must calculate the dollar value of the estimated return for each holding period and compare it with the transactions fee to determine if a gain can be made by investing in the securities. Those calculations and the resultant recommendations follow:

	Recommendation
1. $2,000,000 (.12) (1/12) = $20,000 < $45,000	No
2. $2,000,000 (.12) (2/12) = $40,000 < $45,000	No
3. $2,000,000 (.12) (3/12) = $60,000 > $45,000	Yes
4. $2,000,000 (.12) (6/12) = $120,000 > $45,000	Yes
5. $2,000,000 (.12) (12/12) = $240,000 > $45,000	Yes

b. Let (%) be the required yield. With $2 million to invest for three months we have

$$\$200,000 \; (\%) \; (3/12) = \$ \;\; 45,000$$

$$\$200,000 \; (\%) \qquad\quad = \$180,000$$

$$\$200,000 \; (\%) \qquad\quad = \$180,000/2,000,000 = 9\%$$

The breakeven yield, therefore, is 9%.

Cash-Management Models: Split Between Cash and Near Cash

In this appendix we continue our discussion of the management of the firm's cash position. We have dwelled on the overall objectives of company cash management, described some actual liquid asset holdings of selected industries and firms, and overviewed a wide array of cash-collection and disbursement procedures.

We now consider the problem of properly dividing the firm's liquid asset holdings between cash and near cash.

Liquid Assets: Cash Versus Marketable Securities

Through use of the cash-budgeting procedures outlined in Chapter 13, the financial manager can pinpoint time periods when funds will be in either short or excess supply. If a shortage of funds is expected, then alternative avenues of financing must be explored. Conversely, the cash-budget projections might indicate that large, positive net cash balances in excess of immediate transactions needs will be forthcoming. In this more pleasant situation the financial manager ought to decide on the proper split of the expected cash balances between actual cash holdings and marketable securities. To hold all of the expected cash balances as actual balances would needlessly penalize the firm's profitability.

Let's look at various methods by which the financial manager can develop useful cash balance level benchmarks.

Benchmark 1: When Cash Need Is Certain

A basic method for indicating the proper *average* amount of cash to have on hand involves use of the economic order quantity concept so familiar in discussions of inventory management (Chapter 16).[15] The objective of this analysis is to balance the lost income that the firm suffers from holding cash rather than marketable securities against the transactions costs involved in converting securities into cash. The rudiments of this decision model can easily be introduced by the use of an illustration.

Suppose that the firm knows with certainty that it will need $250,000 in cash for transactions purposes over the next two months and that this much cash is currently available. This transactions demand for cash will be represented by the variable T. Let us assume, for purposes of this illustration, that when the firm requires cash for its transactions needs it

---

[15]The roots of a quantitative treatment of the firm's cash balance as just another type of inventory are found in William J. Baumol, "The Transactions Demand for Cash: An Inventory Theoretic Approach," *Quarterly Journal of Economics* 66 (November 1952), pp. 545–56.

	$30,000	$40,000	$50,000	$60,000	$70,000
1. Cash conversion size (the dollar amount of marketable securities that will be sold to replenish the cash balance)	$30,000	$40,000	$50,000	$60,000	$70,000
2. Number of cash order per time period (the time period is two months in this example) ($250,000 ÷ line 1)	8.33	6.25	5.00	4.17	3.57
3. Average cash balance (line 1 ÷ 2)	$15,000	$20,000	$25,000	$30,000	$35,000
4. Interest income forgone (line 3 × .01)	$150.00	$200.00	$250.00	$300.00	$350.00
5. Cash conversion cost ($50 × line 2)	$416.50	$312.50	$250.00	$208.50	$178.50
6. Total cost of ordering and holding cash (line 4 + line 5)	$566.50	$512.50	$500.00	$508.50	$528.50

will sell marketable securities in any one of five lot sizes, ranging from $30,000 to $70,000. These cash conversion (order) sizes, C, are identified in line 1 of Table 15A–1.

Line 2 shows the number of times marketable securities will be turned into cash over the next two months for a particular order size. For example, should it be decided to liquidate securities in amounts of $40,000, then the number of cash conversions needed to meet transactions over the next two months is $250,000/$40,000 = 6.25. In general, the number of cash withdrawals from the near-cash portfolio can be represented as T/C.

Next, we assume that the firm's cash payments are of constant amounts and are made continually over the two-month planning period. This implies that the firm's cash balance behaves in the sawtooth manner shown in Figure 15A–1. The assertion of regularity and constancy of payments allows the firm's average cash balance over the planning period to be measured as $C/2$ (see Figure 15A–1). When marketable securities are sold and cash flows into the demand deposit account, the cash balance is equal to C. As payments are made on a regular and constant basis, the cash balance is reduced to a level of zero. The average cash balance over the period is then

$$\frac{C + 0}{2} = \frac{C}{2}$$

The average cash balances corresponding to the different cash conversion sizes in our example are noted in line 3 of Table 15A–1.

Line 4 measures the opportunity cost of earnings forgone based on

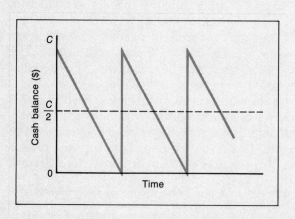

holding the average cash balance recorded on line 3. If the *annual* yield available on marketable securities is 6 percent, then over the *two-month period* we are analyzing, the forfeited interest rate is .06/6 = .01.[16] Multiplying each average cash balance, $C/2$, by the .01 interest rate, i, available over the two-month period produces the opportunity costs entered on line 4.

The very act of liquidating securities, unfortunately, is not without cost. Transacting conversions of marketable securities into cash can involve any of the following activities, each of which require the time of company employees as well as direct payment by the firm for various services:

1. Assistant treasurer's time to order the trade
2. Long-distance phone calls to effect the trade
3. Secretarial time to type authorization letters, make copies of the letters, and forward the letters to the company treasurer
4. Treasurer's time to read, approve, and sign the documents that authorize the trade
5. General accountant's time to record and audit the transaction
6. The value of fringe benefits incurred on the above times
7. The brokerage fee on each transaction

Suppose that the firm has properly studied the transaction costs, similar to those enumerated above, and finds they are of a fixed amount, b, per trade equal to $50. The transaction cost variable, b, is taken to be independent of the size of a particular securities order. Multiplying the transaction cost of $50 per trade by the number of cash orders that will take place during the planning period produces line 5. In general, the cash conversion cost (transaction cost) is equal to $b(T/C)$.

We are now down to the last line in Table 15A–1. This is the sum total of the income lost by holding cash rather than marketable securities and the cash-ordering costs. Line 6, then, is the total of lines 4 and 5. The inventory model seeks to *minimize* these *total costs* associated with holding cash balances. Table 15A–1 tells us, if cash is ordered on five occasions in $50,000 sizes over the two-month period, the total costs of holding an average cash balance of $25,000 will be $500. This is less than the total costs associated with any other cash conversion size.

At the beginning of the two-month planning horizon, all of the $250,000 available for transactions purposes need not be held in the firm's demand deposit account. To minimize the total costs of holding cash, only $50,000 should immediately be retained to transact business. The remaining $200,000 should be invested in income-yielding securities and then turned into cash as the firm's disbursal needs dictate.

It is useful to put our discussion of the inventory model for cash management into a more general form. Summarizing the definitions developed in the illustration, we have

C = The amount per order of marketable securities to be converted into cash

i = the interest rate per period available on investments in marketable securities

---

[16]If we were studying a *one-month* planning period, rather than the two-month period being discussed, the annual yield would have to be stated on a monthly basis or .06/12 = .005.

b = the fixed cost per order of converting marketable securities into cash

T = the total cash requirements over the planning period

TC = the total costs associated with maintenance of a particular average cash balance

As just pointed out, the total costs (TC) of having cash on hand can be expressed as

$$TC = i\left(\frac{C}{2}\right) + b\left(\frac{T}{C}\right)$$

(15A–1)

$\underset{\text{total interest income forgone}}{}$ $\underset{\text{total ordering costs}}{}$

If equation (15A–1) is applied to the $50,000 cash conversion size column in Table 15A–1, the total costs can be computed directly as follows:

$$TC = .01\left(\frac{\$50,000}{2}\right) + 50\left(\frac{\$250,000}{\$50,000}\right)$$

$$= \$250 + \$250 = \$500$$

You can see that the $500 total cost is the same as was found deductively in Table 15A–1. The optimal cash conversion size, C^*, can be found by use of equation (15A–2):

$$C^* = \sqrt{\frac{2bT}{i}}$$

(15A–2)

When the data in our example are applied to equation (15A–2), the optimal cash order size is found to be

$$C^* = \sqrt{\frac{2(50)(250,000)}{.01}} = \$50,000$$

Figure 15A–2 displays this solution to our example problem graphically. Notice that the optimal cash order size of $50,000 occurs at the minimum point of the total cost curve associated with keeping cash on hand.

Inventory Model Implications

The solution to equation (15A–2) tells the financial manager that the optimal cash order size, C^*, varies directly with the square root of the order costs, bT, and inversely with the yield, i, available on marketable securities. Notice that as transactions requirements, T, increase, owing perhaps to an augmented sales demand, the optimal cash order size does *not* rise proportionately.

The model also indicates that as interest rates rise on near-cash investments, the optimal cash order size decreases, with the effect dampened by the square-root sign as equation (15A–2) suggests. With higher

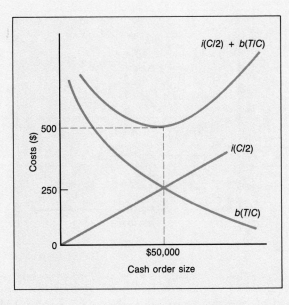

FIGURE 15A-2.
Solution to Inventory Model for Cash Management

yields to be earned on the marketable securities portfolio, the financial manager will be more reluctant to make large withdrawals because of the interest income that will be lost.

Some final perspectives on the use of the economic order quantity model in cash management can be obtained by reviewing the assumptions upon which it is derived. Among the more important of these assumptions are the following:

1. Cash payments over the planning period are (a) of a regular amount, (b) continuous, and (c) certain.

2. No unanticipated cash receipts will be received during the analysis period.

3. The interest rate to be earned on investments remains constant over the analysis period.

4. Transfers between cash and the securities portfolio may occur any time at a fixed cost, regardless of the amount transferred.

Clearly, the strict assumptions of the inventory model are not completely realized in actual business practice. For instance, the amount and timing of cash payments will not be known with certainty; nor are cash receipts likely to be as discontinuous or lumpy as is implied. If relaxation of the critical assumptions is not so prohibitive as to render the model useless, then the model can provide a benchmark for managerial decision making. The model's output is not intended to be a precise and inviolable rule. On the other hand, if the assumptions of the model cannot be reasonably approximated, the financial manager must look elsewhere for possible guides that indicate a proper split between cash and marketable securities.

Benchmark 2: When Cash Balances Fluctuate Randomly

It is entirely possible that the firm's cash balance pattern does *not* at all resemble that indicated in Figure 15A-1. The assumptions of certain regularity and constancy of cash payments may be unduly restrictive when

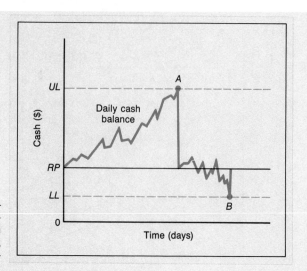

FIGURE 15A–3.
Randomly Fluctuating Cash
Balances

applied to some organizations.[17] Rather, the cash balance might behave more like the jagged line shown in Figure 15A–3. In this figure it is assumed that the firm's cash balance changes in an irregular fashion from day to day. The changes are unpredictable; that is, they are *random*. Further, let us suppose the chances that a cash balance change will be either (1) positive or (2) negative are equal at .5 each.

As cash receipts exceed expenditures, the cash balance moves upward until it hits an upper control limit, *UL*, expressed in dollars. This occurs at point *A* in Figure 15A–3. At such time, the financial officer initiates an investment in marketable securities equal to *UL* − *RP* dollars, where *RP* is the cash return point.

If cash payments exceed receipts, the cash balance moves downward until it hits a lower control limit, *LL*. This situation is noted by point *B* in Figure 15A–3. When this occurs, the financial officer sells marketable securities equal to *RP* − *LL* dollars. This restores the cash balance to the return point, *RP*.

To make this application of control theory to cash management operational, we must determine the upper control limit, *UL*, the lower control limit, *LL*, and the cash return point, *RP*. For the present case in which a net cash increase is as likely to occur as a net cash decrease, use of the following variables will allow computation of the cash return point, *RP*.[18]

b = the fixed cost per order of converting marketable securities into cash

i = the daily interest rate available on investments in marketable securities

σ^2 = the variance of daily changes in the firm's expected cash balances (this is a measure of volatility of cash flow changes over time)

[17]This discussion is based upon Merton H. Miller and Daniel Orr, "A Model of the Demand for Money by Firms," *Quarterly Journal of Economics* 80 (August 1966), pp. 413–35.

[18]Situations in which the probabilities of cash increases and decreases are not equal are extremely difficult to evaluate within the framework of the Miller-Orr decision model. See Miller and Orr, "A Model of the Demand for Money by Firms," *Quarterly Journal of Economics* 80 (August 1966), pp. 427–29, 433–35.

The optimal cash return point, RP, can be calculated as follows:

$$RP = \sqrt[3]{\frac{3b\sigma^2}{4i}} + LL \qquad\qquad \textbf{(15A–3)}$$

The upper control limit, UL, can be computed quite simply:

$$UL = 3RP - 2LL \qquad\qquad \textbf{(15A–4)}$$

The actual value for the lower limit, LL, is set by management. In business practice a minimum is typically established below which the cash balance is not permitted to fall. Among other things, it will be affected by (1) the firm's banking arrangements, which may require compensating balances, and (2) management's risk-bearing tendencies.

To illustrate use of the model, suppose that the annual yield available on marketable securities is 9 percent. Over a 360-day year, i becomes $.09/360 = .00025$ per day. Assume that the fixed cost, b, of transacting a marketable securities trade is $50. Moreover, the firm has studied its past cash balance levels and has observed that the standard deviation, σ, in daily cash balance changes is equal to $800. The firm sees no reason why this variability should change in the future. It is the firm's policy to maintain $1,000 in its demand deposit account (LL) at all times. Finally, the firm has established that each day's actual cash balance is random. The equations that comprise this control limit system can be applied to provide guidelines for cash-management policy.

The optimal cash return point for transactions purposes becomes

$$RP = \sqrt[3]{\frac{3(50)(800)^2}{4(.00025)}} + 1000 = (4579 + 1000) = \$5579$$

The upper cash balance limit that will trigger a transfer of cash to marketable securities is

$$UL = 3(5579) - 2(1000) = \$14{,}737$$

The cash balance control limits derived from this example are graphed in Figure 15A–4. Should the cash balance bump against the upper limit of $14,737 (point A), then the financial officer is instructed to buy $9,158 of marketable securities. At the other extreme, if the cash balance should

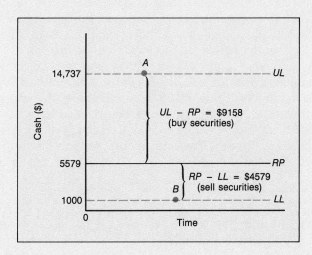

drop to the lower limit of $1,000 (point *B*), then the financial officer is instructed to sell $4,579 of marketable securities to restore the cash balance level to $5,579. As long as the cash balance wanders within the *UL* to *LL* range, no securities transactions take place. By acting in this manner, the financial officer will *minimize* the sum of interest income forgone and the costs of purchasing and selling securities.[19]

Control Limit Model Implications

Use of equation (15A–3) results in determination of the optimal cash return point within the framework of the control limit model. Inspection of this equation indicates to the financial officer that the optimal cash return level, *RP*, will vary directly with the cube root of both the transfer cost variable, *b*, and the volatility of daily cash balance changes, σ^2. Greater transfer costs or cash-balance volatility result in a greater *absolute* dollar spread between the upper control limit and the cash return point. This larger spread between *UL* and *RP* means that securities purchases are made in larger lot sizes. It is further evident that the optimal cash return point varies inversely with the cube root of the lost interest rate.

Similar to the basic inventory model reviewed in the preceding section, the control limit model implies that economies of scale are possible in cash management. In addition, the optimal cash return point always lies well below the midpoint of the range *UL* to *LL*, over which the cash balance is permitted to "walk." This means that the liquidation of marketable securities occurs (1) more frequently and (2) in smaller lot sizes than purchases of securities. This suggests that firms with highly volatile cash balances must be acutely concerned with the liquidity of their marketable securities portfolio.

Benchmark 3: Compensating Balances

An important element of the commercial banking environment that affects corporate cash management deserves special mention. This is the practice of the bank's requiring, either formally or informally, that the firm maintain deposits of a given amount in its demand deposit account. Such balances are referred to as *compensating balances*.

The compensating-balance requirement became typical banking practice after federal action forbade the payment of interest on demand deposits in the early 1930s.[20] In the face of prospective withdrawals the procedure allowed banks to maintain favorable levels of their basic raw material—deposits. Such balances are normally required of corporate customers in three situations: (1) where the firm has an established line of credit (loan commitment) at the bank but it is not entirely used, (2) where the firm has a loan outstanding at the bank, or (3) in exchange for various other services provided by the bank to its customer.

As you would expect, compensating-balance policies vary among commercial banks and, furthermore, are influenced by general conditions in the financial markets. Still, some tendencies can be identified. In the case of the unused portion of a loan commitment, the bank might require that the firm's demand deposits average anywhere from 5 to 10 percent of the commitment. If a loan is currently outstanding with the bank, the requirement will probably be 10 to 20 percent of the unpaid balance.

---

[19]As with the Baumol inventory model, the Miller-Orr control limit model seeks to minimize the total cost of managing the firm's cash balance over a finite planning horizon.
[20]Paul S. Nadler, "Compensating Balances and the Prime at Twilight," *Harvard Business Review* 50 (January–February 1972), p. 112.

During periods when monetary policy is restrictive, so-called tight money periods, the ranges rise by about 5 percent across the board.[21]

Instead of charging directly for certain banking services, the bank may ask the firm to "pay" for them by the compensating-balance approach. These services include check clearing, the availability of credit information, and any of the array of receipts-acceleration or payment-control techniques that we discussed in Chapter 15.

If the bank asks for compensation in the form of balances left on deposit rather than charging unit prices for services rendered, the requirement may be expressed as (1) an absolute amount or (2) an average amount. The latter is preferable to most firms, as it provides for some flexibility in use of the deposits. With the average balance requirement calculated over a month, and in some instances as long as a year, the balance can be low on occasion as long as it is offset with heavy balances in other time periods.

Compensating-Balance Requirement Implications

In the analysis that the financial officer undertakes to determine the split between cash and near cash, explicit consideration must be given to compensating-balance requirements. This information can be used in conjunction with the basic inventory model (benchmark 1) or the control limit model (benchmark 2).

One approach is to use either of the models and in the calculations ignore the compensating-balance requirement. This is logical in many instances. Generally, the compensating balance required by the bank is beyond the firm's control.

In using the models, then, the focus is on the discretionary cash holdings above the required levels. Once the solution to the particular model is found, the firm's optimal average cash balance will be the *higher* of that suggested by the model or the balance requirement set by the bank.

A second approach is to introduce the size of the compensating balance into the format of the cash-management model and carry out the requisite calculations. We noted previously that in the control limit model, the lower control limit (*LL*) could be the compensating-balance requirement faced by the firm as opposed to a value of zero for *LL*. In the basic inventory model the compensating balance can be treated as a safety stock. In Figure 15A–1, then, the cash balance would not touch the zero level and trigger a marketable securities purchase; rather, it would fall to the level of the compensating balance (some amount greater than zero) and initiate the securities purchase. Under ordinary circumstances, the calculated optimal order size of marketable securities is not altered by consideration of compensating balances in either model, so useful information on the proper split between near cash and discretionary cash (cash held in excess of compensating balances) is still provided by these two benchmarks.

Trends indicate that compensating balances are slowly giving way to unit pricing of bank services. Under unit pricing, the bank quotes a stated price for the service. The firm pays that rate only for the services actually used. Such a trend means that the importance of this third benchmark may diminish in the foreseeable future. At the same time, the policies suggested by application of cash-management models may well attract attention.

---

[21]See Howard D. Crosse and George H. Hempel, *Management Policies for Commercial Banks*, 2d ed. (Englewood Cliffs, NJ: Prentice Hall, 1973), pp. 200–202; and E. E. Reed, R. V. Cotter, E. K. Gill, and R. Smith, *Commercial Banking*, 2d ed. (Englewood Cliffs, NJ: Prentice Hall, 1980), pp. 246–47.

STUDY PROBLEMS

15A–1. (*Inventory Model*) The Richard Price Metal Working Company will experience $800,000 in cash payments next month. The annual yield available on marketable securities is 6.5 percent. The company has analyzed the cost of obtaining or investing cash and found it to be equal to $85 per transaction. Because cash outlays for Price Metal Working occur at a constant rate over any given month, the company has decided to apply the principles of the inventory model for cash management to provide answers to several questions.

a. What is the optimal cash conversion size for the Price Metal Working Company?

b. What is the total cost of having cash on hand during the coming month?

c. How often (in days) will the firm have to make a cash conversion? Assume a 30-day month.

d. What will be Price Metal Working's average cash balance?

15A–2. (*Control Limit Model*) The Edinboro Fabric Company manufactures 18 different final products, which are woven, cut, and dyed for use primarily in the clothing industry. Owing to the whimsical nature of the underlying demand for certain clothing styles, Edinboro Fabric has a most difficult time forecasting its cash balance levels. The company maintains $2,000 in its demand deposit account at all times. A detailed study of past cash balance levels has revealed that the standard deviation, σ, in daily cash balance changes has been equal to $600. The nature of the firm is not expected to undergo any structural changes in the foreseeable future, and for this reason the past volatility in cash balance levels is expected to continue in the future. Edinboro has determined that the cost of transacting a marketable securities trade is $85. Marketable securities are yielding 6 percent per annum. The firm always uses a 360-day year in its analysis procedures. Robert Cambridge, Edinboro's treasurer, has just returned from a three-day cash-management seminar in New York City. He has decided to apply the control limit model for cash management to his firm's situation.

a. What is the optimal cash return point for Edinboro?

b. What is the upper control limit?

c. In what lot sizes will marketable securities be purchased? Sold?

d. Graph your results.

CHAPTER *16*

Accounts Receivable and Inventory Management

Accounts Receivable Management • Inventory Management • Just-in-Time Inventory Control

In the two preceding chapters we developed a general overview of working-capital management and took an in-depth look at the management of cash and marketable securities. In this chapter we will focus on the management of two more working-capital items, accounts receivable and inventory. Accounts receivable and inventory make up a large portion of the firm's assets; they actually compose on average 26.50 and 4.88 percent, respectively, of a typical firm's assets. In fact, in several industries, accounts receivable and inventory make up a larger percentage of the firm's assets. For example, accounts receivable typically make up just over 50 percent of the assets of a firm in the motor vehicles manufacturing industry, whereas inventory typically makes up almost 50 percent of the assets of a retail auto dealership. Thus, because of their sheer magnitude any changes in their levels will affect profitability. For example, an increase in accounts receivable—that is, additional extension of trade credit—not only results in higher sales, it also requires additional financing to support the increased investment. The costs of credit investigation and collection efforts are increased, as well as chance of bad debts. A larger investment in inventory leads to more efficient production and speedier delivery, hence increased sales. However, additional financing is required to support the increase in inventory and the handling and carrying costs.

In studying the management of these current assets, we first examine accounts receivable management, focusing on its importance, what determines investment in it, and what the decision variables are and how we determine them. Then we turn to inventory management, examine its importance, and discuss order quantity and order point problems, which in combination determine the level of investment in inventory.

Accounts Receivable Management

All firms by their very nature are involved in selling either goods or services. Although some of these sales will be for cash, a large portion will involve credit. Whenever a sale is made on credit, it increases the firm's accounts receivable. Thus, the importance of how a firm manages its accounts receivable depends on the degree to which the firm sells on credit. Table 16–1 lists, for selected industries, the percentage of total assets made up by accounts receivable.

From Table 16–1 we can see that accounts receivable typically comprise over 25 percent of a firm's assets. In effect, when we discuss management of accounts receivable, we are discussing the management of one-quarter of the firm's assets. Moreover, because cash flows from a sale cannot be invested until the account is collected, control of receivables takes on added importance; efficient collection determines both profitability and liquidity of the firm.

Size of Investment in Accounts Receivable

The size of the investment in accounts receivable is determined by several factors. First, the percentage of credit sales to total sales affects the level of accounts receivable held. Although this factor certainly plays a major role in determining a firm's investment in accounts receivable, it generally is not within the control of the financial manager. The nature of the business tends to determine the blend between credit sales and cash sales. A large grocery store tends to sell exclusively on a cash basis, whereas most construction-lumber supply firms make their sales primarily with credit. Thus, the nature of the business, and not the decisions of the financial manager, tends to determine the proportion of credit sales.

The level of sales is also a factor in determining the size of the investment in accounts receivable. Very simply, the more sales, the greater accounts receivable. As the firm experiences seasonal and permanent growth in sales, the level of investment in accounts receivable will naturally increase. Thus, although the level of sales affects the size of the investment in accounts receivable, it is not a decision variable for the financial manager.

The final determinants of the level of investment in accounts receivable are the credit and collection policies—more specifically, the *terms of sale*, the *quality of customer*, and *collection efforts*. The terms of sale specify both the time period during which the customer must pay and the terms, such as penalties for

TABLE 16–1.
Accounts Receivable as a Percentage of Total Assets for Major Industries

Industry	Accounts Receivable Relative to Total Assets
All industries	26.50%
Motor vehicles and equipment— manufacturing	51.38
General merchandising stores—retail	28.36
Total construction	26.38
Building materials, garden supplies, and mobile home dealers—retail	19.84
Apparel and accessory stores—retail	16.58
Automotive dealers and service stations—retail	13.51
Transportation	13.47
Agricultural, forestry, and fishing	9.26
Food stores	8.60
Hotels and other lodging places	6.98

Source: Internal Revenue Service, U.S. Treasury Department, *Statistics of Income, 1986, Corporate Income Tax Returns* (Washington, DC: Government Printing Office, 1990), pp. 1–47.

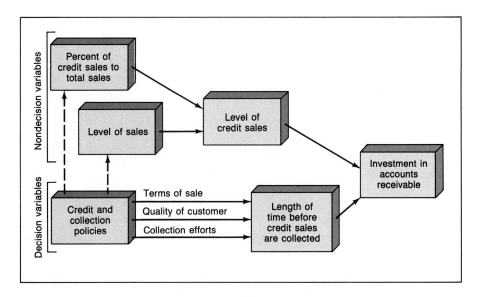

FIGURE 16–1.
Determinants of Investment in
Accounts Receivable

late payments or discounts for early payments. The type of customer or credit policy also affects the level of investment in accounts receivable. For example, the acceptance of poorer credit risks and their subsequent delinquent payments may lead to an increase in accounts receivable. The strength and timing of the collection efforts can affect the period for which past-due accounts remain delinquent, which in turn affects the level of accounts receivable. Collection and credit policy decisions may further affect the level of investment in accounts receivable by causing changes in the sales level and the ratio of credit sales to total sales. However, the three credit and collection policy variables are the only true decision variables under the control of the financial manager. Graphically, this situation is shown in Figure 16–1.

Perspective in Finance

As we examine the credit decision, try to remember that our goal is not to minimize losses but to maximize profits. Although we will spend a good deal of time trying to sort out those customers with the highest probability of default, this analysis is only an input into a decision based on shareholder wealth maximization. Essentially a firm with a high profit margin can tolerate a more liberal credit policy than a firm with a low profit margin.

Terms of Sale—Decision Variable

The **terms of sale** identify the possible discount for early payment, the discount period, and the total credit period. They are generally stated in the form *a/b* net *c*, indicating that the customer can deduct *a* percent if the account is paid within *b* days; otherwise, the account must be paid within *c* days. Thus, for example, trade credit terms of 2/10, net 30 indicate that a 2 percent discount can be taken if the account is paid within 10 days; otherwise it must be paid within 30 days. What if the customer decides to forgo the discount and not pay until the final payment date? If such a decision is made, the customer has the use of the money for the time period between the discount date and the final payment date. However, failure to take the discount represents a cost to the customer. For instance, if the terms are 2/10, net 30, the annualized opportunity cost of passing up this 2 percent discount in order to withhold payment for an additional 20 days is 36.73 percent. This is determined as follows:

$$\left(\begin{array}{c} \text{annualized opportunity cost} \\ \text{of forgoing the discount} \end{array} \right) = \frac{a}{1-a} \times \frac{360}{c-b} \qquad \textbf{(16–1)}$$

Substituting the values from the example, we get

$$36.73\% = \frac{.02}{1 - .02} \times \frac{360}{30 - 10} \qquad \text{(16-2)}$$

In industry the typical discount ranges anywhere from one-half percent to 10 percent, whereas the discount period is generally 10 days and the total credit period varies from 30 to 90 days. Although the terms of credit vary radically from industry to industry, they tend to remain relatively uniform within any particular industry.[1] Moreover, the terms tend to remain relatively constant over time, and they do not appear to be used frequently as a decision variable.

Type of Customer—Decision Variable

A second decision variable involves determining the *type of customer* who is to qualify for trade credit. Several costs always are associated with extending credit to less credit-worthy customers (high-risk firms or individuals). First, as the probability of default increases, it becomes more important to identify which of the possible new customers would be a poor risk. When more time is spent investigating the less credit-worthy customer, the costs of credit investigation increase.

Default costs also vary directly with the quality of the customer. As the customer's credit rating declines, the chance that the account will not be paid on time increases. In the extreme case, payment never occurs. Thus, taking on less credit-worthy customers results in increases in default costs.

Collection costs also increase as the quality of the customer declines. More delinquent accounts force the firm to spend more time and money collecting them. Overall, the decline in customer quality results in increased costs of credit investigation, collection, and default.

In determining whether or not to grant credit to an individual customer, we are primarily interested in the customer's short-run welfare. Thus, liquidity ratios, other obligations, and the overall profitability of the firm become the focal point in this analysis. Credit-rating services, such as Dun & Bradstreet, provide information on the financial status, operations, and payment history for most firms. Other possible sources of information would include credit bureaus, trade associations, Chambers of Commerce, competitors, bank references, public financial statements, and, of course, the firm's past relationship with the customer.

One way in which both individuals and firms are often evaluated as credit risks is through the use of credit scoring. **Credit scoring** involves the numerical evaluation of each applicant. An applicant receives a score based on his or her answers to a simple set of questions. This score is then evaluated according to a predetermined standard, its level relative to the standard determining whether or not credit should be extended. The major advantage of credit scoring is that it is inexpensive and easy to perform. For example, once the standards are set, a computer or clerical worker without any specialized training could easily evaluate any applicant.

The techniques used for constructing credit-scoring indexes range from the simple approach of adding up default rates associated with the answers given to each question, to sophisticated evaluations using multiple discriminate analysis (MDA). MDA is a statistical technique for calculating the appropriate importance to be given to each question used in evaluating the applicant. Figure 16-2 shows a credit "scorecard" used by a large automobile dealer. The weights or scores attached to each answer are based on the auto dealer's past experience with credit sales. For example, the scorecard indicates that individuals with no

[1]Theodore N. Beckman and Ronald S. Foster, *Credits and Collections* (New York: McGraw-Hill, 1969), pp. 697–704.

Telephone / Score

Home	Relative	None				
(5)	1	0				

Living quarters

Own home no mortgage	Own home mortgage	Rent a house	Live with someone	Rent an apartment	Rent a room
6	3	2	1	(0)	0

Bank accounts

None	1	More than 1				
0	4	(6)				

Years at present address

Under 1/2	1/2-2	3-7	8 or more			
(0)	1	3	4			

Size of family including customer

1	2	3-6	7 or more			
2	(4)	3	0			

Monthly income

Under $900	$901-$1100	$1101-$1400	$1401-$1700	More than $1700		
0	1	2	6	(8)		

Length of present employment

Under 1/2 year	1/2-2 years	3-7 years	8 years or more			
0	1	(2)	4			

Percent of selling price on credit

Under 50	50-69	70-84	85-99			
5	3	1	(0)			

Interview discretionary points (+5 to −5)

Total

Credit scorecard

_____
(Customer's name)

_____
(Street address)

_____
(City, State, Zip)

_____
(Home/Office telephone)

_____
(Credit scorer)

Credit scorecard evaluation

Dollar amount: $0-$2000

0-18	19-21	22 or more
Reject	Refer to main credit	Accept

Dollar amount: $2001-$5000

0-21	22-24	25 or more
Reject	Refer to main credit	Accept

Dollar amount: more than $5000

0-23	24–27	27 or more
Reject	Refer to main credit	Accept

If a previous loan customer, were payments received promptly? Yes ☐ No* ☐

Are you willing to take responsibility for authorizing this loan? Yes ☐ No* ☐

*Refer to main credit if answer to either question is _No_.

FIGURE 16–2.
Credit "Scorecard"

telephone in their home have a much higher probability of default than those with a telephone. One caveat should be mentioned: Whenever this type of questionnaire is used to evaluate credit applicants, it should be examined carefully to be sure that it does not contain any illegal discriminatory questions.

Another model that could be used for credit scoring has been provided by Edward Altman, who used multiple discriminant analysis to identify businesses that might go bankrupt. In his landmark study Altman used financial ratios to predict which firms would go bankrupt over the period 1946 to 1965. Using multiple discriminant analysis, Altman came up with the following index:

$$Z = 3.3 \left(\frac{EBIT}{total\ assets} \right) + 1.0 \left(\frac{sales}{total\ assets} \right) + 0.6 \left(\frac{market\ value\ of\ equity}{book\ value\ of\ debt} \right)$$

$$+ 1.4 \left(\frac{retained\ earnings}{total\ assets} \right) + 1.2 \left(\frac{working\ capital}{total\ assets} \right) \qquad \textbf{(16-3)}$$

Altman found that of the firms that went bankrupt over this time period, 94 percent had Z scores of less than 2.7 one year prior to bankruptcy and only 6 percent had scores above 2.7 percent. Conversely, of those firms that did not go bankrupt, only 3 percent had Z scores below 2.7 and 97 percent had scores above 2.7.

Again, the advantages of credit-scoring techniques are low cost and ease of implementation. Simple calculations can easily spot those credit risks that need more screening before credit should be extended to them.

Perspective in Finance

It is tempting to look at the credit decision as a single yes or no decision based on some simple formula. However, simply to look at the immediate future in making a credit decision would be a mistake. If extending a customer credit means that the customer may become a regular customer in the future, it may be appropriate to take a risk that otherwise would not be prudent. In effect, our goal is to ensure that all cash flows affected by the decision at hand are considered, not simply the most immediate cash flows.

Collection Efforts—Decision Variable

The key to maintaining control over collection of accounts receivable is the fact that the probability of default increases with the age of the account. Thus, control of accounts receivable focuses on the control and elimination of past-due receivables. One common way of evaluating the current situation is **ratio analysis.** The financial manager can determine whether or not accounts receivables are under control by examining the average collection period, the ratio of receivables to assets, the ratio of credit sales to receivables (called the accounts receivable turnover ratio), and the amount of bad debts relative to sales over time. In addition, the manager can perform what is called an aging of accounts receivable to provide a breakdown in both dollars and in percentages of the proportion of receivables that are past due. Comparing the current aging of receivables with past data offers even more control. An example of an *aging account* or *schedule* appears in Table 16–2.

Table 16–3 provides a ranking of measures used in monitoring accounts receivable compiled in a survey of Fortune 500 Companies. This survey indicates that the aging account or schedule along with the accounts receivable turnover ratio and average collection period (which are actually variations of each other) serve as the primary tools used in monitoring the payment behavior of customers.

TABLE 16–2.
Aging Account

Age of Accounts Receivable (Days)	Dollar Value (00)	Percent of Total
0–30	$2340	39%
31–60	1500	25
61–90	1020	17
91–120	720	12
Over 120	420	7
Total	$6000	100%

Measure	Number of Responses	Percentage Assigning Rank			
		1	2	3	4
Accounts receivable turnover	52	9.6%	26.9%	63.5%	
Collection period	77	33.8	50.6	15.6	
Aging schedule	92	69.6	27.2	2.2	1.1%
Other	5	20.0	80.0		

Source: K. V. Smith and B. Belt, "Working Capital Management in Practice: An Update," Working Paper No. 951 (West Lafayette, IN: Krannert Graduate School of Management, Purdue University, 1989).

TABLE 16–3.
Ranking of Measures Used in Monitoring Payment Behavior of Customers, 1988

Once the delinquent accounts have been identified, the firm's accounts receivable group makes an effort to collect them. For example, a past-due letter, called a *dunning letter*, is sent if payment is not received on time, followed by an additional dunning letter in a more serious tone if the account becomes 3 weeks past due, followed after 6 weeks by a telephone call. Finally, if the account becomes 12 weeks past due, it might be turned over to a collection agency. Again, a direct tradeoff exists between collection expenses and lost goodwill on one hand and noncollection of accounts on the other, and this tradeoff is always part of making the decision.

Thus far, we have discussed the importance and role of accounts receivable in the firm and then examined the determinants of the size of the investment in accounts receivable. We have focused on credit and collection policies, because these are the only discretionary variables for management. In examining these decision variables, we have simply described their traits. These variables are analyzed in a decision-making process called marginal or incremental analysis.

Credit Policy Changes: The Use of Marginal or Incremental Analysis

Changes in credit policy involve direct tradeoffs between costs and benefits. When credit policies are eased, sales and profits from customers increase. Conversely, easing credit policies can also involve an increase in bad debts, additional funds tied up in accounts receivable and inventory, and additional costs from customers taking a cash discount. Given these costs, when is it appropriate for a firm to change its credit policy? The answer is when the increased sales generate enough in the way of new profit to more than offset the increased costs associated with the change. Determining whether this is so is the job of *marginal or incremental analysis*. In general, there are three categories of changes in credit policy that a firm can consider: a change in the risk class of the customer, a change in the collection process, or a change in the discount terms. To illustrate, let us follow through an example.

EXAMPLE

Assume that Denis Electronics currently has annual sales, all credit, of $8 million and an average collection period of 30 days. The current level of bad debt is $240,000 and the firm's opportunity cost or required rate of return is 15 percent. Further assume that the firm produces only one product, with variable costs equaling 75 percent of the selling price. The company is considering a change in the credit terms from the current terms of net 30 to 1/30 net 60. If this change is made it is expected that half of the customers will take the discount and pay on the 30th day, whereas the other half will pass the discount and pay on the 60th day. This will increase the average collection period from 30 days to 45 days. The major reason Denis Electronics is considering this change is that it will generate additional sales of $1,000,000. Although the sales from these new customers will generate new profits, they will also generate more bad debts; however, it is assumed that the level of bad debts on the original sales will remain constant, and that the level of bad debts on the new sales will be 6 percent of those sales. In addition, to service the new sales, it will be necessary to increase the level of average inventory from $1,000,000 to $1,025,000. ∎

General Procedure

Marginal or incremental analysis involves a comparison of the incremental profit contribution from new sales with the incremental costs resulting from the change in credit policy. If the benefits outweigh the costs, the change is made. If not, the credit policy remains as is. A four-step procedure for performing marginal or incremental analysis on a change in credit policy follows:

Step 1: Estimate the change in profit.

Step 2: Estimate the cost of additional investment in accounts receivable and inventory.

Step 3: Estimate the cost of the discount (if a change in the cash discount is enacted).

Step 4: Compare the incremental revenues with the incremental costs.

To simplify the analysis, Table 16–4 provides a summary of the relevant information concerning Denis's proposed credit change, whereas Table 16–5 provides the results of the incremental analysis.

TABLE 16–4
Denis Electronics: Relevant Information for Incremental Analysis

New sales level (all credit): $9,000,000
Original sales level (all credit): $8,000,000
Contribution margin: 25%
Percent bad debt losses on new sales: 6%
New average collection period: 45 days
Original average collection period: 30 days
Addition investment in inventory: $25,000
Pre-tax required rate of return: 15%
New percent cash discount: 1%
Percent of customers taking the cash discount: 50%

TABLE 16–5.
Denis Electronics: Incremental Analysis of a Change in Credit Policy

Step 1: *Estimate the Change in Profit.* This is equal to the increased sales times the profit contribution on those sales less any additional bad debts incurred.

= (increased sales × contribution margin) −
(increased sales × percent bad debt losses on new sales)
= ($1,000,000 × .25) − ($1,000,000 × .06)
= $190,000

Step 2: *Estimate the Cost of Additional Investment in Accounts Receivable and Inventory.* This involves first calculating the change in the investment in accounts receivable; the new and original levels of investment in accounts receivable are calculated by multiplying the daily sales level times the average collection period. The additional investment in inventory is added to this, and the sum is then multiplied by the pre-tax required rate of return.

$$= \left(\begin{array}{c} \text{additional} \\ \text{accounts} \\ \text{receivable} \end{array} + \begin{array}{c} \text{additional} \\ \text{inventory} \end{array} \right) \times \left(\begin{array}{c} \text{pre-tax required} \\ \text{rate of return} \end{array} \right)$$

First, calculate the additional investment in accounts receivable.

$$\left(\begin{array}{c} \text{additional} \\ \text{accounts} \\ \text{receivable} \end{array} \right) = \left(\begin{array}{c} \text{new level} \\ \text{of daily} \\ \text{sales} \end{array} \right) \times \left(\begin{array}{c} \text{new average} \\ \text{collection} \\ \text{period} \end{array} \right) - \left(\begin{array}{c} \text{original level} \\ \text{of daily} \\ \text{sales} \end{array} \right) \times \left(\begin{array}{c} \text{original averge} \\ \text{collection} \\ \text{period} \end{array} \right)$$

$$= \left(\frac{\$9,000,000}{360} \times 45 \right) - \left(\frac{\$8,000,000}{360} \times 30 \right)$$

$$= \$458,340$$

TABLE 16–5.
cont.

Second, sum additional investments in accounts receivable and inventory ($25,000) and multiply this sum times the pre-tax required rate of return.

$$= (\$458,340 + \$25,000) \times .15$$

$$= \$72,501$$

Step 3: Estimate the Change in the Cost of the Cash Discount (if a Change in the Cash Discount is Enacted). This is equal to the new level of sales times the new percent cash discount, times the percent of customers taking the discount, less the original level of sales, times the original percent cash discount, times percent of customers taking the discount.

$$= \begin{pmatrix} \text{new} \\ \text{level} \\ \text{of} \\ \text{sales} \end{pmatrix} \times \begin{pmatrix} \text{new} \\ \text{percent} \\ \text{cash} \\ \text{discount} \end{pmatrix} \times \begin{pmatrix} \text{percent} \\ \text{of} \\ \text{taking} \\ \text{discount} \end{pmatrix} - \begin{pmatrix} \text{original} \\ \text{level} \\ \text{of} \\ \text{sales} \end{pmatrix} \times \begin{pmatrix} \text{original} \\ \text{percent} \\ \text{cash} \\ \text{discount} \end{pmatrix} \times \begin{pmatrix} \text{original} \\ \text{percent} \\ \text{taking} \\ \text{discount} \end{pmatrix}$$

$$= (\$9,000,000 \times .01 \times .50) - (\$8,000,000 \times .00 \times .00)$$

$$= \$45,000$$

Step 4: Compare the Incremental Revenues with the Incremental Costs.

$$\begin{matrix} \text{net change} \\ \text{in pre-tax} \\ \text{profits} \end{matrix} = \begin{matrix} \text{change} \\ \text{in} \\ \text{profits} \end{matrix} - \begin{pmatrix} \text{cost of new} \\ \text{investment in} \\ \text{accounts receivable} \\ \text{and inventory} \end{pmatrix} + \begin{matrix} \text{cost of} \\ \text{change in} \\ \text{cash} \\ \text{discount} \end{matrix}$$

$$= \text{Step 1} - (\text{Step 2} + \text{Step 3})$$
$$= \$190,000 - (\$72,501 + \$45,000)$$
$$= \$72,499$$

In Step 1 of the analysis, the additional profits less bad debts from the new sales are calculated to be $190,000. In Step 2, the additional investment in accounts receivable and inventory is determined to be $458,340. Because the pre-tax required rate of return is 15 percent, the company's required return on this investment is $72,501. In Step 3, the cost of introducing a cash discount is determined to be $45,000. Finally, in Step 4 the benefits and costs are compared, and the net change in pre-tax profits are determined to be $72,499. Thus, a change in the present credit policy is warranted.

In summary, the logic behind this approach to credit policy is to examine the incremental or marginal benefits from such a change and compare these with the incremental or marginal costs. If the change promises more benefits than costs, the change should be made. If, however, the incremental costs are greater than the benefits, the proposed change should not be made. Figure 16–3 on the next page graphs this process: The point where marginal costs equal marginal benefits occurs at credit policy A.

Perspective in Finance

The calculations associated with the incremental analysis of a change in credit policy illustrate the changes that occur when credit policy is adjusted. On the positive side, a loosening of credit policy should increase sales. On the negative side, bad debts, investment in accounts receivable and inventory, and costs associated with the cash discount all increase. The decision then boils down to whether the incremental benefits outweigh the incremental costs.

Inventory Management

Inventory management involves the control of the assets that are produced to be sold in the normal course of the firm's operations. The general categories of inventory include raw materials inventory, work-in-process inventory, and

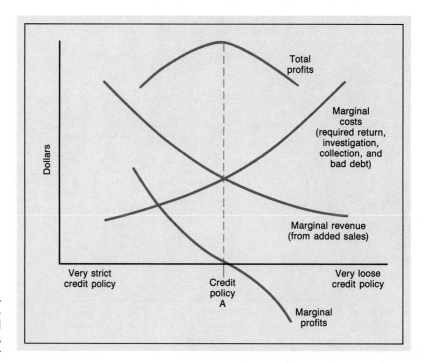

FIGURE 16-3.
Credit Policy Changes and Profits

TABLE 16-6.
Inventory as a Percentage of Total Assets for Major Industries

Industry	Inventory Relative to Total Assets
All industries	4.88%
Automotive dealers and service stations—retail	49.72
Apparel and accessory stores	37.18
Building materials, garden supplies, and mobile home dealers—retail	33.76
Food stores	25.36
Total construction	14.78
Electrical and electronic equipment	13.20
Agriculture, forestry, and fishing	9.22
Eating and drinking places	4.02
Petroleum and coal products	3.58
Hotels and other lodging places	1.56

Source: Internal Revenue Service, U.S. Treasury Department, *Statistics of Income, 1986, Corporate Income Tax Returns* (Washington, DC: Government Printing Office, 1990), pp. 1–47.

finished goods inventory. The importance of inventory management to the firm depends on the extent of the inventory investment. For an average firm, approximately 4.88 percent of all assets are in the form of inventory. However, the percentage varies widely from industry to industry, as Table 16–6 shows. Thus the importance of inventory management and control varies from industry to industry also. For example, it is much more important in the automotive dealer and service station trade, where inventories make up 49.72 percent of total assets, than in the hotel business, where the average investment in inventory is only 1.56 percent of total assets.

Purposes and Types of Inventory

The purpose of carrying inventories is to uncouple the operations of the firm—that is, to make each function of the business independent of each other function—so that delays or shutdowns in one area do not affect the production and sale of the final product. Because production shutdowns result in increased costs, and because delays in delivery can lose customers, the management and control of inventory are important duties of the financial manager.

Decision making in investment in inventory involves a basic tradeoff between risk and return. The risk is that if the level of inventory is too low, the various functions of business do not operate independently, and delays in production and customer delivery can result. The return results because reduced inventory investment saves money. As the size of inventory increases, storage and handling costs as well as the required return on capital invested in inventory rise. Therefore, as the inventory a firm holds is increased, the risk of running out of inventory is lessened, but inventory expenses rise. To illustrate better the uncoupling function that inventories perform, we will look at several general types of inventories.

Raw Materials Inventory

Raw materials inventory consists of basic materials purchased from other firms to be used in the firm's production operations. These goods may include steel, lumber, petroleum, or manufactured items such as wire, ball bearings, or tires that the firm does not produce itself. Regardless of the specific form of the raw materials inventory, all manufacturing firms by definition maintain a raw materials inventory. Its purpose is to uncouple the production function from the purchasing function—that is, to make these two functions independent of each other, so that delays in shipment of raw materials do not cause production delays. In the event of a delay in shipment, the firm can satisfy its need for raw materials by liquidating its inventory. During the 1991 war with Iraq, many firms that used petroleum as an input in production built up their petroleum inventories in anticipation of a slowdown or possibly a stoppage in the flow of oil from the Middle East. This buildup in raw material inventory would have allowed those firms with adequate inventories to continue production even if the war had severely cut the flow of oil.

Work-in-Process Inventory

Work-in-process inventory consists of partially finished goods requiring additional work before they become finished goods. The more complex and lengthy the production process, the larger the investment in work-in-process inventory. The purpose of work-in-process inventory is to uncouple the various operations in the production process so that machine failures and work stoppages in one operation will not affect the other operations. Assume, for example, there are 10 different production operations, each one involving the piece of work produced in the previous operation. If the machine performing the first production operation breaks down, a firm with no work-in-process inventory will have to shut down all 10 production operations. Yet if a firm has such inventory, the remaining 9 operations can continue by drawing the input for the second operation from inventory rather than directly from the output of the first operation.

Finished-Goods Inventory

The *finished-goods inventory* consists of goods on which the production has been completed but that are not yet sold. The purpose of a finished-goods inventory is to uncouple the production and sales functions so that it is not necessary to produce the good before a sale can occur—sales can be made directly out of inventory. In the auto industry, for example, people would not buy from a dealer who made them wait weeks or months, when another dealer could fill the order immediately.

Stock of Cash

Although we have already discussed cash management at some length in Chapter 15, it is worthwhile to mention cash again in the light of inventory management. This is because the *stock of cash* carried by a firm is simply a special type of inventory. In terms of uncoupling the various operations of the firm, the purpose of holding a stock of cash is to make the payment of bills independent of the collection of accounts due. When cash is kept on hand, bills can be paid without prior collection of accounts.

As we examine and develop inventory economic ordering quantity (EOQ) models, we will see a striking resemblance between the EOQ inventory and EOQ cash model; in fact, except for a minor redefinition of terms, they will be exactly the same.

Inventory-Management Techniques

The importance of effective inventory management is directly related to the size of the investment in inventory. Because, on average, approximately 4.88 percent of a firm's assets are tied up in inventory, effective management of these assets is essential to the goal of shareholder wealth maximization. To control the investment in inventory, management must solve two problems: the order quantity problem and the order point problem.

Order Quantity Problem

The *order quantity problem* involves determining the optimal order size for an inventory item given its expected usage, carrying costs, and ordering costs. Aside from a change in some of the variable names, it is exactly the same as the inventory model for cash management (EOQ model) presented in Chapter 15.

The EOQ model attempts to determine the order size that will minimize total inventory costs. It assumes that

$$\text{total inventory costs} = \text{total carrying costs} + \text{total ordering costs} \qquad (16\text{–}4)$$

Assuming that inventory is allowed to fall to zero and then is immediately replenished (this assumption will be lifted when we discuss the order point problem), the average inventory becomes $Q/2$, where Q is inventory order size in units. This can be seen graphically in Figure 16–4.

FIGURE 16–4.
Inventory Level and the Replenishment Cycle

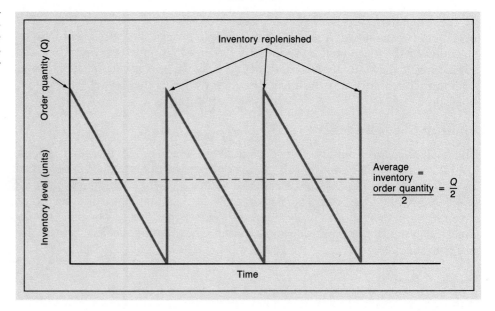

If the average inventory is $Q/2$ and the carrying cost per unit is C, then carrying costs become:

$$\begin{matrix} \text{total} \\ \text{carrying costs} \end{matrix} = \begin{pmatrix} \text{average} \\ \text{inventory} \end{pmatrix} \begin{pmatrix} \text{carrying cost} \\ \text{per unit} \end{pmatrix} \quad \text{(16–5)}$$

$$= \left(\frac{Q}{2}\right) C \quad \text{(16–6)}$$

where Q = the inventory order size in units

C = carrying costs per unit

The carrying costs on inventory include the required rate of return on investment in inventory, in addition to warehouse or storage costs, wages for those who operate the warehouse, and costs associated with inventory shrinkage. Thus, carrying costs include both real cash flows and opportunity costs associated with having funds tied up in inventory.

The ordering costs incurred are equal to the ordering costs per order times the number of orders. If we assume total demand over the planning period is S and we order in lot sizes of Q, then S/Q represents the number of orders over the planning period. If the ordering cost per order is O, then

$$\begin{matrix} \text{total} \\ \text{ordering costs} \end{matrix} = \begin{pmatrix} \text{number} \\ \text{of orders} \end{pmatrix} \begin{pmatrix} \text{ordering cost} \\ \text{per order} \end{pmatrix} \quad \text{(16–7)}$$

$$= \left(\frac{S}{Q}\right) O \quad \text{(16–8)}$$

where S = total demand in units over the planning period

O = ordering cost per order

Thus, total costs in equation (16–4) become

$$\text{total costs} = \left(\frac{Q}{2}\right) C + \left(\frac{S}{Q}\right) O \quad \text{(16–9)}$$

Figure 16–5 illustrates this equation graphically.

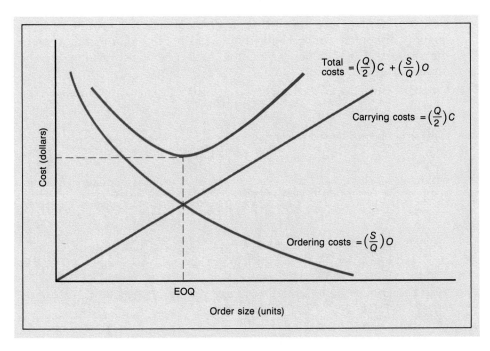

FIGURE 16–5.
Total Cost and EOQ Determination

What we are looking for is the ordering size, Q^*, which provides the minimum total costs. By manipulating equation (16–9), we find that the optimal value of Q—that is, the economic ordering quantity (EOQ)—is[2]

$$Q^* = \sqrt{\frac{2SO}{C}}$$

(16–10)

The use of the EOQ model can best be illustrated through an example.

EXAMPLE

Suppose a firm expects total demand (S) for its product over the planning period to be 5,000 units, whereas the ordering cost per order (O) is $200, and the carrying cost per unit (C) is $2. Substituting these values into equation (16–10) yields

$$Q^* = \sqrt{\frac{2 \cdot 5000 \cdot 200}{2}} = \sqrt{1,000,000} = 1000 \text{ units}$$

Thus, if this firm orders in 1,000-unit lot sizes, it will minimize its total inventory costs. ∎

Examination of EOQ Assumptions

Despite the fact that the EOQ model tends to yield quite good results, there are weaknesses in the EOQ model associated with several of its assumptions. When its assumptions have been dramatically violated, the EOQ model can generally be modified to accommodate the situation. The model's assumptions are as follows:

1. **Constant or uniform demand.** Although the EOQ model assumes constant demand, demand may vary from day to day. If demand is stochastic—that is, not known in advance—the model must be modified through the inclusion of a safety stock.
2. **Constant unit price.** The inclusion of variable prices resulting from quantity discounts can be handled quite easily through a modification of the original EOQ model, redefining total costs and solving for the optimum order quantity.
3. **Constant carrying costs.** Unit carrying costs may vary substantially as the

---

[2]This result can be obtained through calculus.

$$\text{total cost } (TC) = \left(\frac{Q}{2}\right) C + \left(\frac{S}{Q}\right) O$$

The first derivative with respect to Q defines the slope of the total cost curve. Setting this derivative equal to zero specifies the minimum point (zero slope) on the curve. Thus,

$$\frac{dTC}{dQ} = \frac{C}{2} - \frac{SO}{Q^2} = 0$$

$$Q^2 = \frac{2SO}{C}$$

$$Q^* = \sqrt{\frac{2SO}{C}}$$

To verify that a minimum point is being found, rather than a maximum point where the slope would also equal zero, we check for a positive second derivative:

$$\frac{d^2TC}{dQ^2} = \frac{2SO}{Q^3} \geq 0$$

The second derivative must be positive, because SO and Q can only take on positive values; hence, this is a minimum point.

size of the inventory rises, perhaps decreasing because of economies of scale or storage efficiency or increasing as storage space runs out and new warehouses have to be rented. This situation can be handled through a modification in the original model similar to the one used for variable unit price.

4. **Constant ordering costs.** Although this assumption is generally valid, its violation can be accommodated by modifying the original EOQ model in a manner similar to the one used for variable unit price.

5. **Instantaneous delivery.** If delivery is not instantaneous, which is generally the case, the original EOQ model must be modified through the inclusion of a safety stock, that is, the inventory held to accommodate any unusually large and unexpected usage during the delivery time.

6. **Independent orders.** If multiple orders result in cost savings by reducing paperwork and transportation cost, the original EOQ model must be further modified. Although this modification is somewhat complicated, special EOQ models have been developed to deal with it.[3]

These assumptions illustrate the limitations of the basic EOQ model and the ways in which it can be modified to compensate for them. An understanding of the limitations and assumptions of the EOQ model provides the financial manager with more of a base for making inventory decisions.

Order Point Problem

The two most limiting assumptions—those of constant or uniform demand and instantaneous delivery—are dealt with through the inclusion of **safety stock,** which is the inventory held to accommodate any unusually large and unexpected usage during delivery time. The decision on how much safety stock to hold is generally referred to as the **order point problem;** that is, how low should inventory be depleted before it is reordered?

Two factors go into the determination of the appropriate order point: (1) the procurement or delivery-time stock and (2) the safety stock desired. Figure 16–6 graphs the process involved in order point determination. We observe that the order point problem can be decomposed into its two components, the

---

[3]For example, R. J. Tersire, *Material Management and Inventory Control* (New York: Elsevier–North Holland, 1976).

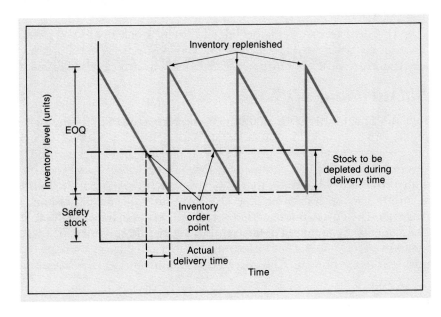

FIGURE 16–6.
Order Point Determination

delivery-time stock—that is, the inventory needed between the order date and the receipt of the inventory ordered—and the safety stock. Thus, the order point is reached when inventory falls to a level equal to the delivery-time stock plus the safety stock.

$$\begin{matrix} \text{inventory order point} \\ [\text{order new inventory} \\ \text{when the level of} \\ \text{inventory falls to} \\ \text{this level}] \end{matrix} = \begin{pmatrix} \text{delivery-time} \\ \text{stock} \end{pmatrix} + \begin{pmatrix} \text{safety} \\ \text{stock} \end{pmatrix} \quad \textbf{(16–11)}$$

As a result of constantly carrying safety stock, the average level of inventory increases. Whereas before the inclusion of safety stock the average level of inventory was equal to EOQ/2, now it will be

$$\text{average inventory} = \frac{\text{EOQ}}{2} + \text{safety stock} \quad \textbf{(16–12)}$$

In general, several factors simultaneously determine how much delivery-time stock and safety stock should be held. First, the efficiency of the replenishment system affects how much delivery-time stock is needed. Because the delivery-time stock is the expected inventory usage between ordering and receiving inventory, efficient replenishment of inventory would reduce the need for delivery-time stock.

The uncertainty surrounding both the delivery time and the demand for the product affects the level of safety stock needed. The more certain the patterns of these inflows and outflows from the inventory, the less safety stock required. In effect, if these inflows and outflows are highly predictable, then there is little chance of any stockout occurring. However, if they are unpredictable, it becomes necessary to carry additional safety stock to prevent unexpected stockouts.

The safety margin desired also affects the level of safety stock held. If it is a costly experience to run out of inventory, the safety stock held will be larger than it would be otherwise. If running out of inventory and the subsequent delay in supplying customers result in strong customer dissatisfaction and the possibility of lost future sales, then additional safety stock is necessary. A final determinant is the cost of carrying additional inventory, in terms of both the handling and storage costs and the opportunity cost associated with the investment in additional inventory. Very simply, the greater the costs, the smaller the safety stock.

The determination of the level of safety stock involves a basic tradeoff between the risk of stock-out, resulting in possible customer dissatisfaction and lost sales, and the increased costs associated with carrying additional inventory.

Inflation and EOQ

Inflation affects the EOQ model in two major ways. First, although the EOQ model can be modified to assume constant price increases, often major price increases occur only once or twice a year and are announced ahead of time. If this is the case, the EOQ model may lose its applicability and may be replaced with **anticipatory buying**—that is, buying in anticipation of a price increase to secure the goods at a lower cost. Of course, as with most decisions, there are tradeoffs. The costs are the added carrying costs associated with the inventory. The benefits, of course, come from buying at a lower price. The second way inflation affects the EOQ model is through increased carrying costs. As inflation pushes interest rates up, the cost of carrying inventory increases. In our EOQ model this means that C increases, which results in a decline in Q^*, the optimal economic order quantity:

$$\downarrow Q^* = \sqrt{\frac{2SO}{C \uparrow}} \qquad (16\text{-}13)$$

EFFECT of INFLATION

Reluctance to stock large inventories because of high carrying costs became particularly prevalent during the late 1970s and early 1980s when inflation and interest rates were at high levels.

Just-in-Time Inventory Control

The **just-in-time inventory control system** is more than just an inventory control system, it is a production and management system. Not only is inventory cut down to a minimum, but the time and physical distance between the various production operations are also reduced. In addition, management is willing to trade off costs to develop close relationships with suppliers and promote speedy replenishment of inventory in return for the ability to hold less safety stock.

The just-in-time inventory control system was originally developed in Japan by Taiichi Okno, a vice-president of Toyota. Originally the system was called the *kanban* system, named after the cards that were placed in the parts bins that were used to call for a new supply. The idea behind the system is that the firm should keep a minimum level of inventory on hand, relying on suppliers to furnish parts "just in time" for them to be assembled. This is in direct contrast to the traditional inventory philosophy of U.S. firms, which is sometimes referred to as a "just-in-case" system, which keeps healthy levels of safety stocks to ensure that production will not be interrupted. Although large inventories may not be a bad idea when interest rates are low, when interest rates are high they become very costly.

Although the just-in-time inventory system is intuitively appealing, it has not proved easy to implement. Long distances from suppliers and plants constructed with too much space for storage and not enough access (doors and

Making Just-in-Time Inventory Systems Work with Maquiladoras: But Do Maquiladoras Exploit Mexican Workers?

In the late 1970s and early 1980s many U.S. firms moved their manufacturing operations to Asian countries in an effort to reduce production costs. One problem firms have encountered for goods produced abroad is long delivery times. This has been particularly troublesome for firms that have implemented just-in-time inventory systems. To reduce the delivery time firms such as Ford, GM, Chrysler, Dale Electronics, Emerson Electric, Zenith, Honeywell, Hitachi, Sanyo, General Electric, Texas Instruments, and many others have built *maquiladoras*. These are assembly plants operated by non-Mexican companies along the Mexican side of the U.S.-Mexican border. In an effort to help develop both sides of what has historically been an impoverished border region, the first maquiladoras were established in 1966 and given special tariff treatment. By early 1992 there were approximately 1,800 maquiladoras employing approximately one-half million Mexican workers; it has been estimated that by the year 2000 up to 3 million workers could be employed.

In the April 18, 1991, *Wall Street Journal*, Lane Kirkland, president of the AFL–CIO, blasted maquiladoras, stating that they cost hundreds of thousands of Americans their jobs *and* that the Mexicans working at the maquiladoras were "joining the ranks of the most crudely exploited human beings on the planet," citing the low wage rate of $3 to $6 per day. The questions are: Do U.S., Japanese, and European corporations take advantage of Mexican workers by operating plants just south of the U.S. border? Are they exporting U.S. jobs?[1]

On one side are those who argue that maquiladoras exploit the large pool of unskilled Mexicans who have migrated north to these border cities to escape the poverty in inner Mexico. These people are desperate for work and are glad to take jobs at wages that are one-tenth those of employees just over the border. U.S.

union officials further charge that maquiladoras took 300,000 U.S. jobs during the 1980s and will increasingly siphon off higher-paid jobs. Additionally, many Mexicans claim that the jobs and money come at too high a social cost; that is, northern Mexico is being Americanized. They are upset by the dilution of Mexican culture created by the spreading use of both English and the U.S. dollar.

The other side of the argument proposes that, far from feeling exploited, Mexican workers often find their clean, air-conditioned work surroundings a relief from their humble homes. Although the pay is low by U.S. standards, these jobs are in high demand and provide an escape from poverty for hundreds of thousands of Mexicans. Moreover, proponents of maquiladoras stress that economics and global competition demand that production seek its lowest cost level. Firms north of the border that fail to transfer operations to gain cost benefits save jobs in the United States only in the short term. In the long term, competition will drive these firms out of business.

Are corporations that build plants south of the border profiting at the expense of exploited Mexican workers and taking jobs away from U.S. workers? What do *you* think?

---

[1] Based on "The Rise of Gringo Capitalism," *Newsweek*, January 5, 1987, pp. 40–41; "The Magnet of Growth in Mexico's North," *Business Week*, June 6, 1988, pp. 48–50; Cheryl D. Hein, "Maquiladoras: Should U.S. Companies Run for the Border?" *The CPA Journal*, September 1991 (New York Society of CPAs), pp. 14–18; Mariah E. deForest, "Are Maquiladoras a Menace to U.S. Workers?" *Business Horizons*, November 1991 (Indiana University), pp. 82–90.
Adapted by permission from Stephen P. Robbins, *Management*, 3d ed. p. 103. Copyright 1991 by Prentice Hall, Inc.

loading docks) to receive inventory have limited successful implementation. But many firms' relationships with their suppliers have been forced to change. Because firms rely on suppliers to deliver high-quality parts and materials immediately, they must have a close long-term relationship with them. Despite the difficulties of implementation, many U.S. firms are committed to moving toward a just-in-time system. General Motors, for example, cut its inventory by 17 percent between 1981 and 1984, saving the company hundreds of millions of dollars a year. National Cash Register reaped similar returns from the implementation of a just-in-time inventory system. In 1980 NCR carried more than $1 billion in inventory with sales of $3.3 billion. By 1990, NCR had doubled sales, whereas the just-in-time inventory method allowed inventory to be cut in half. In fact, between 1977 and 1986 the average level of inventory relative to total assets for all American corporations fell by 46.04 percent. Today, just-in-time inventory techniques had become a fairly common method of inventory control as is shown in Table 16–7.

TABLE 16–7.
Status of "Just-in-Time"
Inventory Technique, 1988

Status	Percent Response
Don't Plan to Use	21.7%
Considering Use	25.0
Using: Questionable Results	12.0
Using: Favorable Results	41.3

Source: S. V. Smith and B. Belt, "Working Capital Management in Practice: An Update," Working Paper No. 951 (West Lafayette, IN: Krannert Graduate School of Management, Purdue University, 1989).

Although the just-in-time system does not at first appear to bear much of a relationship to the EOQ model, it simply alters some of the assumptions of the model with respect to delivery time and ordering costs, and draws out the implications. Actually, it is just a new approach to the EOQ model that tries to produce the lowest average level of inventory possible. If we look at the average level of inventory as defined by the EOQ model, we find it to be

$$\text{average inventory} = \frac{\sqrt{\dfrac{2SO\downarrow}{C}}}{2} + \text{safety stock} \downarrow$$

JUST IN TIME INVENTORY

The just-in-time system attacks this equation in two places. First, by locating inventory supplies in convenient locations, laying out plants in such a way that it is inexpensive and easy to unload new inventory shipments, and computerizing the inventory order system, the cost of ordering new inventory, O, is reduced. Second, by developing a strong relationship with suppliers located in the same geographical area and setting up restocking strategies that cut time, the safety stock is also reduced. The philosophy behind the just-in-time inventory system is that the benefits associated with reducing inventory and delivery time to a bare minimum through adjustment in the EOQ model will more than offset the costs associated with the increased possibility of stock-outs.

SUMMARY

The size of the investment in accounts receivable depends on three factors: the percentage of credit sales to total sales, the level of sales, and the credit and collection policies. However, only the credit and collection policies are decision variables open to the financial manager. The policies that the financial manager has control over include the terms of sale, the quality of customer, and the collection efforts.

Although the typical firm has less assets tied up in inventory (4.88%) than it does in accounts receivable (26.50%), inventory management and control is still an important function of the financial manager. The purpose of holding inventory is to make each function of the business independent of the other functions—that is, to uncouple the firm's operations. Inventory-management techniques primarily involve questions of how much inventory should be ordered and when the order should be placed. The answers directly determine the average level of investment in inventory. The EOQ model is employed in answering the first of these questions. This model attempts to calculate the order size that minimizes the sum of the inventory carrying and ordering costs. The order point problem attempts to determine how low inventory can drop before it is reordered. The order point is reached when the inventory falls to a level equal to the delivery-time stock plus the safety stock. Determining the level of safety stock involves a direct tradeoff between the risk of running out of inventory and the increased costs associated with carrying additional inventory.

The just-in-time inventory control system lowers inventory by reducing the time and distance between the various production functions. The idea behind the system is that the firm should keep a minimum level of inventory on hand and rely on suppliers to furnish parts "just in time" for them to be assembled.

STUDY QUESTIONS

16-1. What factors determine the size of the investment a firm makes in accounts receivable? Which of these factors are under the control of the financial manager?

16-2. What do the following trade credit terms mean?
  a. 1/20, net 50
  b. 2/30, net 60
  c. net 30
  d. 2/10, 1/30, net 60

16-3. What is the purpose of the use of an aging account in the control of accounts receivable? Can this same function be performed through ratio analysis? Why or why not?

16-4. If a credit manager experienced no bad debt losses over the past year, would this be an indication of proper credit management? Why or why not?

16-5. What is the purpose of credit scoring?

16-6. What are the risk–return tradeoffs associated with adopting a more liberal trade credit policy?

16-7. Explain the purpose of marginal analysis.

16-8. What is the purpose of holding inventory? Name several types of inventory and describe their purpose.

16-9. Can cash be considered a special type of inventory? If so, what functions does it attempt to uncouple?

16-10. To control investment in inventory effectively, what two questions must be answered?

16-11. What are the major assumptions made by the EOQ model?

16-12. What are the risk–return tradeoffs associated with inventory management?

16-13. How might inflation affect the EOQ model?

SELF-TEST PROBLEMS

ST-1. (*EOQ Calculations*) A local gift shop is attempting to determine how many sets of wine glasses to order. The store feels it will sell approximately 800 sets in the next year at a price of $18 per set. The wholesale price that the store pays per set is $12. Costs for carrying one set of wine glasses are estimated at $1.50 per year while ordering costs are estimated at $25.
  a. What is the economic order quantity for the sets of wine glasses?
  b. What are the annual inventory costs for the firm if it orders in this quantity? (Assume constant demand and instantaneous delivery and thus no safety stock is carried.)

ST-2. (*EOQ Calculations*) Given the following inventory information and relationships for the F. Beamer Corporation:
  1. Orders can be placed only in multiples of 100 units.
  2. Annual unit usage is 300,000. (Assume a 50-week year in your calculations.)
  3. The carrying cost is 30 percent of the purchase price of the goods.
  4. The purchase price is $10 per unit.
  5. The ordering cost is $50 per order.
  6. The desired safety stock is 1,000 units. (This does not include delivery-time stock.)
  7. Delivery time is two weeks.

Given this information
  a. What is the optimal EOQ level?
  b. How many orders will be placed annually?
  c. At what inventory level should a reorder be made?

16–1A. (*Trade Credit Discounts*) Determine the effective annualized cost of forgoing the trade credit discount on the following terms:
  a. 1/10, net 20
  b. 2/10, net 30
  c. 3/10, net 30
  d. 3/10, net 60
  e. 3/10, net 90
  f. 5/10, net 60

16–2A. (*Altman Model*) The following ratios were supplied by six loan applicants. Given this information and the credit-scoring model developed by Altman (equation [16–3]), which loans have a high probability of defaulting next year?

	$\dfrac{EBIT}{\text{Total Assets}}$	$\dfrac{Sales}{\text{Total Assets}}$	$\dfrac{Market\ Value\ of\ Equity}{\text{Book Value of Debt}}$	$\dfrac{Earnings}{\text{Total Assets}}$	$\dfrac{Working\ Capital}{\text{Total Assets}}$
Applicant 1	.2	.2	1.2	.3	.5
Applicant 2	.2	.8	1.0	.3	.8
Applicant 3	.2	.7	.6	.3	.4
Applicant 4	.1	.4	1.2	.4	.4
Applicant 5	.3	.7	.5	.4	.7
Applicant 6	.2	.5	.5	.4	.4

16–3A. (*Ratio Analysis*) Assuming a 360-day year, calculate what the average investment in inventory would be for a firm, given the following information in each case:
  a. The firm has sales of $600,000, a gross profit margin of 10 percent, and an inventory turnover ratio of 6.
  b. The firm has a cost of goods sold figure of $480,000 and an average age of inventory of 40 days.
  c. The firm has a cost of goods sold figure of $1,150,000 and an inventory turnover ratio of 5.
  d. The firm has a sales figure of $25 million, a gross profit margin of 14 percent, and an average age of inventory of 45 days.

16–4A. (*Marginal Analysis*) The Bandwagonesque Corporation is considering relaxing its current credit policy. Currently the firm has annual sales (all credit) of $5 million and an average collection period of 60 days (assume a 360-day year). Under the proposed change the trade credit terms would be changed from net 60 days to net 90 days and credit would be extended to a riskier class of customer. It is assumed that bad debt losses on current customers will remain at their current level. Under this change, it is expected that sales will increase to $6 million. Given the following information, should the firm adopt the new policy?

> New sales level (all credit): $6,000,000
> Original sales level (all credit): $5,000,000
> Contribution margin: 20%
> Percent bad debt losses on new sales: 8%
> New average collection period: 90 days
> Original average collection period: 60 days
> Additional investment in inventory: $50,000
> Pre-tax required rate of return: 15%

16–5A. (*Marginal Analysis*) The Foxbase Alpha Corporation is considering a major change in credit policy. Managers are considering extending credit to a riskier class of customer and extending their credit period from net 30 days to net 45 days. They do not expect bad debt losses on their current customers to change. Given the following information, should they go ahead with the change in credit policy?

New sales level (all credit): $12,500,000
Original sales level (all credit): $11,000,000
Contribution margin: 20%
Percent bad debt losses on new sales: 9%
New average collection period: 45 days
Original average collection period: 30 days
Additional investment in inventory: $75,000
Pre-tax required rate of return: 15%

16–6A. (*Marginal Analysis*) Nirvana, Inc., has annual sales of $5 million. All sales are credit, and the current credit terms are 1/50 net 70. The company is studying the possibility of relaxing credit terms to 2/60 net 90 in hopes of securing new sales. Managers do not expect bad debt losses on their current customers to change under the new credit policy. Given the following information, should they go ahead with the change in credit policy?

New sales level (all credit): $8,000,000
Original sales level (all credit): $7,000,000
Contribution margin: 25%
Percent bad debt losses on new sales: 8%
New average collection period: 75 days
Original average collection period: 60 days
Additional investment in inventory: $50,000
Pre-tax required rate of return: 15%
New percent cash discount: 2%
Percent of customers taking the new cash discount: 50%
Original percent cash discount: 1%
Percent of customers taking the old cash discount: 50%

16–7A. (*EOQ Calculations*) A downtown bookstore is trying to determine the optimal order quantity for a popular novel just printed in paperback. The store feels that the book will sell at four times its hardback figures. It would therefore sell approximately 3,000 copies in the next year at a price of $1.50. The store buys the book at a wholesale figure of $1. Costs for carrying the book are estimated at $.10 a copy per year, and it costs $10 to order more books.
a. Determine the EOQ.
b. What would be the total costs for ordering the books 1, 4, 5, 10, and 15 times a year?
c. What questionable assumptions are being made by the EOQ model?

16–8A. (*EOQ Calculations*) The local hamburger fast-food restaurant purchases 20,000 boxes of hamburger rolls every month. Order costs are $50 an order, and it costs $.25 a box for storage.
a. What is the optimal order quantity of hamburger rolls for this restaurant?
b. What questionable assumptions are being made by the EOQ model?

16–9A. (*EOQ Calculations*) A local car manufacturing plant has a $75 per-unit per-year carrying cost on a certain item in inventory. This item is used at a rate of 50,000 per year. Ordering costs are $500 per order.
a. What is the EOQ for this item?
b. What are the annual inventory costs for this firm if it orders in this quantity? (Assume constant demand and instantaneous delivery.)

16–10A. (*EOQ Calculations*) Swank Products is involved in the production of camera parts and has the following inventory, carrying, and storage costs:
1. Orders must be placed in round lots of 200 units.
S ~**2.** Annual unit usage is 500,000. (Assume a 50-week year in your calculations.)
3. The carrying cost is 20 percent of the purchase price. C = .40 ¢
4. The purchase price $2 per unit.
5. The ordering cost is $90 per order. — O
6. The desired safety stock is 15,000 units. (This does not include delivery time stock.)
7. The delivery time is one week.
Given the above information:
a. Determine the optimal EOQ level.
b. How many orders will be placed annually?

    c. What is the inventory order point? (That is, at what level of inventory should a new order be placed?)

    d. What is the average inventory level?

16–11A. (*EOQ Calculations*) Toledo Distributors has determined the following inventory information and relationships:

1. Orders can be placed only in multiples of 200 units.
2. Annual unit usage is 500,000 units. (Assume a 50-week year in your calculations.)
3. The carrying cost is 10 percent of the purchase price of the goods.
4. The purchase price is $5 per unit.
5. The ordering cost is $100 per order.
6. The desired safety stock is 5,000 units. (This does not include delivery time stock.)
7. Delivery time is four weeks.

Given this information:

    a. What is the EOQ level?

    b. How many orders will be placed annually?

    c. At what inventory level should a reorder be made?

    d. Now assume the carrying costs are 50 percent of the purchase price of the goods and recalculate (a), (b), and (c). Are these the results you anticipated?

16–12A. (*Comprehensive EOQ Calculations*) Knutson Products, Inc., is involved in the production of airplane parts and has the following inventory, carrying, and storage costs:

1. Orders must be placed in round lots of 100 units.
2. Annual unit usage is 250,000. (Assume a 50-week year in your calculations.)
3. The carrying cost is 10 percent of the purchase price.
4. The purchase price is $10 per unit.
5. The ordering cost is $100 per order.
6. The desired safety stock is 5,000 units. (This does not include delivery time stock.)
7. The delivery time is one week.

Given the above information:

    a. Determine the optimal EOQ level.

    b. How many orders will be placed annually?

    c. What is the inventory order point? (That is, at what level of inventory should a new order be placed?)

    d. What is the average inventory level?

    e. What would happen to the EOQ if annual unit sales doubled (all other unit costs and safety stocks remaining constant)? What is the elasticity of EOQ with respect to sales? (That is, what is the percent change in EOQ divided by the percent change in sales?)

    f. If carrying costs double, what would happen to the EOQ level? (Assume the original sales level of 250,000 units.) What is the elasticity of EOQ with respect to carrying costs?

    g. If the ordering costs double, what would happen to the level of EOQ? (Again assume original levels of sales and carrying costs.) What is the elasticity of EOQ with respect to ordering costs?

    h. If the selling price doubles, what would happen to EOQ? What is the elasticity of EOQ with respect to selling price?

STUDY PROBLEMS (SET B)

16–1B. (*Trade Credit Discounts*) Determine the effective annualized cost of forgoing the trade credit discount on the following terms:

    a. 1/5, net 20

    b. 2/20, net 90

    c. 1/20, net 100

    d. 4/10, net 50

    e. 5/20, net 100

    f. 5/30, net 50

16–2B. (*Altman Model*) The following ratios were supplied by six loan applicants. Given this information and the credit-scoring model developed by Altman (equation [16–3]), which loans have a high probability of defaulting next year and thus should be avoided?

| | EBIT | Sales | Market Value of Equity | Earnings | Working Capital |
	Total Assets	Total Assets	Book Value of Debt	Total Assets	Total Assets
Applicant 1	.3	.4	1.2	.3	.5
Applicant 2	.2	.6	1.3	.4	.3
Applicant 3	.2	.7	.6	.3	.2
Applicant 4	.1	.5	.8	.5	.4
Applicant 5	.5	.7	.5	.4	.6
Applicant 6	.2	.4	.2	.4	.4

16–3B. (*Ratio Analysis*) Assuming a 360-day year, calculate what the average investment in inventory would be for a firm, given the following information in each case.

    a. The firm has sales of $550,000, a gross profit margin of 10 percent, and an inventory turnover ratio of 5.

    b. The firm has a cost of goods sold figure of $480,000 and an average age of inventory of 35 days.

    c. The firm has a cost of goods sold figure of $1,250,000 and an inventory turnover ratio of 6.

    d. The firm has a sales figure of $25 million, a gross profit margin of 15 percent, and an average age of inventory of 50 days.

16–4B. (*Marginal Analysis*) The Hyndford Street Corporation is considering relaxing its current credit policy. Currently the firm has annual sales (all credit) of $6 million and an average collection period of 40 days (assume a 360-day year). Under the proposed change the trade credit terms would be changed from net 40 days to net 90 days and credit would be extended to a riskier class of customer. It is assumed that bad debt losses on current customers will remain at their current level. Under this change, it is expected that sales will increase to $7 million. Given the following information, should the firm adopt the new policy?

New sales level (all credit): $7,000,000

Original sales level (all credit): $6,000,000

Contribution margin: 20%

Percent bad debt losses on new sales: 8%

New average collection period: 90 days

Original average collection period: 40 days

Additional investment in inventory: $40,000

Pre-tax required rate of return: 15%

16–5B. (*Marginal Analysis*) The Northern Muse Corporation is considering a major change in credit policy. Managers are considering extending credit to a riskier class of customer and extending their credit period from net 30 days to net 50 days. They do not expect bad debt losses on their current customers to change. Given the following information, should they go ahead with the change in credit policy?

New sales level (all credit): $18,000,000

Original sales level (all credit): $17,000,000

Contribution margin: 20%

Percent bad debt losses on new sales: 8%

New average collection period: 50 days

Original average collection period: 30 days

Additional investment in inventory: $60,000

Pre-tax required rate of return: 15%

16–6B. (*Marginal Analysis*) Linden Arden, Inc., has annual sales of $10 million. All sales are credit and the current credit terms are 1/30 net 60. The company is studying the possibility of relaxing credit terms to 2/60 net 90 in hopes of securing new sales. Managers do not expect bad debt losses on their current customers to change under the new credit policy. Given the following information, should they go ahead with the change in credit policy?

New sales level (all credit): $10,500,000
Original sales level (all credit): $10,000,000
Contribution margin: 25%
Percent bad debt losses on new sales: 8%
New average collection period: 75 days
Original average collection period: 45 days
Additional investment in inventory: $60,000
Pre-tax required rate of return: 15%
New percent cash discount: 2%
Percent of customers taking the new cash discount: 50%
Original percent cash discount: 1%
Percent of customers taking the original cash discount: 50%

16–7B. (*EOQ Calculations*) A downtown bookstore is trying to determine the optimal order quantity for a popular novel just printed in paperback. The store feels that the book will sell at four times its hardback figures. It would therefore sell approximately 3,500 copies in the next year at a price of $1.50. The store buys the book at a wholesale figure of $1. Costs for carrying the book are estimated at $.20 a copy per year, and it costs $9 to order more books.
   a. Determine the EOQ.
   b. What would be the total costs for ordering the books 1, 4, 5, 10, and 15 times a year?
   c. What questionable assumptions are being made by the EOQ model?

16–8B. (*EOQ Calculations*) The local hamburger fast-food restaurant purchases 21,000 boxes of hamburger rolls every month. Order costs are $55 an order, and it costs $.20 a box for storage.
   a. What is the optimal order quantity of hamburger rolls for this restaurant?
   b. What questionable assumptions are being made by the EOQ model?

16–9B. (*EOQ Calculations*) A local car manufacturing plant has a $70 per-unit per-year carrying cost on a certain item in inventory. This item is used at a rate of 55,000 per year. Ordering costs are $500 per order.
   a. What is the economic order quantity for this item?
   b. What are the annual inventory costs for this firm if it orders in this quantity? (Assume constant demand and instantaneous delivery.)

16–10B. (*EOQ Calculations*) Swank Products is involved in the production of camera parts and has the following inventory, carrying, and storage costs:
   1. Orders must be placed in round lots of 200 units.
   2. Annual unit usage is 600,000. (Assume a 50-week year in your calculations.)
   3. The carrying cost is 15 percent of the purchase price.
   4. The purchase price $3 per unit.
   5. The ordering cost is $90 per order.
   6. The desired safety stock is 15,000 units. (This does not include delivery time stock.)
   7. The delivery time is one week.
   Given the above information:
   a. Determine the optimal EOQ level.
   b. How many orders will be placed annually?
   c. What is the inventory order point? (That is, at what level of inventory should a new order be placed?)
   d. What is the average inventory level?

16–11B. (*EOQ Calculations*) Toledo Distributors has determined the following inventory information and relationships:
   1. Orders can be placed only in multiples of 200 units.
   2. Annual unit usage is 500,000 units. (Assume a 50-week year in your calculations.)
   3. The carrying cost is 9 percent of the purchase price of the goods.
   4. The purchase price is $5 per unit.
   5. The ordering cost is $75 per order.
   6. The desired safety stock is 5,000 units. (This does not include delivery time stock.)
   7. Delivery time is four weeks.
   Given this information:
   a. What is the EOQ level?

b. How many orders will be placed annually?

c. At what inventory level should a reorder be made?

d. Now assume the carrying costs are 50 percent of the purchase price of the goods and recalculate (a), (b), and (c). Are these the results you anticipated?

16–12B. (*Comprehensive EOQ Calculations*) Good Gravy Products, Inc., is involved in the production of tractor parts and has the following inventory, carrying, and storage costs:

1. Orders must be placed in round lots of 100 units.

2. Annual unit usage is 300,000. (Assume a 50-week year in your calculations.)

3. The carrying cost is 10 percent of the purchase price.

4. The purchase price is $12 per unit.

5. The ordering cost is $100 per order.

6. The desired safety stock is 4,000 units. (This does not include delivery time stock.)

7. The delivery time is one week.

Given the above information:

a. Determine the optimal EOQ level.

b. How many orders will be placed annually?

c. What is the inventory order point? (That is, at what level of inventory should a new order be placed?)

d. What is the average inventory level?

e. What would happen to the EOQ if annual unit sales doubled (all other unit costs and safety stocks remaining constant)? What is the elasticity of EOQ with respect to sales? (That is, what is the percent change in EOQ divided by the percent change in sales?)

f. If carrying costs double, what would happen to the EOQ level? (Assume the original sales level of 250,000 units.) What is the elasticity of EOQ with respect to carrying costs?

g. If the ordering costs double, what would happen to the level of EOQ? (Again assume original levels of sales and carrying costs.) What is the elasticity of EOQ with respect to ordering costs?

h. If the selling price doubles, what would happen to EOQ? What is the elasticity of EOQ with respect to selling price?

SELF-TEST SOLUTIONS

SS–1. **a.** The economic order quantity is

$$Q^* = \sqrt{\frac{2SO}{C}}$$

where S = total demand in units over the planning period

           O = ordering cost per order

           C = carrying costs per unit

Substituting the values given in the self-test problem into the EOQ equation we get

$$Q^* = \sqrt{\frac{2 \cdot 800 \cdot 25}{1.50}}$$

$$= \sqrt{26,667}$$

$$= 163 \text{ units per order}$$

Thus, 163 units should be ordered each time an order is placed. Note that the EOQ calculations occur based on several limiting assumptions such as constant demand, constant unit price, and constant carrying costs, which may influence the final decision.

b. Total costs = carrying costs + ordering costs

$$= \left(\frac{Q}{2}\right) C + \left(\frac{S}{Q}\right) O$$

$$= \left(\frac{163}{2}\right) \$1.50 + \left(\frac{800}{163}\right) \$25$$

$$= \$122.25 + \$122.70$$

$$= \$244.95$$

Note that carrying costs and ordering costs are the same (other than a slight difference caused by having to order in whole rather than fractional units). This is because the total costs curve is at its minimum when ordering costs equal carrying costs, as shown in Figure 16–5.

SS–2. **a.**

$$EOQ = \sqrt{\frac{2SO}{C}}$$

$$= \sqrt{\frac{2(300,000)(50)}{3}}$$

= 3,162 units, but because orders must be placed in 100 unit lots, the effective EOQ becomes 3,200 units

b.

$$\frac{\text{Total usage}}{\text{EOQ}} = \frac{300,000}{3,200} = 93.75 \text{ orders per year}$$

c.

Inventory order point = delivery time + safety stock

$$= \frac{2}{50} \times 300,000 + 1,000$$

$$= 12,000 + 1,000$$

$$= 13,000 \text{ units}$$

CHAPTER 17

Short-Term Financing

Estimation of the Cost of Short-Term Credit ● Sources of Short-Term Credit

SHORT TERM < 1YR
INTERMEDIATE = 1 TO 10
LONG TERM > 10 YRS

This chapter is one of four that discuss sources of financing. By convention all sources of financing that must be repaid within one year are considered to be short term, those that must be repaid in one to ten years are intermediate term, and all sources with maturities longer than ten years are classified as long term. Intermediate-term sources are discussed in Chapter 19 in conjunction with financial leases, whereas long-term sources are presented in Chapters 20 and 21.

Two major issues are involved in managing the firm's use of short-term financing: (1) How much short-term financing should the firm use? and (2) What specific sources of short-term financing should the firm select? Chapter 14 used the *hedging principle* of working-capital management to answer the first of these two questions. Basically, the hedging principle describes the process of matching temporary needs for funds with short-term sources of financing and permanent needs with long-term sources.[1] The objective of this chapter is to answer the second of the questions above: How should the financial manager select sources of short-term credit? In general, three basic factors should be considered in selecting a source of short-term credit: (1) the effective cost of credit, (2) the availability of credit in the amount needed and for the period when financing is required, and (3) the influence of the use of a particular credit source on the cost and availability of other sources of financing. We discuss the problem of estimating the cost of short-term credit before introducing the various sources of credit, because the same procedure is used for all sources. We examine credit availability and the impact of short-term credit on the financial plan with a look at individual credit sources.

---

[1]Temporary needs for funds arise in response to a temporary need for current assets. These include current assets that the firm does not plan to hold throughout the indefinite future. Permanent needs for funds arise in conjunction with a permanent need for certain assets. These assets consist of fixed assets plus the firm's minimum level of investment in current assets. Thus, when discussing working-capital management, we abandoned the current fixed asset classification in favor of the more useful concept of temporary and permanent assets.

Estimation of Cost of Short-Term Credit

Approximate Cost-of-Credit Formula

The procedure for estimating the cost of short-term credit is a very simple one and relies on the basic interest equation:

$$\text{interest} = \text{principal} \times \text{rate} \times \text{time} \qquad\qquad (17\text{--}1)$$

where *interest* is the dollar amount of interest on a *principal* that is borrowed at some annual *rate* for a fraction of a year (represented by *time*). For example, a six-month loan for $1,000 at 8 percent interest would require an interest payment of $40:

$$\text{interest} = \$1000 \times .08 \times \frac{1}{2} = \$40$$

We use this basic relationship to solve for the cost of a source of short-term financing or the annual effective rate (RATE) where the interest amount, the principal sum, and the time period for financing are known. Thus, solving the basic interest equation for RATE produces[2]

$$\text{RATE} = \frac{\text{interest}}{\text{principal} \times \text{time}} \qquad\qquad (17\text{--}2)$$

or

$$\text{RATE} = \frac{\text{interest}}{\text{principal}} \times \frac{1}{\text{time}}$$

This equation, called the RATE calculation, is clarified with the following example.

EXAMPLE

The SKC Corporation plans to borrow $1,000 for a 90-day period. At maturity the firm will repay the $1,000 principal amount plus $30 interest. The effective annual rate of interest for the loan can be estimated using the RATE equation, as follows:

$$\text{RATE} = \frac{\$30}{\$1000} \times \frac{1}{90/360}$$

$$= .03 \times \frac{360}{90} = .12, \text{ or } 12\%$$

The effective annual cost of funds provided by the loan is therefore 12 percent. ∎

Annual Percentage Rate Formula

The simple RATE calculation does not consider compound interest. To account for the influence of compounding, we can use the following equation:

$$\text{APR} = \left(1 + \frac{r}{m}\right)^{m} - 1 \qquad\qquad (17\text{--}3)$$

$r = \text{RATE}$

$m = \dfrac{1}{time}$

---

[2]A similar expression was used in Chapter 16 to estimate the effective cost of passing up discounts on trade credit.

where APR is the annual percentage rate, r is the nominal rate of interest per year (12 percent in the above example), and m is the number of compounding periods within a year [$m = 1/\text{TIME} = 1/(90/360) = 4$ in the preceding example]. Thus, the effective rate of interest on the example problem, considering compounding, is

$$\text{APR} = \left(1 + \frac{.12}{4}\right)^4 - 1 = .126, \text{ or } 12.6\%$$

Compounding effectively raises the cost of short-term credit. Because the differences between RATE and APR are usually small, we use the simple interest version of RATE to compute the cost of short-term credit.

Sources of Short-Term Credit

Short-term credit sources can be classified into two basic groups: unsecured and secured. **Unsecured** loans include all those sources that have as their security only the lender's faith in the ability of the borrower to repay the funds when due. There are three major sources of unsecured short-term credit: trade credit, unsecured bank loans, and commercial paper. **Secured** loans involve the pledge of specific assets as collateral in the event the borrower defaults in payment of principal or interest. Commercial banks, finance companies, and factors are the primary suppliers of secured credit. The principal sources of collateral include accounts receivable and inventories.

Unsecured Sources: Accrued Wages and Taxes

Because most businesses pay their employees only periodically (weekly, biweekly, or monthly), firms accrue a wages payable account that is, in essence, a loan from their employees. For example, if the wage expense for the Appleton Manufacturing Company is $450,000 per week and it pays its employees monthly, then by the end of a four-week month the firm will owe its employees $1.8 million in wages for services they have already performed during the month. Consequently, the employees finance their own efforts through waiting a full month for payment.

Similarly, firms generally make quarterly income tax payments for their estimated quarterly tax liability. This means that the firm has the use of the tax monies it owes based on quarterly profits up through the end of the quarter. In addition, the firm pays sales taxes and withholding (income) taxes for its employees on a deferred basis. The longer the period that the firm holds the tax payments, the greater the amount of financing they provide.

Note that these sources of financing *rise and fall spontaneously* with the level of firm sales. That is, as the firm's sales increase so do its labor expense, sales taxes collected, and income tax. Consequently, these accrued expense items provide the firm with automatic or spontaneous sources of financing.

Trade Credit

Trade credit provides one of the most flexible sources of short-term financing available to the firm. In Chapter 14 we noted that trade credit is a primary source of spontaneous, or on-demand, financing. That is, trade credit arises spontaneously with the firm's purchases. To arrange for credit the firm need only place an order with one of its suppliers. The supplier checks the firm's credit and, if it is good, sends the merchandise. The purchasing firm then pays for the goods in accordance with the supplier's credit terms.

Credit Terms and Cash Discounts

Very often the credit terms offered with trade credit involve a cash discount for early payment. For example, a supplier might offer terms of 2/10, net 30, which means that a 2 percent discount is offered for payment within 10 days or the full amount is due in 30 days. Thus, a 2 percent penalty is involved for not paying within 10 days or for delaying payment from the 10th to the 30th day (that is, for 20 days). The effective annual cost of not taking the cash discount can be quite severe. Using a $1 invoice amount, the effective cost of passing up the discount period using the preceding credit terms and our RATE equation can be estimated.

$$\text{RATE} = \frac{\$.02}{\$.98} \times \frac{1}{20/360} = .3673, \text{ or } 36.73\%$$

Note that the 2 percent cash discount is the *interest* cost of extending the payment period an *additional* 20 days. Note also that the principal amount of the credit is $.98. This amount constitutes the full principal amount as of the 10th day of the credit period, after which time the cash discount is lost. The effective cost of passing up the 2 percent discount for two days is quite expensive: 36.73 percent. Furthermore, once the discount period has passed, there is no reason to pay before the final due date (the 30th day). Table 17–1 lists the effective annual cost of a number of alternative credit terms. Note that the cost of trade credit varies directly with the size of the cash discount and inversely with the length of time between the end of the discount period and the final due date.

Credit Terms	Effective Rate
2/10, net 60	14.69%
2/10, net 90	9.18
3/20, net 60	27.84
6/10, net 90	28.72

Stretching on Trade Credit

Some firms that use trade credit engage in a practice called *stretching* of trade accounts. This practice involves delaying payments beyond the prescribed credit period. For example, a firm might purchase materials under credit terms of 3/10, net 60; however, when faced with a shortage of cash, the firm might extend payment to the eightieth day. Continued violation of trade terms can eventually lead to a loss of credit. However, for short periods, and at infrequent intervals, stretching offers the firm an emergency source of short-term credit.

Advantages of Trade Credit

As a source of short-term financing, trade credit has a number of advantages. First, trade credit is conveniently obtained as a normal part of the firm's operations. Second, no formal agreements are generally involved in extending credit. Furthermore, the amount of credit extended expands and contracts with the needs of the firm; this is why it is classified as a spontaneous, or on-demand, source of financing (Chapter 14).

Unsecured Sources: Bank Credit

Commercial banks provide unsecured short-term credit in two basic forms: lines of credit and transaction loans (notes payable). Maturities of both types of loans are usually one year or less, with rates of interest depending on the creditworthiness of the borrower and the level of interest rates in the economy as a whole.

Line of Credit

A **line of credit** is generally an informal agreement or understanding between the borrower and the bank as to the maximum amount of credit that the bank will provide the borrower at any one time. Under this type of agreement there is no *legal* commitment on the part of the bank to provide the stated credit. In a **revolving credit agreement,** which is a variant of this form of financing, a legal obligation is involved. The line of credit agreement generally covers a period of one year corresponding to the borrower's *fiscal* year. Thus, if the borrower is on a July 31 fiscal year, its lines of credit will be based on the same annual period.

Credit terms ■ Lines of credit generally do not involve fixed rates of interest, instead they state that credit will be extended *at ½ percent over prime* or some other spread over the bank's prime rate.[3] Furthermore, the agreement usually does not spell out the specific use that will be made of the funds beyond a general statement, such as *for working-capital purposes.* Figure 17–1 gives an example letter of agreement to extend a line of credit.

Lines of credit usually require that the borrower maintain a minimum balance in the bank throughout the loan period, called a **compensating balance.** This required balance (which can be stated as a percent of the line of credit or the loan amount) increases the effective cost of the loan to the borrower, unless a deposit balance equal to or greater than this balance requirement is ordinarily maintained in the bank.

[3]The *prime rate of interest* is the rate that a bank charges its most creditworthy borrowers.

```
                    City National Bank
                      Snook, Texas


                    July 14, 19XX


Ms. Rebecca Swank
Vice President and Treasurer
Nuland Manufacturing Company
Bryan, Texas 78740

Dear Ms. Swank:

Following an analysis of your request, we have decided to extend
to you a line of credit for working capital purposes in the
amount of $300,000. The credit is extended for your current
fiscal year ending July 31, 19X1. Borrowings under this line will
be at our prime rate prevailing at the time.

This credit is subject only to maintaining the firm's financial
position.

                    Sincerely,



                    Francis L. Prince
                    Executive Vice President
```

FIGURE 17–1.
Letter of Agreement
to Extend a Line of Credit

The effective cost of short-term bank credit can be estimated using the
RATE equation. Consider the following example:

EXAMPLE

M&M Beverage Company has a $300,000 line of credit that requires a compen-
sating balance equal to 10 percent of the loan amount. The rate paid on the loan
is 12 percent per annum, $200,000 is borrowed for a six-month period, and the
firm does not, at present, have a deposit with the lending bank. The dollar cost of
the loan includes the interest expense and, in addition, the opportunity cost of
maintaining an idle cash balance equal to the 10 percent compensating balance.
To accommodate the cost of the compensating balance requirement, assume
that the added funds will have to be borrowed and simply left idle in the firm's
checking account. Thus, the amount actually borrowed (B) will be larger than
the $200,000 needed. In fact, the needed $200,000 will constitute 90 percent of
the total borrowed funds because of the 10 percent compensating balance
requirement, hence $.90B = \$200,000$, such that $B = \$222,222$. Thus, interest is
paid on a $222,222 loan ($\$222,222 \times .12 \times \frac{1}{2} = \$13,333.32$), of which only
$200,000 is available for use by the firm.[4] The effective annual cost of credit
therefore is

$$\text{RATE} = \frac{\$13,333.32}{\$200,000} \times \frac{1}{180/360} = 13.33\%$$

---

[4]The same answer would have been obtained by assuming a total loan of $200,000, of which only 90
percent of $180,000 was available for use by the firm; that is,

$$\text{RATE} = \frac{\$12,000}{\$180,000} \times \frac{1}{180/360} = 13.33\%$$

Interest is now calculated on the $200,000 loan amount ($\$12,000 = \$200,000 \times .12 \times \frac{1}{2}$).

BASIC FINANCIAL MANAGEMENT IN PRACTICE

How Do Banks Lend Money?

It is often quipped that a banker is a person who lends you an umbrella when it is fair, and takes it away when it rains. Actually, bankers utilize two very basic approaches to lending money. The first is commonly referred to as secured lending, which can be loosely translated to mean lending on the borrower's assets, and the second is cash flow lending.

Secured lending involves lending money based upon the borrower's assets as collateral. In *The Merchant of Venice* Shylock demanded a pound of flesh as security for a loan. In practice, banks accept a wide variety of objects as collateral. In any case to be acceptable as collateral the object must have three basic attributes: (i) It must first be worth at least as much as the amount being lent. Of course the worth of any asset is not always known with certainty nor is it assured that its worth will remain constant over the term of the loan. For these reasons banks will vary the percentage of the value of the collateral they will lend in response to their assessment of the riskiness of the collateral asset's value. For instance, if the borrower has a portfolio of U.S. Government securities that it wants to use as collateral, then the bank might advance a loan of up to 90 percent of the face value of these securities, while it might loan as little as 20 percent against the estimated worth of the firm's work in progress inventories. (ii) To be good collateral it must be relatively easy to take possession of the asset. Here it helps if the collateral is not too mobile. For example, following the collapse of the shipping industry beginning in 1982 bankers found themselves with over $10 billion in bad debts that required they quite literally search the ports of the world in search of their *floating security*. (iii) Finally, collateral must be easily identified. This requirement is actually an important element of item (ii) above. For example, although

banks do make loans based on *blanket liens* against all or a portion (for example, inventories) of a firm's assets, they prefer not to since it is more difficult to determine just what assets they hold claim to in the event of default.

An alternative to asset based loans banks also engage in *cash flow lending*, or loans based upon the supposed ability of the debtor to repay the loan. The key to this type of lending is a good estimate of the borrower's normal free cash flow that can serve as the basis for repaying creditors. One commonly used basis for assessing this free cash flow is the sum of the firm's net profit after tax, its depreciation expense, and its interest charges. The idea here is that this sum is the amount of cash the firm could use to meet its principal and interest charges. The ratio of the firm's free cash flow to its interest and principal expenses is generically referred to as the firm's interest cover. What constitutes an acceptable interest cover will vary with the nature of the firm's business, with riskier businesses demanding higher coverage ratios.

All of this sounds very scientific and quantifiable to this point. However, we know from the history of bank failures and crises that the lending process is fraught with uncertainty. In the end there is no substitute for common sense. For example, when the Texas oil boom was in full swing, hind sight tells us that Houston property lenders seldom looked outside their high-rise office towers to count the number of construction cranes on the horizon.

Sources: Based on "How Banks Lend," *The Economist*, (February 4, 1989), pp. 78–79. "Evaluating Commercial Loan Requests," Timothy Koch, *Bank Management* (Chicago: The Dryden Press, 1988), pp. 465–93.

If the firm normally maintains at least $20,000 (or 10 percent of the needed funds) in a demand deposit with the lending bank, then the cost of the credit is

$$\text{RATE} = \frac{\$12,000}{\$200,000} \times \frac{1}{180/360} = 12\%$$

In the M&M Beverage Company example the loan required the payment of principal ($222,222) plus interest ($13,333.32) at the end of the six-month loan period. Frequently, bank loans will be made on a discount basis. That is, the loan interest will be deducted from the loan amount before the funds are transferred to the borrower. Extending the M&M Beverage Company example to consider discounted interest involves reducing the loan proceeds ($200,000) in the previous example by the amount of interest for the full six months ($13,333.32). The effective rate of interest on the loan is now:

$$\text{RATE} = \frac{\$13,333.32}{\$200,000 - \$13,333.32} \times \frac{1}{180/360}$$

$$= .1429, \text{ or } 14.29\%$$

The effect of discounting interest was to raise the cost of the loan from 13.33 to 14.29 percent. This results from the fact that the firm pays interest on the same amount of funds as before (\$222,222); however, this time it gets the use of \$13,333.32 less, or \$200,000 − \$13,333.32 = \$186,666.68.[5]

Transaction Loans

Still another form of unsecured short-term bank credit can be obtained in the form of **transaction loans.** Here the loan is made for a specific purpose. This is the type of loan that most individuals associate with bank credit. The loan is obtained by signing a promissory note similar to the one shown in Figure 17–2.

Unsecured transaction loans are very similar to a line of credit regarding cost, term to maturity, and compensating balance requirements. In both instances commercial banks often require that the borrower *clean up* its short-term loans for a 30- to 45-day period during the year. This means, very simply, that the borrower must be free of any bank debt for the stated period. The purpose of such a requirement is to ensure that the borrower is not using short-term bank credit to finance a part of its permanent needs for funds.

Merchant Banking

The term *merchant banking* is sometimes used to describe the financing activities of traditional commercial banks. A merchant bank is a commercial bank that is willing and able to provide equity as well as debt financing.

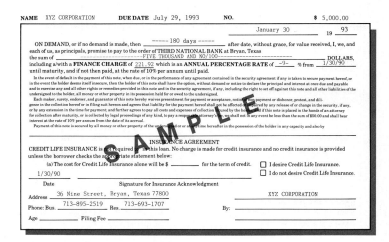

FIGURE 17–2.
Example Short-Term Bank Note

---

[5]If M&M needs the use of a full \$200,000 then it will have to borrow more than \$222,222 to cover both the compensating balance requirement *and* the discounted interest. In fact, the firm will have to borrow some amount B such that

$$B - .10B - (.12 \times \tfrac{1}{2})B = \$200,000$$

$$.84B = \$200,000$$

$$B = \frac{\$200,000}{.84} = \$238,095$$

The cost of credit remains the same at 14.29 percent, as we see below:

$$\text{RATE} = \frac{\$14,285.70}{\$238,095 - \$23,810 - \$14,285.70} \times \frac{1}{180/360}$$

$$= .1429, \text{ or } 14.29\%$$

Historically, the Glass-Stegall act of 1933 prohibited U.S. banks from engaging in equity financing in an attempt to stabilize the banking system in response to the Great Depression. However, in recent years U.S. commercial banks have been increasingly organized as bank holding companies, which have been allowed to make limited equity investments in the commercial bank's clients. This phenomenon is likely to continue to grow in response to increasing international competition from foreign banks, which operate as merchant banks on a regular basis.

Unsecured Sources: Commercial Paper

Only the largest and most creditworthy companies are able to use **commercial paper,** which is simply a short-term *promise to pay* that is sold in the market for short-term debt securities.[6]

Credit Terms

The maturity of this credit source is generally six months or less, although some issues carry 270-day maturities. The interest rate on commercial paper is generally slightly lower (.5 to 1 percent) than the prime rate on commercial bank loans. Also, interest is usually discounted, although sometimes interest-bearing commercial paper is available.

New issues of commercial paper are either placed directly (sold by the issuing firm directly to the investing public) or dealer placed. Dealer placement involves the use of a commercial paper dealer, who sells the issue for the issuing firm. Many major finance companies, such as General Motors Acceptance Corporation, place their commercial paper directly. The volume of direct versus dealer placements is roughly 4 to 1 in favor of direct placements. Dealers are used primarily by industrial firms that either make only infrequent use of the commercial paper market or, owing to their small size, would have difficulty placing the issue without the help of a dealer.

Commercial Paper as a Source of Short-Term Credit

Several advantages accrue to the user of commercial paper:

1. **Interest rate.** Commercial paper rates are generally lower than rates on bank loans and comparable sources of short-term financing. Figure 17–3 displays historical rates of interest on short-term bank credit and commercial paper spanning the 15-month period ending January 16, 1992.
2. **Compensating balance requirement.** No minimum balance requirements are associated with commercial paper. However, issuing firms usually find it desirable to maintain lines of credit agreements sufficient to back up their short-term financing needs in the event that a new issue of commercial paper cannot be sold or an outstanding issue cannot be repaid when due.
3. **Amount of credit.** Commercial paper offers the firm with very large credit needs a single source for all its short-term financing. Because of loan restrictions placed on the banks by the regulatory authorities, obtaining the necessary funds from a commercial bank might require dealing with a number of institutions.[7]

---

[6]A limited discussion of commercial paper is presented here; the topic is discussed in detail in Chapter 15.

---

[7]Member banks of the Federal Reserve System are limited to 10 percent of their total capital, surplus, and undivided profits when making loans to a single borrower. Thus, when a corporate borrower's needs for financing are very large it may have to deal with a group of participating banks to raise the needed funds.

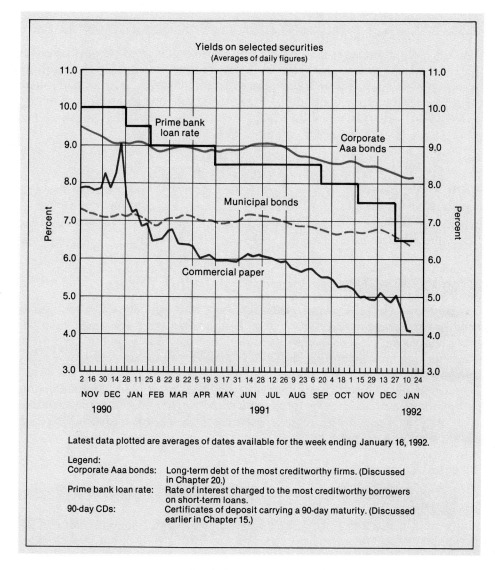

Latest data plotted are averages of dates available for the week ending January 16, 1992.

Legend:
Corporate Aaa bonds: Long-term debt of the most creditworthy firms. (Discussed in Chapter 20.)
Prime bank loan rate: Rate of interest charged to the most creditworthy borrowers on short-term loans.
90-day CDs: Certificates of deposit carrying a 90-day maturity. (Discussed earlier in Chapter 15.)

FIGURE 17–3.
Historical Rates of Interest on Short-Term Bank Credit and Commercial Paper
Source: St. Louis Federal Reserve Bank, U.S. Financial Data, January 16, 1992, p. 6.

4. **Prestige.** Because it is widely recognized that only the most creditworthy borrowers have access to the commercial paper market, its use signifies a firm's credit status.

Using commercial paper for short-term financing, however, involves a very important *risk.* That is, the commercial paper market is highly impersonal and denies even the most creditworthy borrower any flexibility in terms of repayment. When bank credit is used, the borrower has someone with whom he or she can work out any temporary difficulties that might be encountered in meeting a loan deadline. This flexibility simply does not exist for the user of commercial paper.

Estimation of the Cost of Commercial Paper

The cost of commercial paper can be estimated using the simple effective cost of credit equation (RATE). The key points to remember are that commercial paper interest is usually discounted and that if a dealer is used to place the issue, a fee is charged. Even if a dealer is not used, the issuing firm will incur costs associated with preparing and placing the issue, and these costs must be included in estimating the cost of credit.

The EPG Mfg. Company uses commercial paper regularly to support its needs for short-term financing. The firm plans to sell $100 million in 270-day-maturity paper on which it expects to have to pay discounted interest at an annual rate of 12 percent per annum. In addition, EPG expects to incur a cost of approximately $100,000 in dealer placement fees and other expenses of issuing the paper. The effective cost of credit to EPG can be calculated as follows:

$$\text{RATE} = \frac{\$9 \text{ million} + \$100,000}{\$100 \text{ million} - \$100,000 - \$9 \text{ million}} \times \frac{1}{270/360}$$

$$= .1335, \text{ or } 13.35\%$$

where the interest cost is calculated as $100 million × .12 × 270/360 = $9 million. Thus, the effective cost of credit to EPG is 13.35 percent. ■

Secured Sources: Accounts Receivable Loans

Secured sources of short-term credit have certain assets of the firm pledged as collateral to secure the loan. Upon default of the loan agreement, the lender has first claim to the pledged assets in addition to its claim as a general creditor of the firm. Hence the secured credit agreement offers an added margin of safety to the lender.

Generally, a firm's receivables are among its most liquid assets. For this reason they are considered by many lenders to be prime collateral for a secured loan. Two basic procedures can be used in arranging for financing based on receivables: pledging and factoring.

Pledging Accounts Receivable

Under the **pledging** arrangement the borrower simply pledges accounts receivable as collateral for a loan obtained from either a commercial bank or a finance company. The amount of the loan is stated as a percent of the face value of the receivables pledged. If the firm provides the lender with a *general line* on its receivables, then all of the borrower's accounts are pledged as security for the loan. This method of pledging is simple and inexpensive. However, because the lender has no control over the quality of the receivables being pledged, it will set the maximum loan at a relatively low percent of the total face value of the accounts, generally ranging downward from a maximum of around 75 percent.

Still another approach to pledging involves the borrower's presenting specific invoices to the lender as collateral for a loan. This method is somewhat more expensive in that the lender must assess the creditworthiness of each individual account pledged; however, given this added knowledge the lender will be willing to increase the loan as a percent of the face value of the invoices. In this case the loan might reach as high as 85 or 90 percent of the face value of the pledged receivables.

Credit terms ■ Accounts receivable loans generally carry an interest rate 2 to 5 percent higher than the bank's prime lending rate. Finance companies charge an even higher rate. In addition, the lender will usually charge a handling fee stated as a percent of the face value of the receivables processed, which may be as much as 1 to 2 percent of the face value.

The A. B. Good Company sells electrical supplies to building contractors on terms of net 60. The firm's average monthly sales are $100,000; thus, given the firm's two-month credit terms, its average receivables balance is $200,000. The firm pledges all its receivables to a local bank, which in turn advances up to 70 percent of the face value of the receivables at 3 percent over prime and with a 1 percent processing charge on *all* receivables pledged. A. B. Good follows a practice of borrowing the maximum amount possible, and the current prime rate is 10 percent.

The effective cost of using this source of financing for a full year is computed as follows:

$$\text{RATE} = \frac{\$18,200 + \$12,000}{\$140,000} \times \frac{1}{360/360} = 21.57\%$$

where the total dollar cost of the loan consists of both the annual interest expense (.13 × .70 × \$200,000 = \$18,200) and the annual processing fee (.01 × \$100,000 × 12 months = \$12,000). The amount of credit extended is .70 × \$200,000 = \$140,000. Note that the processing charge applies to *all* receivables pledged. Thus, the A. B. Good Company pledges \$100,000 each month, or \$1,200,000 during the year, on which a 1 percent fee must be paid, for a total annual charge of \$12,000.[8] ■

One more point: The lender, in addition to making advances or loans, may be providing certain credit services to the borrower. For example, the lender may provide billing and collection services. The value of these services should *not* be considered a part of the cost of credit. In the preceding example A. B. Good Company may *save* credit department expenses of \$10,000 per year by pledging all its accounts and letting the lender provide those services. In this case, the cost of short-term credit is only

$$\text{RATE} = \frac{\$18,200 + \$12,000 - \$10,000}{\$140,000} \times \frac{1}{360/360} = 14.43\%$$

Advantages and disadvantages of pledging ■ The primary advantage of pledging as a source of short-term credit is the flexibility it provides the borrower. Financing is available on a continuous basis. The new accounts created through credit sales provide the collateral for the financing of new production. Furthermore, the lender may provide credit services that eliminate or at least reduce the need for similar services within the firm. The primary disadvantage associated with this method of financing is its cost, which can be relatively high compared with other sources of short-term credit, owing to the level of the interest rate charged on loans and the processing fee on pledged accounts.

Factoring Accounts Receivable

Factoring accounts receivable involves the outright sale of a firm's accounts to a financial institution called a *factor*. A **factor** is a firm that acquires the receivables of other firms. The factoring institution may be a commercial finance company that engages solely in the factoring of receivables (known as an *old-line factor*) or it may be a commercial bank. The factor, in turn, bears the risk of collection and, for a fee, services the accounts. The fee is stated as a percent of the face value of all receivables factored (usually from 1 to 3 percent).

---

[8]If only one month's accounts are factored and those accounts are collected in 60 days, then the cost of credit can be calculated as follows:

$$\text{RATE} = \frac{\$1,516.67 + \$1000}{\$70,000} \times \frac{1}{(60/360)} = .2157, \text{ or } 21.57\%$$

where interest equals \$100,000 × .70 × .13 × ⅙ = \$1516.67 and the pledging fee equals .01 × \$100,000 = \$1000.

The factor firm typically does *not* make payment for factored accounts until the accounts have been collected or the credit terms have been met. Should the firm wish to receive immediate payment for its factored accounts, it can borrow from the factor, using the factored accounts as collateral. The maximum loan the firm can obtain is equal to the face value of its factored accounts less the factor's fee (1 to 3 percent) less a reserve (6 to 10 percent) less the interest on the loan. For example, if $100,000 in receivables is factored, carrying 60-day credit terms, a 2 percent factor's fee, a 6 percent reserve, and interest at 1 percent per month on advances, then the maximum loan or advance the firm can receive is computed as follows:

Face amount of receivables factored	$100,000
Less: fee (.02 × $100,000)	(2,000)
Reserve (.06 × $100,000)	(6,000)
Interest (.01 × $92,000 × 2 months)	(1,840)
Maximum advance	$ 90,160

Note that interest is discounted and calculated based upon a maximum amount of funds available for advance ($92,000 = $100,000 − $2000 − $6000). Thus, the effective cost of credit can be calculated as follows:

$$\text{RATE} = \frac{\$1840 + \$2000}{\$90,160} \times \frac{1}{60/360}$$

$$= 25.55\%$$

Secured Sources: Inventory Loans

Inventory loans provide a second source of security for short-term secured credit. The amount of the loan that can be obtained depends on both the marketability and perishability of the inventory. Some items, such as raw materials (grains, oil, lumber, and chemicals), are excellent sources of collateral, because they can easily be liquidated. Other items, such as work-in-process inventories, provide very poor collateral because of their lack of marketability.

There are several methods by which inventory can be used to secure short-term financing. These include a *floating* or *blanket lien, chattel mortgage, field warehouse receipt,* and *terminal warehouse receipt.*

Floating Lien Agreement

Under a **floating lien** agreement the borrower gives the lender a lien against all its inventories. This provides the simplest but least secure form of inventory collateral. The borrowing firm maintains full control of the inventories and continues to sell and replace them as it sees fit. Obviously, this lack of control over the collateral greatly dilutes the value of this type of security to the lender. Correspondingly, loans made with floating liens on inventory as collateral are generally limited to a relatively modest fraction of the value of the inventories covered by the lien. In addition, floating liens usually include future as well as existing inventories.

Chattel Mortgage Agreements

The lender can increase its security interest by having specific items of inventory identified (by serial number or otherwise) in the security agreement. Such an arrangement is provided by a **chattel mortgage agreement.** The borrower retains title to the inventory but cannot sell the items without the lender's consent. This type of agreement is costly to implement, because specific items of inventory must be identified. It is used only for major items of inventory such as machine tools or other capital assets.

BASIC FINANCIAL MANAGEMENT IN PRACTICE

The Ins and Outs of Factoring

Getting In

Factors are necessarily selective in the companies they agree to take on as clients. Detailed negotiations take place with prospective clients and their financial advisers; two key items of information that the factor will require are:

- Audited accounts for the past year and the current management accounts.
- A list of the customers and a monthly turnover projection for each.

Commencement date. Once agreement has been reached a date will be arranged for the factor to assume responsibility for the sales ledger.

Introducing the service. At the start of the factoring arrangement, it is useful for the client to send a letter to customers explaining the introduction of the factor. Where appropriate, the factor may speak personally to some customers.

Invoices. Once factoring starts, clients will be encouraged to invoice their customers immediately a valid debt has been created, passing copies of invoices to the factor or, in some cases, passing the invoices to the factor for mailing. Clients must ensure that their invoicing procedure is efficient, with the terms and conditions clearly stated so that they will be understood by customers.

Factoring. With recourse and non-recourse factoring, clients may only draw on a financial facility within the credit limits agreed for each customer. These credit limits must be monitored constantly to ensure they are realistic.

Credit cover. In the case of non-recourse factoring, clients must ensure they have credit approval from the factor before delivering the goods or providing the service. They must seek credit cover for new customers before delivery, and should monitor the level of credit cover on existing customers to ensure that it is adequate.

Management accounts. During the course of the year, a factor will ask to see its client's management accounts, usually at about quarterly intervals, in order to monitor the progress of the business.

Day-to-day operation. A number of routine procedures and associated documentation will be employed in the operation of the factoring arrangement, depend-

ing on the precise system of the factor concerned. Factors will usually supply a concise set of operating instructions to guide the client.

Getting Out

Companies should not be inhibited from entering into factoring arrangements for fear that they may find it difficult to discontinue the service. Indeed they may wish to discontinue for a variety of reasons. For instance:

- Acquisition by a larger parent who does not wish to factor.
- Change in the pattern of business, resulting for example in a significant reduction in customers.
- Replacement from another source of funding at present being taken from the factor.
- Generation of increased profits rendering factoring unnecessary.

A factoring agreement will almost certainly contain a clause relating to the notice requirement—usually about three months on either side. On deciding to withdraw from factoring, clients will need to address themselves to just three principal matters:

- The availability of funds to finance the buying back of the outstanding debts from the factor.
- The setting up of a sales ledger system and the acquisition of necessary sales ledger administration, credit control and collection staff, to be effective from the agreed handing-over date.
- Credit insurance arrangements to replace the credit cover at present provided by the factor in the case of a non-recourse agreement.

Factors have no wish to hold clients to agreements if their services are no longer needed. Indeed they will provide every assistance to effect a smooth change over when client wishes to terminate the arrangement.

Source: Michael Maberly, "Factoring: A Catalyst for Growth and Profits," *Accountancy*, Institute of Chartered Accountants 97 (April 1986), pp. 122–24.

Field Warehouse Financing Agreements

Increased lender control over inventories used as loan collateral can be obtained through the use of a **field warehouse financing agreement.** Here the inventories used as collateral are physically separated from the firm's other inventories and placed under the control of a third-party field warehousing firm. Note that the inventories are not removed from the borrower's premises but are placed under the control of a third party who is responsible for protecting the security interests of the lender. This arrangement is particularly useful when large, bulky items are used as collateral. For example, a refinery might use a part of its inventory of fuel oil to secure a short-term bank loan. Under a field warehousing agreement the oil reserves would be set aside in specific tanks or storage vessels, which would be controlled (monitored) by a field warehousing concern.

The warehousing firm, on receipt of the inventory, takes full control of the collateral. This means that the borrower is no longer allowed to use or sell the inventory items without the consent of the lender. The warehousing firm issues a *warehouse receipt* for the merchandise, which carries title to the goods represented therein. The receipt may be negotiable, in which case title can be transferred through sale of the receipt, or nonnegotiable, whereby title remains with the lender. In a negotiable receipt arrangement the warehouse concern will release the goods to whoever holds the receipt, whereas a nonnegotiable receipt allows the goods to be released only on the written consent of the lender.

The cost of such a loan can be quite high, because the services of the field warehouse company must be paid for by the borrower.

The M. M. Richards Company follows a practice of obtaining short-term credit based on its seasonal finished goods inventory. The firm builds up its inventories of outdoor furniture throughout the winter months for sale in spring and summer. Thus, for the two-month period ended March 31, it uses its fall and winter production of furniture as collateral for a short-term bank loan. The bank lends the company up to 70 percent of the value of the inventory at 14 percent interest plus a fixed fee of $2,000 to cover the costs of a field warehousing arrangement. During this period the firm usually has about $200,000 in inventories, which it borrows against. The annual effective cost of the short-term credit is therefore

$$\text{RATE} = \frac{\$3267 + \$2000}{\$140,000} \times \frac{1}{60/360} = 22.57\%$$

where the financing cost consists of two month's interest

$$(\$140,000 \times .14 \times 60/360 = \$3,267)$$

plus the field warehousing fee of $2,000. ∎

Terminal Warehouse Agreements

The **terminal warehouse agreement** differs from the field warehouse agreement in only one respect. Here the inventories pledged as collateral are transported to a public warehouse that is physically removed from the borrower's premises. The lender has an added degree of safety or security because the inventory is totally removed from the borrower's control. Once again the cost of this type of arrangement is increased because the warehouse firm must be paid by the borrower; in addition, the inventory must be transported to and eventually from the public warehouse.

The same warehouse receipt procedure described earlier for field warehouse loans is used. Again, the cost of this type of financing can be quite high.

There are two basic issues involved in managing the firm's use of short-term financing. The first of these is determining the level of short-term financing the firm should use. This question was first addressed in Chapter 14 through the use of the **hedging principle** of working-capital management. Basically, this principle suggests that short-term financing be used to finance temporary or short-term investments in assets. In this chapter we have sought to answer the second question. How should the financial manager select a source of short-term financing?

Three basic factors provide the key considerations in selecting a source of short-term financing: (1) the effective cost of credit, (2) the availability of financing in the amount and for the time needed, and (3) the effect of the use of credit from a particular source on the cost and availability of other sources of credit.

The various sources of short-term credit can be categorized into two groups: unsecured and secured. Unsecured credit offers no specific assets as security for the loan agreement. The primary sources include trade credit, lines of credit, and unsecured transaction loans from commercial banks, and commercial paper. Secured credit is generally provided to business firms by commercial banks, finance companies, and factors. The most popular sources of security involve the use of accounts receivable and inventories. Loans secured by accounts receivable include pledging agreements, in which a firm pledges its receivables as security for a loan, and factoring agreements, in which the firm sells the receivables to a factor. A primary difference in these two arrangements relates to the ability of the lender to seek payment from the borrower in the event that the accounts used as collateral become uncollectible. In a pledging arrangement the lender retains the right of recourse in the event of default, whereas in factoring a lender is generally without recourse.

Loans secured by inventories can be made using one of several types of security arrangements. Among the most widely used are the floating lien, chattel mortgage, field warehouse agreement, and terminal warehouse agreement. The form of agreement used will depend on the type of inventories pledged as collateral and the degree of control the lender wishes to exercise over the loan collateral.

STUDY QUESTIONS

17-1. What distinguishes short-term, intermediate-term, and long-term debt?

17-2. What considerations should be used in selecting a source of short-term credit? Discuss each.

17-3. How can the formula "interest = principal × rate × time" be used to estimate the effective cost of short-term credit?

17-4. How can we accommodate the effects of compounding in our calculation of the effective cost of short-term credit?

17-5. There are three major sources of unsecured short-term credit. List and discuss the distinguishing characteristics of each.

17-6. What is meant by the following trade credit terms: 2/10, net 30? 4/20, net 60? 3/15, net 45?

17-7. Define the following:
   a. Line of credit
   b. Commercial paper

c. Compensating balance

d. Prime rate

17–8. List and discuss four advantages of the use of commercial paper.

17–9. What risk is involved in the firm's use of commercial paper as a source of short-term credit? Discuss.

17–10. List and discuss the distinguishing features of the principal sources of secured credit based upon accounts receivable.

17–11. List and discuss the distinguishing features of the primary sources of secured credit based upon inventories.

SELF-TEST PROBLEMS

ST–1. (*Analyzing the Cost of a Commercial Paper Offering*) The Marilyn Sales Company is a wholesale machine tool broker which has gone through a recent expansion of its activities resulting in a doubling of its sales. The company has determined that it needs an additional $200 million in short-term funds to finance peak season sales during roughly six months of the year. Marilyn's treasurer has recommended that the firm use a commercial paper offering to raise the needed funds. Specifically, he has determined that a $200 million offering would require 10 percent interest (paid in advance or discounted) plus a $125,000 placement fee. The paper would carry a six-month (180-day) maturity. What is the effective cost of credit?

ST–2. (*Analyzing the Cost of Short-Term Credit*) The Samples Mfg. Co. provides specialty steel products to the oil industry. Although the firm's business is highly correlated with the cyclical swings in oil exploration activity, it also experiences some significant seasonality. The firm currently is concerned with this seasonality in its need for funds. The firm needs $500,000 for the two-month July–August period each year, and as a result the company's vice-president of finance is currently considering the following three sources of financing:

a. Establish a line of credit with the Second State Bank of Granger, Texas. The bank has agreed to provide Samples with the needed $500,000, carrying an interest rate of 14 percent with interest discounted and a compensating balance of 20 percent of the loan balance. Samples does not have a bank account with First State and would have to establish one to satisfy the compensating balance requirement.

b. Samples can forgo its trade discounts over the two months of July and August when the funding will be needed. The firm's discount terms are 3/15, net 30, and the firm averages $500,000 in trade credit purchases during July and August.

c. Finally, Samples could enter into a pledging arrangement with a local finance company. The finance company has agreed to extend Samples the needed $500,000 if it pledges $750,000 in receivables. The finance company has offered to advance the $500,000, with 12 percent annual interest payable at the end of the two-month loan term. In addition, the finance company will charge a one-half of one percent fee based on pledged receivables to cover the cost of processing the company's accounts (this fee is paid at the end of the loan period).

Analyze the cost of each of the alternative sources of credit and select the best one. Note that a total of $500,000 will be needed for a two-month period (July–August) each year.

ST–3. (*Analyzing the Cost of Short-Term Credit*) The treasurer of the Lights-a-Lot Mfg. Company is faced with three alternative bank loans. The firm wishes to select the one that minimizes its cost of credit on a $200,000 note that it plans to issue in the next 10 days. Relevant information for the three loan configurations is found below:

a. An 18 percent rate of interest with interest paid at year-end and no compensating balance requirement.

b. A 16 percent rate of interest but carrying a 20 percent compensating balance requirement. This loan also calls for interest to be paid at year end.

c. A 14 percent rate of interest that is discounted plus a 20 percent compensating balance requirement.

Analyze the cost of each of these alternatives. You may assume that the firm would not normally maintain any bank balance that might be used to meet the 20 percent compensating balance requirements of alternatives (b) and (c).

17-1A. (*Estimating the Cost of Bank Credit*) Paymaster Enterprises has arranged to finance its seasonal working-capital needs with a short-term bank loan. The loan will carry a rate of 12 percent per annum with interest paid in advance (discounted). In addition, Paymaster must maintain a minimum demand deposit with the bank of 10 percent of the loan balance throughout the term of the loan. If Paymaster plans to borrow $100,000 for a period of three months, what is the effective cost of the bank loan?

17-2A. (*Estimating the Cost of Commercial Paper*) On February 3, 199X, the Burlington Western Company plans a commercial paper issue of $20 million. The firm has never used commercial paper before but has been assured by the firm placing the issue that it will have no difficulty raising the funds. The commercial paper will carry a 270-day maturity and will require interest based upon a rate of 11 percent per annum. In addition, the firm will have to pay fees totaling $200,000 in order to bring the issue to market and place it. What is the effective cost of the commercial paper issue to Burlington Western?

17-3A. (*Cost of Trade Credit*) Calculate the effective cost of the following trade credit terms where payment is made on the net due date.
   a. 2/10, net 30
   b. 3/15, net 30
   c. 3/15, net 45
   d. 2/15, net 60

17-4A. (*Annual Percentage Rate*) Compute the cost of the trade credit terms in problem 17-3A using the compounding formula, or annual percentage rate.

17-5A. (*Cost of Short-Term Financing*) The R. Morin Construction Company needs to borrow $100,000 to help finance the cost of a new $150,000 hydraulic crane used in the firm's commercial construction business. The crane will pay for itself in one year and the firm is considering the following alternatives for financing its purchase:
   Alternative A—The firm's bank has agreed to lend the $100,000 at a rate of 14 percent. Interest would be discounted, and a 15 percent compensating balance would be required. However, the compensating balance requirement would not be binding on R. Morin, because the firm normally maintains a minimum demand deposit (checking account) balance of $25,000 in the bank.
   Alternative B—The equipment dealer has agreed to finance the equipment with a one-year loan. The $100,000 loan would require payment of principal and interest totaling $116,300.
   a. Which alternative should R. Morin select?
   b. If the bank's compensating balance requirement were to necessitate idle demand deposits equal to 15 percent of the loan, what effect would this have on the cost of the bank loan alternative?

17-6A. (*Cost of Short-Term Bank Loan*) On July 1, 199X, the Southwest Forging Corporation arranged for a line of credit with the First National Bank of Dallas. The terms of the agreement called for a $100,000 maximum loan with interest set at 1 percent over prime. In addition, the firm has to maintain a 20 percent compensating balance in its demand deposit throughout the year. The prime rate is currently 12 percent.
   a. If Southwest normally maintains a $20,000 to $30,000 balance in its checking account with FNB of Dallas, what is the effective cost of credit through the line-of-credit agreement where the maximum loan amount is used for a full year?
   b. Recompute the effective cost of credit to Southwest if the firm will have to borrow the compensating balance and it borrows the maximum possible under the loan agreement. Again, assume the full amount of the loan is outstanding for a whole year.

17-7A. (*Cost of Commercial Paper*) Tri-State Enterprises plans to issue commercial paper for the first time in the firm's 35-year history. The firm plans to issue $500,000 in 180-day maturity notes. The paper will carry a 10¼ percent rate with discounted interest and will cost Tri-State $12,000 (paid in advance) to issue.
   a. What is the effective cost of credit to Tri-State?
   b. What other factors should the company consider in analyzing whether to issue the commercial paper?

17-8A. (*Cost of Accounts Receivable*) Johnson Enterprises, Inc., is involved in the manufacture and sale of electronic components used in small AM–FM radios. The firm needs $300,000 to finance an anticipated expansion in receivables due to increased sales. Johnson's credit terms are net 60, and its average monthly credit sales are $200,000. In general, the firm's customers pay within the credit period; thus the firm's average accounts receivable balance is $400,000.

Chuck Idol, Johnson's comptroller, approached the firm's bank with a request for a loan for the $300,000 using the firm's accounts receivable as collateral. The bank offered to make the loan at a rate of 2 percent over prime plus a 1 percent processing charge on all receivables pledged ($200,000 per month). Furthermore, the bank agreed to lend up to 75 percent of the face value of the receivables pledged.

a. Estimate the cost of the receivables loan to Johnson where the firm borrows the $300,000. The prime rate is currently 11 percent.

b. Idol also requested a line of credit for $300,000 from the bank. The bank agreed to grant the necessary line of credit at a rate of 3 percent over prime and required a 15 percent compensating balance. Johnson currently maintains an average demand deposit of $80,000. Estimate the cost of the line of credit to Johnson.

c. Which source of credit should Johnson select? Why?

17-9A. (*Cost of Factoring*) MDM, Inc., is considering factoring its receivables. The firm has credit sales of $400,000 per month and has an average receivables balance of $800,000 with 60-day credit terms. The factor has offered to extend credit equal to 90 percent of the receivables factored less interest on the loan at a rate of 1½ percent per month. The 10 percent difference in the advance and the face value of all receivables factored consists of a 1 percent factoring fee plus a 9 percent reserve, which the factor maintains. In addition, if MDM, Inc., decides to factor its receivables, it will sell them all, so that it can reduce its credit department costs by $1,500 a month.

a. What is the cost of borrowing the maximum amount of credit available to MDM, Inc., through the factoring agreement?

b. What considerations other than cost should be accounted for by MDM, Inc., in determining whether or not to enter the factoring agreement?

17-10A. (*Inventory Financing*) In June of each year the Arlyle Publishing Company builds up its inventories for fall sales. The company has explored the possibility of a field warehouse security agreement as collateral for an inventory loan from its bank during the three summer months. During these months inventories average $400,000. The field warehouse arrangement will cost Arlyle a flat fee of $2,000 a month on all its inventory regardless of the amount the firm borrows. The bank has agreed to lend up to 70 percent of the value of the inventory at a rate of 14 percent.

a. If Arlyle borrows $200,000 using the inventory loan for June through August, what is the effective cost of credit?

b. What is the effective cost of borrowing $280,000 for the June through August period?

17-11A. (*Cost of Secured Short-Term Credit*) The Sean–Janeow Import Co. needs $500,000 for the three-month period ending September 30, 199X. The firm has explored two possible sources of credit.

1. S–J has arranged with its bank for a $500,000 loan secured by accounts receivable. The bank has agreed to advance S–J 80 percent of the value of its pledged receivables at a rate of 11 percent plus a 1 percent fee based on all receivables pledged. S–J's receivables average a total of $1 million year-round.

2. An insurance company has agreed to lend the $500,000 at a rate of 9 percent per annum, using a loan secured by S–J's inventory of salad oil. A field warehouse agreement would be used, which would cost S–J $2,000 a month.

Which source of credit should S–J select? Explain.

17-12A. (*Cost of Short-Term Financing*) You plan to borrow $20,000 from the bank to pay for inventories for a gift shop you have just opened. The bank offers to lend you the money at 10 percent annual interest for the six months the funds will be needed.

a. Calculate the effective rate of interest on the loan.

b. In addition, the bank requires you to maintain a 15 percent compensating balance in the bank. Because you are just opening your business, you do not have a demand deposit at the bank that can be used to meet the compensating balance requirement. This means that you will have to put 15 percent of the loan amount from your own personal money (which you had planned to use to help finance the business) in a checking account. What is the cost of the loan now?

c. In addition to the compensating balance requirement in (b), you are told that interest will be discounted. What is the effective rate of interest on the loan now?

17-13A. (*Cost of Factoring*) A factor has agreed to lend the JVC Corporation working capital on the following terms. JVC's receivables average $100,000 per month and have a 90-day average collection period (note that JVC's credit terms call for payment in 90 days and accounts receivable average $300,000 because of the 90-day average collection period). The factor will charge 12 percent interest on any advance (1 percent per month paid in advance), will charge a 2 percent processing fee on all receivables factored, and will maintain a 20 percent reserve. If JVC undertakes the loan it will reduce its own credit department expenses by $2,000 per month. What is the annual effective rate of interest to JVC on the factoring arrangement? Assume that the maximum advance is taken.

17-14A. (*Opportunity Cost of Decreasing Wages Payable*) In June of this year the AMB Manufacturing Company negotiated a new union contract with its employees. One of the provisions of the new contract involved increasing the frequency of its wage payments from once a month to once every two weeks. AMB's biweekly payroll averages $250,000 and the firm's opportunity cost of funds is 12 percent per annum.
  a. What is the annual dollar cost of this new wage payment scheme to AMB?
  b. What is the maximum percentage increase in wages that AMB would have been willing to accept in lieu of the increased frequency of wage payments?

STUDY PROBLEMS (SET B)

17-1B. (*Estimating the Cost of Bank Credit*) Dee's Christmas Trees, Inc., is evaluating options for financing its seasonal working-capital needs. A short-term loan from Liberty Bank would carry a 14 percent annual interest rate, with interest paid in advance (discounted). If this option is chosen, Dee's would also have to maintain a minimum demand deposit equal to 10 percent of the loan balance, throughout the term of the loan. If Dee's needs to borrow $125,000 for the upcoming three months before Christmas, what is the effective cost of the loan?

17-2B. (*Estimating the Cost of Commercial Paper*) Duro Auto Parts would like to exploit a production opportunity overseas, and is seeking additional capital to finance this expansion. The company plans a commercial paper issue of $15 million on February 3, 199X. The firm has never issued commercial paper before, but has been assured by the investment banker placing the issue that it will have no difficulty raising the funds, and that this method of financing is the least expensive option, even after the $150,000 placement fee. The issue will carry a 270-day maturity and will require interest based on an annual rate of 12 percent. What is the effective cost of the commercial paper issue to Duro?

17-3B. (*Cost of Trade Credit*) Calculate the effective cost of the following trade credit terms where payment is made on the net due date.
  a. 2/10, net 30
  b. 3/15, net 30
  c. 3/15, net 45
  d. 2/15, net 60

17-4B. (*Annual Percentage Rate*) Compute the cost of the trade credit terms in problem 17-3B using the compounding formula, or annual percentage rate.

17-5B. (*Cost of Short-Term Financing*) Vitra Glass Company needs to borrow $150,000 to help finance the cost of a new $225,000 kiln to be used in the production of glass bottles. The kiln will pay for itself in one year and the firm is considering the following alternatives for financing its purchase:
  Alternative A—The firm's bank has agreed to lend the $150,000 at a rate of 15 percent. Interest would be discounted, and a 16 percent compensating balance would be required. However, the compensating balance requirement would not be binding on Vitra, because the firm normally maintains a minimum demand deposit (checking account) balance of $25,000 in the bank.
  Alternative B—The kiln dealer has agreed to finance the equipment with a one-year loan. The $150,000 loan would require payment of principal and interest totaling $163,000.
  a. Which alternative should Vitra select?

b. If the bank's compensating balance requirement were to necessitate idle demand deposits equal to 16 percent of the loan, what effect would this have on the cost of the bank loan alternative?

17–6B. (*Cost of Short-Term Bank Loan*) Lola's Ice Cream recently arranged for a line of credit with the Longhorn State Bank of Dallas. The terms of the agreement called for a $100,000 maximum loan with interest set at 2.0 percent over prime. In addition, Lola's must maintain a 15 percent compensating balance in its demand deposit throughout the year. The prime rate is currently 12 percent.

a. If Lola's normally maintains a $15,000-to-$25,000 balance in its checking account with LSB of Dallas, what is the effective cost of credit through the line-of-credit agreement where the maximum loan amount is used for a full year?

b. Recompute the effective cost of credit to Lola's Ice Cream if the firm has to borrow the compensating balance and it borrows the maximum possible under the loan agreement. Again, assume the full amount of the loan is outstanding for a whole year.

17–7B. (*Cost of Commercial Paper*) Luft, Inc., recently acquired production rights to an innovative sailboard design but needs funds to pay for the first production run, which is expected to sell briskly. The firm plans to issue $450,000 in 180-day maturity notes. The paper will carry an 11 percent rate with discounted interest and will cost Luft $13,000 (paid in advance) to issue.

a. What is the effective cost of credit to Luft?

b. What other factors should the company consider in analyzing whether to issue the commercial paper?

17–8B. (*Cost of Accounts Receivable*) TLC Enterprises, Inc., is a wholesaler of toys and curios. The firm needs $400,000 to finance an anticipated expansion in receivables. TLC's credit terms are net 60, and its average monthly credit sales are $250,000. In general, the TLC's customers pay within the credit period; thus the firm's average accounts receivable balance is $500,000.

Kelly Leaky, TLC's comptroller, approached the firm's bank with a request for a loan for the $400,000 using the firm's accounts receivable as collateral. The bank offered to make the loan at a rate of 2 percent over prime plus a 1 percent processing charge on all receivables pledged ($250,000 per month). Furthermore, the bank agreed to lend up to 80 percent of the face value of the receivables pledged.

a. Estimate the cost of the receivables loan to TLC where the firm borrows the $400,000. The prime rate is currently 11 percent.

b. Leaky also requested a line of credit for $400,000 from the bank. The bank agreed to grant the necessary line of credit at a rate of 3 percent over prime and required a 15 percent compensating balance. TLC currently maintains an average demand deposit of $100,000. Estimate the cost of the line of credit.

c. Which source of credit should TLC select? Why?

17–9B. (*Cost of Factoring*) To increase profitability, a management consultant has suggested to the Dal Molle Fruit Company that it consider factoring its receivables. The firm has credit sales of $300,000 per month and has an average receivables balance of $600,000 with 60-day credit terms. The factor has offered to extend credit equal to 90 percent of the receivables factored less interest on the loan at a rate of 1½ percent per month. The 10 percent difference in the advance and the face value of all receivables factored consists of a 1 percent factoring fee plus a 9 percent reserve, which the factor maintains. In addition, if Dal Molle, decides to factor its receivables, it will sell them all, so that it can reduce its credit department costs by $1,400 a month.

a. What is the cost of borrowing the maximum amount of credit available to Dal Molle, through the factoring agreement?

b. What considerations other than cost should be accounted for by Dal Molle, in determining whether or not to enter the factoring agreement?

17–10B. (*Inventory Financing*) In anticipation of summer sales, Ol' Trusty Barbecues, Inc., builds up inventories each year in March. The company has explored the possibility of a field warehouse security agreement as collateral for an inventory loan from its bank during the three spring months. During these months inventories average $400,000. The field warehouse arrangement will cost Ol' Trusty a flat fee of $2,000 a month on all its inventory regardless of the amount the firm borrows. The bank has agreed to lend up to 70 percent of the value of the inventory at a rate of 14 percent.

a. If Ol' Trusty borrows $250,000 using the inventory loan for March through May, what is the effective cost of credit?

b. What is the effective cost of borrowing $180,000 for the March through May period?

17–11B. (*Cost of Secured Short-Term Credit*) DST, Inc., a producer of inflatable river rafts, needs $400,000 for the three-month summer season, ending September 30, 199X. The firm has explored two possible sources of credit.

1. DST has arranged with its bank for a $400,000 loan secured by accounts receivable. The bank has agreed to advance DST 80 percent of the value of its pledged receivables at a rate of 11 percent plus a 1 percent fee based on all receivables pledged. DST's receivables average a total of $1 million year-round.
2. An insurance company has agreed to lend the $400,000 at a rate of 9 percent per annum, using a loan secured by DST's inventory. A field warehouse agreement would be used, which would cost DST $2,000 a month.

Which source of credit should DST select? Explain.

17–12B. (*Cost of Secured Short-Term Financing*) You are considering a loan of $25,000 to finance inventories for a janitorial supply store that you plan to open. The bank offers to lend you the money at 11 percent annual interest for the six months the funds will be needed.
  a. Calculate the effective rate of interest on the loan.
  b. In addition, the bank requires you to maintain a 15 percent compensating balance in the bank. Because you are just opening your business, you do not have a demand deposit at the bank that can be used to meet the compensating balance requirement. This means that you will have to put 15 percent of the loan amount from your own personal money (which you had planned to use to help finance the business) in a checking account. What is the cost of the loan now?
  c. In addition to the compensating balance requirement in (b), you are told that interest will be discounted. What is the effective rate of interest on the loan now?

17–13B. (*Cost of Financing*) Tanglewood Roofing Supply, Inc., has agreed to borrow working capital from a factor on the following terms: Tanglewood's receivables average $150,000 per month and have a 90-day average collection period (note that the firm offers 90-day credit terms and its accounts receivable average $450,000 because of the 90-day average collection period). The factor will charge 13 percent interest on any advance (1 percent per month paid in advance), will charge a 2 percent processing fee on all receivables factored, and will maintain a 15 percent reserve. If Tanglewood undertakes the loan it will reduce its own credit department expenses by $2,000 per month. What is the annual effective rate of interest to Tanglewood on the factoring arrangement? Assume that the maximum advance is taken.

17–14B. (*Opportunity Cost of Decreasing Wages Payable*) In June of this year Becker Services, Inc., negotiated a new union contract with its employees. One of the provisions of the new contract involved increasing the frequency of its wage payments from once a month to once every two weeks. Becker's biweekly payroll averages $300,000 and the firm's opportunity cost of funds is 11 percent per annum.
  a. What is the annual dollar cost of this new wage payment scheme to Becker?
  b. What is the maximum percentage increase in wages that Becker would have been willing to accept in lieu of the increased frequency of wage payments?

SELF-TEST SOLUTIONS

SS–1. The discounted interest cost of the commercial paper issue is calculated as follows:

Interest expense = .10 × $200 million × 180/360 = $10 million

The effective cost of credit can now be calculated as follows:

$$\text{RATE} = \frac{\$10 \text{ million} + \$125,000}{\$200 \text{ million} - \$125,000 - \$10 \text{ million}} \times \frac{1}{180/360}$$

$$.46\%$$

SS–2. a. $\text{Interest for two months} = .14 \times \dfrac{2}{12} \times \$500,000$

$$= \$11,667$$

$\text{Loan proceeds (for \$500,000 loan)} = \$500,000 - (.2 \times \$500,000 + \$11,667)$

$$= \$388,333$$

$$\text{RATE} = \frac{\$11{,}667}{\$388{,}333} \times \frac{12}{2}$$

$$= .030043 \times 6 = .18026, \text{ or } 18.026\%$$

Note that Samples would actually have to borrow more than the needed $500,000 in order to cover the compensating balance requirement. However, as we demonstrated earlier, the effective cost of credit will not be affected by adjusting the loan amount for interest expense changes accordingly.

b. The estimation of the cost of forgoing trade discounts is generally quite straightforward; however, in this case the firm actually stretches its trade credit for purchases made during July beyond the due date by an additional 30 days. If it is able to do this *without penalty*, then the firm effectively forgoes a 3 percent discount for not paying within 15 days and does not pay for an additional 45 days (60 days less the discount period of 15 days). Thus, for the July trade credit, Samples's cost is calculated as follows:

$$\text{RATE} = (.03/.97) \times (360/45) = 24.74\%$$

However, for the August trade credit the firm actually pays at the end of the credit period (the 30th day), so that the cost of trade credit becomes

$$\text{RATE} = (.03/.97) \times (360/15) = 74.22\%$$

c.

$$\frac{\text{Interest for}}{\text{two months}} = .12 \times \frac{2}{12} \times \$500{,}000$$

$$= \$10{,}000$$

$$\text{Pledging fee} = .005 \times \$750{,}000$$

$$= \$3750$$

$$\text{RATE} = \frac{\$10{,}000 + \$3{,}750}{\$500{,}000} \times \frac{12}{2}$$

$$= .0275 \times 6 = .165, \text{ or } 16.5\%$$

SS-3. a.

$$\text{RATE} = \frac{.18 \times \$200{,}000}{\$200{,}000} \times \frac{1}{1}$$

$$= .18, \text{ or } 18\%$$

b.

$$\text{RATE} = \frac{.16 \times \$200{,}000}{\$200{,}000 - .20 \times \$200{,}000} \times \frac{1}{1}$$

$$= .20, \text{ or } 20\%$$

c.

$$\text{RATE} = \frac{.14 \times \$200{,}000}{\$200{,}000 - .14 \times \$200{,}000 - .2 \times \$200{,}000} \times \frac{1}{1}$$

$$= .21212, \text{ or } 21.212\%$$

Alternative (a) offers the lower-cost service of financing, although it carries the highest stated rate of interest. The reason for this, is that there is no compensating balance requirement nor is interest discounted for this alternative.

CONCLUSION

VIDEO CASE 5

The Campeau Bankruptcy: The Sudden Deterioration of Supplier Accounts Receivable

from ABC News, *Business World,* January 7, 1990

The video case described the problems created for many firms in the garment industry by the Campeau retailing empire bankruptcy. Review the questions we considered when Video Case 5 was introduced on page 531.

Rumors about cash problems at Campeau stores appeared in the business press in early 1989. In April 1989, Campeau was forced to refinance some of its debt, a sign that the firm was having cash flow problems. On November 14, 1989, the *Wall Street Journal* reported that Campeau was in the midst of a **working-capital crisis.** Other warnings were given directly to Campeau's suppliers by the factoring companies that act as the financing arm of the garment industry. Offsetting the warnings was the fact that the Campeau stores paid their bills on time through the Christmas buying season. The payment history was indicative of financial health. But even if these small firms had been able to determine the severity of Campeau's problems, that may not have been enough to save them.

Because the garment industry sells goods that are dated, it may be particularly prone to sudden changes in the value of receivables and inventory. This "spoilage" effect puts suppliers over a barrel. If the goods don't sell at Christmas they may not have a second chance to sell except at a deep discount. Then not only would profit margins be squeezed, there would be further delay in receiving the cash (if goods are sold after the Christmas season), which would make the problem worse. This points out why it is important to consider the industry that a firm is in when valuing its inventory and accounts receivable.

The inventories and accounts receivable of suppliers that sold a large portion of their production to the Campeau stores are probably particularly risky. In fact, these firms were probably hurt the most by Campeau's problems. Whenever a single customer makes up a large fraction of a firm's business, that firm is vulnerable. This occurs in more industries than just in the garment industry. Think about automobile suppliers. In the United States they can have only a few customers—GM, Ford, Chrysler, Honda, and so on. Losing one account, or a cutback in purchases by one of those customers, has an immediate and dramatic effect on the supplier's financial health. Firms in that position might think about using their expertise to supply other industries or design contracts that protect them from sudden changes in their major customers' demand.

Discussion questions

1. We discussed how having a single large customer can make a supplier vulnerable. Can you think of ways the customer can exert pressure on the supplier? Does the same degree of bargaining advantage exist if the customer is supplied solely by one supplier as opposed to having several suppliers? What about the capacity of the suppliers?
2. Can you think of other situations in which businesses may be vulnerable to a customer's financial health or even its payment procedures? Examples might be banks and major borrowers or producers with large government contracts. Explain possible problems that might exist in these cases. Do you know of rules that limit such problems?

Suggested reading

GRAHAM, MARY. "Business: Bankrupt and Bullish," *The Atlantic,* March 1992.

PART 6

LONG-TERM FINANCING

The economic importance of corporations is due in part to the ease with which these firms can raise outside capital. This access to funds means that corporations can carry out investments far beyond the reach of partnerships and sole proprietorships. To understand how corporations raise investment funds, one must have an understanding of capital markets and the characteristics of the various types of financial instruments that corporations use to raise capital. Financial or capital markets bring together investors with funds and firms in need of funds. Well-functioning capital markets have helped fuel the unprecedented economic growth of the twentieth century and have done so with an amazing resiliency, surviving confidence-shaking events such as the stock market crashes of 1929 and 1987 as well as the insider trading scandals of the 1980s. Chapter 18 introduces the key players in these markets: commercial bankers, investment bankers, institutional investors (primarily insurance companies and pension funds), rating agencies, and regulators; it describes the various roles each plays in making capital markets work smoothly.

The remaining chapters describe the characteristics, and the advantages and disadvantages of the many varieties of long-term financing available to firms. A firm can acquire the use of a machine through leasing, or it may purchase the same asset using borrowed funds such as a term loan from a bank or long-term debt from the public or private debt market (Chapter 19). Alternatively, the firm may sell stock to investors (Chapter 20). Owning stock in a firm means that an investor's wealth is tied to the prosperity of the firm; wealth increases if the firm prospers and fails if the firm declines. Hybrid securities, such as convertible debt, combine the features of debt and equity (Chapter 21). The futures and options markets provide a unique method of reducing risk (Chapter 22). It seems that the variety of financial instruments is limited only by the imagination of the investment bankers who design them and the willingness of investors to share in them.

INTRODUCTION

VIDEO CASE 6

The Fall of Drexel Burnham Lambert: Investment Banking *in extremis*

from ABC News, *Business World*, February 18, 1990

Investment bankers play a crucial role in funneling funds from investors to firms with worthwhile investment opportunities. Until the 1980s the world of investment bankers was one that few people knew about or understood. Increased competition and the rise of Drexel Burnham Lambert, primarily owing to Michael Milken's junk bond business, changed that. Suddenly the high-stakes world of investment banking was front-page news. Billion-dollar takeovers and LBOs became the norm and seemed to occur almost daily. This video describes how Drexel Burnham Lambert, the investment banking firm with the bad-boy image (and proud of it), changed the nature of corporate finance and even the structure of business enterprise in the United States in the 1980s. It also discusses the "deal-doing" attitude that Drexel's aggressive style helped foster on Wall Street and how the fall of Drexel may affect business in the 1990s.

As you read Chapters 18 through 22, think about the role investment bankers play as intermediaries—helping firms that need funds find investors—and how Drexel's junk bonds facilitated that role. You might also consider the following questions:

- Investment bankers are intermediaries; they help firms that need funds find investors. How did Drexel's junk bonds facilitate that role?
- Are junk bonds intrinsically bad?
- What drives the deal-doing attitude the video portrayed as typical among investment bankers in the 1980s?
- What will happen now that Drexel is not making a market for the junk bonds it underwrote?

At the end of this section we will return to discuss these questions and a few other issues raised by this dramatic period in the financial history of corporate America.

CHAPTER *18*

Raising Funds in the Capital Market

The Mix of Corporate Securities Sold in the Capital Market ● Why Financial Markets Exist ● Financing of Business: The Movement of Funds Through the Economy ● Components of the U.S. Financial Market System ● The Investment Banker ● Private Placements ● Flotation Costs ● Regulation ● More Recent Regulatory Developments

At times internally generated funds will not be sufficient to finance all of the firm's proposed expenditures. In these situations, the corporation may find it necessary to attract large amounts of financial capital externally.[1] This chapter focuses on the market environment in which long-term capital is raised. Ensuing chapters will discuss the distinguishing features of the instruments by which long-term funds are raised. Long-term funds are raised in the capital market. By the term *capital market,* we mean all institutions and procedures that facilitate transactions in long-term financial instruments (like common stocks and bonds).

Business firms in the nonfinancial corporate sector of the U.S. economy rely heavily on the nation's financial market system in order to raise cash. Table 18–1 displays the relative internal and external sources of funds for such corporations over the 1975–1990 period. Notice that the percentage of external funds raised in any given year can vary substantially from that of other years. In 1975, for example, the nonfinancial business sector raised only 19.7 percent of its funds by external means (in the financial markets). This was substantially less than the 33.5 percent raised externally only one year later during 1976. In more recent years the same type of significant adjustment made by financial managers is evident. For example, during 1988 nonfinancial firms raised 31.1 percent of new funds in the external markets. By the end of 1990 this proportion dropped to 18.3 percent.

Such adjustments illustrate an important point: The financial executive is perpetually on his or her toes regarding market conditions. Changes in market conditions influence the precise way that corporate funds will be raised.

The financial market system must be both organized and resilient. Periods of economic recession, for instance, test the financial markets and those firms that continually use the markets. Economic contractions are especially chal-

---

[1] By *externally generated,* we mean that the funds are obtained by means *other* than through retentions or depreciation. Funds from these latter two sources are commonly called *internally generated* funds.

lenging to financial decision makers because all recessions are *unique*. This forces financing policies to become unique.

During the 1981–82 recession, which lasted 16 months, interest rates remained high during the worst phases of the downturn. This occurred because policy makers at the Federal Reserve System decided to wring a high rate of inflation out of the economy by means of a tight monetary policy. Simultaneously, stock prices were depressed. These business conditions induced firms to forgo raising funds via external means. During 1982 we notice that 78.9 percent of corporate funds were generated internally (see Table 18–1).

The ninth recession since the end of World War II began in July 1990. Realized inflation and inflationary expectations were not the main culprits of contraction this time. As a result of loose monetary policy and low inflation rates, both short- and long-term interest rates moved to low levels. Treasury bills of three- and six-month maturities sold at prices that produced yields of less than 4 percent during early 1992. (By contrast during the 1981–82 recession, three-month Treasury bills yielded 10.7 percent for all of 1982 and 14 percent for all of 1981.)

Further, common stock prices rose to all-time *highs* during early 1992. Accordingly, corporate financial managers made more trips to the financial markets with new security issues. The cost of corporate capital was *perceived* as being low. In the midst of such business conditions firms turn to the financial markets and raise a greater proportion of their funds externally. As economic policy shapes the environment of the financial markets, managers must both understand the meaning of the economic ups and downs, and remain flexible in their decision-making processes.

The sums involved in tapping the capital markets can be vast. In two separate issues sold in October 1975 and June 1976, the old American Telephone and Telegraph Company (AT&T) sold a combined total of $1.2 billion of common stock. In March 1984 United Brands Company marketed $100 million of senior subordinated debentures.[2] On March 25, 1987, the U.S. government sold 58,750,000 shares of Consolidated Rail Corporation common stock to the public at $28 per share. This raised $1.65 billion and was a record at the time for an initial public offering. The sale, which took Conrail out of the government domain and placed it in the hands of public investors, was authorized by the Conrail Privatization Act of 1986. This major fund-raising

Year	Total Sources ($ Billions)	Percent Internal Funds	Percent External Funds
1990	$466.7	81.7%	18.3%
1989	548.4	73.9	26.1
1988	586.7	68.9	31.1
1987	545.0	69.0	31.0
1986	521.5	64.6	35.4
1985	464.3	75.8	24.2
1984	491.4	68.5	31.5
1983	431.2	67.8	32.2
1982	313.7	78.9	21.1
1981	375.4	63.6	36.4
1980	320.6	62.3	37.7
1979	324.4	61.2	38.8
1978	313.5	58.6	41.4
1977	256.5	63.4	36.6
1976	211.2	66.5	33.5
1975	155.6	80.3	19.7

Source: *Economic Report of the President,* February 1992, p. 402.

TABLE 18–1.
Nonfinancial Corporate Business Sources of Funds

---

[2]Debentures are long-term, unsecured promissory notes. Chapter 20 discusses the detailed features of corporate debt instruments.

huge underwriting syndicate; the lead investment bankers included Goldman, Sachs & Co.; The First Boston Corporation; Merrill Lynch Capital Markets; Morgan Stanley & Co.; Salomon Brothers, Inc.; and Shearson Lehman Brothers, Inc. Clearly, these are important amounts of money to the companies selling the related securities.

To be able to distribute and absorb security offerings of this size, an economy must have a well-developed financial market system. To use that system effectively, the financial officer must have a basic understanding of its structure. Accordingly, this chapter explores the rudiments of raising funds in the capital market.

Perspective in Finance

In Chapters 9 and 10 we learned how to assess leverage use—both operating and financial leverage. Further, we examined the corporate financing decision in Chapter 10. Portions of those earlier discussions identified financial managers' confirmed preferences for raising funds through new debt contracts. The next section presents some near-term history of that financing behavior.

The Mix of Corporate Securities Sold in the Capital Market

When corporations decide to raise cash in the capital market, what type of financing vehicle is most favored? Many individual investors think that common stock is the answer to this question. This is understandable, given the coverage of the level of common stock prices by the popular news media. All the major television networks, for instance, quote the closing price of the Dow Jones Industrial Average on their nightly news broadcasts. Common stock, though, is not the financing method relied on most heavily by corporations. The answer to this question is **corporate bonds.** *The corporate debt markets clearly dominate the corporate equity markets when new funds are being raised.* This is a long-term relationship—it occurs year after year. Table 18–2 bears this out.

In Table 18–2 we see the total volume (in millions of dollars) of corporate securities sold for cash over the 1975–1990 period. The percentage breakdown

TABLE 18–2.
Corporate Securities
Offered for Cash
(Domestic Offerings)

Year	Total Volume ($ millions)	Percent Common Stock	Percent Preferred Stock	Percent Bonds and Notes
1990	$212,712	9.1%	1.9%	89.0%
1989	213,617	12.2	2.9	84.9
1988	244,670	14.7	2.7	82.6
1987	262,725	16.4	3.9	79.7
1986	248,722	23.7	4.9	71.4
1985	133,460	27.5	5.3	67.2
1984	95,287	23.3	4.5	72.2
1983	103,355	43.9	7.7	48.4
1982	73,397	32.3	6.7	61.0
1981	64,500	39.5	2.6	57.9
1980	65,383	29.7	5.3	65.0
1979	36,117	25.2	5.7	69.1
1978[a]	28,832	27.3	6.1	66.6
1977	54,229	14.8	7.2	78.0
1976	53,314	15.6	5.3	79.1
1975	53,632	13.8	6.4	79.8

Source: *Economic Report of the President,* January 1989, p. 415, and *Federal Reserve Bulletin,* February 1992, p. A32.
[a]Beginning in 1978, security offerings exclude private placement.

among common stock, preferred stock, and bonds is also displayed. We know from our previous discussion on the cost of capital (Chapter 8) and planning the firm's financing mix (Chapter 10) that the U.S. tax system inherently favors debt as a means of raising capital. Quite simply, interest expense is deductible from other income when computing the firm's federal tax liability, whereas the dividends paid on both preferred and common stock are not.

Financial executives responsible for raising corporate cash know this. When they have a choice between marketing new bonds and marketing new preferred stock, the outcome is usually in favor of bonds. The after-tax cost of capital on the debt is less than that incurred on the preferred stock. Likewise, if the firm has unused debt capacity and the general level of equity prices is depressed, financial executives favor the issuance of debt securities over the issuance of new common stock. It is always good to keep some benchmark figures in your head. The average (unweighted) mix of corporate securities sold for cash over the 1978–1990 period follows. This *excludes* private debt placements or the bonds and notes categories would be a bit higher.

Common stock	25%
Preferred stock	5
Bonds and notes	70
Total	100%

Perspective in Finance

When you borrow money from a commercial bank to finance a purchase of stereo equipment or take out a mortgage to pay for a new home, you have used this country's financial market system. The average individual (and you are not that because of your study of financial management) tends to take the reality of the financial markets for granted. But they were not always there, and they have evolved amidst much controversy over a long period.

Recent years have produced heated debates over alterations in our financial system—this just illustrates the dynamic nature of these markets. Much of that debate followed the collapse of the equity markets on Monday, October 19, 1987, when the Dow Jones Industrial Average fell by an unprecedented 508 points. Like banks, the equity markets are another piece of our complex financial market system. One reason why underdeveloped countries are underdeveloped is because they lack a financial market system that has the confidence of those who must use it. Without such a system, real assets (like your home) do not get produced at an adequate rate and the populace suffers. We learn next why financial markets exist.

Why Financial Markets Exist

Financial markets are institutions and procedures that facilitate transactions in all types of financial claims. The purchase of your home, the common stock you may own, and your life insurance policy all took place in some type of financial market. Why do financial markets exist? What would the economy lose if our complex system of financial markets were not developed? We will address these questions here.

Some *economic units,* such as households, firms, or governments, spend *more* during a given period than they earn. Other economic units spend *less* on current consumption than they earn. For example, business firms in the aggregate usually spend more during a specific period than they earn. House-

BASIC FINANCIAL MANAGEMENT IN PRACTICE

Financing Flexibility and Market Awareness

During most of the 1980s nonfinancial businesses levered up their balance sheets issuing significantly more debt securities than common stock. After 1983, in fact, these businesses were net buyers of common equity rather than net issuers. This trend in business financing practices is shown below.

Nonfinancial Business Change in Corporate Equities Outstanding, 1981–90

Year	Billions ($)
1990	− 63.0
1989	−124.2
1988	−129.5
1987	− 75.5
1986	− 85.0
1985	− 84.5
1984	− 79.0
1983	20.0
1982	6.4
1981	− 11.5

Source: *Flow of Funds Accounts, Second Quarter 1991,* Flow of Funds Section (Washington, DC: Board of Governors of the Federal Reserve System, September 1991).

During the early 1990s, with common equities selling at relatively high prices, many firms reversed the trend (above) and began issuing large amounts of equity securities. The following piece highlights the activities of one firm, Kohlberg Kravis Roberts (KKR) that recognized early—to its advantage—the reversal in the investing public's appetite for common stock. KKR is a financial corporation that specializes in several forms of business combinations, acquisitions, and divestitures. The discussion illustrates how the financial executive has to stay in tune with the financial markets.

For every season there is a financial fashion. In the 1980s debt was in vogue and the smart people on Wall Street made fortunes trading debt for the public's equity. Now debt is passé and equity is all the rage, and the same smart people are making second fortunes by selling equity back to the public, at much higher prices than what they paid just a few years ago.

The game is called reverse leveraged buyouts, and no one plays it better than the people at Kohlberg Kravis Roberts. In 1987 and 1988 KKR bought four companies—Duracell International, AutoZone, Owens-Illinois and Stop & Shop. KKR's total equity investment in these four companies was about $690 million. Last year KKR took all four public, racking up an estimated $4.4 billion, mostly in paper profits for itself and for fellow investors in its buyout pools. That's a 600%-plus return in five years. And we're not even counting at least $100 million in fees KKR took for itself before the companies went to the market.

Behind these stunning profits is not theft but the clever use of other people's money. The KKRs of the world have arbitraged brilliantly between two markets—debt and equity—over several years. Back in the 1980s investors were hungry for high-yielding junk bonds and allowed the deal makers to use minimal cash down payments and lots of debt to take companies private. In the early days of the LBO craze, the deal makers even bought equity on the cheap because the markets, particularly in terms of cash flow, were undervaluing the stocks of the publicly traded companies they took private. Only later in the 1980s did the buyout game get so crowded that assets were overpriced and debt undercollaterized—junk bonds really did become junk.

Now the situation has reversed, and the sheep are coming back to be shorn. With interest rates low and stocks high, the new-issues market is providing the deal makers with the cash to wipe their balance sheets clean of some of the high-priced junk debt and to take huge profits on their small equity investments as the market applauds their reequitization.

Source: Richard L. Stern and Tatiana Pouschine, "Junk Equity," *Forbes,* March 2, 1992, p. 40.

holds in the aggregate spend less on current consumption than they earn. As a result, some mechanism is needed to facilitate the transfer of savings from those economic units with a surplus to those with a deficit. That is precisely the function of financial markets. Financial markets exist in order to *allocate* the supply of savings in the economy to the demanders of those savings. The central characteristic of a financial market is that it acts as the vehicle through which the forces of demand and supply for a specific type of financial claim (such as a corporate bond) are brought together.

Now, why would the economy suffer without a developed financial market system? The answer is simple. The wealth of the economy would be less without the financial markets. The rate of capital formation would not be as high if

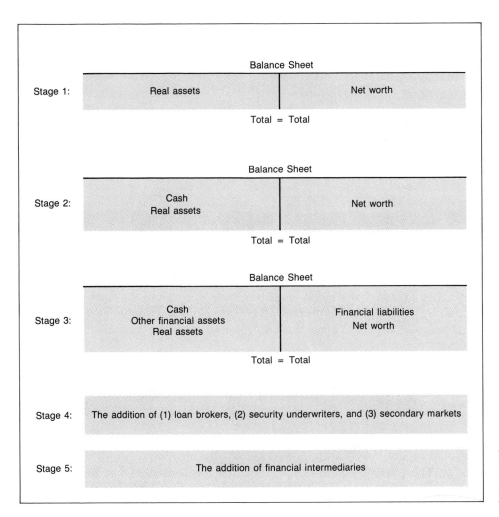

Balance Sheet

Stage 1:

| Real assets | Net worth |

Total = Total

Balance Sheet

Stage 2:

| Cash Real assets | Net worth |

Total = Total

Balance Sheet

Stage 3:

| Cash Other financial assets Real assets | Financial liabilities Net worth |

Total = Total

Stage 4: The addition of (1) loan brokers, (2) security underwriters, and (3) secondary markets

Stage 5: The addition of financial intermediaries

FIGURE 18–1.
Development of a Financial Market System

financial markets did not exist. This means that the net additions during a specific period to the stocks of (1) dwellings, (2) productive plant and equipment, (3) inventory, and (4) consumer durables would occur at lower rates. Figure 18–1 helps clarify the rationale behind this assertion. The abbreviated balance sheets in the figure refer to firms or any other type of economic units that operate in the private as opposed to governmental sectors of the economy. This means that such units cannot issue money to finance their own activities.

At stage 1 in Figure 18–1 only real assets exist in the hypothetical economy. **Real assets** are tangible assets like houses, equipment, and inventories. They are distinguished from **financial assets,** which represent claims for future payment on other economic units. Common and preferred stocks, bonds, bills, and notes all are types of financial assets. If only real assets exist, then savings for a given economic unit, such as a firm, must be accumulated in the form of real assets. If the firm has a great idea for a new product, that new product can be developed, produced, and distributed only out of company savings (retained earnings). Furthermore, all investment in the new product must occur simultaneously as the savings are generated. If you have the idea, and we have the savings, there is no mechanism to transfer our savings to you. This is not a good situation.

At stage 2 paper money comes into existence in the economy. Here, at least, you can *store* your own savings in the form of money. Thus, you can finance your great idea by drawing down your cash balances. This is an improvement over stage 1, but there is still no effective mechanism to transfer our savings to you. You see, we will not just hand you our dollar bills. We will want a receipt.

The concept of a receipt that represents the transfer of savings from one economic unit to another is a monumental advancement. The economic unit with excess savings can lend the savings to an economic unit that needs them. To the lending unit these receipts are identified as "other financial assets" in stage 3 of Figure 18–1. To the borrowing unit, the issuance of financial claims (receipts) shows up as "financial liabilities" on the stage 3 balance sheet. The economic unit with surplus savings will earn a rate of return on those funds. The borrowing unit will pay that rate of return, but it has been able to finance its great idea.

In stage 4 the financial market system moves further toward full development. Loan brokers come into existence. These brokers help locate pockets of excess savings and channel such savings to economic units needing the funds. Some economic units will actually purchase the financial claims of borrowing units and sell them at a higher price to other investors; this process is called **underwriting.** Underwriting will be discussed in more detail later in this chapter. In addition, **secondary markets** develop. Secondary markets simply represent trading in already existing financial claims. If you buy your brother's General Motors common stock, you have made a secondary market transaction. Secondary markets reduce the risk of investing in financial claims. Should you need cash, you can liquidate your claims in the secondary market. This induces savers to invest in securities.

The progression toward a developed and complex system of financial markets ends with stage 5. Here, financial intermediaries come into existence. You can think of financial intermediaries as the major financial institutions with which you are used to dealing. These include commercial banks, savings and loan associations, credit unions, life insurance companies, and mutual funds. Financial intermediaries share a common characteristic: They offer their own financial claims, called **indirect securities,** to economic units with excess savings. The proceeds from selling their indirect securities are then used to purchase the financial claims of other economic units. These latter claims can be called **direct securities.** Thus, a mutual fund might sell mutual fund shares (their indirect security) and purchase the common stocks (direct securities) of some major corporations. A life insurance company sells life insurance policies and purchases huge quantities of corporate bonds. Financial intermediaries thereby involve many small savers in the process of capital formation. This means there are more "good things" for everybody to buy.

A developed financial market system provides for a greater level of wealth in the economy. In the absence of financial markets, savings are not transferred to the economic units most in need of those funds. It is difficult, after all, for a household to build its own automobile. The financial market system makes it *easier* for the economy to build automobiles and all the other goods that economic units like to accumulate.

Perspective in Finance

The movement of financial capital (funds) throughout the economy just means the movement of savings to the ultimate user of those savings. Some sectors of the economy save more than other sectors. As a result, these savings are moved to a productive use—say to manufacture that Corvette you want to buy.

The price of using someone else's savings is expressed in terms of interest rates. The financial market system helps to move funds to the most-productive end use. Those economic units with the most promising projects should be willing to bid the highest (in terms of rates) to obtain the savings. The concepts of financing and moving savings from one economic unit to another are now explored.

Financing of Business: The Movement of Funds through the Economy

The Financing Process

We now understand the crucial role that financial markets play in a capitalist economy. At this point we will take a brief look at how funds flow across some selected sectors of the U.S. economy. In addition, we will focus a little more closely on the process of financial intermediation that was introduced in the preceding section. Some actual data are used to sharpen our knowledge of the financing process. We will see that financial institutions play a major role in bridging the gap between savers and borrowers in the economy. Nonfinancial corporations, we already know, are significant borrowers of financial capital.

Table 18–3 shows how funds were supplied and raised by the major sectors of our economy in 1990. Households were the largest net supplier of funds to the financial markets. This is the case, by the way, year in and year out. In 1990, households made available $160.3 billion in funds to other sectors. That was the excess of their funds supplied over their funds raised in the markets. In the jargon of economics, the household sector is a *savings-surplus* sector.

Likewise in 1990, the nonfinancial business sector is a savings-surplus sector. In 1990 we see that nonfinancial corporations supplied $46.6 billion more in funds to the financial markets than they raised. This was due to extensive repurchases of their own common stock by firms in the marketplace. In fact, during the 11-year period of 1980–90 corporations were *net buyers* (rather than issuers) of common stock on eight occasions. However, during longer periods, such as 20 to 30 years, the nonfinancial business sector is typically a *savings-deficit* sector. That is, this sector raises more financial capital in the markets than it supplies.

Next, it can also be seen that the U.S. government sector was a savings-deficit sector for 1990. In 1990 the federal government raised $217.3 billion in excess of the funds it supplied to the financial markets. This highlights a serious problem for the entire economy and for the financial manager. Persistent federal deficits have increased the role of the federal government in the market for borrowed funds. The last time the federal government posted a budget surplus was 1969; the last time prior to that was 1960. The federal government has thus become a "quasi-permanent" savings-deficit sector. Most financial economists agree that this tendency puts upward pressure on interest rates in the financial marketplace and thereby raises the general (overall) cost of capital to corporations. This phenomenon has become known as *crowding-out:* The private borrower is pushed out of the financial markets in favor of the government borrower.

Sector	[1] Funds Raised	[2] Funds Supplied	[2] - [1] Net Funds Supplied
Households[a]	$259.1	$419.4	$160.3
Nonfinancial corporate business	53.6	100.2	46.6
U.S. government	246.6	29.3	−217.3
State and local governments	20.3	− 8.0	− 28.3
Foreign	72.9	104.5	31.6

[a]Includes personal trusts and nonprofit organizations.
Source: *Flow of Funds Accounts, Second Quarter 1991*, Flow of Funds Section (Washington, DC: Board of Governors of the Federal Reserve System, September 1991).

TABLE 18–3.
Sector View of Flow of Funds in U.S. Financial Markets for 1990 (Billions of Dollars)

Table 18–3 further highlights how important *foreign* financial investment is to the activity of the U.S. economy. As the federal government has become more of a "confirmed" savings-deficit sector, the need for funds has been increasingly supplied by foreign interests. Thus, in 1990, the foreign sector *supplied* a net $31.6 billion to the domestic capital markets. As recently as 1982, the foreign sector *raised*—rather than supplied—$30.8 billion in the U.S. financial markets! This illustrates the dynamic nature of financial management.

Table 18–3 demonstrates that the financial market system must exist to facilitate the orderly and efficient flow of savings from the surplus sectors to the deficit sectors of the economy. The result during long periods is that the nonfinancial business sector is *typically* dependent on the household sector to finance its investment needs. The governmental sectors—especially the federal government—are quite reliant on foreign financing.

As we noted in the preceding section, the financial market system includes a complex network of intermediaries that assist in the transfer of savings among economic units. Two intermediaries will be highlighted here: life insurance companies and pension funds. They are especially important participants in the capital market of the country.

Because of the nature of their business, life insurance firms can invest heavily in long-term financial instruments. This investment tendency arises for two key reasons: (1) life insurance policies usually include a *savings element* in them, and (2) their liabilities liquidate at a very predictable rate. Thus, life insurance companies invest in the "long end" of the securities markets. This means that they favor (1) mortgages and (2) corporate bonds as investment vehicles rather than shorter-term-to-maturity financial instruments like treasury bills. To a lesser extent, they acquire corporate stocks for their portfolios.

Table 18–4 shows the financial asset mix of life insurance companies for the years 1960, 1970, 1980, 1985, and 1991. The box drawn around their holdings of corporate stocks and corporate bonds demonstrates that these firms are major suppliers of financial capital to the nonfinancial business sector. The sum of corporate stocks and bonds held by life insurance companies expressed as a percent of their total investment in financial assets for each of the five selected years in Table 18–4 is listed below:

Year	Percent
1960	46.0%
1970	44.6
1980	48.7
1985	45.3
1991	48.2

TABLE 18–4.
Financial Asset Mix of Life Insurance Companies (Billions of Dollars)

Assets	1960 $	1960 %	1970 $	1970 %	1980 $	1980 %	1985 $	1985 %	1991 $	1991 %
Demand deposits and currency	$ 1.3	1.1%	$ 1.8	0.8%	$ 3.2	0.7%	$ 5.1	0.6%	$ 5.4	0.4%
U.S. government securities	6.5	5.6	4.6	2.3	17.0	3.7	101.1	12.8	221.1	14.8
State and local securities	3.6	3.1	3.3	1.6	6.7	1.4	9.7	1.2	11.9	0.8
Mortgages	41.8	36.1	74.4	37.0	131.1	28.2	171.8	21.7	275.1	18.4
Corporate stocks	5.0	4.3	15.4	7.7	47.4	10.2	77.5	9.8	123.0	8.2
Corporate bonds	48.2	41.7	74.1	36.9	178.8	38.5	280.6	35.5	598.8	40.0
Miscellaneous	9.4	8.1	27.3	13.7	80.0	17.3	145.3	18.4	261.3	17.4
Total financial assets	$115.8	100.0%	$200.9	100.0%	$464.2	100.0%	$791.1	100.0%	$1496.6	100.0%

Source: *Flow of Funds Accounts, Assets and Liabilities Outstanding,* 1959–82 and 1974–91, Flow of Funds Section (Washington, DC: Board of Governors of the Federal Reserve System, August 1983 and January 1992).

TABLE 18–5.
Financial Asset Mix of Private Pension Funds (Billions of Dollars)

Assets	1960 $	1960 %	1970 $	1970 %	1980 $	1980 %	1985 $	1985 %	1991 $	1991 %
Demand deposits and currency	$ 0.5	1.3%	$ 1.1	1.0%	$ 4.2	0.9%	$ 6.2	0.7%	$ 2.4	0.2%
Time deposits	0.0	0.0	0.7	0.6	25.1	5.3	51.7	6.1	107.5	7.9
U.S. government securities	2.7	7.1	3.0	2.7	50.6	10.8	104.5	12.4	187.6	13.8
Corporate stocks	16.5	43.3	67.9	60.6	230.6	49.1	412.4	48.6	663.0	48.8
Corporate bonds	15.7	41.2	29.4	26.3	77.7	16.5	121.0	14.3	116.6	8.6
Mortgages	1.3	3.4	4.2	3.8	3.6	0.8	7.0	0.8	25.1	1.8
Miscellaneous	1.4	3.7	5.7	5.0	77.8	16.6	145.3	17.1	256.7	18.9
Total financial assets	$38.1	100.0%	$112.0	100.0%	$469.6	100.0%	$848.1	100.0%	$1358.9	100.0%

Source: *Flow of Funds Accounts, Financial Year End Assets and Liabilities Outstanding*, 1959–82 and 1974–91, Flow of Funds Section (Washington, DC: Board of Governors of the Federal Reserve System, August 1983 and January 1992).

Over recent years, about 47 percent of the financial assets of life insurance firms are represented by corporate stocks and bonds. We see that life insurance companies are an important financial intermediary. By issuing life insurance policies (indirect securities), they can acquire direct securities (corporate stocks and bonds) for their investment portfolios. Their preference, by far, is for bonds over stocks.

Let us now direct our attention to another financial intermediary, private pension funds. Table 18–5 shows the financial asset mix of the private pension funds in the United States. It is constructed in a manner similar to that of Table 18–4. In comparison with life insurance companies, three factors stand out. First, since 1960, private pension funds have grown at a *much faster rate* than have the insurance companies. Second, a *greater proportion* of the financial asset mix of the pension funds is devoted to corporate stocks and bonds. Third, the pension funds *invest more heavily* in corporate stocks than they do in corporate bonds. The sum of corporate stocks and bonds held by private pension funds expressed as a percent of their total investment in financial assets for each of the five selected years in Table 18–5 is listed below:

Year	Percent
1960	84.5%
1970	86.9
1980	65.6
1985	62.9
1991	57.4

Over recent years, then, about 62 percent of the financial assets of private pension funds have been tied up in corporate stocks and bonds. These financial institutions also are significant sources of business financing in this country. The pension funds play the same intermediary role as does the life insurance subsector of the economy.

Movement of Savings

Figure 18–2 provides a useful way to summarize our discussion of (1) why financial markets exist and (2) the movement of funds through the economy. It also serves as an introduction to the role of the investment banker—a subject discussed in detail later in this chapter.

We see that savings are ultimately transferred to the business firm in need of cash in three ways:

1. The direct transfer of funds. Here the firm seeking cash sells its

3 ways funds are Transfered

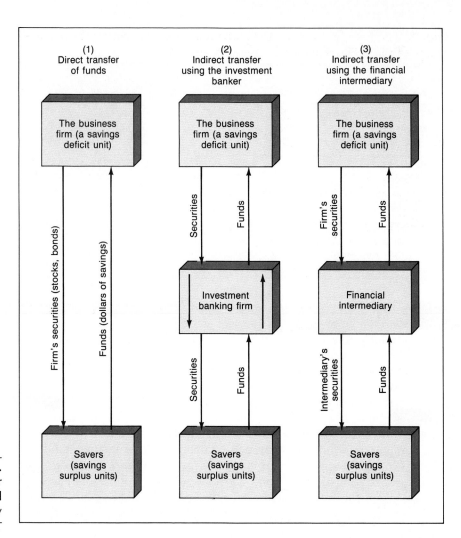

FIGURE 18–2.
Three Ways to Transfer
Financial Capital
in the Economy

securities directly to savers (investors) who are willing to purchase them in hopes of earning a reasonable rate of return. New business formation is a good example of this process at work. The new business may go directly to a saver or group of savers called *venture capitalists*. The venture capitalists will lend funds to the firm or take an equity position in the firm if they feel the product or service the new firm hopes to market will be successful.

2. **Indirect transfer using the investment banker.** In a common arrangement under this system, the managing investment banking house will form a syndicate of several investment bankers. The syndicate will buy the entire issue of securities from the firm that is in need of financial capital. The syndicate will then sell the securities at a higher price than it paid for them to the investing public (the savers). Merrill Lynch Capital Markets and Kidder, Peabody & Co. are examples of investment banking firms. They tend to be called "houses" by those who work in the financial community. Notice that under this second method of transferring savings, the securities being issued just pass through the investment banking firm. They are *not* transformed into a different type of security.

3. **Indirect transfer using the financial intermediary.** This is the type of system life insurance companies and pension funds operate within. The financial intermediary collects the savings of individuals and issues its own (indirect) securities in exchange for these savings. The intermediary then

uses the funds collected from the individual savers to acquire the business firm's (direct) securities, such as stocks and bonds.

We all benefit from the three transfer mechanisms displayed in Figure 18–2. Capital formation and economic wealth are greater than they would be in the absence of this financial market system.

Perspective in Finance

Because the United States enjoys such a developed system of financial markets, the terms used to discuss operations in those markets are numerous—some would say limitless. The financial executive, and those who work close to the financial executive, need to master a basic understanding of the commonly used terms and financing situations. There is just no getting around this requirement. But, if you can learn the terminology of baseball, basketball, or football—you can do the same relative to the financial markets. It may, in fact, pay off in a much wealthier fashion for you.

Components of the U.S. Financial Market System

Numerous approaches exist for classifying the securities markets. At times, the array can be confusing. An examination of four sets of dichotomous terms can help provide a basic understanding of the structure of the U.S. financial markets.

Public Offerings and Private Placements

When a corporation decides to raise external capital, those funds can be obtained by making a public offering or a private placement. In a **public offering** both individual and institutional investors have the opportunity to purchase the securities. The securities are usually made available to the public at large by a managing investment banking firm and its underwriting (risk-taking) syndicate. The firm does not meet the ultimate purchasers of the securities in the public offering. The public market is an impersonal market.

In a **private placement,** also called a **direct placement,** the securities are offered and sold to a limited number of investors. The firm will usually hammer out, on a face-to-face basis with the prospective buyers, the details of the offering. In this setting the investment banking firm may act as a finder by bringing together potential lenders and borrowers. The private placement market is a more personal market than its public counterpart. Both investment banking and private placements are explored in more detail later in this chapter.

Primary Markets and Secondary Markets

Primary markets are those in which securities are offered for the *first* time to potential investors. A new issue of common stock by AT&T is a primary market transaction. This type of transaction increases the total stock of financial assets outstanding in the economy.

As mentioned in our discussion of the development of the financial market system, **secondary markets** represent transactions in currently outstanding securities. If the first buyer of the AT&T stock subsequently sells it, he or she does so in the secondary market. All transactions after the initial purchase take place in the secondary market. The sales do *not* affect the total stock of financial assets that exist in the economy. Both the money market and the capital market, described next, have primary and secondary sides.

Money Market and Capital Market

Money Market

The key distinguishing feature between the money and capital markets is the maturity period of the securities traded in them. The **money market** refers to all institutions and procedures that provide for transactions in short-term debt instruments generally issued by borrowers with very high credit ratings. By financial convention, *short term* means maturity periods of one year or less. Notice that equity instruments, either common or preferred, are not traded in the money market. The major instruments issued and traded are U.S. Treasury bills, various federal agency securities, bankers' acceptances, negotiable certificates of deposit, and commercial paper. Detailed descriptions of these instruments as elements of the firm's marketable securities portfolio are given in Chapter 15. Commercial paper as a short-term financing vehicle is discussed in Chapter 17. Keep in mind that the money market is an intangible market. You do not walk into a building on Wall Street that has the words "Money Market" etched in stone over its arches. Rather, the money market is primarily a telephone market where trading does not occur at any specific location. Most agree, however, that New York City is the center of this market because of the city's corresponding strength in the capital market.

Capital Market

The **capital market** refers to all institutions and procedures that provide for transactions in long-term financial instruments. *Long-term* here means having maturity periods that extend beyond one year. In the broad sense this encompasses term loans and financial leases, corporate equities, and bonds. All these financing modes are discussed in Chapters 19, 20, and 21. The funds that comprise the firm's capital structure are raised in the capital market. Important elements of the capital market are the organized security exchanges and the over-the-counter markets.

Organized Security Exchanges and Over-the-Counter Markets

Organized security exchanges are tangible entities; they physically occupy space (such as a building or part of a building), and financial instruments are traded on their premises. The **over-the-counter markets** include all security markets *except* the organized exchanges. The money market, then, is an over-the-counter market. Because both markets are important to financial officers concerned with raising *long-term capital*, some additional discussion is warranted.

Organized Security Exchanges

For practical purposes there are seven major security exchanges in the United States.[3] These are the (1) New York Stock Exchange, (2) American Stock Exchange, (3) Midwest Stock Exchange, (4) Pacific Stock Exchange, (5) Philadelphia Stock Exchange, (6) Boston Stock Exchange, and (7) Cincinnati Stock Exchange. The New York Stock Exchange (NYSE) and the American Stock Exchange (AMEX) are called *national* exchanges, whereas the others are loosely described as *regionals*.

---

[3]Others include (1) The Honolulu Stock Exchange, which is unregistered; (2) the Board of Trade of the City of Chicago, which does not now trade stocks; and (3) the Chicago Board Options Exchange, Inc., which deals in options rather than stocks. The cities of Colorado Springs, Salt Lake City, and Spokane also have small exchanges. From time to time you may hear of the New York Futures Exchange (NYFE). This subsidiary of the NYSE was incorporated on April 5, 1979. Trading on the NYFE is in futures contracts and options contracts.

All of these seven active exchanges are registered with the Securities and Exchange Commission (SEC). Firms whose securities are traded on the registered exchanges must comply with reporting requirements of both the specific exchange and the SEC. About 85 percent of the annual dollar volume of transactions on the *registered* exchanges takes place on the NYSE. In 1977 the dollar trading volume on the Midwest exchange actually exceeded that of the AMEX, which usually runs second to the NYSE.[4] Together, the NYSE, the AMEX, and the Midwest account for about 94 percent of the annual dollar volume transacted on the registered exchanges. In 1985 the NYSE accounted for 81.6 percent of all *shares* sold on registered exchanges in the United States, with the AMEX accounting for 5.7 percent, and all others 12.7 percent.[5]

Another indication of the importance of the NYSE to our financial market system is reflected in something known as "consolidated tape volume." The Consolidated Tape prints all of the transactions on stocks that are listed on the NYSE and are traded on other organized markets. These markets include the seven exchanges mentioned earlier plus two over-the-counter markets. In 1990, the NYSE accounted for 82.9 percent of consolidated volume.[6]

The business of an exchange, including securities transactions, is conducted by its **members.** Members are said to occupy "seats." There are 1,366 seats on the NYSE, a number that has remained constant since 1953. Major brokerage firms own seats on the exchanges. An officer of the firm is designated to be the member of the exchange, and this membership permits the brokerage house to use the facilities of the exchange to effect trades. During 1990 the prices of seats that were exchanged for cash ranged from a low of $250,000 to a high of $430,000.[7] The record price, by the way, was $1.15 million paid on September 21, 1987—just prior to the October 19 market debacle.

Stock exchange benefits ■ Both corporations and investors enjoy several benefits provided by the existence of organized security exchanges. These include

1. **Providing a continuous market.** This may be the most important function of an organized security exchange. A continuous market provides a series of continuous security prices. Price changes from trade to trade tend to be smaller than they would be in the absence of organized markets. The reasons are that there is a relatively large sales volume in each security, trading orders are executed quickly, and the range between the price asked for a security and the offered price tends to be narrow. The result is that price volatility is reduced. This enhances the liquidity of security investments and makes them more attractive to potential investors. While it is difficult to prove, it seems logical that this market feature probably reduces the cost of capital to corporations.

2. **Establishing and publicizing fair security prices.** An organized exchange permits security prices to be set by competitive forces. They are not set by negotiations off the floor of the exchange, where one party might have a bargaining advantage. The bidding process flows from the supply and demand underlying each security. This means the specific price of a security is determined in the manner of an auction. In addition, the security prices determined at each exchange are widely publicized. Just read the pages of most newspapers, and the information is available to you. By contrast, the prices and resulting yields on the private placements of securities are more difficult to obtain.

---

[4]Jonathan R. Laing, "Shaky Floor: Problems Multiply at Midwest Exchange, but Chief Is Optimistic," *Wall Street Journal,* April 4, 1978, p. 1, 20.
[5]New York Stock Exchange, *Fact Book* (New York, 1986), p. 74.
[6]New York Stock Exchange, *Fact Book* (New York, 1991), p. 22.
[7]New York Stock Exchange, *Fact Book* (New York, 1991), p. 67.

3. Helping business raise new capital. Because a continuous secondary market exists where prices are competitively determined, it is easier for firms to float new security offerings successfully. This continuous pricing mechanism also facilitates the determination of the offering price of a new issue. This means that comparative values are easily observed.

Listing requirements ■ To receive the benefits provided by an organized exchange, the firm must seek to have its securities listed on the exchange. An application for listing must be filed and a fee paid. The requirements for listing vary from exchange to exchange; those of the NYSE are the most stringent. The general criteria for listing fall into these categories: (1) profitability; (2) size, (3) market value, and (4) public ownership. To give you the flavor of an actual set of listing requirements, those set forth by the NYSE are displayed in Table 18–6.[8]

Over-the-Counter Markets

Many publicly held firms do not meet the listing requirements of major stock exchanges. Others may want to avoid the reporting requirements and fees required to maintain listing. As an alternative their securities may trade in the over-the-counter markets. On the basis of sheer numbers (not dollar volume), more stocks are traded over-the-counter than on organized exchanges. As far as secondary trading in corporate bonds is concerned, the over-the-counter markets are where the action is. In a typical year, more than 90 percent of corporate bond business takes place over-the-counter.

Most over-the-counter transactions are done through a loose network of security traders who are known as broker-dealers and brokers. Brokers do not purchase securities for their own account, whereas dealers do. Broker-dealers stand ready to buy and sell specific securities at selected prices. They are said to "make a market" in those securities. Their profit is the spread or difference between the price they will pay for a security (bid price) and the price at which they will sell the security (asked price).

Price quotes ■ The availability of prices is not as continuous in the over-the-counter market as it is on an organized exchange. Since February 8, 1971, however, when a computerized network called NASDAQ came into existence, the availability of prices in this market has improved substantially. **NASDAQ** stands for National Association of Security Dealers Automated Quotation System. It is a telecommunications system that provides a national information link among the brokers and dealers operating in the over-the-counter markets. Subscribing traders have a cathode-ray terminal that allows them to obtain representative bids and ask prices for thousands of securities traded over-the-counter. NASDAQ is a quotation system, not a transactions system. The final trade is still consummated by direct negotiation between traders.

TABLE 18–6.
NYSE Listing Requirements

Profitability
Earnings before taxes (EBT) for the most recent year must be at least $2.5 million. For the two years preceding that, EBT must be at least $2.0 million.

Size
Net tangible assets must be at least $18.0 million.

Market Value[a]
The market value of publicly held stock must be at least $18.0 million.

Public Ownership
There must be at least 1.1 million publicly held common shares. There must be at least 2000 holders of 100 shares or more.

[a]The market value test is tied to the level of common stock prices prevailing in the marketplace at the time of the listing application. From time to time the $18.0 million requirement noted above may be lessened. Under current regulations of the NYSE, the requirement can never be less than $9.0 million.

[8]New York Stock Exchange, *Fact Book* (New York, 1991), p. 26.

NASDAQ price quotes for many stocks are published daily in the *Wall Street Journal*. This same financial newspaper also publishes prices on hundreds of other stocks traded over-the-counter. Local papers supply prices on stocks of regional interest. Finally, the National Quotation Bureau publishes daily "pink sheets," which contain prices on about 8,000 securities; these sheets are available in the offices of most security dealers.

Perspective in Finance

We touched briefly on the investment banking industry and the investment banker earlier in this chapter when we described various methods for transferring financial capital (see Figure 18–2). The investment banker *is to be distinguished from the* commercial banker *in that the former's organization is not a permanent depository for funds. Later it will be shown, however, that a trend is under way in this country to let commercial banks perform more functions and services that since 1933 have belonged almost exclusively to the investment banking industry. For the moment, it is important for you to learn about the role of the investment banker in the funding of commercial activity.*

The Investment Banker

Most corporations do not raise long-term capital frequently. The activities of working-capital management go on daily, but attracting long-term capital is, by comparison, episodic. The sums involved can be huge, so these situations are considered of great importance to financial managers. Because most managers are unfamiliar with the subtleties of raising long-term funds, they enlist the help of an expert. That expert is an investment banker.[9]

Definition

The **investment banker** is a financial specialist involved as an intermediary in the merchandising of securities. He or she acts as a "middle person" by facilitating the flow of savings from those economic units that want to invest to those units that want to raise funds. We use the term investment banker to refer both to a given individual and to the organization for which such a person works, variously known as an **investment banking firm** or an **investment banking house.** Although these firms are called investment bankers, they perform no depository or lending functions. The activities of commercial banking and investment banking as we know them today were separated by the Banking Act of 1933 (also known as the Glass-Steagall Act of 1933). Just what does this middleman role involve? That is most easily understood in terms of the basic functions of investment banking.

Functions

The investment banker performs three basic functions: (1) underwriting, (2) distributing, and (3) advising.

Underwriting

The term **underwriting** is borrowed from the field of insurance. It means "assuming a risk." The investment banker assumes the risk of selling a security issue at a satisfactory price. A satisfactory price is one that will generate a profit for the investment banking house.

---

[9]Some structural, managerial, and operational changes in the investment banking industry are described in "The Traders Take Charge," *Business Week*, February 20, 1984, pp. 58–61, 64.

The procedure goes like this. The managing investment banker and its syndicate will buy the security issue from the corporation in need of funds. The **syndicate** is a group of other investment bankers who are invited to help buy and resell the issue. The managing house is the investment banking firm that originated the business because its corporate client decided to raise external funds. On a specific day, the firm that is raising capital is presented with a check in exchange for the securities being issued. At this point the investment banking syndicate owns the securities. The corporation has its cash and can proceed to use it. The firm is now immune from the possibility that the security markets might turn sour. If the price of the newly issued security falls below that paid to the firm by the syndicate, the syndicate will suffer a loss. The syndicate, of course, hopes that the opposite situation will result. Its objective is to sell the new issue to the investing public at a price per security greater than its cost.

Distributing

Once the syndicate owns the new securities, it must get them into the hands of the ultimate investors. This is the distribution or selling function of investment banking. The investment banker may have branch offices across the United States, or it may have an informal arrangement with several security dealers who regularly buy a portion of each new offering for final sale. It is not unusual to have 300 to 400 dealers involved in the selling effort. The syndicate can properly be viewed as the security wholesaler, and the dealer organization can be viewed as the security retailer.

Advising

The investment banker is an expert in the issuance and marketing of securities. A sound investment banking house will be aware of prevailing market conditions and can relate those conditions to the particular type of security that should be sold at a given time. Business conditions may be pointing to a future increase in interest rates. The investment banker might advise the firm to issue its bonds in a timely fashion to avoid the higher yields that are forthcoming. The banker can analyze the firm's capital structure and make recommendations as to what general source of capital should be issued. In many instances the firm will invite its investment banker to sit on the board of directors. This permits the banker to observe corporate activity and make recommendations on a regular basis.

Distribution Methods

Several methods are available to the corporation for placing new security offerings in the hands of final investors. The investment banker's role is different in each of these. Sometimes, in fact, it is possible to bypass the investment banker. These methods are described in this section. Private placements, because of their importance, are treated separately later in the chapter.

Negotiated Purchase

In a negotiated underwriting, the firm that needs funds makes contact with an investment banker, and deliberations concerning the new issue begin. If all goes well, a *method* is negotiated for determining the price the investment banker and the syndicate will pay for the securities. For example, the agreement might state that the syndicate will pay $2 less than the closing price of the firm's common stock on the day before the offering date of a new stock issue. The negotiated purchase is the most prevalent method of securities distribution in the private sector. It is generally thought to be the most profitable technique as far as investment bankers are concerned.[10]

Competitive Bid Purchase

The method by which the underwriting group is determined distinguishes the competitive bid purchase from the negotiated purchase. In a competitive underwriting, several underwriting groups bid for the right to purchase the new issue from the corporation that is raising funds. The firm does not directly select the investment banker. The investment banker that underwrites and distributes the issue is chosen by an auction process. The syndicate willing to pay the greatest dollar amount per new security will win the competitive bid.[11]

Most competitive bid purchases are confined to three situations, compelled by legal regulations: (1) railroad issues, (2) public utility issues, and (3) state and municipal bond issues. The argument in favor of competitive bids is that any undue influence of the investment banker over the firm is mitigated and the price received by the firm for each security should be higher. Thus, we would intuitively suspect that the cost of capital in a competitive bid situation would be less than in a negotiated purchase situation. Evidence on this question, however, is mixed.[12] One problem with the competitive bid purchase as far as the fundraising firm is concerned is that the benefits gained from the advisory function of the investment banker are lost. It may be necessary to use an investment banker for advisory purposes and then by law exclude the banker from the competitive bid process. In the 1960s and 1970s, many utilities obtained exemptions from the Federal Power Commission to permit them to raise capital by negotiated underwriting.

Commission or Best-Efforts Basis

Here, the investment banker acts as an agent rather than as a principal in the distribution process. The securities are *not* underwritten. The investment banker attempts to sell the issue in return for a fixed commission on each security actually sold. Unsold securities are returned to the corporation. This arrangement is typically used for more speculative issues. The issuing firm may be smaller or less established than the investment banker would like. Because the underwriting risk is not passed on to the investment banker, this distribution method is less costly to the issuer than a negotiated or competitive bid purchase. On the other hand the investment banker only has to give it his or her "best effort." A successful sale is not guaranteed.

Privileged Subscription

Occasionally, the firm may feel that a distinct market already exists for its new securities. When a new issue is marketed to a definite and select group of investors, it is called a **privileged subscription.** Three target markets are typically involved: (1) current stockholders, (2) employees, or (3) customers. Of these, distributions directed at current stockholders are the most prevalent. Such offerings, called rights offerings, are discussed in detail in Chapter 20. In a privileged subscription the investment banker may act only as a selling agent. It

---

[10]Samuel L. Hayes, III, "Investment Banking: Power Structure in Flux," *Harvard Business Review* 49 (March–April 1971), p. 138.

[11]An excellent description of this process is found in Ernest Bloch, "Pricing a Corporate Bond Issue: A Look Behind the Scenes," *Essays in Money and Credit* (New York: Federal Reserve Bank of New York, December 1964), pp. 72–76.

[12]Gary D. Tallman, David F. Rush, and Ronald W. Melicher, "Competitive versus Negotiated Underwriting Cost of Regulated Industries," *Financial Management* 3 (Summer 1974), pp. 49–55.

is also possible that the issuing firm and the investment banker might sign a **standby agreement,** which would obligate the investment banker to underwrite the securities that are not accepted by the privileged investors.

Direct Sale

In a **direct sale** the issuing firm sells the securities directly to the investing public without involving an investment banker. Even among established corporate giants this procedure is relatively rare. A variation of the direct sale, though, has been used more frequently in the 1970s than in previous decades. This involves the private placement of a new issue by the fundraising corporation *without* the use of an investment banker as an intermediary. Texaco, Mobil Oil, and International Harvester (now Navistar) are examples of large firms that have followed this procedure.[13]

Negotiated Purchase Sequence

The negotiated purchase is the distribution method most likely to be used by the private corporation. It makes sense, then, to cover in some detail the sequence of events that comprise the negotiated underwriting.

1. **Selection of an investment banker.** The firm initiates the fundraising process by choosing an investment banker. On some occasions a third party, called a **finder,** may direct the firm to a specific investment banker. Typically, the finder receives a fee from the fundraising firm if an underwriting agreement is eventually signed. Use of a finder is one way of gaining access to a quality investment banker.

2. **Preunderwriting conferences.** A series of preunderwriting conferences are held between the firm and the investment banker. Key items discussed are (1) the amount of capital to be raised, (2) whether the capital markets seem to be especially receptive at this time to one type of financing instrument over another, and (3) whether the proposed use of the new funds appears reasonable. At these conferences it is confirmed that a flotation will, in fact, take place, and that this particular investment banker will manage the underwriting. The investment banker then undertakes a complete financial analysis of the corporation and assesses its future prospects. The final outcome of the preunderwriting conferences is the **tentative underwriting agreement.** This details (1) the approximate price the investment banker will pay for the securities and (2) the **upset price.** The upset price is a form of escape mechanism for the benefit of the issuing firm. If the market price of the firm's securities should drop in a significant fashion just before the new securities are to be sold, the price the investment banker is to pay the firm might drop below the upset price. In this situation the new offering would be aborted.

3. **Formation of the underwriting syndicate.** An *underwriting syndicate* is a temporary association of investment bankers formed to purchase a security issue from a corporation for subsequent resale, hopefully at a profit to the underwriters. The syndicate is formed for very sound reasons. First, the originating investment bank probably could not finance the entire underwriting itself. Second, the use of a syndicate reduces the risk of loss to any single underwriter. Third, the use of a syndicate widens the eventual distribution effort. Each underwriter has its own network of security dealers who will purchase a portion of the participation in the offering. Most syndicates contain 10 to 60 investment banking houses. Because each house has its own distribution network, the selling group can often

[13]See Wyndham Robertson, "Future Shock at Morgan Stanley," *Fortune* 97 (February 27, 1978), pp. 88, 90.

consist of 100 to 600 dealers. An agreement signed by all members of the syndicate binds them to certain performance standards. This agreement details their participation (amount they can purchase) in the offering and their liability for any portion of the issue unsold by their fellow underwriters.

4. **Registering the securities.** Before a new public issue can be offered to prospective investors, it must be registered with the Securities and Exchange Commission (SEC). Securities that are exempt from registration will be discussed later in this chapter when we examine the regulation of the securities markets. Most new issues must comply with the requirements of the **Securities Act of 1933.** This dictates that a **registration statement** must be submitted to the SEC; this statement is aimed at disclosing all facts relevant to the new issue that will permit an investor to make an informed decision.[14] The SEC itself does *not* judge the investment quality of securities. The registration statement is a lengthy document containing (1) historical, (2) financial, and (3) administrative facts about the firm. The details of the new offering are presented, as well as the proposed use of the funds that are being raised. During a 20-day waiting period, the SEC examines the statement for errors or omissions. While this examination process is being carried out, the investment banking syndicate *cannot* offer the security for sale. Part of the package presented to the SEC for scrutiny is a document called a **prospectus.** Once approved, it is the official advertising vehicle for the offering. During the waiting period a **preliminary prospectus,** outlining the important features of the new issue, may be distributed to potential investors. The preliminary prospectus contains no selling price information or offering date. In addition, a stamped red-ink statement on the first page tells the reader that the document is *not* an official offer to sell the securities. In the jargon of finance, this preliminary prospectus is called a **red herring.** Once the registration statement is approved by the SEC, the security can be offered for sale provided the prospectus is made available to all concerned parties.

5. **Formation of the selling group.** In order to distribute the securities to final investors, a selling group is formed. The dealers comprising the selling group purchase portions of the new issue from the syndicate members with whom they regularly do business. They pay for each security a price higher than that paid by the syndicate member, but less than the offering price to the investing public. The responsibilities and rewards of the selling group are contained in the **selling group agreement.** Formation of the selling group completes the distribution network for the new offering. The structure of such a network is diagrammed in Figure 18–3.

6. **The due diligence meeting.** This is a "last-chance" gathering to get everything in order before taking the offering to the public. Usually, all members of the syndicate are present, along with key officers of the issuing firm. Any omissions from the prospectus should be caught at this meeting. Most important, the final price to be paid by the syndicate to the firm is settled at this meeting. As we said earlier, if the issue is additional common stock, the underwriting price may be a fixed amount below the closing price of the firm's outstanding stock on the day prior to the new offering. Capital market conditions are discussed, and the security's offering price to the public is set in light of those conditions. The "go ahead" is given to print the final prospectus, which now contains all relevant price information. The offering is usually made the next day after the meeting.

7. **Price-pegging.** Once the issue has been offered for sale, the managing

---

[14]See the section on shelf registration at the end of this chapter.

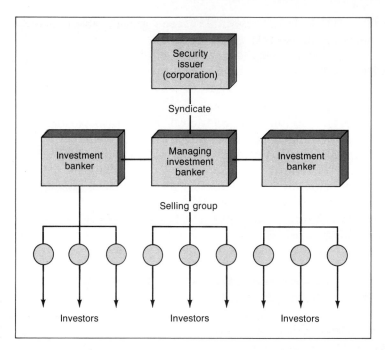

FIGURE 18–3.
Distributing New Securities

STABILIZE the PRICE →

underwriter attempts to mitigate downward price movements in the secondary market for the security by placing orders to buy at the agreed-on public offering price. The objective is to stabilize the market price of the issue so it can be sold at the initial offering price. The syndicate manager's intention to perform this price maintenance operation must be disclosed in the registration statement.

8. **Syndicate termination.** A contractual agreement among the underwriters identifies the duration of the syndicate. The syndicate is dissolved when the issue has been fully subscribed. If the demand for the issue is great, it may be sold out in a few days. If the issue lingers on the market, without much buyer interest, the remaining inventory may be sold at the existing secondary market price. The name of the game in investment banking is not margin, but turnover. Should the issue go sour, the underwriters will quickly absorb the loss and get on to the next underwriting.

Industry Leaders

All industries have their leaders, and investment banking is no exception. We have discussed investment bankers in general at some length in this chapter. Table 18–7 gives us some idea who the major players are within the investment

TABLE 18–7.
Leading U.S. Investment
Bankers, 1991

Firm	Underwriting Volume (Billions of Dollars)	Number of Issues	Percent of Market
1. Merrill Lynch	$100.0	1180	17.2%
2. Goldman, Sachs	72.7	1013	12.5
3. Lehman Brothers	67.6	1336	11.7
4. First Boston	56.8	944	9.8
5. Kidder, Peabody	50.0	1705	8.6
6. Morgan Stanley	48.0	564	8.3
7. Salomon Brothers	43.7	626	7.5
8. Bear, Stearns	33.9	1087	5.8
9. Prudential Securities	18.2	613	3.1
10. Donaldson, Lufkin & Jenrette	11.2	324	1.9

Source: IDD Information Services as reported in the *New York Times*, January 2, 1992, p. C6.

banking industry. It lists the top 10 houses in 1991 based upon the dollar volume of security issues that were managed. The number of issues the house participated in as lead manager is also identified, along with its share of the market.

Private Placements

Private placements are an alternative to the sale of securities to the public or to a restricted group of investors through a privileged subscription. Any type of security can be privately placed (directly placed). This market, however, is clearly dominated by debt issues. Thus, we restrict this discussion to debt securities. From year to year the volume of private placements will vary. Table 18–8 shows, though, that the private placement market is always a significant portion of the U.S. capital market.

The major investors in private placements are large financial institutions. Based on the volume of securities purchased, the three most important investor groups are (1) life insurance companies, (2) state and local retirement funds, and (3) private pension funds.

In arranging a private placement the firm may (1) avoid the use of an investment banker and work directly with the investing institutions or (2) engage the services of an investment banker. If the firm does not use an investment banker, of course, it does not have to pay a fee. Conversely, investment bankers can provide valuable advice in the private placement process. They are usually in contact with several major institutional investors; thus, they will know if a firm is in a position to invest in its proposed offering, and they can help the firm evaluate the terms of the new issue.

Private placements have both advantages and disadvantages compared with public offerings. The financial manager must carefully evaluate both sides of the question. The advantages associated with private placements are these:

1. **Speed.** The firm usually obtains funds more quickly through a private placement than a public offering. The major reason is that registration of the issue with the SEC is *not* required.

2. **Reduced flotation costs.** These savings result because the lengthy registration statement for the SEC does not have to be prepared, and the

Year	Total Volume ($million)	Percent Publicly Placed	Percent Privately Placed
1990	$276,259	68.5%	31.5%
1989	298,813	60.7	39.3
1988	329,919	61.3	38.7
1987	301,447	69.5	30.5
1986	313,502	74.2	25.8
1985	165,754	72.1	27.9
1984	109,903	66.9	33.1
1983	68,370	69.1	30.9
1982	53,636	81.7	18.3
1981	45,092	84.5	15.5
1980	53,206	78.2	21.8
1979	40,139	64.3	35.7
1978	36,872	53.7	46.3
1977	42,015	57.3	42.7
1976	42,262	62.6	37.4
1975	42,756	76.2	23.8

Source: *Federal Reserve Bulletin*, various issues.

TABLE 18–8.
Publicly and Privately Placed Corporate Debt Placed Domestically (Gross Proceeds of All New U.S. Corporate Debt Issues)

investment banking underwriting and distribution costs do not have to be absorbed.

3. **Financing flexibility.** In a private placement the firm deals on a face-to-face basis with a small number of investors. This means that the terms of the issue can be tailored to meet the specific needs of the company. For example, all of the funds need not be taken by the firm at once. In exchange for a commitment fee the firm can "draw down" against the established amount of credit with the investors. This provides some insurance against capital market uncertainties, and the firm does not have to borrow the funds if the need does not arise. There is also the possibility of *renegotiation*. The terms of the debt issue can be altered. The term to maturity, the interest rate, or any restrictive covenants can be discussed among the affected parties.

The following disadvantages of private placements must be evaluated:

1. **Interest costs.** It is generally conceded that interest costs on private placements exceed those of public issues. Whether this disadvantage is enough to offset the reduced flotation costs associated with a private placement is a determination that the financial manager must make. There is some evidence that on smaller issues, say $500,000 as opposed to $30 million, the private placement alternative would be preferable.[15]

2. **Restrictive covenants.** Dividend policy, working-capital levels, and the raising of additional debt capital may all be affected by provisions in the private-placement debt contract. That is not to say that such restrictions are always absent in public debt contracts. Rather, the financial officer must be alert to the tendency for these covenants to be especially burdensome in private contracts.

3. **The possibility of future SEC registration.** If the lender (investor) should decide to sell the issue to a public buyer before maturity, the issue must be registered with the SEC. Some lenders, then, require that the issuing firm agree to a future registration at their option.

Flotation Costs

The firm raising long-term capital incurs two types of **flotation costs:** (1) the underwriter's spread and (2) issuing costs. Of these two costs, the underwriter's spread is the larger. The **underwriter's spread** is simply the difference between the gross and net proceeds from a given security issue expressed as a percent of the gross proceeds. The **issue costs** include (1) printing and engraving, (2) legal fees, (3) accounting fees, (4) trustee fees, and (5) several other miscellaneous components. The two most significant issue costs are printing and engraving and legal fees.

Data published by the SEC have consistently revealed two relationships about flotation costs. First, the costs associated with issuing common stock are notably greater than the costs associated with preferred stock offerings. In turn, preferred stock costs exceed those of bonds. Second, flotation costs (expressed as a percent of gross proceeds) decrease as the size of the security issue increases.

In the first instance, the stated relationship reflects the fact that issue costs are sensitive to the risks involved in successfully distributing a security issue.

[15]John D. Rea and Peggy Brockschmidt, "The Relationship between Publicly Offered and Privately Placed Corporate Bonds," *Monthly Review, Federal Reserve Bank of Kansas City* (November 1973), p. 15.

Common stock is riskier to own than corporate bonds. Underwriting risk is, therefore, greater with common stock than with bonds. Thus, flotation costs just mirror these risk relationships. In the second case, a portion of the issue costs is fixed. Legal fees and accounting costs are good examples. So, as the size of the security issue rises, the fixed component is spread over a larger gross proceeds base. As a consequence, average flotation costs vary inversely with the size of the issue.

Perspective in Finance

Since late 1986, there has been a renewal of public interest in the regulation of the country's financial markets. The key event was a massive insider trading scandal that made the name Ivan F. Boesky one of almost universal recognition —but, unfortunately, in a negative sense. This was followed by the October 19, 1987, crash of the equity markets. More recently, in early 1990, the investing community (both institutional and individual) became increasingly concerned over a weakening in the so-called "junk bond market." The upshot of all of this enhanced awareness is a new appreciation of the crucial role that regulation plays in the financial system. The basics are presented below.

Regulation

Following the severe economic downturn of 1929–32, congressional action was taken to provide for federal regulation of the securities markets. State statutes (blue sky laws) also govern the securities markets where applicable, but the federal regulations are clearly more pressing and important. The major federal regulations are reviewed here.

Primary Market Regulations

The new issues market is governed by the Securities Act of 1933. The intent of the act is important. It aims to provide potential investors with accurate, truthful disclosure about the firm and the new securities being offered to the public. This does *not* prevent firms from issuing highly speculative securities. The SEC says nothing whatsoever about the possible investment worth of a given offering. It is up to the investor to separate the junk from the jewels. The SEC does have the legal power and responsibility to enforce the 1933 act.

Full public disclosure is achieved by the requirement that the issuing firm file a registration statement with the SEC containing requisite information. The statement details particulars about the firm and the new security being issued. During a minimum 20-day waiting period, the SEC examines the submitted document. In numerous instances the 20-day wait has been extended by several weeks. The SEC can ask for additional information that was omitted in order to clarify the original document. The SEC can also order that the offering be stopped.

During the registration process a preliminary prospectus (the red herring) may be distributed to potential investors. When the registration is approved, the final prospectus must be made available to the prospective investors. The prospectus is actually a condensed version of the full registration statement. If, at a later date, the information in the registration statement and the prospectus is found to be lacking, purchasers of the new issue who incurred a loss can sue for damages. Officers of the issuing firm and others who took part in the registration and marketing of the issue may suffer both civil and criminal penalties.

Generally, the SEC defines public issues as those that are sold to more than 25 investors. Some public issues need not be registered. These include

1. Relatively small issues where the firm sells less than $1.5 million of new securities per year.
2. Issues that are sold entirely intrastate.
3. Issues that are basically short-term instruments. This translates into maturity periods of 270 days or less.
4. Issues that are already regulated or controlled by some other federal agency. Examples here are the Federal Power Commission (public utilities) and the Interstate Commerce Commission (railroads).

Secondary Market Regulations

Secondary market trading is regulated by the **Securities Exchange Act of 1934.** This act created the SEC to enforce federal securities laws. The Federal Trade Commission enforced the 1933 act for one year. The major aspects of the 1934 act can be best presented in outline form:

1. Major security exchanges must register with the SEC. This regulates the

exchanges and places reporting requirements upon the firms whose securities are listed on them.

2. Insider trading is regulated. Insiders can be officers, directors, employees, relatives, major investors, or anyone having information about the operation of the firm that is not public knowledge. If an investor purchases the security of the firm in which the investor is an insider, he or she must hold it for at least six months before disposing of it. Otherwise, profits made from trading the stock within a period of less than six months must be returned to the firm. Furthermore, insiders must file with the SEC a monthly statement of holdings and transactions in the stock of their corporation.[16]

3. Manipulative trading of securities by investors to affect stock prices is prohibited.

4. The SEC is given control over proxy procedures.

5. The Board of Governors of the Federal Reserve System is given responsibility for setting margin requirements. This affects the flow of credit into the securities markets. Buying securities on margin simply means using credit to acquire a portion of the subject financial instruments.

More Recent Regulatory Developments

Securities Acts Amendments of 1975

The Securities Acts Amendments of 1975 touched on three important issues. First, Congress mandated the creation of a national market system (NMS). Only

---

[16]On November 14, 1986, the SEC announced that Ivan F. Boesky had admitted to illegal inside trading after an intensive investigation. Boesky at the time was a very well known Wall Street investor, speculator, and arbitrageur. Boesky was an owner or part owner in several companies, including an arbitrage fund named Ivan F. Boesky & Co. L. P. Boesky agreed to pay the U.S. government $50 million, which represented a return of illegal profits, another $50 million in civil penalties, to withdraw permanently from the securities industry, and to plead guilty to criminal charges. The far-reaching investigation continued into 1987 and implicated several other prominent investment figures.

The chairman of the SEC during this period was John S. R. Shad. Shad suggested that security trades would be considered illegal if they were based on "material, non-public information." As you would expect, this insider trading case garnered a lot of attention in the popular business press and led to renewed discussions of ethics in business schools. See "Who'll Be the Next to Fall?" *Business Week,* December 1, 1986, pp. 28–30; "Wall Street Enters the Age of the Supergrass," *The Economist,* November 22–28, 1986, pp. 77–78; "Going After the Crooks," *Time,* December 1, 1986, pp. 48–51; and "The Decline and Fall of Business Ethics," *Fortune* 114, December 8, 1986, pp. 65–66, 68, 72.

BASIC FINANCIAL MANAGEMENT IN PRACTICE

Focus on Regulation

In the latter half of 1989, Mr. Richard Breeden, a lawyer, became chairman of the SEC. He has been involved in Washington, D.C., circles for several years. In early 1990, Mr. Breeden was interviewed by *Institutional Investor*—a respected trade magazine for the investments and corporate financing industries. Parts of that interview follow.

Notice Mr. Breeden's references to the 1934 act, insider trading, and the *international dimension* of corporate financing.

Richard Breeden on Securities Regulation

Q: You have pressed for functional regulation—assigning regulatory authority on the basis of the activity being regulated, regardless of what institution is carrying out the activity—for the past eight years. How would this change the SEC's jurisdiction?

A: We generally favor letting anybody who wants to compete in the securities business do so. But they all ought to have to operate by the same set of rules and regulations. The level playing field for all companies—their public reporting, their disclosure requirements—should be the (1934 Securities Exchange Act) with SEC oversight. Then their subsidiary companies, whether they're in the insurance or the banking business or the broker-dealer business, should be regulated by the appropriate regulatory authority.

Q: What are your enforcement priorities going to be?

A: Clean markets.

Q: Insider trading?

A: I've said before, and I'm happy to say again, I consider insider trading to be a serious matter. But I don't think that should be our exclusive enforcement focus. I'm also very troubled by the types of pennystock frauds that we see where individual investors are defrauded, sometimes of their entire life savings. And the types of practices that were appearing (during congressional hearings on the collapse of Lincoln Savings & Loan

Association): We had some very tragic testimony from individuals who went into the lobby of an S&L thinking they were going to get an insured deposit and came out with a junk bond, and ended up losing savings that were vital to them. That undercuts people's confidence and willingness to participate in the market.

Q: Are we going to need a new kind of regulation for the various automated trading systems?

A: It depends on what you mean by a new kind of regulation. We are blessed with having a marketplace that is innovative and creative, where new products are developed frequently, and that calls for a regulatory system that will evolve along with the markets. The contrary approach is to expect the markets to meet the bureaucratic needs of the regulatory agencies.

But the objectives of regulation don't change. We want to see a stable marketplace in which competition can flourish.

Q: But do you have any specific ideas of how regulation might have to change as more and more market activity and trading go through computers instead of exchange floors and the public markets?

A: There are a lot of different people who have a lot of different hypotheses about how the markets will evolve. I don't know that the SEC knows what the markets five years from now will look like.

Q: How else will the markets change in the 1990s?

A: I think certainly one of the big factors of the '90s will be an increased international dimension to everything we do and everything that's done in the marketplace. So we also have to recognize that the volume of cross-border transactions will continue to grow and so will our need to work closely with the Securities Bureau in Japan and with regulatory authorities in London, Frankfurt and around the world.

Source: "The World According to Richard Breeden," *Institutional Investor*, January 1990, p. 110.

broad goals for this national exchange were identified by Congress. Implementation details were left to the SEC and, to a much lesser extent, the securities industry in general. Congress was really expressing its desire for (1) widespread application of auction market trading principles, (2) a high degree of competition across markets, and (3) the use of modern electronic communication systems to link the fragmented markets in the country into a true NMS. The NMS is still a goal toward which the SEC and the securities industry are moving. Agreement as to its final form and an implementation date have not occurred.

A second major alteration in the habits of the securities industry also took place in 1975. This was the elimination of fixed commissions (fixed brokerage rates) on public transactions in securities. This was closely tied to the desire for an NMS in that fixed brokerage fees provided no incentive for competition among brokers. A third consideration of the 1975 amendments focused on such financial institutions as commercial banks and insurance firms. These financial institutions were prohibited from acquiring membership on stock exchanges in order to reduce or save commissions on their own trades.

Shelf Registration

On March 16, 1982, the SEC began a new procedure for registering new issues of securities. Formally it is called SEC Rule 415; informally the process is known as a **shelf registration,** or a **shelf offering.** The essence of the process is rather simple. Rather than go through the lengthy, full registration process each time the firm plans an offering of securities, it can get a blanket order approved by the SEC. A master registration statement that covers the financing plans of the firm over the coming two years is filed with the SEC. Upon approval, the firm can market some or all of the securities over this two-year period. The securities are sold in a piecemeal fashion, or "off the shelf." Prior to each specific offering, a short statement about the issue is filed with the SEC.

Corporations raising funds approve of this new procedure. The tedious, full registration process is avoided with each offering pulled off the shelf. This should result in a saving of fees paid to investment bankers. Moreover, an issue can more quickly be brought to the market. Also, if market conditions change, an issue can easily be redesigned to fit the specific conditions of the moment.

- ADVANTAGES of SHELF REGISTRATION

As is always the case—there is another side to the story. Recall that the reason for the registration process in the first place is to give investors useful information about the firm and the securities being offered. Under the shelf registration procedure some of the information about the issuing firm becomes old as the two-year horizon unfolds. Some investment bankers feel they do not have the proper amount of time to study the firm when a shelf offering takes place. This is one of those areas of finance where more observations are needed before any final conclusions can be made. Those observations will only come with the passage of time.[17]

- DISADVANTAGE

SUMMARY

This chapter centers on the market environment in which corporations raise long-term funds, including the structure of the U.S. financial markets, the institution of investment banking, and the various methods for distributing securities.

Mix of Corporate Securities Sold

When corporations go to the capital market for cash, the most favored financing method is debt. The corporate debt markets clearly dominate the equity markets when new funds are raised. The U.S. tax system inherently favors debt capital as a fundraising method. In an average year over the 1972–85 period, bonds and notes made up 69 percent of external cash that was raised.

Why Financial Markets Exist

The function of financial markets is to allocate savings efficiently in the economy to the ultimate demander (user) of the savings. In a financial market the forces of supply and demand for a specific financial instrument are brought together. The wealth of an economy would not be as great as it is without a fully developed financial market system.

---

[17]A study of the issue costs associated with Rule 415 is provided by M. Wayne Marr and G. Rodney Thompson, "Rule 415: Preliminary Empirical Results," *Working Paper No. 24* (Department of Finance, Virginia Polytechnic Institute and State University, October 1983). For an overview of the negative side of the matter, see "Shelf Offerings Still Worry Wall Street," *Business Week*, March 5, 1984, p. 83.

Financing of Business

Every year households are a net supplier of funds to the financial markets. The nonfinancial business sector is always a net borrower of funds. Both life insurance companies and private pension funds are important buyers of corporate securities. In the economy savings are ultimately transferred to the business firm seeking cash by means of (1) the direct transfer, (2) the indirect transfer using the investment banker, or (3) the indirect transfer using the financial intermediary.

Components of U.S. Financial Market System

Corporations can raise funds through public offerings or private placements. The public market is impersonal in that the security issuer does not meet the ultimate investors in the financial instruments. In a private placement, the securities are sold directly to a limited number of institutional investors.

The primary market is the market for new issues. The secondary market represents transactions in currently outstanding securities. Both the money and capital markets have primary and secondary sides. The money market refers to transactions in short-term debt instruments. The capital market, on the other hand, refers to transactions in long-term financial instruments. Trading in the money and capital markets can occur in either the organized security exchanges or the over-the-counter market. The money market is exclusively an over-the-counter market.

Investment Banker

The investment banker is a financial specialist involved as an intermediary in the merchandising of securities. He or she performs the functions of (1) underwriting, (2) distributing, and (3) advising. Major methods for the public distribution of securities include (1) the negotiated purchase, (2) the competitive bid purchase, (3) the commission or best-efforts basis, (4) privileged subscriptions, and (5) direct sales. The direct sale bypasses the use of an investment banker. The negotiated purchase is the most profitable distribution method to the investment banker. It also provides the greatest amount of investment banking services to the corporate client.

Private Placements

Privately placed debt provides an important market outlet for corporate bonds. Major investors in this market are (1) life insurance firms, (2) state and local retirement funds, and (3) private pension funds. Several advantages and disadvantages are associated with private placements. The financial officer must weigh these attributes and decide if a private placement is preferable over a public offering.

Flotation Costs

Flotation costs consist of the underwriter's spread and issuing costs. The flotation costs of common stock exceed those of preferred stock, which, in turn, exceed those of debt. Moreover, flotation costs as a percent of gross proceeds are inversely related to the size of the security issue.

Regulation

The new issues market is regulated at the federal level by the Securities Act of 1933. It provides for the registration of new issues with the SEC. Secondary market trading is regulated by the Securities Exchange Act of 1934. The Securities Acts Amendments of 1975 placed on the SEC the responsibility for devising a national market system. This concept is still being studied. The shelf registration procedure (SEC Rule 415) was initiated in March 1982. Under this regulation and with the proper filing of documents, firms that are selling new issues do not have to go through the old, lengthy registration process each time the firm plans an offering of securities.

STUDY QUESTIONS

18–1. What are financial markets? What function do they perform? How would an economy be worse off without them?

18–2. Define in a technical sense what we mean by *financial intermediary*. Give an example of your definition.

18–3. Distinguish between the money and capital markets.

18–4. What major benefits do corporations and investors enjoy because of the existence of organized security exchanges?

18–5. What are the general categories examined by an organized exchange in determining whether an applicant firm's securities can be listed on it? (Specific numbers are not needed here, but rather areas of investigation.)

18–6. Why do you think most secondary market trading in bonds takes place over-the-counter?

18–7. What is an investment banker, and what major functions does he or she perform?

18–8. What is the major difference between a negotiated purchase and a competitive bid purchase?

18–9. Why is an investment banking syndicate formed?

18–10. Why might a large corporation want to raise long-term capital through a private placement rather than a public offering?

18–11. As a recent business school graduate, you work directly for the corporate treasurer. Your corporation is going to issue a new security and is concerned with the probable flotation costs. What tendencies about flotation costs can you relate to the treasurer?

18–12. You own a group of five clothing stores, all located in southern California. You are about to market $200,000 worth of new common stock. Your stock trades over-the-counter. The stock will be sold only to California residents. Your financial advisor informs you that the issue must be registered with the SEC. Is the advisor correct?

18–13. When corporations raise funds, what type of financing vehicle (instrument or instruments) is most favored?

18–14. What is the major (most significant) savings-surplus sector in the U.S. economy?

18–15. Identify three distinct ways that savings are ultimately transferred to business firms in need of cash.

CASE PROBLEM

In this chapter we study the Securities Exchange Act of 1934 and learn that this act enables the SEC to regulate insider trading. The following ethics case problem touches on some of the difficult areas of enforcement and definition that surround the insider trading concept.

PROFITING ON COLUMNS PRIOR TO PUBLICATION

In April 1984, R. Foster Winans, who wrote *The Wall Street Journal*'s highly influential stock-market column, "Heard on the Street," was fired from the paper after admitting to federal investigators that he had improperly taken advantage of his position. The thirty-six-year-old business analyst confirmed that he had leaked information about upcoming columns to associates who were able to profit from the information by buying or selling stock.

On May 17, the Securities and Exchange Commission charged Winans with violating federal law by failing to disclose to readers that he had financial interests in the securities he wrote about. Winans, whose tips about columns prior to publication helped two stockbrokers net about half a million dollars, also was charged with personally profiting from the material.

The basis of the charges was an SEC rule that prohibits anyone from omitting to state a material fact regarding the purchase or sale of securities. But applicability of the SEC rule to Winans's case is unclear. Professor of journalism Gilbert Cranberg phrases the ambiguity this way: "Is the ownership by a reporter of stock in a company about which he writes a 'material fact' to readers sufficient to require disclosure, or must the reporter also intend to profit from the story?"[1] Ambiguous or not, the SEC's action has convinced some legal scholars that the media must disclose the financial holdings of their financial analysts.

Even before the Winans case, some publications had formulated explicit policies designed to leave no doubt in reporters' minds about the impropriety of trading on knowledge of stories. For example, the *Washington Post* requires that all its financial and business reporters submit to their editors a confidential statement outlining their stock holdings. *Post* policy prohibits writers from either writing about companies in which they have an interest or buying stock in companies they have written about. *The New York Times* has a similar policy, and *Forbes* magazine and the *Chicago Tribune* require editorial employees to divulge their corporate investments. Ralph Schulz, senior vice president at McGraw-Hill's publication unit, says his company has a conflict-of-interest policy based on the premise that "nobody who writes about a company ought to own stock in it."[2] And *The Wall Street Journal*'s three-and-a-half-page conflict-of-interest policy warns employees against trading in companies immediately before or after a *Journal* piece on that company. The policy reads in part:

> It is not enough to be incorruptible and act with honest motives. It is equally important to use good judgment and conduct one's outside activities so that no one—management, our editors, an SEC investigator with power of subpoena, or a political critic of the company—has any grounds for even raising the suspicion that an employee misused a position with the company.[3]

But such written policies remain the exception, as shown by an informal survey of the country's media conducted by *The Wall Street Journal*. Although many newspapers have formal dress codes, few have formal rules about stock trading. Moreover, few news executives show any concern about insider trading by noneditorial employees, although sensitive investigative reports generally are accessible to any employee in the newsroom.

The Wall Street Journal survey also reveals general indifference among media executives to stock trading by subjects of interviews, as in the case of G. D. Searle & Co. Early in 1984, the SEC began investigating unusual activity in options on that company's stock just before the mid-January "CBS Evening News" report that raised questions about NutraSweet, Searle's new low-calorie sweetener. The SEC charged that an Arizona scientist interviewed by CBS for the report bought "put" options in Searle's NutraSweet before the story aired, convinced that the stock would tumble as a result of negative comments by himself and others. "I honestly believe I had a right to do it," says the Arizona scientist. He adds, "I don't think it's unethical. It's the American way."[4] The scientist's lawyer and some CBS employees also were targets of the SEC investigation.

Syndicated financial columnist Dan Dorman admits that his stories may affect the price of stocks, and by implication, shrewd subjects of interviews could stand to benefit on the stories. But he doesn't think there's anything he can do about that. "It's not my job to police," Dorman says. "My job is to get information."[5]

John G. Craig, Jr., editor of the *Pittsburg Post Gazette*, agrees. In his view, preventing sources from trading on an article "is an ethical responsibility a newspaper can't assume."[6]

And yet James Michaels, the editor of *Forbes*, recalls once holding out a story when he learned that one of the sources had sold stock short, betting the article would have a negative impact. And *The Wall Street Journal* admits to killing stories upon learning that investors were using their knowledge of it to wheel and deal on Wall Street.

---

[1]Gilbert Cranberg, "*Wall Street Journal* Case Could Bring Overreaction," *Los Angeles Times*, June 4, 1984, p. II-5.

[2]See "Media Policies Vary on Preventing Employees and Others from Profiting on Knowledge of Future Business Stories," *Wall Street Journal*, March 2, 1984, p. 8.

[3]Ibid.

[4]"Market Leaks: Illegal Insider Trading Seems to Be on Rise," *Wall Street Journal*, March 2, 1984, p. 8.

[5]"Media Policies," *Wall Street Journal*, p. 8.

[6]Ibid.

In the meantime, the government pressed its case against R. Foster Winans. In September 1984, the Justice Department brought a sixty-one-count indictment for fraud and conspiracy against him and two alleged collaborators. Among other things, the indictment charged that, in the first half of 1983, Winans and his roommate speculated on stocks about to be mentioned in forthcoming columns. They made about a $3,000 profit on a $3,000 investment.[7] Although Winans describes his role in these deals as "stupid" and "wrong," he denies he broke any law. After a long and technical legal battle, the Supreme Court in November 1987 upheld the Justice Department's contention that what he did was not just imprudent but criminal.

Professor Cranberg fears that the Winans case may ultimately make bad law. Although he thinks that the time has come for reporters and editors to report outside compensation and financial interests, he worries that the SEC and the courts may equate business-news reporters with investment advisers and, as a result, wield undue influence on the press.

Cranberg fears that such a development not only threatens freedom of the press but would have a chilling effect on press coverage of corporate America. "Not every problem has, or should have, a legal solution," Cranberg points out. "Most problems involving the press are best handled by voluntary measures. The way for the press to show that it can keep its house in order is to do it. More actions and less self-satisfied ridicule of concern about conflicts of interest would be signs that the press can and will."[8]

Michael Missal, a lawyer for the SEC, thinks such fears are unfounded. "We don't expect every journalist to disclose all financial relationships," he says. Instead, the government wishes to prevent profiteering on advance knowledge of stories. That, Missal says, is what the Winans case is all about.[9]

QUESTIONS

1. In your opinion, did Winans engage in insider trading? Did he do something wrong?

2. Do you believe that media financial analysts should disclose to their audience any financial interests they have in the securities they write about? Do you think they should be required to make such disclosures? If so, should the requirement take the form of an institutional policy, law, or both?

3. Would you say that, as long as reporters do not intend to profit from their stories, they cannot and should not be held guilty of insider trading? Or do you think that a reporter can engage in insider trading even if he or she does not intend to profit personally?

4. Do you think that McGraw-Hill's policy—that "nobody who writes about a company ought to own stock in it"—is fair? Or do you think it is an unreasonable encroachment on the employee's right to profit through investments?

5. Do you agree that the Arizona scientist had a "right" to trade on the information before it was broadcast?

6. Under what circumstances does a company have a right to know about the financial investments of its employees?

[7]See William A. Henry III, "Impropriety or Criminality?" *Time*, September 10, 1984, p. 45.

[8]Cranberg, "Case Could Bring Overreaction," p. 5.

[9]Henry, "Impropriety or Criminality?" p. 43.

Adapted by permission from William Shaw and Vincent Barry, *Moral Issues in Business*, 5th ed., pp. 384–86. © 1992 by Wadsworth Inc.

CHAPTER *19*

Term Loans and Leases

Term Loans • Leases

For discussion purposes we generally categorize the sources of financing available to the business firm into three groups, distinguished on the basis of the maturity of the financing agreement. These maturities are not exact but represent generally accepted guidelines for categorizing sources of financing. Short-term sources of financing, which have a maturity of 1 year or less, were discussed in Chapter 17. Intermediate-term financing, which includes all financing arrangements whose final maturities are longer than 1 year but no longer than 10 years, is the subject of this chapter. Long-term financing, which is defined as all forms of financing with final maturities longer than 10 years, is discussed in Chapters 20 and 21.

The principal sources of intermediate-term financing include term loans and leases. We will look first at the primary sources of term loans and their characteristics. Then we will discuss lease financing including the types of leasing arrangements, the accounting treatment of financial leases, the lease versus purchase decision, and the potential benefits from leasing.

Term Loans

Term loans generally share three common characteristics: They (1) have maturities of 1 to 10 years, (2) are repaid in periodic installments (such as quarterly, semiannual, or annual payments) over the life of the loan, and (3) are usually secured by a chattel mortgage on equipment or a mortgage on real property. The principal suppliers of term credit are commercial banks, insurance companies, and to a lesser extent pension funds.

We will consider briefly some of the more common characteristics of term loan agreements.

Maturities

Commercial banks generally restrict their term lending to 1- to 5-year maturities. Insurance companies and pension funds with their longer-term liabilities generally make loans with 5- to 15-year maturities. Thus, the term lending activities of commercial banks actually complement rather than compete with those of insurance companies and pension funds. In fact, commercial banks very often cooperate with both insurance companies and pension funds in providing term financing for very large loans.

Collateral

Term loans are generally always backed by some form of collateral. Shorter-maturity loans are frequently secured with a *chattel mortgage,* or a mortgage on machinery and equipment, or with securities such as stocks and bonds. Longer-maturity loans are frequently secured by mortgages on real estate.

Restrictive Covenants

In addition to requiring collateral, the lender in a term loan agreement often places restrictions on the borrower that, when violated, make the loan immediately due and payable. These restrictive covenants are designed to prohibit the borrower from engaging in any activities that would increase the likelihood of loss on the loan. Some common restrictions are discussed subsequently.

1. **Working-capital requirement.** This restriction requires that the borrower maintain a minimum amount of working capital. Very often this restriction takes the form of a minimum current ratio, such as 2 to 1 or 3½ to 1, or a minimum dollar amount of net working capital. The actual requirement would reflect the norm for the borrower's industry, as well as the lender's desires.

2. **Additional borrowing.** Generally this type of restriction requires the lender's approval before any additional debt can be issued. Furthermore, a restriction on additional borrowing is often extended to long-term lease agreements, which are discussed later in this chapter.

3. **Periodic financial statements.** A standard covenant in most term loan agreements includes a requirement that the borrower supply the lender with financial statements on a regular basis. These generally include annual or quarterly income statements and balance sheets.

4. **Management.** Term loan agreements sometimes include a provision that requires prior approval by the lender of major personnel changes. In addition, the borrower may be required to insure the lives of certain key personnel, naming the lender as beneficiary.

We have presented only a partial listing of restrictions commonly found in term loan agreements. The number and form of such provisions are limited only by legality and the imagination of the parties involved. It should be noted, however, that restrictive covenants are subject to negotiation. The specific agreement that results reflects the relative bargaining strengths of the borrower and lender. Marginal borrowers are more likely to find their loan agreements burdened with restrictive covenants than more creditworthy borrowers.

Term loan agreements can be very technical and are generally tailored to the situation. Therefore, it is difficult to generalize about their content. However, many banks rely on *worksheets* or *checksheets* to aid in the preparation of the document.

Repayment Schedules

Term loans are generally repaid with periodic installments, which include both an interest and a principal component. Thus, the loan is repaid over its life with equal annual, semiannual, or quarterly payments.

To illustrate how the repayment procedure works, let us assume that a firm borrows $15,000, which is to be repaid in five annual installments. The loan will carry an 8 percent rate of interest, and payments will be made at the end of each of the next five years. The following diagram shows the cash flows to the lender:

| Year | | | | | |
0	1	2	3	4	5
$(15,000)	A_1	A_2	A_3	A_4	A_5

The $15,000 cash flow at period zero is placed in parentheses to indicate an outflow of cash by the lender, whereas the annual installments, A_1 through A_5, represent cash inflows (of course, the opposite is true for the borrower). The lender must determine the annual installments that will give an 8 percent return on the outstanding balance over the life of the loan. This problem is very similar to the internal rate of return problem encountered in Chapter 6, where we discussed capital-budgeting decisions. There we had to determine the rate of interest that would make the present value of a stream of future cash flows equal to some present sum. Here we want to determine the future cash flows whose present value, when discounted at 8 percent, is equal to the $15,000 loan amount. Thus, we must solve for those values of A_1 through A_5 whose present value when discounted at 8 percent is $15,000. In equation form,

$$\$15,000 = \sum_{t=1}^{5} \frac{A_t}{(1 + .08)^t} \tag{19-1}$$

Where we assume equal annual installments, A, for all 5 years, we can solve for A as follows:

$$\$15,000 = A \sum_{t=1}^{5} \frac{1}{(1 + .08)^t}$$

Thus,

$$A = \frac{\$15,000}{\sum_{t=1}^{5} \frac{1}{(1 + .08)^t}} \tag{19-2}$$

The term as it is divided into the $15,000 loan functions as the present value factor for a five-year annuity carrying an 8 percent rate of interest. Thus,

$$A = \frac{\$15,000}{3.993} = \$3756.57$$

Therefore, if the borrower makes payments of $3,756.57 each year, then the lender will receive an 8 percent return on the outstanding loan balance. To verify this assertion, check Table 19-1, which contains the principal and interest components of the annual loan payments. We see that the $3,756.57 installments truly provide the lender with an 8 percent return on the outstanding balance of a $15,000 loan.

TABLE 19–1.
Term Loan Amortization
Schedule

End of Year t	Installment Payment[a] A	Interest[b] I_t	Principal Repayment[c] P_t	Remaining Balance[d] RB_t
0	—	—	—	$15,000.00
1	$3,756.57	$1,200.00	$2,556.57	12,443.43
2	3,756.57	995.47	2,761.10	9,682.33
3	3,756.57	774.59	2,981.98	6,700.35
4	3,756.57	536.03	3,220.54	3,479.81
5	3,756.57	278.38	3,478.19	1.62[e]

[a]The annual installment payment, A, is found as follows:

$$A = \frac{\$15,000}{\sum_{t=1}^{5} \frac{1}{(1 + .08)^t}} = \$3756.57$$

[b]Annual interest expense is equal to 8 percent of the outstanding loan balance. Thus, for year 1 the interest expense, I_1, is found as follows:

$$I_1 = .08(\$15,000) = \$1200$$

[c]Principal repayment for year t, P_t, is the difference in the loan payment, A, and interest for the year. Thus, for year 1 we compute

$$P_1 = A - I_1 = \$3756.57 - \$1200 = \$2556.57$$

[d]The remaining balance of the end of year 1, RB_1, is the difference in the remaining balance for the previous year, RB_0, and the principal payment in year 1, P_1. Thus, at the end of year 1,

$$RB_1 = RB_0 - P_1 = \$15,000 - \$2556.57 = \$12,443.43$$

[e]The $1.62 difference in RB_4 and P_5 is due to rounding error.

Loan Participations among Banks

The demand for loans is not evenly dispersed across banks; heavier demand is placed on large money center banks and banks in regions of the country that are experiencing strong economic growth. This frequently means that these banks cannot provide all the necessary funds, so they share the loan demand with one or more participating banks. This shared lending has grown rapidly in recent years and has served to promote the flow of funds from banks with excess lending capacity to those with excess loan demand. The participating banks work out an agreement and receive a certificate of participation, which states that the lead bank will pay a portion of the loan cash flows as they are received.

Eurodollar Loans

Eurodollar loans are intermediate term loans made by major international banks to businesses based on foreign deposits that are denominated in dollars. These loans are generally made in amounts ranging from $1 million to $1.5 billion with the rate based on a certain amount above the London Interbank Offered Rate (LIBOR). The rate on these loans is adjusted periodically (generally every six months), and there is a wide range of maturities. Eurodollar lending has become a major source of commercial lending with the total volume of lending being measured in trillions of dollars.[1]

Perspective in Finance

Leasing provides an alternative to buying an asset to acquire its services. Although some leases involve maturities of more than 10 years, most do not. Thus, lease financing is classified as a source of intermediate term credit. Today, virtually any type of asset can be acquired through a lease agreement. The recent growth in lease financing has been phenomenal, with more than $200 billion in assets (based on original cost) now under lease in the United States.

[1]For a description of the workings of the Eurodollar market see E. W. Reed, R. V. Cotter, E. K. Gill, and R. K. Smith, *Commercial Banking*, 3rd ed. (Englewood Cliffs, NJ: Prentice Hall, 1984).

Leases

We begin our discussion by defining the major types of lease arrangements. Next we briefly renew the history and describe the present practice of the accounting treatment of leases. We examine the lease versus purchase decision, and we conclude by investigating the potential benefits of leasing.

Types of Lease Arrangements

There are three major types of lease agreements: direct leasing, sale and leaseback, and leveraged leasing. Most lease agreements fall into one of these categories. However, the particular lease agreement can take one of two forms. (1) The **financial lease** constitutes a noncancelable contractual commitment on the part of the firm leasing the asset (the lessee) to make a series of payments to the firm that actually owns the asset (the lessor) for use of the asset. (2) The **operating lease** differs from the financial lease only with respect to its cancelability. An operating lease can be canceled after proper notice to the lessor any time during its term. Thus, operating leases are by their very nature sources of short-term financing. The balance of this chapter is concerned with the financial lease, which provides the firm with a form of intermediate-term financing most comparable with debt financing.

Direct Leasing

In a *direct lease* the firm acquires the services of an asset it did not previously own. Direct leasing is available through several financial institutions including manufacturers, banks, finance companies, independent leasing companies, and special-purpose leasing companies.[2] In the lease arrangement, the lessor purchases the asset and leases it to the lessee. In the case of the manufacturer lessor, however, the acquisition step is not necessary.

Sale and Leaseback

A **sale and leaseback arrangement** arises when a firm sells land, buildings, or equipment that it already owns to a lessor and simultaneously enters into an agreement to lease the property back for a specified period under specific terms. The lessor involved in the sale and leaseback varies with the nature of the property involved and the lease period. When land is involved and the corresponding lease is long term, the lessor is generally a life insurance company. If the property consists of machinery and equipment, then the maturity of the lease will probably be intermediate term, and the lessor could be an insurance company, commercial bank, or leasing company.

The lessee firm receives cash in the amount of the sales price of the assets sold and the use of the asset over the term of the lease. In return, the lessee must make periodic rental payments through the term of the lease and give up any salvage or residual value to the lessor.

Net and Net-Net Leases

In the jargon of the leasing industry, a financial lease can take one of two basic forms: a **net lease** or a **net-net lease.** In a net lease agreement the lessee firm assumes the risk and burden of ownership over the term of the lease. That is, the lessee must maintain the asset, as well as pay insurance and taxes on the asset. A net-net lease requires that the lessee meet all the requirements of the net lease

---

[2]Many leasing companies specialize in the leasing of a single type of asset. For example, several firms lease computers exclusively, and others lease only automobiles.

as well as return the asset, still worth a *preestablished value,* to the lessor at the end of the lease term.

Leveraged Leasing

In the leasing arrangements discussed thus far only two participants have been identified: the lessor and lessee. In **leveraged leasing** a third participant is added. The added party is the lender who helps finance the acquisition of the asset to be leased. From the viewpoint of the lessee there is no difference in a leveraged lease, direct lease, or sale and leaseback arrangement. However, with a leveraged lease the method of financing used by the lessor in acquiring the asset receives specific consideration. The lessor generally supplies equity funds up to 20 to 30 percent of the purchase price and borrows the remainder from a third-party lender, which may be a commercial bank or insurance company. In some arrangements the lessor firm sells bonds, which are guaranteed by the lessee. This guarantee serves to reduce the risk and thus the cost of the debt. The majority of financial leases are leveraged leases.

Accounting for Leases

Before January 1977 most financial leases were not included in the balance sheets of lessee firms. Instead, they were reported in the footnotes to the balance sheet.[3] However, in November 1976 the Financial Accounting Standards Board reversed its position with *Statement of Financial Accounting Standards No. 13,* "Accounting for Leases."[4] The board adopted the position that the economic effect of the transaction should govern its accounting treatment.[5] In this regard, the FASB asserted that "a lease that transfers substantially all the benefits and risks incident to the ownership of property should be accounted for as the acquisition of an asset and the incurrence of an obligation by the lessee."[6] Specifically, Statement No. 13 requires that any lease that meets one or more of the following criteria is a **capital lease** and must be included in the body of the balance sheet of the lessee. All other lease agreements are classified as **operating leases** for accounting purposes. In a capital lease

1. The lease transfers ownership of the property to the lessee by the end of the lease term.
2. The lease contains a bargain repurchase option.
3. The lease term is equal to 75 percent or more of the estimated economic life of the leased property.
4. The present value of the minimum lease payments equals or exceeds 90 percent of the excess of the fair value of the property over any related investment tax credit retained by the lessor.[7]

---

[3]Before January 1977 the guiding accounting principles regarding the treatment of leases were *Opinion No. 5* and *Opinion No. 31* of the Accounting Principles Board (APB). Opinion No. 5 stated that only in the case in which a lease "is in substance a purchase" should an asset and a liability appear on the lessee's balance sheet. In response to requests from various groups of statement users, the APB expanded its disclosure requirements in *Opinion No. 31.* See American Institute of Certified Public Accountants (AICPA), *Accounting Principles Board Opinion No. 5,* "Reporting of Leases in Financial Statements of Lessee" (New York: AICPA, September 1964), and *Accounting Principles Board Opinion No. 31,* "Disclosure of Lease Commitments by Lessees" (New York: AICPA, June 1973). Finally, FASB Standard No. 98, "Accounting for Leases: Sale-Leaseback Involving Real Estate, Sales-Type Leases of Real Estate, Definition of the Lease Term, and Initial Direct Costs of Direct Financing Leases," appeared in May 1988.

[4]Financial Accounting Standards Board, *Statement of Accounting Standards No. 13,* "Accounting for Leases" (Stamford, CT: FASB, November 1976).

[5]Ibid., p. 49.

[6]Ibid.

[7]Ibid., pp. 9–10.

Assets	
Current assets	$14
Plant and equipment	20
Leased property (capital leases)	4
Total	$38
Liabilities and stockholders' equity	
Current liabilities	8
Long-term debt	9
Capital lease obligations	4
Stockholders' equity	17
Total	$38

The last two requirements are the most stringent elements in the board's statement. The first two have been applicable to most leases for many years because of the Internal Revenue Service's "true" lease requirements.[8] However, the last two apply to most financial leases written in the United States. As a result, the board now requires capitalization of all leases meeting one or more of these criteria.

Figure 19–1 is a sample balance sheet for the Alpha Mfg. Company. Alpha has entered into capital leases whose payments have a present value of $4 million.

Note that the asset "leased property" is matched by a liability, "capital lease obligations." The specific entries recorded for the lease obligation equal the present value of minimum lease payments the firm must pay over the term of the lease. The discount rate used is the lower of either the lessee's incremental borrowing rate or the lessor's implicit interest rate (where that rate can be determined).

Operating leases are not disclosed in the body of the balance sheet. Instead, these lease obligations must be reported in a footnote to the balance sheet.

The Lease versus Purchase Decision

The lease versus purchase decision is a hybrid capital-budgeting problem that forces the analyst to consider the consequences of alternative forms of financing on the investment decision. When we discussed capital budgeting in Chapter 6 and the cost of capital in Chapter 8, we assumed that all new financing would be undertaken in accordance with the firm's optimal capital structure. When analyzing an asset that is to be leased, the analysis must be altered to consider financing through leasing as opposed to the use of the more traditional debt and equity sources of funds. Thus, the lease versus purchase decision requires a standard capital-budgeting type of analysis, as well as an analysis of two alternative financing *packages*. The lease–purchase decision involves the analysis of two basic issues.

1. Should the asset be purchased using the firm's optimal financing mix?
2. Should the asset be financed using a financial lease?

The answer to the first question can be obtained through an analysis of the project's *NPV* following the method laid out in Chapter 6. However, regardless

---

[8]The Economic Recovery Tax Act of 1981 effectively suspended the true lease requirements of Rev. Rul. 55–540, 1955 C.B. 41; however, these changes were largely reversed by the Tax Equity and Fiscal Responsibility Act of 1982. This act did create a "finance lease," which for tax purposes is classified as a lease. However, unlike the true lease requirements of the pre-ERTA, a finance lease *can* include a purchase option (equal to a minimum of 10 percent of the original purchase price of the leased asset), and it *can* be used to finance "limited use" property (property that can only be used by the lessee).

of whether the asset should or should not be purchased, it may be advantageous for the firm to lease it. That is, the cost savings accruing through leasing might be great enough to offset a negative net present value resulting from the purchase of an asset. For example, the Alpha Mfg. Co. is considering the acquisition of a new computer-based inventory and payroll system. The computed net present value of the new system based on normal purchase financing is −$40, indicating that acquisition of the system through purchasing or ownership is not warranted. However, an analysis of the cost savings resulting from leasing the system (referred to here as the *net advantage of leasing—NAL*) indicates that the lease alternative will produce a present value cost saving of $60 over normal purchase financing. Therefore, the net present value of the system if leased is $20 (the net present value if leased equals the *NPV* of a purchase *plus* the net advantage of leasing, or − $40 + $60). Thus, the system's services should be acquired via the lease agreement.

In the pages that follow we will (1) review briefly the concept of a project's net present value, which we will refer to as the *net present value of purchase*, or *NPV(P)*; (2) introduce a model for estimating the net present value advantage of leasing over normal purchase financing, which we will refer to as the *net advantage of lease financing*, or *NAL*; (3) present a flow chart that can be used in performing lease–purchase analyses based on *NPV(P)* and *NAL*; and (4) provide a comprehensive example of a lease–purchase analysis.

The Lease–Purchase Algorithm

Answers to both questions posed above can be obtained using the two equations found in Table 19–2. The first equation is simply the net present value of purchasing the proposed project, discussed in Chapter 6. The second equation calculates the net present value advantage of leasing. *NAL* represents an accumulation of the cash flows (both inflows and outflows) associated with leasing *as opposed* to purchasing the asset. Specifically, through leasing the firm avoids certain operating expenses, O_t, but incurs the after-tax rental expense, $R_t(1 - T)$. By leasing, furthermore, the firm loses the tax-deductible expense associated with interest, $T \cdot I_t$, and depreciation, $T \cdot D_t$. Finally, the firm does not receive the salvage value from the asset, V_n, if it is leased, but it does not have to make the initial cash outlay to purchase the asset, IO. Thus, *NAL* reflects the cost savings associated with leasing, net of the opportunity costs of not purchasing.

Note that the before-tax cost of new debt is used to discount the *NAL* cash flows other than the salvage value, V_n. This is justified because the affected cash flows are very nearly riskless and certainly no more risky than the interest and principal accruing to the firm's creditors (which underlie the rate of interest charged to the firm for its debt).[9] Because V_n is not a risk-free cash flow but depends on the market price for the leased asset in year n, a rate higher than r is appropriate. Because the salvage value of the leased asset was discounted using the cost of capital when determining *NPV(P)*, we use this rate here when calculating *NAL*.

---

[9]The argument for using the firm's borrowing rate to discount these tax shelters goes as follows: The tax shields are relatively free of risk in that their source (depreciation, interest, rental payments) can be estimated with a high degree of certainty. There are, however, two sources of uncertainty regarding these tax shelters: (1) the possibility of a change in the firm's tax rate and (2) the possibility that the firm might become bankrupt at some future date. If we attach a very low probability to the likelihood of a reduction in the tax rate, then the prime risk associated with these tax shelters is the possibility of bankruptcy wherein they would be lost forever (certainly, all tax shelters after the date of bankruptcy would be lost). We now note that the firm's creditors also faced the risk of the firm's bankruptcy when they lent the firm funds at the rate r. If this rate, r, reflects the market's assessment of the firm's bankruptcy potential as well as the time value of money, then it offers an appropriate rate for discounting the interest shelters generated by the firm. Note also that the O_t cash flows are generally estimated with a high degree of certainty (in the case in which they represent insurance premiums they may be contractually set) such that r is appropriate as a discount rate here also. Of course, r is adjusted for taxes to discount the after-tax cash flows.

TABLE 19–2.
Lease–Purchase Model

Equation One—Net present value of purchase *[NPV(P)]*:

$$NPV(P) = \sum_{t=1}^{n} \frac{ACF_t}{(1 + K)^t} - IO \qquad (19\text{--}3)$$

where ACF_t = the annual after-tax cash flow in period t resulting from the asset's purchase (note that ACF_n also includes any after-tax salvage value expected from the project).

K = the firm's cost of capital applicable to the project being analyzed and the particular mix of financing used to acquire the project.

IO = the initial cash outlay required to purchase the asset in period zero (now).

n = the productive life of the project.

Equation Two—Net Advantage of Leasing *(NAL)*:

$$NAL = \sum_{t=1}^{n} \frac{O_t(1 - T) - R_t(1 - T) - T \cdot I_t - T \cdot D_t}{(1 + r_b)^t} - \frac{V_n}{(1 + K_s)^n} + IO \qquad (19\text{--}4)$$

where O_t = any operating cash flows incurred in period t that are incurred only when the asset is purchased. Most often this consists of maintenance expenses and insurance that would be paid by the lessor.

R_t = the annual rental for period t.

T = the marginal tax rate on corporate income.

I_t = the tax-deductible interest expense forfeited in period t if the lease option is adopted. This represents the interest expense on a loan equal to the full purchase price of the asset being acquired.[a]

D_t = depreciation expense in period t for the asset.

V_n = the after-tax salvage value of the asset expected in year n.

K_s = the discount rate used to find the present value of V_n. This rate should reflect the risk inherent in the estimated V_n. For simplicity the after-tax cost of capital (K) is often used as a proxy for this rate. Also, note that this rate is the same one used to discount the salvage value in $NPV(P)$.

IO = the purchase price of the asset, which is not paid by the firm in the event the asset is leased.

r_b = the after-tax rate of interest on borrowed funds (i.e., $r_b = r (1 - T)$ where r is the before-tax borrowing rate for the firm). This rate is used to discount the relatively certain after-tax cash flow savings that accrue through the leasing of the asset.

[a]This analysis makes the implicit assumption that a dollar of lease financing is equivalent to a dollar of loan. This form of equivalence is only one of several that might be used. The interested reader is referred to A. H. Ofer, "The Evaluation of the Lease Versus Purchase Alternatives," *Financial Management* 5 (Summer 1976), pp. 67–74.

Figure 19–2 contains a flow chart that can be used in performing lease–purchase analyses. The analyst first calculates *NPV(P)*. If the project's net present value is positive, then the left-hand branch of Figure 19–2 should be followed. Tracing through the left branch we now compute *NAL*. If *NAL* is positive, the lease alternative offers a positive present-value cost advantage over normal purchase financing, and the asset should be leased. Should *NAL* be negative, then the purchase alternative should be selected. Return to the top of Figure 19–2 once again. This time we assume that *NPV(P)* is negative, and the analyst's attention is directed to the right-hand side of the flow chart. The only hope for the project's acceptance at this point is a favorable set of lease terms. In this circumstance the project would be acceptable and thus leased *only* if *NAL* were large enough to offset the negative *NPV(P)* (i.e., where *NAL* was greater than the absolute value of *NPV[P]* or, equivalently, where *NAL* + *NPV[P]* ≥ 0).[10]

Case Problem in Lease–Purchase Analysis

The Waynesboro Plastic Molding Company (WPM) is now deciding whether to purchase an automatic casting machine. The machine will cost $15,000 and for tax purposes will be depreciated toward a zero salvage value over a five-year

---

[10]That is, *NAL* = *NPV(L)* − *NPV(P)*, where *NPV(L)* is the net present value of the asset if leased. Thus, the sum of *NPV(P)* and *NAL* is the net present value of the asset if leased. See Lawrence D. Schall, "The Lease-or-Buy and Asset Acquisition Decisions," *Journal of Finance* 29 (September 1974), pp. 1203–14, for a development of net present value of leasing and purchasing equations.

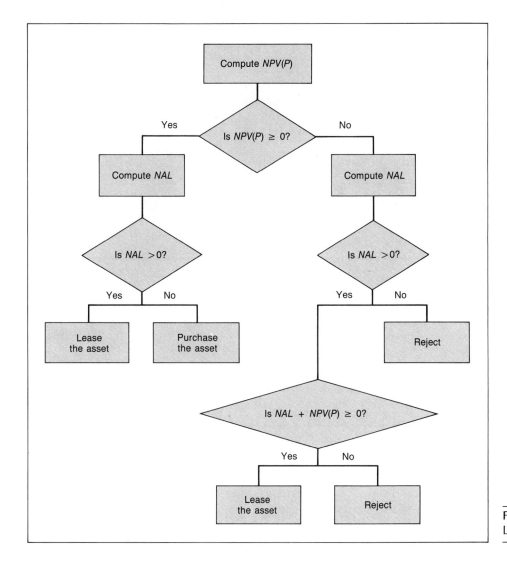

FIGURE 19–2.
Lease–Purchase Analysis

period. However, at the end of five years the machine actually has an expected salvage value of $2,100. Because the machine is depreciated toward a zero book value at the end of five years, the salvage value is fully taxable at the firm's marginal tax rate of 50 percent. Hence, the after-tax salvage value of the machine is only $1,050.[11] The firm uses the straight-line depreciation method to depreciate the $15,000 asset toward a zero salvage value. Furthermore, the project is expected to generate annual cash revenues of $5,000 per year over the next five years (net of cash operating expenses but before depreciation and taxes). For projects of this type WPM has a target debt ratio of 40 percent that is impounded in its after-tax cost-of-capital estimate of 12 percent. Finally, WPM can borrow funds at a before-tax rate of 8 percent.

Step 1: Computing NPV(P)—Should the Asset Be Purchased? The first step in analyzing the lease–purchase problem involves computing the net present value under the purchase alternative. The relevant cash flow computations are presented in Table 19–3.

The *NPV(P)* is found by discounting the annual cash flows *(ACFₜ)* in Table 19–3 back to the present at the firm's after-tax cost of capital of 12 percent, adding this sum to the present value of the salvage value, and subtracting the initial cash

---

[11]The problem example is a modification of the well-known example from R. W. Johnson and W. G. Lewellen, "Analysis of the Lease-or-Buy Decision," *Journal of Finance* 27 (September 1972), pp. 815–23.

TABLE 19-3.
Computing Project Annual After-Tax Cash Flows (ACF_t) Associated with Asset Purchase

| | Year | | | | | | | | | |
| | 1 | | 2 | | 3 | | 4 | | 5 | |
	Book Profits	Cash Flow	Book Profits	Cash Flow	Book Profits	Cash Flow	Book Profits	Cash Flow	Book Profits	Cash Flow
Annual cash revenues	$5000	$5000	$5000	$5000	$5000	$5000	$5000	$5000	$5000	$5000
Less: depreciation	(3000)	—	(3000)	—	(3000)	—	(3000)	—	(3000)	—
Net revenues before taxes	$2000	$5000	$2000	$5000	$2000	$5000	$2000	$5000	$2000	$5000
Less: taxes (50%)	(1000) →	(1000)	(1000) →	(1000)	(1000) →	(1000)	(1000) →	(1000)	(1000) →	(1000)
Annual after-tax cash flow		$4000		$4000		$4000		$4000		$4000

TABLE 19-4.
Calculating NPV(P)

Year t	Annual Cash Flow ACF_t	Discount Factor for 12 Percent	Present Value
1	$4000	.893	$3572
2	4000	.797	3188
3	4000	.712	2848
4	4000	.636	2544
5	4000	.567	2268
5 (Salvage — V_n)	1050	.567	595.35

Present value of ACFs and V_n = $15,015.35

NPV(P) = $15,015.35 − $15,000 = $ 15.35

outlay. These calculations are shown in Table 19–4. The project's *NPV(P)* is a positive $15.35, indicating that the asset should be acquired.

The second question concerns whether the asset should be leased. This can be answered by considering the net advantage to leasing *(NAL)*.

Step 2: Computing NAL—Should the Asset Be Leased? The computation of *NAL* is shown in Table 19–5. The resulting *NAL* is a negative $(1,121), which indicates that leasing is not preferred to the normal debt–equity method of financing. In fact, WPM will be $(1,121) worse off, in present value terms, if it chooses to lease rather than purchase the asset.

Calculating *NAL* involves solving equation (19–4) presented earlier in Table 19–2. To do this, we first estimate all those cash flows that are to be discounted at the firm's after-tax cost of debt, r_b. These include $o_t(1 − T)$, $R_t(1 − T)$, $l_t \cdot T$, and $T \cdot D_t$.

The operating expenses associated with the asset that will be paid by the lessor if we lease—that is, the O_t—generally consist of certain maintenance expenses and insurance. WPM estimates them to be $1,000 per year over the life of the project. The annual rental or lease payments, R_t, are given and equal $4,200.

The interest tax shelter lost because the asset is leased and not purchased must now be estimated. This tax shelter is lost because the firm does not borrow any money if it enters into the lease agreement. Table 19–1 contains the principal and interest components for a 5-year $15,000 loan. Note that the interest column supplies the needed information for the interest tax shelter that is lost if the asset is leased, I_t.[12]

---

[12]Technically the firm does not lose the interest tax shelter on a $15,000 loan if it leases. In fact, the firm would lose the tax shelter on only that portion of the $15,000 purchase price that it would have financed by borrowing, for example, 40 percent of the $15,000 investment, or $6,000. However, if the firm leases the $15,000 asset, it has effectively used 100 percent levered (nonowner) financing. This means that the leasing of this project uses not only its 40 percent allotment of levered (debt) financing, but an additional 60 percent as well. Thus, by leasing the $15,000 asset the lessee forfeits the interest tax shelter on a 40 percent or $6,000 loan plus an additional 60 percent of the $15,000 purchase price, or an additional $9,000 loan. In total, leasing has caused the firm to forgo the interest tax savings on a loan equal to 100 percent of the leased asset's purchase price. Once again, we note that this analysis presumes $1 of lease financing is equivalent to $1 of loan financing. See footnote *a* to Table 19–2.

TABLE 19-5.
Computing *NAL*

Overview: To solve for *NAL* we use equation (19-4), which was discussed in Table 19-2. This equation contains three terms and is repeated below for convenience.

$$NAL = \sum_{t=1}^{n} \frac{O_t(1-T) - R_t(1-T) - I_t \cdot T - D_t \cdot T}{(1+r_b)^t} - \frac{V_n}{(1+K_s)^n} + IO$$

Term 1   Term 2   Term 3

Step 1: Solving for Term 1 = $\sum_{t=1}^{n} \dfrac{O_t(1-T) - R_t(1-T) - I_t \cdot T - D_t \cdot T}{(1+r_b)^t}$

Year t	After-Tax Operating Expenses Paid by Lessor[a] $O_t(1-T)$	−	After-Tax Rental Expense[b] $R_t(1-T)$	−	Tax Shelter on Loan Interest[c] I_tT	−	Tax Shelter on Deprecia- tion[d] D_tT	=	Sum	×	Discount Factor[e] DF	=	Present Value PV
1	$500		$2100		$600		$1500		−$3700		.962		−$3,558
2	500		2100		498		1500		−3598		.925		−3,326
3	500		2100		387		1500		−3487		.889		−3,100
4	500		2100		268		1500		−3368		.855		−2,879
5	500		2100		140		1500		−3240		.822		−2,662

−15,525

Step 2: Solving for term 2 = $-\left[\dfrac{V_n}{(1+K)^n}\right] = -\dfrac{\$1050}{(1+.12)^5} \times -\$1050 \times .567^f =$ −596

Step 3: Term 3 = *IO* $15,000

Step 4: Calculate *NAL* = − $13,961 − $595 + $15,000 =   −$1,121

[a]After-tax lessor-paid operating expenses are found by $O_t(1-T) = \$1000(1-.5) = \$500$.
[b]After-tax rent expense for year 1 is computed as follows: $R_t(1-T) = \$4200(1-.5) = \$2100$.
[c]Interest expense figures were calculated in Table 18-1 for a $15,000 loan. For year 1 the interest tax shelter is $0.5 \times \$1200 = \$600$.
[d]The tax shelter from depreciation is found as follows: $D_1T = \$3000 \times 0.5 = \$1500$.
[e]Based on the after-tax borrowing rate, i.e., $.08(1-.5) = .04$.
[f]K_s was estimated to be the same as the firm's after-tax cost of capital, 12 percent.

The next step in calculating *NAL* involves finding the present value of the after-tax salvage value. Earlier when we computed *NPV(P)*, we found this to equal $15.35. Now, substituting the results of our calculations into equation (19-4) produces the *NAL* of $(1,121).

Note that the lease payments used in this example were made at the end of each year. In practice lease payments are generally made at the beginning of each year (i.e., they constitute an *annuity due* rather than an ordinary annuity as used here). The *NAL* for the example used here is even more negative if we assume beginning of year lease payments. That is, with beginning of year payments *NAL* = −$1,495. You can easily verify this result as follows: Note first that changing from a regular annuity to an annuity due affects only the first and last annuity payments. In this example this means that the first lease payment of $2,100 (after tax) is paid immediately such that its present value is $2,100. However, the final lease payment is now made at the beginning of year 5 (or at the end of year 4). The present value of the fifth year after-tax lease payment is therefore $2100 × .822 = $1,726. To summarize, by changing from a regular annuity set of lease payments to an annuity due, we must include a −$2,100 immediate cash flow at time *t* = 0, and we exchange this for the 5th year present-value after-tax lease payment of $1,726. Therefore, the *NAL* with annuity due lease payments is *NAL* (annuity due) = (1,121) + 1,726 − 2,100 = (1,495). Hence, if the lease payments are an annuity due, the asset should be purchased (because *NPV[P]* = $15.35) and not leased (because *NAL* = −$1,495).

To summarize the lease-purchase analysis: First the project's net present value was computed. This analysis produced a positive *NPV(P)* equal to $15.35, which indicated that the asset should be acquired. On computing the net advantage to leasing, we found that the financial lease was not the preferred method of financing the acquisition of the asset's services. Thus, the asset's services should be purchased using the firm's normal financing mix.

Potential Benefits from Leasing[13]

Several purported advantages have been associated with leasing as opposed to debt financing. These benefits include flexibility and convenience, lack of restrictions, avoiding the risk of obsolescence, conservation of working capital, 100 percent financing, tax savings, and availability of credit. However, before we discuss the relative merits of each purported advantage, let's review briefly the economic character of leasing and purchasing.

Figure 19–3 is a diagram that can be used to summarize the participants and transactions involved in leasing (the right-hand side of the figure) and purchasing (the left-hand side). In purchasing, the asset is financed via the sale of securities and the purchaser acquires title to the asset (including both the use and salvage value of the asset). In leasing, the lessee acquires the use value of the asset but uses the lessor as an *intermediary* to finance and purchase the asset. The key feature of leasing as opposed to purchasing is the interjection of a financial intermediary (the lessor) into the scheme used to acquire the asset's services. Thus, the basic question that arises in lease–purchase analysis is one of "Why does adding another financial intermediary (the lessor) save the lessee money?" Some of the traditional answers to this question are discussed subsequently. As you read through each, simply remember that the lessee is *hiring* the lessor to perform the functions associated with ownership that he or she would perform if the asset were purchased. Thus, for the lease to be "cheaper" than owning, the lessor must be able to perform these functions of

FIGURE 19–3.
Comparison of Purchasing with Simple Financial Lease Agreement

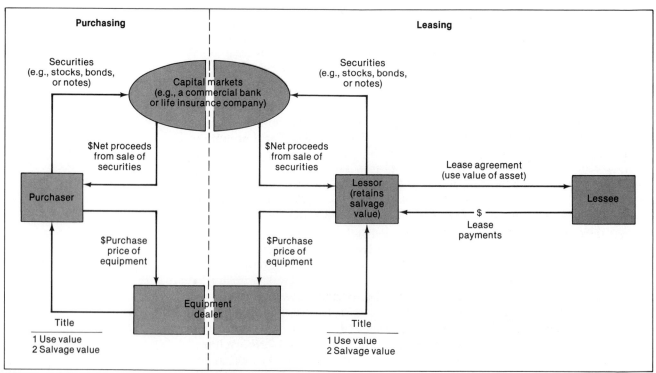

[13]The contributions of Paul F. Anderson in the preparation of this discussion are gratefully acknowledged.

ownership at a lower cost than the lessee could perform them, and be willing to pass these savings along to the lessee in the form of lower rental rates.

Flexibility and Convenience

A variety of potential benefits are often included under the rubric of flexibility and convenience. It is argued, for example, that leasing provides the firm with flexibility because it allows for piecemeal financing of relatively small asset acquisitions. Debt financing of such acquisitions can be costly and difficult to arrange. Leases, conversely, may be arranged more quickly and with less documentation.

Another flexibility argument notes that leasing may allow a division or subsidiary manager to acquire equipment without the approval of the corporate capital-budgeting committee. Depending on the firm, the manager may be able to avoid the time-consuming process of preparing and presenting a formal acquisition proposal.

A third flexibility advantage relates to the fact that some lease payment schedules may be structured to coincide with the revenues generated by the asset, or they may be timed to match seasonal fluctuations in a given industry. Thus, the firm is able to synchronize its lease payments with its cash cycle—an option rarely available with debt financing.

Arguments for the greater convenience of leasing take many forms. It is sometimes stated that leasing simplifies bookkeeping for tax purposes because it eliminates the need to prepare time-consuming depreciation tables and subsidiary fixed asset schedules. It is also pointed out that the fixed-payment nature of lease rentals allows more accurate forecasting of cash needs. Finally, leasing allows the firm to avoid the "problems" and "headaches" associated with ownership. Executives often note that leasing "keeps the company out of the real estate business." Implicit in this argument is the assumption that the firm's human and material resources may be more profitably allocated to its primary line of business and that it is better to allow the lessor to deal with the obligations associated with ownership.

It is difficult to generalize about the validity of the various arguments for greater flexibility and convenience in leasing. Some companies, under specific conditions, may find leasing advantageous for some of the reasons listed earlier. In practice, the tradeoffs are likely to be different for every firm. The relevant issue is often that of shifting functions. By leasing a piece of capital equipment, the firm may effectively shift bookkeeping, disposal of used equipment, and other functions to the lessor. The lessee will benefit in these situations if the lessor is able to perform the functions at a lower cost than the lessee and is willing to pass on the savings in a lower lease rate.

The arguments that follows should be viewed in a similar vein. The lessee must attempt to determine the price it is paying for greater flexibility and convenience. In many cases the benefits the firm is able to attain are not worth the cost. Compounding the problem is the fact that it is often difficult for a lessee firm to quantify such cost–benefit tradeoffs.

Lack of Restrictions

Another suggested advantage relates to the lack of restrictions associated with a lease. Unlike term loan agreements or bond indentures, lease contracts generally do not contain protective covenant restrictions. Furthermore, in calculating financial ratios under existing covenants, it is sometimes possible to exclude lease payments from the firm's debt commitments. Once again, the extent to which lack of restrictions benefits a lessee will depend on the price it must pay. If a lessor views its security position to be superior to that of a lender, it may not require a higher return on the lease to compensate for the lack of restrictions on the lessee. Conversely, if the prospective lessee is viewed as a marginal credit risk, a higher rate may be charged.

Avoidance of Risk of Obsolescence

Similar reasoning applies to another popular argument for leasing. This argument states that a lease is advantageous because it allows the firm to avoid the risk that the equipment will become obsolete. In actuality, the risk of obsolescence is passed on to the lessee in any financial lease. Because the original cost of the asset is fully amortized over the basic lease term, all of the risk is borne by the lessee. Only in a cancelable operating lease is it sometimes possible to avoid the risk of obsolescence.

A related argument in favor of leasing states that a lessor will generally provide the firm with better and more reliable service to maintain the resale value of the asset. The extent to which this is true depends on the lessor's own cost–benefit tradeoff. If the lessor is a manufacturing or a leasing company that specializes in a particular type of equipment, it may be profitable to maintain the equipment's resale value by ensuring that it is properly repaired and maintained. Because of their technical and marketing expertise, these types of lessors may be able to operate successfully in the secondary market for the equipment. Conversely, bank lessors or independent financial leasing companies would probably find it too expensive to follow this approach.

Conservation of Working Capital

One of the oldest and most widely used arguments in favor of leasing is the assertion that a lease conserves the firm's working capital. Indeed, many managers within the leasing industry consider this to be the number one advantage of leasing.[14] The conservation argument runs as follows: Because a lease does not require an immediate outflow of cash to cover the full purchase price of the asset, funds are retained in the business.

It is clear that a lease does require a lower initial outlay than a cash purchase. However, the cash outlay associated with the purchase option can be reduced or eliminated by borrowing the downpayment from another source. This argument leads us directly into the next purported advantage of lease financing.

One Hundred Percent Financing

Another alleged benefit of leasing is embodied in the argument that a lease provides the firm with 100 percent financing. It is pointed out that the borrow-and-buy alternative generally involves a downpayment, whereas leasing does not. Given that investors and creditors are reasonably intelligent, however, it is sensible to conclude that they consider similar amounts of lease and debt financing to add equivalent amounts of risk to the firm. Thus, a firm uses up less of its capacity to raise nonequity funds with debt than with leasing. In theory, it could issue a second debt instrument to make up the difference—that is, the downpayment.

Tax Savings

It is also argued that leasing offers an economic advantage in that the tax shield generated by the lease payments usually exceeds the tax shield from depreciation that would be available if the asset were purchased. The extent to which leasing provides a tax-shield benefit is a function of many factors. The *NAL*

---

[14]For example, see L. Rochwarger, "The Flexible World of Leasing," *Fortune* 39 (November 1974), pp. 56–59.

equation (19–4), discussed earlier, is the basis for weighing these differences in tax shields.

Ease of Obtaining Credit

Another purported advantage of leasing is that firms with poor credit ratings are able to obtain assets through leases when they are unable to finance the acquisitions with debt capital. The counterargument is that the firm will certainly face a high lease interest rate to compensate the lessor for bearing the risk of default.

Why Do Firms Lease?

Several researchers have asked firms why they use financial leases as opposed to purchasing. For example, in a study by Ferrara, Thies, and Dirsmith[15] the following factors were found to affect the leasing decision:

Factor	Rank	Percent of Respondents
Implied interest rate	1	52
Threat of obsolescence	2	37
Income taxes	3	33
Maintain flexibility	4	12
Conserve working capital	5	12
Less restrictive financing	6	6
Off balance sheet finance	7	7

Interestingly, the factor most often mentioned was the implied cost of financing. That is, 52 percent of the lessees considered the cost of lease financing to be an important factor in determining their decision to use lease financing. This factor was followed by concern over the risk of obsolescence followed by tax considerations. In light of the theoretical significance given to tax considerations in the theoretical literature on lease financing, it is interesting to note that only 33 percent of the respondents felt that tax considerations were a factor in their decision to lease.

Ferrara, Thies, and Dirsmith also provide evidence concerning the motives underlying a firm's decision to use lease financing and its financial characteristics.[16] Specifically, they observed that smaller and financially weaker firms tended to justify the use of lease financing based on qualitative benefits. These included flexibility, the conservation of working capital, financing restrictions, off balance sheet financing, and transference of the risk of obsolescence. Conversely, larger and financially stronger firms tended to base their leasing decisions on more quantitative considerations. That is, this latter group tended to use more formal comparisons of the cost of leasing versus other forms of intermediate-term financing.

---

[15]W. L. Ferrara, J. B. Thies, and M. W. Dersmith, "The Lease-Purchase Decision," National Association of Accountants, 1980. Cited in "Leasing—A Review of the Empirical Studies," *Managerial Finance* 15, nos. 1 & 2 (1989), pp. 13-20.

[16]Anderson and Bird, also investigated the reasons why lessees lease. They used a survey in which the respondents were asked to indicate both the extent to which they agreed or disagreed with the advantages attributed to leasing and the extent to which a particular advantage was important to their lease decisions. One of the purported advantages to leasing was the following: "All things considered, leasing is less expensive than debt as a means of acquiring equipment." The respondents accorded the lowest agreement rating to this statement (i.e., they disagreed that this was true), yet they ranked this same statement third in overall importance in terms of their decision to lease. The authors interpret this finding as evidence that lessees believe that it is important that the cost of leasing be less than the cost of debt financing, but they do not expect to find this to be so in practice.

SUMMARY

Intermediate credit, or simply term credit, is any source of financing with a final maturity greater than 1 year but less than 10. The two major sources of term credit are term loans and financial leases.

Term loans are available from commercial banks, life insurance companies, and pension funds. Although the specifics of each agreement vary, they share a common set of general characteristics. These include

1. A final maturity of 1 to 10 years
2. A requirement of some form of collateral
3. A body of restrictive covenants designed to protect the security interests of the lender
4. A loan amortization schedule whereby periodic loan payments, comprised of both principal and interest components, are made over the life of the loan

There are three basic types of lease arrangements:

1. Direct lease
2. Sale and leaseback
3. Leveraged lease

The lease agreement can further be classified as a financial or operating lease; we focused on the financial lease. Recent statements by the FASB virtually ensure the inclusion of all financial leases in the body of the lessee firm's balance sheet.

The lease versus purchase decision is a hybrid capital-budgeting problem wherein the analyst must consider both the investment and financing aspects of the decision. Many and varied factors are often claimed as advantages of leasing as opposed to the use of the firm's usual debt–equity financing mix. Many of the arguments have been found to be at least partly fallacious. However, a complete lease–purchase analysis using a model similar to the one discussed here should provide a rational basis for uncovering the true advantages of lease financing.

STUDY QUESTIONS

19–1. What characteristics distinguish intermediate-term debt from other forms of debt instruments?

19–2. List and discuss the major types of restrictions generally found in the covenants of term loan agreements.

19–3. Define each of the following:
   a. Direct leasing
   b. Sale and leaseback arrangement
   c. Leveraged leasing
   d. Operating lease

19–4. How are financial leases handled in the financial statements of the lessee firm?

19–5. List and discuss each of the potential benefits from lease financing.

SELF-TEST PROBLEMS

ST–1. (*Analyzing a Term Loan*) Calculate the annual installment payment and the principal and interest components of a five-year loan carrying a 10 percent rate of interest. The loan amount is $50,000.

ST–2. (*Analyzing an Installment Loan*) The S. P. Sargent Sales Company is contemplating the purchase of a new machine. The total cost of the machine is $120,000 and the firm plans to make a $20,000 cash downpayment. The firm's bank has offered to finance the remaining $100,000 at a rate of 14 percent. The bank has offered two possible loan repayment plans. Plan A involves equal annual installments payable at the end of each of the next five years. Plan B requires five equal annual payments plus a balloon payment of $20,000 at the end of year 5.

   a. Calculate the annual payment on the loan in plan A.
   b. Calculate the principal and interest components of the plan A installment loan.
   c. Calculate the annual installments for plan B where the loan carries a 14 percent rate.

ST–3. (*Lease Versus Purchase Analysis*) Jensen Trucking, Inc., is considering the possibility of leasing a $100,000 truck-servicing facility. This newly developed piece of equipment facilitates the cleaning and servicing of diesel tractors used on long-haul runs. The firm has evaluated the possible purchase of the equipment and found it to have an $8,000 net present value. However, an equipment leasing company has approached Jensen with an offer to lease the equipment for an annual rental charge of $24,000 payable at the beginning of each of the next five years. In addition, should Jensen lease the equipment it would receive insurance and maintenance valued at $4,000 per year (assume that this amount would be payable at the beginning of each year if purchased separately from the lease agreement). Also, for simplicity you may assume that tax savings are realized immediately. Additional information pertaining to the lease and purchase alternatives is found in the following table:

Acquisition price	$100,000
Useful life (used in analysis)	5 years
Salvage value (estimated)	$0
Depreciation method	Straight-line
Borrowing rate	12%
Marginal tax rate	40%
Cost of capital (based on a target debt/total asset ratio of 30%)	16%

   a. Calculate the net advantage of leasing (*NAL*) the equipment.
   b. Should Jensen lease the equipment?

STUDY PROBLEMS (SET A)

19–1A. (*Installment Payments*) Compute the annual payments for an installment loan carrying an 18 percent rate of interest, a five-year maturity, and a face amount of $100,000.

19–2A. (*Principal and Interest Components of an Installment Loan*) Compute the annual principal and interest components of the loan in problem 19–1A.

19–3A. (*Cost of an Intermediate-Term Loan*) The J. B. Marcum Company needs $250,000 to finance a new minicomputer. The computer sales firm has offered to finance the purchase with a $50,000 down payment followed by five annual installments of $59,663.11 each. Alternatively, the firm's bank has offered to lend the firm $250,000 to be repaid in five annual installments based on an annual rate of interest of 16 percent. Finally, the firm has arranged to finance the needed $250,000 through a loan from an insurance company requiring a lump-sum payment of $385,080, in five years.

   a. What is the effective annual rate of interest on the loan from the computer sales firm?
   b. What will the annual payments on the bank loan be?
   c. What is the annual rate of interest for the insurance company term loan?
   d. Based on cost considerations only, which source of financing should Marcum select?

19–4A. (*Cost of Intermediate-Term Credit*) Charter Electronics is planning to purchase a $400,000 burglar alarm system for its southwestern Illinois plant. Charter's bank has offered to lend the firm the full $400,000. The note would be paid in one payment at the end of four years and would require payment of interest at a rate of 14 percent compounded annually. The manufacturer of the alarm system has offered to finance the $400,000 purchase with an installment loan. The loan would require four annual installments of $140,106 each. Which method of financing should Charter select?

19–5A. (*Lease Versus Purchase Analysis*) Early in the spring of 1991 the Jonesboro Steel Corporation (JSC) decided to purchase a small computer. The computer is designed to handle the inventory, payroll, shipping, and general clerical functions for small manufacturers like JSC. The firm estimates that the computer will cost $60,000 to purchase and will last four years, at which time it can be salvaged for $10,000. The firm's marginal tax rate is 50 percent, and its cost of capital for projects of this type is estimated to be 12 percent. Over the next four years the management of JSC thinks the computer will reduce operating expenses by $27,000 a year before depreciation and taxes. JSC uses straight-line depreciation and plans to depreciate the asset toward its expected salvage value of $10,000.

JSC is also considering the possibility of leasing the computer. The computer sales firm has offered JSC a four-year lease contract with annual payments of $18,000. In addition, if JSC leases the computer, the lessor will absorb insurance and maintenance expenses valued at $2,000 per year. Thus, JSC will save $2,000 per year if it leases the asset (on a before-tax basis).

  a. Evaluate the net present value of the computer purchase. Should the computer be acquired via purchase? (*Hint:* Refer to Tables 19–3 and 19–4.)
  b. If JSC uses a 40 percent target debt to total assets ratio, evaluate the net present value advantage of leasing. JSC can borrow at a rate of 8 percent with annual installments paid over the next four years. (*Hint:* Recall that the interest tax shelter lost through leasing is based on a loan equal to the full purchase price of the asset or $60,000.)
  c. Should JSC lease the asset?

19–6A. (*Lease versus Purchase Analysis*) S. S. Johnson Enterprises (SSJE) is evaluating the acquisition of a heavy-duty forklift with 20,000- to 24,000-pound lift capacity. SSJE can purchase the forklift through the use of its normal financing mix (30 percent debt and 70 percent common equity) or lease it. Pertinent details follow:

Acquisition price of the forklift	$20,000
Useful life	4 years
Salvage value (estimated)	$4000
Depreciation method	Straight-line
Annual before-tax and depreciation cash savings from the forklift	$6000
Rate of interest on a 4-year installment loan	10 percent
Marginal tax rate	50 percent
Annual rentals (4-year lease)	$6000
Annual operating expenses included in the lease	$1000
Cost of capital	12 percent

  a. Evaluate whether the forklift acquisition is justified through purchase.
  b. Should SSJE lease the asset?

19–7A. (*Installment Loan Payment*) Calculate the annual installment payments for the following loans:
  a. A $100,000 loan carrying a 15 percent annual rate of interest and requiring 10 annual payments.
  b. A $100,000 loan carrying a 15 percent annual rate of interest with quarterly payments over the next five years. (*Hint:* Refer to Chapter 10 for a discussion of semiannual compounding and discounting.)
  c. A $100,000 loan requiring annual installments for each of the next five years at a 15 percent rate of interest. However, the annual installments are based on a 30-year loan period. In year 5 the balance of the loan is due in a single (balloon) payment. (*Hint:* Calculate the installment payments using $n = 30$ years. Next use the procedure given in Table 19–1 to determine the remaining balance of the loan at the end of the fifth year.)

STUDY PROBLEMS (SET B)

19–1B. (*Installment Payments*) Compute the annual payments for an installment loan carrying a 16 percent rate of interest, a seven-year maturity, and a face amount of $100,000.

19–2B. (*Principal and Interest Components of an Installment Loan*) Compute the annual principal and interest components of the loan in problem 19–1B.

19–3B. (*Cost of an Intermediate Loan*) Azteca Freight Forwarding Company of Laredo, Texas, needs $300,000 to finance the construction of several prefabricated metal warehouses. The firm that produces the warehouses has offered to finance the purchase with a $50,000 downpayment followed by five annual installments of $69,000 each. Alternatively, Azteca's bank has offered to lend the firm $300,000 to be repaid in five annual installments based on an annual rate of interest of 16 percent. Finally, the firm could finance the needed $300,000 through a loan from an insurance company requiring a lump-sum payment of $425,000 in five years.

   a. What is the effective annual rate of interest on the loan from the warehouse producer?
   b. What will the annual payments on the bank loan be?
   c. What is the annual rate of interest for the insurance company term loan?
   d. Based on cost considerations only, which source of financing should Azteca select?

19–4B. (*Cost of Intermediate-Term Credit*) Powder Meadows, a western ski resort, is planning to purchase a $500,000 ski lift. Powder Meadows' bank has offered to lend it the full $500,000. The note would be paid in one payment at the end of four years and would require payment of interest at a rate of 14 percent compounded annually. The manufacturer of the ski lift has offered to finance the $500,000 purchase with an installment loan. The loan would require four annual installments of $175,000 each. Which method of financing should Powder Meadows select?

19–5B. (*Lease Versus Purchase Analysis*) Early in the spring of 1992 Lubin Landscaping, Inc., decided to purchase a truck-mounted lawn fertilizer tank and spray unit. The truck would replace its hand-held fertilizer tanks, providing substantial reductions in labor expense. The firm estimates that the truck will cost $65,000 to purchase and will last four years, at which time it can be salvaged for $8,000. The firm's marginal tax rate is 50 percent, and its cost of capital for projects of this type is estimated to be 14 percent. Over the next four years the management of Lubin feels the truck will reduce operating expenses by $29,000 a year before depreciation and taxes. Lubin uses straight-line depreciation and plans to depreciate the asset toward its expected salvage value of $8,000.

   Lubin is also considering the possibility of leasing the truck. The truck sales firm has offered Lubin a four-year lease contract with annual payments of $20,000. In addition, if Lubin leases the computer, the lessor will absorb insurance and maintenance expenses valued at $2,250 per year. Thus, Lubin will save $2,250 per year if it leases the asset (on a before-tax basis).

   a. Evaluate the net present value of the truck purchase. Should the truck be acquired via purchase? (*Hint:* Refer to Tables 19–3 and 19–4.)
   b. If Lubin uses a 40 percent target debt to total assets ratio, evaluate the net present value advantage of leasing. Lubin can borrow at a rate of 8 percent with annual installments paid over the next four years. (*Hint:* Recall that the interest tax shelter lost through leasing is based on a loan equal to the full purchase price of the asset or $65,000.)
   c. Should Lubin lease the asset?

19–6B. (*Lease versus Purchase Analysis*) KKR Live, Inc., a carnival operating firm based in Laramie, Wyoming, is considering the acquisition of a new German-made carousel, with a passenger capacity of 30. KKR can purchase the carousel through the use of its normal financing mix (30 percent debt and 70 percent common equity) or lease it. Pertinent details follow:

Acquisition price of the carousel	$25,000
Useful life	4 years
Salvage value	$5000
Depreciation method	Straight-line
Annual before-tax and depreciation cash savings from the carousel	$7000
Rate of interest on a 4-year installment loan	11 percent
Marginal tax rate	50 percent
Annual rentals (4-year lease)	$7000
Annual operating expenses included in the lease	$1250
Cost of capital	13 percent

   a. Evaluate whether the carousel acquisition is justified through purchase.
   b. Should KKR lease the asset?

19–7B. (*Installment Loan Payment*) Calculate the annual installment payments for the following loans:

a. A $125,000 loan carrying a 13 percent annual rate of interest and requiring 12 annual payments.

b. A $125,000 loan carrying a 13 percent annual rate of interest with quarterly payments over the next six years. (*Hint:* Refer to Chapter 10 for a discussion of semiannual compounding and discounting.)

c. A $125,000 loan requiring annual installments for each of the next 5 years at a 13 percent rate of interest. However, the annual installments are based on a 30-year loan period. In year 5 the balance of the loan is due in a single (balloon) payment. (*Hint:* Calculate the installment payments using $n = 30$ years. Next use the procedure given in Table 19–1 to determine the remaining balance of the loan at the end of the 5th year.)

SELF-TEST SOLUTIONS

SS–1.

Time	Payment	Principal	Interest	Remaining Balance
0				$50,000.00
1	$13,189.83	$ 8,189.83	$5,000.00	41,810.17
2	13,189.83	9,008.81	4,181.02	32,801.36
3	13,189.83	9,909.69	3,280.14	22,891.67
4	13,189.83	10,900.66	2,289.17	11,991.01
5	13,189.83	11,990.73	1,199.10	0.28

SS–2. **a.** Payment $= \$100,000 \div \sum_{t=1}^{5} \dfrac{1}{(1.14)^t}$

$= \$29,128.35$

b.

Time	Payment	Principal	Interest	Remaining Balance
0	—	—	—	$100,000
1	$29,128.35	$15,128.35	$14,000.00	84,871
2	29,128.35	17,246.32	11,882.03	67,625
3	29,128.35	19,660.80	9,467.55	47,964
4	29,128.35	22,413.32	6,715.03	25,551
5	29,128.35	25,551.18	3,577.17	.03[a]

[a]Rounding error.

c. Because the plan B loan includes a $20,000 balloon payment, the five annual installments have a present value of only

$$\$89,613 = \$100,000 - \$20,000/(1.14)^5$$

Therefore, the annual installments can be calculated as follows:

$$\text{Payment} = \$89,613 \div \sum_{t=1}^{5} \frac{1}{(1.14)^t}$$

$$= \$26,102.79$$

SS–3. **a.** *NAL* = $1,772.69.

b. The *NAL* is positive, indicating that the lease would offer cost savings over a purchase and therefore should be used.

Year	After-Tax Operating Expenses Paid by Lessor[a]	After-Tax Rental Expense[b]	Tax Shelter on Depreciation[c]	Tax Shelter on Loan Interest[d]			Discount Factor at Borrowing Rate (12%)		Present Value
t	$O_t(1-T)$ −	$R_t(1-T)$ −	D_tT −	I_tT =	Sum	×	DF	=	PV
0	$2400	−$14400.000			−$12000.000		1.000		−$12,000.00
1	2400	− 14400.000	−$8000.000	−4800.00	− 24800.000		0.933		− 23,134.33
2	2400	− 14400.000	− 8000.000	−4044.43	− 24044.433		0.870		− 20,923.05
3	2400	− 14400.000	−8000.000	−3198.20	− 23198.199		0.812		− 18,830.85
4	2400	− 14400.000	− 8000.000	−2250.42	− 22250.416		0.757		− 16,848.41
5			− 8000.000	−1188.90	− 9188.899		0.706		− 6,490.67

Total	−$ 98,227.31
Plus: initial outlay	100,000.00
NAL	=$ 1,772.69

[a]$4000 (1 − .4) = $2400. For simplicity we assume that the tax shields on expenses paid at the beginning of the year are realized immediately.

[b]$14,400 = $24,000 (1 − .4).

[c]The machine has a zero salvage value. Thus, its annual depreciation expense is $100,000/5 = $20,000.

[d]Based on a $100,000 loan with four end-of-year installments and a 12 percent rate of interest. The loan payments equal $27,740.97.

CHAPTER *20*

Long-Term Debt, Preferred Stock, and Common Stock

Bonds or Long-Term Debt • Preferred Stock • Common Stock

In this chapter we concern ourselves with the three major sources of long-term and permanent funds for the firm: long-term debt, preferred stock, and common stock. In Chapters 5 and 10 we discussed the valuation and theory behind the use of long-term sources for funds. In this chapter we devote our attention to the terminology and basic features common to these securities; we will focus on their similarities and differences, as well as their advantages and disadvantages, as sources of financing to the firm.

Bonds or Long-Term Debt

A **bond** is any long-term (10 years or more) promissory note issued by the firm. In examining bonds we will first outline bond terminology and features, then examine types of bonds (both secured and unsecured), methods of retiring debt, bond refunding, and advantages and disadvantages of financing with long-term debt.

Basic Bond Terminology and Characteristics

Par Value

The **par value** of a bond is its face value that is returned to the bondholder at maturity. In general, most corporate bonds are issued in denominations of $1,000, although there are some exceptions to this rule. When bond prices are quoted, either by financial managers or in the financial press, prices are generally expressed as a percentage of the bond's par value. For example, a Detroit Edison bond that pays $90 per year interest, and matures in 1999, was recently quoted in The *Wall Street Journal* as selling for 95⅛. That does not mean you can buy the bond for $95.125. It does mean that this bond is selling for 95⅛ percent of its par value, which happens to be $1,000. Hence, the market price of this bond is actually $951.25. At maturity in 1999, the bondholder will receive the $1,000.

Coupon Interest Rate

The **coupon interest rate** on a bond indicates what percentage of the par value of the bond will be paid out annually in the form of interest. Thus, regardless of what happens to the price of a bond with an 8 percent coupon interest rate and a $1,000 par value, it will pay out $80 annually in interest until maturity.

Maturity

The **maturity** of a bond indicates the length of time until the bond issuer returns the par value to the bondholder and terminates the bond.

Indenture

An **indenture** is the legal agreement between the firm issuing the bonds and the bond trustee who represents the bondholders. The indenture provides the specific terms of the loan agreement, including a description of the bonds, the rights of the bondholders, the rights of the issuing firm, and the responsibilities of the trustees. This legal document may run 100 pages or more in length, with the majority of it devoted to defining protective provisions for the bondholder. The bond trustee, usually a banking institution or trust company, is then assigned the task of overseeing the relationship between the bondholder and the issuing firm, protecting the bondholder, and seeing that the terms of the indenture are carried out.

Typically, the restrictive provisions included in the indenture attempt to protect the bondholder's financial position relative to that of other outstanding securities. Common provisions involve (1) prohibitions on the sale of accounts receivable, (2) constraints on the issuance of common stock dividends, (3) restrictions on the purchase or sale of fixed assets, and (4) constraints on additional borrowing. Prohibitions on the sale of accounts receivable are specified because such sales would benefit the firm's short-run liquidity position at the expense of its future liquidity position. Constraints on common stock dividends generally means limiting their issuance when working capital falls below a specified level, or simply limiting the maximum dividend payout to 50 or 60 percent of earnings under any circumstance. Fixed-asset restrictions generally require lender permission before the liquidation of any fixed asset or prohibit the use of any existing fixed asset as collateral on new loans. Constraints on additional borrowing are usually in the form of restrictions or limitations on the amount and type of additional long-term debt that can be issued. All these restrictions have one thing in common: They attempt to prohibit action that would improve the status of other securities at the expense of bonds and to protect the status of bonds from being weakened by any managerial action.

Current Yield

The **current yield** on a bond refers to the ratio of the annual interest payment to the bond's market price. If, for example, we are examining a bond with an 8 percent coupon interest rate, a par value of $1,000, and a market price of $700, it would have a current yield of

$$\text{current yield} = \frac{\text{annual interest payments}}{\text{market price of the bond}} \tag{20-1}$$

$$= \frac{.08 \times \$1000}{\$700} = \frac{\$80}{\$700} = 11.4 \text{ percent}$$

Yield to Maturity

CH. 5 →

The **yield to maturity** refers to the bond's internal rate of return. It incorporates into the analysis both the annual interest payments and capital gains or losses. Mathematically, the yield to maturity is the discount rate that equates the present value of the interest and principal payments with the current market price of the bond.[1]

Bond Ratings

John Moody first began to rate bonds in 1909; since that time three rating agencies—Moody's, Standard and Poor's, and Fitch Investor Services—have provided **ratings** on corporate bonds. These ratings involve a judgment about the future risk potential of the bond. Although they deal with expectations, several historical factors seem to play a significant role in their determination.[2] Bond ratings are favorably affected by (1) a low utilization of financial leverage, (2) profitable operations, (3) a low variability in past earnings, (4) large firm size, and (5) little use of subordinated debt. In turn, the rating a bond receives affects the rate of return demanded on the bond by the investors. The poorer the bond rating, the higher the rate of return demanded in the capital markets. An example and description of these ratings is given in Table 20–1. Thus, for the financial manager, bond ratings are extremely important. They provide an indicator of default risk that in turn affects the rate of return that must be paid on borrowed funds.

TABLE 20–1. Standard and Poor's Corporate Bond Ratings	
AAA	This is the highest rating assigned by Standard and Poor's debt obligation and indicates an extremely strong capacity to pay principal and interest.
AA	Bonds rated AA also qualify as high-quality debt obligations. Their capacity to pay principal and interest is very strong, and in the majority of instances they differ from AAA issues only in small degree.
A	Bonds rated A have a strong capacity to pay principal and interest, although they are somewhat more susceptible to the adverse effects of changes in circumstances and economic conditions.
BBB	Bonds rated BBB are regarded as having an adequate capacity to pay principal and interest. Whereas they normally exhibit adequate protection parameters, adverse economic conditions or changing circumstances are more likely to lead to a weakened capacity to pay principal and interest for bonds in this category than for bonds in the A category.
BB B CCC CC	Bond rated BB, B, CCC, and CC are regarded, on balance, as predominantly speculative with respect to the issuer's capacity to pay interest and repay principal in accordance with the terms of the obligation. BB indicates the lowest degree of speculation and CC the highest. While such bonds will likely have some quality and protective characteristics, these are outweighed by large uncertainties or major risk exposures to adverse conditions.
C	The rating C is reserved for income bonds on which no interest is being paid.
D	Bonds rated D are in default, and payment of principal and/or interest is in arrears.
	Plus (+) or Minus (−): To provide more detailed indications of credit quality, the ratings from "AA" to "BB" may be modified by the addition of a plus or minus sign to show relative standing within the major rating categories.
	Provisional Ratings: A provisional rating assumes the successful completion of the project being financed by the issuance of the bonds being rated and indicates that payment of debt service requirements is largely or entirely dependent upon the successful and timely completion of the project. This rating, however, while addressing credit quality subsequent to completion, makes no comment on the likelihood of, or the risk of default upon failure of, such completion. Accordingly, the investor should exercise his judgment with respect to such likelihood and risk.

Source: *Standard and Poor's Fixed Income Investor,* Vol. 8 (1980). Reprinted by permission.

---

[1]See Chapter 5 for illustrative example.

[2]See Thomas F. Pogue and Robert M. Soldofsky, "What's in a Bond Rating?" *Journal of Financial and Quantitative Analysis* 4 (June 1969), pp. 201–28; and George E. Pinches and Kent A. Mingo, "A Multivariate Analysis of Industrial Bond Ratings," *Journal of Finance* 28 (March 1973), pp. 1–18.

Determinants of the Cost of Long-Term Debt

In Chapter 13 we computed an investor's required rate of return for debt financing to the firm. We now focus on the factors that determine the required rate of return that investors demand on this debt. The total cost of debt that the firm will pay depends primarily on five factors: (1) the size of the issue, (2) the issue's maturity, (3) the issue's riskiness or rating, (4) the restrictive requirements of the issue, and (5) the current riskless interest rate. To a large extent the administrative costs of issuing debt are fixed, and they will decrease in percentage terms as the size of the issue increases. In effect, economies of scale are associated with the issuance of debt. The issue's maturity also affects the cost of debt. Borrowers prefer to borrow for long periods to lock in interest rates and avoid the problem of frequent refinancing, whereas lenders would rather not tie up their money for long periods. In order to bring about equilibrium between supply and demand for funds, long-term debt generally carries a higher interest rate than short-term debt. This tends to encourage some borrowers to borrow for shorter periods and some investors to lend for longer periods.

Investors also desire additional return for taking on added risk. Thus, the less risky the bond or the higher the bond rating, the lower will be the interest rate. We can see this by looking at the movement of bond yields for four different ratings during 1991, as shown in Table 20–2.

The restrictive requirements and rights of both issuer and holder also affect the interest rate paid on the bond. The more the bondholder requires in the way of protection and rights, the lower will be the rate of return earned. Conversely, the more rights the issuer demands—for example, the right to repurchase the debt at a predetermined price (called a *call provision* and discussed later in detail)—the higher will be the rate that the issuer will have to offer in order to convince investors to purchase the bond.

Finally, the current riskless interest rate plays a major role in determining the cost of debt. As the riskless rate of interest moves up and down, corporate bond rates move in parallel. The determination of the riskless interest rate is generally deferred to courses on money and banking, and financial institutions. We note here that one of the major factors affecting the riskless interest rate is the anticipated rate of inflation.

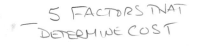

5 FACTORS THAT DETERMINE COST

	Ratings			
	Least Risk			Most Risk
	AAA	AA	BBB	B
January	9.01%	9.45%	11.62%	19.63%
February	8.71	9.12	10.67	19.04
March	8.95	9.24	10.43	16.86
April	8.84	9.13	10.23	15.84
May	8.87	9.16	10.19	15.03
June	9.08	9.37	10.24	14.42
July	8.78	9.29	10.10	14.28
August	8.47	8.98	9.81	14.38
September	8.49	8.81	9.69	14.42
October	8.41	8.73	9.55	14.99
November	8.42	8.74	9.56	14.68
December	8.24	8.49	9.34	12.91
Monthly averages	8.69%	9.04%	10.12%	15.54%

Source: Standard and Poor's Corporation, *Bond Guide,* January 1992.

Claims on Assets and Income

In the case of insolvency, claims of debt are honored before those of both common stock and preferred stock. However, different types of debt may also have a hierarchy among themselves as to the order of their claim on assets.

Bonds also have a claim on income that comes ahead of common and preferred stock. If interest on bonds (other than income bonds, to be discussed later) is not paid, the bond trustees can classify the firm insolvent and force it into bankruptcy. Thus, the bondholder's claim on income is more likely to be honored than that of common and preferred stockholders, whose dividends are paid at the discretion of the firm's management.

Types of Bonds

Debentures

The term **debentures** applies to any unsecured long-term debt. Because these bonds are unsecured, the earning ability of the issuing corporation is of great concern to the bondholder. They are also viewed as being more risky than secured bonds and as a result must provide investors with a higher yield than secured bonds provide. Often the issuing firm attempts to provide some protection to the holder through the prohibition of any additional encumbrance of assets. This prohibits the future issuance of secured long-term debt that would further tie up the firm's assets and leave the bondholders less protected. To the issuing firm, the major advantage of debentures is that no property has to be secured by them. This allows the firm to issue debt and still preserve some future borrowing power.

Subordinated Debentures

Many firms have more than one issue of debentures outstanding. In this case a hierarchy may be specified, in which some debentures are given subordinated standing in the case of insolvency. The claims of the **subordinated debentures** are honored only after the claims of secured debt and unsubordinated debentures have been satisfied.

Income Bonds

An **income bond** requires interest payments only if earned, and failure to meet these interest payments cannot lead to bankruptcy. In this sense income bonds are more like preferred stock (which is discussed in a later section) than bonds. They are generally issued during the reorganization of a firm facing financial difficulties. The maturity of income bonds is usually much longer than that of

SIMILAR TO
Preferred stock

other bonds to relieve pressure associated with the repayment of principal. While interest payments may be passed, unpaid interest is generally allowed to accumulate for some period and must be paid before the payment of any common stock dividends. This cumulative interest feature provides the bondholder with some security.

Mortgage Bonds

A **mortgage bond** is a bond secured by a lien on real property. Typically, the value of the real property is greater than that of the mortgage bonds issued. This provides the mortgage bondholders with a margin of safety in the event the market value of the secured property declines. In the case of foreclosure, the trustees have the power to sell the secured property and use the proceeds to pay the bondholders. In the event that the proceeds from this sale do not cover the bonds, the bondholders become general creditors, similar to debenture bondholders, for the unpaid portion of the debt.

Floating Rate or Variable Rate Bonds

Floating rate or **variable rate bonds,** for many years popular in Europe, appeared in this country in July 1974, when Citicorp issued $850 million of debt with the interest rate set at 1 percent above the 90-day Treasury bill rate. In periods of unstable interest rates this type of debt offering becomes appealing to issuers and investors. To banks and finance companies, whose revenues go up when interest rates rise and decline as interest rates fall, this type of debt eliminates some of the risk and variability in earnings that accompany interest rate swings. To the investor, it eliminates major swings in the market value of the debt that would otherwise have occurred if interest rates had changed.

As an example, in July 1989 Memorex Telex corporation issued $155 million of floating rate bonds due in 1996. The interest rate on these bonds is subject to quarterly adjustments and is reset at 300 basis points (3 percent) above the three-month London Interbank Offered Rate. The London Interbank Offered Rate, or LIBOR as it is often called, is the rate that most creditworthy international banks charge each other for large loans and is often used as a benchmark to which variable rate loans are pegged. Thus, if the LIBOR was 9 percent, the Memorex Telex bonds would pay 12 percent, and, if the LIBOR rose to 9½ percent at the time of the next three-month adjustment, the Memorex Telex bonds would be adjusted to pay 12½ percent. In late 1991 and early 1992, several firms including Clark Oil, Reynolds Metals, KeyCorp, RJR Nabisco Holdings, and DuPont called in their floating rate bonds and replaced them with fixed rate bonds. This was because interest rates had fallen, and the firms wanted to lock in the favorable rates that existed at the time.

While every floating rate bond is a bit different, these bonds generally possess common characteristics:

1. After an initial period of 3 to 18 months during which a minimum interest rate is guaranteed, the coupon is allowed to float. Then weekly, every 3 months, or every 6 months the coupon rate changes to a new level, usually 0.5 to 3.0 percent above the preceding week's average Treasury bill rate or the LIBOR.

2. The bondholder generally has the option of redeeming the bond at par value every 6 months.

3. The issuer is generally, although not always, a bank, bank holding company, or finance company whose revenues are subject to swings with interest rate fluctuations.

There are, of course, exceptions and variations in the concept of floating rate bonds. Two of the more interesting are bonds issued by Petro-Lewis, a Texas oil firm, and Sunshine Mining Company, a silver-mining firm. In 1980 Petro-

TABLE 20-3.
Floating Rate (or Floating Principal) Bonds

Issuer	Maturity (Year)	Initial Interest Rate	Terms of Adjustment
First Interstate Bancorp	1994	6-month LIBOR plus 0.20%	Adjusted quarterly to 20 basis points (0.20%) above the 6-month LIBOR
General Chemical Corporation	1994	3-month LIBOR plus 2.00%	Adjusted quarterly to 200 basis points (2.00%) above the 3-month LIBOR
Continental Bank	1994	3-month LIBOR plus 0.15%	Adjusted quarterly to 15 basis points (0.15%) above the 3-month LIBOR
Petro-Lewis	2000	13.00%	Adjusted quarterly and tied to the price of crude oil. The rate is allowed to vary between 13.00% and 15.00%.
Sunshine Mining Co.	1995 or whenever redemption value exceeds $2000 for a period of 30 consecutive days.	8.00%	Interest rate is fixed; however, the redemption value at maturity is equal to the greater of $1000 or the market price of 50 ounces of silver.

Lewis issued bonds in which the interest rate was tied to the price of crude oil from West Texas. If the oil price rose more than 10 percent, the bonds' interest rate would also rise. The Sunshine Mining Company debt was issued in February 1983 and carried a coupon interest rate of 8 percent, with the principal tied to the price of silver. The common feature of all the variable rate bonds is that an attempt is made to counter uncertainty by allowing the interest rate (or in the case of the Sunshine Mining Bonds the principal) to float. In this way a decline in cash inflows to the firm should be offset by a decline in interest payments. Table 20-3 gives several examples of variations of floating rate bonds.

Junk Bonds

Junk or **low-rated bonds** are bonds rated BB or below. Originally, the term was used to describe bonds issued by "fallen angels"; that is, firms with sound financial histories that were facing severe financial problems and suffering from poor credit ratings. Today, junk bonds refer to any bond with a low rating. The major participants in this market are new firms that do not have an established record of performance, although junk bonds have been issued to finance corporate buyouts. Still, the backbone of the junk bond market involves young firms without established records of performance. Before the mid-1970s these new firms simply did not have access to the capital markets because of the reluctance of investors to accept speculative grade bonds. However, by the late 1980s junk bonds grew to the point that they represented between 10 and 20 percent of the total public bond issuances by U.S. corporations. As the economy slowed in the late 1980s and early 1990s, junk bonds were issued less frequently. This growth is illustrated in Table 20-4, which shows the proliferation of new issues of junk bonds. Today, with the leveraged buyout movement of the late 1980s over, junk bonds play a smaller role in corporate finance than they had. The bankruptcy of Drexel Burnham Lambert, the jailing of the "king of junk bonds" Michael Milken, and the realization that high leverage is dangerous have all contributed to a shrinkage of this market. As we look forward to the mid- and late 1990s and the century ahead it appears that although the role of junk bonds may be reduced, they will continue to play an important role for new firms raising capital for the first time.

Since junk bonds are of speculative grade, they carry a coupon interest rate of between 3 to 5 percent more than AAA grade long-term debt.

Perspective in Finance

The cost advantages that U.S. firms have been able to achieve in the Eurobond market are very difficult to explain given the fact that the financial markets are relatively well integrated. In integrated markets the flow of capital between

TABLE 20–4.
New Issues of Junk Bonds
(Billions of Dollars)

Year	(1) Newly Issued Public Straight Junk Bonds[a]	(2) Exchange Offers and Private Issues Going Public[b]	(3) Total Junk Bond Issuance (1) + (2)	(4) Total Public Bond Issues by U.S. Corporations[b]	(5) (1) as % of (4)	(6) (3) as % of (4)
1987	28.9	n.a.	n.a.	219.1	13.2	n.a.
1986	34.3	11.3	45.6	232.5	14.8	19.6
1985	15.4	4.4	19.8	119.6	12.9	16.6
1984	14.8	0.9	15.7	73.6	20.1	21.3
1983	8.0	0.5	8.5	47.6	16.8	17.9
1982	2.7	0.5	3.2	44.3	6.1	7.2
1981	1.4	0.3	1.7	38.1	3.7	4.5
1980	1.4	0.7	2.1	41.6	3.4	5.0
1979	1.4	0.3	1.7	25.8	5.4	6.6
1978	1.5	0.7	2.2	19.8	7.6	11.1
1977	0.6	0.5	1.1	24.1	2.5	4.6

[a]From Drexel, Burnham, Lambert (1987). 1987 figure from *Investment Dealer's Digest.*
[b]From *Federal Reserve Bulletin.* 1987 figure from *Investment Dealer's Digest.*
Source: Kevin J. Perry and Robert A. Taggart, Jr., "The Growing Role of Junk Bonds," *Journal of Applied Corporate Finance,* 1 (Spring 1988), p. 38.

countries should keep interest rates approximately equal in different countries. One possible explanation for the low interest rates in the Eurobond market centers on the value to investors of the anonymity conferred by the fact that the holder of a Eurobond does not have to register his or her name anywhere. This makes it easier for the bondholder to cheat on taxes.

Eurobonds

Eurobonds are not so much a different type of security as they are securities, in this case bonds, issued in a country different from the one in whose currency the bond is denominated. For example, a bond that is issued in Europe or in Asia by an American company and that pays interest and principal to the lender in U.S. dollars would be considered a Eurobond. Thus, even if the bond is not issued in Europe, it merely needs to be sold in a country different from the one in whose currency it is denominated to be considered a Eurobond. The Eurobond market actually had its roots in the 1950s and 1960s as the U.S. dollar became increasingly popular because of its role as the primary international reserve. In recent years as the U.S. dollar has gained a reputation for being one of the most stable currencies, demand for Eurobonds has increased. The primary attraction to borrowers, aside from favorable rates, in the Eurobonds market is the relative lack of regulation (Eurobonds are not registered with the SEC), less rigorous disclosure requirements than those of the SEC, and the speed with which they can be issued. Interestingly, not only are Eurobonds not registered with the SEC, but U.S. citizens and residents may not be offered them during their initial distribution.

The use of Eurobonds by U.S. firms to raise funds has fluctuated dramatically, with the relative interest rates and abundance or lack of funds in the European markets dictating the degree to which they are used. Without question, cost considerations have pushed U.S. firms into this market. The *International Financial Management* box, "Wayne Marr and John Trimble on Eurobond Borrowing," discusses the growth of this market.

Zero and Very Low Coupon Bonds

Zero and very low **coupon bonds** allow the issuing firm to issue bonds at a substantial discount from their $1,000 face value with a zero or very low coupon. The investor receives a large part (or all on the zero coupon bond) of the return from the appreciation of the bond. For example, in April 1983 Homestead Savings issued $60 million of debt maturing in 1995 with a zero

Kevin J. Perry and Robert A. Taggart, Jr., on the Role
of Junk Bonds in Corporate Financial Policy

Given that junk bonds have established a solid position in the corporate debt market, we now examine their role in corporate financial policy. When should a corporation consider issuing junk bonds?

Stewart Myers' "pecking order" theory provides a useful starting point.[3] Myers notes that a firm's managers typically know more about its true value than other capital market participants. If the managers act in the interests of their existing shareholders, they will thus try to issue securities at times when they know them to be overvalued. Recognizing this incentive, however, market participants will then interpret securities issues as a sign that they are overvalued. That in turn reduces the amounts they are willing to pay for the securities.

This problem of unequal information gives rise to a pecking order of sources of funds. Internally generated funds are unaffected by the problem, since their use entails no new securities issues. The closer a company's debt securities are to being riskless, the less severe is this problem as well. This is because the value of riskless securities will be unaffected by revisions in the estimated value of the company's assets. Riskier securities such as equity, however, will clearly be affected by investors'

perceptions of firm value. Since the mere fact of their issuance is likely to lead to downward revisions in their value, managers will be reluctant to issue these securities.

The pecking order, then, implies the following rules for financial policy: (1) Use internal funds first, until these have been exhausted; (2) to the extent that external funds must be relied upon, issue debt first, the less risky the better; (3) issue common stock only as a last resort, after all debt capacity has been exhausted.

Junk bonds occupy an intermediate position in this pecking order. They are more susceptible to the investor information problem than investment grade debt, but less so than common stock. For a firm that needs large amounts of external financing for its current investment plan, junk bonds can allow the firm to fully use its available debt capacity and thus avoid an equity issue.

Source: Kevin J. Perry and Robert A. Taggart, Jr., "The Growing Role of Junk Bonds," *Journal of Applied Corporate Finance* 1 (Spring 1988), pp. 37–45.

coupon rate. These bonds were sold at a 75 percent discount from their par value; that is, investors only paid $250 for a bond with a $1,000 par value. Investors who purchased these bonds for $250 and hold them until they mature in 1995 will receive an 11.50 percent yield to maturity, with all of this yield coming from appreciation of the bond. Homestead Savings, on the other hand, will have no cash outflows until these bonds mature; however, at that time it will have to pay back $60 million even though it only received $15 million when the bonds were first issued.

As with any form of financing, there are both advantages and disadvantages of issuing zero or very low coupon bonds. The disadvantages are, first (as already mentioned), when the bonds mature Homestead Savings will face an extremely large nondeductible cash outflow, much greater than the cash inflow it experienced when the bonds were first issued. Second, discount bonds are not callable and can only be retired at maturity. Thus, if interest rates fall, Homestead Savings cannot benefit. The advantages of zero and low coupon bonds are, first, that annual cash outflows associated with interest payments do not occur with zero coupon bonds and are at a relatively low level with low coupon bonds. Second, because there is relatively strong investor demand for this type of debt, prices tend to be bid up and yields tend to be bid down. That is to say, Homestead Savings was able to issue zero coupon bonds at about half a percent less than it would have been if they had been traditional coupon bonds. Finally, Homestead Savings is able to deduct the annual amortization of the discount, which will provide a positive annual cash flow to Homestead.

[3]See "The Capital Structure Puzzle," *Journal of Finance* 39 (June 1984), pp. 575–92. Reprinted in *Midland Corporate Finance Journal* 3 (Fall 1985), pp. 6–18.

INTERNATIONAL FINANCIAL MANAGEMENT

Wayne Marr and John Trimble on Eurobond Borrowing

Between 1975 and 1988, the volume of U.S. corporate borrowing in the Eurodollar bond market grew at the astonishing rate of 63 percent annually. In 1975 U.S. firms borrowed approximately $30 million overseas, which accounted for less than one percent of total U.S. corporate borrowing. In 1987 they borrowed nearly $17 billion overseas, which represented roughly 17 percent of total U.S. corporate borrowing. This amount, moreover, was sharply down from the 1985 high of $42 billion, accounting for 42 percent of total corporate borrowing.

What is behind this huge increase in overseas borrowing? According to the chief financial officers of U.S. companies, it is extraordinarily favorable borrowing rates. Many CFOs, in fact, report interest cost savings between 25 and 100 basis points in the Eurodollar as compared with the domestic market.[4] Though intermittent, such savings have been available often enough to provide a significant advantage. And, harder to believe, the reported savings at times have been much larger than 100 basis points. On September 11, 1984, for example, Coca Cola issued $100 million of seven-year Eurodollar bonds priced at 80 basis points below comparable U.S. Treasury notes.[5] And, while interest cost savings as large as Coca Cola's are clearly an aberration, recent academic research provides support for claims in the financial press of substantial corporate savings in the Eurobond market.[6]

Besides cost considerations, there could be other reasons why U.S. companies choose to issue Eurobonds. They may wish, for example, to broaden the market for their securities and attract investors who would not otherwise purchase securities registered in the United States. Or they may wish to avoid the disclosure requirements of regulations. But surely the predominant reason for the large volume of Eurodollar bonds is that U.S. companies perceive some cost advantage to borrowing overseas.[7]

In two recent studies we found that, in fact Eurodollar bonds have offered issuers remarkable savings relative to comparable domestic bonds. Using a sample of 229 new debt issues sold by U.S. public utility firms between January 1979 and December 1983, we found that the average gross yield on 38 Eurodollar bond issues was approximately 58 basis points less than yields on 191 comparable domestic issues.[8] In a more recent study we found an even larger 104 basis points saving for 118 industrial firms issuing Eurodollar bonds (relative to 198 domestic issues) during this same period. These are indeed significant savings. For a typical $100 million bond issue, for example, 104 basis points translates into a reduction in debt service cost of $1.04 million a year.

Source: Wayne Marr and John Trimble, "The Persistent Borrowing Advantage of Eurodollar Bonds: A Plausible Explanation," *Journal of Applied Corporate Finance* 1 (Summer 1988), pp. 65–70.

Retiring Debt

Because bonds have a maturity date, their retirement is a crucial matter. Bonds can be retired at maturity, at which time the bondholder receives the par value

---

[4]See W. Cooper, "Some Thoughts About Eurobonds," *Institutional Investor* (February 1985), pp. 157–58; S. Lohr, "The Eurobond Market Boom," *New York Times*, December 31, 1985, p. 31; F. G. Fisher, *The Eurodollar Bond Market* (London: Euromoney Publications Limited, 1979); R. Karp, "How U.S. Companies Are Catching the Eurobond Habit," *Institutional Investor* (August 1982), pp. 208–12; M. S. Mendelson, *Money on the Move* (New York: McGraw-Hill, 1980); Orion Royal Bank Limited, *The Orion Royal Guide to the International Capital Markets* (London: Euromoney Publications Limited, 1982); Securities Industry Association, *The Importance of Access to Capital Markets Outside the United States* (May 1983); and D. W. Starr, "Opportunities of U.S. Corporate Borrowers in the International Bond Markets," *Financial Executive* (June 1979), pp. 50–59.

[5]See W. Cooper, "Some Thoughts About Eurobonds," *Institutional Investor* (February 1985), pp. 157–58.

[6]See M. W. Marr and J. L. Trimble, "Domestic versus Euromarket Bond Sale: A Persistent Borrowing Cost Advantage," University of Tennessee, Department of Finance Working Paper, 1988.

[7]Two empirical studies have documented the savings. They are D. S. Kidwell, M. W. Marr, and G. R. Thompson, "Eurodollar Bonds: Alternative Financing for U.S. Companies," *Financial Management* (Winter 1985), pp. 18–27. A correction to the above study appears in *Financial Management* (Spring 1986), pp. 78–79; and M. W. Marr and J. Trimble, "Domestic versus Euromarket Bond Sale: A Persistent Borrowing Cost Advantage," University of Tennessee, Department of Finance Working Paper, 1988.

[8]Ibid.

of the bond, or they can be retired prior to maturity. Early redemption is generally accomplished through the use of a call provision or a sinking fund.

Call Provision

A **call provision** entitles the corporation to repurchase or "call" the bonds from their holders at stated prices over specified periods. This feature provides the firm with the flexibility to recall its debt and replace it with lower-cost debt if interest rates fall. The terms of the call provision are provided in the indenture and generally state the call price above the bond's par value. The difference between the call price and the par value is referred to as the **call premium.** The size of this premium changes over time, becoming smaller as the date of call approaches the bond's scheduled maturity. It is also common to prohibit calling the bond during its first years. Obviously, a call provision works to the disadvantage of the bondholder, who for this reason is generally compensated by a higher rate of return on the bond.

Sinking Fund

A **sinking fund** requires the periodic repayment of debt, thus reducing the total amount of debt outstanding. When a sinking fund is set up, the firm makes annual payments to the trustee, who can then purchase the bonds in the capital markets or use the call provision. The advantage is that the annual retirement of debt through a sinking fund reduces the amount needed to retire the remaining debt at maturity. Otherwise the firm would face a major payment at maturity. If the firm were experiencing temporary financial problems when the debt matured, both the repayment of the principal and the firm's future could be jeopardized. The use of a sinking fund and its periodic retirement of debt eliminates this potential danger.

Perspective in Finance

The bond-refunding decision is actually nothing more than a capital-budgeting decision. While a casual glance at the calculations may appear intimidating, all that the financial manager really does is determine the present value of the annual net cash benefits from the refund and subtract out the initial outlay.

Bond Refunding

The *bond-refunding* decision—that is, whether or not to call an entire issue of bonds—is similar to the capital-budgeting decision. The present value of the stream of benefits from the refunding decision is compared with the present value of its costs. If the benefits outweigh the costs, the refunding is done.

The benefits from refunding generally involve interest savings, achieved by replacing older, high-cost debt with less expensive debt as interest rates drop. In addition, tax benefits come about because the unamortized flotation costs and discount on the old bonds, if any, as well as the call premium are treated as expenses during the year of the refunding. The costs include issuing and recalling expenses and any interest expenses during the bond overlap period. An *overlap period,* generally occurs because firms wish to obtain the funds from the new issue before calling the old bonds. During this period, when the new bonds have been issued and the old bonds have not yet been called, the risk of a rise in interest rates or a drying up of funds in the capital markets is eliminated. Thus, the cost associated with the additional interest payment can be viewed as the cost of elimination of this risk.

Although the calculations associated with a bond-refunding decision appear to be quite complex, remember that we are merely determining the net present value of this decision. The major difference between the refunding decision and capital budgeting, as presented in Chapter 6, is that the discount rate used in refunding is the after-tax cost of borrowing on the new bonds rather than the firm's cost of capital. This is because in a refunding decision, as opposed to a normal investment decision, the costs and benefits are known with complete certainty. In effect, a refunding decision is an example of a riskless investment. The only risk involved is the risk of the firm's defaulting on the interest or principal payments. Thus, because the after-tax cost of borrowing on the new bonds takes into account this default risk, it is the appropriate discount rate. The following example will illustrate and explain these calculations.[9]

EXAMPLE

Suppose that interest rates have just fallen and that a firm in the 34 percent tax bracket has a $50 million, 9 percent debenture issue outstanding with 20 years remaining to maturity. The unamortized flotation costs and discount on the old bonds total $3 million. These bonds contain a call provision and can be called at $104 (that is, $104 for each $100 of par). Let us assume that they could be replaced with a $50 million issue of 8 percent 20-year bonds providing the firm with $48 million after flotation costs. That is to say, the discount on the new bonds is $2 million ($50 million − $48 million). Let us further assume that an additional $400,000 in issuing expenses would be incurred. The overlap period during which both issues will be outstanding is expected to be one month. Finally, since the marginal corporate tax rate is 34 percent, the appropriate discount rate is 8% $(1 - .34) = 5.28$ percent.

The procedure for arriving at a decision involves first determining the initial outlay and the differential cash flows. Then all the flows are discounted back to the present and the net present value of the refunding decision is determined. Table 20–5 illustrates these calculations. In this example the net present value of the refunding decision is $944,971. Because this is positive, the refunding proposal should be accepted.

TABLE 20–5.
Calculations Illustrating the Bond-Refunding Decision

Step 1: Calculate the *initial outlay*.
  (a) Determine the difference between the inflow from the new issue and the outflow from retiring the old issue:

Cost of calling old bonds ($50,000,000 × 1.04)		$52,000,000
Proceeds, after flotation costs, from new issue		48,000,000
Difference between inflow and outflow		$ 4,000,000

  (b) Determine total issuing and overlap expenses:

Issuing expense on new bonds	$ 400,000	
Interest expense on old bonds during overlap period	375,000	775,000
(c) Add the items above to determine the gross initial outlay		$ 4,775,000

  (d) Determine tax-deductible expenses incurred:

Interest expenses during overlap period	$ 375,000	
Unamortized flotation costs and discount on the old bonds	3,000,000	
Call premium (call price less par value)	2,000,000	
Total tax-deductible expenses	$5,375,000	

  (e) Less tax savings:

Marginal tax rate (34% × total tax-deductible expenses)	× .34	1,827,500
(f) Equals net *initial* cash outflow		$ 2,947,500

---

[9]The subject of the appropriate discount rate to be used in discounting the benefits of a bond refund back to present has received considerable attention. See, for example, Thomas H. Mayor and Kenneth G. McCoin, "The Rate of Discounting in Bond Refunding," *Financial Management* 3 (Autumn 1974), pp. 54–58; and Aharon R. Ofer and Robert A. Taggart, Jr., "Bond Refunding: A Clarifying Analysis," *Journal of Finance* 32 (March 1977), pp. 21–30. Ofer and Taggart show that the relevant discount rate is the after-tax cost of the refunding bonds when new bonds are used to replace the existing bonds.

TABLE 20–5.
Cont.

Step 2: Calculate the *annual cash benefit* from eliminating the old bonds through refunding.

(a) Determine annual interest expense:
9% interest on $50,000,000 — $ 4,500,000

(b) Determine tax-deductible expenses incurred:

Annual interest expense	$4,500,000	
Annual amortization of flotation costs and discount on old bonds ($3,000,000/20)	150,000	
Total annual tax-deductible expenses	$4,650,000	

(c) Less annual tax savings:
Marginal tax rate (34%) × total annual tax-deductible expenses — × .34 — 1,581,000

(d) Equals annual cash benefit from elimination of old bonds — $ 2,919,000

Step 3: Calculate the *annual cash outflow* from issuing the new bonds.

(a) Determine the annual interest expense:
8% interest on $50,000,000 — $ 4,000,000

(b) Determine tax deductible expenses incurred:

Annual interest expense	$4,000,000	
Annual amortization of bond discount ($2,000,000/20)	100,000	
Annual amortization of issuing expenses ($400,000/20)	20,000	
Total annual tax-deductible expenses	$4,120,000	

(c) Less annual tax savings:
Marginal tax rate (34%) × total annual tax-deductible expenses — × .34 — 1,400,800

(d) Equals annual net cash outflow from issuing new bonds — $ 2,599,200

Step 4: Calculate the *annual net cash benefits* (that is, difference between the annual benefits and costs) from the refunding decision.

(a) Add benefits:
Annual cash benefits from eliminating the old bonds (from Step 2) — $ 2,919,000

(b) Less costs:
Annual cash outflows from issuing the new debt (from Step 3) — 2,599,200

(c) Equals annual net cash benefits — $ 319,800

Step 5: Calculate the *present value of the annual net cash benefits.*

(a) Discount the 20-year $319,800 annuity (from Step 4) back to the present at the after-tax cost of borrowing on the new bonds of 5.28 percent — $ 3,892,471

Step 6: Calculate the *refunding decision's net present value.*

(a) Present value of the annual net cash benefits (from Step 5) — $ 3,892,471

(b) Less present value of initial outlay (from Step 1) — 2,947,500

(c) Equals net present value — $ 944,971

A typical complication in the analysis of the bond-refunding decision involves a difference in the maturities of the new and old bonds. The old bonds, which have been outstanding for some length of time, may have a shorter maturity than the proposed new bonds that are intended to replace them. Actually, this complication is quite easy to accommodate. The only alteration in the analysis is that *only* the net benefits up to the maturity of the old bonds are considered; after the old bonds terminate, the analysis terminates.

Advantages and Disadvantages

The corporate financing decision is complicated by the various tradeoffs among alternative financial instruments. To better understand the role of long-term debt in this decision process, we will examine its advantages and disadvantages.

Advantages to the Firm

1. Long-term debt is generally less expensive than other forms of financing because (a) investors view debt as a relatively safe investment alternative

and demand a lower rate of return, and (b) interest expenses are tax deductible.

2. Bondholders do not participate in extraordinary profits; the payments are limited to interest.

3. Bondholders do not have voting rights.

4. Flotation costs on bonds are generally lower than those on common stock.

Disadvantages to the Firm

1. Debt (other than income bonds) results in interest payments that, if not met, can force the firm into bankruptcy.

2. Debt (other than income bonds) produces fixed charges, increasing the firm's financial leverage. Although this may not be a disadvantage to all firms, it certainly is for some firms with unstable earnings streams.

3. Debt must be repaid at maturity and thus at some point involves a major cash outflow.

4. The typically restrictive nature of indenture covenants may limit the firm's future financial flexibility.

Preferred Stock

Preferred stock is often referred to as a hybrid security because it has many characteristics of both common stock and bonds. Preferred stock is similar to common stock in that it has no fixed maturity date, the nonpayment of dividends does not bring on bankruptcy, and dividends are not deductible for tax purposes. On the other hand, preferred stock is similar to bonds in that dividends are limited in amount.

The size of the preferred stock dividend is generally fixed either as a dollar amount or as a percentage of the par value. For example, Texas Power and Light has issued $4 preferred stock, while Toledo Edison has some 4.25 percent preferred stock outstanding. The par value on the Toledo Edison preferred stock is $100, hence each share pays 4.25% × $100, or $4.25 in dividends annually. Because these dividends are fixed, preferred stockholders do not share in the residual earnings of the firm but are limited to their stated annual dividend.

In examining preferred stock we will first discuss several features common to almost all preferred stock. Next we will investigate less frequently included features and take a brief look at methods of retiring preferred stock. We will close by examining its advantages and disadvantages.

Features of Preferred Stock

Although each issue of preferred stock is unique, several characteristics are common to almost all issues. These traits include the ability to issue multiple classes of preferred stock, the claim on assets and income, and the cumulative and protective features.

Multiple Classes

If a company desires, it can issue more than one series or class of preferred stock, and each class can have different characteristics. In fact, it is quite common for firms that issue preferred stock to issue more than one series. For example, Philadelphia Electric has 13 different issues of preferred stock outstanding. These issues can be further differentiated by the fact that some are convertible into common stock while others are not, and they have varying priority status with respect to assets in the event of bankruptcy.

Adjustable Rate

In the early 1980s, another new financing alternative was developed aimed at providing investors with some protection against wide swings in principal that occur when interest rates move up and down. This financing vehicle is called *adjustable rate preferred stock*. With adjustable rate preferred stock, quarterly dividends fluctuate with interest rates under a formula that ties the dividend payment at either a premium or discount to the highest of (1) the three-month Treasury bill rate, (2) the 10-year Treasury bond constant maturity rate, or (3) the 20-year Treasury bond constant maturity rate. While adjustable rate preferred stock allows interest rates to be tied to the rates on Treasury securities, it also provides a maximum and a minimum level to which they can climb or fall called the *dividend rate band*. The purpose of allowing the interest rate on this preferred stock to fluctuate is, of course, to minimize the fluctuation in the principal of the preferred stock. In times of high and fluctuating interest rates, this is a very appealing feature indeed. In Table 20–6 several issues of adjustable rate preferred stock are identified.

In the late 1980s *auction rate preferred stock* began to appear. Auction rate preferred stock is actually variable rate preferred stock in which the dividend rate is set by an auction process. In the case of auction rate preferred, the dividend rate is set every 49 days. At each auction, buyers and sellers place bids for shares, specifying the yield they are willing to accept for the next seven-week period. The yield is then set at the lowest level necessary to match buyers and sellers. As a result, the yield offered on auction rate preferred stock accurately reflects current interest rates, while keeping the market price of these securities at par.

Convertibility

Much of the preferred stock that is issued today is **convertible** at the discretion of the holder into a predetermined number of shares of common stock. In fact, today about one-third of all preferred stock issued has a convertibility feature. The convertibility feature is, of course, desirable and thus reduces the cost of the preferred stock to the issuer. The characteristics common to this type of preferred stock will be discussed in detail in Chapter 21.

TABLE 20–6.
Adjustable Rate Preferred Stock

Issuer	Amount of Offering ($000)	Dividend Rate at Offering	Dividend Rate Thereafter (Applicable Rate)[a]	Dividend Rate Band	Call Protection
Bank America Corp.	$400,000	9.25%	Adjusted quarterly to 4.00% below the applicable rate	6%–12%	No call allowed for the first 5 years
J. P. Morgan & Co., Inc.	250,000	9.25	Adjusted quarterly to 4.875% below the applicable rate	5%–11½%	No call allowed for the first 3 years
Integrated Resources, Inc.	100,000	12.50	Adjusted quarterly to 0.75% higher than the applicable rate	8%–15%	No call allowed for the first 5 years
Liberty National Corp.	25,000	11.00	Adjusted quarterly at the applicable rate	6½%–13%	No call allowed for the first 5 years
Reading & Bates Corp.	37,500	13.00	Adjusted quarterly to 0.75% higher than the applicable rate	7%–14%	No call allowed for the first 5 years
Gulf States Utilities Corp.	30,000	11.50	Adjusted quarterly to 0.65% higher than the applicable rate	7%–13%	No call allowed for the first 5 years

[a]In all cases the "applicable rate" refers to the highest of (1) the 3-month Treasury bill rate, (2) the 10-year Treasury bond maturity rate, or (3) the 20-year Treasury bond constant maturity rate.

Claim on Assets and Income

Preferred stock has priority over common stock with respect to claims on assets in the case of bankruptcy. The preferred stock claim is honored after that of bonds and before that of common stock. Multiple issues of preferred stock may be prioritized. Preferred stock also has a claim on income prior to common stock. That is, the firm must pay its preferred stock dividends before it pays common stock dividends. Thus, in terms of risk, preferred stock is safer than common stock because it has a prior claim on assets and income. However, it is riskier than long-term debt because its claims on assets and income come after those of bonds.

Cumulative Feature

Most preferred stock carries a **cumulative feature** that requires all past unpaid preferred stock dividends be paid before any common stock dividends are declared. The purpose is to provide some degree of protection for the preferred stock shareholder. Without a cumulative feature there would be no reason why preferred stock dividends would not be omitted or passed when common stock dividends were passed. Because preferred stock does not have the dividend enforcement power of interest from bonds, the cumulative feature is necessary to protect the rights of preferred stockholders.

Protective Provisions

In addition to the cumulative feature, protective provisions are common to preferred stock. These protective provisions generally allow for voting rights in the event of nonpayment of dividends, or they restrict the payment of common stock dividends if sinking-fund payments are not met or if the firm is in financial difficulty. In effect, the protective features included with preferred stock are similar to the restrictive provisions included with long-term debt.

To examine typical protective provisions, let us look at Tenneco and Reynolds Metals preferred stock. The Tenneco preferred stock has a protective provision that provides preferred stockholders with voting rights whenever six quarterly dividends are in arrears. At that point the preferred shareholders are given the power to elect a majority of the board of directors. The Reynolds Metals preferred stock includes a protective provision that precludes the payment of common stock dividends during any period in which the preferred stock sinking fund is in default. Both provisions, which yield protection beyond that provided for by the cumulative provision and thereby reduce shareholder risk, are desirable. They reduce the cost of preferred stock to the issuing firm.

Participation

Although participating features are infrequent in preferred stock, their inclusion can greatly affect its desirability and cost. The *participation feature* allows the preferred stockholder to participate in earnings beyond the payment of the stated dividend. This is usually done in accordance with some set formula. For example, Borden Series A preferred stock currently provides for a dividend of no less than 60 cents per share, to be determined by the board of directors. Preferred stock of this sort actually resembles common stock as much as it does normal preferred stock. Although a participating feature is certainly desirable from the point of view of the investor, it is infrequently included in preferred stock.

PIK Preferred

One by-product of the levered buyout boom of the late 1980s was the creation of pay-in-kind (PIK) preferred stock. With PIK preferred, investors receive no dividends initially; they merely get more preferred stock, which in turn pays dividends in even more preferred stock. Eventually, usually after five or six years if all goes well for the issuing company, cash dividends should replace the preferred stock dividends. Needless to say, the issuing firm has to offer hefty dividends, generally ranging from 12 percent to 18 percent, to entice investors to purchase PIK preferred.

Retirement of Preferred Stock

Although preferred stock does not have a set maturity associated with it, issuing firms generally provide for some method of retirement. If preferred stock could not be retired, issuing firms could not take advantage of falling interest rates.

Calling Preferred Stock

Most preferred stock has some type of call provision associated with it. In fact, the Securities and Exchange Commission discourages the issuance of preferred stock without some call provision. The SEC has taken this stance on the grounds that if a method of retirement is not provided, the issuing firm will not be able to replace its preferred stock if interest rates fall.

The call feature on preferred stock usually involves an initial premium above the par value or issuing price of the preferred of approximately 10 percent. Then, over time, the call premium generally falls. For example, Quaker Oats in 1976 issued $9.56 cumulative preferred stock with no par value for $100 per share. This issue was not callable until 1980 and then was callable at $109.56. After that the call price gradually drops to $100 in the year 2000, as shown in Table 20–7.

By setting the initial call price above the initial issue price and allowing it to decline slowly over time, the firm protects the investor from an early call that carries no premium. A call provision also allows the issuing firm to plan the retirement of its preferred stock at predetermined prices.

Using Sinking Funds Provisions

A **sinking-fund** provision requires the firm periodically to set aside an amount of money for the retirement of its preferred stock. This money is then used to purchase the preferred stock in the open market or through the use of the call provision, whichever method is cheaper. Although preferred stock does not have a maturity date associated with it, the use of a call provision in addition to a sinking fund can effectively create a maturity date. For example, the Quaker Oats issue we just examined has associated with it an annual sinking fund, operating between the years 1981 and 2005, which requires the annual elimination of a minimum of 20,000 shares and a maximum of 40,000. The minimum payments are designed so that the entire issue will be retired by the year 2005. If any sinking-fund payments are made above the minimum amount, the issue will be retired prior to 2005. The Quaker Oats issue of preferred stock has a maximum life of 30 years, and the size of the issue outstanding decreases each year after 1981.

TABLE 20–7.
Call Provision of Quaker Oats
$9.56 Cumulative Preferred
Stock

Date		Call Price
Date of issue until 7/19/80		Not callable
7/20/80	until 7/19/85	$109.56
7/20/85	until 7/19/90	107.17
7/20/90	until 7/19/95	104.78
7/20/95	until 7/19/00	102.39
After 7/19/00		100.00

Advantages and Disadvantages

Because preferred stock is a hybrid of bonds and common stock, it offers the firm several advantages and disadvantages by comparison with bonds and common stock.

Advantages to the Firm

1. Preferred stock does not have any default risk to the issuer. That is, the nonpayment of dividends does not force the firm into bankruptcy, as does the nonpayment of interest on debt.
2. The dividend payments are generally limited to a stated amount. Preferred stock does not participate in excess earnings, as does common stock.
3. Preferred stockholders do not have voting rights except in the case of financial distress. Therefore, the issuance of preferred stock does not create a challenge to the owners of the firm.
4. Although preferred stock does not carry a specified maturity, the inclusion of call features and sinking funds provides the ability to replace the issue if interest rates decline.

Disadvantages to the Firm

1. Because preferred stock is riskier than bonds and because its dividends are not tax deductible, its cost is higher than that of bonds.
2. Although preferred stock dividends can be omitted, their cumulative nature makes their payment almost mandatory.

Common Stock

Common stock involves ownership in the corporation. In effect, bondholders and preferred stockholders can be viewed as creditors, while the common stockholders are the true owners of the firm. Common stock does not have a maturity date, but exists as long as the firm does. Nor does common stock have an upper limit on its dividend payments. Dividend payments must be declared by the firm's board of directors before they are issued. In the event of bankruptcy the common stockholders, as owners of the corporation, cannot exercise claims on assets until the bondholders and preferred shareholders have been satisfied.

In examining common stock, we will look first at several of its features or characteristics. Then we will focus on the process of raising funds through rights offerings. Finally, we will investigate the advantages and disadvantages of the use of common stock.

Perspective in Finance

Recently, stock repurchases, takeovers, and going private transactions have severely eaten into the outstanding amount of corporate equity. In fact, between 1983 and 1988, the level of publicly traded corporate equity fell by at least 5 percent per year as a result of these transactions. At the current rate, it has been estimated that in the year 2003 the last individually owned share of publicly traded common stock will be sold. Although the likelihood of this occurring is extremely remote, it does give some perspective on how much corporate equity recently has diminished.

Features or Characteristics

We now examine common stock's claim on income and assets, stockholder voting rights, and the meaning and importance of its limited-liability feature.

Claim on Income

As the owners of the corporation, the common shareholders have the right to the residual income after bondholders and preferred stockholders have been paid. This income may be paid directly to the shareholders in the form of dividends or retained and reinvested by the firm. Although it is obvious the shareholder benefits immediately from the distribution of income in the form of dividends, the reinvestment of earnings also benefits the shareholder. Plowing back earnings into the firm results in an increase in the value of the firm, in its earning power, and in its future dividends. This action in turn results in an increase in the value of the stock. In effect, residual income is distributed directly to shareholders in the form of dividends or indirectly in the form of capital gains on their common stock.

The right to residual income has both advantages and disadvantages for the common stockholder. The advantage is that the potential return is limitless. Once the claims of the most senior securities—that is, bonds and preferred stock—have been satisfied, the remaining income flows to the common stockholders in the form of dividends or capital gains. The disadvantage is that if the bond and preferred stock claims on income totally absorb earnings, common shareholders receive nothing. In years when earnings fall, it is the common shareholder who suffers first.

Claims on Assets

Just as common stock has the residual claim on income, it also has a residual claim on assets in the case of liquidation. Only after the claims of debt holders and preferred stockholders have been satisfied do the claims of common shareholders receive attention. Unfortunately, when bankruptcy does occur, the claims of the common shareholders generally go unsatisfied. In effect, this residual claim on assets adds to the risk of common stock. Thus, while common stock has historically provided a large return, averaging 10 percent annually since the late 1920s, it also has large risks associated with it.

Voting Rights

The common stock shareholders are entitled to elect the board of directors and are in general the only security holders given a vote. Early in this century it was not uncommon for a firm to issue two classes of common stock, which were identical except that only one carried voting rights. For example, both the Parker Pen Co. and the Great Atlantic and Pacific Tea Co. (A&P) had two such classes of common stock. This practice was virtually eliminated by (1) the Public Utility Holding Company Act of 1935, which gave the Securities and Exchange Commission the power to require that newly issued common stock carry voting rights, (2) the New York Stock Exchange's refusal to list common stock without voting privileges, and (3) investor demand for the inclusion of voting rights. However, with the merger boom of the eighties dual classes of common stock with different voting rights again emerged, this time as a defensive tactic used to prevent takeovers. The *Financial Management in Practice* box, "Gregg A. Jarrell on Dual-Class Recapitalizations," speaks to this.

Common shareholders not only have the right to elect the board of directors, they also must approve any change in the corporate charter. A typical charter change might involve the authorization to issue new stock or perhaps a merger proposal.

Voting for directors and charter changes occurs at the corporation's annual meeting. While shareholders may vote in person, the majority generally vote by proxy. A **proxy** gives a designated party the temporary power of attorney to vote for the signee at the corporation's annual meeting. The firm's management generally solicits proxy votes and, if the shareholders are satisfied with its performance, has little problem securing them. However, in times of financial distress or when management takeovers are threatened, *proxy fights*—battles between rival groups for proxy votes—occur.

While each share of stock carries the same number of votes, the voting procedure is not always the same from company to company. The two procedures commonly used are majority and cumulative voting. Under *majority voting*, each share of stock allows the shareholder one vote, and each position on the board of directors is voted on separately. Because each member of the board of directors is elected by a simple majority, a majority of shares has the power to elect the entire board of directors.

With *cumulative voting*, each share of stock allows the shareholder a number of votes equal to the number of directors being elected. The shareholder can then cast all of his or her votes for a single candidate or split them among the various candidates. The advantage of a cumulative voting procedure is that it gives minority shareholders the power to elect a director.

Perspective in Finance

In theory, the shareholders pick the corporate board of directors, generally through proxy voting, and the board of directors in turn pick the management. Unfortunately, in reality the system frequently works the other way around. Management selects both the issues and the board of director nominees and then distributes the proxy ballots. In effect, shareholders are offered a slate of nominees selected by management from which to choose. The end result is that management effectively selects the directors who then may have more allegiance to the managers than to the shareholders. This in turn sets up the potential for agency problems in which a divergence of interests between managers and shareholders is allowed to exist, with the board of directors not monitoring the managers on behalf of the shareholders as they should.

Limited Liability

Although the common stock shareholders are the actual owners of the corporation, their liability in the case of bankruptcy is limited to the amount of their investment. The advantage is that investors who might not otherwise invest their funds in the firm become willing to do so. This limited-liability feature aids the firm in raising funds.

Preemptive Rights

The **preemptive right** entitles the common shareholder to maintain a proportionate share of ownership in the firm. When new shares are issued, common shareholders have the first right of refusal. If a shareholder owns 25 percent of the corporation's stock, then he or she is entitled to purchase 25 percent of the new shares. Certificates issued to the shareholders giving them an option to purchase a stated number of new shares of stock at a specified price during a 2- to 10-week period are called **rights.** These rights can be exercised, generally at a price below the common stock's current market price, can be allowed to expire, or can be sold in the open market.

Rights Offering

We will look first at the dates surrounding a rights offering and then examine the process of raising funds and the value of a right.

Dates Surrounding a Rights Offering

Let us examine the announcement of a rights offering by a hypothetical corporation. On March 1 the firm announces that all "holders of record" as of April 6 will be issued rights, which will expire on May 30 and will be mailed to them on April 25. In this example March 1 is the **announcement date,** April 6 the **holder-of-record date,** and May 30 the **expiration date.** While this seems rather straightforward, it is complicated by the fact that if the stock is sold a day or two before the holder-of-record date, the corporation may not have time to record the transaction and replace the old owner's name with that of the new owner; the rights might then be sent to the wrong person. To deal with this problem an additional date has been created, the **ex-rights date.** The ex-rights date occurs four trading days before the holder-of-record date.

On or after the ex-rights date the stock sells without the rights. Whoever owns the stock on the day prior to the ex-rights date receives the rights. Thus, if the holder-of-record date is April 6 and four trading days earlier is April 2, anyone purchasing the stock on or before April 1 will receive the rights, whereas anyone purchasing the stock on or after April 2 will not. The price of the stock prior to the ex-rights date is referred to as the **rights-on price,** whereas the price on or after the ex-rights date is the **ex-rights price.** The timing of this process and the terminology are shown in Table 20–8.

Raising of Funds Through Rights Offerings

Three questions and theoretical relationships must be explained about rights offerings. First, how many rights are required to purchase a share of new stock? Second, what is the theoretical value of a right? Finally, what effect do rights offerings have on the value of the common stock outstanding?

TABLE 20–8.
Illustration of Timing
of Rights Offering

Stock sells rights-on	{	March 1 —Announcement date
		April 1 —The owner of the stock as of this date receives the rights
Stock sells ex-rights	{	April 2 —Ex-rights date } four trading days
		April 6 —Holder-of-record date }
		April 25 —Mailing date
		May 30 —Expiration date

Let us continue with the example of our hypothetical corporation and assume it has 600,000 shares of stock outstanding, currently selling for $100 per share. To finance new projects, this firm needs to raise an additional $10,500,000 and wishes to do so with a rights offering. Moreover, the subscription price on the new stock is $70 per share. The subscription price is set below the current market price of the stock to ensure a complete sale of the new stock. To determine how many shares must be sold to raise the desired funds, we divide the desired funds by the subscription price:

$$\text{new shares to be sold} = \frac{\text{desired funds to be raised}}{\text{subscription price}}$$

$$= \frac{\$10,500,000}{\$70} \qquad \textbf{(20-2)}$$

$$= 150,000 \text{ shares}$$

We know each share of common stock receives one right, and 150,000 new shares of common stock must be sold. Therefore, to determine the number of rights necessary to purchase one share of stock, we simply divide the original number of shares outstanding by the new shares to be sold:

$$\begin{array}{l}\text{number of rights necessary to} \\ \text{purchase one share of stock}\end{array} = \frac{\begin{array}{c}\text{original number of} \\ \text{shares outstanding}\end{array}}{\text{new shares to be sold}}$$

$$= \frac{600,000 \text{ shares}}{150,000 \text{ shares}} \qquad \textbf{(20-3)}$$

$$= 4 \text{ rights}$$

This indicates that if a current shareholder wishes to purchase a share of the new stock, he or she needs four rights plus $70:

$$\begin{array}{l}\text{price of a share} \\ \text{of new stock}\end{array} = \begin{array}{c}\text{subscription} \\ \text{price}\end{array} + \begin{array}{c}\text{number of rights} \\ \text{necessary to purchase} \\ \text{one share of stock}\end{array}$$
$$\qquad \textbf{(20-4)}$$
$$= \$70 + 4 \text{ rights}$$

Because the subscription price is well below the current market value, there is clearly some value to a right.

The theoretical value of the right obviously depends upon (1) the relationship between the market price of the stock and the subscription price and (2) the number of rights necessary to purchase one share of stock. To determine the value of a right in the preceding example, first let us determine the market value of the corporation. Originally, the firm had 600,000 shares of stock outstanding, selling at $100 each, for a total value of $60,000,000. Let us now assume that the market value of the firm went up by exactly the amount raised by the rights offering, $10,500,000, making the new market value of the firm $70,500,000. In reality the market value of the firm will go up by more than this amount if investors feel the firm will earn more than its required rate of return on these funds.

Taking the new market value for the firm, $70,500,000, and dividing by the total number of shares outstanding, 750,000, we find that the new market value for the stock will be $94 per share. That is to say, after all the new stock has been issued, the market value of the stock will fall to $94 per share. Because it takes four rights and $70 to purchase one share of stock that will end up worth $94, the value of a right is equal to the savings made ($24—that is, you can buy a $94 share of stock for $70), divided by the number of rights necessary to purchase one share of stock:

$$\text{theoretical value of one right} = \frac{\left(\begin{array}{c}\text{market price}\\ \text{of stock ex rights}\end{array}\right) - \left(\begin{array}{c}\text{subscription}\\ \text{price}\end{array}\right)}{\begin{array}{c}\text{number of rights}\\ \text{necessary to purchase}\\ \text{one share of stock}\end{array}} \qquad \textbf{(20-5)}$$

$$R = \frac{P_{\text{ex}} - S}{N}$$

$$= \frac{\$94 - \$70}{4} \qquad \textbf{(20-6)}$$

$$= \$6$$

where R = value of one right

P_{ex} = ex-rights price of the stock

$\quad S$ = subscription price

$\quad N$ = number of rights necessary to purchase one share of stock

If the stock were selling rights-on—that is, before the ex-rights date—the theoretical value of a right could be determined from the following equation:[10]

$$R = \frac{P_{\text{on}} - S}{N + 1} \qquad \textbf{(20-12)}$$

where P_{on} is the rights-on price of the stock. Substituting in the values from our example, we find:

$$R = \frac{\$100 - \$70}{4 + 1} = \$6$$

We found the same theoretical value for the right from both equations because the second equation is derived directly from the first.

If we think about the mathematical operations we have just performed, we can see that stockholders do not benefit or lose from a rights offering. They receive something of value, the right, but lose exactly that amount in the form of a stock price decline. Of course, if they do not exercise or sell their rights, they lose, but if the rights are not ignored, then they neither lose nor gain from a rights offering. Examination of the behavior of stockholders shows that only a small percentage neglect to exercise or sell their rights.

At this point it also should be clear that the subscription price is irrelevant in a rights offering. The main concern in selecting a subscription price is setting it low enough so that the price of the stock will not fall below it. As long as the subscription price is set far enough below the price of the stock to ensure that

---

[10]This equation is derived from the preceding equation as follows. We know that

$$P_{\text{ex}} = P_{\text{on}} - R \qquad \textbf{(20-7)}$$

Substituting $(P_{\text{on}} - R)$ for P_{ex} in equation (20-6) yields

$$R = \frac{P_{\text{on}} - R - S}{N} \qquad \textbf{(20-8)}$$

Simplifying,

$$RN = P_{\text{on}} - R - S \qquad \textbf{(20-9)}$$

$$RN + R = P_{\text{on}} - S \qquad \textbf{(20-10)}$$

$$R(N + 1) = P_{\text{on}} - S \qquad \textbf{(20-11)}$$

$$R = \frac{P_{\text{on}} - S}{N + 1} \qquad \textbf{(20-12)}$$

the rights maintain a positive value, the offering should be successful and the shareholders should not benefit or lose from the offering.

You have probably noticed that in our discussion of rights valuation we have said we are looking at the *theoretical* value of a right. The actual value may differ from the theoretical value for several reasons. One common reason is that transactions costs can limit investor arbitrage that would otherwise push the market price of the right to its theoretical value. A second reason is that speculation and irregular sale of rights over the subscription period may cause shifts in supply that push the market price of the right above or below its theoretical value. It should also be noted that transaction or flotation costs, particularly on smaller issues, can be quite large. Although not shown in this table, flotation costs also vary with diffusion of share ownership. This table also illustrates that flotation costs associated with rights offerings are largely fixed costs; hence the larger the rights offering, the lower the flotation costs as a percent of the amount of funds raised.

Advantages and Disadvantages

The raising of new funds with common stock offers the firm several advantages and disadvantages by comparison with bonds and preferred stock.

Advantages to the Firm

1. The firm is not legally obligated to pay common stock dividends. Thus, in times of financial distress there need not be a cash outflow associated with common stock, while there must be with bonds.

2. Because common stock has no maturity date, the firm does not have a cash outflow associated with its redemption. If the firm desires, it can repurchase its stock in the open market, but it is under no obligation to do so.

3. By issuing common stock the firm increases its financial base and thus its future borrowing capacity. Conversely, issuing debt increases the financial base of the firm, but also cuts into the firm's borrowing capacity. If the firm's capital structure is already overburdened with debt, a new debt offering may preclude any future debt offering until the existing equity base is enlarged. Thus, financing with common stock increases the firm's financing flexibility.

Disadvantages to the Firm

1. Because dividends are not tax deductible, as are interest payments, and because flotation costs on equity are larger than those on debt, common stock has a higher cost than does debt.

2. The issuance of new common stock may result in a change in the ownership and control of the firm. Although the owners have a preemptive right to retain their proportionate control, they may not have the funds to do so. If this is the case, the original owners may see their control diluted by the issuance of new stock.

SUMMARY

Bonds are any long-term promissory note issued by a firm. The legal agreement between the issuing firm and the bond trustee who represents the bondholders is called the indenture. The indenture states the specific terms of the issue, the rights of the bondholders and issuing firm, and the responsibilities of the trustee. In the case of insolvency the claims of debt are honored before those of both common and preferred stock. Bonds also have a claim on income before those of common and preferred stock.

The major types of unsecured debt include debentures, subordinated debentures, and income bonds, while the major types of secured debt include mortgage, first mortgage, second mortgage, blanket mortgage, closed-end mortgage, and open-end mortgage bonds. Because bonds have a maturity date, they must be retired or refunded. Bonds may be retired at maturity, or they may be retired before maturity through the use of a call provision or a sinking fund. We also examined the bond-refunding decision.

Preferred stock is called a hybrid security because it possesses many characteristics of both common stock and bonds. With respect to its claim on assets in the case of bankruptcy and its claim to income for dividends, it takes priority over common stock and yields priority to debt. Most preferred stock also has a cumulative feature, requiring that all past unpaid preferred stock dividends be paid before any common stock dividends are declared. Although preferred stock does not have a maturity date, its retirement is usually provided for through the use of call provisions and sinking funds.

Although debt holders and preferred stockholders can be viewed as creditors, the common stockholders are the true owners of the company. As such, they cannot exercise a claim on assets in the event of bankruptcy until the bondholders and preferred stockholders have been satisfied. The common stockholders have the right to elect the board of directors. They have the further right to maintain their proportionate share in the firm, called the preemptive right. To allow common shareholders to maintain this proportionate ownership, new funds are often raised through rights offerings.

STUDY QUESTIONS

20-1. Explain the difference between mortgage bonds and debentures.

20-2. Why are income bonds regarded as more risky than debentures?

20-3. Under what circumstances will a bond's current yield equal its yield to maturity? How is it possible for a bond's current yield to be greater than its yield to maturity? How is it possible for a bond's current yield to be less than its yield to maturity?

20-4. What factors affect the cost of long-term debt?

20-5. Explain why there might be cost advantages to Eurobonds.

20-6. Bondholders often prefer the inclusion of a sinking fund in their bond issue. Why?

20-7. Although the bond-refunding decision is analyzed in much the same way as the capital-budgeting decision, one major difference is the discount rate used. What discount rate is used in the refunding decision, and what is the rationale behind this?

20-8. Why is preferred stock referred to as a hybrid security? It is often said to combine the worst features of common stock and bonds. What is meant by this statement?

20-9. Since preferred stock dividends in arrears must be paid before common stock dividends, should they be considered a liability and appear on the right-hand side of the balance sheet?

20-10. What are the advantages and disadvantages of the common stockholders' residual claim on income from the point of view of the investor?

20-11. What is a proxy? What is a proxy fight? Why do they occur?

20-12. Explain the difference between majority voting and cumulative voting. If you were a majority shareholder, which would you favor? Why? If you were a minority shareholder, which would you favor? Why?

20-13. Since a rights offering allows common shareholders to purchase common stock at a price below the current market price, why is it not of value to the common shareholder?

ST-1. (*Rights Offering*) A firm is considering a rights offering to raise $30 million. Currently this firm has 3 million shares outstanding selling for $60 per share. The subscription price on the new shares would be $40 per share.
  a. How many shares must be sold to raise the desired funds?
  b. How many rights are necessary to purchase one share of stock?
  c. What is the value of one right?

STUDY PROBLEMS (SET A)

20-1A. (*Bankruptcy Distribution*) The Hayes Corporation is facing bankruptcy. The market value of its mortgaged assets is $30 million and of all other assets $50 million. Hayes currently has outstanding $40 million in mortgaged bonds, $20 million in subordinated debentures, and $20 million in preferred stock, and the par value of the common stock outstanding is $40 million. If the corporation goes bankrupt, how will the distribution be made?

20-2A. (*Refunding Decision*) The A. Fields Wildcats Corporation currently has outstanding a 20-year $10 million bond issue with a 9¼ percent interest rate callable at $103. The unamortized flotation costs and the discount on these bonds currently total $600,000. Because of a decline in interest rates, Fields would be able to refund the issue with a $10 million issue of 8 percent 20-year bonds, providing the firm with $9.3 million after flotation costs. The issuing expenses would claim an additional $200,000. The overlap period during which both issues would be expected to be outstanding is one month. Assuming a 34 percent marginal corporate tax rate, determine whether or not this bond issue should be refunded. (*Note:* The present value of an annuity of $1 for 20 years at 5.28 percent is 12.172.)

20-3A. (*Refunding Decision*) Three years ago the R. Wittman Corporation issued a 30-year $50 million bond issue with a 7 percent interest rate callable at $108. Because of the discount and flotation costs this issue initially raised only $48 million. The discount and flotation costs are being amortized using the straight-line method. During the past three years interest rates have fallen, allowing the Wittman Corporation to replace this bond issue with a 27-year $50 million bond issue with a coupon rate of 6 percent. The new issue will provide the firm with $49 million after flotation costs. Issuing expenses will drain an additional $400,000. The overlap period during which both issues are expected to be outstanding is one month. Assuming a 34 percent marginal corporate tax rate, determine whether or not the refunding decision should be made. (*Note:* The present value of an annuity of $1 for 27 years at 3.96 percent is 16.4031.)

20-4A. (*Zero Coupon Bond—Valuation*) Power Supply Corporation has issued zero coupon bonds that mature in 20 years. These bonds pay $1,000 at maturity. What is their price if they provide an 8 percent return per year?

20-5A. (*Zero Coupon Bond—Determination of Yield to Maturity*) Linkous Corporation has zero coupon bonds outstanding that pay $1,000 at maturity and mature in 20 years. If these bonds are selling for $104, what is their yield to maturity?

20-6A. (*Bond Indenture Research Project*) As a research project obtain several bond indentures. These can be obtained directly from the corporation issuing the bond or perhaps through a local stockbroker. Examine the restrictive covenants—in particular, prohibitions on the sale of accounts receivable, constraints on common stock dividends, fixed asset restrictions, and constraints on additional borrowing—and determine the reason for their inclusion.

20-7A. (*Rights Offering*) The L. Turner Corporation is considering raising $12 million through a rights offering. It has one million shares of stock outstanding, currently selling for $84 per share. The subscription price on the new stock will be $60 per share.
  a. How many shares must be sold to raise the desired funds?
  b. How many rights are necessary to purchase one share of stock?
  c. What is the value of one right?

20-8A. (*Rights Offering*) The E. Muransky Corporation is considering a rights offering to raise $35 million to finance new projects. It currently has 2 million shares of stock outstanding, selling for $50 per share. The subscription price on the new shares would be $35 per share.
  a. How many shares must be sold to raise the desired funds?
  b. How many rights are necessary to purchase one share of stock?
  c. What is the value of one right?

20-9A. (*Rights Offerings*) The B. Fuller Corporation is in the process of selling common stock through a rights offering. Prior to the rights offering, the firm had 500,000 shares of common stock outstanding. Through the rights offering, it plans on issuing an additional 100,000 shares at a subscription price of $30. After the stock went ex-rights, the market price was $40. What was the price of the B. Fuller common stock just prior to the rights offering? (*Hint:* Set equation (20-6) equal to equation (20-12) and solve for P_{on}.)

STUDY PROBLEMS (SET B)

20-1B. (*Bankruptcy Distribution*) The Finky Corporation is facing bankruptcy. The market value of its mortgaged assets is $40 million and of all other assets $35 million. Finky currently has outstanding $45 million in mortgaged bonds, $15 million in subordinated debentures, and $20 million in preferred stock, and the par value of the common stock outstanding is $35 million. If the corporation goes bankrupt, how will the distribution be made?

20-2B. (*Refunding Decision*) The Hook'ems Corporation currently has outstanding a 20-year $12 million bond issue with a 9.5 percent interest rate callable at $103. The unamortized flotation costs and the discount on these bonds currently total $600,000. Because of a decline in interest rates, Hook'ems would be able to refund the issue with a $12 million issue of 8 percent 20-year bonds, providing the firm with $11.3 million after flotation costs. The issuing expenses would claim an additional $250,000. The overlap period during which both issues would be expected to be outstanding is one month. Assuming a 34 percent marginal corporate tax rate, determine whether or not this bond issue should be refunded. (*Note:* The present value of an annuity of $1 for 20 years at 5.28 percent is 12.172.)

20-3B. (*Refunding Decision*) Three years ago the Boulder Corporation issued a 30-year $45 million bond issue with a 6.75 percent interest rate callable at $108. Because of the discount and flotation costs this issue initially raised only $43 million. The discount and flotation costs are being amortized using the straight-line method. During the past 3 years interest rates have fallen, allowing the Boulder Corporation to replace this bond issue with a 27-year $45 million bond issue with a coupon rate of 6 percent. The new issue will provide the firm with $44 million after flotation costs. Issuing expenses will drain an additional $350,000. The overlap period during which both issues are expected to be outstanding is one month. Assuming a 34 percent marginal corporate tax rate, determine whether or not the refunding decision should be made. (*Note:* The present value of an annuity of $1 for 27 years at 3.96 percent is 16.4031.)

20-4B. (*Zero Coupon Bond—Valuation*) Walker Corporation has issued zero coupon bonds that mature in 15 years. These bonds pay $1,000 at maturity. What is their price if they provide a 9 percent return per year?

20-5B. (*Zero Coupon Bond—Determination of Yield to Maturity*) Beeks Corporation has zero coupon bonds outstanding that pay $1,000 at maturity and mature in 15 years. If these bonds are selling for $183, what is their yield to maturity?

20-6B. (*Junk Bond Indenture Research Project*) As a research project obtain several junk bonds and AA rated bonds indentures. These can be obtained directly from the corporation issuing the bonds or perhaps through a local stockbroker. Examine the restrictive covenants—do you notice a difference in the restrictive nature of the restrictions on junk versus "normal" bonds? Why do you think this is so?

20-7B. (*Rights Offering*) The Good Gravy Corporation is considering raising $15 million through a rights offering. It has one million shares of stock outstanding, currently selling for $86 per share. The subscription price on the new stock will be $60 per share.

    a. How many shares must be sold to raise the desired funds?
    b. How many rights are necessary to purchase one share of stock?
    c. What is the value of one right?

20–8B. (*Rights Offering*) The Utlonghorns Corporation, a film company responsible for the hit movie "Revenge of the Nightmare Police Academy the Thirteenth Part VI," is considering a rights offering to raise $75 million to finance new projects. It currently has 1.5 million shares of stock outstanding, selling for $35 per share. The subscription price on the new shares would be $25 per share.
    a. How many shares must be sold to raise the desired funds?
    b. How many rights are necessary to purchase one share of stock?
    c. What is the value of one right?

20–9B. (*Rights Offerings*) The Gold Castle Corporation is in the process of selling common stock through a rights offering. Prior to the rights offering, the firm had 600,000 shares of common stock outstanding. Through the rights offering, it plans on issuing an additional 100,000 shares at a subscription price of $37. After the stock went ex-rights, the market price was $42. What was the price of the Gold Castle common stock just prior to the rights offering? [*Hint:* Set equation (20–6) equal to equation (20–12) and solve for P_{on}.]

SELF-TEST SOLUTION

SS–1. **a.** new shares to be sold $= \dfrac{\text{desired funds to be raised}}{\text{subscription price}}$

$$= \frac{\$30,000,000}{\$40}$$

$$= 750,000 \text{ shares}$$

    b. number of rights
necessary to purchase $= \dfrac{\text{original number of shares outstanding}}{\text{new shares to be sold}}$
one share of stock

$$= \frac{3,000,000}{750,000}$$

$$= 4 \text{ rights}$$

    c. value of one right $= \dfrac{P_{on} - S}{N + 1}$

$$= \frac{\$60 - \$40}{4 + 1}$$

$$= \frac{\$20}{5}$$

$$= \$4$$

CHAPTER 21

Convertible Securities and Warrants

Convertible Securities ● Warrants

In earlier chapters we concerned ourselves with methods of raising long-term funds through the use of common stock, preferred stock, and short- and long-term debt. In this chapter we will examine how convertibles and warrants can be used to increase the attractiveness of these securities. We have grouped convertibles and warrants together in our discussion because both can be exchanged at the owner's discretion for a specified number of shares of common stock. In investigating each financing alternative we look first at its specific characteristics and purpose; then we focus on any special considerations that should be examined before the convertible security or the warrant is issued.

Convertible Securities

A **convertible security** is a preferred stock or a debt issue that can be exchanged for a specified number of shares of common stock at the will of the owner. It provides the stable income associated with preferred stock and bonds in addition to the possibility of capital gains associated with common stock. This combination of features has led convertibles to be called *hybrid* securities.

When the convertible is initially issued, the firm receives the proceeds from the sale, less flotation costs. This is the only time the firm receives any proceeds from issuing convertibles. The firm then treats this convertible as if it were normal preferred stock or debentures, paying dividends or interest regularly. If the security owner wishes to exchange the convertible for common stock, he or she may do so at any time according to the terms specified at the time of issue. The desire to convert generally follows a rise in the price of the common stock. Once the convertible owner trades the convertibles in for common stock, the owner can never trade the stock back for convertibles. From then on the owner is treated as any other common stockholder and receives only common stock dividends.

Characteristics and Features of Convertibles

Conversion Ratio

The number of shares of common stock for which the convertible security can be exchanged is set out when the convertible is initially issued. On some convertible issues this **conversion ratio** is stated directly. For example, the convertible may state that it is exchangeable for 15 shares of common stock. Some convertibles give only a **conversion price,** stating, for example, that the security is convertible at $39 per share. This tells us that for every $39 of par value of the convertible security one share of common stock will be received.

$$\text{conversion ratio} = \frac{\text{par value of convertible security}}{\text{conversion price}} \qquad \textbf{(21-1)}$$

For example, in 1987 Union Carbide issued $350 million of convertible debentures that mature in 2012. These convertibles have a $1,000 par value, a 7½ percent coupon interest rate, and a conversion price of $35.50. Thus, the conversion ratio—the number of shares to be received upon conversion—is $1000/$35.50 = 28.169 shares. The security owner has the choice of holding the 7½ percent convertible debenture or trading it in for 28.169 shares of Union Carbide common stock.

Conversion Value

The **conversion value** of a convertible security is the total market value of the common stock for which it can be exchanged. This can be calculated as follows:

$$\begin{matrix}\text{conversion} \\ \text{value}\end{matrix} = \begin{pmatrix}\text{conversion} \\ \text{ratio}\end{pmatrix} \times \begin{pmatrix}\text{market value per share} \\ \text{of the common stock}\end{pmatrix} \qquad \textbf{(21-2)}$$

If the Union Carbide common stock were selling for, say, $24 per share, then the conversion value for the Union Carbide convertible would be (28.169)($24.00) = $676.06, that is, the market value of the common stock for which the convertible could be exchanged would be $676.06. Thus, regardless of what this convertible debenture was selling for, it could be converted into $676.06 worth of common stock.

Security Value

The **security value** (or bond value, as it is sometimes called) of a convertible security is the price the convertible security would sell for in the absence of its conversion feature. This is calculated by determining the required rate of return on a straight (nonconvertible) issue of the same quality and then determining the present value of the interest and principal payments at this rate of return. For example, the Union Carbide convertible has a Standard and Poor's BB− rating, and on a given day BB− issues were yielding approximately 10 percent. In determining the security value of this issue, we are answering the question, What must this Union Carbide bond, which pays 7½ percent semiannually and is rated BB− with 20 years to maturity, sell at in order to yield 10 percent? Since this bond pays 7½ percent semiannually, it gives the investor $37.50 every six months for the next 20 years for a total 40 $37.50 payments, and at the end of 20 years (after 40 six-month periods) it pays the investor its par value of $1,000. As shown in equation (3−7), in determining the present value of this bond we use a discount rate of 10/2, or 5 percent. Thus, the value of this bond with semiannual payments is determined as follows:

$$SV = \sum_{t=1}^{2n} \frac{\frac{IP}{2}}{\left(1 + \frac{i}{2}\right)^t} + \frac{P}{\left(1 + \frac{i}{2}\right)^{2n}} \qquad \textbf{(21-3)}$$

where SV = the security value

I = the coupon interest rate

P = the par value

n = the number of years to maturity

i = the required rate of return on a straight issue of the same quality

Then the value of the Union Carbide security as a straight debenture yields the following:

$$SV = \sum_{t=1}^{40} \frac{\$37.50}{(1 + .05)^i} + \frac{\$1000}{(1 + .05)^{40}}$$
$$= \$37.50 (17.159) + \$1000 (.142)$$
$$= \$643.46 + \$142.00$$
$$= \$785.46$$

Thus, regardless of what happens to the value of Union Carbide's common stock, the lowest value to which the convertible can drop, assuming there is no change in interest rates, is its value as a straight bond, or is $785.46.

Conversion Period

On some issues the time period during which the convertible can be exchanged for common stock is limited. Many times conversion is not allowed until a specified number of years have passed, or is limited by a terminal conversion date. Still other convertibles may be exchanged at any time during their life. In either case the **conversion period** is specified when the convertible is originally issued.

Conversion Parity Price

The **conversion parity price** is the price at which the investor, in effect, buys the company's stock:

$$\frac{\text{conversion}}{\text{parity price}} = \frac{\begin{array}{c}\text{market price}\\ \text{of convertible security}\end{array}}{\text{conversion ratio}} \qquad \textbf{(21-4)}$$

If the Union Carbide bond is selling for $910.00 and the investor can exchange the bond for 28.169 shares of Union Carbide common stock, then the conversion parity price is ($910.00/28.169) = $32.31. Thus, if the investor purchases this convertible and converts it to common stock, he or she is in effect buying that stock for $32.31 per share.

Conversion Premium

The **conversion premium** is the difference between the convertible's market price and the higher of its security value and its conversion value. It can be expressed as an absolute dollar value, in which case it is defined as

$$\frac{\text{conversion}}{\text{premium}} = \left(\begin{array}{c}\text{market price of}\\ \text{the convertible}\end{array}\right) - \left(\begin{array}{c}\text{higher of the security value}\\ \text{and conversion value}\end{array}\right) \qquad \textbf{(21-5)}$$

Alternatively, the conversion premium can be expressed as a percentage, in which case it is defined as

TABLE 21-1.
Summary of Convertible Terminology

Conversion ratio: the number of shares for which the convertible security can be exchanged.

$$\frac{\text{Conversion}}{\text{ratio}} = \frac{\text{par value of convertible security}}{\text{conversion price}} \qquad (21\text{-}1)$$

Conversion value: the total market value of the common stock for which the covertible can be exchanged.

$$\frac{\text{Conversion}}{\text{value}} = \left(\begin{array}{c}\text{conversion} \\ \text{ratio}\end{array}\right) \times \left(\begin{array}{c}\text{market value per} \\ \text{share of the common stock}\end{array}\right) \qquad (21\text{-}2)$$

Security value: the price the convertible security would sell for in the absence of its conversion feature.

Conversion period: the time period during which the convertible can be exchanged for common stock.

Conversion parity price: the price the investor is in effect paying for the common stock.

$$\frac{\text{Conversion}}{\text{parity price}} = \frac{\text{market price of convertible security}}{\text{conversion ratio}} \qquad (21\text{-}4)$$

Conversion premium: the difference between the convertible's market price and the higher of its security value and its conversion value.

$$\frac{\text{Conversion}}{\text{premium}} = \left(\begin{array}{c}\text{market price} \\ \text{of the} \\ \text{convertible}\end{array}\right) - \left(\begin{array}{c}\text{higher of the} \\ \text{security value and} \\ \text{conversion value}\end{array}\right) \qquad (21\text{-}5)$$

$$\frac{\text{percentage}}{\text{conversion}} = \frac{\left(\begin{array}{c}\text{market price of} \\ \text{convertible bond}\end{array}\right) - \left(\begin{array}{c}\text{higher of the security value} \\ \text{and the conversion value}\end{array}\right)}{\text{higher of the security value and the conversion value}} \qquad \textbf{(21-6)}$$

The Union Carbide convertible's market price was \$910 while its security value was \$785.46 and its conversion value was \$676.06. Thus, its conversion premium was

$$\frac{\$910.00 - \$785.46}{\$785.46} = 15.9 \text{ percent}$$

In effect, an investor was willing to pay a 15.9 percent premium over the higher of its security and conversion values in order to have the possibility of capital gains from stock price advances coupled with the security of the fixed interest payments associated with a debenture.

In describing convertibles, we have introduced a number of terms. To eliminate confusion, Table 21–1 summarizes them.

Perspective in Finance

As you recall the agency problem deals with conflicts of interest between stockholders, bondholders, and managers. Convertible bonds, which allow bondholders to benefit from the price appreciation of equity, help align the interests of stockholders and bondholders and reduce the agency problem.

Reasons Given for Issuing Convertibles

There are several reasons financial managers tend to give for choosing to issue convertibles rather than straight debt, preferred stock, or common stock. These reasons include "sweetening" the long-term debt issue to make it more attractive, delayed equity financing, financing corporate mergers, and the fact that interest rates on convertibles are indifferent to the issuing firm's risk level.

Sweetening Long-Term Debt

Before World War II the major reason for adding a convertible feature to preferred stock or debt was to make the security attractive enough to ensure a market for it. At that time convertibles were primarily limited to firms of lower credit standings that would have had a difficult time issuing straight debt or preferred stock. For these firms, adding a convertible feature would increase the attractiveness of the issue and thereby guarantee its success. Since World War II firms of higher credit standing have also entered the convertible market, issuing convertibles for other reasons, whereas weaker firms have continued to use convertibles as sweeteners.

Delayed Equity Financing

Often a company would rather issue common stock than either preferred stock or debentures; however, it resorts to convertible securities because management feels the current stock price is temporarily depressed or is worried that issuing additional common stock will temporarily drive the stock's earnings per share down and result in a lower stock price. Management's hope is that, after a short period of time, the common stock price will rise and investors will trade their convertibles in for common stock. For example, if the price of Union Carbide's common stock rose and investors subsequently exchanged their convertibles for common stock, they would have in effect purchased the common stock for the conversion parity price, $32.31. That is, for every share of stock Union Carbide exchanged for convertibles, investors originally received $32.31. Because Union Carbide has set its conversion parity price above the stock's market price, the firm will have to give up fewer shares of common stock when the securities are converted than if it raised funds via a common stock offering originally. In effect, equity financing is provided only if the market value of the common stock rises. If it does not, financing remains in the form of lower-cost debt or preferred stock.

Although this may be an explanation financial managers commonly give to explain their use of convertible debt, it should be noted that it would be just as appropriate, in rationalizing why convertibles are issued, to look at what the firm's alternatives would have been if the stock price increased and straight debt had been chosen. In that case the firm might have been better off as it could then replace the short-term debt with stock that may be selling well in excess of the conversion price.

Financing Corporate Mergers

If the stockholders of an acquired company take cash or debt in exchange for their common stock, they incur an immediate tax liability on any capital gains on their investment. If, however, the exchange is made for common, preferred, or convertible preferred stock, the tax liability is postponed, since the transaction is regarded as a tax-free exchange. Thus, many mergers are financed with common or convertible preferred stock.

Convertible preferred stock frequently provides the most attractive terms possible for the exchange. Holders of stock in the company being acquired can be offered the stable income and limited risk of preferred stock, plus the chance for capital gains afforded by the convertible feature. The issuing company also benefits from the use of convertible preferred stock rather than common stock in that less dilution of earnings occurs. The reason is that investors would have demanded additional common stock if the exchange had been made for straight common stock.

Interest Rate Indifference to the Issuing Firm's Risk Level

While higher risk and uncertainty bring on higher interest costs in straight debt, this is not necessarily the case with convertibles. If we think about a convertible as a package of straight debt and a convertible feature allowing the holder to purchase common stock at a set price, an increase in risk and uncertainty certainly raises the cost of the straight-debt portion of the convertible. However, the convertibility feature benefits from this increase in risk and uncertainty and the increase in stock price volatility that follows. In effect the conversion feature only has value if the stock price rises; otherwise it has zero value. The more risk and stock price volatility, the greater the likelihood that the conversion feature will be of value at some point before the expiration date. As a result, more risk and uncertainty increase the value of the conversion feature of the convertible. Thus, the negative effect of an increase in risk and uncertainty on the straight-debt portion of a convertible is partially offset by the positive effect on the conversion feature. The result of all this is that the interest rate associated with convertible debt is, to an extent, indifferent to the risk level of the issuing firm. The coupon rates for medium and high-risk companies issuing convertibles and straight debt might be as follows:

	Company Risk	
	Medium	High
Convertible debt	8%	8.25%
Straight debt	11	13

Thus, for companies with a high level of risk, convertible debt may allow them to raise funds at a relatively favorable rate.

Perspective in Finance

Given what you have learned so far about convertibles, it makes sense that convertibles tend to be issued most frequently by smaller firms with lower bond ratings, high growth rates, and more than average leverage. In addition, convertibles tend to be subordinated and unsecured.

Other Factors to Be Considered

Overhanging Issue

An *overhanging* issue occurs when the firm cannot force conversion because the common stock has not risen sufficiently to justify it. The overhanging issue's major disadvantage to the firm is that it limits financing flexibility. Not only does it make additional financing with convertible securities practically impossible, but it may also make long-term debt unacceptable to investors if the firm has been relying on a successful conversion to bring its financial structure back to normal. If this is the case, the conversion has been thwarted by an insufficient rise in the common stock price; the only available alternative may be a common stock offering. However, this too may be unacceptable or at least undesirable to the firm's management if it feels the common stock price is temporarily depressed.

Forced Conversion

While investors have full legal control over the exercise of a convertible security, the firm can often force them into conversion by calling the convertibles or establishing step-up conversion prices. If, for example, the conversion value of a security exceeds its call price, the firm need only call the security to force any rational investor to convert. A second way of inducing conversion is to provide for increasingly larger conversion prices and thus lower conversion ratios over the years. A convertible debenture with a $1,000 par value could have a conversion price of $50 per share for the first five years and $60 per share after that. In this case if the price of the common stock had risen to $100 per share after five years, an investor would have the choice of converting the security into 20 shares of common stock worth $2,000 or not converting and watching the conversion value of the security drop to $1,666.67 as the conversion price is increased to $60 per share. In most cases a step-up conversion price provides enough incentive to induce conversion as long as the conversion value is greater than the security value of the convertible.

Valuation of a Convertible

The valuation of a convertible depends primarily upon two factors: the value of the straight debenture or preferred stock and the value of the security if it were converted into common stock. Complicating the valuation is the fact that investors are in general willing to pay a premium for the conversion privilege, which allows them to hedge against the future. If the price of the common stock should rise, the investor would participate in capital gains; if it should decline, the convertible security will fall only to its value as a straight debenture or preferred stock.

In examining the Union Carbide convertible debenture we found that if it were selling as a straight debenture, its price would be $785.46. Thus, regardless of what happens to its common stock, the lowest value the convertible can drop to is $785.46. The conversion value, on the other hand is, $676.06. Thus, this convertible is worth more as common stock than if it were straight debt. However, the real question is, Why are investors willing to pay a conversion premium of 15.9 percent over its security or conversion value for this Union Carbide debenture? Quite simply because investors are willing to pay for the chance for capital gains without the large risk of loss.

Figure 21–1 graphically depicts the relationship between the value of the convertible and the price of its common stock. The bond value of the convertible serves as a floor for the value of the investment: When the conversion value reaches the convertible's security value (point *A*), the value of the convertible becomes dependent upon its conversion value. *In effect the convert-*

FIGURE 21–1.
Relationship Between the Market Price of the Common Stock and the Market Price of the Convertible Security

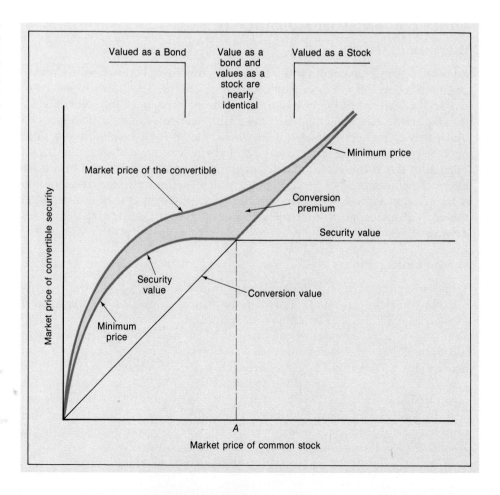

ible security is valued as a bond when the price of the common stock is low and as common stock when the price of the common stock rises. Of course, if the firm is doing poorly and in financial distress, both the common stock price and the security value will suffer. In the extreme, when the firm's total value falls to zero both the common stock and any debt that the firm had issued would have no value. Although the minimum price of the convertible is determined by the higher of either the straight bond or preferred stock price or the conversion value, investors also pay a premium for the conversion option. Again, this premium results because convertible securities offer investors stable income from debenture or preferreds—and thus less risk of price decline due to adverse stock conditions—while retaining capital gains prospects from stock price gains. In effect, downside stock price variability is hedged away, whereas upside variability is not.

Less RISKY (minimize or Protect against a loss)

Perspective in Finance

As you look at the convertible and warrant markets, as well as the options and futures markets covered in the next chapter, keep in mind the fact that these markets are continuously evolving. For example, recently a variation of the convertible debenture called an exchangeable debenture has gained popularity. An exchangeable debenture is similar to a convertible debenture except that it can be exchanged at the option of the holder for the common stock of another company. For example, in late 1989 Millicom Inc. issued $60 million of subordinated exchangeable debentures due in 2014. These debentures are identical to convertibles except that they can be exchanged for stock in Racal Electronics of which Millicom owns 30 million shares. The point here is that in these two chapters we are only describing several basic securities of which there are unlimited variations in the financial markets.

Warrants

A **warrant** provides the investor with an option to purchase a fixed number of shares of common stock at a predetermined price during a specified time period. Warrants have been used in the past primarily by weaker firms as sweetener attachments to bonds or preferred stock to improve their marketability. However, in April 1970, when AT&T included them as a part of a major financing package, warrants achieved a new level of respectability.

Only recently have warrants been issued in conjunction with common stock. Their purpose is essentially the same as when they are issued in conjunction with debt or preferred stock; that is, to improve the reception in the market of the new offering or make a tender offer too attractive to turn down. An example of issuing warrants occurred in 1992 when Hyal Pharmaceutical issued $12,750,000 of units each containing one share of common stock and one half warrant. The warrants were exercisable at any time before the end of 1995, entitling the holder to purchase one share of common stock at a fixed price per share.

Although warrants are similar to convertibles in that both provide investors with a chance to participate in capital gains, the mechanics of the two instruments differ greatly. From the standpoint of the issuing firm there are two major differences. First, when convertibles are exchanged for common stock, debt is eliminated and fixed finance charges are reduced; whereas when warrants are exchanged fixed charges are not reduced. Second, when convertibles are exchanged there is no cash inflow into the firm—the exchange is merely one type of security for another. But with warrants, since they are merely an option to buy the stock at a set price, a cash flow accompanies the exchange.

Characteristics and Features of Warrants

Exercise Price

The **exercise price** is that at which the warrant allows its holder to purchase the firm's common stock. The investor trades a warrant plus the exercise price for common stock. Typically, when warrants are issued the exercise price is set above the current market price of the stock. Thus, if the stock price does not rise above the exercise price, the warrant will never be converted. In addition there can also be a step-up exercise price where the warrant's exercise price changes over time.

Expiration Date

Although some warrants are issued with no **expiration date,** most warrants are set to expire after a number of years. In issuing warrants as opposed to convertibles, the firm gives up some control over when the warrants will be exercised. With convertibles the issuing company can force conversion by calling the issue or using step-up conversion prices, whereas with warrants only the approach of the expiration date or the use of step-up exercise prices can encourage conversion.

Detachability

Most warrants are said to be **detachable** in that they can be sold separately from the security to which they were originally attached. Thus, if an investor purchases a primary issuance of a corporate bond with a warrant attached, he or she has the option of selling the bond alone, selling the warrant alone, or selling the combination intact. *Nondetachable warrants* cannot be sold separately from the security to which they were originally attached. Such a warrant can be separated from the senior security only by being exercised.

Exercise Ratio

The **exercise ratio** states the number of shares that can be obtained at the exercise price with one warrant. If the exercise ratio on a warrant were 1.5, one warrant would entitle its owner to purchase 1.5 shares of common stock at its exercise price.

Reasons for Issuing Warrants

Sweetening Debt

Warrants attached to debt offerings provide a feature whereby investors can participate in capital gains while holding debt. The firm can thereby increase the demand for the issue, increase the proceeds, and lower the interest costs. Attaching warrants to long-term debt is a sweetener, performing essentially the same function that the convertibility feature on debt performs; that is, giving investors something they want and thereby increasing the marketability and demand for the bonds.

Additional Cash Inflow

If warrants are added to sweeten a debt offering, the firm will receive an eventual cash inflow when and if the warrants are exercised; a convertibility feature would not provide this additional inflow.

Other Factors to Be Considered

Nonextinguishment of Debt

When warrants are exercised, the debt or security to which they were originally attached remains in existence. The warrant exercise process provides an additional cash inflow, but it does not provide for the elimination of the original security. With convertible debt, on the other hand, when the convertible is exercised no cash flow occurs, but the original security is eliminated. Thus, the decision between convertible and warrant financing becomes one of tradeoffs —elimination of debt versus additional cash inflows.

CONVERTIBLE   WARRANT

Dilution and Flexibility

Because present accounting standards provide that earnings per share be stated as if all the warrants outstanding had been exercised, warrants have the effect of reducing the firm's reported earnings per share. This potential dilution of   DISADVANTAGE
earnings per share may reduce the firm's financing flexibility. Because of previously issued warrants, the issuance of additional common stock may be hindered or even prohibited. The market's reluctance to accept further equity offerings may be due not only to the potential earnings per share dilution effect of the outstanding warrants, but also to a feeling that only weaker firms have to resort to warrant financing to sweeten their senior security offerings.

Valuation of a Warrant

Because the warrant is an option to purchase a specified number of shares of stock at a specified price for a given length of time, the market value of the warrant will be primarily a function of the common stock price. To understand the valuation of warrants we must define two additional terms, the minimum price and the premium. Let us look at the Hyal Pharmaceutical warrants issued in 1992 in conjunction with common stock with an expiration date of December 31, 1995, an exercise ratio of 1.00, and let's assume an exercise price of $80 through the expiration date. This means that any time until expiration on December 31, 1995, an investor with one warrant can purchase one share of Hyal Pharmaceutical stock at $80 regardless of the market price of that stock. Let's assume these Hyal Pharmaceutical warrants were selling at $5.50, and the Hyal Pharmaceutical stock was selling for $56.75 per share.

Minimum price ■ The *minimum price* of a warrant is determined as follows:

$$\text{minimum price} = \left(\begin{array}{c} \text{market price of} \\ \text{common stock} \end{array} - \begin{array}{c} \text{exercise} \\ \text{price} \end{array} \right) \times \text{exercise ratio} \qquad \textbf{(21–7)}$$

In the Hyal Pharmaceutical example the exercise price is greater than the price of the common stock ($80 as opposed to $56.75). In this case the minimum price of the warrant is considered to be zero, because things simply do not sell for negative prices [($56.75 − $80) × 1.00 = −$23.25]. If, for example, the price of the Hyal Pharmaceutical common stock rose to $86 per share, the minimum price on the warrant would become ($86 − $80) × 1.00 = $6. This would tell us that this warrant could not fall below a price of $6.00, because if it did, investors could realize immediate trading profits by purchasing the warrants and converting them along with the $80 exercise price into common stock until the price of the warrant was pushed up to the minimum price. This process of simultaneously buying and selling equivalent assets for different prices is called *arbitrage*.

Premium ■ The *premium* is the amount above the minimum price for which the warrant sells:

$$\text{premium} = \left(\begin{array}{c} \text{market price} \\ \text{of warrant} \end{array} \right) - \left(\begin{array}{c} \text{minimum price} \\ \text{of warrant} \end{array} \right) \qquad \textbf{(21–8)}$$

In the case of the Hyal Pharmaceutical warrant the premium is $5.50 − $0 = $5.50. Investors are paying a premium of $5.50 above the minimum price for the warrant. They are willing to do so because the possible loss is small, since the warrant price is only about 9.69 percent that of the common stock; in turn, the possible return is large, because, if the price of the common stock climbs the value of the warrant also will climb.

Figure 21–2 graphs the relationships among the warrant price, the minimum price, and the premium. Point A represents the exercise price on the warrant. Once the price of the stock is above the exercise price, the warrant's minimum price takes on positive (or nonzero) values.

A hypothetical numerical example based upon Figure 21–2 is provided in Table 21–2. Looking at the graphic representation of the warrant and the example, we find that the warrant premium tends to drop off as the ratio of the stock price to the exercise price climbs. Why? As the stock price climbs, the warrant loses its leverage ability. Looking at the numerical example, assume an investor purchased $1,000 worth of warrants and $1,000 worth of common stock when the common stock price was $40 and the warrant price was $10; then the price of the stock went up 50 percent to $60 per share, which caused the price of the warrant to go up 150 percent to $25 per share. This leverage feature—the fact that the value of the warrant increases and declines by larger percentages than the value of the underlying stock and thus a small investment

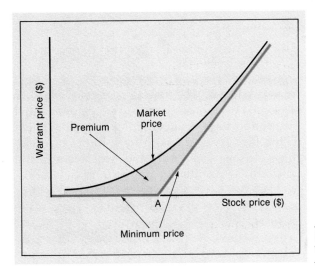

FIGURE 21–2.
Valuation of Warrants

has large possible returns—encourages investors to purchase warrants. However, as the stock price rises, the leverage ability of the warrant declines. For example, assume that an investor purchases $1,000 worth of common stock selling at $110 per share and $1,000 worth of warrants selling for $71 per share. If the stock price went up to $130, the stock investment would have returned 18 percent, whereas the warrant price would have risen to $90 for a return of 27 percent. In the first example when the stock price rose from $40 to $60 per share, the warrant resulted in profits three times greater than on the common stock. In the second example the warrant provided profits only about one and one-half times larger than the common stock. Thus, the warrant premium tends to drop off as the ratio of the stock price to the exercise price climbs and the leverage ability of the warrant declines.

INCREASE IN STOCK PRICE = DECREASE IN PREMIUM

While the stock price/exercise price ratio is one of the most important factors in determining the size of the premium, several other factors also affect it. One such factor is the time left to the warrant expiration date. As the warrant's expiration date approaches, the size of the premium begins to shrink, approaching zero. A second factor is investors' expectations concerning the capital gains potential of the stock. If they feel favorably about the prospects for price increases in the common stock, a large warrant premium will result, because a stock price increase will effect a warrant price increase. Finally, the degree of price volatility on the underlying common stock affects the size of the warrant premium. The more volatile the common stock price, the higher the warrant premium. As price volatility increases, so does the probability of and potential size of profits.

TABLE 21–2.
Hypothetical Warrant Example

Stock Price, SP	Exercise Price, EP	Exercise Ratio, ER	Minimum Price: $(SP - EP) \times ER$ = MP	Hypothetical Warrant Price, WP	Premium, WP − MP	Stock Price/ Exercise Price Ratio, SP/EP
$ 30	$40	1	$ 0	$ 5	$ 5	75%
40	40	1	0	10	10	100
50	40	1	10	16	6	125
60	40	1	20	25	5	150
70	40	1	30	34	4	175
80	40	1	40	43	3	200
90	40	1	50	52	2	225
100	40	1	60	62	2	250
110	40	1	70	71	1	275
120	40	1	80	81	1	300
130	40	1	90	90	0	325

SUMMARY

Convertible securities are preferred stock or debentures that can be exchanged for a specified number of shares of common stock at the will of the owner. They are issued by corporations to sweeten debt and thereby make it more marketable, as a form of delayed equity financing, and because they allow companies with a high level of risk to raise funds at a relatively favorable rate. Although these reasons can justify the use of convertibles, the risks involved in the possibility of an overhanging issue should also be weighed. In the case of an overhanging issue, conversion does not occur and the firm cannot force it, because the common stock price has not risen sufficiently; financing flexibility is reduced, since, depending on the firm's financial structure, investors might react negatively toward an additional offering of either debt or equity. The valuation of convertible securities is a function of both its value as a straight bond and its value if converted into common stock. Because the convertible provides the security of debt with the capital gains potential of common stock, it generally sells for a premium above the higher of its bond or conversion value.

A warrant is an option to purchase a fixed number of shares of common stock at a predetermined price during a specified period. Although in general warrants are issued in association with debt, most warrants are detachable in that they can be bought and sold separately from the debt to which they were originally attached. They are generally issued as a sweetener to debt in order to make it more marketable and lower the interest costs. In addition, unlike convertibles, warrants provide for an additional cash inflow when they are exercised. Conversely, the exercise of convertibles results in the elimination of debt, whereas the exercise of warrants does not. Thus, there is a tradeoff—additional cash inflow versus elimination of debt—involved in the warrants versus convertibles decision. Because a warrant is an option to purchase a specified number of shares of stock during a given period, its market value is primarily a function of the price of the common stock. Warrants generally sell above their minimum price; the size of the premium is determined by the degree of leverage they provide, the time left to expiration, investors' expectations as to the future movement of the stock price, and the stock's price volatility.

STUDY QUESTIONS

21–1. Define the following terms:
  a. Conversion ratio
  b. Conversion value
  c. Conversion parity price
  d. Conversion premium

21–2. What are some reasons commonly given for issuing convertible securities?

21–3. Why does a convertible bond sell at a premium above its value as a bond or common stock?

21–4. Convertible bonds are said to provide the capital gains potential of common stock and the security of bonds. Explain this statement both verbally and graphically. What happens to the graph when interest rates rise? When they fall?

21–5. Convertible bonds generally carry lower coupon interest rates than do nonconvertible bonds. If this is so, does it mean that the cost of capital on convertible bonds is lower than on nonconvertible? Why or why not?

21–6. Since convertible securities allow for the conversion price to be set above the current common stock price, is it true that the firm is actually issuing its common stock at a price above the current market price?

21–7. In light of our discussion of the common stockholders' preemptive right in Chapter 20, explain why convertibles are often sold on a rights basis.

21-8. Although only the holder of a convertible has the right to convert the security, firms are often able to force conversion. Comment on this statement.

21-9. Explain the difference between a convertible security and a warrant.

21-10. How do firms force the exercising of warrants?

21-11. Explain the valuation of warrants both verbally and graphically.

21-12. What factors affect the size of the warrant premium? How?

ST-1. (*Convertible Terminology*) In 1993 Winky's Cow Paste, Inc., issued $10 million of $1,000 par value, 10 percent semiannual convertible debentures that come due in 2008. The conversion price on these convertibles is $16.75 per share. The common stock was selling for $14¾ per share on a given date shortly after these convertibles were issued. These convertibles have a B− rating, and straight B− debentures were yielding 14 percent on that date. The market price of the convertible was $970 on that date. Determine the following:
  a. Conversion ratio
  b. Conversion value
  c. Security value
  d. Conversion parity price
  e. Conversion premium in absolute dollars
  f. Conversion premium in percentage

ST-2. (*Warrant Terminology*) Petro-Tech, Inc., currently has some warrants outstanding that allow the holder to purchase, with one warrant, one share of common stock at $18.275 per share. If the common stock was selling at $25 per share and the warrants were selling for $9.50, what would be the
  a. Minimum price?
  b. Warrant premium?

21-1A. (*Convertible Terminology*) In 1993 the Andy Fields Corporation of Delaware issued some $1,000 par value, 6 percent convertible debentures that come due in 2013. The conversion price on these convertibles is $40 per share. The price of the common stock is now $27.25 per share. These convertibles have a BBB rating, and straight BBB debentures are now yielding 9 percent. The market price of the convertible is now $840.25. Determine the following (assume bond interest payments are made annually):
  a. Conversion ratio
  b. Conversion value
  c. Security value
  d. Conversion parity price
  e. Conversion premium in absolute dollars
  f. Conversion premium in percentage

21-2A. (*Convertible Terminology*) The L. Padis, Jr., Corporation has an issue of 5 percent convertible preferred stock outstanding. The conversion price on these securities is $27 per share to 9/30/97. The price of the common stock is now $13.25 per share. The preferred stock is selling for $17.75. The par value of the preferred stock is $25 per share. Similar quality preferred stock without the conversion feature is currently yielding 8 percent. Determine the following:
  a. Conversion ratio
  b. Conversion value
  c. Conversion premium (in both absolute dollars and percentages)

21-3A. (*Warrant Terminology*) The T. Kitchel Corporation has a warrant that allows the purchase of one share of common stock at $30 per share. The warrant is currently selling at $4 and the common stock is priced at $25 per share. Determine the minimum price and the premium of the warrant.

21-4A. (*Warrant Terminology*) Cobra Airlines has some warrants outstanding that allow the purchase of common stock at the rate of one warrant for each share of common stock at $11.71 per share.

    a. Given that the warrants were selling for $3 each and the common stock was selling for $10 per share, determine the minimum price and warrant premium as of that date.

    b. Given that the warrants were selling for $9.75 each, and the common stock was selling for $16.375 per share, determine the minimum price and warrant premium as of that date.

21–5A. (*Warrant Terminology*) International Corporation has some warrants outstanding that allow the purchase of common stock at the price of $22.94 per share. These warrants are somewhat unusual in that one warrant allows for the purchase of 3.1827 shares of common stock at the exercise price of $22.94 per share. Given that the warrants were selling for $6.25 each, and the common stock was selling for $7.25 per share, determine the minimum price and the warrant premium as of that date.

21–6A. (*Warrants and Their Leverage Effect*) A month ago you purchased 100 Bolster Corporation warrants at $3 each. When you made your purchase, the market price of Bolster's common stock was $40 per share. The exercise price on the warrants is $40 per share while the exercise ratio is 1.0. Today, the market price of Bolster's common stock has jumped up to $45 per share, while the market price of Bolster's warrants has climbed to $7.50 each. Calculate the total dollar gain that you would have received if you had invested the same dollar amount in common stock versus warrants. What is this in terms of return on investment?

STUDY PROBLEMS (SET B)

21–1B. (*Convertible Terminology*) In 1993 the P. Mauney Corporation of Virginia issued some $1,000 par value, 7 percent convertible debentures that come due in 2013. The conversion price on these convertibles is $45 per share. The price of the common stock is now $26 per share. These convertibles have a BBB rating, and straight BBB debentures are now yielding 9 percent. The market price of the convertible is now $840.25. Determine the following (assume bond interest payments are made annually):

    a. Conversion ratio
    b. Conversion value
    c. Security value
    d. Conversion parity price
    e. Conversion premium in absolute dollars
    f. Conversion premium in percentage

21–2B. (*Convertible Terminology*) The Ecotosleptics Corporation has an issue of 6 percent convertible preferred stock outstanding. The conversion price on these securities is $28 per share to 9/30/97. The price of the common stock is now $14 per share. The preferred stock is selling for $20.00. The par value of the preferred stock is $25 per share. Similar quality preferred stock without the conversion feature is currently yielding 8 percent. Determine the following:

    a. Conversion ratio
    b. Conversion value
    c. Conversion premium (in both absolute dollars and percentages)

21–3B. (*Warrant Terminology*) The Megacorndoodles Corporation has a warrant that allows the purchase of one share of common stock at $32 per share. The warrant is currently selling at $5 and the common stock is priced at $24 per share. Determine the minimum price and the premium of the warrant.

21–4B. (*Warrant Terminology*) Taco Fever has some warrants outstanding that allow the purchase of common stock at the rate of one warrant for each share of common stock at $11.75 per share.

    a. Given that the warrants were selling for $4 each and the common stock was selling for $9 per share, determine the minimum price and warrant premium as of that date.

    b. Given that the warrants were selling for $7 each, and the common stock was selling for $15.375 per share, determine the minimum price and warrant premium as of that date.

21–5B. (*Warrant Terminology*) Fla'vo'phone Corporation has some warrants outstanding that allow the purchase of common stock at the price of $22.94 per share. These warrants are somewhat unusual in that one warrant allows for the purchase of 4.257 shares of common stock at the exercise price of $22.94 per share.

  a. Given that the warrants were selling for $6.75 each, and the common stock was selling for $8 per share, determine the minimum price and the warrant premium as of that date.

21–6B. (*Warrants and Their Leverage Effect*) A month ago you purchased 100 Annie Kay's Corporation warrants at $2.75 each. When you made your purchase, the market price of Annie Kay's common stock was $35 per share. The exercise price on the warrants is $35 per share while the exercise ratio is 1.0. Today, the market price of Annie Kay's common stock has jumped up to $40 per share, while the market price of Annie Kay's warrants has climbed to $6.75 each. Calculate the total dollar gain that you would have received if you had invested the same dollar amount in common stock versus warrants. What is this in terms of return on investment?

SELF-TEST SOLUTIONS

SS–1. a. $\text{conversion ratio} = \dfrac{\text{par value of convertible security}}{\text{conversion price}}$

$\quad\quad = \dfrac{\$1000}{\$16.75}$

$\quad\quad = 59.70 \text{ shares}$

  b. $\text{conversion value} = \begin{pmatrix}\text{conversion} \\ \text{ratio}\end{pmatrix} \times \begin{pmatrix}\text{market value per share} \\ \text{of common stock}\end{pmatrix}$

$\quad\quad = 59.70 \text{ shares} \times \$14.75/\text{share}$

$\quad\quad = \$880.58$

  c. $\text{security value} = \displaystyle\sum_{t=1}^{40} \dfrac{\$50}{(1+.07)^t} + \dfrac{\$1000}{(1+.07)^{40}}$

$\quad\quad = \$50(13.332) + \$1000(.067)$

$\quad\quad = \$666.60 + \$67$

$\quad\quad = \$733.60$

  (*Note:* Because this debenture pays interest semiannually, $t = 20 \text{ years} \times 2 = 40$ and $i = 14\%/2 = 7\%$ in the calculations.)

  d. $\text{conversion parity price} = \dfrac{\text{market price of convertible security}}{\text{conversion ratio}}$

$\quad\quad = \dfrac{\$970.00}{59.70}$

$\quad\quad = \$16.25$

  e. $\begin{matrix}\text{conversion premium} \\ \text{in absolute dollars}\end{matrix} = \begin{pmatrix}\text{market price of} \\ \text{the convertible}\end{pmatrix} - \begin{pmatrix}\text{higher of the bond value} \\ \text{and conversion value}\end{pmatrix}$

$\quad\quad = \$970.00 - \$880.58$

$\quad\quad = \$89.42$

$$\textbf{f. } \begin{array}{c}\text{conversion premium} \\ \text{in percentage}\end{array} = \frac{\left(\begin{array}{c}\text{market price of} \\ \text{the convertible}\end{array}\right) - \left(\begin{array}{c}\text{higher of the bond value} \\ \text{and conversion value}\end{array}\right)}{\left(\begin{array}{c}\text{higher of the bond value} \\ \text{and conversion value}\end{array}\right)}$$

$$= \frac{\$970.00 - \$880.58}{\$880.58}$$

$$= 10.15\%$$

SS–2. a. $\text{minimum price} = \left(\begin{array}{c}\text{market price of} \\ \text{common stock}\end{array} - \begin{array}{c}\text{exercise} \\ \text{price}\end{array}\right) \times \left(\begin{array}{c}\text{exercise} \\ \text{ratio}\end{array}\right)$

$$= (\$25.00 - \$18.275) \times (1.0)$$

$$= \$6.725$$

b. $\text{warrant premium} = \left(\begin{array}{c}\text{market price} \\ \text{of warrant}\end{array}\right) - \left(\begin{array}{c}\text{minimum price} \\ \text{of warrant}\end{array}\right)$

$$= \$9.50 - \$6.725)$$

$$= \$2.775$$

CHAPTER 22

The Use of Futures and Options to Reduce Risk

Futures • Options • How Financial Managers Use Options and Futures

---

Futures

In the previous chapter we examined two financial instruments, convertible securities and warrants, created by the firm. We now look at two additional financial instruments that are similar to convertibles and warrants but are not created by the firm: futures and options. Despite the fact that these instruments are not issued by the firm, it is important for us to be familiar with them for two reasons. First, these instruments can be used to reduce the risks associated with interest and exchange rate and commodity price fluctuations. Second, as you will see in future finance courses, an understanding of the pricing of options is extremely valuable because many different financial assets can be viewed as options. In fact, warrants, convertible bonds, risky bonds, common stock, and the abandonment decision can all be thought of as types of options.

Perspective in Finance

Although there are many uses for futures and options, our interest focuses on how financial managers use them to reduce risk. Keeping this in mind, you will see how they can be used to effectively offset future movements in the price of commodities or interest rates. Remember, options can be used to eliminate the effect of unfavorable price movements, whereas futures eliminate the effect of both favorable and unfavorable price movements.

Commodity and financial futures are perhaps the fastest-growing and in many respects most exciting new financial instrument today. Financial managers who only a few years ago would not have considered venturing into the futures market are now actively using this market to eliminate risk. As the number of participants in this market has grown, so has the number of items on which future contracts are offered, jumping to nearly 100 contracts ranging from the old standbys like coffee and soybeans to newer ones like U.S. Treasury bonds, sorghum, and municipal bonds.

A **future,** or **futures contract,** is a contract to buy or sell a stated commodity (such as soybeans or corn) or financial claim (such as U.S. Treasury bonds) at a specified price at some future specified time. It is important to note here that this is a contract that *requires* its holder to buy or sell the asset, regardless of what happens to its value during the interim. The importance of a futures contract is that it can be used by financial managers to lock in the price of a commodity or an interest rate and thereby eliminate one source of risk. For example, if a corporation is planning on issuing debt in the near future and is concerned about a possible rise in interest rates between now and when the debt would be issued, it might sell a U.S. Treasury bond futures contract with the same face value as the proposed debt offering and a delivery date the same as when the debt offering is to occur. Alternatively, with the use of a futures contract, Ralston-Purina or Quaker Oats can lock in the future price of corn or oats whenever they wish. Because a futures contract locks in interest rates or commodity prices, the costs associated with any possible rise in interest rates or commodity prices are completely offset by the profits made by writing the futures interest rate contract. In effect, futures contracts allow the financial manager to lock in future interest and exchange rates or prices for a number of agricultural commodities like corn and oats.

As the use of futures contracts becomes more common in the financial management of the firm, it is important for the financial manager to be familiar with the operation and terminology associated with these financial instruments.

An Introduction to Futures Markets

The origins of the futures markets historically go back to medieval times. England, France, and Japan all developed futures markets of their own. Here in the United States several futures markets sprang up in the early years, but it was not until the establishment of the Chicago Board of Trade (CBT) in 1848 that the futures markets were provided with their true roots. As we will see, although this market has been in operation for almost 150 years, it was not until the early 1970s, when the futures markets expanded from agricultural commodities to financial futures, that financial managers began to regularly venture into this market.

To develop an understanding for futures markets, let us examine several features that distinguish futures contracts from simple forward contracts. To begin with, a *forward contract* is any contract for delivery of an asset in the future. A futures contract is a specialized form of a forward contract distinguished by (1) an organized exchange, (2) a standardized contract with limited price changes and margin requirements, (3) a clearinghouse in each futures market, and (4) daily resettlement of contracts.

The Organized Exchange

Although the Chicago Board of Trade is the oldest and largest of the futures exchanges, it is certainly not the only exchange. In fact, there are more than 10 different futures exchanges in operation in the United States today. The importance of having organized exchanges associated with the futures market is that they provide a central trading place. If there were no central trading place, then there would be no potential to generate the depth of trading necessary to support a secondary market, and in a very circular way the existence of a secondary market encourages more traders to enter the market and in turn provides additional liquidity.

An organized exchange also encourages confidence in the futures market by allowing for the effective regulation of trading. The various exchanges set and enforce rules and collect and disseminate information on trading activity and the commodities being traded. Together, the liquidity generated by having a central trading place, effective regulation, and the flow of information through the organized exchanges has effectively fostered their development.

Standardized Contracts

To develop a strong secondary market in any security, there must be many identical securities—or in this case, futures contracts—outstanding. In effect, standardization of contracts leads to more frequent trades on that contract, leading to greater liquidity in the secondary market for that contract, which in turn draws more traders into the market. It is for this reason that futures contracts are highly standardized and very specific with respect to the description of the goods to be delivered and the time and place of delivery. Let's look at a Chicago Board of Trade oats contract. This contract calls for the delivery of 5,000 bushels of No. 2 heavy or No. 1 grade oats to Chicago or to Minneapolis–St. Paul at a 7.5 cents per bushel discount. In addition, these contracts are written to come due in March, May, July, September, and December. Through this standardization of contracts, trading has built up in enough identical contracts to allow for the development of a strong and highly liquid secondary market.

To encourage investors to participate in the futures market, daily price limits are set on all futures contracts. Without these limits, it is thought that there would be more price volatility on most futures contracts than many investors would be willing to accept. These daily price limits are set to protect investors, maintain order on the futures exchanges, and encourage the level of trading volume necessary to develop a strong secondary market. For example, the Chicago Board of Trade imposes a 10 cents per bushel ($500 per contract) price movement limit above and below the previous day's settlement price of oats contracts. This limit protects against runaway price movements. These daily price limits do not halt trading once the limit has been reached, but they do provide a boundary within which trading must occur. The price of an oats contract may rise 10 cents very early in the trading day—"up the limit" in futures jargon. This will not stop trading; it only means that no trade can take place above that level. As a result, any dramatic shifts in the market price of a futures contract must take place over a number of days, with the price of the contract going "up the limit" each day.

Futures Clearinghouse

The main purpose of the futures clearinghouse is to guarantee that all trades will be honored. This is done by having the clearinghouse interpose itself as the buyer to every seller and the seller to every buyer. Because of this substitution of parties, it is not necessary for the original seller (or buyer) to find the original buyer (or seller) when he or she decides to clear his or her position. As a result, all an individual has to do is make an equal and opposite transaction that will provide a net zero position with the clearinghouse and cancel out that individual's obligation.

Because no trades occur directly between individuals, but between individuals and the clearinghouse, buyers and sellers realizing gains in the market are assured that they will be paid. Because futures contracts are traded with minimal "good faith" money, as we will see in the next section, it is necessary to provide some security to traders so that when money is made, it will be paid. There are other important benefits of a clearinghouse, including providing a mechanism for the delivery of commodities and the settlement of disputed trades, but these benefits also serve to encourage trading in the futures markets and thereby create a highly liquid secondary market.

Daily Resettlement of Contracts

Another safeguard of the futures market is a margin requirement. Although margin requirements on futures resemble stock margin requirements in that there is an initial margin and a maintenance margin that comes into play when the value of the contract declines, similarities between futures and stock margins end there.

Before we explore margin requirements on futures it would be helpful to develop an understanding of the meaning of a margin on futures. The concept of a margin on futures contracts has a meaning that is totally different from its usage in reference to common stocks. The margin on common stocks refers to the amount of equity the investor has invested in the stocks. With a futures contract, no equity has been invested, because nothing has been bought. All that has happened is that a contract has been signed obligating the two parties to a future transaction and defining the terms of that transaction. This is an important thought: There is no actual buying or selling occurring with a futures contract; it is merely an agreement to buy or sell some commodity in the future. As a result, the term *futures margin* refers to "good faith" money the purchaser puts down to ensure that the contract will be carried out.

The initial margin required for commodities (deposited by both buyer and seller) is much lower than the margin required for common stock, generally amounting to only 3 to 10 percent of the value of the contract. For example, if September oats contracts on the CBT were selling at $1.65 per bushel, then one contract for 5,000 bushels would be selling for $1.65 × 5000 = $8250. The initial margin on oats is $400 per contract, which represents only about 4.85 percent of the contract price. Needless to say, the leverage associated with futures trading is tremendous—both on the up and down sides. Small changes in the price of the underlying commodity result in very large changes in the value of the futures contract, since very little has to be put down to "own" a contract. Moreover, for many futures contracts, if the financial manager can satisfy the broker that he or she is not engaged in trading as a speculator, but as a hedger, the manager can qualify for reduced initial margins. Because of the low level of the initial margin, there is also a *maintenance* or *variation margin* requirement that forces the investor or financial manager to replenish the margin account to a level specified by the exchange after any market loss.

One additional point related to margins deserves mention. The initial margin requirement can be fulfilled by supplying Treasury bills instead of cash. These Treasury bills are valued at 90 percent of their value for margin purposes so it takes $100,000 worth of Treasury bills to provide a $90,000 margin. The advantage of using Treasury bills as margin is that the investor earns money on them, whereas brokerage firms do not pay interest on funds in commodity cash accounts. Moreover, if the financial manager is going to carry Treasury bills anyway, he or she can just deposit the Treasury bills with the broker and purchase the futures contracts with no additional cash outlay.

Suppose you are a financial manager for Ralston-Purina. You are in charge of purchasing raw materials—in particular, oats. Currently, a September futures contract for the delivery of oats has a price of $1.65 per bushel. You need oats in September and feel that this is an exceptional price and that oats will probably be selling for more than that per bushel in September. Thus, you want to lock in this price, and to do this you purchase one contract for 5,000 bushels at 165 cents or $1.65 per bushel. On purchasing the September oats contract the only cash you would have to put up would be the initial margin of $400. Let's further assume that the price of oats futures then falls to a level of 161 cents per bushel the day after you make your purchase. In effect, you have incurred a loss of 4 cents per bushel on 5,000 bushels, for a total loss on your investment of $200.

At this point the concept of daily resettlement comes into play. What this means is that all futures positions are brought to the market at the end of each trading day and all gains and losses, in this case a loss, are then settled. You have lost $200, which is then subtracted from your margin account, lowering it to $200 ($400 initially less the $200 loss). Because the margin account has fallen below the maintenance margin on oats, which is $250, you would have to replenish the account back to its initial level of $400. If on the following day the price of September oats contracts fell another cent to 160 cents per bushel, you would have lost another 1 cent on 5,000 bushels for a loss of $50. This would then be subtracted from your margin account during the daily resettlement at the end of the trading day, leaving $350 in the account. Because your margin account would not be below the maintenance margin requirement of $250, you would not have to add any additional funds to the account. Let's carry our example one day further, this time to the upbeat side and put some profits in. Let's assume on the third day the price of September oats contracts is up 5 cents per bushel. This means that you have made 5 cents on 5,000 bushels, for a total profit of $250. This brings your margin account up from $350 to $600, which is $200 above the initial margin of $400. You can withdraw this $200 from your margin account.

Obviously, the purpose of margin requirements is to provide some measure of safety for futures traders, and despite the very small level of margin requirements imposed, they do a reasonable job. They are set in accordance with the historical price volatility of the underlying commodity in such a way that it is extremely unlikely that a trader will ever lose more than is in his or her margin account in any one day.

Commodity Futures

In general, when people talk about commodities they are referring to nonfinancial futures. This includes agricultural commodities as well as metals, wood products, and fibers. Although there are several new commodity futures contracts now being traded, such as lumber and orange juice, much of the trading in the commodities futures markets involves such traditional favorites as corn and wheat. For the financial manager these markets provide a means of offsetting the risks associated with future price changes. Here the financial manager is securing a future price for a good that is currently in production, or securing a future price for some commodity that must be purchased in the future. In either case, the manager is using the futures market to eliminate the effects of future price changes on the future purchase or sale of some commodity.

Financial Futures

Financial futures come in a number of different forms, including Treasury bills, notes and bonds, GNMAs, certificates of deposit, Eurodollars, foreign currencies, and stock indices. These financial newcomers first appeared in 1972, when foreign currencies were introduced; interest rate futures did not appear until 1975. The growth in financial futures has been phenomenal, and today they dominate the futures markets. Figure 22–1 shows the volume distribution of financial futures as a proportion of volume on the Chicago Board of Trade. Our discussion of financial futures will be divided into three sections: (1) interest rate futures, (2) foreign exchange futures, and (3) stock index futures.

Interest rate futures ■ Currently, Treasury bond futures are the most popular of all futures contracts in terms of contracts issued. In fact on October 15, 1987, 659,487 contracts were traded with a face value of $65.94 billion! Although Treasury, or T-bond futures, as they are called, are just one of several interest rate futures contracts, the fact that they are risk-free, long-term bonds with a maturity of at least 15 years has been the deciding factor in making them the most popular of the interest rate futures.

For the financial manager, interest rate futures provide an excellent means

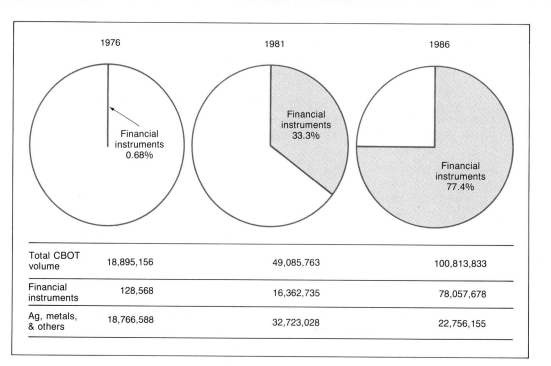

	1976	1981	1986
Total CBOT volume	18,895,156	49,085,763	100,813,833
Financial instruments	128,568	16,362,735	78,057,678
Ag, metals, & others	18,766,588	32,723,028	22,756,155

FIGURE 22–1.
CBOT Volume Distribution by Product Complex Source: CBOT Financial Instruments Guide: (Chicago, IL: Chicago Board of Trade, 1987)

for eliminating the risks associated with interest rate fluctuations. As we learned earlier, there is an inverse relationship between bond prices in the secondary market and yields—that is, when interest rates fall bond prices rise, and when interest rates rise bond prices fall. If you think back to the chapter on valuation, you will recall that this inverse relationship between bond prices and yield is a result of the fact that when bonds are issued, their coupon rate is fixed. However, once the bond is issued it must compete in the market with other financial instruments. Because new bonds are issued to yield the current interest rates, yields on old bonds must adjust to remain competitive with the newer issues. Thus, when interest rates rise, the price of an older bond with a lower coupon interest rate must decline to increase the yield on the old bond, making it competitive with the return on newly issued bonds.

Interest rate futures offer investors a very inexpensive way of eliminating the risks associated with interest rate fluctuations. For example, banks, pension funds and insurance companies all make considerable use of the interest rate futures market to avoid paper losses that might otherwise occur when interest rates unexpectedly increase. Corporations also use interest rate futures to lock in interest rates when they are planning to issue debt. If interest rates rise before the corporation has the opportunity to issue the new debt, the profits on the interest rate futures contracts they have sold will offset the increased costs associated with the proposed debt offering. Several possible uses for Treasury bond futures are given in Table 22–1.

Foreign exchange futures ■ Of all the financial futures, foreign exchange futures have been around the longest, first appearing in 1972. Foreign exchange futures work in the same way as other futures, but in this case the commodity is German marks, British pounds, or some other foreign currency. As we will see, the similarities between these futures and the others we have examined are great. Not only do foreign exchange futures work in the same way as other futures, but they also are used by financial managers for the same basic reasons—to hedge away risks, in this case exchange rate risks. One of the major participants in the foreign exchange futures market is the exporter who will receive foreign currency when its exported goods are finally received and who uses this market to lock in a certain exchange rate. As a result, the exporter is unaffected by any exchange rate fluctuations that might occur before it receives payment. Foreign exchange futures are also used to hedge away possible fluctuations in the value of earnings of foreign subsidiaries.

TABLE 22–1.
How Treasury Bond Futures Are Used

Protect Portfolio Value and Return: Pension funds, banks, corporations, insurance companies and individual investors can use 10-year Treasury futures as a hedge against losses incurred on fixed-income portfolios when interest rates rise and prices decline. Careful timing in the placement of a hedge can protect the holding period return of a portfolio containing notes and other related instruments. Futures offer flexibility to money managers by allowing them to adapt to a changing market.

Protect Issuance Costs: Corporations that plan to issue intermediate-term debt can control their interest cost by selling 10-year Treasury futures and offsetting the position when the issue comes to market. By hedging, the issuer can take advantage of today's lower rates, thus lessening the cost of raising capital.

Transfer Risk: Underwriters of corporate issues can sell futures to transfer the risk between the time they buy the debt securities until the time they are sold to dealers and investors.

Hedge Participation in Treasury Auctions: Primary government securities dealers can use the new contract to hedge participation in 7- and 10-year note auctions. Ten-year Treasury futures allow government securities dealers to remain competitive and offer a better price to their customers.

Lock in a Favorable Rate of Return: Portfolio managers can hedge the reinvestment rate of coupon income. If interest rates decline, the reinvestment rate will diminish for note holders. Buying futures today as a substitute for later investments allows the investor to hedge a drop in rates. If rates *fall,* the decreased return on reinvestment will be offset by a gain in the futures position. If rates *rise,* the loss on the futures position will be offset by a higher return on investment.

Source: *Ten Year Treasury Futures* (Chicago: Chicago Board of Trade, 1983).

In the 1980s, fluctuations in exchange rates became common. With exchange rate futures a financial manager could eliminate the effects—good or bad—of exchange rate fluctuation with a relatively small investment. The extremely high degree of leverage that was available coupled with the dramatic fluctuations in foreign exchange rates in the 1980s encouraged many financial managers to consider entering the exchange rate futures market. One example of a dramatic price movement came as the British pound dropped to a value of just over $1.07 in early 1985. To get a feel for the degree of leverage experienced in the foreign exchange futures market and the large profits and losses that can occur in this market let's look at Figure 22–2, which examines profits and losses resulting from buying and selling British pound futures.

As can be seen in Figure 22–2, fortunes could have been lost and made by those investing in British pound futures. Some firms no doubt saved themselves enormous losses by hedging away exchange rate risk, whereas others would have benefited by the dramatic swing in the exchange rate. Over just five trading days, the value of an investment in British pound futures went up almost threefold, whereas the return on the initial margin investment for those selling British pounds dropped almost threefold. Needless to say, the foreign exchange futures market is a very risky market, characterized by extreme leverage both on the up and down side and periodic major movements in the underlying values of the foreign exchange currencies. To the financial manager, this market provides a perfect mechanism for eliminating the effect of exchange rate fluctuations.

Stock index futures ■ Stock indexes have been around for many years, but it has only been recently that financial managers and investors have had the opportunity to trade them directly. In fact, despite only first appearing in February 1982, by 1984 they became the second most widely traded futures contract of all, exceeded in trading volume only by T-bond futures contracts.

At this point, after looking at other futures contracts, the workings of stock index futures should be clear. They work basically the same way, with one major exception: Stock index futures contracts allow only for cash settlement. There is no delivery, because what is being traded is the *future price* of the index, not the underlying stocks in the index. Currently there are several stock index futures available, with futures on the S&P 500 index clearly dominating in terms of volume. Four of these indexes are compared in Table 22–2.

Let's examine exactly what an S&P 500 index futures contract involves. The S&P 500 index is a broad-based index made up of 400 industrials, 40 utilities, 20 transportations, and 40 financial companies on the NYSE. These

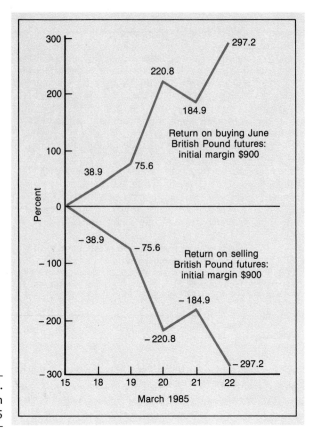

FIGURE 22–2.
Profits and Losses on British
Pound Futures in March 1985

companies represent about 80 percent of the value of all issues traded on the NYSE. This is a value-weighted index; the weight each stock takes on in the index is determined by the market value of that stock. The contract size or value of each contract is 500 times the S&P 500 index, which put it at about $210,000 in mid-1992.

Just as with currency futures, when there is a major fluctuation in the stock market, entire fortunes can be made or lost in the stock index futures market. Take for example trading on October 22, 1987, during the week of the great crash. That day one trader, Albert "Bud" Furman III made $900,000 in 90 seconds by buying 303 S&P 500 futures contracts at $196.00 a contract and selling 300 futures contracts 90 seconds later at $202.00 per contract (500 × $6/contract × 300 contracts = $900,000).

After the 1987 crash a system of shock absorber limits and circuit breakers were introduced to most index futures markets. These serve the same purpose as do daily price limits, but they are not as strict. For example, the New York Futures Exchange has 10-minute, 30-minute, one- and two-hour trading halts that result from wide swings in the stock market. The purpose of these programmed trading halts is to allow investors to rationally appraise the market during periods of large price swings.

To the financial manager, the great popularity of these financial newcomers lies in their ability to reduce or eliminate systematic risk. When we talked about the variability or risk associated with common stock returns we said that there were two types of risk: systematic and unsystematic risk. Unsystematic risk, although accounting for a large portion of the variability of an individual security's returns, is largely eliminated in large portfolios through random diversification, leaving only systematic or market risk in a portfolio. As a result, we said that a portfolio's returns are basically determined by market movements, as modified by the portfolio's beta. Before the introduction of stock index futures, a portfolio or pension fund manager was forced to adjust the portfolio's beta if he or she anticipated a change in the direction of the market. Stock index futures allow the portfolio or pension fund manager to eliminate or

TABLE 22–2.
Characteristics of Stock Index Futures Contracts

Feature	Kansas City Board of Trade	Chicago Mercantile Exchange	New York Futures Exchange	Chicago Board of Trade
Location	Kansas City	Chicago	New York	Chicago
Underlying market index	Value Line Composite Average (VLA). This is an equally weighted index of approximately 1700 stocks. Geometric average is used.	Standard & Poor's 500 Index (S&P 500). This is a value weighted index of 500 stocks. Arithmetic average is used.	NYSE Composite Index. This is a value-weighted average of all common stocks listed on the NYSE. Arithmetic average is used.	20 major blue chip stocks.
Contract size (value of contract)	Five hundred times the Value Line average.	Five hundred times the S&P index.	Five hundred times the NYSE composite index.	Five hundred times the major market index.
Minimum price change	Tick size is 0.01 points. The minimum change would cause the value of the contract to change by $5.	Tick size is 0.05 points. This represents a change of $25 per tick.	Tick size is 0.05 points. This represents a change of $25 per tick.	Tick size is ⅛ points. This represents a change of $12.50 per tick.
Margins (minimum customer margin set by the exchange)	Initial Margin $7500 / Maintenance Margin $7500	Initial Margin $12,000 / Maintenance Margin $6000	Initial Margin $6500 / Maintenance Margin $3000	Initial Margin $8000 / Maintenance Margin $5000
Delivery concept	Cash settlement. Actual value of VLA determines the payment. Final settlement is the last trading day of the expiring month.	Cash settlement. Actual value of S&P 500 index determines the payment. Final settlement of open contracts occurs on the third Thursday of the delivery month.	Cash settlement. Actual value of NYSE composite determines the payment. Settlement is based on the difference between the settlement price on the next to the last day of trading in the month and the value of NYSE composite index at the close of trading.	Cash settlement. Actual value of MMI determines the payment. Final settlement of contract occurs on the third Friday of the trading month.

When you think of Federal Bureau of Investigations (FBI) sting operations you normally think of drug busts, the mafia, or the U.S. Senate, but on January 17, 1989, the FBI began handing down indictments to 48 commodity futures traders as a result of a sting operation on the Chicago Board of Trade and the Chicago Mercantile Exchange. As of mid-1992, 22 of the 48 indicted pleaded guilty, and 13 others have been convicted.

To understand what happened and how the futures markets were able to shield their illegal trades, one must understand the way transactions occur in the futures markets. In the futures markets there is no computerized entry of trades or any orderly lines; traders simply congregate around trading pits. Trades are then made between traders 30 to 40 feet away from each other, with traders "talking" through hand signals, eye contact, or simply throat-wrenching shouts. This method of trading is called the "open outcry" system. You've probably seen footage of it on TV, or in the movie *Trading Places*, but it really looks more like a chaotic, uncontrolled argument than an organized exchange. It was this noise and confusion of the futures markets that offered cover for the fraud and illegal trading that occurred.

Much of what the FBI found centered around "bucket trading." To better explain what happened let's use an example of an order to buy 100 U.S. Treasury bond futures contracts, keeping in mind that each contract is for $100,000 worth of bonds. First, a trader receives a customer's order to buy the contracts at the market price. The trader then signals his partner in crime, known as a "bagman," to buy the contracts. Let's say that the market price of the bonds associated with each contract is $104,000, for a total value for the 100 contracts of $10,400,000. If the price of the bonds associated with each contract rises to $104,100, in the next few minutes, the broker buys again (a second set of contracts) and fills the customer's order at this new price. The customer is led to believe that he or she has received a fair price in a volatile market, and the bagman now takes the first set of contracts he bought and sells them at the new price for a gain of $100 per contract on 100 contracts for a total of $10,000, which is then split between the bagman and the trader. If the bond prices had dropped instead of risen, the trader would have simply repurchased the contracts from the bagman at the original higher price of $104,000, and the traders would have suffered no losses. The customer would not have benefited from the drop in Treasury bond prices.

When all the FBI charges are examined, it appears that the futures markets are, in general, run quite honestly, with a few bad apples making the news. Still, for the financial markets to work they must be totally rid of all corruption, and the public must have total confidence in them. In effect, the financial markets must live by Caesar's rule: "You must not only be virtuous, you must also be seen to be virtuous."

mute the effects of swings in the market without the large transactions costs that would be associated with the trading needed to modify the portfolio's beta. Unfortunately, although stock index futures allow for the elimination of the unwanted effects of market downswings, they also eliminate the effects of market upswings. In other words, they allow the portfolio or pension fund manager to eliminate as much of the effect of the market as he or she wishes from his or her portfolio.

Options

An **option,** or **option contract,** gives its owner the right to buy or sell a fixed number of shares at a specified price over a limited time period. Although trading in option contracts has existed for many years, it was not until the Chicago Board Options Exchange (CBOE) began trading in listed options in 1973 that the volume of trading reached any meaningful level. During the years since the CBOE first listed options on 16 stocks, volume has grown at a phenomenal rate, with over 10,000 different active option contracts on over 800 stocks listed today. Trading volume has also grown to such an extent that on a typical day, trading in options involves numbers equal to half the volume of trading on the NYSE. Still, to many financial managers, options remain a mystery, viewed as closer to something one would find in Las Vegas than on Wall Street.

Obviously, there is too much going on in the options markets not to pay attention to them. Financial managers are just beginning to turn to them as an effective way of eliminating risk for a small price. As we will see, they are fascinating, but they are also confusing—with countless variations and a language of their own. Moreover, their use is not limited to speculators; options are also used by the most conservative financial managers to eliminate unwanted risk. In this section we will discuss the fundamentals of options, their terminology, and how they are used by financial managers.

The Fundamentals of Options

Although the market for options seems to have a language of its own, there are only two basic types of options: puts and calls. Everything else involves some variation. A **call option** gives its owner the right to purchase a given number of shares of stock or some other asset at a specified price over a given period. Thus, if the price of the underlying common stock or asset goes up, a call purchaser makes money. This is essentially the same as a "rain check" or guaranteed price. You have the option to buy something, in this case common stock, at a set price. In effect a call option gives you the right to buy, but it is not a promise to buy. A **put,** on the other hand, gives its owner the right to sell a given number of shares of common stock or some other asset at a specified price over a given period. A put purchaser is betting that the price of the underlying common stock or asset will drop. Just as with the call, a put option gives its holder the right to sell the common stock at a set price, but it is not a promise to sell. Because these are just options to buy or sell stock or some other asset, they do not represent an ownership position in the underlying corporation, as does common stock. In fact, there is no direct relationship between the underlying corporation and the option. An option is merely a contract between two investors.

Because there is no underlying security, a purchaser of an option can be viewed as betting against the seller or *writer* of the option. For this reason the options markets are often referred to as a zero sum game. If someone makes money, then someone must lose money; if profits and losses were added up, the total for all options would equal zero. If commissions are considered, the total becomes negative, and we have a "negative sum" game. As we will see, the options markets are quite complicated and risky. Some experts refer to them as legalized institutions for transferring wealth from the unsophisticated to the sophisticated.

The Terminology of Options

In order to continue with our discussion, it is necessary to define several terms that are unique to options.

The contract ■ To understand the discussion of options, it is necessary to point out that when an option is purchased it is nothing more than a contract that allows the purchaser to either buy in the case of a call, or sell in the case of a put, the underlying stock or asset at a predetermined price. That is, no asset has changed hands, but the price has been set for a future transaction that will occur *only if and when* the option purchaser wants it to. In this section we will refer to the process of selling puts and calls as *writing*. Often, selling options is referred to as *shorting* or *taking a short position* in those options, while buying an option is referred to as *taking a long position*.

The exercise or striking price ■ This is the price at which the stock or asset may be purchased from the writer in the case of a call or sold to the writer in the case of a put.

Option premium ■ The option premium is merely the price of the option. It is generally stated in terms of dollars per share rather than per option contract, which covers 100 shares. Thus, if a call option premium is $2, then an option contract would cost $200 and allow the purchase of 100 shares of stock at the exercise price.

Perspective in Finance

Remember that the option premium is what the option purchaser pays for the option, and that the option writer keeps this payment regardless of whether or not the option is ever exercised. In addition, the option premium is not a downpayment on the stock's exercise price—the terms of the option do not change when the option premium is paid.

Expiration date ■ This is the date on which the option contract expires. An American option is one that can be exercised any time up to the expiration date. A European option can be exercised only on the expiration date.

Covered and naked options ■ If a call writer owns the underlying stock or asset on which he or she writes a call, the writer is said to have written a *covered call*. Conversely, if the writer writes a call on a stock or asset that he or she does not own, he or she is said to have written a *naked call*. The difference is that if a naked call is exercised, the call writer must deliver stock or assets that he or she does not own.

Open interest ■ The term *open interest* refers to the number of option contracts in existence at a point in time. The importance of this concept comes from the fact that open interest provides the investor with some indication of the amount of liquidity associated with that particular option.

In-, out-of, and at-the-money ■ A call (put) is said to be out-of-the-money if the underlying stock is selling below (above) the exercise price of the option. Alternatively, a call (put) is said to be in-the-money if the underlying stock is selling above (below) the exercise price of the option. If the option is selling at the exercise price, it is said to be selling at-the-money. For example, if Ford Motor's common stock was selling for $52 per share, a call on Ford with an exercise price of $50 would be in-the-money, while a call on Ford with an exercise price of $60 would be out-of-the-money.

Intrinsic and time (or speculative) value ■ The term *intrinsic value* refers to the minimum value of the option—that is, the amount by which the stock is in-the-money. Thus, for a call the intrinsic value is the amount by which the stock price exceeds the exercise price. If the call is out-of-the-money—that is, the exercise price is above the stock price—then its intrinsic value is zero. Intrinsic values can never be negative. For a put, the intrinsic value is again the minimum value the put can sell for, which is the exercise price less the stock price. For example, the intrinsic value on a Ford April 50 put, that is, a put on Ford Stock with an exercise price of $50 that expires in April, when Ford's common stock was selling for $42 per share would be $8. If the put was selling for anything less than $8, investors would buy puts and sell the stock until all profits from this strategy were exhausted. Arbitrage, this process of buying and selling like assets for different prices, keeps the price of options at or above their intrinsic value. If an option is selling for its intrinsic value, it is said to be selling at *parity*.

The *time value*, or speculative value, of an option is the amount by which the option premium exceeds the intrinsic value of the option. The time value represents the amount above the intrinsic value of an option that an investor is willing to pay to participate in capital gains from investing in the option. At expiration, the time value of the option falls to zero and the option sells for its intrinsic value, because the chance for future capital gains has been exhausted. These relationships are as follows:

call intrinsic value = stock price − exercise price

put intrinsic value = exercise price − stock price

call time value = call premium − (stock price − exercise price)

put time value = put premium − (exercise price − stock price)

Perhaps the easiest way to gain an understanding of the pricing of options is to look at them graphically. Figure 22-3 presents a profit and loss graph for the purchase of a call on Ford stock with an exercise price of $50 that is bought for $4. This is termed a Ford 50 call. In Figure 22-3, and all other profit and loss graphs, the vertical axis represents the profits or losses realized on the option's expiration date, and the horizontal axis represents the stock price on the expiration date. Remember that, because we are viewing the value of the option at expiration, the option has no time value and therefore it sells for exactly its intrinsic value. To keep things simple, we will also ignore any transaction costs.

For the Ford 50 call shown in Figure 22-3, the call will be worthless at expiration if the value of the stock is less than the exercise or striking price. This is because it would make no sense for an individual to exercise her call option to purchase Ford stock for $50 per share if she could buy the same Ford stock from her broker at a price less than $50. Although the option will be worthless at expiration if the stock price is below the exercise price, the most that an investor can lose is the option premium, that is, how much she paid for the option, which in this case was $4. Although this may be the entire investment in the option, it is also generally only a fraction of the stock's price. Once the stock price climbs above the exercise price, the call option takes on a positive value and increases in a linear one-to-one basis as the stock price increases. Moreover, there is no limit on how high the profits can climb. In the case of the Ford 50 call, once the price of the Ford stock rises above $50 the call begins taking on value, and once it hits $54 the investor breaks even. The investor has earned enough in the way of profits to cover the $4 premium she paid for the option in the first place.

To the call writer, the profit and loss graph is the mirror image of the call purchaser's graph. As we noted earlier, the options market is a zero sum game in which one individual gains at the expense of another. Figure 22-4 shows the profits and losses at expiration associated with writing a call option. Once again we will look at the profits and losses at expiration, because at that point in time options have no time value. The maximum profit to the call writer is the premium, or how much the writer received when the option was sold, whereas the maximum loss is unlimited.

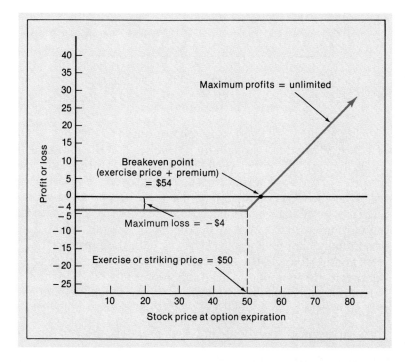

FIGURE 22-3.
Purchase a Call on Ford Stock with an Exercise Price of $50 for a Premium of $4

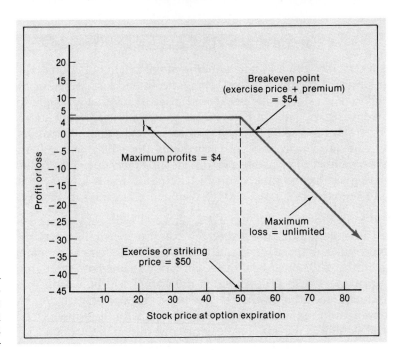

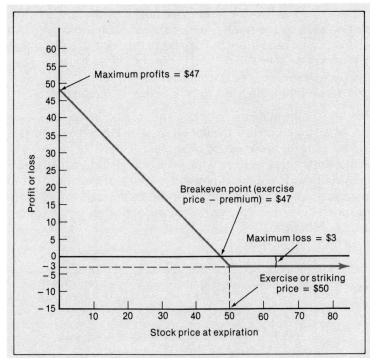

Looking at the profit and loss graph presented in Figure 22–5 for the purchase of a Ford 50 put that is bought for $3, we see that the lower the price of the Ford stock, the more the put is worth. Here the put only begins to take on value once the price of the Ford stock drops below the exercise price, which in this case is $50. Then for every dollar that the price of the Ford stock drops, the put increases in value by one dollar. Once the Ford stock drops to $47 per share, the put purchaser breaks even by making $3 on the put, which exactly offsets what was initially paid for the put. Here, as with the purchase of a call option, the most an investor can lose is the premium, which although small in dollar value relative to the potential gains, still represents 100% of the investment. The maximum gain associated with the purchase of a put is limited only by the fact that the lowest a stock's price can fall to is zero.

To a put writer, the profit and loss graph is the mirror image of the put

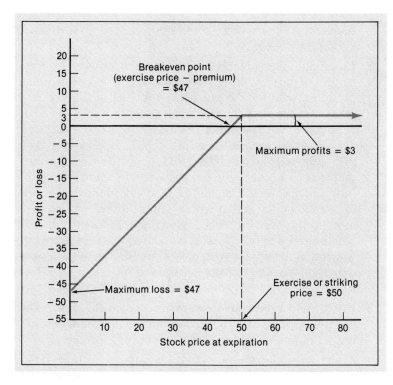

FIGURE 22-6.
Write a Put on Ford Stock with an Exercise Price of $50 for a Premium of $3

purchaser's graph. This is shown in Figure 22–6. Here the most a put writer can earn is the premium or amount for which the put was sold. The potential losses for the put writer are limited only by the fact that the stock price cannot fall below zero.

All of our graphs have shown the price of the option at expiration. When we reexamine these relationships at a time before expiration, we find that the options now take on some time value. In other words, investors are willing to pay more than the intrinsic value for an option because of the uncertainty of the future stock price. That is, although the stock price may fluctuate, the possible losses on the option are limited, whereas the possible gains are almost unlimited. ■

Perspective in Finance

The most you can ever lose when you purchase a put or call option is the premium, or what you paid for it. Although this may seem rather small relative to the price of the stock, it is still 100 percent of your investment.

Characteristics of Options

As we examine options from the viewpoint of the financial manager, we will see that they have some attractive features that help explain their popularity. There are three reasons for the popularity of options:

1. **Leverage.** Calls allow the financial manager the chance for unlimited capital gains with a very small investment. Because a call is only an option to buy, the most a financial manager can lose is what was invested, which is usually a very small percentage of what it would cost to buy the stock itself, while the potential for gain is unlimited. As we will see, when a financial manager owns a call, he or she controls or benefits directly from any price increases in the stock. The idea of magnifying the potential return is an example of leverage. It is similar to the concept of leverage in physics, where a small amount of force can lift a heavy load. Here a small investment is doing the work of a much larger investment. Unfortunately, leverage is a double-edged sword: Small price increases can produce a large percentage profit, but small price decreases can produce large

percentage losses. With an option, the maximum loss is limited to the amount invested.

2. **Financial insurance.** For the financial manager, this is the most attractive feature of options. A put can be looked on as an insurance policy, with the premium paid for the put being the cost of the policy. The transactions costs associated with exercising the put can then be looked on as the deductible. When a put with an exercise price equal to the current stock price is purchased, it insures the holder against any declines in the stock price over the life of the put. Through the use of a put, a pension fund manager can reduce the risk exposure in a portfolio with little in cost and little change to the portfolio. One dissimilarity between a put and an insurance policy is that with a put an investor does not need to own the asset, in this case the stock, before buying the insurance. A call, because it has limited potential losses associated with it, can also be viewed as an investment insurance policy. With a call, the investor's potential losses are limited to the price of the call, which is quite a bit below the price of the stock itself.

3. **Investment alternative expansion.** From the viewpoint of the investor, the use of puts, calls, and combinations of them can materially increase the set of possible investment alternatives available.

Again, an understanding of the popularity of both puts and calls to the financial manager involves understanding (1) the concept of leverage—in the case of calls unlimited and in the case of puts very large potential gains with limited and relatively small maximum potential losses—and (2) the concept of financial insurance. These two factors combined allow for an expansion of the available investment alternatives. Remember, both puts and calls are merely options to buy or sell the stock at a specified price. The worst that can happen is that the options become worthless and the financial manager loses the investment.

The Chicago Board Options Exchange

Prior to 1973, when the CBOE opened, there was no central marketplace for put and call options. At that time put and call options transactions took place on the over-the-counter market through what was called the Put and Call Dealers Association, with only about 20 active brokers and dealers in the market. Through a telephone hookup, these dealers acted as middlemen, matching up potential writers and purchasers of options.

Because the specifics of each option were negotiated directly between the writer and the purchaser of the option, very seldom were any two options alike. Generally, every option written had a different expiration date and a different exercise price. As a result, there was little in the way of a secondary market for these individualized options, and the writers and purchasers generally had to hold their position until expiration or until the options were exercised.

With the creation of the CBOE, all this began to change. In 1973 the CBOE began trading listed options on 16 different stocks. Today there are four different exchanges that list and trade options—the CBOE, the AMEX, the Philadelphia, and the Pacific—with over 800 different stocks having listed options. Although the over-the-counter market run by the Put and Call Association is still in operation for stocks that are not listed on the CBOE or any other exchange, it now handles less than 10 percent of all traded options.

This dramatic growth in the trading of options is almost entirely due to the several developments brought on by exchange-listed trading that the CBOE initiated, including the following:

1. **Standardization of the option contracts.** Today, the expiration dates for all options are standardized. As a result, there is only one day per month on which a listed option on any stock can expire. The number of shares that a

call allows its owner to purchase, and a put allows its owner to sell, has also been standardized to 100 shares per option contract. In addition, the striking prices have been standardized, generally at five-point intervals, so that there are more identical options. Through this standardization the number of different option contracts on each stock is severely limited. The result is that more options are identical and the secondary market is made more liquid.

2. **Creation of a regulated central marketplace.** The exchange listing of options provides a central location for continuous trading in options, both newly issued and in the secondary market. The CBOE and the exchanges that followed in listing options also imposed strong surveillance and disclosure requirements.

3. **Creation of the options clearinghouse corporation (OCC).** The OCC bears full responsibility for honoring all options issued on the CBOE. In effect, all options held by individuals have been written by the OCC, and alternatively all options written by individuals are held by the OCC. The purpose of creating a buffer between individual buyers and sellers of options is to provide investors with confidence in the market, in addition to facilitating the clearing and settlement of options. Because of the importance of the OCC, let us look for a moment at its operation.

    When an options transaction is agreed on, the seller writes an option contract to the OCC, which in turn writes an identical option contract to the buyer. If the buyer later wants to exercise the option, he or she gives the OCC the exercise price associated with the option, which in turn provides the buyer with stock. To get the stock to cover the option, the OCC simultaneously exercises a call option it has on this stock. Because of the operation of the OCC and the strong secondary market created by the CBOE, options are not exercised very frequently but are generally sold. Rather than exercise an option, an investor or financial manager usually just sells the option to another investor and realizes the profits in that manner. Writers of options clear their position by buying an option identical to the one they wrote. As a result the writer has two identical contracts on both sides of the market with the OCC. These positions then cancel each other out.

4. **Trading was made certificateless.** Instead of issuing certificates, the OCC maintains a continuous record of traders' positions. In addition to making the clearing of positions (the canceling out of an option writer's obligation when an identical option is purchased) easier, it has also allowed for an up-to-date record of existing options to be maintained.

5. **Creation of a liquid secondary market with dramatically decreased transactions costs.** There also has been a self-fulfilling generation of volume adding to the liquidity of the secondary market. That is, the innovations created a liquid secondary market for options, and this liquid secondary market attracted more investors into the options market, which in turn created even more liquidity in the secondary market.

Innovations in Options Market

Recently, four additional variations of the traditional option have appeared: the stock index option, the interest rate option, the foreign currency option, and the Treasury bond futures option.

Stock index options ▪ The options on stock indexes were first introduced on the CBOE in 1983 and have since proved extremely popular. Although there are a variety of different index options, based on several different broad stock market indexes and also industry indexes such as a computer industry index, it has been the broader stock market indexes that have carried the bulk of the popularity of index options. While the industry-based index options have received a somewhat mixed reception, stock index options, in particular the S&P 100 index on the CBOE, have proved to be extremely popular. In fact, more than 80 percent of all stock index options trading involves the S&P 100 index. Currently it accounts for over half of the volume of all option trading, and has made the CBOE the second largest U.S. securities market, with daily trading occasionally reaching nearly 700,000 contracts (remember each contract involves an option on 100 "shares" of the index).

The reason for this popularity is quite simple. These options allow portfolio managers and other investors holding broad portfolios cheaply and effectively to eliminate or adjust the market risk of their portfolio. When we talked about systematic and unsystematic risk, we noted that in a large and well-diversified portfolio unsystematic risk was effectively diversified away, leaving only systematic risk. Thus, the return on a large and well-diversified portfolio was a result of the portfolio's beta and the movement of the market. As a result, because the movements of the market cannot be controlled, portfolio managers periodically attempt to adjust the beta of the portfolio when they think a change in the market's direction is at hand. Index options allow them to make this change without the massive transaction costs that would otherwise be incurred.

In general, stock index options are used in exactly the same way traditional options are used: for leverage and for investment insurance. However, because of the unusual nature of the "underlying stock," these concepts take on a different meaning. In the case of leverage, the portfolio manager is speculating that the market will head either up or down and is able to cash in on any market volatility with a relatively small investment. In fact, the ability to enjoy the leverage of an option while being concerned with broad market movements has resulted in much of the popularity of stock index options, as small changes in the market can result in very large changes in the price of these options. To get an idea of exactly what we mean, let us look at what happened in early 1985, when the stock market moved ahead.

On January 21, 1985, when the S&P 100 was at 169.27, an investor could have bought a February call with an exercise price of 170 and paid 2¾, or $275.00, as shown in Figure 22–7. Ten days later it was worth 9⅜, or $937.50, when the index closed at 178.14. Conversely, an investor who purchased a put for 3¼, or $325, would have had the value of the investment drop to $25. All this dramatic price movement was the result of only a 5.24 percent change in the underlying index.

In the case of the investment insurance motive for holding index options, the financial manager is really using them to eliminate the effects of a possible downward movement in the market. For example, a portfolio manager who wants to insure the portfolio against a downturn in the market might purchase a put on the S&P 100 or S&P 500 index. Thus, if the market declines, the put will appreciate in value, it is hoped, offsetting the loss in the investor's portfolio.

In effect, index options can be used in the same way as the more traditional options. The only difference is that here the profits or losses depend on what happens to the value of the index rather than to one stock.

Interest rate options ■ Options on 30-year Treasury bonds are also traded on the CBOE. Although the trading appeal of interest rate options is somewhat limited, they do open some very interesting doors to the financial manager. In terms of the insurance and leverage traits, they allow the financial manager to insure against the effects of future changes in interest rates. We know that as interest rates rise the market value of outstanding bonds falls; thus, through the purchase of an interest rate put, the market value of a portfolio manager's bonds can be protected. Alternatively, a financial manager who is about to raise new capital through a debt offering and who is worried about a possible rise in interest rates before the offering occurs may purchase an interest rate put. This

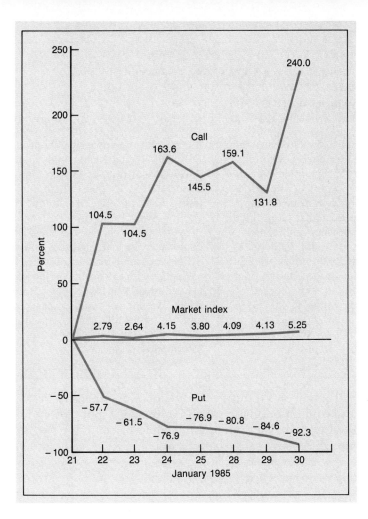

FIGURE 22–7.
February 170 Options
on the S&P 100

would have the effect of locking in current interest rates at the maximum level that the firm would have to pay.

Foreign currency options ■ Foreign currency options are the same as the other options we have examined except the underlying asset is the British pound, the Japanese yen, or some other foreign currency. Although foreign currency options are limited to the Philadelphia Exchange, there is a considerable amount of interest in them largely because of the wide fluctuations foreign currency has had in recent years relative to the dollar. In terms of the insurance and leverage traits, these options allow multinational firms to guard against fluctuations in foreign currencies that might adversely affect their operations. The leverage trait allows investors to speculate in possible future foreign currency fluctuations with a minimum amount of exposure to possible losses.

Perspective in Finance

An option on a Treasury bond future really holds little advantage over an option on a Treasury bond in terms of ability to reduce interest rate risk. Its advantages stem mainly from the great depth of the Treasury bond futures market.

Options on Treasury bond futures ■ Options on Treasury bond futures work the same way as any other option. The only difference between them and other bond options is that they involve the acquisition of a futures position rather than the delivery of actual bonds. To the creative financial manager, they provide a flexible tool to insure against adverse changes in interest rates while retaining the opportunity to benefit from any favorable interest rate movement that might occur. Although a futures contract establishes an obligation for both parties to buy and sell at a specified price, an option only establishes a right. It is therefore exercised only when it is to the option holder's advantage to do so. In effect, a call option on a futures contract does not establish a price obligation, but rather a maximum purchase price. Conversely, a put option on a futures contract is used to establish a minimum selling price. Thus, *the buyer of an option on a futures contract can achieve immunization against any unfavorable price movements, whereas the buyer of a futures contract can achieve immunization against any price movements regardless of whether they are favorable or unfavorable.*

In their short history, options on U.S. Treasury bond futures have proved to be extremely popular, with the majority of institutions choosing to trade options on bond futures rather than options on actual bonds. Their extreme popularity can be traced to several important advantages they possess:

1. Efficient price determination of the underlying instrument. The U.S. Treasury bond futures contract on the Chicago Board of Trade is the most widely traded futures contract of all. As a result, there is a continuous stream of market-determined price information concerning these contracts. Conversely, price information on most other bonds is generally somewhat sketchy at best, with substantial time between trades and generally a wide gap between existing bid and ask prices.

2. Unlimited deliverable supply. Because the Clearing Corporation can create as many futures contracts as are needed, the process of exercising an option is made extremely simple. When an option on a futures contract is exercised, the buyer simply assumes a futures position at the exercise price of the option. Because the Clearing Corporation can create as many futures contracts as are needed, the market price of these contracts is not affected by the exercise of the options on them. Conversely, if an option holder on an actual bond were to exercise his or her option, he or she would have to take delivery of the underlying bond. Because the supply of any particular bond is limited, a serious price pressure might be placed on that bond, provided the bond does not enjoy sufficient liquidity. Thus, because of the unlimited deliverable supply of futures contracts, the exercise of options on futures does not affect the price of those futures.

3. Greater flexibility in the event of exercise. If the option proves to be profitable, the purchaser or writer can settle the transaction in cash by offsetting the futures position acquired by exercise, or do nothing temporarily and assume the futures position and make or take delivery of the actual bonds when the futures contract comes due.

4. Extremely liquid market. Because of the other advantages of options on Treasury bond futures, a great number of these options have been created and are traded daily. As a result of the large volume, options on Treasury bond futures have developed a very liquid and active secondary market, which has encouraged other traders to enter this market.

Financial institutions seem to be major participants in the options on Treasury bond futures market, although there are many potential users of financial futures. They use futures options to alter the risk–return structure of their investment portfolios and actually reduce their exposure to downside risk. A common strategy is to purchase put options and thereby eliminate the possibility of large losses while retaining the possibility of large gains. There is a cost associated with this strategy, because the option premium must be paid regardless of whether or not the option is exercised. An additional return is also generated by those who write call options against a bond portfolio. With this strategy, the premium increases the overall return if bond yields remain stable or rise; however, a maximum return is also established for the portfolio, because it is this tail of the distribution that is sold with the option.

How Financial Managers Use Options and Futures

The use of options and financial futures by financial managers is in the early stages. In a survey of the Fortune 500, 19.2 percent of firms that responded reported that they used either futures or options in the conduct of their financial affairs.[1] There also seemed to be some relationship between the size of the firm and the utilization rate. For example, among large firms (over $1 billion in assets), 23.7 percent used interest rate futures. However, among smaller firms, only 5.36 percent did.

Of the various options and futures available, by far the most popular were Treasury bill futures and Eurodollar futures. This is shown in Table 22–3. Of those firms that did not use financial futures and options, the reasons most commonly cited were the resistance of top management and lack of knowledge on the part of the financial manager. It would seem that these two reasons for not using futures and options go together. It also would seem that as the advantages of using financial futures and options to hedge away interest rate and exchange rate risk become more widely understood, their use will become more common.

Security	Category	Number of Firms Utilizing the Instrument
Treasury bill	Future	16
Eurodollar	Future	14
Certificate of deposit	Future	7
Treasury bond	Future	4
Treasury bill	Option	4
Treasury bond	Option	4
Treasury note	Future	2
Treasury note	Option	1
GNMA	Future	1
Total		53

Source: Stanley B. Block and Timothy J. Gallagher, "The Use of Interest Rate Futures and Options by Corporate Financial Managers," *Financial Management* 15 (Autumn 1986), pp. 73–78.

TABLE 22–3.
Financial Futures and Options Most Frequently Used

[1]See Stanley B. Block and Timothy J. Gallagher, "The Use of Interest Rate Futures and Options by Corporate Financial Managers," *Financial Management* 15 (Autumn 1986), pp. 73–78.

SUMMARY

A *futures contract* is a contract to buy or sell a stated commodity (such as soybeans or corn) or financial claim (such as U.S. Treasury bonds) at a specified price at some future specified time. This contract requires its holder to buy or sell the asset regardless of what happens to its value during the interim. The importance of a futures contract is that it can be used by financial managers to lock in the price of a commodity or an interest rate and thereby eliminate one source of risk. A futures contract is a specialized form of a forward contract distinguished by (1) an organized exchange, (2) a standardized contract with limited price changes and margin requirements, (3) a clearinghouse in each futures market, and (4) daily resettlement of contracts.

A *call option* gives its owner the right to purchase a given number of shares of stock at a specified price over a given period. Thus, if the price of the underlying common stock goes up, a call purchaser makes money. A *put*, conversely, gives its owner the right to sell a given number of shares of common stock at a specified price over a given period. Thus, a put purchaser is betting that the price of the underlying common stock will drop. Because these are just options to buy or sell stock, they do not represent an ownership position in the underlying corporation, as does common stock.

STUDY QUESTIONS

22-1. What is the difference between a commodity future and financial future? Give an example of a commodity future and a financial future.

22-2. Describe a situation in which a financial manager might use a commodity future. Assume that during the period following the transaction the price of that commodity went up. Describe what happened. Now assume that the price of that commodity went down. Now what happened?

22-3. Describe a situation in which a financial manager might use an interest rate future. Assume that during the period following the transaction the interest rates went up. Describe what happened. Now assume that interest rates went down following the transaction. Now what happened?

22-4. Define a call option.

22-5. Define a put option.

22-6. What innovative developments were brought on by exchange-listed trading that the CBOE initiated that led to the dramatic growth in the trading of options?

22-7. What is an option on a futures contract? Give an example of one.

22-8. Compare the two strategies of buying a call and writing a put. What are the differences between the two?

22-9. Draw a profit or loss graph (similar to Figure 22-3) for the purchase of a call contract with an exercise price of $65 for which a $9 premium is paid. Identify the breakeven point, maximum profits, and maximum losses. Now draw the profit or loss graph assuming an exercise price of $70 and a $6 premium.

22-10. Repeat problem 22-9, but this time draw the profit or loss graph (similar to Figure 22-4) for the call writer.

22-11. Draw a profit or loss graph (similar to Figure 22-5) for the purchase of a put contract with an exercise price of $45 for which a $5 premium is paid. Identify the breakeven point, maximum profits, and maximum losses.

22-12. Repeat problem 22-11, but this time draw the profit or loss graph (similar to Figure 22-6) for the put writer.

CONCLUSION

VIDEO CASE 6

The Fall of Drexel Burnham Lambert: Investment Banking *in extremis*

from ABC News, *Business World*, February 18, 1990

When we introduced Video Case 6 on page 671, we asked a list of questions that you should now review.

Junk bonds served a valuable purpose for some firms, especially smaller corporations that did not have access to the public debt markets. Junk bonds, or as they are sometimes called *high-yield securities,* allowed riskier companies to raise funds when traditional funding sources such as banks would not consider them. Junk bonds, in and of themselves, are not *bad.* Sadly, they were put to bad uses. Savings-and-loan (S & L) associations invested in junk bonds with little thought about the inherent risk of these securities. The attraction of high yield blinded the S & L executives to the obvious risk. Junk bonds also were used to finance some acquisitions with at best questionable economic value. The ease with which funds could be raised by Milken's junk-bond department made debt the preferred security for acquisitions and going-private transactions. In some cases more debt was piled onto the assets than could be supported.

The deal-doing mentality of the 1980s was summed up by Michael Milken in this video: "There's very few people in the merger and acquisitions department that ever saw a bad deal. Every deal is a great deal; every deal is a good credit. Why? Because they [the investment bankers] usually get their fees up front." And what fees they are. In the RJR-Nabisco buyout the investment banking, attorney, and accountant fees totaled $1.15 *billion!*

What happens now? As several commentators in the video mentioned, junk bonds will continue to be used, though certainly not to the extent they were in the 1980s. The evaluation of transactions and credit quality will be more conservative, so fewer deals will be done. The biggest effect will likely be in the market for junk bonds. Drexel was the primary market maker; that is, Drexel created much of the liquidity in the junk bond market. Without Drexel acting as the intermediary, holders of junk bonds may find it very difficult to sell those bonds, or they may be able to sell them only at a low price. This has had a profound effect on the S & Ls that were ordered to divest their portfolios of junk bonds. In fact, one economist estimates the cost of not having Drexel as a market maker for junk bonds at $640 million (*Wall Street Journal*, March 4, 1992, p. A12).

Discussion questions

1. Economists have documented that small firms are increasingly responsible for new product development. How do you think the contraction of the junk-bond market affects this important source of innovation?
2. It has been argued that many firms using junk bonds switched from bank loans. Are junk bonds and bank loans substitutes for one another? How do they differ, and which source is likely to provide the largest amount of funds?

Suggested readings

BRUCK, CONNIE. *The Predator's Ball: The Junk Bond Raiders and the Man Who Staked Them.* New York: Simon & Schuster, 1988.

STONE, DAN. *April Fools: An Insider's Account of the Rise and Collapse of Drexel Burnham.* New York: Donald I. Fine & Co., 1990.

SPECIAL TOPICS IN FINANCIAL MANAGEMENT

In the 1980s it would have been almost impossible to have missed the news about megamergers, leveraged buyouts, enormous firms going bankrupt, and the ascent of foreign capital markets and the global economy. In Part 7 we discuss these topics, as well as that of small-business finance.

Synergy, tender offer, poison pills, white knights, and *golden parachutes* are just a few of the terms that have become permanently associated with corporate mergers and acquisitions (Chapter 23). Besides spawning a new vocabulary, the restructuring wave of the 1980s changed corporate America in several fundamental ways. Although some of these changes were forced on the economy by global competition, much of the restructuring occurred as investors demanded more responsive management and more efficient use of corporate resources.

Students of financial management need to understand the process of business failure, even if they never experience it (Chapter 24). Business failure does not always mean bankruptcy. Sometimes debt contracts can be renegotiated or securities exchanged so that technical default is eliminated.

Chapter 25 provides a brief introduction to some of the key concepts in the fast-growing world of international finance. Although many of these concepts are similar to the lessons we have already learned, international finance has some unique aspects, such as currency exchange risk and political risk, that must be understood if a firm is to succeed in the global marketplace.

Small firms are not just big firms with lower sales. There are unique costs and benefits associated with small size. Raising capital is difficult, for example, but changes in focus or strategy are more easily implemented. In Chapter 26 we describe some of these differences and discuss some of the more important aspects of small-business financial management.

INTRODUCTION

VIDEO CASE 7

The USX Proxy Contest: Putting a Divestiture Decision to a Shareholder Vote

from ABC News, *Business World*, May 6, 1990

In 1981 the United States Steel Corporation acquired Marathon Oil for $6.4 billion. In 1985 it bought another energy company, Texas Oil & Gas. These acquisitions shifted U.S. Steel from a steel company to a diversified steel and energy company. Along the way the firm's name also changed to USX. Since making these acquisitions USX has had more than its share of problems. The energy industry has performed poorly; oil prices have been flat since 1985, and natural gas prices have actually fallen (see *Time*, March 16, 1992, for a discussion of the energy industry's problems). Making USX's problems more serious has been fierce competition in the steel industry from both foreign competitors and domestic minimills.

In response to the acquisitions and subsequent poor performance of the firm, some shareholders want changes in the way USX is structured. This video describes investor Carl Icahn's efforts to divide USX into two separate companies—the old U.S. Steel and a separate energy company. Carl Icahn is leading a proxy battle to demand the reorganization of the firm. In a proxy contest a shareholder (or group of shareholders) puts a proposal on the annual meeting agenda for shareholder vote. In the most extreme proxy contests the dissident shareholder group proposes an entirely different slate of directors. If elected the new board will fire the current management team and hire new managers. The objectives of less far-reaching proxy proposals include activating anti-takeover devices such as poison pills, or implementation of confidential voting. In the USX case the proposal is to *spin off* or divest USX of its steel business. Separate shares would be issued for the steel division and current USX shareholders would receive shares in the new company equal to their share ownership in USX.

In the video the costs and benefits of the divestiture are discussed. Predictably, management sees only costs arising from the reorganization, and members of the dissident shareholder group see only benefits. Financial analysts are uncertain whether the value of the two separate firms will exceed the current value of USX.

As you read Chapter 23, consider these questions:

- Which argument makes more sense: Two separate firms would be more costly to manage, so shareholders will suffer from the divestiture; or two separate firms will be more attractive to investors, so the divestiture will enhance shareholder wealth?

- If you think that the divestiture will increase shareholder value, explain the source of the gains.

- Do you think that proxy contests such as this one are likely to be successful?

CHAPTER 23

Corporate Restructuring: Combinations and Divestitures

Mergers and Acquisitions: A Historical Perspective ● Why Mergers Might Create Wealth ● Determination of a Firm's Value ● Financing and Corporate Restructuring ● Tender Offer ● Resistance to the Merger ● Divestitures

Corporate restructuring in the past decade has dramatically affected the perceptions most of us have about business and finance—not to mention the significant change in the number and structure of firms that existed only a few years ago. In the United States alone, the total value of assets changing hands in the past decade was $1.3 trillion. Of the 500 largest industrial corporations in the U.S. in 1980, 28 percent had been acquired by other firms by 1989. The decade was well known even to the most casual observer as the period of the **hostile takeover,** meaning that managers of the acquired firm resisted being taken over by investors who might be less than friendly to the current management. These years were also characterized by the use of large amounts of leverage in acquiring other companies; this process came to be known as a **leveraged buyout** (LBO). In addition, management buyouts (MBOs), in which managers used large amounts of borrowed funds to buy the firms they managed, occurred with increasing frequency. In short, the mergers and acquisitions of the last 10 years have created a great amount of excitement and emotion, including anxiety, and represent an area of keen interest in our study of finance. We have six objectives in our study of corporate restructuring.

1. Provide a bit of history of the merger and acquisition phenomenon in the United States
2. Understand why mergers may create value
3. Identify and explain the basic factors that determine the value of an acquisition target
4. Examine the techniques used in financing an acquisition
5. Explain the use of tender offers in acquiring a new business
6. Study the methods managers use to resist an undesired suitor wanting to acquire their firm

We also study divestitures, focusing on the different options available to management in divesting part of the firm.

796

Mergers and Acquisitions: A Historical Perspective[1]

Corporate growth and restructuring through the acquiring of and merging with other companies has long been part of the Anglo-American business tradition, going back to the 1800s. For the most part, however, there have been four identifiable periods in which activity in mergers and acquisitions was particularly accentuated. In all four cases, the increased activity coincided with economic expansion. Invariably, firms were responding to new investment and profit opportunities arising out of changing economic conditions and technological innovations.

The first merger wave occurred at the turn of this century, mostly between 1895 and 1904. Despite the Sherman Antitrust Act of 1890, which made illegal collusive agreements between firms, a company was still allowed to capture up to 90 percent of the market share in their industry. During this brief time, many industries were merged into near monopolies. For example, U.S. Steel, founded by J. P. Morgan (who later joined with Andrew Carnegie), had as much as 75 percent of the U.S. steel-making capacity at one time. American Tobacco had a 90 percent market share. Standard Oil, owned by John D. Rockefeller, captured about 85 percent of the U.S. retail oil market. The merger movement of these barons eventually came to an end when a severe recession occurred in 1903.

The second merger wave, as did the first, began with an economic upturn in 1922, and ended with the collapse of the stock market and the economy in 1929. If the first merger wave can be associated with monopolies, the second is closely related to the creation of oligopolies (industries dominated by a few firms). The public utilities and banking industries, along with food processing, chemicals, and mining were the most frequent players during this period. Many of the mergers represented product or market extensions, and included the creation of such firms as IBM, General Foods, and Allied Chemical. During this time, developments in transportation, communications, and merchandising fostered the growth. Improved transportation allowed firms to reach markets that had been inaccessible, and the radio allowed firms to differentiate their products with potential customers.

In the 1950s, the government's antitrust policy (manifested by the Celler-Kefauver Act of 1950) became increasingly antagonistic toward mergers between firms within the same industry. No longer permitted to acquire firms within their own industries, companies with excess cash (at a time when there was a favorable market for equity issues) actively began acquiring companies outside their industries. The union of dissimilar firms into one corporate entity has come to be known as the **conglomerate.** The middle of this century was a time when control of businesses was shifted by takeovers from entrepreneurs who started their own firms to professional managers of the conglomerates. The creation of a conglomerate was thought to be an efficient way of monitoring individual businesses by subjecting them to regular quantitative evaluations by the central office. The conglomerate allowed funds to be reallocated from slowly growing subsidiaries that generated cash, such as insurance and finance, to fast-growing, high-technology businesses that required investment funds.

With hindsight we now see that conglomerate acquisitions have for the most part proven unsuccessful. The evidence suggests that buyers often paid too much to acquire the businesses, and that mergers were frequently followed by declines in earnings. It is estimated that 60 percent of the cross-industry

[1]Many of the comments in this section come from an article by Andrei Shleifer and Robert W. Vishny, "The Takeover Wave of the 1980s," *Journal of Applied Corporate Finance* (Fall 1991), pp. 49–56, and from J. Fred Weston, Kwang S. Chung, and Susan Hoag, *Mergers, Restructuring, and Corporate Control* (Englewood Cliffs, NJ: Prentice Hall, 1990).

acquisitions occurring between 1970 and 1982 were sold or divested (broken up) by 1989.

Why have conglomerates failed? Perhaps the most important reason may have been a disregard for the principle that specialization raises productivity. Many important business decisions were made by managers with only limited information who had to divide their attention and resources between multiple businesses. For example, Kraft supposedly ignored its Duracell battery division to give priority to its cheese product lines. Likewise, Revlon suffered as its management dedicated its scarce resources to expanding its health care business, at the expense of its basic cosmetics business. Also, conglomerates developed large and expensive central offices for the purpose of monitoring the various businesses. Monitoring by central offices usually proved to be less effective than the market discipline to which stand-alone businesses are generally subjected. Because the subsidiaries of conglomerates are insulated from market forces, they can afford to lose money and be subsidized by other divisions. They simply do not have to raise external capital and, as a result, do not have to be as competitive.

The most recent merger wave, which we have already discussed in our introduction to the chapter, has been called the *decade of the deal*. The 1980s provided favorable equity markets and the availability of large amounts of debt financing, amounts previously not thought possible. One consequence was a strong demand for expansion through acquisitions. At the same time, the Reagan administration consciously relaxed enforcement of antitrust provisions in an effort to encourage growth. As a result, intraindustry acquisitions became possible on a large scale for the first time in 30 years. The significance of this era is shown in Table 23–1, which shows that, of the 20 largest mergers, listed according to 1991 prices, 16 occurred after 1980.

In the 1980s, several large investors such as T. Boone Pickens and Carl Icahn, who came to be known as *corporate raiders,* and several of the major investment banking houses became the brokers of the merger and acquisition activities. The pattern became that of acquiring a conglomerate, breaking it up into its individual business units, and selling off the units to large corporations in the same businesses. Several firms created in this process were temporary organizations intended to last only as long as was required to divest the pieces of the acquired firm to other corporations. Any remaining businesses were then

TABLE 23-1
Twenty Largest U.S. Mergers
(Billions of Dollars)

Acquirer	Target	Date	Price Actual	1991 Dollars
KKR	RJR Nabisco	1989	$24.7	$27.0
U.S. Steel	11 firms	1901	1.4	22.1
Chevron	Gulf	1984	13.3	17.3
Philip Morris	Kraft	1988	12.6	14.1
Bristol-Myers	Squibb	1989	12.5	13.4
Time Warner	Warner Communications	1990	12.6	13.4
Texaco	Getty Oil	1984	10.1	13.3
Du Pont	Conoco	1981	6.9	10.0
British Petroleum	Standard Oil	1987	7.6	9.0
Beecham Group	SmithKline Beckman	1989	8.3	9.0
U.S. Steel	Marathon Oil	1982	6.2	8.8
KKR	Beatrice	1986	6.3	7.8
Dow Chemical	Marion Laboratories	1989	7.1	7.6
General Electric	RCA	1986	6.1	7.6
American Tobacco	7 firms	1903	0.5	7.5
Campeau	Federated Department Stores	1988	6.5	7.4
Mobil	Superior Oil	1984	5.7	7.4
Royal Dutch/Shell	Shell Oil	1985	5.7	7.1
Philip Morris	General Foods	1985	5.6	7.0
Atlantic Richfield	Sinclair Oil	1969	1.9	6.8

Sources: Mergers & Acquisitions Database; Ralph L. Nelson, "Merger Movements in American Industry, 1985–1956."

offered to the public, especially when the business unit's value had been enhanced by improvements in the firm's operations.

The *decade of the deal* came to an end in the late 1980s, largely because the huge amounts of debt financing used to fund many of the acquisitions dried up. Also, a recession developed, which resulted in some major firms not being able to meet their debt obligations.

What may we conclude about this era of takeovers, a time when Michael Milken and Carl Icahn became household names? Some believe that it was a time of excesses and greed. Hostile takeovers and management buyouts, particularly, have been blamed for a multitude of problems including massive layoffs. The fear of being taken over by the likes of T. Boone Pickens is thought to have caused managers to reduce significantly their planning horizons. The large debt loads of many of the acquiring and acquired firms have, according to some, increased the instability of the economy and resulted in the general decline of U.S. competitiveness. For these reasons, many states have all but banned hostile takeovers.

Whatever we believe about takeovers during the 1980s, they undoubtedly did include some excesses and greed. After all was said and done, however, the evidence suggests that takeovers during the 1980s represented a return to more specialized and focused firms after years of diversification. Most acquisitions during the latter years involved companies buying other firms in their own lines of business. Most often, firms were taken over, and their various business lines were sold off to different buyers in the same line of business. To a significant extent, hostile takeovers and leveraged buyouts that attracted so much public attention facilitated this process of deconglomeration. Some of the most common objections to takeovers, such as a reduction of competition and cutbacks in employment, investment, and R & D, are not supported by the data.[2]

[2]See, for example, Amar Bhide, "The Causes and Consequences of Hostile Takeovers," *Journal of Applied Corporate Finance* (Summer 1989), pp. 36–59.

Although the jury is still out as to the long-term consequences of the 1980s era of acquisitions, the mere fact that the conglomerates failed to deliver as they promised could mean that the performance of many firms as they gain increased focus will improve. We shall see in time.

Perspective in Finance

Mergers and acquisitions are usually justified by management on the grounds that merging diversifies the firm, thus reducing risk. However, it may be that the stockholder can diversify personally with more ease and less expense by buying stock in the two companies. There must be other reasons for the merger.

Why Mergers Might Create Wealth

Clearly, for a merger to create wealth it would have to provide shareholders with something they could not get by merely holding the individual shares of the two firms. Such a requirement is the key to the creation of wealth under the capital

1986 (CONT.)

October	Icahn announces a $7.8 billion bid for USX.
November	Robert Campeau acquires Allied Stores for $3.6 billion.
November	Ivan Boesky agrees to pay $100 million penalty for insider trading.
December	Revco goes private for $1.3 billion to elude the Haft family.

1987

January	Goodyear Tire does a $2 billion leveraged recapitalization to fight off Goldsmith.
February	Henry Kravis's KKR leads $3.6 billion LBO of Owens-Illinois.
April	Merrill Lynch leads a $4.2 billion LBO of Borg-Warner.
May	Cain Chemical formed from seven petrochemical plants in a $1 billion LBO.
June	Morgan Stanley leads a $2.5 billion LBO of Burlington Industries.
July	Harcourt Brace Jovanovich does a $3 billion leveraged recap to fight off a takeover bid from Robert Maxwell.

1988

January	Eastman Kodak acquires Sterling Drug for $5.1 billion.
April	Campeau acquires Federated Department Stores for $6.6 billion.
April	Texaco pays Pennzoil $3 billion to settle suit arising from Getty takeover.
May	USG does a leveraged recap to fend off a takeover bid by Desert Partners.
June	KKR and management buy Duracell from Kraft for $1.8 billion in an LBO.
July	Revco becomes first major LBO to file for Chapter 11.
September	Michael Milken and Drexel are charged with insider trading, fraud, and stock parking.
October	Ross Johnson proposes a $17 billion management buyout of RJR Nabisco.
October	Philip Morris acquires Kraft for $13 billion.
November	KKR does $25 billion LBO for RJR Nabisco, the biggest deal ever.
December	Kroger pays a special dividened as part of its leveraged recap to fend off takeover bids from KKR and the Haft family.

1989

July	Bristol-Myers and Squibb agree to a $12.6 billion merger.
July	Time, Inc., acquires Warner Communications.
September	Junk bond prices start to plunge.
September	Sony acquires Columbia Pictures for $3.4 billion.
September	Drexel pleads guilty to mail and securities fraud.
October	United Airlines buyout collapses.

Source: Adapted from Edmund Faltermayer, "The Deal Decade: Verdict in the '80s," *Fortune*, August 26, 1991, pp. 58–76. Used by permission.

asset pricing model. Restating the question: What benefits are there to shareholders from holding the stock of a new, single firm that has been created through a merger as opposed to holding stock in the two individual firms prior to their merger? Let's consider some of these benefits.

Tax Benefits

If a merger were to result in a reduction of taxes that is not otherwise possible, then wealth is created by the merger. This can be the case with a firm that has lost money and thus generated tax credits but does not currently have a level of earnings sufficient to use those tax credits. You will recall that losses can be carried back 3 years and forward a total of 15 years. As a result, tax credits that cannot be used and have no value to one firm can take on value when that firm is acquired by another firm that has earnings sufficient enough to employ the tax credits. In addition, a merger allows for previously depreciated assets to be revaluated; thus, wealth is created from the tax benefits arising from the increased depreciation associated with this revaluation of assets.

Reduction of Agency Costs

As we know, the agency problem can occur when the management and ownership of the firm are separate. To compensate for the agency problem, stockholders and bondholders impose a premium on funds supplied to the firm to compensate them for any inefficiency in management. A merger, particularly when it results in a holding company or conglomerate organizational form, may reduce the significance of this problem, because top management is created to monitor the management of the individual companies making up the conglomerate. As a result, management of the individual companies can be effectively monitored without any forced public announcement of proprietary information, such as new product information that might aid competitors. If investors recognize this reduction in the agency problem as material, they may provide funds to the firm at a reduced cost, no longer charging as large an "agency problem premium."

Alternatively, it can be argued that the creation of a conglomerate might result in increased agency costs. Shareholders in conglomerates may think they have less control over the firm's managers as a result of the additional layers of management between them and the decision makers. Moreover, the resultant expenditures necessary to monitor conglomerates, because of their multi-industry nature, may give further rise to agency cost.

Free Cash Flow Problem: A Specific Case of the Agency Problem

The "free cash flow" problem was first identified by Michael Jensen in 1986. Free cash flow refers to the operating cash flow in excess of what is necessary to fund all profitable investments available to the firm; that is, to fund all projects with a positive net present value. As we know from our discussion of shareholder-wealth maximization, this free cash flow should be paid out to shareholders; otherwise it would be invested in projects returning less than the required rate of return, in effect less than shareholders could earn elsewhere.

Unfortunately, managers may not wish to pass these funds to the shareholders because they may think that their power would be reduced. Moreover, if they return these surplus funds, they may be forced to go outside for financing if more profitable investment opportunities are identified at a later date. Certainly, what we are describing here is a form of the agency problem; still, we need to see these actions in the context of the corporate management culture rather than as an attempt by the managers to maintain their own position. That is to say, as economic conditions change, managers who have successfully managed firms over the years of growing markets may have difficulty in adjusting their financial strategies to conditions in which not all cash flows can be invested at the required rate of return. Jensen argues that this was the case in oil and gas industry in the late 1970s and resulted in much of the merger activity that took place in those markets during that period.[3] A merger can create wealth by allowing the new management to pay this free cash flow out to the shareholders, thus allowing them to earn a higher return on this excess than would have been earned by the firm.

Economies of Scale

Wealth can also be created in a merger through economies of scale. For example, administrative expenses including accounting, data processing, or simply top-management costs, may fall as a percentage of total sales as a result of sharing these resources.

[3]Michael C. Jensen, "The Takeover Controversy: Analysis and Evidence," *Midland Corporate Finance Journal* 4 (2) (Summer 1986), pp. 6–32.

The sharing of resources can also lead to an increase in the firm's productivity. For example, if two firms sharing the same distribution channels merge, distributors carrying one product may now be willing to carry the other, thereby increasing the sales outlets for the products. In effect, wealth would be created by the merger of the two firms and shareholders should benefit.

Unused Debt Potential

Some firms simply do not exhaust their debt capacity. If a firm with unused debt potential is acquired, the new management can then increase debt financing, and reap the tax benefits associated with the increased debt.

Complementarity in Financial Slack

When cash-rich bidders and cash-poor targets are combined, wealth may be created as a result of the positive NPV projects taken by the merged firm that the cash-poor firm would have passed up. Thus, although these cash-poor firms are selling at a firm price, the discounted value of their future cash flow is below their potential price. In effect, a merger allows positive NPV projects to be accepted that would have been rejected if the merger had not occurred.

Removal of Ineffective Management

Any time a merger can result in the replacement of inefficient operations, whether in production or management, wealth should be created. If a firm with ineffective management can be acquired, it may be possible to replace the current management with a more efficient management team, and thereby create wealth. This may be the case with firms that have grown from solely production into production and distribution companies, or R & D firms that have expanded into productions and distribution; the managers simply may not know enough about the new aspects of the firm to manage it effectively.

Increased Market Power

The merger of two firms can result in an increase in the market or monopoly power of the two firms. Although this can result in increased wealth, it may also be illegal. The Clayton Act, as amended by the Celler-Kefauver Amendment of 1950, makes any merger illegal that results in a monopoly or substantially reduces competition. The Justice Department and the Federal Trade Commission monitor all mergers to ensure that they do not result in a reduction of competition.

Reduction in Bankruptcy Costs

There is no question that firm diversification, when the earnings from the two firms are less than perfectly positively correlated, can reduce the chance of bankruptcy. The question is whether or not there is any wealth created by such an activity. Quite obviously, in the real world there is a cost associated with bankruptcy. First, if a firm fails, its assets in general cannot be sold for their true economic value. Moreover, the amount of money actually available for distribution to stockholders is further reduced by selling costs and legal fees that must be paid. Finally, the opportunity cost associated with the delays related to the legal process further reduces the funds available to the shareholder. Therefore, because costs are associated with bankruptcy, reduction of the chance of bankruptcy has a very real value to it.

The risk of bankruptcy also entails indirect costs associated with changes in the firm's debt capacity and the cost of debt. As the firm's cash flow patterns stabilize, the risk of default will decline, giving the firm an increased debt capacity and possibly reducing the cost of the debt. Because interest payments are tax deductible, whereas dividends are not, debt financing is less expensive than equity financing. Thus, monetary benefits are associated with an increased debt capacity. These indirect costs of bankruptcy also spread out into other areas of the firm, affecting things like production and the quality and efficiency of management. Firms with higher probabilities of bankruptcy may have a more difficult time recruiting and retaining quality managers and employees because jobs with that firm are viewed as less secure. This in turn may result in less productivity for these firms. In addition, firms with higher probabilities of bankruptcy may have a more difficult time marketing their product because of customer concern over future availability of the product. In short, there are real costs to bankruptcy. If a merger reduces this possibility of bankruptcy, it creates some wealth.

"Chop-Shop" Approach—Buying Below Replacement Cost

The "chop-shop" approach, which will be discussed more fully later, suggests that the individual parts of a firm are worth more than the current value of the firm as a whole. In the 1980s, many corporate raiders were driven by the fact that it was less expensive to purchase assets through an acquisition than it was to obtain those assets in any other way. This was particularly true of both conglomerates and oil companies. For conglomerates, corporate raiders found that they often sold for less than the sum of the market value of their parts. Much of the merger and acquisition activity associated with oil companies was driven by the fact that it was cheaper to acquire new oil reserves by purchasing a rival oil company than it was through exploration. If assets are mispriced, as this approach seems to suggest, then identifying those assets and revealing this information about the undervalued assets to investor may result in the creation of wealth.

It should be noted that the free cash flow theory could explain this creation of wealth as easily as a mispricing theory. In particular, the oil industry was characterized in the late 1970s and early 1980s by overexploration and drilling activity in the face of reduced consumption while oil price increases created large cash flows. During this period, managers attempted to increase reserves to protect them from possible future market fluctuations. In effect, the free cash flow problem appeared to exist in the oil industry. As mergers and restructuring raged through the oil industry, wealth was created. Again, this creation of wealth did not necessarily come about through any correction of mispricing. It may have been the elimination of wasted expenditures that created the wealth.

Determination of a Firm's Value

One of the first problems in analyzing a potential merger involves placing a value on the acquired firm. This task is not easy. The value of a firm depends not only on its cash flow generation capabilities, but also upon the operating and financial characteristics of the acquiring firm. As a result, no single dollar value exists for a company. Instead, a range of values is determined that would be economically justifiable to the prospective acquirer. The final price within this range is then negotiated by the two managements.

To determine an acceptable price for a corporation, several factors are carefully evaluated. We know that the objective of the acquiring firm is always maximization of the stockholders' wealth (stock price). However, quantifying the relevant variables for this purpose is difficult at best. For instance, the primary reason for a merger might be to acquire managerial talent, or to complement a strong sales staff with an excellent production department. This potential *synergistic effect* is difficult to measure using the historical data of the companies involved. Even so, several quantitative variables are frequently used in an effort to estimate a firm's value. These factors include (1) book value, (2) appraisal value, (3) market price of the firm's common stock, and (4) expected cash flows.

Book Value

The **book value** of a firm's net worth is the balance sheet amount of the assets less its outstanding liabilities, or in other words, the owners' equity. For example, if a firm's historical cost less accumulated depreciation is $10 million and the firm's debt totals $4 million, the aggregate book value is $6 million. Furthermore, if 100,000 shares of common stock are outstanding, the book value per share is $60 ($6 million ÷ 100,000 shares).

Book value does not measure the true market value of a company's net worth because it is based on the historical cost of the firm's assets. Seldom do such costs bear a relationship to the value of the organization or its ability to produce earnings.

Although the book value of an enterprise is clearly not the most important factor, it should not be overlooked. It can be used as a starting point to be compared with other analyses. Also, a study of the firm's working capital is particularly important to acquisitions involving a business consisting primarily of liquid assets such as financial institutions. Furthermore, in industries where the ability to generate earnings requires large investments in such items as steel, cement, and petroleum, the book value could be a critical factor, especially where plant and equipment are relatively new.

Appraisal Value

An **appraisal value** of a company may be acquired from an independent appraisal firm. The techniques used by appraisers vary widely; however, this value is often closely tied to replacement cost. This method of analysis is not adequate by itself, since the value of individual assets may have little relation to the firm's overall ability to generate earnings, and thus the going-concern value of the firm. However, the appraised value of an enterprise may be beneficial when used in conjunction with other valuation methods. Also, the appraised value may be an important factor in special situations, such as in financial companies, natural resource enterprises, or organizations that have been operating at a loss.[4]

The use of appraisal values does yield several additional advantages. The value according to independent appraisers may permit the reduction of accounting goodwill by increasing the recognized worth of specific assets. *Goodwill* results when the purchase price of a firm exceeds the value of the individual assets. Consider a company having a book value of $60,000 that is purchased for $100,000 (the $40,000 difference is goodwill). The $60,000 book value consists of $20,000 in working capital and $40,000 in fixed assets. However, an appraisal might suggest that the current values of these assets are $25,000 and $55,000, respectively. The $15,000 increase ($55,000 − $40,000) in fixed assets permits the acquiring firm to record a larger depreciation expense than would otherwise be possible, thereby reducing taxes. A second reason for an appraisal is to provide a test of the reasonableness of results obtained through methods based upon the going-concern concept. Third, the appraiser may uncover strengths and weaknesses that otherwise might not be recognized, such as in the valuation of patents, secret processes, and partially completed R & D expenditures.

---

[4]The assets of a financial company and a natural resources firm largely consist of securities and natural reserves, respectively. The value of these individual assets has a direct bearing on the firm's earning capacity. Also, a company operating at a loss may only be worth its liquidation value, which would approximate the appraisal value.

BASIC FINANCIAL MANAGEMENT IN PRACTICE

Corporate Restructuring: The New Thinking

The fundamental assumptions about how businesses should be organized have changed significantly from what they were several years ago. Financial market behavior, economic logic and plain common sense suggest that focusing on a single business, or on a very small number of genuinely linked businesses, is the only way to build the value of a company in the long term. The tempting, even seductive, aphorisms of the past—diversify to reduce risk; diversify for higher growth; manage a balanced portfolio of businesses—are about as useful on today's corporate battlefield as is a horse cavalry in a modern tank war. Sadly, these old assumptions are still cherished by some corporate managers today.

The Financial Rules of the Game

The financial markets, however, have imposed their own set of rules on corporate management. Two key points highlight the difference between the old and new thinking:

(1) Managements cannot create value by doing what shareholders can do for themselves. Unless there are real economic and business connections that lead to sustainable improvements in operating performance, managements do nothing by making acquisitions that investors cannot do for themselves by making a telephone call to a broker. Investors can diversify their risks by investing at the market price. They do not want corporate managements to do it for them by paying acquisition premiums of 50–100% above the going rate.

This sounds straightforward enough, but it actually strikes at the heart of many, if not most, of the reasons given for corporate acquisitions in the US and UK. Many managements seem to operate under the illusion that they should act as a substitute for the capital markets, making resource-allocation decisions that take them well beyond the activities in which they enjoy true operating advantages.

Few topics have been subjected to as much measurement and analysis as corporate diversification, and there is a large body of evidence that points to one conclusion: Unless an acquired business gains a sustainable operating advantage from becoming part of another company, no value for the acquiror's shareholders will be created by the acquisition. The fact that two businesses operate in adjacent or apparently similar areas of activity is not enough to justify the acquisition of one by the other. In fact, much of the restructuring we have seen over the past several years has been the unwinding of grandiose schemes devised by those self-deluding managements that have confused their own role with that of the financial markets. The markets are now exhibiting a healthy impatience with such fantasies.

(2) Shareholders will unlock values suppressed by management. If investors notice that a particular company's strategy is causing it to trade at a discount to its true value, the defenses installed by managements will not, in the long run, stop the investors from getting their way. Investors can be misled, and they frequently misprice securities; however, years of bitter experience and their increasing sophistication (particularly in the US) have made investors far less willing to accept management rationales for diversifying acquisitions. They are much more likely to seek ways to evade the various barriers erected by managements to protect their empires.

Furthermore, size is no longer a barrier. Some corporate managements acquire businesses as part of a defensive strategy, believing that bigger is, if not better, at least tougher to knock over. However, unless such acquisitions achieve sustainable operating advantages for the company, they only put off the evil day. Indeed, all such acquisitions really do is increase the size of the discount in absolute dollars and make the acquiring company even more attractive to well-financed or imaginative predators.

Thus, the appraisal procedure is generally worthwhile if performed with additional evaluation processes. In specific instances, it may be an important instrument for valuing a corporation.

Stock Market Value

The **stock market value,** as expressed by stock market quotations, is another approach to estimating the net worth of a business. If the stock is listed on a major securities exchange, such as the New York Stock Exchange, and is widely traded, an approximate value can be established on the basis of the market value. The justification is based on the fact that the market quotations indicate the consensus of investors as to a firm's cash flow potential and the corresponding risk.

The New Business Environment

The changes in the ground rules mentioned above show that if companies do not restructure themselves, the financial markets will do it for them. Even without the prodding from the financial markets, however, there are compelling business reasons for companies to restructure:

(1) Competition. In a fiercely competitive environment, a broad span of businesses is a luxury that is less and less affordable. Indeed, today's managers are seeing a heightened sense of competitor performance. Absolute measures of success mean much less. Whatever the subject—whether product cost or quality, the rate of innovation, quality of service, or almost any other dimension of business—it is all relative to the competition.

(2) Flexibility. The quick and the dead. Rapidity of response is becoming crucial to corporate survival and success. Technological developments in information, production and distribution systems and an increased consumer demand for variety are causing major shifts in the pattern of business activity. As a result, diversified firms are in for a tough time. It is hard to jump in several directions at once.

(3) Excessive corporate overhead. Too much value is absorbed by unnecessary corporate expense. Such expense is often worse than unnecessary; it can be positively damaging. In order to justify their existence, corporate headquarters frequently embark upon acquisition programs that create no value for their shareholders. After all, acquisitions are exciting, dramatic and glamorous.

For example, the financial statements of one major diversified corporation reveal an item called "corporate expense" that totals slightly under $200 million. Compare this amount to the company's net income, which (after various adjustments for extraordinary items) totals about $1.3 billion. While adjusted net income has grown at slightly under 15% per annum over the past few years, corporate expense has been growing at the staggering rate of just under 50% per annum over the same period. Adjusting the corporate expense to an aftertax figure and applying the company's price/earnings ratio to the net expense produces a cost of over $1.4 billion. Even assuming that some of the expense is necessary, there is clearly a lot of value being wasted by excessive overhead. (Editor's note: The company in question is RJR Nabisco. Duffy's article was written prior to the recent buyout.)

The Role of Finance

Under these new ground rules, the CFO must play a more active role in planning the direction of the company. However, good finance is not a substitute for good strategy and operations. The CFO's role is overlapping more and more with those of the CEO and COO because of the growing interconnectedness of finance, strategy and operations. Unless this interconnectedness is acknowledged and encouraged, the best finance function in the world will not be able to make up for poor strategy or inferior performance.

Therefore, the CFO needs to be centrally involved in strategy formulation, not just to ensure that the strategy is financially sound, but to bring a financial market perspective and ensure that strategic plans translate directly into shareholder value. He also needs to be more closely involved in operations, if only to ensure that the operators are fully aware of the financial dimension of operating decisions and make certain that the real causes of poor financial performance are addressed and remedied.

Source: Simon Duffy, "Corporate Restructuring: The New Thinking," *Business International Money*, January 9, 1989, pp. 1–3.

The market-value approach is the one most frequently used in valuing large corporations. However, this value can change abruptly. Analytical factors compete with purely speculative influences and are subject to people's sentiments and personal decisions. Thus,

> [T]he market is not a weighing machine, on which the value of each issue is recorded by an exact and impersonal mechanism, in accordance with the specific qualities. Rather should we say that the market is a voting machine, whereon countless individuals register choices which are the product partly of reason and partly of emotion.[5]

---

[5]Benjamin Graham, David L. Dodd, and Sidney Cottle, *Security Analysis*, 4th ed. (New York: McGraw-Hill, 1962), p. 42.

In short, the market-value approach is probably the one most widely used for determining the worth of a firm; a 10 to 20 percent premium above the market price is often required as an inducement for the current owners to sell their stock. Even so, executives who place their entire reliance upon this method are subject to an inherent danger of market psychology.

The "Chop-Shop" Value

The "chop-shop" approach to valuation was first proposed by Dean Lebaron and Lawrence Speidell of Batterymarch Financial Management. Specifically, it attempts to identify multi-industry companies that are undervalued and would be worth more if separated into their parts. This approach conceptualizes the practice of attempting to buy assets below their replacement cost.

Any time we confront a technique that suggests that stocks may be inefficiently priced, we must be a bit skeptical. In the case of a multi-industry firm, inefficiency in pricing may be brought on by the high cost of obtaining information. Alternatively, these firms may be worth more if split up because of agency problems. Shareholders of multi-industry companies may feel they have less control of the firm's managers, since additional layers of management may have developed with multi-industry firms. These agency costs may take the form of increased expenditures necessary to monitor the managers, costs associated with organizational change, and opportunity costs associated with poor decisions made as a result of the manager acting in his or her own best interests rather than the best interest of the shareholders.

The "chop-shop" approach attempts to value companies by their various business segments. As it is implemented by Batterymarch, it first attempts to find "pure-play" companies—that is, companies in a single industry—from which it computes average "valuation ratios." The ratios frequently used compare total capitalization (debt plus equity) to total sales, to assets, and to income. In effect, these ratios represent the average value of a dollar of sales, a dollar of assets, and a dollar of income for a particular industry based on the average of all pure companies in that industry. Assuming that these ratios hold for the various business segments of a multi-industry firm, the firm can then be valued by its parts.

For the chop-shop valuation technique to be feasible, we must naturally have information about the various business segments within the firm. This requirement is fulfilled, at least in part, by the reporting rules set forth in Statement 14 of the Financial Accounting Standards Board (the public accountants' governing group). This standard requires that firms provide detailed accounting statements along the various lines of business or what is called Standard Industrial Codes (SIC). Of course, we know that not all firms in the same industry are in fact the same—some simply have more potential growth or earnings ability than others. As such, this methodology should be viewed cautiously. However, it is in use by financial managers, and we should have an understanding of it.

The "chop-shop" approach is actually a three-step process.

Step 1: Identify the firm's various business segments and calculate the average capitalization ratios for firms in those industries.

Step 2: Calculate a "theoretical" market value based upon each of the average capitalization ratios.

Step 3: Average the "theoretical" market values to determine the "chop-shop" value of the firm.

EXAMPLE

To illustrate the chop-shop approach, consider Cavos, Inc., with common stock currently trading at a total market price of $13 million. For Cavos, the accounting data set forth four business segments: industrial specialties, basic chemicals, consumer specialties, and basic plastics. Data for these four segments are as follows:

Business Segment	Segment Sales ($000)	Segment Assets ($000)	Segment Income ($000)
Industrial specialties	$2,765	$2,206	$186
Basic chemicals	5,237	4,762	165
Consumer specialties	2,029	1,645	226
Basic plastics	1,506	1,079	60
Total	$11,537	$9,692	$637

The three steps for valuing Cavos would be

Step 1: We first identify "pure" companies, that being firms that operate solely in one of above industries; we then calculate the average capitalization ratios for those firms. This could easily be done using a computer data base, such as the Computstat tapes, which provide detailed financial information on most publicly traded firms. Assume the average capitalization ratios for the four business segments that Cavos is active in have been determined and are as shown in Table 23–2.

Step 2: Once we have calculated the average market capitalization ratios for the various market segments, we need only multiply Cavos' segment values (that is, segment sales, segment assets, and segment income) times the capitalization ratios to determine the theoretical market values. This is done in Table 23–3.

Business Segment	Capitalization Sales	Capitalization Assets	Capitalization Operating Income
Industrial specialties	0.61	1.07	21.49
Basic chemicals	2.29	2.43	17.45
Consumer specialties	3.58	2.92	19.26
Basic plastics	1.71	2.18	15.06

TABLE 23–2.
Average Capitalization Ratios for Industries in Which Cavos, Inc., Is Active

TABLE 23–3.
Calculation of the "Theoretical Values" for Cavos, Inc., Using Market Capitalization Ratios

Value Based on Market Capitalization/Sales

Business Segment	(A) Market Capitalization Sales	(B) Segment Sales	(A) X (B) Theoretical Market Value
Industrial specialties	0.61	$2,765	$1,686.7
Basic chemicals	2.29	5,237	11,992.7
Consumer specialties	3.58	2,029	7,263.8
Basic plastics	1.71	1,506	2,575.3
Total			$23,518.5

Value Based on Market Capitalization/Assets

Business Segment	(A) Market Capitalization Assets	(B) Segment Assets	(A) X (B) Theoretical Market Value
Industrial specialties	1.07	$2,206	$2,360.4
Basic chemicals	2.43	4,762	11,571.7
Consumer specialties	2.92	1,645	4,803.4
Basic plastics	2.18	1,079	2,352.2
Total			$21,087.7

Value Based on Market Capitalization/Income

Business Segment	(A) Market Capitalization Income	(B) Segment Income	(A) X (B) Theoretical Market Value
Industrial specialties	21.49	$186	$3,997.1
Basic chemicals	17.45	165	2,879.3
Consumer specialties	19.26	226	4,352.8
Basic plastics	15.06	60	903.6
Total			$12,132.8

Step 3: Finally, the theoretical values must be averaged to calculate the "chop-shop" value of the firm. The average of the three theoretical values in Table 23–3 is $18,923,000, computed as follows:

$$\frac{\text{value based on sales} + \text{value based on assets} + \text{value based on income}}{3}$$

or

$$\frac{(\$23,518,500 + \$21,087,700 + \$12,132,800}{3}$$

$$= \$18,913,000$$

Hence, Cavos, Inc. is selling for significantly less than its chop-shop value, $13 million compared with $18.9 million.

The major limitation of a valuation model such as the chop-shop approach is that it is not derived from any theoretical basis. What it does is assume that average industry capitalization relationships—in this case, ratios of capitalization to sales, assets, and operating income—hold for all firms or conglomerate subsidiaries in that particular industry. Of course, this is frequently not the case. It is easy to identify specific companies that simply produce superior products and whose future earnings growth is, as a result, brighter. These companies, because of their expected future growth, should have their sales, assets, and operating income valued higher. This only makes sense because, as we know, the valuation of any asset is based on the market's expectations.

Given this limitation of the chop-shop valuation approach, why have we dealt with it in such detail? The reason is that it reflects a view among some investors and corporate raiders that the replacement value of a firm's assets may exceed the value placed on the firm as a whole in the market. It attempts to value the multi-industry firm by its parts. Moreover, as we will see as we explore the cash flow approach to valuation, there simply is no way to estimate the value of a takeover candidate with complete confidence. Thus, this method may provide the decision maker with additional information. ■

The Cash Flow Value

Our last look at valuation models should be familiar to us, given our prior work in finding the present value of cash flows, as we did in our studies in capital budgeting. Using the cash flow approach to merger valuation requires that we estimate the incremental net cash flows available to the bidding firm as a result of the merger or acquisition. The present value of these cash flows then will be determined, and this will be the maximum amount that should be paid for the target firm. The initial outlay then can be subtracted out to calculate the net present value from the merger. Although this is very similar to a capital-budgeting problem, there are differences, particularly in estimating the initial outlay.

Finding the present value of the cash flows for a merger involves a five-step process:

Step 1: Estimate the incremental cash flows available from the target firm. This estimation of incremental after-tax cash flows includes all synergistic cash flows (including those to both the bidding and target firms) created as a result of the acquisition. It should also be noted that interest expenses are not included in these cash flows, as they are accounted for in the required rate of return.

Step 2: Estimate the risk-adjusted discount rate associated with cash flows from the target firm. The target firm's, not the bidding firm's, required rate of return is appropriate here. If there is any anticipated change in financing associated with the target firm as a result of the acquisition, this change should be considered.

Step 3: Calculate the present value of the incremental cash flows from the target firm.

Step 4: Estimate the initial outlay associated with the acquisition. The initial outlay is defined here as the market value of all securities and cash paid out plus the market value of all debt liabilities assumed.

Step 5: Calculate the net present value of the acquisition by subtracting the initial outlay from the present value of the incremental cash flows from the target firm.

Estimation of the incremental after-tax cash flows resulting from an acquisition is extremely difficult. There is a certain lack of precision that is inherent in these calculations because of the problem of estimating the synergistic gains from combining the two firms. For example, it is very difficult to estimate the gains that might be expected from any reduction in bankruptcy costs, increased market power, or reduction in agency costs that might occur. Still, it is imperative to estimate these gains if we are to place a value on the target firm. Once the required rate of return is determined, the present value of the incremental cash flows from acquiring the target firm can then be calculated. The final step then becomes the calculation of the initial outlay associated with the acquisition.

Let's look at the example of Tabbypaw Pie, Inc., which is being considered as a possible takeover target by ALF, Inc. Currently, Tabbypaw Pie uses 30 percent debt in its capital structure, but ALF plans on increasing the debt ratio to 40 percent (we will assume that only debt and equity are used) once the acquisition is completed. The after-tax cost of debt capital for Tabbypaw Pie is estimated to be 7 percent, and we will assume that this rate does not change as Tabbypaw's capital structure changes. The cost of equity after the acquisition is expected to be 20.8 percent. The current market value of Tabbypaw's debt outstanding is $110 million, all of which will be assumed by ALF. Also, let's assume that ALF intends to pay $260 million in cash and common stock for all of Tabbypaw Pie's stock in addition to assuming all of Tabbypaw's debt. Currently, the market price of Tabbypaw Pie's common stock is $210 million. ∎

Step 1: Estimate the incremental cash flows from the target firm, including the synergistic flows, such as any possible flows from tax credits. This estimation for Tabbypaw is provided in Table 23–4. Here we are assuming that any cash flows after 1996 will be constant at $75 million. Also, we subtract any funds that must be reinvested in the firm in the form of capital expenditures that are required to support the firm's increasing profits.

	1993	1994	1995	1996	1997 and Thereafter
Net sales	$496	$536	$606	$670	$731
Cost of goods sold	354	385	444	500	551
Administrative and selling expenses	28	30	32	35	38
Earnings before depreciation and interest	114	121	130	135	142
Depreciation	39	40	41	42	43
Earnings before interest and taxes	75	81	89	93	99
Taxes (incremental)	27	30	34	36	39
Net income	48	51	55	57	60
+Depreciation	39	40	41	42	43
−Capital Expenditures	24	25	26	27	28
Net after-tax cash flow (before interest)	$63	$66	$70	$72	$75

TABLE 23–4.
Estimated Incremental Cash Flows from Tabbypaw Pie, Inc. ($ millions)

Step 2: Determine an appropriate risk-adjusted discount rate for evaluating Tabbypaw. Here we will use the weighted cost of capital (WCC) for Tabbypaw as our discount rate, where the weighted cost of capital is calculated as

$$WCC = W_d K_d + W_c K_c$$

where W_d, W_c = the percentage of funds provided by debt and common, respectively

K_d, K_c = the cost of debt and common, respectively

For Tabbypaw,

$WCC = (.40)(.07) + (.60)(.208) = .1528$, or 15.28%

Step 3: Next we must calculate the present value of the incremental cash flows expected from the target firm, as given in Table 23–4. Assuming that cash flows do not change after 1997, but continue at the 1997 level in perpetuity, and discounting these cash flows at the 15.28 percent, we get

$$\begin{pmatrix} \text{present value} \\ \text{of all cash flows} \end{pmatrix} = \begin{pmatrix} \text{present value} \\ \text{of 1993–1996} \\ \text{cash flows} \end{pmatrix} + \begin{pmatrix} \text{present value} \\ \text{of cash flows} \\ \text{after 1996} \end{pmatrix}$$

that will affect the cash flow and profitability of their business. Making these guesses as an outsider is like playing blind man's bluff. Merging two organisations with thousands of employees resentful at being bought and sold like chattels is always more difficult than bosses imagine it will be. Such problems can cause even friendly acquisitions by normally super-cautious companies to flop. Bridgestone, Japan's biggest tyre maker, has struggled for three years to digest America's Firestone. It is difficult to see how Sony or Matsushita will ever earn the returns needed to justify the billions of dollars which they have spent buying Hollywood film studios.

This does not mean that all takeovers are a bad idea. Everything businessmen do involves some sort of risk; doing nothing can be the riskiest strategy of all. Taking over another company to gain quick access to a new technology or a new market, to achieve economies of scale, or simply to reap the benefits of running it better than its existing managers, will always be an option worth considering. And the threat of takeover is a valuable discipline for managers of all publicly held firms.

But too often the risks of a merger are underestimated, the promised rewards inflated. The pyramid of guesses needed to justify any merger means that the potential benefits had better be colossal. Most bids put the spotlight on the target company, whose strengths and weaknesses are then scrutinised by analysts, journalists and its own shareholders. In the coming wave of takeovers, the lights should be turned on the bidder.

Source: *The Economist*, December 28, 1991, pp. 19–20. Used by permission.

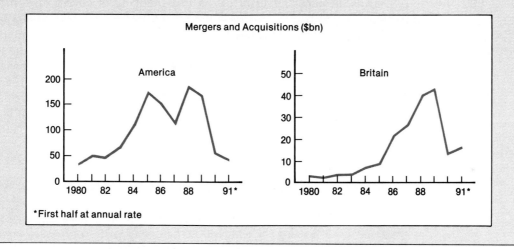

where the present value of cash flows for the first four years of 1993 through 1996 would be $190.772 million, determined as follows:

$$\frac{\$63}{(1+.1528)} + \frac{\$66}{(1+.1528)^2} + \frac{\$70}{(1+.1528)^3} + \frac{\$72}{(1+.1528)^4} = \$190.772$$

and the present value of the $75 million cash flow stream, beginning in 1997, is computed to be $277.921 million.[6]

$$\frac{\frac{\$75}{.1528}}{(1+.1528)^4} = \$277.921$$

Thus, the present value of the cash inflows associated with the acquisition of Tabbypaw Pie by ALF is $468.693 million, or $468,693,000; that is, the sum of $190.772 million and $277.921 million.

---

[6]Remember that we find the present value of an infinite stream of cash flows, where the amount is constant in each year, as follows:

$$\text{value} = \frac{\text{annual cash flow}}{\text{required rate of return}}$$

Because the cash flows do not begin until the fifth year, our equation is finding the value at the end of the fourth year; thus, we must discount the value back for four years.

Step 4: Next, we estimate the initial outlay associated with the acquisition. As already noted, the initial outlay is defined as the market value of all securities and cash paid out plus the market value of all debt liabilities assumed. In this case, the market value of the debt obligations is $110 million. This amount, along with the acquisition price of $260 million, comprise the initial outlay of $370 million.

Step 5: Finally, the net present value of the acquisition is calculated by subtracting the initial outlay (calculated in step 4) from the present value of the incremental cash flows from the target firm (calculated in step 3):

$$\text{NPV acquisition} = \text{PV inflows} - \text{initial outlay}$$

$$= \$468,693,000 - \$370,000,000$$

$$= \$98,693,000$$

Thus, this acquisition should be undertaken because it has a positive net present value. In fact, ALF could pay up to $468.693 million for Tabbypaw Pie.

Financing and Corporate Restructuring[7]

In recent years, we have seen significant changes in the financing practices of U.S. firms, in part the result of the restructuring of corporate America. The outstanding debt of many companies increased as they borrowed heavily to finance restructuring activity. As part of this restructuring, three popular types of highly leveraged transactions have developed: MBO, LBO, and the leveraged Employee Stock Ownership Plan (ESOP). How significant are these financing techniques? The use of LBOs increased from less than $5 billion in 1983 to more than $60 billion in 1989. These three financing approaches are described subsequently.[8] Following a discussion of these techniques, we will look at the use of a bond that has drawn great attention during the 1980s—the junk bond.

MBOs

A MBO occurs when a group of investors form a shell corporation to acquire the target firm or buy the target firm directly. The distinguishing features of a MBO are (1) the group of investors includes members of the management of the target company; (2) following the acquisition the newly formed company goes private; and (3) the acquisition is financed primarily by debt, so the resulting firm is much more highly leveraged than most publicly traded companies.

LBOs

A LBO is a more general type of restructuring device that can be distinguished from a MBO in that the new owners do not necessarily have to include members of the original management team, and the firm is not necessarily taken private following the acquisition. Most LBOs are also MBOs, and the term *LBO* is more generally used in describing high-leverage acquisitions and restructurings. Table 23–5 illustrates the process of an LBO, using the events surrounding the RJR Nabisco LBO as an example.

Leveraged ESOPs

In a leveraged ESOP the rank-and-file employees participate with management in the purchase of stock in their corporation. In these arrangements, a special

---

[7]The ideas in this section come largely from Leland Crabbe, Margaret Pickering, and Stephen Prowse, "Recent Developments in Corporate Finance," *Federal Reserve Bulletin* (August 1990), pp. 595–603.

[8]Taken from John D. Martin and John W. Kensinger, *Exploring the Controversy Over Corporate Restructuring* (Morristown, NJ: Financial Executive Institute Research Foundation, 1990), p. 46.

TABLE 23-5
An LBO: The Case of RJR
Nabisco Corp.

First indication	October 21, 1988, F. Ross Johnson, CEO of RJR, announced a proposed MBO for $75 per share.
Completion date	December 1, 1988, KKR won a bidding war for RJR for $109 per share.

Major events

10/21/88	RJR announced a proposed MBO.
10/27/88	KKR began a $20.8 billion tender offer for RJR.
11/8/88	RJR management was joined by Shearson Lehman Hutton and Salomon on a buyout offer of $21.16 billion ($92 per share). RJR opened the bidding process for sealed bids.
11/30/88	KKR appeared to have won the bidding contest for RJR with a bid of $23.7 billion ($103 per share).
12/1/88	KKR officially named the winner of the bidding war with a bid of $109 per share, or $25 billion.
2/7/89	Swiss Bank and J. P. Morgan (Switzerland) demanded that RJR call its Swiss Franc Bonds at face value because of losses incurred by bondholders due to the LBO financing.
2/10/89	KKR completed the takeover.
3/23/89	Swiss court issues temporary order to stop the completion of the RJR takeover. The order is on behalf of Swiss bondholders who have seen the value of their RJR bonds decrease due to the buy out.
4/6/89	RJR plans to sell $5.5 to $6 billion in assets. RJR also files prospectus for $4 billion bond issue. These bonds are to be used to pay interest on current debt.
4/28/89	Shareholders vote final approval of RJR buyout.
5/12/89	$4 billion bridge loan refinanced.
6/1/89	Federal judge rejects Metropolitan Life's claims that RJR had violated an unwritten requirement to treat bondholders fairly.
6/7/89	RJR sells five of its European food businesses for $2.5 billion.
6/12/89	Federal judge rules that RJR can sell off assets to help pay debt incurred by LBO. Met Life files suit to protect bondholder's rights.
6/21/89	Chung King sold for $52 million.
7/6/89	Three corporate planes sold for $46.4 million.
7/28/89	Scandinavian food unit sold for $20.4 million.
8/1/89	Several corporate apartments and houses sold for $8.6 million.
9/7/89	Del Monte Tropical Fruit sold for $875 million. Negotiations underway for the sale of Del Monte Foods canned food unit for $1.5 billion.

Source: John D. Martin and John W. Kensinger, *Exploring the Controversy over Corporate Restructuring* (Morristown, NJ: Financial Executive Institute Research Foundation, 1990), p. 11.

trust is formed to borrow money to purchase the firm's stock. The loan is then repaid from the employees' retirement funds, and the shares are credited to the employees' retirement account. The employer corporation typically guarantees the loan. The stock is held in trust until the participating employee retires or terminates employment. There are three distinct tax advantages with an ESOP: (1) Dividends paid by the company to stock owned by an ESOP are tax deductible; (2) the institution lending the money to create the ESOP has to pay income tax on only half of the interest received from the ESOP, and thus the plan allows borrowing at low interest rates; and (3) the employer corporation is allowed to make tax-deductible contributions of cash or stock to the ESOP.

Junk Bonds

Junk bonds, which have been described in several earlier chapters, have been closely linked to the large, and at times unsuccessful, mergers of the 1980s. The use of these bonds has been viewed as a common element in some of the country's worst financial disasters in the late 1980s. Examples include the failure of the Campeau retailing empire and the bankruptcy of Drexel, Burnham, Lambert.

Some critics blame many of the market ills on junk bonds. According to these critics, junk bonds fueled the merger mania of the 1980s, caused the excessive use of debt, and created instability in the financial markets. Although these opinions are certainly understandable, the evidence does not support these extreme charges against junk bonds.[9] Junk bonds align with our expectations, as studied in Chapter 4, in terms of risk and expected returns. They are not inherently different from other securities—they have greater risk but also greater expected return. Also, the junk bond market, although significant, was too small to have caused the 1980s merger boom, nor was it large enough to account directly for the growth in corporate debt. Junk bonds in fact accounted for only 14 percent of the growth in corporate debt during the 1980s. Nevertheless, the financing that had been available through the junk bond market essentially evaporated at the conclusion of the 1980s. Merger activity accordingly declined noticeably during the first part of 1990 as a consequence of the virtual unavailability of new financing in the low-grade bond market. Also, the more cautious attitude of commercial banks and the weakening in the market for asset sales contributed to the decline. Nevertheless, well-structured acquisition proposals, especially those aimed at enhancing a firm's competitive position within its own lines of business, were still being well received by investors as we entered the 1990s.

Tender Offer

As an alternative approach in purchasing another firm, the acquiring corporation may consider using a **tender offer.** A tender offer involves a bid by an interested party for controlling interest in another corporation. The prospective purchaser approaches the stockholders of the firm, rather than the management, to encourage them to sell their shares, typically at a premium over the current market price. For instance, in late 1990, AT&T made a $6.1 billion tender offer for NCR, or $90 per share. NCR's management quickly responded by telling the stockholders they should refuse the offer because the stock was worth $125, even though it had only been selling for $48 per share before AT&T's tender offer. After a real dog fight, the final agreement was for $110 per share.

Because the tender offer is a direct appeal to the stockholders, prior approval is not required by the management of the target firm. However, the acquiring firm may choose to approach the management of the target firm. If the two managements are unsuccessful in negotiating the terms, a tender offer may then be attempted. Alternatively, a firm's management interested in acquiring control of a second corporation may try a surprise takeover without contacting the management of the latter company. T. Boone Pickens of Mesa Petroleum is a prime example of someone who has used the tender offer in his efforts to acquire such firms as Cities Service and Gulf.

Resistance to the Merger

In response to unfriendly merger attempts, especially tender offers, the management of the firm under attack will frequently strike back. Several defense tactics are used to counter tender offers. These defensive maneuvers include white knights, PacMans, shark repellents, poison pills and golden parachutes. Let us examine these more closely.

A **white knight** is a company that comes to the rescue of a corporation that

[9]These ideas come from Sean Beckett, "The Truth About Junk Bonds," Federal Reserve Bank of Kansas City, *Economic Review* (July–August 1990), pp. 45–54.

is being targeted for a takeover. For example, when Pennzoil made a tender offer for Getty Oil, the Getty management opposed the Pennzoil attempt. To prevent the takeover, Texaco, at the encouragement of Getty's management, made its own tender offer for Getty at a higher price. Texaco was the white knight for Getty. However, Pennzoil later received a $10 billion judgment against Texaco for its action in the Getty acquisition.

PacMan, the name taken from the video game, is another defensive tactic to tender offers, where the firm under attack becomes the attacker. For instance, Bendix Corporation tried to take control of Martin-Marietta by a tender offer. When the takeover effort failed, Martin-Marietta counterattacked by buying Bendix stock in an attempt to take control of Bendix. Martin-Marietta became the PacMan. To recounter, Bendix successfully courted Allied Corporation to come to its rescue. Allied bought Bendix so that Martin-Marietta could not buy enough for control. Allied was a white knight.

Shark repellents are policy changes or legal manipulations that can be used to discourage unfriendly takeovers. As an example, a firm may revise its bylaws to stagger the terms of directors so that only a few come up for election in any one year. A firm making a tender offer would have to wait at least two years before gaining a majority of board members. Another ploy is to reincorporate in a state with rules that favor existing management. Gulf Oil was incorporated in Pennsylvania, where minority stockholders could use cumulative voting to gain a voice on the board of directors. When T. Boone Pickens began buying major blocks of Gulf stock, Gulf reincorporated in Delaware, where cumulative voting could not be used, making it more difficult for Pickens to have any impact on the management of Gulf.

Another tactic is the **poison pill,** an action initiated automatically if an unfriendly party tries to acquire the firm. For instance, management might devise a plan whereby all the firm's debt becomes due if the management is removed. Still another tactic is the **golden parachute,** which stipulates that the acquiring company must pay the executives of the acquired firm a substantial sum of money to "let them down easy" as new management is brought into the company.

The disadvantages of the unfriendly takeover are readily apparent from the preceding examples. If the target firm's management attempts to block it, the costs of executing the offer may increase significantly. Also, the purchasing company may fail to acquire a sufficient number of shares to meet the objective of controlling the firm. Conversely, if the offer is not strongly contested, it may possibly be less expensive than the normal route for acquiring a company, in that it permits control by purchasing a smaller portion of the firm. Also, the tender offer has proven somewhat less susceptible to judicial inquiries regarding the fairness of the purchase price, because each stockholder individually decides the fairness of the price.

Divestitures

Although the mergers-and-acquisition phenomenon has been a major influence in restructuring the corporate sector, **divestitures,** or what we might call "reverse mergers," may have become an equally important factor. In fact, preliminary research to date would suggest that we may be witnessing a "new era" in the making—one where the public corporation has become a more efficient vehicle for increasing and maintaining stockholder wealth.[10] Chew calls it the "new math," when he writes that

---

[10]See G. Alexander, P. Benson, and J. Kampmeyer, "Investigating the Valuation Effects of Voluntary Corporate Sell-offs," *Journal of Finance* 39 (1984), pp. 503–17; and D. Hearth, "Voluntary Divestitures and Value," *Financial Management* (1984).

a new kind of arithmetic has come into play. Whereas corporate management once seemed to behave as if 2 + 2 were equal to 5, especially during the conglomerate heyday of the 60's, the wave of reverse mergers seems based on the counter proposition that 5 − 1 is 5. And the market's consistently positive response to such deals seems to be providing broad confirmation of the "new math."[11]

A successful divestiture allows the firm's assets to be used more efficiently and therefore to be assigned a higher value by the market forces. It essentially eliminates a division or subsidiary that does not fit strategically with the rest of the company; that is, it removes an operation that does not contribute to the company's basic purposes.

The different types of divestitures may be summarized as follows:

1. **Selloff.** A selloff is the sale of a subsidiary, division, or product line by one company to another. For example, Radio Corporation of America (RCA) sold its finance company and General Electric sold its metallurgical coal business.

2. **Spinoff.** A spinoff involves the separation of a subsidiary from its parent, with no change in the equity ownership. The management of the parent company gives up operating control of the subsidiary, but the shareholders retain the same percentage ownership in both firms. New shares representing ownership in the diverted assets are issued to the original shareholders on a pro-rata basis.

3. **Liquidation.** A liquidation in this context is not a decision to shut down or abandon an asset. Rather, the assets are sold to another company, and the proceeds are distributed to the stockholders.

[11]Joel M. Stern, and Donald H. Chew, Jr. (eds.), *The Revolution in Corporate Finance* (New York: Basis Blackwell, 1986), p. 416.

4. Going private. A company goes private when its stock that has traded publicly is purchased by a small group of investors, and the stock is no longer bought and sold on a public exchange. The ownership of the company is transferred from a diverse group of outside stockholders to a small group of private investors, usually including the firm's management. The leveraged buyout is a special case of going private. As noted earlier in the chapter, the existing shareholders sell their shares to a small group of investors. The purchasers of the stock use the firm's unused debt capacity to borrow the funds to pay for the stock. Thus, the new investors acquire the firm with little, if any, personal investment. However, the firm's debt ratio may increase by as much as tenfold.

SUMMARY

Business combinations historically have represented a major influence in the growth of firms within the United States. This avenue for growth has been particularly important during select periods, such as in the 1980s.

The assertion that merger activity creates wealth for the shareholder cannot be maintained with certainty. Only if the merger provides something that the investor cannot do on his or her own can a merger or acquisition be of financial benefit. There may in fact be certain benefits that accrue to the shareholders, but we must be careful to take a position that can be justified.

Valuing a Firm

Determining the worth of a firm is a difficult task. In addition to projecting the firm's future profitability, which is a cornerstone in valuation, the acquirer must consider the effects of joining two businesses into a single operation. What may represent a good investment may not be a good merger.

In estimating a firm's worth several factors are frequently considered, including (1) the firm's book value, (2) the appraisal value, (3) the stock market value of a firm's common shares, (4) the chop-shop value, and (5) the present value of future free cash flows.

Financing the Merger

Financial innovation frequently has come in conjunction with corporate restructuring; most notable examples include MBOs, LBOs, and leveraged ESOPs. Certainly these concepts are not new, but the extent of their application has increased significantly. In more recent years, we have seen a marked increase in the use of debt. Before the takeovers of the 1980s, managers strove to maintain a targeted capital structure mix. In the 1980s, the use of an LBO sometimes meant that an acquired firm's debt might be increased 10-fold; the intent was not to maintain that high level of debt but rather to bring it down to more acceptable norms as soon as possible. As the 1990s began, the failure of some large firms to meet their large debt obligations brought on by mergers has caused the use of equity currently to be the favored way to finance a merger.

Tender Offers

Normally, the invested purchaser approaches the management of the firm to be acquired. Alternatively, the purchasing firm can directly approach the stockholders of the firm under consideration. This bid for ownership, called a tender offer, has been used with increasing frequency. This approach may be cheaper, but often the managers of the target firm attempt to block it.

Divestitures

A divestiture represents a variety of ways to let go of a portion of the firm's assets. It has become an important vehicle in restructuring the corporation into a more efficient operation.

STUDY QUESTIONS

23-1. Describe the major merger waves that have occurred in the United States.

23-2. What have we learned from history about centralizing activities versus specialization?

23-3. What factors contributed to the reduction in the number of mergers in 1969 and 1970 and again in the late 1980s?

23-4. Why might merger activities create wealth?

23-5. Why is book value alone not a significant measure of the worth of a company?

23-6. What advantages are provided by the use of an appraisal value in valuing a firm?

23-7. What is the concept of the chop-shop valuation procedure?

23-8. Compare the NPV approach used in valuing a merger with the same approach in capital budgeting.

23-9. Describe an MBO, LBO, and leveraged ESOP.

23-10. What are the disadvantages of the tender offer?

23-11. Explain the different types of divestitures.

SELF-TEST PROBLEM

ST-1. Using the chop-shop approach, assign a value for the Calvert Corporation, where its common stock is currently trading at a total market price of $5 million. For Calvert, the accounting data set forth two business segments: auto sales and auto specialties. Data for the firm's two segments are as follows:

Business Segment	Segment Sales ($000)	Segment Assets ($000)	Segment Income ($000)
Auto sales	$3,000	$1,000	$150
Auto specialties	2,500	3,000	500
Total	$5,500	$4,000	$650

Industry data for "pure-play" firms have been compiled and are summarized as follows:

Business Segment	Capitalization Sales	Capitalization Assets	Capitalization Operating Income
Auto sales	1.40	3.20	18.00
Auto specialties	.80	.90	8.00

23–1A. (*Chop-Shop Valuation*) Using the chop-shop approach, assign a value for Dabney, Inc., whose common stock is currently trading at a total market price of $7 million. For Dabney, the accounting data sets forth three business segments: consumer wholesaling, specialty services, and retirement centers. Data for the firm's three segments are as follows:

Business Segment	Segment Sales ($000)	Segment Assets ($000)	Segment Income ($000)
Consumer wholesaling	$2000	$1500	$175
Specialty services	1000	500	100
Retirement centers	3500	4000	600
Total	$6500	$6000	$875

Industry data for "pure-play" firms have been compiled and are summarized as follows:

Business Segment	Capitalization Sales	Capitalization Assets	Capitalization Operating Income
Consumer wholesaling	0.80	.70	12.00
Specialty services	1.20	1.00	6.00
Retirement centers	1.20	.70	7.00

23–2A. (*Chop-Shop Valuation*) Using the chop-shop method, determine a value for Aramus, Inc., whose common stock is trading at a total market price of $15 million. For Aramus, the accounting data are divided into three business segments: sunglasses distribution, reading glasses distribution, and technical products. Data for the firm's three segments are as follows:

Business Segment	Segment Sales ($000)	Segment Assets ($000)	Segment Income ($000)
Sunglasses distribution	$ 3,500	$ 1,000	$ 350
Reading glasses distribution	2,000	1,500	250
Technical products	6,500	8,500	1,200
Total	$12,000	$11,000	$1,800

Industry data for "pure-play" firms have been computed and are summarized as follows:

Business Segment	Capitalization Sales	Capitalization Assets	Capitalization Operating Income
Sunglasses distribution	1.0	.8	8.0
Reading glasses distribution	.9	.8	10.0
Technical products	1.2	1.0	7.0

23–3A. (*Free Cash Flow Valuation*) The Argo Corporation is viewed as a possible takeover target by Hilary, Inc. Currently, Argo uses 20 percent debt in its capital structure, but Hilary plans to increase the debt ratio to 30 percent if the acquisition is consummated. The after-tax cost of debt capital for Argo is estimated to be 8 percent, which holds constant. The cost of equity after the acquisition is expected to be 18 percent. The current market value of Argo's debt outstanding is $40 million, all of which will be assumed by Hilary. Hilary intends to pay $250 million in cash and common stock for all of Argo's stock in addition to assuming all of Argo's debt. Currently, the market price of Argo's common stock is $200 million. Selected items from Argo's financial data are as follows:

	1993	1994	1995	1996	Thereafter
			(Millions)		
Net sales	$200	$225	$240	$250	$275
Administrative and selling expenses	15	20	27	28	30
Depreciation	10	15	17	20	24
Capital expenditures	12	13	15	17	20

In addition, the cost of goods sold runs 60 percent of sales and the marginal tax rate is 34 percent. Compute the net present value of the acquisition.

23–4A. (*Free Cash Flow Valuation*) The Prime Corporation is viewed as a possible takeover target by Big Boy, Inc. Currently, Prime uses 25 percent debt in its capital structure, but Big Boy plans to increase the debt ratio to 40 percent if the acquisition is consummated. Prime's after-tax cost of debt is 10 percent, which should hold constant. The cost of equity after the acquisition is expected to be 20 percent. The current market value of Prime's debt outstanding is $30 million, all of which will be assumed by Big Boy. Big Boy intends to pay $150 million in cash and common stock for all of Prime's stock in addition to assuming all of its debt. Currently, the market price of Prime's common stock is $125 million. Selected items from Prime's financial data are as follows:

	1993	1994	1995	1996	Thereafter
			(Millions)		
Net sales	$300	$330	$375	$400	$425
Administrative and selling expenses	40	50	58	62	65
Depreciation	25	30	35	38	40
Capital expenditures	30	37	45	48	50

In addition, the cost of goods sold runs 60 percent of sales, and the marginal tax rate is 34 percent. Compute the NPV of the acquisition.

STUDY PROBLEMS (SET B)

23–1B. (*Chop-Shop Valuation*) Using the chop-shop approach, assign a value for Cornutt, Inc., whose common stock is currently trading at a total market price of $4 million. For Cornutt, the accounting data set forth three business segments: consumer wholesaling, specialty services, and retirement centers. Data for the firm's three segments are as follows:

Business Segment	Segment Sales ($000)	Segment Assets ($000)	Segment Income ($000)
Consumer wholesaling	$1500	$750	$100
Specialty services	800	700	150
Retirement centers	2000	3000	600
Total	$4300	$4450	$850

Industry data for "pure-play" firms have been compiled and are summarized as follows:

Business Segment	Capitalization Sales	Capitalization Assets	Capitalization Operating Income
Consumer wholesaling	0.75	.60	10.00
Specialty services	1.10	.90	7.00
Retirement centers	1.00	.60	6.00

23–2B. (*Chop-Shop Valuation*) Using the chop-shop method, determine a value for Wrongway, Inc., whose common stock is trading at a total market price of $10 million. For Wrongway, the accounting data are divided into three business segments: sunglasses distribution, reading glasses distribution, and technical products. Data for the firm's three segments are as follows:

Business Segment	Segment Sales ($000)	Segment Assets ($000)	Segment Income ($000)
Sunglasses distribution	$2,200	$ 600	$200
Reading glasses distribution	1,000	700	150
Technical products	3,500	5,000	500
Total	$6,700	$6,300	$850

Industry data for "pure-play" firms have been computed and are summarized as follows:

Business Segment	Capitalization Sales	Capitalization Assets	Capitalization Operating Income
Sunglasses distribution	.8	1.0	8.0
Reading glasses distribution	1.2	.9	10.0
Technical products	1.2	1.1	12.0

23–3B. (*Free Cash Flow Valuation*) The Brown Corporation is viewed as a possible takeover target by Cicron, Inc. Currently, Brown uses 20 percent debt in its capital structures, but Cicron plans to increase the debt ratio to 25 percent if the acquisition is consummated. The after-tax cost of debt capital for Brown is estimated to be 8 percent, which should not change. The cost of equity after the acquisition is expected to be 22 percent. The current market value of Brown's debt outstanding is $75 million, all of which will be assumed by Cicron. Cicron intends to pay $225 million in cash and common stock for all of Brown's stock in addition to assuming all of Brown's debt. Currently, the market price of Brown's common stock is $200 million. Selected items from Brown's financial data are as follows:

	1993	1994	1995	1996	Thereafter
			(Millions)		
Net sales	$260	$265	$280	$290	$300
Administrative and selling expenses	25	25	25	30	30
Depreciation	15	17	18	23	30
Capital expenditures	22	18	18	20	22

In addition, the cost of goods sold runs 50 percent of sales and the marginal tax rate is 34 percent. Compute the net present value of the acquisition.

23-4B. (*Free Cash Flow Valuation*) The Little Corp. is viewed as a possible takeover target by Big, Inc. Currently, Little uses 20 percent debt in its capital structure, but Big plans to increase the debt ratio to 50 percent if the acquisition goes through. The after-tax cost of debt for Little is 15 percent, which should hold constant. The cost of equity after the acquisition is expected to be 25 percent. The current market value of Little's debt outstanding is $12 million, all of which will be assumed by Big. Big intends to pay $25 million in cash and common stock for all of Little's stock in addition to assuming all of Little's debt. Currently, the market price of Little's common stock is $20 million. Selected items from Little's financial data are as follows:

	1993	1994	1995	1996	Thereafter
			(Millions)		
Net sales	$200	$220	$245	$275	$300
Administrative and selling expenses	30	35	38	40	45
Depreciation	18	20	22	25	30
Capital expenditures	20	22	25	28	30

In addition, the cost of goods sold is 70 percent of sales, and the marginal tax rate is 34 percent. Compute the NPV of the acquisition.

SELF-TEST SOLUTION

SS-1

	Capital-to-Sales	Segment Sales	Theoretical Values
Auto sales	1.40	$3000	$4200
Auto specialties	0.80	2500	2000
			$6200

	Capital-to-Assets	Segment Assets	Theoretical Values
Auto sales	3.20	$1000	$3200
Auto specialties	0.90	3000	2700
			$5900

	Capital-to-Income	Segment Income	Theoretical Values
Auto sales	18.00	$150	$2700
Auto specialties	8.00	500	4000
			$6700

Theoretical value based on	
Sales	$6200
Assets	5900
Income	6700
Average value	$6267

CHAPTER 24

Failure and Reorganization

What Failure Is • Who Fails? • Frequent Causes of Failure • Symptoms of Bankruptcy •
Voluntary Remedies to Insolvency • Reorganization • Liquidation

Decline and embarrassment—hardly topics we like to discuss, especially when we are personally involved. We much prefer to address growth and success. In ancient Greece, people frequently blamed their failures on the whims of the gods. In our own age, failure is for many a crushing disgrace, which probably contributes to our tendency to avoid the subject or to hold on to a bad idea beyond the point of rationality. But despite our aversion to the subject, we can learn from failure. The learning process may help us avoid losses and insolvency. More than likely, a financial manager will eventually be called on to work with a customer who is having severe financial problems. So managers must be aware of the issues associated with failure in business.

In this chapter, we have several objectives.

1. Explain the general terms of business failure
2. Identify frequent causes of company failures
3. Identify the financial characteristics that generally develop within a firm facing possible bankruptcy
4. Explain the procedural aspects for reorganizing or liquidating a business

What Failure Is

The term *failure* is used in a variety of contexts. **Economic failure** suggests that the company's costs exceed its revenues. Stated differently, the internal rates of return on investments are less than the firm's cost of capital. **Insolvency** also is frequently used to specify serious financial problems. A firm is *technically insolvent* when it can no longer honor its financial obligations. Although the book value of assets may exceed total liabilities, indicating a positive net worth, the company simply does not have sufficient liquidity to pay its debts. This condition may be temporary, and reorganization may be possible, or irreversible. Another term used is *insolvency in bankruptcy*. In this case the company's liabilities are greater than the fair valuation of its assets, which means a negative net worth. Regardless of the liquidity of its assets, the company is completely and unquestionably unable to meet maturing obligations. This situation generally indicates that liquidation rather than a reorganization of the firm is necessary.

Who Fails?

During 1990, over 60,000 businesses failed, which is close to the all-time high in 1986 of more than 61,000. Both these years are a bit staggering when we realize that only a decade earlier less than 7,000 firms failed. The number of failures in

FIGURE 24–1.
Business Failure Profile Source: Dun & Bradstreet, Inc.,
The 1990 Dun & Bradstreet Business Failure Record (New York, 1991).

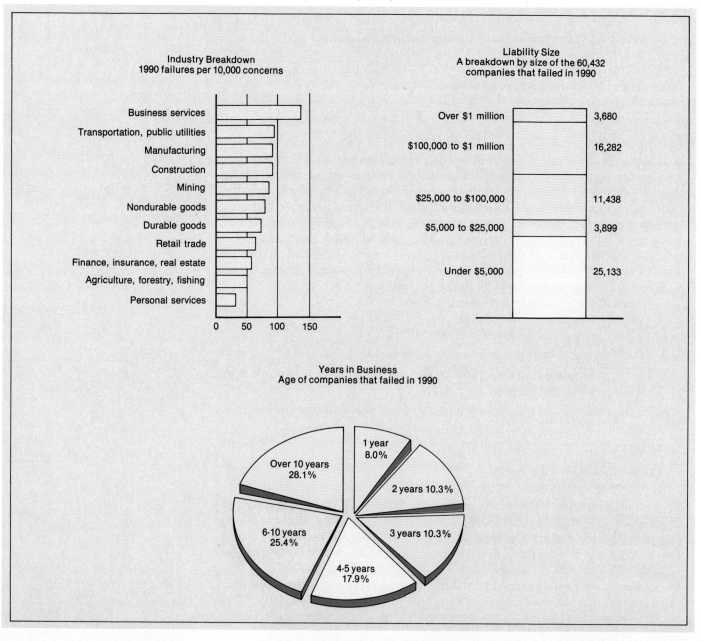

recent years overshadows the statistics of the Great Depression,[1] when the number of failures approached 32,000 in 1932. Of course, we quickly recognize that many more firms exist today than did in the 1930s. Thus, we need to use a relative measure, that is, the number of failures compared with the total number of firms. When we adjust our comparison to business failures per 10,000 firms, no year has had more failures than 1932, when there were 154 failures. However, 1986 came closer than any year since, when 120 firms per 10,000 companies went into bankruptcy. In 1990, the latest year for which data are available, there were 75 failures per 10,000 firms, a decline of 38 percent from 1986.

A profile of the firms experiencing failure is presented in Figure 24–1, which shows the industry, age, and size of the failed companies. The industry most prone to failure has been business services. The services industry long has had a tendency to encounter failure, largely because services are among the first businesses to be affected by economic recessions.

In terms of age, we would expect the majority of firms that fail to be relatively young and, consequently, small. Experience certainly verifies our intuition, in that 47 percent of the companies that have failed had been in existence for five years or less. Equally significant, 72 percent of all failures happened within the first 10 years of a firm's life. As we also would expect, small firms account for the preponderance of failures, with 67 percent of the failing firms having less than $100,000 in liabilities, and 94 percent having $1 million or less, still a small firm in today's world. Thus, business failures are predominantly characteristic of young and small companies. Bankruptcy, however, is not restricted to small companies. Table 24–1 lists the 20 largest bankruptcies in the United States, all of which occurred after 1980, with the exception of Penn Central and W. T. Grant.

Although the probability is much less, large corporations are subject to failure. In fact, the failure statistics do not include large corporations that for all practical purposes failed but either were merged into another company or

| | | Liabilities | |
	Date	Actual	1991 Prices
Texaco	1987	21.6	25.8
Penn Central	1970	3.3	11.4
Campeau	1990	9.9	10.5
Lomas Financial	1989	6.1	6.6
Continental Air	1990	6.2	6.2
LTV	1986	4.7	5.8
Southmark	1989	4.0	4.3
Eastern Air Lines	1989	3.2	3.5
Southland	1990	3.4	3.4
Drexel Burnham Lambert	1990	3.0	3.2
Wickes	1982	2.0	2.8
Itel	1981	1.7	2.6
W. T. Grant	1975	1.0	2.5
Pan Am	1991	2.4	2.4
Hills Department Stores	1991	2.3	2.3
Interco	1991	2.2	2.2
Global Marine	1986	1.8	2.2
Baldwin-United	1983	1.6	2.1
Laventhal & Horwath	1990	2.0	2.0
PS New Hampshire	1988	1.7	2.0
Note: Excludes banks			

TABLE 24–1.
Big U.S. Bankruptcies, 1991

[1]*The 1990 Dun & Bradstreet Business Failure Record* (New York: Dun & Bradstreet, Inc., 1991).

received governmental assistance. For example, the collapse of Douglas Aircraft was avoided only by a merger with McDonnell. Chrysler and Lockheed would have failed if the federal government had not provided aid. Thus, while small companies have a much greater chance of failure relative to large corporations, the issue is real for both.

Frequent Causes of Failure

Although causes of business failure vary from firm to firm, we can identify several common ones. The predominant cause of failure is managerial incompetence. The following key structural problems within management may appear:[2]

1. An imbalance of skills within the top echelon. A manager tends to attract other managers of similar skills. For example, the corporate management may consist principally of individuals having a background in sales, when managers with production experience also are needed.

2. A chief executive who dominates a firm's operations without regard for the advice of peers.

3. An inactive or ill-informed board of directors. For instance, the board of directors for Penn Central, even including the members who were bankers, supposedly did not become aware of the firm's impending financial disaster until a few weeks before its declaration of insolvency.

4. A deficient finance function within the firm's management. Not infrequently, the only substantial input provided by the financial officer occurs when the budget is submitted to the board. A company may have an effective financial information system; however, this information is of no avail if it does not flow to the board through a strong financial officer.

5. The absence of responsibility for the chief executive officer. Although all other managers with a company are responsible to a superior, the chief executive seldom must account for his or her actions. While this person is responsible to the stockholders, the link between management and stockholders may be tenuous or altogether lacking.

The deficiencies render the firm vulnerable to several mistakes. First, management may be negligent in developing effective accounting systems. Second, the company may be unresponsive to change—unable to adjust to a general recession and unfavorable industry developments. Third, management may be inclined to undertake an investment that is disproportionately large relative to firm size. If the project fails, the probability of insolvency is greatly increased. Finally, management may come to rely so heavily on debt financing that even a minor problem can place the firm in a dangerous position.

Dun & Bradstreet, Inc., each year samples a large number of companies that have experienced failure.[3] The reasons given for these business casualties are shown in Table 24–2. Clearly, the primary causes relate to economic factors beyond management's control and management-induced financial problems, such as excessive use of debt and insufficient capital.

---

[2]John Argenti, *Corporate Collapse: The Causes and Symptoms* (New York: Wiley, 1976), pp. 123–26.
[3]*The 1990 Dun & Bradstreet Business Failure Record* (New York: Dun & Bradstreet, Inc., 1991), 19.

TABLE 24–2.
Causes of Business Failures
in 1990

	Manufacturers	Wholesalers	Retailers	Construction	All-firm Total
Neglect	1.9%	2.0%	2.0%	1.9%	1.6%
Disaster	.6	.6	.6	.4	.4
Fraud	.6	.5	.4	.2	.3
Economic factors	67.7	70.7	71.2	72.8	71.7
Lack of experience	18.4	17.1	20.1	19.4	20.3
Sales problems	10.4	10.2	13.0	11.9	11.1
Expense problems	6.4	5.6	5.8	6.0	8.1
Customer problems	.8	.7	.3	.8	.4
Excessive assets	.2	.2	.3	.2	.2
Capital problems	.6	.5	.7	.6	.5
Total[a]	100.0%	100.0%	100.0%	100.0%	100.0%

[a]Since some failures are attributable to a combination of causes, the totals may exceed 100 percent.
Source: *The 1990 Dun & Bradstreet Business Failure Record* (New York: Dun & Bradstreet Inc., 1991), 19.

Symptoms of Bankruptcy

As a company enters the final stages prior to failure, a pattern may develop in terms of a changing financial profile. Although bankruptcy or insolvency cannot be predicted with certainty, several financial ratios have proven to be useful indicators of impending disaster. A study by Altman[4] developed a statistical model that found the financial ratios best predicting bankruptcy. Based on Altman's sample of bankrupt firms, the study yielded an equation that used five ratios to predict bankruptcy:

$$\text{bankruptcy score} = 1.2X_1 + 1.4X_2 + 3.3X_3 + .6X_4 + .999X_5$$

where X_1 = (net working capital ÷ total assets)   – CURRENT ASSETS

X_2 = (retained earnings ÷ total assets)   – PROFITABILITY TO TIME

X_3 = (earnings before interest and taxes ÷ total assets)   – GENERAL EARNING POWER

X_4 = (total market value of stock ÷ book value of total debt) – FINANCIAL LEVERAGE POSITION

X_5 = (sales ÷ total assets)   – ASSET TURNOVER RATIO

With this equation, the criterion for separating firms with a strong likelihood of bankruptcy from those that probably will not fail should be as follows. If the score exceeds 2.99, no concern for bankruptcy should exist. On the other hand, a score less than 1.81 suggests that the firm is a likely candidate for failure. Values between 1.81 and 2.99 are difficult to classify. However, although a firm in this "gray area" can easily be misclassified in terms of the final outcome, the best way to set up a dividing line is to predict that a company will fail if its score is less than 2.675. Alternatively, a score exceeding 2.675 may be used as an indicator that success is more likely than failure. These guidelines are shown in Table 24–3.

We may conclude that a potentially failing corporation begins to invest less in current assets (X_1). Because X_2 is a cumulative indicator of profitability relative to time, the findings suggest that younger companies have a greater

[4]Edward I. Altman, *Corporate Bankruptcy in America* (Lexington, MA: Heath Lexington Books, 1971).

TABLE 24–3.
Altman's Bankruptcy Criterion

| | Bankruptcy Score | |
Less than 1.81	Between 1.81 and 2.99	Greater than 2.99
Probability of failure is high	Probability of failure is difficult to determine	Probability of failure is remote
Predict failure	Less than 2.675—predict failure Greater than 2.675—predict success	Predict success

chance of bankruptcy. Variable X_3 reflects the firm's general earnings power. Deterioration in this factor was shown to be the best single indicator that bankruptcy may be forthcoming. Variable X_4 depicts the firm's financial leverage position. Finally, X_5, the asset turnover ratio, measures management's ability to generate sales from the firm's assets.

Although the financial information flowing from a firm helps us identify problems, the predictions we make with it certainly are not perfect. Owing to factors unique to the firm, as well as to the tendency for managements of problem firms to do some "window dressing" of the financial statements, the ratios will not always effectively identify corporations that face bankruptcy within the near future. Even so, they will help us assess the likelihood of bankruptcy.

When a firm faces severe problems, either the problems must be resolved or the firm must be liquidated. At such a point, an important question has to be answered: Is the firm worth more dead or alive? A decision to continue operating has to be based upon the feasibility and fairness of reorganizing the firm as opposed to the benefits of liquidating the business. As shown in Figure 24–2, when technical insolvency occurs, management must either modify the operating and financial conditions or terminate the firm's life. If the decision is made to alter the company in the hopes of revitalizing its operations, either voluntary agreements with the investors or a formal court-arranged reorganization must be used. If, conversely, the difficulties are believed to be insurmountable, a liquidation will take place, either by assignment of the assets to an independent party for liquidation or by formal bankruptcy proceedings.

FIGURE 24–2.
Reorganization Versus Liquidation

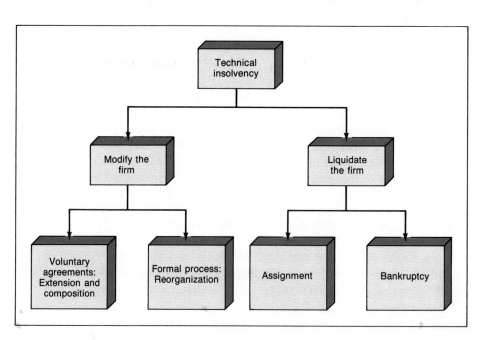

Voluntary Remedies to Insolvency

If a company finds itself in financial distress, management must seek a remedy that is acceptable to the creditors. If the evidence suggests that the company's going-concern value is greater than its liquidation value, management may attempt to arrange for a voluntary reorganization. These arrangements may allow the firm an extension of time to pay the debts, or even reduce the amount ultimately to be paid.

Prerequisites

Voluntary remedies avoid the necessity of a court settlement. However, participation must be unanimous; any creditor who refuses to participate may legally prohibit the arrangement for the remaining creditors. Such action that reaches the courts may result in a smaller settlement; thus, general agreement by the creditors is the key to the success of a voluntary remedy. Whether a reasonable chance exists for the creditors to finalize such a plan is based on (1) the debtor's proven honesty and integrity, (2) the firm's potential for recovery, and (3) the economic prospects for the industry.

Procedure

Most frequently, the debtor confers with the creditors to explain the firm's financial condition and to request that they consider developing a plan that would be beneficial to all parties involved. This meeting is generally planned under the guidance of an adjustment bureau associated with a local credit association or a trade association. The creditors appoint a committee to represent both the large and small claimants. If the committee decides a feasible plan can be developed, the committee, in conjunction with the firm and the adjustment bureau, constructs an agreement. This voluntary agreement may be classified as an extension, a composition, or some combination thereof.

Extension

An **extension** requires that the debtor pay the amount owed in full. However, an extension in time is provided. For instance, the agreement may stipulate that all new purchases are to be made on a cash basis, and the outstanding balance from prior purchases is to be paid over an extended period. Also, the contract may place the existing debt in subordination to new liabilities during the extension period. Clearly, the creditors must have confidence in the company's management and in the economic conditions affecting the firm; otherwise they would not agree to such concessions.

Although the creditors' basis for an extension does depend on their trust in the present management, several control mechanisms may be used during this period of uncertainty. For example, the plan may prohibit any dividend payments to the stockholders until the firm is financially sound again. In fact, the stockholders may have to place their shares in escrow with the creditors' committee. Also, the agreement may require that the firm's assets be assigned to the creditors' committee for the duration of the extension period. Finally, a requirement may be incorporated into the contract stipulating that a member of the creditors' committee countersign checks.

Composition

A **composition** permits the debtor to pay less than the full balance owed the creditors. In other words, the creditors receive a pro-rated share of their claims.

The amount received represents final settlement of the indebtedness. The creditors' agree to a partial payment because the only remaining option is bankruptcy proceedings, the costs of which can quickly deplete the firm's resources. Negotiations between debtor and creditors hinge on the savings that may be expected by avoiding the legal costs associated with bankruptcy. Also, the debtor avoids the stigma attached to bankruptcy.

Evaluation of Voluntary Remedies

The primary advantages of voluntary remedies relate to the minimization of costs and the informality of the process. A significant amount of legal, investigative, and administrative expenses may be avoided, resulting in a higher return to the creditors. Also, the bargaining process is greatly simplified, and a more congenial atmosphere typically prevails than in the bankruptcy courts.

One of the difficulties in arranging a voluntary remedy is that a creditor may refuse to participate. To encourage participation and cooperation of the firm's creditors, a composition generally allows for the payment in full of small claims. For instance, the terms of the agreement may state that all creditors are to receive $50 plus a pro-rated share of the remaining claim. This provision eliminates the small claims. However, it means that the larger creditors partially underwrite the amounts payable to small creditors.

Another disadvantage, particularly for the extension, is that the debtor maintains control of the business. If the underlying problems confronting the business are not corrected, the company's assets may continue to erode in value, which clearly works to the detriment of the creditors. However, as already explained, controls may be initiated to minimize any potential losses due to continued inefficient management.

Reorganization

If a voluntary remedy, such as an extension or composition, is not workable, a company can declare or be forced by its creditors into bankruptcy. As a part of this process, the firm is either reorganized or dissolved. Reorganization under the Bankruptcy Act is similar to an extension or composition; the objective is to revitalize the firm by changing its operating procedures and the capital structure. However, the procedure is more formal and it is administered by the bankruptcy courts. Chapter 11 of the Bankruptcy Act provides the guidelines for an orderly reorganization of a business.

The Petition to Reorganize

Under Chapter 11, a case is initiated when a petition is filed with the bankruptcy courts. The petition may be filed by the firm's management (voluntary) or by its creditors (involuntary). To initiate an involuntary reorganization, the creditors must show that the debtor company is generally not paying its debts as they come due. When the debtor has more than 12 creditors, the law requires at least three creditors with claims totaling $5,000 or more file the petition. If there are fewer than 12 creditors, the petition must be filed by two creditors or a single creditor who is owed at least $5,000.

When a petition is filed, either voluntary or involuntary, a committee of unsecured creditors—usually the seven creditors with the largest claims—is appointed by the court to work with the court in reorganizing the company's operations and possibly restructuring its financial mix. The plan must be approved by a majority of the creditors holding at least two-thirds of the dollar claims. Under Chapter 11, the debtor continues to operate the business unless a reason exists for a trustee to be given managerial control. Reasons may be fraud, dishonesty, incompetence, or gross mismanagement.

Before recent changes in the law, the SEC played a significant role in the bankruptcy process. Although it did not possess any decision-making authority, the SEC was charged with rendering a critical evaluation of the reorganization plan, including an opinion as to the fairness and feasibility of the plan. When there was a difference between the trustee's plan and that of the SEC, the latter usually suggested alternative guidelines. Today the role of the SEC as the public's representative has diminished significantly in an effort to add expediency to the reorganization process. For example, it no longer makes petitions to the courts to change a plan of reorganization.

The Reorganization Decision

In the reorganization process, the trustee has to establish the going-concern value for the debtor's business after the reorganization. This procedure requires an estimation of the company's future earnings. With this projection in hand, a capitalization rate (or equivalently a price/earnings ratio) for a similar but prosperous firm is determined. When this rate is applied to the earnings, a going-concern value may be approximated. For example, assume that a corporation may reasonably expect to make $1 million in annual earnings after the reorganization. If the price/earnings multiple for a comparable firm is 8, the going-concern value is $8 million ($1 million earnings × 8 price/earnings).

After a going-concern value has been estimated, the trustee devises a reorganization plan, including a way of reformulating the capital structure to meet the criteria of fairness and feasibility. In developing this recommendation, the trustee evaluates what changes are necessary to place the company in a more profitable posture. Also, in revamping the capital structure, the firm's ability to cover the financial fixed charges—interest, principal repayments, and preferred dividends—is evaluated.

If the facts indicate that a reorganization is fair and feasible to the respective creditors and the stockholders, new securities are issued to reflect the revised capital structure. The principal guideline in this procedure has generally been the **rule of absolute priority,** which simply indicates that the company must completely honor senior claims on assets before settling junior claims. However, plans are frequently based on a blend of *absolute* and *relative* priorities, where a junior claim receives partial payment even though a senior claim has not been paid in its entirety. Such a compromise is at times necessary to satisfy small creditors who might otherwise vote against a proposed plan.

EXAMPLE

To illustrate the priorities that might be used in a reorganization plan, consider the Paine Corporation, which is currently undergoing a reorganization. Table 24–4 presents the firm's balance sheet. The creditors have filed a petition for reorganization. The court has named a trustee who is developing a possible plan of organization. Based on the trustee's evaluation, an internal reorganization is considered to be both fair and feasible to the investors. The trustee has projected the company's earnings and by using an appropriate price/earnings multiple has estimated the firm's going-concern value to be $8 million, as compared with a $6 million liquidation value (the approximate amount that would be received if the business were terminated and the assets sold individually).

Table 24–5 gives the proposed plan for reorganizing the company. The first portion of the table specifies the amounts of the distribution to be made to each group of creditors. Since the going-concern value is $8 million, only 50 percent of the $16 million in debt can be honored. As a result, the common stockholders

TABLE 24–4.
Paine Corporation Balance
Sheet

Assets	
Current assets	$ 2,000,000
Net plant and equipment	15,500,000
Other assets	1,000,000
Total assets	$18,500,000
Liabilities and equity	
Current liabilities	
Accounts payable	$ 1,000,000
Notes payable	3,000,000
Total current liabilities	$ 4,000,000
Long-term liabilities	
Mortgage bonds (8% due in 1995)	$ 4,000,000
Subordinated debentures (9½% due in 1995)[a]	8,000,000
Total long-term liabilities	$12,000,000
Total liabilities	$16,000,000
Equity	
Common stock (par $5)	500,000
Paid-in capital	14,000,000
Retained earnings	(12,000,000)
Total equity	$ 2,500,000
Total liabilities and equity	$18,500,000

[a]Subordinated to the mortgage bonds.

TABLE 24–5.
Paine Corporation
Reorganization Plan

Creditors	Amount of Claim	50 Percent of Claim	New Claim After Subordination
Accounts payable	$ 1,000,000	$ 500,000	$ 500,000
Notes payable	3,000,000	1,500,000	1,500,000
Mortgage bonds	4,000,000	2,000,000	4,000,000
Subordinated debentures[a]	8,000,000	4,000,000	2,000,000
	$16,000,000	$8,000,000	$8,000,000

[a]Subordinated to the mortgage bonds.

will not be entitled to any of the distribution. Also, the subordinated debentures are not to participate in the reorganization until the mortgage bondholders have been repaid in full. Consequently, the $4 million in securities that would have been distributed to the owners of the debentures has to be reduced by $2 million. The final distribution, after recognizing the subordination, is shown in the last column of Table 24–5.

The lower section of Table 24–5 reflects the trustee's proposed changes in the firm's capital structure. The objective is to reduce the financial leverage to a

New Securities Issued in the Reorganization

Old Security	New Securities	
Accounts payable	Accounts payable	$ 250,000
	Common stock	250,000
Notes payable	Preferred stock	750,000
	Common stock	750,000
Mortgage bonds	Mortgage bonds (8%)	2,000,000
	Subordinated debentures (9½%)	1,000,000
	Preferred stock (10%)	1,000,000
Subordinated debentures	Common stock	2,000,000
		$8,000,000

Accounts payable	$ 250,000	
Mortgage bonds (8%)	2,000,000	
Subordinated debentures (9½%)	1,000,000	
Preferred stock (10%)	1,750,000	
Common stock	3,000,000	
	$8,000,000	

TABLE 24–6.
Paine Corporation Liabilities
and Equity After Reorganization

point commensurate with the company's ability to cover the fixed financial charges from earnings. For example, the original accounts payable balance is reduced to $500,000, with the creditors entitled to a short-term claim of $250,000 and $250,000 in new common stock. The final capital structure, if the trustee's plan is adopted, is provided in Table 24–6. ■

Continental Airlines Reorganization

A recent example of a major firm that has reorganized under Chapter 11 is Continental Airlines. The reorganization occurred following the deregulation of the airline industry in the late 1970s—no doubt, a time of adjustment for all the carriers. Continental actually filed for protection under Chapter 11 on September 25, 1983. Because of deregulation of the industry in 1978, Continental had reported losses of $500 million. During the first half of 1983 alone, its losses were equal to $84 million and the firm's net worth was essentially nonexistent. One of the major reasons for Continental's decision to seek relief under Chapter 11 was the inability to reach appropriate labor agreements to help mitigate the firm's financial distress.

Almost two years after the filing, on September 6, 1985, Continental's reorganization plan was approved by the firm's creditors. In the following summer of 1986, the bankruptcy courts approved the plan. The basic parts of the plan are presented in Table 24–7. The claimants for the most part involved creditors and employees; nothing went to equity. Even the employees were required to delay receipt of the major part of their claims.

Continental's problems continued, and its management again filed a reorganization plan in February 1992; this new plan would essentially eliminate the preferred stock and common stock.[5] As proposed, the plan would make its unsecured creditors its new owners by swapping their debt for equity in the company. Although the corporate makeup of Continental still may change, its operations are expected to remain essentially the same. The plan required the approval of unsecured creditors holding at least two-thirds of the claims against the firm.

Claims to Be Resolved

Of the approximately $925 million in debt outstanding, $142 million was to be paid within 10 days of the effective date of the plan, with the balance to be paid with interest over three to 10 years. The breakdown of this debt and the planned repayment schedule are as follows:

1. Unsecured creditors were to be paid the entire $125 million of the principal owed to them, but they would receive a low 6 percent interest rate on the claims from the time of the initial Chapter 11 filing until the final court approval in 1986. After the 1986 approval of the plan, they were to be paid an interest rate of the prime plus 2 percent. Total payout was to be over the ensuing five years.

2. Secured bank lenders were to receive all principal owed and interest at the prime plus 1 percent over the next eight years.

3. Employee claims: $20 million of the $80 million owed employees claims were to be paid immediately, with the remainder being settled over an extended number of years.

TABLE 24–7.
Continental Airlines
Reorganization Plan

---

[5]See Bridget O'Brian, "Continental Air Reorganization Plan Erases Stock, Makes Creditors Owners," *The Wall Street Journal*, February 7, 1992. p. A7.

Liquidation

If the likelihood is small that reorganization of an insolvent firm will result in a profitable business, the firm should be dissolved. In this situation the liquidation value exceeds the going-concern value, and it is to the investor's advantage to terminate the business. Continuing the operation at this point generally results only in further losses. Complete termination of the company can be accom-

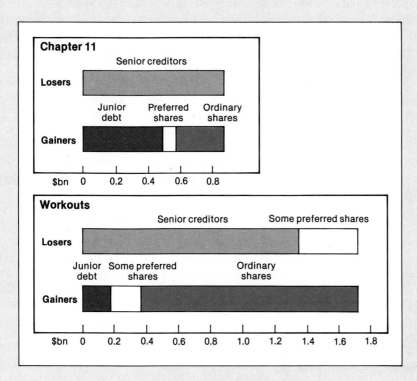

The Bankruptcy Game: Distribution of Gains[a] and Losses in Rescue Deals, 1983–90

deal it likes, the firm will simply file for chapter 11 protection. So in workouts, too, creditors may be willing to give up their seniority rights. This, the study finds, is the case. In fact, senior creditors give up even more in workouts than in chapter 11 deals, although the write-downs of their claims tend to be a lot less. Of the $1.7 billion shifted from losers to gainers in workouts, senior creditors gave up $1.3 billion. This is less odd than it looks: it pays creditors to avoid the delays and legal costs of chapter 11.

In effect, then, chapter 11 says it is better to keep a firm running than to honour debt agreements. This is fine for managers and employees, who (or many of whom) keep their jobs, and for shareholders, who would otherwise face large losses. It is also good for politicians, who are spared having to explain job losses, and, as ever, for lawyers. Yet it may be bad for other firms, even sound ones, since lenders will become increasingly wary, and may charge higher interest rates overall to make up for their higher risks.

One answer would be for the judges ruling on applications for chapter 11 to get tough in backing creditors' claims against the firm. There is some sign of this. The academics had earlier studied chapter 11 between 1978 and 1984; the amounts gained by share-holders at the expense of senior creditors were even higher then than in the more recent cases.

Alternatively America could move towards a more British system of receivership, which puts creditors before shareholders, and is more likely to end in the firm simply ceasing to trade. That is not as bad as it sounds. Worthwhile parts of the firm will be bought by some other firm that can make use of them—perhaps better use than the existing management.

*Julian Franks and Walter Torous, "How Firms Fare in Workouts and Chapter 11 Reorganisations." London Business School working paper, May 1991.

Source: *The Economist*, May 25, 1991, p. 83. Used by permission

plished through assignment or by declaring bankruptcy. The objective of either procedure is to distribute any proceeds from the liquidation to the creditors.

Liquidation by Assignment

If an **assignment** is used to liquidate a business, the final settlement is done privately with a minimum amount of court involvement. The debtor transfers title of the firm's assets to a third party who has been appointed by the creditors or by the court. This individual, known as an **assignee** or **trustee,** administers the liquidation process and sees that an appropriate distribution of the proceeds is made. Under an assignment, the debtor is not automatically discharged of the remaining balance due a creditor unless a notation appears on the checks indicating that endorsement of the check represents the creditor's acceptance of the money as full settlement of the claim. However, a creditor can refuse to accept the payment, considering that his or her interests would be better served by a court-administered liquidation.

Because of the possibility that one or more creditors may not accept the assignment, the debtor may attempt to reach a prior agreement with the creditors that the assignment will represent a complete settlement of claims. If the agreement is made, a creditors' committee will usually recommend that the debtor be released from all claims after final execution of the assignment.

An assignment has several advantages over a formal bankruptcy procedure. The assignment is usually quicker, is less expensive, and requires less legal formality. The assignee is provided greater discretion and flexibility in liquidating the assets than a court-appointed trustee in bankruptcy. He or she can take quicker action to avoid further depletion in the value of inventories and equipment and typically is more familiar with the debtor's business, which should improve the final results. However, the assignment does not legally discharge the debtor from the responsibility of unpaid balances, and the creditor is not protected against fraud; consequently, formal bankruptcy proceedings may be preferred by either the debtor or creditors.

Liquidation by Bankruptcy

The Liquidation Process

A petition for a company to be declared bankrupt may be filed in the bankruptcy courts. Subject to the provisions in Chapter 7 of the Bankruptcy Act, the petition can be initiated either by the debtor (voluntary) or by the creditors (involuntary). A voluntary declaration of bankruptcy by the debtor is usually taken when management believes further delays are detrimental to the stockholders' position. The rules for creditors wishing to initiate an involuntary bankruptcy are the same as those given for an involuntary reorganization. The creditors must show that the debtor is not paying liabilities on a timely basis. Also, if more than 12 creditors exist, at least three creditors must sign the petition for bankruptcy. For firms with fewer than 12 creditors, only two creditors must petition, or one creditor if at least $5,000 is owed the petitioning creditor.

After the filing and approval of the bankruptcy petition, the court adjudges the debtor bankrupt and names a **referee in bankruptcy.** In turn, the referee may appoint a **receiver** to serve as interim caretaker of the company's assets until a trustee can be designated by the creditors. The referee then requests from the debtor a list of assets and liabilities.

The referee calls a meeting of the creditors. At the meeting, the creditors elect a trustee and appoint a creditors' committee. Also, the debtor may be questioned for additional information relevant to the proceedings.

The trustee and the creditors' committee initiate plans to liquidate the company's assets. As a part of this conversion process, individuals owing money to the debtor are contacted in an effort to collect these outstanding balances. Appraisers are selected to determine a value for the property, and these values are used as guidelines in liquidating assets. Specifically, the trustee may not sell an asset at less than 75 percent of its appraised value without the approval of the court. After all assets have been converted into cash through private sales or public auctions, all expenses incurred in the bankruptcy process are paid. The remaining cash is distributed on a pro-rated basis to the creditors. The trustee provides a final accounting to the creditors and the referee. The bankruptcy filing is then discharged, and the debtor is relieved of all responsibility for prior debts.

BASIC FINANCIAL MANAGEMENT IN PRACTICE

Life After Chapter 11 for Six Big Survivors

Company (Business)	Date Filed for Chapter 11 and Why	What Company Did to Reorganize	Date Emerged from Chapter 11	What's Happened Since (1990 Figures Are Estimates)
Allegheny International (conglomerate)	2/20/88. Unable to pay $500 million in debt despite its divestitures, including Wilkinson Sword.	Two former Goldman Sachs partners bought company for $655 million. Name changed to Sunbeam-Oster, after its major consumer product brands.	9/28/90	Revenues: $1 billion Loss: more than $43 million Stock not yet trading
Baldwin-United (financial services)	9/26/83. Had more than $600 million in debt and some insurance subsidiaries faced insolvency.	Settled more than 8,300 claims. Assets shrank from $9 billion to $490 million. Renamed Phlcorp. Leucadia National, a financial services company, buys control.	11/13/86	Revenues: $350 million Profits: $35 million Stock price: $13.50
Manville (building and forest products)	8/26/82. Potential $2.5 billion asbestos liability for damages to customers and employees.	Set up a $3.6 billion trust, much of it funded from company stock, and a profit-sharing plan to pay claims. Sold asbestos operations. Kept fiberglass and forest products.	11/28/88	Trust finds it tough to pay claims Revenues: $2.2 billion Profits: $108 million Stock price: $4.38
Storage Technology (computer hardware)	10/31/84. Unable to pay $645 million of debt and obtain working capital.	Sold $60 million of assets, including a chip factory. Refocused business on computer storage systems.	7/28/87	Revenues: $1.1 billion Profits: $70 million Stock price: $23.50
Texaco (oil)	4/12/87. To prevent Pennzoil from collecting the $11 billion jury award against Texaco's purchase of Getty Oil.	Paid Pennzoil $3 billion and creditors $2.5 billion. Sold more than $6 billion worth of assets. Fought off raider Carl Icahn's hostile proxy bid; repurchased $500 million of own stock.	4/7/88	Revenues: $41 billion Profits: $1.5 billion Stock price: $58.00
Wheeling-Pittsburgh Steel	4/16/85. After modernizing plants, unable to pay $535 million of debt.	Terminated pension plans. Sold integrated steel plant for $45 million, limiting business to sheet steel production.	1/3/91	Revenues: $1 billion Profits: small loss after write-off Stock price: $7.86

Source: "Strategies for the 1990s: Bankruptcy," *Fortune*, February 11, 1991, p. 13.

Priority of Claims

Following the rule of absolute priority, claims are honored in the following order:

1. Secured creditors, with the proceeds from the sale of the specific property going first to these creditors. If any portion of the claim remains unpaid, the balance is treated as an unsecured loan.
2. Expenses incurred in administering the bankrupt estate.
3. Expenses incurred after the bankruptcy petition has been filed but before a trustee has been appointed.
4. Salaries and commissions not exceeding $2,000 per employee that were earned within the three months preceding the bankruptcy petition.
5. Federal, state, and local taxes.
6. Unsecured creditors.
7. Preferred stock.
8. Common stock.

An example will illustrate the order of payments from a liquidation. The Poverty Stricken Corporation has been judged bankrupt; its balance sheet is shown in Table 24–8. Although the historical cost of the assets was $100 million, the trustee in bankruptcy was able to realize only $44 million from their sale. In addition, costs of $8 million were incurred in administering the bankruptcy.

The order of settling the claims is listed in Table 24–9. As the table shows, the first mortgage bondholders are entitled to receive the net proceeds resulting from the sale of specific property identified in the lien (an office building). We are assuming that the sale price of this property is $10 million, which leaves an unpaid balance of $4 million to be treated as an unsecured claim. Next, the

Assets			
Current assets			$ 20,000
Net plant and equipment			80,000
Total assets			$100,000
Liabilities			
Current liabilities			
Accounts payable	$22,000		
Accrued wages[a]	600		
Notes payable	20,000		
Federal taxes	2,500		
State taxes	500		
Total current liabilities		$45,600	
Long-term liabilities			
First mortgage bonds[b]	$14,000		
Subordinated debentures[c]	10,000		
Total long-term liabilities		24,000	
Total liabilities			69,600
Equity			
Preferred stock	$ 4,000		
Common stock	26,400		
Total equity			30,400
Total liabilities and equity			$100,000

TABLE 24–8.
Poverty Stricken Corporation
Balance Sheet ($000)

[a]No single claim exceeds $2,000.
[b]These bonds have a first lien on an office building.
[c]Subordinated to the notes payable.

TABLE 24–9.
Poverty Stricken Corporation
Priority of Claims ($000)

Distribution of Proceeds		
Liquidation value of assets		$44,000
Priority of claims:		
1. First mortgage receipts from the sale of an office building	$10,000	
2. Administrative expenses	8,000	
3. Salaries due employees	600	
4. Taxes	3,000	
Total prior claims		21,600
Amount available for settling claims of general creditors		$22,400

TABLE 24–10.
Poverty Stricken Corporation
Claims of General Creditors

General Claims	Claim	40% of Claims	Adjustment for Subordination
Accounts payable	$22,000,000	$ 8,800,000	$ 8,800,000
Notes payable	20,000,000	8,000,000	12,000,000
Remaining portion of first mortgage bond	4,000,000	1,600,000	1,600,000
Subordinated debenture	10,000,000	4,000,000	–0–
Totals	$56,000,000	$22,400,000	$22,400,000

administrative costs associated with filing and executing the bankruptcy petition, the employees' salaries, and the tax liabilities are to be paid.

After all payments have been made for prior claims, $22,400,000 is available for general unsecured creditors, whose claims total $56 million; dividing 22.4 by 56, we find that the claimants are entitled to 40 percent of the original loan. This percentage is computed from the amount available for general creditors, $22,400,000, relative to the total claims of $56 million. However, an adjustment must be made to recognize the subordination of the debentures to the notes payable. In essence, the owners of debentures must relinquish their right to any money until the notes payable have been settled in full. In this situation, $12 million of the note balance remains unpaid. As a consequence, the $4 million originally shown to be received by the debentures must be paid to the investors owning the note payable. The actual distributions to the unsecured creditors are shown in the last column of Table 24–10.

SUMMARY

Facing financial adversity is never easy, but managers need to be aware of the implications and consequences of financial trouble. This information may prove useful if reorganization or liquidation is on the horizon for the firm or if similar action becomes necessary for one of the firm's customers.

Business failure is principally the result of incompetent management or a deficiency in the management structure, such as an imbalance of skills. The symptoms of the weaknesses that lead to insolvency are often readily identifiable in the firm's financial statements. The company in trouble can be seen to generally decrease its investment in liquid assets, while its profitability declines. Also, the use of financial leverage increases significantly. Finally, management's efficient use of assets, as depicted by the asset turnover ratio, may deteriorate.

When a business becomes technically insolvent, one of two decisions must be made. The firm has to be reorganized or liquidated. In either case, the process may be relatively informal or closely controlled by the court. In the reorg-

SIGNS of BANKRUPTCY

anization of a firm, voluntary agreements may be arranged, taking the form of either an extension or a composition. If, however, these plans are not acceptable to the creditors, a court-administered reorganization may be necessary. If the company's liquidation value is thought to exceed its going-concern value, the firm should be dissolved.

In the liquidation process, a firm's assets may be assigned to a third party to sell and distribute the funds according to the rule of absolute priority. Such an assignment aims to avoid the more costly court-ordered bankruptcy filing. Yet, if the debtor or creditors consider formal bankruptcy proceedings preferable, voluntary or involuntary bankruptcy may be requested. If the debtor is judged to be bankrupt, a referee is selected to liquidate the firm's assets and distribute the proceeds in accordance with the rule of absolute priority.

STUDY QUESTIONS

24-1. Explain the following terms: *economic failure, technical insolvency,* and *insolvency in bankruptcy.*

24-2. What are the most frequent causes of business failure?

24-3. To what potential mistakes is a firm vulnerable if it is experiencing any of the deficiencies cited in question 24-2?

24-4. What are the prerequisites to a successful voluntary remedy?

24-5. What procedure is usually followed in arranging a voluntary agreement?

24-6. Compare an extension with a composition.

24-7. What are the advantages and disadvantages of voluntary remedies?

24-8. Explain the process of liquidation by assignment.

SELF-TEST PROBLEMS

ST-1. (*Predicting Bankruptcy*) You are studying five companies and have decided to use Altman's model to predict the probability of bankruptcy for each. The data needed are given below. What are the bankruptcy scores for these companies and how are they interpreted?

			Variables		
Company	X_1	X_2	X_3	X_4	X_5
A	15%	20%	35%	335%	1.60×
B	25	45	40	175	1.95
C	20	25	15	125	.75
D	15	12	10	110	.55
E	40	35	30	175	1.50

ST-2. (*Reorganization*) Brogham, Inc., is filing for bankruptcy. The trustee has estimated the firm's liquidation value to be $1,260,000. Given the liabilities and equity from the balance sheet, compute the distributions of proceeds.

Brogham, Inc.

Liabilities and equity	
Current liabilities	
Accounts payable	$ 120,000
Notes payable	300,000
Total current liabilities	$ 420,000

Brogham, Inc. (Cont.)

Long-term liabilities		
Long-term notes payable	$ 420,000	
Subordinated debentures[a]	1,260,000	
Total long-term liabilities	$1,680,000	
Total liabilities	$2,100,000	
Equity		
Common stock (par $10)	$ 500,000	
Paid-in capital	2,000,000	
Total equity	$2,500,000	
Total liabilities and equity	$4,600,000	

[a]Subordinated to the long-term notes payable.

ST–3. (*Distribution of Proceeds in Bankruptcy*) Pioneer Enterprises is bankrupt and being liquidated. The liabilities and equity portion of its balance sheet are given below. The book value of the assets was $60 million, but the realized value when liquidated was only $31.58 million, of which $7.55 million came from the sale of the firm's office building. Administrative expenses associated with the liquidation were $4.8 million. Determine the distribution of the proceeds.

Pioneer Enterprises Liabilities and Equities

Current liabilities		
Accounts payable	$ 6,500,000	
Accrued wages[a]	400,000	
Notes payable	15,000,000	
Federal taxes	3,000,000	
State taxes	1,250,000	
Total current liabilities		$26,150,000
Long-term debt		
First mortgage bonds[b]	$14,000,000	
Subordinated debentures[c]	8,500,000	
Total long-term debt		22,500,000
Equity		
Preferred stock	$ 2,350,000	
Common stock	9,000,000	
Total equity		11,350,000
Total liabilities and equity		$60,000,000

[a]No single claim exceeds $2,000.
[b]Have first lien on an office building.
[c]Subordinated to the first mortgage bonds.

24–1A. (*Predicting Bankruptcy*) You are considering investing in the securities of three companies. Using the Altman model and the information given below, compute the bankruptcy score for each company. Which companies would you invest in?

	Company		
	A	B	C
Sales	$1,500,000	$ 800,000	$3,000,000
Total assets	4,000,000	1,000,000	4,500,000
Net working capital	1,100,000	650,000	2,000,000

	Company (cont.)		
	A	B	C
Earnings before interest and taxes	1,000,000	500,000	1,000,000
Retained earnings	800,000	350,000	1,500,000
Stock market value	1,250,000	500,000	2,200,000
Debt book value	750,000	100,000	1,250,000

24-2A. (*Reorganization*) The trustee for the reorganization of the Rose Corporation has established the going-concern value at $7.5 million. The creditors and the amounts owed are given below. As part of the reorganization plan, the accounts payable are to be settled by renewal of $500,000 of the accounts, with a due date of six months. Any remaining amount to be received by these claimants is to be realized in the form of long-term notes payable. The current owners of the firm's notes are to be paid in preferred stock. The mortgage bondholders will receive half of their adjusted claim under the reorganization in the form of newly issued bonds, with the remainder given in common stock. The investors owning the subordinated debentures are to receive common stock in settlement of their claim. What will Rose's liabilities and equity be after reorganization?

Rose Corporation

Creditors	Amount of Claims
Accounts payable	$ 2,000,000
Notes payable	1,000,000
Mortgage bonds	4,000,000
Subordinated debentures[a]	3,000,000
	$10,000,000

[a]Subordinated to the mortgage bonds.

24-3A. (*Reorganization*) Pepertyme, Inc., has filed for voluntary reorganization. The firm's liabilities are shown below. The firm has an estimated going-concern value of $1,825,000 and a liquidation value of $1,400,000. What will Pepertyme's liabilities and equity be after reorganization if the following rules are applied?
   a. Accounts payable are to receive 50 percent of their claim in accounts payable due in 30 days and 50 percent in 90-day notes payable.
   b. Notes payable are to receive 50 percent of their claim in short-term notes payable and 50 percent in long-term notes payable.
   c. Mortgage bondholders will receive half of their claim in new bonds and half in common stock.
   d. Subordinated debentures will receive their claim as 50 percent preferred stock and 50 percent common stock.

Pepertyme, Inc.

Creditors	Amount of Claims
Accounts payable	$ 650,000
Short-term notes payable	500,000
Mortgage bonds	1,000,000
Subordinated debentures[a]	1,500,000
	$3,650,000

[a]Subordinated to the mortgage bonds.

24-4A. (*Distribution of Proceeds in Bankruptcy*) Loggins Industries has filed a bankruptcy petition and is in the process of being liquidated. Its liabilities and equity are shown below. The book value of the assets is $80 million, but the liquidation value is $42 million. Administrative expenses of the liquidation procedures were $2 million. What is the distribution of proceeds?

Loggins Industries Liabilities and Equity

Current debt		
Accounts payable	$10,000,000	
Accrued wages[a]	1,000,000	
Notes payable	17,000,000	
Federal taxes	3,000,000	
State taxes	1,000,000	
Total current debt		$32,000,000
Long-term debt		
Bonds (10-year 8%)	$25,000,000	
Subordinated debentures (7-year 10%)[b]	18,000,000	
Total long-term debt		43,000,000
Equity		
Preferred stock	$ 1,000,000	
Common stock	4,000,000	
Total equity		5,000,000
Total debt and equity		$80,000,000

[a]No single claim exceeds $2,000.
[b]Subordinated to notes payable.

24–5A. (*Distribution of Proceeds in Bankruptcy*) Heinburner, Inc., a local manufacturing concern, is bankrupt and is being liquidated. The book value of the assets is $1.5 million. When the firm was liquidated, $1.25 million was realized. Administrative costs for the liquidation were $150,000. Determine the distribution of proceeds.

Heinburner, Inc., Liabilities and Equity

Current debt		
Accounts payable	$200,000	
Accrued wages[a]	10,000	
Notes payable	350,000	
State and federal taxes	140,000	
Total current debt		$ 700,000
Long-term debt		300,000
Equity		
Preferred stock	$100,000	
Common stock	400,000	
Total equity		500,000
Total debt and equity		$1,500,000

[a]No single claim exceeds $2,000.

24–6A. (*Predicting Bankruptcy*) You are considering investing in the securities of three companies. Using the Altman model and the information given below, compute the bankruptcy score for each company. In which company would you invest?

	Company		
	A	B	C
Sales	$2,000,000	$6,000,000	$3,500,000
Total assets	3,000,000	13,000,000	5,000,000
Net working capital	1,400,000	4,500,000	2,200,000
EBIT	1,500,000	3,000,000	2,500,000
Retained earnings	1,000,000	2,500,000	1,800,000
Stock market value	1,600,000	5,000,000	2,800,000
Debt book value	900,000	3,200,000	1,500,000

24-7A. (*Reorganization*) Juarez, Inc., is going through a voluntary reorganization. The corporation's liabilities are shown below. The firm has an estimated going-concern value of $8,400,000 and a liquidation value of $6,500,000. What will the liabilities and equity of Juarez, Inc., be after reorganization if the following rules are applied?

a. Accounts payable are due to receive one-third of their claim in accounts payable due in 30 days and the remainder in long-term notes payable.

b. Notes payable are to receive 50 percent in short-term notes payable and 50 percent in preferred stock.

c. Mortgage bondholders will receive half of their claim in new bonds and half in common stock.

d. Subordinated debentures will receive common stock in settlement of their claim.

Juarez, Inc.

Creditors	Amount of Claims
Accounts payable	$ 3,000,000
Notes payable	2,000,000
Mortgage bonds	2,000,000
Subordinated debentures[a]	5,000,000
	$12,000,000

[a]Subordinated to the mortgage bonds.

24-8A. (*Distribution of Proceeds in Bankruptcy*) Sanchez Firefighting, Inc., is bankrupt and is being liquidated. The book value of the assets is $3,750,000, but the liquidation value totals only $3,125,000. Administrative costs for the liquidation process totaled $375,000. What is the distribution of proceeds?

Sanchez Firefighting, Inc.

Current debt		
Accounts payable	$550,000	
Accrued wages[a]	20,000	
Notes payable	950,000	
State and federal taxes	280,000	
Total current debt		$1,800,000
Long-term debt		700,000
Equity		
Preferred stock	500,000	
Common stock	700,000	
Total equity		1,200,000
Total debt and equity		$3,700,000

[a]No single claim exceeds $2,000.

STUDY PROBLEMS (SET B)

24-1B. (*Predicting Bankruptcy*) You are considering investing in the securities of three companies. Using the Altman model and the information given below, compute the bankruptcy score for each company. In which companies would you invest?

	Company		
	A	B	C
Sales	$1,550,000	$ 900,000	$2,750,000
Total assets	4,000,000	1,000,000	4,500,000
Net working capital	1,100,000	650,000	2,000,000

	Company (cont.)		
	A	B	C
Earnings before interest and taxes	975,000	500,000	1,000,000
Retained earnings	800,000	350,000	1,500,000
Stock market value	1,150,000	550,000	2,000,000
Debt book value	750,000	100,000	1,300,000

24–2B. (*Reorganization*) The trustee for the reorganization of Hester Corporation has established the going-concern value at $7 million. The creditors and the amounts owed are given below. As part of the reorganization plan, the accounts payable are to be settled by renewal of $500,000 of the accounts, with a due date of six months. Any remaining amount to be received by these claimants is to be realized in the form of long-term notes payable. The current owners of the firm's notes are to be paid in preferred stock. The mortgage bondholders will receive half of their adjusted claim under the reorganization in the form of newly issued bonds, with the remainder given in common stock. The investors owning the subordinated debentures are to receive common stock in settlement of their claim. What will Hester's liabilities and equity be after reorganization?

Hester Corporation

Creditors	Amount of Claims
Accounts payable	$ 2,250,000
Notes payable	1,000,000
Mortgage bonds	3,750,000
Subordinated debentures[a]	3,250,000
	$10,250,000

[a]Subordinated to the mortgage bonds.

24–3B. (*Reorganization*) Topher, Inc., has filed for voluntary reorganization. The firm's liabilities are shown below. The firm has an estimated going-concern value of $1,900,000 and a liquidation value of $1,500,000. What will Topher's liabilities and equity be after reorganization if the following rules are applied?

a. Accounts payable are to receive 50 percent of their claim in accounts payable due in 30 days and 50 percent in 90-day notes payable.

b. Notes payable are to receive 50 percent of their claim in short-term notes payable and 50 percent in long-term notes payable.

c. Mortgage bondholders will receive half of their claim in new bonds and half in common stock.

d. Subordinated debentures will receive their claim as 50 percent preferred stock and 50 percent common stock.

Topher, Inc.

Creditors	Amount of Claims
Accounts payable	$ 575,000
Notes payable	520,000
Mortgage bonds	1,250,000
Subordinated debentures[a]	1,500,000
	$3,845,000

[a]Subordinated to the mortgage bonds.

24–4B. (*Distribution of Proceeds in Bankruptcy*) Grigsby Industries has filed a bankruptcy petition and is in the process of being liquidated. Its liabilities and equity are shown below. The book value of the assets is $84 million, but the liquidation value is $43 million. Administrative expenses of the liquidation procedures were $2 million. What is the distribution of proceeds?

Grigsby Industries Liabilities and Equity

Current debt		
Accounts payable	$12,000,000	
Accrued wages[a]	1,000,000	
Notes payable	17,000,000	
Federal taxes	3,000,000	
State taxes	1,000,000	
Total current debt		$34,000,000
Long-term debt		
Bonds (10-year 8%)	$25,000,000	
Subordinated debentures (7-year 10%)[b]	20,000,000	
Total long-term debt		45,000,000
Equity		
Preferred stock	$ 1,000,000	
Common stock	4,000,000	
Total equity		5,000,000
Total debt and equity		$84,000,000

[a]No single claim exceeds $2,000.
[b]Subordinated to notes payable.

24–5B. (*Distribution of Proceeds in Bankruptcy*) Scoggins, Inc., a local manufacturing concern, is bankrupt and is being liquidated. The book value of the assets is $1.5 million. When the firm was liquidated, $1.25 million was realized. Administrative costs for the liquidation were $150,000. Determine the distribution of proceeds.

Scoggins, Inc., Liabilities and Equity

Current debt		
Accounts payable	$190,000	
Accrued wages[a]	12,000	
Notes payable	350,000	
State and federal taxes	140,000	
Total current debt		$ 692,000
Long-term debt		250,000
Equity		
Preferred stock	$100,000	
Common stock	500,000	
Total equity		600,000
Total debt and equity		$1,542,000

[a]No single claim exceeds $2,000.

24–6B. (*Predicting Bankruptcy*) You are considering investing in the securities of three companies. Using the Altman model and the information given below, compute the bankruptcy score for each company. In which company would you invest?

	Company		
	A	B	C
Sales	$3,000,000	$2,000,000	$3,200,000
Total assets	4,000,000	4,500,000	5,500,000
Net working capital	2,500,000	1,800,000	2,000,000
EBIT	2,000,000	900,000	1,800,000
Retained earnings	1,800,000	800,000	1,400,000
Stock market value	2,300,000	1,700,000	2,900,000
Debt book value	1,400,000	1,100,000	1,300,000

24-7B. (*Reorganization*) Insuba, Inc., is going through a voluntary reorganization. The corporation's liabilities are shown below. The firm has an estimated going-concern value of $3,800,000 and a liquidation value of $3,200,000. What will the liabilities and equity of Insuba, Inc., be after reorganization if the following rules are applied?

    a. Accounts payable are due to receive two-thirds of their claim in accounts payable due in 30 days and the remainder in long-term notes payable.

    b. Notes payable are to receive 40 percent in short-term notes payable and 60 percent in preferred stock.

    c. Mortgage bondholders will receive two-fifths of their claim in new bonds and three-fifths in common stock.

    d. Subordinated debentures will receive common stock in settlement of their claim.

Insuba, Inc.

Creditors	Amount of Claims
Accounts payable	$1,200,000
Notes payable	1,000,000
Mortgage bonds	1,000,000
Subordinated debentures[a]	2,500,000
	$5,700,000

[a]Subordinated to the mortgage bonds.

24-8B. (*Distribution of Proceeds in Bankruptcy*) Outaluk, Inc., is bankrupt and is being liquidated. The book value of the assets is $8,400,000, but the liquidation value totals only $7,850,000. Administrative costs for the liquidation process total $900,000. What is the distribution of proceeds?

Outaluk, Inc.

Current debt		
Accounts payable	$2,450,000	
Accrued wages[a]	60,000	
Notes payable	3,150,000	
State and federal taxes	560,000	
Total current debt		$6,220,000
Long-term debt		450,000
Equity		
Preferred stock	1,200,000	
Common stock	2,800,000	
Total equity		4,000,000
Total debt and equity		$10,670,000

[a]No single claim exceeds $2,000.

SELF-TEST SOLUTIONS

SS-1. Bankruptcy score $= 1.2X_1 + 1.4X_2 + 3.3X_3 + 0.6X_4 + 0.999X_5$

    where $X_1 =$ (net working capital ÷ total assets)

           $X_2 =$ (retained earnings ÷ total assets)

           $X_3 =$ (earnings before interest and taxes ÷ total assets)

           $X_4 =$ (market value of stock ÷ book value of debt)

           $X_5 =$ (sales ÷ total assets)

Company A

    $1.2(.15) + 1.4(.20) + 3.3(.35) + 0.6(3.35) + 0.999(1.60) = 5.22$

Company B

    $1.2(.25) + 1.4(.45) + 3.3(.40) + 0.6(1.75) + 0.999(1.95) = 5.25$

Company C

$$1.2(.20) + 1.4(.25) + 3.3(.15) + 0.6(1.25) + 0.999(.75) = 2.58$$

Company D

$$1.2(.15) + 1.4(.12) + 3.3(.10) + 0.6(1.10) + 0.999(.55) = 1.88$$

Company E

$$1.2(.40) + 1.4(.35) + 3.3(.30) + 0.6(1.75) + 0.999(1.50) = 4.51$$

Interpretation of results:

Score < 1.81—Likely candidate for failure

Score > 2.99—No concern of bankruptcy

1.81 < Score < 2.675—Probability of failure greater than success

2.675 < Score < 2.99—Probability of success greater than failure

The probability of failure is greater than that of success for companies C and D. Companies A, B, and E need not be concerned with bankruptcy.

SS–2. Brogham, Inc., Reorganization Plan

Creditors	Amount	60% of Claim	Claim After Subordination
Accounts payable	$ 120,000	$ 72,000	$ 72,000
Notes payable	300,000	180,000	180,000
Mortgage bonds	420,000	252,000	420,000
Subordinated debentures	1,260,000	756,000	588,000
	$2,100,000	$1,260,000	$1,260,000

Percentage of claim = going-concern value ÷ total liabilities

= $1,260,000 ÷ $2,100,000

= 60%

SS–3. Pioneer Enterprises

Distribution of Proceeds

Liquidation value of assets		$31,580,000
Priority of claims		
1. Administrative expenses	$4,800,000	
2. Wages payable	400,000	
3. Taxes	4,250,000	
4. First mortgage receipts from building sale	7,550,000	
Total prior claims		17,000,000
Amount available to general creditors		$14,580,000

Claims of General Creditors

Creditors	Amount	40% of Claim	Claim After Subordination
Accounts payable	$ 6,500,000	$ 2,600,000	$ 2,600,000
Notes payable	15,000,000	6,000,000	6,000,000
Remainder of first mortgage bonds	6,450,000	2,580,000	5,980,000
Subordinated debentures	8,500,000	3,400,000	–0–
	$36,450,000	$14,580,000	$14,580,000

$$\text{Percentage of claims} = \left(\begin{array}{c}\text{amount available to}\\\text{general creditors}\end{array}\right) \div \left(\begin{array}{c}\text{amount of}\\\text{claims}\end{array}\right)$$

= $14,580,000 ÷ $36,450,000

= 40%

CHAPTER 25

International Business Finance

The Globalization of Product and Financial Markets • Exchange Rates • Interest Rate Parity Theory • Purchasing Power Parity • Exposure to Exchange Rate Risk • Multinational Working-Capital Management • International Financing and Capital Structure Decisions • Direct Foreign Investment

Thus far, although we have examined international examples, we primarily have discussed financial management in the domestic economy of the United States. Many firms conduct business activities in more than one country, and they need to consider additional factors in their foreign operations. In addition, because of the increasing international integration of product and financial markets, all firms are subject to and are influenced by international events and by global economic forces. Thus, managers of all companies must be sensitive to the international aspects of business finance.

Firms can operate internationally in various ways. In the simplest instance, a firm exports to (or imports from) a single foreign country. Other export or import firms operate in many countries simultaneously. For example, banks conduct business in many countries, lending in some currencies and borrowing in others. Many manufacturing companies set up production facilities in foreign countries, to sell abroad or to import the output back to the home country.

Some companies have more elaborate international operations. A United States automobile company may have a plant in Germany for manufacturing engines, another plant in France for drive trains, a third in Belgium for other components, and an assembly plant in Italy. The final product, the automobile, may be destined for all markets in Europe, Asia, and Africa. This is an example of a **multinational corporation (MNC)**.

The basic problems facing international companies differ from those facing domestic companies. Examples of additional complexities of conducting international business would include the following:

1. **Multiple currencies.** Revenues may be denominated in one currency, costs in another, assets in a third, liabilities in a fourth, and stock price in a fifth. Thus, maximization of the wealth of the owners must consider changing currency values.

2. **Differing legal and political environments.** International variations exist in tax laws, depreciation allowances and other accounting practices, as

well as in government regulation and control of business activity. Repatriation of profits may be a problem in certain countries.[1]

3. **Differing economic and capital markets.** The extent of government regulation and control of the economy and capital markets may differ greatly across nations. For example, the ability of a foreign company to raise different types and amounts of capital may be restricted.

4. **Internal control challenge.** It may be difficult to organize, evaluate, and control different divisions of a company when they are separated geographically and when they operate in different environments.

Perspective in Finance

This chapter highlights multiple currencies as a major additional dimension of international finance that firms must consider. Effective strategies for the reduction of foreign exchange risk are discussed. Working-capital management and capital structure decisions in the international context are also covered. For the international firm, direct foreign investment is a capital-budgeting decision—with some additional complexities.

The Globalization of Product and Financial Markets

World trade has grown much faster over the last few decades than world aggregate output (global gross national product [GNP]). Global exports and imports were about one-fifth of global aggregate output in 1962. This figure had increased to about one-fourth by 1972, to more than one-third by 1982, and it continues to increase. The dollar value of world exports has grown from $129.5 billion in 1962 to $3.3 *trillion* in 1990. This remarkable increase in international trade is reflected in the increased openness of almost all national economies to international influences. For example, the proportion of U.S. GNP accounted for by exports and imports (about one-fifth) is now double what it was two decades ago, and is even higher for manufactured goods (see Figure 25–1). The

FIGURE 25–1.
U.S. Trade as a Share of U.S. Manufacturing Output
Source: U.S. Department of Labor, Bureau of Labor Statistics, 1991;
Organization for Economic Cooperation and Development, 1991

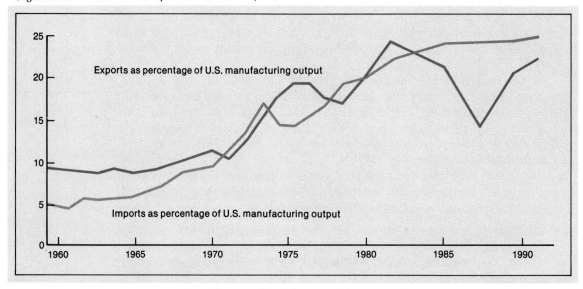

---

[1]Repatriation of profits refers to the withdrawal of profits from foreign operations to the home country of the MNC.

U.S. Department of Commerce estimates that the United States exports about a fifth of its industrial production and that about 70 percent of all U.S. goods compete directly with foreign goods.

Some industries and states are highly dependent on the international economy. For example, the electronic consumer products and automobile industries are widely considered to be global industries. Ohio ranks fourth in terms of manufactured exports, and more than half of all Ohio workers are employed by firms that depend to some extent on exports.

There has also been a rise in the global level of international portfolio and direct investment. Both direct and portfolio investment in the United States have been increasing faster than U.S. investment overseas. **Direct investment** occurs when the MNC has control over the investment, such as when it builds an off-shore manufacturing facility. **Portfolio investment** involves financial assets with maturities greater than one year, such as the purchase of foreign stocks and bonds. Total foreign investment in the U.S. now exceeds such U.S. investment overseas.

A major reason for long-run overseas investments of United States companies is the high rates of return obtainable from these investments. The amount of United States *direct foreign investments (DFI)* abroad is large and growing. Significant amounts of the total assets, sales, and profits of American MNCs are attributable to foreign investments and foreign operations. Direct foreign investment is not limited to American firms. Many European and Japanese firms have operations abroad, too. During the last decade these firms have been increasing their sales and setting up production facilities abroad, especially in the United States.

Capital flows between countries for international financial investment purposes have also been increasing. Many firms, investment companies, and individuals invest in the capital markets in foreign countries. The motivation is twofold: to obtain returns higher than those obtainable in the domestic capital markets and to reduce portfolio risk through international diversification. The increase in world trade and investment activity is reflected in the recent globalization of financial markets. The Eurodollar market is larger than any domestic financial market. U.S. companies are increasingly turning to this market for funds. Even companies and public entities that have no overseas presence are beginning to rely on this market for financing.

In addition, most national financial markets are becoming more integrated with global markets because of the rapid increase in the volume of interest rate and currency swaps ($2.4 trillion in 1989). Because of the widespread availability of these swaps, the currency denomination and the source country of financing for many globally integrated companies are dictated by accessibility and relative cost considerations regardless of the currency ultimately needed by the firm.

The foreign exchange markets have also grown rapidly, and the weekly trading volume in these globally integrated markets, between $3 and $5 trillion, exceeds the annual trading volume on the world's securities markets. Even a *purely domestic firm* that buys all its inputs and sells all its output in its home country is not immune to foreign competition, nor can it totally ignore the workings of the international financial markets.

Exchange Rates

Recent History of Exchange Rates

Between 1949 and 1970 the exchange rates between the major currencies were fixed. All countries were required to set a specific *parity rate* for their currency vis-à-vis the United States dollar. For example, consider the German currency, the Deutsche mark (DM). In 1949 the parity rate was set at 4.0 DM to $1. The actual exchange rate prevailing on any day was allowed to lie within a narrow band around the parity rate. The DM was allowed to fluctuate between 4.04 and 3.96 per dollar. A country could effect a major adjustment in the exchange rate by changing its parity rate with respect to the dollar. When the currency was made cheaper with respect to the dollar, this adjustment was called a *devaluation.* A *revaluation* resulted when a currency became more expensive with respect to the dollar. In 1969 the DM parity rate was adjusted to 3.66 per dollar. This adjustment was a revaluation of the DM parity by 9.3 percent. The new bands around the parity were 3.7010 and 3.6188 DM per dollar. The DM strengthened against the dollar since fewer DM were needed to buy a dollar.

Since 1973 a *floating-rate* international currency system has been operating. For most currencies, there are no parity rates and no bands within which the currencies fluctuate.[2] Most major currencies, including the United States dollar, fluctuate freely, depending upon their values as perceived by the traders in foreign exchange markets. The country's relative economic strengths, its level of exports and imports, the level of monetary activity, and the deficits or surpluses in its balance of payments (BOP) are all important factors in the determination of exchange rates.[3] Short-term, day-to-day fluctuations in exchange rates are caused by changing supply and demand conditions in the foreign exchange market.

The Foreign Exchange Market

The foreign exchange market provides a mechanism for the transfer of purchasing power from one currency to another. This market is not a physical entity like the New York Stock Exchange; it is a network of telephone and cable connections among banks, foreign exchange dealers, and brokers. The market operates simultaneously at three levels. At the first level, customers buy and sell foreign exchange (i.e., foreign currency) through their banks. At the second level, banks buy and sell foreign exchange from other banks in the same commercial center. At the last level, banks buy and sell foreign exchange from banks in commercial centers in other countries. Some important commercial centers for foreign exchange trading are New York, London, Zurich, Frankfurt, Hong Kong, Singapore, and Tokyo.

An example will illustrate this multilevel trading. A trader in Texas may buy foreign exchange (pounds) from a bank in Houston for payment to a British supplier against some purchase made. The Houston bank, in turn, may purchase the foreign currency (pounds) from a New York bank. The New York bank may buy the pounds from another bank in New York or from a bank in London.

Because this market provides transactions in a continuous manner for a very large volume of sales and purchases, the currency markets are **efficient.** In other words, it is difficult to make a profit by shopping around from one bank to another. Minute differences in the quotes from different banks are quickly eliminated. Because of the arbitrage mechanism (discussed later), simultaneous quotes to different buyers in London and New York are likely to be the same.

Two major types of transactions are carried out in the foreign exchange markets: *spot* and *forward transactions.*

Spot Exchange Rates

A typical spot transaction involves an American firm buying foreign currency from its bank and paying for it in dollars. The price of foreign currency in terms

[2]The system of floating rates is referred to as the "floating-rate regime."

[3]The balance of payments for the U.S. reflects the difference between the imports and exports of goods (the trade balance) and services. Capital inflows and outflows are tabulated in the capital account.

of the domestic currency is the *exchange rate*. Another type of spot transaction is when an American firm receives foreign currency from abroad. The firm typically would sell the foreign currency to its bank for dollars. These are both **spot transactions,** because one currency is exchanged for another currency today. The actual exchange rate quotes are expressed in several different ways, as discussed later. To allow time for the transfer of funds, the *value date* when the currencies are actually exchanged is two days after the spot transaction occurs. Four banks could easily be involved in the transactions: the local banks of the buyer and seller of the foreign exchange, and the money-center banks that handle the purchase and sale in the interbank market. Perhaps the buyer or seller will have to move the funds from one of its local banks to another, bringing even more banks into the transaction.

On the spot exchange market the quoted exchange rate is typically called a direct quote. A *direct quote* indicates the number of units of the home currency required to buy one unit of the foreign currency. That is, in New York the typical exchange-rate quote indicates the number of dollars needed to buy one unit of a foreign currency: dollars per pound, dollars per mark, and so on. The spot rates in columns 2 and 3 of Table 25–1 are the direct exchange quotes taken from the

TABLE 25–1.
Foreign Exchange Rates
Reported on January 2, 1992

Country	U.S. $ equiv.		Currency[a] per U.S. $	
	Tues.	Mon.	Tues.	Mon.
Argentina (Austral)	.0001010	.0001008	9905.01	9918.67
Australia (Dollar)	.7600	.7600	1.3158	1.3158
Austria (Schilling)	.09363	.09359	10.68	10.69
Bahrain (Dinar)	2.6525	2.6525	.3770	.3770
Belgium (Franc)	.03197	.03196	31.28	31.29
Brazil (Cruzeiro)	.00096	.00095	1040.00	1056.40
Britain (Pound)	1.8695	1.8675	.5349	.5355
30-Day Forward	1.8587	1.8635	.5380	.5366
90-Day Forward	1.8388	1.8368	.5438	.5444
180-Day Forward	1.8098	1.8078	.5525	.5532
Canada (Dollar)	.8654	.8632	1.1555	1.1585
30-Day Forward	.8632	.8613	1.1585	1.1611
90-Day Forward	.8590	.8570	1.1642	1.1699
180-Day Forward	.8538	.8516	1.1713	1.1743
Czechoslovakia (Koruna)				
Commercial rate	.0366300	.0362845	27.3000	27.5600
Chile (Peso)	.002743	.002753	364.50	363.27
China (Renminbi)	.185185	.183993	5.4000	5.4350
Colombia (Peso)	.001739	.001709	575.00	585.00
Denmark (Krone)	.1694	.1692	5.9020	5.9100
Ecuador (Sucre)				
Floating rate	.000804	.000804	1244.01	1244.01
Finland (Markka)	.24207	.24198	4.1310	4.1325
France (Franc)	.19305	.19292	5.1800	5.1835
30-Day Forward	.19205	.19188	5.2070	5.2115
90-Day Forward	.19015	.19000	5.2590	5.2632
180-Day Forward	.18742	.18721	5.3357	5.3415
Germany (Mark)	.6601	.6590	1.5150	1.5175
30-Day Forward	.6570	.6560	1.5220	1.5245
90-Day Forward	.6511	.6501	1.5358	1.5383
180-Day Forward	.6425	.6414	1.5565	1.5590
Greece (Drachma)	.005714	.005780	175.00	173.00
Hong Kong (Dollar)	.12858	.12853	7.7770	7.7800
Hungary (Forint)	.0133156	.0133333	75.1000	75.0000
India (Rupee)	.03876	.03879	25.80	25.78
Indonesia (Rupiah)	.0005040	.0005013	1984.01	1995.01
Ireland (Punt)	1.7524	1.7510	.5706	.5711
Israel (Shekel)	.4464	.4394	2.2400	2.2760
Italy (Lira)	.0008715	.0008697	1147.50	1149.80
Japan (Yen)	.008013	.007962	124.80	125.60
30-Day Forward	.008006	.007955	124.91	125.71
90-Day Forward	.007983	.007932	125.26	126.07
180-Day Forward	.007957	.007907	125.67	126.47
Jordan (Dinar)	1.4859	1.4859	.6730	.6730
Kuwait (Dinar)	3.5186	3.5156	.2842	.2845

TABLE 25–1.
(Continued)

Country	U.S. $ equiv.		Currency[a] per U.S. $	
	Tues.	Mon.	Tues.	Mon.
Lebanon (Pound)	.001138	.001138	879.00	879.00
Malaysia (Ringgit)	.3676	.3660	2.7205	2.7320
Malta (Lira)	3.2000	3.3058	.3125	.3025
Mexico (Peso)				
Floating rate	.0003237	.0003262	3089.00	3066.01
Netherland (Guilder)	.5858	.5845	1.7070	1.7110
New Zealand (Dollar)	.5400	.5412	1.8519	1.8477
Norway (Krone)	.1676	.1672	5.9675	5.9800
Pakistan (Rupee)	.0407	.0407	24.60	24.60
Peru (New Sol)	.9500	.9358	1.05	1.07
Philippines (Peso)	.03824	.03839	26.15	26.05
Poland (Zloty)	.0009524	.00009259	10500.00	10800.30
Portugal (Escudo)	.007485	.007413	133.60	134.90
Saudi Arabia (Riyal)	.26667	.26667	3.7500	3.7500
Singapore (Dollar)	.6171	.6135	1.6205	1.6300
South Africa (Rand)				
Commercial rate	.3648	.3645	2.7413	2.7433
Financial rate	.3153	.3145	3.1720	3.1800
South Korea (Won)	.0013180	.0013148	758.70	760.60
Spain (Peseta)	.010354	.010336	96.58	96.75
Sweden (Krona)	.1807	.1802	5.5355	5.5500
Switzerland (Franc)	.7372	.7377	1.3565	1.3555
30-Day Forward	.7349	.7355	1.3607	1.3597
90-Day Forward	.7298	.7303	1.3703	1.3693
180-Day Forward	.7225	.7231	1.3840	1.3830
Taiwan (Dollar)	.039216	.039124	25.50	25.56
Thailand (Baht)	.03992	.03957	25.05	25.27
Turkey (Lira)	.0001990	.0001997	5025.00	5008.01
United Arab (Dirham)	.2723	.2723	3.6725	3.6725
Uruguay (New Peso)				
Financial	.000407	.000403	2457.00	2481.40
Venezuela (Bolivar)				
Floating rate	.01645	.01622	60.80	61.65
SDR[b]	1.43043	1.42899	.69909	.69979
ECU[c]	1.34093	1.34130	—	—

[a]**Exchange Rates:** Tuesday, December 31, 1991. The New York foreign exchange selling rates apply to trading among banks in amounts of $1 million and more, as quoted at 3 p.m. Eastern time by Bankers Trust Co., Telerate Systems, Inc. and other sources. Retail transactions provide fewer units of foreign currency per dollar.
[b]Special Drawing Rights (SDR) are based on exchange rates for the U.S., German, British, French and Japanese currencies. Source: International Monetary Fund.
[c]European Currency Unit (ECU) is based on a basket of community currencies. Source: European Community Commission.

Wall Street Journal on January 2, 1992. To buy one pound on December 31, 1991, 1.8695 dollars were needed. To buy one franc and one mark, 19.305 cents and 66.01 cents were needed, respectively. The quotes in the spot market in Paris are given in terms of francs and those in Frankfurt in terms of Deutsche marks.

An *indirect quote* indicates the number of units of foreign currency that can be bought for one unit of the home currency. This reads as pounds per dollar, francs per dollar, and so on. Indirect quotes are given in the last two columns of Table 25–1.

In summary, a direct quote is the dollar/foreign currency rate ($/FC), and an indirect quote is the foreign currency/dollar rate (FC/$). Therefore, an indirect quote is the reciprocal of a direct quote and vice versa. The following example illustrates the computation of an indirect quote from a given direct quote.

EXAMPLE

Suppose you want to compute the indirect quotes from the direct quotes of spot rates for pounds, francs, and marks given in column 2 of Table 25–1. The direct quotes are: pound, 1.8695; French franc, .19305; and deutsche mark, .6601. The related indirect quotes are calculated as the *reciprocal* of the direct quote as follows:

$$\text{indirect quote} = \frac{1}{\text{direct quote}}$$

Thus

pounds:

$$\frac{1}{\$1.8695/\pounds} = \pounds.5349/\$$$

francs:

$$\frac{1}{\$.19305/FF} = FF5.1800/\$$$

deutsche marks:

$$\frac{1}{\$.6601/DM} = DM1.5150/\$ \quad \blacksquare$$

Notice that the above direct quotes and indirect quotes are identical to those shown in columns 2 and 4 of Table 25–1.

Direct and indirect quotes are useful in conducting international transactions, as the following examples show.

EXAMPLE

An American business must pay 1,000 marks to a German firm on December 31, 1991. How many dollars will be required for this transaction?

$$\$.6601/DM \times DM1000 = \$660.10 \quad \blacksquare$$

EXAMPLE

An American business must pay \$2,000 to a British resident on December 31, 1991. How many pounds will the British resident receive?

$$\pounds.5349/\$ \times \$2000 = \pounds1059.80 \quad \blacksquare$$

Exchange Rates and Arbitrage

The foreign exchange quotes in two different countries must be in line with each other. The direct quote for U.S. dollars in London is given in pounds/dollar. Because the foreign exchange markets are efficient, the direct quotes for the United States dollar in London, on December 31, 1991, must be very close to the indirect rate of .5349 pounds/dollar prevailing in New York on that date.

If the exchange-rate quotations between the London and New York spot exchange markets were *out of line*, then an enterprising trader could make a profit by buying in the market where the currency was cheaper and selling it in the other. Such a buy-and-sell strategy would involve a zero net investment of funds and no risk bearing yet would provide a sure profit. Such a person is called an **arbitrager**, and the process of buying and selling in more than one market to make a riskless profit is called **arbitrage**. Spot exchange markets are efficient in the sense that arbitrage opportunities do not persist for any length of time. That is, the exchange rates between two different markets are quickly brought *in line*, aided by the arbitrage process. *Simple arbitrage* eliminates exchange rate differentials across the markets for a single currency, as in the preceding example for the New York and London quotes. *Triangular arbitrage* does the same across the markets for all currencies. Covered interest arbitrage eliminates differentials across currency and interest rate markets.

Suppose that London quotes £.5500/\$ instead of £.5349/\$. If you simultaneously bought a pound in New York for £.5349/\$ and sold a pound in London for £.5500/\$, you would have (1) taken a zero net investment position since you bought one pound and sold one pound, (2) locked in a sure profit of £.0151/\$ *no matter which way* the pound subsequently moves, and (3) set in motion the forces that will eliminate the different quotes in New York and London. As others in the marketplace learn of your transaction, they will attempt to make the same transaction. The increased demand to buy pounds in New York will lead to a higher quote there and the increased supply of pounds will lead to a lower quote in London. The workings of the market will produce a new spot rate that lies between £.5349/$ and £.5500/$ and is the same in New York and in London.

Asked and Bid Rates

In the spot exchange market two types of rates are quoted: the asked and the bid rates. The *asked rate* is the rate the bank or the foreign exchange trader "asks" the customer to pay in home currency for foreign currency when the bank is selling and the customer is buying. The asked rate is also known as the *selling rate* or the *offer rate*. The *bid rate* is the rate at which the bank buys the foreign currency from the customer by paying in home currency. The bid rate is also known as the *buying rate*. Note that Table 25–1 contains only the selling, offer, or asked rates, and not the buying rate.

The bank sells a unit of foreign currency for more than it pays for it. Therefore, the direct asked quote ($/FC) is greater than the direct bid quote. The difference is known as the **bid-asked spread.** When there is a large volume of transactions and the trading is continuous, the spread is small and can be less than .5% (.005) for the major currencies. The spread is much higher for infrequently traded currencies. The spread exists to compensate the banks for holding the risky foreign currency and for providing the service of converting currencies.

Cross Rates

A **cross rate** is the computation of an exchange rate for a currency from the exchange rates of two other currencies. The following example illustrates how this works.

EXAMPLE

Taking the dollar/pound and the mark/dollar rates from columns 2 and 4 of Table 25–1, we can determine the mark/pound and pound/mark exchange rates.

We see that

$$(\$/£) \times (DM/\$) = (DM/£)$$

or

$$1.8695 \times 1.5150 = DM2.8323/£$$

Thus, the pound/mark exchange rate is

$$1/2.8323 = £.3531/DM$$

Cross-rate computations make it possible to use quotations in New York to compute the exchange rate between pounds, marks, and francs. Arbitrage conditions hold in cross rates, too. For example, the pound exchange rate in Frankfurt (the direct quote marks/pound) must be 2.8323. The mark exchange rate in London must be .3531 pounds/mark. If the rates prevailing in Frankfurt and London were different from the computed cross rates, using quotes from New York, a trader could use three different currencies to lock in arbitrage profits through a process called *triangular arbitrage.*

Forward Exchange Rates

A *forward exchange contract* requires delivery, at a specified future date, of one currency for a specified amount of another currency. The exchange rate for the forward transaction is agreed on today; the actual payment of one currency and the receipt of another currency take place at the future date. For example, a 30-day contract on March 1 is for delivery on March 31. Note that the forward rate is not the same as the spot rate that will prevail in the future. The actual spot rate that will prevail is not known today; only the forward rate is known. The actual spot rate will depend on the market conditions at that time; it may be more or less than today's forward rate. **Exchange-rate risk** is the risk that tomorrow's exchange rate will differ from today's rate.

As indicated earlier, it is extremely unlikely that the future spot rate will be exactly the same as the forward rate quoted today. Assume that you are going to receive a payment denominated in pounds from a British customer in 30 days. If you wait for 30 days and exchange the pounds at the spot rate, you will receive a dollar amount reflecting the exchange rate 30 days hence (i.e., the future spot rate). As of today, you have no way of knowing the exact dollar value or your future pound receipts. Consequently, you cannot make precise plans about the use of these dollars. If, conversely, you buy a future contract, then you know the exact dollar value of your future receipts, and you can make precise plans concerning their use. The forward contract, therefore, can reduce your uncertainty about the future, and the major advantage of the forward market is that of *risk reduction*.

Forward contracts are usually quoted for periods of 30, 90, and 180 days. A contract for any intermediate date can be obtained, usually with the payment of a small premium. Forward contracts for periods longer than 180 days can be obtained by special negotiations with banks. Contracts for periods greater than one year can be costly.

Forward rates, like spot rates, are quoted in both direct and indirect form. The direct quotes for the 30-day and 90-day forward contracts on pounds, francs, and marks are given in column 2 of Table 25–1. The indirect quotes for forward contracts, like spot rates, are reciprocals of the direct quotes. The indirect quotes are indicated in column 4 of Table 25–1. The direct quotes are the dollar/foreign currency rate, and the indirect quotes are the foreign currency/dollar rate similar to the spot exchange quotes.

The 30-day forward quote for pounds is $1.8587 per pound. This means that if one purchases the contract for forward pounds on December 31, 1991, the bank will deliver a pound against the payment of $1.8587 on January 30, 1992. The bank is contractually bound to deliver the pound at this price, and the buyer of the contract is legally obligated to buy it at this price on January 30, 1992. Therefore, this is the price the customer must pay regardless of the actual spot rate prevailing on January 30, 1992. If the spot price of the pound is less than $1.8587, then the customer pays *more* than the spot price. If the spot price is greater than $1.8587, then the customer pays *less* than the spot price.

The forward rate is often quoted at a **premium** to or **discount** from the existing spot rate. For example, the 30-day pound forward rate may be quoted as .0108 discount (1.8587 forward rate − 1.8695 spot rate). If the forward contract is selling for more dollars than the spot—that is, a larger direct quote—the pound is said to be selling at a premium. Note that the dollar is expected to strengthen against the pound. The market expects that in the future fewer dollars will be required to buy a pound. Conversely, the pound is expected to be worth fewer dollars in the future. When the forward contract sells for fewer dollars than the spot—a smaller direct quote—the pound is said to be at a discount from the dollar. Notice in column 2 of Table 25–1 that the forward contracts are selling at a discount for pounds, Deutsche marks, and French francs. This premium or discount is also called the *forward-spot differential*. Notationally, the relationship may be written as

$$F - S = p \text{ (or } d) \tag{25-1}$$

where F = the forward rate, direct quote

S = the spot rate, direct quote

p = the premium, if $F > S$

d = the discount, if $S > F$

The premium or discount can also be expressed as an annual percentage rate, computed as follows:

$$\frac{F - S}{S} \times \frac{12}{n} \times 100 = P \text{ (or } D) \tag{25-2}$$

where n = the number of months of the forward contract

P = the annualized percentage premium, if $F > S$

D = the annualized percentage discount, if $S > F$

EXAMPLE

Compute the percent-per-annum premium on the 30-day forward pound.

Step 1: Identify F, S, and n.
$$F = 1.8587, \quad S = 1.8695, \quad n = 1 \text{ month}$$

Step 2: Because S is greater than F, we compute D:
$$D = \frac{1.8587 - 1.8695}{1.8695} \times \frac{12 \text{ months}}{1 \text{ month}} \times 100$$

$$= -6.93\%$$

The percent-per-annum discount on the 30-day pound is −6.93 percent.

The percent-per-annum discount on the 30-day and 90-day pound, franc, and mark contracts are computed similarly. The results are given in Table 25–2.

TABLE 25–2.
Percent-per-Annum (Discount)

	30-Day	90-Day
British pound	−6.93%	−6.57%
French franc	−6.22	−6.01
Deutsche mark	−5.64	−5.45

Examples of Exchange Rate Risk

The concept of exchange rate risk applies to all types of international businesses. The measurement of these risks, and the type of risk, may differ among businesses. Let us see how exchange risk affects international trade contracts, international portfolio investments, and direct foreign investments.

Exchange Rate Risk in International Trade Contracts

The idea of exchange rate risk in trade contracts is illustrated in the following situations.

Case I ■ An American automobile distributor agrees to buy a car from the manufacturer in Detroit. The distributor agrees to pay $6,500 on delivery of the car, which is expected to be 30 days from today. The car is delivered on the 30th day and the distributor pays $6,500. Notice that, from the day this contract was written until the day the car was delivered, the buyer knew the *exact dollar amount* of the liability. There was, in other words, *no uncertainty* about the value of the contract.

Case II ■ An American automobile distributor enters into a contract with a British supplier to buy a car from the United Kingdom for 3,500 pounds. The amount is payable on the delivery of the car, 30 days from today. From Figure 25–2, we see the range of spot rates that we believe can occur on the date the contract is consummated. On the 30th day, the American importer will pay some amount in the range of $5,843.25 (3,500 × 1.6695) to $7,243.25 (3,500 × 2.0695) for the car. Today, the American firm is not certain what its future dollar outflow will be 30 days hence. That is, the *dollar value of the contract is uncertain*.

These two examples help illustrate the idea of foreign exchange risk in international trade contracts. In the domestic trade contract (Case I), the exact dollar amount of the future dollar payment is known today with certainty. In the case of the international trade contract (Case II), where the *contract is written in the foreign currency*, the exact dollar amount of the contract is not known. The variability of the exchange rate induces variability in the future cash flow.

Exchange rate risk exists when the contract is written in terms of the foreign currency or *denominated* in foreign currency. There is no direct exchange risk if the international trade contract is written in terms of the domestic currency. That is, in Case II, if the contract were written in dollars, the American importer would face *no* direct exchange risk. With the contract written in dollars, the British exporter would bear *all* the exchange risk because the British exporter's future pound receipts would be uncertain. That is, the British exporter would receive payment in dollars, which would have to be converted into pounds at an unknown (as of today) pound–dollar exchange rate. In international trade contracts of the type discussed here, at least one of the two parties to the contract *always* bears the exchange risk.

Certain types of international trade contracts are denominated in a third currency, different from either the importer's or the exporter's domestic

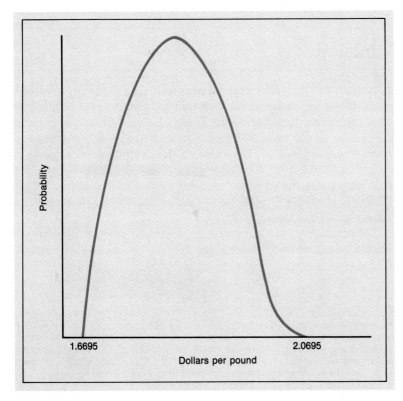

FIGURE 25–2.
A Subjective Probability Distribution of the Pound Exchange Rate, 30 Days in the Future

currency. In Case II the contract might have been denominated in, say, the Deutsche mark. With a mark contract, both importer and exporter would be subject to exchange rate risk.

Exchange risk is not limited to the two-party trade contracts; it exists also in foreign portfolio investments and direct foreign investments.

Exchange Risk in Foreign Portfolio Investments

Let us look at an example of exchange risk in the context of portfolio investments. An American investor buys a German security. The exact return on the investment in the security is unknown. Thus, the security is a risky investment. The investment return in the holding period of, say, three months stated in marks could be anything from −2 to +8 percent. In addition, the mark–dollar exchange rate may depreciate by 4 percent or appreciate by 6 percent in the three-month period during which the investment is held. The return to the American investor, in dollars, will therefore be in the range of −6 to +14 percent.[4] Notice that the return to a German investor, in marks, is in the range of −2 to +8 percent. Clearly, for the American investor, the exchange factor induces a greater variability in the dollar rate of return. Hence, the *exchange rate fluctuations may increase the riskiness* of the investments.

Exchange Risk in Direct Foreign Investment

The exchange risk of a direct foreign investment (DFI) is more complicated. In a DFI the parent company invests in assets denominated in a foreign currency. That is, the balance sheet and the income statement of the subsidiary are written in terms of the foreign currency. The parent company receives the repatriated profit stream in dollars. Thus, the exchange risk concept applies to fluctuations in the dollar value of the *assets* located abroad as well as to the fluctuations in the home-currency-denominated *profit stream*. Exchange risk not only affects immediate profits, it may affect the future profit stream as well.

Although exchange rate risk can be a serious complication in international business activity, remember the principle of the risk–return tradeoff: Traders and corporations find numerous reasons that the returns from international transactions outweigh the risks.

Interest Rate Parity Theory

Forward rates generally entail a premium or a discount relative to current spot rates. However, these forward premiums and discounts differ between currencies and maturities (see Table 25–2). These differences depend solely on the difference in the level of interest rates between the two countries, called the *interest rate differential*. The value of the premium or discount can be theoretically computed from the **interest rate parity (IRP)** theory. This theory states that (except for the effects of small transactions costs) the forward premium or discount should be equal to the difference in the national interest rates for securities of the same maturity.

Specifically, the premium or discount on the percent-per-annum basis should be equal to the following:

$$P \text{ (or } D) = \left(-\frac{I^f - I^d}{1 + I^f} \right) = \left(\frac{I^d - I^f}{1 + I^f} \right) \qquad \textbf{(25–3a)}$$

---

[4]*Example:* Assume the spot exchange rate is .50 dollars per mark. In three months the exchange rate would be .50 × (1 − .04) = .48 to .50 × (1 + .06) = .53. A $50 investment today is equivalent to a 100-mark investment. The 100-mark investment would return 98 to 108 marks in three months. The return, in the worst case, is 98 marks × .48 = $47.04. The return, in the best case, is 108 marks × .53 = $57.24. The holding-period return, on the $50 investment, will be between −6 percent ($47.04 − $50)/$50) and + 14 percent ($57.24 − $50)/$50).

where P (or D) = the percent-per-annum premium (or discount) on the forward rate

I^f = the annualized interest rate on a foreign instrument having the same maturity as the forward contract

I^d = the annualized interest rate on a domestic instrument having the same maturity as the forward contract

To compute the forward premium on, say, a 30-day forward pound contract, we need the 30-day Treasury-bill (T-bill) rate in the United States and its counterpart in the United Kingdom, both expressed as annual rates.

IRP states that the P (or D) calculated by the use of equation (25–3a) should be the same as the P (or D) calculated by using equation (25–2), except for small variations owing to political and commercial risks and transactions costs. When the interest rates are relatively low, equation (25–3a) can be approximated by:

$$P \text{ (or } D) \cong -(I^f - I^d) = (I^d - I^f) \qquad \textbf{(25–3b)}$$

Notice in Table 25–2 that the 30-day forward pound is selling at a discount of approximately −6.93 percent. IRP says that the 30-day interest rate in the United Kingdom must be approximately −6.93 percent (annualized) greater than the 30-day Treasury bill rate in the United States, as indicated by equation (25–3a).

Covered Interest Arbitrage

The rationale for IRP is provided by the *covered interest arbitrage* argument. This argument states that if the premiums (or discounts) in forward rates are not exactly equal to the interest rate differential, then arbitrage or riskless profits can be made.[5] The arbitrage mechanics involved here are substantially more complicated than the simple and triangular arbitrage discussed earlier. The covered interest arbitrage argument is explained by the following examples.

EXAMPLE

The pound spot and 30-day forward rates are $1.8695 and $1.8587, respectively, on December 31, 1991. The 30-day U.S. T-bill rate on December 31, 1991, expressed as an annual rate was approximately 3.68 percent. Assume now that the rate on 30-day United Kingdom instruments on December 31, 1991, was 9.14 percent, annualized. Given these data, does a riskless profit (or arbitrage) opportunity exist?

Step 1: Compute the forward premium using equation (25–2). $D = -6.93$ percent, as solved in a previous example.

Step 2: Compute the interest rate differential by equation (25–3).

$$D = \frac{.0368 - .0914}{1 + .0914} = \frac{-.0546}{1.0914} = -.0500 = -5.00\%$$

The premiums computed by the use of the two equations are not identical. IRP is violated. Arbitrage opportunities exist.

What can the arbitrager do to make a profit? A United States arbitrager can take the following steps:

---

[5]The interest rate differential is approximately equal to the right-hand side of equation (25–3b).

On December 31, 1991:

Step 1: Borrow 1 million pounds for 30 days from the United Kingdom money markets at a 9.14 percent annual rate of interest. For 30 days the interest is .76 percent.[6] On January 30, 1992, the arbitrager will need to repay 1 million pounds × 1.0076 = 1,007,600 pounds.

Step 2: Exchange the borrowed pounds into dollars at the spot exchange rate of $1.8695 per pound on December 31, 1991. He receives 1 million pounds × $1.8695 = $1,869,500.

Step 3: Invest the dollars in the United States money market for 30 days at 3.68 percent annual rate. For 30 days the rate is .31 percent. Receive, on January 30, 1992, $1,869,500 × 1.0031 = $1,875,233.

Step 4: Enter into a 30-day forward contract to buy 1,007,600 pounds on January 30, 1992. On January 30, 1992, the arbitrager will need to pay 1,007,600 × 1.8587 = $1,872,826 to receive the 1,007,600 pounds needed to repay the loan principal and interest on the 1 million pound loan taken in step 1.

On January 30, 1992, the arbitrage position is closed out as follows:

1. *Receive* $1,875,233 from the United States money market investment.

2. *Pay* $1,872,826 to the bank to *obtain* 1,007,600 pounds at a 1.8587 exchange rate.

3. *Pay* 1,007,600 pounds toward the principal and interest on the 1 million pound loan. ∎

On January 30, 1991, the United States arbitrager's net position is no liability and no assets. However, a net profit has been made of $2,407 ($1,875,233 − $1,872,826). None of the arbitrager's own funds were invested, there was no risk (since the arbitrager knew payments and receipts exactly on December 31, 1991), yet the arbitrager made a net profit of $2,407. This arbitrage was accomplished by *simultaneously borrowing* in one market, *investing* in another money market, and *covering* the exchange position in the forward exchange market. The entire process is known as covered interest arbitrage.

Note that the arbitrage profit was possible because the forward premium was not equal to the interest rate differential. Under such circumstances, arbitragers enter the market, increase the demand for the forward foreign currency, and drive up the price of the forward contract. The equilibrium price of the forward contract would then obey the IRP theory.

EXAMPLE

Assume that the interest rates indicated in the previous example are the actual rates prevailing in the United States and the United Kingdom. What should be the "correct" price of the forward contract, consistent with the interest rates in the two countries?

Step 1: Compute the discount using equation (25–3a).

$$D = \frac{.0368 - .0914}{1 + .0914} = -.0500 \text{ or } -5.00\%$$

Step 2: Using this premium in equation (25–2), compute the forward rate, *F*.

$$\frac{F - 1.8695}{1.8695} \times \frac{12}{1} \times 100 = -5.00\%$$

$$F = 1.8617$$ ∎

The example illustrates the technique for computing the *correct* price of the forward contract. If the quote is *less* than the computed price, the forward contract is *undervalued*. If the quote is *greater* than the computed price, the

[6]The 30-day rate, as an approximation, is equal to the annual rate × ¹⁄₁₂.

forward contract is *overvalued*. In our example, the forward contract is undervalued.

The forward markets are *efficient* is the sense that the quotes in the market represent the "correct" price of the contract. The markets' efficiency also implies that no profit can be made by computing the prices at every instant and buying the forward contract when they appear undervalued. Some minor deviations from the computed correct price may exist for short periods. These deviations, however, are such that after the transactions costs involved in the four separate arbitrage steps have been recognized, no net profit can be made. Numerous empirical studies attest to the efficiency of the forward markets.

In the previous example the correct price of the forward pound was computed under the assumption that the 30-day interest rate in the United Kingdom was 9 percent. All the other data for the examples were obtained from the actual market quotes in New York. We now ask, given the data on spot rate, forward rate, and the United States Treasury bill rate, can we compute the interest rate for the 30-day United Kingdom instrument? The answer is given in the next example.

EXAMPLE

The spot rate and forward rate for the pound are 1.8695 and 1.8587, respectively. The 30-day U.S. T-bill rate is 3.68 percent annualized. What is the 30-day United Kingdom rate?

Step 1: Compute the premium using equation (25–2). From previous computations,

$$D = -6.93\%$$

Step 2: Using equations (25–3a), solve for the unknown foreign interest rate.

$$-.0693 = \frac{.0368 - I^f}{1 + I^f}$$

$$I^f = .1140, \text{ or } 11.40\%$$ ■

Purchasing Power Parity

Long-run changes in exchange rates are influenced by international differences in inflation rates and the purchasing power of each nation's currency. Exchange rates of countries with high rates of inflation will tend to decline. According to the purchasing power parity (PPP) theory, exchange rates will tend to adjust in such a way that each currency will have the same purchasing power (especially in terms of internationally traded goods). Thus, if the United Kingdom experiences a 10 percent rate of inflation in a year that Germany experiences only a 6 percent rate, the U.K. currency (the pound) will be expected to decline in value approximately by 4 percent (10% − 6%) against the German currency (the Deutsche mark). More accurately, according to the PPP

$$S_{t+1} = S_t (1 + P_d)/(1 + P_f)^n$$

$$\cong S_t (1 + P_d - P_f)^n$$

where S_t = the direct exchange rate (units of domestic currency per unit of the foreign currency) at time t

P_f = the foreign inflation rate

P_d = the domestic inflation rate

n = number of time periods

Thus, if the beginning value of the mark was £0.40, with a 6 percent inflation rate in Germany and a 10 percent inflation rate in the United Kingdom, according to the PPP, the expected value of the Deutsche mark at the end of that year will be £.40 × [1.10/1.06], or £.4151.

The Law of One Price

Underlying the PPP relationship is the Law of One Price. This law is actually a proposition that in competitive markets where there are no transportation costs or barriers to trade, the same good sold in different countries sells for the same price if all the different prices are expressed in terms of the same currency. The idea is that the worth, in terms of marginal utility, of a good does not depend on where it is bought or sold. Because inflation will erode the purchasing power of any currency, its exchange rate must adhere to the PPP relationship if the Law of One Price is to hold over time. The following example illustrates the workings of this proposition.

EXAMPLE

Given the information above, assume that today a widget costs DM 100.00 in Germany and £40.00 in the United Kingdom. At the current exchange rate the Law of One Price appears to be holding since Germans can buy British widgets for DM 100.00 (× £.40/DM = £40.00), and the British can buy German widgets for £40.00 (÷ £.40/DM = DM 100.00). It is possible to determine how the exchange rate must change for the Law of One Price holds in *relative* form—for example, over the next year. We might expect that the exchange rate will change to reflect the decline in each currency's *domestic* purchasing power caused by next year's inflation. Today we know:

$$DM\ 100.00 = 1\ widget = £40.00$$

At this point, Germans would be indifferent between buying German widgets or British widgets. Given that inflation in the United Kingdom is expected to be 10 percent, one British widget can be expected to cost £44.00 = (£40.00)(1 + 0.10). At the current exchange rate, in one year British widgets would cost Germans DM 110.00.

$$DM\ 110.00 = 1\ widget = £44.00$$
$$= £44.00 ÷ £.40/DM$$

We will ignore the effects of German inflation for the moment. Germans would not buy British widgets for DM 110.00 in one year; they would buy German widgets for DM 100.00. Thus, *at the current exchange rate*, PPP would not hold. Germans might, however, be willing to continue spending DM 100.00 one year from now for British widgets. This could happen only if the DM were to strengthen against the pound. The new exchange rate suggested by the United Kingdom inflation is

$$DM\ 100.00 = 1\ widget = £44.00$$
$$(£/DM) = £44.00/DM\ 100.00 = £.44/DM$$

or:

$$(£/DM) = £.40 × (1 + P_{U.K.}) = £.40 × 1.10$$

Note that the **terms of trade** are important—Germans want the same amount of goods for the same number of DM before and after the British inflation. After the British inflation, the DM buys more pounds *at the new exchange rate*. Note also that the British also will be paying £40.00 per widget in *today's* pounds—all British goods will cost 10 percent more next year because of inflation. That is, although widgets will cost more in *nominal* terms next year in the United Kingdom, the *real* cost of widgets will be unchanged.

Now we will consider German inflation. Because the DM's purchasing power is also expected to decline over the next year, Germans would be willing to pay DM 106.00 (= DM 100.00 × (1 + P_{Ger}) for a British widget in one year because this is what they would have to pay for a German widget at that time. The new exchange rate becomes the same as the PPP estimate calculated earlier.

$$\text{DM } 106.00 = 1 \text{ widget} = £44.00$$
$$(£/\text{DM}) = £44.00/\text{DM } 106.00 = £.4151/\text{DM}$$

or:

$$(£/\text{DM}) = £.40 \times (1 + P_{\text{U.K.}})/(1 + P_{\text{Ger}}) = £.4151/\text{DM} \qquad ■$$

International Fisher Effect

According to the domestic Fisher effect (FE), interest (I) rates reflect the expected inflation rate (P) and a real rate of return (I_r). In other words

$$1 + I = (1 + P)(1 + I_r)$$

and

$$I_r = P + I_r + PI_r$$

While there is mixed empirical support for the FE internationally (IFE), it is widely thought that, for the major industrial countries, I_r is about 3 percent when a long-term period is considered. In such a case, with the previous assumption regarding inflation rates, interest rates in the United Kingdom and Germany would be (1 + 0.10)(1 + 0.03) − 1 or 13.3 percent and (1 + 0.06)(1 + 0.03) − 1 or 9.18 percent, respectively.

In addition, according to IRP, the expected premium for the Deutsche mark forward rate should be (0.133 − 0.0918)/1.0918 or 3.774 percent (rounded off). Starting with a value of £.40 gives us a one-year forward rate of £.40 (1.03774) = £.4151. As you may notice, this one-year forward rate is exactly the same as the PPP expected spot rate one year from today. In other words, if the real rate (I_r) is the same in both Germany and the United Kingdom and expectations regarding inflation rates hold true, today's one-year forward rate is likely to be the same as the future spot rate one year from now. Thus, in efficient markets, with rational expectations, the forward rate is an unbiased (not necessarily accurate) forecast of the future spot rate (UFR). These relationships between inflation and interest rates, and spot and forward rates are depicted in Figure 25–3.

The actual (not forecasted) future spot rate, as of today, is a *random variable*. In Figure 25–2 we indicate a possible hypothetical distribution of the pound spot rate on January 30, 1992. This distribution is what we, on December 31, 1991, subjectively believe the future spot rate to be. Notice in Figure 25–2 that the exchange rate may be as low as 1.6695 dollars or as high as 2.0695 dollars per pound with different probabilities.

Yet given the available information, we have done our best to forecast accurately. As we will see in the next section, such forecasts are useful in eliminating exchange risk for near-term international transactions, a process called *hedging*. However, there is no easy way to hedge long-term cash flows for international operations. As will be discussed in the next section and in the section on direct foreign investment, the problem is that the terms of trade *can* also change. Exchange rate changes can go beyond PPP-induced changes, leading to real exchange rate changes.

If PPP holds, and if there are no real exchange rate changes, currency gains and losses from nominal exchange rate changes will generally be offset over time by differences in relative rates of inflation between two countries, as we saw in the preceding widget example. Real exchange rate changes lead to real

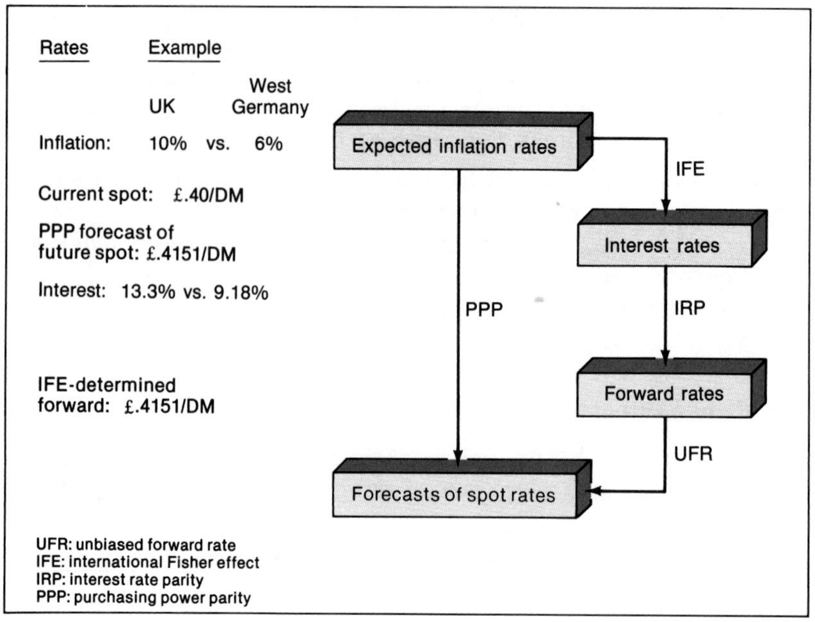

Rates
Example
UK
West Germany
Inflation: 10% vs. 6%
Current spot: £.40/DM
PPP forecast of future spot: £.4151/DM
Interest: 13.3% vs. 9.18%
IFE-determined forward: £.4151/DM
Expected inflation rates
IFE
Interest rates
IRP
Forward rates
UFR
PPP
Forecasts of spot rates
UFR: unbiased forward rate
IFE: international Fisher effect
IRP: interest rate parity
PPP: purchasing power parity

FIGURE 25–3. Efficient Foreign Exchange Market Relationships

exchange gains and losses: Consider the situation of Japanese auto makers selling subcompacts in the United States between 1986 and 1988. Assuming U.S. inflation to be about 5 percent annually over this period, and using actual 1986 and 1988 \$/yen exchange rates leads to the following situation:

	U.S. Price of Subcompact	*\$/Yen*	*Yen-Equivalent Price*
1986	\$10,000	.004988	¥2,004,811
1988	11,000	.007974	1,379,483

Because the yen strengthened far beyond what the PPP forecast would suggest, the yen's value increased in real terms. To the extent that revenues were dollar based and costs were yen based (the cars were made in Japan), the Japanese auto makers were at a competitive disadvantage relative to U.S. auto makers—their costs did not change while their yen-equivalent revenues fell by one-third. It is interesting that some of the Japanese auto makers have created *economic hedges* to control for this risk by building auto plants in the United States—these auto makers now have dollar-based revenues *and* dollar-based costs.

Exposure to Exchange Rate Risk

An asset denominated or valued in terms of foreign currency cash flows will lose value if that foreign currency declines in value. It can be said that such an asset is exposed to exchange rate risk. However, this possible decline in asset value may be offset by the decline in value of any liability that is also denominated or valued in terms of that foreign currency. Thus, a firm would normally be interested in its net exposed position (exposed assets − exposed liabilities) for each period in each currency.

While expected changes in exchange rates can often be included in the cost–benefit analysis relating to such transactions, in most cases there is an unexpected component in exchange rate changes and often the cost–benefit analysis for such transactions does not fully capture even the expected change in the exchange rate. For example, price increases for the foreign operations of many MNCs often have to be less than those necessary to offset exchange rate changes fully owing to the competitive pressures generated by local businesses, as the Japanese car makers found in 1988 for their U.S. sales.

Three measures of foreign exchange exposure are translation exposure, transactions exposure, and economic exposure. Translation exposure arises because the foreign operations of MNCs have accounting statements denominated in the local currency of the country in which the operation is located. For U.S. MNCs, the *reporting currency* for its consolidated financial statements is the dollar, so the assets, liabilities, revenues, and expenses of the foreign operations must be translated into dollars. International transactions often require a payment to be made or received in a foreign currency in the future, so these transactions are exposed to exchange-rate risk. Economic exposure exists over the long term because the value of future cash flows in the reporting currency (i.e., the dollar) from foreign operations are exposed to exchange rate risk. Indeed, the whole stream of future cash flows is exposed. The Japanese automaker situation highlights the effect of economic exposure on a MNC's revenue stream. The three measures of exposure now are examined more closely.

Translation Exposure

Foreign currency assets and liabilities are considered exposed if their foreign currency value for accounting purposes is to be translated into the parent company currency using the current exchange rate—the exchange rate in effect on the balance sheet date. Other assets and liabilities and equity amounts that are translated at the historic exchange rate—the rate in effect when these items were first recognized in the company's accounts—are not considered to be exposed. The rate (current or historic) used to translate various accounts depends on the translation procedure used. For U.S. companies, Financial Accounting Standard Board (FASB) Statement No. 52 specifies the translation procedure to be used.

While transaction exposure can result in exchange rate change-related losses and gains that are realized and have an impact on both reported and taxable income, translation exposure results in exchange rate losses and gains that are reflected in the company's accounting books, but are unrealized and have little or no impact on taxable income. Thus, if financial markets are efficient and managerial goals are consistent with owner wealth maximization (and if agency and signaling costs are negligible), a firm should not have to waste real resources hedging against possible paper losses caused by translation exposure. However, if there are significant agency or information costs or if markets are not efficient (that is, if translation losses and gains raise information costs for investors, or if they endanger the firm's ability to satisfy debt or other covenants, or if the evaluation of the firm's managers depends on translated accounting data), a firm may indeed find it economical to hedge against translation losses or gains.

Transactions Exposure

Receivables, payables, and fixed-price sales or purchase contracts are examples of foreign currency transactions whose monetary value was fixed at a time different from the time when these transactions are actually completed. *Transactions exposure* is a term that describes the net contracted foreign currency transactions for which the settlement amounts are subject to changing exchange rates. A company normally must set up an additional reporting system to track transactions exposure, because several of these amounts are not recognized in the accounting books of the firm.

Exchange risk may be neutralized or hedged by a change in the asset and liability position in the foreign currency. An exposed asset position (e.g., an account receivable) can be *hedged* or *covered* by creating a liability of the same amount and maturity denominated in the foreign currency (e.g., a forward contract to *sell* the foreign currency). An exposed liability position (e.g., an account payable) can be covered by acquiring assets of the same amount and maturity in the foreign currency (e.g., a forward contract to *buy* the foreign currency). The objective is to have a zero net asset position in the foreign currency. This eliminates exchange risk, since the loss (gain) in the liability (asset) is exactly offset by the gain (loss) in the value of the asset (liability) when the foreign currency appreciates (depreciates). Two popular forms of hedge are the money market hedge and the exchange market or forward market hedge. In both types of hedge the *amount* and the *duration* of the asset (liability) positions are *matched*. Note as you read the next two subsections how IRP theory assures that each hedge provides the same cover.

Money-Market Hedge

In a money-market hedge, the exposed position in a foreign currency is offset by borrowing or lending in the money market. Consider the case of the American firm with a net liability position (i.e., the amount it owes) of 3,000 pounds. The firm knows the exact amount of its pound liability in 30 days, but it does not know the liability in dollars. Assume that the 30-day money market rates in both the United States and United Kingdom are, respectively, 1 percent for lending and 1.5 percent for borrowing. The American business can take the following steps:

Step 1: Calculate the present value of the foreign currency liability (3,000 pounds) that is due in 30 days. Use the money market rate applicable for the foreign country (1 percent in the United Kingdom). The present value of 3,000 pounds is 2,970.30 pounds, computed as follows: 3000/(1 + .01).

Step 2: Exchange dollars on today's spot market to obtain the 2,970.30 pounds. The dollar amount needed today is $5,552.97 (2970.30 × $1.8695).

Step 3: Invest 2,970.30 pounds in a United Kingdom one-month money market instrument. This investment will compound to exactly 3,000 pounds in one month. The future liability of 3,000 pounds is covered by the 2,970.30 pounds investment.[7]

Note: If the American business does not own this amount today, it can borrow $5,552.97 from the United States money market at the going rate of 1.5 percent. In 30 days the American business will need to repay $5,636.26 [$5,552.97 × 1 + .015].

Assuming that the American business borrows the money, its management may base its calculations on the knowledge that the British goods, on delivery in 30 days, will cost it $5,636.26. The British business will receive 3,000 pounds. The American business need not wait for the future spot exchange rate to be revealed. On today's date, the future dollar payment of the contract is known with certainty. This certainty helps the American business in making its pricing and financing decisions.

Many businesses hedge in the money market. The firm needs to borrow (creating a liability) in one market, lend or invest in the other money market, and use the spot exchange market on today's date. The mechanics of *covering a net asset position* in the foreign currency are the exact *reverse* of the mechanics of covering the *liability position*. With a net asset position in pounds: Borrow in the United Kingdom money market in pounds, convert to dollars on the spot exchange market, invest in the United States money market. When the net assets

[7]Observe that 2970.30 pounds × (1 + .01) = 3000 pounds.

converted into pounds (i.e., when the firm receives what it is owed), pay off the loan and the interest. The cost of hedging in the money market is the cost of doing business in three different markets. Information about the three markets is needed, and analytical calculations of the type indicated here must be made.

Many small and infrequent traders find the cost of the money market hedge prohibitive, owing especially to the need for information about the market. These traders use the exchange or the forward market hedge, which has very similar hedging benefits.

The Forward Market Hedge

The forward market provides a second possible hedging mechanism. It works as follows: A net asset (liability) position is covered by a liability (asset) in the forward market. Consider again the case of the American firm with a liability of 3,000 pounds that must be paid in 30 days. The firm may take the following steps to cover its liability position.

Step 1: Buy a forward contract today to purchase 3,000 pounds in 30 days. The 30-day forward rate is, $1.8587 per pound.

Step 2: On the thirtieth day pay the banker $5,576.10 (3000 × $1.8587) and collect 3,000 pounds. Pay these pounds to the British supplier.

By the use of the forward contract the American business knows the exact worth of the future payment in dollars ($5,576.10). The exchange risk in pounds is totally eliminated by the net asset position in the forward pounds. In the case of a net asset exposure, the steps open to the American firm are the exact opposite: Sell the pounds forward, and on the future day receive and deliver the pounds to collect the agreed-on dollar amount.

The use of the forward market as a hedge against exchange risk is simple and direct. That is, match the liability or asset position against an offsetting position in the forward market. The forward market hedge is relatively easy to implement. The firm directs its banker that it needs to buy or sell a foreign currency on a future date, and the banker gives forward quote.

The forward hedge and the money market hedge give an identical future dollar payment (or receipt) if the forward contracts are priced according to the interest rate parity theory. The alert student may have noticed that the dollar payments in the money market hedge and the forward market hedge examples were, respectively, $5,536.26 and $5,576.10. Recall from our previous discussions that in efficient markets, the forward contracts do indeed conform to IRP theory. However, the numbers in our example are not identical because the forward rate used in the forward hedge is not exactly equal to the interest rates in the money market hedge.

Currency Future and Option Contracts

The forward market hedge is not adequate for some types of exposure. If the foreign currency asset or liability position occurs on a date for which forward quotes are not available, the forward hedge cannot be accomplished. In certain cases the forward hedge may cost more than the money market hedge. In these cases a corporation with a large amount of exposure may prefer the money market hedge. In addition to forward and money market hedges, a company can also hedge its exposure by buying (or selling) some relatively new instruments —foreign currency futures contracts and foreign currency options. Although futures contracts are similar to forward contracts in that they provide fixed prices for the *required* delivery of foreign currency at maturity, options *permit* fixed (strike) price foreign currency transactions anytime before maturity. Futures contracts and options differ from forward contracts in that, unlike forward contracts, which are customized regarding amount and maturity date, futures and options are traded in standard amounts with standard maturity dates. In addition, although forward contracts are written by banks, futures and options are traded on organized exchanges, and individual traders deal with the exchange-based clearing organization rather than with each other. The purchase of futures requires the fulfillment of margin requirements (about 5 to 10 percent of the face amount), whereas the purchase of forward contracts requires only good credit standing with a bank. The purchase of options requires an immediate outlay that reflects a premium above the strike price and an outlay equal to the strike price when and if the option is exercised.

Economic Exposure

The economic value of a company can vary in response to exchange rate changes. This change in value may be caused by a rate-change-induced decline in the level of expected cash flows and/or by an increase in the riskiness of these cash flows. *Economic exposure* refers to the overall impact of exchange rate changes on the value of the firm and includes not only the strategic impact of changes in competitive relationships that arise from exchange rate changes, but also the economic impact of transactions exposure and, if any, of translation exposure.

Economic exposure to exchange rate changes depends on the competitive structure of the markets for a firm's inputs and its outputs and how these markets are influenced by changes in exchange rates. This influence, in turn, depends on several economic factors, including price elasticities of the products, the degree of competition from foreign markets and direct (through prices) and indirect (through incomes) impact of exchange rate changes on these markets. Assessing the economic exposure faced by a particular firm thus depends on the ability to understand and model the structure of the markets for its major inputs (purchases) and outputs (sales).

A company need not engage in any cross-border business activity to be exposed to exchange rate changes, because product and financial markets in most countries are related and influenced to a large extent by the same global forces. The output of a company engaged in business activity only within one country may be competing with imported products, or it may be competing for its inputs with other domestic and foreign purchasers. For example, a Canadian chemical company that did no cross-border business nevertheless found that its profit margins depended directly on the United States dollar–Japanese yen exchange rate. The company used coal as an input in its production process, and the Canadian price of coal was heavily influenced by the extent to which the Japanese bought United States coal, which in turn depended on the dollar–yen exchange rate.

Although translation exposure need not be managed, it might be useful for a firm to manage its transaction and economic exposures because they affect firm value directly. In most companies, transaction exposure is generally tracked and managed by the office of the corporate treasurer. Economic exposure is difficult to define in operating terms, and very few companies manage it actively. In most companies, economic exposure is generally considered part of the strategic planning process, rather than as a treasurer's or finance function.

Multinational Working-Capital Management

The basic principles of working-capital management for a multinational corporation are similar to those for a domestic firm. However, tax and exchange rate factors are additional considerations for the MNC. For an MNC with subsidiaries in many countries, the optimal decisions in the management of working capital are made by considering the company as a whole. The global or centralized financial decision for an MNC is superior to the set of independent optimal decisions for the subsidiaries. This is the *control* problem of the MNC. If the individual subsidiaries make decisions that are best for them individually, the consolidation of such decisions may not be best for the MNC as a whole. To effect *global* management, sophisticated computerized models—incorporating many variables for each subsidiary—are solved to provide the best overall decision for the MNC.

Before considering the components of working-capital management, we examine two techniques that are useful in the management of a wide variety of working-capital components.

Leading and Lagging

Two important risk-reduction techniques for many working-capital problems are called **leading** and **lagging.** Often, forward and money market hedges are not available to eliminate exchange risk. Under such circumstances, leading and lagging may be used to *reduce* exchange risk.

Recall that a net asset (long) position is not desirable in a weak or potentially depreciating currency. If a firm has a net asset position in such a currency, it should expedite the disposal of the asset. The firm should get rid of the asset earlier than it otherwise would have, or *lead*, and convert the funds into assets in a relatively stronger currency. By the same reasoning, the firm should *lag*, or delay the collection against a net asset position in a strong currency. If the firm has a net liability (short) position in the weak currency, then it should delay the payment against the liability, or lag, until the currency depreciates. In the case of an appreciating or strong foreign currency and a net liability position, the firm should lead the payments—that is, reduce the liabilities earlier than it would otherwise have.

These principles are useful in the management of working capital of an MNC. They cannot, however, eliminate the foreign exchange risk. When exchange rates change continuously, it is almost impossible to guess whether or when the currency will depreciate or appreciate. This is why the risk of exchange rate changes cannot be eliminated. Nevertheless, the reduction of risk, or the increasing of gain from exchange rate changes, via the lead and lag is useful for cash management, accounts receivable management, and short-term liability management.

Cash Management and Positioning of Funds

Positioning of funds takes on an added importance in the international context. Funds may be transferred from a subsidiary of the MNC in country A to another subsidiary in country B such that the foreign exchange exposure and the tax liability of the MNC as a whole are minimized. It bears repeating that, owing to the *global strategy* of the MNC, the tax liability of the subsidiary in country A may be greater than it would otherwise have been, but the overall tax payment for all units of the MNC is minimized.

The transfer of funds among subsidiaries and the parent company is done by royalties, fees, and transfer pricing. A *transfer price* is the price a subsidiary or a parent company charges other companies that are part of the MNC for its goods or services. A parent that wishes to transfer funds from a subsidiary in a depreciating-currency country may charge a higher price on the goods and services sold to this subsidiary by the parent or by subsidiaries from strong-currency countries.

Centralized cash management of all the affiliates at the global level, achieved with the help of computer models, reduces both the overall cost of holding cash and the foreign exchange exposure of the MNC as a whole with respect to cash. The excess cash balance of one subsidiary is transferred to a cash-deficit subsidiary in the form of a loan. The optimal holdings of cash in different currencies are calculated in a manner similar to the optimal portfolio problem discussed in Chapter 13.

International Financing and Capital Structure Decisions

An MNC has access to many more financing sources than a domestic firm. It can tap not only the financing sources in its home country that are available to its domestic counterparts, but also sources in the foreign countries in which it operates. Host countries often provide access to low-cost subsidized financing to attract foreign investment. In addition, the MNC may enjoy preferential credit standards because of its size and investor preference for its home currency. An MNC may be able to access third-country capital markets—countries in which it does not operate but which may have large, well-functioning capital markets. Finally, an MNC can also access external currency markets: Eurodollar, Eurocurrency, or Asiandollar markets. These external markets are unregulated, and because of their lower spread, can offer very attractive rates for financing *and* for investments. With the increasing availability of interest rate and currency swaps, a firm can raise funds in the lowest-cost maturities and currencies and swap them into funds with the maturity and currency denomination it requires. Because of its ability to tap a larger number of financial markets, the MNC may have a lower cost of capital, and because it may better be able to avoid the problems or limitations of any one financial market, it may have a more continuous access to external finance compared to a domestic company.

Access to national financial markets is regulated by governments. For example, in the United States, access to capital markets is governed by SEC regulations. Access to Japanese capital markets is governed by regulations issued by the Ministry of Finance. Some countries have extensive regulations; other countries have relatively open markets. These regulations may differ depending on the legal residency terms of the company raising funds. A company that cannot use its local subsidiary to raise funds in a given market will be treated as foreign. In order to increase their visibility in a foreign capital market, a number of MNCs are now listing their equities on the stock exchanges of many of these countries.

The external currency markets are predominantly centered in Europe, and about 80 percent of their value is denominated in terms of the U.S. dollar. Thus, most external currency markets can be characterized as Eurodollar markets. Such markets consist of an active short-term money market and an intermediate-term capital market with maturities ranging up to 15 years and averaging about 7 to 9 years. The intermediate-term market consists of the Eurobond and the Syndicated Eurocredit markets. Eurobonds are usually issued as unregistered bearer bonds and generally tend to have higher flotation costs but lower coupon rates compared to similar bonds issued in the United States. A Syndicated Eurocredit loan is simply a large term loan that involves contributions by a number of lending banks. Most large U.S. banks are active in the external currency markets.

In arriving at its capital-structure decisions, an MNC has to consider a number of factors. First, the capital structure of its local affiliates is influenced by local norms regarding capital structure in that industry and in that country. Local norms for companies in the same industry can differ considerably from country to country. Second, the local affiliate capital structure must also reflect corporate attitudes toward exchange rate and political risk in that country, which would normally lead to higher levels of local debt and other local capital. Third, local affiliate capital structure must reflect home country requirements with regard to the company's consolidated capital structure. Finally, the optimal MNC capital structure should reflect its wider access to financial markets, its ability to diversify economic and political risks, and its other advantages over domestic companies.

Direct Foreign Investment

An MNC often makes direct foreign investments abroad in the form of plants and equipment. The decision process for this type of investment is very similar to the capital-budgeting decision in the domestic context—with some additional twists. Most real-world capital-budgeting decisions are made with uncertain future outcomes. Recall that a capital-budgeting decision has three major components: the estimation of the future cash flows (including the initial cost of the proposed investment), the estimation of the risk in these cash flows, and the choice of the proper discount rate. We will assume that the NPV criterion is appropriate as we examine (1) the risks associated with direct foreign investment and (2) factors to be considered in making the investment decision that may be unique to the international scene.

Risks in Direct Foreign Investments

Risks in domestic capital budgeting arise from two sources: business risk and financial risk. The international capital-budgeting problem incorporates these risks as well as political risk and exchange risk.

Business Risk and Financial Risk

International business risk is due to the response of business to economic conditions in the foreign country. Thus, the U.S. MNC needs to be aware of the business climate in both the United States and the foreign country. Additional business risk is due to competition from other MNCs, local businesses, and imported goods. Financial risk refers to the risks introduced in the profit stream by the firm's financial structure. The financial risks of foreign operations are not very different from those of domestic operations.

Political Risk

Political risk arises because the foreign subsidiary conducts its business in a political system different from that of the home country. Many foreign governments, especially those in the Third World, are less stable than the U.S. government. A change in a country's political setup frequently brings a change in policies with respect to businesses—and especially with respect to foreign businesses. An extreme change in policy might involve nationalization or even outright expropriation of certain businesses. These are the political risks of conducting business abroad. A business with no investment in plants and equipment is less susceptible to these risks. Some examples of political risk are listed below:

1. Expropriation of plants and equipment without compensation
2. Expropriation with minimal compensation that is below actual market value
3. Nonconvertibility of the subsidiary's foreign earnings into the parent's currency—the problem of *blocked funds*
4. Substantial changes in the laws governing taxation

5. Governmental controls in the foreign country regarding the sale price of the products, wages, and compensation to personnel, hiring of personnel, making of transfer payments to the parent, and local borrowing

6. Some governments require certain amounts of local equity participation in the business. Some require that the majority of the equity participation belong to their country.

All these controls and governmental actions introduce risks in the cash flows of the investment to the parent company. These risks must be considered before making the foreign investment decision. The MNC may decide against investing in countries with risks of types 1 and 2. Other risks can be borne—provided that the returns from the foreign investments are high enough to compensate for them. Insurance against some types of political risks may be purchased from private insurance companies or from the U.S. government Overseas Private Investment Corporation. It should be noted that although an MNC cannot protect itself against all foreign political risks, political risks are also present in domestic business.

Exchange Risk

The exposure of the fixed assets is best measured by the effects of the exchange rate changes on the firm's future earnings stream: that being *economic* exposure rather than *translation* exposure. For instance, changes in the exchange rate may adversely affect sales by making competing imported goods cheaper. Changes in the cost of goods sold may result if some components are imported and their price in the foreign currency changes because of exchange rate fluctuations. The thrust of these examples is that the effect of exchange rate changes on income statement items should be properly measured to evaluate exchange risk. Finally, exchange risk affects the dollar-denominated profit stream of the parent company, whether or not it affects the foreign-currency profits.

If the foreign sales volume is expected to be low, the MNC may consider setting up a *sales office* in the foreign country. The product may be exported to the foreign country from production facilities in the home country or from some other foreign subsidiary. An NPV calculation may now be employed. The acceptance of this scheme is ensured, because no direct capital investment is needed. If the estimated sales levels are high enough that the establishment of a plant in the foreign country appears profitable, owing to the potential savings in the transportation costs, yet the NPV of the DFI is negative, the MNC may consider *licensing* or *an affiliate arrangement* with a local company. The MNC provides the technology, and the interested domestic firm finances and sets up the plant. The MNC does not bear the risks of a DFI, but receives a royalty payment from the sales of the affiliate company instead.

SUMMARY

The growth of our global economy, the increasing number of multinational corporations, and the increase in foreign trade itself underscore the importance of the study of international finance.

Exchange rate mechanics are discussed in the context of the prevailing floating rates. Under this system, exchange rates between currencies vary in an apparently random fashion in accordance with the supply and demand conditions in the exchange market. Important economic factors affecting the level of exchange rates include the relative economic strengths of the countries involved, the balance-of-payments mechanism, and the countries' monetary policies. Several important exchange-rate terms are introduced. These include the asked and the bid rates, which represent the selling and buying rates of currencies. The direct quote is the units of home currency per unit of foreign currency, and the indirect quote is the reciprocal of the direct quote. Cross-rate computations reflect the exchange rate between two foreign currencies. Finally, simple arbitrage for indirect quote and triangular arbitrage for cross rates are shown to hold. The efficiency of spot exchange markets implies that no arbitrage (riskless) profits can be made by buying and selling currencies in different markets.

The forward exchange market provides a valuable service by quoting rates for the delivery of foreign currencies in the future. The foreign currency is said to sell at a premium (discount) forward from the spot rate when the forward rate is greater (less) than the spot rate, in direct quotation. The computation of the percent-per-annum deviation of the forward from the spot rate was used to demonstrate the interest rate parity (IRP) theory, which states that the forward contract sells at a discount or premium from the spot rates, owing solely to interest rate differential between the two countries. The IRP theory was shown to hold by means of the covered interest arbitrage argument. In addition, the influences of purchasing power parity (PPP) and the international Fisher effect (IFE) in determining the exchange rate are discussed. In rational and efficient markets, forward rates are unbiased forecasts of future spot rates that are consistent with the PPP.

Exchange risk exists because the exact spot rate that prevails on a future date is not known with certainty today. The concept of exchange risk is applicable to a wide variety of businesses including export–import firms and firms involved in making direct foreign investments or international investments in securities. Exchange exposure is a measure of exchange risk. There are different ways of measuring the foreign exposure including the net asset (net liability) measurement. Different strategies are open to businesses to counter the exposure to this risk including the money market hedge, the forward market hedge, futures contracts, and options. Each involves different costs.

In discussing working-capital management in an international environment we find leading and lagging techniques useful in minimizing exchange risks and increasing profitability. In addition, funds positioning is a useful tool for reducing exchange risk exposure. The MNC may have a lower cost of capital because it has access to a larger set of financial markets than a domestic company. In addition to the home, host, and third-country financial markets, the MNC can tap the rapidly growing external currency markets. In making capital-structure decisions, the MNC must consider political and exchange risks and host and home county capital-structure norms.

The complexities encountered in the direct foreign investment decision include the usual sources of risk—business and financial—and additional risks associated with fluctuating exchange rates and political factors. Political risk is due to differences in political climates, institutions, and processes between the home country and abroad. Under these conditions the estimation of future cash flows and the choice of the proper discount rates are more complicated than for the domestic investment situation. Rejection of a DFI proposal may lead either to the setting up of a sales office abroad or to an affiliate arrangement with a foreign company.

STUDY QUESTIONS

25-1. What additional factors are encountered in international as compared with domestic financial management? Discuss each briefly.

25-2. What different types of businesses operate in the international environment? Why are the techniques and strategies available to these firms different?

25-3. What is meant by *arbitrage profits?*

25-4. What are the markets and mechanics involved in generating (a) simple arbitrage profits, (b) triangular arbitrage profits, (c) covered interest arbitrage profits?

25-5. How do the purchasing power parity, interest rate parity, and the Fisher effect explain the relationships between the current spot rate, the future spot rate, and the forward rate?

25-6. What is meant by (a) exchange risk, (b) political risk?

25-7. How can exchange risk be measured?

25-8. What are the differences between transaction, translation and economic exposures? Should all of them be ideally reduced to zero?

25-9. What steps can a firm take to reduce exchange risk? Indicate at least two different techniques.

25-10. How are the forward market and the money market hedges affected? What are the major differences between these two types of hedges?

25-11. In the New York exchange market, the forward rate for the Indian currency, the rupee, is not quoted. If you were exposed to exchange risk in rupees, how could you cover your position?

25-12. Compare and contrast the use of forward contracts, futures contracts, and options to reduce foreign exchange exposure. When is each instrument most appropriate?

25-13. Indicate two working-capital management techniques that are useful for international businesses to reduce exchange risk and potentially increase profits.

25-14. How do the financing sources available to an MNC differ from those available to a domestic firm? What do these differences mean for the company's cost of capital?

25-15. What risks are associated with direct foreign investment? How do these risks differ from those encountered in domestic investment?

25-16. How is the direct foreign investment decision made? What are the inputs to this decision process? Are the inputs more complicated than those to the domestic investment problem? If so, why?

25-17. A corporation desires to enter a particular foreign market. The DFI analysis indicates that a direct investment in the plant in the foreign country is not profitable. What other course of action can the company take to enter the foreign market? What are the important considerations?

25-18. What are the reasons for the acceptance of a sales office or licensing arrangement when the DFI itself is not profitable?

SELF-TEST PROBLEMS

The data for self-test Problems ST–1 and ST–2 are given in the following table:

Selling Quotes for the German Mark in New York

Country	Contract	$/Foreign Currency
Germany — mark	Spot	.3893
	30-day	.3910
	90-day	.3958

ST-1. You own $10,000. The dollar rate on the German mark is $2,5823/DM. The German mark rate is given in the table above. Are arbitrage profits possible? Set up an arbitrage scheme with your capital. What is the gain (loss) in dollars?

ST-2. If the interest rates on the 30-day instruments in the United States and Germany are 14 and 10 percent (annualized), respectively, what is the correct price of the 30-day forward mark?

The data for Study Problems 25–1A through 25–11A are given in the following table:

Selling Quotes for Foreign Currencies in New York

Country	Contract	$/Foreign Currency
Canada—dollar	Spot	.8437
	30-day	.8417
	90-day	.8395
Japan—yen	Spot	.004684
	30-day	.004717
	90-day	.004781
Switzerland—franc	Spot	.5139
	30-day	.5169
	90-day	.5315

25–1A. An American business needs to pay (a) 10,000 Canadian dollars, (b) 2 million yen, and (c) 50,000 Swiss francs to businesses abroad. What are the dollar payments to the respective countries?

25–2A. An American business pays $10,000, $15,000, and $20,000 to suppliers in, respectively, Japan, Switzerland, and Canada. How much, in local currencies, do the suppliers receive?

25–3A. Compute the indirect quote for the spot and forward Canadian dollar, yen, and Swiss franc contracts.

25–4A. The spreads on the contracts as a percent of the asked rates are 2 percent for yen, 3 percent for Canadian dollars, and 5 percent for Swiss francs. Show, in a table similar to the one above, the bid rates for the different spot and forward rates.

25–5A. You own $10,000. The dollar rate in Tokyo is 216.6743. The yen rate in New York is given in the previous table. Are arbitrage profits possible? Set up an arbitrage scheme with your capital. What is the gain (loss) in dollars?

25–6A. Compute the Canadian dollar/yen and the yen/Swiss franc spot rate from the data in the table above.

25–7A. Compute the simple premium (discount) on the 30-day and 90-day yen, Swiss franc, and Canadian dollar quotes. Tabulate the percent-per-annum deviations as in Table 25–2.

25–8A. Assume that the interest rate on the United States 30-day T-bill is 15 percent (annualized). The corresponding Canadian rate is 18 percent. The spot and the forward rates are shown in the previous table. Can an American trader make arbitrage profits? If the trader had $100,000 to invest, indicate the steps he or she would take. What would be the net profit? (Ignore transactions and other costs.)

25–9A. If the interest rates on the 30-day instruments in the United States and Japan are 15 and 12 percent (annualized), respectively, what is the correct price of the 30-day forward yen? Use the spot rate from the table.

25–10A. The 30-day T-bill rate in the United States is 15 percent annualized. Using the 30-day forward quotes, compute the 30-day interest rates in Canada, Switzerland, and Japan.

The data for Study Problems 25–1B through 25–11B are given in the following table:

Selling Quotes for Foreign Currencies in New York

Country	Contract	$/Foreign Currency
Canada—dollar	Spot	.8439
	30-day	.8410
	90-day	.8390
Japan—yen	Spot	.004680
	30-day	.004720
	90-day	.004787
Switzerland—franc	Spot	.5140
	30-day	.5179
	90-day	.5335

25–1B. An American business needs to pay (a) 15,000 Canadian dollars, (b) 1.5 million yen, and (c) 55,000 Swiss francs to businesses abroad. What are the dollar payments to the respective countries?

25–2B. An American business pays $20,000, $5,000, and $15,000 to suppliers in, respectively, Japan, Switzerland, and Canada. How much, in local currencies, do the suppliers receive?

25–3B. Compute the indirect quote for the spot and forward Canadian dollar, yen, and Swiss franc contracts.

25–4B. The spreads on the contracts as a percent of the asked rates are 4 percent for yen, 3 percent for Canadian dollars, and 6 percent for Swiss francs. Show, in a table similar to the previous one, the bid rates for the different spot and forward rates.

25–5B. You own $10,000. The dollar rate in Tokyo is 216.6752. The yen rate in New York is given in the table above. Are arbitrage profits possible? Set up an arbitrage scheme with your capital. What is the gain (loss) in dollars?

25–6B. Compute the Canadian dollar/yen and the yen/Swiss franc spot rate from the data in the table above.

25–7B. Compute the simple premium (discount) on the 30-day and 90-day yen, Swiss franc, and Canadian dollar quotes. Tabulate the percent-per-annum deviations as in Table 25–2.

25–8B. Assume that the interest rate on the United States 30-day T-bill is 14 percent (annualized). The corresponding Canadian rate is 17 percent. The spot and the forward rates are shown in the table above. Can an American trader make arbitrage profits? If the trader had $100,000 to invest, indicate the steps he or she would take. What would be the net profit? (Ignore transactions and other costs.)

25–9B. If the interest rates on the 30-day instruments in the United States and Japan are 16 and 13 percent (annualized), respectively, what is the correct price of the 30-day forward yen? Use the spot rate from the table.

25–10B. The 30-day T-bill rate in the United States is 16 percent annualized. Using the 30-day forward quotes, compute the 30-day interest rates in Canada, Switzerland, and Japan.

SELF-TEST SOLUTIONS

SS–1. The German rate is 2.5823 marks/$1, while the (indirect) New York rate is 1/.3893 = 2.5687 marks/$.

Assuming no transaction costs, the rates between German and New York are out of line. Thus, arbitrage profits are possible.

Step 1: Because the mark is cheaper in Germany, buy $10,000 worth of marks in Germany. The number of marks purchased would be

$$\$10,000 \times 2.5823 = 25,823 \text{ marks}$$

Step 2: Simultaneously sell the marks in New York at the prevailing rate. The amount received upon the sale of the marks would be:

$$25,823 \text{ marks} \times \$.3893/\text{mark} = \$10,052.89$$

$$\text{net gain is } \$10,052.89 - \$10,000 = \underline{\$52.89}$$

SS–2. *Step 1:* Compute the percent-per-annum premium on the forward rate using equation (25–3a):

$$P = \frac{I^d - I^f}{1 + I^f} \qquad \qquad \textbf{(25–3a)}$$

where I^d = the annualized interest rate on a domestic instrument having the same maturity as the forward contract

I^f = the annualized interest rate on a foreign instrument having the same maturity as the forward contract

Thus,

$$P = \frac{.14 - .10}{1 + .10} = \frac{.04}{1.10} = 0.0364$$

Step 2: Using this premium in equation (25–2), compute the forward rate F:

$$\frac{F - S}{S} \times \frac{12}{n} \times 100 = P \qquad \qquad \textbf{(25–2)}$$

where F = the forward rate, direct quote

S = the spot rate, direct quote

n = the number of months of the forward contract

P = the annualized percent premium

$$\frac{F - 0.3893}{0.3893} \times \frac{12}{1} \times 100 = 0.364$$

$$\frac{1200F - 467.16}{0.3893} = .0364$$

$$1200F - 467.16 = 1.417052$$

$$F = .3905$$

Thus the correct price of the forward rate is .3905.

CHAPTER 26

Financial Management: A Small-Firm Perspective

Small Versus Large: Is There a Difference? ● Capital Budgeting in the Small Firm ● Financing of the Small Firm

Small companies have been a major driving force of the American economy, creating most of the new jobs and technological innovation. The majority of the more than 20 million new jobs added during the past decade have come from small businesses. Practically every innovation in the computer industry since the development of the mainframe has been started or commercialized by companies financed by venture capitalists. Examples include the microprocessor, the personal computer, the minicomputer, workstations, the supercomputer, and most of the accompanying software. Large American corporations have lost their leadership in key industries ranging from consumer electronics to steel. Management flexibility has become more important than the long-touted economies of scale in research, production, and marketing.

As evidence of the new role of the small firm, consider the fact that in 1988 large firms were more profitable, as measured by the return on equity, than small firms in only four of the 67 industries represented by the *Business Week* Top 1000. Some of the smaller steelmakers can produce a ton of steel with about one-third of the labor used by their larger competitors. In computing, the smaller firms can develop a new computer three to five times faster than can the "giants." Even management guru Peter Drucker, who often used General Motors as an example of a successful large corporation, now believes that large companies have essentially outlived their usefulness, noting that most of the recent growth and innovation in American business has come from midsize companies that employ 200 to 4,000 people. Drucker states that, "A penalty of size is that you try to do everything, and no one can do everything well."[1]

Although "small is beautiful," in the eyes of many, there are some skeptics. Some would argue that small firms will not be able to withstand the increasing global competition. The large corporation, combined with government support, is thought to be the key to long-term competitiveness. Smaller companies are thought to have many limitations. For example, they could not commit money to

[1]Peter Drucker quoted by John A. Byrne, "Is Your Company Too Big?" *Business Week*, March 27, 1989, pp. 84–94.

AT&T Chopping up six major businesses into 19 or more smaller groups. Goals: eliminate turf wars, deemphasize management by committee, encourage individual risk-taking, improve focus on individual markets	
GENERAL ELECTRIC Chairman Jack Welch attacks "big company encumbrances" by cutting management layers between factory floor to executive suite from nine to as few as four. Staff should be "facilitator, adviser, and partner," not "monitors, checkers, kibitzers, approvers"	
GENERAL MOTORS Chairman Roger Smith vows to dismantle entrenched bureaucracies by stripping out layers of management; seeks ideas from customers and suppliers; develops technological advances through acquisitions	**FIGURE 26–1**
HEWLETT-PACKARD To give managers "self-direction and ownership," President John Young divvies up the company's businesses into 50 units with own profit-loss, planning, and support responsibilities	When Big Companies Try to Act Small
McDONALD'S Building on structure as far-flung collection of independent entrepreneurs; boasts a vice-president for individuality to "make the company feel small" through incentives and awards; autonomous franchisees credited with such innovations as McD.L.T. and Egg McMuffin	
Source: John A. Byrne, "Is Your Company Too Big?" *Business Week*, March 27, 1989, p. 88.	

a project that requires five years to complete. Some undertakings inherently necessitate size and staying power. Still, the corporate restructuring that is pervasive in the American economy is largely an effort to reduce the many layers of middle management that have developed in the large corporations and to encourage managers to "think small." Examples of large companies trying to gain the advantages of smallness are presented in Figure 26–1.[2]

The debate about size will long be with us, but the fact remains that small firms are a major part of the economy and deserve some of our attention as we study finance. This chapter examines financial management from the perspective of the owner-manager of a small firm. We first identify financial attributes often characteristic of the small business. Next, we consider the capital-budgeting issue for the small firm. Finally, we look at an overview of the financing of small firms.

Small Versus Large: Is There a Difference?

We might reasonably question the rationale for studying small business apart from large business. That is, is the financial management of a small firm different from that of a large firm?

A study conducted by Walker and Petty evaluated the financial differences between large and small firms, as measured by various financial ratios.[3] To compare these two groups, financial data were gathered for a sample of growth manufacturing firms with sales not exceeding $5 million. The small firm sample consisted of businesses that had filed prospectuses with state securities regulatory bodies in an effort to "go public." Thus, Walker and Petty were looking at operations involving successful closely held companies that were trying to tap the public equity markets. Similar data for a sample of large companies in the same industries were also compiled. The results are compared in Table 26–1.

In examining Table 26–1 we see that there clearly are some differences between small and large firms. The most prominent difference is the disparity in dividend policies. For example, dividends as a percent of earnings are approxi-

---

[2]This introduction comes from John Byrne, "Is Your Company Too Big?" *Business Week*, March 27, 1989, pp. 84–94.
[3]Ernest W. Walker and J. William Petty II, "Financial Differences between Large and Small Firms," *Financial Management* (Winter 1978), pp. 61–68.

TABLE 26–1.
Financial Data for Small
and Large Companies

	Average Values	
	Small Firms	Large Firms
Liquidity indicators		
Current ratio	2.00×	2.77×
Accounts receivable turnover	7.04×	6.40×
Inventory turnover	8.47×	5.31×
Current liabilities/total debt	83.70%	62.99%
Profitability indicators		
Operating profit margin	10.91%	9.20%
Accounts receivable turnover	7.04×	6.40×
Inventory turnover	8.47×	5.31×
Fixed assets turnover	9.40×	3.50×
Financing indicators		
Debt/total assets	49.00%	38.05%
Current liabilities/total debt	83.70%	62.99%
Fixed charges coverage	33.16×	22.47×
Business risk indicator		
Variability of operating income	21.94%	7.71%
Dividend policy indicator		
Dividend/earnings	2.9%	40.52%

Source: Ernest W. Walker and J. William Petty II, "Financial Differences Between Large and Small Firms," *Financial Management* (Winter 1978), pp. 61–68.

mately 3 percent and 40 percent for small and large firms, respectively. The low dividend payout ratio, which is generally thought to be typical of small firms, is seen to be characteristic even of small firms entering the public markets. In fact, 74 percent of the small firms made no distribution in the form of cash dividends in the year preceding the offering. Thus, the incentive, as well as the opportunity, for small firms to pay dividends in anticipation of a favorable impact on the common stock when entering the marketplace is in no way apparent. The investors purchasing such securities must have believed that these securities represented shares in "growth companies." They were evidently willing to rely almost solely on the capital gains potential from their investment.

The second major difference between small and large firms is liquidity. Large firms have more liquidity, as reflected by the current ratio. The difference would seem to be the result of two factors. First, small firms retain smaller amounts of accounts receivable and inventory, as reflected by higher accounts receivable and inventory turnovers. Second, small firms rely more heavily on current liabilities, as shown by the current liabilities/total debt ratio. Thus, small firms typically maintained less liquidity.

The apparent difference in liquidity between the large and small firms lends further support to the belief that a working-capital shortage is a problem for small firms. The difference could be the result of at least two factors. First, the small firm's limited access to the capital markets may impose the need for more economy in the use of working capital. Second, the management style of the entrepreneur could have a bearing on the working-capital decisions within the small firm. If the managers of small firms are willing to assume greater risk, as experience would suggest, their attitude may well be reflected in the small firm's liquidity position.

Business risk and financial risk also help distinguish between small and large firms. Business risk, as measured by the variability of earnings before interest and taxes, is greater for small firms. The inability to diversify across investments, as well as geographically, increases the small firm's volatility of profits. Also, the small firm's capital structure is more debt oriented, with an even greater tendency for using short-term credit. This heavy use of debt is usually perceived as one of the basic characteristics of managing a small firm.

Unquestionably there are differences in the financial management of small and large businesses. Based on the Walker-Petty study, these differences may be summarized as follows:

1. Small firms are less liquid than their larger counterparts, and short-term cash flow patterns become critical to the success of the small business.

2. Small companies have more volatile profits and cash flows over time, owing to the greater business and financial risk experienced by smaller entities.

3. Small firms use relatively large amounts of debt in the financing of the business, which may be the consequence of entrepreneurs' greater propensity to assume risk. However, it is more likely that the issue relates to the small company's inaccessibility to the public capital markets, especially the equity markets.

4. The inaccessibility of the small corporation to the capital markets means the value of the firm is more difficult to determine. Also, the absence of market data for the firm's securities makes determining the cost of capital a difficult, if not impossible, job.

Table 26–1 reveals some differences between the large and small firm in terms of their financial data. There are some underlying reasons for these differences. It has been said that "a small company is not just a little big business"—the issue is more than a matter of the number of zeros.[4] In other words, there are reasons why traditional financial analysis may not tell the whole story at times. We cite a few of these reasons.

1. The owner may not always be a value maximizer. There may be some personal goals that are of equal if not greater importance. Personal life-styles realized through the company may distort the economic content of the financial statements, such as when the firm owns a house on the lake. Also, because the small firm, in a way, is an extension of the owner, it becomes difficult to separate the firm from the owner in a financial context without causing distortions. For example, in making an investment decision the need to develop autonomy outside the firm may be as important as the investment's net present value.

2. For the small company, the goal of survival may supersede *ideal* financial practices, owing largely to the small firm's limited access to the public capital markets and bankers' insistence on looking to the owner's personal guarantees in addition to the firm's financial position.

3. Traditional definitions of debt and equity, as we have studied them, may not apply. For instance, loans to the owners may in reality be a form of equity, because there is no intent for the firm to repay the loan. Also, the owner's personal preference for financial risk, rather than the goal of minimizing the firm's cost of capital, is more important in determining the desired level of debt.

4. The concept that cash flows equal income plus depreciation is an illusion for small high-growth firms or companies experiencing rapid change. For the small firm, "cash is king." The owner absolutely must understand the nature of the firm's cash flows.

[4]See J. A. Welsh, and J. F. White, "A Small Business Is Not a Little Big Business," *Harvard Business Review* (July-August 1981), pp. 18–32; and Richard Levin and Virginia Travis, "Small Company Finance: What the Books Don't Say," *Harvard Business Review* (November-December 1987), pp. 30–35.

The implications of these differences are truly significant to the small owner. In making financial decisions, the owner should seek to maximize the total value of both corporate and individual wealth, subject to personal life-style preferences. Second, small-business owners should make every effort to maintain flexibility when dealing with bankers and other providers of capital. Finally, the owner should always prepare a cash budget along with the income statement, and contingency planning should be a constant.

Capital Budgeting in the Small Firm

We studied capital-budgeting techniques in Chapters 6 and 7, where we developed an understanding of the discounted cash flow (DCF) techniques in valuing capital projects. Now we consider (1) how the managers-owners of small firms actually evaluate capital investments and (2) how ought they to do so, given the nature of the small firm.

Capital-Budgeting Practices of Small Firms

In 1963, Robert Soldofsky studied a large number of small firms in Iowa, where, among other things, he asked the owners how they went about analyzing capital-budgeting projects.[5] The response would not be encouraging to a finance professor, with 50 percent of the respondents saying they use the payback technique; and even worse, 40 percent of the firms used no formal analysis at all. In defense of DCF techniques, we would quickly note that these findings are extremely dated, going back almost 30 years. Even the large firms, for the most part, would not have been using discounted cash flow techniques to any great extent so long ago; so we need to find a more recent study.

Next we look at a 1983 study by L. R. Runyon, who studied more than 200 small companies with net worths between $500,000 and $1 million.[6] In probing into their approaches for evaluating the merits of proposed capital investments, he learned that only 14 percent of the firms used any form of a discounted cash flow technique; 70 percent indicated they used no DCF approach at all; and 9 percent used no formal analysis of any form. Surprisingly, we may judge that time has had little impact on the investment decision-making process within small firms. Although we may be encouraged that the practice of not relying on any formal analysis has declined significantly, little use is made of any market-value rules afforded by present value analysis.

Why are the findings of the preceding studies so dismal? Why has there been so little change in 20 years? Have small-firm decision makers not been taught? Maybe, but we believe that the issue is bigger than training. Because Runyon was dealing with the "smaller of the smalls," with net worths not exceeding $1 million, there probably are a significant number who have not been exposed to financial theory. However, the cause for such limited use of DCF tools probably rests more with the nature of the small firm itself. We would argue that several more important reasons exist, among them the following:

1. As previously stated, for many owners of small firms, the business is an extension of their lives. As a consequence, nonfinancial variables may play a significant part in their decisions. For instance, the desire to be viewed as a respected part of the community may be more important to the owner than the present value of a decision.

[5]Robert M. Soldofsky, "Capital Budgeting Practices in Small Manufacturing Companies," in Dudley G. Luckett, ed., *Studies in the Factor Markets for Small Business Firms* (Washington, DC: Small Business Administration, 1964).

[6]L. R. Runyon, "Capital Expenditure Decision Making in Small Firms," *Journal of Business Research* (September 1983), pp. 389–97.

2. The frequent undercapitalization and liquidity problems of the small firm impact directly on the decision-making process within the small firm, where survival becomes the top priority.

3. The greater uncertainty of cash flows within the small firm makes long-term forecasts and planning unappealing, and even viewed as a waste of time. The owner simply has no confidence in his or her ability to reasonably predict cash flows beyond two or three years. Thus, calculating the cash flows for the entire life of a project is viewed as an effort in futility.

4. Because the value of a closely held firm is not as observable as a publicly held firm, where the market value of the firm's securities are actively traded in the marketplace, the owner of the small firm may consider the market-value rule of maximizing net present values irrelevant. In this environment, estimating the firm's cost of capital is also difficult. If computing the large firm's cost of capital is difficult at best, the measurement for the small firm becomes virtually impossible.

5. The smaller size of projects of a small firm may make net-present-value computations not feasible in a practical sense. Much of the time and costs required to analyze a capital investment are fixed; thus, the small firm incurs a diseconomy of scale in evaluation costs.

6. Management talent within a small firm is a scarce resource. Also, the training of the owner-managers is frequently of a technical nature, as opposed to a business or finance orientation. The perspective of these owners is influenced greatly by their backgrounds.

The foregoing characteristics of the small firm, and equally important the owners, have a significant impact on the decision-making process within the small firm, whether or not we agree with the logic. The result is a short-term mind set, somewhat by necessity and partly by choice. Nevertheless, given the nature of the environment, what could we recommend to the owner-managers of the small firm? That is, what would be the ideal process for making investment decisions for the firm?

A Better Way of Capital Budgeting for the Small Firm

We may recall from several earlier chapters that an agency problem can develop in large firms where management is more concerned with its own priorities than serving the owners' best interests—thus becoming wealth satisfiers, rather than wealth maximizers. If potential conflicts of interest develop, they cannot and should not be ignored. However, the small firm has a different situation. If the owner-managers are one and the same, the decision to be wealth satisfiers rather than wealth maximizers cannot be criticized. If the owners are maximizing their utility, which includes more than financial considerations, who is to say they are wrong? What finance *can* do, however, is address the potential need of the small firm to consider liquidity on an equal footing with value maximization, as well as the problem of estimating cash flows in the long-term future. Also, we may at least partially resolve the difficulty in measuring the firm's cost of capital.

The Need for Liquidity

While not an ideal answer, a case may be developed for the small firm to use a discounted payback period in evaluating a proposed investment.[7] From our study of the payback method in Chapter 6, we remember that the method does

---

[7]See Richard Wacht, "Capital Investment Analysis for the Small Firm," Working Paper (February 1988).

have some real limitations. However, it does provide us an indication of how long our funds are tied up in an investment. As such, it does give us some measure of liquidity, which in turn may be vitally important for the small firm. Also, although we had faulted the payback approach for ignoring cash flows beyond the payback period, such a limitation may have less significance for the small firm, because the cash flows are more uncertain over the long run.

EXAMPLE

To illustrate the use of the discounted payback period, we have estimated the cash flows for a project for the first five years of its life. The project is expected to cost $50,000, and the owners have a required rate of return of 15 percent. The expected cash flows for the first five years are as follows:

Years	Expected Cash Flows	Cumulative Cash Flows	Present Value of Expected Cash Flows	Cumulative Present Values
1	$12,000	$12,000	$10,435	$10,435
2	14,000	26,000	10,586	21,021
3	17,000	43,000	11,178	32,199
4	20,000	63,000	11,435	43,634
5	20,000	83,000	9,944	53,578
		Total present value		$53,578

The payback period for the investment would be 3.35 years ($43,000 received in three years and the remaining $7,000 recouped in .35 years, i.e., $7,000/ $20,000). However, when we recognize the owner's required rate of return of 15 percent, we find the present value of the first five years' expected cash flows to be $53,578. Using these present values, we see that the owners recoup their investment on a present value basis in 4.64 years ($43,634 of the investment received in four years and the remaining $6,366 in .64 year, i.e., $6366/$9944). By comparing projects in this manner, we give consideration both to the present value criterion and the liquidity of the project. ■

A Direct Approach to Measuring the Cost of Capital

The methodology used in Chapter 8 for measuring the cost of capital is not totally applicable for the small firm. We simply do not have access to market data for the small firm as we do for the large corporation whose stock is traded on the New York Stock Exchange. Thus, we might better resort to some alternative method.

As noted in Chapter 8, the cost of capital is an opportunity-cost concept. Stockholders should receive from their investment in the firm an amount at least equal to the rate of return available in the capital markets, given the level of risk. We use the market data of the firm's securities to estimate these opportunity costs. However, no such information is available for most small companies. We therefore need to modify our approach.

A small business either is family owned or the stock is owned by a small group of investors, who are relatively close to the situation. Consequently, we need not use market data in the absence of knowing the investors. With a board of directors who would also be major investors in the company, we may inquire directly about the desired rates of return. They only need to be informed about competitive rates in the marketplace and then set the required rate of return as the owners. We would then suggest using the "residual NPV approach," which compares the cash flows going to the stockholders to their required rate of return, rather than using a weighted cost of capital for all investors.

The Residual Net Present Value

The residual net present value is a slight modification of the conventional weighted cost-of-capital approach. Rather than computing the present value of the expected cash flows going to all investors discounted at the weighted cost of capital, we estimate the cash that will flow to the owners after all debt and preferred stockholders have been paid their returns. We then discount these flows at the owners' required rate of return. Thus we would recommend the following method:

1. Determine a target position for the firm's debt–equity ratio.

2. Compute the residual after-tax cash flows available to the owners of the company, net of interest expense, debt principal repayment, and preferred dividend payments. In Chapter 6, we used after-tax operating cash flows (cash flows available to all investors of the firm, that is, debt, preferred stock, and common stock) in our net-present-value calculations. However, with the weighted cost of capital, our discount rate recognized the required rates of return for all these investors as well.

3. Have the owners of the company decide what is a fair rate of return for the project, given its level of business risk. This rate may be somewhat subjective; however, an appropriate rate can be determined by allowing for any alternative uses of the funds and by considering personal factors that affect the owners' total utility from operating the business.

4. Calculate the present value of the residual cash flows going to the owners and determine the project's discounted payback period. Use these results to evaluate the proposed investment against other investments under consideration or that have been recently accepted.[8]

EXAMPLE

Assume the Arganes Corporations is contemplating an investment that costs $55,000. The project would have an expected life of about 15 years; however, the uncertainty of these cash flows makes management uncomfortable to project the flows beyond six years. The firm has a 40 percent target debt ratio; the interest rate on the debt is expected to be 10 percent; and the principal on the debt is to be repaid over 10 years by reducing the balance by 10 percent at the end of each year. For tax purposes, the asset will be depreciated on a

[8]If the discounted project payback period is shorter than the expected life of the investment, we may be assured that the project will have a positive NPV.

TABLE 26–2.
Arganes Corporation Project
Analysis

	Year					
	1	2	3	4	5	6
Operating income	$20,000	$23,000	$25,000	$25,000	$27,000	$27,000
Interest	2,640	2,376	2,112	1,540	1,320	1,100
Earnings before tax	17,360	20,624	22,888	23,460	25,680	25,900
Taxes	6,944	8,250	9,155	9,384	10,272	10,360
Earnings after tax	10,416	12,374	13,733	14,076	15,408	15,540
Depreciation	5,500	5,500	5,500	5,500	5,500	5,500
Cash before debt payment	15,916	17,874	19,233	19,576	20,908	21,040
Debt payment	2,200	2,200	2,200	2,200	2,200	2,200
Cash flow to owners	$13,716	$15,674	$17,033	$17,376	$18,708	$18,840
Present value	$11,927	$11,852	$11,199	$ 9,935	$ 9,301	$ 8,145
Cumulative present value	$11,927	$23,779	$34,978	$44,913	$54,214	$62,359

straight-line basis over 10 years, with no salvage recognized. The firm's tax rate is 40 percent. The resulting cash flows going to the owners in each year are computed in Table 26–2.

Beginning with the expected operating income for each of the six years, we subtract the interest expense, which is 12 percent of the remaining debt balance each year. A $2,200 payment on the debt principal is made at the end of each year, which is subtracted from the cash flows from operations and after interest expense. The remaining amount is the cash flow accruing to the owners of the firm. Using a 15 percent required rate of return, the present value of these residual cash flows is calculated and shown in the last row in Table 26–2.

From the present values of the annual cash flows in Table 26–2, we can determine the discounted payback period as follows:

$$\text{discounted payback period} = \left(\begin{array}{c} \text{5 years of cash flows} \\ \text{with present value} \\ \text{of \$54,214} \end{array} \right)$$

$$+ \left(\begin{array}{c} \text{.097 years to receive} \\ \text{remaining cash flow of \$786} \\ \text{or } \dfrac{\$786}{\$8145} \end{array} \right)$$

$$= 5.097 \text{ years}$$

Thus, in 5.097 years, the owners may expect to recoup their original investment, while earning their required rate of return of 15 percent. The decision to accept or reject the project would come only after comparing it with other alternative uses of the funds and the impact on the project of key nonfinancial variables that only the owners can know. ■

Financing of the Small Firm

In studying how a small firm is financed, we restrict our discussion to the financing stages a firm experiences during its business life. As shown in Figure 26–2 on page 892, the business firm goes through three primary financing stages in the earlier segment of its business life cycle. Phase one, the *initial investment*, consists of the owner's personal capital, the credit provided by the

BASIC FINANCIAL MANAGEMENT IN PRACTICE

Small-Firm Financial Markets

What might be called the small business and entrepreneurial finance market is really four markets. . . . Here is an outline of the make-up of these markets and what influences them, the sources of the data, and the implications for jobs.

Professional Venture Capital

This is the market everyone talks about—investments in new and growing companies by professional venture capital firms.

Venture Economics Publishing Co. of Needham, Mass., keeps tally of the venture capital industry's annual investments stretching from 1970 to the present. The industry itself dates to the early '50s and as late as 1977 disbursed only a few hundred million dollars a year to portfolio companies. Investments mushroomed after the 1978 Steiger Amendment lowered the effective capital gains tax to 28% from 35%, and even more after the 1981 Tax Act dropped it to 20%. Passing $1 billion for the first time in 1980 (all figures are in 1991 dollars), venture capital disbursements peaked at $4.8 billion in 1987. By 1990, commitments had fallen to $2.1 billion.

Initial Public Offerings

Going public is usually considered the last stage of venture financing, although some professionals argue that later public offerings are often part of the entrepreneurial support process.

Prof. Jay Ritter of the University of Illinois has assembled authoritative annual totals on Initial Public Offerings for the years from 1960 to 1990.

The IPO market took off in the mid-1960s, reached $9.7 billion in 1969 (as always, figures are in 1991 dollars), but then collapsed to $2.8 billion in 1970, after Congress increased the capital-gains tax rate. The market recovered briefly in 1971 and 1972 (when $8.9 billion was raised), as a debased dollar and price controls created a bubble in all equity markets, but collapsed again in 1973. By 1974, the IPO market had shrunk to a near-death $142 million, and it remained near death until the Steiger Amendment resurrected it. Then, with setbacks in the 1982 recession and 1984, it zoomed upward to $24.1 billion in 1986 only to expire once more after the boosting of the capital gains tax. Last year IPOs raised only $6 billion.

The financial press has heralded a recent flurry of IPOs. Mr. Ritter believes, however, that when real estate and closed-end mutual funds are screened out, this year's market will prove only a little larger than last's.

Angels

The term comes from Broadway's name for people who back shows. This market is made up of private individuals who back new companies. Although nearly invisible, it provides most outside investment for start-ups, says University of New Hampshire professor William E. Wetzel, Jr., its leading authority. Angels tend to be upper-middle class (median family income, $97,000), and many are successful entrepreneurs. Seven out of 10 angels put their money into companies within 50 miles of their homes or offices. According to Professor Wetzel, virtually all firms receiving angel financing are incorporated, making it easier to cash out for a capital gain if all goes well.

In 1988 the Small Business Administration published a study of the angel market titled "The Informal Supply of Capital." Findings were derived from three regional surveys conducted between late 1985 and mid-1987. The study estimates the average annual angel investment over these years at $40.9 billion (as before, 1991 dollars) or about 10 times the size of the venture capital market.

The angel market appears to have contracted since 1986. Specialists in public financings for emerging biotechnology firms have noticed that the typical company they take public has less angel capital than before, and many have none.

And a new kind of angel financing has appeared—foreign money. People involved in all parts of entrepreneurial finance report that Asians and Europeans have stepped forward, particularly for high-technology projects with international applications. Foreign investors are taxed at home, where capital gains taxes either don't exist or are lower than here.

Moms & Pops

This market is where the middle class puts its entrepreneurial capital, and like the middle class, it is where most of the money is. Amounts cited here are for yearly capital expenditures of proprietorships and partnerships (not for working capital raised or capital for financial investments), and yet in 1986 the total came to almost twice that of the three other markets combined.

While Mesa Petroleum fits in this group, more typical are small service firms, law and accounting firms (those that aren't professional corporations) and most new businesses.

Source: Clark S. Judge, *Wall Street Journal*, June 24, 1991, pp. A12, 13.

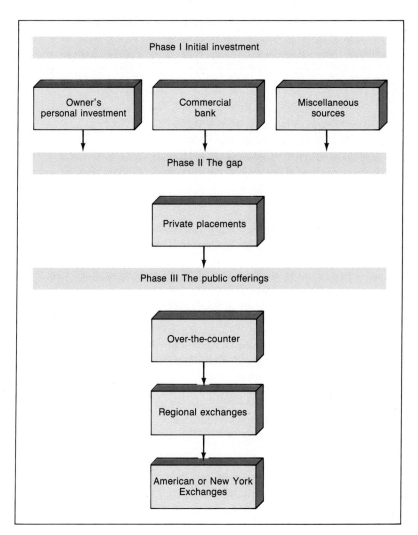

Phase I Initial investment

| Owner's personal investment | Commercial bank | Miscellaneous sources |

Phase II The gap

Private placements

Phase III The public offerings

Over-the-counter

Regional exchanges

American or New York Exchanges

FIGURE 26–2.
Business Financing Stages
Source: Ernest W. Walker
and J. William Petty II,
*Financial Management
of the Small Firm* (Englewood
Cliffs, NJ: Prentice Hall, 1984).

commercial banker, and a host of miscellaneous sources. Examples of miscellaneous sources in this phase would include (1) savings and loan associations, (2) the Small Business Administration, (3) friends and relatives, (4) leasing companies, and (5) commercial finance companies.

Phase two of a young firm's financial existence may be referred to as *the gap*. During this period the firm has grown to the level beyond which the owners have the capability to finance all investments; however, the firm is not large enough to justify a public offering. At this point it must sell securities to private individuals or groups. As shown in Figure 26–3, several sources for private placements exist and may be directly placed through an investment banker. For instance, financial institutions (banks and savings and loan associations), private investor groups, and venture capitalists may be approached either directly or through an investment banker acting as a liaison.[9] Large corporations may provide financing for a small firm but are generally approached directly. Furthermore, the kind of financing available from these respective sources varies, with financial institutions providing primarily debt financing and large corporations providing equity financing. Between the two extremes, a mixture of debt and equity capital would be available.

[9]The term *venture capitalist* is used to describe professional investors interested in investing in high-risk firms with potentially large returns. A more detailed explanation is provided in the next section.

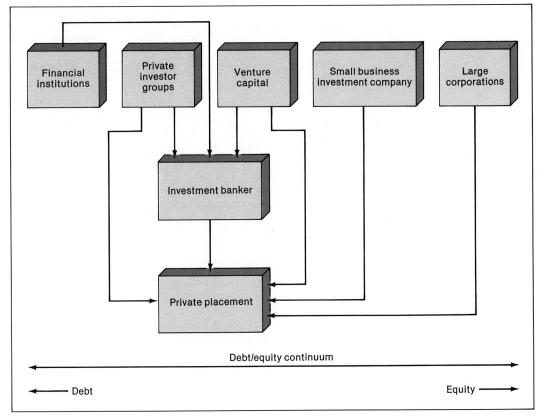

FIGURE 26–3.
Sources of Private Placements
Source: Ernest W. Walker and J. William Petty II, *Financial Management of the Small Firm*
(Englewood Cliffs, NJ: Prentice Hall, 1984).

The final stage of development for the small firm in terms of financing sources is the point at which funds are raised in the public markets. As explained in Chapter 18, a firm's stock is first traded publicly over-the-counter, then on a regional exchange, and finally on the American Stock Exchange or the New York Stock Exchange.

SUMMARY

In this chapter, we consider briefly how a small-business owner's perspective on finance may differ from that of a Fortune 500 company. We observe that small firms characteristically (1) tend to rely more heavily on the retention of earnings as a way to build equity, (2) have less liquidity, (3) use greater amounts of debt, and (4) experience more business risk. We then consider the implications of these differences for the small-firm owner. Finally, we take a bird's-eye view of the financing of the small firm as it matures over time.

STUDY QUESTIONS

26–1. Describe the financial difference between a small and a large firm.

26–2. What factors unique to the small firm must be considered in analyzing capital investments?

26–3. Explain the stages of financing that a firm may experience during its growth.

VIDEO CASE 7

The USX Proxy Contest: Putting a Divestiture Decision to a Shareholder Vote

from ABC News, *Business World*, May 6, 1990

When we introduced Video Case 7 on page 795, we asked some questions that you should now review.

Studies examining divestitures similar to the one proposed by Carl Icahn for USX have found that on average shareholders are helped by such transactions. The sum of the prices of the two separate firms exceeds the price of the single combined firm. There are several possible reasons for these results: Increased disclosure for the separate firms allow investors to know more about each unit, so they can value them more accurately; compensation plans can be designed to improve incentives in the spunoff subsidiary; divestitures result in pure equity plays in which investors can more precisely fine-tune their portfolios; cross-subsidizations between units are curtailed, so unprofitable units are not supported by profitable units.

Several of these rationales apply to the USX case. As one of the commentators mentions, the steel division has been riding on the cash flows of the energy division. Divesting the steel unit would expose this lack of profitability and possibly force the steel unit's management to make changes. As long as the energy division provides cash to help the steel unit survive hard times, managers have limited incentive to make difficult choices. The *pure play* rationale is also applicable. If you own USX shares you own a fixed mix of steel and energy in your portfolio. Most investors will not want to own steel and oil in those proportions. Investors can diversify their portfolios more efficiently by buying shares in a *pure* steel company and a *pure* energy company until they get the proportions that fit their risk–return profile. Investors will discount USX shares because those shares force an undesirable mix of energy and steel on their portfolios.

In the USX case, the divestiture proposal received about 42 percent of the vote and was rejected. However, within six months USX management decided to carry out a similar divestiture plan. On the day when the decision to separate the steel and energy divisions was announced, USX stock jumped $2.38 or 8.2 percent—a sure sign that investors approved of the plan. USX stock sold for about $29 per share in January and February of 1991. In May the separate shares of USX–U.S. Steel and USX–Marathon Oil sold for $25.25 and $31.75, respectively, or for a combined value of $57. Shareholders benefited to the tune of $27 per share from the separation of the two business units.

Proxy contests such as this one are seldom immediately successful. Interestingly, there is some evidence that within three years after a proxy contest there is about a 50 percent chance that the CEO will be replaced, or the firm will be taken over or restructured in some other way. Although the proxy contest may not appear to be successful, it apparently sets forces in motion that create major changes in the firm.

Discussion question

1. The rules of proxy contests favor incumbent managers who can use firm resources to defeat the proxy initiative. Moreover, it is very costly for dissident shareholders to mount a proxy contest, and most shareholders do not own enough stock for the costs to be offset by the potential benefits of the proposed changes. Given these facts is there just enough, too little, or too much monitoring carried out by shareholders? Can you think of changes that might improve this situation?

Suggested reading

DeAngelo, Harry and Linda. "Proxy Contests and the Governance of Publicly Held Corporations," *The Journal of Finance*, 1990.

SELECTED REFERENCES

CHAPTER 1

Anthony, Robert N. "The Trouble with Profit Maximization," *Harvard Business Review* 38 (November–December 1960), 126–34.

Barnea, Amir, Robert A. Haugen, and Lemma W. Senbet. *Agency Problems and Financial Contracting.* Englewood Cliffs, NJ: Prentice Hall, 1985.

———. "Market Imperfections, Agency Problems, and Capital Structure: A Review," *Financial Management* 10 (Summer 1981), 7–22.

Beranek, William. "Research Directions in Finance," *Quarterly Review of Economics and Business* 21 (Spring 1981), 6–24.

Bowle, Norman E., and Ronald F. Duska. *Business Ethics,* 2d ed. Englewood Cliffs, NJ: Prentice Hall, 1990.

Branch, Ben. "Corporate Objectives and Market Performance," *Financial Management* 2 (Summer 1973), 24–29.

Buhholz, Rogene A. *Fundamental Concepts and Problems in Business Ethics.* Englewood Cliffs, NJ: Prentice Hall, 1989.

Cisel, David H., and Thomas M. Carroll. "The Determinants of Executive Salaries: An Econometric Survey," *Review of Economics and Statistics* 62 (February 1980), 7–13.

Cooley, Phillip L. "Managerial Pay and Financial Performances of Small Business," *Journal of Business* (September 1979), 267–76.

Donaldson, Gordon. "Financial Goals: Management vs. Stockholders," *Harvard Business Review* 41 (May–June 1963), 116–29.

Findlay, M. Chapman, III, and G. A. Whitmore. "Beyond Shareholder Wealth Maximization," *Financial Management* 3 (Winter 1974), 25–35.

Findlay, M. Chapman, III, and E. E. Williams. "A Positivist's Evaluation of the New Finance," *Financial Management* 9 (Summer 1980), 7–17.

Friedman, Milton. "The Social Responsibility of Business Is to Increase Its Profits," *New York Times Magazine* (September 13, 1970), 33, 122–26.

Hand, John H., William P. Lloyd, and Robert B. Rogow. "Agency Relationships in the Close Corporation," *Financial Management* 11 (Spring 1982), 25–30.

Jensen, Michael, and William H. Meckling. "Theory of the Firm: Managerial Behavior, Agency Costs, and Ownership Structure," *Journal of Financial Economics* 2 (October 1976), 305–60.

Pindyck, Robert S., and Daniel L. Ruben-feld. *Microeconomics,* 2d ed. New York: Macmillan, 1992.

Simkowitz, Michael A., and Charles P. Jones. "A Note on the Simultaneous Nature of Finance Methodology," *Journal of Finance* 27 (March 1972), 103.

Solomon, Ezra. *The Theory of Financial Management,* chaps. 1 and 2. New York: Columbia University Press, 1963.

Weston, J. Fred. "Developments in Finance Theory," *Financial Management* 10 (1981), 5–22.

———. *The Scope and Methodology of Finance.* Englewood Cliffs, NJ: Prentice Hall, 1966.

CHAPTER 2

Amihud, Yakov, and Haim Mendelson. "Liquidity, Maturity, and the Yields on U.S. Treasury Securities," *Journal of Finance* 46 (September 1991), 1411–26.

Carleton, Willard T., and Ian A. Cooper. "Estimation and Uses of the Term Structure of Interest Rates," *Journal of Finance* 31 (September 1976), 1067–84.

Collins, J. Markham, and Roger P. Bey. "The Master Limited Partnership: An Alternative to the Corporation," *Financial Management* 15 (Winter 1986), 5–14.

Culbertson, John M. "The Term Structure of Interest Rates," *Quarterly Journal of Economics* 71 (November 1957), 499–502, 507–509.

Echols, Michael E., and Jan Walter Elliott. "A Quantitative Yield Curve Model for Estimating the Term Structure of Interest Rates," *Journal of Financial and Quantitative Analysis* 11 (March 1976), 87–114.

Estrella, Arturo, and Gikas A. Hardouvelis. "The Term Structure as a Predictor of Real Economic Activity," *Journal of Finance* 46 (June 1991), 555–76.

Fama, Eugene F., and Michael C. Jensen. "Separation of Ownership and Control," *Journal of Law and Economics* 26 (June 1983), 301–25.

Fisher, Irving. "Appreciation and Interest," *Publications of the American Economic Association* 11 (August 1986), 23–29.

Jensen, Michael C. "Eclipse of the Public Corporation," *Harvard Business Review* (September–October 1989), 61–75.

Martin, John, Samuel Cox, and Richard MacMinn. *The Theory of Finance: Evidence and Applications.* Hinsdale, IL: Dryden Press, 1988.

McCulloch, J. Huston. "Measuring the Term Structure of Interest Rates," *Journal of Business* 44 (January 1971), 19–31.

1991 Federal Tax Course. New York: Commerce Clearing House, 1992.

1991 Federal Tax Course. Englewood Cliffs, NJ: Prentice Hall, 1992.

Rose, Andrew K. "Is the Real Interest Rate Stable?" *Journal of Finance* 43 (December 1988), 1095–1112.

Van Horne, James C. *Financial Market Rates and Flows,* 2d ed. Englewood Cliffs, NJ: Prentice Hall, 1984.

CHAPTER 3

Greynolds, Elbert B., Jr., Julius S. Aronofsky, and Robert J. Frame. *Financial Analysis Using Calculators: Time Value of Money.* New York: McGraw-Hill, 1980.

Hart, William L. *Mathematics of Investment,* 5th ed. Lexington, MA: D. C. Health, 1975.

Shao, Stephen P. *Mathematics for Management and Finance,* 6th ed. Cincinnati, OH: South-Western Publishing, 1990.

Tobias, Andrew. *Money Angles,* New York: Linden Press, 1984.

CHAPTER 4

Altman, Edward I., New York University. "Setting the Record Straight on Junk Bonds: A Review of the Research on Default Rates and Returns," *Journal of Applied Corporate Finance* (Summer 1990), 82.

Bower, D., R. Bower, and D. Logue. "Arbitrage Pricing and Utility Stock Returns," *Journal of Finance* (September 1984), 1041–54.

———. "Equity Screening Rates Using Arbitrage Pricing Theory," in C. F. Lee, ed., *Advances in Financial Planning.* Greenwich, CT: JAI Press, 1984.

Blume, Marshall E., Donald B. Keim, and Sandeep A. Patel. "Returns and Volatility of Low-Grade Bonds, 1977–1989," *Journal of Finance* (March 1991), 49–74.

Butler, J. S., and Barry Schachter. "The Investment Decision: Estimation Risk and Risk Adjusted Discount Rates," *Journal of Financial Management* (Winter 1989), 13.

Chen, N. "Some Empirical Tests of the Theory of Arbitrage Pricing," *Journal of Finance* 38 (December 1983), 1393–1414.

Cochrane, John H. "Production-Based Asset Pricing and the Link Between Stock Returns and Economic Fluctuations," *Journal of Finance* (March 1991), 209–38.

Fama, Eugene, and Kenneth French. "The Cross Section of Expected Stock Returns," University of Chicago Center for Research in Security Prices, 1991.

Haugen, Robert A., Eli Talmor, and Walter

N. Torous. "The Effect of Volatility Changes on the Level of Stock Prices and Subsequent Expected Returns," *Journal of Finance* (July 1991), 985–1008.

Ibbotson, R. G., and R. A. Sinquefield. *Stocks, Bonds, Bills and Inflations: Historical Return (1926–1907)*. Chicago: Dow Jones-Irwin, 1991.

Keim, D. "Size-Related Anomalies and Stock Market Seasonality: Further Empirical Evidence," *Journal of Financial Economics* (June 1983), 13–32.

Lanstein, R., and W. Sharpe. "Duration and Security Risk," *Journal of Financial and Quantitative Analysis* (November 1978), 653–68.

Levy, H. "Tests of Capital Asset Pricing Hypotheses," *Research in Finance* 1 (1979), 115–223.

Macaulay, F. R. *Some Theoretical Problems Suggested by Movements of Interest Rates, Bond Yields, and Stock Prices since 1856*. New York: National Bureau of Economic Research, 1938.

Markowitz, Harry M. "Foundations of Portfolio Theory," *Journal of Finance* (June 1991), 469–78.

Martin, John, Samuel Cox, and Richard MacMinn. *The Theory of Finance: Evidence and Applications*, chaps. 15–17. Hinsdale, IL: Dryden Press, 1988.

Modigliani, E., and G. Pogue. "An Introduction to Risk and Return," *Financial Analysts Journal* (March–April and May–June 1974), 68–80, 69–86.

Piper, Thomas R., and William E. Fruhan, Jr. "Is Your Stock Worth Its Market Price?" *Harvard Business Review* (May–June 1981), 124–32.

Rappaport, Alfred, *Creating Shareholder Wealth*. New York: The Free Press, 1986.

———. "Stock Market Signals to Managers," *Harvard Business Review* (November–December 1987), 57–62.

Reinganum, Marc R. "The Anatomy of a Stock Market Winner," *Financial Analysts Journal* (March–April 1988), 16–28.

Roll, R. "A Critique of the Asset Pricing Theory's Tests," *Journal of Financial Economics* (March 1977), 126–76.

———. "Performance Evaluation and Benchmark Errors," *Journal of Portfolio Management* 6 (Summer 1980), 5–12.

Roll, R., and S. Ross. "The Arbitrage Pricing Theory Approach to Strategic Portfolio Planning," *Financial Analysts Journal* (May–June 1984), 14–26.

———. "An Empirical Investigation of the Arbitrage Pricing Theory," *Journal of Finance* (December 1980), 1073–1103.

Rosenberg, B. "The Capital Asset Pricing Model and the Market Model," *Journal of Portfolio Management* (Winter 1981), 5–16.

Snow, Karl N. "Diagnosing Asset Pricing Models Using the Distribution of Asset Returns," *Journal of Finance* (July 1991), 955–84.

Stewart, G. Bennett, III. "Announcing the Stern Stewart Performance 1,000: A New Way of Viewing Corporate America," *Journal of Applied Corporate Finance* (Summer 1990), 38.

CHAPTER 5

Arzac, Enrique R. "Do Your Business Units Create Shareholder Value?" *Harvard Business Review* (January–February 1986), 121–26.

Balachandran, Bala V., Nandu J. Nagarajan, and Alfred Rappaport. "Threshold Margins for Creating Economic Value," *Financial Management* 15 (Spring 1986), 68–77.

Banz, Rolf W. "The Relationship Between Return and Market Value of Common Stocks," *Journal of Financial Economics* 9 (March 1981), 3–18.

Basu, Snajoy. "The Relationship Between Earnings' Yield, Market Value and Return for NYSE Common Stocks: Further Evidence," *Journal of Financial Economics* 12 (June 1983), 129–56.

Fuller, Russell J., and Chi-Cheng Hsia. "A Simplified Common Stock Valuation Model," *Financial Analysts Journal* 40 (September–October 1984), 49–56.

Gordon, Myron. *The Investment, Financing and Valuation of the Corporation*. Homewood, IL: Richard D. Irwin, 1963.

Hector, Gary. "What Makes Stock Prices Move?" *Fortune* (October 10, 1988), 69–76.

———. "Yes, You Can Manage Long Term," *Fortune* (November 21, 1988), 63.

Hickman, Kent, and Glenn H. Petry. "A Comparison of Stock Predictions Using Court Accepted Formulas, Dividend Discount, and P/E Models," *Journal of Financial Management* (Summer 1990), 76.

Malkiel, Burton G. *A Random Walk Down Wall Street*. New York: Norton, 1985.

Marsh, Terry A., and Robert C. Merton. "Dividend Variability and Variance Bounds Tests for the Rationality of Stock Market Prices," *American Economic Review* (June 1986), 483–98.

Piper, Thomas R., and William E. Fruhan, Jr. "Is Your Stock Worth Its Market Price?" *Harvard Business Review* (May–June 1981), 124–32.

Rappaport, Alfred. *Creating Shareholder Wealth*, New York: Free Press, 1986.

———. "Stock Market Signals to Managers," *Harvard Business Review* (November–December 1987), 57–62.

Reinganum, Marc R. "The Anatomy of a Stock Market Winner," *Financial Analysts Journal* (March–April 1988), 16–28.

Ryngaert, Michael D. "Firm Valuation, Takeover Defenses, and the Delaware Supreme Court," *Journal of Financial Management* (Autumn 1989), 20.

Shiller, Robert J. "Do Stock Prices Move Too Much to Be Justified by Subsequent Changes in Dividends," *American Economic Review* (June 1981), 421–36.

Timme, Stephen G., and Peter C. Eisemann. "On the Use of Consensus Forecasts of Growth in the Constant Growth Model: The Case of Electric Utilities," *Journal of Financial Management* (Winter 1989), 23.

Williams, John B. *The Theory of Investment Value*. Cambridge, MA: Harvard University Press, 1938.

CHAPTER 6

Agmon, Tamir. "Capital Budgeting and Unanticipated Changes in the Exchange Rate," *Advances in Financial Planning and Forecasting* (1990), Part II, 295–314.

Alpin, Richard D., and George L. Casler. *Capital Investment Analysis*. Columbus, OH: Grid, 1973.

Bodie, Zvi. "Compound Interest Depreciation in Capital Investment," *Harvard Business Review* 60 (May–June 1982), 58–60.

Cheung, Joseph K., and John Heaney. "A Contingent-Claim Integration of Cost-Volume-Profit Analysis with Capital Budgeting," *Contemporary Accounting Research* 6 (1990), Part II, 738–60.

Dorfman, Robert. "The Meaning of Internal Rates of Return," *Journal of Finance* 36 (December 1981), 1011–21.

Gitman, Lawrence J., and John R. Forrester, Jr. "Forecasting and Evaluation Practices and Performance: A Survey of Capital Budgeting," *Financial Management* 6 (Fall 1977), 66–71.

Herbst, Anthony. "The Unique, Real Internal Rate of Return: Caveat Emptor!" *Journal of Financial and Quantitative Analysis* 13 (June 1978), 363–70.

Hoskins, Colin G., and Glen A. Mumey. "Payback: A Maligned Method of Asset Ranking?" *Engineering Economist* 25 (Fall 1979), 53–65.

Ingersoll, Jonathan E., Jr., and Stephen A. Ross. "Waiting to Invest: Investment and Uncertainty," *Journal of Business* 65 (1992), 1–29.

Jessell, Kenneth A., and Daniel E. McCarty. "A Note on Marginal Analysis, NPV Criterion and Wealth Maximization," *Journal of Financial Education* 16 (1987), 12–15.

Keane, Simon M. "The Internal Rate of Return and the Reinvestment Fallacy," *Journal of Accounting and Business Studies* 15 (June 1979), 48–55.

Kim, Suk H. "Capital Budgeting Practices in Large Corporations and Their Impact on Over-all Profitability," *Baylor Business Studies* (November–December 1978, January 1979), 48–66.

———. "Current Capital Budgeting Practices," *Management Accounting* 28 (June 1981), 26–30.

Kim, Suk H., Trevor Crick, and Sesung H. Kim. "Do Executives Practice What Academics Teach?" *Management Accounting* 33 (November 1986), 49–52.

Kim, Suk H., and E. J. Farragher. "Capital Budgeting Practices in Large Industrial Firms," *Baylor Business Studies*, (November 1976), 19–25.

Kim, Suk H., and Larry Guin. "A Summary of Empirical Studies on Capital Budgeting Practices," *Business and Public Affairs* 13 (Fall 1986), 21–25.

Klammer, Thomas. "The Association of Capital Budgeting Techniques with Firm Performance," *Accounting Review* (April 1973), 535–64.

———. "Empirical Evidence of the Adoption of Sophisticated Capital Budgeting Techniques," *Journal of Business* (July 1972), 387–97.

Kwan, Clarence C. Y., and Yufei Yuan. "Optimal Sequential Selection in Capital Budgeting: A Shortcut," *Financial Management* 17 (Spring 1988), 54–59.

Logue, Dennis E., and T. Craig Tapley. "Performance Monitoring and the Timing of Cash Flows," *Financial Management* 14 (Autumn 1985), 34–39.

Lorie, James H., and Leonard J. Savage. "Three Problems in Rationing Capital," *Journal of Business* 28 (October 1955), 229–39.

McConnell, John J., and Chris J. Muscarella. "Corporate Capital Expenditure Decisions and the Market Value of the Firm," *Journal of Financial Economics* 14 (September 1985), 399–422.

Mehta, Dileep R., Michael D. Curley, and Hung-Gay Fung. "Inflation Cost of Capital and Capital Budgeting Procedures," *Financial Management* 13 (Winter 1984), 48–54.

Merrett, A. J., and Allen Sykes. *Capital Budgeting and Company Finance*, London: Longmans, 1966.

Myers, Stewart C. "Notes on an Expert System for Capital Budgeting," *Financial Management* 17 (Autumn 1988), 23–31.

Narayanan, M. P. "Observability and the Payback Criterion," *Journal of Business* 58 (July 1985), 309–323.

Petty, J. William, and Oswald D. Bowlin. "The Financial Manager and Quantitative Decision Models," *Financial Management* 4 (Winter 1976), 32–41.

Petty, J. William, David F. Scott, Jr., and Monroe M. Bird. "The Capital Expenditure Decision-Making Process of Large Corporations," *Engineering Economist* 20 (Spring 1975), 159–72.

PonArul, Richard. "Treatment of Flotation Cost of Equity in Capital Budgeting," *Journal of Financial Education* 19 (1990), 44–45.

Porter, Michael E. *Competitive Advantage.* New York: Free Press, 1985.

Rappaport, Alfred, and Robert A. Taggart, Jr. "Evaluation of Capital Expenditure Proposals under Inflation," *Financial Management* 11 (Spring 1982), 5–13.

Rosenblatt, Meir J. "A Survey and Analysis of Capital Budgeting Decision Process in Multi-Division Firms," *Engineering Economist* 25 (Summer 1980), 259–73.

Ross, Marc. "Capital Budgeting Practices of Twelve Large Manufacturers," *Financial Management* 15 (Winter 1986), 15–22.

Schall, Laurence D., Gary L. Sundem, and William R. Geljsbeek, Jr. "Survey and Analysis of Capital Budgeting Methods," *Journal of Finance* 33 (March 1978), 281–87.

Solomon, Ezra. "The Arithmetic of Capital-Budgeting Decisions," *Journal of Business* 29 (April 1956), 124–29.

Statman, Meir, and David Caldwell. "Applying Behavioral Finance to Capital Budgeting: Project Terminations," *Financial Management* 16 (Winter 1987), 7–15.

Statman, Meir, and Tyzoon T. Tyebjee. "Optimistic Capital Budgeting Forecasts," *Financial Management* 14 (Autumn 1985), 27–33.

Teichroew, Daniel, Alexander A. Robichek, and Michael Montalbano. "An Analysis of Criteria for Investment and Financing Decisions under Certainty," *Management Science* 12 (November 1965), 151–79.

Thompson, Arthur A., Jr. *Economics of the Firm: Theory and Practice.* Englewood Cliffs, NJ: Prentice Hall, 1989.

Turner, Leslie D. "Improved Measures of Manufacturing Maintenance in a Capital Budgeting Context: An Application of Data Envelopment Analysis Efficiency Measures," *Journal of Management Accounting Research* 2 (1990), 127–33.

Viscione, Jerry, and John Neuhauser. "Capital Expenditure Decisions in Moderately Sized Firms," *Financial Review* (1974), 16–23.

Weaver, Samuel C., Donald Peters, Roger Cason, and Joe Daleiden. "Capital Budgeting: Panel Discussions on Corporate Investments," *Financial Management* 18 (Spring 1989), 10–17.

Woods, John C., and Maury R. Randall. "The Net Present Value of Future Investment Opportunities: Its Impact on Shareholder Wealth and Implications for Capital Budgeting Theory," *Financial Management* 18 (Summer 1989), 85–92.

CHAPTER 7

Aggarwal, Raj, and Lue A. Soenen. "Project Exit Value as a Measure of Flexibility and Risk Exposure," *Engineering Economist* 35 (Fall 1989), 39–54.

Balachandran, Bala V., Nandu J. Nagarajan, and Alfred Rappaport. "Threshold Margins for Creating Economic Value," *Financial Management* 15 (Spring 1986), 68–77.

Bierman, Harold, Jr., and Vithala R. Rao. "Investment Decisions with Sampling," *Financial Management* 7 (Autumn 1978), 19–24.

Brennan, Michael J. "Latent Assets," *Journal of Finance* 45 (July 1990), 709–30.

Brennan, Michael J., and Eduardo S. Schwartz. "A New Approach to Evaluating Natural Resource Investments," *Midland Corporate Finance Journal* 3 (Spring 1985), 37–47.

Butler, J. S., and Barry Schachter. "Estimation Risk and Risk Adjusted Discount Rates," *Financial Management* 18 (Winter 1989), 13–22.

Cozzolina, John M. "A New Method of Risk Analysis," *Sloan Management Review* 20 (Spring 1979), 53–65.

Dixit, Avinash. "Entry and Exit Decisions Under Uncertainty," *Journal of Political Economy* 97 (June 1989), 620–38.

Galai, Dan, and Ronald W. Masulis. "The Option Pricing Model and the Risk Factor of Stock," *Journal of Financial Economics* 3 (January–March 1976), 66–69.

Hertz, David B. "Investment Policies that Pay Off," *Harvard Business Review* 46 (January–February 1968), 96–108.

———. "Risk Analysis in Capital Investment," *Harvard Business Review* 42 (January–February 1964), 95–106.

Hillier, Frederick S. "A Basic Model for Capital Budgeting of Risky Interrelated Projects," *Engineering Economist* 17 (Fall 1971), 1–30.

———. "The Derivation of Probabilistic Information for the Evaluation of Risky Investments," *Management Science* 9 (April 1963), 443–57.

Hodder, James E., and Henry E. Riggs. "Pitfalls in Evaluating Risky Projects," *Business Review* 63 (January–February 1985), 128–35.

Jarrett, Jeffrey E. "An Abandonment Decision Model," *Engineering Economist* 19 (Fall 1973), 35–46.

Lewellen, Wilbur G., and Michael S. Long. "Simulation versus Single-Value Estimates in Capital Expenditure Analysis," *Decision Sciences* 3 (1972), 19–33.

Magee, J. F. "How to Use Decision Trees in Capital Investment," *Harvard Business Review* 42 (September–October 1964) 79–96.

Marshuetz, Richard J. "How American Can Allocates Capital," *Harvard Business Review* 63 (January–February 1985), 82–91.

Osteryoung, Jerome S., Elton Scott, and Gordon S. Roberts. "Selecting Projects with the Coefficient of Variation," *Financial Management* 6 (Summer 1977), 65–70.

Petty, J. William, David F. Scott, Jr., and Monroe M. Bird. "The Capital Expenditure Decision-Making Process of Large Corporations," *Engineering Economist* 20 (Spring 1975), 159–72.

Schall, Lawrence D., and Gary L. Sundem. "Capital Budgeting Methods and Risk: A Further Analysis," *Financial Management* 9 (Spring 1980), 7–11.

Schall, Lawrence D., Gary L. Sundem, and William R. Geijsbeek, Jr. "Survey and Analysis of Capital Budgeting Methods," *Journal of Finance* 33 (March 1978), 281–87.

Sick, Gordon A. "A Certainty-Equivalent Approach to Capital Budgeting," *Financial Management* 15 (Winter 1986), 23–32.

Spahr, Ronald W., and Stanley A. Martin. "Project Pricing in Limited Diversification Portfolios," *Engineering Economist* 26 (Spring 1981), 207–22.

CHAPTER 8

Amihud, Yakov, and Haim Mendelson. "Liquidity and Cost of Capital: Implications for Corporate Management," *Journal of Applied Corporate Finance* (Fall 1989), 65–73.

Ang, James S., and Wilbur G. Lewellen. "Risk Adjustment in Capital Investment Project Evaluations," *Financial Management* 11 (Summer 1982), 5–14.

Beaver, William H., Paul Kettler, and Myron Scholes. "The Association between Market Determined and Accounting Determined Risk Measures," *Accounting Review* (October 1970), 654–82.

Blume, Marshall E., Irwin Friend, and Randolph Westerfield. "Impediments to Capital Formation: Summary Report of a Survey of Nonfinancial Corporations." Working Paper (Philadelphia: Wharton School, University of Pennsylvania), 1980.

Bowman, Robert G. "The Theoretical Relationship between Systematic Risk and Financial (Accounting) Variables," *Journal of Finance* (June 1979), 617-30.

Chambers, D. R., Robert S. Harris, and John J. Pringle. "Treatment of Financing Mix in Analyzing Investment Opportunities," *Financial Management* 11 (Summer 1982), 24-41.

Chen, Carl R. "Time Series Analysis of Beta Stationarity and Its Determinants: A Case of Public Utilities," *Financial Management* (Autumn 1982), 64-70.

Conine, Thomas E., Jr., and Maury Tamarkin. "Division Cost of Capital Estimation: Adjusting for Leverage," *Financial Management* 14 (Spring 1985), 54-58.

Cooley, Philip L. "A Review of the Use of Beta in Regulatory Proceedings," *Financial Management* (Winter 1981), 75-81.

Diamond, Douglas W., and Robert E. Verrecchia. "Disclosure, Liquidity, and the Cost of Capital," *The Journal of Finance* (September 1991), 1325-60.

Durand, David. "Afterthoughts on a Controversy with MM, Plus New Thoughts on Growth and the Cost of Capital," *Journal of Financial Management* (Summer 1989), 12.

Elliott, J. Walter. "The Cost of Capital and U.S. Investment," *Journal of Finance* 35 (September 1980), 981-1000.

Ezzell, John R., and R. Burr Porter. "Flotation Costs and the Weighted Average Cost of Capital," *Journal of Financial and Quantitative Analysis* 11 (September 1976), 403-13.

Frankel, Jeffrey A. "The Japanese Cost of Finance: A Survey," *Journal of Financial Management* (Winter 1991), 95.

Fuller, Russell J., and Halbert S. Kerr. "Estimating the Divisional Cost of Capital: An Analysis of the Pure-Play Technique," *Journal of Finance* 36 (December 1981), 997-1009.

Gehr, Adam K., Jr. "Risk-Adjusted Capital Budgeting Using Arbitrage," *Financial Management* 10 (Winter 1981), 14-19.

Gitman, Lawrence J., and Vincent A. Mercurio. "Cost of Capital Techniques Used by Major U.S. Firms: Survey and Analysis of Fortune's 1000," *Financial Management* 11 (Winter 1982), 21-29.

Gup, Benton E., and Samuel W. Norwood III. "Divisional Cost of Capital: A Practical Approach," *Financial Management* 11 (Spring 1982), 20-24.

Harris, Robert S., and John J. Pringle. "A Note on the Implications of Miller's Argument for Capital Budgeting," *Journal of Financial Research* (Spring 1983), 13-23.

———. "Risk-Adjusted Discount Rates—Extensions from the Average-Risk Case," *Journal of Financial Research* 8 (Fall 1985), 237-44.

Miles, James A., and John R. Ezzell. "The Weighted Average Cost of Capital, Perfect Capital Markets, and Project Life: A Clarification," *Journal of Financial and Quantitative Analysis* 15 (September 1980), 719-30.

Modigliani, F., and M. Miller. "The Cost of Capital, Corporation Finance, and the Theory of Investment," *American Economic Review* 48 (June 1958), 261-96.

Nantell, Timothy J., and C. Robert Carlson. "The Cost of Capital as a Weighted Average," *Journal of Finance* (December 1975), 1343-55.

Pettway, Richard H., and Bradford D. Jordon. "Diversification, Double Leverage, and the Cost of Capital," *Journal of Financial Research* (Winter 1982), 289-301.

Rosenberg, Barr, and Andrew Rudd. "The Corporate Use of Beta", *Issues in Corporate Risk Management* (New York: Stern, Stewart, Putman & Macklis, Inc., 1983), 42-45.

Scott, David F., Jr., and J. William Petty. "Determining the Cost of Common Equity Capital: The Direct Method," *Journal of Business Research* 8 (March 1980), 89-103.

Van Horne, James C. "An Application of the Capital Asset Pricing Model to Divisional Required Returns," *Financial Management* 9 (Spring 1980), 14-19.

CHAPTER 9

Adar, Zvi, Amir Barnea, and Baruch Lev. "A Comprehensive Cost-Volume-Profit Analysis under Uncertainty," *Accounting Review* 52 (January 1977), 137-49.

Berkovitch, Elazar, and E. Han Kim. "Financial Contracting and Leverage Induced Over- and Under- Investment Incentives," *The Journal of Finance* 45 (July 1990), 765-94.

Bowlin, Oswald D., John D. Martin, and David F. Scott Jr. *Guide to Financial Analysis*, 2d ed., Chap. 11. New York: McGraw-Hill, 1990.

Brigham, Eugene F., and T. Craig Tapley. "Financial Leverage and Use of the Net Present Value Investment Criterion: A Re-examination," *Financial Management* 14 (Summer 1985), 48-52.

Choi, Jongmoo J., Frank J. Fabozzi, and Uzi Yaari. "Optimum Corporate Leverage with Risky Debt: A Demand Approach," *Journal of Financial Research* 12 (Summer 1989), 129-42.

Chung, Kee H. "The Impact of the Demand Volatility and Leverages on the Systematic Risk of Common Stocks," *Journal of Business Finance and Accounting* 16 (Summer 1989), 343-60.

Clark, John J., Margaret T. Clark, and Andrew G. Verzilli. "Strategic Planning and Sustainable Growth," *Columbia Journal of World Business* 20 (Fall 1985), 51.

Conine, Thomas E., Jr. "A Pedagogical Note on Cash Break-even Analysis," *Journal of Business Finance and Accounting* 14 (Autumn 1987), 437-41.

Dammon, Robert M., and Lemma W. Senbet. "The Effect of Taxes and Depreciation on Corporate Investment and Financial Leverage," *Journal of Finance* 43 (June 1988), 357-74.

Dugan, Michael T., and Keith A. Shriver. "The Effects of Estimation Period, Industry, and Proxy on the Calculation of the Degree of Operating Leverage," *The Financial Review* 24 (February 1989), 109-22.

Gamble, Richard H. "Deleveraging: Relief from a Big Debt Hangover," *Corporate Cashflow* 12 (January 1991), 24-30.

Gahlon, James M., and James A. Gentry. "On the Relationship between Systematic Risk and the Degrees of Operating and Financial Leverage," *Financial Management* 11 (Summer 1982), 15-23.

Ghandi, J. K. S. "On the Measurement of Leverage," *Journal of Finance* 21 (December 1966), 715-26.

Gilbert, Nathaniel. "Living on Leverage: Can U.S. Business Survive Its Passion for Debt?" *Management Review* 79 (April 1990), 50-55.

Golbe, Devra L., and Barry Schachater. "The Net Present Value Rule and an Algorithm for Maintaining a Constant Debt-Equity Ratio," *Financial Management* 14 (Summer 1985), 53-58.

Gritta, Richard D. "The Effect of Financial Leverage on Air Carrier Earnings: A Break-Even Analysis," *Financial Management* 8 (Summer 1979), 53-60.

Gupta, Atul, and Leonard Rosenthal. "Ownership Structure, Leverage, and Firm Value: The Case of Leveraged Recapitalizations," *Financial Management* 20 (Autumn 1991), 69-83.

Haslem, John A. "Leverage Effects on Corporate Earnings," *Arizona Business Review* 19 (March 1970), 7-11.

Helfert, Erich A. *Techniques of Financial Analysis*, 5th ed. Chap. 6. Homewood, IL: Richard D. Irwin, 1982.

Higgins, Robert C. *Analysis for Financial Management*, Chap. 7. Homewood, IL: Richard D. Irwin, 1984.

Hunt, Pearson. "A Proposal for Precise Definitions of Trading on the Equity and Leverage," *Journal of Finance* 16 (September 1961), 377-86.

Jaedicke, Robert K., and Alexander A. Robichek. "Cost-Volume-Profit Analysis under Conditions of Uncertainty," *Accounting Review* 39 (October 1964), 917-26.

Janjigian, Vahan. "The Leverage Changing Consequences of Convertible Debt Financing," *Financial Management* 16 (Autumn 1987), 15-21.

Leibowitz, Martin L., and Stanley Kogelman. "The Franchise Factor for Leveraged Firms," *Financial Analysts Journal* 47 (November–December 1991), 29-43.

Leibowitz, Martin L., Stanley Kogelman, and Eric B. Lindenberg. "A Shortfall Approach to the Creditor's Decision: How Much Leverage Can a Firm Support?" *Financial Analysts Journal* 46 (May–June 1990), 43-52.

Lev, Baruch. "On the Association between Operating Leverage and Risk," *Journal of Financial and Quantitative Analysis* 9 (September 1974), 627-42.

Lewellen, Wilbur G., and William A. Kracaw. "Inflation, Corporate Growth, and Corporate Leverage," *Financial Management* 16 (Winter 1987), 29-36.

McConoughey, Deborah J. "Breakeven Analysis for Maturity Decisions in Cash Management," *Journal of Cash Management* 5 (January–February 1985), 18-21.

Miller, Merton H. "Leverage," *The Journal of Finance* 46 (June 1991), 479–88.

O'Brien, Thomas J., and Vanderheiden, Paul A. "Empirical Measurement of Operating Leverage for Growing Firms," *Financial Management* 16 (Spring 1987), 45–53.

Osteryoung, Jerome S., and Daniel E. McCarty. *Analytical Techniques for Financial Management*, Chap. 11. Columbus, OH: Grid, 1980.

Percival, John R. "Operating Leverage and Risk," *Journal of Business Research* 2 (April 1974), 223–27.

Phillips, Aaron L. "An Empirical Study of Asset Size, Financial Leverage, and Stock Market Anomalies," *Akron Business and Economic Review* 20 (Fall 1989), 40–54.

Prezas, Alexandros P. "Effects of Debt on the Degree of Operating and Financial Leverage," *Financial Management* 16 (Spring 1987), 39–44.

Reinhardt, U. E. "Break Even Analysis for Lockheed's Tri Star: An Application of Financial Theory," *Journal of Finance* 28 (September 1973), 821–38.

Remolona, Eli M. "Understanding International Differences in Leverage Trends," *Federal Reserve Bank of New York Quarterly Review* 15 (Spring 1990), 31–42.

Shalit, Sol S. "On the Mathematics of Financial Leverage," *Financial Management* 4 (Spring 1975), 57–66.

Shashua, Leon, and Yaaqov Goldschmidt. "Break-even Analysis Under Inflation," *Engineering Economist* 32 (Winter 1987), 79–88.

Siegel, Frederick W., and James P. Hoban. "Measuring Risk Aversion: Allocation, Leverage, and Accumulation," *Journal of Financial Research* 14 (Spring 1991), 27–35.

Sullivan, Timothy G. "Market Power, Profitability and Financial Leverage," *Journal of Finance* 29 (December 1974), 1407–14.

Thode, Stephen F., Ralph E. Drtina, and James A. Largay III. "Operating Cash Flows: A Growing Need for Separate Reporting," *Journal of Accounting, Auditing and Finance* 1 (Winter 1986), 46–57.

Tsurumi, Yoshi, and Hiroki Tsurumi. "Value-Added Maximizing Behavior of Japanese Firms and Roles of Corporate Investment and Finance," *Columbia Journal of World Business* 20 (Spring 1985), 29–35.

Viscione, Jerry A. *Financial Analysis: Principles and Procedures*, Chap. 4. Boston: Houghton Mifflin, 1977.

Wiggins, James B. "The Relation between Risk and Optimal Debt Maturity and the Value of Leverage," *Journal of Financial and Quantitative Analysis* 25 (September 1990), 377–86.

Zimmer, Steven A. "Event Risk Premia and Bond Market Incentives for Corporate Leverage," *Federal Reserve Bank of New York Quarterly Review* 15 (Spring 1990), 15–30.

CHAPTER 10

Barges, Alexander. *The Effect of Capital Structure on the Cost of Capital*. Englewood Cliffs, NJ: Prentice Hall, 1963.

Barnea, Amir, Robert A. Haugen, and Lemma W. Senbet. "Market Imperfections, Agency Problems, and Capital Structure: A Review," *Financial Management* 10 (Summer 1981), 7–22.

Barton, Sidney L., Ned C. Hill, and Srinivasan Sundaram. "An Empirical Test of Stakeholder Theory Predictions of Capital Structure," *Financial Management* 18 (Spring 1989), 36–44.

Baskin, Jonathan. "An Empirical Investigation of the Pecking Order Hypothesis," *Financial Management* 18 (Spring 1989), 26–35.

Baumol, William, and Burton G. Malkiel. "The Firm's Optimal Debt-Equity Combination and the Cost of Capital," *Quarterly Journal of Economics* 81 (November 1967), 547–78.

Baxter, Nevins D. "Leverage, Risk of Ruin, and the Cost of Capital," *Journal of Finance* 22 (September 1967), 395–404.

Belkaoui, Ahmed. "A Canadian Survey of Financial Structure," *Financial Management* 4 (Spring 1975), 74–79.

Bhide, Amar. "Why Not Leverage Your Company to the Hilt?" *Harvard Business Review* 66 (May/June 1988), 92–98.

Bowen, Robert M., Lane A. Daley, and Charles C. Huber, Jr. "Evidence on the Existence and Determinants of Inter-Industry Differences in Leverage," *Financial Management* 11 (Winter 1982), 10–20.

Brick, Ivan E., and S. Abraham Ravid. "Interest Rate Uncertainty and the Optimal Debt Maturity Structure," *Journal of Financial and Quantitative Analysis* 26 (March 1991), 63–82.

Brigham, Eugene F., and Myron J. Gordon. "Leverage, Dividend Policy, and the Cost of Capital," *Journal of Finance* 23 (March 1968), 85–104.

Castanias, Richard. "Bankruptcy Risk and Optimal Capital Structure," *Journal of Finance* 38 (December 1983), 1617–35.

Chang, Rosita P., and S. Ghon Rhee. "The Impact of Personal Taxes on Corporate Dividend Policy and Capital Structure Decisions," *Financial Management* 19 (Summer 1990), 21–35.

Chatterjee, Sris, and James H. Scott, Jr. "Explaining Differences in Corporate Capital Structure: Theory and New Evidence," *Journal of Banking and Finance* 13 (May 1989), 283–310.

Cherry, Richard T., and Larry W. Spradley. "Further Tests of Industry Influence on Capital Structure," *The Review of Business and Economic Research* 25 (Spring 1990), 58–66.

Cornell, Bradford, and Alan C. Shapiro, "Corporate Stakeholders and Corporate Finance," *Financial Management* 16 (Spring 1987), 5–14.

Donaldson, Gordon. *Corporate Debt Capacity*. Boston: Division of Research, Graduate School of Business Administration, Harvard University, 1961.

———. "New Framework for Corporate Debt Policy," *Harvard Business Review* 40 (March–April 1962), 117–31.

———. "Strategy for Financial Emergencies," *Harvard Business Review* 47 (November–December 1969), 67–79.

———. *Strategy for Financial Mobility*. Boston: Division of Research, Graduate School of Business Administration, Harvard University, 1969.

Durand, David. "Costs of Debt and Equity Funds for Business: Trends and Problems of Measurement," *Conference on Research in Business Finance*. New York: National Bureau of Economic Research, 1952, pp. 215–47.

Easterwood, John C., and Palani-Rajan Kadapakkam. "The Role of Private and Public Debt in Corporate Capital Structures," *Financial Management* 20 (Autumn 1991), 49–57.

Ferri, Michael G., and Wesley H. Jones. "Determinants of Financial Structure: A New Methodological Approach," *Journal of Finance* 34 (June 1979), 631–44.

Fischer, Edwin O., Robert Heinkel, and Josef Zechner. "Dynamic Capital Structure Choice: Theory and Tests," *Journal of Finance* 44 (March 1989), 19–40.

Fletcher, Ralph H., Jr., and Stephen D. Gray. "Private Placements' Big Screen Success," *Corporate Cashflow* 11 (March 1990), 32–37.

Frankel, Jeffrey A. "The Japanese Cost of Finance: A Survey," *Financial Management* 20 (Spring 1991), 95–127.

Greenfield, Robert L., Maury R. Randall, and John C. Woods. "Financial Leverage and Use of the Net Present Value Criterion," *Financial Management* 12 (Autumn 1983), 40–44.

Hamada, Robert S. "The Effect of the Firm's Capital Structure on the Systematic Risk of Common Stocks," *Journal of Finance* 27 (May 1972), 435–52.

Harris, John M., Jr., Rodney L. Roenfeldt, and Philip L. Cooley. "Evidence of Financial Leverage Clienteles," *Journal of Finance* 38 (September 1983), 1125–32.

Harris, Milton, and Artur Raviv. "Capital Structure and the Informational Role of Debt," *The Journal of Finance* 45 (June 1990), 321–49.

———. "The Theory of Capital Structure," *The Journal of Finance* 46 (March 1991), 297–355.

Haugen, Robert A., and Lemma W. Senbet. "The Insignificance of Bankruptcy Costs to the Theory of Optimal Capital Structure," *Journal of Finance* 33 (May 1978), 383–93.

Huggins, Nancy J. "Where Can the Middle Market Find Capital?" *Financial Executive* 7 (May/June 1991), 24–29.

Israel, Ronen. "Capital Structure and the Market for Corporate Control: The Defensive Role of Debt Financing," *The Journal of Finance* 46 (September 1991), 1391–1409.

Jalilvand, Abolhassan, and Robert S. Harris. "Corporate Behavior in Adjusting to Capital Structure and Dividend Targets: An Econometric Study," *Journal of Finance* 39 (March 1984), 127–45.

Jensen, Michael C., and William E. Meckling. "Theory of the Firm: Managerial Behavior, Agency Costs and Ownership

Structure," *Journal of Financial Economics* 3 (October 1976), 305–60.

Kane, Alex, Alan J. Marcus, and Robert L. McDonald. "Debt Policy and the Rate of Return Premium to Leverage," *Journal of Financial and Quantitative Analysis* 20 (December 1985), 479–99.

Kim, E. Han. "A Mean-Variance Theory of Optimal Financial Structure and Corporate Debt Capacity," *Journal of Finance* 33 (March 1978), 45–64.

———. "Miller's Equilibrium, Shareholder Leverage Clienteles, and Optimal Capital Structure," *Journal of Finance* 37 (May 1982), 301–19.

Litzenberger, Robert H. "Some Observations on Capital Structure and the Impact of Recent Recapitalizations on Share Prices," *Journal of Financial and Quantitative Analysis* 21 (March 1986), 59–71.

Marsh, Paul. "The Choice between Equity and Debt: An Empirical Study," *Journal of Finance* 37 (March 1982), 121–44.

Martin, John D., and David F. Scott, Jr. "A Discriminant Analysis of the Corporate Debt-Equity Decision," *Financial Management* 3 (Winter 1974), 71–79.

———. "Debt Capacity and the Capital Budgeting Decision," *Financial Management* 5 (Summer 1976), 7–14.

———. "Debt Capacity and the Capital Budgeting Decision: A Revisitation," *Financial Management* 9 (Spring 1980), 23–26.

Miller, Merton H. "Debt and Taxes," *Journal of Finance* 32 (May 1977), 261–75.

Modigliani, Franco, and Merton H. Miller. "Corporate Income Taxes and the Cost of Capital: A Correction," *American Economic Review* 53 (June 1963), 433–43.

———. "The Cost of Capital, Corporation Finance and the Theory of Investment," *American Economic Review* 48 (June 1958), 261–97.

Myers, Stewart C. "Determinants of Corporate Borrowing," *Journal of Financial Economics* 5 (1977), 147–75.

Picker, Ida. "Getting Smarter About Debt," *Institutional Investor* 24 (February 1990), 87–90.

Piper, Thomas R., and Wolf A. Weinhold. "How Much Debt Is Right for Your Company?" *Harvard Business Review* 60 (July-August 1982), 106–14.

Roderick, Pamela H. "Cracking the Debt Market: Tough Nut, Cheap Funds," *Corporate Cashflow* 12 (August 1991), 24–30.

Schwartz, Eli, and J. Richard Aronson. "Some Surrogate Evidence in Support of the Concept of Optimal Capital Structure," *Journal of Finance* 22 (March 1967), 10–18.

Scott, David F., Jr. "Evidence on the Importance of Financial Structure," *Financial Management* 1 (Summer 1972), 45–50.

Scott, David F., Jr., and Dana J. Johnson. "Financing Policies and Practices in Large Corporations," *Financial Management* 11 (Summer 1982), 51–59.

Scott, David F., Jr., and John D. Martin. "Industry Influence on Financial Structure," *Financial Management* 4 (Spring 1975), 67–73.

Scott, James H., Jr. "A Theory of Optimal Capital Structure," *Bell Journal of Economics* 7 (Spring 1976), 33–54.

Senbet, Lemma A., and Robert A. Taggert, Jr. "Capital Structure Equilibrium under Market Imperfections and Incompleteness," *Journal of Finance* 39 (March 1984), 93–103.

Shrieves, Ronald E., and Mary M. Pashley. "Evidence on the Association Between Mergers and Capital Structure," *Financial Management* 13 (Autumn 1984), 39–48.

Solomon, Ezra. "Leverage and the Cost of Capital," *Journal of Finance* 18 (May 1963), 273–79.

Taggart, Robert A. "Capital Budgeting and the Financing Decision: An Exposition," *Financial Management* 6 (Summer 1977), 59–64.

———. "Corporate Financing: Too Much Debt?" *Financial Analysts Journal* 41 (May-June 1986), 35–42.

Titman, Sheridan, and Roberto Wessels. "The Determinants of Capital Structure Choice," *Journal of Finance* 43 (March 1988), 1–20.

Zechner, Josef, and Peter Swoboda. "The Critical Implicit Tax Rate and Capital Structure," *Journal of Banking and Finance* 10 (October 1986), 327–41.

CHAPTER 11

Asquith, Paul, and David Mullins. "The Impact of Initiating Dividend Payments on Shareholders' Wealth," *Journal of Business* 56 (January 1983), 77–99.

———. "Signalling with Dividends, Stock Repurchases, Equity Issues," *Financial Management* 15 (Autumn 1986), 27–45.

Baker, H. K., G. E. Farrelly, and R. B. Edelman. "A Survey of Management's Views on Dividend Policy," *Financial Management* (Autumn 1985), 78–84.

Benesh, G. A., A. J. Keown, and J. M. Pinkerton. "An Examination of the Market Reaction to Substantial Shifts in Dividend Policy," *Journal of Financial Research* (Summer 1984), 131–42.

Black, F. "The Dividend Puzzle," *Journal of Portfolio Management* 2 (Winter 1976).

Black, F., and M. Scholes. "The Effects of Dividend Yield and Dividend Policy on Common Stock Prices and Returns," *Journal of Financial Economics* 1 (May 1974), 1–22.

Brickley, James A. "Shareholder Wealth, Information Signalling, and the Specially Designated Dividend: An Empirical Study," *Journal of Financial Economics* 12 (1983), 287–309.

Chang, Rosita P., and S. Ghon Rhee. "The Impact of Personal Taxes on Corporate Dividend Policy and Capital Structure Decisions," *Journal of Financial Management* (Summer 1990), 21.

Crutchley, Claire E., and Robert S. Hansen. "A Test of the Agency Theory of Managerial Ownership, Corporate Leverage, and Corporate Dividends," *Journal of Financial Management* (Winter 1989), 36.

Dyl, E. A., and J. R. Hoffmeister. "A Note on Dividend Policy and Beta," *Journal of Business Finance and Accounting* (Spring 1986), 107–15.

Feldstein, M., and J. Green. "Why Do Companies Pay Dividends?" National Bureau of Economic Research, Conference Paper No. 54 (October 1980).

Gonedes, N. "Corporate Signaling, External Accounting and Capital Market Equilibrium: Evidence on Dividends, Income, and Extraordinary Items," *Journal of Accounting Research* (Spring 1978), 26–79.

Grinblatt, M. S., R. W. Masulis, and S. Titman. "The Valuation Effects of Stock Splits and Stock Dividends," *Journal of Financial Economics* 13 (December 1984), 461–90.

Hakansson, Nils H. "To Pay or Not to Pay Dividends," *Journal of Finance* 37 (May 1982), 415–28.

Hess, P. "The Ex-Dividend Behavior of Stock Returns: Further Evidence on Tax Effects," *Journal of Finance* 37 (May 1982), 445–56.

John, Kose, and Larry H. P. Lang. "Insider Trading around Dividend Announcements: Theory and Evidence," *The Journal of Finance* (September 1991), 1361–90.

Lintner, J. "Distribution of Incomes of Corporations Among Dividends, Retained Earnings, and Taxes," *American Economic Review* 46 (May 1956), 97–113.

Litzenberger, R. H., and K. Ramaswamy. "The Effect of Personal Taxes and Dividends on Capital Asset Prices: Theory and Empirical Evidence," *Journal of Financial Economics* 7 (June 1979), 163–95.

Michaely, Roni. "Ex-Dividend Day Stock Price Behavior: The Case of the 1986 Tax Reform Act," *The Journal of Finance* (July 1991), 845–60.

Miller, M. H. "Behavioral Rationality: The Case of Dividends," *Journal of Business* 59 (October 1986), 5451–68.

———. "The Informational Content of Dividends," in *Macroeconomics: Essays in Honor of Franco Modigliani*, ed. J. Bossons, R. Dornbusch, and S. Fischer. Cambridge, MA: MIT Press, 1987.

Miller, M. H., and Franco Modigliani. "Dividend Policy, Growth, and the Valuation of Shares," *Journal of Business* 34 (October 1961), 411–33.

Miller M. H., and K. Rock. "Dividend Policy under Asymmetric Information," *Journal of Finance* 40 (September 1985), 1031–51.

Morgan, I. G. "Dividends and Capital Asset Prices," *Journal of Finance* 37 (September 1982), 1071–86.

Penman, S. H. "The Predictive Content of Earnings Forecasts and Dividends," *Journal of Finance* (September 1983), 1181–99.

Shefrin, H., and M. Statman. "Explaining Investor Preference for Cash Dividends, *Journal of Financial Economics* 13 (June 1984), 253–82.

Talmor, Eli, and Sheridan Titman. "Taxes and Dividend Policy," *Journal of Financial Management* (Summer 1990), 32.

Woolridge, J. R. "Dividend Changes and Security Prices," *Journal of Finance* 38 (December 1983), 1607–15.

———. "Stock Dividends as Signals," *Journal of Financial Research* 6 (Spring 1983), 1–12.

CHAPTER 12

Altman, Edward I. "Financial Ratios, Discriminant Analysis and the Prediction of Corporate Bankruptcy," *Journal of Finance* 23 (September 1968), 598–609.

Altman Edward I., R. G. Haldeman, and P. Narayanan. "Zeta Analysis: A New Model to Identify Bankruptcy Risk of Corporations," *Journal of Banking and Finance* 1 (June 1977), 29–54.

Bedingfield, J. P., P. M. J. Reckers, and A. J. Stagliano. "Distributions of Financial Ratios in the Commercial Banking Industry, *Journal of Financial Research* (Spring 1985), 77–81.

Benishay, Haskell. "Economic Information in Financial Ratio Analysis," *Accounting and Business Research* 2 (Spring 1971), 174–79.

Bowlin, Oswald D., John D. Martin, and David F. Scott, Jr. *Guide to Financial Analysis*, 2d ed., Chap. 2. New York: McGraw-Hill, 1990.

Chen, Kung H., and T. A. Shimerda. "An Empirical Analysis of Useful Financial Ratios," *Financial Management* 10 (Spring 1981), 51–60.

Collins, R. A. "An Empirical Comparison of Bankruptcy Prediction Models," *Financial Management* (Summer 1980), 52–57.

Frecka, T., and C. F. Lee. "Generalized Ratio Generation Process and Its Implications," *Journal of Accounting Research* (Spring 1983), 308–16.

Gordon, Gus. *Understanding Financial Statements*. Cincinnati: South-Western Publishing, 1992.

Harrington, D. R., and B. D. Wilson. *Corporate Financial Analysis*, Chap. 1. Plano, TX: BPI, Inc., 1986.

Helfert, Erich. *Techniques of Financial Analysis*, Chap. 2–3. Homewood, IL: Richard D. Irwin, 1991.

Kamath, Ravindra. "How Useful Are Commonly Used Liquidity Measures?" *Journal of Cash Management* 9 (January/February 1989), 24–28.

Kieso, Donald E., and Jerry J. Weygandt. *Intermediate Accounting*, 6th ed. New York: Wiley, 1989.

Maness, Terry S., and James W. Henderson. "A Framework for Analyzing the Statement of Cash Flows," *Journal of Cash Management* (May/June 1989), 19–22.

Murray, Roger F. "The Penn Central Debacle: Lessons for Financial Analysis," *Journal of Finance* 26 (May 1971), 327–32.

Robert Morris Associates. *Annual Statement Studies*. Philadelphia, PA: Updated annually.

Rose, J. T., and D. F. Cunningham. "Industry Analysis in Individual Credit Decision-Making: A Comparison of RMA and D&B Benchmark Data," Working paper. Waco, TX: Baylor University, 1991.

Stickney, Clyde P. *Financial Statement Analysis*. San Diego: Harcourt Brace Jovanovich, 1990.

CHAPTER 13

Beyer, William E. "Liquidity Measurement in Corporate Forecasting," *Journal of Cash Management* (November–December 1988), 14–16.

Carleton, W. T., C. L. Dick, and D. H. Downes. "Financial Policy Models: Theory and Practice," *Journal of Financial and Quantitative Analysis* 8 (December 1973), 691–710.

Chambers, John C., Satinder K. Mullick, and Donald D. Smith. "How to Choose the Right Forecasting Technique," *Harvard Business Review* 49 (July–August 1971), 45–74.

Parker, G. G. C., and E. L. Segura. "How to Get a Better Forecast," *Harvard Business Review* 49 (March–April 1971), 99–109.

Seed, A. H., III. "Measuring Financial Performance in an Inflationary Environment," *Financial Executive* (January 1982), 40–50.

Weston, J. Fred. "Forecasting Financial Requirements," *Accounting Review* 33 (July 1958), 427–40.

CHAPTER 14

Burns, Richard, and Joe Walker. "A Survey of Working Capital Policy Among Small Manufacturing Firms," *Journal of Small Business* 1: 1 (1991), 61–74.

Gentry, J. A., "State of the Art of Short-Term Financial Management," *Financial Management* (Summer 1988), 30–37.

Hawawini, Gabriel, Claude Viallett, and Ashok Vora. "Industry Influence on Corporate Working Capital Decisions," *Sloan Management Review* (Summer 1986), 15–24.

Hill, N. C., and W. L. Sartoris. *Short-Term Financial Management*. New York: Macmillan, 1988.

Knight, W. D. "Working Capital Management—Satisficing Versus Optimization," *Financial Management* 1 (Spring 1972), 33–40.

Richards, V. D., and E. J. Laughlin. "A Cash Conversion Cycle Approach to Liquidity Analysis," *Financial Management* (1980), 32–38.

Sartoris, W. L., and N. C. Hill. "A Generalized Cash Flow Approach to Short-Term Financial Decisions," *Journal of Finance* 38 (May 1983), 349–60.

Smith, Keith V. *Management of Working Capital*, 2d ed. New York: West, 1980.

Smith, Keith V., and Brian Belt. "Working Capital Management in Practice," in *Readings in the Management of Working Capital*, 2d ed. ed. K. V. Smith New York: West, 1980.

Smith, Keith V., and Brian Belt. "Working Capital Management in Practice: An Update." Paper No. 951, Institute for Research in the Behavioral, Economic, and Management Sciences, Krannert Graduate School of Management, Purdue University, West Lafayette, IN (March 1989).

Smith, K. V., and G. W. Gallinger. *Readings on Short-Term Financial Management*, 3rd ed. St. Paul MN: West, 1988.

Walker, Ernest W. "Toward a Theory of Working Capital," *Engineering Economist* 9 (January–February 1964), 21–35.

CHAPTER 15

An Analytical Record of Yields and Yield Spreads. New York: Salomon Brothers, 1977–1989.

Anderson, Paul F., and R. D. Boyd Harman. "The Management of Excess Corporate Cash," *Financial Executive* 32 (October 1964), 26–30, 51.

Archer, Stephen H. "A Model for the Determination of Firm Cash Balances," *Journal of Financial and Quantitative Analysis* 1 (March 1966), 1–11.

Arthur, William J. "Cash Flow Yardstick: Here's One Way to Make the Cash Flow Statement More Useful," *Financial Executive* 54 (October 1986), 35–40.

Aziz, Abdul, and Gerald H. Lawson. "Cash Flow Reporting and Financial Distress Models: Testing of Hypotheses," *Financial Management* 18 (Spring 1989), 55–63.

Bagamery, Bruce D. "On the Correspondence Between the Baumol-Tobin and Miller-Orr Optimal Cash Balance Models," *The Financial Review* 22 (May 1987), 313–38.

Batlin, C. A., and Susan Hinko. "Lockbox Management and Value Maximization," *Financial Management* 10 (Winter 1981), 39–44.

Baumol, William J. "The Transactions Demand for Cash: An Inventory Theoretic Approach," *Quarterly Journal of Economics* 66 (November 1952), 545–56.

Bennett, Barbara. "Standby Letters of Credit," Federal Reserve Bank of San Francisco, *Weekly Letter* (May 23, 1986), 1–3.

Briscoe, Carl G., II, and Arlene F. Perkins. "Automating the Cash Management Transaction Processing Cycle," *Journal of Cash Management* 11 (March–April 1991), 27–30.

Brunell, Kateri T. "Cash Management Practices of Small Firms," *Journal of Cash Management* 10 (November–December 1990), 52–55.

Budin, Morris, and Robert J. Van Handel. "A Rule-of-Thumb Theory of Cash Holdings by Firms," *Journal of Financial and Quantitative Analysis* 10 (March 1975), 85–108.

Campbell, Tim, and Leland Brendsel. "The Impact of Compensating Balance Requirements on the Cash Balances of Manufacturing Corporations: An Empirical Study," *Journal of Finance* 32 (March 1977), 31–40.

Carraro, Kenneth C., and Daniel L. Thornton. "The Cost of Checkable Deposits in the United States," Federal Reserve Bank of St. Louis, *Review* 68 (April 1986), 19–27.

"Cash Management: The New Art of Wringing More Profit from Corporate Funds," *Business Week* (March 13, 1978), 62–68.

Collins, J. Markham, and Alan W. Frankle. "International Cash Practices of Large U.S. Firms," *Journal of Cash Management* 5 (July–August 1985), 42–48.

Cook, Timothy Q., and T. D. Rowe, eds. *Instruments of the Money Market*, 6th ed.

Richmond, VA: Federal Reserve Bank of Richmond, 1986.

Dalessandro, Glen K. "Cash Transaction Distribution Method," *Journal of Cash Management* 10 (September–October 1990), 15–17.

Desalvo, Alfred. "Cash Management Converts Dollars into Working Assets," *Harvard Business Review* 50 (May–June 1972), 92–100.

Emery, Gary W. "Some Empirical Evidence on the Properties of Daily Cash Flow," *Financial Management* 10 (Spring 1981), 21–28.

Etzel, Thomas J. "How Retailers Can Maximize the Utility of Bank Cash Management Services," *Journal of Cash Management* 11 (July–August 1991), 22–24.

Fabozzi, Frank J., and Leslie N. Masonson. *Corporate Cash Management.* Homewood, IL: Dow Jones-Irwin, 1985.

Ferguson, Daniel M. "Optimize Your Firm's Lockbox Selection System," *Financial Executive* 51 (April 1983), 8–12, 14–15, 18–19.

Gentry, James A. "State of the Art of Short-Run Financial Management," *Financial Management* 17 (Summer 1988), 41–57.

Gentry, James A., R. Vaidyanathan, and Hei Wai Lee. "A Weighted Cash Conversion Cycle," *Financial Management* 19 (Spring 1990), 90–99.

Gitman, Lawrence J., and Mark D. Goodwin. "An Assessment of Marketable Securities Management Practices," *Journal of Financial Research* 2 (Fall 1979), 161–69.

Gombola, Michael J., Mark E. Haskins, J. Edward Ketz, and David D. Williams. "Cash Flow in Bankruptcy Prediction," *Financial Management* 16 (Winter 1987), 55–65.

Grahman, Richard P. "Investment Management in the Turbulent 1990s," *Journal of Cash Management* 11 (NCCMA Conference 1991), 51–56.

Joehnk, Michael D., Oswald D. Bowlin, and J. William Petty II. "Preferred Dividend Rolls: A Viable Strategy for Corporate Money Managers?" *Financial Management* 9 (Summer 1980), 78–87.

Johnson, James M., David R. Campbell, and Leonard M. Savoie. "Corporate Liquidity: A Comparison of Two Recessions," *Financial Executive* 51 (October 1983), 18–22.

Jones, Reginald H. "Face to Face with Cash Management: How One Company Does It," *Financial Executive* 37 (September 1969), 37–39.

Kamath, Ravindra. "How Useful Are Common Liquidity Measures?" *Journal of Cash Management* 9 (January/February 1989), 24–28.

Lordan, James F. "A Profile of Corporate Cash Management," *Magazine of Bank Administration* 48 (April 1972), 15–19.

Maier, Steven F., and Larry A. Meeks. "Applications and Models: When Is the Right Time to Do a Lockbox Study?" *Journal of Cash Management* 6 (March–April 1986), 32–34.

Maier, Steven F., and James H. Vander Weide. "A Practical Approach to Short-Run Financial Planning," *Financial Management* 7 (Winter 1978), 10–16.

———. "What Lockbox and Disbursement Models Really Do," *Journal of Finance* 38 (May 1983), 361–71.

McConoughey, Deborah J. "Breakeven Analysis for Maturity Decisions in Cash Management," *Journal of Cash Management* 5 (January–February 1985), 18–21.

Miller, Merton H., and Daniel Orr. "The Demand for Money by Firms: Extension of Analytic Results," *Journal of Finance* 23 (December 1968), 735–59.

———. "A Model of the Demand for Money by Firms," *Quarterly Journal of Economics* 80 (August 1966), 413–35.

Miller, Tom W., and Bernell K. Stone. "Daily Cash Forecasting and Seasonal Resolution: Alternative Models and Techniques for Using the Distribution Approach," *Journal of Financial and Quantitative Analysis* 20 (September 1985), 335–51.

Myers, Stewart C. *Modern Developments in Financial Management,* Part 4. New York: Praeger, 1976.

Nauss, Robert M., and Robert E. Markland. "Solving Lock Box Location Problems," *Financial Management* 8 (Spring 1979), 21–27.

Pohlman, Randolph A., Emmanuel S. Santiago, and F. Lynn Markel. "Cash Flow Estimation Practices of Large Firms," *Financial Management* 17 (Summer 1988), 71–79.

Richards, Verlyn D., and Eugene J. Laughlin. "A Cash Conversion Cycle Approach to Liquidity Analysis," *Financial Management* 9 (Spring 1980), 32–38.

Rinne, Heikki, Robert A. Wood, and Ned C. Hill. "Reducing Cash Concentration Costs by Anticipatory Forecasting," *Journal of Cash Management* 6 (March–April 1986), 44–50.

Sartoris, William L., and Ned C. Hill. "A Generalized Cash Flow Approach to Short-Term Financial Decisions," *Journal of Finance* 38 (May 1983), 349–60.

Scott, David F., Jr., Laurence J. Moore, Andre Saint-Denis, Edouard Archer, and Bernard W. Taylor III. "Implementation of a Cash Budget Simulator at Air Canada," *Financial Management* 8 (Summer 1979), 46–52.

Searby, Frederick W. "Use Your Hidden Cash Resources," *Harvard Business Review* 46 (March–April 1968), 71–80.

Seidner, Alan G. "Investing Excess Corporate Cash," *Financial Executive* 7 (January–February 1991), 38–41.

Senchack, Andrew J., and Don M. Heep. "Auction Profits in the Treasury Bill Market," *Financial Management* 4 (Summer 1975), 45–52.

Stone, Bernell K. "The Ongoing Evolution of Corporate Cash Management," *Journal of Cash Management* 10 (NCCMA Conference 1990), 45–54.

Stone, Bernell K., and Ned C. Hill. "Cash Transfer Scheduling for Efficient Cash Concentration," *Financial Management* 9 (Autumn 1980), 35–43.

Stone, Bernell K., and Tom W. Miller. "Daily Cash Forecasting with Multiplicative Models of Cash Flow Patterns," *Financial Management* 16 (Winter 1987), 45–54.

Stone, Bernell K., and Robert A. Wood. "Daily Cash Forecasting: A Simple Method for Implementing the Distribution Approach," *Financial Management* 6 (Fall 1977), 40–50.

Syron, Richard, and Sheila L. Tschinkel. "The Government Securities Market: Playing Field for Repos," Federal Reserve Bank of Atlanta, *Economic Review* 70 (September 1985), 10–19.

Thornrose, Carl N. "Electronic Payments: Making the Promise Hatch," *Corporate Cashflow* 12 (March 1991), 28–31.

Vickson, R. G. "Simple Optimal Policy for Cash Management: The Average Balanced Requirement Case," *Journal of Financial and Quantitative Analysis* 20 (September 1985), 353–69.

White, George C. "'Marrying' Checks and EFT: Moving Toward Same Day Collection," *Journal of Cash Management* 11 (May–June 1991), 52–53.

CHAPTER 16

Altman, Edward I. "Financial Ratios, Discriminate Analysis and the Prediction of Corporate Bankruptcy," *Journal of Finance* 23 (September 1968), 589–609.

Atkins, Joseph C., and Yong H. Kim. "Comment and Correction: Opportunity Cost in the Evaluation of Investment in Accounts Receivable," *Financial Management* 6 (Winter 1977), 71–74.

Beranek, William. "Financial Implications of Lot-Size Inventory Models," *Harvard Business Review* 47 (January–February 1969), 72–90.

Brennan, Michael, J., Vojislav Maksimovic, and Josef Zechner. "Vendor Financing," *Journal of Finance* 43 (December 1988), 1127–41.

Brick, Ivan E., and William K. H. Fung. "The Effect of Taxes on the Trade Credit Decision," *Financial Management* 13 (Summer 1984), 24–30.

Brooks, Leroy D. "Risk-Return Criteria and Optimal Inventory Stocks," *Engineering Economist* 25 (Summer 1980), 275–99.

Brosky, John J. *The Implicit Cost of Trade Credit and Theory of Optimal Terms of Sale.* New York: Credit Research Foundation, 1969.

Carpenter, Michael D., and Jack E. Miller. "A Reliable Framework for Monitoring Accounts Receivable," *Financial Management* 8 (Winter 1979), 37–40.

Celec, Stephen E., and Joe D. Icerman. "A Comprehensive Approach to Accounts Receivable," *Financial Management* 15 (Spring 1980), 23–34.

Dyl, Edward A. "Another Look at the Evaluation of Investments in Accounts Receivable," *Financial Management* 6 (Winter 1977), 67–70.

Emery, Gary W. "A Pure Financial Explanation for Trade Credit," *Journal of Financial and Quantitative Analysis* 19 (September 1984), 271–85.

Halloren, John A., and Howard P. Lanser. "The Credit Policy Decision in an Inflationary Environment," *Financial Management* 10 (Winter 1981), 31–38.

Herbst, Anthony F. "Some Empirical Evidence on the Determinants of Trade Credit at the Industry Level of Aggregation," *Journal of Financial and Quantitative Analysis* 9 (June 1974), 377–94.

Hill, Ned C., and Kenneth D. Riener. "Determining the Cash Discount in the Firm's Credit Policy," *Financial Management* 8 (Spring 1979), 68–73.

Kim, Yong H., and Joseph C. Atkins. "Evaluating Investments in Accounts Receivable: A Wealth Maximization Framework," *Journal of Finance* 33 (May 1978), 403–12.

Kim, Yong H., and Kee H. Chung. "An Integrated Evaluation of Investment in Inventory and Credit," *Journal of Business Finance and Accounting* 17 (1990), 381–90.

Long, Michael S. "Credit Screening System Selection," *Journal of Financial and Quantitative Analysis* 11 (June 1976), 313–28.

Mehta, Dileep. "The Formulation of Credit Policy Models," *Management Science* 15 (October 1968), 30–50.

Mian, Shedzad L., and Clifford Smith. "Accounts Receivable Management Policy: Theory and Evidence," *Journal of Finance* 47 (March 1992), 169–200.

Oh, John S. "Opportunity Cost in the Evaluation of Investment in Accounts Receivable," *Financial Management* 6 (Summer 1976), 32–36.

Sachdeva, Kanwal S. "Accounts Receivable Decisions in a Capital Budgeting Framework," *Financial Management* 10 (Winter 1981), 45–49.

Smith, Keith V. *Management of Working Capital*, 2d ed. New York: West Publishing, 1980.

Smith, Keith V., and Brian Belt. "Working Capital Management in Practice: An Update," Working Paper No. 951. West Lafayette, IN: Krannert Graduate School of Management, Purdue University, 1989.

Soldofsky, Robert M. "A Model for Accounts Receivable Management," *N.A.A. Bulletin* (January 1966), 55–58.

Srinivasan, Venkat, and Yong H. Kim. "Granting: A Comparative Analysis of Classification Procedures," *Journal of Finance* 42 (July 1987), 665–81.

Vander Weide, J., and S. F. Maier. *Managing Corporate Liquidity*. New York: Wiley, 1985.

Walia, Tirlochan S. "Explicit and Implicit Cost of Changes in the Level of Accounts Receivable and the Credit Policy Decision of the Firm," *Financial Management* 6 (Winter 1977), 75–78.

Weston, J. Fred, and Pham D. Tuan. "Comment on Analysis of Credit Policy Changes," *Financial Management* 9 (Winter 1980), 59–63.

CHAPTER 17

Besley, S., and J. S. Osteryoung. "Survey of Current Practices in Establishing Trade-Credit Limits," *Financial Review* (February 1985), 70–81.

Emery, G. W. "A Pure Financial Explanation for Trade Credit," *Journal of Financial*

and *Quantitative Analysis* 19 (September 1984), 271–86.

Hill, Ned C. Robert A. Wood, and Dale R. Sorenson. "Factors Influencing Credit Policy: A Survey," *Journal of Cash Management* 1 (December 1981), 38–47.

Korsvik, W. J., and C. O. Mailburg. *The Loan Officer's Handbook*. Homewood, IL: Dow Jones-Irwin, 1986.

Loosigian, Allan M. "Hedging Commercial Paper Borrowing Costs with Treasury Bill Futures," *Journal of Cash Management* 2, no. 2 (June 1982), 50–57.

Pizzo, T. V. "Factoring as a Management Tool," *Credit and Financial Management* (December 1979), 16–18.

Santomero, Anthony M. "Fixed Versus Variable Rate Loans," *Journal of Finance* 38 (December 1983), 1363–80.

Stigham, M. *The Money Market: Myth, Reality and Practice*. Homewood, IL: Richard D. Irwin, 1983.

Stone, Bernell K. "The Cost of Bank Loans," *Journal of Financial and Quantitative Analysis* 7 (December 1972), 2077–86.

Wort, D. H. "The Trade Discount Decision: A Markov Chain Approach," *Decision Sciences* (Winter 1985), 43–56.

CHAPTER 18

Affleck-Graves, John, and Robert E. Miller. "Regulatory and Procedural Effects on the Underpricing of Initial Public Offering," *The Journal of Financial Research* 12 (Fall 1989), 183–92.

Asquith, Paul, and David W. Mullins, Jr. "Equity Issues and Offering Dilution," *Journal of Financial Economics* 15 (January–February 1986), 61–89.

Bae, Sung C., and Haim Levy. "The Valuation of Firm Commitment Underwriting Contracts for Seasoned New Equity Issues: Theory and Evidence," *Financial Management* 19 (Summer 1990), 48–59.

Barry, Christopher B., Chris J. Muscarella, and Michael R. Vetsuypens. "Underwriting Warrants, Underwriter Compensation, and the Costs of Going Public," *Journal of Financial Economics* 29 (March 1991), 113–35.

Bhagat, S., M. Wayne Marr, and G. Rodney Thompson. "The Rule 415 Experiment: Equity Markets," *Journal of Finance* 40 (December 1985), 1385–1401.

Booth, James R., and Richard L. Smith, II. "Capital Raising, Underwriting and the Certification Hypothesis," *Journal of Financial Economics* 15 (January–February 1986), 261–81.

Bower, Nancy L. "Firm Value and the Choice of Offering Method in Initial Public Offerings," *Journal of Finance* 44 (July 1989), 647–62.

Carter, Richard B., and Frederick H. Dark. "The Use of the Over Allotment Option in Initial Public Offerings," *Financial Management* 19 (Autumn 1990), 55–64.

Collins, Bruce M., and Frank J. Fabozzi. "A Methodology for Measuring Transaction Costs," *Financial Analysts Journal* 47 (March–April 1991), 27–36.

Conroy, Robert M., and Robert L. Winkler. "Market Structure: The Specialist as Deal-

er and Broker," *Journal of Banking and Finance* 10 (March 1986), 21–36.

Cooper, S. Kerry, Donald R. Fraser, and Gene C. Uselton. *Money, the Financial System, and Economic Policy*. Reading, MA: Addison-Wesley, 1983.

Eckbo, B. Espen. "Valuation Effects of Corporate Debt Offerings," *Journal of Financial Economics* 15 (January–February 1986), 119–51.

Ederington, Louis H. "Negotiated versus Competitive Underwritings of Corporate Bonds," *Journal of Finance* 31 (March 1976), 17–28.

Edmister, Robert O. *Financial Institutions, Markets and Management*, 2d ed. New York: McGraw-Hill, 1986.

Fabozzi, Frank J., and Frank G. Zarb, eds. *Handbook of Financial Markets*. Homewood, IL: Dow Jones-Irwin, 1981.

Feldstein, Martin, ed. *The American Economy in Transition*. Chicago: University of Chicago Press, 1980.

Friedman, Benjamin M., ed. *The Changing Roles of Debt and Equity in Financing U.S. Capital Formation*. Chicago: University of Chicago Press, 1982.

Goulet, Waldemar M. "Price Changes, Managerial Actions and Insider Trading at the Time of Listing," *Financial Management* 3 (Spring 1974), 30–36.

Hansell, Saul. "The Six-Month Corporate Underwriting Sweepstakes," *Institutional Investors* 24 (September 1991), 87–88.

Hansen, Robert S., Beverly R. Fuller, and Vahan Janjigian. "The Over-Allotment Option and Equity Financing Costs: An Empirical Investigation," *Financial Management* 16 (Summer 1987), 24–32.

Haubrich, Joseph G. "Financial Intermediation: Delegated Monitoring and Long-Term Relationships," *Journal of Banking and Finance* 13 (March 1989), 9–20.

Hayes, Samuel L., III. "Investment Banking: Power Structure in Flux," *Harvard Business Review* 49 (March–April 1971), 136–52.

Henning, Charles N., William Pigott, and Robert H. Scott. *Financial Markets and the Economy*, 4th ed. Englewood Cliffs, NJ: Prentice Hall, 1984.

Houston, Arthur L., Jr., and Carol Olson Houston. "Financing With Preferred Stock," *Financial Management* 19 (Autumn 1990), 42–54.

Humphrey, Joseph J. H. "Investment Banking—1989," *Journal of Cash Management* 9 (September–October 1989), 26–34.

Johnson, James M., and Robert E. Miller. "Investment Banker Prestige and the Underpricing of Initial Public Offerings," *Financial Management* 17 (Summer 1988), 19–29.

Johnson, Keith B., Gregory T. Morton, and M. Chapman Findlay III. "An Empirical Analysis of the Flotation Cost of Corporate Securities, 1971–1972," *Journal of Finance* 30 (June 1975), 1129–33.

Light, J. O., and William L. White. *The Financial System*. Homewood, IL: Richard D. Irwin, 1979.

Logue, Dennis E., and John R. Lindvall. "The Behavior of Investment Bankers: An

Econometric Investigation," *Journal of Finance* 29 (March 1974), 203–15.

Logue, Dennis E., John R. Lindvall, and Robert A. Jarrow. "Negotiation vs. Competitive Bidding in the Sale of Securities by Public Utilities," *Financial Management* 7 (Autumn 1978), 31–39.

Marr, M. Wayne, and G. Rodney Thompson. "Rule 415: Preliminary Empirical Results," *Working Paper No. 24*, Department of Finance, Virginia Polytechnic Institute and State University, October 1983.

Miller, Robert E., and Frank K. Reilly. "An Examination of Mispricing, Returns, and Uncertainty for Initial Public Offerings," *Financial Management* 16 (Autumn 1987), 29–35.

Ratner, David L. *Securities Regulation in a Nutshell*. St. Paul, MN: West Publishing, 1978.

Retkwa, Rosalyn. "Cultivating Equity: Growing New Capital in a Post-Debt Era," *Corporate Cashflow* 11 (February 1990), 29–31.

Rose, Peter S., and Donald R. Fraser. *Financial Institutions*, 3d ed. Dallas: Business Publications, 1984.

Ross, Stephen A. "Institutional Markets, Financial Marketing, and Financial Innovation," *Journal of Finance* 44 (July 1989), 541–56.

Seward, James K. "Corporate Financial Policy and the Theory of Financial Intermediation," *The Journal of Finance* 45 (June 1990), 351–77.

Smith, Clifford W., Jr. "Investment Banking and the Capital Acquisition Process," *Journal of Financial Economics* 15 (January–February 1986), 3–29.

Stulz, Rene M. "Managerial Discretion and Optimal Financing Policies," *Journal of Financial Economics* 26 (July 1990), 3–27.

Tallman, Gary D., David R. Rush, and Ronald W. Melicher. "Competitive versus Negotiated Underwriting Cost of Regulated Industries," *Financial Management* 3 (Summer 1974), 49–55.

Welch, Ivo, "Seasonal Offerings, Imitation Costs, and the Underpricing of Initial Public Offerings," *Journal of Finance* 44 (June 1989), 421–50.

West, Richard R., and Seha M. Tinic. "Corporate Finance and the Changing Stock Market," *Financial Management* 3 (Autumn 1974), 14–23.

Wiesen, Jeremy L. *Regulating Transactions in Securities*. St. Paul, MN: West Publishing, 1975.

Zent, Charles H. "Pricing an IPO: An Accurate Way to Set Share Value When Going Public," *Corporate Cashflow* 11 (February 1990) 32–35.

CHAPTER 19

Anderson, Paul F., and John D. Martin. "Lease vs. Purchase Decisions: A Survey of Current Practice," *Financial Management* (Spring 1977), 41–47.

Ang, J., and P. Peterson. "The Leasing Puzzle," *Journal of Finance* 39 (September 1984), 1055–65.

Blose, Laurence E., and John D. Martin. "Federal Government Leasing," *Public Budgeting and Finance* 9 (Summer 1989), 66–75.

Bower, Richard S., and George S. Oldfield, Jr. "Of Lessees, Lessors, and Discount Rates and Whether Pigs Have Wings," *Journal of Business Research* 9 (March 1981), 29–38.

Braud, Steven L. "Leasing—A Review of the Empirical Studies," *Managerial Finance* 15, nos. 1 & 2 (1989), 13–20.

Cason, R. L., "Leasing, Asset Lives and Uncertainty: A Practitioner's Comments," *Financial Management* 16 (Summer 1987), 13–16.

Clark, T. M. "The Leverage of Leasing—An International Perspective," *Managerial Finance* 15, nos. 1 & 2 (1989), 44–47.

Copeland, T., and J. F. Weston. "A Note on the Evaluation of Cancellable Operating Leases," *Financial Management* 11 (Summer 1982), 60–67.

Crawford, Peggy J., Charles P. Harper, and John J. McConnell. "Further Evidence on the Terms of Financial Leases," *Financial Management* 10 (Autumn 1981), 7–14.

Doenges, R. Conrad. "The Cost of Leasing," *Engineering Economist* 17 (Fall 1971), 31–44.

Drury, Colin. "Evaluating the Lease or Purchase Decision," *Managerial Finance* 15 nos. 1 & 2 (1989), 26–38.

Fabozzi, F., and U. Yaari. "Valuation of Safe Harbor Tax Benefit Transfer Leases," *Journal of Finance* 38 (May 1983), 595–606.

Grimlund, R., and R. Capettini. "A Note on the Evaluation of Leveraged Leases and Other Investments," *Financial Management* 11 (Summer 1982), 68–72.

Hodges, Stewart D. "Variable Rate Leases," *Managerial Finance* 15, nos. 1 & 2 (1989), 39–43.

Idol, Charles R. "A Note on Specifying Debt Displacement and Tax Shield Borrowing Opportunities in Financial Lease Valuation Models," *Financial Management* 9 (Summer 1980), 24–29.

Johnson, Robert W., and Wilbur G. Lewellen. "Analysis of the Lease-or-Buy Decision," *Journal of Finance* 27 (September 1972), 815–23.

Martin, John D. "Leasing," in *The Handbook of Corporate Finance*, ed. Edward Altman. New York: Wiley, 1986.

Martin, John D., Paul F. Anderson, and Chester L. Allen. "A Pragmatic Approach to the Estimation Problems Encountered in Lease Purchase Analyses," in *Risk, Capital Costs, and Project Financing Decisions*, eds. Frans G. J. Derkinderen and Roy L. Crum, pp. 254–73. Boston: Martinus Nijhoff Publishing, 1981.

McConnell, J. J., and J. S. Schallheim. "Valuation of Asset Leasing Contracts," *Journal of Financial Economics* 12 (August 1983), 237–61.

Mukherjee, T. K. "A Survey of Corporate Leasing Analysis," *Financial Management* 20 (Autumn 1991), 96–107.

Reed, E. W., R. V. Cotter, E. K. Gill, and R. K. Smith. *Commercial Banking*, 3d ed. Englewood Cliffs, NJ: Prentice Hall, 1984.

Schall, L. D. "Analytic Issues in Lease Versus Purchase Decisions," *Financial Management* 16 (Summer 1987), 17–20.

———. "The Lease-or-Buy and Asset Acquisition Decisions," *Journal of Finance* 29 (September 1974), 1203–14.

Smith, B. "Accelerated Debt Repayment in Leveraged Leases," *Financial Management* 11 (Summer 1982), 73–80.

Smith, C. W., and L. M. Wakeman. "Determinants of Corporate Leasing Policy," *Journal of Finance* 40 (3) (July 1985), 896–908.

Weingartner, H. M. "Leasing, Asset Lives and Uncertainty: Guides to Decision Making," *Financial Management* 16 (Summer 1987), 5–12.

CHAPTER 20

Agmon, T., A. R. Ofer, and A. Tamir. "Variable Rate Debt Instruments and Corporate Debt Policy," *Journal of Finance* 36 (March 1981), 113–26.

Alderson, Michael J., Keith C. Brown, and Scott L. Lummer. "Dutch Auction Rate Preferred Stock," *Financial Management* 6 (Summer 1987), 68–73.

Allen, David S., Robert E. Lamy, and G. Rodney Thompson. "The Shelf Registration of Debt and Self Selection Bias," *Journal of Finance* 45 (1990), 275–88.

Altman, Edward I. "Setting the Record Straight on Junk Bonds: A Review of the Research on Default Rates and Returns," *Journal of Applied Corporate Finance* 3 (1990), 82–95.

Ang, James S. "The Two Faces of Bond Refunding," *Journal of Finance* 30 (June 1975), 869–74.

Bhagat, Sanjai, James A. Brickley, and Ronald C. Lease. "The Authorization of Additional Common Stock: An Empirical Investigation," *Financial Management* 15 (Autumn 1986), 45–53.

Billingsley, Randall S., Robert E. Lamy, and David M. Smith. "Units of Debt with Warrants: Evidence of the 'Penalty-Free' Issuance of an Equity-Like Security," *Journal of Financial Research* 13 (1990), 187–200.

Bowlin, Oswald D. "The Refunding Decision: Another Special Case in Capital Budgeting," *Journal of Finance* 21 (March 1966), 55–68.

Brennan, Michael J., and Eduardo S. Schwartz. "Savings Bonds, Retractable Bonds and Callable Bonds," *Journal of Financial Economics* 5 (1977), 66–88.

Brown, Keith, and Donald J. Smith. "Forward Swaps, Swap Options, and the Management of Callable Debt," *Journal of Applied Corporate Finance* 2 (1990), 59–71.

Chang, Rosita P., Peter E. Koveos, and S. Ghon Rhee. "Financial Planning for International Long-Term Debt Financing," *Advances in Financial Planning and Forecasting* 5, Part I (1990), 33–58.

Cornell, Bradford, and Alan C. Shapiro. "Financing Corporate Growth," *Journal of Applied Corporate Finance* 1 (Summer 1988), 6–22.

Emery, Douglas R. "Overlapping Interest in Bond Refunding: A Reconsideration,"

Financial Management 17 (Summer 1978), 19–20.

Hansen, Robert S., and Claire E. Crutchley. "Corporate Earnings and Financing: An Empirical Analysis," *Journal of Business* 63 (1990), 347–71.

Hansen, Robert S., Beverly R. Fuller, and Vahan Janjigian. "The Over-Allotment Option and Equity Financing Flotation Costs: An Empirical Investigation," *Financial Management* 16 (Summer 1987), 24–32.

Hansen, Robert S., and John M. Pinkerton. "Direct Equity Financing: A Resolution of a Paradox," *Journal of Finance* 37 (June 1982), 651–65.

Harris, Robert S. "The Refunding of Discounted Debt: An Adjusted Present Value Analysis," *Financial Management* 9 (Winter 1980), 7–12.

Heinkel, Robert, and Josef Zechner. "The Role of Debt and Preferred Stock as a Solution to Adverse Investment Incentives," *Journal of Financial and Quantitative Analysis* 25 (1990), 1–24.

Houston, Arthur L., Jr., and Carol Olson Houston. "Financing with Preferred Stock," *Financial Management* 19 (1990), 42–54.

Jarrell, Greg A. "Financial Innovation and Corporate Mergers," in *The Merger Boom*, ed. Lynn E. Browne and Eric S. Rosengren. Boston: Federal Reserve Bank of Boston, 1987.

Kao, Chihwa, and Chunchi Wu. "Sinking Funds and the Agency Costs of Corporate Debt," *Financial Review* 25 (1990), 95–114.

Kolodny, Richard. "The Refunding Decision in Near Perfect Markets," *Journal of Finance* 29 (December 1974), 1467–78.

Marr, Wayne, and John Trimble. "The Persistent Borrowing Advantage of Eurodollar Bonds: A Plausible Explanation," *Journal of Applied Corporate Finance* 1 (Spring 1988), 65–70.

Marshall, William J., and Jess B. Yawitz. "Optimal Terms of the Call Provision on a Corporate Bond," *Journal of Financial Research* 2 (Fall 1980), 203–11.

Mayor, Thomas H., and Kenneth G. McCoin. "The Rate of Discount in Bond Refunding," *Financial Management* 3 (Autumn 1974), 54–58.

McConnell, John J., and Gary G. Schlarbaum. "Returns, Risks, and Pricing of Income Bonds, 1956–76," *Journal of Business* 54 (January 1981), 33–57.

Ofer, Aharon R., and Robert A. Taggart, Jr. "Bond Refunding: A Clarifying Analysis," *Journal of Finance* 32 (March 1977), 21–30.

Perry, Kevin J., and Robert A. Taggart, Jr. "The Growing Role of Junk Bonds," *Journal of Applied Corporate Finance* 1 (Spring 1988), 37–45.

Riener, Kenneth D. "Financial Structure Effects on Bond Refunding," *Financial Management* 9 (Summer 1980), 18–23.

Sibley, A. M. "Some Evidence on the Cash Flow Effects of Bond Refunding," *Financial Management* 3 (Autumn 1974), 50–53.

Smith, Clifford W., Jr., and Jerold B. Warner. "On Financial Contracting: An Analysis of Bond Covenants," *Journal of Financial Economics* 7 (June 1979), 117–61.

Wansley, James W., Fayez A. Elayan, and Brian A. Maris. "Preferred Stock Returns, CreditWatch, and Preferred Stock Rating Changes," *Financial Review* 25 (1990), 265–86.

White, R. W., and P. A. Lusztig. "The Price Effects of Rights Offerings," *Journal of Financial and Quantitative Analysis* 15 (March 1980), 25–40.

Wigmore, Barrie A. "The Decline in Credit Quality of New-Issue Junk Bonds," *Financial Analysts Journal* 46 (1990), 53–62.

Winger, Bernard J., Carl R. Chen, John D. Martin, J. William Petty, and Steven C. Hayden. "Adjustable Rate Preferred Stock," *Financial Management* 15 (Spring 1986), 48–57.

Wingler, Tony R., and G. Donald Jud. "Premium Debt Tenders: Analysis and Evidence," *Financial Management* 19 (1990), 58–67.

CHAPTER 21

Alexander, Gordon J., and David B. Kuhnau. "Market Timing Strategies in Convertible Debt Financing," *Journal of Finance* 34 (March 1979), 143–55.

Alexander, Gordon J., and Robert D. Stover. "The Effect of Forced Conversion on Common Stock Prices," *Financial Management* 9 (Spring 1980), 39–45.

———. "Pricing in the New Issue Convertible Debt Market," *Financial Management* 6 (Fall 1977), 35–39.

Bacon, Peter W., and Edward L. Winn, Jr. "The Impact of Forced Conversion on Stock Prices," *Journal of Finance* 24 (December 1969), 871–74.

Baumol, William J., Burton G. Malkiel, and Richard E. Quandt. "The Valuation of Convertible Securities," *Quarterly Journal of Economics* 80 (February 1966), 48–59.

Billingsley, Randall S., Robert E. Lamy, and David M. Smith. "Units of Debt with Warrants: Evidence of the 'Penalty-Free' Issuance of an Equity-Like Security," *Journal of Financial Research* 13 (1990), 187–200.

Billingsley, Randall S., Robert E. Lamy, and G. Rodney Thompson. "Valuation of Primary Issue Convertible Bonds," *Journal of Financial Research* 9 (1986), 251–59.

Brennan, Michael J., and Eduardo S. Schwartz. "Analyzing Convertible Bonds," *Journal of Financial and Quantitative Analysis* 15 (November 1980), 907–29.

———. "The Case for Convertibles," *Journal of Applied Corporate Finance* 1 (Spring 1988), 55–64.

———. "Convertible Bonds: Valuation and Optimal Strategies for Call and Conversion," *Journal of Finance* 32 (December 1977), 1699–1715.

Constantinides, George M. "Warrant Exercise and Bond Conversion in Competitive Markets," *Journal of Financial Economics* 13 (September 1984), 371–97.

Cowan, Arnold R., Nandkumar Nayar, and Ajai K. Singh. "Stock Returns Before and After Calls of Convertible Bonds," *Journal of Financial and Quantitative Analysis* 25 (1990), 549–54.

Dann, Larry Y., and Wayne H. Mikkelson. "Convertible Debt Issuance, Capital Structure Change, and Financing-Related Information: Some New Evidence," *Journal of Financial Economics* 13 (June 1984), 157–87.

Emanuel, David C. "Warrant Valuation and Exercise Strategy," *Journal of Financial Economics* 12 (August 1983), 211–35.

Fooladi, Iraj, and Gordon S. Roberts. "On Preferred Stock," *Journal of Financial Research* 9 (Winter 1986), 319–24.

Frank, Werner G., and Charles O. Kroncke. "Classifying Conversions of Convertible Debentures over Four Years," *Financial Management* 3 (Summer 1974), 33–42.

Galai, Dan, and Mier I. Schneller. "Pricing of Warrants and the Value of the Firm," *Journal of Finance* 33 (December 1978), 1333–42.

Green, Richard C. "Investment Incentives, Debt and Warrants," *Journal of Financial Economics* 13 (March 1984), 115–36.

Harris, Milton, and Arthur Raviv. "A Sequential Signaling Model of Convertible Debt Policy," *Journal of Finance* 40 (December 1985), 1263–81.

Janjigian, Vahan. "The Leverage Changing Consequences of Convertible Debt Financing," *Financial Management* 16 (Autumn 1987), 15–21.

Jennings, Edwards H. "An Estimate of Convertible Bond Premiums," *Journal of Financial and Quantitative Analysis* 9 (January 1974), 33–56.

Lauterbach, Beni, and Paul Schultz. "Pricing Warrants: An Empirical Study of the Black–Scholes Model and Its Alternatives," *Journal of Finance* 45 (1990), 1181–1209.

Leonard, David C., and Michael E. Solt. "On Using the Black–Scholes Model of Value Warrants," *Journal of Financial Research* 13 (1990), 81–92.

Lewellen, Wilbur G., and George A. Racette. "Convertible Debt Financing," *Journal of Financial and Quantitative Analysis* 7 (December 1973), 777–92.

Long, Michael S., and Stephan E. Sefcik. "Participation Financing: A Comparison of the Characteristics of Convertible Debt and Straight Bonds Issued in Conjunction with Warrants," *Financial Management* 19 (1990), 23–34.

Marr, M. Wayne, and G. Rodney Thompson. "The Pricing of New Convertible Bond Issues," *Financial Management* 13 (Summer 1984), 31–37.

Pinches, George E. "Financing with Convertible Preferred Stocks, 1960–1967," *Journal of Finance* 25 (March 1970), 53–64.

Rush, David F., and Ronald W. Melicher. "An Empirical Examination of Factors Which Influence Warrant Prices," *Journal of Finance* 29 (December 1974), 1449–66.

Samuelson, Paul A. "Rational Theory of Warrant Pricing," *Industrial Management Review* 6 (Spring 1965), 13–31.

Schwartz, Eduardo S. "The Valuation of Warrants: Implementing a New Approach," *Journal of Financial Economics* 4 (January 1977), 79–93.

Soldofsky, Robert M. "Yield-Risk Performance of Convertible Securities," *Financial Analysts Journal* 39 (March–April 1971), 61–65.

CHAPTER 22

Billingsley, Randall S., and Don M. Chance. "Options Market Efficiency and the Box Spread Strategy," *Financial Review* 20 (1985), 287–301.

Billingsley, Randall S., and Don M. Chance. "The Pricing and Performance of Stock Index Futures Spreads," *Journal of Futures Markets* 8 (1988), 303–10.

Black, Fisher. "Fact and Fantasy in the Use of Options," *Financial Analysts Journal* (July–August 1975), 61–72.

———. "The Pricing of Commodity Contracts," *Journal of Financial Economics* 3 (January–March 1976), 167–79.

Black, Fischer, Emanuel Derman, and William Toy. "A One-Factor Model of Interest Rates and Its Application to Treasury Bond Options," *Financial Analysts Journal* 46 (1990), 33–39.

Black, Fisher, and M. Scholes. "The Pricing of Options and Corporate Liabilities," *Journal of Political Economy* 81 (May–June 1973), 637–54.

———. "The Valuation of Option Contracts and a Test of Market Efficiency," *The Journal of Finance* (May 1972), 399–418.

Block, Stanley B., and Timothy J. Gallagher. "The Use of Interest Rate Futures and Options by Corporate Financial Managers," *Financial Management* 15 (Autumn 1986), 73–78.

Chance, Don M. "Boundary Condition Tests of Bid and Ask Prices of Index Call Options," *Journal of Financial Research* 11 (1988), 21–32.

———. "Option Volume and Stock Market Performance," *Journal of Portfolio Management* 16 (1990), 42–51.

———. *An Introduction to Options and Futures*, 2d. ed. Chicago, IL: Dryden Press, 1991.

Cheung, C. Sherman, Clarence C. Y. Kwan, and Patrick C. Y. Yip. "The Hedging Effectiveness of Options and Futures: A Mean-Gini Approach," *Journal of Futures Markets* 10 (1990), 61–74.

Courtadon, George. "The Pricing of Options on Default-Free Bonds," *Journal of Financial and Quantitative Analysis* 17 (March 1982), 75–100.

Fabozzi, Frank J., and Gregory M. Kipnis (eds.). *Stock Index Futures*. Homewood, IL: Dow Jones–Irwin, 1984.

Fishe, Raymond P. H., Lawrence G. Goldberg, Thomas F. Gosnell, and Sujata Sinha. "Margin Requirements in Futures Markets: Their Relationship to Price Volatility," *Journal of Futures Markets* 10 (1990), 541–54.

Followill, Richard A., and Billy P. Helms. "Put-Call-Futures Parity and Arbitrage Opportunity in the Market for Options on Gold Futures Contracts," *Journal of Futures Markets* 10 (1990), 339–52.

French, Kenneth R. "Pricing Financial Futures Contracts: An Introduction," *Journal of Applied Corporate Finance* 1 (Winter 1989), 59–66.

Hein, Scott E., Christopher K. Ma, and S. Scott MacDonald. "Testing Unbiasedness in Futures Markets: A Clarification," *Journal of Futures Markets* 10 (1990), 555–62.

Jordan, James V., and George Emir Morgan. "Default Risk in Futures Markets: The Customer-Broker Relationship," *Journal of Finance* 45 (1990), 909–34.

Kaufman, Perry J. *Handbook of Futures Markets*. New York: Wiley Interscience, 1984.

Loosigian, Allan M. *Foreign Exchange Futures*. Homewood, IL: Dow Jones–Irwin, 1981.

———. *Interest Rate Futures*. Homewood, IL: Dow Jones–Irwin, 1980.

MacBeth, James D., and Larry J. Merville. "Tests of the Black–Scholes and Cox Call Option Valuation Models," *Journal of Finance* (May 1980), 285–300.

Martell, Terrence F., and Ruben C. Trevino. "The Intraday Behavior of Commodity Futures Prices," *Journal of Futures Markets* 10 (1990), 661–72.

Rothstein, Nancy H. (ed.) *The Handbook of Financial Futures*. New York: McGraw-Hill, 1984.

Rubinstein, Mark, and John C. Cox. *Option Markets*. Englewood Cliffs, NJ: Prentice Hall, 1982.

Smith, C., Jr. "Option Pricing: A Review," *Journal of Financial Economics* (January–March 1976), 1–51.

Sterk, W. "Comparative Performance of the Black–Scholes and the Roll–Geske–Whaley Option Pricing Models," *Journal of Financial and Quantitative Analysis* (September 1983), 345–54.

———. "Tests of Two Models for Valuing Call Options on Stocks with Dividends," *Journal of Finance* 37 (December 1982), 1229–37.

Stoll, Hans R. "The Relationship Between Put and Call Option Prices," *Journal of Finance* (December 1969), 802–24.

Stoll, Hans R., and Robert E. Whaley. "The Dynamics of Stock Index and Stock Index Futures Returns," *Journal of Financial and Quantitative Analysis* 25 (1990), 441–68.

Strong, Robert A. *Speculative Markets: Options, Futures and Hard Assets*. Chicago, IL: Longman Financial Services Publishing, 1989.

Whaley, R. "On the Valuation of American Call Options on Stocks with Known Dividends," *Journal of Financial Economics* 9 (June 1981), 207–11.

———. "Valuation of American Call Options on Dividend-Paying Stocks: Empirical Tests," *Journal of Financial Economics* 10 (March 1982), 29–58.

CHAPTER 23

Alexander, G., P. Benson, and J. Kampmeyer. "Investigating the Valuation Effects of Voluntary Corporate Sell-offs," *Journal of Finance* 39 (1984), 503–17.

Altman, Edward I. "Setting the Record Straight on Junk Bonds: A Review of the Research on Default Rates and Returns," *Journal of Applied Corporate Finance* (Summer 1990), 82–95.

Asquith, P. "Merger Bids, Uncertainty, and Stockholder Returns," *Journal of Financial Economics* 11 (April 1983).

Bhide, Amar. "Reversing Corporate Diversification," *Journal of Applied Corporate Finance* (Summer 1990), 70–81.

Brown, David T., and Michael D. Ryngaert. "The Mode of Acquisition in Takeovers: Taxes and Asymmetric Information," *The Journal of Finance* (June 1991), 653–70.

Choi, Dosoung, and George C. Philippatos. "An Examination of Merger Synergism," *Journal of Financial Research* 6 (Fall 1983), 239–56.

DeAngelo, H., L. DeAngelo, and E. Rice. "Going Private: Minority Freezeouts and Stockholder Wealth," *Journal of Law Economics* (October 1984).

Fridson, Martin S. "What Went Wrong with the Highly Leveraged Deals? (Or, All Variety of Agency Costs)," *Journal of Applied Corporate Finance* (Fall 1991), 57–67.

Giliberto, S. Michael, and Nikhil P. Varaiya, "The Winner's Curse and Bidder Competition in Acquisitions: Evidence from Failed Bank Auctions," *The Journal of Finance* (March 1989), 59–76.

Hearth, D., and J. Zaima. "Voluntary Divestitures and Value," *Financial Management* 13 (Spring 1984), 10–16.

Jarrell, Gregg A., and Annette B. Poulsen. "The Returns to Aquiring Firms in Tender Offers: Evidence from Three Decades," *Journal of Financial Management* (Autumn 1989), 12–19.

Kohlberg Kravis Roberts and Co. (with Deloitte Haskins and Sells). "Leveraged Buyouts," *Journal of Applied Corporate Finance* 2(1) (Spring 1989), 64–70.

Little, William B., and Steven B. Klinsky. "How Leveraged Buyouts Can Really Work: A Look at Three Cases," *Journal of Applied Corporate Finance* 2(1) (Spring 1989), 71–75.

Loderer, Claudio, and Kenneth Martin. "Corporate Acquisitions by Listed Firms: The Experience of a Comprehensive Sample," *Journal of Financial Management* (Winter 1990), 17–33.

Mohan, Nancy, and Carl R. Chen. "A Review of the RJR-Nabisco Buyout," *Journal of Applied Corporate Finance* (Summer 1990), 102–8.

Ryngaert, Michael D. "Firm Valuation, Takeover Defenses, and the Delaware Supreme Court," *Journal of Financial Management* (Autumn 1989), 20–28.

Schipper, K., and A. Smith. "Effects of Recontracting on Shareholder Wealth: The Case of Voluntary Spin-offs," *Journal of Financial Economics* 12 (1983), 437–67.

Shleifer, Andrei. "The Takeover Wave of the 1980s," *Journal of Applied Corporate Finance* (Fall 1991), 49–56.

Thompson, Steve, Mike Wright, and Ken Robbie. "Management Buyouts, Debt, and Efficiency: Some Evidence from the U.K.," *Journal of Applied Corporate Finance* 2(1) (Spring 1989), 76–86.

Wansley, James W., William R. Lane, and Salil Sarkar. "Managements' View on Share Repurchase and Tender Offer Premiums," *Journal of Financial Management* (Autumn 1989), 97–110.

Wansley, James W., William R. Lane, and Ho C. Yang. "Abnormal Returns to Acquired Firms by Type of Acquisition and Method of Payment," *Financial Management* 12 (Autumn 1983), 16–22.

Wansley, James W., Rodney L. Roenfeldt, and Philip L. Cooley. "Abnormal Returns from Merger Profiles," *Journal of Financial and Quantitative Analysis* 18 (June 1983), 149–62.

Wright, Mike, Ken Robbie, and Steve Thompson. "Corporate Restructuring, Buy-Outs, and Managerial Equity: The European Dimension," *Journal of Applied Corporate Finance* (Winter 1991), 46–58.

CHAPTER 24

Altman, Edward I. "Corporate Bankruptcy Potential, Stockholder Returns and Share Valuation," *Journal of Finance* 24 (December 1969), 887–900.

———. *Corporate Financial Distress.* New York: John Wiley, 1983.

———. "A Further Empirical Investigation of the Bankruptcy Cost Question," *Journal of Finance* 39 (September 1984), 1067–89.

Altman, Edward I., and Menachem Brenner. "Financial Ratios, Discriminant Analysis and the Prediction of Corporate Bankruptcy," *Journal of Finance* 23 (September 1968), 589–609.

Ang, James S., Jess H. Chua, and John J. McConnell. "The Administrative Costs of Corporate Bankruptcy: A Note," *Journal of Finance* 37 (March 1982), 219–26.

Argenti, John. *Corporate Collapse: The Causes and Symptoms.* New York: Wiley, 1976.

Edmister, Robert O. "An Empirical Test of Financial Ratio Analysis for Small Business Failure Prediction," *Journal of Financial and Quantitative Analysis* 7 (March 1972), 1477–93.

Gilson, Stuart C. "Managing Default: Some Evidence on How Firms Choose Between Workouts and Bankruptcy," *Journal of Applied Corporate Finance* (Summer 1991), 62–70.

Gombola, Michael J., Mark E. Haskins, J. Edward Ketz, and David D. Williams. "Cash Flow in Bankruptcy Prediction," *Financial Management* 16 (Winter 1987), 55–65.

Kalaba, Robert E., Terence C. Langetieg, Nima Rasakhoo, and Mark I. Weinstein. "Estimation of Implicit Bankruptcy Costs," *Journal of Finance* 39 (July 1984), 629–42.

Morse, Dale, and Wayne Shaw. "Investing in Bankrupt Firms," *Journal of Finance* 43 (December 1988), 1193–1206.

Paroush, Jacob. "The Domino Effect and the Supervision of the Banking System," *Journal of Finance* 43 (December 1988), 1207–18.

Rohman, Mark C., "Financing Chapter 11 Companies in the 1990s," *Journal of Ap-* plied *Corporate Finance* (Summer 1990), 96–101.

Scott, James. "The Probability of Bankruptcy," *Journal of Banking and Finance* 5 (September 1981), 317–44.

Weiss, Lawrence A. "The Bankruptcy Code and Violations of Absolute Priority," *Journal of Applied Corporate Finance* (Summer 1991), 71–78.

White, Michelle J. "Bankruptcy Costs and the New Bankruptcy Code," *Journal of Finance* 38 (May 1983), 477–88.

Wruck, Karen H. "What Really Went Wrong at Revco," *Journal of Applied Corporate Finance* (Summer 1991), 79–92.

CHAPTER 25

Adler, Michael, and Bernard Dumas. "International Portfolio Choice and Corporate Finance: A Synthesis," *Journal of Finance* 38 (June 1983), 925–84.

Aggarwal, Raj. "Distribution of Exchange Rates and Risk Premia," *Decision Sciences* 21 (Summer 1990).

———. "International Differences in Capital Structure Norms," *Management International Review* 21 (1981), 75–88.

Aggarwal, Raj, and Cheng-Few Lee (eds.). *Advances in International Financial Planning and Forecasting.* Greenwich, CT: JAI Press, 1990.

Aggarwal, Raj, and Luc Soenen. "Cash and Foreign Exchange Management: Theory and Practice," *Journal of Business Finance and Accounting* 16 (Winter 1989), 599–619.

———. "Managing Persistent Real Changes in Exchange Rates," *Columbia Journal of World Business* 24 (Fall 1989).

Beidleman, Carl (ed.). *The Handbook of International Investing.* Chicago: Probus, 1987.

Caves, Richard. *Multinational Enterprises and Economic Analysis.* Cambridge, England: Cambridge University Press, 1982.

Choi, Fred D. S., and Gerhardt Mueller. *An Introduction to Multinational Accounting.* Englewood Cliffs, NJ: Prentice Hall, 1984.

Eiteman, David K., and Arthur I. Stonehill. *Multinational Business Finance.* Reading, MA: Addison-Wesley, 1989.

Folks, William R., and Raj Aggarwal. *International Dimensions of Financial Management.* Boston: Kent Publishing Company, 1988.

Goodman, Lauri S. "Pricing of Syndicated Eurocurrency Credits," *Federal Reserve Bank of New York Quarterly Review* (Summer 1980), 39–49.

Grabbe, J. Orlin. *International Financial Markets.* New York: Elsevier, 1986.

Hodder, James E. "Evaluation of Manufacturing Investments: A Comparison of U.S. and Japanese Practices," *Financial Management* 15 (Winter 1986), 17–24.

Kelly, Marie W. *Foreign Investment Practices of U.S. Multinational Corporations.* Ann Arbor, MI: UMI Research Press, 1981.

Kobrin, Steven J. *Environmental Assessment in the International Firm.* Berkeley: University of California Press, 1982.

Levich, Richard M. *The International Money Market: An Assessment of Forecasting Techniques and Market Efficiency.* Greenwich, CT: JAI Press, 1979.

Owens, E. A. *International Aspects of U.S. Income Taxation.* Cambridge, MA: Harvard Law School, 1980.

Shapiro, Alan C. *Multinational Financial Management.* Boston: Allyn and Bacon, 1988.

Stern, Joel M., and Donald H. Chew (eds.). *New Developments in International Finance.* Cambridge, MA: Basil Blackwell, 1988.

CHAPTER 26

Aggarwal, Reena, and Pietra Rivoli. "Fads in the Initial Public Offering Market?" *Journal of Financial Management* (Winter 1990), 45–54.

Ang, James S. "Small Business Uniqueness and the Theory of Financial Management," *Journal of Small Business Finance* (Spring 1991), 1–14.

Beedles, William L. "Size, Liquidity, and the Cost of Equity," *Journal of Small Business Finance* (Spring 1991), 29–44.

Barry, Christopher, Chris J. Muscarella, John W. Peavy III, and Michael R. Vetsuypens. "The Role of Venture Capital in the Creation of Public Companies," *Journal of Financial Economics* (October 1990), 448–71.

Bygrave, William D. "The Entrepreneurship Paradigm: I. A Philosophical Look at Its Research Methodologies," *Entrepreneurship: Theory and Practice* (Fall 1989), 7–26.

Churchill, W. C., and V. L. Lewis. "The Five Stages of Small Business Growth," *Harvard Business Review* (November–December 1983), 30ff.

Cornell, Bradford, and Alan Shapiro. "Financing Corporate Growth," *Journal of Applied Corporate Finance* (Summer 1988), 6–22.

Finegan, Patrick T. "Maximizing Share Value at the Private Company," *Journal of Applied Corporate Finance* (Spring 1991), 30–45.

Florida, R. L., and M. Kenney. "Venture Capital-Financed Innovation and Technological Changes in the U.S.," *Research Policy* 17, no. 3, (1988), 119–37.

Freear, John, and William E. Wetzel, Jr. "The Informal Venture Capital Market in the Year 2000," presented at the State of the Art Entrepreneurship Conference, The Frank Hawkins Kenan Institute of Private Enterprise, The University of North Carolina, Chapel Hill, October 1990.

Gorman, Michael, and William A. Sahlman. "What Do Venture Capitalists Do?" *Frontiers of Entrepreneurship Research* (1986), 414–436.

Levin, Richard, and Virginia Travis. "Small Company Finance: What the Books Don't Say," *Harvard Business Review* (November–December 1987), 30–35.

Ritter, Jay. "The Long-Run Performance of Initial Public Offerings," *The Journal of Finance* (March 1991), 3–28.

Sahlman, William, "Aspects of Financial Contracting in Venture Capital," *Journal* of *Applied Corporate Finance* (Summer 1988), 23–36.

Sahlman, William, "The Structure and Governance of Venture-Capital Organizations," *Journal of Financial Economics* (October 1990), 473–521.

Stoll, Hans R. *Small Firms' Access to Public Equity Financing.* Washington, DC: Interagency Task Force on Small Business Finance, December 1981.

Walker, Ernest W., and J. William Petty II. "Financial Differences between Large and Small Firms," *Financial Management* (Winter 1978), 61–68.

Welsh, J. A., and J. F. White. "A Small Business Is Not a Little Big Business," *Harvard Business Review* (July–August 1981), 18–32.

APPENDIXES

APPENDIX A
Using a Calculator
(a tutorial on the Hewlett-Packard HP 17BII)

As you prepare for a career in business, the ability to use a financial calculator is essential, whether you are in the finance division or the marketing department. For most positions, it will be assumed that you can use a calculator in making computations that at one time were simply not possible without extensive time and effort. The following examples let us see what is possible, but they represent only the beginning of using the calculator in finance.

With just a little time and effort, you will be surprised at how much you can do with the calculator, such as calculating a stock's beta, or determining the value of a bond on a specific day, given the exact date of maturity, or finding net present values and internal rates of return, or calculating the standard deviation. The list is almost endless.

In demonstrating how calculators may make our work easier, we must first decide which calculator to use. The options are numerous and largely depend on personal preference. We have chosen to demonstrate the Hewlett-Packard HP 17BII.

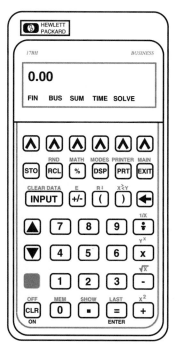

We will limit our discussion to the following issues:

I. Introductory Comments
II. A Good Starting Point
III. Calculating Table Values for:
    A. Appendix B (Compound sum of $1)
    B. Appendix C (Present value of $1)
    C. Appendix D (Sum of an annuity of $1 for *n* periods)
    D. Appendix E (Present value of an anuity of $1 for *n* periods)
IV. Calculating Present Values
V. Calculating Future Values (Compound sum)
VI. Calculating the Number of Payments or Receipts
VII. Calculating the Payment Amount
VIII. Calculating the Interest Rate
IX. Bond Valuation
    A. Computing the value of a bond
    B. Calculating the yield to maturity on a bond
X. Computing the Net Present Value and Internal Rate of Return
    A. Where future cash flows are equal amounts in each period (annuity)
    B. Where future cash flows are unequal amounts in each period

I. Introductory Comments

In the examples that follow, you are told (1) which keystrokes to use, (2) the resulting appearance of the calculator display, and (3) a supporting explanation.

The keystrokes column tells you which keys to press. The keystrokes shown in an unshaded box tell you to use one of the calculator's dedicated or "hard" keys. For example, if $+/-$ is shown in the keystrokes instruction column, press that key on the keyboard of the calculator. To use a function printed in gold lettering above a dedicated key, always press the gold key ▮ first, then the function key. For example, keying in 2 and pressing ▮ $\sqrt{x}$ calculates the square root of 2.

When the calculator is on, a set of labels appears across the bottom of the display. This is called a *menu*, because it presents you with the choices of what you can do next. Press the key directly beneath the menu label to access that function. Menu keys are represented with a shaded box in the keystrokes column. For example, **TIME** displays the current date and time, and the other TIME menu options.

II. An Important Starting Point

Purpose: Before each new calculation, clear the variables, and if need be, change the number of digits displayed, the number of payments per period, and the beginning or end mode.

Example: You want to display four numbers to the right of the decimal.

Keystrokes	Display	Explanation
DSP	Select display format.	Sets display to show four numbers to the right of the decimal
FIX 4 INPUT	0.0000	
CLR	0.0000	Clears display

Example: You want to display two payments per year to be paid at the end of each period.

Keystrokes	Display	Explanation
FIN TVM OTHER 2 P/YR END EXIT	2 P/YR END MODE	Sets number of payments per year at 2 and timing of payment at the end of each period

III. Calculating Table Values for:

A. The compound sum of $1 (Appendix B)

Purpose: Compute the table values for Appendix B, the future value of $1.

Method: Solve for the future value of $1: $FVIF_{i,n} = \$1(1 + i)^n$

Example: What is the table value for the compound sum of $1 for 5 years at a 12 percent annual interest rate?

Keystrokes	Display	Explanation
FIN TVM		Displays TVM menu
OTHER 1 P/YR END EXIT		Sets 1 payment per year; END mode
CLEAR DATA	1 P/YR	Clears TVM variables
1 +/− PV	PV = − 1.0000	Stores initial $1 as a negative present value. Otherwise the answer will appear as a negative
5 N	N = 5.0000	Stores number of periods
12 I%YR	I%YR = 12.0000	Stores interest rate
FV	FV = 1.7623	Table value

B. The present value of $1 (Appendix C)

Purpose: Compute the table values for Appendix C, the present value of $1.

Method: Solve for the present value of $1: $PVIF_{i,n} = \dfrac{\$1}{(1 + i)^n}$

Example: What is the table value for the present value of $1 for 8 years at a 10 percent annual interest rate?

Keystrokes	Display	Explanation
FIN TVM CLEAR DATA		Clears TVM variables; verifies the correct number of payments per year and the BEG or END mode
1 +/− FV	FV = − 1.0000	Stores future amount as negative value
8 N	N = 8.0000	Stores number of periods
10 I%YR	I%YR = 10.0000	Stores interest rate
PV	PV = 0.4665	Table value

C. The sum of an annuity of $1 for n periods (Appendix D)

Purpose: Compute the table values for Appendix D, the sum of an annuity of $1.

Method: Solve for the future value of an annuity of $1:

$$FVIFA_{i, n} = \$1 \sum_{t=0}^{n-1} (1 + i)^t,$$

which may also be solved as $FVIFA_{i, n} = \dfrac{(1 + i)^n - 1}{i}$.

Example: What is the table value for the compound sum of an annuity of $1 for 6 years at a 14 percent annual interest rate?

Keystrokes	Display	Explanation
FIN TVM CLEAR DATA		Clears TVM variables; verifies the correct number of payments per year and the BEG or END mode
1 +/− PMT	PMT = − 1.0000	Stores annual payment (annuity) as a negative number. Otherwise the answer will appear as a negative
6 N	N = 6.0000	Stores number of periods
14 I%YR	I%YR = 14.0000	Stores interest rate
FV	FV = 8.5355	Table value

D. The present value of an annuity of $1 for n periods (Appendix E)

Purpose: Compute the table values for Appendix E, the present value of an annuity of $1.

Method: Solve for the present value of an annuity of $1:

$$PVIFA_{i, n} = \sum_{t=1}^{n} \frac{\$1}{(1 + i)^t},$$

which may also be solved as $PVIFA_{i, n} = \dfrac{1 - [1/(1 + i)^n]}{i}$.

Example: What is the table value for the present value of an annuity of $1 for 12 years at a 9 percent annual interest rate?

Keystrokes	Display	Explanation
FIN TVM CLEAR DATA		Clears TVM variables; and verifies the correct number of payments per year and the BEG or END mode
1 +/− PMT	PMT = − 1.0000	Stores annual payment (annuity) as a negative number. Otherwise the answer will appear as a negative

12 N	N = 12.0000	Stores number of periods
9 I% YR	I%YR = 9.0000	Stores interest rate
PV	PV = 7.1607	Table value

IV. Calculating Present Values

Purpose: Be able to compute the present value of a future cash flow stream (CF_t) involving equal amounts plus an additional amount to be received at the end of the period (FV_n).

Method: Solve for the present value of:

$$PV_n = \sum_{t=1}^{n} \frac{CF_t}{(1+i)^t} + \frac{\$FV_n}{(1+i)^n}$$

Example: You are considering the purchase of a franchise of quick oil-change locations, which you believe will provide an annual cash flow of $50,000. At the end of ten years, you believe that you will be able to sell the franchise for an estimated $900,000. Calculate the maximum amount you should pay for the franchise (present value) in order to realize at least an 18 percent annual yield.

Keystrokes	Display	Explanation
FIN TVM CLEAR DATA		Clears TVM variables; and verifies the correct number of payments per year and the BEG or END mode
10 N	N = 10.0000	Stores n, the holding period
18 I%YR	I%YR = 18.0000	Stores i, the required rate of return
50,000 PMT	PMT = 50,000.0000	Stores PMT, the annual cash flow to be received
900,000 FV	FV = 900,000.0000	Stores FV, the cash flow to be received at the end of the project
PV	PV = −396,662.3350	The present value, given a required rate of return of 18 percent. (*Note:* The present value is displayed with a minus sign since it represents cash paid out.)

V. Calculating Future Values (Compound Sum)

Purpose: Compute the future value of expected cash flows (CF_t) involving equal amounts each year.

Method: Solve for the compound sum value of:

$$FV_n = \$CF_t \sum_{t=1}^{n} (1+i)^t,$$

Example: If you deposit $300 a month (at the beginning of each month) into a new account that pays 6.25% annual interest compounded monthly, how much will you have in the account after 5 years?

Keystrokes	Display	Explanation
FIN TVM CLEAR DATA		Clears TVM variables; and verifies the correct number of payments per year and the BEG or END mode
OTHER BEG 12 P/YR EXIT	12 P/YR	Sets 12 payments per year; begin mode (BEG) assumes cash flows are at the beginning of each month
60 N	N = 60.0000	Stores n, the number of months for the investment

Keystrokes	Display	Explanation
6.25 I%YR	I%YR = 6.2500	Stores i, the annual interest rate
300 +/− PMT	PMT = − 300.0000	Stores PMT, the monthly amount invested (with a minus sign for cash paid out)
FV	FV = 21,175.7613	The future value after 5 years

VI. Calculating the Number of Payments or Receipts

Purpose: Compute the number of payments for a given future value.

Method: Solve for n in the equation: $FV_n = \$CF_t \sum_{t=1}^{n} (1 + i)^t$

Example: If you wish to retire with $500,000 saved, and can only afford payments of $500 each month, how long will you have to contribute toward your retirement if you can earn a 10 percent return on your contributions?

Keystrokes	Display	Explanation
FIN TVM CLEAR DATA		Clears TVM variables; and verifies the correct number of payments per year and the BEG or END mode
OTHER BEG 12 P/YR EXIT	12 P/YR	Sets 12 payments per year; begin mode (BEG) assumes cash flows are at the beginning of each month
10 I%YR	I%YR = 10.0000	Stores i, the interest rate
500 +/− PMT	PMT = − 500.0000	Stores PMT, the monthly amount invested (with a minus sign for cash paid out)
500,000 FV	FV = 500,000.0000	The value we want to achieve
N	N = 268.2539	Number of months (since we considered monthly payments) required to achieve our goal

VII. Calculating the Payment Amount

Purpose: Compute the amount of equal payments needed to achieve a given future value in a known period of time.

Method: Solve for $\$CF$ in the equation:

$$FV_n = \$CF_t \sum_{t=1}^{n} (1 + i)^t$$

Example: Suppose your retirement needs were $750,000. If you are currently 25 years old and plan to retire at age 65, how much will you have to contribute each month for retirement if you can earn 12.5% on your savings?

Keystrokes	Display	Explanation
FIN TVM CLEAR DATA		Clears TVM variables; and verifies the correct number of payments per year and the BEG or END mode
OTHER BEG 12 P/YR EXIT	12 P/YR	Sets 12 payments per year; begin mode (BEG) assumes cash flows are at the beginning of each month
12.5 I%YR	I%YR = 12.5000	Stores i, the interest rate

480 **N**	N = 480.0000	Stores *n*, the number of periods until we stop contributing (40 years × 12 months/years = 480 months)
750,000 **FV**	FV = 750,000.0000	The value we want to achieve
PMT	PMT = − 53.8347	Monthly contribution required to achieve our ultimate goal (shown as negative since it represents cash paid out)

VIII. Calculating the Interest Rate

Purpose: Compute the nominal annual interest rate of investments made in future periods.

Method: Solve for *i* in the equation: $FV_n = \$CF_t \sum_{t=0}^{n-1} (1+i)^t$

Example: If you invest \$300 at the end of each month for six years (72 months) for a promised \$30,000 return at the end, what interest rate are you earning on your investment?

Keystrokes	Display	Explanation
FIN **TVM** **CLEAR DATA**		Clears TVM variables; and verifies the correct number of payments per year and the BEG or END mode
OTHER **END** 12 **P/YR** **EXIT**	12 P/YR	Sets 12 payments per year; end mode (END) assumes cash flows are at the end of each month
72 **N**	N = 72.0000	Stores N, the number of deposits (investments)
300 1 **+/−** **PMT**	PMT = − 300.0000	Stores PMT, the monthly amount invested (with a minus sign for cash paid out)
30,000 **FV**	FV = 30,000.0000	Stores the future value to be received in 6 years
I%YR	I%YR = 10.5892	The annual interest rate earned on the investment

IX. Bond Valuation

A. Computing the value of a bond

Purpose: Calculate the value of a bond.

Method: Assuming the maturity value, *M*, (also face or par value) of a bond is \$1,000 and interest, I_t, is paid semiannually for *n* years, solve for the value that the bond should sell for, V_b, given the investor's required rate of return, R_b; that is,

$$V_b = \sum_{t=1}^{2n} \frac{\$I_t/2}{(1 + R_b/2)^t} + \frac{\$M}{(1 + R_b/2)^{2n}}$$

Example: Assume the current date is January 1, 1993, and that you want to know the value of a bond that matures in 10 years and has a coupon rate of 9 percent (4.5% semiannually). Your required rate of return is 12 percent.

Keystrokes	Display	Explanation
FIN **TVM** **CLEAR DATA**		Clears TVM variables; and verifies the correct number of payments per year and the BEG or END mode

Keystrokes	Display	Explanation
OTHER **END** 2 **P/YR** **EXIT**	2 P/YR	Sets 2 payments per year; end mode (END) assumes cash flows are at the end of each 6-month period
20 **N**	N = 20.0000	Stores the number of semiannual periods (10 years × 2)
12 **I%YR**	I%YR = 12.0000	Stores annual rate of return
45 **PMT**	PMT = 45.0000	Stores the semiannual interest payments
1,000 **FV**	FV = 1,000.0000	Stores the bond's maturity or par value
PV	PV = − 827.9512	Value of the bond, expressed as a negative number

Solution using the bond feature:

Keystrokes	Display	Explanation
MAIN **FIN** **BOND** **CLEAR DATA**	30/360 SEMI- ANNUAL	Clears BOND variables
9 **CPN%**	CPN% = 9.0000	Stores the coupon interest rate
1.011993 **SETT**	SETT = 01/01/1993 FRI	Stores the current date (month, day, year)
1.012003 **MAT**	MAT = 01/01/2003 WED	Stores the maturity date in 10 years
MORE 12 **YLD%**	YLD% = 12.0000	Stores the investor's required rate of return
PRICE	PRICE = 82.7951	Value of bond as a % of par value; i.e., value of bond is $827.95

B. Computing the yield to maturity on a bond

Purpose: Calculate the yield to maturity on a bond, given its current market value.

Method: Assuming the maturity value, M, (also face or par value) of a bond is $1,000 and interest, I_t, is paid semiannually for n years, and the bond is selling for V_b, solve for the yield to maturity (YTM); that is,

$$V_b = \sum_{t=1}^{2n} \frac{\$I_t/2}{(1 + YTM/2)^t} + \frac{\$M}{(1 + YTM/2)^{2n}}$$

Example: Assume the current date is January 3, 1994, and that you want to know your yield to maturity on a bond that matures in 8 years and has a coupon rate of 12 percent (6% semiannually). The bond is selling for $1,100.

Keystrokes	Display	Explanation
FIN **TVM** **CLEAR DATA**	2 P/YR	Clears TVM variables; and verifies the correct number of payments per year and the BEG or END mode
16 **N**	N = 16.0000	Stores the number of semiannual periods (8 years × 2)
1100 **+/−** **PV**	PV = − 1,100.0000	Value of the bond, expressed as a negative number

60 PMT	PMT = 60.0000	Stores the semiannual interest payments
1,000 FV	FV = 1,000.0000	Stores the bond's maturity or par value
I%YR	I%YR = 10.1451	The yield to maturity, expressed on an annual basis

Solution using the bond feature:

MAIN FIN BOND CLEAR DATA	30/360 SEMI-ANNUAL	Clears BOND variables
12 CPN%	CPN% = 12.0000	Stores coupon interest rate
1.031994 SETT	SETT = 01/03/1994 MON	Stores the current date (month, day, year)
1.032002 MAT	MAT = 01/03/2002 THU	Stores maturity date in 8 years
MORE 110 PRICE	PRICE = 110.0000	Stores the bond value as a percentage of par value
YLD%	YLD% = 10.1451	Bond's yield to maturity

X. Computing the Net Present Value and Internal Rate of Return

Purpose: Determine the net present value (*NPV*) and the internal rate of return (*IRR*) for a capital investment where the cash flows are equal amounts in each of the future periods.

Method: Solve for the *NPV* of the project, given the investment outlay (*IO*), the project's future cash flows (*CF_t*), the life of the project (*n*), and the firm's required rate of return or cost of capital (*K*), using the following equation:

$$NPV = \sum_{t=1}^{n} \frac{\$CF_t}{(1 + K)^t} - IO$$

Then solve for the discount rate that results in a zero net present value, which is the internal rate of return.

A. Where future cash flows are equal amounts in each period (annuity)

Example: The firm is considering a capital project that would cost $80,000. The firm's cost of capital is 12 percent. The project life is 10 years, during which time the firm expects to receive $15,000 per year. Calculate the NPV and the IRR.

Keystrokes	Display	Explanation
FIN TVM CLEAR DATA		Clears TVM variables; and verifies the correct number of payments per year and the BEG or END mode
OTHER 1 P/YR END EXIT	1 P/YR	Sets 1 payment per year; end mode (END) assumes cash flows are at the end of each year
15,000 PMT	PMT = 15,000.0000	Stores the annual cash flows of $15,000
10 N	N = 10.0000	Stores the life of the project

Keystrokes	Display	Explanation
12 I%YR	I%YR = 12.0000	Stores the cost of capital
PV	PV = −84,753.3454	Calculates present value
+ 80000 = +/−	4,753.3454	Calculates net present value by adding back the initial investment and changing signs
80000 +/− PV I%YR	PV = −80,000.0000 I% YR = 13.4344	Calculates the IRR

B. Where future cash flows are unequal amounts in each period

Example: The firm is considering a capital project that would cost $110,000. The firm's cost of capital is 15 percent. The project life is 5 years, with the following expected cash flows: $−25,000, $50,000, $60,000, $60,000, and $70,000. In addition, you expect to receive $30,000 in the last year from the salvage value of the equipment. Calculate the NPV and the IRR.

Keystrokes	Display	Explanation
FIN CFLO		Clears CFLO variables
CLEAR DATA YES	CLEAR THE LIST ? FLOW(0) = ?	
110,000 +/− INPUT	FLOW(1) = ? −110,000.0000 #TIMES(1) = 1	Stores CF_0, the initial investment (with a minus sign for a negative cash flow)
25,000 +/− INPUT	#TIMES(1) = 1 1.0000	Stores CF_1, the first year's cash flow (with a minus sign for a negative cash flow)
INPUT	FLOW(2) = ?	Stores the number of years CF_1 is repeated (in this case, one year only)
50,000 INPUT	#TIMES(2) = 1 1.0000	Stores CF_2
INPUT	FLOW(3) = ? 1.0000	Stores the number of years CF_2 is repeated
60,000 INPUT	#TIMES(3) = 1 1.0000	Stores CF_3
2 INPUT	FLOW(4) = ? 2.0000	Stores the number of years CF_3 is repeated (here, two years, so our response is 2 to the "#TIMES(3)=" prompt)
100,000 INPUT	#TIMES(4) = 1 1.0000	Stores CF_5, $70,000, plus expected $30,000
INPUT	FLOW(5) = ? 1.0000	Stores the number of years CF_4 is repeated
EXIT		Ends storage of individual cash flows
CALC	NPV, NUS, NFV NEED I%	Displays calculation menu, so that operations may be performed on the cash flow sequence just entered
15 I%	I% = 15.0000	Stores interest rate
NPV	NPV = 29,541.8951	Calculates the project's NPV at the stated interest rate
IRR%	IRR% = 22.0633	Calculates the project's IRR

APPENDIX B. Compound Sum of $1

n	1%	2%	3%	4%	5%	6%	7%	8%	9%	10%
1	1.010	1.020	1.030	1.040	1.050	1.060	1.070	1.080	1.090	1.100
2	1.020	1.040	1.061	1.082	1.102	1.124	1.145	1.166	1.188	1.210
3	1.030	1.061	1.093	1.125	1.158	1.191	1.225	1.260	1.295	1.331
4	1.041	1.082	1.126	1.170	1.216	1.262	1.311	1.360	1.412	1.464
5	1.051	1.104	1.159	1.217	1.276	1.338	1.403	1.469	1.539	1.611
6	1.062	1.126	1.194	1.265	1.340	1.419	1.501	1.587	1.677	1.772
7	1.072	1.149	1.230	1.316	1.407	1.504	1.606	1.714	1.828	1.949
8	1.083	1.172	1.267	1.369	1.477	1.594	1.718	1.851	1.993	2.144
9	1.094	1.195	1.305	1.423	1.551	1.689	1.838	1.999	2.172	2.358
10	1.105	1.219	1.344	1.480	1.629	1.791	1.967	2.159	2.367	2.594
11	1.116	1.243	1.384	1.539	1.710	1.898	2.105	2.332	2.580	2.853
12	1.127	1.268	1.426	1.601	1.796	2.012	2.252	2.518	2.813	3.138
13	1.138	1.294	1.469	1.665	1.886	2.133	2.410	2.720	3.066	3.452
14	1.149	1.319	1.513	1.732	1.980	2.261	2.579	2.937	3.342	3.797
15	1.161	1.346	1.558	1.801	2.079	2.397	2.759	3.172	3.642	4.177
16	1.173	1.373	1.605	1.873	2.183	2.540	2.952	3.426	3.970	4.595
17	1.184	1.400	1.653	1.948	2.292	2.693	3.159	3.700	4.328	5.054
18	1.196	1.428	1.702	2.026	2.407	2.854	3.380	3.996	4.717	5.560
19	1.208	1.457	1.753	2.107	2.527	3.026	3.616	4.316	5.142	6.116
20	1.220	1.486	1.806	2.191	2.653	3.207	3.870	4.661	5.604	6.727
21	1.232	1.516	1.860	2.279	2.786	3.399	4.140	5.034	6.109	7.400
22	1.245	1.546	1.916	2.370	2.925	3.603	4.430	5.436	6.658	8.140
23	1.257	1.577	1.974	2.465	3.071	3.820	4.740	5.871	7.258	8.954
24	1.270	1.608	2.033	2.563	3.225	4.049	5.072	6.341	7.911	9.850
25	1.282	1.641	2.094	2.666	3.386	4.292	5.427	6.848	8.623	10.834
30	1.348	1.811	2.427	3.243	4.322	5.743	7.612	10.062	13.267	17.449
40	1.489	2.208	3.262	4.801	7.040	10.285	14.974	21.724	31.408	45.258
50	1.645	2.691	4.384	7.106	11.467	18.419	29.456	46.900	74.354	117.386

n	11%	12%	13%	14%	15%	16%	17%	18%	19%	20%
1	1.110	1.120	1.130	1.140	1.150	1.160	1.170	1.180	1.190	1.200
2	1.232	1.254	1.277	1.300	1.322	1.346	1.369	1.392	1.416	1.440
3	1.368	1.405	1.443	1.482	1.521	1.561	1.602	1.643	1.685	1.728
4	1.518	1.574	1.630	1.689	1.749	1.811	1.874	1.939	2.005	2.074
5	1.685	1.762	1.842	1.925	2.011	2.100	2.192	2.288	2.386	2.488
6	1.870	1.974	2.082	2.195	2.313	2.436	2.565	2.700	2.840	2.986
7	2.076	2.211	2.353	2.502	2.660	2.826	3.001	3.185	3.379	3.583
8	2.305	2.476	2.658	2.853	3.059	3.278	3.511	3.759	4.021	4.300
9	2.558	2.773	3.004	3.252	3.518	3.803	4.108	4.435	4.785	5.160
10	2.839	3.106	3.395	3.707	4.046	4.411	4.807	5.234	5.695	6.192
11	3.152	3.479	3.836	4.226	4.652	5.117	5.624	6.176	6.777	7.430
12	3.498	3.896	4.334	4.818	5.350	5.936	6.580	7.288	8.064	8.916
13	3.883	4.363	4.898	5.492	6.153	6.886	7.699	8.599	9.596	10.699
14	4.310	4.887	5.535	6.261	7.076	7.987	9.007	10.147	11.420	12.839
15	4.785	5.474	6.254	7.138	8.137	9.265	10.539	11.974	13.589	15.407
16	5.311	6.130	7.067	8.137	9.358	10.748	12.330	14.129	16.171	18.488
17	5.895	6.866	7.986	9.276	10.761	12.468	14.426	16.672	19.244	22.186
18	6.543	7.690	9.024	10.575	12.375	14.462	16.879	19.673	22.900	26.623
19	7.263	8.613	10.197	12.055	14.232	16.776	19.748	23.214	27.251	31.948
20	8.062	9.646	11.523	13.743	16.366	19.461	23.105	27.393	32.429	38.337
21	8.949	10.804	13.021	15.667	18.821	22.574	27.033	32.323	38.591	46.005
22	9.933	12.100	14.713	17.861	21.644	26.186	31.629	38.141	45.923	55.205
23	11.026	13.552	16.626	20.361	24.891	30.376	37.005	45.007	54.648	66.247
24	12.239	15.178	18.788	23.212	28.625	35.236	43.296	53.108	65.031	79.496
25	13.585	17.000	21.230	26.461	32.918	40.874	50.656	62.667	77.387	95.395
30	22.892	29.960	39.115	50.949	66.210	85.849	111.061	143.367	184.672	237.373
40	64.999	93.049	132.776	188.876	267.856	378.715	533.846	750.353	1051.642	1469.740
50	184.559	288.996	450.711	700.197	1083.619	1670.669	2566.080	3927.189	5988.730	9100.191

APPENDIX B. Compound Sum of $1 *(continued)*

n	21%	22%	23%	24%	25%	26%	27%	28%	29%	30%
1	1.210	1.220	1.230	1.240	1.250	1.260	1.270	1.280	1.290	1.300
2	1.464	1.488	1.513	1.538	1.562	1.588	1.613	1.638	1.664	1.690
3	1.772	1.816	1.861	1.907	1.953	2.000	2.048	2.097	2.147	2.197
4	2.144	2.215	2.289	2.364	2.441	2.520	2.601	2.684	2.769	2.856
5	2.594	2.703	2.815	2.932	3.052	3.176	3.304	3.436	3.572	3.713
6	3.138	3.297	3.463	3.635	3.815	4.001	4.196	4.398	4.608	4.827
7	3.797	4.023	4.259	4.508	4.768	5.042	5.329	5.629	5.945	6.275
8	4.595	4.908	5.239	5.589	5.960	6.353	6.767	7.206	7.669	8.157
9	5.560	5.987	6.444	6.931	7.451	8.004	8.595	9.223	9.893	10.604
10	6.727	7.305	7.926	8.594	9.313	10.086	10.915	11.806	12.761	13.786
11	8.140	8.912	9.749	10.657	11.642	12.708	13.862	15.112	16.462	17.921
12	9.850	10.872	11.991	13.215	14.552	16.012	17.605	19.343	21.236	23.298
13	11.918	13.264	14.749	16.386	18.190	20.175	22.359	24.759	27.395	30.287
14	14.421	16.182	18.141	20.319	22.737	25.420	28.395	31.691	35.339	39.373
15	17.449	19.742	22.314	25.195	28.422	32.030	36.062	40.565	45.587	51.185
16	21.113	24.085	27.446	31.242	35.527	40.357	45.799	51.923	58.808	66.541
17	25.547	29.384	33.758	38.740	44.409	50.850	58.165	66.461	75.862	86.503
18	30.912	35.848	41.523	48.038	55.511	64.071	73.869	85.070	97.862	112.454
19	37.404	43.735	51.073	59.567	69.389	80.730	93.813	108.890	126.242	146.190
20	45.258	53.357	62.820	73.863	86.736	101.720	119.143	139.379	162.852	190.047
21	54.762	65.095	77.268	91.591	108.420	128.167	151.312	178.405	210.079	247.061
22	66.262	79.416	95.040	113.572	135.525	161.490	192.165	228.358	271.002	321.178
23	80.178	96.887	116.899	140.829	169.407	203.477	244.050	292.298	349.592	417.531
24	97.015	118.203	143.786	174.628	211.758	256.381	309.943	374.141	450.974	542.791
25	117.388	144.207	176.857	216.539	264.698	323.040	393.628	478.901	581.756	705.627
30	304.471	389.748	497.904	634.810	807.793	1025.904	1300.477	1645.488	2078.208	2619.936
40	2048.309	2846.941	3946.340	5455.797	7523.156	10346.879	14195.051	19426.418	26520.723	36117.754
50	13779.844	20795.680	31278.301	46889.207	70064.812	104354.562	154942.687	229345.875	338440.000	497910.125

n	31%	32%	33%	34%	35%	36%	37%	38%	39%	40%
1	1.310	1.320	1.330	1.340	1.350	1.360	1.370	1.380	1.390	1.400
2	1.716	1.742	1.769	1.796	1.822	1.850	1.877	1.904	1.932	1.960
3	2.248	2.300	2.353	2.406	2.460	2.515	2.571	2.628	2.686	2.744
4	2.945	3.036	3.129	3.224	3.321	3.421	3.523	3.627	3.733	3.842
5	3.858	4.007	4.162	4.320	4.484	4.653	4.826	5.005	5.189	5.378
6	5.054	5.290	5.535	5.789	6.053	6.328	6.612	6.907	7.213	7.530
7	6.621	6.983	7.361	7.758	8.172	8.605	9.058	9.531	10.025	10.541
8	8.673	9.217	9.791	10.395	11.032	11.703	12.410	13.153	13.935	14.758
9	11.362	12.166	13.022	13.930	14.894	15.917	17.001	18.151	19.370	20.661
10	14.884	16.060	17.319	18.666	20.106	21.646	23.292	25.049	26.924	28.925
11	19.498	21.199	23.034	25.012	27.144	29.439	31.910	34.567	37.425	40.495
12	25.542	27.982	30.635	33.516	36.644	40.037	43.716	47.703	52.020	56.694
13	33.460	36.937	40.745	44.912	49.469	54.451	59.892	65.830	72.308	79.371
14	43.832	49.756	54.190	60.181	66.784	74.053	82.051	90.845	100.509	111.19
15	57.420	64.358	72.073	80.643	90.158	100.712	112.410	125.366	139.707	155.567
16	75.220	84.953	95.857	108.061	121.713	136.968	154.002	173.005	194.192	217.793
17	98.539	112.138	127.490	144.802	164.312	186.277	210.983	238.747	269.927	304.911
18	129.086	148.022	169.561	194.035	221.822	253.337	289.046	329.471	375.198	426.875
19	169.102	195.389	225.517	260.006	299.459	344.537	395.993	454.669	521.525	597.625
20	221.523	257.913	299.937	348.408	404.270	468.571	542.511	627.443	724.919	836.674
21	290.196	340.446	398.916	466.867	545.764	637.256	743.240	865.871	1007.637	1171.343
22	380.156	449.388	530.558	625.601	736.781	865.668	1018.238	1194.900	1400.615	1639.878
23	498.004	593.192	705.642	838.305	994.653	1178.668	1394.986	1648.961	1946.854	2295.829
24	652.385	783.013	938.504	1123.328	1342.781	1602.988	1911.129	2275.564	2706.125	3214.158
25	854.623	1033.577	1248.210	1505.258	1812.754	2180.063	2618.245	3140.275	3761.511	4499.816
30	3297.081	4142.008	5194.516	6503.285	8128.426	10142.914	12636.086	15716.703	19517.969	24201.043
40	49072.621	66519.313	89962.188	121388.437	163433.875	219558.625	294317.937	393684.687	525508.312	700022.688

APPENDIX C. Present Value of $1

n	1%	2%	3%	4%	5%	6%	7%	8%	9%	10%
1	.990	.980	.971	.962	.952	.943	.935	.926	.917	.909
2	.980	.961	.943	.925	.907	.890	.873	.857	.842	.826
3	.971	.942	.915	.889	.864	.840	.816	.794	.772	.751
4	.961	.924	.888	.855	.823	.792	.763	.735	.708	.683
5	.951	.906	.863	.822	.784	.747	.713	.681	.650	.621
6	.942	.888	.837	.790	.746	.705	.666	.630	.596	.564
7	.933	.871	.813	.760	.711	.665	.623	.583	.547	.513
8	.923	.853	.789	.731	.677	.627	.582	.540	.502	.467
9	.914	.837	.766	.703	.645	.592	.544	.500	.460	.424
10	.905	.820	.744	.676	.614	.558	.508	.463	.422	.386
11	.896	.804	.722	.650	.585	.527	.475	.429	.388	.350
12	.887	.789	.701	.625	.557	.497	.444	.397	.356	.319
13	.879	.773	.681	.601	.530	.469	.415	.368	.326	.290
14	.870	.758	.661	.577	.505	.442	.388	.340	.299	.263
15	.861	.743	.642	.555	.481	.417	.362	.315	.275	.239
16	.853	.728	.623	.534	.458	.394	.339	.292	.252	.218
17	.844	.714	.605	.513	.436	.371	.317	.270	.231	.198
18	.836	.700	.587	.494	.416	.350	.296	.250	.212	.180
19	.828	.686	.570	.475	.396	.331	.277	.232	.194	.164
20	.820	.673	.554	.456	.377	.312	.258	.215	.178	.149
21	.811	.660	.538	.439	.359	.294	.242	.199	.164	.135
22	.803	.647	.522	.422	.342	.278	.226	.184	.150	.123
23	.795	.634	.507	.406	.326	.262	.211	.170	.138	.112
24	.788	.622	.492	.390	.310	.247	.197	.158	.126	.102
25	.780	.610	.478	.375	.295	.233	.184	.146	.116	.092
30	.742	.552	.412	.308	.231	.174	.131	.099	.075	.057
40	.672	.453	.307	.208	.142	.097	.067	.046	.032	022
50	.608	.372	.228	.141	.087	.054	.034	.021	.013	.009

n	11%	12%	13%	14%	15%	16%	17%	18%	19%	20%
1	.901	.893	.885	.877	.870	.862	.855	.847	.840	.833
2	.812	.797	.783	.769	.756	.743	.731	.718	.706	.694
3	.731	.712	.693	.675	.658	.641	.624	.609	.593	.579
4	.659	.636	.613	.592	.572	.552	.534	.516	.499	.482
5	.593	.567	.543	.519	.497	.476	.456	.437	.419	.402
6	.535	.507	.480	.456	.432	.410	.390	.370	.352	.335
7	.482	.452	.425	.400	.376	.354	.333	.314	.296	.279
8	.434	.404	.376	.351	.327	.305	.285	.266	.249	.233
9	.391	.361	.333	.308	.284	.263	.243	.225	.209	.194
10	.352	.322	.295	.270	.247	.227	.208	.191	.176	.162
11	.317	.287	.261	.237	.215	.195	.178	.162	.148	.135
12	.286	.257	.231	.208	.187	.168	.152	.137	.124	.112
13	.258	.229	.204	.182	.163	.145	.130	.116	.104	.093
14	.232	.205	.181	.160	.141	.125	.111	.099	.088	.078
15	.209	.183	.160	.140	.123	.108	.095	.084	.074	.065
16	.188	.163	.141	.123	.107	.093	.081	.071	.062	.054
17	.170	.146	.125	.108	.093	.080	.069	.060	.052	.045
18	.153	.130	.111	.095	.081	.069	.059	.051	.044	.038
19	.138	.116	.098	.083	.070	.060	.051	.043	.037	.031
20	.124	.104	.087	.073	.061	.051	.043	.037	.031	.026
21	.112	.093	.077	.064	.053	.044	.037	.031	.026	.022
22	.101	.083	.068	.056	.046	.038	.032	.026	.022	.018
23	.091	.074	.060	.049	.040	.033	.027	.022	.018	.015
24	.082	.066	.053	.043	.035	.028	.023	.019	.015	.013
25	.074	.059	.047	.038	.030	.024	.020	.016	.013	.010
30	.044	.033	.026	.020	.015	.012	.009	.007	.005	.004
40	.015	.011	.008	.005	.004	.003	.002	.001	.001	.001
50	.005	.003	.002	.001	.001	.001	.000	.000	.000	.000

APPENDIX C.   Present Value of $1 *(continued)*

n	21%	22%	23%	24%	25%	26%	27%	28%	29%	30%
1	.826	.820	.813	.806	.800	.794	.787	.781	.775	.769
2	.683	.672	.661	.650	.640	.630	.620	.610	.601	.592
3	.564	.551	.537	.524	.512	.500	.488	.477	.466	.455
4	.467	.451	.437	.423	.410	.397	.384	.373	.361	.350
5	.386	.370	.355	.341	.328	.315	.303	.291	.280	.269
6	.319	.303	.289	.275	.262	.250	.238	.227	.217	.207
7	.263	.249	.235	.222	.210	.198	.188	.178	.168	.159
8	.218	.204	.191	.179	.168	.157	.148	.139	.130	.123
9	.180	.167	.155	.144	.134	.125	.116	.108	.101	.094
10	.149	.137	.126	.116	.107	.099	.092	.085	.078	.073
11	.123	.112	.103	.094	.086	.079	.072	.066	.061	.056
12	.102	.092	.083	.076	.069	.062	.057	.052	.047	.043
13	.084	.075	.068	.061	.055	.050	.045	.040	.037	.033
14	.069	.062	.055	.049	.044	.039	.035	.032	.028	.025
15	.057	.051	.045	.040	.035	.031	.028	.025	.022	.020
16	.047	.042	.036	.032	.028	.025	.022	.019	.017	.015
17	.039	.034	.030	.026	.023	.020	.017	.015	.013	.012
18	.032	.028	.024	.021	.018	.016	.014	.012	.010	.009
19	.027	.023	.020	.017	.014	.012	.011	.009	.008	.007
20	.022	.019	.016	.014	.012	.010	.008	.007	.006	.005
21	.018	.015	.013	.011	.009	.008	.007	.006	.005	.004
22	.015	.013	.011	.009	.007	.006	.005	.004	.004	.003
23	.012	.010	.009	.007	.006	.005	.004	.003	.003	.002
24	.010	.008	.007	.006	.005	.004	.003	.003	.002	.002
25	.009	.007	.006	.005	.004	.003	.003	.002	.002	.001
30	.003	.003	.002	.002	.001	.001	.001	.001	.000	.000
40	.000	.000	.000	.000	.000	.000	.000	.000	.000	.000
50	.000	.000	.000	.000	.000	.000	.000	.000	.000	.000

n	31%	32%	33%	34%	35%	36%	37%	38%	39%	40%
1	.763	.758	.752	.746	.741	.735	.730	.725	.719	.714
2	.583	.574	.565	.557	.549	.541	.533	.525	.518	.510
3	.445	.435	.425	.416	.406	.398	.389	.381	.372	.364
4	.340	.329	.320	.310	.301	.292	.284	.276	.268	.260
5	.259	.250	.240	.231	.223	.215	.207	.200	.193	.186
6	.198	.189	.181	.173	.165	.158	.151	.145	.139	.133
7	.151	.143	.136	.129	.122	.116	.110	.105	.100	.095
8	.115	.108	.102	.096	.091	.085	.081	.076	.072	.068
9	.088	.082	.077	.072	.067	.063	.059	.055	.052	.048
10	.067	.062	.058	.054	.050	.046	.043	.040	.037	.035
11	.051	.047	.043	.040	.037	.034	.031	.029	.027	.025
12	.039	.036	.033	.030	.027	.025	.023	.021	.019	.018
13	.030	.027	.025	.022	.020	.018	.017	.015	.014	.013
14	.023	.021	.018	.017	.015	.014	.012	.011	.010	.009
15	.017	.016	.014	.012	.011	.010	.009	.008	.007	.006
16	.013	.012	.010	.009	.008	.007	.006	.006	.005	.005
17	.010	.009	.008	.007	.006	.005	.005	.004	.004	.003
18	.008	.007	.006	.005	.005	.004	.003	.003	.003	.002
19	.006	.005	.004	.004	.003	.003	.003	.002	.002	.002
20	.005	.004	.003	.003	.002	.002	.002	.002	.001	.001
21	.003	.003	.003	.002	.002	.002	.001	.001	.001	.001
22	.003	.002	.002	.002	.001	.001	.001	.001	.001	.001
23	.002	.002	.001	.001	.001	.001	.001	.001	.001	.000
24	.002	.001	.001	.001	.001	.001	.001	.001	.000	.000
25	.001	.001	.001	.001	.001	.000	.000	.000	.000	.000
30	.000	.000	.000	.000	.000	.000	.000	.000	.000	.000
40	.000	.000	.000	.000	.000	.000	.000	.000	.000	.000

APPENDIX D. Sum of an Annuity of $1 for *n* Periods

n	1%	2%	3%	4%	5%	6%	7%	8%	9%	10%
1	1.000	1.000	1.000	1.000	1.000	1.000	1.000	1.000	1.000	1.000
2	2.010	2.020	2.030	2.040	2.050	2.060	2.070	2.080	2.090	2.100
3	3.030	3.060	3.091	3.122	3.152	3.184	3.215	3.246	3.278	3.310
4	4.060	4.122	4.184	4.246	4.310	4.375	4.440	4.506	4.573	4.641
5	5.101	5.204	5.309	5.416	5.526	5.637	5.751	5.867	5.985	6.105
6	6.152	6.308	6.468	6.633	6.802	6.975	7.153	7.336	7.523	7.716
7	7.214	7.434	7.662	7.898	8.142	8.394	8.654	8.923	9.200	9.487
8	8.286	8.583	8.892	9.214	9.549	9.897	10.260	10.637	11.028	11.436
9	9.368	9.755	10.159	10.583	11.027	11.491	11.978	12.488	13.021	13.579
10	10.462	10.950	11.464	12.006	12.578	13.181	13.816	14.487	15.193	15.937
11	11.567	12.169	12.808	13.486	14.207	14.972	15.784	16.645	17.560	18.531
12	12.682	13.412	14.192	15.026	15.917	16.870	17.888	18.977	20.141	21.384
13	13.809	14.680	15.618	16.627	17.713	18.882	20.141	21.495	22.953	24.523
14	14.947	15.974	17.086	18.292	19.598	21.015	22.550	24.215	26.019	27.975
15	16.097	17.293	18.599	20.023	21.578	23.276	25.129	27.152	29.361	31.772
16	17.258	18.639	20.157	21.824	23.657	25.672	27.888	30.324	33.003	35.949
17	18.430	20.012	21.761	23.697	25.840	28.213	30.840	33.750	36.973	40.544
18	19.614	21.412	23.414	25.645	28.132	30.905	33.999	37.450	41.301	45.599
19	20.811	22.840	25.117	27.671	30.539	33.760	37.379	41.446	46.018	51.158
20	22.019	24.297	26.870	29.778	33.066	36.785	40.995	45.762	51.159	57.274
21	23.239	25.783	28.676	31.969	35.719	39.992	44.865	50.422	56.764	64.002
22	24.471	27.299	30.536	34.248	38.505	43.392	49.005	55.456	62.872	71.402
23	25.716	28.845	32.452	36.618	41.430	46.995	53.435	60.893	69.531	79.542
24	26.973	30.421	34.426	39.082	44.501	50.815	58.176	66.764	76.789	88.496
25	28.243	32.030	36.459	41.645	47.726	54.864	63.248	73.105	84.699	98.346
30	34.784	40.567	47.575	56.084	66.438	79.057	94.459	113.282	136.305	164.491
40	48.885	60.401	75.400	95.024	120.797	154.758	199.630	295.052	337.872	442.580
50	64.461	84.577	112.794	152.664	209.341	290.325	406.516	573.756	815.051	1163.865

n	11%	12%	13%	14%	15%	16%	17%	18%	19%	20%
1	1.000	1.000	1.000	1.000	1.000	1.000	1.000	1.000	1.000	1.000
2	2.110	2.120	2.130	2.140	2.150	2.160	2.170	2.180	2.190	2.200
3	3.342	3.374	3.407	3.440	3.472	3.506	3.539	3.572	3.606	3.640
4	4.710	4.779	4.850	4.921	4.993	5.066	5.141	5.215	5.291	5.368
5	6.228	6.353	6.480	6.610	6.742	6.877	7.014	7.154	7.297	7.442
6	7.913	8.115	8.323	8.535	8.754	8.977	9.207	9.442	9.683	9.930
7	9.783	10.089	10.405	10.730	11.067	11.414	11.772	12.141	12.523	12.916
8	11.859	12.300	12.757	13.233	13.727	14.240	14.773	15.327	15.902	16.499
9	14.164	14.776	15.416	16.085	16.786	17.518	18.285	19.086	19.923	20.799
10	16.722	17.549	18.420	19.337	20.304	21.321	22.393	23.521	24.709	25.959
11	19.561	20.655	21.814	23.044	24.349	25.733	27.200	28.755	30.403	32.150
12	22.713	24.133	25.650	27.271	29.001	30.850	32.824	34.931	37.180	39.580
13	26.211	28.029	29.984	32.088	34.352	36.786	39.404	42.218	45.244	48.496
14	30.095	32.392	34.882	37.581	40.504	43.672	47.102	50.818	54.841	59.196
15	34.405	37.280	40.417	43.842	47.580	51.659	56.109	60.965	66.260	72.035
16	39.190	42.753	46.671	50.980	55.717	60.925	66.648	72.938	79.850	87.442
17	44.500	48.883	53.738	59.117	65.075	71.673	78.978	87.067	96.021	105.930
18	50.396	55.749	61.724	68.393	75.836	84.140	93.404	103.739	115.265	128.116
19	56.939	63.439	70.748	78.968	88.211	98.603	110.283	123.412	138.165	154.739
20	64.202	72.052	80.946	91.024	102.443	115.379	130.031	146.626	165.417	186.687
21	72.264	81.698	92.468	104.767	118.809	134.840	153.136	174.019	197.846	225.024
22	81.213	92.502	105.489	120.434	137.630	157.414	180.169	206.342	236.436	271.028
23	91.147	104.602	120.203	138.295	159.274	183.600	211.798	244.483	282.359	326.234
24	102.173	118.154	136.829	158.656	184.166	213.976	248.803	289.490	337.007	392.480
25	114.412	133.333	155.616	181.867	212.790	249.212	292.099	342.598	402.038	471.976
30	199.018	241.330	293.192	356.778	434.738	530.306	647.423	790.932	966.698	1181.865
40	581.812	767.080	1013.667	1341.979	1779.048	2360.724	3134.412	4163.094	5529.711	7343.715
50	1668.723	2399.975	3459.344	4994.301	7217.488	10435.449	15088.805	21812.273	31514.492	45496.094

n	21%	22%	23%	24%	25%	26%	27%	28%	29%	30%
1	1.000	1.000	1.000	1.000	1.000	1.000	1.000	1.000	1.000	1.000
2	2.210	2.220	2.230	2.240	2.250	2.260	2.270	2.280	2.290	2.300
3	3.674	3.708	3.743	3.778	3.813	3.848	3.883	3.918	3.954	3.990
4	5.446	5.524	5.604	5.684	5.766	5.848	5.931	6.016	6.101	6.187
5	7.589	7.740	7.893	8.048	8.207	8.368	8.533	8.700	8.870	9.043
6	10.183	10.442	10.708	10.980	11.259	11.544	11.837	12.136	12.442	12.756
7	13.321	13.740	14.171	14.615	15.073	15.546	16.032	16.534	17.051	17.583
8	17.119	17.762	18.430	19.123	19.842	20.588	21.361	22.163	22.995	23.858
9	21.714	22.670	23.669	24.712	25.802	26.940	28.129	29.369	30.664	32.015
10	27.274	28.657	20.113	31.643	33.253	34.945	36.723	38.592	40.556	42.619
11	34.001	35.962	38.039	40.238	42.566	45.030	47.639	50.398	53.318	56.405
12	42.141	44.873	47.787	50.895	54.208	57.738	61.501	65.510	69.780	74.326
13	51.991	55.745	59.778	64.109	68.760	73.750	79.106	84.853	91.016	97.624
14	63.909	69.009	74.528	80.496	86.949	93.925	101.465	109.611	118.411	127.912
15	78.330	85.191	92.669	100.815	109.687	119.346	129.860	141.302	153.750	167.285
16	95.779	104.933	114.983	126.010	138.109	151.375	165.922	181.867	199.337	218.470
17	116.892	129.019	142.428	157.252	173.636	191.733	211.721	233.790	258.145	285.011
18	142.439	158.403	176.187	195.993	218.045	242.583	269.885	300.250	334.006	371.514
19	173.351	194.251	217.710	244.031	273.556	306.654	343.754	385.321	431.868	483.968
20	210.755	237.986	268.783	303.598	342.945	387.384	437.568	494.210	558.110	630.157
21	256.013	291.343	331.603	377.461	429.681	489.104	556.710	633.589	720.962	820.204
22	310.775	356.438	408.871	469.052	538.101	617.270	708.022	811.993	931.040	1067.265
23	377.038	435.854	503.911	582.624	673.626	778.760	900.187	1040.351	1202.042	1388.443
24	457.215	532.741	620.810	723.453	843.032	982.237	1144.237	1332.649	1551.634	1805.975
25	554.230	650.944	764.596	898.082	1054.791	1238.617	1454.180	1706.790	2002.608	2348.765
30	1445.111	1767.044	2160.459	2640.881	3227.172	3941.953	4812.891	5873.172	7162.785	8729.805
40	9749.141	12936.141	17153.691	22728.367	30088.621	39791.957	52570.707	69376.562	91447.375	120389.375

n	31%	32%	33%	34%	35%	36%	37%	38%	39%	40%
1	1.000	1.000	1.000	1.000	1.000	1.000	1.000	1.000	1.000	1.000
2	2.310	2.320	2.330	2.340	2.350	2.360	2.370	2.380	2.390	2.400
3	4.026	4.062	4.099	4.136	4.172	4.210	4.247	4.284	4.322	4.360
4	6.274	6.362	6.452	6.542	6.633	6.725	6.818	6.912	7.008	7.104
5	9.219	9.398	9.581	9.766	9.954	10.146	10.341	10.539	10.741	10.946
6	13.077	13.406	13.742	14.086	14.438	14.799	15.167	15.544	15.930	16.324
7	18.131	18.696	19.277	19.876	20.492	21.126	21.779	22.451	23.142	23.853
8	24.752	25.678	26.638	27.633	28.664	29.732	30.837	31.982	33.167	34.395
9	33.425	34.895	36.429	38.028	39.696	41.435	43.247	45.135	47.103	49.152
10	44.786	47.062	49.451	51.958	54.590	57.351	60.248	63.287	66.473	69.813
11	59.670	63.121	66.769	70.624	74.696	78.998	83.540	88.335	93.397	98.739
12	79.167	84.320	89.803	95.636	101.840	108.437	115.450	122.903	130.822	139.234
13	104.709	112.302	120.438	129.152	138.484	148.474	159.166	170.606	182.842	195.928
14	138.169	149.239	161.183	174.063	187.953	202.925	219.058	236.435	255.151	275.299
15	182.001	197.996	215.373	234.245	254.737	276.978	301.109	327.281	355.659	386.418
16	239.421	262.354	287.446	314.888	344.895	377.690	413.520	452.647	495.366	541.985
17	314.642	347.307	383.303	422.949	466.608	514.658	567.521	625.652	689.558	759.778
18	413.180	459.445	510.792	567.751	630.920	700.935	778.504	864.399	959.485	1064.689
19	542.266	607.467	680.354	761.786	852.741	954.271	1067.551	1193.870	1334.683	1491.563
20	711.368	802.856	905.870	1021.792	1152.200	1298.809	1463.544	1648.539	1856.208	2089.188
21	932.891	1060.769	1205.807	1370.201	1556.470	1767.380	2006.055	2275.982	2581.128	2925.862
22	1223.087	1401.215	1604.724	1837.068	2102.234	2404.636	2749.294	3141.852	3588.765	4097.203
23	1603.243	1850.603	2135.282	2462.669	2839.014	3271.304	3767.532	4336.750	4989.379	5737.078
24	2101.247	2443.795	2840.924	3300.974	3833.667	4449.969	5162.516	5985.711	6936.230	8032.906
25	2753.631	3226.808	3779.428	4424.301	5176.445	6052.957	7073.645	8261.273	9642.352	11247.062
30	10632.543	12940.672	15737.945	19124.434	23221.258	28172.016	34148.906	41357.227	50043.625	60500.207

APPENDIX E.   Present Value of an Annuity of $1 for n Periods

n	1%	2%	3%	4%	5%	6%	7%	8%	9%	10%
1	.990	.980	.971	.962	.952	.943	.935	.926	.917	.909
2	1.970	1.942	1.913	1.886	1.859	1.833	1.808	1.783	1.759	1.736
3	2.941	2.884	2.829	2.775	2.723	2.673	2.624	2.577	2.531	2.487
4	3.902	3.808	3.717	3.630	3.546	3.465	3.387	3.312	3.240	3.170
5	4.853	4.713	4.580	4.452	4.329	4.212	4.100	3.993	3.890	3.791
6	5.795	5.601	5.417	5.242	5.076	4.917	4.767	4.623	4.486	4.355
7	6.728	6.472	6.230	6.002	5.786	5.582	5.389	5.206	5.033	4.868
8	7.652	7.326	7.020	6.733	6.463	6.210	5.971	5.747	5.535	5.335
9	8.566	8.162	7.786	7.435	7.108	6.802	6.515	6.247	5.995	5.759
10	9.471	8.983	8.530	8.111	7.722	7.360	7.024	6.710	6.418	6.145
11	10.368	9.787	9.253	8.760	8.306	7.887	7.499	7.139	6.805	6.495
12	11.255	10.575	9.954	9.385	8.863	8.384	7.943	7.536	7.161	6.814
13	12.134	11.348	10.635	9.986	9.394	8.853	8.358	7.904	7.487	7.103
14	13.004	12.106	11.296	10.563	9.899	9.295	8.746	8.244	7.786	7.367
15	13.865	12.849	11.938	11.118	10.380	9.712	9.108	8.560	8.061	7.606
16	14.718	13.578	12.561	11.652	10.838	10.106	9.447	8.851	8.313	7.824
17	15.562	14.292	13.166	12.166	11.274	10.477	9.763	9.122	8.544	8.022
18	16.398	14.992	13.754	12.659	11.690	10.828	10.059	9.372	8.756	8.201
19	17.226	15.679	14.324	13.134	12.085	11.158	10.336	9.604	8.950	8.365
20	18.046	16.352	14.878	13.590	12.462	11.470	10.594	9.818	9.129	8.514
21	18.857	17.011	15.415	14.029	12.821	11.764	10.836	10.017	9.292	8.649
22	19.661	17.658	15.937	14.451	13.163	12.042	11.061	10.201	9.442	8.772
23	20.456	18.292	16.444	14.857	13.489	12.303	11.272	10.371	9.580	8.883
24	21.244	18.914	16.936	15.247	13.799	12.550	11.469	10.529	9.707	8.985
25	22.023	19.524	17.413	15.622	14.094	12.783	11.654	10.675	9.823	9.077
30	25.808	22.397	19.601	17.292	15.373	13.765	12.409	11.258	10.274	9.427
40	32.835	27.356	23.115	19.793	17.159	15.046	13.332	11.925	10.757	9.779
50	39.197	31.424	25.730	21.482	18.256	15.762	13.801	12.234	10.962	9.915

n	11%	12%	13%	14%	15%	16%	17%	18%	19%	20%
1	.901	.893	.885	.877	.870	.862	.855	.847	.840	.833
2	1.713	1.690	1.668	1.647	1.626	1.605	1.585	1.566	1.547	1.528
3	2.444	2.402	2.361	2.322	2.283	2.246	2.210	2.174	2.140	2.106
4	3.102	3.037	2.974	2.914	2.855	2.798	2.743	2.690	2.639	2.589
5	3.696	3.605	3.517	3.433	3.352	3.274	3.199	3.127	3.058	2.991
6	4.231	4.111	3.998	3.889	3.784	3.685	3.589	3.498	3.410	3.326
7	4.712	4.564	4.423	4.288	4.160	4.039	3.922	3.812	3.706	3.605
8	5.146	4.968	4.799	4.639	4.487	4.344	4.207	4.078	3.954	3.837
9	5.537	5.328	5.132	4.946	4.772	4.607	4.451	4.303	4.163	4.031
10	5.889	5.650	5.426	5.216	5.019	4.833	4.659	4.494	4.339	4.192
11	6.207	5.938	5.687	5.453	5.234	5.029	4.836	4.656	4.487	4.327
12	6.492	6.194	5.918	5.660	5.421	5.197	4.988	4.793	4.611	4.439
13	6.750	6.424	6.122	5.842	5.583	5.342	5.118	4.910	4.715	4.533
14	6.982	6.628	6.303	6.002	5.724	5.468	5.229	5.008	4.802	4.611
15	7.191	6.811	6.462	6.142	5.847	5.575	5.324	5.092	4.876	4.675
16	7.379	6.974	6.604	6.265	5.954	5.669	5.405	5.162	4.938	4.730
17	7.549	7.120	6.729	6.373	6.047	5.749	5.475	5.222	4.990	4.775
18	7.702	7.250	6.840	6.467	6.128	5.818	5.534	5.273	5.033	4.812
19	7.839	7.366	6.938	6.550	6.198	5.877	5.585	5.316	5.070	4.843
20	7.963	7.469	7.025	6.623	6.259	5.929	5.628	5.353	5.101	4.870
21	8.075	7.562	7.102	6.687	6.312	5.973	5.665	5.384	5.127	4.891
22	8.176	7.645	7.170	6.743	6.359	6.011	5.696	5.410	5.149	4.909
23	8.266	7.718	7.230	6.792	6.399	6.044	5.723	5.432	5.167	4.925
24	8.348	7.784	7.283	6.835	6.434	6.073	5.747	5.451	5.182	4.937
25	8.442	7.843	7.330	6.873	6.464	6.097	5.766	5.467	5.195	4.948
30	8.694	8.055	7.496	7.003	6.566	6.177	5.829	5.517	5.235	4.979
40	8.951	8.244	7.634	7.105	6.642	6.233	5.871	5.548	5.258	4.997
50	9.042	8.305	7.675	7.133	6.661	6.246	5.880	5.554	5.262	4.999

n	21%	22%	23%	24%	25%	26%	27%	28%	29%	30%
1	.826	.820	.813	.806	.800	.794	.787	.781	.775	.769
2	1.509	1.492	1.474	1.457	1.440	1.424	1.407	1.392	1.376	1.361
3	2.074	2.042	2.011	1.981	1.952	1.923	1.896	1.868	1.842	1.816
4	2.540	2.494	2.448	2.404	2.362	2.320	2.280	2.241	2.203	2.166
5	2.926	2.864	2.803	2.745	2.689	2.635	2.583	2.532	2.483	2.436
6	3.245	3.167	3.092	3.020	2.951	2.885	2.821	2.759	2.700	2.643
7	3.508	3.416	3.327	3.242	3.161	3.083	3.009	2.937	2.868	2.802
8	3.726	3.619	3.518	3.421	3.329	3.241	3.156	3.076	2.999	2.925
9	3.905	3.786	3.673	3.566	3.463	3.366	3.273	3.184	3.100	3.019
10	4.054	3.923	3.799	3.682	3.570	3.465	3.364	3.269	3.178	3.092
11	4.177	4.035	3.902	3.776	3.656	3.544	3.437	3.335	3.239	3.147
12	4.278	4.127	3.985	3.851	3.725	3.606	3.493	3.387	3.286	3.190
13	4.362	4.203	4.053	3.912	3.780	3.656	3.538	3.427	3.322	3.223
14	4.432	4.265	4.108	3.962	3.824	3.695	3.573	3.459	3.351	3.249
15	4.489	4.315	4.153	4.001	3.859	3.726	3.601	3.483	3.373	3.268
16	4.536	4.357	4.189	4.033	3.887	3.751	3.623	3.503	3.390	3.283
17	4.576	4.391	4.219	4.059	3.910	3.771	3.640	3.518	3.403	3.295
18	4.608	4.419	4.243	4.080	3.928	3.786	3.654	3.529	3.413	3.304
19	4.635	4.442	4.263	4.097	3.942	3.799	3.664	3.539	3.421	3.311
20	4.657	4.460	4.279	4.110	3.954	3.808	3.673	3.546	3.427	3.316
21	4.675	4.476	4.292	4.121	3.963	3.816	3.679	3.551	3.432	3.320
22	4.690	4.488	4.302	4.130	3.970	3.822	3.684	3.556	3.436	3.323
23	4.703	4.499	4.311	4.137	3.976	3.827	3.689	3.559	3.438	3.325
24	4.713	4.507	4.318	4.143	3.981	3.831	3.692	3.562	3.441	3.327
25	4.721	4.514	4.323	4.147	3.985	3.834	3.694	3.564	3.442	3.329
30	4.746	4.534	4.339	4.160	3.995	3.842	3.701	3.569	3.447	3.332
40	4.760	4.544	4.347	4.166	3.999	3.846	3.703	3.571	3.448	3.333
50	4.762	4.545	4.348	4.167	4.000	3.846	3.704	3.571	3.448	3.333

n	31%	32%	33%	34%	35%	36%	37%	38%	39%	40%
1	.763	.758	.752	.746	.741	.735	.730	.725	.719	.714
2	1.346	1.331	1.317	1.303	1.289	1.276	1.263	1.250	1.237	1.224
3	1.791	1.766	1.742	1.719	1.696	1.673	1.652	1.630	1.609	1.589
4	2.130	2.096	2.062	2.029	1.997	1.966	1.935	1.906	1.877	1.849
5	2.390	2.345	2.302	2.260	2.220	2.181	2.143	2.106	2.070	2.035
6	2.588	2.534	2.483	2.433	2.385	2.339	2.294	2.251	2.209	2.168
7	2.739	2.677	2.619	2.562	2.508	2.455	2.404	2.355	2.308	2.263
8	2.854	2.786	2.721	2.658	2.598	2.540	2.485	2.432	2.380	2.331
9	2.942	2.868	2.798	2.730	2.665	2.603	2.544	2.487	2.432	2.379
10	3.009	2.930	2.855	2.784	2.715	2.649	2.587	2.527	2.469	2.414
11	3.060	2.978	2.899	2.824	2.752	2.683	2.618	2.555	2.496	2.438
12	3.100	3.013	2.931	2.853	2.779	2.708	2.641	2.576	2.515	2.456
13	3.129	3.040	2.956	2.876	2.799	2.727	2.658	2.592	2.529	2.469
14	3.152	3.061	2.974	2.892	2.814	2.740	2.670	2.603	2.539	2.477
15	3.170	3.076	2.988	2.905	2.825	2.750	2.679	2.611	2.546	2.484
16	3.183	3.088	2.999	2.914	2.834	2.757	2.685	2.616	2.551	2.489
17	3.193	3.097	3.007	2.921	2.840	2.763	2.690	2.621	2.555	2.492
18	3.201	3.104	3.012	2.926	2.844	2.767	2.693	2.624	2.557	2.494
19	3.207	3.109	3.017	2.930	2.848	2.770	2.696	2.626	2.559	2.496
20	3.211	3.113	3.020	2.933	2.850	2.772	2.698	2.627	2.561	2.497
21	3.215	3.116	3.023	2.935	2.852	2.773	2.699	2.629	2.562	2.498
22	3.217	3.118	3.025	2.936	2.853	2.775	2.700	2.629	2.562	2.498
23	3.219	3.120	3.026	2.938	2.854	2.775	2.701	2.630	2.563	2.499
24	3.221	3.121	3.027	2.939	2.855	2.776	2.701	2.630	2.563	2.499
25	3.222	3.122	3.028	2.939	2.856	2.776	2.702	2.631	2.563	2.499
30	3.225	2.124	3.030	2.941	2.857	2.777	2.702	2.631	2.564	2.500
40	3.226	3.125	3.030	2.941	2.857	2.778	2.703	2.632	2.564	2.500
50	3.226	3.125	3.030	2.941	2.857	2.778	2.703	2.632	2.564	2.500

APPENDIX F
Check Figures for Selected End-of-Chapter Problems

CHAPTER 2
2-1A. 11.28%
2-3A. 12.35%
2-5A. Taxable income = $526,800
Tax liability = $179,112
2-7A. Taxable income =$365,000
Tax liability = $124,100
2-9A. Taxable income = ($38,000)
Tax liability = $0
2-11A. Taxable income =$153,600
Tax liability = $43,154
2-13A. Taxable income = $370,000
Tax liability = $125,800
2-15A. Taxable income =$1,813,000
Tax liability = $616,420
2-17A. 1987 $ 6,000 pay   1991 $10,000 pay
1988 $ 6,000 refund 1992 $19,450 refund
1989 $ 1,500 pay   1993 $ 7,500 pay
1990 $15,450 pay   1994 $11,250 refund

CHAPTER 3
3-1A. **a.** $12,970
c. $3,019.40
3-2A. **a.** n = 15 years
3-3A. **b.** 5%
c. 9%
3-4A. **b.** PV = $235.20
3-5A. **a.** $6,289
c. $302.89
3-6A. **c.** $1,562.96
3-7A. **a.** FV_1 = $10,600
FV_5 = $13,380
FV_{15} = $23,970
3-9A. **a.** $6,690
b. Semiannual: $6,720
Bimonthly: $6,740
3-11A. Year 1: 18,000 books
Year 2: 21,600 books
Year 3: 25,920 books
3-13A. $6,108.11
3-15A. 8%
3-17A. $658,197.85
3-21A. **b.** $8,333.33
3-22A. $824.36
3-26A. $6,509
3-28A. 22%
3-29A. $6,934.81
3-32A. **a.** $1,989.73
3-35A. $15,912
3-37A. 36.47%

CHAPTER 4
4-1A. $\overline{X}$ = 9.1%; σ = 3.06%
4-3A. Security A: $\overline{X}$ = 16.7%; σ = 10.12%
Security B: $\overline{X}$ = 9.2%: σ = 3.57%

4-5A. About 0.50
4-7A. 10.56%
4-9A.

Time	*Asman* *Return*
2	20.0%
3	−8.3
4	18.2

4-11A. **a.** Expected Return = 15.8%
b. Beta = 0.95
4A-1. Alpha 1.31%
Beta 0.72
Arka:
Average return: 12.25%
Standard deviation: 5.32%
S&P 500:
Average return: 15.25%
Standard deviation: 7.37%

CHAPTER 5
5-1A. $752.52
5-3A. $1,058.34; $1,057.23
5-5A. 4.63%
5-7A. $51.50
5-9A. $24.50
5-11A. **a.** 21.24%
b. $52.34
5-13A. $39.96
5-15A. 9.65%
5-17A. **a.** 7.06%
b. $847.48
5-19A. **a.** 14.07%
b. $57.02

CHAPTER 6
6-1A. **a.** $6,800
b. $3,400
c. No taxes
d. $1,020
6-3A. **a.** 2.75 years
b. $10,628.16
6-5A. **a.** IRR = 7%
b. IRR = 17%
6-7A. **a.** IRR = approximately 19%
6-9A. **a.** $560,000
b. Cash flow after tax: $116,170
6-11A. **a.** Payback: 3.10
b. NPV = $34,697
6-13A. **b.** NPV = $17,371.76
6-15A. IRR_A = slightly over 23%
IRR_B = 8%
6-17A. **a.** $40,100
e. 2.37 years
6-19A. $NPV_{POINT\ BLANK}$ = $29,260

CHAPTER 7

7-1A. **a.** $NPV_A = \$136.30$
$NPV_B = \$454.$
b. $PI_A = 1.2726$
$PI_B = 1.0908$
c. $IRR_A = 40\%$
$IRR_B = 20\%$
7-3A. **a.** Payback A = 1.589 years
Payback B = 3.019 years
b. $NPV_A = \$8,743$
$NPV_B = \$11,615$
c. $IRR_A = 40\%$
$IRR_B = 30\%$
e. $EAA_A = \$3,830$
$EAA_B = \$2,098$
7-7A. **b.** $NPV_A = \$53,212.50$
$NPV_B = \$58,265$
7-9A. NVP = \$-330
7-11A. $NPV_A = \$9,813.25$

CHAPTER 8

8-1A. **a.** $K_d = 6.53\%$
b. $K_{nc} = 14.37\%$
c. $K_c = 15.14\%$
d. $K_p = 8.77\%$
e. $K_d = 7.92\%$
8-3A. **a.** $K_d = 5.28\%$
b. $K_{nc} = 9.85\%$
c. $K_d = 7.63\%$
d. $K_p = 8.24\%$
e. $K_c = 11.90\%$
8-5A. $K_d = 7.23\%$
8-7A. $K_d = 8.48\%$
8-9A. $K_c = 18.74\%$
8-11A. **a.** $V_b = \$1,320.52$
b. $NP_o = \$1,181.87$
c. 423 bonds
d. $K_d = 7.21\%$
8-13A. $K_o = 15.07\%$
8-15A. K_o (internal only) = 10.09%;
K_o (external only) = 10.22%
8-17A. *$Breaks in Weighted Marginal Cost Curve*
Debt $750,000
Preferred $625,000; $1,250,000
Common $1,000,000
Weighted Cost of Capital
$0–$625,000   10.88%
$625,001–$750,000   10.96%
$750,001–$1,000,000   11.56%
8-19A. Cost of debt 5.28%; 5.94%; 6.93%
Cost of preferred 10.625%; 11.333%
Cost of common 13.16%; 13.90%; 14.20%
Weighted Cost of Capital
$0–$250,000   10.543%
$250,001–$500,000   10.987%
$500,001–$625,000   11.185%
8-21A. *Required Rate*
A: 16.30%
B: 14.35%

CHAPTER 9

9-1A. **a.** Jake's EBIT = $154,067.40
Sarasota = 480,000
Jefferson = 28,970
b. Jake's = 8,232
Sarasota = 1,789
Jefferson = 8,310
c. Jake's = 1.78 times
Sarasota = 2.77 times
Jefferson = 4.09 times
d. Jefferson Wholesale would suffer the largest decline in profitability.
9-3A. **a.** 6,296 pairs of shoes
b. $534,591.19
c. At 7,000, EBIT = $19,000
At 9,000, EBIT = $73,000
At 15,000, EBIT = $235,000
d. 9.95 times; 3.33 times; 1.72 times
9-4A. **a.** 9,000 units
b. $1,620,000
9-6A. **a.** $85,416.67
b. 7,030 units; $189,815
9-8A. **a.** 1.94 times
9-10A. **a.** 10,000 units
b. $1,800,000
9-12A. **a.** F = $173,333.33
b. 14,444 units; S* = $288,888.88
9-18A. **a.** 5,000 units
b. $125,000
c. −$10,000; $10,000; $30,000
9-20A. 5 times
9-22A. 1,400,000 units
9-24A. **a.** 3 times
b. 1.25 times
c. 3.75 times
d. $8 million
9-26A. **b.** 35%
c. $84,000

CHAPTER 10

10-1A. **a.** EBIT = $2,000,000
b. EPS will be $1.00 for each plan.
d. Plan B
10-3A. **a.** EBIT = $240,000
b. EPS will be $1.80 for each plan.
10-4A. **a.** EBIT = $220,000
b. Plan B.
10-6A. **a.** $640,000
b. EPS = $3.20
10-8A. **a.** $300,000
b. EPS = $3.00
10-10A. **a.** Plan A = $7.68
b. 10.378
10-14A. **a.** $20,000,000
b. $k_c = 25\%$; $k_o = 25\%$
10-16A. **a.** Plan A vs. Plan B = $9,000
Plan A vs. Plan C = $18,000

A. 95,238 shares

11-3A. Equity financing needed = $384,000
Dividend = $16,000

11-5A. Price for Plan A or Plan B = $31.76

11-7A. **a.** Value before split = $122,500
b. Net gain = $24,500

11-8A. **a.** Year 1 = $.70; Year 3 = $.93
b. $.90
c. Year 1 = $.50; Year 3 = $.68

11-9A. **a.** $52.00
b. 9,615 shares

11-11A. Equity financing needed = $360,000;
Dividend = $90,000

CHAPTER 12

12-1A. $500,000.00

12-3A. **a.** Return on total assets = 10%
b. Sales growth = 20%
c. Return on equity = 17.1%

12-5A.

	Beginning	End
Current Ratio	6x	4x
ACP	135 days	106 days
Fixed Asset T/O	1x	1.04x
Net Profit Margin	10%	12.4%

12-7A. Cash flow from:

Operations	$87,000
Investing	(142,500)
Financing	63,000

12-9A. **a.** 25%; 2.25×; 11.11%
b. 19.5%
c. 14.5%

CHAPTER 13

13-1A. Total assets = $1.8 million

13-3A. Total assets = $2 million
Long-term debt = $.4 million

13-5A.

	July	Aug.	Sept
Net Monthly Change	$(10,600)	(600)	7,800
Cumulative Borrowing	10,600	11,306	3,619

13-7A. **a.** Accounts receivable = $22,222
b. Accounts receivable = $31,111

13-11A. **a.** Average collection period = 40 days
b. Reduction in accounts receivable = $100,000

13-13A.

	Jan.	Feb.	March
Net Monthly Change	$38,300	($900)	($91,500)
Cumulative Borrowing	$-0-	$-0-	$52,100

CHAPTER 14

14-1A. **a.** Return on equity = 19.48%
b. Return on equity = 14.05%

14-3A. Net operating income = $195,666
Net income = $101,200

CHAPTER 15

15-1A. **a.** Yes; the company will save $160,199 annually.

15-3A. **a.** Yes; the firm will generate $35,288 in net annual savings.

b. 5.01%

15-4A. **b.** 15%

15-5A. **a.** $2,625,000
b. $241,500

15-6A. Yes; annual savings = $211,000

15-8A. 0.5322 days

15-10A. **b.** 12%

15-12A. Net annual savings = $3,375

15-14A. 0.4106 days

15-16A. $10,667

15-18A. $14,247

15-25A. **a.** $912.44
b. $87.56
c. $17.59

15-27A. **b.** 10.185%

15A-1. **a.** $158,698
b. $856.97
c. 5.95 days
d. $79,349

CHAPTER 16

16-1A. **a.** 36.36%
b. 36.73%

16-3A. **a.** $90,000
b. $53,333

16-5A. $56,875

16-7A. **a.** 775 units

16-9A. **a.** 816 units
b. $61,237

16-11A. **b.** 35.2 orders per year

CHAPTER 17

17-1A. Rate = 13.79%

17-3A. **a.** Rate = 36.73%
b. Rate = 74.23%

17-7A. **a.** Rate = 16.27%

17-11A. Pledging: Rate = 16%
Inventory loan: Rate = 13.8%

17-13A. Rate = 12.37%

CHAPTER 19

19-1A. **a.** $31,977.78

19-3A. **a.** 15%
b. Payment = $76,359
c. 9%

19-5A. **a.** *NPV(P)* = $6,340.75

19-7A. **a.** $19,925.20
c. $15,229.97

CHAPTER 20

20-3A. Yes, *NPV* = $1,709,901

20-5A. *i* = 12.098%

CHAPTER 21

21-1A. **a.** 25 shares
b. $681.25

21-3A. **b.** $4

21-5A. Warrant premium = $6.25

CHAPTER 23

23-1A. Average theoretical value: $6,083

23-3A. Net present value: −$29.87

CHAPTER 24

24-1A. Bankruptcy score for company A = 2.810
Bankruptcy score for company B = 6.719
Bankruptcy score for company C = 3.455

24-3A. *Corporate Structure After Reorganization*

Accounts Payable	$162,500
Short-term Notes Payable	287,500
Long-term Note Payable	125,000
Mortgage Bonds	500,000
Preferred Stock	125,000
Common Stock	625,000

24-5A. Final distribution to:

Accounts payable	$200,000
Notes payable	350,000
Long-term debt	300,000

Preferred stock	100,000
Common stock	0

CHAPTER 25

25-1A. **a.** $8,437
b. $9,368
c. $25,695

25-3A. Canada: 1.1853; 1.1881; 1.1912
Japan: 213.4927; 211.9992; 209.1613
Switzerland; 1.9459; 1.9346; 1.8815

25-5A. Net gain = $149.02

25-7A. Canada: (2.85%); (1.99%)
Japan: 8.45%; 8.28%
Switzerland: 7%; 13.7%

25-9A. $.0046945/yen

GLOSSARY

Accelerated Cost Recovery System. A means of accelerated depreciation for assets acquired after 1981, whereby assets are assigned to specific property classifications and depreciated accordingly.

Accelerated Depreciation Techniques. Techniques that allow the owner of the asset to take greater amounts of depreciation during the early years of its life, thereby deferring some of the taxes until later years.

Accounting Rate of Return (AROR). A capital-budgeting criterion that relates the returns generated by the project, as measured by average accounting profits after tax, to the average dollar size of the investment required.

Accrual Method. A method of accounting whereby income is recorded when earned, whether or not the money has been received at that time, and expenses are recorded when incurred, whether or not any money has actually been paid out.

Accumulated Earnings Credit. The greater of (1) the profits for the year retained for reasonable business needs, and (2) $150,000 less the retained earnings shown in the balance sheet.

Accumulated Taxable Income. The firm's taxable income less dividends paid and accrued during the year, and less an **accumulated earnings credit.**

Acid Test Ratio. (Current assets − inventories) ÷ current liabilities. This ratio is a more stringent measure of liquidity than the current ratio in that it subtracts inventories (the least liquid current asset) from current assets.

Acquisition. A combination of two or more businesses into a single operational entity.

ACRS. Accelerated Cost Recovery System.

Affiliated Group. A group of firms related by affiliation, expressed in terms of one firm's owning, either directly or indirectly, 80 percent of the firm paying the dividend.

Agency Costs. The costs, such as a reduced stock price, associated with potential conflict between managers and investors when these two groups are not the same.

Amortized Loans. Loans that are paid off in equal periodic payments.

Annuity. A series of equal dollar payments for a specified number of years.

Appraisal Value. The value of a company as stated by an independent appraisal firm.

Arbitrage-Pricing Model. A theory that relates stock returns and risk. The theory maintains that security returns vary from their expected amounts when there are unanticipated changes in basic economic forces. Such forces would include unexpected changes in industrial production, inflation rates, term structure of interest rates, and the difference between interest rates of high-and-low risk bonds.

Arbitrageur. A person involved in the process of buying and selling in more than one market to make a riskless profit.

Arrangement. A reorganizational plan involving a petition to the court requesting that the firm be required to make only partial or a delayed payment to its creditors.

Arrearage. An overdue payment, generally referring to omitted preferred stock dividends.

Assignee. The third party responsible for disposal of the debtor firm's assets and distribution of the proceeds to the creditors in an assignment.

Assignment. A method of liquidating a business that has been declared insolvent. To minimize court involvement (and therefore costs), a third party receives title for the firm's assets and is responsible for the disposal of the assets and distribution of the proceeds. Creditors have the right to refuse such a settlement, and if they so choose, to force the debtor into a court-administered liquidation.

Automated Depository Transfer System. A system that moves funds from local bank accounts to concentration accounts electronically. This eliminates the mail float from the local banks to the concentration banks.

Average Collection Period. Accounts receivable/(annual credit sales/360). A ratio that expresses how rapidly the firm is collecting its credit accounts.

Average Tax Rate. The rate calculated by dividing the total tax liability by the entity's taxable income.

Balance Sheet. A basic accounting statement that represents the financial position of a firm on a given date.

Balance Sheet Leverage Ratios. Financial ratios used to measure the extent of a firm's use of borrowed funds calculated using information found in the firm's balance sheet.

Bankers' Acceptances. A draft (order to pay) drawn on a specific bank by a seller of goods in order to obtain payment for goods that have been shipped (sold) to a customer. The customer maintains an account with that specific bank.

Bank Wire. A private wire service used and supported by approximately 250 banks in the United States for transferring funds, exchanging credit information, or effecting securities transactions.

Beta. The relationship between an investment's returns and the market returns. This is a measure of the investment's nondiversifiable risk.

Bird-in-the-Hand Dividend Theory. The belief that dividend income has a higher value to the investor than does capital gains income, since dividends are more certain than capital gains.

Bond. A long-term (ten-year or more) promissory note issued by the borrower, promising to pay the owner of the security a predetermined and fixed amount of interest each year.

Bond Par Value. The face value appearing on the bond, which is to be returned to the bondholder at maturity.

Book Value. The depreciated value of a company's assets (original cost less accumulated depreciation) less the outstanding liabilities.

Book-Value Weights. The percentage of financing provided by different capital sources as measured by their book values from the company's balance sheet.

Break-Even Analysis. An analytical technique used to determine the quantity of output or sales that results in a zero level of earnings before interest and taxes (EBIT). Relationships among the firm's cost structure, volume of output, and EBIT are studied.

Business Risk. The relative dispersion or variability in the firm's expected earnings before interest and taxes (EBIT). The nature of the firm's operations causes its business risk. This type of risk is affected by the firm's cost structure, product demand characteristics, and intra-industry competitive position. In capital-structure theory, business risk is distinguished from financial risk. See **Financial Risk.**

Call Option. A call option gives its owner the right to purchase a given number of shares of stock or some other asset at a specified price over a given time period.

Call Premium. The difference between the call price and the security's par value.

Call Provision. A provision that entitles the corporation to repurchase its bonds or preferred stock from their holders at stated prices over specified periods.

Capital Asset. All property used in conducting a business other than assets held primarily for sale in the ordinary course of business or depreciable and real property used in conducting a business.

Capital Asset Pricing Model. An equation stating that the expected rate of return on a project is a function of (1) the risk-free rate, (2) the investment's systematic risk, and (3) the expected risk premium in the market.

Capital Budgeting. The decision-making process with respect to investment in fixed assets. Specifically it involves measuring the incremental cash flows associated with investment proposals and evaluating those proposed investments.

Capital Gain or Loss. As defined by the revenue code, a gain or loss resulting from the sale or exchange of a capital asset.

Capital Market. All institutions and procedures that facilitate transactions in long-term financial instruments.

Capital Rationing. The placing of a limit by the firm on the dollar size of the capital budget.

Capital Structure. The mix of long-term sources of funds used by the firm. This is also called the firm's **capitalization.** The relative total (percentage) of each type of fund is emphasized.

Cash Breakdown Analysis. Another version of break-even analysis that includes only the cash costs of production within the cost components. This means noncash expenses, like depreciation, are omitted in the analysis.

Cash Budget. A detailed plan of future cash flows. This budget is composed of four elements: cash receipts, cash disbursements, net change in cash for the period, and new financing needed.

Cash Flow Process. The process of cash generation and disposition in a typical business setting.

Certainty Equivalents. The amount of cash a person would require with certainty to make him indifferent between this certain sum and a particular risky or uncertain sum.

Characteristic Line. The line of "best fit" through a series of returns for a firm's stock relative to the market returns. The slope of the line, frequently called beta, represents the average movement of the firm's stock returns in response to a movement in the market's returns.

Chattel Mortgage Agreement. A loan agreement in which the lender can increase his security interest by having specific items of inventory identified in the loan agreement. The borrower retains title to the inventory but cannot sell the items without the lender's consent.

Chop-Shop Value. A valuation approach that values a firm based on its various business segments. It is an attempt to identify multi-industry companies that are undervalued and would be worth more if separated into their parts.

Clientele Effect. The belief that individuals and institutions that need current income will invest in companies that have high dividend payouts. Other investors prefer to avoid taxes by holding securities that offer only small dividend income, but large capital gains. Thus, we have a "clientele" of investors.

Commercial Paper. Short-term unsecured promissory notes sold by large businesses in order to raise cash. Unlike most other money market instruments, commercial paper has no developed secondary market.

Common Size Financial Statements. Financial statements that have been converted to a percent of either sales in the case of the income statement or total assets in the case of the balance sheet. The information within the common size statements is standardized and consequently can be used to compare firms of very different sizes.

Compensating Balance. A balance of a given amount that the firm maintains in its demand deposit account. It may be required by either a formal or informal agreement with the firm's commercial bank. Such balances are usually required by the bank (1) on the unused portion of a loan commitment, (2) on the unpaid portion of an outstanding loan, or (3) in exchange for certain services provided by the bank, such as check-clearing or credit information. These balances raise the effective rate of interest paid on borrowed funds.

Composition. A voluntary remedy to insolvency in which the creditors receive a portion of the amounts originally owed to them. This may be preferable to forcing bankruptcy due to the high costs of bankruptcy courts and the possibility that the insolvent firm's resources may be further depleted by the bankruptcy proceedings.

Compounding. The process of determining the future value of a payment or series of payments when applying the concept of compound interest.

Compound Interest. The situation in which interest paid on the investment during the first period is added to the principal and, during the second period, interest is earned on the original principal plus the interest earned during the first period.

Concentration Bank. A bank where the firm maintains a major disbursing account.

Conglomerate. A multifaceted corporation involved in a variety of products and services.

Constant Dividend Payout Ratio. A dividend payment policy in which the percentage of earnings paid out in dividends is held constant. The dollar amount fluctuates from year to year as profits vary.

Contractual Interest Rate. The interest rate to be paid on a bond expressed as a percent of par value.

Contribution Margin. The difference between a product's selling price and its unit variable costs. It is usually measured on a per unit basis.

Conversion Parity Price. The price for which the investor in effect purchases the company's common stock when purchasing a convertible security. Mathematically it is the market price of the convertible security divided by the conversion ratio.

Conversion Ratio. The number of shares of common stock for which a convertible security can be exchanged.

Convertibles. Preferred stock or debentures that can be exchanged for a specified number of shares of common stock at the will of the owner.

Corporate Bylaws. Regulations that govern the internal affairs of the corporation, designating such items as the time and place of the shareholders' meetings, voting rights, the election process for selecting members of the board of directors, the procedures for issuing and transferring stock certificates, and the policies relating to the corporate records.

Corporation. An entity that *legally* functions separate and apart from its owners.

Cost Budgets. Budgets prepared for every major expense category of the firm, such as production cost, selling cost,

administrative cost, financing cost, and research and development cost.

Cost of Capital. The rate that must be earned in order to satisfy the required rate of return of the firm's investors. It may also be defined as the rate of return on investments at which the price of the firm's common stock will remain unchanged. The cost of capital is based on the opportunity cost of funds as determined in the capital markets.

Cost of Common Stock. The rate of return the firm must earn in order for the common stockholders to receive their required rate of return. The rate is based on the opportunity cost of funds for the common stockholders in the capital markets.

Cost of Debt. The rate that has to be received from an investment in order to achieve the required rate of return for the creditors. The cost is based on the debtholders' opportunity cost of debt in the capital markets.

Cost of Preferred Stock. The rate of return that must be earned on the preferred stockholders' investment to satisfy their required rate of return. The cost is based on the preferred stockholders' opportunity cost of preferred stock in the capital markets.

Cost-Volume-Profit Analysis. Another way of referring to ordinary break-even analysis.

Coupon Interest Rate. The interest to be paid annually on a bond as a percent of par value, which is specified in the contractual agreement.

Coverage Ratios. A group of ratios that measure a firm's ability to meet its recurring fixed charge obligations, such as interest on long-term debt, lease payments, and/or preferred stock dividends.

Credit Scoring. The numerical evaluation of credit applicants where the score is evaluated relative to a predetermined standard.

Cross Rates. The indirect computation of the exchange rate of one currency from the exchange rates of two other currencies.

Cumulative Feature. A requirement that all past unpaid preferred stock dividends can be paid before any common stock dividends are declared.

Current Ratio. Current assets/current liabilities. A ratio that indicates a firm's degree of liquidity by comparing its current assets to its current liabilities.

Date of Record. Date at which the stock transfer books are to be closed for determining the investor to receive the next dividend payment. See **Ex-Dividend Date.**

Debenture. Any unsecured long-term debt.

Debt Capacity. The maximum proportion of debt that the firm can include in its capital structure and still maintain its lowest composite cost of capital.

Debt Ratio. Total liabilities/total assets. A ratio that measures the extent to which a firm has been financed with debt.

Declaration Date. The date upon which a dividend is formally declared by the board of directors.

Default Risk. The uncertainty of expected returns from a security attributable to possible changes in the financial capacity of the security issuer to make future payments to the security owner. Treasury securities are considered to be default-free. Default risk is also referred to as "financial risk" in the context of marketable securities management.

Degree of Combined Leverage. The percentage change in earnings per share caused by a percentage change in sales. It is the product of the degree of operating leverage and the degree of financial leverage.

Depository Transfer Checks. A means for moving funds from local bank accounts to concentration accounts. The depository transfer check itself is an unsigned, nonnegotiable instrument. It is payable only to the bank of deposit for credit to the firm's specific account.

Depreciation. The means by which an asset's value is expensed over its useful life for federal income tax purposes.

Direct Quotes. The exchange rate that indicates the number of units of the home currency required to buy one unit of foreign currency.

Disbursing Float. Funds available in the company's bank account until its payment check has cleared through the banking system.

Discount Bond. A bond that sells at a discount below par value.

Discounting. The inverse of compounding. This process is used to determine the present value of a cash flow.

Discount Rate. The interest rate used in the discounting process.

Diversifiable Risk. See **Unsystematic Risk.**

Divestitures. The removal of a division or subsidiary from the company. Typically, the part of the firm being separated is viewed as not contributing to the company's basic purposes.

Dividend Payout Ratio. The amount of dividends relative to the company's net income or earnings per share.

Dividend Yield. The dividend per share divided by the price of the security.

Double-Declining Balance Depreciation. A method for computing declining balance depreciation expense in which the constant percentage is equal to 2/N, where N represents the depreciable life of the asset.

Dunning Letters. Past-due letters sent out to delinquent accounts.

Duration. A measure of responsiveness of the bond price to a change in interest rates.

EBIT. Common financial notation for **earnings before interest and taxes.**

EBIT-EPS Indifference Point. The level of earnings before interest and taxes (EBIT) that will equate earnings per share (EPS) between two different financing plans.

Economic Failure. Situation in which the company's costs exceed its revenues. Stated differently, the internal rates of return on investments are less than the firm's cost of capital.

Efficient Market. A market in which the values of all assets and securities at any instant in time fully reflect all available information.

EPS. Typical financial notation for **earnings per** (common) **share.**

Equivalent Annual Annuity (EAA). An annuity cash flow that yields the same present value as the project's NPV. It is calculated by dividing the project's NPV by the appropriate $PVIFA_{1\%,n\ yr}$.

ERTA. Economic Recovery Tax Act of 1981.

Eurodollar Market. This is a banking market in U.S. dollars outside the U.S. Large sums of U.S. dollars can be borrowed or invested in this unregulated financial market. Similar external markets exist in Europe and Asia and for other major currencies.

Exchange Risk. The variability in future cash flows caused by variations in the exchange rates.

Ex-Dividend Date. The date upon which stock brokerage companies have uniformly decided to terminate the right of ownership to the dividend, which is four days prior to the record date.

Exercise Price. The price at which a warrant allows its holder to purchase the firm's common stock.

Exercise Ratio. The number of shares of stock that can be obtained at the exercise price with one warrant.

Expected Rate of Return. The arithmetic mean or average of all possible outcomes where those outcomes are weighted by the probability that each will occur.

Extension. An arrangement requiring that the debtor pay the amount owed in full, but providing an extension in time.

Ex-Rights Date. The date on or after which the stock sells without rights.

External Common Equity. A new issue of common stock.

Factor. A firm that acquires the receivables of other firms. A commercial finance company that engages solely in the factoring of receivables is known as an old-line factor.

Factoring of Accounts Receivable. The outright sale of a firm's accounts to another party (the factor) without recourse. The factor, in turn, bears the risk of collection.

Fair Value. The present value of an asset's expected future cash flows.

Federal Agency Securities. Debt obligations of corporations and agencies created to carry out the lending programs of the U.S. government.

Federal Reserve System. The U.S. central banking system.

Field Warehouse Financing Agreement. A security agreement in which inventories are used as collateral, physically separated from the firm's other inventories, and placed under the control of a third-party field warehousing firm.

Financial Analysis. The assessment of a firm's financial condition or well being. Its objectives are to determine the firm's financial strengths and to identify its weaknesses. The primary tool of financial analysis is the financial ratio.

Financial Assets. Claims for future payment by one economic unit upon another.

Financial Intermediaries. Major financial institutions, such as commercial banks, savings and loan associations, credit unions, life insurance companies, and mutual funds, that assist the transfer of savings from economic units with excess savings to those with a shortage of savings.

Financial Lease. A noncancellable contractual commitment on the part of the firm leasing the asset (the lessee) to make a series of payments to the firm that actually owns the asset (the lessor) for the use of the asset.

Financial Leverage. The use of securities bearing a fixed (limited) rate of return to finance a portion of the firm's assets. Financial leverage can arise from the use of either debt or preferred stock financing. The use of financial leverage exposes the firm to **financial risk.**

Financial Markets. Institutions and procedures that facilitate transactions in all types of financial claims (securities).

Financial Risk. The added variability in earnings available to the firm's common shareholders, and the added chance of insolvency caused by the use of securities bearing a limited rate of return in the firm's financial structure. The use of financial leverage gives rise to financial risk.

Financial Structure Design. The activity of seeking the proper mixture of a firm's short-term, long-term, and permanent financing components to minimize the cost of raising a given amount of funds.

Financial Structure. The mix of *all* funds sources that appear on the right-hand side of the balance sheet.

Fixed Asset Turnover. Sales/fixed assets. A ratio indicating how effectively a firm is using its fixed assets to generate sales.

Fixed Costs. Charges that do **not** vary in total amount as sales volume or the quantity of output changes over some relevant range of output.

Flotation Costs. The underwriter's spread and issuing costs associated with the issuance and marketing of new securities.

Foreign Direct Investment. Physical assets, such as plant and equipment, acquired outside a corporation's home country but operated and controlled by that corporation.

Formal Control. Control vested in the stockholders having the majority of the voting common shares.

Forward Exchange Contract. A contract which requires delivery of one currency at a specified future date for a specified amount of another currency.

Free Cash Flow Value. The value of a firm based on the cash flows available for distributing to any investors, both debt and equity. The free cash flows equal operating cash flows less any incremental investments made to support a firm's future growth. The value of these flows is equal to their present value.

Functional Control. Control executed by the corporate officers in conducting the daily operations.

Futures Contract. A futures contract is a contract to buy or sell a stated commodity (such as soybeans or corn) or financial claim (such as U.S. Treasury bonds) at a specified price at some future, specified time.

General Partnership. A partnership in which all partners are fully liable for the indebtedness incurred by the partnership.

Golden Parachute. A target management's attempt to ensure its own future in the event of an acquisition; stipulations regarding severance pay, extension of benefits, and other "extras" to be provided to outgoing management by the acquirer.

Gross Income. The firm's dollar sales from its product or services less the cost of producing or acquiring the product or service.

Gross Profit Margin. Gross profit/net sales. A ratio denoting the gross profit of the firm as a percentage of net sales.

Hedge. A means to neutralize exchange risk on an exposed asset position, whereby a liability of the same amount and maturity is created in a foreign currency.

Hedging Principle. A working capital management policy which states that the cash flow generating characteristics of a firm's investments should be matched with the cash flow requirements of the firm's sources of financing. Very simply, short-lived assets should be financed with short-term sources of financing while long-lived assets should be financed with long-term sources of financing.

Holding-Period Return. The return an investor would receive from holding a security for a designated period of time. For example, a monthly holding-period return would be the return for holding a security during a particular month.

Hostile Takeover. A merger or acquisition in which management resists the group initiating the transaction.

Hurdle Rate. The required rate of return used in capital budgeting.

Income Bond. A bond that requires interest payments only if earned. Failure to meet these interest payments will not result in bankruptcy.

Income Statement. A basic accounting statement that measures the results of a firm's operations over a specified period, commonly one year. Also known as the profit and loss statement. The bottom line of the income statement shows the firm's profit or loss for the period.

Increasing-Stream Hypothesis of Dividend Policy. A smoothing of the dividend stream in order to minimize the effect of company reversals. Corporate managers make every effort to avoid a dividend cut, attempting instead to develop a gradually increasing dividend series over the long-term future.

Incremental Cash Flows. The cash flows that result from the acceptance of a capital-budgeting project.

Indenture. The legal agreement between the firm issuing the bonds and the bond trustee who represents the bondholders, providing the specific terms of the loan agreement.

Indirect Quote. The exchange rate that expresses the required number of units of foreign currency to buy one unit of home currency.

Information Asymmetry. The difference in accessibility to information between managers and investors, which may result in a lower stock price than would be true if we had conditions of certainty.

Insolvency. The inability to meet interest payments or to repay debt at maturity.

Interest-Rate Parity Theory. States that (except for the effect of small transaction costs) the forward premium or discount should be equal and opposite in size to the difference in the national interest rates for securities of the same maturity.

Interest-Rate Risk. The uncertainty that envelops the expected returns from a security caused by changes in interest rates. Price changes induced by interest-rate changes are greater for long-term than for short-term financial instruments.

Internal Common Equity. Profits retained within the business for investment purposes.

Internal Growth. A firm's growth rate in earnings resulting from reinvesting company profits rather than distributing the earnings in the form of dividends. The growth rate is a function of the amount retained and the return earned on the retained funds.

Internal Rate of Return (IRR). A capital-budgeting technique that reflects the rate of return a project earns. Mathematically it is the discount rate that equates the present value of the inflows with the present value of the outflows.

Intrinsic Value. The present value of the investment's expected future cash flows, discounted at the investor's required rate of return.

Inventory Loans. Loans secured by inventories. Examples include floating or blanket lien agreements, chattel mortgage agreements, field warehouse receipt loans, and terminal warehouse receipt loans.

Inventory Turnover Ratio. Cost of goods sold/inventory. A ratio that measures the number of times a firm's inventories are sold and replaced during the year. This ratio reflects the relative liquidity of inventories.

Investment Banker. A financial specialist who underwrites and distributes new securities and advises corporate clients about raising new funds.

Investor's Required Rate of Return. The minimum rate of return necessary to attract an investor to purchase or hold a security.

Junk Bonds. Any bond rated BB or below.

Just-in-Time Inventory Control. A production and man-agement system in which inventory is cut down to a minimum through adjustments to the time and physical distance between the various production operations. Under this system the firm keeps a minimum level of inventory on hand relying upon suppliers to furnish parts "just-in-time" for them to be assembled.

Lead and Lag Strategies. Techniques used to reduce exchange risk where the firm maximizes its asset position in the stronger currency and its liability position in the weaker currency.

Least-Squares Regression. A procedure for "fitting" a line through a scatter of observed data points in a way that minimizes the sum of the squared deviations of the points from the fitted line.

Leveraged Buyout. A corporate restructuring where the existing shareholders sell their shares to a small group of investors. The purchasers of the stock use the firm's unused debt capacity to borrow the funds to pay for the stock.

Leveraged Leasing. A leasing arrangement in which the lessor will generally supply equity funds of 20 to 30 percent of the purchase price and borrow the remainder from a third-party lender.

Limited Partnership. A partnership in which one or more of the partners has limited liability, restricted to the amount of capital he invests in the partnership.

Line of Credit. Generally an informal agreement or understanding between the borrower and the bank as to the maximum amount of credit the bank will provide the borrower at any one time. Under this type of agreement there is no "legal" commitment on the part of the bank to provide the stated credit. See **Revolving Credit Agreement.**

Liquidation by Assignment. A proceeding in which the debtor transfers title of the firm's assets to a third party, who has been appointed either by the creditors or by the court. This individual, known as an assignee or trustee, administers the liquidation process and sees that an appropriate distribution is made of the proceeds.

Liquidation Value. The dollar sum that could be realized if an asset were sold independently of the going concern.

Liquidity. A firm's ability to pay its bills on time. Liquidity is related to the ease and quickness with which a firm can convert its noncash assets into cash, as well as the size of the firm's investment in noncash assets vis-à-vis its short-term liabilities.

Liquidity Preference Theory. The shape of the term structure of interest rates is determined by an investor's additional required interest rate in compensation of additional risks.

Liquidity Ratios. Financial ratios used to assess the ability of a firm to pay its bills on time. Examples of liquidity ratios include the current ratio and the acid test ratio.

Loan Amortization Schedule. A breakdown of the interest and principle payments on an amortized loan.

Long-Term Residual Dividend Policy. A dividend plan

by which the residual capital is distributed smoothly to the investors over the planning period.

Mail Float. Funds tied up during the time that elapses from the moment a customer mails his remittance check until the firm begins to process it.

Marginal Cost of Capital. The cost of capital that represents the weighted cost of each additional dollar of financing from all sources, debt, preferred stock, and common stock.

Marginal Tax Rate. The tax rate that would be applied to the next dollar of income.

Market Equilibrium. The situation in which expected returns equal required returns.

Market Risk. See **Systematic Risk**

Market Segmentation Theory. The shape of the term structure of interest rates implies that the rate of interest for a particular maturity is determined solely by demand and supply for a given maturity. This demand is independent of the demand and supply for securities having different maturities.

Market Value. The value observed in the market place, where buyers and sellers negotiate a mutually acceptable price for the asset.

Market-Value Weights. The percentage of financing provided by different capital sources, measured by the current market prices of the firm's bonds and preferred and common stock.

Marketable Securities. Security investments that the firm can quickly convert into cash balances.

Maturity Date. The date upon which a borrower is to repay a loan.

Merger. A combination of two or more businesses into a single operational entity.

Money Market. All institutions and procedures that facilitate transactions in short-term instruments issued by borrowers with very high credit ratings.

Money Market Mutual Funds. Investment companies that purchase a diversified array of short-term, high-grade (money market) debt instruments.

Monitoring Costs. A form of agency costs. Typically these costs arise when bond investors take steps to ensure that protective convenants in the bond indenture are adhered to by management.

Mortgage Bonds. Bonds secured by a lien on real property.

Multinational Corporation. A corporation with holdings and/or operations in more than one country.

Mutually Exclusive Projects. A set of projects that perform essentially the same task, so that acceptance of one will necessarily mean rejection of the others.

Negotiable Certificates of Deposit. Marketable receipts for funds deposited in a bank for a fixed period. The deposited funds earn a fixed rate of interest. More commonly, these are called CDs.

Net Income. A figure representing the firm's profit or loss for the period. It also represents the earnings available to the firm's common *and* preferred stockholders.

Net Income Available to Common Equity (Also Net Common Stock Earnings). Net income after interest taxes and preferred dividends.

Net Operating Loss Carryback and Carryforward. A tax provision that permits the taxpayer first to apply the loss against the profits in the three prior years (carryback). If the loss has not been completely absorbed by the profits in these three years, it may be applied to taxable profits in each of the seven following years (carryforward).

Net Present Value (NPV). A capital-budgeting concept defined as the present value of the project's annual net cash flows after tax less the project's initial outlay.

Net Profit Margin. Net income/sales. A ratio that measures the net income of the firm as a percent of sales.

Net Working Capital. The difference between the firm's current assets and its current liabilities.

Non-Diversifiable Risk. See **Systematic Risk.**

Nominal Interest Rate. The interest rate paid on debt securities without an adjustment for any loss in purchasing power.

Normal Probability Distribution. A special class of bell-shaped distributions with symmetrically decreasing density, where the curve approaches but never reaches the **X** axis.

Operating Income Return on Investment. The ratio of net operating income divided by total assets.

Operating Lease. A contractual commitment on the part of the firm leasing the asset (the lessee) to make a series of payments to the firm that actually owns the asset (the lessor) for use of the asset. An operating lease differs from a financial lease in that it can be canceled at any time after proper notice has been given to the lessor.

Operating Leverage. The responsiveness to sales changes of the firm's earnings before interest and taxes. This responsiveness arises from the firm's use of fixed operating costs.

Operating Profit Margin. Net operating income/sales. A firm's earnings before interest and taxes. This ratio serves as an overall measure of operating effectiveness.

Opportunity Cost of Funds. The next best rate of return available to the investor for a given level of risk.

Opportunity Set. The return-risk relationship available for an investor interested in the purchase or sale of securities.

Optimal Capital Structure. The capital structure that minimizes the firm's composite cost of capital (maximizes the common stock price) for raising a given amount of funds.

Optimal Range of Financial Leverage. The range of various capital structure combinations that yield the lowest overall cost of capital for the firm.

Option Contract. An option contract gives its owner the right to buy or sell a fixed number of shares at a specified price over a limited time period.

Organized Security Exchanges. Formal organizations involved in the trading of securities. Such exchanges are tangible entities that conduct auction markets in listed securities.

Over-the-Counter Markets. All security markets **except** the organized exchanges. The money market is an over-the-counter market. Most corporate bonds also are traded in this market.

Pac Man. A defensive tactic to a tender offer where the firm under attack becomes the attacker.

Partnership. An association of two or more individuals joining together as co-owners to operate a business for profit.

Par Value. On the face of a bond, the stated amount that the firm is to repay upon the maturity date.

Payable-Through Draft. A legal instrument that has the physical appearance of an ordinary check but is not drawn on a bank. A payable-through draft is drawn on and paid by the issuing firm. The bank serves as a collection point and passes the draft on to the firm.

Payback Period. A capital-budgeting criterion defined as the number of years required to recover the initial cash investment.

Payment Date. The date on which the company mails a dividend check to each investor.

Percent of Sales Method. A method of financial forecasting that involves estimating the level of an expense, asset, or liability for a future period as a percent of the sales forecast.

Perfect Markets. Hypothetical markets under the assumptions that (1) information is readily available to all investors at no cost, (2) there are no transaction costs, (3) investment opportunities are readily accessible to all prospective investors, and (4) financial distress and bankruptcy costs are nonexistent.

Permanent Investment. An investment that the firm expects to hold longer than one year. The firm makes permanent investments in fixed and current assets. Contrast with **Temporary Investments.**

Perpetuity. An annuity with an infinite life.

Physical Budgets. Budgets for unit sales, personnel or manpower, unit production, inventories, and physical facilities. These budgets are used as the basis for generating cost and profit budgets.

Pledging Accounts Receivable. A loan the firm obtains from a commercial bank or a finance company using its accounts receivable as collateral.

Poison Pill. A tactic used by the target of a hostile takeover; an unfavorable event, such as immediate repayment of all outstanding debt, triggered by an unfriendly party's acquisition of significant stock holdings.

Portfolio Beta. The relationship between a portfolio's returns and the market returns. It is a measure of the portfolio's nondiversifiable risk.

Portfolio Diversification Effect. The fact that variations of the returns from a portfolio or combination of assets may be less than the sum of the variation of the individual assets making up the portfolio.

Preauthorized Checks (PACs). A check that resembles the ordinary check but does not contain or require the signature of the person on whose account it is being drawn. A PAC is created only with the individual's legal authorization. The PAC system is advantageous when the firm regularly receives a large volume of payments of a fixed amount from the same customer over a long period.

Preemptive Right. The right entitling the common shareholder to maintain his proportionate share of ownership in the firm.

Present Value. The value in today's dollars of a future payment discounted back to present at the required rate of return.

Present Value of Dividend Growth (PVDG). The net present value of any dividend growth resulting from the reinvestment of future earnings.

Price/Earnings Ratio (P/E). The price the market places on $1 of a firm's earnings. For example, if a firm has an earnings per share of $2, and a stock price of $30, its price/earnings ratio is 15 ($30 ÷ $2).

Price Pegging. Buying orders placed by an underwriting syndicate manager for the security being marketed by his selling group. The objective is to stabilize the market price of the new issue.

Probability Tree. A schematic representation of a problem in which all possible outcomes are graphically displayed.

Processing Float. Funds tied up during the time required for the firm to process remittance checks before they can be deposited in the bank.

Profit Budget. A budget of forecasted profits based on information gleaned from the cost and sales budgets.

Profit Margins. Financial ratios (sometimes simply referred to as margins) that reflect the level of firm profits relative to sales. Examples include the gross profit margin (gross profit divided by sales), operating profit margin (operating earnings divided by sales), and the net profit margin (net profit divided by sales).

Profitability Index (PI). A capital budgeting criterion defined as the ratio of the present value of the future net cash flows to the initial outlay.

Pro Forma Income Statement. A statement of planned profit or loss for a future period.

Prospectus. A condensed version of the full registration statement filed with the Securities and Exchange Commission that describes a new security issue.

Proxy. A means of voting in which a designated party is provided with the temporary power of attorney to vote for the signee at the corporation's annual meeting.

Purchasing Power Parity. In the long run, exchange rates adjust so that the purchasing power of each currency tends to remain the same and, thus, exchange rate changes tend to reflect international differences in inflation rates. Countries with high rates of inflation tend to experience declines in the value of their currency.

Put Option. A put option gives its owners the right to sell a given number of shares of common stock or some other asset at a specified price over a given time period.

Real Assets. Tangible assets like houses, equipment, and inventories; real assets are distinguished from financial assets.

Real Interest Rate. The nominal rate of interest less any loss in purchasing power of the dollar during the time of the investment.

Red Herring. Finance jargon for a preliminary prospectus, which outlines the important features of a new issue without specifying the selling price and offering date.

Refunding. The process of replacing an old debt issue with the sale of new debt.

Registration Statement. A lengthy document filed with the Securities and Exchange Commission containing pertinent facts about a firm planning to sell new securities.

Remote Disbursing. A cash management service specifically designed to extend disbursing float.

Reorganization. A procedure, administered by the courts, that attempts to revitalize a firm by changing its operating procedures and capital structure.

Repurchase Agreements. Legal contracts that involve the sale of short-term securities by a borrower to a lender of funds. The borrower commits to repurchase the securities at a later date at the contract price plus a stated interest charge.

Required Rate of Return. The minimum rate of return necessary to attract an investor to purchase or hold a security. It is also the discount rate that equates the present value of the cash flows with the value of the security.

Residual Dividend Theory. A theory asserting that the dividends to be paid should equal the equity capital **left over** after the financing of profitable investments.

Restrictive Covenants. Provisions in the loan agreement that place restrictions on the borrower and make the loan immediately payable and due when violated. These restrictive covenants are designed to maintain the borrower's financial condition on a par with that which existed at the time the loan was made.

Return on Common Equity. Net income available to the common stockholders/common equity. A ratio relating earned income to the common stockholder's investment.

Return on Total Assets. Net income/total assets. This ratio determines the yield on the firm's assets by relating net income to total assets.

Return-Risk Line. A specification of the appropriate required rates of return for investments having different amounts of risk.

Revolving Credit Agreement. An understanding between the borrower and the bank as to the amount of credit the bank will be legally obligated to provide the borrower. See **Line of Credit.**

Right. A certificate issued to common stockholders giving them an option to purchase a stated number of new shares at a specified price during a two- to ten-week period.

Risk. The possible variation associated with the expected return measured by the standard deviation or coefficient of variation.

Risk-Adjusted Discount Rate. A method for incorporating the project's level of risk into the capital budgeting process, in which the discount rate is adjusted upward to compensate for higher-than-normal risk or downward to compensate for lower-than-normal risk.

Riskless Rate of Return. The rate of return on risk-free investments, such as the interest rate on short-term U.S. government securities.

Risk Premium. The additional return expected for assuming risk.

Rule of Absolute Priority. Rule that the company must completely honor senior claims on assets before settling junior claims.

Sale and Leaseback Arrangement. An arrangement arising when a firm sells land, buildings, or equipment that it already owns and simultaneously enters into an agreement to lease the property back for a specified period, under specific terms.

Salvage Value. The value of an asset or investment project at the end of its usable life.

Scatter Diagram Method. A method of financial forecasting that involves visually "fitting" a line through a scatter of points so that the distance of points about the line is minimized.

Scenario Analysis. Simulation analysis that focuses on an examination of the range of possible outcomes.

Secondary Market. Transactions in currently outstanding securities. This is distinguished from the new issues or primary market.

Secured Credit. Sources of credit that require security in the form of pledged assets. In the event the borrower defaults in payment of principal or interest the lender can seize the pledged assets and sell them to settle the debt.

Securities and Exchange Commission (SEC). The federal agency created by the Securities Exchange Act of 1934 to enforce federal securities laws.

Securities Exchange Act of 1933. A regulation that requires registration of certain new issues of public securities with the Securities and Exchange Commission (SEC). The registration statement should disclose all facts relevant to the new issue that will permit an investor make an informed decision.

Securities Exchange Act of 1934. This act enables the SEC to enforce federal securities laws. The major aspects of the 1934 act include: 1. Major securities exchanges are required to register with the SEC; 2. insider-trading is regulated; 3. stock price manipulation by investors is prohibited; 4. the SEC has control over proxy procedures; 5. the Board of Governors of the Federal Reserve System is given the responsibility of setting margin requirements.

Security Market Line. The return line that reflects the attitudes of investors regarding the minimal acceptable return for a given level of systematic risk.

Sell-Off. The sale of a subsidiary, division, or product line by one company to another.

Selling Group. A collection of securities dealers that participates in the distribution of new issues to final investors. A selling group agreement links these dealers to the underwriting syndicate.

Semivariable Costs. Charges that behave as variable costs over certain ranges of output and as fixed costs over other ranges of output.

Shark Repellents. Any of a variety of legalistic means used to counteract a tender offer by the firm under attack.

Shelf Registration (SEC Rule 415). A procedure for issuing new securities where the firm gets a master registration statement approved by the SEC. For the next 2 years the firm can sell securities in a piecemeal fashion against this "blanket order."

Simulation. The process of imitating the performance of an investment project through repeated evaluations, usually using a computer. In the general case, experimentation upon a mathematical model that has been designed to capture the critical realities of the decision-making situation.

Sinking Fund. A required annual payment that allows for the periodic retirement of debt.

Skewed Distribution. A distribution that has a longer "tail" to the right or left.

Sole Proprietorship. A business owned by a single individual.

Spin-Off. The separation of a subsidiary from its parent, with no change in the equity ownership. The management of the parent company gives up operating control over the subsidiary, but the shareholders maintain their same percentage ownership in both firms. New shares representing ownership in the averted company are issued to the original shareholders on a pro-rata basis.

Spontaneous Financing. The trade credit and other accounts payable that arise "spontaneously" in the firm's day-to-day operations.

Spot Transaction. A transaction made immediately in the market place at the market price.

Stable Dollar Dividend per Share. A dividend policy that maintains a relatively stable dollar dividend per share over time.

Standard Deviation. A statistical measure of the spread of a probability distribution calculated by squaring the difference between each outcome and its expected value, weighting each value by its probability, summing over all possible outcomes, and taking the square root of this sum.

Statement of Changes in Financial Position. A basic accounting statement, also known as a sources and uses of funds statement, identifying how the firm acquired its funds for the period and what it did with those funds.

Stock Dividend. A distribution of shares of up to 25 percent of the number of shares currently outstanding, issued on a pro-rata basis to the current stockholders.

Stock Market Value. (See **Market Value**.)

Stock Split. A stock dividend exceeding 25 percent of the number of shares currently outstanding.

Stock Repurchases. The repurchase of common stock by the issuing firm for any of a variety of reasons resulting in a reduction of shares outstanding.

Straight-Line Depreciation. A method for computing depreciation expenses in which the cost of the asset is divided by the asset's useful life.

Stretching on Trade Credit. Failing to pay within the prescribed credit period. For example, under credit terms of 2/10, net 30, a firm would be stretching its trade credit if it failed to pay by the 30th day and paid on the 60th day.

Subchapter S Corporation. A corporation that, because of specific qualifications, is taxed as though it were a partnership.

Subscription Price. The price for which the security may be purchased in a rights offering.

Synergistic Effect. An often-used reason for mergers; the benefit derived from the combination of the acquirer's operations (or financing capabilities) with the target's. Also referred to as "the sum of the parts equalling more than the whole."

Systematic Risk (Nondiversifiable Risk or Market Related Risk). The portion of variations in investment returns that cannot be eliminated through investor diversification. These variations result from factors that affect all stocks.

Target Debt Ratio. A desired proportion of long-term debt in the firm's capital structure. Alternatively, it may be the desired proportion of total debt in the firm's financial structure.

Taxable Income. Gross income from all sources, except for allowable exclusions, less any tax deductible expenses.

Tax Liability. The amount owed the federal, state, or local taxing authorities.

TBL Leases. Tax benefit transfer leases created under the Tax Act of 1981 and eliminated in 1982.

Technical Insolvency. Situation in which the firm can no longer honor its financial obligations. Although its assets may exceed its total liabilities, thereby indicating a positive net worth, the company simply does not have sufficient liquidity to pay its debts.

Temporary Financing. Financing (other than spontaneous sources) that will be repaid within a period of one year or less. Included among these sources of short-term debt are secured and unsecured bank loans, commercial paper, loans secured by accounts receivable, and loans secured by inventories.

Temporary Investments. These investments are comprised of the firm's investment in current assets that will be liquidated and not replaced within a period of one year or less. Examples include seasonal expansions in inventories and accounts receivable.

Tender Offer. A bid by an interested party, usually a corporation, for controlling interest in another corporation.

Terminal Warehouse Agreement. A security agreement in which the inventories pledged as collateral are transported to a public warehouse that is physically removed from the borrower's premises. This is the safest (and a costly) form of financing secured by inventory.

Term Loans. Loans that have maturities of one to ten years and are repaid in periodic installments over the life of the loan. Term loans are usually secured by a chattel mortgage on equipment or a mortgage on real property.

Term Structure of Interest Rates. The relationship between interest rates and the term to maturity, where the risk of default is held constant.

Times Interest Earned Ratio. Earnings before interest and taxes (EBIT)/interest expense. A ratio that measures the firm's ability to meet its interest payments from its annual operating earnings.

Total Asset Turnover. Sales/total tangible assets. An overall measure of the relation between the firm's tangible assets and the sales they generate.

Trade Credit. Credit made available by a firm's suppliers in conjunction with the acquisition of materials. Trade credit appears on the balance sheet as accounts payable.

Transaction Loan. A loan where the proceeds are designated for a specific purpose—for example, a bank loan used to finance the acquisition of a piece of equipment.

Transit Float. Funds tied up during the time necessary for a deposited check to clear through the commercial banking system and become usable funds to the company.

Treasury Bills. Direct debt obligations of the U.S. government sold on a regular basis by the U.S. Treasury.

Trend Analysis. An analysis of a firm's financial ratios over time.

Trustee. (See **Assignee**.)

Unbiased Expectations Theory. The shape of the term structure of interest rates is determined by an investor's expectations about future interest rates.

Uncommitted Earnings per Share. Earnings per share **minus** sinking-fund payments per share.

Underwriting. The purchase and subsequent resale of a new security issue. The risk of selling the new issue at a satisfactory (profitable) price is assumed by the investment banker.

Underwriting Syndicate. A temporary association of investment bankers formed to purchase a new security issue and quickly resell it at a profit. Formation of the syndicate spreads the risk of loss among several investment bankers, thereby minimizing the risk exposure of any single underwriter.

Undiversifiable Risk. The portion of the variation in investment returns that cannot be eliminated through investor diversification.

Unique Risk. See **Unsystematic Risk**.

Unlisted Securities. Securities that are not traded on an organized security exchange.

Unsecured Credit. All sources of credit that have as their security only the lender's faith in the borrower's ability to repay the funds when due.

Unsystematic Risk (Firm-Specific Risk or Unique Risk). The portion of the variation in investment returns that can be eliminated through investor diversification. These variations result from factors that are unique to the particular firm.

Value of a Bond. The present value of the interest payments, I_t in period t, plus the present value of the redemption or par value of the indebtedness, M, at the maturity date.

Value of a Security. The present value of all future cash inflows expected to be received by the investor owning the security.

Variable Costs. Charges that vary in total as output changes. Variable costs are fixed per unit of output.

Venture Capitalists. Investors interested in supplying capital to particularly high-risk situations, such as start-ups or firms denied conventional financing.

Voluntary Remedy. A voluntary reorganization that is acceptable to the creditors.

Warrant. An option to purchase a fixed number of shares of common stock at a predetermined price during a specified time period.

Weighted Cost of Capital. A composite of the individual costs of financing incurred by each capital source. A firm's weighted cost of capital is a function of (1) the individual costs of capital, (2) the capital structure mix, and (3) the level of financing necessary to make the investment.

Weighted Marginal Cost of Capital. The composite cost for each additional dollar of financing. The marginal cost of capital represents the appropriate criterion for making investment decisions.

White Knight. A defensive tactic to a tender offer whereby an able company comes to the rescue of the firm targeted for takeover.

Working Capital. A concept traditionally defined as a firm's investment in current assets. Net working capital refers to the difference between current assets and current liabilities.

Yield to Maturity. The rate of return the investor will earn if the bond is held to maturity.

Zero Balance Accounts. A cash management tool that permits centralized control over cash outflow while maintaining divisional disbursing authority. Objectives include: 1. Achieve better control over cash payments; 2. reduce excess cash balances held in regional banks for disbursing purposes; and 3. increase disbursing float.

INDEXES

Subject Index

Corporate near-sightedness, 291
Corporate raiders, 798
Corporate restructuring. *See* Mergers/acquisitions
Corporate takeovers, executive views on, 381
Corporation, defined, 40–41
Cost advantage(s), 184, 185–86
Cost budgets, 497
Cost of capital. *See also* Weighted cost of capital
  corporation survey of, 294–95
  defined, 266–67
  international comparisons, 389–91
  saucer-shaped curve of, 365–66
Cost of debt, 274–75
Cost of goods sold
  accounting for, 23–24
  defined, 26
Costs, assumed behavior of, 318–20
Coupon interest rate, 140
Coverage ratios, 377, 457–58
  cash flow overall coverage ratio, 457–58
  times interest earned ratio, 457
Covered options, 782
Credit scoring, 622
Cross rates, 858
Crowding-out, 679
Current assets
  defined, 26, 532
  risk-return tradeoff and, 533
Current liabilities
  advantages
    flexibility, 534
    interest cost, 534
  defined, 26
  disadvantages, 534–35
  risk-return tradeoff and, 535–36
Current ratio, 453
Current yield, 727

D

Date of record, dividend payment and, 427
Dean, Joel, 5
Debentures, defined, 26, 730
Debt capacity, 268, 383
  defined, 365–66
Debt financing, 337, 372
  explicit cost of capital in, 361
  implicit cost of debt in, 361
Debt policy, executive views on, 381
Debt ratio, 456
Debt retirement, 735–38
Decade of the deal, 798, 799, 800, 801
Declaration date, dividend payment and, 427
Deferred income taxes, defined, 26

Delivery-time stock, 634
De Lorean, John, 381
Dependence hypothesis (NI theory), 361–63
Depository Institutions Act of 1982, 583
Depository transfer checks, 563–65
Depreciable life, defined, 26
Depreciation
  calculation, by simplified straight-line method, 180–81
  Tax Reform Act of 1986 and, 180
Depreciation expense
  defined, 26
  methods for computing, 48–49, 60–63
Depreciation of fixed assets, 24, 48–49, 60–63
  accelerated cost recovery system (ACRS), 61
    example of, 62
  asset depreciation range (ADR), 61–62
  averaging conventions, 63
  double-declining balance (DDB), 61
  straight-line (SL), 24, 61
Dersmith, M.W., 719
Devaluation, 854
Dewing, Arthur S., 4
Differential after-tax cash flow, 174, 176
  over project's life, 179–81
Dion, Phillip J., 381
Dionne, Joseph L., 357
Direct costs, 319
Direct foreign investment (DFI), 853
  risks in
    business/financial, 875
    exchange, 876
    political, 875–76
Direct investment, 853
Direct leasing, 708
Direct quote, 855
Direct sale distribution method, 689
Direct securities, 678
Disbursement float, 558
  remote disbursing and, 568–69
Discount rate, 584
  changes in, 585
  defined, 73
Discretionary sources of financing, 495–96
Diversification. *See* Risk
Divestitures, 817–19. *See also* Mergers/acquisitions
  types of
    going private, 819
    liquidation, 818
    selloff, 818

    spinoff, 818
Dividend, defined, 26
Dividend decision making, 422–26
  factors in
    earnings predictability, 423
    inflation, 424
    lack of financing sources, 423
    legal restrictions, 423
    liquidity position, 423
    ownership control, 424
    payment patterns, 424–26
      constant dividend payout ratio, 425
      small regular dividend plus year-end extra, 425
      stable dollar dividend per share, 425–26
Dividend exclusion, 48
Dividend-growth approach, estimating cost of equity by, 277–79, 295
Dividend payment procedures, 426–27
  date of record, 427
  declaration date, 427
  ex-dividend date, 427
  payment date, 427
Dividend payout ratio, 409
Dividend policy
  common stock prices and, 408–22
  decision making about, 422–26
  payment procedures, 426–27
  stock dividends/stock splits, 428–30
  stock repurchases, 430–32
Dividend policy and common stock prices, 408–22
  agency costs, 419
  clientele effect, 417–18
  contrasting views of
    dividend irrelevance, 410–13, 415
    high dividends, 413–14
    low dividends, 414
  expectations theory, 419–20
  financial managers' views of, 420–22
  guidelines for, 422
  information effect, 418–19
  residual dividend theory, 416–17
Dividend rate band, 740
Donaldson, Gordon, 379
Double-declining balance (DDB) method, 48, 61
Double-declining balance depreciation, defined, 26
Drucker, Peter, 882
Dual-class recapitalizations, 745
Due diligence meeting, 691

Dun & Bradstreet financial ratios, 450
Dunning letter, 625
Dunphy, Dermot, 424

E

Earnings
    defined, 26
    value and, 169–72
Earnings after taxes (EAT), defined, 26
Earnings before interest and taxes (EBIT). *See* EBIT
Earnings before taxes (EBT), defined, 26
Earnings per share (EPS), defined, 26
EBIT
    breakeven analysis and, 317–25
    business risk and, 315–16
    financial leverage and, 331–34
    financial risk and, 317
    operating leverage and, 326–30
EBIT-EPS analysis, 374–77
    computing indifference points, 376
        uncommitted earnings per share in, 376–77
    graphic analysis, 375–76
    primary weakness of, 377
Economic exposure, 872
Economic failure, 825
Economic order quantity (EOQ) model
    cash management and, 609–13
    inflation and, 634–35
    inventory management and, 630–35, 637
Edelman, Richard B., 421
Effective cost-of-credit formula (RATE), 647–48, 649, 651–53, 654, 657, 658, 660
Efficiency ratios, 453–55
    accounts receivable turnover ratio, 454
    average collection period ratio, 454
    fixed asset turnover ratio, 455
    inventory turnover ratio, 454–55
    total asset turnover ratio, 455
Efficient markets, 9–10, 137, 854
Einhorn, Steven, 386
Electronic funds transfer (EFT), 569
Entry barriers
    cost advantages, 184, 185–86
    product differentiation, 184–85
EOQ model. *See* Economic order quantity (EOQ) model
Equity financing, defined, 26
Equivalent annual annuity (EAA) approach, 226–27
Ethics/ethical behavior, 11–13

bond covenants and, 729
in capital budgeting, 201
Congress and, 649
early tycoons and, 798
in futures markets, 780
guidelines, 35
Ivan Boesky and, 697
managerial choice and, 271
social responsibility of corporations and, 13, 201
whistleblowers and, 449
worker exploitation and, 636
Eurobonds, 733
Eurodollar loans, 707
Exchange-rate risk, 859
    examples of, 860–62
    exposure to, 868–72
        economic exposure, 872
        transactions exposure, 869–71
        translation exposure, 896
Exchange rates
    arbitrage and, 857–58
    asked/bid rates, 858
    cross rates, 858
    exchange-rate risk, 859, 860–62
    foreign exchange market, 854
    forward exchange rates, 859–60
    interest rate parity theory and, 862–65
    purchasing power parity (PPP) and, 865–68
    recent history of, 853–54
    spot exchange rates, 854–57
Ex-dividend date, 427
Exercise price, 762, 781
Exercise ratio, 762
Expectations theory, 419–20
Expected rates of return, bond/stock valuation and, 149–54
Expiration date
    of options, 782
    of rights offering, 746
    of warrants, 762
Explicit cost of capital, 361
Ex-rights date, 746
Ex-rights price, 746
Extension, insolvency and, 831
External common equity, 276
Extraordinary item, defined, 26

F

Factor/factoring, 657–58, 659
Factoring accounts receivable, 657–58
Failure. *See* Business failure
Fair value, 137
Fama, Eugene, 116
Farrelly, Gail E., 421
Federal agency securities, 577

Federal funds rate, 584
Federal Home Loan Banks (FHLB), 577
Federal income taxation, 44–53
    accumulated earnings tax, 50
    capital gains/losses, 49
    corporate tax computations, 46–51
        taxable income, 46
        taxes owed, 46–48
    debt financing, 337
    depreciation, 48–49
    dividend exclusion, 48
    financial decision making and, 51–53
    net operating loss deduction, 49
    objectives, 44
    security investments and, 574–75
    Subchapter S Corporation, 50–51
    types of taxpayers, 45–46
Federal Intermediate Credit Banks, 577
Federal Land Banks, 577
Federal National Mortgage Association (FNMA), 577
Federal Open Market Committee (FOMC), 584
Federal Power Commission, 689, 696
Federal Reserve System
    float and, 572
    interest rates and, 584–86
Federal Reserve Wire System, 565
Federal Trade Commission, 696, 803
Ferrara, W.L., 719
Fiduciaries, 45
Field warehouse financing agreement, 659
FIFO, 23–24
    defined, 26
Financial Accounting Standards Board (FASB), 447
    Standard 13, 709
    Standard 95, 444, 448
    Statement 14, 808
    Statement 52, 869
Financial analysis
    basic financial statements for, 443–49
        balance sheet, 442, 443–44
        income statement, 442, 444
        statement of cash flows, 447–49
        statement of changes in financial position, 444–47
    financial ratios in, 449–64
    limitations, 468–70
    methods for analyzing, 450–68
Financial assets, 677
Financial decisions
    risk-return relationships and, 9
    tax role in, 51–53
        on capital investment, 52–53

Keynes, John Maynard, 552
Kirkland, Lane, 636

L

Lagging, as risk-reduction technique, 873
Lanier, J.L., Jr., 381
Last-in, first-out (LIFO), 23–24
  defined, 27
Lavery, John, 201
Law of the One Price, 866
Leading, as risk-reduction technique, 873
Lease(s)/leasing
  accounting for, 709–10
  defined, 27
  direct, 708
  financial, 708
  lease vs. purchase decision, 710–16
    case problem analysis, 712–16
    lease-purchase algorithm, 711–12
  leveraged, 709
  net/net-net, 708–9
  operating, 708
  potential benefits from, 716
    avoidance of obsolescence risk, 718
    ease of obtaining credit, 719
    flexibility/convenience, 717
    lack of restrictions, 717–18
    one hundred percent financing, 718
    tax savings, 718–19
    working capital conservation, 718
  rationale for, 719
  sale and leaseback, 708
Lebaron, Dean, 808
Legal forms of business organization
  comparison criteria, 41–43
    attractiveness for raising capital, 43
    business continuity, 42
    income taxes, 43
    management control/regulations, 43
    owner liability, 42
    ownership transferability, 42
    requirements/costs, 41–42
  corporation, 40–41
  economic significance of, 36–38
  limited liability company (LLC), 44–45
  partnership, 39–40
    general, 39
    limited, 39
    master limited, 40
  sole proprietorship, 39

Lerner, Teena, 763
Leveraged buyouts, 796, 814
Leveraged Employee Stock Ownership Plan (LESOPs), 814–15
Leveraged leasing, 709
Leverage ratios, 455–58
  balance sheet leverage ratios, 456
  cash flow overall coverage ratio, 457–58
  debt ratio, 456
  long-term debt to total capitalization ratio, 456–57
  times interest earned ratio, 457
Liability, defined, 27
LIFO, 23–24
  defined, 27
Limited liability company (LLC), 44
Limited partnership, 39
Line of credit
  terms, 650
Lintner, John, 425
Liquid assets. See also Cash; Cash management; Marketable securities management
  cash vs. marketable securities, 609–17
  defined, 27, 550
  variations in holdings of, 554–55
Liquidation, 836–41
  by assignment, 837–38
  by bankruptcy, 838, 840–41
    priority of claims, 840–41
    process, 838
Liquidation value, defined, 137
Liquidity, securities portfolio and, 574
Liquidity management. See Working capital management
Liquidity preference theory, 34–35
Liquidity premium, 35
Liquidity ratios, 452–53
  acid test ratio, 453
  current ratio, 453
Lock-box arrangement, 558–61
Logue, Dennis E., 132
London Interbank Offered Rate (LIBOR), 707, 731
Long-term debt, defined, 27
Long-term debt to total capitalization ratio, 456–57
Long-term financing. See also specific topics
  bonds, 726–39
  common stock, 743–49
  convertible securities, 754–61
  futures, 771–80
  options, 780–91
  preferred stock, 739–43
  warrants, 761–65

Loy, David, 590

M

MacArthur, John, 291
Mail float, 557. See also Depository transfer checks; Lock-box arrangement; Preauthorized checks (PACs)
Management buyouts (MBOs), 796
Maquiladoras, 636
Marginal analysis, 625–27
Marginal cost of capital, 284. See also Weighted cost of capital
  calculation of, 285–86
    example, 286–92
  effect of new financing on, 285
Marginal tax rate, 47
Margin requirements, futures contracts and, 774
Marketable securities, defined, 27, 550
Marketable securities management. See also Cash management
  portfolio composition
    bankers' acceptances, 578–79
    commercial paper, 580
    federal agency securities, 577
    money market deposit accounts (MMDAs), 583
    money market mutual funds, 581–83
    negotiable certificates of deposit (CDs), 579
    repurchase agreements (repos), 580–81
    U.S. Treasury bills, 576
  portfolio selection criteria, 571–76
    financial risk, 571, 573, 576
    interest rate risk, 573–74, 576
    liquidity, 574, 576
    taxability, 574–75, 576
    yields, 575–76
  portfolio yield structure, 586–89
  practices, studies of, 589–90
Market portfolio, 107
Market-related risk, 106
Market segmentation theory, 35–36
Market value, defined, 137
Marr, Wayne, 733, 735
Master limited partnership (MLP), 40
Matching principle, 23
Mathur, Ike, 589–90
Maturity date of bonds, 140, 727
Maturity matching. See Hedging principle
Maxwell, Robert, 812
McCauley, Robert N., 390
Merchant banking, 653–54
Mergers/acquisitions. See also Divestitures

Corporate Name Index

A

Abbott Labs, 6
Airborne Express, 185
Airbus, 229
A. L. Williams Corporation, 763
Allegheny International, 839
Allegheny Power, 554
Allen-Bradley, 184
Allied Chemical, 797
Allied Corporation, 817
American Electric Power, 554
American Hospital Supply, 133
American Telephone and Telegraph
    Company. *See* AT&T
American Tobacco, 797
Amoco, 555
Apple Computer, 178
Armour, 185
AT&T, 144–45, 382, 673, 761, 883
AutoZone, 676

B

Baldwin-United, 839
Batterymarch Financial
    Management, 808
Beechcraft, 790
Beech-Nut Nutrition, 201
Bendix Corporation, 817
Bethlehem Steel, 150
Blanks Engraving, 137
Boeing, 229
Borden, 741
Bristol-Myers Squibb Co., 12
British Bio-Technology, 6

C

Campbell Soup Co., 9
Caterpillar Tractor, 184
CBS, 133
CBS Records, 390
Chevron, 555
Chrysler Corporation, 554, 555, 636,
    828
Chugai, 6
CitiCorp, 141–42
Clark Oil, 731
Coca-Cola Company, 128–30, 334,
    355
Colgate-Palmolive, 150
Columbia Pictures, 390
Consolidated Rail Corporation
    (Conrail), 673
Continental Airlines, 835

D

Dale Electronics, 636
Delta Airlines, 427
Domino's Pizza, 185
Douglas Aircraft, 828
Drexel, Burnham, Lambert, 11, 732,
    815
Dun & Bradstreet, Inc., 450, 622,
    828
Dupont, 731
Duracell International, 676

E

Emerson Electric, 636
Emery/Purolator, 185
Exxon, 555

F

FANUC, Ltd., 184
Federal Express, 185
Fiberboard Corporation, 382
First Boston Corporation, 579, 580,
    674
Fitch Investor Services, 728
Ford Motor Company, 173, 228, 554,
    555, 636
Fujisawa, 6

G

GE Fanuc Automation Corp., 184
General Electric, 184, 636, 883
General Foods, 174, 797
General Motors, 173, 425, 636, 883
Genetics Institute, Inc., 6
Gen-Probe, Inc., 6
Gerber Products, 201
Getty Oil Company, 106, 817
Goldman, Sachs & Co., 580, 674
Great Atlantic and Pacific Tea Co.
    (A&P), 744
Gulf Oil, 817

H

H. J. Heinz, 201
Hewlett-Packard, 883
Hitachi, 229, 636
Hoffman-La Roche, 184
Honeywell, 636
Hyal Pharmaceutical, 761

I

IBM, 5, 178, 558, 559, 797
Immunex Corporation, 763
Inland Steel, 229
International Business Machines. *See*
    IBM
International Harvester, 690
Iowa Beef Packers, 185

J

J. C. Penney, 137
J and S Corporation, 46–47
Johnson & Johnson, 230–31, 239

K

Kellogg's, 174
KeyCorp, 731
Kidder, Peabody & Co., 682
Kohlberg Kravis Roberts (KKR), 676,
    818
Kraft, 798

L

Leucadia National, 839
L. F. Rothschild Company, 763
Limited, The, 636
Lockheed, 828
LyphoMed, 6

M

Manville, 839
Martin-Marietta, 817
McDonald's, 185, 883
McGraw-Hill, Inc., 357
Memorex Telex, 731
Merrill Lynch, Pierce, Fenner &
    Smith, 579, 580
Merrill Lynch Capital Markets, 674,
    682
Mobil Oil, 690
Moody's Investors Service, 728, 763
Morgan Stanley & Co., 674

N

National Cash Register, 636
National Data Corporation, 564
Navistar, 690
Nestle, 201
Nippon Steel, 229

O

Octagon Communications Limited
    Liability Co., 44
Owens-Illinois, 676

P

Parker Pen Co., 744
Penn Central, 828